Encyclopedia of Beasts
and Monsters in Myth,
Legend and Folklore

Encyclopedia of Beasts and Monsters in Myth, Legend and Folklore

Theresa Bane

McFarland & Company, Inc., Publishers

Jefferson, North Carolina

Library of Congress Cataloguing-in-Publication Data [new form]

Names: Bane, Theresa, 1969– author.
Title: Encyclopedia of beasts and monsters in myth, legend and folklore /
Theresa Bane.
Description: Jefferson, North Carolina : McFarland & Company, Publishers,
2015. | Includes bibliographical references and index.
Identifiers: LCCN 2015043160 | ISBN 9780786495054 (softcover : acid free paper)
Subjects: LCSH: Animals, Mythical—Encyclopedias. | Monsters—Encyclopedias.
Classification: LCC GR825 .B275 2015 | DDC 001.944—dc23
LC record available at http://lccn.loc.gov/2015043160

ISBN (print) 978-0-7864-9505-4
ISBN (ebook) 978-1-4766-2268-2

British Library cataloguing data are available

Printed in the United States of America

McFarland & Company, Inc., Publishers
Box 611, Jefferson, North Carolina 28640
www.mcfarlandpub.com

To Athena, my beloved canine companion.
You are where "abomination" and "fairy hound" meet.

Table of Contents

Preface
5

Introduction
7

The Encyclopedia
11

Bibliography
349

Index
383

Preface

To date this encyclopedic work on mythological creatures is my largest undertaking, written with the needs of other authors and researchers in mind. Numerous books already cover the subject of folkloric, imaginary, and mythological creatures, but I believe this one to be unique in its completeness and the breadth of its sources. I was determined to include every possible creature, leaving no culture, religion, or time period untouched.

This volume does not contain any fictional creations—those animals invented purely from the imagination of an author for a work of strict fiction, such as the Ravenous Bugblatter Beast of Traal from the late Douglas Adams's *Hitchhiker's Guide to the Galaxy*. Although references to the universe's most profoundly unintelligent animal are made commonly in some circles, it originated from a radio show turned novel turned TV show turned movie. The RBBoT is neither folkloric nor mythological but entirely fictional; it cannot be encountered in the most remote part of this (or any other) planet nor does it exist anywhere except in the fiction of the author who created it and the many works of Adams fan fiction circulating on the internet and convention circuits. No reasonable person is funding an expedition to look for one and to date, it has never been sighted nor has its blurry photograph been published anywhere I could discover.

Additionally, this book does not contain any cryptozoological animals or beings like the phantom kangaroos sighted in England, France, and throughout America. The kangaroo is a real animal, and although the idea of one hopping down a Parisian back alley or living in troops in the American west is delightful, interesting, and even possible, it is in all likelihood an urban legend. The overwhelming opportunities for evidence to be collected if these animals were present would be there for the taking; the fact that over a hundred years have passed and one has yet to be captured, dead or alive, is evidence enough for their lack of presence (but perhaps the flotilla of alligators in the sewers keep their number low). The Mothman, Springheel Jack, and their ilk are also not represented here. These beings are not cryptids, folkloric, nor mythological in origin; at best they are pop culture urban legends who come in and out of vogue as the media sees fit.

Also not included are the many extra-terrestrial species of aliens who abduct us, visit us, and make crop circles for our consideration. These beings from distant galaxies have been sighted and reported for many years, hundreds even, but their existence is akin to the aforementioned alligators in the sewers and phantom kangaroos. ETs are not a part of mythology although some religions assert their gods descended to earth in vehicles "from the stars." If I am ever given the opportunity to write an encyclopedia of gods and goddesses, those beings may appear in that work.

Furthermore, at no point in the book do I ever speculate about what the creature "could be" or what the ancient author was "probably" looking upon. By following this strict guideline, the book is a far more useful research tool for authors and academics, as I do not pollute their thoughts with my interpretation of the material.

The goal of this work is to include as many mythological and folkloric creatures as I could discover so fellow researchers can utilize it as their initial "go to" book; hopefully they will read their desired entry and get the information they seek or have an idea of how to begin their own research if they so desire. It is a nearly impossible task to include every mythological being ever imagined by man and to fully detail every nuance of its aspect and history, but I hope this book comes closer to achieving this goal than any before it.

Each entry contains the country of origin or the name of the people from which the creature originated. Wherever possible a physical description and preferred prey are included. Some entries also have a pronunciation of the name and summation of the mythological history of the creature included if one was attached. Naturally, some entries are longer than others, as some creatures were more fleshed out, so to speak, than others.

The entries are arranged in alphabetical order. Some authors have grouped the creatures by country or according to the six main classes of animals (amphibians, birds, fishes, invertebrates, mammals, and reptiles). This method leaves much to be desired; for instance, a creature may appear in the mythologies of many countries, as is the case with the DRAGON and the UNICORN, so there is no single geographical location by which to place it. Similarly, many chimerical creatures have physical descriptions containing features from two or more of the animal classes. For these reasons, I kept to the tried and true traditional alphabetical listing and method of collation. If a researcher wants to know what creatures hail from a specific country, there is an exhaustive index that will serve the purpose.

Over time the spellings of words change, as they do when a myth travels from country to country and is translated time and again. Because of this, some creatures' names have many variant forms. All are included in the index to ensure access by any version of the name.

As some mythologies are older and more thoroughly explored than others, as is the case with Greek, Hindu, and Norse mythologies, many beings are entangled in one another's stories. Words in SMALL CAPS signal that there is more to the story as well as where to find it cross referenced in the book.

The resources I utilized for this work were primarily other research books and academic articles written by my predecessors. I relied heavily on Google Books for access to the 19th century works as they are difficult to come by otherwise. Apart from my personal library made up of a lifetime's collection of books I also visited the many public and private libraries in the various cities and towns I have lived in over the years.

In conclusion, I would be remiss if I did not express my deep appreciation to those who assisted me with this commission: beta-readers and index assistants, Angela McGill, Pam Paarisi and Jeanie Bone; my morale officer Amedeo C. Falcone who would daily ask for reports on my progress and encourage me to soldier on; and especially my devoted and supporting husband, T. Glenn Bane, who enables me to pursue this career. Without this dedicated cadre of overworked individuals, this book would not have been possible.

Introduction

"Here there be Dragons!"

This notation was often placed at the edge of a map to indicate the end of civilization and the known world; it may conjure up images of far-off distant lands where undiscovered races of people hunt never-before-seen species of creatures. The archetypal Hero or Merchant may go to these places, risking life and livelihood to return victorious from battle or with bundles of foreign goods along with adventurous stories of how they were so cleverly acquired. Both brave adventurers will tell tales of a simpler place, a bucolic wonderland, filled with magic, miracles, and mysteries—of beautifully landscaped forests, musically-inclined wildlife, and sights too surreal to properly do justice in the retelling.

It sounds all well and good, but can you honestly imagine living in a world filled with the mythological creatures in this book?

Assuming you are of the working class of people, your first thoughts of the day are not of "coffee" but rather of the need to complete all of your chores before the sun sets and the truly monstrous creatures leave their lairs to hunt prey. While simultaneously offending neither your ANCESTRAL SPIRITS who watch your every move nor the NATURE SPIRITS who live in virtually every rock and tree—both of which are ready to pass harsh judgment on even a slight transgression—you'll need to scrape together enough firewood without enraging the NYMPHS to cook a small meal, followed by collecting water from the riverbank without being spotted by an ARANDA. Hopefully you'll be able to outsmart the local CURUPIRA who makes hunting for game difficult under the best of circumstances.

Working the fields requires one to be ever vigilant against the attack of a CORN SPIRIT while minding where the children are lest a PONTARF or some other NURSERY BOGIE swallows them whole. Even if none of these creatures are on the hunt, there is always a chance the local DRAGON picks today to ravage the countryside while the knights are off on some quest, like hunting the wild boar TWRCH TRWYTH.

When twilight arrives, sounded by the mournful cry of a SQUONK, you must ignore the twinkling lights of the dragon lanterns (see DRAGON, OCCIDENTAL) and herd in the lambs or else a BOOBRIE will make a meal of them. Inside your home, once the HOUSE-SPIRIT is properly placated and a daily offering is left behind on the stove so the brownie (a species of domestic fairy or HOUSE-SPIRIT from Scottish fairy folklore) won't become bogarts (an injurious species of fairy), a meager meal may finally be consumed by any surviving family members. Then, if your luck holds throughout the night, an INCUBUS or SUCCUBUS won't attack your family while they sleep nor will a DWARF or CORPAN SIDE slip into the home and steal your newborn child, leaving a miserable and squalling CHANGELING in its place. After a night's rest, you get to wake up and do it all over again—after all ... tomorrow is another day!

How miserable existence would be if the smallest percentage of the nearly three thousand mythological creatures in this book actually existed. Fortunately, none of them are real; they only exist in our folklore, imaginations, legends, and mythologies.

For clarity, folklore and folktales are those traditional stories that are told and are well known among the people in a community or society. Most often they are from an oral tradition and only recently (i.e., within the last few centuries) committed to paper. Very often these tales teach a lesson, be it of morality or social behavior; the messages include advice and cautionary tales on how to be a good parent as well as how to be a wise and just king. These tales clearly lay out the consequences of failing to heed their advice. Fairy tales fall into this category. The word *lore* is commonly used, and although there is less of a story connected with the attached warning, it is basically an interchangeable word for *folklore*.

A legend is a traditional story which seems to be plausible on a historical level; elements of it may have a folkloric feel but may also include miraculous events and supernatural beings. Animals in these tales, generally speaking, tend to be far less conversational, helpful, or bent on random destruction; they tend to act much more animalistic and are far more concerned with their base animal needs or fulfilling a task eternally assigned to them, such as filling their bellies, guarding a treasure hoard, or monitoring the amount of rainfall.

Angels, demi-gods, demons, divine messengers, gods, and goddesses all appear in myths. These stories are of a religious nature and tightly interwoven into a culture's beliefs and their opinion of the world in which they live. These mythological tales exemplify the attitudes and values people hold in the utmost of importance as the tales not only explain the origin of many of their traditions, but also the origin of their world and universe as well as their place in it. Myths give an account of a society's standards, their social taboos, and the consequences to be suffered by divine justice if those things are broken. Myths also enumerate epic battles fought between their beloved heroes and their most hated villains.

A large number of entries in this work derive from Norse mythology. There are numerous good sources available, as the ancient Norse people had a tendency to name everything they perceived relevant as they fleshed out every aspect of their religion. The Norse had a name for everything and everyone, a developed personality, and detailed descriptions of what these named beings looked like, even going so far as to single out specific articles of clothing, boulders, and jewelry. Everything in their pantheon had a backstory and was almost always connected to someone or something else.

Sources were much scarcer for many other cultures. Some entries are rather sizeable but have only one or two sources listed; this is because although the books cited are considered to be reputable resources, other books on the subject either had the same exact information (sometimes duplicated word for word) or did not cover the creature at all.

There is staggeringly little information available on creatures from Inuit folklore and mythology; even when utilizing a book on this culture, there is seldom a mention of such creatures. Many of the Inuit entries thus cite only one source that I considered reliable. The importance of revealing these creatures to a larger audience seemed to outweigh the drawback of having no other sources to corroborate or expand on the information. It is a rich and wonderful culture, and in many ways, a completely original mythology.

When an entry is only a sentence or two long, as many are, I chose to include it because the source material was, in my opinion, reputable. I did not want to dismiss a creature simply because available information was thin. If all we know of FOLKVIR is its name but the animal is mentioned repeatedly throughout a mythology, even if no other information is ever given about the beast, I consider it important enough to include. As excavations of ancient sites continue to turn up new information, the lost history of FOLKVIR may eventually emerge.

Not included in this book are those animals and beings which fall into the category of cryptozoology, the study of unknown animals. This is a field of science (or pseudoscience to some) which delves into those beasts whose existence is not proven but may nevertheless be true; the bulk of evidence that such animals exist is based largely on personal testimonials, unclear photographs and video imagery, and physical evidence such as a plaster cast of a suspected footprint, suspected nesting locations, and calls or cries in the night which are not identifiable or recognized to be from any known creature, regional or otherwise.

Cryptozoology is considered by many scientists to be at best an inaccurate attempt at zoology as the cryptids (the animals in question) have traditionally only existed in a culture's mythology or folktales. Adding to this, many of the field researchers do not follow the scientific method when collecting data. For the purpose of this book, cryptids such as Bigfoot and the Loch Ness Monster are not included solely because they are cryptids, and also because there is no folklore or mythology attached to them. By contrast the THUNDERBIRD is contained within; although it is considered to be a cryptid by some cryptozoologists there are many traditional and tribal stories of these birds from many of the native people of the American southwest. It also appears in the mythology of some of the Arabic and Russian tribes. If you were hoping to read of cryptids here, you will find only those with folkloric or mythological origins, and in those circumstances I do not delve into the reports of alleged sightings and scientific studies attempted on the subject in question.

Another example of an accepted cryptid would be the MAMLAMBO, a supernatural creature, the FAMILIAR of a witch according to the Xhosa people of Africa, as well as the name of an alleged river monster. In instances like this, where the creature crossed the line from fantasy into pending factual discoveries, I only wrote about the supernatural creature and its related features omitting the cryptozoographic aspects. In order to retain the original and initial point of this book it was necessary to focus only on those creatures of myth and legend and not the cryptozoological ones. If the reader is interested in the subject of cryptozoology, I highly suggest reading Michael Newton's *Encyclopedia of Cryptozoology: A Global Guide to Hidden Animals and Their Pursuers* (McFarland, 2005, 2014). This excellent book on the subject responsibly and thoroughly covers cryptids, regardless of their origin.

Alien beings and extra-terrestrials said to have been discovered and catalogued by UFOlogists are also, not surprisingly, excluded from this work. Apart from my personal feelings on the existence of such life-forms, they are clearly not in line with the purpose of this book. Although I am sure there must be an excellent book on the subject listing such entities, I cannot with good conscience recommend any, as this is far from my field of expertise.

When reading an entry, it may be helpful to keep in mind that if I did not mention, for instance, the breeding habits of a creature, it is because I did not come upon such information. A reader may choose to assume an equine-like creature breeds as any real-world equine does, but unless I came across specific information, I did not address the subject. There is actually a species of UNICORN which reproduces by means of spontaneous generation. This is not to say all UNICORNS do.

Those who have read my encyclopedias on demons, fairies, and vampires will note the occasional overlap of an entry in this book. When this occurs those entries are updated for inclusion. This process is only applied to those entries representing a demonic, fairy, or vampiric creature. Individual, named, and singular beings from my previous books were not duplicated in this work. Although named individual beings are presented here, they are of a classification I have not previously written about and are not found in my other works.

It was the decision of the publisher, and one I strongly agree with, not to include any pictures in this book. To show a drawing of a creature which does not exist seems innocent enough but I feel otherwise. A drawing is a work of art and the product of the artist's interpretation. The reader is equally able to imagine how a creature would look from the available description.

In the interest of posterity, I attempted to be as accurate as well as succinct as possible with each entry; while some have a longer synopsis of their legends than others, I did my best to uphold all the relevant highlights while maintaining their cultural significance. Additionally, whenever presented with the opportunity to correct a longstanding misconception, I took advantage of it; for instance, it is a popular misconception the god of the Roman underworld is Pluto. In fact, Pluto was a god of wealth (or luck); it was Dis who was the god of the underworld, as is confirmed by the resources I have provided.

My research relied on old, traditional methods of gathering and collecting information. A perfect example is the entry entitled DOGS OF ACTÆON. I happened upon these creatures in a book published in 1833. No other source I found mentions the names let alone the number of hounds in this Greek hero's pack although many mention his adoptive father, the CENTAUR, CHEIRON. Apparently at one point folks knew their names and numbers and no longer saw fit to repeat the information. Time passed and the data was not passed along to future generations; methods of education changed, interest in the matter was lost, and eventually the names and numbers of the dogs were forgotten. Art and sculpture only ever pictured poor Actæon being consumed by one or two of his beloved dogs. But in the huge number of books listed in my bibliography only one had all the names of all the dogs as well as the briefest description for most of them. I felt lucky to have come across this information and included it here. In regards to having entries with only one line of information and one source cited, this is why that happens. These nuggets of information are being lost to us and I am delving through what printed materials are left to discover more before they are gone forever.

The Encyclopedia

Aarvak (AHR-vak)

Variations: Aarak, Aavak, Arvak, Árvak, Arvaka, Arvakr, Árvakr, Avak, Arawker, Arwakr, Hrim Faxi ("frost mane"), Hrimfaxe

Pulling the chariot of the Norse god Sol across the sky, Aarvak ("early awake" or "early waker") and his companion, ALSVID ("fleet one"), were born in Muspellsheim, the divine realm of warmth and brightness; together the team represented the dawn. Magical runes were carved on Aarvak's ears. As the horses pulled the chariot, the shield, Svalin, protected them from the harmful rays of the sun.

Source: Coulter, *Encyclopedia of Ancient Deities*, 5; Grimes, *Norse Myths*, 255; Norroena Society, *Asatrii Edda*, 25; Rose, *Giants, Monsters, and Dragons*, 178

Ab-Esh-Imy-Duat

Variations: AB-SHE, Aken

According to ancient Egyptian mythology, Ab-Esh-Imy-Duat ("to split" or "to wear out the eyes") was a crocodile, monstrous in size and appearance; it was the guardian of the seventh section, or hour, of Tuat, the Underworld. As the sun god Ra passed it by, he would utter a magical spell which would allow him to pass. Then the god Osiris, who lies beneath the ground under Ab-Esh-Imy-Duat, rises up and looks upon Ra as he passes.

Source: Avant, *Mythological Reference*, 143; Coulter, *Encyclopedia of Ancient Deities*, 5, 33; Mercatante, *Who's Who in Egyptian Mythology*, 2

Ab-She

A monstrous crocodile from the mythology of the ancient Egyptians, Ab-She was said to eat the souls of those who became lost in the seventh section, or hour, of Tuat, the Underworld.

Source: Avant, *Mythological Reference*, 143; Mercatante, *Who's Who in Egyptian Mythology*, 2

Ab-Ta

In ancient Egyptian mythology Ab-Ta was a monstrous serpent which guarded the entrance way to the ninth section, or hour, of Tuat, the Underworld. In *The Text of Unas* there is a magical spell which when performed will cause the destruction of monstrous beasts and serpents alike; Ab-Ta would be affected by this spell.

Source: Avant, *Mythological Reference*, 144, Coulter, *Encyclopedia of Ancient Deities*, 32; Mercatante, *Who's Who in Egyptian Mythology*, 2

Ababil

A species of gigantic birds from Korean folklore, the ababil ("flocks") were said to have dropped *sijjil* stones upon the army of elephants sent by the king of Yemen to attack Mecca in the year 571 when Mohammed, the prophet, was born. The ababil are described as having dark feathers, green necks, sharp claws, and yellow beaks.

Source: Matthews, *Element Encyclopedia of Magical Creatures*, 5; Raheem, *Muhammad the Prophet*, 48–49; Zell-Ravenheart, *Wizard's Bestiary*, 14

Abada

Variations: Äbädä

In Tatar mythology the abada is a shy NATURE SPIRIT in the African Congo; it is described as having two small crooked horns which are alleged to be able to be made into a powerful antidote against poisons. Sometimes, in old texts on Indonesia and Malaya mythologies, the abada is likened to a female UNICORN.

Source: Bartlett, *Quarterly Review*, Volume 60, 52; Reade, *Savage Africa*, 373; Rose, *Giants, Monsters, and Dragons*, 1; Zell-Ravenheart, *Wizard's Bestiary*, 14

Abaia

A gigantic eel-like sea creature (see SEA SERPENT) from Melanesian mythology, the lake dwelling abaia is very territorial, fiercely protecting all of the fish in its lake as it considers them its children. Known to cause tidal waves with its tail, the abaia will take the life of anyone who catches a glimpse of it.

Source: Coulter, *Encyclopedia of Ancient Deities*, 6; Hargreaves, *New Illustrated Bestiary*, 43; Rose, *Giants, Monsters, and Dragons*, 2; Zell-Ravenheart, *Wizard's Bestiary*, 14

Abakur

Abakur ("hot one") was one of the favorite warhorses of King Sunna, according to Scandinavian mythology.

Source: Brewer, *Dictionary of Phrase and Fable*, 624

Abas

Abas was a CENTAUR from ancient Greek mythology; he may have been one of the CENTAURS who attended the wedding of Pirithous, became drunk on wine, and following the lead of EURYTUS who assaulted Hippodame, began to assault and rape any woman they could grab. A great Centauromachy then followed. Abas was noted for being an excellent hunter by the Roman poet Ovid (43 BC–AD 17) in his work *Metamorphoses*.

Source: *Commentary, Mythological, Historical, and Geographical on Pope's Homer*, 55; Lemprière, *Classical Dictionary*, 15

Abaster

One of the four black horses of the god of the Underworld, Hades (Dis), from ancient Greek mythology, Abaster ("away from the stars") and his stable mates, ABATOS, AETON, and NOMOS, pulled the god's chariot.

Source: Bell, *Bell's New Pantheon*, 2; Brewer, *Wordsworth Dictionary of Phrase and Fable*, 565; Rubin, *Writer's Companion*, 868; Ruthven, *Shaman Pathways*, n.pag.

Abath

Originating in the Malay Peninsula, the abath was described by the European travelers of the sixteenth century as being a female UNICORN, as it had an alicorn (a single horn), brownish-grey in color and growing from the center of its forehead. This horn was highly coveted as it was believed to be both a powerful antidote against poisons as well as an aphrodisiac.

Source: Markham, *Voyages of Sir James Caldwell to the East Indies*, 14–15; Matthews, *Element Encyclopedia of Magical Creatures*, 6; Rose, *Giants, Monsters, and Dragons*, 2; Zell-Ravenheart, *Wizard's Bestiary*, 15

Abatos

One of the four black horses of the god of the Underworld, Hades (Dis), from ancient Greek mythology, Abatos ("inaccessible") and his stable mates, ABASTER, AETON, and NOMOS, pulled the god's chariot.

Source: Brewer, *Dictionary of Phrase and Fable*, 624; Rubin, *Writer's Companion*, 868; Ruthven, *Shaman Pathways*, n.pag.

Abchanchu

A shape-shifting vampiric creature from Bolivian folklore, the abchanchu preys upon the kindness of strangers. Pretending to be an old man, helpless and lost, it waits for someone to offer their assistance; when opportunity presents itself the creature reveals its true form and attacks. To prevent falling victim to the abchanchu, travelers wear an amulet containing a small amount of garlic oil which will ward it off.

Source: Lavine, *Ghosts the Indians Feared*, 14–15; Maberry, *Vampire Universe*, 1–2

Abdu

Variations: Abtu, Abuk

In ancient Egyptian mythology Abdu and INET were the two fish which swam on either side of the boat of the sun god, Ra; their duty was to chase away any evil being approaching the vessel.

Source: Avant, *Mythological Reference*, 144; Coulter, *Encyclopedia of Ancient Deities*, 9; Mercatante, *Who's Who in Egyptian Mythology*, 2

Abere

Variations: Abele, Obere

From Melanesian folklore comes the singular demonic creature known as Abere ("maiden"). Described as a beautiful young woman as well as a provocative seductress, she is a known cannibal and preys exclusively upon men. Abere will use her feminine guile to lure a man into the lake or swampy region she calls home. Once there, she strips naked and slides into the water, hiding just out of full sight in the mimia reeds; from her hidden position, she calls, enticing the man to follow. If her prey is foolish enough to do so, Abere will stealthily hunt him down, and, using her power over the reeds, will tangle and trap him there, after which she will drown him and consume his flesh. In addition to having control over the water reeds, she also commands several young and nearly as beautiful female companions.

Source: Carlyon, *A Guide to the Gods*, 365; Herdt, *Ritualized Homosexuality in Melanesia*, 284–5; Riesenfeld, *Megalithic Culture of Melanesia*, 469–70; Rose, *Giants, Monsters, and Dragons*, 2; Turner, *Dictionary of Ancient Deities*, 7

Abhac

Variations: Abac, Adanc, Addanc, Addane, Afanc ("beaver"), Avanc

Originating in Welsh folklore and spreading into British, the abhac is a lake monster (see SEA SERPENT) of varying descriptions including a beaver, a crocodile, a demon, and a DWARF. There are also numerous lakes which are alleged to be where the creature lives, such as Llyn Barfog, Llyn Llion, and Llyn yr Afanc. Sources vary in opinion as to whether this is a singular creature or a species of FUATH.

There are various stories regarding the abhac's destruction, as the abhac is powerless when it is out of the water; many of these stories involve a young maiden luring it up onto the lake's shore. One such tale tells how Hu Gadarn used oxen to drag it out of the water and slay it; other tales say it was lured out of the water where it fell asleep on her lap, was bound up in chains, and then either dragged off to Lake Cwm Ffynnon or slain by Peredur.

According to *Llyfr Coch Hergest* (*Red Book of Hergest*), written between 1382–1410, and *Llyfr Gwyn Rhydderch* (*White Book of Rhydderch*), written in 1350, the thrashing of the abhac had once caused massive flooding, which drowned all the original inhabitants of Britain except for Dwyfan and Dwyfach, who went on to found a new race of British people.

Source: Gettings, *Dictionary of Demons*, 21; Lewis, *Gomer's Dictionary for Young People*, 141; McCoy, *Celtic Myth and Magick*, 252

Abiku

Variations: Ogbanje

In Dahomey mythology the abiku ("one who is born, dies") is a type of otherworld being, part human and part spirit, which is locked into a continuous cycle of life, death, and rebirth. This belief is particularly strong in southern Nigeria where it is said the abiku begins the cycle in the spirit world; there, among its companions, it makes a pact to leave the realm but sets a date on which it will return. The abiku enters the world via a woman's womb and is given birth from her; it then lives a short life, willing its own death to happen before the abiku can complete a full and natural life-cycle; the process is then repeated, with the abiku often returning to the world by use of the same mother.

While it is alive in our world, the cantankerous abiku has great power over its parents, who live in constant fear of its too early demise. Typically, this creature is seen as having a mental state somewhere between eccentric and insane as it is often observed having long conversations with its invisible spirit companions. Prone to fights and unpredictable behavior, this creature is also perennially sick and in need of ongoing medical attention. Should the creature die within days of its birth the body must be whipped into a mutilated condition in order to prevent it from returning—especially to the same mother.

It is possible to sever the link the abiku has with the spirit world and permanently bind it to its earthly home if its magic token is found and destroyed; this item is said to be buried in a secret location in a remote area. Another method is to find the abiku's "sealed words," its secret oath containing the circumstances, method, and time of its return

to the spirit world. If a *babalawo* (witch doctor) can discover this item, he will be able to break the abiku of its death wish. There are some tales of an abiku choosing to break its own sacred oath in order to remain in the world of the living; when this occurs its spirit world companions will try to lure it back, first by means of persuasion and then by force.

The West African Yoruba translation for abiku means "children born of the spirit world" or "ancestral soul being reborn" (see ANCESTRAL SPIRIT). Here, the belief is that an abiko is the returning soul of a child who died prematurely. Mothers will cut a notch in the ear of a child so if it should die they will have an easier time finding it upon its return.

Source: Falola, *Historical Dictionary of Nigeria*, 4; Lim, *Infinite Longing for Home*, 63–4; Matthews, *Element Encyclopedia of Magical Creatures*, 2

Abonsam

Vampiric creatures living along the African coast, the abonsam come inland at night to prey upon crabs but are said to occasionally supplement their diet by attacking sleeping children, men, and women; when this occurs, the creature inadvertently infects them with a "wasting" disease. Those afflicted by the abonsam will slowly waste away unless they visit a witch doctor for a charm which will ward the creature off from its nightly visits. A fire is lit in the room of the ill person and as the embers die out, they are mixed with a special medicine during a special ceremony. The air has now been made putrid to the senses of the abonsam forcing the creature to return to its usual food source, crabs, allowing the victim to safely recover.

The abonsam is described as looking exactly like a normal and typical person from the village so long as it keeps its skin on; when one of these creatures is discovered, one is advised to wait until it has removed its skin and departed for its nightly feeding or orgy; then slather the hide with ground red chili peppers. When the abonsam returns and tries to don its skin, the pepper will prove to be too much of an irritant, forcing the creature to abandon its pelt and flee the village.

Source: Freeman, *Travels and Life in Ashanti and Jaman*, 291–93; Jordan, *Dictionary of Gods and Goddesses*, 2

Aboulomri

Variations: Ak-Baba, KERKES

In Muslim mythology, the aboulomri is a bird, comparable in appearance to a vulture, which has the ability to live for 1,000 years; it is similar to the PHOENIX and the ROC.

Source: Stewart, *Dictionary of Images and Symbols in Counselling*, 16

Abraxas

Variations: Therbeeo

In ancient Greek mythology, Abraxas, one of the HIPPOI ATHANATOI, was one of the four immortal horses belonging to the god of the sun and second generation Titan, Helios (Sol), pulling his chariot, Quadriga, across the sky.

Source: Brewer, *Dictionary of Phrase and Fable*, 624; Gemondo, *Animal Totems*, 60

Abzu (AB-zoe)

Variations: APSU, Apsû, Engur

In the Babylonian creation epic, *Enuma Elish* (twelfth-century BC), Abzu was a primal demonic creature made up of freshwater; he was the lover of TIAMAT, a creature of saltwater. Abzu was the demon of semen, wisdom, and the Watery Abyss, a vast freshwater ocean beneath the earth which served as the source of all lakes, rivers, springs, streams, and wells.

Source: Black, *Gods, Demons, and Symbols of Ancient Mesopotamia*, 34, 57, 134; Bossieu, *Academy, Issue 14*, 13–14; Cunningham, *Deliver me from Evil*, 11–2, 38; Sorensen, *Possession and Exorcism in the New Testament and Early Christianity*, 27–8

Achlis

Described by Pliny the Elder, the Roman author, natural philosopher, naturalist, and army and naval commander in his work, *Natural History* (AD 77), the achlis was styled as being elk-like in appearance; it was said to have such an extensive upper lip that it forced the creature to graze while walking backward least it crop back into its own mouth. Although it was said to be rather "fleet of foot" the achlis lacked joints in its hindquarters which prevented it from being able to lie down; because of this anomaly, it was necessary for this animal to lean against a tree at night while it slept.

Source: Jennison, *Animals for Show and Pleasure in Ancient Rome*, 188; Matthews, *Element Encyclopedia of Magical Creatures*, 7; Rose, *Giants, Monsters, and Dragons*, 3; Zell-Ravenheart, *Wizard's Bestiary*, 15

Acipenser

Medieval fishing tales of the North sea describe a gigantic fish called an acipenser; its scales faced in the opposite direction, turned toward its head; this unique abnormality caused it to swim slowly but because it was so large, no one was ever able to catch one.

Source: Hulme, *Myth-land*, 158; Matthews, *Element Encyclopedia of Magical Creatures*, 7; Zell-Ravenheart, *Wizard's Bestiary*, 15

Actaeon (Ak-tigh-on)

Variations: Actæon

One of the many winged horses from the classical mythology of the ancient Greeks and Romans, Actaeon ("effulgence") was one of the horses which pulled the golden chariot Quadriga, made by Hephaistos (Vulcan) for the sun god and second generation Titan, Helios (Sol). Like the other horses on his team, Actaeon was of the purest white and had flared nostrils from which he could breathe fire. Each morning the Horae—nymphs of time—would harness up the team. At dusk, the horses grazed upon magical herbs which grew on the island of the Blessed.

Source: Berens, *Myths and Legends of Ancient Greece and Rome*, 91; Matthews, *Element Encyclopedia of Magical Creatures*, 8; Rose, *Giants, Monsters, and Dragons*, 7

Acthon

Variations: Aethon

According to the Roman poet Ovid (43 BC–AD 17), Acthon, EOUS, PHLEGON, and PYROIS are the horses harnessed to the chariot pulling the sun across the heavens.

Source: Hargreaves, *Hargreaves New Illustrated Bestiary*, 67; Matthews, *Element Encyclopedia of Magical Creatures*, 8; Rose, *Giants, Monsters, and Dragons*, 7

Adar Llwch Gwin

Similar to the GRIFFIN, the adar llwch gwin of Welsh folklore were fierce, gigantic, magical birds with the ability to perfectly understand human speech and to do exactly as their master commanded. These birds were given as a gift to the cultural hero Drudwas ap Tryffin by his fairy wife. According to the folklore, Drudwas ap Tryffin took the adar llwch gwin with him on the day he went to do battle against King Arthur, giving his birds the command "kill the first man to enter the battle." The king was delayed and the birds—being perfectly obedient—followed their orders, tearing their master to pieces. In medieval poetry, the adar llwch gwin were described as being brave men, falcons, and hawks.

Source: Matson, *Celtic Mythology A to Z*, 46; Matthews, *Element Encyclopedia of Magical Creatures*, 8; Zell-Ravenheart, *Wizard's Bestiary*, 15

Adaro

A species of malevolent SEA SERPENT or NATURE SPIRIT from Polynesian mythology, the adaro actually lived in the sun and came to earth by traveling down rainbows. These beings were described as looking like men with gills behind their ears, a horn like a shark fin, a pike on their head like a sword fish or sawfish, and tail-fins for feet. Unlike MERMAIDS, adaro were always dangerous to mankind, shooting them with flying fish and causing at least unconsciousness if they successfully struck their target. If a flying fox is immediately thrown into the water after an assault, the act will magically awaken the person rendered unconscious and give the would-be victim temporary immunity from further assaults. It is believed an adaro is created when the evil part of a man's soul lingers on after his death. The chief of the adaro, NGORIERU, lives off the San Cristobal coast.

Source: Andrews, *Dictionary of Nature Myths*, 4; Avant, *Mythological Reference*, 413; Parker, *Mythology*, 374; Zell-Ravenheart, *Wizard's Bestiary*, 15

Aderyn y Corph

Variations: Corpse Bird, Derwyn Corph

In Welsh folklore the aderyn y corph was a bird whose appearance was considered to be a psychopomp (death omen). Tradition says it chirps at the door of a person who is about to die; its cry sounds like the Welsh word for "come," *dewch*. In the most ancient version of this folklore, the aderyn y corph has no feathers or wings but still has the ability of flight. When not upon the earth, this creature lived in Cymry Fu, the land of fantasy and illusions.

Source: Sikes, *British Goblins*, 212–13; Spurrell, *Dictionary of the Welsh Language*, 4; Williams, *Collections Historical and Archaeological Relating to Montgomeryshire*, Volume 22, 327

Al Adha

The swiftest camel belonging to the Muslim prophet Mahomet, al Adha ("the slit-eared") was said to have made the journey from Jerusalem to Meca in four bounds. As a reward for this miraculously quick journey, al Adha was given the promise of a place in Heaven; there the animal would be joined with BORAK, the prophet's horse, the ASS OF BALAAM, the dog of Tobit, and KATMIR, the dog of the seven sleepers. In all, ten animals were allowed to enter into Muslim Paradise.

Source: Brewer, *Dictionary of Phrase and Fable*, 12, 205; Brewer, *Character Sketches of Romance, Fiction and the Drama*, Volumes 5–6, 377; Irving, *Life of Mahomet*, 176

Adhunall

In Irish mythology Adhunall was a FAIRY ANIMAL, one of the many hunting dogs of the cultural hero Finn Mac Cumhaill; his other dogs were BRAN, LUATH LUCHAR, SCEOLAN, and SEAR DUGH.

Source: Gregory, *Gods and Fighting Men*, 238, 398; Monaghan, *Encyclopedia of Celtic Mythology and Folklore*, 3

Adissechen (d-dts'i-ken)

Variations: Adis'sechen

A thousand-headed serpent of Hindu mythology, Adissechen was used as a gigantic rope around the Mandriguiri Mountain so the gods could churn the Sea of Milk. When Adissechen's body could no longer take the abuse, he expired, fire shooting out of his eyes, his thousand mouths hissing so loudly as to shake the earth, his tongues hung black and pulsated, and he vomited forth copious amounts of poison. The god Vishnu rubbed his body with the poison, dyeing his flesh blue.

Source: Hulme, *Myth-land*, 146; Southey, *Southey's Common-place Book*, Volume 4, 250

Adro

In Lugbaran mythology, the epitome of all evil and the master of witches and wizards, for the people who live in the West Nile region of Uganda. Adro is an *onzi* ("bad") earth NATURE SPIRIT which separated itself from the *onyiru* ("good") Adroa Ba' during the creation of the earth. Adro appears as a whirlwind and its cries can be heard during grass fires. Having the ability to cause illness and possess young women, it will also kidnap and consume people. Oftentimes Adro will take on the appearance of a pale or translucent humanlike being which has torn its own body in half vertically. Its offspring, the ADROANZI (water snakes), drown and eat people.

Source: Asante, *Encyclopedia of African Religion*, Volume 1, 344; Jones, *Evil in Our Midst*, 147; Lynch *African Mythology, A to Z*, 4, 121

The Adroanzi

Variations: Adro Onzi ("bad god")

In Lugbaran mythology there is a race of snake creatures called the Adroanzi. Born the offspring of the evil earth spirit, ADRO, the Adroanzi, found in streams, trees, and near rocks, easily pass themselves off as common water snakes but are aggressive about attacking and consuming people. When the Adroanzi hunt at night, they appear as a human, walk up behind their intended victim, and attack the moment the intended prey steals a glance over their shoulder; so long as their prey walks fearlessly ahead they are safe from the Adroanzi.

Source: Chopra, *Academic Dictionary of Mythology*, 10; Cotterell, *Dictionary of World Mythology*, 239; Lynch *African Mythology, A to Z*, 4

Aegipanes

Variations: Panes, Paniski

Minor forest beings or NATURE SPIRITS in the mythology of the ancient Greeks, the aegipanes were the loyal goat-footed followers of the god Pan (Faunus). In some texts, it was only the females of the species which were referred to as paniski.

Source: Avant, *Mythological Reference*, 210; Bennett, *Gods and Religions of Ancient and Modern Times*, Volume 2, 77; Murray, *Manual of Mythology*, 137, 139

Aello

Variations: Ællo

A dog from ancient Greek mythology, Aello ("rainstorm," "storm wind," stormy," "squall," or "whirlwind") was one of the DOGS OF ACTÆON, the unfortunate youth who was raised by the CENTAUR, CHEIRON. Aello was a noted stout runner.

Source: Leeming, *World of Myth*, 111; Murray, *Classical Manual*, 160; Naso, *Fasti, Tristia*, 93–5

Aeternae

Variations: Aeternae

The collective name for the animals said to have inhabited the northern plains of India during the fourth century, BC, the aeternae were described as having a saw-edged bonelike protrusion jutting out from the center of their forehead, a weapon they used to attack with. It is said that several of the soldiers in the army of Alexander the Great were slain by the aeternae when they were provoked to attack.

Source: Barber, *Dictionary of Fabulous Beasts*, n.pag.; Rose, *Giants, Monsters, and Dragons*, 4; Zell-Ravenheart, *Wizard's Bestiary*, 15

Aethenoth

Aethenoth ("noble audacity") was, according to folklore, the name of the horse Lady Godiva (Godgifu) rode upon while naked through the town of Coventry.

Source: Hartston, *Encyclopedia of Useless Information*, 159

Aethiops (e-thi-o-pes)

In classical Greek and Roman mythology Aethiops was one of the many winged horses belonging to Helios (Sol) which assisted in pulling the sun across the sky. According to Apollodorus, Aethiops and EOUS were stallions and the trace horses (the outside horse on a chariot team in which more than two horses are driven abreast); Aethiops, like a flame, was said to cause the grain to ripen as he flew through the sky.

Source: Apollodorus, *Apollodorus' Library and Hyginus' Fabulae*, 158; Parada, *Genealogical Guide to Greek Mythology*, 35; Rose, *Giants, Monsters, and Dragons*, 178

Aethlem

In Arthurian folklore, Aethlem was one of the many hounds accompanying King Arthur on the quest to hunt the boar TWRCH TRWYTH; however, it was only one of three dogs which were required to be present by a special condition placed by the GIANT Ysbaddaden as he was trying to make obtaining the object as difficult as possible for Cylhwch (see ANED, and DRUDWYN). It was part of the provision that a special handler was to be obtained for Aethlem— Cynedyr the Wild—which the King eventually had to provide. Aethlem had a reputation for never failing to kill an animal it was set upon; no leash in the world could hold him at bay unless it was made from the beard hairs of Dissul, son of Eurei, the bearded GIANT. The hunt ended when AETHLEM and Aned chased TWRCH TRWYTH into the ocean and into the Underworld, never to be seen again.

Source: Bruce, *Arthurian Name Dictionary*, 5, 137, 477; Ellis, *Celtic Myths and Legends*, 385, 395

Aethon

Variations: Æthon

Throughout ancient Greek and Roman mythology, Aethon ("blazing," "burning," "fiery red" or "shining") was an epithet applied to many animals, mostly horses as it denoted a reddish-brown or tawny color.

In Virgil's epic Latin poem, *Aeneid*, the warhorse pulling the blood-stained chariot of Pallas was called Aethon, denoting the animal's fiery spirit.

In the Latin narrative poem *Metamorphoses* (2.153) written by the Roman poet Ovid, the sun god and second generation Titan, Helios (Sol), had his golden chariot, Quadriga, pulled across the sky by the flying horses Aethon, ASTROPE, BRONTE, CHRONOS, EOUS, LAMPON, PHAETHON, PHLEGON, and PYROIS. All of these horses are described as being pure white and having flaring nostrils which can breathe forth flame, and they were counted among the HIPPOI ATHANATOI.

Source: Breese, *God's Steed*, 86; Guirand, *Larousse Encyclopedia of Mythology*, 160; Paschalis, *Virgil's Aeneid*, 371

Aeton

Variations: Æton, A'eton

One of the four black horses of the god of the Underworld, Hades (Dis), from ancient Greek mythology, Aeton ("swift as an eagle") and his stable mates, ABATOS, ABASTER, and NOMOS, pulled the god's chariot.

Source: Brewer, *Wordsworth Dictionary of Phrase and Fable*, 565; Rubin, *Writer's Companion*, 868; Ruthven, *Shaman Pathways*, n.pag.

Afrasiab (Ah-FRAS-ee-abh)

Variations: Afra-Sia-Ab ("past the black river"), Afrosiyob, Alp Er Tonga ("courageous tiger man"), Efrasiyab

Afrasiab is the name of a Scythian, demonic creature which looks like a snake. It is also the name of an ancient city, several historical hero-kings, and a tribe of ancient people.

Source: Bonnefoy, *Asian Mythologies*, 324, 337; Carus, *History of the Devil and the Idea of Evil*, 53; Johnson, *Dictator and the Devil*, 304

Agdistis

Variations: Acdestis, Cybele, Kubba, Kubile, Kybele

A monster from the mythology of ancient Phrygia and Sumeria, the monstrous and hermaphroditic Agdistis ("she of the rock") was dangerously wild and uncontrollable. One day while bathing in his pool, Agdistis was drugged with wine by the gods and while he slept had his genitals tied to a tree. Awaking with a start, he castrated himself. In the Greek version of this tale, it is said a pomegranate tree grew up from the remnants of his genitals while in other versions, it was said to be an almond tree. After his castration, Agdistis became known as the goddess Cybele.

Source: Chopra, *Academic Dictionary of Mythology*, 12; Daly, *Greek and Roman Mythology, A to Z*, 39; Edwards, *Cambridge Ancient History*, Volumes 1–4, 435–36

Aghasura

Variations: Agha the Asura

Aghasura was the gigantic serpent form assumed by the demon Agha in Hindu folklore. Sent by Kasna to Gokula to kill Krishna and his companions, this KRAVYAD shape-shifted himself into a boa-constrictor of monstrous size, four *yojanas* long. Krishna and his cowherds mistook his open mouth for a cave entrance and entered it, but fortunately Kasna detected the trap and stretched himself out, blocking Aghasura's throat and choking him to death.

The measure of a single *yojanas* has never been clear; some scholars say it is approximately four and a half miles while other say it ranges between seven and nine miles.

Source: Dowson, *Classical Dictionary of Hindu Mythology and Religion, Geography, History, and Literature*, 6; Garg, *Encyclopaedia of the Hindu World*, Volume 1, 207

Agloolik

A NATURE SPIRIT from Inuit mythology, Agloolik lived beneath the ice; when properly prayed to, he would give his assistance to fishermen and lead hunters to seal holes.

Source: Andrews, *Dictionary of Nature Myths*, 14; Bilby, *Among Unknown Eskimo*, 72; Drew, *Wiccan Bible*, 278; Rose, *Spirits, Fairies, Gnomes, and Goblins*, 5

Agre

A dog from ancient Greek mythology, Agre ("catcher") was one of the DOGS OF ACTÆON, the unfortunate youth who was raised by the CENTAUR, CHEIRON. Agre was noted for her keen sense of smell.

Source: Leeming, *World of Myth*, 111; Murray, *Classical Manual*, 160; Naso, *Fasti, Tristia*, 93–5

Agriodus

A dog from ancient Greek mythology, Agriodus ("wild tooth") was one of the DOGS OF ACTÆON,

the unfortunate youth who was raised by the CENTAUR, CHEIRON. Agriodus was cross-bred of a Cretan mother and a Spartan father, just like fellow pack member LEBROS.

Source: Leeming, *World of Myth*, 111; Murray, *Classical Manual*, 160; Naso, *Fasti, Tristia*, 93–5

Agriogourouno   (Ah-ghree-oh-GHOO-roo-no)

In Macedonian folklore it is believed Turkish people who have led very wicked lives and have never eaten pork will become an agriogourouno ("wild boar") upon death. As much a WERE-CREATURE as a vampire, this shape-shifting being is well known for its gluttonous appetite for human blood.

Source: Holton, *Greek*, 247; Jackson, *Compleat Vampyre*, 56

Ahi

Variations: Vitra, Vritra ("enclose"), Vrtra

In Hindu mythology Ahi was a gigantic serpent or drought-DRAGON slain by Trita, an early god of war who was later replaced with the god Indra. According to the story, Ahi was so large he was capable of drinking all the water of the earth, and after doing so, curled himself up around the peaks of a mountain to sleep. While Ahi slept, Trita (or Indra depending on the age of the story) came upon the sleeping creature and slew it with his devastating thunderbolts, releasing the water, and restoring fertility and life to the world.

Source: Conway, *Barons of the Potomack and the Rappahannock*, 191; Matthews, *Element Encyclopedia of Magical Creatures*, 11; Skyes, *Who's Who in Non-Classical Mythology*, 4

Ahool

A bat-like creature from the folklore of the people of western Java, the ahool is said to fly through the sky on wings some twelve feet across. Described as having simian-like (monkey-like) head, a dark-grey fur covered body, large dark eyes, and claw-tipped wings, the typically timid ahool hunts and feeds off of fish and small game. These creatures are believed to live behind waterfalls and were named onomatopoeically after the sound of their call, "ahool, ahool, ahool!"

Source: Eberhart, *Mysterious Creatures*, 7; Maberry, *Vampire Universe*, 11; Shuker, *Beasts That Hide from Man*, 86–7; Zell-Ravenheart, *Wizard's Bestiary*, 15–6

Ahuitazotl

Variations: Ahuizotl, Ahuitzotl, Sun Dog

In ancient Aztec Mexican folklore, Ahuitazotl ("water monster," "water possum") was described as being about the size of a teui dog, having slick and slippery black skin, a human hand on the tip of its tail, prehensile fingers, small pointed ears, and a simian face. This creature would lie in wait just below the surface of the water, waving its hand-like tail breaking the water's surface in the hope of luring a person to the bank of the river. When its tail was grabbed, the ahuitazotl would pull the victim into the water, drowning them. Three days later the body would surface missing its eyes, nails, and teeth, the only parts the ahuitazotl consumes.

Source: Austin, *Tamoanchan, Tlalocan*, 34; Bahr, *Collier's Encyclopedia* Volume 16, 479; Rosen, *Mythical Creatures Bible*, 113; Zell-Ravenheart, *Wizard's Bestiary*, 16

Äi

An äi was a class of DRAGON or serpent living in the forests and woods in the folklore of southern Estonia; they are said to cause and spread disease.

Source: De Kirk, *Dragonlore*, 38; Rose, *Giants, Monsters, and Dragons*, 8

Ai Tojon

From the mythology of the Yakuts people who live along the Lena River in Serbia, the ai tojon is described as being a gigantic two-headed eagle living atop the teetering world tree where he spreads sunlight.

Source: Matthews, *Element Encyclopedia of Magical Creatures*, 12; Rose, *Giants, Monsters, and Dragons*, 8; Zell-Ravenheart, *Wizard's Bestiary*, 16

Aiatar

Variations: Ajatar, Ajattarais, Ajattaro

From Finnish folklore, the Aiatar ("devil of the woods") is an evil, female forest NATURE SPIRIT taking the form of a DRAGON. Its children assume the form of small snakes and can cause illness to anyone who looks upon them.

Source: De Kirk, *Dragonlore*, 38; Matthews, *Element Encyclopedia of Magical Creatures*, 12; Rose, *Spirits, Fairies, Leprechauns, and Goblins*, 6

Aicha Kandida

A DJINN from Moroccan folklore, Aicha Kandida, wife to HAMOU UKAIOU, is said to live in and around the banks of the Sebu River near Marrakech; she is also said to wander the sultan's palace grounds. Assuming the form of a beautiful woman this creature will approach men who are traveling alone at night, calling them by name. Aicha Kandida hates mankind and takes delight in drowning her prey; however, it is said that if a man can sexually gratify her, she sets him free laden down with gifts.

Source: Legey, *Folklore of Morocco*, 73; Matthews, *Element Encyclopedia of Magical Creatures*, 12–13; Rose, *Spirits, Fairies, Leprechauns, and Goblins*, 6

Aigikampoi

Variations: Aigicampoi, Aigokeros, Capricorn, CAPRICORNUS

Although used in the art of the ancient Greeks, the aigikampoi was a creature from the folklore of the ancient Etruscans; it was described as having the forequarters of a goat and the hind-section of a dolphin or fish.

Source: Breverton, *Breverton's Phantasmagoria*, n.pag.; Cook, *God of the Dark Sky*, 938; Robertson, *Christianity and Mythology*, 348

Aillen Trechenn

A three-headed monster from Irish folklore, Aillen Trechenn ("triple-headed Aillen") hated all of humanity but would regularly attack the regional capital of Emain Macha in Ulster as it particularly despised its warriors. Stories vary as to the gender of the monster but it is consistently said to live in a cave named Oweynagat, which was located in the Connacht capital of Cruachan. Aillen Trechenn was eventually slain by the poet Amairgin.

Source: Matthews, *Element Encyclopedia of Magical Creatures*, 14; Monaghan, *Encyclopedia of Celtic Mythology and Folklore*, 10; Rose, *Giants, Monsters, and Dragons*, 9; Zell-Ravenheart, *Wizard's Bestiary*, 16

Airapadam

Variations: Aïrapadam

A white elephant from Hindu mythology, Airapadam is one of the eight elephants who support the earth and protect the eight zones of the universe; he is responsible for the eastern zone. Airapadam is depicted on the side of temples to Vishnu as having four tusks and being lavishly decorated.

Source: Balfour, *Cyclopædia of India and of Eastern and Southern Asia*, Volume 1, 60; Brewer, *Dictionary of Phrase and Fable*, 25

Airavat

Variations: Airavana, Airavata ("a fine elephant"), Airavati, Ardha-Matanga ("elephant of the clouds"), Arkasodara ("brother of the sun"), Iravat ("produced from water"), Naga-malla ("fighting elephant"), Sada-Dana ("always in rut"), Madambara ("covered in ichor")

Created at the Churning of the Ocean, the winged white elephant Airavat was appropriated by the god Indra as his *vahan* ("vehicle"). As the king of the elephants, he was born the son of Kasyapa and his wife Kadru. He was also one of the DIGGAJAS, guardians of the eight points of the compass—he protected the East. The name of Airavat's wife was Abhramu.

Airavata is a much used name in Hindu folklore. Originally, Airavata ("son of Iravat") was a snake demon in Hindu mythology; however, he later became known as the elephant of the god Indra.

Another Airavata was a demon slain by Krsna. It is also the name of a land as well as an architectural term used to describe a five-story building.

Source: Balfour, *Cyclopædia of India and of Eastern and Southern Asia*, Volume 1, 60; Dowson, *Classical Dictionary of Hindu Mythology and Religion*, 9, 127; Garg, *Encyclopaedia of the Hindu World*, Volume 1, 256

Airitech

In the folklore of the Goidelic Celts Airitech was a creature from the Otherworld with three beautiful lycanthrope daughters; at will or by their father's bidding, they could shape-shift into vicious werewolves killing sheep (see WEREWOLF). The daughters lived in Cave Cruachan which, presumably, had an opening into the Otherworld.

The bard and cultural hero Cas Corach, son of Caincinde, played a tune on his harp so sweet it lulled the sisters into a stupor; while in this altered state, Cas Corach slew the daughters of Airitech, running them through their breasts with his spear and beheading the bodies.

Source: Maberry, *They Bite*, 180; Stokes, *Acallamh na Seanórach Acallamh na Senórach*, Volume 4, 264–66

Aithe

In the ancient Greek epic poem, the *Iliad* ("Song of Ilion") (1240 BC), attributed to Homer, Aithe was the mare ridden by Agamemnon; she was given to him by Ankhises's son, Ekhepolos, and was described as being swift and having a fair mane.

Source: *Contemporary Review*, Volume 27, 810; Homer, *Iliad of Homer*, 485, 492

Aithon

One of the HIPPOI ATHANATOI, this fire-breathing horse from the mythology of the ancient Romans, Aithon ("fire"), belonged to Ares (Mars), the god of war; his stable mates were CONABOS ("tumult"), PHLOGIOS ("flame"), and PHOBOS ("terror"). According to the ancient Greek epic poem, the *Iliad* ("Song of Ilion") (1240 BC), attributed to Homer, Aithon was the mount of Hector, the foremost Trojan warrior.

Source: *Contemporary Review*, Volume 27, 810; Coulter, *Encyclopedia of Ancient Deities*, dccxv; Gemondo, *Animal Totems*, 60

Aithops

One of the fire-breathing horses from the mythology of the ancient Romans as well as one of the HIPPOI ATHANATOI, Aithops ("blazing") belonged to Ares (Mars), the god of war. According to the Roman poet Ovid (43 BC–AD 17), Aithops,

along with EOUS, PHLEGON, and PYROIS, were the winged horses harnessed to the chariot pulling the sun across the heavens.

Source: Cook, *Zeus*, 195; Hard, *Routledge Handbook of Greek Mythology*, 45; Rose, *Handbook of Greek Mythology*, 25

Aitvaras

Variations: Altviksas, Damavikas ("HOUSE-SPIRIT"), Damvaykas, Gausinelis, KAUKAS, Pisuhand, Koklikas, Pukis ("DRAGON" or a toy kite), Puuk, Spay-ius, Spirukas, Tulihand

In Lithuania, prior to the introduction of Christianity, Aitvaras was a NATURE SPIRIT living in the sky or in the woods. It was said when it flew through the night sky, it looked like a meteorite. Aitvaras was once considered to be a noble and divine being regulating human wealth and relations. However, under the influence of Christianity, the aitvaras was demonized and used as an antagonist in parables regarding ambition and greed. The aitvaras became a type of demonic creature under the command of the Devil himself. It would make a nest for itself behind the stove and once it claimed a place as a home, it was very difficult to remove.

Now as demonic creature it is often made into a FAMILIAR who is either given to a person by the Devil in exchange for their soul, or was patiently hatched from a seven-year-old rooster egg. If the aitvaras is given as a FAMILIAR, it will provide its master with the corn, milk, and money it steals from people.

When indoors aitvaras are described as looking like a black cat or black rooster; when outside they take on the appearance of a fiery snake or flying DRAGON. They have the ability to heal themselves by touching earth. Infernal, immortal creatures, the aitvaras cannot be destroyed but can be prevented from attack by leaving offerings of food (they are partial to eating omelets).

Source: DePorte, *Lithuanaia in the Last 30 Years*, 409; Grimal, *Larousse World Mythology*, 421; Icon, *Demons*, 136; Larson, *Myth in Indo-European Antiquity*, 89; Zell-Ravenheart, *Wizard's Bestiary*, 16

Aja Akapad

Variations: Aja Ekapad

In Hindu mythology Aja Akapad ("he who has one foot") was a lightning fast one-legged goat; it was the personification of the force of lightning, striking the earth with a single kick.

Source: Macdonell, *Vedic Mythology*, 73, 151; Zell-Ravenheart, *Wizard's Bestiary*, 16

Ak-Kula

In Turkic mythology Ak-Kula ("light Isabel") the TULPAR (winged horse) was utilized by the hero

Manas; it was described as being similar in appearance to a PEGASUS and was conceived by its mother on a foggy, moonless night sired by a racing whirlwind. Ak-Kula was said to have been slain in a battle against Chinese forces.

Source: Hainsworth, *Traditions of Heroic and Epic Poetry*, 76, 102; Kruger, *Uralic and Altaic Series*, Volume 111, 76–7

Akaname (AH-kah-NAH-may)

Variations: Bathtub Licker

The akaname ("filth licker" or "red licker"), a YŌKAI of Japanese folklore, is a hideous looking monster having long tangled hair, a long pointed tongue, and unnaturally red skin. Although traditionally these creatures are only interested in consuming the mildew, mold, and slime from bathtubs and the rooms they are located in, modern tales claim their tongue is coated in poison and leaves behind a residue which will cause both cancer and pneumonia. The akaname is the personification of the fear of using an unlit bathroom late at night; traditionally Japanese homes have one room for their toilet and another for their tub. Some tales claim the akaname are afraid of badgers, but there are even fewer tales of anyone keeping a badger in their bathroom to ward them away.

Source: Frater, *Com's Ultimate Book of Bizarre Lists*, 533; Maberry, *Cryptopedia*, 227; Yoda, *Yokai Attack*, 86–9

Akandoji (äh-kän-dōj)

In the Japanese fairy tale "Momotaro, the Little Peachling," the hero, Momotaro ("little peachling"), decided to cross over to the Island of the Devils and take their treasures as his own. There he confronted the chief of the spirits, Akandoji. Moimotaro grappled the spirit to the ground and defeated it soundly, binding it up tightly with rope, and held it until Akandoji agreed to surrender his treasury. Once Momotaro left the island to return home with his winnings, the devils, OGRES, and spirits of the island took up Akandoji and threw him into the ocean where he then drowned.

Source: Antropov, *Fairy tales*, Volume 4874, 52–54; Mabie, *Young Folks' Treasury*, 431–32; Williston, *Japanese Fairy Tales*, 73

Akeneh

Akeneh was a demonic-like serpent mentioned in a magical formula written by the ancient Egyptian king Unas; he ruled during the fifth dynasty BC (2450–2290, Old Kingdom).

Source: Avant, *Mythological Reference*, 145; Mercatante, *Who's Who in Egyptian Mythology*, 4

Akerbeltz

Originally worshiped as a god by witches in the sixteenth and seventeenth centuries, Akerbeltz ("black billy-goat") is in Basque folklore the representative of the god Mari. Portrayed as a black male goat, Akerbeltz was a protector of animals; oftentimes a black goat was kept on a farm to protect the stock from sickness and plague.

Source: Lurker, *Dictionary of Gods and Goddesses, Devils and Demons*, 7; Miguel de Barandiarán, *Selected Writings of José Miguel De Barandiarán*, 107–08

Akhekh

Regarded as a form of the evil god Set from the mythology of the ancient Egyptians, Akhekh was described as a GRIFFIN-like chimerical creature; it had the body of an antelope, wings, and the head of a bird upon which three *uraeu* (cobras) sat.

Source: Coulter, *Encyclopedia of Ancient Deities*, 33; Mercatante, *Who's Who in Egyptian Mythology*, 4; Remler, *Egyptian Mythology, A to Z*, 5

Akhekhu

A species of DRAGON from ancient Egyptian mythology, the four-legged, serpentine, and wingless akhekhu were considered to be semi-divine beings; they are mentioned in the *Egyptian Book of the Dead*, chapter XCVIII.

Source: Davis, *Egyptian Book of the Dead*, 121; De Kirk, *Dragonlore*, 56; Hargreaves, *Hargreaves New Illustrated Bestiary*, 57; Zell-Ravenheart, *Wizard's Bestiary*, 16

Akhen

Variations: AB-ESH-IMY-DUAT, AB-SHE

Guarding the entrance to the seventh section, or hour, of Tuat, the Underworld, according to the mythology of the ancient Egyptians, was the monstrous serpent Akhen ("to split" or "to wear out the eyes"). In *The Text of Unas* there is a magical spell which when performed will cause the destruction of monstrous beasts and serpents alike; Akhen would be affected by this spell.

Source: Avant, *Mythological Reference*, 145; Coulter, *Encyclopedia of Ancient Deities*, 32, 33; Mercatante, *Who's Who in Egyptian Mythology*, 4

Akhlut

In the folklore of the Inuit Yup'ik people, Akhlut is a vicious orca who has the ability of therianthropy, enabling it to shape-shift into the form of a wolf; in doing so, it would then hunt on land for both animals and people. Akhlut's tracks can be differentiated from other wolf tracks because the paw prints it leaves in the snow lead directly up to the water's edge and then disappear, presumably having entered into the Bering Sea.

Source: Haksteen, *Searching for Power*, 25; Lynch, *Native American Mythology A to Z*, 3; Stookey, *Thematic Guide to World Mythology*, 13

Akkorokamui

In the seas off the coast of Hokkaido in Northern Japan, the mythological SEA SERPENT, Akkorokamui, has been blamed for attacking small fishing boats for generations. This gigantic fish, octopus, or squid is described as being bright red in color and as long as 360 feet (110 meters).

Source: Steiger, *Real Monsters, Gruesome Critters, and Beasts from the Darkside*, 273

Aksar

A fierce and gigantic python from Greek folklore appearing in many medieval bestiaries, Aksar was said to be sixty cubits long and had once terrified Moses.

Source: Flaubert, *Temptation of St. Anthony*, 255; Gilmore, *Monsters*, 40

Akupara

Variations: Father of All Turtles, Kurma

According to Hindu mythology, Akupara is the name of the gigantic, immortal king of the tortoises who lives in Lake Indradyumna in the Himalayas; upon his back, the earth rests, the carapace of its shell is the vault of the sky, and its plastron is the foundation of the earth. During the Churning of the Ocean, Kurma dove to the bottom of the sea to support the mountain the gods were using as a dash (or churning tool). The story of how this cosmic turtle recognized the reincarnated King Indradyumna is told in the *Mahabharata*.

Source: Buitenen, *Mahabharata*, Volume 2: Book 2, 606; Garg, *Encyclopaedia of the Hindu World*, Volume 1, 314; Rose, *Giants, Monsters, and Dragons*, 11

Al

Variations: Elk

A race of hairy anthropoids of Armenian, Libyan, and Persian folklore, the Al were described as having boar-like tusks protruding from their mouths, brass claws, fiery eyes, iron teeth, and shaggy serpentine hair; they lived in dark and damp places such as in the corners of stables, wet houses, and swamps. The Al, one of the KHRAFSTRA, attack humans who enter into their territory; they are especially fond of women who are incapacitated by childbirth as infants are their favorite food; they are even said to carry scissors on them to cut the umbilical cord. The Al will also steal the woman's liver and consume the organ once it has returned to the safety of its lair.

In the folklore of Afghanistan the Al is said to be a GHUL-like female creature, having long floating hair and talons for fingernails; they consume human corpses.

Source: Zell-Ravenheart, *Wizard's Bestiary*, 16

Ala

In Mesopotamian demonology an ala is a nocturnal demonic creature. Stalking the streets, it freely enters into a person's home. Appearing like an amorphous, cloud-like being, it preys upon sleeping men, causing them to have nocturnal emissions. If it envelopes a person in its cloud-like form, it will cause them to suffer from insomnia. Signs that a person has been attacked by this sort of demon include depression and loss of appetite.

Source: Boulay, *Flying Serpents and Dragons*, 255; Pick, *Dreams and History*, 42; Sorensen, *Possession and Exorcism in the New Testament and Early Christianity*, 27–8

Ala-muki

In Hawaiian mythology, Ala-muki is a DRAGON goddess, a descendant of the primordial DRAGON goddess, MO-O-INANEA.

Source: Monaghan, *Encyclopedia of Goddesses and Heroines*, 155; Westervelt, *Legends of Gods and Ghosts*, 258

Alan

Variations: Balbal, Mananananggal, Mananggal, Wak Wak

A species of winged creatures from Filipino folklore, the alan live in the deep forest and spend much of their time hanging upside down from trees; some tales say they have homes constructed on the ground made of pure gold. Described as being human in appearance, half bird and half man, they also are said to have a long tongue, scaly arms, curved claws, fingers on their feet, and toes on their hands; all their digits also point backward. The alan are generally benign toward humans but there are tales of them acting both maliciously and mischievously. Typically they assist heroes on their quests.

Source: Eberhart, *Mysterious Creatures: N-Z*, 8; Rose, *Giants, Monsters, and Dragons*, 11; Worcester, *Philippine Islands and Their People*, 109; Zell-Ravenheart, *Wizard's Bestiary*, 17

Alarabi

A NATURE SPIRIT of the mountains, Alarabi is a TÁRTALO ("CYCLOPS") or evil spirit from Basque mythology in the region of Marquina; it is said to live in a cave.

Source: Miguel de Barandiarán, *Selected Writings of José Miguel De Barandiarán*, 92

Albotritch

Originating in the lumberjack communities of the developing United States of America, the albotritch is one of the many named FEARSOME CRITTERS of which, beyond a name, there is nothing else known.

Source: Rose, *Giants, Monsters, and Dragons*, 119

Alce

Variations: Anthalops, Alcida, Calopus, Keythong, Panthalops, Tapopus

In heraldic symbology the alce is a wingless, male GRIFFIN with rays or spikes of gold protruding from several parts of its body; on occasion it also sports two long straight horns atop its head. A pair of such creatures is present on the coat of arms of the Earl of Ormande.

Source: Elvin, *Dictionary of Heraldry*, 4; Epstein, *Medieval Haggadah*, 57–8; Planché, *Pursiuvant of Arms*, 183; Zell-Ravenheart, *Wizard's Bestiary*, 18–9

Alce, dog

A dog from ancient Greek mythology, Alce ("strong") was one of the DOGS OF ACTÆON, the unfortunate youth who was raised by the CENTAUR, CHEIRON.

Source: Leeming, *World of Myth*, 111; Murray, *Classical Manual*, 160; Naso, *Fasti, Tristia*, 93–5

Alecto (ah-LECK-too)

Variations: Alekto, Allecto

One of the three FURIES from classical Greek mythology, Alecto ("envy" or "never ending") was the sister who specialized in maintaining justice. She, like her sisters, MEGAERA ("envious anger" or "slaughter") and TISIPHONE ("face of retaliation" or "rage"), was described as looking like an old hag with bat wings, bloodshot eyes, and snakes in her hair; sometimes they were confused for being a GORGON.

The ancient Greek tragedian Aeschylus (525 BC–456 BC) claimed the sisters were the daughters of Night while the tragedian Sophocles (497 BC–406 BC) said they were the daughters of Skotos, the personification of darkness and the earth.

Source: Chopra, *Academic Dictionary of Mythology*, 112, 284; Drury, *Dictionary of the Esoteric*, 93; Hard, *Routledge Handbook of Greek Mythology*, 39

Alerion

Variations: Aleiron, Allerion, Avelerion, Ilerion

In the medieval era, *The Alerion* was an allegorical dissertation on bad and good love by the use of ravenous birds of prey which were differentiated by their relative nobility in the sport of hunting birds. The poem is divided into five sections: the sparrow hawk, the alerion part one, the eagle, the gerfalc, and the alerion part two. In art the alerion was depicted as a small eagle without beak or claws; its use as a heraldic symbol was rare.

Prester John, the legendary Christian king, described in a letter to the Byzantine Emperor Manuel I Conmenus (circa 1150) the various exotic birds in his country, one of which was the alerion, said to be the color of fire, much larger than an eagle, and having razor sharp wings. The letter went on to claim only one pair of these birds existed at a time and every 60 years a set of twin eggs were laid. After six days the eggs would hatch; the parents would fly out to sea and drown themselves, leaving their young to be raised by the other birds of the region. Once the new pair of alerion was old enough to fly, they could see to their own needs.

Source: Eason, *Fabulous Creatures, Mythical Monsters, and Animal Power Symbols*, 58; Kelly, *Medieval Imagination*, 151; Whitney, *Century Dictionary and Cyclopedia*, Volume 1, 147

Alicanto

Variations: Allicanto

In Chilean mythology, the alicanto, a bird of the Atacama Desert, is said to feed off of gold and silver. Described as having plumage with a metallic sheen and eyes shining as it flies through the night sky, the alicanto is considered to be an omen of good fortune. Living in caves of gold and silver ore, the alicanto are sought after by miners who hope to follow the bird back to its cave; however, if the alicanto detects it is being followed it will lead the miner to a cliff where he may fall to his death.

Source: Nozedar, *Secret Language of Birds*, 33; Rose, *Giants, Monsters, and Dragons*, 12; Sanders, *Revealing the Heart of the Galaxy*, 130; Zell-Ravenheart, *Wizard's Bestiary*, 17

Alicha

Variations: Alklha

The cosmic DRAGON of Siberian mythology, Alicha was described as being extremely large; its wings, when unfurled, would partially cover the sun, making sunny days appear dark and overcast. Alicha would nibble away at the moon each night until it was, over the course of a month, finally consumed; however, the moon was too much of an irritant on its stomach, so each month Alicha would vomit it back up. This DRAGON would also make daily attempts on consuming the sun, but it being too hot to keep down, would come back up each day. The markings on the moon which are visible to the naked human eye are said to have been made by Alicha's claws.

Source: De Kirk, *Dragonlore*, 38; Dixon-Kennedy, *Encyclopedia of Russian and Slavic Myth and Legend*, 6; McCutcheon, *Wordsworth Word Finder*, 413; Rose, *Giants, Monsters, and Dragons*, 12

Alkonost

Possibly originating in Persian folklore as one of the KHRAFSTRA, the alkonost of Russian and Slavic folklore is a SIRIN, a bird with the chest, face, and head of a woman, who torments the damned. Living in Rai, the land of the dead, the song the alkonost continuously sings to those who have led evil lives keeps them perpetually awake. It is said if an alkonost lays her eggs in the sea it will be a calm ocean for six or seven days; however, when the eggs hatch, there will be a storm at sea.

Source: Dixon-Kennedy, *Encyclopedia of Russian and Slavic Myth and Legend*, 6; Kubesh, *Mythological Creatures Around the World*, 9; Porter, *Animals in Folklore*, 187–88

Alkuntane

A species of highly dangerous vampiric mosquitoes from the folklore of the Pacific northwest, the alkuntane are said to look and sound just like regular mosquitoes; however if they manage to crawl into your ear they will then burrow and drill through your head until they reach your brain. The only way to prevent their attack is to keep your ears covered at all times; if ever you should happen to see a dark blue bubble emerging from someone's ear, it is an indicator they are under the attack of an alkuntane—grab the bubble and quickly yank it out, then cover your own ears.

Source: Sierra, *Gruesome Guide to World Monsters*, 8

Allghoi Khorkhoi

Variations: Mongolian Death Worm

A huge serpentine creature said to live in the sand dunes of the southern Gobi desert, the allghoi khorkhoi ("intestine worm") is such a fast and efficient killer, there are but a handful of stories of those who have encountered the creature and survived the experience. Its lethal venom, which is spat at targets over a great distance, is described as acting like a neurotoxin; the poison, yellow in color, is powerful enough to corrode metal. The strength of the poison begins to lose its potency in June and by the end of the year it is believed it may be possible for a strong man to survive a poisonous attack. Additionally, the allghoi khorkhoi has the ability to emit a fatal electrical discharge powerful enough to kill a horse and have its flesh already cooked most of the way through before the body hits the ground.

First sighted in 1929, the allghoi khorkhoi is said to have a purplish-red hide from which it secretes a poisonous oily substance powerful enough to kill anyone who touches it. It moves in a cork-screw-like motion, swimming beneath the surface of the sand as it hunts for camels and horses to consume.

Source: Eberhart, *Mysterious Creatures: N-Z*, 350; Maberry, *Vampire Universe*, 13; Mackerle, *Far Out Adventures*, 198

Allocamelus

Variations: Ass Camel

In the medieval English heraldic symbology, the allocamelus was a mythological creature emblazoned on many families' coats of arms; it was depicted as a hybrid of a camel and a donkey or a camel and a llama. One source describes the allocamelus as standing two yards tall and stretching five feet from tip to tail, having the ears, head, and neck of a mule with a camel's body and the feet of an ostrich. Having no horns, the animal's neck was as white as a swan's while the rest of its body was a sort of yellow; interestingly, the males of the species were said to discharge their urine backwards.

Source: Boreman, *Description of Three Hundred Animals*, 22; Elvin, *Elvin's Dictionary of Heraldry*, 5; Parker, *Glossary of Terms Used in Heraldry*, 413; Rose, *Giants, Monsters, and Dragons*, 13

Alloes

Described in the sixteenth century work *Comography* by the French cosmographer, explorer, and Franciscan priest André de Thevet, the alloes was said to be a sea creature (see SEA SERPENT), a hybrid of a goose and fish as it had a long bird-like neck and flippers rather than wings and feet.

Source: Zell-Ravenheart, *Wizard's Bestiary*, 17

Alp (Alp)

Variations: Alb, Alf, Alfemoe, Alpdaemon, Alpen, Alpes, Alpmann, Apsaras, Bockshexe, Bocksmarte, Cauquemare, Chauche Vieille, Dochje, Dockele, Dockeli, Doggi, Druckerl, Drude, Drut, Drutt, Elbe, Fraueli, Inuus, Leeton, Lork, Maar, Mahr, Mahrt, Mahrte, Mar, Mara, Mare, Märt, Moor, Mora, Morous, Mura, Murawa, Nachtmaennli, Nachtmahr, Nachtmanndli, Nachtmännlein, Nachtmerrie, Nachtschwalbe, Nachttoter, Nielop, Nightmare, Night Terror, Old Hag, Quauquemaire, Racking One, Rätzel, Schrätlein, Schrättel, Schrättele, Schrätteli, Schrattl, Schrettele, Schrötle, Schrötlein, Schrsttel, Stampare, Stampen, Stampfen, Stempe, Sukkubus, Toggeli, Trampling, Trempe, Trud, Trude, Trutte, Tryd, Tudd, Vampyr, Walrider, Walriderske, Wichtel, and numerous others through history and geographic region

Originating from Germany, this demonic, vampiric creature does not have a single true form. Throughout the ages the only consistency in its description is it is said to wear a white hat. Generally the alp is said to be male, and although there are a scant few reports of it being female, it should be noted this creature has exceptional shapeshifting abilities by use of its therianthropy. An alp can assume the form of any animal it pleases, but it is said to prefer birds, cats, demon dogs, dogs, mist, pigs, and snakes. It is very strong, can become invisible, can fly, and has the unique ability to spit butterflies and moths from its mouth. Because of its shape-shifting ability, the alp has been linked to WEREWOLF folklore in Cologne, Germany.

Typically a demon is an infernal, immortal being and was never human, but this is not the case for the lecherous and ravenous alp. In fact, it became what it is through one of a few fairly mundane acts, such as when a newborn male child dies, when a child whose mother went through a particularly long and painful childbirth dies, or when a family member dies and his spirit simply returns with no further explanation added.

At night the alp seeks out its most common prey, a sleeping woman, although it has been known to occasionally attack men and young boys as well as cattle, geese, horses, and rabbits. Once the prey is selected, the alp shape-shifts into mist and slips into the person's home completely undetected. Next, it sits upon the victim's chest and compresses the air out of their lungs so they cannot scream. Then the alp will drink blood (and milk if the victim is a woman who is lactating), which will cause her to have both horrible nightmares and erotic dreams. The next day the victim will have vivid memories of the attack and be left feeling drained of energy and miserable. The attack event in its entirety is called an *alpdrücke*. It is interesting to note that if a woman calls an alp to her, then the creature will be a gentle lover with her.

The alp, when it attacks a horse, is usually referred to as a *mare*. It will mount up and ride the animal to death. The alp, however, may also choose to crush the animal instead, as it is known to do when it crushes geese and rabbits to death in their pens. When an alp crushes cattle to death, it is called a *schrattl* attack.

Fortunately, as powerful as the alp is, its attacks can be fairly easily thwarted. To protect horses and cattle from being ridden and/or crushed to death, simply hang a pair of crossed measuring sticks in the barn or place a broom in the animal's stall.

There are numerous ways to prevent yourself or others from being attacked by an alp. According to folklore, the alp's power is linked to its hat. If you can steal the hat off its head, it will lose its superhuman strength and the ability to become invisible. Desperate to have its hat back, the alp will greatly reward anyone who returns it, although with what or how this will happen specifically is not known.

Another way to keep an alp at bay is to draw a magical hexagram on your bedroom door with chalk and imbue it with the names of the three magi who visited the Christ child after his birth: Balthasar, Caspar, and Melchior, during the Festival of the Three Kings (January 6). Variations of this preventative method say the head of the household must make a pentagram on the bedroom door and empower it with names of the patriarchic prophets, Elias and Enoch.

Burying a stillborn child under the front door of your home will protect all the occupants who sleep there not only from alp attacks, but also from attacks by other species of vampires as well.

A less invasive defensive method is to keep your shoes at the side of your bed at night when you fall asleep. If the toes are pointed toward the bedroom door, it will keep the alp from entering. Also, sleeping with a mirror upon your chest will scare it off should it somehow manage to enter into the room.

At one time there was the practice of singing a specific song at the hearth before the last person in the house went to bed for the night. Sadly, this method is no longer with us, as the words, melody, and even the name of the song have been lost to history; only the memory of once doing so remains.

If despite your best attempts all preventative measures have been taken and alp attacks persist, there is hope to fend it off yet. If you should awaken during the attack and find yourself being pressed down upon by an alp, put your thumb in your hand and it will flee.

Occasionally a witch binds an alp to her in order to inflict harm upon others. Witches who have an alp in their possession have the telltale sign of letting their eyebrows grow together. They allow this to happen because the alp, in this instance, lives inside the witch's body when not in use. When it leaves her through an opening in her eyebrow, it takes on the guise of a moth or white butterfly. If it ever happens you awaken in the night and see such an insect upon your chest, say to it, "Trud, come back tomorrow and I will lend you something." The insect should immediately fly away and the next day the alp, appearing as a human, will come to your home looking to borrow something. When this happens, give it nothing but say to it, "Come back tomorrow and drink with me." The alp will leave and the following day the witch who sent the alp to attack you will come to your home, seeking a drink. Give it to her and the attacks should stop.

Sometimes an alp will return night after night to assault the same person. Fortunately, there is a powerful, if not bizarre, way to prevent this from continuing to happen. The victim needs to urinate into a clean, new bottle, which is then hung in a place where the sun can shine upon it for three days.

Then, without saying a single word, carry the bottle to a running stream and throw it over your head into the water.

For all the trouble an alp can prove to be, it is as easy to kill as most every other form of vampire. Once it is captured, place a lemon in its mouth and set the creature ablaze.

Source: Grimm, *Teutonic Mythology*, 423, 442, 463; Jones, *On the Nightmare*, 126; Nuzum, *Dead Travel Fast*, 234, Riccardo, *Liquid Dreams*, 139

Alp-Luachra

Normally, the alp-luachra ("joint eater") of Irish folklore was harmless to humans except in one particular circumstance: should a person fall asleep beside a stream and accidentally swallow a newt. If this singular event should occur, then the alp-luachra—the newt in disguise—would cause its victim to be compelled to eat but prevent him from gaining any nourishment from the food consumed. When not in its newt form, this creature was completely invisible and unable to be detected until it was too late to help the victim.

In Douglas Hyde's *Beside the Fire*, one victim was able to rid himself of the alp-luachra by ingesting great quantities of salted beef without drinking any water. Then he went back to the stream he acquired the FAIRY ANIMAL from and fell back asleep. The alp-luachra, desperate and thirsty, returned of its own accord to the water.

Source: Hyde, *Beside the Fire*, 51–60; Monaghan, *Encyclopedia of Celtic Mythology and Folklore*, 15; Rose, *Spirits, Fairies, Leprechauns, and Goblins*, 10, 351

Alphyn

In the medieval English heraldic symbology the alphyn, a mythological creature emblazoned on many families' coats of arms, was depicted as a hybrid between a GRIFFIN and a stocky tiger with big ears, eagle claws on his hind feet, a long, thin tongue, and a knotted, tufted tail. It is similar in appearance to the TYGER.

Source: Franklyn, *Shield and Crest*, 479; Friar, *Basic Heraldry*, 166; Zell-Ravenheart, *Wizard's Bestiary*, 17

Alsvid

Variations: Alswid

Pulling the chariot of the Norse god Sol, across the sky, Alsvid ("all swift" or "fleet one") and his companion, AARVAK ("early awake"), were born in Muspellsheim, the divine realm of warmth and brightness; together the team represented the dawn. As the horses pulled the chariot, the shield, Svalin, protected them from the harmful rays of the sun (see also AVAK, AARVAK, HRIMFAXI, and SKINFAXI).

Source: Coulter, *Encyclopedia of Ancient Deities*, 38; Daly,

Norse Mythology A to Z, 3; Grimes, *Norse Myths*, 254; Rose, *Giants, Monsters, and Dragons*, 178

Alsvider (AL-svith-r)

Variations: All Strong, All Swift, All-Strong, All-Swift, Alsvid, Alsvider, Alsvidr, Alsvidur ("rapid one"), Alsvin, Alsvinnr, Alsvith, Alswider, Fjosvartnir

In Norse mythology Alsvider ("all swift") was the horse pulling Mani (Maane), the moon, in a cart across the night sky. Magical runes were carved on his hooves.

Source: Brewer, *Dictionary of Phrase and Fable*, 624; Coulter, *Encyclopedia of Ancient Deities*, 5; Grimes, *Norse Myths*, 254

Aluga (Ah-lou-ga, A-luga)

Variations: Alouqâ, Alouque, Alukah, Aluqa, Aulak

The aluga takes its name from the Hebrew word synonymous with vampirism and translates to mean "leech." A vampiric creature originating from Mediterranean folklore, the aluga is considered by some sources to be nothing more than a blood-drinking demon while others claim it to be the very name of the demonic king of vampires. A handful of references say it is nothing more than a flesh-eating GHOUL.

The aluga is mentioned in the Bible, Proverbs 30:15: "*The horseleech hath two daughters, crying Give, give. There are three things that are never satisfied, yea, four things say not, It is enough: (16) The grave; and the barren womb; the earth that is not filled with water; and the fire that saith not, It is enough.*"

Source: Bunson, *Vampire Encyclopedia*, 5; Hyatt, *Book of Demons*, 63; Preece, *New Encyclopaedia Britannica*, 461

Amalthea (am-al-THEE-ah)

Variations: Amaltheia

The sacred fine-haired goat from classical Greek mythology, Amalthea ("tender") suckled the infant god Zeus (Jupiter) while he lived on the island of Crete and was raised by the Melissae. Zeus (Jupiter) had broken off one of her horns and in doing so created the cornucopia, a horn with the magical ability of filling with anything the wielder desired. The aegis of Zeus (Jupiter) was made for him by Hephaistos (Vulcan) from the hide of Amalthea; whenever he shook it, he could control and produce intense darkness, storms, and tempests.

In gratitude for her services, when he ascended to the throne of Olympus, he set Amalthea among the stars as the constellation Capricornus.

Source: Berens, *Myths and Legends of Ancient Greece and Rome*, 7, 16, 106; Daly, *Greek and Roman Mythology, A to Z*, 8; Olcott, *Star Lore of All Ages*, 116

Amamehagi

Variations: Amahage

Similar to the NAMAHAGE, the amamehagi is a ceremonial purifying demon in Hokuriku, Japan. On the first full moon of the new year, moving in groups, the leader carrying a wand of white paper strips, the assembly barges into a home unannounced and while one of the amamehagi purifies the family altar, the others chase the children around the home. Once the head of the household offers them rice cakes, the demons leave.

Source: Bocking, *Popular Dictionary of Shinto*, 98; Plutschow, *Matsuri*, 35

Aman

Variations: Amamet, Amamet the Devourer, Amemait, Amemet, Amermait, Amit, Amit the Devourer, Am-Mit, Ammet, Ammit, Ammut, Amunet, the Devourer of Amenti, Eater of the Dead

In ancient Egyptian mythology Aman ("bone eater," "water") was believed to be an iatrical part of the Judgment of the Dead ceremony which took place in the afterlife. Described as having the body of a lion, the forequarters of a crocodile, and the hindquarters of a hippopotamus, Aman would wait at the base of the scales used to weigh the deceased's *ba*, or soul; if the *ba* was too heavy with sin, it was tossed over to the awaiting Aman who would devour it in an instant. Interestingly, there has yet to be found a record of Aman having devoured the soul of anyone making their Negative Confession.

Source: Coulter, *Encyclopedia of Ancient Deities*, n.pag.; Mercatante, *Who's Who in Egyptian Mythology*, 5–6; Remler, *Egyptian Mythology, A to Z*, 112; Zell-Ravenheart, *Wizard's Bestiary*, 18

Amanojaku

A singular and specific ONI from Japanese folklore, Amanojaku was said to kidnap, flay, and consume girls by means of his expert impersonations; after his meal, he would wear his victim's skin. Amanojaku takes great delight in causing havoc.

Source: Maberry, *Cryptopedia*, 227; Mayer, *Yanagita Kunio Guide to the Japanese Folk Tale*, 6–7

Amarok

Variations: Waheela

A gigantic wolf from the folklore of the Inuit people of Canada and the Unites States, Amarok is a lone predator who stalks those who hunt during the night. A solitary creature living without a pack, it is known for removing the head of its victims.

Source: Maberry, *They Bite*, 180; Rose, *Giants, Monsters, and Dragons*, 15; Zell-Ravenheart, *Wizard's Bestiary*, 17, 100

Amarum

To the Quicha people of Ecuador, Amarum is a formidable demonic creature; this singular entity appearing as a gigantic water-boa is the father of witchcraft. The souls of sorcerers reside within its body.

Source: Bonnerjea, *Allborough New Age Guide*, 19

Ambize

Variations: Angula, Angulo, Hog Fish

Said to live off of the West African coast, the ambize is a species of SEA SERPENT described as having the body of an enormous fish, the head of a pig or an ox, humanoid hands in place of flippers, and a flat tail like a beaver's. Fishermen in the Congo said the flesh of the ambize was most delicious, similar to pork, and its body fat was rendered into lard; however, these 500-pound creatures are notoriously difficult to catch. The ambize never leaves the water but will graze upon the grass growing along the riverbanks.

Source: Baudler, *Collection of Voyages and Travels*, 532–33; Rose, *Giants, Monsters, and Dragons*, 15; Zell-Ravenheart, *Wizard's Bestiary*, 17

Amefurashi

A monster from Japanese folklore, the amefurashi ("the rain harbinger") is child-like in appearance; it has control over the rain.

Source: Pauley, *Pauley's Guide*, 4

Amen

According to ancient Egyptian mythology Amen was one of the creature guardians of Osiris while the god was in his form known as Osiris the Seeker. In *The Text of Unas* there is a magical spell which when performed will cause the destruction of monstrous beasts and serpents alike; Amen would be inadvertently affected by this spell.

Source: Coulter, *Encyclopedia of Ancient Deities*, 32, 418

Ametha

In classical Greek and Roman mythology Ametha ("no loiterer") was one of the many winged horses said to assist pulling the sun chariot, Quadriga, belonging to the second generation Titan, Helios (Sol) across the sky and was counted among the HIPPOI ATHANATOI.

Source: Brewer, *Wordsworth Dictionary of Phrase and Fable*, 565; Rose, *Giants, Monsters, and Dragons*, 178

Amhuluk

A humanoid lake monster from the folklore of the Kalapuya Indians, Oregon, United States of America, Amhuluk was greatly feared. Other than having hairless legs and a rack of beautifully spotted horns of enormous size upon his head, there is nothing else to add to his physical description. Originally the creature wanted to reside on the fertile plains of Atfalati but decided they were too small a territory. After an extended search he settled on Forked Mountain. Amhuluk prefers to linger about in pools of stagnant water he keeps cluttered with the crowns of the trees near the water. When there is a thick fog over the water, this creature is most active.

According to folklore, every living being that has ever seen Amhuluk has died apart from the dogs he keeps, a single child, and its father from an old tale. In other telling's, Amhuluk is not a singular being but rather a species of lake monster (see SEA SERPENT). In these versions of the story the serpentine creatures have the ability of therianthropy, enabling them to shape-shift into other forms; the water they live in can also transform any animal which falls into it into a monster.

Source: De Kirk, *Dragonlore*, 48; Gatschet, *Journal of American Folk-lore*, Volume 4, Parts 1–2, 141–43; Rose, *Giants, Monsters, and Dragons*, 15; Zell-Ravenheart, *Wizard's Bestiary*, 17

Amikiri

A creature from Japanese folklore, the amikiri is described as looking like a bird, lobster, and snake chimerical hybrid; rather than actually harming people, it cuts holes in fishing and mosquito nets.

Source: Hardin, *Supernatural Tales from Around the World*, 304; Maberry, *Cryptopedia*, 227; Zell-Ravenheart, *Wizard's Bestiary*, 17

Amphimedon

A CENTAUR from ancient Greek mythology, Amphimedon was a comrade of Phineus in his battle against the hero Perseus; he was slain when the hero drove his sword between the ribs of Amphimedon and into Phineus' neck.

Source: Bell, *Bell's New Pantheon*, 58; Simpson, *Metamorphoses of Ovid*, 80

Amphion (AM-fi-on)

In ancient Greek mythology, Amphion was one of the CENTAURS slain by the demi-god and cultural hero Hercules (Heracles) while visiting his friend, a CENTAUR named PHOLUS, between the conclusion of his third Labor and the onset of his fourth. When an old and particularly fragrant hogshead of wine was opened, the aroma carried on the air and drove the local CENTAURS into a fury. Amphion, ARGEIUS, DAPHNIS, DUPO, HIPPOTION, ISOPLES, MELANCHETES, OREUS, PHRIXUS, and

THEREUS were slain by Hercules (Heracles) as he defended himself from their violent and unwarranted assault.

Source: Barthell, *Gods and Goddesses of Ancient Greece*, 187; Berens, *Myths and Legends of Ancient Greece and Rome*, 33; Diodorus, *Historical Library of Diodorus the Sicilian*, Volume 1, 229–30

Amphiptere

Variations: IACULI, Jaculus

Described as a small, legless, winged serpent, the amphiptere ("javelin snake") was described by Pliny as having two tongues, one serpent-like and the other shaped like an arrow; it resembles the GUIVRE of French folklore and heraldry. Rarely depicted in European heraldry, the amphiptere as a creature was feared.

Source: Fox-Davies, *Complete Guide to Heraldry*, 231; Rose, *Giants, Monsters, and Dragons*, 16; Rosen, *Mythical Creatures Bible*, 88

Amphisbaena

Variations: Amfivena, Amphisbaina, Amphisbainai, Amphisbene, Amphisboena, Amphisbona, Amphista, Amphivena (feminine form), Anksymen, Anphine, Anphivena (feminine, "mother of ants")

A creature from heraldic symbology, the amphisbaena ("goes both ways") is depicted as a legless, winged serpent with a head on each end of its body. In medieval paintings it is shown as having wings but also two feet and horns upon it heads.

In the folklore of classical Greek and Roman mythology it was believed the amphisbaena could cause a woman to have a miscarriage if she stepped over one; however, if she kept a deceased one in a jar she would then be able to safely step over a living one which would enable her to have an easy childbirth. Should a pregnant woman ever step over a living amphisbaena without carrying her jarred deceased one, she would not miscarry so long as she quickly returned with her jar and stepped over the living amphisbaena again for the magical powers of the deceased creature could counteract the abilities of the living one.

According to the Roman author Claudius Aelianus, a teacher of rhetoric, the amphisbaena, in addition to having the ability to move backward or forward as needed, if the creature was wrapped around a walking stick it would ward off not only snakes but all other creatures which kill by striking. Saint Isidore of Seville, the last historian of the ancient world, described the amphisbaena as having eyes shining like lanterns and as being the only serpent known to venture out into the cold.

Source: Bettini, *Women and Weasels*, 133; Fox-Davies, *Complete Guide to Heraldry*, 231; Breverton, *Breverton's Phan-*

tasmagoria, 69; Elvin, *Elvin's Dictionary of Heraldry*, 5; Zell-Ravenheart, *Wizard's Bestiary*, 18

Amphisien

Variations: Amphisien-Cockatrice, COCKATRICE

The amphisien is the alternative name used for the COCKATRICE in reference to European heraldry; its depiction upon the shield of a medieval knight would have been a fearsome sight. The amphisien is depicted very much like a COCKATRICE; however, it has a second head on the tip of its tail. The glance of this creature was enough to kill its adversary, or, at the very least, turn them to stone.

Source: Elvin, *Elvin's Dictionary of Heraldry*, 5; Rose, *Giants, Monsters, and Dragons*, 16; Zell-Ravenheart, *Wizard's Bestiary*, 18

Amphiteres

A legless, feather-winged serpent with a dragonesque head, typically found in European heraldry, the amphiteres is very similar in appearance to the AMPHIPTERE. Its eyes were described as looking like the tail of a peacock, its body between six and nine feet long, and covered in heavy scales. The amphiteres, also found in Mesoamerican mythology, was represented as the gods Kulkulcan and Quetzalcoatl.

Source: De Kirk, *Dragonlore*, 39; Breverton, *Breverton's Phantasmagoria*, 306; Woodward, *Treatise on Heraldry, British and Foreign*, Volume 1, 454

Amycus (am-i-cus)

A CENTAUR from ancient Greek mythology, Amycus was born the son of Ophion. According to Ovid's *Metamorphoses*, Amycus was one of the CENTAURS who attended the wedding of Pirithous, became drunk on wine and, following the lead of EURYTUS, who assaulted Hippodame, began to assault and rape any woman they could grab. A great Centauromachy then followed. After Theseus slew EURYTUS with a heavy wine bowl, Amycus became enraged and led a counter assault against Theseus and the men who sought to stop them. Hefting up a blazing candelabra from the wedding shrine, Amycus used it as a weapon, striking Celadon the Lapith so soundly in the face it left his visage an unrecognizable mass of bone and flesh. Pelates of Pella broke a leg off of a table made from maple wood and struck Amycus with it, knocking him to his knees. While Amycus was dazed from the blow, Pelates beat him to death.

Source: Berens, *Myths and Legends of Ancient Greece and Rome*, 219; Lemprière, *Bibliotheca Classica*, 694; Simpson, *Metamorphoses of Ovid*, 204

Analopos

Variations: Antelope, Aptaleon

According to Saint Albertus, the analopos was a creature with horns sharp enough to cut down trees but unable able to slash its way through viney undergrowth. When the analopos became entangled in the underbrush it would send out a call of alarm alerting predators, both animal and human, of its dire situation; upon discovery, entangled and unable to defend itself, the analopos was easily slain.

Source: Albertus, *Man and the Beasts*, 71; Bone, *Atlantic Monthly*, Volume 33, 272; Zell-Ravenheart, *Wizard's Bestiary*, 19

Anansi

Variations: Ananse-Sem, Ananse, Anansi-Tori, Aunt Nancy, Kweku Ananse

Portrayed intermittently as both a human and a creature, Anansi ("spider") of West African folklore is a cultural hero and an atypical trickster. In Caribbean island folklore and the akan-speaking tribes of West Africa, Anansi is associated with spiders and is often described as such. In these tales he is described as being a large and long-legged husky crab-spider. Tales of the wise and wily Anansi are popular in spite of the fact he is a treacherous liar, a murderer, and a thief. In most of his folktales Anansi is pitted against Canary, Lion, and Turtle, and in these tales he is portrayed as a spider. His most dangerous enemy is Tiger. Other animals he is pitted against are Agouti, Ass, Boa Constrictor (*Abona*), Caiman, Cat, Cock, Cockroach, Cow, Cricket (*Sen-Sen*), Deer, Dog, Elephant, Fly, Goat, Hen, Horse, Howling Monkey, Rat, Snail, Snake, Toad, Vulture, Whale, and Wren. However, when he is dealing with people, Anansi is humanoid in appearance.

Born as the son of the god of the sky, Nyame, mortal Anansi often acts as an intermediary between his father and the earth. He taught mankind how to sow grain, married a princess, possessed endless resources, and was the owner of a magical stone whose name, if ever said aloud, would kill the person who spoke it. He also has the ability to decrease or increase his size whenever he chooses.

Source: Haase, *Greenwood Encyclopedia of Folktales and Fairy Tales*, 31; Penard, *Journal of American Folk-lore*, Volume 7, 241–42

Ananta Boga

Variations: Ananta Sesha, Ananta Shisha, Anantaboga ("serpent king"), Naga Anantaboga, Sesha, Shesha the Endless

In the Hindu mythology from India Ananta Boga ("endless" or "infinity") is an immense cosmic serpent having a thousand heads; each is venomous and has the ability to spit fire. At the end of each *kalpa* (period of time) Ananta Boga destroys all of creation. By churning up the ocean, Anata Boga created the Elixir of Immortality.

In the Javanese *wayang* ("shadow theater") mythology, Ananta Boga is the king of the DRAGONS.

Source: De Kirk, *Dragonlore*, 32; Jones, *Instinct for Dragons*, 166; Leeming, *Dictionary of Asian Mythology*, 22; Rose, *Giants, Monsters, and Dragons*, 16–17

Anaskelades

In the folklore from the island of Crete the anaskelades ("upside-down-ones") was a type of creature said to resemble a donkey prepped and ready to be ridden; as soon as it was mounted, the beast would increase its size until it was as large as a mountain. Then, once it was as tall as it could grow, the anaskelades would buck its rider off, letting the fall kill them.

Source: Rose, *Giants, Monsters, and Dragons*, 16–17

Anaye

Variations: Alien Gods, Child of the Waters

In the Navajo folklore of the United States of America, the anaye ("evil gods" or "monsters") is the collective name for four types of supernatural beings: the limbless BINAYE AHANI, the feathered TSANAHALE, the headless THELGETH, and the last remains unnamed. The chief of the anaye was the scaly GIANT, Yeitso. Anaye are the product of evil women, conceived without a human father; folklore says all anaye are the progeny of the god, Sun Bearer. These gigantic and monstrous beings cause fear, misery, and wickedness throughout the world. According to the folklore the anaye were eventually defeated by the two sons of the sun and water, Nayanezgani ("slayer of alien gods") and Thobadzistshini ("child born of water"); however, the siblings of the anaye, Cold, Famine, Lice Man, Old Age, Poverty, and Sleep, continue to plague mankind.

Source: Cotterell, *Dictionary of World Mythology*, 220; Coulter, *Encyclopedia of Ancient Deities*, 51; Leviton, *Encyclopedia of Earth Myths*, n.pag.; Rose, *Giants, Monsters, and Dragons*, 18

Ancestral Spirit

Ancestral spirits are common in many of the world's mythologies, folklores, religions, and spiritual beliefs, but are most prevalent in Buddhism, China, Hinduism, indigenous religions of Africa, Japan, Korea, Native America, Native Australia, and Oceania. This belief is most common in societies where kinship is important, such as with tribal groups. Those who believe in the interaction of ancestral spirits do not necessary worship them, although it is present in most religions in some fashion even if it manifests only as a remembrance, offering of prayer, or simply lighting a candle. Veneration is given to those who in life held a position of importance or rank, for example, clan leaders, heads of families, heroes, kings, lineage founders, political leaders, royalty, tribal elders, and other such groups. Common forms of venerations are attendance of the gravesite and monuments, commemorative services, festivals of honor, maintenance of moral standards, offerings, prayers, and sacrifices.

Ancestral spirits are best described as being the deceased members of one's family or tribe and are similar to ANGELS, bodhisattvas, lesser gods, NATURE SPIRITS, and saints; they may even share similar abilities, features, and responsibilities. These spirits concern themselves with looking after the well-being of their descendants; this manifests as blessing those who keep with traditions and reverence and punishing those unworthy progenies who break social and spiritual laws, practices, or taboos.

Often, shamans or comparable figures are utilized to speak with these spirits in order to seek guidance or discover what had occurred to offend them. Ancestral spirits, like lesser gods with mighty powers, have the ability to cause illness and misfortune, manifesting in a number of ways; they expect to receive proper treatment and to be shown respect. When this occurs, the people are blessed with health and material happiness.

Source: Doniger, *Merriam-Webster's Encyclopedia of World Religions*, 54; Ellwood, *Encyclopedia of World Religions*, 14–5

The Ancient One

A SEA SERPENT from Piute mythology, the Ancient One is said to live in Lake Pyramid in Nevada, United States of America. Like AMHULUK, the Ancient One snatches people from the shore and, dragging them into the water, drowns them. The Piute say a whirlpool in the lake is the Ancient One lurking about looking for prey.

Source: De Kirk, *Dragonlore*, 48; Rose, *Giants, Monsters, and Dragons*, 18

Andandara

From the sixteenth century Spanish folklore comes the andandara, a race of evil were-cats that would seek out women to rape in order to produce a line of feline-human offspring. In addition to having deadly claws and teeth, the andandara were said to have the ability to kill with their intense stare. The presence of one of these creatures can cause crop failure, disease, and ill fortune.

The Azande people of Africa describe the andandara as a race of malevolent wild cats, having bright bodies and gleaming eyes; these creatures have intercourse with women who then will give birth to both a child and a kitten. Similar to the Spanish folklore, the African version of this monster has the Evil Eye; its presence can cause misfortune and to hear its cry in the brush is considered to be an unlucky omen.

Source: Bharati, *Agents and Audiences*, Volume 1, 43; Guiley, *Encyclopedia of Vampires, Werewolves, and Other Monsters*, 5; Maberry, *Vampire Universe*, 17

Andaokut

The Tsimshian are a people who live along the Pacific Northwest Coast of Alaska and British Columbia, and from their folklore comes the story of Andaokut ("mucous boy"), a HOMUNCULUS-like being created from the accumulation of mucus a woman generated while mourning the loss of her child who was stolen by the Great Woman of the Wood, Malahas. This witch was well known for abducting children and smoking them alive over a fire pit so she could eat them at her leisure. The creation grew very fast and soon asked its new parents for a bow and an arrow. After discovering why his foster mother cried so often, Andaokut set out to find Malahas. Through a series of carefully played tricks he managed to kill the old witch the only way she could be—by finding her small black heart where she hid it and piercing it with an arrow. Once Malahas was destroyed, Andaokut gathered up the bodies of the children, laid them out carefully on the ground, and urinated all over them, which brought them back to life.

Source: Boas, *Tsimshian Mythology*, 903–07

Androsphinx

Variations: Andro-Sphinx

In ancient Egyptian mythology there were three types of Sphinxes: the androsphinx, the CRIO-SPHINX, and the HIERACOSPHINX. Each of these variations represented the king and was a token of respect to the god whose head they most resembled. The androsphinx had the head of a man and the body of a lion and represented the union of intellectual and physical power; it therefore was associated with the human-headed gods Amon, Khem, Pthah, and Osiris.

Source: Audsley, *Popular Dictionary of Architecture and the Allied Arts*, Volume 1, 98; Wilkinson, *Manners and Customs of the Ancient Egyptians*, Volume 5, 200–01

Andura

Variations: Hoga

Believed to have lived in the deep freshwater lake outside of the city of Themistitan, Mexico, the andura of Mexican folklore was described as being as large as a sea-cow with swine-like head and ears and whiskers a foot and half long, giving birth to live young, and having a hide which could change color between green, red, and yellow; it was particularly delicious to eat. Found dwelling near the edge of the lake feeding off of the leaves of the Hoga tree, the toothy andura was said to be savage in killing fish to eat, even ones much large than itself.

Source: Pare, *On Monsters and Marvels*, 121; Rose, *Giants, Monsters, and Dragons*, 18, 175

Aned

In Arthurian folklore, Aned was one of the many hounds accompanying King Arthur on the quest to hunt down the boar, TWRCH TRWYTH; however, it was only one of three dogs which were required to be present by a special condition placed by the GIANT, Ysbaddaden, as he was trying to make obtaining the goal as difficult as possible for Cylhwch (see AETHLEM and DRUDWYN). Part of the provision required a special handler to be obtained for Aned—Cynedyr the Wild—which the King eventually had to provide. Aned had a reputation for never failing to kill an animal it is set upon; no leash in the world could hold him at bay unless it was made from the beard hairs of Dissul, son of Eurei, the bearded GIANT. The hunt ended when AETHLEM and Aned chased TWRCH TRWYTH into the ocean and into the Underworld, never to be seen again.

Source: Bruce, *Arthurian Name Dictionary*, 23, 137, 477; Ellis, *Celtic Myths and Legends*, 385, 395

Angel

Variations: The Fiery Ones, the Holy Ones, Malak YHWH ("messenger of the Lord"), Sons of God

The word *angel* likely derives from the Sanskrit word *angiras*, a type of divine spirit. However, it may have come from the Persian word *angaros*, which means *courier*, or even from the Greek word *angelos*, meaning *a messenger* or *a person sent*. In both Hebrew and Arabic, the Hebrew word *malakh*, meaning *messenger*, is used; literally translated it means "on going" or "one sent."

The Hebrews developed their idea of angelic beings from the Babylonians and the Persians. Gabriel and Michael, the only two named angels in the Old Testament, were lifted from Babylonian mythology. A third angel, Raphael, appears, but only in the apocryphal *Book of Tobit*. Enoch named many angels and demons alike, but his works are considered apocryphal and were largely unknown to the general populace until recently. Arguments could be made to include Abaddon, the Angel of the Bottomless Pit mentioned in the Book of Revelations; Wormwood, the angel referred to as a star; Rahab, the Angel of the Sea; and Satan, who goes by the title *ha-satan* ("adversary") and does not become a fallen angel or even evil until he appears in Christian and post-biblical writings.

In early pre–Christian times the word *angel* and the Greek word *daimon* were interchangeable, most notably in the writings of John and Paul. It was not until much later that *daimon* came to take on negative connotations. Angels were always a part of the beliefs of Christianity, and early church leaders oftentimes struggled in deciding how much attention they merited and how significant their role would be in dogma. The council of Nicea in AD 325 officially ruled in favor of angels playing a part in Christian beliefs, although Saint Paul was against their veneration.

Roman Catholic folklore teaches that angels were created *tota simul* ("all at once") in the early days of Creation. Beliefs vary between angels already having existed and dwelt in the void with God, having been created on the second day, or having been created on the fifth day. In Jewish folklore it is believed the angels are born "new every morning" and are continuously reformed with every breath taken by God.

The stereotypical imagery depicts angels as winged men and women dressed in long gowns and having a light or halo on or around their heads. More traditional descriptions of angels have them as bodiless, immaterial intelligences, and being immaterial, they are not subject to the boundaries of space and time. In their true form they are said to be more than two-thousand parasangs tall, about 7,760 miles. They are described as beings of pure light, or made of fire, or fully encompassed in light. They are assumed to be "good" and not subject to evil compulsions.

Angels are assumed by the public at large to be "good" and not subject to evil impulses. Although this idea is basically correct, angels are not wholly benign or without the ability to fight and defend themselves. Biblical descriptions have them holding drawn swords, brandishing weapons, and riding upon horses; one angel even carries an ink-horn. On occasion, angelic countenance is said to be "terrible" and causing "great fear to behold," their voices almost too unbearable to hear. They bear swords or destroying weapons in their hands. They are militant minded and capable combatants, as one lone angel destroyed in a single night a whole Assyrian army of 185,000 men (2 Kings 19:35).

As frightful and powerful as angels are, they have also been gifted with the knowledge of all earthly events, are correct in their judgment, and are holy and wise but not infallible. It is commonly accepted angels do not have envy or hatred within them and live without a free-will of their own; however, if this is completely true, it does not account for fallen angels, the War of Heaven, or the Divine Laws angels alone are subject to.

It has come to popular belief angels are, generally speaking, divine supernatural beings acting as an intermediary between God and mankind. Traditionally, in addition to being the messenger of God and fulfilling His will on earth, they also sit at His throne and act as His divine council. They accompany Him as His attendants when He appears before man. They travel between Heaven and Earth and report to God the events which are happening.

In the Bible, angels appear to mankind as fellow humans but of noticeable beauty; on several occasions, they are not recognizable as being an angel until they reveal themselves. Biblical angels can consume sacrifices in fire by touching them, disappear in sacrificial fires, fly through the air of their own power or on a chariot of fire, become invisible, and appear in flames as an APPARITION.

The number of angels is unknown but unquestionably prodigious. Revelation 5:11 said the angels number "ten thousand times ten thousand, and thousands of thousands," but it should be noted this is not meant to be an exact number but rather a way of expressing an unimaginably large number. Cabalists in the 14th century conducted a census of the angels; their best efforts estimated the angelic population at 301,655,722, adding they reproduced "like flies."

Sources: Rahner, *Encyclopedia of Theology*, 8–12; Smith, *Dictionary of Christian Biography, Literature, Sects and Doctrines*, 13

Angka

A species of gigantic bird of Arabic folklore, the angka were said to be able to sweep down and snatch up an elephant. Similar to the PHOENIX, the angka were believed to live for seventeen hundred years and then their bodies would ignite, become consumed in ashes, reform, and rise anew. Associated with the ROC because of their size, these creatures were believed to have been created as the perfect bird, but over the eons began to devour all of the animals on earth and then began hunting human children. The people of the world prayed to God for deliverance and He made the angka unable to reproduce, eventually causing the species to become extinct.

Source: Leviton, *Encyclopedia of Earth Myths*, n.pag.; Zell-Ravenheart, *Wizard's Bestiary*, 18

Angont

In the traditional beliefs of the Wyandot (Huron) people of North America, Angont was believed to be a gigantic, venomous, and vicious horned snake (see HORNED SERPENT) with fiery eyes living in desolate and lonely places in caves, forests, lakes, and rivers; from these locations it was able to affect the world with its massive coils and bring disaster and disease to mankind. Medicine men would sometimes go in search of it in order to create powerful medicine but because it was so poisonous no good ever came from it or anyone who wore its talisman.

Source: De Kirk, *Dragonlore*, 48; Eberhart, *Mysterious Creatures*, 19; Rose, *Giants, Monsters, and Dragons*, 19; Zell-Ravenheart, *Wizard's Bestiary*, 18

Anguta

A creature from the Inuit underworld, Adlivun, Anguta took the souls of the deceased into the afterlife where he lived with his daughter, the beautiful and desirous goddess of the sea, Sedna.

According to folklore, Sedna was courted by a seabird, the chief of the fulmars, but she was miserable in his filthy tent and his inability to provide enough food; for a year and a day she cried out to her father to save her. Arriving on a warm wind he appeared, killed the fulmar, and fled with his daughter. When the fulmars discovered the fate of their leader they flew out to sea until they discovered the father and daughter escaping in a boat. The birds caused a great storm to arise and in an attempt to save himself, Anguta tossed his daughter overboard. As Senda tried to climb back into the boat, her father, Anguta, cut off her fingers, which—as they fell into the ocean—became the first whales. Eventually the storm ended and she managed to climb back into the boat. No longer loving her father, Sedna had her hunting dogs attack Anguta and they chewed off his hands and feet.

Source: Leeming, *Dictionary of Creation Myths*, 218; Lynch, *Native American Mythology A to Z*, 5

Animalitos (On-ah-ma-lee-toes)

In Spanish folklore, the *animalitos* ("little animals") are a species of vampiric creatures described as having the head of a lizard and the mouth of a dog. Standing only about four inches tall, they hunt in natural water sources and pools where bathers and swimmers frequent. This is one of the few vampiric creatures proven helpful to mankind. According to folklore, centuries ago animalitos were captured by healers and tamed in order to be used in treatment methods which otherwise would have required the use of leeches. Only the most skilled healers would utilize an animalitos in their practice, for it was believed if the creature drank too much blood and killed the patient, the person's soul would immediately descend straight into Hell.

Source: Dominicis, *Repase y escriba*, 206; Espinosa, *Spanish Folk-Tales*, 66, 179; Maberry, *Vampire Universe*, 18

Aniukha (On-you-khah)

This vampiric creature has more in common with the CHUPACABRA of Mexico than the undead shaman of Mongolia, who shares its name. This vampiric animal was first sighted in Siberia immediately after the Second World War. Numerous members of the Jewish community claimed to have seen it, describing it as a small woodland animal ranging in size between a large grasshopper and a small rabbit. Although the aniukha ran on all four legs, it could also stand erect and was said to be able to leap with the skill and grace of a cat. Its body was described as having plated skin and intermittent patches of thick, brown fur; huge, black eyes; pointed ears; and a short snout housing a mouth full of short, jagged, little teeth. As oddly as this chimerical creature is described, it has no extraordinary physical capabilities; rather, it uses its cleverness and acts of trickery to snare prey—small children and the elderly. Luckily the aniukha is repelled by garlic. By smearing some on your chest or even along the doorways of your home, its aroma will keep the creature at bay. The only way to completely destroy the aniukha is to cremate the body, rendering it to ashes.

Source: *Encyclopaedia of Religion and Ethics*, Volume 3, 8; Lopatin, *Cult of the Dead*, 60; Maberry, *Vampire Universe*, 19

Aniwye

In Ojibwa folklore in Canada and the United States of America, aniwye is described as being an enormous skunk which craves human flesh, killing its prey with its powerful spray. Fortunately this creature is large enough to see a great distance away and can be avoided. It is easy to communicate with and understands mankind; in one story, it was strong enough to rip the roof off of a house.

Source: Rose, *Giants, Monsters, and Dragons*, 19; Sierra, *Gruesome Guide to World Monsters*, 14; Zell-Ravenheart, *Wizard's Bestiary*, 18

Anjana

Variations: Anja

One of the DIG-GAJAS from Hindu mythology, Anjana is one of the eight elephant protectors of the eight compass points; he guards the west and his mate is named Anjanavati. Symbols of protection, stability, and strength, they were born of the halves of the cosmic golden egg, Hiranyagarbha, which hatched the sun.

Source: Dowson, *Classical Dictionary of Hindu Mythology and Religion, Geography, History, and Literature*, 92, 180; Gupta, *Elephant in Indian Art and Mythology*, 7

Anjing Ajak

A particularly ferocious and vicious lycanthrope from Indonesian folklore, the anjing ajak lives the life of a man by day but at night he transforms into a vicious creature, part man and part wolf (see WEREWOLF). Walking on its hind legs, this creature hunts humans and kills them savagely with its claws and teeth. Clever as well as smart, the anjing ajak may be slain by shooting it through the brain or heart.

Source: Knappert, *Pacific Mythology*, 19, 322; Maberry, *Vampire Universe*, 19–20; Rose, *Giants, Monsters, and Dragons*, 19

Ankh-Aapau

Variations: Amamet, Am-Mit

In ancient Egyptian mythology Ankh-Aapau was described as being a monstrous serpent living in the fifth section, or hour, of Tuat, the Underworld; it lived upon the flames it emanated from its mouth. Ankh-Aapau and TEPAN are watched over by two SPHINXES; before Ankh-Aapau are four seated gods who have the emblems of "hidden symbols" of the god Seker upon their knees. In *The Text of Unas* there is a magical spell which when performed will cause the destruction of monstrous beasts and serpents alike; Ankh-Aapau would be affected by this spell.

Source: Budge, *Gods of the Egyptians*, 222; Coulter, *Encyclopedia of Ancient Deities*, 32; Mercatante, *Who's Who in Egyptian Mythology*, 10

Ankhi

In ancient Egyptian mythology Ankhi is a monstrous serpent; it is described as having a bearded mummy-form god growing out from each side of its body.

Source: Budge, *Gods of the Egyptians*, 200; Mercatante, *Who's Who in Egyptian Mythology*, 11

Ankou (Ahn-koo)

Variations: Death, Father Time, Grim Reaper

In the Breton folklore tradition Ankou ("reaper of the dead") is the personification of Death; it is described as looking like a tall, thin, white-haired person carrying a scythe, wearing a felt hat, and dressed in either black clothing or a shroud. Sometimes he is said to look like a skeleton. Ankou's head can rotate three-hundred-sixty degrees; he drives a *karrigell an Ankou* ("carriage of Ankou") pulled by skeletal horses and has a servant called *mevel an Ankou*. In some parts of Brittany, it is believed the last person who died in the previous year is the current year's Ankou.

Ankou is said to travel the countryside collecting the souls of the dead and dying, although there is some confusion over what he does with the souls once he has them. Some tales say he delivers them to Anaon, the king of the Underworld, takes them across the sea, or delivers them to face their Final Judgment.

Source: Koch, *Celtic Culture*, 67; McCoy, *Witch's Guide to Faery Folk*, 175; Van Scott, *Encyclopedia of Hell*, 19

Anmalfrosh

In Albanian-Italian mythology, anmalfrosh ("wild beast") was a ferocious being known to the Albanians residing in Calabria and Sicily.

Source: Elsie, *Dictionary of Albanian Religion, Mythology, and Folk Culture*, 9

Annwn, Hounds of

Variations: Cwn Annwn, Herla's Hounds, Hounds of the Hills

The hounds of Annwn were the spectral fairy hounds (see FAIRY ANIMAL) associated with Annwn, the underworld in Welsh mythology. Owned by Arawn, Lord of Annwn, the pack was usually sent out on their own to retrieve souls for Annwn or to reveal and occasionally consume a corpse. In the *First Branch of the Mabinogi* (*Pedair Cainc y Mabinogi*), the hounds were described as being shining white with red ears, but other sources say they were small, grey hounds with red speckles. Considered to be a psychopomp (death omen), to see them was an omen of death.

After the introduction of Christianity the Hounds of Annwn were reclassified as hell hounds; however, Annwn itself was more accurately defined as a paradise.

Source: Conway, *Magickal, Mystical Creatures*, 147; Green, *Animals in Celtic Life and Myth*, 168, 190; Illes, *Encyclopedia of Spirits*, 188–9

Anqa

Variations: Anqä, Anqu Mughrib, Al-Mas'udi, SEEMURG, Simurgh

In Turkish folklore, the anqa is an enormous bird said to inhabit the Caucasus mountain range; it is attracted to fire and has been associated with the sun and the mythological bird, the PHOENIX.

When the female anqa lays its eggs, it becomes very sick and the male anqa brings her water it carries in its beak. Once the egg is laid the female leaves and the male broods upon it for 125 years, after which the mother returns, the egg will hatch, and an adult anqa emerges. If the hatchling is a female then its mother collects great quantities of wood and striking her bill against the male's creates a spark which will ignite a fire. The mother then allows her body to be consumed in the flames and the female hatchling becomes the male's new mate. If the hatchling is male, then the process is repeated, except it is the father who immolates.

Source: Bonnerjea, *Allborough New Age Guide*, 22; Lawrence, *Shahrastani on the Indian Religions*, 127, 129–30; Skyes, *Who's Who in Non-Classical Mythology*, 166

Antaf

A much feared serpent from ancient Egyptian mythology, Antaf ("he who ends life") was well known to attack the deceased in their tombs. In *The Text of Unas* there is a magical spell which when performed will cause the destruction of monstrous beasts and serpents alike; Antaf would be affected by this spell.

Source: Budge, *Gods of the Egyptians*, 23; Coulter, *Encyclopedia of Ancient Deities*, 32,

Antelopes with Six Legs

In Siberian mythology the antelopes with six legs were said to be too fast for humans to hunt and impossible to catch. The divine huntsman, Tunkpoj, made a pair of skates from a sacred tree and cut off the animals' rear-most legs thereby making the animals easier to hunt.

Source: Borges, *Book of Imaginary Beings*, 22

Antholops

Variations: Yahmur

A species of fierce bovines with saw-like horns, the antholops were powerful enough to cut down oak trees. The antholops were too clever to be slain by hunters who stalked after them but they were often slain when they would go to the river to drink; they would play in the soft branches and vines along the riverbanks where they would become entangled. Once trapped in the flora, hunters could easily approach and shoot. The antholops were described as being fast runners; their reddish, solid horns shed annually like those of a deer.

Source: Torrance, *Encompassing Nature*, 580; Wiener, *Contributions Toward a History of Arabico-Gothic Culture*, Volume 4, 68

Antlion

Variations: Ant-Lion, Formicaleon, Formicaleun, Mirmicioleon, Mermicoleon ("lion among ants"), Myrmecoleon, Myrmecoles

According to *Physiologus*, a didactic Greek text of natural folklore compiled by an unknown Christian author sometime in the second century, AD, an antlion is a creature born of the union between a male lion and a female ant; it is described as having the face of a lion and the fore- and hindquarters of an ant. Eventually all antlions die of starvation because their dual nature will not allow them to eat either animal flesh or plants.

Source: Curley, *Physiologus*, 49; Flaubert, *Temptation of St. Anthony*, 255; Rosen, *Mythical Creatures Bible*, 173; Zell-Ravenheart, *Companion for the Apprentice Wizard*, 178

Antukai

Variations: Atunkai

In the folklore of the Kalapuya Indians, Oregon, United States of America, the antukai is a monstrous otter-like creature. According to folklore a bear once wandered too close to the water occupied by an AMHULUK, who in its anger, transformed the bear into the antukai.

Source: Gatschet, *Journal of American Folk-lore*, 260; Rose, *Giants, Monsters, and Dragons*, 21; Zell-Ravenheart, *Wizard's Bestiary*, 19

Anxo

Variations: Ancho, Antxo

A NATURE SPIRIT of the mountains, Anxo is a CYCLOPS or evil spirit from Basque mythology in the region of Marquina; it is said to live in a cave.

Source: Miguel de Barandiarán, *Selected Writings of José Miguel De Barandiarán*, 92

Anzu

Variations: Anzu Bird, Imgig Bird, Imdugud, Imndugud, Zu

The personal guard to the god Enlil in Sumerian mythology, Anzu was a large eagle or vulture sometimes said to have a lion head. Originally he was benign and faithful, representing the power of thunderstorms, and in the Old Sumerian period he was depicted as an animal-man hybrid; however, around 2000 BC, a story of Anzu's rebellion against the gods and his becoming evil came forth. This was particularly prevalent in Akkadian folklore where ancient literature described him as "aggressive."

According to the story, Anzu waited for Enlil to take his daily ritual bath and then stole the Tablets of Destiny in order to control the destinies and the powers of the gods. In the end, Anzu was slain by the hero Ninurta for his treachery; the hero cut off his pinions with an arrowhead and before Anzu could speak the spell to restore them, was slain. Anzu is listed as one of the SLAIN HEROES.

Source: Ataç, *Mythology of Kingship in Neo-Assyrian Art*, 185; Andrews, *Dictionary of Nature Myths*, 97; Leick, *Dictionary of Ancient Near Eastern Mythology*, 9–10; Zell-Ravenheart, *Wizard's Bestiary*, 19

Ao Ao

In the folklore of Argentina, Brazil, Bolivia, and Paraguay, the carnivorous ao ao is a nocturnal predator hunting humans. It has been described as looking like a porcine (piglike) monster or a sheep with fangs; when on the hunt it makes a cry from which its onomatopoeia name was given "ao, ao, ao, ao." It is relentless in pursuit of its prey, never giving up until it has captured its quarry. The only means by which to escape an ao ao is to climb up a palm tree; if safety is sought in any other species of tree the ao ao will dig at its roots until the tree falls over.

Source: Maberry, *Wanted Undead Or Alive*, 137; O'Rourke, *Give War a Chance*, 49

Ao Bing

Variations: Ao Ping

In ancient Chinese mythology, Ao Bing was a DRAGON and the third son of the DRAGON KING, AO KUANG; he was described as having the head of a fish and the body of a human. Ao Bing was slain by the violent, cultural warrior Nezha (Nazha, Nuozha) while trying to retrieve an apology from him for his having slain two of his father's messengers. After his death, Nezha had the tendons removed and woven into a belt to commemorate his great victory.

Source: Roberts, *Chinese Mythology, A to Z*, 3, 4, 36

Ao Ch'in

Variations: Ao Chin, Ao K'in, Ao Qin

In ancient Chinese mythology, Ao Ch'in was one of the four DRAGON KINGS, collectively they controlled the rain and sea water; each has its own dominion. Ao Ch'in watched over the Southern Sea of China.

Source: De Kirk, *Dragonlore*, 25–6; Roberts, *Chinese Mythology, A to Z*, 35, 36; Rose, *Giants, Monsters, and Dragons*, 21

Ao Jun

Variations: Ao Guang, Ao Ji

In ancient Chinese mythology, Ao Jun was one of the four DRAGON KINGS; collectively they controlled the rain and sea water; each has its own dominion; Ao Jun watched over the Western Sea of China. He possessed an impressive treasure trove of both magical items and wealth.

Source: De Kirk, *Dragonlore*, 25–6; Roberts, *Chinese Mythology, A to Z*, 34; Rose, *Giants, Monsters, and Dragons*, 21

Ao Kuang

Variations: Ao Guang

In ancient Chinese mythology, Ao Kuang was one of the four DRAGON KINGS. Collectively they controlled the rain and sea water, each having its own dominion. Ao Kuang watched over the Eastern Sea of China. Ao Kuang's third son, AO BING, was slain by the child warrior Nezha (Nuozha). Upon learning of his son's death, Ao Kuang demanded an apology from Nezha who refused to give it; instead the overly proud warrior confronted the grieving father, trampled his body, and skinned him alive. Wailing in pain, Ao Kuang begged for mercy and his life was spared on the condition he transform into a blue snake and live as a pet in the sleeve of Nezha (Nuozha).

Source: De Kirk, *Dragonlore*, 25–6; Roberts, *Chinese Mythology A to Z*, 31; Rose, *Giants, Monsters, and Dragons*, 21

Ao Shun

Variations: Ao Ghun, Ao Ming

In ancient Chinese mythology, Ao Shun was one of the four DRAGON KINGS. Collectively they controlled the rain and sea water, each having its own dominion. Ao Shun watched over the Northern Sea of China.

Source: De Kirk, *Dragonlore*, 25–6; Rose, *Giants, Monsters, and Dragons*, 21

Aobōzu

In Japanese folklore the aobōzu ("blue priest") is a YŌKAI possibly created by the eighteenth century artist Toriyama Sekien in his book *Gazu Hyakki Yakō*; it was depicted as a one-eyed Buddhist priest standing next to a thatched hut. It is possible the aobōzu was the inspiration for the one-eyed YŌKAI priest HITOTSUME-KOZŌ.

Source: Murakami, *Yōkai Jiten*, 3–4, 164; Tada, *Edo Yōkai Karuta*, 18

Aonbarr

Variations: Aonbharr, Enabarr ("foam" or "froth")

In Irish mythology, Aonbarr ("unique supremacy") was the loyal white steed of the hero Mannann mac Lir; he was said to be able to gallop fast enough to travel over sea as easily as he could over land.

Source: Andrews, *Dictionary of Nature Myths*, 115; Rose, *Giants, Monsters, and Dragons*, 22

Aosagibi

Variations: Aosaginohi

A monstrous, animal-like YŌKAI from Japanese folklore, the aosagibi ("blue heron fire") was created by the eighteenth century artist Toriyama Sekien in his book *Gazu Hyakki Yakō*; it was depicted as a night heron with an illuminated body.

Source: Mizuki, *Mujara 5*, 70

Apa

Variations: Apa Atua

In Polynesian mythology there were two species of apa; the apa atua were minor gods and acted as the messengers of the other gods. The other apa was a whirlwind, the bodily form of the apa atua. The apa, in general, were the messengers and servitors of the MAREIKURA and the WHATUKURA.

Source: Whatahoro, *Lore of the Whare-wānanga*, xv

Apalala

Variations: Apala

A NAGA from Buddhist folklore, Apalala lived in the Swat River in what is now Pakistan; this huge and benign DRAGON was capable of controlling the flow of the river and the amount of rain which fell in the area; the local farmers would show their appreciation for this and his willingness to keep evil DRAGONS who would try to causes droughts, floods, and rainstorms out of the area by making an offering of grain to him each season. Apalala was very good at protecting the valley, so much so that the people there began to take him for granted and their tribute to him stopped; this neglect caused him to become angry and vengeful. Apalala caused a great flood to sweep through the valley one year and then the next caused a terrible drought. The Buddha came to Swat and, filled with compassion for the people who could reliably grow their crops, went to speak with the angered NAGA. The Buddha was so convincing in showing Apalala the error of his ways the NAGA converted and became a Buddhist himself. He stopped tormenting the people of the valley and they promised to deliver to him a large tribute every twelve years to celebrate his kindness.

Source: De Kirk, *Dragonlore*, 36; McCall, *Dragons*, 22–23; Niles, *Dragons*, 104–05; Zell-Ravenheart, *Wizard's Bestiary*, 19

Aphareus

According to Ovid's *Metamorphoses*, Aphareus was one of the CENTAURS who attended the wedding of Pirithous, became drunk on wine and, following the lead of EURYTUS, who assaulted Hippodame, began to assault and rape any women they could grab. During the ensuing Centauromachy, Aphareus was throwing boulders.

Source: Combe, *Description of the Collection of Ancient Marbles in the British Museum*, 9; Ovid, *Metamorphoses*, 215

Aphidas

A CENTAUR from ancient Greek mythology, Aphidas was one of the CENTAURS who attended the wedding of Pirithous, became drunk on wine and, following the lead of EURYTUS, who assaulted Hippodame, began to assault and rape any women they could grab. Aphidas had passed out drunk before the Centauromachy started but he was seen by Pirithous who took advantage of the situation and threw a spear at him, piercing him through the neck and killing the CENTAUR without ever awakening him.

Source: *Commentary, Mythological, Historical, and Geographical on Pope's Homer*, 55; Ovid, *Metamorphoses*, 336

Apli

Apli ("calf") was one of the oxen named in Thorgrimr's *Rhymes* in *Prose Edda*, written by Snorri Sturluson (1179–1241), the Icelandic historian, poet, and politician.

Source: Jennbert, *Animals and Humans*, 49; Sturluson, *Prose Edda*, Volume 5, 213

Apophis

Variations: Aaapef, Aphophis, Apep

The name *Apophis* is the Greek form of the ancient Egyptian name *Aaapef*, a gigantic night-demon serpent; it is the most commonly used name of the creature. According to some scholars, Apophis was a form taken by the god of darkness and evil, Set.

According to the mythology, each night Apophis would battle the sun god Ra just before he would ascend into Tuat, the Underworld. Using his flames and magical spells, Ra destroyed him.

The *Book of the Overthrowing of Apophis* describes a ritual which was performed daily in the temple of Ra. The spell describes in great detail the fate of Apophis, who was gashed and speared before every bone in his body was removed with red-hot knives. Then, his head, legs, and tail were singed, scorched, and consumed by fire. NAK and SEBAU, as well as all the other monstrous helpers, offspring, shadows, and spirits, suffered this same demise.

Source: Davis, *Egyptian Book of the Dead*, 30; Mercatante, *Who's Who in Egyptian Mythology*, 13–14

Apotamkin

Variations: Ponca

The Maliseet-Passamaquoddy people of the northeastern coast of the Unites States of America have in their mythology a FAIRY ANIMAL called an apotamkin. Described as looking like an extremely hairy humanoid with enormous teeth, it preys on children who wander out on thin ice, venture onto the beach alone, or otherwise misbehave; this essentially makes it a NURSERY BOGIE.

Source: Malinowski, *Gale Encyclopedia of Native American Tribes*, 108, 225; Rose, *Giants, Monsters, and Dragons*, 7

Apotharni

Described by the Alsatian humanist and encyclopedist Conrad Lycosthenes (1518–1561) in his

1557 work, *Prodigorum ac ostentorum chronicon*, the apotharni were a hybrid race, half horse and half human. Similar to the CENTAURS of Greek mythology, which were almost always male, the marsh-dwelling apotharni were of both genders; the females were described as being baldheaded but having whiskers upon their chin resembling a beard.

Source: Ashman, *Fabulous Beasts*, 54; Rose, *Giants, Monsters, and Dragons*, 24; Zell-Ravenheart, *Wizard's Bestiary*, 19

Apparition

The field of parapsychology loosely defines an apparition as the perceptual experience of an animal or person which is not physically present, cannot be communicated with, and has been ruled out as hallucination. It also makes a clear separation of apparitions and spirit forms. Apparitions are the supernatural visual presence of a substantial presence which may be a ghost, a spirit, or simply the image of a person, be they deceased or living.

Source: Irwin, *Introduction to Parapsychology*, 192–93; Joyce, *Weiser Field Guide to the Paranormal*, 10–11

Après

Variations: Apree, Apres

Seldom seen outside of heraldic text-books, the après is depicted as a creature with a body similar to a bull but has the tail of a bear.

Source: Elvin, *Elvin's Dictionary of Heraldry*, 6; Fox-Davies, *Complete Guide to Heraldry*, 231; Zell-Ravenheart, *Wizard's Bestiary*, 19

Apsaras (Aps-sa-rahs)

Similar to the ALP of German folklore, the apsaras ("from the water") of India is a female vampiric celestial creature; they were created when Vishnu used Mount Mandara as a churning rod in the *Churning of the Ocean* folklore. As he did so, aside from the other fabulous creatures and treasures he created, 35 million apsaras came forth.

Known for their goddess-like beauty and charms, artistic talents, excessive love of wine and dice as well as their love of dance, the apsaras are sent to earth to defile virtuous men, particularly those seeking to become even more virtuous. The creature will seduce such a man off his path, causing him to use up the merit he had previously accumulated.

An apsaras has a wide array of talents and abilities at its disposal to assist in carrying out its tasks, such as the capability to cause insanity, having complete control over the animals of the forest, inspiring a warlike fury in a man, making frighteningly accurate predictions, shape-shifting into various forms, and sending inspiration to lovers. Although apsaras can also perform minor miracles, they do not have the power to grant a boon like the Devas or the gods.

Occasionally, an apsaras will enjoy the task it has been sent on. Should it succeed in breaking the man's will and finds him to be a pleasurable lover, it may offer him the reward of immortality. However, if despite its best efforts the apsaras cannot make the man succumb, it will either cause him to go insane or have his body torn apart by the wild animals of the forest.

Collectively, the apsaras are mated to the gandharvas, who can play music as beautifully as the apsaras can dance; however, there have been times when an apsaras has fallen in love with the man it was sent to seduce. Rather than cause his ruin, she would marry him. Stories say they make for an excellent wife and mother.

When not seeking to undo righteous men, the apsaras fly about the heads of those who will be great warriors on the battlefield. If one of these warriors dies with his weapon still in hand, the apsaras will carry his soul up and into Paradise.

Source: Bolle, *Freedom of Man*, 69, 74–75; Dowson, *Classical Dictionary*, 19; Hopkins, *Epic Mythology*, 28, 45, 164; Meyer, *Mythologie der Germanen*, 138, 142, 148; Turner, *Dictionary of Ancient Deities*, 63

Apsasu

In ancient Sumerian mythology, the apsasu were the female human-headed, winged bull and lion colossi guarding the gateways of Assyrian and Hittite palaces and temples; the corresponding males were called *aladlammu*.

Source: Black, *Gods, Demons and Symbols of Ancient Mesopotamia*, 115; Cherry, *Mythical Beasts*, 113

Aqrabuamelu

Variations: Girtablilu, Scorpion Man

In ancient Akkadian mythology the aqrabuamelu—human-scorpion hybrids—acted as the guardians to the gate of Kurnugi, an underworld. The only known man-made structure where the aqrabuamelu appear is as a relief on a wall of the Tell Halaf palace; it dates from the late tenth or early ninth century BCE.

Source: Ornan, *Orbis Biblicus et Orientalis*, 124; Wilson, *The Devil*, 23

Aqueous Devils

In Francesco Maria Guazzo's book, *Compendium Maleficarum* (*Compendium of Witches*, 1628), he described seven different types of demons, one of which is the aqueous, or aquatic devil. He writes as a species they appear as generally beautiful and seductive women who prey upon mankind, striking whenever an opportunity presents itself. They have the ability to drown swimmers, cause storms at sea, and sink ships. Naturally, one would encounter such a creature in lakes, oceans, and other bodies of water where they must live.

Source: Kipfer, *Order of Things*, 255; Paine, *Hierarchy of Hell*, 69; Simons, *Witchcraft World*, 78; Summers, *Witchcraft and Black Magic*, 77

Aquila

An eagle from ancient Greek mythology, Aquila ("eagle") carried the thunderbolts of the god Zeus (Jupiter) for him into battle against the Titans.

Source: Dixon-Kennedy, *Encyclopedia of Greco-Roman Mythology*, 41

Arachne (a-rak-ne)

In Ovid's *Metamorphose*, Arachne was born the daughter of Idmon of Colophone; a beautiful young woman who was a highly skilled weaver. Arachne was proud and boastful of her skill, claiming she was more talented than Athena (Minerva), the goddess of weaving. One day the goddess assumed the form of an old woman and visited Arachne, advising her to act and speak more modestly. When Arachne replied with a rude quip the virgin goddess revealed herself and challenged the mortal to a weaving contest. Athena's tapestry depicted a scene of the twelve Olympian gods punishing those who challenged their authority; Arachne's depicted the exploitative and unjust behavior the gods showed the mortals. Arachne's tapestry was flawlessly constructed but in her anger, Athena (Minerva) ripped it apart and struck the young woman with her shuttle. When Arachne later tried to hang herself, the goddess decided to make an example of her and transformed her into a spider so she may artlessly and eternally spin.

Source: Fox, *Greek and Roman*, 78; Roman, *Encyclopedia of Greek and Roman Mythology*, 78; Simpson, *Metamorphoses of Ovid*, 94–7

Aralez

Variations: Arlez, Jaralez

In Armenian folklore, the sacred dogs of the gods, the aralez ("to lick" or "take blood"), have the ability to lick the wounds of the brave warriors who fell in battle or died by the hand of a treacherous foe. In their licking, they would heal the body and restore it to life as they did in the unrequited love story between Ara the beautiful and Shamiram.

Source: Bonnefoy, *American, African, and Old European Mythologies*, 267; Chahin, *Kingdom of Armenia*, 74; Gray, *Mythology of All Races* Volume 7, 90

Aranda

An enormous river-serpent from Emianga folk-lore, a region of Australia, the aranda lives in the depths of the river where the currents are so deep they do not disturb the surface. It consumes people in a single gulp who come along the riverbanks to fish.

Source: De Kirk, *Dragonlore*, 59; Rose, *Giants, Monsters, and Dragons*, 24

Arassas

Variations: Arasses

In French Alps folklore the arassas is described as being a serpentine DRAGON, having the forequarters of a lizard but the head of a cat; it is similar to the TAZZLEWORM of Austria, Bavaria, and the Swiss Alps.

Source: De Kirk, *Dragonlore*, 39, 46; Rose, *Giants, Monsters, and Dragons*, 24

Arcadian Hind

Variations: Akadian Hind, Cerneian Hind, Cerynean Hind, Ceryneia Hind, Cerynitian Hind, Hind of Ceryneia, Kerynitian Hind

In ancient Greek mythology the capture of the Arcadian hind was the fourth (or third, sources vary) of the twelve Labors the demi-god and cultural hero Hercules (Heracles) had to perform in order to cleanse himself of having killed his wife and children and to simultaneously gain his immortality. He was to capture it and return it to Eurystheus in Mycenae. The hind lived near the Kernites River on Mount Kernites in north-eastern Arcadia; a sacred animal to the goddess Artemis (Diana), Hercules did not want to anger the goddess, so attempted to capture the hind alive; it ran so quickly it took Hercules (Heracles) a year to track it from Oenoe to Mount Artemisius in Argolis; there, he shot it non-lethally with an arrow just as it was about to jump across the river Ladon. Hercules then carried the wounded hind, alive, to Mycenae, a distance of nearly fifty miles (80 kilometers). The hind, sacred to the goddess Artemis (Diana), was described as being beautiful, having antlers shining like gold and feet of bronze.

Source: Daly, *Greek and Roman Mythology, A to Z*, 69; Hard, *Routledge Handbook of Greek Mythology*, 259; Roman, *Encyclopedia of Greek and Roman Mythology*, 210

Arctophonos

Variations: Aretophonus

In classical Greek mythology, Arctophonos ("bear-killer") and PTOOPHAGOS were the two hunting dogs of the GIGANTE, Orion. Arctophonos was said to have enough endurance and strength to kill a bear.

Source: Brewer, *Character Sketches of Romance, Fiction and the Drama*, Volume 3, 131; Rose, *Giants, Monsters, and Dragons*, 25

Arctus

A CENTAUR from ancient Greek mythology, Arctus attended the wedding of Prince of Pirithous to Hippodame. The epic Greek poem *The Shield of Heracles* written by the Greek poet Hesiod, records the Centauromachy between the Lapith soldiers and the CENTAURS which took place when fellow CENTAUR EURYTUS became drunk and attempted to rape the bride during the reception. Upon the surface of the intricately worked shield are representatives of each army; on one side are the Lapith soldiers, Prince Caeneus, Dryas, Exadius, Hopleus, Phalerus, King Pirithous, and Prolochusc, and rushing at them are the CENTAURS ASBOLUS, black-maned MIMAS, PETRAEUS, and UREUS. The men, armed with spears, were met by the CENTAURS who ripped up fir trees and used them as weapons, swatting at them with the trunks.

Source: Hesiod, *Works of Hesiod, Callimachus and Theognis*, 59; Westmoreland, *Ancient Greek Beliefs*, 202

Areion (Ariôn)

Variations: Areion of the Black Mane, Arion

In classical Greek mythology, Areion was an immortal horse born to the goddess Demeter (Ceres) after she had been raped by the god of the sea, Poseidon (Neptune), who had assumed the form of a horse; the resulting colt was one of the HIPPOI ATHANATOI. Areion was first owned by Ogkios, then Hercules (Heracles), and finally by Adrestos, a Trojan warrior who was slain by Agamemnon in Homer's *Iliad* (book six). Areion was noted for having extraordinary qualities, such as human speech.

According to the Greek grammarian and poet Antimachus, Areion was the offspring of Gaea; in other traditions, Poseidon (Neptune) or Zephyrus (the west wind) begot the horse by a HARPY. In one story, Poseidon (Neptune) created the horse while competing in a contest with Athena (Minerva).

Source: Brewer, *Character Sketches of Romance, Fiction and the Drama*, Volumes 8, 266; *Contemporary Review*, Volume 27, 809; Smith, *Dictionary of Greek and Roman Biography and Mythology*, n.pag.

Areop Enap

Variations: Ancient Spider, Yelafaz

In Nauruan mythology the primordial spider Areop Enap ("old spider") was caught by a clam while looking for food; within it she came upon RIGI the caterpillar and cast a magical spell making him temporarily strong so he might be able to force the clam open. During the attempt RIGI sweated so much salt water that the clam was forced to open or die. From the top of the shell Areop Enap created the sky and from the bottom, the earth. A snail—

also trapped within the clam—became the moon; the flesh of the clam became the islands. Sadly, RIGI died from exhaustion so Areop Enap wove a cocoon around his body and suspended him in the sky, creating the sun.

Source: Bartlett, *Mythology Bible*, 176; Tresidder, *Complete Dictionary of Symbols*, 45; Zell-Ravenheart, *Wizard's Bestiary*, 19

Areos

A CENTAUR from classical Greek mythology, Areos attended the wedding of Pirithous, became drunk on wine and, following the lead of EURYTUS, who assaulted Hippodame, began to assault and rape any women they could grab. During the ensuing Centauromachy, Areos, along with IMBRIUS and LYCIDAY, was slain by the the Lapith soldier, Dryas.

Source: Dymock, *Bibliotheca Classica*, 98; Simpson, *Metamorphoses of Ovid*, 481

Arfr

Variations: Arf

Arfr ("bull") was one of the oxen named in Thorgrimr's *Rhymes* in the Icelandic historian, poet, and politician Snorri Sturluson's (1179–1241) *Prose Edda*.

Source: Jennbert, *Animals and Humans*, 49; Sturluson, *Prose Edda*, Volume 5, 213

Arfuni

Arfuni ("heir") was one of the oxen named in Thorgrimr's *Rhymes* in the Icelandic historian, poet, and politician Snorri Sturluson's (1179–1241) *Prose Edda*.

Source: Jennbert, *Animals and Humans*, 49; Sturluson, *Prose Edda*, Volume 5, 213

Argeius

In classical Greek mythology, Argeius was one of the CENTAURS slain by the demi-god and cultural hero Hercules (Heracles) while visiting his friend, a CENTAUR named PHOLUS, between the conclusion of his third Labor and the onset of his fourth. When an old and particularly fragrant hogshead of wine was opened, its aroma carried on the air and drove the local CENTAURS into a fury. Argeius, AMPHION, DAPHNIS, DUPO, HIPPOTION, ISOPLES, MELANCHETES, OREUS, PHRIXUS, and THEREUS were slain by Hercules (Heracles) as he defended himself from their violent and unwarranted assault.

Source: Barthell, *Gods and Goddesses of Ancient Greece*, 187; Diodorus, *Historical Library of Diodorus the Sicilian*, Volume 1, 229–30

Argopelter

One of the FEARSOME CRITTERS from the lumberjack folklore of the United States of America, the argopelters were creatures which lived inside of hollow trees and would assault passersby with swinging branches and wood splinters; their aim was typically flawless. In spite of their common assaults, the argopelters were never seen so there is no description of them.

Source: Botkin, *American People*, 2; Godfrey, *Monsters of Wisconsin*, 131; Rose, *Giants, Monsters, and Dragons*, 25

Argos

In *The Odyssey*, the epic Greek poem attributed to Homer, the greatest of Greek epic poets, Argos was the faithful dog of Odysseus. After a 20 year adventure Odysseus finally manages to make his way back home to Ithaca; he approaches his home in disguise and is recognized by no one save for his dog, Argos. Once known for his speed, strength, and tracking skills, the dog—which had been neglected—is sitting upon a pile of cow manure, tired and covered with lice. The dog recognizes his master immediately and although he is too weak to get up and greet him, Argos is able to drop his ears and wag his tail. In order to maintain his disguise Odysseus passes by his old friend, shedding a tear; as he enters his home's hall, Argos passes away.

Source: Berens, *Myths and Legends of Ancient Greece and Rome*, 209, 216; Homer, *The Odyssey*, 319–21; Segal, *Singers, Heroes, and Gods in the Odyssey*, 56

Argus Fish

Named after Argus Panoptes of Greek mythology, the SEA SERPENT known as the argus fish was depicted in Olaus Magnus' *Monstrum in Oceano Germanica* ("Monsters of the North Sea," 1537); it was said to be over 70 feet long and had numerous sets of eyes upon its flanks.

Source: Zell-Ravenheart, *Wizard's Bestiary*, 19

Ariels

In the King James interpretation of the Bible, the ariels were leonine (lion-like) men, humans whose faces were similar to a lion's because they were descendants of the NEPHILIM. Behaiah, one of the thirty mighty men of King David, was said to have slain two ariels who came from Moab.

Source: Comay, *Who's Who in the Old Testament*, 57; DeLoach, *Giants*, 17, 77

Aries

Variations: Khrysomallos, Krios

In classical Greek mythology, Aries, a golden-fleeced and winged ram, was given as a gift by the god Hermes to the goddess (or NYMPH, sources vary), Nephele. According to folklore the goddess was wed to King Athamas and had two children

with him, but she eventually decided to return to Mount Olympus. The king remarried and his new wife, Ino, despised the children of her predecessor, Helle and Phrixus; the new queen arranged to have the children offered up in sacrifice. On the day the ritual was to take place, Nephele sent Aries to rescue her children. As they flew over the Black Sea, Helle lost her grip and fell. Upon arriving in Colchis, the ram shed its coat and flew up into the sky where it became the dim constellation, Aries. Phrixus hung the shed coat on a tree branch in a sacred grove. Another version of the folklore says Phrixus sacrificed the ram to Zeus (Jupiter) in thanks for his life being spared; the hide of the animal was offered to King Aeetes as a gift and Zeus (Jupiter) set Aries in the night sky as a constellation.

Source: Andrews, *Dictionary of Nature Myths*, 16; Hard, *New Handbook of Greek Mythology*, 379; Zell-Ravenheart, *Wizard's Bestiary*, 20

Arion (uh RY uhn)

In classical Greek mythology, the fabulous horse Arion and his sister, the goddess Despoina ("mistress"), were born of the rape of the goddess Demeter (Ceres, "earth mother") by the god Poseidon (Neptune). Not desirous of his attentions, the goddess attempted to escape him by use of therianthropy, shape-shifting herself into various forms; it was when she had become a mare and he a stallion that Poseidon (Neptune) caught up with her.

In the Roman version of the origin of Arion, the god of the sea, Neptune, raised Arion up from the ground by striking the earth with his trident. Another version says the horse was born of the union between the god and the FURY, Erynnes; yet another said he was conceived during the rape of Ceres while she was in the form of a mare attempting to escape Neptune.

No matter his origin, Arion, who had the feet of a man and was capable of human speech, was raised by the nereids (golden-haired sea nymphs); sometimes he was hitched to the chariot of Neptune and with his incredible speed, pulled him through the ocean. Arion had three masters in his life: King Capreus of Haliartus, the demi-god Hercules (Heracles), and finally King Adrastus of Argos.

Source: Bell, *Bell's New Pantheon*, 93; Monaghan, *Encyclopedia of Goddesses and Heroines*, 399; Room, *Naming of Animals*, 134; Zell-Ravenheart, *Wizard's Bestiary*, 19, 147

Arius

A CENTAUR from ancient Greek mythology, Arius was one of the CENTAURS slain by the demi-god and cultural hero Hercules (Heracles) while visiting his friend, a CENTAUR named PHOLUS, between the conclusion of his third Labor and the onset of his fourth.

Source: *Commentary, Mythological, Historical, and Geographical on Pope's Homer*, 55

Arkan Sonney

Variations: Fairy Pig of Man, Lucky Piggies, Lucky Piggy, Tucky Piggy

Arkan Sonney was a FAIRY ANIMAL from the folklore of the Isle of Man. Like the Hounds of Annwn from Welsh mythology, Arkan Sonney was described as a white pig with red ears; it also had the ability to change its size at will (see ANNWN, HOUNDS OF). Although it was a difficult undertaking, it was considered to be very lucky to catch one of these creatures. According to the folklore, if you did, you would find a piece of silver in your pocket.

Source: Briggs, *Encyclopedia of Fairies*, 10; Monaghan, *Encyclopedia of Celtic Mythology and Folklore*, 51; Smith, *W.B. Yeats and the Tribes of Danu*, 126

Arktos

In ancient Greek mythology Arktos ("mountain bear") was the name of one of the CENTAURS who attended the wedding of Pirithous, became drunk on wine and, following the lead of EURYTUS, who assaulted Hippodame, began to assault and rape any women they could grab. A great Centauromachy then followed.

Source: Colvin, *Cornhill Magazine*, Volume XXXVIII, 296; D'Angour, *Greeks and the New*, 76

Arneus

A CENTAUR from ancient Greek mythology, Arneus was one of the CENTAURS slain by the demigod and cultural hero Hercules (Heracles) while visiting his friend, a CENTAUR named PHOLUS, between the conclusion of his third Labor and the onset of his fourth.

Source: *Commentary, Mythological, Historical, and Geographical on Pope's Homer*, 55; Lemprière, *Bibliotheca Classica*, 694

Arngnasiutik

A type of anthropoid monster from Inuit folklore, the arngnasiutik ("woman chaser") was associated with the tree-line; these creatures are recognized for having humanoid behavior and motivations and therefore were not considered as animals such as one would hunt, but a type of "other," or creature.

Source: Halpin, *Manlike Monsters on Trial*, 205

Arundel

In British folklore Arundel was the mount of Sir Bevis of Southampton; he was said to not only be the best horse in all of England, but unmatched in speed and strength; once in a seven mile race, he did not begin to run until the others were two miles into the race and he still managed to win. Arundel was virtually unridable by anyone but his own knight, and when lent out to another, refused the rider and threw him, causing the man great harm. When he was stolen by King Edgar's son, indignant Arundel refused his new owner and kicked in the prince's brains; charged with murder, he and sir Bevis were banished from England.

Source: Brewer, *Character Sketches of Romance, Fiction and the Drama*, Volumes 1–2, 75; Ellis, *Saxon Romances*, 112, 125, 152–3

Arusha

In Hindu mythology Arusha ("bright" or "red") is the remarkable red stallion and lead horse pulling the chariot of the sun god, Suraya; of the six mares also harnessed but unnamed, the lead mare is known as Arushi ("dawn").

Source: Müller, *Vedic Hymns*, 24; Rose, *Giants, Monsters, and Dragons*, 27, 178

Aryaka

A NAGARAJA in Hindu mythology, Aryaka was the grandfather of the handsome Sumukha who had slain the father of GARUDA, a divine creature and the mount of the god, Vishnu. Matali, the charioteer of the god Indra, wanted to marry his daughter, Gunakesi, to Sumukha and sought Aryaka's permission; sadly, the NAGA reported GARUDA had declared his intent to consume his grandson for the slaying. Wanting to make the match, both Aryaka and Matali approached Indra and Vishnu with the dilemma; the gods gave them a draught of amrita, the Elixir of Immortality, to give to Sumukha to drink. Once the potion was consumed, the young man was made impervious to GARUDA's assault and able to marry his beloved.

Source: Menon, *Mahabharata*, 101–04; Vogel, *Indian Serpent-lore*, 93–4

Arzshenk

In Zoroastrian mythology and Persian folklore, Arzshenk was the king of Ahermanabâd; there he lived in an enchanted castle filled with plundered treasure; he was described as looking like a grotesque humanoid monster with the head of a bull, making him one of the KHRAFSTRA. Answerable only to the demonic and evil Ahriman, his army was commanded by the DEEV, SEFEED, and they would do constant battle against the forces of good. It has been foretold the hero Roostem (Rustam) will, in the final battle, decapitate Arzshenk.

Source: Keightley, *World Guide to Gnomes, Fairies, Elves, and Other Little People*, 18; Richardson, *Dictionary, Persian, Arabic and English*, Volume 1, Liv, Lv; Richardson, *Dissertation on the Languages*, 144; Yardley, *Supernatural in Romantic Fiction*, 53

Asag

Variations: ABZU, Asakku, DRAGON of the Abyss

The Sumerian mythological poem *Lugale (Lugal-e u me-lam-bi nir-gal, The Feats and Exploits of Ninurta)* mentions the demonic, underworld creature aptly named Asag ("demon that causes sickness"). Conceived on Earth and born from the union between the gods An and Ki, Asag was born a hideous, monstrous DRAGON. Although the poem speaks of him as if he were an actual being, it gives no true or definable description other than to say he is so repulsive his very presence in the water could boil fish. Asag commands an army of rock demons, his very own offspring created from his mating with a mountain. Asag was considered to be one of the SLAIN HEROES.

The personification of the frigid cold of winter and a demon of disease and sickness, Asag attacks and kills mankind through drought, head fevers, and migraines. He also restrains and withholds the Primal waters which fill the Abyss, keeping them from flooding the earth.

Asag was said to live in the Abyss, or in the mountains; the poem *Lugale* alluded to both places as his home. Asag's fate is unclear. The poem reveals he was attacked by the god Ninurta with his weapon, Sharur, but it never goes on to explain if Asag survived the assault or was slain.

Source: Ataç, *Mythology of Kingship in Neo-Assyrian Art*, 185; Bienkowski, *Dictionary of the Ancient Near East*, 214; *Journal of Near Eastern Studies, Sumerian Mythology: A Review Article*, 128–152; Lurker, *Dictionary of Gods and Goddesses*, 38; Wakeman, *God's Battle with the Monster*, 7–8

Asavan

In Zoroastrian mythology Asavan was said to be a three-legged, nine-mouthed, and six-eyed white mule with a golden alicorn (a single horn) atop its head; it would stride purposefully around the sea, Vourukasa. Asavan feeds upon *menong* (spiritual food) and when it drinks, it destroys all harmful creatures in the water; in fact, evil fails and eventually dies in its righteous presence. Ambergris is its dung, a substance highly valued by perfumers.

Source: Boyce, *History of Zoroastrianism*, 89

Asbolus

In ancient Greek mythology Asbolus ("sooty") was a CENTAUR who was not only a surgeon but also skilled in ornithomancy, divination by the flight patterns of birds. He was present at the wedding of the Prince of Pirithous to Hippodame when fellow CENTAUR EURYTUS became drunk and attempted to rape the bride during the reception. The epic Greek poem *The Shield of Heracles* written by the Greek poet Hesiod records the Centauromachy between the Lapith soldiers and the CENTAUR. Upon the surface of the intricately worked shield are representatives of each army; on one side are the Lapith soldiers, Prince Caeneus, DRYAS, Exadius, Hopleus, Phalerus, King Pirithous, and Prolochusc, and rushing at them are the CENTAURS ARCTUS, ASBOLUS, black-maned MIMAS, PETRAEUS, and UREUS.

Source: Hesiod, *Works of Hesiod, Callimachus and Theognis*, 59; Smith, *New Classical Dictionary of Greek and Roman Biography*, 113; Westmoreland, *Ancient Greek Beliefs*, 202

Asbolus, dog

A dog from ancient Greek mythology, Asbolus ("soot") was one of the DOGS OF ACTÆON, the unfortunate youth who was raised by the CENTAUR, CHEIRON. Asbolus was noted for his coat of all-black fur.

Source: Leeming, *World of Myth*, 111; Murray, *Classical Manual*, 160; Naso, *Fasti, Tristia*, 93–5

Asbsar

Believed to live on the islands located in the China Sea, the asbsar ("resembling a horse") is a creature, tall of stature, having a head like a horse but the body of a man and a set of wings.

Source: Qazvīnī, *Zoological Section of the Nuzhatu-l-qulūb of Ḥamdullāh al-Mustaufi al-Qazwīnī*, 48

Asdeev

A DEV from Persian folklore who could take the form of a white DRAGON, Asdeev, one of the KHRAFSTRA, was slain by the cultural hero, Roostem (Rustam).

Asdeev is also the name of a species of DRAGON believed to be the guardians of the subterranean treasures of the earth; they are similar to the FUT'SANG of Chinese mythology.

Source: De Kirk, *Dragonlore*, 33; Keightley, *World Guide to Gnomes, Fairies, Elves, and Other Little People*, 81; Rose, *Giants, Monsters and Dragons*, 27

Asena

Variations: Sena

In Turkish mythology Asena ("wolf") was the grey wolf with a sky-blue mane who, after a battle, discovered an injured young boy and nursed him back to health. The young man recovered and he impregnated the wolf who gave birth to ten human-wolf hybrids. Ashina, one of these offspring, went on to become the leader of his siblings and founded the Orhon speaking Göktürks ("blue turks" or "sky turks").

Source: Kaylan, *Kemalists*, 55; Walsh, *Journal of the Royal Asiatic Society of Great Britain and Ireland*, 660

Ash-Hrau

A monstrous five-headed serpent from the mythology of ancient Egypt, Ash-Hrau ("lots of faces") resided in the sixth section, or hour, of Tuat, the Underworld; it was described as having its body bent into an irregular oval in such a way so its tail almost touched one of its heads. In *The Text of Unas* there is a magical spell which when performed will cause the destruction of monstrous beasts and serpents alike; Ash-Hrau would be affected by this spell.

Source: Coulter, *Encyclopedia of Ancient Deities*, 32, 72; Mercatante, *Who's Who in Egyptian Mythology*, 14

Ashiarai Yashiki (AH-shee ah-rye YASH-key)

An ancient YŌKAI from Japanese folklore, ashiarai yashiki ("foot-washing mansion") is a gigantic disembodied muddy foot and hairy leg capable of speech; in some tales, it is blood covered. This being crashes through the roof of an affluent home in the dead of night demanding to be washed. If the foot is washed, it will leave as it came but if ignored it will rampage through the home destroying as much as it can before leaving; on occasion the owner of the home is killed during the attack but is not necessarily singled out. Some scholars believe the ashiarai yashiki is not one of the YŌKAI at all but rather an illusion sent by a TANUKI.

Source: Yoda, *Yokai Attack*, 130–33

Ashmog

A DRAGON from Zoroastrian mythology, Ashmog, "the two-footed serpent of evil," was described in the sacred text *Yend-Avesta* as having the neck of a camel. In Kabalistic texts Ashmog was referred to as the "flying camel."

Source: Blavatsky, *Theosophical Glossary*, 34; Dempster, *Essays*, 185

Ashtadikkaranis

According to Hindu mythology there are eight divine elephants collectively known as the Ashtadikkaranis who, together, each support one of the eight cardinal points. Their mates are known as the DIG-GAJAS. Abhramu is the mate of AIRAVATA who supports the East; Angina is the mate of SARVA-BHAUMA who supports the North; Anjanavati is the mate of SU-PRATIKA who supports the North East; Anupama is the mate of KUMUDA who supports the South West; Kapila is the mate of PUNDARIKA who supports the South East; Pingala is the mate of VAMANA who supports the South; Subhradanti is the mate of PUSHPA-DANTA who supports the North West; and Tamrakarni is the mate of ANJANA who supports the West.

Source: Dalal, *Hinduism*, 43

Asin

In the Alsean folklore of the Pacific Northwest comes the legend of the asin, a being described as both a demon in human form and as a monstrous creature of the woods, feminine in form but covered in hair with claw-like hands and wolf-like teeth. Common to the folklore of a NURSERY BOGIE, the asin hunts children who stray too far from home, snatching them up, and disappearing into the woods with them, moving at incredible speeds. It also has the magical ability to enchant the huckleberry bush so any child who eats its fruit falls under the asin's enchantment and wanders off into the woods. Although this cannibal prefers to consume children, it will eat whoever it can catch. Often before it strikes, its laughter can be heard. It is believed if a medicine man dreams of the asin a great misfortune is about to occur in the community.

Source: Maberry, *Vampire Universe*, 24; Rose, *Giants, Monsters, and Dragons*, 27

Asipatra

A monstrous bird from Hindu mythology Asipatra ("the blade of a sword") is believed to live in Yamapura, the city of death, perched upon the branches of trees made of spears as it watches for its prey. Although this KRAVYAD looks like a regular bird Asipatra has talons like knives and its wingtips are extremely sharp and used like a scythe as it flies through the air, swooping down, and attacking, condemning, and torturing its prey, those sinners who disobeyed the orders of their guru.

Source: Knappert, *Indian Mythology*, 40; Rose, *Giants, Monsters, and Dragons*, 28; Zell-Ravenheart, *Wizard's Bestiary*, 20

Askefruer

NATURE SPIRITS of the forest, the askefruer ("ash women") are the hamadryads (the nymphs of oak trees in Greek mythology) of ash trees in Danish mythology; they are described as being covered with hair, having wrinkled faces, pendulous breasts, and wearing clothing of moss. The askefruer have the magical ability to cure diseases.

Source: Bonnerjea, *Allborough New Age Guide*, 27; Hastings, *Encyclopaedia of Religion and Ethics*, Volume 4, 634

Aso Zusta

In Persian folklore aso zusta ("being loved of Asa") was a species of bird capable of speaking Holy Scripture in its own language, enabling it to scare off devils, even when encountered in barren and isolated places. Nail clippings are offered to the aso zusta to guard over as it can prevent the clippings from being stolen by demons and turned into hostile weapons against the person they came from.

Source: Boyce, *History of Zoroastrianism*, 90; Yar-Shater, *Encyclopaedia Iranica*, Volume 4, 507

Asootee

The gigantic world serpent of Hindu mythology, the Asootee is believed to encircle the universe with its tail in its mouth; included within its coils are the DIG-GAJAS, ANANTA BOGA, CHUKWA, and the earth.

Source: Deane, *Worship of the Serpent Traced Throughout the World*, 72; Zell-Ravenheart, *Wizard's Bestiary*, 20

Aspidochelone

Variations: Asp Turtle, Aspidochelon, Aspidodelone, Aspido-Tortoise, FASTITOCALON ("devil whale"), Floater on Ocean Streams, Zaratan

A gigantic creature from European medieval traveler folklore, the aspidochelone ("shield turtle," "snake turtle") has in fact been written about since the time of the ancient Egyptians and Greeks. It has throughout the ages been described as a fish, turtle, and whale but it is consistently described as being so large it was often mistaken for an island. The aspidochelone had a stony body, its shelled back was covered with soil and trees, and was said to live on a diet of fish which it lures into its open mouth with its sweet smelling breath. In some tales sailors would land upon it, make camp, and build cooking fires before being alerted to their mistake, as when the island began to move, shake, and submerge itself in order to extinguish the flames.

Source: Eberhart, *Mysterious Creatures*, 172–3; Hargreaves, *Hargreaves New Illustrated Bestiary*, 14; Rose, *Giants, Monsters, and Dragons*, 28; Zell-Ravenheart, *Wizard's Bestiary*, 20

Ass-Bittern

A creature from the symbology of British heraldry, the ass-bittern was depicted as a hybrid of an ass and a large water-fowl; it was depicted on the Asbitter family arms.

Source: Lower, *Curiosities of Heraldry*, 103; Rose, *Giants, Monsters, and Dragons*, 29; Zell-Ravenheart, *Wizard's Bestiary*, 20

Ass of Balaam

Variations: Balaam's Ass, She-ass of Balaam

One of the ten animals allowed entry into Paradise in Muslim mythology, the story of the ass of Balaam is also told in the Old Testament, Numbers 22:21–33. Balaam, who was acting perversely in the eyes of the Lord, left his home riding upon his ass. An angel of the Lord was sent to slay Balaam but the animal saw the ANGEL and veered its course to save its master's life; however, each time it did so, Balaam struck the animal. After the third time the Lord enabled the animal to speak and it questioned its owner's harsh treatment; then the Lord allowed Balaam to see the ANGEL himself.

Source: Brewer, *Dictionary of Phrase and Fable*, 205; Gilhus, *Animals, Gods and Humans*, 162

Ass with Three Legs

In Zoroastrian mythology the Avesta describes an ass as large as a mountain with three legs, six eyes, nine mouths, and an alicorn (a single horn) atop its head; this proto-UNICORN-like creature stands in the middle of the sea and purifies the water.

Source: Hargreaves, *Hargreaves New Illustrated Bestiary*, 16; Sax, *Mythical Zoo*, 14

Asterion

Variations: Asterius

In ancient Greek mythology Asterion ("starry") was the name of the MINOTAUR born from the wife of King Minos, Pasiphae; it was condemned to inhabit the labyrinth constructed by the great inventor Daedalus on the island of Cnossus.

Source: Coulter, *Encyclopedia of Ancient Deities*, 76

Astrope

In the Latin narrative poem *Metamorphoses* (2.153), written by the Roman poet Ovid (43 BC–AD 17), the sun god and second generation Titan, Helios (Sol), had his golden chariot, Quadriga, pulled across the sky by the flying horses AETHON, Astrope, BRONTE, CHRONOS, EOUS, LAMPON, PHAETHON, PHLEGON, and PYROIS. All of these horses are described as being pure white and having flaring nostrils which can breathe forth flame.

Source: Breese, *God's Steed*, 86; Coulter, *Encyclopedia of Ancient Deities*, 76; Rose, *Giants, Monsters, and Dragons*, 178

Astyle

A CENTAUR from ancient Greek mythology, Astyle was one of the CENTAURS slain by the demigod and cultural hero Hercules (Heracles) while visiting his friend, a CENTAUR named PHOLUS, between his conclusion of his third Labor and the onset of his fourth.

Source: *Commentary, Mythological, Historical, and Geographical on Pope's Homer*, 55

Aswang (Az-wang)

In Philippine mythology the word *aswang* ("dog") is applied to anything and everything considered to be a vampire or vampire-like. There are six different species of aswang vampires: the aswang mandurugo, aswang mannananggal, aswang shape-shifter, aswang tik-tik, aswang tiyanak, aswang witch, and the tanggal.

The Capiz province, Philippines, is known as a haven for witches and a species of elusive demonic vampires known as the aswang mandurugo. These creatures appear as a beautiful woman by day, but at night their true form, a monstrous winged being, is revealed. When it can, it will marry to ensure a constant supply of blood. It will "kiss" the sustenance it needs nightly from its husband prey by inserting its barbed tongue into the victim's mouth and draining off the blood it requires. The only symptom the husband may present is a gradual and unexplainable weight loss. There is no test or discernable way to ascertain beforehand if a bride-to-be is an aswang mandurugo, but a preventative measure may be taken. If the husband sleeps with a knife under his pillow, he may awake in time to witness his attacker. If he is fast enough to draw the knife and stab the vampire in the heart, it will be destroyed.

The aswang mannananggal, is a type of vampiric witch which gets its name from a derivative of the Tagalog word *tanggal*, which means "to separate." This creature creates more of its own kind by tricking a woman into drinking the cooked blood of another person. Once the victim has been converted and transformed, it will look like a woman with long hair during the day but on nights of the full moon it will transform into its true form. Sprouting large, leathery bat-like wings with long clawed hands and a maw full of fanged teeth, the aswang mannananggal rips its upper body away from its lower and takes flight to hunt out its prey—unborn children from their mother's womb. Should it not be able to find a suitable meal, it will temporarily sate its appetite by dining on human entrails.

The aswang mannananggal is vulnerable only when it is not conjoined. To destroy this vampiric creature, find its lower body and rub it with garlic or salt, as this will destroy the appendage. When the upper and otherwise invulnerable half returns at dawn to rejoin itself, it will be unable to. Then, when the sun rises, the upper half will revert to its human form and die.

The aswang shape-shifter is found throughout the Philippines. It can look either male or female but typically appears as an old woman with bloodshot eyes, long black hair, and a long black tongue. A sorcerer can decide to become this vampiric creature by performing a magical ceremony, but should it ever decide to convert someone against their will, all the vampire would have to do is simply blow down the person's back. Fortunately, there is a type of healer called a *mananambal* who knows how to brew a potion which will restore an aswang unwillingly converted. Naturally the vampire will resist, so the potion is forcibly poured down its throat. The aswang will immediately begin to vomit up all sorts of objects, like eggs or live birds. When the purging has stopped, the victim is cured. Sadly, the transformed willing sorcerer cannot be reverted back to human.

The aswang shape-shifter is so named because of its amazing transformation abilities. Not only can it change to look like any animal or person, but also inanimate objects as well. It is possible to detect if this aswang is near, but it requires brewing a very complex oil which can only be made on Good Friday. When the vampire is near, the oil will begin to boil.

This species of aswang is particularly cruel, not just because it preys on children, women, and those who are ill, but because of its hunting methods. Once the aswang shape-shifter has selected its prey, it may decide to attack while the victim is asleep. If so, it will emit a strong odor which will paralyze the person, in case they wake up. Otherwise, the aswang will stalk and physically overpower him. In either case, once it has its prey, it will create a replica of its victim out of banana leaves, grass, and sticks. Then, using its magic, the vampire animates the facsimile. Over the course of the next few days, the replacement will become sick and die. The only way to tell if the sick person is real is to look closely into their eyes. If you can see your reflection there, it is who you believed it to be. However, if your reflection is upside-down, it is the animated replacement. In the meantime, the aswang has returned to its lair with its captive. Taking its time, the vampire slowly and torturously consumes its food. It is particularly fond of the liver.

As if this vampire did not have enough predatory advantages, it can also fly due to an oily substance secreted through glands in its armpits.

The onomatopeically named aswang tik-tik gets is so called from the small owl which accompanies it; the owl makes a cry of alarm sounding like "tik-tik," alerting a potential sleeping victim.

This aswang only hunts at night when it shape-shifts from its human guise into a bird. It flies to the house of its intended victim, usually a child, and perches on the roof directly over the spot where its prey lies sleeping. Then it sends its long, thin, tube-like tongue into the house. Using a barb on the end of its tongue, it pierces a small hole in the flesh and sips up its meal. When the vampire has finished eating, the breasts of its bird form will be large and swollen with blood. It then flies back to its home where it breastfeeds its own children. In some tellings of the myth, it is said rather than shape-shifting into a bird, the aswang tik-tik maintains its human appearance while hunting and feeding. Rather than looking like a bird with plump breasts, it looks like a pregnant woman. If this species of aswang licks the shadow of a person, he will die.

The aswang tiyanak is a vampiric demon born the offspring of a woman and a demon, but it can also come into being when a child dies without having been baptized. Another way an aswang tiyanak can be created happens when a mother aborts a fetus. In this instance, it springs into life and brings nothing but hardship and misery to the woman who should have been its mother.

The aswang tiyanak is described as having red skin, no hair, and glowing red eyes. It hunts women by shape-shifting into an adorable baby and placing itself somewhere it will be found. When it is discovered, the aswang tiyanak waits until it has been taken home. Then when its would-be rescuer is asleep, the vampire will assume its true form and attack, draining the victim dry of blood.

The aswang witch is a living vampiric witch, born a human female who is then trained in the art of magic and witchcraft. As she ages, the witch learns to make a magical ointment that when applied makes her look young and beautiful. In her youthful guise she then finds suitable prey and lures him to a secluded place. Once alone, the aswang witch tears him apart, drinking the blood and consuming the heart and liver. Although her means of utilizing the seduction-lure works well, it is said that the witch prefers her food to come from children.

Apart from her magical ointment, the aswang witch is a mortal woman and can be slain in any method which would kill a human.

The tanggal ("comes apart") is a vampiric sorcerer known and feared throughout Cambodia, Indonesia, Malaysia, Melanesia, and the Trobriand Islands. By day, it looks like an ordinary woman, but at night it detaches its head from its body and flies off by undulating its intestines and flapping its ears and lungs. It attacks people for their blood and feces, which it feeds on. The tanggal is easily repelled by garlic, salt, and spices.

Source: Alip, *Political and Cultural History*, 77–78; Anima, *Witchcraft, Filipino-Style*, 53–54; Buenconsejo, *Songs and Gifts*, 92; Cannell, *Power and Intimacy*, 144–45, 277; Curran, *Vampires*, 35–44; Demetrio, *Encyclopedia of Philippine Folk Beliefs*, 398; Demetrio, *Myths and Symbols Philippines*, 170; Garcia, *Philippine Gay Culture*, 176–77, 179; Guiley, *Complete Vampire Companion*, 26; Hastings, *Encyclopedia of Religion and Ethics Part 13*, 237; Hufford, *Terror That Comes*, 236–37; Jocano, *Folk Medicine*, 109, 169; Lopez, *Handbook of Philippine Festivals*, 146, 221, 227; McAndrew, *People of Power*, 92; Ramos, *Aswang Syncrasy*, 3, 8, 38–9, 69; Ramos, *Creatures of Philippine*, 15, 28, 66, 118, 130; Roces, *Culture Shock*, 214; Serag, *Remnants of the Great Ilonggo*, 60; Spence, *Encyclopædia of Occultism*, 93–94; University of San Carlos, *Philippine Quarterly*, Volume 10–11, 213; University of the Philippines, *Asian Studies*, 297; Woods, *Philippines*, 28–29

Athach

Athach ("GIANT" or "monster") is a species of FAIRY ANIMAL living in isolated glens and lochs in the Irish highlands.

Source: Campbell, *Popular Tales of the West Highlands*, Volume 3, 365; Ellis, *Chronicles of the Celts*, 223–4; Rose, *Giants, Monsters, and Dragons*, 30

Atoosh

In Inuit mythology of the Cree and Witiko people the atoosh is a cannibal monster, similar to the ATSHEN and the WINDIGO; it captures people and eats them raw.

Source: Henriksen, *I Dreamed the Animals*, 27; Preston, *Cree Narrative*, 112

Atraoimen

In Caribbean island mythology a monster known as the atraoimen is responsible for the scattering of the people across the islands. Once a very popular and social *kalinago* ("very peaceful man") had sons so jealous of his life they murdered him and discarded his body in the ocean. As the body decomposed the soul of the gentle-natured man became corrupt, twisted, and entered into a fish, transforming it into a fierce man-killer which became known as the atraoimen. This monster fish (see SEA SERPENT) hunted the murderous sons, slaughtering anyone who got in its way. The people fled, hoping when they scattered they would escape the monster's wrath.

Source: Maberry, *Vampire Universe*, 27–28

Atshen

Variations: Acten, Atce'n

In the Inuit mythology of the Innu people, an atshen was once a member of the tribe who became a "wild person" and then a cannibalistic monster (see WILD MAN); the more human flesh it devoured the larger in size it grew. A small atshen is known as an *athsheniss*. Stories about the atshen are not considered by the Innu to be myth (*atanukans*) but rather the retelling of actual events within contemporary memory (*tipatshimuns*). To destroy an atshen it needs to be captured and held in a secure location, deprived of food and water until it dies; then, the body must be burned.

Source: Henriksen, *I Dreamed the Animals*, 27, 157–8

Audhumbla (Aud-hum'-bla or Owd-hoom-lah or OUTH-hum-la)

Variations: Audhumla, Audumla, Audumbla

In Norse mythology Audhumbla ("darkness nourishes," "hornless wealth-cow") was the primordial cow which nourished the JOTUN Ymir with her milk prior to the creation of the nine worlds; she was created by Surt from the melting droplets of the Ginnungagap ice of the primordial void. Audhumbla lived off Niflheim ice, licking hoar frost and salt from it; while licking the ice she formed Buri (Bure), who fathered Bor, and was the grandfather of the gods Odin, Vili, and Ve.

Source: Anderson, *Norse Mythology*, 174, 441–2; Daly, *Norse Mythology A to Z*, 7, 39; Grimes, *Norse Myths*, 4–6; Jennbert, *Animals and Humans*, 49; Oehlenschläger, *Gods of the North*, xxxiv

Aufhocker (Off-hocker), plural: Aufhöcker

From German folklore comes the tale of the aufhocker ("leap upon"), a huge and black vampiric dog which walks upon its hind legs and singles out those who travel alone at night, typically attacking them at a crossroads and ripping out the throat of its victim. The aufhocker is said to have the ability of therianthropy allowing it to shape-shift into other animals and on rare occasions it can assume human form. Although it cannot be killed, it can be driven off by the pealing of church bells; it will also retreat with the rising of the sun.

Source: Grimm, *German Legends*, 342, 359; Maberry, *Vampire Universe*, 28; Petzoldt, *Demons*, 23; Rose, *Giants, Monsters, and Dragons*, 30; Wurmser, *Jealousy and Envy*, 94

Aughisky

In Irish folklore the aughisky was a species of water-horse very similar to the EACH UISCE of Scottish Highlands folklore, the Welsh CEFFYL DWFR, and the SHOOPILTEE from the Shetlands except it was never seen galloping along the shores of the inland lakes where it lived. It was also different from the Scottish KELPIE which inhabited running water.

Unlike the beautiful lake-dwelling horse belonging to the cultural hero Cúchulainn, the aughisky could not be permanently tamed. If a halter was placed on one, the aughisky would be a faithful mount so long as it never laid eyes on its lake. Should this happen, the fairy horse (see FAIRY ANI-MAL) would make a dash for its old home, taking its rider with it; there, it would tear its former master into bloody pieces. Once wild again, it would return to its normal diet of eating cattle.

Most sightings of this creature were made in the month of November when they left their lake to come on land to graze. Generally regarded as being a benign, stories say most people will not to go in a lake reported to be the home of an aughisky after dark.

Source: Briggs, *Encyclopedia of Fairies*, 13; Conway, *Magickal, Mystical Creatures*, 45; Froud, *Faeries*, 108; Kölbing, *Englische Studien*, Volume 5, 396

Aunyaina

In Brazilian folklore, especially from the Tupari people, the aunyaina was believed to be a gigantic, cannibalistic sorcerer and monster; it was described as being humanoid in appearance, with boar tusks protruding from his mouth. Although it would hunt and consume anyone, it was particularly fond of preying on children who wandered just outside of camp and into the forest.

Source: Dixon-Kennedy, *Native American Myth and Legend*, 28; Rose, *Giants, Monsters, and Dragons*, 32

Autochthon

In Greek mythology, an autochthon ("earth-sprung") is a being having the upper body of a man but the lower body of a DRAGON or snake, similar to the NAGA of India. Ekhion, the father of Pentheus, was one such creature, as was CECROPS, the legendary first king of Athens.

Source: Antoninus, *Metamorphoses of Antoninus Liberalis*, 119; Komar, *Reclaiming Klytemnestra*, 21; Watkins, *How to Kill a Dragon*, 363

Avagrah

Variations: Gara, Graha, Nyan, Tanti–Gaha

In Burmese mythology the avagrah is a monstrous serpentine creature living in rivers; it is described as being between one and two hundred fathoms long (approximately 550 and 1,100 feet), and looking like an earthworm. This predatory creature is extraordinarily strong and is even said to attack elephants.

Source: Gould, *Dragons, Unicorns, and Sea Serpents*, 336; Rose, *Giants, Monsters, and Dragons*, 32; Zell-Ravenheart, *Wizard's Bestiary*, 74

Avak

Variations: Aavak

In Norse mythology Avak, along with AARVAK, ALSVID, HRIMFAXI, and SKINFAXI, was one of the many winged horses said to assist in pulling the sun across the sky.

Source: Rose, *Giants, Monsters, and Dragons*, 178

Axehandle Hound

Variations: Axhandle Hound, Ax-Handle Hound, Axe-Handle Hound

In the folklore of Minnesota and Wisconsin, Unites States of America, the axehandle hound was a creature said to harry lumberjacks throughout the nineteenth and early twentieth centuries; it was described as having short, squat legs, a long and thin body in the shape of an axehandle, and a head resembling a hatchet. It lived off a diet of unattended axehandles.

The axehandle hound was a member of the FEARSOME CRITTERS, a collection of creatures from lumberjack folklore who were spoken of around campfires and whose stories explained the mysterious noises heard at night.

Source: Borges, *Book of Imaginary Beings*, 83; Rose, *Giants, Monsters, and Dragons*, 32

Axex

Appearing in the 17th dynasty, the axex ("dawn") of the ancient Egyptian mythology was depicted as a winged lion with the head of a hawk.

Source: Wilkinson, *Manners and Customs of the Ancient Egyptians*, Volume 3, 312; Zell-Ravenheart, *Wizard's Bestiary*, 20

Ayakashi

In Japanese mythology the ayakashi was a gigantic SEA SERPENT said to live off of Saikoku ("four countries"), southwest of Japan's main island, Honshu; it is said to secrete an oily substance from its body and will rise up from the water and crawl over a ship. As the ayakashi makes its way over the vessel, it leaves behind this oily substance; if the crew is not fast in removing it, the vessel will sink.

Source: Japan Society of London, *Transactions and Proceedings of the Japan Society*, Volume 9, 40; Temple, *Traditional Themes in Japanese Art*, 226

Az-I–Wu-Gum-Ki-Mukh-Ti

Variations: Az-i-wA'-giimki-mukh'tt, Walrus Dog

In Inuit mythology the fearsome az-i-wu-gum-ki-mukh-ti was described as having a long and thin body covered with shiny black scales not too difficult to pierce with a spear, sturdy canine legs, and the head of a heavily fanged dog; it was so strong one blow of its long, round tail was powerful enough to kill a man instantly. The az-i-wu-gum-ki-mukh-ti followed the large lek (or herds) of walrus and was a known man-killer.

Source: Eberhart, *Mysterious Creatures*, Volume 1, 577; Nelson, *Annual Reports*, Volume 18, Part 1, 459; Rose, *Giants, Monsters, and Dragons*, 33; Zell-Ravenheart, *Wizard's Bestiary*, 21

Azaban (Ahz-bahn)

Variations: Asban, Azban, Azeban

A trickster hero spirit from the folklore of the Abenaki people of Southern Quebec, the clever Azaban ("raccoon") is always using his wits to get food from the other animals. Azaban received his distinctive mask as a punishment; haven eaten all of Grandmother's acorns she hit him with a fire poker, leaving a burn mark on his face.

Source: Caduto, *Keepers of the Animals*, 247; Lynch, *Native American Mythology A to Z*, 9, 86

Azcatl

In Aztec mythology Azcatl ("ant") discovered the source of maize, Tonacatepetl ("mount of subsistence"); he shared the location of it with the plumed serpent Quetzalcoatl and together they retrieved some to bring back to the young gods to eat.

Source: Bancroft, *Native Races of the Pacific States*, 193–4; Recinos, *Popol Vuh*, 166

Azeman (Oz-amen)

Variations: Azéman

In Suriname folklore the azeman is the name of both a type of WEREWOLF and vampire. Should a woman become infected with azeman blood she would be transformed into one. By day the victim would appear to be a regular person but at night she would transform into an APPARITION, a bat, or some nocturnal predatory animal.

To prevent attack from an azeman, sprinkling seeds on the ground will cause it to stop whatever it is doing to count them, as it is inexplicably compelled to do so. To prevent it from entering into your home, simply prop a broom across the doorway, as it will create a mystical barrier the azeman cannot cross.

Source: American Folklore Society, *Journal of American Folklore*, Volume 30, 242; Benjamins, *Encyclopaedie van Nederlandsch West-Indië*, 63, 140; Rose, *Giants, Monsters, and Dragons*, 32; Shepard, *Encyclopedia of Occultism*, 116

Azi

In Altaic Buryat mythology, azi ("molar" or "tusk") are red-headed NATURE SPIRITS which seem to enjoy human company, music, tea, and tobacco. Forest azi behave differently than mountain azi but neither will allow their cattle, the wild game, to be hunted and killed without reason. Those who infuriate the azi are said to lose their soul.

Source: Boĭkova, *Kinship in the Altaic World*, 107; Grimal, *Larousse World Mythology*, 437

Azi Dahaka

Variations: Ahi ("throttle"), Az Dahak, Azdahak, Azhdak, Azhi, Azhi Dahaka, Azidahaka, Azi

Dahaka, Azhi Dahaki, Azi, Azi-Dahak, Bivar-Asp, Dahag, Dahak, Dahhak, Vishapa ("whose saliva is poisonous"), Zahhak, Zohak

A three headed anthropophagous (man-eating) DRAGON from Persian folklore, Azi Dahaka ("biting snake" or "fiendish snake"), one of the KHRAFS-TRA, was created by the principal of Evil, Angra Mainya. Zoroastrian texts describe Azi Dahaka as having six eyes, three mouths, and a thousand skills; its wings were so large they hide the stars when spread and it had three heads: anguish, death, and pain. If ever Azhi Dahaka were to be cut open he would spill forth enough lizards, scorpions, snakes, spiders, and other venomous creatures, to completely cover the earth. He offered scarifies to Ardvi Sura Anahita in the hopes of ridding the world of men.

Zoroastrian text describes two battles the DRAGON took place in: the first was against Atar, a principal of Fire who was created by the principal of Good, Spenta Mainyu. Azi Dahaka threatens to extinguish Atar but the principal counters with a threat of his own, promising to send a jet of flame up and into Azi Dahaka's anus and out of each of his three mouths; the DRAGON concedes the fight and leaves. The second battle Azi Dahaka is involved in is against the young hero Thraetaona. Although the battle is not described in the text it is known that each time nine-year old Thraetaona strikes Azi Dahaka he releases a horde of harmful creatures into the world. Eventually the young hero wins by binding up the DRAGON and burying him alive beneath Mount Demavend. Azhi Dahaka will stay there until the end of time when the beginning of the battle between Good and Evil takes place. At this time the principal Atar will kill Azhi Dahaka and scatter his ashes into oblivion but not before the DRAGON is able to destroy one third of the human population and one third of all the vegetation.

Source: Boyce, *History of Zoroastrianism*, 91; Ogden, *Drakon*, 13–4; Chopra, *Academic Dictionary of Mythology*, 44; Coulter, *Encyclopedia of Ancient Deities*, n.pag.; Guiley, *Encyclopedia of Demons and Demonology*, 21; Sarianidi, *Margiana and Protozoroastrism*, 172

Azi Sruvara

Variations: Aži Sruvara ("yellow DRAGON"), Aži Zairita

In Zoroastrian mythology Azi Sruvara is a horned, yellowy-green DRAGON said to consume horses and men; it uses its poison to lay waste to the land. Azi Sruvara was a classification of creature known as KHRAFSTRA, a monster opposed by heroic humans.

Source: Boyce, *History of Zoroastrianism*, 91; Sarianidi, *Margiana and Protozoroastrism*, 172

Aži Višāpa

According to Zoroastrian mythology Aži Višāpa ("DRAGON of poisonous slaver") consumed the offerings made between sunset and sunrise.

Source: Boyce, *History of Zoroastrianism*, 91; Selbie, *Encyclopædia of Religion and Ethics*, Volume 1, 800

Azukiarai (AH-zoo-key AH-rye)

Variations: Azuki Arai ("red bean washer"), Azuki-koshi, Azukitogi, Azuki-toge, Azuki-togi

In Japanese mythology the azukiarai ("bean washer") is an elusive and rare YŌKAI to happen upon; living in the mountains this creature sits along a riverbank washing red beans in a bamboo colander singing a song: *"Azuki togou ka? Hito tottekuou ka? Shoki shoki."* ("Should I grind my azuki beans? Or should I snatch a person to eat?") *Shoki shoki* is the sound of the beans being washed in the water). Should a person try to follow the sound and catch a glimpse of the azukiarai they will quickly find themselves disoriented, lose their footing, and end up falling into the river; other than this mishap, the azukiarai is harmless but is said to enjoy watching the event unfold.

Source: Yoda, *Yokai Attack*, 90–3

Ba She

Variations: Bashe, Ba-Snake

In Chinese mythology the ba she is said to be a snake large enough to consume an elephant; it takes the creature three years to digest the body and pass the bones; ancient sources vary as to its description but generally it is described as being python-like, black with a green head, or black, green, red, and yellow. Folklore claims if a person carries a bit of the ba she's hide next to their skin they will not suffer from heart or lung ailments.

Source: Strassberg, *Chinese Bestiary*, 190

Babai

Variations: Babi, the Master of Darkness, Babi, Bebi, Bibi

A creature living in the Egyptian Underworld, Babai assists Ammut, the Eater of the Dead (see AMAN), in consuming and disposing of the souls which fail the test of the Treasure of Truth. As the first born son of the god Osiris, his appearance is said to be similar to a bull and his fiendish nature is comparable to the god, Seth.

Source: Müller, *Egyptian [mythology]*, 131; Von Dassow, *Egyptian Book of the Dead*, 173; Zell-Ravenheart, *Wizard's Bestiary*, 21

Babayka

A NURSERY BOGIE from Russian folklore, parents will warn their children of babayka, a BOGEYMAN who "gets" children who misbehave.

Source: Leen, *International Perspectives on Chicana/o Studies*, 72

Bacchis

Variations: Bacis, Bash, Basis, Pacis, Onuphis, Sacred Bull of Hermonthis

In Egyptian mythology Bacchis was a sacred bull believed to be the physical manifestation of the god of the sun, Ra; it was described as having long black hair which grew backward and changed its color every hour of the day.

Source: Remler, *Egyptian Mythology, A to Z*, 34; Wilkinson, *Manners and Customs of the Ancient Egyptians*, 197–8

Bäckahästen

Variations: Nykur

The bäckahästen ("brook horse") was a beautiful white fairy horse from Scandinavian folklore (see FAIRY ANIMAL). Very similar to the KELPIE from Scottish folklore, the näcken (a species of male, solitary, water fairy in Scandinavia folklore), and nixen of Polish folklore, it rose up from the river and lurked along the banks looking too magnificent to not be ridden. Anyone who climbed upon its back would find they would not be able to climb off again as the bäckahästen charged headlong into the water, drowning its rider. In the Middle Ages there was the belief in saying "*Bäckahästen go back to your watery place and set me free in the name of our Lady and the Holy Trinity*" three times the rider would be allowed to dismount before being murdered.

There are stories of it being harnessed and made to plow but sometimes this is because it was all part of the bäckahästen's plan while other times its domestication came about because it was tricked by the hero of the story.

Source: Craigie, *Scandinavian Folk-Lore*, 233; Eason, *Fabulous Creatures, Mythical Monsters, and Animal Power Symbols*, 142; Scales, *Poseidon's Steed*, n.pag.

Baconaua

Variations: Bakonaua, Bakonawa, Bakunawa

In Filipino folklore, Baconaua ("bent serpent," "man eater," and "moon eater") is an immense silver DRAGON said to live in the sea but has gigantic bat-like membranous wings enabling it to fly through the sky. According to the myth, in the earth's ancient past the planet once had seven moons but greedy Baconaua consumed six of them. Each time there is an eclipse occurring it is believed Baconaua is attempting to eat the remaining moon. In order to prevent this from happening, local people would gather together and make loud noises banging metal objects together hoping to scare him back into the sea.

Source: Eason, *Fabulous Creatures, Mythical Monsters, and Animal Power Symbols*, 141; Ramos, *Creatures of Philippine Lower Mythology*, 199; Redfern, *Most Mysterious Places on Earth*, 112

Badabada

Humanoids from Melanesian folklore, the Badabada ("largest") are said to have only one leg and must move about with the assistance of a staff; larger than the natives, they usually live in the tree branches from where they can safely throw projectiles at anyone who gets too near to their location. It is unknown what the Badabada eat and it is suspected they may not require any food.

Source: Seligman, *Melanesians of British New Guinea*, 649

Badhava

Variations: Haya-Siras ("horse head")

In Hindu mythology Badhava ("mare, the submarine fire") was created, according to the *Mahabharata*, when the sage Aurva removed his anger and cast it into the sea; his anger then became a being, a horse-faced creature composed of flame.

Source: Bonnerjea, *Allborough New Age Guide*, 31; Dowson, *Classical Dictionary of Hindu Mythology and Religion, Geography, History, and Literature*, 33, 39, 120

Badigui

Variations: Diba, Ngakoula-Ngou ("water devil"), Songo

A gigantic snake from Ubangi folklore, the badigui is said to graze in the upper tree branches of the Ubangi Shari waterways without having to leave the water; it is known to strangle hippopotamuses in its coils but does not consume them.

Source: Eberhart, *Mysterious Creatures*, 29; Zell-Ravenheart, *Wizard's Bestiary*, 21

Bagat

In Filipino folklore the bagat are large monstrous dogs which prey on those individuals who harm dogs; they are seldom encountered as they prefer to hunt in remote areas only during the full moon when it is storming. Although not malicious by nature a bagat will become savagely enraged if a dog within its territory is injured.

Source: Jocano, *Growing up in a Philippine Barrio*, 108; Maberry, *Vampire Universe*, 28–29

Baginis

Variations: Diba, Ngakoula-Ngou

In Australian aboriginal folklore the baginis are a species of beautiful hybrid women, part human and part animal; they are described as having claw-like fingers and toes; sometimes they are considered to be spirits and beings from Dreamtime. The baginis are known for abducting, raping, and then releasing men, if they were not kept and consumed as food.

Source: Coleman, *Dictionary of Mythology*, 122; Zell-Ravenheart, *Wizard's Bestiary*, 21

Bagwyn

In the symbology of heraldry, a bagwyn is a chimerical creature with the head of an antelope, having long, backward curving horns over its ears, but with the body and tail of a horse.

Source: Fox-Davies, *Complete Guide to Heraldry*, 231; Parker, *Glossary of Terms Used in Heraldry*, 34; Sloane-Evans, *Grammar of British Heraldry*, 144

Bahamut

Variations: Labuna

In Islamic mythology Bahamut is an immensely large creature supporting the earth; it has been described as looking like a magnificently bright fish with the head of an elephant or hippopotamus. In one account it was created to support a gigantic bull, KUJATA, who in turn supported a ruby upon which stood an ANGEL holding six hells and above which rested the earth and seven heavens. In another version Bahamut upheld a layer of sand upon which stood a gigantic bull whose forehead was the location of a mountain which held back the water in which the Earth was located. Beneath Bahamut, suffering the fires of Hell, is the monstrously vast serpent of hell, called FALAK.

No matter the description, the size of Bahamut is so great no human mind can even begin to comprehend its scope. In the tale *One-Thousand and One Arabian Nights*, in the 496th tale, we are told Isa (Jesus) was granted the great privilege of being able to see Bahamut in all his size and scope.

Source: Borges, *Book of Imaginary Beings*, 26; Rose, *Giants, Monsters, and Dragons*, 37; Zell-Ravenheart, *Wizard's Bestiary*, 21, 59

Bahri

In Islamic mythology the bahri is a bird-like creature with the head of a man.

Source: Hargreaves, *Hargreaves New Illustrated Bestiary*, 67; Rose, *Giants, Monsters, and Dragons*, 37; Zell-Ravenheart, *Wizard's Bestiary*, 21

Bai Ze

Variations: Bei Zi, Hakutaku, Kutabe

In Chinese mythology the divine bai ze ("white marsh") is described as looking like a large lion but having either one or two horns atop its head; in some descriptions it has an extra set of eyes on its back or face. According to folklore, while on patrol in Mount Hengshan, the Yellow emperor happened across the creature. Intelligent, well-read, and well-spoken, the bai ze explained to the ruler he only appeared to the most auspicious of sovereigns. In speaking with one another the emperor discovered the creature knew all about supernatural creatures and how to overcome them. Lacking this knowledge the Yellow Emperor asked the bai ze to share what he knew; the creature wrote a book entitled *Bai Ze Tu*; it contained 11,520 entries. Although no complete copy of the book exists, fragments of its information appear in many other works.

Source: Bates, *29 Chinese Mysteries*, 87–8; Yuan, *Dragons and Dynasties*, 37–8

Baital (Bay-till)

Variations: Baitala, Baitel, Baitol, Bay Valley, Katakhanoso, Vetal, Vetala

A divine vampiric race first mentioned in *The Tibetan Book of the Dead*, the baital are described as being half man and half bat. They are said to have a short, stubby tail and stand anywhere between four and seven feet tall. In ancient artwork the baital has been depicted as holding drinking cups made of human skulls and filled with human blood up to its mouth, about to drink. These beings are so horrific to behold, to look fully upon one will cause a person to lock up in fear, growing weak and dizzy; some people even faint. When not consuming the human flesh offered to it in sacrifice, the baital can be found at rest, hanging upside down from trees in the jungle, usually near cemeteries. Despite their horrific appearance and taste for human flesh, the baital are not mindless monsters.

Capable of possession, they are known to animate corpses so they can involve themselves in human affairs. The vampire from the Indian story *Vikram and the Vampire* is a baital. In the story, the vampire decided to help the hero, Rajah Vikram, by giving him a reminder that the GIANT's advice should be taken seriously and the sorcerer should be slain. Vikram was frightened by the baital's attempt to help, as the vampire had possessed the body of a murder victim, causing the hero to think it to be a devil.

Source: Burton, *Vikram and the Vampire*, 11; Icon Group, *Hanging: Webster's Quotations*, 400; Making of America Project, *The Atlantic Monthly*, Volume 49, 69–72

Bâjang (Bha-jang)

Variations: Bajang

Witches and sorcerers in Malaysia can bring forth a vampiric demonic-creature through a magical ceremony involving the body of a stillborn child or the corpse of a family member. If the demon is male, it is called a bâjang; the female of the species is called a langsuir. If the caster is strong enough, he can bind the creature to him as a FAMILIAR which can then be passed down through the generations. The witch will then keep their FAMILIAR in a specially constructed container called a *tabong*; it is made of bamboo, sealed with leaves, and locked with a magical charm.

The person who possesses the bâjang must personally feed it a diet of milk and eggs or else it will turn on its owner and start eating its favorite food—children.

The bâjang can by use of therianthropy shapeshift into three different forms: a cat, a weasel, or a large lizard. In its cat form, if it mews at a baby, the child will die.

The witch will oftentimes send its FAMILIAR out to do its bidding. When it is sent out to harm a person, the bâjang will inflict upon its intended victim a mysterious disease for which there is no cure. The person will grow weak, suffering from convulsions and fainting spells until they eventually die.

There is no known way to destroy a bâjang, but there are charms which can be made or purchased to keep it at bay. Probably the best way to tackle the problem of a bâjang would be to deal with the witch who commands it.

Source: Clifford, *Dictionary of the Malay Language*, 121; Gimlette, *Malay Poisons and Charm*, 47; Hobart, *People of Bali*, 116–17; Winstedt, *Malay Magician*, 25

Baka

Variations: Baka-Asura

In the Sanskrit epic of ancient India, the *Mahābhārata*, the baka ("crane" or "stork") is a cannibalistic ASURA who is terrorizing the Brahman town of Ekachakrapura, demanding each family in turn sacrifice to him a driver with a cartload of rice and two buffalos. This creature is described as having glowing red eyes, a terrible anger, a roar which could shake the earth, and the strength to rip a tree up from the ground by its roots and throw it as a projectile. Baka is slain by Bhima, the second son of the wind god Vayu and the goddess Kunti.

Source: Evans, *Epic Narratives in the Hoysaḷa Temples*, 132; Rao, *Mahabharata*, 45–6

Bakemono

Variations: Obake, O-bake, O-bakemono

Supernatural creatures from Japanese folktales, folklore, and mythology, the bakemono ("a changed thing") have an array of evil powers, such as deception and being eaters of human flesh, although they themselves are not necessarily evil. Female bakemono are exceptionally creepy, turning beauty and seduction into unadulterated horror while male bakemono are just naturally terrifying. Nearly all bakemono were once humans who, after their death, were transformed into a hideous physical manifestation of their nature. All bakemono have the ability to become invisible and visible at will and can also change the solidity of their substance and mass or have none at all.

Source: Brown, *Complete Idiot's Guide to the Paranormal*, n.pag.; Roberts, *Japanese Mythology A to Z*, 24

Bakeneko

A YŌKAI from Japanese mythology, the supernatural creature known as a bakeneko ("ghost cat" or "monster cat") began life as an ordinary house cat which was fed too much and became unusually large; once reaching an immense size, the animal begins to display magical abilities or supernatural powers such as therianthropy, making it a shapeshifter.

Source: Bush, *Asian Horror Encyclopedia*, 19; Smith, *Complete Idiot's Guide to World Mythology*, 250

Bakezori

The bakezori ("ghost sandal"), a YŌKAI of Japanese folklore is a sandal with two arms and legs but only one eye. Typically this TSUKOMOGAMI is harmless; they haunt homes out of boredom; during the night they run through the home yelling "*Kararin, kororin, kankororin! Two eyes, three eyes and two teeth!*" If there are other YŌKAI present in the home, the bakezori will group with them, otherwise, it will wander off in its own time.

Source: Haustein, *Mythologien der Welt: Japan, Ainu, Korea*, 9

Bakhtak

A humanoid ursidae (bear-like) KHRAFSTRA from Iranian mythology, the bakhtak ("nightmare") would creep into a person's room at night and settle upon a person's chest, pressing down, causing the sleeper to have nightmares, similar to the ALP of German folklore; in extreme cases, the bakhtak kills its victim and then eats the remains.

Source: Guppy, *Blindfold Horse*, 82

Bal-bal

All of the tribes in the Philippines have their version of a WEREWOLF, and among the Muslim Mormo, theirs is the bal-bal; it is described as a creature with the body of a man and having wings like a bird; it eats the livers out of unburied corpses.

Source: Dalton, *Rough Guide to the Philippines*, 512; Hurley, *Swish of the Kris*, 259

Baladeva

Variations: Bala Bhardra

A NAGARAJA from Hindu mythology, Baladeva, the elder brother of Krishna, is considered to be an incarnation of SESHA, the World Serpent.

Source: Vogel, *Indian Serpent-Lore*, 42, 191

Balâm the Ox

According to the Koran, Balâm the ox, along with NUN the fish, will present themselves as the food to be consumed in Paradise; the lobes of the livers of Balâm and Nun will feed 70,000 saints.

Source: Sale, *Koran*, 72

Balaur

The word *balaur*, according to *National Legends of Roumania*, in Wallach refers to creatures with the body of a serpent that are capable of human speech; they are guardians of hidden treasures. Wallachian folklore says precious gems are formed from the froth of the balaur's mouth.

Source: Daniels, *Encyclopedia of Superstitions, Folklore, and the Occult Sciences of the World*, 1419–20

Balbal (Bawl-bawl)

A vampiric, GHUL-like creature from Tagbanua, Philippines, the balbal ("one who licks up") can be found in or near Muslim villages. When hunting, the balbal glides through the air and alights upon a home with a thatched roof. Then, using its long, curved nails, it rips open the roof and snatches up its sleeping prey with its very long, thick tongue. After it kills and feeds, the balbal returns with a facsimile of its prey made of banana leaves and places it in the home.

Source: Dumont, *Visayan Vignettes*, 13, 121; Parais, *Balete Book*, 40; Ramos, *Creatures of Midnight*, 47; Ramos, *Creatures of Philippine*, 69, 72

Balena

In late medieval European sailor and traveler folklore the balena was described as being a female SEA SERPENT. Authors from the time borrowed descriptions from the second century didactic text, *Physiologus*, written by an unknown author in Alexandria while others were inspired to embellish upon the already fanciful descriptions given in bestiaries of the day; therefore there is no consistent description of the balena although it was said to be able to spout water up into the air at a great height.

Source: Rose, *Giants, Monsters, and Dragons*, 38; Szabo, *Monstrous Fishes and the Mead-Dark Sea*, 47; Zell-Ravenheart, *Wizard's Bestiary*, 21

Balios (BAY-lee-yose)

Variations: Balius

According to Greek mythology Balios ("dappled," a piebald) was an immortal horse, one of the HIPPOI ATHANATOI; he and his brother, the stallion XANTHOS, were the offspring of the god of the wind Zephyros and the HARPY, PODARGE. In the ancient Greek epic poem the *Iliad* ("*Song of Ilion,*" 1240 BC), attributed to Homer, Balios was the horse ridden by heroic and semi-divine Achilles, the Myrmidon leader, as well as the horse who drew his chariot during the Trojan War. Both horses are described as having manes long enough to touch the ground.

Source: *Contemporary Review*, Volume 27, 810; Homer, *Iliad of Homer*, 338, 420; Markman, *Horse in Greek Art*, 5; Room, *Naming of Animals*, 134

Ball-Tailed Cat

Originating in the lumberjack communities of the developing United States of America, the ball tailed cat, one of the FEARSOME CRITTERS, was one of the many imaginary creatures invented to explain both natural and unexplained events experienced in the wilderness as well as to entertain. The ball tailed cat was described as looking much like a mountain lion except for having an exceptionally long tail at the end of which was a bulbous mass used as a weapon to strike its prey.

Source: Rose, *Giants, Monsters, and Dragons*, 119; Tryon, *Fearsome Critters*, 7

Balubaale, singular lubaale

In Gandan mythology the god Katonda exerts his control over the natural world by use of NATURE SPIRITS called balubaale; there are over 50 named balubaale, some of which have been deified as heroes while other are the personification of natural phenomena or daily human activities. For instance, the balubaale of death is WALUMBE and the balubaale of war is KIBUKA.

Source: Bauckham, *Epistle to the Hebrews and Christian Theology*, 327; Cotterell, *Dictionary of World Mythology*, 246

Bangma

Variations: Bulbul Hezar

In Indian folklore the bangma is a fabulous bird that not only is capable of human speech but is also an oracle who gives advice; the female of the species is called a *bangmi*.

Source: Bonnerjea, *Allborough New Age Guide*, 32, 49;

Banw

In Arthurian folklore, Banw was one of the seven piglets acting as part of the warrior entourage for the boar, TWRCH TRWYTH. For many days and nights King Arthur and his men fought the boar and piglets in the valley Dyffryn Amanw; although some of the men died, all of the piglets were slain. Banw and BENNWIG died in the battle which took place in Dyffryn Amanw. At this point in the hunt, the only piglets remaining were GRUGYN GWRYCH EREINT and LLWYDAWG GOVYNNYAD.

Source: Bruce, *Arthurian Name Dictionary*, 57, 477; Kibler, *Medieval Arthurian Epic and Romance*, 96

Bapet

In Ute folklore and legends in the Great Basin region of the United States of America, there was a race of monstrous humanoids known as the SIATS; the females of the species were known as bapets. These cannibals would kidnap children to consume but were also known to suckle a child with their enormous breasts filled with poisonous milk. Under normal conditions, bapets were immortal but could be killed only if fatally shot with an obsidian tipped arrow.

Source: Rose, *Giants, Monsters, and Dragons*, 39

Bar Yachre

Variations: Bar Juchne, GRIFFIN

In Rabbinical folklore the bar yachre was a gigantic bird similar to the ROC; it was described as being eagle-like in appearance and consumed herds of cattle. In the Middle Ages, Rabi Benjamin of Tudela wrote of the bar yachre, claiming when sailors were lost at sea near China they would stitch themselves up in hides and wait for the gigantic eagle to come and swoop them up and carry them to land believing the parcels to be its natural food. One hundred years later, Marco Polo wrote of the bar yachre in his travel notes having heard of the creature while in Madagascar.

Source: Lee, *English Charlemagne Romances*, 806; Rose, *Giants, Monsters, and Dragons*, 39

Barbioletes

A mythological animal mentioned in Chrétien de Troyes's *Erec and Enide*, the barbioletes was described only as having a multicolored pelt and survived on a diet of cinnamon, fresh clove, and spices. The back of the barbiolete was red, its belly green, its head all white, its neck pure black, and its tail a dark blue. There is no description or any indication of its shape or size given.

Source: Hurst, *Comparative Criticism: Volume 1*, 59–60; Karr, *King Arthur Companion*, 148

Bardha

Similar to the ZANA of Romanian folklore, the bardha ("white ones") of Albanian mythology are NATURE SPIRITS described as looking like white maidens living in the mist up in the mountains as well as in the Underworld. Typically the bardha are indifferent to humanity but when they are spoken badly of or otherwise angered, such as by stepping on one, they can paralyze the person or cause them to become mute. Whenever a person falls off their horse it is said it happened because the animal trod upon one of the bardha. To appease their anger and keep them content and indifferent, offerings of cake, honey, and sugar are left for them with a few words of kindness.

Source: Elsie, *Dictionary of Albanian Religion, Mythology, and Folk Culture*, 22; Lurker, *Dictionary of Gods and Goddesses, Devils and Demons*, 30; Rose, *Spirits, Fairies, Leprechauns, and Goblins*, 35

Barguest

Variations: Bargeist, Bargest, Bargheist, Bargtjest, Barguist, Bo-guest

Originating in Yorkshire folklore, England, the barguests were a species of shape-shifting FAIRY ANIMAL. Although they could take any form they pleased, combining such features as claws, fiery eyes, horns, and vicious teeth, they usually took on the appearance of a mastiff dog or some other domestic animal. Its name likely originated from the words *barn ghaist* meaning "barn spirit." In Manchester, England, the barguest was said to be headless.

Haunting the wastelands between Headingley Hill near Leeds and Wreghorn in west Yorkshire, the barguest, like the banshee (an Irish ANCESTRAL SPIRIT), was most active at the death of a notable person or prominent figure. It gathered together all the dogs of the community and lead them on a howling procession through the streets. To see a barguest was a psychopomp (death omen) and those who saw it died within a few days; to catch a fleeting glimpse would allow the viewer to live on, but only for a few months.

Source: Chisholm, *Encyclopædia Britannica*, Volume 3, 399; Keightley, *World Guide to Gnomes, Fairies, Elves, and Other Little People*, 317, 442; Rose, *Spirits, Fairies, Leprechauns, and Goblins*, 35

Bariaua

From Tubetube and Wagawaga folklore of Melanesia comes the bariaua, a race of benign and shy NATURE SPIRITS. Keeping far from humans they live deep in the forest within the trunks of ancient trees. It is said they are incapable of making any sort of water-going vessel and on occasion will borrow a person's canoe. Bariaua abhor the very thought of being seen by human eyes and if they are ever spotted they disappear instantly.

Source: Renner, *Primitive Religion in the Tropical Forests*, 84; Rose, *Spirits, Fairies, Leprechauns, and Goblins*, 35; Seligman, *Melanesians of British New Guinea*, 647

Barnacle Goose

Variations: Annes de la mer, Barchad, Barnacha, Bernekke, Bernaca, Bernicle, Bernicle Goose, Goose Tree, Tree Goose

In the Middle Ages it was believed the barnacle goose, a bird smaller in size than a common wild goose weighing only about five pounds, began its life as a crustacean, the barnacle. In 1187 the chronicler and clergyman Giraldus Cambrensis wrote these geese grew from small *bernacae* attached to fir timber adrift at sea. As the *bernacae* developed and grew the bird within, the creature could be seen within descended from the wood by its bill, hanging downward. Upon reaching full development it broke free and took to the sky. Cambrensis, in addition to having witness this first hand, also said the barnacle goose was the only bird in the world to be conceived without intercourse between the parents or developed in a nest.

Source: Ashton, *Curious Creatures in Zoology*, 104; Findlater, *Chambers's Encyclopædia*, Volume 1, 746; Isaacs, *Animals in Jewish Thought and Tradition*, 179; Zell-Ravenheart, *Wizard's Bestiary*, 21

Barometz

Variations: Barbary Lamb, Borametz, Borometz, Jeduah, Little Lamb, Lycopodium, Scythian Lamb, Tartar, Tartary Lamb, Vegetable Lamb of Tartary

As early as the eleventh century it was believed there was a tree which grew in central Asia capable of growing zoophyle (animal-plant creature) much the same way other trees grew fruit; one such plant which grew sheep was known as the barometz. In the earliest versions of the myth, there were two distinct variations of the plant. The first variant described a tall bush or small tree where the lamb grew from its branches in a pod, similar to a bean. These lambs have no horns but their wool is very desirable for cloth; their flesh is said to taste like fish and their blood like honey.

In the other version of the legend the animal was connected by a vine-like umbilical cord to the plant. The lamb would graze the area around the base of its plant; when all of the accessible foliage had been consumed, the lamb, and shortly thereafter the plant, would die. The lamb, although connected to and grown from a plant, was said to be made of flesh and blood and was a favorite meal of wolves. According to Hebrew folklore, when the barometz was slain, people would gather certain bones and by placing them in their mouth were then briefly possessed by prophesying spirits, making predictions of the future.

Source: Ashton, *Curious Creatures in Zoology*, 98–9; Bar-ber, *Dictionary of Fabulous Beasts*, 150; Large, *Tree Ferns*, 306; Zell-Ravenheart, *Wizard's Bestiary*, 22

Barushka Matushka

Variations: Borushka Matushka, Kosmatushka, Sivushko

A magical and magnificent horse from Russian folklore, Barushka Matushka ("little mother") was the mount of the cultural hero, the bogatyr, Il'ya Muromets. A gift from his mother, Barushka Matushka would carry Il'ya safely so long as he kept his promise to her to protect the peasantry.

Source: Dixon-Kennedy, *Encyclopedia of Russian and Slavic Myth and Legend*, 42; Hubbs, *Mother Russia*, 156; Rose, *Giants, Monsters, and Dragons*, 40

Basilisk (baz'-uh-lisk)

Variations: Basilcoc, Basil Cock, Basili-Coc, Basilisci Serpentis ("Basilisk Serpent"), Basilishrkoi, Basilicok, Bazalicek, COCKATRICE, Regulus, SKOFFIN

A basilisk ("little king") was a highly poisonous reptile from ancient Greek mythology; it was so lethal it could kill not just by looking at its prey, but also by breathing on or touching them. Described as having the body of a large golden colored snake with two arms protruding from the top of its head, it hated mankind.

Although the basilisk originated in Greek mythology, it did not figure much into it. Pliny the Elder, a Roman author, army and naval commander, natural philosopher, and naturalist, wrote of the basilisk in his book, *Naturalis Historia*; in it he inscribed it was a small creature native to the province of Cyrenaica, had a white diamond shape mark on its head, and was only about twelve inches long. Pliny goes on to say the basilisk was so poisonous it could kill bushes, scorch grass, and cause rocks to burst. Pliny claimed the basilisk could split rocks and walked upright upon a rear set of legs—not slither along the ground as snakes do.

In European and Middle Eastern folklore the basilisk, in its earliest descriptions, was described as being small (lengths given vary between six inches and two feet) and venomous; this yellow colored snake, had a crown shaped crest upon its head and in some tellings two or three bony protrusions, like a crown. Not only was the bite of this creature fatal but it was capable of killing any living thing it breathed upon, glanced upon, or touched. The sound of its hissing drove away other snakes. Where the basilisk stood, the grass burned and destroyed the land; it preferred warm weather and was found in the desert.

In the eleventh and twelfth centuries the basilisk's

description grew not only in size but also in capability; not only was it now much larger but it also had the ability to breath fire and generate a sonic attack, killing with the sound of its voice. Medieval travelers were advised to carry a crystal globe or mirror on their person in the event they happened upon this creature, as the basilisk is so poisonous it could only be killed by seeing its own reflection. The sound of a cock crowing would cause the basilisk to have a deadly seizure and the mongoose and weasel was its only natural enemies. It was believed if a person saw a basilisk before the creature saw them, they could hold up an empty bottle and mystically capture the invisible transference of its poison before it entered into the person and killed them. If they were successful in doing this, the action would in turn kill the creature.

In the fourteenth century the English author Geoffrey Chaucer used the basilisk in one of the stories in his *Canterbury Tales*; his spelling of the creature's name, *basilicok*, evolved into the word COCKATRICE. This new creature had the serpentine head of the basilisk but the legs, head, and neck of a cockerel. Later descriptions added DRAGON wings and a human face.

Source: Conway, *Magickal, Mystical Creatures*, 184–5; Eason, *Fabulous Creatures, Mythical Monsters, and Animal Power Symbols*, 30; Lehner, *Big Book of Dragons, Monsters, and Other Mythical Creatures*, 73; Magnanini, *Fairy-Tale Science*, 126; Pliny, *Natural History of Pliny*, Volume 2, 282; Rosen, *Mythical Creatures Bible*, 92–3

Basmu

In Akkadian mythology the DRAGON Basmu is described as being a HORNED SERPENT with two forelegs; he appears in the *Story of the Slaying of Labbu* which recounts the victory of the god Tishpak over Basmu, LABBU, and MUSHUSSU, servants of TIAMAT. Venomous, Basmu roams the countryside devouring birds, fish, men, and wild asses. Eventually he is slain by Nergal.

Source: Kuehn, *Dragon in Medieval East Christian and Islamic Art*, 170; Wiggermann, *Mesopotamian Protective Spirits*, 166–7

Batibat

Variations: Bangungot ("nightmare"), Fat Old Woman of the Post

From Ilocano demonology of the Philippines comes the demonic creatures of nightmares, the batibat ("nightmare"). Assuming the form of a huge, old, obese woman, these nocturnal demons prey upon those who cut down the tree they live in so the wood may be used as a support beam in a house or as a bedpost. They are territorial and vengeful demons who will not let anyone sleep near their home; if anyone should they will sit on their chest and suffocate them in their sleep. Batibat prefer to attack those individuals who sleep in a room alone.

Should the tree a batibat lives in be cut down and used as a support beam in a house, the demon will not leave its tree but take its vengeance out on the inhabitants of the home, at the very least inflicting them with nightmares if not trying to kill them outright in their sleep. During a batibat-induced nightmare it is advised to bite your thumb or wiggle your toes to wake up and save yourself. Should a person survive a batibat attack, they are said to have become a *naluganan* ("something has taken hold") and have gained the ability to see and hear the supernatural.

Source: Ramos, *Creatures of Philippine Lower Mythology*, 25, 30; Rosen, *Mythical Creatures Bible*, 220; Rubino, *Ilocano*, 222

Baubas

Variations: Bauba ("bugbear")

In Lithuanian mythology the baubas ("one who frightens children") is a type of malevolent monster, NURSERY BOGIE, or witch said to carry off naughty children; they are associated with the ancient goddess of death.

Source: Dexter, *Varia on the Indo-European Past*, 147; Gimbutas, *Living Goddesses*, 29

Bawa

Variations: Baconawa

A massive bird from Philippine mythology, the bawa has a beak and talons of steel and is covered with feathers as long and strong as a sword. This animal is the guardian of Caliludan, the cave of the sky, which is covered by a veil of blue smoke.

Source: Demetrio, *Towards a Survey of Philippine Folklore and Mythology*, 43, 91; Redfern, *Most Mysterious Places on Earth*, 113

Bayard

Bayard was the enchanted horse belonging to the French hero, Maugis Renadu, who quested and won him (see FAIRY ANIMAL). The horse was said to understand the human language and possessed supernatural intelligence, loyalty, power, and speed. Bayard, a beautiful white charger, was able to bear the weight of three riders and still perform perfectly in combat as a warhorse. When fighting Charlemagne's army and faced with starvation, Bayard knelt before his master and offered up his life so the men of the army could eat his flesh. When Charlemagne tried to drown the animal in the River Meuse, the horse broke the millstone tied to him, swam to the opposite side of the river, escaped pursuit through the woods, and joined his handler.

Bayard was also the name of one of the HIPPOI ATHANATOI from ancient Greek mythology; it was one of a pair of horses given to the king of Athens, Erekhtheus (see PODARKES).

Source: Akehurst, *Stranger in Medieval Society*, 112–3; Hausman, *Mythology of Horses*, 216–8; Keightley, *World Guide to Gnomes, Fairies, Elves, and Other Little People*, 33

Bayardo

The charger of the hero Rinaldo, Bayardo was originally found by the knight wizard Malagigi in a grotto where the horse, along with a suite of armor and the sword, Fusberta, were under the watch of a DRAGON. After Malagigi dispatched the creature he gave the horse to his cousin, Rinaldo.

Source: Ariosto, *Orlando Furioso*, Volume 1, 35; Brewer, *Dictionary of Phrase and Fable*, 625

Baykok

In the Great Lakes region of the United States of America, the Ojibwa folklore includes a being known as the Baykok ("skin draped bones" or "skeletal decomposed remains"); it is undead and wanders the woods at night compelled by hunger, attacking only lone travelers and eating their livers. Wielding a bludgeoning club and invisible spirit arrows, Baykok will incapacitate his victims before consuming them. According to folklore a highly skilled and proud hunter became hopelessly lost in the woods while tracking a large buck. Unable to find his way home or catch any food to eat, the hunter began to die of starvation. The hunter swore with his last breath his spirit would never leave his body. Sometime after his death a hunting party passed by his remains and roused his spirit. Baykok attacked the group, eating them; thereafter he wandered the woods, continuing his hunt for more to eat.

Source: Brown, *Complete Idiot's Guide to Zombies*, n.pag.; Ingpen, *Ghouls and Monsters*, 43

Beannach-Nimhe

A monster in Scottish folklore, the beannach-nimhe ("horned poison") is a gigantic creature roaming the highlands of Scotland.

Source: Forbes, *Gaelic Names of Beasts*, 5, 188, 190; Rose, *Giants, Monsters, and Dragons*, 42

Beast Jasconius

Variations: Jasconius ("fish")

Mentioned in the story of the voyage of Saint Brendan, the beast Jasconius was said to be a fish so large it was mistaken for an island. Once a year for seven consecutive years, Saint Brendan and his companion of monks would return to the same place in the ocean where the gigantic fish was resting, spend Holy Saturday night encamped upon it

singing songs, on Easter Morning celebrate mass, and then peacefully leave. On the seventh year, however, the fish began to swim after mass taking the Saint and his companions to the Island of Birds.

Source: Mackley, *Legend of St. Brendan*, 110; Sprague de Camp, *Lands Beyond*, 117; Zell-Ravenheart, *Wizard's Bestiary*, 53

Beast of Gevaudin

Variations: La Bèstia de Gavaudan, La Bête du Gévaudan, Wild Beast of Gevaudin

In the folklore of eighteenth century France the Beast of Gevaudin was said to be a monstrous creature roaming the countryside between 1764 and 1767. Described as looking like a shaggy-coated, long-legged hyena with glowing eyes or a WEREWOLF, this creature was accredited with the deaths of over 100 people.

Source: Rose, *Giants, Monsters, and Dragons*, 394

Beathach mbr Loch Odha

Variations: Big Beast of Lochawe

In the Scottish Highlands there is the folklore of a twelve-legged creature known as Beathach mbr Loch Odha ("big beast of Lochawe"); although other details of its appearance vary greatly between an eel and a horse, it is commonly believed it can be heard in the winter floundering about atop of the ice breaking it up.

Source: Campbell, *Superstitions of the Highlands and Islands of Scotland*, 218; Spence, *Magic Arts in Celtic Britain*, 95

Bed Cat

Originating in the lumberjack communities of the developing U.S., the bed cat, one of the FEARSOME CRITTERS, was said to have extremely warm fur. In the Wisconsin region where these animals lived, their pelt was used to trim the nightgowns of ladies to keep them warm in the harsh winter months.

Source: Rose, *Giants, Monsters, and Dragons*, 119; Wyman, *Wisconsin Folklore*, Volume 3, 18

Beigad

In the folklore and literature of Iceland, Beigad ("fear-bringer" or "terrifier") is a boar both admired and feared by the people; tales of him are told in both the medieval work *Landnamabok* and in the saga, *Vatnsdœla*. According to folklore, when word had reached the people Beigad was loose among Ingimund's sows and had killed ten of his pigs, they gathered a hunting party to catch him. Eventually they chased the boar to the sea where the animal dove in and began to swim. Beigad tired but "swam till his hooves fell off"; eventually he made his way to shore, exhausted, and drug himself up a hill, later named Beigadarhill, where he died.

Source: Pálsson, *Book of Settlements*, 85; Rose, *Giants, Monsters, and Dragons*, 43–4

Beigorri

In Basque mythology Beigorri is a red-haired bull who is one of the guardians and minions of the goddess Mari; his primary function is to protect her home and her sanctuaries. Beigorri is believed to live in the caves found in the countryside.

Source: Miguel de Barandiarán, *Selected Writings of José Miguel De Barandiarán*, 94

Yn Beisht Kione

In the folklore from the Isle of Man, Great Britain, the yn beisht kione ("beast with the black head") is said to live in the waters off of the south side of the island.

Source: Rose, *Giants, Monsters, and Dragons*, 44

Beithir

A black-scaled water DRAGON from Scottish folklore, the fiery-eyed Beithir ("bear," beast," or "serpent") was believed to live in the lakes and caves around Loc a' Mhuillidh in Scotland.

Source: Armstrong, *Gaelic Dictionary in Two Parts*, 60; De Kirk, *Dragonlore*, 39; Eberhart, *Mysterious Creatures*, 44; Zell-Ravenheart, *Wizard's Bestiary*, 23

Bhainsasura

Variations: Mahisha, Mahishasura

In the Hindu folklore of India this denomic creature lives in Lake Barewa in Mirzapur. He appears, accompanied by NAGAS, at the time of the rice harvest; if not given an offering of a pig and shown respect, this KRAVYAD will destroy crops and fertile fields and terrorize the village. Bhainsasura is said to look like an enormous elephantine creature with the head of a water buffalo.

Fishermen will make offerings of eggs, fowl, and goats to gain permission to fish safely in Lake Barewa. A story tells that while a herdsman was watering his buffalos, a flood swept through and drowned them all. Because Bhainsasura's evil had permeated the water, they returned as demonic creatures.

It should be noted the demonic creature Bhainsasura is a derivative of another creature in Hindu mythology known as Mahisha; it was slain by the goddess Durga or the hero Skanda.

Source: Crooke, *Popular Religion and Folk-Lore of Northern India*, 44; Hastings, *Encyclopedia of Religion and Ethics*, Part 24, 716; Rose, *Giants, Monsters, and Dragons*, 47; Zell-Ravenheart, *Wizard's Bestiary*, 23

Bhardra

In Hindu mythology, Bhardra was one of the four mountainous elephants who supported the weight of the world upon their heads; he guarded the North. MAHA-PUDMA guarded the South, SAUMANASA guarded the West, and VIRUPAKSHA guarded the East.

Source: Vālmīki, *Ramayana: Book 1*, 223

Bi-Blouk

Folktale of the Khoikhoi people of south Africa tell of the bi-blouk, a dangerous female creature; it is described as having only half of a human body—one arm, leg, and half of a head with one eye, half a nose and mouth. The bi-blouk is a cannibal and hunts for its prey by leaping with its powerful leg. The male version of this creature is called HAI-URI.

Source: Knudsen, *Fantastical Creatures and Magical Beasts*, 28

Bialozar

Variations: KREUTZET

A THUNDERBIRD from Polish and Russian folklore, the bialozar is described as looking like a gigantic eagle; it is similar to the ROC.

Source: Barber, *Dictionary of Fabulous Beasts*, 95; Rose, *Giants, Monsters, and Dragons*, 312; Zell-Ravenheart, *Wizard's Bestiary*, 23

Biarki

Biarki was a bear named in Thorgrimr's *Rhymes* and in Snorri Sturluson's (1179–1241) *Prose Edda*. In Icelandic folklore and mentioned in the *Biarkarimur*, there is the tale of a hero named Biarki who is in service to King Hrolf; this warrior had the ability of therianthropy, enabling it to shape-shift into a white bear that was nearly impervious to blades.

Source: Jennbert, *Animals and Humans*, 50; Olrik, *Heroic Legends of Denmark*, 76

Biasd Bheulach

Variations: The Beast of Odail Pass

The biasd bheulach was one of the ATHACH, a strict nocturnal FAIRY ANIMAL living in the Odail Pass on the Isle of Skye in the Scottish Highlands. Sometimes it appeared as a greyhound or a man with only one leg. It was said to make a horrific wail; some stories claimed the biasd bheulach was a spirit of a vengeful ghost of a murdered man, on the hunt and hungry for revenge. Victims of this creature were found dead on the roadside with two piercing wounds on their side and one on their leg; a hand was said to be pressed to each wound.

Source: Avant, *Mythological Reference*, 79; Briggs, *Encyclopedia of Fairies*, 23, Campbell, *Witchcraft and Second Sight in the Highlands and Islands of Scotland*, 207–8; Zell-Ravenheart, *Wizard's Bestiary*, 23

Biasd na Srogaig

Variations: The Beast of the Lowering Horn

Said to live on the Isle of Sky, the biasd na srogaig is described as a large animal with long legs, an awkward gait, tall, and an alicorn (a single horn) on his forehead. This creature lived in the water much like a moose or water buffalo.

Source: Campbell, *Superstitions of the Highlands and Islands of Scotland*, 218; Spence, *Magic Arts in Celtic Britain*, 95

Bicha

In Spanish folklore the bicha was a monstrous bull with a human head; its image has been depicted since ancient times.

Source: Rose, *Giants, Monsters, and Dragons*, 48; Zell-Ravenheart, *Wizard's Bestiary*, 23

Bicorne

Variations: Bicouaine ("to be in a bad mood"), En Bicouaine ("to be wrong-headed"), La Bincouaine ("confusion"), Bulchin

According to medieval British folklore the bicorne ("two horns") was a panther-like creature with a woman's face which fed upon husbands who were berated and bullied by their wives. All bicornes were female and obese; their male counterparts were known as the CHICHEVACHE.

Source: Bois, *Jersey Folklore and Superstitions Volume Two*, 34–5; Chaucer, *Canterbury Tales*, 495; Rose, *Giants, Monsters, and Dragons*, 48

Bida

Appearing in the *Epic of the Dausi* from West African mythology, Bida was a DRAGON bound to the city of Wagadoo. When King Dinga tried to his pass on the secret of his rule to his eldest son, the man would not appear in court, but his youngest son, Lagarre, came right away. The king told the young man to wash from nine specific jars of water and then to take the drum Tabele into the northern desert and strike it. When the son did as he was told a city rose up from the sand and with it the DRAGON Bida. Lagarre and Bida struck an accord: every year one maiden (or ten; sources vary) was sacrificed to the DRAGON and it would gift the city with a shower of gold three times a year. The arrangement stood for three generations until a young maiden named Sia Jatta Bari was scheduled to be sacrificed. Her lover, Mamadi Sefe Dekote, caught Bida off-guard as he rose up from his lake, beheading the DRAGON. Unfortunately, the blow was not clean and Bida was able to curse the city before he died; for seven years, seven weeks, and seven days, it would not rain gold. Sadly, Sida tricked Mamadi into cutting off one of his fingers and toes then claimed she could not love an incomplete man. Mamadi turned to a witch for a love potion and tricked Sida into first drinking it

and then into sleeping with a servant. Sida, upon realizing what she had done, died of shame.

Source: De Kirk, *Dragonlore*, 57, 103–04; Knappert, *African Mythology*, 95

Big Ears

Big Ears is a monstrous, catlike creature originating in the folklore of the Scottish Highlands. It was summoned through use of the Taghairm, an ancient magical rite, for the purpose of granting wishes. For four consecutive days cats were roasted alive over an open fire until the creature Big Ears appeared. Stones with deep ruts in them were said to be places where Big Ears manifested, his claw marks left behind as evidence of his presence. Described as having evil-looking yellow eyes and gigantic ears, it was believed to be the king of the Underworld cats. Big Ears was sometimes associated to the CAIT SITH, a witch transformed into a cat.

Source: Avant, *Mythological Reference*, 86, 89; Briggs, *Encyclopedia of Fairies*, 23; Conway, *Mysterious, Magickal Cat*, 88

Big Fish

Variations: Big Fish of Iliamna

In the lakes throughout Tanaina, Alaska, is the legendary Big Fish, a species of large fish living in various lakes. These creatures are said to be exceptionally strong and capable of biting out the bottoms of boats; as a rule they hate the color red and will attack anything in the water bearing the color.

Source: Rose, *Giants, Monsters, and Dragons*, 48; Sturtevant, *Handbook of North American Indians: Subarctic*, 635

Big Head

Variations: Flying Head

Vampiric creatures from Iroquois mythology in the northeastern United States of America, the big heads are described as large flying humanoid heads covered with stringy hair, having fiery eyes, and rows of sharp teeth in their mouths with lockable jaws. Having wings where their ears should be, the big heads fly through stormy skies keeping aloft by the undulation of their hair as they look for prey. Once a target has been selected, it swoops down and snatches it up in its toothy maw.

Big Heads are not particularly intelligent and can be easily lured to the ground where they can be slain. First the Iroquois would roast chestnuts over an open fire made up of many red hot coals; next they would make loud exclamations of how particularly delicious they tasted. The big head would swoop down and grab a mouthful of the red hot coals before locking up its jaws. The coals would immediately begin to burn and soon, the big head would ignite and combust into flames.

Source: Beauchamp, *Iroquois Trail*, 95; Canfield, *Legends of the Iroquois*, 125–26; McLeish, *Myths and Legends of the World Explored*, 199; Rose, *Giants, Monsters and Dragons*, 124; Wonderley, *Oneida Iroquois Folklore*, 92

Big Owl

In Apache mythology Big Owl is a gigantic owl whose description varies according to tradition. Among the Chiricahua and the Mescalero Apache, it is an evil GIANT. To the Jacarillo Apache he is an owl cannibal with the ability to paralyze humans with his evil stare; his cry caused fear in everyone who heard it and his voice was like thunder causing things to quake. The White Mountain Apache claim Big Owl is son of the Sun and brother of their cultural hero, He. When he was slain, his body hit the earth sending his feathers flying off in every direction; these feathers transformed into the owls which now live in the forests.

Source: Goodwin, *Myths and Tales of the White Mountain Apache*, 24; Opler, *Myths and Tales of the Jicarilla Apache Indians*, 74; Rose, *Giants, Monsters, and Dragons*, 48

Billdad

The billdad, a FEARSOME CRITTER from the folklore of northwest Maine, lives only in Boundary Pound in Hurricane Township. A shy animal and increasingly rare, the billdad is most often heard rather than seen but it has been described as being about the size of a beaver with short front legs and kangaroo-like hind-quarters; it has webbed feet and a heavy bill reminiscent of a hawk. When hunting for fish, the billdad will perch upon a grassy point overlooking the water; when a trout rises to the surface the billdad leaps and brings its heavy tail down on the surface of the water. The smack will stun the fish making it easy for the billdad to pick it out of the water.

Source: Cox, *Fearsome Creatures of the Lumberwoods*, 43; Rose, *Giants, Monsters, and Dragons*, 119; Theitic, *Witches' Almanac*, Issue 34, 17

Biloko

In the folklore of the Democratic Republic of the Congo there is a vampiric creature called a biloko ("food") said to live in the deepest sections of the rainforest within hollowed out trees. The biloko is said to be covered with grass and uses leaves as its clothing; it has long, sharp claws, piercing eyes, and a snout-like nose. The biloko rings its magical bell and anyone who hears it will fall asleep; it will then pick up its prey and swallow the person whole. The biloko, because of its magical bell, is often appointed as the guardian of a hidden treasure. Fortunately, amulets and fetishes can be made to protect the wearer from the bell's magic.

Source: Chopra, *Dictionary of Mythology*, 53; Knappert, *Bantu Myths and Other Tales*, 142; Knappert, *Myths and Legends of the Congo*, 130

Bimbam

Originating in the lumberjack communities of the developing United States of America, the bimbam was one of the FEARSOME CRITTERS. Unfortunately, there is no additional information on this creature other than its name, causing writers of the time, 1841–1861, to believe it had gone extinct.

Source: Mencken, *American Language Supplement 1*, 251

Binaye Ahani

Variations: Ahani, Binaye Albani

In the folklore of the Navajo people, the binaye ahani ("the people who slay with their eyes") was one of the ANAYE, one of four races of gigantic and monstrous supernatural beings causing fear, misery, and wickedness throughout the world. Binaye ahani are described as being limbless twins conjoined at the torso, full of hate, and related to the feathered TSANAHALE and the headless THELGETH; these creatures are similar to the HARPIES of Greek mythology.

Source: Cotterell, *Dictionary of World Mythology*, 220; Dixon-Kennedy, *Native American Myth and Legend*, 23; Rose, *Giants, Monsters, and Dragons*, 49; Zell-Ravenheart, *Wizard's Bestiary*, 15

Bingbuffer

In the American folklore from the Ozark Mountains, the bingbuffer is said to be a lacertilian (lizard-like) monster killing people by throwing rocks at them.

Source: Cavendish, *Man, Myth and Magic*, Volume 5, 2101; Hendrickson, *Facts on File Dictionary of American Regionalisms*, 344; Rose, *Giants, Monsters, and Dragons*, 49

Bird Griffin

Usually depicted with scales covering its body, the bird griffin is considered by some scholars, such as Heinz Adolf Mode (August 15, 1913–July 6, 1992), a former professor of Oriental archaeology at University of Halle, as being a variant of the DRAGON while others, like H. Prinz, see it as being its own unique mythological species along with the SNAKE GRIFFIN and the lion griffin. The bird griffin was said to have the body of a lion covered with scales, the neck and head of a bird, and wings.

Source: Mode, *Fabulous Beasts and Demons*, 128–9; South, *Mythical and Fabulous Creatures*, 87

Bird Man

A creature in Japanese folklore and mythology, bird man is described as being humanoid with a bird shaped head, a beak, cock's comb, human ears, wattles, and human hands on the tips of its wings. It dresses in traditional Japanese clothing.

Source: Rose, *Giants, Monsters, and Dragons*, 49

Birds of Mount Gurayu

The fourth of four deadly monsters in the Moro tradition were the birds of Mount Gurayu; they had seven heads each and preyed upon the people of Nindanao. These birds were so destructive and ravenous it took little time for them to nearly deplete the resources of the area and cause the few remaining people to live hidden in caves behind waterfalls.

Source: Hurley, *Swish of the Kris*, 264; Roque, *Tales from Our Malay Past*, 83

Birds of Rhiannon

The birds of Rhiannon were FAIRY ANIMALS of British folklore; typically their number was given as three. These birds were wonderful musicians with the ability to sing the dead back to life. According to the "*Mabinogi of Branwen, Daughter of Llyr*" a warrior came upon the birds and was so enchanted by their song he stopped and listened to them sing for 80 consecutive years; there are many versions of this story.

Source: Evans-Wentz, *Fairy Faith in Celtic Countries*, 334; Parker, *Mythology*, 214; Sikes, *British Goblins*, 89

Bisan

A species of female NATURE SPIRITS from the folklore of the Malay people of West Malaysia, the bisan are the guardians of, specifically, the camphor-bearing trees (*Cinnamonium camphora*); at night they make a shrill cry identical to the call of the cicadas. Appearing to humans in the form of the cicada these creatures must be approached using the correct method, such as only speaking *bahasa kapor* (camphor language), sacrificing a white rooster, and leaving a small offering of food. While hunting for camphor-bearing trees one must eat his trail rations without any form of condiment or the bisan will be offended.

Source: Rose, *Spirits, Fairies, Leprechauns, and Goblins*, 41; Skeat, *Malay Magic*, 213; Watts, *Dictionary of Plant Lore*, 55

Bishop Fish

Variations: Monachi Marini, Sea Bishop, Seabishop, SEA MONK, Squatina Angelus

Depicted in the medieval bestiary *Historia Animalium* (1551–1558) by Swiss naturalist Konrad von Gesner, the bishop fish was depicted as a large fish with its head shaped like a bishop's miter, its pectoral fins drawn as claw-like fingers, and its tail resembling fishermen's boots. According to the accompanying folklore, the fish was first captured in the Baltic Sea in the thirteenth century and presented to the king of Poland. Another was caught off the coast of Poland in 1531. When presented to a gathering of bishops the fish gestured with its claw-like hands to be set free. The bishops agreed and the fish, making the sign of the cross, dove back into the water. A final fish was captured off the coast of Germany and held in captivity; the fish refused to eat and after being held for three days, died.

Source: Bassett, *Legends and Superstitions of the Sea and Of Sailors in All Lands and At All Times*, 206–07; Breverton, *Breverton's Phantasmagoria*, 189; Rosen, *Mythical Creatures Bible*, 143

Bison Bull

In ancient Sumerian mythology, Bison Bull was one of the many monsters slain by the warrior god, Ninurta. Little is known of this creature other than Gudea, a ruler of Lagash (c.a. 2100 BC), referred to it and the other monsters vanquished by Ninurta as the SLAIN HEROES; he elevated them all to the status of god and made a place of worship for them in the temple.

Source: Ataç, *Mythology of Kingship in Neo-Assyrian Art*, 185; Salem, *Near East, the Cradle of Western Civilization*, 102–3; Sherman, *Storytelling*, 332

Bistern Dragon

Said to have ravished and terrorized the countryside of Hampshire, England, during the sixteenth century the Bistern Dragon was confronted by Sir Moris Barkley (Sir Maurice de Berkeley), a knight who had covered his armor with bits of broken glass, and took with him his faithful pack of hunting dogs. Although the DRAGON was slain, neither Barkley nor his dogs survived the confrontation. The Berkeley family coat of arms and family crest were changed to reflect and remember Sir Moris' heroic deed.

Source: De Kirk, *Dragonlore*, 39; Hart, *Secret of the Dragon's Eye*, 62; Rose, *Giants, Monsters, and Dragons*, 49

Bitje

In the mythology of ancient Egypt, Bitje was a monstrous serpent described as having a head at each end of its body; it was said to live in the ninth section, or hour, of Tuat, the Underworld. In *The Text of Unas* there is a magical spell which when performed will cause the destruction of monstrous beasts and serpents alike; Bitje would be affected by this spell.

Source: Coulter, *Encyclopedia of Ancient Deities*, 32, 102; Mercante, *Who's Who in Egyptian Mythology*, 24

Bitoso

Variations: The Faster

A species of demonic creatures from ancient Roman folklore, the four-headed worms known as the bitoso were said to cause ear-aches, loss of appetite, stomach aches, and tooth aches.

Source: Wall, *Meyer Brothers Druggist*, Volume 31, 141; Zell-Ravenheart, *Wizard's Bestiary*, 23

Biwa-Bokuboku (BEE-wah BOH-koo BOH-koo)

Variations: Biwa Monk

One of the YŌKAI of Japanese folklore, the biwa-bokubboku ("Biwa monk") is a sub-species of the TSUKOMOGAMI, as it is an old musical instrument which has taken on a humanoid form. Depicted as wearing a kimono and having a lute for a head, the creature has its eyes tightly closed, as traditionally many lute players were blind. The head of this YŌKAI is said to be a fusion of two legendary and long lost instruments known as the Bokuba and the Genjo. This being can create music so beautiful it can calm even an ONI. Its presence in and of itself is not dangerous but is believed to be an omen of an impending calamity, such as a fire. In art the biwa-bokubboku is typically shown with the KOTO-FURUNUSHI and the SHAMISEN-CHORO. If encountered, these beings are willing to have a musician play them, but if not, they are more than willing to play themselves.

Source: Meyer, *Night Parade of One Hundred Demons*, 212; Yoda, *Yokai Attack*, 106–10

Bixie

A species of CHIMERA from Chinese folklore, the bixie ("to ward off evil spirits") is described as looking like a winged lion with horns upon its head. The images of these creatures were carved of stone and placed near the entrance of tombs to frighten off malevolent intrusions.

Source: Watt, *China*, 104; Zell-Ravenheart, *Wizard's Bestiary*, 24

Black Angus

Variations: BARGUEST, Cu Sith ("fairy dog"), Cwn Annw, Gurt Dog

A black angus is a hound from the folklore of England and Scotland; it is uncertain if this is a species of FAIRY ANIMAL or an individual being. Appearing as a large black dog with yellow glowing eyes and a maw full of sharp teeth, it roams the countryside as a psychopomp (death omen), as anyone who sees it will die within a fortnight. Reports of Black Angus sightings date back as far as the seventeenth century.

Source: Conway, *Magickal, Mystical Creatures*, 139; Jones, *Modern Science and the Paranormal*, 61; McCoy, *Witch's Guide to Faery Folk*, 147, 185

Black Dog

Variations: Bakgest, Barghest, BARGUEST, CAPELTHWAITE, Choin Dubh ("muckle black tyke"), Devil Dog, BLACK ANGUS, BLACK SHUCK, Black Shug, Gurt Dog, GWYLLGI, Gytrash, HELLHOUND, Hounds of Annwn (see ANNWN, HOUNDS OF), Mauthe Dhoog, Morphing Shuck, PADFOOT, Pooka, Rizos, Rongeur d'Os, SKRIKER, Shuck, Suicide Shuck, Tchian du Bouolay, TRASH

There are many different species of black dogs in mythology, especially in the British Isles; generally these injurious FAIRY ANIMALS are described as being large and fierce, typically with a black coat. Their eyes are said to glow red or yellow, their mouth filled with vicious teeth. To see one or hear its howl is a psychopomp (death omen); only a few rare stories exist of a black dog playing the role of a guardian and protector. Black dogs patrol deserted roads, usually invisible right up until the moment they attack; otherwise, only the clicking of their claws can be heard. Crossroads and midnight are also common themes to black dog folklore.

In the British Isles the black dog is shaggy and the size of a calf while in German folklore it is every bit as large but its coat is more akin to a poodle's. Appearance and size differ only slightly from region to region; black dogs are reported in some fashion or another throughout the world.

Although traveling alone is never a good idea at night, having a companion offers no protection from the black dog, as one person may see and hear it while the other does not. According to folklore, the best protection from one of these creatures is to travel with a descendant of Ean MacEndroe of Loch Ewe, as he once reportedly saved the life of a fairy who in return gave him and his family line perpetual and eternal immunity from black dogs.

Source: Bois, *Jersey Folklore and Superstitions*, 103; Budd, *Weiser Field Guide to Cryptozoology*, 98–9; Choron, *Planet Dog*, 28; Godfrey, *Mythical Creatures*, 92–3

Black Shanglan

A FAIRY ANIMAL, Black Shanglan was a warhorse from Irish folklore; along with WOMAN RULER, they lived invisibly inside their fairy fort. This duo appears only when it involves the freeing of Ireland in order to aid and comfort the people during a national uprising.

Sources: Wallace, *Folk-lore of Ireland*, 81

Black Shuck

Variations: Doom Dog, Galleytrot, MODDEY DHOO of Norfolk, Old Shock, Old Shuck, Shucky Dog, Shukir

Black Shuck is the name given to the BLACK DOG (see BARGUEST) roaming the lonely roads in East Anglia, Essex, Norfolk, and the Suffolk coastline of England. Sightings of this HELLHOUND are still made periodically; folklore of him dates back thousands of years to the time of Viking invasions. It has been speculated Black Shuck was named after Shukir, the war dog of Odin and Thor, although it is equally possible the name was derived from the local dialect word *shucky*, which means "hairy" or "shaggy."

Black Shuck has been described in appearance in a number of ways; he is said to have two large saucer-like glowing green or red eyes, sometimes it is said he has only a single eye. Reports vary to his size, in one case he is as large as a horse while in another he is just as big as any large-sized dog, but headless. What apparently sets this particular BLACK DOG apart from others is its haunting of a specific region and that he has very seldom been credited with doing anything more than frightening people nearly to their death. Nevertheless, sightings of this psychopomp (death omen) are still considered to be horrific, as those who encounter him will die within a year.

Appearing just before bad weather and most active on stormy nights when the sea is dark and roiling, Black Shuck will sound out, its cry being carried out over the roar of the waves.

Sources: Dutt, *Highways and Byways in East Anglia*, 216; Eberhart, *Mysterious Creatures*, Volume 1, 63; Guiley, *Encyclopedia of Witches, Witchcraft and Wicca*, 24; Mitchell, *Slow Norfolk and Suffolk*, 47

Black Sow

Variations: Tailless Black Sow ("hwch ddu gwta")

During the Celtic agricultural festival of Beltaine (Ceshamain) bonfires were made atop of hills consisting of ferns, gorse, straw, and thorn bushes; after the fires were lit and while the people danced in a sunwise direction around them, herds of cattle were driven between the bonfires so as to magically prevent them from diseases. As the fires died the participants would run away to escape the frightening appearance of the black sow; its presence could terrify even the bravest of men, as it was often seen as a manifestation of the Devil himself.

Source: Baker, *Celtic Mythological Influences on American Theatre*, 26–7; Ross, *Folklore of Wales*, 29

Black Worm

In Teutonic mythology the tale of a DRAGON guarding a treasure hoard is common; the tale of the black worm is similar to those. The black worm is a gigantic snake or serpentine DRAGON guarding a massive hoard of gold; it wraps its body around the base of its treasure heap but is not quite large enough to coil around it all. While it sleeps, an adventurer enters into its domain and fills his pockets and packs with gold but inevitably greedy, he calls out to his companions to do the same. This call wakes the worm who rears up roaring; panicking, the man drops his ill-gotten gains and flees. The black worm and his treasure then sink into the earth, never to be seen again.

Source: Grimm, *Teutonic Mythology*, 978

Blakkr (BLAK-r)

Variations: Blakk

In Norse mythology Blakkr ("black") was the horse ridden by Bjorn ("bear"), one of the many aliases of the god, Odin. Thrgan ("freeman"), the son of Karl the Yeoman and Snoer, also rode a horse by this name.

Source: Grimes, *Norse Myths*, 258, 301; Norroena Society, *Asatrii Edda*, 339; Sturluson, *Prose Edda*, Volume 5, 212

Bledlochtana

Bledlochtana ("monster") is the collective name for the terrifying monsters of Irish folklore and mythology; they manifest on the anniversary of the Battle of Mag Tuired and let loose with a horrific cry which causes fear in anyone who hears it.

Source: MacCulloch, *Celtic Mythology*, Volume 3, 25; Rose, *Giants, Monsters, and Dragons*, 52

Bledmall

Variations: Bladmall, Bledmail

A SEA SERPENT of Celtic folklore, the bledmall was feared by fishermen off the coast of Ireland and northern waters because it had the uncanny ability to capsize sturdy longships.

Source: Beorh, *Pirate Lingo*, 15; Eberhart, *Mysterious Creatures*, 478; Zell-Ravenheart, *Wizard's Bestiary*, 24

Blóðughófi (BLOHTH-ug-hohv-i)

Variations: Blodughofi, Blodug-hofi, Blodinghofi

The horse of the god of rain and sun, Freyr, from Norse mythology, Blóðughófi ("bloody hoof") was said to be able to understand human speech and run through fire and total darkness. Although Blóðughófi was an exceedingly fast horse he was not able to run as fast as the golden-red boar GULLINBORSTI or jump as high as the eight-legged horse, SLEIPNIR.

Source: Grimes, *Norse Myths*, 66, 164, 258; Norroena Society, *Asatrii Edda*, 25

Blood Dogs

Variations: Scots Hounds

In the legends of northern England and Scotland

there are massive hounds said to haunt the locations of battlefields and lick up the blood of the fallen soldiers; they are most often seen in the misty mornings. Many believe these spectral hounds belong to Charles Edward Stuart (1720–1788; also known as "Bonnie Prince Charlie"). Blood hounds are described as being massive with dark red eyes, fiery breath, and grey colored coats.

Source: Maberry, *Vampire Universe*, 42

Bloody Bones

Variations: Old Bloody Bones

Bloody-Bones is a NURSERY BOGIE primarily from the folklore of England and the United States of America. Ugly beyond description with his bloody and raw flesh exposed, Bloody Bones and his companion, RAWHEAD, were often used as NURSERY BOGIES by parents to trick children into good behavior or for avoiding a certain activity or area, whichever was appropriate.

Source: Brewer, *Reader's Handbook of Famous Names in Fiction*, 129, 743; Monaghan, *Encyclopedia of Celtic Mythology and Folklore*, 450; Wright, *Rustic Speech and Folk-Lore*, 198

Bmola

Variations: Bumole, Pomol, Wind Bird, Wind Eagle

A fearful flying creature from Abenaki mythology, the bmola was said to live on certain islands and on the top of Mount Katahdin where it generated bad weather, cold winds, and storms. The cultural hero Gluskab captured the bird-like creature and bound its wings; however, after the mountain air became too hot to be tolerable to the animals and humans who lived upon the mountain, he allowed it to use its wings to cool the air. Traditional folklore says no one who ever ascended the mountain lived to return because the bmola would kill and consume them.

Source: Bennett, *White Mountains*, 21; Thoreau, *Maine Woods*, 48

Boar of Ben Bulbain

Variations: Wild Boar of Ben Bulben

In Celtic folklore, Gulben, the half-brother of the hero and warrior Dermot (also known as Diarmaid and Diarmait) was accidentally crushed to death by Donn, Dermot's father, while in the camp of the Fianna; Roc, the boy's father, used his magic wand and transformed the corpse of his son into a white boar with no ears or tail. As soon as it was created the boar rose to its feet and fled off to Ben Bulbain Mountain in Sligo to live out its life. This boar was particularly fierce and had slain many men in the course of its life. Dermot was placed under a *geis*

(an individual vow of obligation which if broken curses the person) not to hunt boar as his half-brother was now one.

Fionn and his Fianna were in the Ben Bulben Mountains and found themselves being hunted by the boar; 30 of his men had already been slain when they happened upon Dermot, the third best warrior of all Fianna. Dermot joined the party but only as an extra, refusing to hunt. Eventually Fionn's men killed the white boar and he ordered it measured. Dermot did so (it measured sixteen feet from snout to rump) and discovered it was his half-brother who had been slain. While measuring the beast one of the boar's poisonous bristles pierced the bottom of his foot, his only vulnerable place; eventually he died from the ever-bleeding wound.

Source: Matson, *Celtic Mythology A to Z*, 227; Mountain, *Celtic Encyclopedia*, Volume 3, 549

Boas

A species of large snake described by Pliny the Elder, the Roman author, natural philosopher, naturalist, and army and naval commander in his work *Natural History* (AD 77), the boas was said to be native to Italy and of an incredibly vast weight. Following behind the flocks of cattle and gazelles, they would drink from the udders of the animals until full and then kill the animal. Later descriptions added large ears, two legs, and wings.

Source: Nigg, *Book of Fabulous Beasts*, 88; Zell-Ravenheart, *Wizard's Bestiary*, 25

Bobbi Bobbi

A gigantic serpent, similar to the RAINBOW SERPENT, the Bobbi Bobbi from the mythology of the Binbinga people of northern Australia used to look kindly upon mankind from his home in the Dreamtime. When he saw the people were hungry he sent down to earth *kitiaquantj* (flying foxes) for them to hunt and eat; unfortunately the *kitiaquantj* flew too high in the air for the people to catch by hand. Still wanting to help, Bobbi Bobbi removed one of his ribs and sent it to earth as the first boomerang. Two men, not content with the assistance Bobbi Bobbi had already given mankind, tricked him with flattery into allowing them to come to heaven; they threw the boomerang at the great snake and hit him squarely in the head. During its flight, the weapon also cut a gash in the sky and Bobbi Bobbi fell through it. He came crashing down to the earth and landed on the two men, killing them. Although uninjured by the attack and the fall, Bobbi Bobbi had inadvertently introduced death to the world; he refused to lend his assistance to man ever again.

Source: Bartlett, *Mythology Bible*, 244; De Kirk, *Dragonlore*, 59

Bocanach

In the folklore of Ireland, the bocanach ("bent" or "hooked") was a gigantic goat which menaced people who traveled alone at night on isolated roads.

Source: Macleod, *Dictionary of the Gaelic Language*, 75; Rose, *Giants, Monsters, and Dragons*, 54; Zell-Ravenheart, *Wizard's Bestiary*, 25

Bockman

A SATYR-like NURSERY BOGIE from German folklore, the bockman is used by parents to keep their children from entering into the woods alone.

Source: Rose, *Giants, Monsters, and Dragons*, 54

Bogeyman

Variations: Boggelman, Bogieman, Boogerman, Boogermonster, Boogeyman, Boogie Man, Boogyman, Bumann, NURSERY BOGIE

A creature in many cultures from all historical periods, the bogeyman is basically a type of horrific and terrifying NURSERY BOGIE, a being used to prevent the members of society from committing an act considered socially unacceptable; the indiscretion which can trigger an assault from this being can range from something as simple as walking into the woods alone, venturing too near the edge of a lake or pond, having premarital relations, or wandering the roads alone at night. Dangerous and evil, the bogeyman is not a mischief-maker or a troublesome spirit but rather a malignant and murderous creature which exists on the cultural boundaries between what is perceived as socially right and what is seen as unacceptable, evil, and wrong; it is the epitome of the chaos which can exist when a cultural boundary is crossed. Many tales of the bogeyman have to do with unruly children.

Source: Krensky, *Bogeyman*, 8; Phillips, *Projected Fears*, 132–3

Bokwus

Bokwus ("WILD MAN of the woods") is a NATURE SPIRIT found in the folklore of the Kwakiutl people of the northwest United States of America. Described as a skeletal being and wearing fearsome war paint it uses the sound of rushing water to mask its movement through the spruce wood forest, then, sneaking up on an unsuspecting fisherman it pushes him in the water and tries to drown him. If he succeeds, Bokwus captures his soul. If ever Bokwus offers a person a piece of dried salmon they should not accept it, as in truth it is actually a piece of dried tree bark; if it is eaten, it will transform the person into a ghost under his control.

Source: Avant, *Mythological Reference*, 497; Eason, *Complete Guide to Faeries and Magical Being*, 197; Ingpen, *Ghouls and Monsters*, 43

Bolla

Variations: Bullar

A gigantic, demonic DRAGON from Albanian folklore, Bolla, a singular creature, is described as being serpentine, with a long serpentine body, having four legs, silver faceted eyes, and a pair of small wings. By the time it is twelve years old, it has grown nine tongues, horns, larger wings, spines down its back, and has fully developed its fire-breathing ability. At this point the creature is called a KULSHEDRA. Once a year, on Saint George's Day, Bolla opens its eyes and will attack and consume the first person it sees upon awakening. Most countries which celebrate Saint George's Day do so on April 23, the traditionally accepted day of his death. However, May 6 and November 23 are also days assigned to the Saint.

Source: Elsie, *Dictionary of Albanian Religion*, 46–7; Lurker, *Dictionary of Gods and Goddesses*, 66; Rose, *Giants, Monsters, and Dragons*, 54; Zell-Ravenheart, *Wizard's Bestiary*, 25

Bolman

A NURSERY BOGIE from the Netherlands folklore, the bolman is utilized by parents whose children will not go to sleep at night. Bolman lives beneath a child's bed and using his claws and teeth will attack any child who leaves their bed at night; grabbing them, he will pull them under the bed and consume them.

Source: Frater, *Listverse*, 579

Bolton Ass

In British folklore the Bolton ass was a creature said to chew tobacco and take snuff; adding this to his diet was said to have made him as swift as a racing horse.

Source: Brewer, *Character Sketches of Romance, Fiction and the Drama*, Volumes 1–2, 148; Doran, *Miscellaneous Works*, Volume 2, 17

Bonhomme Sept-Heures

A BOGEYMAN from the folklore of Quebec, Canada, Bonhomme Sept-Heures ("mister seven o'clock") comes around seven o'clock in the evening to gather up all the children who are not in bed. The ones he catches, he takes back to his cave and eats.

Source: Frater, *Listverse*, 580; Krensky, *Bogeyman*, 43; Timmins, *French Fun*, 44

Bonito Maidens

The MERMAIDS of the Melanesian people of southeastern Solomon Islands, the Bonito maidens are the protectors and guardians of the sacred bonito fish. These fish will seek out the bonito maidens in the deep waters so they may remove the hooks from their mouth, having escaped the fisherman's line. Bonito maidens are seldom seen but exceedingly beautiful, adorned with the jewels of the ocean: ivory, pearls, and shells.

Source: Knight, *Goth Magick*, 132; Oliver, *Oceania*, 683

Bonnacon

Variations: Bonachus, Bonacon, Bonaconn, Bonasus

Depicted in medieval bestiaries, the bonnacon was a chimerical type of bull or oxen with large inward curved horns atop its head, a horse-like mane running down its neck, and the noted ability to discharge acidic dung as it ran to dissuade predators from attack; it can in this way cover an area of two acres with its debris and stench. Pliny the Elder (AD 23–79), the Roman author and natural philosopher, wrote of the bonnacon in his work *Historia Naturalis* (AD 77). Gaius Julius Solinus, the Latin grammarian and compiler (early 3rd century), Albert the Great (1206–1280), and Edward Topsell (1572–1625), an English cleric best known for his Topsell treatise bestiary, also included the bonnacon in their documents.

Source: Hassig, *Mark of the Beast*, 130–31; Rose, *Giants, Monsters, and Dragons*, 55; Zell-Ravenheart, *Wizard's Bestiary*, 25

Boobrie

The boobrie is a FAIRY ANIMAL from the Scottish Highlands haunting lakes and salt-water wells; it is said to fly through the water. Its favorite foods are cattle and sheep and it will attack any ship carrying them. The boobrie mimics the sound of a calf or lamb in the hopes of luring an adult animal to the side of the ship; if successful, it will use its long talons to grab the animal, drag it underwater, and drown it. When cows and sheep are not available, it eats otters.

The boobrie has the power of therianthropy, enabling it to shape-shift into a horse; in this form it can run across the surface of the water and when it does so, its hoofbeats sound as if it were running over solid ground. It also can shape-shift into the form of a large insect with tentacles and feeds off horse blood. The foot-print of the boobrie looks like the imprint of an antler.

Source: Briggs, *Encyclopedia of Fairies*, 34; Campbell, *Popular Tales of the West Highland*, 307–8; Howey, *Horse in Magic and Myth*, 146; Mccoy, *Witch's Guide to Faery Folk*, 88–9; Monaghan, *Encyclopedia of Celtic Myth and Folklore*, 53

Al Borak (baw'rak)

Variations: Alborak, Al-Buraaq, Borak, Boraq, Burak ("bright and shining"), Burak the Horse of Abraham, Buraq

According to Islamic mythology in the story of the *Miraj* (ascent into Heaven), one of the ten animals allowed to enter into Paradise in the Muslim mythology was the chimerical al Borak ("the lightning"), a gift from the ANGEL Gabriel to the prophet Mahomet; the animal was intended to carry Mahomet to the seventh heaven upon a saddle made of rubies. Al Borak was a horse (or donkey and mule hybrid, sources conflict) described as being milk-white, winged, and having the face of a human but the cheeks of a horse, eyes like twinkling jacinth, and the ability to speak with a human voice. In the Koran, he was said to be "larger than a donkey but smaller than a mule." In addition to carrying Mahomet to heaven al Borak let Abraham ride him when he wanted to visit his son Ishmael.

Source: Brewer, *Dictionary of Phrase and Fable*, 205, 624; Irving, *Mahomet and his Successors*, 26; Renard, *Islam and the Heroic Image*, 208

Boraro

Humanoid monsters in Tukano mythology in the Amazon, the boraro ("white ones") are hairy-chested, pallid, tall beings with backward-facing feet, an enormous phallus, glowing red eyes, protruding ears, and no knees. They also have a powerful sounding jaguar-like roar. These cannibals use stone weapons when hunting and tracking unwary humans. To subdue its prey the boraro will urinate on them or beat them severely with stone weapons; once the person is incapacitated, it will suck out all of their internal organs through a hole it chews in the top of the victim's head.

Source: Rose, *Giants, Monsters, and Dragons*, 56; Smith, *Enchanted Amazon Rain Forest*, 55

Boraspati Ni Tano

In the Batak mythology the Boraspati Ni Tano is a NATURE SPIRIT. Sacrifices are made to it whenever a new home is constructed; traditionally the offering would be the life of a slave. Associated with fertility, Boraspati Ni Tano manifests in the form of a lizard.

Source: Chopra, *Academic Dictionary of Mythology*, 55; Savill, *Pears Encyclopaedia of Myths and Legends*, 81

Boreas (bo-re-ass)

In ancient Greek mythology the god of the north wind, Boreas, took the form of a horse and would pull the chariot of the god, Zeus (Jupiter); in this form he was considered to be one of the foundation stallions of the HIPPOI ATHANATOI. Boreas when he happened upon the heard of Dardanus consisting of 3,000 mares became so enamored he assumed his horse form and through twelve of the mares sired offspring so swift they could run over water as easily as they could over land.

Source: Andrews, *Dictionary of Nature Myths*, 93; Berens, *Myths and Legends of Ancient Greece and Rome*, 171; Lemprière, *Classical Dictionary*, 134

Boreyne

In heraldic symbology the boreyne was a chimerical creature depicted as having a barbed tongue, curly horns, dorsal fin, forelegs of a lion, and the hindquarters of an eagle.

Source: Coleman, *Dictionary of Mythology*, 161; Zell-Ravenheart, *Wizard's Bestiary*, 25

Boroboro-Ton (BOH-roh Boh-roh tohn)

A YŌKAI from Japanese mythology boroboro-ton ("hunted comforter") is described as an animated futon cover or comforter; apart from being able to move of its own accord it is not known to do anything more than give people a good scare.

Source: Yoda, *Yokai Attack*, 182–5

Boroka

A chimerical monster and witch from Filipino folklore, the boroka is HARPY-like in appearance, as it is described as having the face and torso of a woman, four legs, the hooves of a horse, and the wings of an eagle. A malicious cannibal, this NURSERY BOGIE will track and consume any children who wander into its territory; it is especially fond of the liver. When children are not available, it will consume anyone it happens upon.

Source: Fansler, *Filipino Popular Tales*, Volume 12, 279; Rose, *Giants, Monsters, and Dragons*, 7; Zell-Ravenheart, *Wizard's Bestiary*, 25

Bouders

Variations: Boudons

A tribe of evil DJINN and GIANTS from Indian mythology, the Bouders are the guardians of the god, Shiva.

Source: Brewer, *Dictionary of Phrase and Fable*, 167; Wildridge, *Grotesque in Church Art*, 66

Brahmaparush (Bram-ah-pa-rosh)

Variation: Brahmaparus, Brahmaparusha, Brahmeparush, Bramaparush

A particularly cruel vampire from India, the brahmaparush has a very specific and highly ritualized means of killing its victims, usually travelers. It is described as a floating head with intestines hanging down from the neck and carrying a drinking cup made from a human skull in the tangle of its entrails. Once it has captured a person, the brahmaparush begins the killing ritual by first nibbling a small hole in the person's head to drink up their blood as it trickles out. Then it gnaws a section of skull away and begins to slurp up the brains, carefully keeping the person alive for as long as possible. Next, it does a bizarre dance, lashing at the corpse and eventually entangling itself in the corpse's intestines. Finally, the brahmaparush will play in the offal and has even been known to make a turban out of the viscera and wear it on its head.

Source: Belanger, *Sacred Hunger*, 113; Guiley, *Complete Vampire Companion*

Bran

Bran ("avalanche") and his littermate brother SGEOLAN were the two faithful hunting dogs of the cultural hero, Finn Mac Cumhaill; his other dogs were ADHUNALL, Luath Luchar, SCEOLAN, and SEAR DUGH. As a CU-SITH, or fairy hound, this ferocious dog has been described as being as large as a two year old stirk (a bullock or heifer), overall a dark green but lighter towards his yellow feet with black sides and a white belly and chest. Bran's ears were pointed and blood red upon his small head. He had claws like a wolf, eyes like a DRAGON, the venom of a serpent, and the vigor of a lion. Fast and smart, this sleek-haunch hound was also wise and seemed to possess human knowledge as well as an understanding of the fay (see FAIRY ANIMAL).

The mother of the two dogs was Fionn's own aunt, Turen, who was changed into a CU-SITH herself by a bean sith. In some versions of the story she was changed back into a human just after SGEOLAN'S birth, so Bran was born human while his brother was a dog. Accounts of Bran's death vary. One says he was killed with witchcraft, another says although he had a venomous bite he himself was not immune to his own poison and accidentally bit himself. Another version says while hunting a goddess who had assumed the shape of a deer he followed her relentlessly; when she took a running dive off a cliff, she was able to transform into a bird while the dog mindlessly followed and fell to his death.

Source: Forbes, *Gaelic Names of Beasts*, 139–40; Gregory, *Gods and Fighting Men*, 238, 398; Mountain, *Celtic Encyclopedia*, Volume 3, 682

Brigadore (Brig' adore)

Variations: Brigliadore (bril-yar-dore)

The horse of Sir Guyon in Spencer's *Faerie Queen*, Brigadore ("golden bridle") was known for a distinguishing black spot in its mouth shaped like a horseshoe.

Source: Brewer, *Dictionary of Phrase and Fable*, 624; Farrar, *Magical History of the Horse*, 195; Tozer, *Horse in History*, 195–6

Brigliadoro (bril-ya-do-ro)

The favorite horse of the hero Roland, nephew of Charlemagne, the charger Brigliadoro ("golden bridle") was second in speed and power only to the charger BAYARDO. Brigliadoro was described as a noble beast, always ready to canter across the fields or for an encounter on the battlefield or tournament. He would always neigh with pleasure at the sight of his master.

Source: Baldwin, *Story of Roland*, 191, 337; Brewer, *Dictionary of Phrase and Fable*, 625

The Brinsop Dragon

According to British folklore the Brinsop Dragon was the DRAGON slain by the knight and regional hero, Saint George; it was said to have lived in a well south of the local church in Duck's Pool Meadow, Brinsop, England. The field where the battle between the DRAGON and the knight took place was called Lower Stanks.

Source: Simpson, *British Dragons*, 47; Whitlock, *In Search of Lost Gods*, 28

Brize (BRY-zee)

The gadfly sent by the goddess Hera (Juno) to torment Io, Brize ("gadfly") was described as being as large as a sparrow and having a stinger comparable in size to a dagger. Zeus (Jupiter) had taken the princess of Argos on as his lover, much to his wife's dismay. When the goddess discovered her husband's latest tryst Zeus (Jupiter) transformed Io into a beautiful black and white heifer with polished horns and large, soulful eyes. Brize tormented the cow, stinging it day and night until the animal lost its senses and ran into the ocean seeking relief. Io was rescued by the god Hermes who slew Brize.

Source: Daly, *Greek and Roman Mythology, A to Z*, 71; Evslin, *Gods, Demigods and Demons*, n.pag.

Bronte (bron-teez)

Variations: Bronie ("thunder")

In classical Greek and Roman mythology Bronte ("thunderer") was one of the many winged horses said to assist in pulling the sun across the sky; it was one of the HIPPOI ATHANATOI. In the Latin narrative poem, *Metamorphoses* (2.153), written by the Roman poet Ovid (43 BC–AD 17), the sun god and second generation Titan, Helios (Sol), had his golden chariot, Quadriga, pulled across the sky by the flying horses AETHON, ASTROPE, Bronte, CHRONOS, EOUS, LAMPON, PHAETHON, PHLEGON, and PYROIS. All of these horses are described as being pure white and having flaring nostrils which can breathe forth flame.

Source: Berens, *Myths and Legends of Ancient Greece and Rome*, 16; Breese, *God's Steed*, 86; Brewer, *Dictionary of Phrase and Fable*, 624; Rose, *Giants, Monsters, and Dragons*, 178

Bronzomarte

In Arthurian folklore Bronzomarte, "a mettlesome sorrel" was the favored horse of Sir Lancelot Greaves as he believed the animal to have a generous sensibility, be inspired with reason, and pity virtue in distress. Bronzomarte showed the joy he felt to have such an accomplished master astride his back by curveting and neighing when mounted.

Source: Brewer, *Dictionary of Phrase and Fable*, 624; Smollett, *Miscellaneous Works of Tobias Smollett*, 146, 176

Broxa (BROKES-sa)

There is a creature in Hasidic folklore also named broxa, described as a bird which attacks she-goats during the night, drinking their milk. It has been speculated by some scholars that over time the broxa bird myth evolved into the broxa vampiric witch of medieval Portugal.

Source: Gaster, *Myth, Legend, and Custom*, 580; Masters, *Eros and Evil*, 181; Monaghan, *Women in Myth and Legend*, 51; Trachtenberg, *Jewish Magic*, 43

Brucha

The Irish pseudepigraph *Epistil Isu* ("Sunday Letters"), written by an anonymous author, describes five kinds of monsters which will descend upon those individuals and heathens who do not keep holy the Lord's Day, Sunday. The brucha ("wingless locusts"), the first of the tormentors mentioned, are described as coming from the East and having fiery eyes. These horrid insects with iron-like bristles upon their bodies attack vineyards, cutting the vines and robbing the grapes which they take back to their lair.

Source: Olsen, *Monsters and the Monstrous in Medieval Northwest Europe*, 69–70; Zell-Ravenheart, *Wizard's Bestiary*, 26

Bruckee

Variations: Broc Sidh ("fairy badger")

In Celtic folklore, particularly in the region of Rath Blathmaic near Inchiquin, Ireland, living in Loch Shandangan, is a gigantic four-legged lake monster known as the bruckee. Said to consume both cattle and men, the bruckee resisted the prayers and exorcism of six local saints who tried driving it from the area.

Source: Rose, *Giants, Monsters, and Dragons*, 59; Westropp, *Folklore of Clare*, 27

Buata

A monstrous creature from the West Melanesia island folklore of the island of New Britain, the buata looks like a gigantic boar and having tusks as long as swords, hunts people, consuming them whole. Immensely strong and fast, the buata has rudimentary intelligence and can speak in simple sentences. Like many low intelligence monsters, it can be easily tricked into not eating its prey or may become lost in the woods. The buata is similar to the PUGUT of Filipino folklore.

Source: Maberry, *Vampire Universe*, 60; Rose, *Giants, Monsters, and Dragons*, 59; Zell-Ravenheart, *Wizard's Bestiary*, 26

Buba

Variations: Trashalka

A serpentine creature from Albanian, Armenian, and Bulgarian folklore, the buba come out of their lair in the middle of the day and frighten children, particularly noisy ones, likening it to a NURSERY BOGIE. In southern Albania the buba was said to hunt and consume small farm animals while in Tirana, Albania, it was said to take and hide things.

Source: Elsie, *Dictionary of Albanian Religion, Mythology, and Folk Culture*, 48

Bubák

Variations: Bubak

A NURSERY BOGIE from Wend mythology, the bubák ("goblin") was used to frighten children into behaving properly.

Source: Bonnerjea, *Allborough New Age Guide*, 48; Jonáš, *Bohemian and English Dictionary*, 40; Wolff, *Odd Bits of History*, 152

Bucentaur

A creature from ancient Greek mythology, the bucentaur is a chimerical being, half man and half ox; it is often depicted in art wrestling with the demi-god, Hercules (Heracles), being smothered in his arms. The bucentaur is symbolic man's duality of nature, but with an emphasis on his more base or animalistic needs. It was depicted as having the head and upper body of a man with the legs and lower body and tail of an ox.

Source: Cirlot, *Dictionary of Symbols*, 33; Eason, *Fabulous Creatures, Mythical Monsters, and Animal Power Symbols*, 82; Zell-Ravenheart, *Wizard's Bestiary*, 26

Bucephalus

Variations: Bucephalas, Bukephalos

The beloved horse of Alexander the Great, Bucephalus ("oxen-headed"), purchased for thirteen talents by King Philip, was described as being incredibly large, having a UNICORN's ivory horn or alicorn growing out of his forehead, and the tail of a peacock. The oracles at Delphi had predicted the master of the known-world would ride upon a horse bearing the mark of an ox-head, and in art the black charger is shown having a white ox-head on its brow. According to folklore the horse was unable to be ridden by anyone in the King's employ; a young Alexander discovered the animal was bolting at the sight of its own shadow and, after placing a wager with his father, turned the horse toward the sun, jumped upon his back, and rode off. Although Alexander had other warhorses, Bucephalus was his favorite, as not only was he anthropophagous—a man eater, biting savagely into its enemies and pulling away with mouthfuls of flesh—but also the animal's presence on the battlefield inspired his army. The warhorse was said to have died at the age of thirty, having succumbed to wounds received on the battlefield. He was given a state's funeral and the city of Bucephala was founded for his honor atop his grave.

Source: Jarymowycz, *Cavalry from Hoof to Track*, 14–15; Smith, *New Classical Dictionary of Greek and Roman Biography, Mythology and Geography*, 152

Buckland Shag

In Devon County England folklore, the buckland shag was a water horse with a shaggy coat, similar to the numerous FUATH of Scottish folklore, which would chase down hapless victims and trample them to death; the red flecks upon the stones in the area were said to the be the blood splatter stains of its victims. People were afraid to travel alone until a local vicar was said to have exorcised it by use of bell, book, and candle.

Source: Rose, *Giants, Monsters, and Dragons*, 59; Westwood, *Lore of the Land*, 712

Budas

Variations: Intigre, Tebbib

A were-hyena or WEREWOLF from ancient Abyssinia mythology, the communal-living budas were a cadre of iron workers and potters who had acquired the knowledge of therianthropy enabling them to shape-shift. The budas, who would rob graves at midnight, were capable of spreading bad luck, convulsions, death, and sickness. They distinguished themselves by wearing a golden earing in their ear; when the budas assumed their animal form it was said the earring was still visible on the animal.

Source: Baring-Gould, *Book of Were-Wolves*, 68–9; Maberry, *Vampire Universe*, 61–62

Bujanga

In Javanese folklore the bujanga is a winged creature or DRAGON protecting the forest and jungle; it has the ability to understand the language of all the animals living in its domain. In Hindu traditions the bujanga ("those creeping-on-their-shoulders") is a NAGA.

Source: Daniélou, *Myths and Gods of India*, 308; Rose, *Giants, Monsters, and Dragons*, 60

Bukavac (bukavats)

From Slavic mythology comes the demonic creature known as Bukavac ("noisy"). With its gnarled horns and six legs, this nocturnal demon leaves its watery home, a lake or pool, at night, making a tremendous amount of noise. It leaps upon animals and people alike and strangles them to death.

Source: Hlobil, *Before You*, 106

Bulaing

In Karadjeri mythology of Australia, the bulaing are a species of water snakes living in the Dreamtime and are similar to the RAINBOW SERPENT MAIANGARE but are not connected with rainbows in any way whatsoever.

Source: Buchler, *Rainbow Serpent*, 4, 102; Rose, *Giants, Monsters, and Dragons*, 60; Zell-Ravenheart, *Wizard's Bestiary*, 26

Bull of Heaven

At the request of the goddess Ishtar, Anu released the Bull of Heaven (the constellation of Taurus) to kill the hero Gilgamesh for rejecting her offer of love; the hero knows the goddess has slain all of her lovers, both human and animal. She led the heavenly animal to Uruk and through the gates to the river; there the Bull snorted, drying up the marsh and river, cracking open the earth, and causing 100 men to fall to their death. Then the Bull snorted a second time, drying up more of the water, cracking open the earth again, and causing 200 men to fall to their death. The third snort of the Bull caused ENKIDU to double over in pain but he recovered quickly and grabbed the Bull of Heaven by the horns. While the animal was held, Gilgamesh ran his sword between the nape of its neck and the horns, slaying it. The duo then removed the heart of the Bull and offered it up to Shamash. The goddess Ishtar leapt to the wall of Uruk and began to utter a curse upon Gilgamesh but ENKIDU ripped the right hind leg off of the Bull of Heaven and waved it in her face, exclaiming how he wished he could do worse to her than he did to the Bull. For his hubris, ENKIDU was made sick and eventually died in pain.

Source: Casey, *After Lives*, 46–7; Sanders, *Epic of Gilgamesh*, 88

Bull of Inde

A monstrous ox from Indian folklore, the Bull of Inde was gigantic, having yellow hair growing in a tangled mass over a hide no weapon could pierce and horns which pivoted atop its head so they could face in the direction they were most needed. The malevolent Bull of Inde was almost impossible to capture, but if thought it was about to be trapped, it would gore itself to death rather than be captured.

Source: Hargreaves, *Hargreaves New Illustrated Bestiary*, 22; Rose, *Giants, Monsters, and Dragons*, 60

Bunyip

Variations: Buneep, Dongus, Kajanprati, Moolgewanke

An Australian FAIRY ANIMAL standing only about four feet tall, the shy and seldom seen bunyip ("devil" or "spirit") looks like a small, plump human with backward facing feet. Living in lakes, rivers, and swamplands, these mud-covered fairies will bark out a warning if danger is near although there are some stories in which it will attack anyone who enters into its territory.

The first sighting of the bunyip came in the New South Wales area in 1800 and continued on into the twentieth century. It is believed by the aboriginals Lake Bathurst and Lake George are sacred to the bunyip however after a dam was built across the Murray River in the 1920s and 1930s, sightings of the bunyip all but stopped. Although most native bunyip drawings depict this creature in a wide array of shapes and sizes, most often it is shown as having flippers, walrus-like tusks, and a horse-like tail; it has been speculated the bunyip are nothing more than fur-seals.

Source: Coleman, *Cryptozoology A to Z*, 49–50; Ho, *Mysteries Unwrapped*, 26–7; McCoy, *Witch's Guide to Faery Folk*, 194–5; Newton, *Encyclopedia of Cryptozoology*, 76

Bura-Bura (BOO-rah BOO-rah)

Variations: Bake-Chochin

A class of YŌKAI known as TSUKOMOGAMI, the bura-bura is depicted as a flying garish paper lantern with a leering face; sometimes the face is more human than others but it is always lit from within, like a jack-o-lantern. Basically harmless, the bura-bura mostly hides in a dark place and pops out when a person is near in order to frighten them, razzing its tongue, and making eerie sounds.

Source: Meyer, *Night Parade of One Hundred Demons*, 174; *Yokai Attack*, 110–14

Burach Bhadi

Variations: Wizard's Shackle

An eel or species of leech said to live in the fords

of the western highlands of Scotland, the burach bhadi ("wizard's shackle") is described as having nine eyes on his head and back, all of which squint. This creature would wrap itself around the feet of passing horses and trip them up, causing them to fall into the water where it would then drain them dry of their blood.

Source: Hargreaves, *Hargreaves New Illustrated Bestiary*, 43; Spence, *Magic Arts in Celtic Britain*, 95; Zell-Ravenheart, *Wizard's Bestiary*, 26

Burko

Variations: Burushko

In Russian folklore Burko is a name commonly applied to any magical horse which is ultimately essential for completing a task. The *bogatry* (hero) Dobrynya Nikitich rode upon a horse name Burko who had been the faithful mount of both his father and grandfather. It had stood in its stall for 15 years and was covered up in manure to its knees. This was the horse Dobrynya rode when he went up Saracen Mountain to rescue prisoners and to stomp a nest of baby DRAGONS to death. SIVKO BURKO was the magical horse gifted to Ivan the Fool.

Source: Bailey, *Anthology of Russian Folk Epics*, 89–91; Haney, *Complete Russian Folktale*, 77–9

Buru

A shy DRAGON from Himalayan folklore, the buru is described as having a triangular-shaped head and four prominent fangs. Said to be about 15 feet long, the buru's body is covered with dark blue armor plating and its short and sturdy legs have vicious claws.

Source: Cox, *Spooky Spirits and Creepy Creatures*, 27; De Kirk, *Dragonlore*, 34; Zell-Ravenheart, *Wizard's Bestiary*, 26

Buruburu

Variations: Ghost of Fear, Okubyohgami, Zoku-zokugami

The buruburu ("to shudder") of Japanese folklore lives in rural forests in the guise of an old man or an old woman with one eye shaking with palsy. The creature does not attack its victim in its disguised form but rather drops the disguise and becomes both intangible and invisible, then it attaches to their spine causing goose-bumps to appear and the feeling of a sudden chill. Soon after the assault, the victim dies in a state of terror.

In some versions of the folklore the buruburu does not kill its prey but rather possesses the person and causes them to become overwhelmed with fear; the person locks themselves in their house, suddenly afraid of anything and everything. Sadly, in these cases, the person commits suicide.

Source: Maberry, *Vampire Universe*, 63–4; Plaut, *Japanese Conversation-Grammar*, 255

Bushtra

Variations: Lebushter ("female dog, bitch")

A swamp-dwelling creature from Albanian folklore, a bushtra has the ability of therianthropy, enabling it to shape-shift into the form of a hag as well as being able to spit brimstone and fire; bushtra live to do harm to others.

Source: Elsie, *Dictionary of Albanian Religion, Mythology, and Folk Culture*, 49

Busse

A chimerical creature from medieval European folklore, the busse was described as looking like a small brown-grey bull but having the head and antlers of a stag. This creature, said to live in the region between Greece and Scythia, modern-day Turkey, had the ability to change the color of its coat when it was being hunted or pursued.

Source: Rose, *Giants, Monsters, and Dragons*, 62; Zell-Ravenheart, *Wizard's Bestiary*, 26

Bussemand, plural: bussemend

A BOGEYMAN from Dutch folklore, the busse-mand ("nose pick") is said to live beneath children's beds and snatch up the one who will not go to sleep at bedtime.

Source: Holmen, *Danish-English, English-Danish Dictionary*, 385; Krensky, *Bogeyman*, 43

Butatsch-Ah-Ilgs

In Swiss folklore, the butatsch-ah-ilgs was an enormous amorphous mass-like monster said to be living in the depths of Lake Luschersee near Grisons (see SEA SERPENT); this place was supposedly also a hell-mouth, an entranceway into Hell itself. The creature was described as looking like a gigantic stomach covered with eyes capable of emitting flames. Fishermen would not fish here nor would shepherds allow their flocks to graze on the nearby hills.

Source: Rose, *Giants, Monsters, and Dragons*, 62; Zell-Ravenheart, *Wizard's Bestiary*, 26

Buxenwolf

A lycanthrope (see WEREWOLF) from German folklore, the bloodthirsty and vicious buxenwolf is created when a person makes a pact with the Devil in order to gain power, secret knowledge, and wealth. The individual is given a magical belt which when worn will magically transform the individual into a wolf and in addition to it having enhanced senses, speed, and stamina,will allow them to retain their rational human mind. Should a buxenwolf ever get caught or become trapped, holding iron or steel over its head will break it mystical connection with Hell, remove its human intellect replacing it with a wolf's, and compel the creature to give its name.

Source: Maberry, *Vampire Universe*, 65

Buzawosj

A NURSERY BOGIE from Wend mythology, the buzawosj is a BOGEYMAN used to frighten children into good behavior.

Source: Wolff, *Odd Bits of History*, 152

Byakko

Variations: Chien Ping

In Chinese folklore when a capital city is constructed, it was believed it should be designed to the Four God principal: on each side of the city, representation of each god is present in the form of their respective creatures. In the east is SEIRYU, the blue DRAGON; to the north is GENBU, a snake and turtle hybrid; in the south is SUZAKU, depicted as a red PHOENIX-like bird, and in the west, Byakko, a white tiger, is dominant in autumn.

Source: Bates, *10,000 Chinese Numbers*, 108; Brown, *Genius of Japanese Carpentry*, n.pag.; Grafetstätter, *Islands and Cities in Medieval Myth, Literature, and History*, 119

Cabal

Variations: Cafal, Cafall, Cavall

In Arthurian folklore, Cabal was the dog of King Arthur; it was utilized by him to hunt the great boar TWRCH TRWYTH which it killed in the tale *"How Culhwch Won Olwen"* from *The Mabinogion*. The GIANT Ysbaddaden demanded the hunting dogs AETHLEM, ANED, and DRUDWYN—who had to be held with a special leash, collar, and chain—must take part in the hunt.

Source: Bruce, *Arthurian Name Dictionary*, 477; Jones, *King Arthur in History and Legend*, 24, 25; Reno, *Arthurian Figures of History and Legend*, 57

Caballucos del Diablo

In the folklore of Cantabria, Spain, it is believed that on Saint John's Eve, June 23, the seven-winged Caballucos del Diablo ("Devil's small horses") appear with a loud cry from a smoking fire; these tiny horses mounted by demons are each a different color representing a different but specific sin. The black colored horse represents a hermit who played tricks on people; the blue one a dishonest innkeeper; the orange one is a little child who abused his parents; the red horse, the leader of the caballucos del Diablo is the strongest of them all, a man who would lend money to farmers and then by use of trickery steal their land; the white one a

miller who stole thousands of of gold coins from his master; and the yellow one is a corrupt judge. The text reference does not give an explanation of the green horse.

On this one night of the year the caballucos del Diablo fly about seeking out four-leafed clovers in order to destroy them so no one may be able to find one and benefit from its luck.

Source: Lomas, *Mitología y Supersticiones de Cantabria*, 113, 311

Cabyll-Ushtey

Variations: Glashtinhe

In Manx folklore the pale grey cabyll-ushtey ("water horse") is a species of water horse similar to the Scottish EACH UISCE, although not as injurious. Occasionally this FAIRY ANIMAL will prey upon cattle and humans alike, ripping them to pieces, stampede horse herds, and steal children. The cabyll-ushtey also has the ability to shape-shift into a handsome young man.

Source: Briggs, *Encyclopedia of Fairies*, 57; Conway, *Magickal, Mystical Creatures*, 45; Monaghan, *Encyclopedia of Celtic Mythology and Folklore*, 67

Cactus Cat

In the folklore from the southwestern state of Arizona, United States of America, the cactus cat (*Cactifelinus inebrius*), one of the FEARSOME CRITTERS, is said to live among the cholla and palo verde trees. It has been described as having thorny hairs covering its body, a forked tail, and sharp, knife-like bones protruding from its forepaws. The cactus cat uses these natural weapons to slash open the base of the gigantic cactus so the sap will seep out; the cat will spend the better part of its day going from cactus to cactus slashing up as many plants as it can. During the course of the day, the sap ferments in the heat of the sun; at night the cactus cat revisits each location and laps up its intoxicating mescal. The rest of the evening the animal spends crying out drunkenly.

Source: Cox, *Fearsome Creatures of the Lumberwoods*, 27; Rose, *Giants, Monsters, and Dragons*, 63; Theitic, *Witches' Almanac, Issue 34*, 17

Cadejo (cah-day-ho)

A cow-sized dog from Central American folklore, the cadejo is described as having a shaggy coat of either black or white hair and cloven feet. If you should happen to see a white cadejo it is said good fortune is heading your way and the creature will protect you while you travel on a dangerous journey. There is never a good situation in which seeing a black-haired cadejo is beneficial; there are three species of black cadejo: the first is the Devil himself assuming this form, and anyone who he catches will not only be slain but their souls will be immediately dragged to Hell. The second species of black cadejo is a terrible anthropophagous (man-eating) monster. The third variation of the cadejo is a hybrid of the first two, a dangerous, frightening, and strong creature which may be killed by a well-armed individual.

In a variation of the folklore, the cadejo is a large black dog with a shaggy coat and white spot of fur on its chest. Only ever seen at night near burial places, if left unmolested, the cadejo will walk ahead of the traveler in the middle of the road; otherwise it will attack without mercy. No matter how its sighting is resolved, it is always a psychopomp (death omen), either for the person who sees it or someone in his family.

Source: Gatschet, *Journal of American Folk-lore*, Volume 4, 38; Maberry, *They Bite*, 139–40; Thompson, *Cuentos Folklóricos Mayas*, 123

Cafre

Variations: Kafre, Kafar, Pugot, Pugut

In Filipino folklore the cafre is an enormous monster similar in appearance to a boar but with much larger tusks; it is faster, stronger, and covered in jet-black hair. Having the ability to walk upright on its hind legs, the cafre can also speak and understand human language. Known for its ability to tirelessly track humans through the jungle to capture and consume, the cafre is not especially intelligent and may easily be tricked, thereby losing its prey. The cafre is similar to the BUATA of New Britain and the PUGUT of Filipino folklore.

Source: Knappert, *Pacific Mythology*, 193; Rose, *Giants, Monsters, and Dragons*, 64; Zell-Ravenheart, *Wizard's Bestiary*, 54

Cagrino

Variations: Buccubu, Chagrin, Guecubu, Harginn, Huecuvu ("the wanderer without")

Originally from the Gypsy demonology from northwestern India comes the demonic fey-like creature, Cagrino. Looking like a small yellow hedgehog a foot and a half both long and wide, he is known to mount horses and ride them to exhaustion, leaving them sick and weary with their manes tangled and their bodies covered in sweat.

To prevent Cagrino from stealing off with your horse, tie the animal to a stake which has been covered with garlic juice and then lay a red thread on the ground in the shape of a cross. Another method is to take some of the horse's hair, salt, meal, and the blood of a bat, make bread with it, and rub it on the horse's hoof. Then, take the bowl in which the mixture was made and hide it in a tree, saying the words *"Tarry, pipkin, in this tree, till such time as full ye be."*

Source: Banis, *Charms, Spells, and Curses for the Millions*, 87; Leland, *Gypsy Sorcery and Fortune Telling*, 91; Spence, *Encyclopedia of Occultism*, 88

Cait Sith

Variations: Cat SÍDHE, Cat Sith, Elfin Cats

The cait sith ("fairy cat") is spoken of in both Irish and Scottish folklore. Described as looking like a black cat with a white mark on the center of its chest, this FAIRY ANIMAL is said to be somewhere between the size of a large dog and a small calf. Large and ferocious, especially if surprised, the cait sith are said to have a king among their kind named BIG EARS.

In the Scottish Highlands it is a popular belief the cait sith is not a FAIRY ANIMAL at all but a transformed witch. It has been proposed by some that the cait sith is a hybrid animal between the European wildcats and the domestic cats only found in Scotland; these large black hybrids are typically called Kellas Cats. These animals cannot be domesticated.

Source: Avant, *Mythological Reference*, 86; Briggs, *Encyclopedia of Fairies*, 60; Campbell, *Superstitions of the Highlands and Islands of Scotland*, 5, 32

Caladrius

Variations: Chaladrius, Charadrius, Caladre

First appearing in the *Physiologus*, a didactic text traditionally dated to about the second century AD, the caladrius was described as being a white bird which had the ability to predict if a sick person would die or recover from their illness. The bird was placed next to the sick person; if the creature looked away, there was no hope of their recovery. However, if the bird looked at the person, it would absorb the illness into its own body and then take flight into the sky where it would burn off the illness and scatter it harmlessly into the wind.

A medieval bestiary added to the myth by saying to look directly at the bird was a cure for jaundice and its droppings were able to increase the strength of poor eyes if not outright cure blindness.

Source: Allaby, *Animals*, 93; Prioreschi, *Medieval Medicine*, 588; Zell-Ravenheart, *Wizard's Bestiary*, 26

Calag

A creature from Filipino folklore, the calag ("soul") has no physical description, as the slightest noise frightens it away. When a person dies, coconut oil is traditionally poured into and over the mouth; this prevents putrefaction and allows the calag to pass into the place of punishment. If after three days the body was not buried the calag would cause the stomach to burst and a fever-bearing stench would be released from the corpse.

Source: California Folklore Society. *Western Folklore*, Volumes 27–28, 186–87; Ramos, *Creatures of Philippine Lower Mythology*, 72

La Calchona

Variations: Chiludo

A species of WILD MAN from South American folklore, la calchona ("bogey" or "ghost") is described as looking like a large bearded man whose body is covered with sheep-like wool. A nocturnal creature living in the fields and hills of the countryside, it is reported as doing little more than scaring horses and travelers. In Chile the calchona is described as looking like a large wooly dog with a tangled coat; said to live in the mountains where it frightens travelers and their horses, it occasionally steals their food.

Source: Eberhart, *Mysterious Creatures*, 82; Rose, *Giants, Monsters, and Dragons*, 65; Zell-Ravenheart, *Wizard's Bestiary*, 27

Callitrice

Variations: Callitrix

In medieval European folklore the callitrice were said to be SATYR-like creatures with overly long beards and long, thick tails. Living in the most desolate regions of Ethiopia, these creatures hid from humans for although they were difficult to find they were said to be easy to capture.

Source: Cherry, *Mythical Beasts*, 170; Clark, *Medieval Book of Beasts*, 133–4; Rose, *Giants, Monsters, and Dragons*, 65

Calopus

Variations: Aptaleon, Caleps, Chatloup, Catwolfe

In the medieval English heraldic symbology the chimerical calopus was a horned animal which seemed to be related to the wolf, having a wolf-like body, feet, and tail but the face of a cat and serrated goat horns; it was, at one time, the badge of the Foljambe family.

Source: Dennys, *Heraldic Imagination*, 153; Fox-Davies, *Complete Guide to Heraldry*, 232; Zell-Ravenheart, *Wizard's Bestiary*, 19, 27

Calydonian Boar

Variations: Aetolian Boar, Ætolian Boar, Aper Calydonius, Hus Kalydonios, Kalydonian Boar

In the classical mythology of the ancient Greeks and Romans, the gigantic Calydonian boar was sent by the goddess Artemis (Diana) to punish the people of the Aetolian area of Greece; the king, Oeneus, had failed to offer her sufficient honors and sacrifices. Meleager, a hero, was tasked with the respon-sibility of saving the ravaged countryside and to assist him in the task he called upon the greatest heroes of the time. Together this band of warriors hunted the boar but in the end it was the woman-warrior Atalanta (Atalante) who laid the creature low with an arrow shot from her bow; Meleager delivered the death blow with his spear and offered her its carcass as a gift. The present caused an argu-ment among the warriors who wanted a division of the spoils and in the ensuing battle Meleager was slain.

Source: Coleman, *Dictionary of Mythology*, 187; Matthews, *Element Encyclopedia of Magical Creatures*, 9; Rose, *Giants, Monsters, and Dragons*, 22

Calygreyhound

In heraldic symbology the chimerical calygrey-hound had the body of an antelope, front claws of a cat, head of a wildcat, and hindquarters of an ox; oftentimes it was also given the horns of a ram. The calygreyhound was symbolic of swiftness.

Source: Coleman, *Dictionary of Mythology*, 187; Dennys, *Heraldic Imagination*, 153; Rose, *Giants, Monsters, and Dragons*, 66; Zell-Ravenheart, *Wizard's Bestiary*, 27

Camahueto

In Araucanian (Mapuchen) mythology of south central Chile, they believe a camahueto ("sea ele-phant") is a young bull, silver in color, with a golden alicorn (a single horn) atop its head, and having sharp claws and teeth; it spends it youth in marshes and shallow lakes but when it is fully grown relo-cates to the sea. During its migration, the camahueto destroys gardens and landscaping. Only a wizard can safely lead the bull to sea by wrapping kelp around his neck and leading the way. Once the camahueto has made it to the sea, it is feared as a SEA CREATURE which wrecks ships.

Source: Bingham, *South and Meso-American Mythology A to Z*, 21; Eberhart, *Mysterious Creatures*, 82; Van Scott, *Encyclopedia of Hell*, 189

Cambions (CAM-bee-ins)

Variations: Campions

From post-medieval European demonology comes the belief in the existence of a demonic hybrid offspring called a cambion. It was believed to be created when an INCUBUS and a human woman or when a SUCCUBUS and a human male had a child together. A cambion child can be eas-ily detected as it will be born with a deformity of some sort. Twins are especially suspect of being cambions.

The hybrid will develop the same as any child would, but before the age of seven they show little to no signs of life. These demonic offspring are not considered to be truly alive until they reach the age of seven years, and until that time, it is perfectly acceptable for a witch hunter to kill it. A simple test one may perform would be to have a holy person touch it, as a cambion will cry out.

As it grows into adulthood the cambion will develop a strong and incredibly dense physical form, growing tall and becoming well-muscled. Its physical deformity, if not too severe to begin with, may well disappear altogether. By nature, the cambion will be bold, arrogant, and wicked; however, there are some cambions who are not inclined to be evil and will live among humans peaceably enough. All cambions have some level of supernatural ability and they are likely to become wizards or sorcerers. Cambions usually find themselves prejudiced against because of the circumstances surrounding their conception.

Throughout history there have been several famous individuals who were said to be cambions: Alexander the Great, Caesar Augustus, Martin Luther, Merlin (of King Arthur folklore), Plato, Romulus and Remus, Scipio Africanus, and the father of William the Conqueror. All were suspected of having been fathered by an INCUBUS. Angela de Labarthe of Toulouse, France, was burned at the stake for allegedly giving birth to a child born with a wolf's head and a snake's tail in 1275; the reason given for her execution was only a creature from hell, like an INCUBUS, could have been the father.

Source: Aylesworth, *Servants of the Devil*, 33; Buckland, *Weiser Field Guide to Ghosts*, 143, 145; Hugo, *Toilers of the Sea*, 47, 49; Maberry, *They Bite*, 301; Masters, *Eros and Evil*, 131; Spence, *Encyclopedia of Occultism*, 93

Cameleopardel

Variations: Camel-Leopard, Camelo-Pard, Camelo-Pardalis, Ziraafa ("assemblage of animals")

First described by the ancient Romans, the chimerical cameleopardel was said to look like a camel and pard (leopard) hybrid, having a long neck, a camel head, feet and legs of an ox, and a brown coat with white spots. It was described in the traveler tales of Arabs, Egyptians, Ethiopians, and Indians.

Source: Palmer, *Folk-Etymology*, 49; Rosen, *Mythical Creatures Bible*, 100

Camp Chipmunk

Originating in the lumberjack communities of the developing United States of America, the camp chipmunk, one of the FEARSOME CRITTERS, was originally a part of the folklore connected with Paul Bunyan tales. According to the story, these creatures were once normal sized but they ate the tons of prune pits left behind by the camp cook. The chipmunks grew fierce and large and killed all of the bears and mountain lions in the area so Paul and his men hunted them down as if they were tigers, shooting them all.

Source: Botkin, *American People: Stories, Legends, Tales, Traditions, and Songs*, 251; Rose, *Giants, Monsters, and Dragons*, 119

Campacti

Variations: Cipatli

In Aztec folklore Campacti was said to be a vast primordial Piscean DRAGON; once defeated, its body was used to create the earth.

Source: Rose, *Giants, Monsters, and Dragons*, 66; Zell-Ravenheart, *Wizard's Bestiary*, 27

Campe

Variations: Kampe

A monstrous DRAKAINA from classical Greek mythology, Campe was sent by Cronus (Uranus) to guard the CYCLOPS and the Hecatonchires ("Hundred-Handed") in Tartarus. She was eventually slain by the god Zeus (Jupiter) who was advised by his mother and Metis that if the CYCLOPS were freed and sided with him, he would be able to defeat Cronus.

Source: Apollodorus, *Library of Greek Mythology*, 27; Avant, *Mythological Reference*, 232; McClintock, *Cyclopaedia of Biblical, Theological, and Ecclesiastical Literature*, Volume 1, 757

Camphurcii

An amphibious sea creature (see SEA SERPENT) from Indonesian folklore, the camphurcii is a chimerical being, having the body and forelegs of a deer, a single three-foot long alicorn emerging from the middle of its head similar to a UNICORN, and the hindquarters and webbed feet of a goose. The horn of this creature was believed by the inhabitants of the Island of Molucca to be a cure for poison. The camphurcii was carnivorous, living on a diet of fish.

Source: Rose, *Giants, Monsters, and Dragons*, 67; Zell-Ravenheart, *Wizard's Bestiary*, 28

Camros

Variations: Camrus

In ancient Persian mythology the camros was a bird-like creature mentioned in the story of Apam Napat; it was said to peck non-Iranians as if they were grain. Camros would gather up the seeds of Gao-kerena, the Tree of Life, and take them to the god of rain, Tishtar, who would use them to make the rainfall which provided the people of Iran with vegetation. As the worthiest of all birds, it assisted in the annual task of distributing seeds from the Tree of All Healing.

Source: Boyce, *History of Zoroastrianism*, 43; Ward, *Seal Cylinders of Western Asia*, 236; Yar-Shater, *Encyclopaedia Iranica*, Volume 2, 148

Camulatz

According to the Quiche people's creation myth recorded in the *Popol Vuh*, the Mayans' sacred book, Camulatz was one of four birds which played a significant role in the destruction of the first race of people created by the god of the wind, Hurakan. The creation myth says after the gods made the animals, earth, moon, sky, and sun, they created a race of people made of wood who were meant to appreciate the gods and see to the well-being of the animals.

This first attempt of humanity was a failure as the wooden people insulted the gods and abused the animals. Hurakan sent a great flood to drown the wooden people and Camulatz bit off the heads of the ones who treaded water as they drowned. CATZBALAM pecked away their flesh; TECUMBALAM broke their bones and sinews, and then ground their bodies into powder; and XECOTCOVACH tore out their eyes.

Source: Bingham, *South and Meso-American Mythology A to Z*, 21–2; Spence, *Arcane Secrets and Occult Lore of Mexico and Mayan Central America*, 241

Canache

Variations: Canace

A dog from ancient Greek mythology, Canache ("barker") was one of the DOGS OF ACTÆON, the unfortunate youth who was raised by the CENTAUR, CHEIRON.

Source: Leeming, *World of Myth*, 111; Murray, *Classical Manual*, 160; Naso, *Fasti*, *Tristia*, 93–5

Canchu

Variations: Pumapmicuc

In pre–Columbian Peruvian mythology the mountain dwelling canchu hunted only the strongest warriors, but attacked them when they were unarmed and unarmored while they slept. The canchu would visit their prey each night and take a small amount of blood, returning each evening until their victim died. In modern times the canchu are said to prey upon any reasonably healthy person in lieu of a prime warrior.

Source: Maberry, *Vampire Universe*, 69; McNally, *In Search of Dracula*, 117

Capacti

Variations: Cipactil-Caiman

The *Codex Borgia* (also known as the *Codex Yoalli Ehēcatl*), the Mesoamerican divinatory and ritual manuscript, describes Capacti as a DRAGON which was intrinsically involved in the creation of the world. Capacti can appear either male or female and began its life as a crocodile-like fish. Its body was used to create the earth.

Source: Cooper, *Symbolic and Mythological Animals*, 47; Garlock, *Tao of the Alligator and the Crocodile*, n.pag.

Le Capalu

Variations: Capalus, Cath Palug ("bog cat"), Chapalu

In the French Arthurian folklore of the late twelfth and early thirteenth centuries le Capalu was a man who had been transformed into a large feline; in one poem of the era it confronted King Arthur in a bog, pushed him into a swampy area, and having the upper hand took advantage of the situation, attacking the warrior king, slaying him in battle. In the British and Celtic version of this story Cath Palug, as he is better known, is not only a female cat but is slain by Sir Cai (Kay). In the 1332 poem *Ogier le Danois*, Ogier, a knight in the service of Charlemagne, confronts the feline monster-knight Capalu (Chapalu of *La Bataille Loquifer*, 1170) and defeats him in fair combat.

Source: Larrington, *King Arthur's Enchantresses*, 94; Ross, *Folklore of Wales*, n.pag.

Capelthwaite

Capelthwaite is a FAIRY ANIMAL, a BLACK DOG said to be the size of a calf; it roams Westmorland, an area in North West England and the adjacent Yorkshire. With the ability to assume any quadrupedal form it likes, the capelthwaite prefers its canine visage. When one takes up residence on a farm it will help round-up and herd sheep and will pleasantly regard the residing family; however, it will be injurious and malicious to strangers.

Source: Briggs, *Encyclopedia of Fairies*, 62; Henderson, *Notes on the Folk-Lore of the Northern Counties of England and the Borders*, 275–6; Monaghan, *Encyclopedia of Celtic Mythology and Folklore*, 47

Capricornus (CAP-rih-CORN-us)

Variations: Capricorn

Adopted into ancient Greek mythology from Mesopotamian mythology, the chimerical Capricornus ("goat fish") was said to have been created when the god Pan, fleeing into Egypt to escape the GIGANTE (a race of beings born of the goddess Gaea), Typhoeus, dove into the Nile River where his hindquarters were transformed into the lower half of a fish and his upper body was transformed into a goat. Zeus (Jupiter) confronted the monster on the riverbanks and was able to defeat it, burying Typhoeus under Mount Aetna where it rumbles and writhes to this day causing earthquakes. Unfortunately before the monster was defeated it managed to pull the muscles off of Zeus' legs; with the assistance of Hermes (Mercury), Pan (Faunus) was able to restore the wounded god to his former glory. As a reward for his assistance, Zeus (Jupiter) placed Pan (Faunus) in his new form in the night sky as the constellation Capricorn.

In another version of the Capricornus myth, when the infant Zeus (Jupiter) was being hidden on the isle of Crete he was attended by two NYMPHS, Adrastia and Ida; the goat which furnished the god with his daily milk was named AMALTHEA. As a reward for its service in nourishing the infant god, Zeus (Jupiter) made the goat an immortal and transformed her into the constellation Capricornus.

Source: Andrews, *Dictionary of Nature Myths*, 31; Hard, *Routledge Handbook of Greek Mythology*, 85

Carbuncle Snake

Variations: Carbuncle, Carbunkel, Carrabuncle

In the European folklore of sixteenth century South America, Carbuncle was said to be the name of a creature with a carbuncle stone, or ruby, embedded in the middle of its forehead. In a folktale from Rhode Island, United States of America, a tribe of Indians who originally occupied the area knew of a gigantic snake having a carbuncle embedded in the top of its head; the stone glowed red unless the snake was in danger, then it would change color to green and alert the snake to impending doom. For many years the Indians would try to capture the snake to gain its magical gem. The tribe who had possession of the gem was able to defend themselves from their enemies for many generations. When Europeans came into the area and learned of the carbuncle they assaulted the tribe relentlessly until only its chief was left. Not wanting the gem to fall into his enemies' hands, he threw it into a pond where the local NATURE SPIRITS keep it hidden.

Source: Ignasher, *Forgotten Tales of Rhode Island*, 45–7; Rose, *Giants, Monsters, and Dragons*, 69; Zell-Ravenheart, *Wizard's Bestiary*, 28

Carcinus

Variations: Karkinos

In ancient Greek mythology Carcinus ("crayfish") was a gigantic crab whose only appearance was during the battle between the demigod Hercules (Heracles) and the HYDRA when he was undertaking his second Labor. While the hero was battling the monster, Carcinus grabbed him by the foot in order to interfere with his footwork and hoping to give the HYDRA the advantage. Before the tide of battle could turn, however, Hercules managed to crush the crustacean to death beneath his feet. The goddess Hera (Juno), an enemy of Hercules, decided to honor the brave crab and took it up into the heavens where she made it into the constellation known as Cancer.

Source: Lewis, *Encyclopedia of Heavenly Influences*, 114; Olcott, *Star Lore of All Ages*, 88

Caretyne

A creature from heraldic symbology, the caretyne was depicted as having the body and horns of a bull with a porcine snout; the body was yellow and spotted.

Source: Dennys, *Heraldic Imagination*, 153; Zell-Ravenheart, *Wizard's Bestiary*, 28

Caristae

A caristae was said to be a bird believed to have the ability to fly through flames without burning its body or singeing its feathers.

Source: Nigg, *Book of Fabulous Beasts*, 143; Zell-Ravenheart, *Wizard's Bestiary*, 28

Carrog

In Welsh folklore there is believed to be a monster living in Conway Valley known as the carrog ("torrent"); when roused, this creature has the ability to flood the valley from end to end.

Source: Rose, *Giants, Monsters, and Dragons*, 69; Zell-Ravenheart, *Wizard's Bestiary*, 28

Cartazonon

A species of very aggressive UNICORN said to live in the desert wastes and mountainous regions of India and Northern Africa; they were described as looking like a horse or wild ass, having a black alicorn, a boar's tail, and a long mane, and being yellowish-red in color. The horn grows from between the animals' eyebrows and has a natural twist to it, ending in a point. An enemy of the lion, the cartazonon was able to be slain by hunters but could never be taken alive.

Source: Gould, *Mythical Monsters*, 340–41; Rose, *Giants, Monsters, and Dragons*, 69

Carthaginian Serpent

A 120-foot-long serpentine DRAGON from ancient Roman mythology, it was said to have been confronted by the Roman army led by Regulus as he attempted to take the city of Carthage in 250 BC. As they approached the walled city along the Bagrada River the DRAGON appeared. After it was slain by use of siege ballista and skinned, its pelt was kept in a Roman temple until its mysterious disappearance in 133 BC.

Source: De Kirk, *Dragonlore*, 40, 77–8; Walker, *Selection of Curious Articles from the Gentleman's Magazine*, Volume 1, 511

Castalides

Variations: The Muses

In Greek mythology, the castalides were the muses who lived in the sacred Castalian spring on Mount Parnassus.

Source: Dixon-Kennedy, *Encyclopedia of Greco-Roman Mythology*, 79; Murray, *Classical Manual*, 67

Cat-Fish

Variations: Cat Fish

A hybrid from the folklore of medieval Europe, the cat-fish was said to have the front half of a cat's body and lower half of a fish; it seems to have originated from the idea that for each animal on the land, there was a counterpart for it in the sea. It serves today as a chimerical figure of heraldry.

Source: Lower, *Curiosities of Heraldry*, 104; Rose, *Giants, Monsters, and Dragons*, 70

Cath Palug

Variations: Capalu, Capalus, Cath Balug, Cath Balwg, Cath Paluc, Chapalu, Palug's Cat

A large and fearsome cat from Celtic mythology, Cath Palug ("clawing cat" or "Palug's cat") was born from the enchanted sow, HEN WEN, and soon after birth was thrown into the ocean near the Menai Strait by the sow's keeper. The animal was described as having a smooth and glossy, striped coat. Somehow the feline made its way to Anglesey where it was found and raised by the sons of Palug, whom it eventually turned upon and killed. According to an early Welsh poem, *Pa gur yu y Poraru*, the hero Cei (Kay) went to the Isle of Anglesey specifically for the purpose of "destroying lions." There he confronted Cath Palug and slew the creature.

In the French version of the tale Cath Palug, there known as Chapalu, confronted King Arthur, killed him, and claimed the crown, declaring itself king. Later it is slain by the hero Renoart.

Source: Avant, *Mythological Reference*, 185; Bruce, *Arthurian Name Dictionary*, 111; Pughe, *Dictionary of the Welsh Language*, 394

Catoblepas

Variations: Catablepon, GORGON

A monstrous animal from ancient Greek mythology, the catoblepas ("that which looks downward") has a head so heavy it cannot raise it up; if not for this physical shortcoming it was said this animal would have destroyed all life, as its blood-shot eyes and horrid breath each had the ability to kill in the same way as the BASILISK. This sluggish taurine creature was said to have been found in Africa; it feeds upon poisonous bushes and shrubs.

Source: Avant, *Mythological Reference*, 4; Pliny the Elder, *Natural History of Pliny*, Volume 6, 281

Cattywampus

Originating in the lumberjack communities of the developing United States of America, the cattywampus ("askew") was one of the FEARSOME CRITTERS. Unfortunately, there is no additional information on this creature other than its name causing writers of the time, 1841–1861, to believe it had gone extinct.

Source: Mencken, *American Language Supplement 1*, 251

Caucasus Eagle

Variations: Aetos Kaukasios

One of the children of ECHIDNA, the Caucasus eagle of ancient Greek mythology was utilized by the god Zeus (Jupiter) to punish Prometheus. The Titan was chained to a rock in the Caucasus Mountains; each day the eagle would fly to Prometheus, claw and rip its way into his body, and consume his liver. With each sunrise the organ was restored, the wound healed, and the eagle returned. Eventually, the Caucasus eagle was slain by the demi-god and hero, Hercules.

Source: Beolens, *Eponym Dictionary of Mammals*, 120; Hesiod, *Homeric Hymns and Homerica*, 117

Caumas

A CENTAUR from ancient Greek mythology, Caumas was one of the CENTAURS slain by the demigod and cultural hero Hercules (Heracles) while visiting his friend, a CENTAUR named PHOLUS, between his conclusion of his third Labor and the onset of his fourth.

Source: *Commentary, Mythological, Historical, and Geographical on Pope's Homer*, 55; Lemprière, *Bibliotheca Classica*, 694

Cawthorne Dragon

Variations: Cawthorne Wyrm

A flying DRAGON said to have lived in a well in South Yorkshire, England, the Cawthorne dragon of British folklore would, when aggravated, fly out of his well in a rage and soar over Cawthorner Park.

Source: Fanthorpe, *Satanism and Demonology*, n.pag.

Caypor

A NATURE SPIRIT from Brazilian folklore, the caypor is a frightful demon-like being, described as having red skin and a deformed body partially covered with long, shaggy red hair. Similar to the CURUPIRA, he is both feared and worshiped by the Tupi tribe.

Source: Adams, *Amazon and Its Wonders*, 76; Roth, *Annual Report of the Bureau of American Ethnology to the Secretary of the Smithsonian Institution*, 174

Ccoa

A malicious creature from the mythology of the Quechua people of Peru, the ccoa is associated with the destruction and ruination of crops and as being the animal companion to the god of the mountain, Inkarri. It is described as looking like a grey and black-striped, large-bodied domestic cat with an over-large head and fiery eyes; it is said to have the ability to spit hail. To prevent its anger, regular offerings are made but because the ccoa is demanding, typically only the more wealthy people can leave enough to placate it, causing it to blight the crops of the poor.

Source: Bingham, *South and Meso-American Mythology A to Z*, 23; Rose, *Giants, Monsters, and Dragons*, 70; Zell-Ravenheart, *Wizard's Bestiary*, 28

Ceasg

Variations: Maighdean Mhara ("maid of the sea"), Maighdean na Tuinne ("maid of the wave")

In the Scottish Highlands the ceasg ("tuft") is a MERMAID, having the upper body of a woman and the lower body of a salmon. Injurious by nature, the only way to kill this creature is to discover where it has hidden its soul, usually in an egg or shell, and then destroy it. To see one while out on the sea is considered to be an ill omen. Fishermen would take the chance of confronting this FAIRY ANIMAL for if they were successful in capturing one it was compelled to grant its captor three wishes. If the fisherman is kind hearted, good looking, and can convince the ceasg to live with him, his luck would be perpetual; the ceasg will shape-shift into a beautiful woman and be his wife. There are some Scottish families who claim to be descendants of a male fisherman and a ceasg mother.

Sources: Conway, *Magickal Mermaids and Water Creatures*, 60; Evans-Wentz, *Fairy Faith in Celtic Countries*, 25; Monaghan, *Encyclopedia of Celtic Mythology and Folklore*, 80; Snow, *Incredible Mysteries and Legends of the Sea*, 112

Cecrops

The legendary first king of Attica, Cecrops was, according to the ancient Greek historian and mythographer Apollodorus, an AUTOCHTHON, meaning he had the upper body of a man but the lower body of a DRAKON or snake.

Source: Apollodorus, *Apollodorus: The Library*, Volume 2, 77; Komar, *Reclaiming Klytemnestra*, 21

Ceffyl-Dwr

Variations: Ceffyl Dŵr

In Welsh folklore the ceffyl-dwr ("water horse") is a water-horse, similar to the Scottish EACH UISGUE and KELPIE. Described as looking like a small but beautiful horse grazing alongside the riverbank, it will tempt the unwary to climb up on its back; as soon as it is mounted the ceffyl-dwr will jump into the air, fly about, and buck its rider off from a fatal height. There are a few stories of one of these creatures being put successfully under the bridle and used as a cart horse, but eventually it breaks free and plunges back to its watery domain.

In South Wales the ceffyl-dwr appeared as a small horse; it allowed weary travelers to ride upon its back and after a wild ride, unceremoniously dumped them in a river; it was described as being a luminous and sometimes winged steed. However, in North Wales this FAIRY ANIMAL was a shape-shifter with a murderous agenda; there it was described as being dark and having fiery eyes. Most often the ceffyl-dwr was seen along the coastal shore appearing as having a dappled grey or sand colored coat. Its hoofs were pointed backward and if it could entice someone to ride it, it would plunge its rider into the ocean foam.

In various locations all throughout Wales the ceffyl-dwr is said to be a large, hulking chestnut or piebald horse trotting along the coast after a storm. Prior to a storm this water horse is said to be seen as a dapple, grey, or white horse clumsily stomping about in the ocean waves, possibly brewing up the very storm its sightings precede. In storm seasons, the ceffyl-dwr always appears with a sea-foam white coat.

Sources: Evans, *History of Llangynwyd Parish*, 170; Palmer, *Dragons, Unicorns, and Other Magical Beasts*, 14; Radford, *Tales of South Wales*, 148–9; Trevelyan, *Folk-Lore and Folk-Stories of Wales*, 64–5

Celeris

Variations: XANTHUS

In Greek mythology, Celeris ("swift") was the pure white equine brother of the winged stallion, PEGASUS; it is believed he was given by the god Hermes (Mercury) as a gift to the skilled equestrian, Castor, the twin brother of Pollux and sibling to Helen of Troy. Celeris was known for his speed.

Source: Olcott, *Star Lore of All Ages*, 297; Simpson, *Guidebook to the Constellations*, 100; Virgil, *Georgics*, Volume 2, 55

Celestial Cock

Variations: Bird of the Dawn, Cock of Dawn, Cock of Heaven, THREE-LEGGED BIRD

In Chinese mythology the celestial cock is described as a three-legged golden bird with a majestic bearing and a sonorous voice; it lays eggs and its chicks are born with a red crest. Folklore says cocks which crow with the dawn and in the evening are descendants of the celestial cock.

Source: Werner, *Myths and Legends of China*, 103–04

Celestial Horse

Variations: DRAGON Horse, Tianma

In Chinese mythology, originally the celestial horse was said to live in the Horse-Succeeds Mountains and was described as looking like a white dog but having a black head; shy, whenever it saw a person it would fly away making a call which sounded like its onomatopoeian name, "*tianma*." As the DRAGON HORSE, it was described only as being "strange looking" and was said to have lived in the waters of U-wa and in lake Kara-omo in the town of Ansi in Kansu provenance. According to folklore, one such DRAGON HORSE was presented to Emperor Wu-ti; impressed with it, he deemed it a supernatural being and called it a celestial horse because it was said to have been caught near the Celestial Mountains.

However, during the Han Dynasty (206 BC–AD 220) a celestial horse was understood to mean the powerful horses acquired from Central Asia and ridden by Chinese nobility, a breed called Hanxue Ma ("a horse that sweats blood").

Source: Allen, *Journal of the Royal Asiatic Society of Great Britain and Ireland*, Volume 22, 520; Strassberg, *Chinese Bestiary*, 130; Zell-Ravenheart, *Wizard's Bestiary*, 28

Celestial Stag

According to Chinese mythology, the Celestial Stag lives underground and interacts on occasion with miners; having the ability to both comprehend and speak human languages, this animal will beseech miners to take it to the surface and in exchange will tell where to find the richest veins of ore. Once above ground, the celestial stag cannot maintain its form and will quickly lose its cohesion, becoming first an amorphous and gelatinous blob of jelly-like substance containing many diseases then shriveling up into dusty flakes.

Source: Bush, *Asian Horror Encyclopedia*, 29; Rose, *Giants, Monsters, and Dragons*, 71; Willoughby-Meade, *Chinese Ghouls and Goblins*, 166–67

Celphie

In medieval Europe the celphie was said to live in the wastelands of Ethiopia; this chimerical creature was described as having the body of a cow but five legs, each of which was human from the elbow down so it had hands rather than cloven hooves.

Source: Rose, *Giants, Monsters, and Dragons*, 71; Zell-Ravenheart, *Wizard's Bestiary*, 29

Centaur

Variations: Centauren, Hippocentaur, Kentaure ("bull killer"), Kentauros, Kentauroi, Polkonj, Sagittary

In the classical Greek and Roman myths the centaurs were entangled with issues of sexual boundaries and promiscuity; a creature half-animal and half-human, they were a conflict of cultural and social boundaries. Centaurs, originally called hippocentaurs ("horse centaur") or simply "wild beasts," first appeared as guardians of limits on Kassite boundary stones and were more man than animal, having a full male form grafted to the hind quarters of a horse.

According to the myth the centaurs were born of Ixion, the man who married Dia but refused to pay her bride price; instead he set a trap for his father-in-law and killed him with burning coals. Eventually Ixion became a suppliant for the god Zeus (Jupiter) and quickly began to seduce the god's wife, Hera (Juno). While Hera was in her cloud form, known as the goddess Nephele ("cloud"), Ixion completed his seduction and she gave birth to Centauros who had intercourse with a mare who in turn gave birth to the first centaur.

Living in the wild and uncultivated areas of the mountains alongside the NYMPHS and SATYRS, the centaurs were hyper-masculine with a passion for violence, wine, and women; they were a popular subject for authors and poets. Centauromachy ("Battle with Centaurs") was a popular subject for artists.

Zeus (Jupiter) appointed twelve centaurs to guard the infant god Bacchus (Dionysos) against the conspiracies of the goddess Hera (Juno); their names were: Aisakos, Amphithemis, Eurybios, Gleneus, Keteus, Nomeion, Orthaon, Petraios, Phanes, Phaunos, Rhiphonos, and Spargeus.

Throughout Greek myths the centaurs were against the sanctity of marriage, often disrupting ceremonies and carrying off brides; they were also unable to enjoy wine without becoming aggressively and riotously drunk and raping women. When not being disruptive or sexually harassing women, centaurs were generally depicted as being generous, hospitable, kind, sporting, and wise.

In Slovenian folklore the centaur is known as *polkonji* ("to whip water") and is considered to be the personification of churning and frothing water as it is an untamable force of nature. They are described as having a human body joined at the waist to the body of a horse where its neck would begin; they were said to live in groups near water or in hills which were frequently flooded.

In medieval times, the centaur was often depicted in churches and said to be symbolic of the suffering Christ endured as a man; it was also said to depict the duplicitous nature of man as both a bestial and pious being.

Source: DuBois, *Centaurs and Amazons*, 27–9; Hansen, *Handbook of Classical Mythology*, 132–34; Kropej, *Supernatural Beings from Slovenian Myth and Folktales*, 100, 218; Mol-

lett, *Illustrated Dictionary of Words Used in Art and Archaeology*, 170; Rose, *Giants, Monsters, and Dragons*, 72

Centaurides

Variations: Kentaurides

Female CENTAURS, known as Centaurides, of
classical Greek mythology, were very similar to their
male counterparts, having a female body joined at
the waist to the body of a horse where its neck
would have been, but they also had horse ears. The
centaurides did not play a role in mythology and
prior to the fourth century did not even appear on
pottery. Based on a fragment of writing from Philostratus the Elder (190 BC) as he commented on a
painting, it can be assumed the centaurides had a
less bestial nature than the CENTAURS. Philostratus
described them as being beautiful, bare-chested
women growing out of the body of wonderfully colored and cared for horses; he even described a fair
skinned woman attached to a magnificent black mare.

Source: Hansen, *Handbook of Classical Mythology*, 132;
Maberry, *They Bite*, 335

Centichora

In the Greek didactic text *Physiologus*, written by
an unknown author and dated to the second century AD, the centichora is described as the cruelest
beast upon the earth and having two horns upon
its head, each more than four arm-lengths long and
sharper than a spear. Using a fighting method similar to the EALE, the centichora engages in combat
by first laying one of its twin horns down along its
back and protruding the other forward. Chimerical,
the centichora has a barrel-like head ending in a
rounded muzzle, the chest and thighs of a lion, the
tail of an elephant, the body and feet of a horse, and
a man's voice.

The natural enemy of the centichora is the
BASILISK; whenever this poisonous reptile finds a
centichora asleep, it will stalk up upon it and deliver
a blow between its eyes so they will swell up and
eventually drop out of the centichora's head before
the creature dies from the poison.

Source: Amor, *Beasts and Bawdy*, 51; Druce, *Archaeological
Journal*, Volume 68, 185

Centicore

Described in a thirteenth century French bestiary, the chimerical centicorn was a variation of the
EALE; it is depicted as having the body of a horse,
hooved feet, a mane on the top of its head going
down its neck, a tapered tail, and two long horns
growing from the top of its head, one horn pointing
forward and the other lying across its back.

Source: Druce, *Archaeological Journal*, Volume 68, 185

Centipede of Biwa

A monstrous anthropophagous (man-eating)
creature from Japanese folklore, this gigantic centipede was said to have lived in the mountains near
Lake Biwa, Japan; it was described as being longer
than the mountain it lived upon. According to the
story, the cultural hero and famed monster-slayer,
Hidesato, was beseeched by the local DRAGON KING
Ryujin to slay the monster for him. Hidesato
dipped an arrowhead in his own saliva and shot it
into the brain of the centipede, killing it instantly.
The hero was rewarded with a bag of never-ending
rice said to have fed his family line for centuries; a
cauldron which could cook without fire; a gigantic
bell; and an inexhaustible roll of brocade.

Source: Ashkenazi, *Handbook of Japanese Mythology*, 270;
Roberts, *Japanese Mythology A to Z*, 22

Central American Whintosser

Originating in the lumberjack communities of
the developing United States of America, the Central American whintosser, one of the FEARSOME
CRITTERS, was not a particularly large animal but
was mean and always on the lookout for causing or
finding trouble. The whintosser, found in the coastal
ranges of California, has a long, triangular-shaped
body with three complete sets of legs jutting out on
all sides; in the event of an earthquake, the animal
is not disturbed, even if the floor should suddenly
become the ceiling, or vice versa. To further aid in
this adaptation, its head and tail are each connected
to the body by a swiveling joint allowing the
appendage to rotate as fast as a hundred revolutions
a minute. The hair of the whintosser is forward facing and bristly.

It has been said the whintosser has more lives
than a cat, as it cannot be clubbed, piked, or shot
in any fashion which may kill it. The only known
method of destruction for this foul tempered beast
is to force it into a flume pipe making sure all of its
feet are touching a surface. When the pipe gets hot
enough the animal will attempt to run in three
directions at once, ripping itself apart.

Source: Cox, *Fearsome Creatures of the Lumberwoods*, 41;
Rose, *Giants, Monsters, and Dragons*, 119

Centycore

Variation: Centicore

A creature from ancient Greek mythology, the
centycore is chimerical, having a ten-point rack of
antlers on its forehead, a bear's muzzle, elephant
ears, horse hooves, and the legs of a lion. In spite of
its ability to speak with a human voice, this creature
was said to be extremely vicious and completely
without mercy.

Source: Eason, *Fabulous Creatures, Mythical Monsters, and Animal Power Symbols*, 82; Spencer, *Bibliotheca Spenceriana*, 241; Zell-Ravenheart, *Wizard's Bestiary*, 29

Cepus

A species of dog sacred to the ancient Babylonians and appearing in many medieval bestiaries, the cepus was said to "pour out the blue milk of its teats upon the rocks." It was chimerical, described as having a face like a SATYR and "the rest of a dog and a bear." Pliny describes the cepus as having forelegs ending in human hands and hind legs resembling human feet and thighs.

Source: Flaubert, *Temptation of St. Anthony*, 255; Wilkinson, *Second Series of the Manners and Customs of the Ancient Egyptians*, 114, 131

Cerastes

Variations: Hornworm

The Greek grammarian, physician, and poet Nicander of Colophon (second century AD) described the cerastes ("having horns") as a species of extremely flexible viper about a foot and half long with two or four horns upon its head; its bite was capable of killing a man in as little as three hours or causing him to linger for as long as nine days.

Source: Paulus, *Seven Books of Paulus Aegineta*, 188–89; Perry, *History of Greek Literature*, 774; Zell-Ravenheart, *Wizard's Bestiary*, 29

Cerberus

Variations: Kerberos

The eleventh Labor of the Greek hero and demigod Hercules (Heracles) was to capture the three-headed guard dog of the underworld (Hades), Cerberus, and take it to Eurystheus; the animal was born as one of the many monstrous offspring of ECHIDNA and Typhoeus (see CHIMAERA, HYDRA, and SPHINX). In most tales, Cerberus was said to have three heads, one for the past, one for the present, and one for the future, but the Greek poet Hesiod (750 and 650 BC) wrote he had fifty. Sometimes the dog was also described as having a serpent for a tail and claws like a lion. Cerberus' saliva was exceedingly toxic; wherever it fell upon the ground it would cause aconite to spring up. Newcomers were advised to carry *baklava* (honey cakes) with them as they entered into the underworld, as Cerberus would spitefully bite the shades as they entered.

Hades (Dis), the god of the underworld, said he would allow the hero to take his guardian on the condition he defeat the dog without using any of his weapons. Hercules (Heracles) agreed and eventually managed to subdue Cerberus by grasping him around the necks until he passed out. Once his quest was completed, Hercules (Heracles) returned Cerberus to Hades (Dis).

Source: Dixon-Kennedy, *Encyclopedia of Greco-Roman Mythology*, 82–3; Roman, *Encyclopedia of Greek and Roman Mythology*, 211

Cercopes

Variations: Kerkopes

In ancient Greece, it was believed the twin sons born of Oceanus and Theia were vampiric creatures. Collectively referred to as the *cercopes*, meaning the "tailed ones," they were renowned as being liars and thieves. The names of the brothers vary depending on the source—some say their names were Acmon and Passalus, another claims their names were Eurybatus and Olus, and a third claims the names were Sillus and Triballus. However, all the sources do agree in that the cercopes' physical appearance was of a short and squat simian (monkey-like) due to living in the forest. Very fast and particularly dangerous if trapped, the cercopes will use their amazing stealth to creep into the room of a sleeping child, where they will drink blood from the child's arms and legs.

Source: Barber, *Dictionary of Fabulous Beasts*, 37; Hesiod, *Hesiod, the Homeric Hymns, and Homerica*, 153–54, 539; Lurker, *Dictionary of Gods and Goddesses*, 348; Mahaffy, *History of Classical Greek Literature*, 114, 116; Rose, *Giants, Monsters, and Dragons*, 73

Cerus

In Greek mythology, Cerus ("fit") was a horse said to be owned by Adrastos the King of Argos; it was described as being swifter than the wind.

Source: Brewer, *Dictionary of Phrase and Fable*, 624; Room, *Naming of Animals*, 134

Cetus

Variations: Ketos

A SEA SERPENT from classical Greek mythology, Cetus was under the dominion of the god of the sea, Poseidon (Neptune); it was the personification of the vaporous clouds which would often rise up over the sea, dissipating the sun's light. Chimerical Cetus was described as being limbless but having token membranous flippers along its dolphin-like torso, a fiery red crest atop its hound-like head, forked tail, and two walrus-like tusks protruding from its maw. According to the Greek historian and mythographer Apollodorous (born circa 180 BC) when Cassiopeia bragged her daughter, Andromeda, was more beautiful than the nereids (golden-haired sea nymphs), Poseidon (Neptune) demanded retribution for the slight. The god decided to send his SEA SERPENT Cetus to attack the city of Aethiopia; however, an oracle proclaimed if Andromeda was to be sacrificed to Cetus the city would be saved. The hero and god of the sun, Perseus, had fallen in love with the maiden and was promised by her parents should he save their daughter from her fate, they would permit them to marry. Perseus quested for a means to save his love; he was able to slay the GORGON MEDUSA and while astride his winged horse, PEGASUS, revealed the head of the GORGON, turning Cetus into stone.

Source: Andrews, *Dictionary of Nature Myths*, 11–12, 174; De Kirk, *Dragonlore*, 40; Dixon-Kennedy, *Encyclopedia of Greco-Roman Mythology*, 84; Zell-Ravenheart, *Wizard's Bestiary*, 30

Chakora

A red partridge in Hindu mythology, the chakora ("crow pheasant") bird is said to eat nothing but moonbeams as it sits upon the edge of lotus petals; it is happy all night long as it can eat at its leisure but is miserable by day as it starves. In *bhakti* (devotional) poetry, the chakora is symbolic for a devotee; in court poetry it is symbolic for a cultured and discriminating person who enjoys the finer things in life.

Source: Lochtefeld, *Illustrated Encyclopedia of Hinduism: A-M*, 137; Ranade, *Mysticism in India*, 120

Chamrosh

Variations: Cynogriffin

In ancient Mesopotamia and Persian mythology, the chamrosh was a chimerical creature said to be the chief and protector of birds; this animal was said to have lived atop the summit of Mount Albur but folklore also claims it lived upon the ground beneath the soma tree which was also the roost of SENMURV. The chamrosh was described as having the body of a dog but the head and wings of a bird. According to folklore, whenever SENMURV would take flight, it would shake the tree, knocking down the ripe seeds which were then collected by the chamrosh who would distribute them throughout the earth.

Source: Leviton, *Encyclopedia of Earth Myths*, n.pag.; Nozedar, *Secret Language of Birds*, 36; Rose, *Giants, Monsters, and Dragons*, 76; Zell-Ravenheart, *Wizard's Bestiary*, 30

Chan

Ancient Chinese folklore and legends tell of a monstrous clam of immense proportions called Chan. According to a historical treatise written by Ssu-ma Ch'ien (c. 145–85 BC), Chan's exhalations were made of a substance which created a vast palace underwater.

Source: Rose, *Giants, Monsters, and Dragons*, 76; Zell-Ravenheart, *Wizard's Bestiary*, 30

Chancha Con Cadenas

Variations: Chancho De Lata ("tin pig")

A creature of Argentinean folklore said to lurk in the riverside towns and slums of Buenos Aires and Cordoba, the chancha con cadenas ("sow harnessed with chains") is said to be a large sow wrapped in chains which runs along the railroad tracks and telegraph lines making an earsplitting racket; however, as soon as a person turns to look, the chancha con cadenas disappears.

Source: Zell-Ravenheart, *Wizard's Bestiary*, 30

Ch'ang Hao

Formerly a commander of the army of the emperor, Chou Wang, who traditionally was said to rule from 1154 to 1122 BC, king of the snakes, Ch'ang Hao used his serpentine powers to defeat his master's enemies until he was slain by Yang Chien in the celestial Battle of Mu between the gods and the immortals. Ch'ang Hao had the ability to change his size, either to grow to enormous proportions or shrink down very small.

Source: Rose, *Giants, Monsters, and Dragons*, 76; Savill, *Pears Encyclopaedia of Myths and Legends: The Orient, Book 3*, 233

Charaxus

A CENTAUR from classical Greek mythology, Charaxus was one of the CENTAURS slain by the demi-god and cultural hero Hercules (Heracles) while visiting his friend, a CENTAUR named PHOLUS, between his conclusion of his third Labor and the onset of his fourth.

A blond-haired CENTAUR from ancient Greek mythology also by the name of Charaxus was, according to Ovid's *Metamorphoses*, one of the guests at the wedding of Pirithous, who became drunk on wine and, following the lead of EURYTUS, who assaulted Hippodame, began to assault and rape any women they could grab. In the ensuing Centauromachy, Charaxus received a glancing blow to his forehead from RHOETUS who struck him with a red-hot fire brand. Although the blow was not lethal, the wound was set ablaze and drove him into a frenzy. Mad with pain he hefted up over his head a stone threshold said to weigh more than a ton but was unable to throw it at his opponent. When Charaxus could hold the stone no longer he let it slip from his grasp where it fell onto the head of his CENTAUR comrade, COMETES, killing him instantly. Now, half-burned from his wound Charaxus was unable to defend himself against RHOETUS who beat him to death with four mighty blows, shattering his skull into his brains.

Source: Commentary, Mythological, Historical, and Geographical on Pope's Homer, 55; Simpson, Metamorphoses of Ovid, 205

Charybdis

Variations: Kharybdis

One of two monsters from ancient Greek mythology who were believed to live in the Straits of Messina located between the island of Sicily and the mainland of Italy, Charybdis lived on the Sicilian side of the Strait beneath a large fig tree. Three times a day, she would swallow up the sea and vomit it back out again creating a boiling and dangerous whirlpool.

The monster who resided on the other side of the Straits of Messina was SCYLLA.

Charybdis was born the daughter of the gods Zeus (Jupiter) and Gaea; she was naturally monstrous and notably greedy, so much so her own father was sickened by it and threw her into the Straits of Messina. Whenever a ship comes too close to her, she greedily attempts to swallow it up with her whirlpool.

Source: Andrews, Dictionary of Nature Myths, 171; Daly, Greek and Roman Mythology, A to Z, 116–17

Cheiron

Variations: Chiron, Kheiron

Unlike all other CENTAURS from classical Greek mythology, the immortal Cheiron, and best known of the PHILYRIDES, was civilized and tamed, as he and the rest of his breed, the PHILYRIDES, were born of the union between Cronos (Kronos) and Philyra. Living upon Mount Pelion, cloth-wearing Cheiron was a skilled alchemist, doctor, gymnast, hunter, musician, and prophet who taught not only the gods Apollo and Artemis (Diana) but also the twenty-one heroes including Achilles, ACTAEON, Asclepios, Castor, Hercules (Heracles), Hippolytos, Jason, Meleager, Nestor, Odysseus, Palamedes, Peleus, and Polydeuces. He even assisted Peleus in escaping the wild and untamed CENTAURS and then how to win the hand of the beautiful nereid (golden-haired sea nymphs), Thetis. Cheiron was married to a NYMPH named Chariklo, but other than her name, nothing else of her is known. When their daughter Euippe had become pregnant by Aeolus, the son of Hellen, she was transformed into a horse; his granddaughter was named Melanippe.

Cheiron was accidentally shot by Hercules (Heracles) during his battle with the CENTAURS of Arcadia. Immortal Cheiron was in tremendous pain but could not die; rather than suffer for all eternity, he gave up his immortality to PROMETHEUS. To honor his half-brother Cheiron, Zeus (Jupiter) placed his likeness in the night sky as the constellation Centaurus or Sagittarius.

Source: Dixon-Kennedy, Encyclopedia of Greco-Roman Mythology, 85, 127; DuBois, Centaurs and Amazons, 28–30; Hansen, Handbook of Classical Mythology, 76, 135; Hollenbaugh, Nessus the Centaur, 159

Cherufe

Variations: Cherruve

In Mapuche mythology there is a demonic creature named Cherufe living in the magma pools of the volcanoes in Chile. Cherufe was said to cause earthquakes and volcanic eruptions unless offered a virgin human, who would be thrown into his volcano as a sacrifice. After consuming the choicest parts of his offering, he would ignite the head of his victim and launch it from the volcano.

It should be noted there are actually some cryptozoologists who believe this creature is based on actual sightings of an undiscovered and undocumented creature which can survive in pools of molten rock.

Source: Faron, Mapuche Indians of Chile, 70; Lurker, Dictionary of Gods and Goddesses, 81; Maberry, Vampire Universe, 72; Porterfield, Chile, 44; Zell-Ravenheart, Wizard's Bestiary, 30

Ch'i-Lung

From Chinese folklore the Ch'i-lung species of DRAGON are described as being multicolored, appearing predominantly in green, red, and white; typically their ears and mane are red. These hornless DRAGONs, related to the HAN-RIU, are stuck in the KIAO-LUNG stage of development. When they exhale their breath, it comes out as a cloud of mist.

Source: De Kirk, Dragonlore, 25; Gould, Dragons, Unicorns, and Sea Serpents, 405

Chi Lung Wang

A beneficent celestial DRAGON KING from Chinese folklore, Chi Lung Wang ("the fire-engine DRAGON KING") is under the dominion of the DRAGON KING, Lung Wang, the great DRAGON provider of the earth's water. Chi Lung Wang was responsible for providing domestic water, and because of this was propitiated for support in providing enough water and working pumps when there is a house fire.

Source: Bahr, Collier's Encyclopedia, Volume 16, 478; Rose, Giants, Monsters, and Dragons, 79; Shryock, Temples of Anking and Their Cults, 117

Chiai Tung

Variations: Hai Chai, Hai Chiai, KAI TSI, Kai Tsu, Sin You, Sin U

A type of UNICORN from Chinese folklore, the chiai tung ("spiritual lamb") was described as having a fleshy alicorn (a single horn) growing out of its forehead and a head covered with hair. According to ancient texts such as the *Si Yang Y Shu*, when two parties were at a legal impasse the judge would bring forth the chiai tung who, with its ability to see right and wrong, would gore the guilty party.

Source: Gould, *Mythical Monsters*, 359; Rose, *Giants, Monsters, and Dragons*, 79; Zell-Ravenheart, *Wizard's Bestiary*, 89

Chiang-Liang

A chimerical creature from Chinese folklore, the chiang-liang was described as having the body of a panther but with long legs ending in hooves; it had the head of a tiger but the face of a human. It was often depicted holding a snake in its teeth.

Source: Borges, *Book of Imaginary Beings*, 81; Rose, *Giants, Monsters, and Dragons*, 79; Zell-Ravenheart, *Wizard's Bestiary*, 30

Chiao

Variations: Chiao-Lung ("HORNED DRAGON"), Kiao

A rare species of scaled DRAGON from Chinese mythology, the chiao are Piscean in appearance for the first thousand years of their life and live in rivers; after a millennium has passed, they begin to transform into a more traditional looking DRAGON. A sixteenth century illustrated encyclopedia described the chiao as a four-legged snake with a thin neck covered with white swellings; it does not have the ability to cause rain, but it can split mountains.

Source: Ball, *Animal Motifs in Asian Art*, 11; Ching, *Sages and Filial Sons*, 138, 157

Chichevache

Variations: Chichiface, Chiehe'uaehe

According to medieval British folklore the chichevache ("lean," "meager-looking cow," "thin," "ugly") was an emaciated bovine-like creature which fed upon faithful, obedient, patient wives. The chichevache, frequently depicted as decoration on church furniture, was also known as the BICORNE.

Source: Bois, *Jersey Folklore and Superstitions Volume Two*, 34–5; Chaucer, *Canterbury Tales*, 495; Rose, *Giants, Monsters, and Dragons*, 48; Zell-Ravenheart, *Wizard's Bestiary*, 30

Chickcharney

Variations: Chick Charnie, Chickcharnee, Chickcharnie

A small feathered and furred bird-like creature from deep within the forests of the Andros Islands, Bahamas, the chickcharney would make its nest where two tree-tops would cross. Old tales say if one of the trees which held its nest was cut down the chickcharney would curse the woodsman with hardship and misery. Other folklore regarding the chickcharney says it is a NATURE SPIRIT or half-animal and half-man, appearing only at night, having blood-red eyes and long arms ending in three fingers. As it walks, it casts no shadow.

Source: Coulter, *Encyclopedia of Ancient Deities*, 124; Pavlidis, *On and Off the Beaten Path*, 85; Porter, *Frommer's Bahamas*, 160

Chi'en Tang

Variations: Great Chi'en Tang

The master of all river DRAGONS in Chinese mythology, Chi'en Tang is described as being over 900 feet long, having flaming red scales and a fiery mane.

Source: De Kirk, *Dragonlore*, 27

Chikura

A NAGA from Hindu mythology, he was the father of the great SUMUKHA. Chikura was "reduced to the five elements" (slain) by Vinata's son, GARUDA.

Source: Debroy, *Mahabharata*, 426; Vogel, *Indian Serpent-Lore*, 83

Chimera

Variations: Chimaera ("goat"), Khimaira

Born the daughter of Typhoeus and ECHIDNA, according to the ancient Greek poet Hesiod, Chimera ("she goat") was a fire-breathing chimerical monster who caused a great deal of havoc in Lycia and the surrounding countries. Described as having the fore-body of a lion, the hindquarters of a DRAGON, and the mid-section of a goat, she also had three heads, one of each creature. Some descriptions add between one and three snakes as her tail. Eventually, Chimera was killed by the Corinthian cultural hero Bellerophon while astride the winged horse PEGASUS. The hero, after discovering arrows had no effect, had managed to get a bar of lead down Chimera's fire-breathing throat where the heat melted it and caused her to choke to death.

In some tellings of the myth by classical authors, Chimera is said to be the child of the HYDRA; she is also said to be the mother of the NEMEAN LION by ORTHRUS, the two-headed hound and brother of CERBERUS as well as the mother of the SPHINX.

Source: Apollodorus, *Gods and Heroes of the Greeks*, 71; Conner, *Everything Classical Mythology Book*, 200–01; Smith, *New Classical Dictionary of Greek and Roman Biography, Mythology and Geography*, 197–8

Chinese Dragon

Variations: Imperial Dragons, Shen-Lung

Considered to be divine, the Chinese dragon is an essential part of the culture and mythology of China from ancient times to modern; it is said the first emperor of China was the DRAGON, YU.

For the most part, all Asiatic dragons live for about a millennium and go through many physical transformations throughout their lifetime. A Chinese dragon lives much longer; it is hatched after a thousand years from a brilliant gemlike egg and looks very much like an eel or snake. When the creature is about 500 years old, the young dragon's head will take on the shape of a carp; this stage of development is known as *Kiao*. When the dragon reaches the age of 1,500 years it transforms into its next stage, the KIAO-LUNG, where it develops four stubby legs with four claws on each paw; it will also have an elongated head and tail and sport a long beard. At 2,000 years old the kiao-lung will have grown horns. The final stage of development is called YING-LUNG; this happens when the dragon is 3,000 years old.

The French secular priest Leon Joly (1847–1909) described the mature Chinese dragon as having nine distinctive features in his work "*Le christianisme et l'Extreme-Orient*"; there he describes the dragon as the largest of the scaly animals, having ears like a bull, a head like a camel, scales like carp (piscine), horns like a deer, claws like an eagle, eyes like a hare, neck like an iguana, and paws like a tiger. It had nine times nine scales (eighty-one), usually gold or silver in color, as this is the extreme of a lucky number; the scales of its throat being reversed. On the sides of its mouth are whiskers and under its chin is a bright pearl; on the top of its head the poh shan (or "foot-rule") is found, without which it cannot ascend to heaven. In front of its antlers it carries a pearl of bluish color striated with parallel lines. Its breath transforms into clouds from which can come either fire or rain. The dragon is fond of the flesh of sparrows and swallows; however it dreads the centipede and silk dyed of five colors. It is also afraid of iron.

Source: De Kirk, *Dragonlore*, 23–4; Ingersoll, *Dragons and Dragon Lore*, 75–6

Chinese Fox

Variations: Huli Jing ("fox essence"), Hu Hsien ("fox fairy"), Huxian ("fox transcendent"), Kitsune-Tsuki

Appearing as a common fox, the Chinese fox of folklore is a trickster by nature, often considered to be an ill omen, and having a lifespan between 800 and 1,000 years; a skilled shape-shifter, it would often take the form of an old man, a scholar, or a young woman. Each part of its body was supposed to have a magical ability, such as its tail, which when struck upon the ground, could start a fire. The Chinese fox is seen in graveyards; it is believed the souls of the dead can transmigrate into its body. Typically in folklore the Chinese fox had two basic motives, to show its powerful shape-shifting ability by assuming the form of a person or demon to achieve its second motive: that of revenge for some crime it perceived, real or imagined.

Source: Avant, *Mythological Reference*, 104; Walravens, *Der Fuchs in Kultur, Religion und Folklore Zentral- und Ostasiens, Part 1*, 35

Chinthe (chin dhei)

In Buddhist mythology the chinthe is a winged lion or lion-dog said to stand guard at the base of pagodas all throughout Burma; they are symbolic of authority, ferocity, protection, and unrelenting loyalty to Buddhism.

Source: Skidmore, *Karaoke Fascism*, 128

Chio-Tuan

A species of KI-LIN (UNICORN), the chio-tuan looks like a green-furred deer with an alicorn (a single horn) on its head. According to folklore, when Genghis Khan was preparing to invade India his army encountered one of these creatures in the desert; the chio-tuan spoke to them saying "it is time for your master to return to his land." When the event was reported, Genghis Khan called off his invasion.

Source: Rose, *Giants, Monsters, and Dragons*, 80; Zell-Ravenheart, *Wizard's Bestiary*, 31

Chivato

Variations: ENCERRADOS ("captive" or "recluse")

In the mythology of the Araucanian (Mapuchen) people of Chile the chivato ("young goat") is believed to be a monstrous humanoid; once a child, this person was kidnapped by witches and over the course of several years was physically transformed into this cannibalistic beast. According to folklore, the chivato was fed by one of the witches' servants, an INVUNCHE or a TRELQUEHUECUVE who captured young girls while they were drawing water. Chivato live in the caverns near the towns of Ancud and Chiloc; there is believed to be a passageway or tunnel on the island lake which goes to the lair of the creatures.

Source: Meurger, *Lake Monster Traditions*, 280–81; Rose, *Giants, Monsters, and Dragons*, 80

Chōchinobake

Variations: Chochinobake

One of YŌKAI known as TSUKOMOGAMI of Japanese mythology, the chōchinobake ("lantern-shaped goblin") is an animated paper lamp; after a household item is in use for about a hundred years it is believed the item can gain consciousness and enough magical ability to move and think on its own. Generally, the chōchinobake is benign.

Source: Maberry, *Cryptopedia*, 227

Choko

Variations: Osa-gitsume

A HULI JING from Japanese mythology, Choko ("fox chief") was the king of all foxes and a descendant of KIKO MYOJIN.

Source: Picken, *Essentials of Shinto*, 124

Chollima

Variations: Chonma ("flying horse")

The chollima ("flying horse") is the name used in Korean mythology for a legendary winged horse so elegant and fast no mortal man can ride upon it. According to the folklore, Chollima, the one-thousand-li-horse, was able to travel 249 (400 km) miles a day (one *li* is approximately four kilometers).

Source: Dotan, *Watercraft on World Coins*, 287; Kurnitzky, *Chollima Korea*, 29

Chonchon (Chon-chin)

Variations: Piguechen ("vampire")

The Araucanian (Mapuchen) people of Chile have the belief in which through a mere act of will, a person can become a chonchon, growing wings out of their ears and flapping so hard the head tears free of the body and flies away. Some sources say this only happens after the person is deceased. The Mapuche Indians in the same area say the chonchon is a bird with the head of a *kalku*, a sorcerer. Its cry is said to sound like "tui-tui-tui." Whether it is a flying head or a bird, it feeds on human blood and can shape-shift to look like a person with large ears.

Source: Alexander, *Latin-American*, 329; Edwards, *My Native Land*, 395; Van Scott, *The Encyclopedia of Hell*, 287; Zell-Ravenheart, *Wizard's Bestiary*, 31

Ch'ou-T'i

A chimerical creature from Chinese mythology, the ch'ou-t'i appeared in a book published in AD 981 entitled *T'ai P'ing Kuang Chi* ("Great Records Made in the Period of Peace and Prosperity"); the creature was described as having the body of an animal (unspecified as to which animal) and a head at each end.

Source: Borges, *Book of Imaginary Beings*, 81; Rose, *Giants, Monsters, and Dragons*, 80

Chronos, the Dragon

Variations: Drakon Chronos, Heracles, Unaging Chronos

Not to be confused with the demi-god, god, and flying horse of the same name, the DRAGON Chronos ("time") is a chimerical three-headed monster from ancient Greek mythology of the Orphic tradition; it was born of an egg. This creature has the head of a bull on one side and the head of a lion on the other, and the head of a god in the middle, although the myth does not specify which god the face resembles. Upon its shoulders it has wings. Chronos the DRAGON, although male, produces eggs which hatch his children, each of which has three aspects to them: they are composed of chaos, ether, and Erebus (the Underworld).

Source: Edmonds, *Redefining Ancient Orphism*, 171; Ogden, *Dragons, Serpents, and Slayers in the Classical and Early Christian Worlds*, 36–8

Chthonius

A spear-wielding CENTAUR from ancient Greek mythology, Chthonius was, according to Ovid's *Metamorphoses*, one of the CENTAURS who attended the wedding of Pirithous, became drunk on wine and, following the lead of EURYTUS, who assaulted Hippodame, began to assault and rape any women they could grab. A great Centauromachy then followed.

Source: *Commentary, Mythological, Historical, and Geographical on Pope's Homer*, 55; Simpson, *Metamorphoses of Ovid*, 205

Ch'uan-t'ou

In Chinese mythology, the ch'uan-t'ou were believed to be a race of flying humanoids, having the head of a bird and the wings of a bat. The ch'uan-t'ou were described in a book published in AD 981 entitled *T'ai P'ing Kuang Chi* ("Great Records Made in the Period of Peace and Prosperity"). When seen, it was when they were catching fish from the river and sea.

Source: Borges, *Book of Imaginary Beings*, 102; Eberhart, *Mysterious Creatures*, 176; Rose, *Giants, Monsters, and Dragons*, 82

Chudo-Yudo

A fire-breathing HYDRA-like DRAGON from Russian folklore, Chudo-Yudo, a son of the witch Baba Yaga, is the aggressive guardian of the Waters of Life and Death. A brother of KASHCHEI the Deathless, Chudo-Yudo is associated with times of drought as he had the power to control the weather.

Source: De Kirk, *Dragonlore*, 40; Dixon-Kennedy, *Encyclopedia of Russian and Slavic Myth and Legend*, 27, 52

Chukwa

In Hindu mythology, Chukwa is the gigantic tortoise which the great elephant MAHA-PUDMA stands upon which in turn, supports the world we live on. Beneath the feet of Chukwa is an endless line of tortoises standing upon one another.

Source: Brewer, *Wordsworth Dictionary of Phrase and Fable*, 1086; Loy, *World Is Made of Stories*, 4

Chupacabra (Chew-pa-cob-rha)

The *chupacabra*, the well-known "goat sucker" of Mexico, is one of the best-known vampiric creatures. The first recorded sighting of the beast was by the governor of New Galicia in April of 1540. He described one as being a small, dark-scaled man who carried a torch and a spear, and when it attacked, did so in large numbers. It was also reported the creature was an excellent jumper and could cover a great distance in a single leap. As time passed, the description of the chupacabra changed, and each one varied widely from a chimerical foxlike animal with bat wings, cat eyes, and blue skin to a thick-bodied, furless, quadruped-type canine. There have also been a number of different theories as to what the chupacabra is exactly. Ideas range from an extraterrestrial creature and escaped genetic hybrid to the more mundane explanation of it merely being an animal of the natural world previously unrecorded or a known animal suffering from a bad case of mange and is therefore unfamiliar looking. What is not in dispute is the chupacabra, regardless of what it is or where it came from, is a reputed blood-drinking creature.

To date, all of the known victims of the chupacabra have been an array of domestic animals: chickens, cows, goats, and sheep. It is said the chupacabra uses its amazing stealth to sneak up on the animal, killing it quickly and from surprise before it can sound an alarm. In the morning, the animal's carcass is found with the smallest of bite marks on its body and completely drained of blood, not a single drop to be found anywhere on the ground. Interestingly, in the year 2000, campers and other nature enthusiasts claimed to have seen the chupacabra in their campsites at night and when they awoke in the morning, they discovered their water bottles had been stolen.

This creature, as steeped in folklore and mystery as it is, has also been attributed to having other supernatural powers, such as never leaving tracks or a scent trail, the ability to shape-shift into an old man, and the ability to be non-photogenic or trapped. Fortunately, all the myths and stories surrounding this bloodthirsty creature describe it as being afraid of humans, running off as soon as opportunity presents itself.

Source: Burnett, *Conspiracy Encyclopedia*, 311; Candelaria, *Encyclopedia of Latino Popular Culture*, 161–62; Davis, *Ecology of Fear*, 268–70; Szasz, *Larger Than Life*, 197–98

Cigouave

In Haitian folklore, the cigouave is a creature appearing in Vodou religious beliefs; similar to the MANTICORA, the cigouave has the body of a lion or panther and the head of a human.

Source: Rose, *Giants, Monsters, and Dragons*, 83; White, *Book of Beasts*, 52; Zell-Ravenheart, *Wizard's Bestiary*, 31

Cinnamologus

Variations: Cinnamulgus, Cinnamon Bird, Cirenus Bird, Cynamolgus

A large bird described from mediaeval bestiaries, the cinnamologus of Arabia was said to make its nest from the cinnamon quills it gathered from parts unknown in the top most branches of trees. It was said locals would leave carrion meat out knowing the cinnamologus would take chunks of it back to its nest where the added weight would cause the very fragile nest to break apart and fall to the ground; then, locals would pick up the quills at their leisure. Another way to harvest the nest of the cinnamologus was to shoot the nest with a lead tipped arrow so the weight of it would cause the nest to break the branches supporting it.

Source: Arnott, *Birds in the Ancient World from A to Z*, 145; Eason, *Fabulous Creatures, Mythical Monsters, and Animal Power Symbols*, 59

Cipactli

Variations: Tlaltecuhtli

In ancient Aztec mythology Cipactli ("serpent of knives") was an amphibious female SEA SERPENT or monster depicted as having a monster's body much like a crocodile but with a shark's tail and a strange appendage similar to the rostrum of a sawfish; this bony rostrum was known as Cipactli's sword or striker. She was often depicted with claws upon her knees and elbows, a grinning deathlike face, and a skull on her back. Cipactli was an ancient creature, existing before the beginning of time, swimming through the stars and heavens looking for human flesh to eat.

Cipactli wrestled with four gods who were busy creating the world; the god ripped the creature in half and used the top half to make the heavens and the lower half to make the earth. Paralyzed, she took on the identity of Tlaltecuhtli ("earth lord").

Source: Bingham, *South and Meso-American Mythology A to Z*, 109; Eilperin, *Demon Fish*, 27–8

Circhos

A three-toed humanoid monster from Scandinavian folklore, Circhos is described as having both crusty and soft skin colored black and red; its right foot is very small but its left is long. When Circhos walks it leans on the left side and draws his right foot after itself. It is said when the sky is cloudy and the winds blow, Circhos sits upon the rocks and remains there, unmovable.

Source: Ashton, *Curious Creatures in Zoology*, 247; Rose, *Giants, Monsters, and Dragons*, 83

Cirein Croin

Variations: Cirein Cròin, Curtag Mhor a' Chuain ("the great whirlpool of the ocean"), Mial Mhor a' Chuain ("the beast of the ocean"), Uile Bheisd a' Chuain ("monster of the ocean")

A SEA SERPENT from Celtic and Scottish folklore, Cirein Croin ("grey crest") was said to be the largest of all creatures, able to consume seven whales for its breakfast meal.

Source: Bonnerjea, *Allborough New Age Guide*, 59; De Kirk, *Dragonlore*, 40; Rose, *Giants, Monsters, and Dragons*, 83–4; Zell-Ravenheart, *Wizard's Bestiary*, 31

Cithaeronian

Variations: The Cithaeronian Lion, NEMEAN LION

The lion, Cithaeronian, from ancient Greek mythology was a man-eater, having slain many people including the son of King Megareus, Euippus. The king had promised whoever killed Cithaeronian would marry his daughter and become his heir, succeeding him to the throne. Many tried, but it was the son of Pelops, Alcathous, who hunted and overcame the lion.

Source: Bell, *Place Names in Classical Mythology: Greece*, 81–2; Pausanias, *Pausanias Description of Greece*, Volume 1, 219

Clanis

A CENTAUR from ancient Greek mythology, Clanis was, according to Ovid's *Metamorphoses*, one of the CENTAURS who attended the wedding of Pirithous, became drunk on wine and, following the lead of EURYTUS, who assaulted Hippodame, began to assault and rape any women they could grab. A great Centauromachy then followed. Clanis was slain, just as IPHINOUS was, in up-close, personal combat by Peleus.

Source: *Commentary, Mythological, Historical, and Geographical on Pope's Homer*, 55; Simpson, *Metamorphoses of Ovid*, 207

Clytus

A CENTAUR from ancient Greek mythology, Clytus was one of the CENTAURS slain by the demi-god and cultural hero Hercules (Heracles) while visiting his friend, a CENTAUR named PHOLUS, between the conclusion of his third Labor and the onset of his fourth.

Source: *Commentary, Mythological, Historical, and Geographical on Pope's Homer*, 55; Simpson, *Metamorphoses of Ovid*, 81

The Coca

A fire-breathing DRAGON from Spanish folklore, the coca ("she bogey") is likely derived from the TARASQUE from the folklore of southwestern France; it is remembered annually during the feast of Corpus Christi where a papier-mâché version of it engages in mock battles against Saint George.

Source: Rose, *Giants, Monsters, and Dragons*, 84; Warner, *Monsters of Our Own Making*, 113

Cock-Fish

In European heraldic symbology the cock-fish is a hybrid creature having the forebody of a cockerel and hind body of a fish.

Source: Dennys, *Heraldic Imagination*, 68; Rose, *Giants, Monsters, and Dragons*, 85; Zell-Ravenheart, *Wizard's Bestiary*, 32

Cock of Heaven

In Muslim folklore the cock of Heaven is a divine animal made by God; its morning call rouses every living creature to summon them to morning prayers. It was described as living in the first heaven and being so gigantic in size its crest touched the second heaven. On the morning this bird ceases to call, the Day of Judgment is at hand.

Source: Leeming, *Dictionary of Creation Myths*, 264

Cockatrice

Variations: Basil Cock, Cockatrix

In the fourteenth century the English author Geoffrey Chaucer used the BASILISK in one of the stories in his *Canterbury Tales*; his spelling of the creature's name, *basilicok*, evolved into the word *cockatrice*. This new creature had the serpentine head of the BASILISK but the legs, head, and neck of a cockerel. Later descriptions added DRAGON wings and a human face. Medieval writers claimed the chimerical cockatrice was hatched by a reptile from a yolkless egg laid from a nine-year-old chicken during the hot and sultry days of the Dog Star (from July 24 to August 24). Virtually identical to the BASILISK, the cockatrice would wander the countryside killing with its venomous glance; its only natural enemy was the weasel. Although the cockatrice killed anything it saw, the only defense against it was to see the animal first. According to medieval Christian folklore, the SERPENT OF ISA was the prodigy of the cockatrice.

Source: Conway, *Magickal, Mystical Creatures*, 185; Pedrini, *Serpent Imagery and Symbolism*, 121; Rosen, *Mythical Creatures Bible*, 92–3

Coic Biasta Mora Grannai

In the Irish pseudepigraph *Epistil Isu* ("*Sunday Letters*"), written by an anonymous author, describes five kinds of monsters which will descend upon those individuals and heathens who do not keep holy the Lord's Day, Sunday. The coic biasta mora grannai is the fifth and final of the tormentors to Sunday transgressors. These demonic and infernal creatures are huge and horrible and desire nothing more than to rise to the surface of the earth and punish those who do not keep holy the Lord's Day. Fortunately, according to the folklore, the love God has for mankind is reflected in His mercy by not allowing these monstrosities to escape the confines of Hell to terrorize humanity.

Source: Olsen, *Monsters and the Monstrous in Medieval Northwest Europe*, 69–70

Colo-Colo (Col-o col-o)

Variations: Basilisco, Colocolo

A vampiric creature in the mythology of the Araucanian (Mapuchen) people of Chile, this monstrous being is born of an egg from a cockerel and preys on those asleep. At night, it hovers over them, drinking up their saliva and thereby draining the body of all moisture. The victim of such an attack will awake with a high fever which is always followed by death.

Source: Edwards, *My Native Land*, 395; Guirand, *Larousse Encyclopedia of Mythology*, 453; Rose, *Giants, Monsters and Dragons*, 86

Columbia River Sand Squink

Originating in the lumberjack communities of the developing United States of America, the Columbia River sand squink, one of the FEARSOME CRITTERS, was described as having the front end of a coyote and the back end of a bobcat with a spotted rump; it is capable of emitting an electrical discharge. The sand squink is an egg-laying creature; its eggs are made of a plastic-like material so as to protect the unborn young within from the mother's electrical discharge.

Source: Blackman, *Field Guide to North American Monsters*, 144; Rose, *Giants, Monsters, and Dragons*, 119; Tryon, *Fearsome Critters*, 11

Come-at-a-Body

Originating in the lumberjack communities of the developing United States of America, the come-at-a-body, one of the FEARSOME CRITTERS, is said to be a species of small woodchuck-like animal with very soft, kitten-like, velvety fur. The come-at-a-body is not found outside of the White Mountains.

Source: Dorson, *Man and Beast in American Comic Legend*, 93; Rose, *Giants, Monsters, and Dragons*, 119; Tryon, *Fearsome Critters*, 13

Cometes

A CENTAUR from ancient Greek mythology, Cometes was, according to Ovid's *Metamorphoses*, one of the guests at the wedding of Pirithous, who became drunk on wine and, following the lead of EURYTUS, who assaulted Hippodame, began to assault and rape any women they could grab. In the ensuing Centauromachy, CHARAXUS, the companion of Cometes, received a blow to his forehead from RHOETUS with a red-hot fire brand. The wound was set ablaze, and mad with pain, he hefted up over his head a stone said to weigh more than a ton. Unfortunately, CHARAXUS managed to throw the unwieldy stone and it fell onto the head of Cometes, killing him instantly.

Source: *Commentary, Mythological, Historical, and Geographical on Pope's Homer*, 55; Simpson, *Metamorphoses of Ovid*, 205

Comrade

The horse of Fortunio, Comrade was capable of human speech and had knowledge of those who were fairy-blessed, as he was able to point out to his master: Boisterer, who could work a windmill with a single breath; Fine-Ear, a man blessed with perfect hearing; Gormand, who could eat a thousand loaves of bread in a single mouthful; Lightfoot, who could run ten times faster than the fastest deer; Marksman, who could not only see the distance of a thousand miles but was also an expert marksman; Strong-Back, the man who could carry any weight he chose upon his back; and Tippler, who could drink up entire rivers in a single gulp. Comrade was instrumental in his master's succeeding in his quest to marry the princess. He was an invaluable asset to Fortunio and was frequently consulted on all matters, especially those involving the movements and conflict involving the army.

Source: Aldrich, *Young Folks' Library*, 143–56; Brewer, *Character Sketches of Romance, Fiction and the Drama*, Volumes 8, 266

Con-Ma-Dau

In the Ananmese folklore of Vietnam there is a group of demonic disease-carrying beings known as the con-ma-dau; they are associated with bringing smallpox.

Source: Rose, *Spirits, Fairies, Leprechauns, and Goblins, an Encyclopedia*, 71

Con Tram Nu' O' C

Variations: Con tram nu'o'c

In Annamese folklore Con Tram Nu' O' C is a gigantic water buffalo which can move quite quickly in spite of its massive size. It is believed anyone who carried one of its hairs will have the ability to walk across rivers without getting wet.

Source: Leach, *Funk and Wagnalls Standard Dictionary of Folklore, Mythology, and Legend*, n.pag.; Zell-Ravenheart, *Wizard's Bestiary*, 32

Conabos

Variations: Konabos

One of the HIPPOI ATHANATOI from ancient Greek mythology, the fire-breathing Conabos ("flame") belonged to Ares (Mars), the god of war; his stable-mates were AITHON ("fire"), PHLOGIOS ("flame"), and PHOBOS ("terror").

Source: Coulter, *Encyclopedia of Ancient Deities*, dccxv; Gemondo, *Animal Totems*, 60

Conopenii

In Persian folklore and mythology the conopenii was a hybrid creature, having the body of a horse but the head of an ass; more interesting than the slight difference of its physical appearance is the conopenii had the ability to breathe fire from both its mouth and nostrils.

Source: Barber, *Dictionary of Fabulous Beasts*, n.pag.; Rose, *Giants, Monsters and Dragons*, 86; Zell-Ravenheart, *Wizard's Bestiary*, 32

Corc-Chluasask

In Scottish folklore the corc-chluasask ("split ears") was a type of freshwater FAIRY ANIMAL described only as looking like a gigantic calf with split ears. Born the offspring of the TAIRBH-UISGE, the corc-chluasask were known for their ability to cause trouble; tradition said it was best to kill these animals on sight as they are known for causing misfortunes which build up to a disaster.

Source: Eberhart, *Mysterious Creatures*, 580; Meurger, *Lake Monster Traditions*, 127; Rose, *Giants, Monsters and Dragons*, 180, 353; Zell-Ravenheart, *Wizard's Bestiary*, 32

Cornu

An early Irish Christian folklore of undetermined date involving Saint Patrick takes place in a location known as Saint Patrick's Purgatory on Lough Derg; it is there the story claims the holy man transformed the local deity, or demon, into a great black raven named Cornu.

Source: Haren, *Medieval Pilgrimage to St Patrick's Purgatory*, 161; Rose, *Giants, Monsters, and Dragons*, 87; Tomlinson, *Demons, Druids and Brigands on Irish High Crosses*, 41

Corpan Side

Variations: Siodbrad, Siod Brad

In Irish folklore the corpan side is a species of CHANGELING that, when it is between one and two thousand years old, is left in the place of a newborn infant.

Source: Knight, *Celtic Traditions*, 139; Rose, *Spirits, Fairies, Leprechauns, and Goblins, an Encyclopedia*, 73

Corynthus

A CENTAUR from ancient Greek mythology, Corynthus was one of the CENTAURS slain by the demi-god and cultural hero Hercules (Heracles) while visiting his friend, a CENTAUR named PHOLUS, between his conclusion of his third Labor and the onset of his fourth.

Source: *Commentary, Mythological, Historical, and Geographical on Pope's Homer*, 55

Cotzbalam

According to the Quiche people's creation myth recorded in the *Popol Vuh*, the Mayans' sacred book, Cotzbalam was one of four birds which played a significant role in the destruction of the first race of people created by the god of the wind, Hurakan. The creation myth says after the gods made the animals, earth, moon, sky, and sun, they created a race of people made of wood who were meant to appreciate the gods and see to the well-being of the animals. This first attempt of humanity was a failure as the wooden people insulted the gods and abused the animals. Hurakan sent a great flood to drown the wooden people and Cotzbalam, who pecked the flesh away from their bodies. CAMULATZ bit off the heads of the ones who treaded water as they drowned; TECUMBALAM broke their bones and sinews, and then ground their bodies into powder; and XECOTCOVACH tore out their eyes.

Source: Bingham, *South and Meso-American Mythology A to Z*, 21–2; Spence, *Arcane Secrets and Occult Lore of Mexico and Mayan Central America*, 241

Cougar Fish

In the regional folklore of Wisconsin, United States of America, the cougar fish, one of the FEARSOME CRITTERS, is a vicious species of predator which will attack small boats and canoes; using the claws at the ends of their fins, they pull men into the water. Their teeth are like a saw and can cut through flesh and bone in an instant.

Source: Baughman, *Type and Motif-Index of the Folktales of England and North America*, 534; Botkin, *American People*, 254; Godfrey, *Monsters of Wisconsin*, 132;

Cretan Bull

Variations: Marathonian Bull

In ancient Greek mythology the Cretan bull was generally believed to be the very same bull sent up from the sea by the god Poseidon (Neptune) which King Minos was supposed to sacrifice but instead sent into his herds. Poseidon (Neptune), angry when the promise was broken, not only inflicted madness on the bull but caused Queen Pasiphae to have carnal relations with it, a union which created the MINOTAUR ASTERION.

For his seventh (or eighth, sources conflict) Labor, the demi-god and cultural hero Hercules (Heracles) had to capture the Cretan bull and return with it. Using an old technique, by grabbing the horns and squeezing them together, the bull became calm enough for him to tie the feet together in order for him to carry it back to King Eurystheus. The bull was eventually slain by Theseus.

According to the ancient Greek logographer and mythographer Acusilaus of Argos, this was the same bull which had carried Europa across the sea.

Source: Daly, *Greek and Roman Mythology, A to Z*, 69; Leeming, *Oxford Companion to World Mythology*, 86; Roman, *Encyclopedia of Greek and Roman Mythology*, 210

Criosphinx

Variations: Crio-Sphinx

In ancient Egyptian mythology there were three types of Sphinxes, the ANDROSPHINX, the criosphinx, and the HIERACOSPHINX. Each of these variations represented the king as well as a token of respect to the god whose head they most resembled. The chimerical criosphinx had the head of a ram and the body of a lion and therefore was associated with the god Neph.

Source: Faulkner, *Handy Classical and Mythological Dictionary for Popular Use*, 48; Wilkinson, *Manners and Customs of the Ancient Egyptians*, Volume 5, 200–01

Crocotta

Variations: Akabo, Alazbo, Corocotta, Crocotte, Crocuta, Curcrocute, Cynolycus, Kynolykos, Leucrota, Lupus Vesperitinus, Rosomacha, Zabo

Described by Pliny the Elder, the Roman author, natural philosopher, naturalist, and army and naval commander in his work *Natural History* (AD 77), the crocotta of Ethiopia was said to be the hybrid offspring of a dog and a wolf. Its most notable feature was its amazing bite, as the strength of its jaw combined with the power of its teeth had the ability to bite through anything and chew it into pulp. Other naturalists have claimed the crocotta was the product of the union of a hyena and a lioness and added on to the description saying the crocotta had the ability to perfectly mimic human speech and the call of cattle. Its gaze was always fixed and it did

not have gums in its maw, as the jaw and teeth were one continuous piece of bone.

Source: Ashton, *Curious Creatures in Zoology*, 72; Borges, *Book of Imaginary Beings*, 54; Zell-Ravenheart, *Wizard's Bestiary*, 33

Crodh Mara

Variations: Crodh Sidhe

Less dangerous than the EACH UISCE, the crodh mara ("cattle of the sea") from the Scottish Highlands are a breed of FAIRY-cattle described as being dun colored and hummel ("hornless"), although those in Skye they are said to be black or red (see FAIRY ANIMAL). On occasion one of the bulls will mate with a mortal cow and greatly improve the bloodline. If a crodh mara cow joins a mortal herd they will instinctually follow her; should the fairy-cow return to her *knowe*, the herd will follow her in, never to return.

As the crodh sidhe ("fairy cow"), this breed of friendly fairy-cow is typically described as being hummel, round eared, and white bodied with red speckles, similar to the GWARTHEG Y LLYN. Dwelling in the sea and living on seaweed, the crodh sidhe would sometimes join up with a mortal herd to improve the stocks quality but eventually, they would always make their way back home to the sea.

Sources: Briggs, *Encyclopedia of Fairies*, 81; Eberhart, *Mysterious Creatures*, 580; Monaghan, *Encyclopedia of Celtic Mythology and Folklore*, 105

Cromis

A CENTAUR from ancient Greek mythology, Cromis was, according to Ovid's *Metamorphoses*, one of the guests at the wedding of Pirithous, who became drunk on wine and, following the lead of EURYTUS, who assaulted Hippodame, began to assault and rape any women they could grab. In the ensuing Centauromachy, he and LYCUS were slain by Pirithous.

Source: *Commentary, Mythological, Historical, and Geographical on Pope's Homer*, 55; Simpson, *Metamorphoses of Ovid*, 206

Crommyonian Sow

Variations: Hus Klazomenaios, Phaea ("shining one"), Phaia, the Sow of Crommyon, Sow of Krommyon

Born one of the children of the DRAKAINA, ECHIDNA and Typhoeus, the feral Crommyonian sow of ancient Greek mythology ran wild throughout the Corinth countryside. It is possible she was the mother of the CALYDONIAN BOAR slain by the hero Meleager. Eventually the sow was slain by the hero and king of Athens, Theseus, who did so to prove not all of his exploits were done out of necessity as he was of the opinion it was the duty and responsibility of brave men to not only confront and conquer villainous men but to also slay beasts.

Source: Coulter, *Encyclopedia of Ancient Deities*, 125, 135; Plutarch, *Plutarch's Lives of Illustrious Men*, Volume 1, 8

Le Croque-Mitaine

A French BOGEYMAN, le croque-mitaine ("hand-cruncher" or "mitten biter") is used by parents to frighten children into good behavior with sayings like "the croque-mitaine will have you if you are naughty; he will come to take you." It is unsure as to what sort of being the croque-mitaine is; there is speculation it may be a sort of unlucky or voracious fairy, Fate, or goblin (a general term for any of the grotesque, small but friendly beings among the fay) which grinds its teeth or possibly a species of feline humanoid who is savage one moment and sly the next.

Source: Bois, *Jersey Folklore and Superstitions Volume Two*, 20–1

Cu Bird

A bird from Mexican folklore the mythical and onomatopoeian named cu bird tells the tale of why the owl comes out at night and how its call originated. Owl, kind and wise, asked the other birds each to make a loan of a feather so Cu would not be cold in the winter. A great collection was made and owl delivered the feathers, sure to tell cu the feathers were hers for the winter only. Cu took great pride in placing in her multi-colored feathers and was so pleased with the results she flew off into the woods calling back she may never return. Owl, who had given his word to the other birds their feathers would be returned, was too ashamed to show his face, so he only comes out at night to search for the larcenous cu, calling out her name, "cu, cu, cu."

Source: Kroll, *Wings and Tales*, 103–05; Nozedar, *Secret Language of Birds*, 37

Cu Sith

Variations: Ce Sith, Cusith, Cu Sìth

Cu Sith is a FAIRY ANIMAL from Scottish Highland folklore described as having huge feet, long and shaggy dark green hair, and a long but coiled-up tail resting on its back. It is different from other fairy dogs which are typically described as being white with red ears, such as the Hounds of Annwn (see ANNWN, HOUNDS OF). Cu sith is as large as a two-year old bull but this monstrous canine whose feet were as broad as a man's chest glided along the earth in near silence, traveling in straight lines. When it hunts unlike other dogs the cu sith does not cry out continuously but rather gives three

sharp barks which could be heard by ships out to sea.

Sources: Briggs, *Encyclopedia of Fairies*, 83; Campbell, *Superstitions of the Highlands and Islands of Scotland*, 141–3; Rosen, *Mythical Creatures Bible*, 114

Cuba

Originating in the lumberjack communities of the developing United States of America, the cuba, one of the FEARSOME CRITTERS, was believed to have been specific to the New England region. The Reverend Samuel Peters in his book *General History of Connecticut* gives an excellent description of the animal's temperament and relationship to its mate but not a hint as to its physical appearance other than being "about as large as a cat." It may be assumed by the reader of his work the cuba is some sort of small rodent as its write-up appears between the woodchuck and the skunk.

The male cuba is highly aggressive and courageous, having four long tusks as sharp as razors it will use without restraint while defending itself. If in the course of action it has the opportunity to kill a dog, it will. The male of the species is devoted to its mate and once it has forged a bond to one, it is unbreakable.

The female cuba is virtually harmless and very peaceable; she uses her temperament to calm and direct her mate's actions. If the female perceives a threat she will alert her mate to defend them but if she later feels the threat too great, she will rush to her mate and cling to its neck crying out her distress; together they will then run off to their burrow.

Source: Peters, *General History of Connecticut*, 183–4; Rose, *Giants, Monsters, and Dragons*, 119

Cubilon

In the country of Grenada it is a popular custom to name one's dog CUBILON, LUBINA, or MELAMPO after one of the three dogs who, according to folkloric belief, accompanied the shepherds to look upon the newborn Christ child at Bethlehem. Tradition claims any dog having one of these names will never go mad (contract rabies).

Source: Bates, *Outlook*, Volume 120, 100; Finch, *Gentleman's Magazine* Volume CCLXXIX, 528

Cuco

Variations: Abuelo ("grandfather"), Calaca ("skeleton"), Chamucho, Chumcho, Coca, Coco, Coco Man, Cuca, Cucui, Cucuy

The cuco is a BOGEYMAN or NURSERY BOGIE found in many Hispanic- and Lusophone-speaking countries. Parents will tell their children if they do not go to sleep the cuco will take them away. There is no consistent description of this FAIRY ANIMAL but traditionally it is represented by a jack-o-lantern, a lantern carved from a pumpkin. The coca, the female version of this creature, is represented as a DRAGON in Galician and Portuguese folklore.

Sources: Herrera-Sobek, *Chicano Folklore*, 223, 226; Landy, *Tropical Childhood*, 34, 129; Maberry, *They Bite*, 337

El Cucuy

A species of BOGEYMAN from Mexican folklore, el cucuy is used by parents to frighten children into good behavior; it is described as being a small creature which hides in closets and under beds. The cucuy can be spotted in the darkness by its glowing red eyes.

Source: Herrera-Sobek, *Celebrating Latino Folklore*, 290; Krensky, *Bogeyman*, 43; Garza, *Creepy Creatures and Other Cucuys*, 1

Cuélebre

Variations: Culebre

A vicious fire-breathing DRAGON from the folklore of the Cantabrian region of northern Spain, Cuélebre ("snake") was described as having a long, sinuous, serpentine body and a set of powerful leathery wings. Cuélebre also had the ability to breathe poisonous gas and was known to prey upon humans. This DRAGON was attracted to gold, jewels, and all things shiny, and managed to collect a massive treasure hoard. In some translations Cuélebre was not an individual DRAGON but rather a rare species of DRAGON with the same description, adding only that they were difficult to find and nearly impossible to slay.

Source: Maberry, *Vampire Universe*, 88–89; Rose, *Giants, Monsters, and Dragons*, 89–90

El Cuelebre

A gigantic winged serpent from Spanish folklore, el cuelebre is said to be the guardian of a great treasure kept hidden in a cave or beneath a waterfall; it is said anyone who discovers the location of the treasure and goes to claim it, never returns.

Source: Rose, *Giants, Monsters, and Dragons*, 89; Zell-Ravenheart, *Wizard's Bestiary*, 32

Cuero

Variations: El Bien Peinado ("smooth-headed one"), Cuero Unudo, Hide, Huecu, Lafquen Trilque, Manta ("blanket"), el Trelquehuecuve

A species of gigantic octopus, the legendary Cuero ("cow hide") had a leathery appearance and was said to live in the freshwater of Lago Lacar in the southern Andes where its strange tracks could be seen on the muddy beach. Unique for an *octopoda* Cuero had clawed hands on the end of each of its tentacles and upon his enormous head was a set of oversized ears covered with eyes. Interestingly, the eyes of this monster have the ability to change size, growing large when it needs to see a great distance away and small when hunting for food in dark places. It is believed Cuero would attack and consume a human, either in the water or on the nearby shore when it crawled upon the beach to sun itself, if the opportunity presented. When it was ready to return to the water, it summoned up a gale storm to wash it back into the water. Any carcass which washed ashore and looked as if it had been torn apart and eaten of was said to be the remains of one of Cuero's kills.

Source: Eberhart, *Mysterious Creatures*, 116–17, Grey, *Mythology of all Races*, Volume 11, 328; Maberry, *Vampire Universe*, 88; Zell-Ravenheart, *Wizard's Bestiary*, 33, 65

Cughtagh

In Scottish folklore the cughtagh is said to be a creature or spirit of sea which occupies the caves along the shore of the Isle of Man; from within, these beings unendingly sing for the sheer joy of it, their song oftentimes barely audible over the crash of the waves surrounding the rocky crags they live within. Shy by nature, the cughtagh was only ever glimpsed during storms, never when the water was calm; however, on those days, if one dared to get near the rocky shore, its breathing may be heard.

Source: Herbert, *Isle of Man*, 183; Mountain, *Celtic Encyclopedia*, Volume 5, 1105

Cwn Annwfn

Variations: Cwn Annwn ("hounds of Annwn," see ANNWN, HOUNDS OF), Cwn Cyrff, Cwn Mamau, Cwn y Wybr ("dogs that haunt the air"), Cwn Wyber, GABRIEL HOUNDS

The cwn annwfn ("the dogs of the In-World"), most often seen on the mountains of Cadair Idris, are the red-eared and white bodied fairy-hounds of the underworld in Welsh fairy mythology (see FAIRY ANIMAL). These hounds specialize in revenge, hunting down those who have overhunted the area or run an animal to death; they will find the guilty party and chase him until he can run no more, only then moving in for the kill.

It is said their bays carry off the mountain at night. The growling of the cwn annwfn is very misleading, as it is at its loudest when they are far off; as they near, the sound decreases as their attack becomes more and more imminent. When not hunting, the cwn annwfn fly through the sky and hover over houses where a death will soon occur, acting like a psychopomp (death omen).

Ownership of the cwn annwfn has fallen to both Bran the Blessed and Gwyn Ap Nudd (the Devil); no matter who they answer to, the pack goes out with their master to partake on the Wild Hunt on the eves of All Saints' Day, Christmas, Good Friday, New Year, Saint Agnes' Day, Saint David's Day, Saint John's Day, Saint Martin's Day, and Saint Michael the ARCHANGEL's Day.

Sources: Hastings, *Encyclopedia of Religion and Ethics*, Part 8, 575; Lindahl, *Medieval Folklore*, 190; Matthews, *Encyclopaedia of Celtic Myth and Legend*, 484; Monaghan, *Encyclopedia of Celtic Mythology and Folklore*, 112

Cyclops (SI-clops), plural, Cyclopes

Variations: Kyclops

One-eyed GIGANTES (a race of beings born of the goddess Gaea) from ancient Greek mythology, the Cyclopes ("one-eyed") was the collective name for the three children born of the Titan Uranus ("heaven") and the Earth, Gaea, who had a single eye in the middle of their forehead; the brothers were individually named Arges ("flashing" or "thunderbolt"), Brontes ("thunder"), and Steropes ("thunder-clouds"). When Zeus (Jupiter) and his siblings waged war against Cronus the Cyclops, identified as storm spirits, they forged the lightning and thunderbolts used by Zeus (Jupiter) and continued to do so after he assumed power and established Olympus. They also forged weapons for the other gods, such as Hades'(Dis) helmet, which went on to become the symbols of their power. Later legends say they worked at Hephaistos (Vulcan)'s forge in Mount Aetna.

In *The Odyssey*, the epic Greek poem attributed to Homer, the greatest of Greek epic poets, the Cyclopes (see CYCLOPS, YOUNGER) were said to be "overbearing and lawless" in addition to being aggressive pastoralists prone to cannibalism. Polyphemus had captured the hero Odysseus and the crew of his ship, but was blinded in his eye when tricked into falling into a drunken stupor and allowed his prisoners to escape. Although Odysseus managed to flee, he earned the eternal hatred of Polyphemus' father, the god of the sea, Poseidon (Neptune).

Source: Cotterell, *Dictionary of World Mythology*, 136–137; Daniels, *Encyclopedia of Superstitions, Folklore, and the Occult Sciences of the World*, 1376; Grimal, *Larousse World Mythology*, 106, 108, Jordan, *Encyclopedia of Gods*, 285

Cyclops, Elder

Variations: Kyklopes, Uranian Cyclopes

From classical Greek mythology, Arges ("flashing" or "thunderbolt"), along with Brontes ("thunder") and Steropes ("thunder-clouds"), are the three elder CYCLOPES, the sons of Uranus ("heaven") and Gaea; each was born exceedingly strong and with a single eye in the middle of their foreheads. They were the siblings of the Hecatoncheires ("Hundred-Handed") and the Titans. Uranus hated his children and banished them to Tartarus but his wife eventually convinced him to release them. The youngest of the Titans, Cronus, revolted against his father; once he defeated Uranus he banished the three CYCLOPES back to Tartarus. The Olympian god Zeus (Jupiter) learned from a prophecy he would not be able to defeat Cronus without the assistance of the three CYCLOPE brothers so he freed them from Tartarus; in return they assisted Zeus (Jupiter) in overthrowing his father and created a great many treasures for the Olympians. The three brothers were slain by the god Apollo because they created the thunderbolt which killed his son, Asclepius.

Source: Daly, *Greek and Roman Mythology, A to Z*, 39–40; Daniels, *Encyclopedia of Superstitions, Folklore, and the Occult Sciences of the World*, 1375–8

Cyclops, Younger

Variations: Kyklopes

In the ancient Greek mythology the younger Cyclopes were, as described by Homer, "overbearing and lawless"; as well as being highly territorial herdsmen, these younger Cyclopes were also cannibals and lived apart from ordered law and religion in a region which had never been settled by humans or plowed in any fashion. These newer generation of CYCLOPES were gigantic, nomadic barbarians who raised goats.

Source: Daly, *Greek and Roman Mythology, A to Z*, 40; Homer, *Eight Books of Homer's Odyssey*, 60–61; Roman, *Encyclopedia of Greek and Roman Mythology*, 125–26

Cyllaros

Variations: Cillaros, Cyll'aros, Cyprian

A prized horse from ancient Greek mythology, Cyllaros, one of the HIPPOI ATHANATOI, has uncertain ownership; the ancient Roman poet Virgil assigns him to Pollux who named him after Cylla in Troas, but according to Ovid, another poet of ancient Rome, it was Castor's steed. Claudian the Latin poet and Seneca, the Roman dramatist, statesman, and Stoic philosopher, give Cyllaros to Pollux's brother, Castor. No matter his owner, Cyllaros and his stablemate HARPAGOS, the horse from Harpagium in Phrygia, common to both brothers, were each alleged to be immortal. Cyllaros was described as being coal black with a gleaming coat.

Source: Brewer, *Wordsworth Dictionary of Phrase and Fable*, 313; Room, *Naming of Animals*, 134; Tozer, *Horse in History*, 99

Cyllarus

According to Ovid's *Metamorphoses*, Cyllarus and HYLONOME were a young CENTAUR couple who were deeply in love. Cyllarus was described as being the most handsome of his species, having long blond hair and a matching beard. During the battle which takes place at the wedding of Pirithous to Hippodame, Cyllarus and HYLONOME fought bravely side-by-side. During the Centauromachy, a spear lands directly in Cyllarus' chest, and although it is a small wound, it pierces his heart. As he lies dying HYLONOME rushes to his side and presses her lips against the wound to keep his soul from escaping his body, but sadly, she is too late. After muttering something unheard by anyone and therefore unrecorded, she uses the spear to kill herself, collapsing into his arms.

Source: *Commentary, Mythological, Historical, and Geographical on Pope's Homer*, 55; Simpson, *Metamorphoses of Ovid*, 206

Cyllarus, horse

In Greek mythology, Cyllarus was a magnificent horse given as a gift by the goddess Hera (Juno) to Pollux, the twin brother of the skilled equestrian Castor. Hera had been given the horse as gift from Poseidon (Neptune).

Source: Simpson, *Guidebook to the Constellations*, 100; Virgil, *Georgics*, Volume 2, 55

Cymelus

Variations: Kymelos

A CENTAUR from ancient Greek mythology, Cymelus was one of the CENTAURS slain by the demi-god and cultural hero Hercules (Heracles) while visiting his friend, a CENTAUR named PHOLUS, between the conclusion of his third Labor and the onset of his fourth.

Source: *Commentary, Mythological, Historical, and Geographical on Pope's Homer*, 55; Simpson, *Metamorphoses of Ovid*, 204

Cynoprosopi

Similar to the YING-LONG of China, the cynoprosopi from Mediterranean folklore is described as having the winged, fur-covered body of a DRAGON but the head of a dog with a profuse beard. These creatures communicate with one another through hissing and sharp calls as they prey upon the antelopes and goats of the northern Saharan desert.

Source: De Kirk, *Dragonlore*, 35; Rose, *Giants, Monsters, and Dragons*, 92; Zell-Ravenheart, *Wizard's Bestiary*, 33

Cyprius

A dog from ancient Greek mythology Cyprius was one of the DOGS OF ACTÆON, the unfortunate youth who was raised by the CENTAUR CHEIRON.

Source: Leeming, *World of Myth*, 111; Murray, *Classical Manual Being a Mythological, Historical, and Geographical Commentary on Pope's Homer, and Dryden's Aeneid of Virgil*, 160

Da

Variations: The Rainbow Snake

In the kingdom formerly known as Dahomey ("the womb of Da") which thrived from the sixteenth through nineteenth centuries, Da was a cosmic rainbow serpent in the mythology of the Fon people; they claimed to be able to see a glimpse of him whenever there was a rainbow in the sky or a sheen of iridescence in the water. Da was described as being both male and female, as he was red from his nose to his midsection and then faded into a blue which ran to the end of his tail; however he was also able to change his hue according to the time of day.

Within the seven-thousand coils of Da were the primordial oceans; the waves were made by the undulation of its body; his breath supported the heavens. He has 3,500 coils above the earth and the same number beneath it. The earth was created as Da carried the god Mawu across the universe; as the pair rested, Da's excrement created the mountains and when he moved, created the earth. Currently, Da is said to be supporting the four pillars of the earth, one at each of the cardinal points.

Source: Avant, *Mythological Reference*, 12; Cotterell, *Dictionary of World Mythology*, 249; Rose, *Giants, Monsters, and Dragons*, 93

Dabbatu 'L-Arz

A monster which will, according to the mythology of Islam, rise up from the mountain of Sufah and call out to the people of the planet saying they had not believed in the revelations of God. When Dabbatu 'L-Arz ("reptile of the earth") arrives it will be holding the staff of Moses and the Seal of Solomon. With the staff it will point out the non-believers and with the seal it will leave a mark on their face which shows them to be an infidel. The appearance of Dabbatu 'L-Arz is the third sign of the coming resurrection; it is also the second beast mentioned in the book of Revelations from the Christian New Testament.

Source: Balfour, *Cyclopædia of India and of Eastern and Southern Asia, Commercial, Industrial and Scientific*, Volume 1, 872; Hughes, *Dictionary of Islam*, 64

Dadhikra

Variations: Dadhikravan

In Hindu mythology Dadhikra ("scattering cured milk") was one of the noted celestial winged horses said to assist in pulling the sun across the sky. Swift as the wind, he is the first horse at the head of the chariot; he is often compared to an eagle in his speed, strength of wing, and swooping. When he runs along the ground he can navigate perfectly along a precipice at top speed, making sharp turns and jumps. Dadhikra is often associated with the deity Usas.

Source: Macdonell, *Vedic Mythology*, 148–49; Rose, *Giants, Monsters, and Dragons*, 178; Zell-Ravenheart, *Wizard's Bestiary*, 34, 147

Dagwanoenyent

Variations: Dagwano'ĕñ'iĕn, Flying Heads, Hatdedases

Dagwanoenyent ("what habitually hits or knocks our heads") are flying NATURE SPIRITS from the mythology of the Seneca people of North America, one of the five Iroquois tribes; they are the personification of the cyclone or whirlwind. These creatures have voracious appetites and will eat anything when they are hungry, even rocks; when they do, the crunching sound of it can be heard for miles. Sometimes Dagwanoenyent are portrayed in stories as a singular individual, an elderly female witch.

Source: Avant, *Mythological Reference*, 36; Hewitt, *Seneca Fiction, Legends, and Myths*, 85, 800; Maberry, *Cryptopedia*, 56

Dahdahwat

The dahdahwat are a class of creatures from the mythology of the Seneca people, United States of America. According to the stories, these creatures bit and pursued the cultural hero Ganyadjigowa until he died; they were also responsible for the death of Shodieonskon. The dahdahwat appear in various forms, depending on the story.

Source: Curtin, *Seneca Fiction, Legends, and Myths*, 239, 244; Rose, *Giants, Monsters, and Dragons*, 93

Dahdk

Variations: Dahhak

The Zoroastrian mythology, the Avesta, describes Dahdk as a three-headed, three-mouthed, and six-eyed DRAGON chief among those Ahriman created with the destruction of the world in mind. Although Dahdk is immortal and cannot be slain, the hero Threatona was able to defeat it in combat, chaining it beneath a mountain. According to prophecy, in the final day of the Earth, Dahdk will finally break free of his prison and cause devastating damage worldwide.

Source: Brewer, *Reader's Handbook of Allusions, References, Plots and Stories*, 271; Rose, *Giants, Monsters, and Dragons*, 93

Dahu

In French folklore the dahu is the creature who is often the prey in a pratical joke. Similar to the snipe of the American snipe-hunt, someone is taken into the woods at night with a baton, a lantern, and a sack to hunt a dahu. The companions say they are moving ahead to drive the dahu, but in fact they are abandoning their companion. The dahu is described as a lacertilian (lizard-like) creature with legs shorter on one side of its body than the other to better enable it to move through the mountains. In Northern England and Scotland a similar creature is called Haggis.

Source: Brunvand, *American Folklore*, 831; Facaros, *Northern Spain*, 131

Dain (DAH-in)

Variations: Daain, Dainn, Dáinn

Dain ("dead one") was one of the harts (male Red Deer) or stags named in Thorgrimr's *Rhymes* in Snorri Sturluson's (1179–1241) *Prose Edda*; the other stags were DUNEYR, DURATHROR, and DVALIN. The stags all lived in the branches of the World Tree, Ygdrasil, eating its branches and leaves. It was from the antlers of these animals honey-dew fell to the earth and supplied the water for all of the rivers of the world.

Source: Daly, *Norse Mythology A to Z*, 19; Guerber, *Hammer of Thor*, 9; Jennbert, *Animals and Humans*, 50

Daitengu

Variations: Dai Tengu

In Japanese mythology the daitengu are the most powerful class of TENGU; each one of them lives on its own mountain. These creatures are generally considered to be demons, but they are not all evil or even evil by nature; rather they are sought out by heroes and scholars who wish to be taken in as students and taught forgotten knowledge, legendary skills such as stamina or swordsmanship, to receive magical amulets, spells, or weapons.

The king of the TENGU is SOJOBO, who lived upon Mount Kurama and is often depicted in art as riding upon a boar.

Source: Ashkenazi, *Handbook of Japanese Mythology*, 97, 271; Ball, *Animal Motifs in Asian Art*, 127

Daldah

Variations: FADDA

According to Muslim folklore, Daldah was the name of the Prophet Muhammad's favorite white mule; he performed some of his miracles while astride it, such as the falling of a palm date when Daldah was hungry and the sudden production of milk from a dry goat.

Source: Brewer, *Reader's Handbook of Allusions, References, Plots and Stories*, 288; Reading, *Complete Prophecies of Nostradamus*, 110

Dama Dagenda

In the mythology of the Huli people of Papua New Guinea, the dama dagenda are a species of NATURE SPIRIT which create nose bleeds and painful open sores on the bodies of anyone who invades their territory. The only known means by which one may protect oneself from their attack is to have a shaman teach you a language the dama dagenda do not know and then, using it, speak to yourself as you traverse their terrain.

Sources: Chopra, *Academic Dictionary*, 79; Page, *Encyclopedia of Things That Never Were*, 58; Parratt, *Papuan Belief and Ritual*, 7

Daphnis

In classical Greek mythology, Daphnis was one of the CENTAURS slain by the demi-god and cultural hero Hercules (Heracles) while visiting his friend, a CENTAUR named PHOLUS, between the conclusion of his third Labor and the onset of his fourth. When an old and particularly fragrant hogshead of wine was opened its aroma carried on the air and drove the local CENTAURS into a fury. Daphnis, ARGEIUS, AMPHION, DUPO, HIPPOTION, ISOPLES, MELANCHETES, OREUS, PHRIXUS, and THEREUS were slain by Hercules (Heracles) as he defended himself from their violent and unwarranted assault.

Source: Barthell, *Gods and Goddesses of Ancient Greece*, 187; Diodorus, *Historical Library of Diodorus the Sicilian*, Volume 1, 229–30

Dard

Variations: Cat-Headed Snake

A chimerical lizard from western European folklore, the dard ("forked tongue") is described as having a catlike head and a horse-like mane running the length of its back. The four-legged dard has a short tail, similar to a viper.

Source: Eberhart, *Mysterious Creatures*, 121; Meurger, *Lake Monster Traditions*, 266; Rose, *Giants, Monsters, and Dragons*, 94

Dea

Variations: Stellio, Stellione

A species of reptilian creature with a weasel's head which appeared in an English bestiary dating from 1220, the dea was described as looking like a SALAMANDER and capable of consuming fire. It was believed the dea was so deadly to scorpions the sight of one was enough to paralyze it with fear.

Source: Barber, *Bestiary*, 117, 140; Rose, *Giants, Monsters, and Dragons*, 95; Zell-Ravenheart, *Wizard's Bestiary*, 34, 91

Death Worm

Variations: Allergorhai Horhai ("bloodfilled intestine worm"), Allghoi Khorkhoi ("intestine worm"), Olgoj Chorchoj, Mongolian Death Worm, Shar Khorkhoi

In the Gobi Desert of Mongolia there is, according to folklore, a large, bright red, wormlike creature living beneath the sands known as the death worm. Not only has it been reported killing people by squirting or spitting its corrosive venom but this animal is so toxic to touch it is fatal, even if the touch is indirect. Reports claim those who have struck the death worm with a weapon have died from its venom which traveled through the weapon and into the person, killing them; additionally, the weapon is destroyed in the process.

The death worm is described as being between two and six feet long, as thick as a man's arm, and having no discernable eyes, nostrils, or mouth. Its tail is not tapered but rather ends abruptly, as if it were cut off. The skin of this creature is blood-red and looks much like cattle intestines. The death worm spends most of its life underground asleep, only coming to the surface during the hottest months of the year, June and July, and only after a rain when the ground is wet. It moves by undulating its body and rolling about with little grace. When it has been sighted it has been in hot, desolate valleys where the saxaul plant grows.

Source: Budd, *Weiser Field Guide to Cryptozoology*, 17–20; Eberhart, *Mysterious Creatures*, 350; Shuker, *Beasts That Hide from Man*, 23–24, 26; Zell-Ravenheart, *Wizard's Bestiary*, 69

Deerhurst Dragon

Variations: Dragon of Deerhurst

A large and venomous DRAGON from British folklore the Deerhurst DRAGON was said to plague the people of Deerhurst near Tewkesbury, England, by killing their cattle and poisoning the people with its breath. The people petitioned the king to rid the land of the monster and a royal title was offered as well as the estate on Walton Hill to anyone who could slay it. A blacksmith by the name of John Smith placed a large quantity of milk in an area he knew the DRAGON frequented and waited until the monster consumed the milk, grew sleepy, and lay down in a patch of sunlight to nap and rest. While it was asleep with its scales ruffled up, Smith approached and cut off the DRAGON's head with an ax.

Source: Ingersoll, *Dragons and Dragon Lore*, 151; Walford, *Antiquary*, Volume 38, 140–41

Deimos

One of the fire-breathing horses from the mythology of the ancient Romans, Deimos ("affright") belonged to Ares (Mars), the god of war; his stable mates were AITHON ("fire"), CONABOS ("tumult"), PHLOGIOS ("flame"), and PHOBOS ("terror").

Source: *Contemporary Review*, Volume 27, 809; Dixon-Kennedy, *Encyclopedia of Greco-Roman Mythology*, 199

Delgeth

A species of primordial and predatory anthropophagous (man-eating) antelope from Navajo folklore, the delgeth were hunted down and slain to the last by the cultural heroes, the twins Nagenatzani and Tjhobadesstchin.

Source: Dixon-Kennedy, *Native American Myth and Legend*, 23; Monaghan, *Encyclopedia of Goddesses and Heroines*, 36; Rose, *Giants, Monsters, and Dragons*, 95

Delphinus

Variations: Delphin, Delphinos

A dolphin from ancient Greek mythology Delphinus ("dolphin") was chosen by the god of the sea, Poseidon (Neptune), to go to Nereus and plead his suit for permission to marry his daughter Amphitrite; Nereus consented and in gratitude the god transferred the animal into the constellation which now bears his name.

In another tale of Delphinus, when the poet Arion dove off a ship at sea to avoid being raped, robbed, and murdered by the sailors, the animal carried him safely to shore before the ship could reach the harbor. This gave Arion enough time to report the offense to the authorities who met the vessel as it came into port. As a reward the gods took Delphinus up into the heavens and transformed him into a constellation.

Source: Condos, *Star Myths of the Greeks and Romans*, 107; Dixon-Kennedy, *Encyclopedia of Greco-Roman Mythology*, 107

Delphyne

Variations: Delphyyna, Drakaina, Python

In ancient Greek mythology Delphyne ("womb") was a beardless, female DRAKAINA born the daughter of Gaea and Tartarus who, according to the ancient Greek historian and mythographer Apollodorus, was the guardian of the tendons stolen by Typhoeus from the body of the god Zeus (Jupiter). She is described by Apollodorus as having the upper body of a woman but the lower half of a gigantic serpent. The tendons were wrapped in bearskin and hidden in her Corycian cave until Aegipan and Hermes managed to sneak in unobserved and escape with the tendons. When the god Apollo assumed power over Delphi, the people pleaded with him to slay Delphyne as she had been terrorizing the land and consuming their herds. He eventually slew her with his poisonous arrows.

Source: Apollodorus, *Apollodorus: The Library*, Volume 1, 49; Ogden, *Dragons, Serpents, and Slayers in the Classical and Early Christian Worlds*, 41; Westmoreland, *Ancient Greek Beliefs*, 717

Demoleon

A CENTAUR from ancient Greek mythology, Demoleon was, according to Ovid's *Metamorphoses*, one of the CENTAURS who attended the wedding of Pirithous, became drunk on wine and following the lead of EURYTUS, who assaulted Hippodame, began to assault and rape any women they could grab. During the Centauromachy, Demoleon could no longer tolerate how successful Theseus was in battle against his comrades and in a rage attempted to uproot an ancient pine tree. Unable to do so, he did manage to break off the top portion of the tree and throw it, spear-like, at the hero. Warned by Pallas, Theseus dodged the missile and let it strike Crantor, shearing his head and chest off of his body.

Source: *Commentary, Mythological, Historical, and Geographical on Pope's Homer*, 55; Simpson, *Metamorphoses of Ovid*, 206

Dendan

A gigantic, black scaled fish from Arabic folklore, the dendan were said to be fierce but would die if they came into any contact with a human; even hearing the sound of a person's voice was fatal to them. In the story *The Thousand and One Nights*, it was said a dendan was large enough to eat a camel or an elephant in a single bite and the liver-fat of this fish was similar to beef fat, yellow and sweet.

Source: Poole, *Thousand and One Nights*, 631; Zell-Ravenheart, *Wizard's Bestiary*, 34

Derketo

Variations: Atargatis, Ceto, Dercetis, Derceto

In the mythology of ancient Babylonia and Mesopotamia Derketo was described as a whale with the forequarters of a DRAGON; it was created by the goddess Ishtar and caused a great flood which covered the earth. As Atargatis, Derketo is worshiped as a goddess of vegetation and moisture.

Source: Monaghan, *New Book of Goddesses and Heroines*, 33; Rose, *Giants, Monsters, and Dragons*, 96

Dev

Variations: Devi, Divs (Div), Drauga, DRUJ, Durugh

In Persian mythology a dev is a demon (DJINN) of war. They were created by ANGRA MAINYU, are immoral and ruthless, and intended to be the counterparts to the Amesha Spentas.

In present day Armenia, a dev is described as a gigantic being with an oversized head and eyes as large as bowls; some of them have only one eye but traditionally they had up to seven heads.

Source: Ananikean, *Armenian Mythology*, 101; Blavatsky, *Isis Unveiled*, 482; Ford, *Luciferian Witchcraft*, 288; Turner, *Dictionary of Ancient Deties*, 147–8

Devalpa

In Arabic folklore the devalpa is described as appearing as a decrepit and pathetic looking old man who is standing on the side of the road, deeply sighing sadly to himself. He will ask those who pass by to carry him on their shoulders; if anyone should comply, once he is seated, numerous serpentine legs suddenly erupt out from his abdomen and entwine around the body of his would-be helper demanding they work for him. The only way to be rid of this creature is to trick it into drinking copious amounts of wine. Once it passes out, the devalpa can be shrugged off.

Source: Cronin, *Last Migration*, 201; Mack, *Field Guide to Demons, Vampires, Fallen Angels, and Other Subversive Spirits*, 162–63

Devil-Bird

Variations: Ulama

In the folklore of Sri-Lanka the devil-bird was a species of bird, seldom seen but often heard, which came into being when, according to the lore, a man killed his own child because he was dubious of its parentage; he then used the remains of the child to make curry. The mother discovered what her husband had done while she was eating the curry and transformed instantly into the devil-bird making a cry of grief which sounds exactly like "a boy in torture whose screams are being strangled into silence."

Source: Eberhart, *Mysterious Creatures*, 126; Newton, *Hidden Animals*, 104; Shuler, *From Flying Toads to Snakes with Wings*, 104

Devil Whale

Variations: Jasconius, Teufelwal, Trol, Zaratan

According to Conrad Gessner, a Swiss bibliographer, botanist, classical linguist, naturalist, and physician, the devil whale was a sea creature (see SEA SERPENT) so gigantic, when it slept adrift on surface of the ocean it resembled an island. Because of its size, this creature was not particularly inclined to move when sailors would anchor to it and take leave atop its back; it was only when a fire was lit upon it did the devil whale wake up and begin to submerge. This story, or one very similar to it, is told in the first tale of Sindbad the Sailor as well as by the sixth-century figure Saint Brendan and his seventeen monk companions.

Source: Ashton, *Curious Creatures in Zoology*, 217–18; Heuvelmans, *Kraken and the Colossal Octopus*, 91; Mackley, *Legend of St. Brendan*, 107

Dew Mink

Originating in the lumberjack communities of the developing United States of America, the dew mink, one of the FEARSOME CRITTERS, was described in *General History of Connecticut* as being a species of black and white birds about the size of an English robin whose flesh was delicious. This bird was onomatopoeically named because the sound of its cry resembled the words "dew mink."

Source: Peters, *General History of Connecticut*, 186; Rose, *Giants, Monsters, and Dragons*, 96

Dexamenus

Variations: Dexamenos

In Greek mythology Dexamenus ("the hospitable"), a CENTAUR, was the king of Olenus and the father of the Deianeira (Mnesimache), a woman whom the godling and hero Hercules (Heracles) had fallen in love with while staying with the royal family. Hercules promised to marry Deianeira when he returned, but during his absence the CENTAUR EURYTION sued for the maiden's hand; out of fear, Dexamenus consented to the match. On the day of the wedding Hercules returned and in his anger, slew EURYTION.

Source: Apollodorus, *Apollodorus: The Library*, Volume 1, 197; Grant, *Who's who in Classical Mythology*, 174; Smith, *Dictionary of Greek and Roman Biography and Mythology*, 995

Dhakhan

In the mythology of the Kabi people of the Queensland coast of northwestern Australia the dhakhan is described as being a gigantic serpent with the tail of a fish; it is glimpsed on occasion in the sky as a rainbow, as this is the method of how it moves from one waterhole to the next.

Source: Rose, *Spirits, Fairies, Leprechauns, and Goblins, an Encyclopedia*, 96

Dhananjaya

The legendary NAGARAJA of Indraprastha ("city of Indra") from Hindu mythology, Dhananjaya was renowned for his skill in gambling.

Source: Vogel, *Indian Serpent-Lore*, 144, 191, 295

Dhembesuta

A deaf and enfeebled mare from Albanian folklore, the archetypal dhembesuta ("tooth hind") is ridden in tales to escape from danger.

Source: Elsie, *Dictionary of Albanian Religion, Mythology, and Folk Culture*, 69

Dhinnabarrada

A monstrous tribe of people from the folklore of the Kamilaroi peoples of Australia, the Dhinnabarrada were described as having the body of a man but the legs and feet of an emu. Never moving any-where alone but always in at least a small group, the Dhinnabarrada sustained themselves on grubs and made boomerangs from the wood of the gidyer tree.

Source: Rose, *Giants, Monsters, and Dragons*, 97; Woodgate, *Kamilaroi and Assimilation*, 59

Dhrana

An extremely large seven-headed HYDRA of Indian myth, Dhrana is the king of the serpents as well as the guardian of the god Parsva. Dhrana was the successor of King KALIYA.

Source: De Kirk, *Dragonlore*, 35; Rose, *Giants, Monsters, and Dragons*, 98

Dhritarashtra

Variations: The Blind King of KAURAVYAS

A NAGARAJA from Hindu mythology, Dhri-tarashtra was the first of all the NAGAS, the brother of Iravata, and the father of the Kaurava princes; he was said to have lived in the country of Kosala, a region well known for its numerous snakes.

Source: Royal Asiatic Society of Great Britain and Ireland, *Journal of the Royal Asiatic Society of Great Britain and Ireland*, Volume 21, 291; Vogel, *Indian Serpent-Lore*, 191

Dhuldul

In Muslim folklore Dhuldul was the "peerless" horse of Ali, the son-in-law of the prophet Mohammed.

Source: Brewer, *Dictionary of Phrase and Fable*, 626; Tozer, *Horse in History*, 87

Dhumarna

A NAGA from Hindu mythology, Dhumarna ("smoke colored") is said to be the king of the SEA SERPENTS.

Source: Zell-Ravenheart, *Wizard's Bestiary*, 34

Di-Di

Variations: Dai-Dai, Didi-Aguiri, Dru-Didi

On the northern coast of South America, in British Guyana (Guiana), there is the folkloric belief of a species of hairy simian-like (monkey-like) humanoids known as the di-di which are feared although very seldom seen. Legend says these crea-tures are covered with brown fur and live in pairs. Killing one is very dangerous, as its mate is said to be naturally vengeful and will stalk out its spouse's killer and strangle them one night while they sleep.

Source: Eberhart, *Mysterious Creatures*, 131; Sanderson, *Abominable Snowmen*, 180–81; Zell-Ravenheart, *Wizard's Bestiary*, 35

Dictys (dic-tiss)

A CENTAUR from ancient Greek mythology, Dic-tys was, according to Ovid's *Metamorphoses*, one of the CENTAURS who attended the wedding of Pirit-hous, became drunk on wine and following the lead of EURYTUS, who assaulted Hippodame, began to assault and rape any women they could grab. Dur-ing the ensuing Centauromachy, while running in terror from Pirithous, Dictys slipped and fell from a cliff and struck an ancient ash tree, impaling him-self.

Source: Berens, *Myths and Legends of Ancient Greece and Rome*, 205; *Commentary, Mythological, Historical, and Geo-graphical on Pope's Homer*, 55; Simpson, *Metamorphoses of Ovid*, 206

El Dientudo

From the folklore of Buenos Aries, Argentina, it is said in the dense forest lives a dark-furred humanoid standing approximately seven feet tall called el dientudo ("big teeth"). Smelling of rotting flesh, this creature is seen dragging people off into the woods leaving little behind but bloodied clothes and bits of broken bone.

Source: Eberhart, *Mysterious Creatures*, 132; Maberry, *Vampire Universe*, 107–08

Dig-Gajas

Variations: Ashtadiggajas, Diggajas, Dik-Gajas, Lokapala Elephants

In Hindu mythology and post–Vedic legend, dig-gajas ("space elephants") is the collective name for the eight cardinal elephants and their respective mates protecting the eight points of the compass or *lokapala*; upon the back of each elephant is a corre-sponding god. The pachyderms are: AIRAVAT (east) and his mate Abhramu with the god Indra; ANJANA (west) and his mate Anjanā with the god Varuna; KUMUDA (southwest) and his mate Anupama with the god Surya; PUNDARIKA (southeast) and his mate Kapila with the god Yama; PUSHPA-DANTA (northwest) and his mate Anjanavati with the god Vayu; SARVA-BHAUMA (north) and his mate Tam-rakarna with the god Kubera; SU-PRATIKA (north-east) and his mate Subhadanti with the god Prthivi; VAMANA (south) and his mate Pingala with an unspecified god.

The dig-gajas also simultaneously support the four quarters of the universe as well as the four points in-between. These symbols of protection, stability, and strength were born of the two halves of the cosmic golden egg, Hiranyagarbha, which hatched the sun. The dig-gajas stand upon the shelled back of the cosmic turtle AKUPARA.

Source: Dalal, *Hinduism*, 43; Dowson, *Classical Dictionary of Hindu Mythology and Religion, Geography, History, and Lit-erature*, 92, 180; Gupta, *Elephant in Indian Art and Mythology*, 7; Zimmer, *Myths and Symbols in Indian Art and Civilization*, 105; Zell-Ravenheart, *Wizard's Bestiary*, 62

Dilipa

A NAGARAJA from Hindu mythology, Dilipa is one of the many NAGAS mentioned only by name in Vedic mythology.

Source: Hopkins, *Epic Mythology*, 24; Vogel, *Indian Serpent-Lore*, 191

Dilong

In Chinese mythology the dilong are one of the four different classifications of DRAGONS; they are the earth DRAGONS, they marked out the course of rivers and streams, and are the rulers of the ocean. Dilong ("earth DRAGON") are described as being massive, yellow-colored, and hornless, with the body of a lion but having a humanoid face. Living beneath the surface of the earth, the dilong's movements cause earthquakes and were responsible for the creation of the rapids known as DRAGON's Gate. In autumn, they live beneath the sea.

Source: Forbes, *Illustrated Book of Dragons and Dragon Lore*, n.pag.; Giddens, *Chinese Mythology*, 48; Rosen, *Mythical Creatures Bible*, 63

Ding Ball

Originating in the lumberjack communities of the developing United States of America, the ding ball, one of the FEARSOME CRITTERS, is a large feline, similar to a panther, except it has a mace-like tail it uses to smash in the skulls of its human victims. It lures it prey into dark places with its alluring SIREN-like song.

Source: Dorson, *Man and Beast in American Comic Legend*, 11; Rose, *Giants, Monsters, and Dragons*, 119

Dinos (di-nos)

Variations: Deinos ("the terrible")

In classical Greek mythology, Dinos ("dreadful" or "the marvel") was one of the four MARES OF DIOMEDES, King of Aetolia (or the GIGANTE Diomedes, sources conflict; see LAMPON, PHOLGIOS, and XANTHOS), which made up his chariot team. Although the horses are female, the Latin author Hyginus (64 BC–AD 17), the only author who ever named them, gave them all masculine names. In his eighth Labor the demi-god Hercules (Heracles) was charged with the capture and return of theses savage mares which pulled the chariot of the king and were fed a diet of human flesh.

Source: Brewer, *Dictionary of Phrase and Fable*, 419; Hard, *Routledge Handbook of Greek Mythology* 262; Ruthven, *Shaman Pathways*, n.pag.; Webster, *Historic Magazine and Notes and Queries*, 581

Dip

In Catalonian mythology, Dip is a HELLHOUND, a hairy, injurious, blood-drinking doglike creature similar to the BLACK DOGS of the British Isles. Like many evil beings, he is lame in one leg.

Source: Maberry, *They Bite*, 145

Dipsa

Variations: Situla ("bucket")

According to the Greek folklore and the poet Lucan, the dipsa is a serpent so small it is not seen when it is stepped upon and its body is completely destroyed but not before it is able to deliver its fatal bite. The venom of this snake acts so fast it was believed the person died before they ever felt the pain of the bite or the reaction of the poison. However, there is also the belief, as per the Aesopic fable, that the bite of the dipsa causes the victim to die with a terrible thirst.

Source: Clark, *Medieval Book of Beasts*, 198; White, *Book of Beasts*, 181; Zell-Ravenheart, *Wizard's Bestiary*, 35

Direach

Variations: Direach Ghlinn Eitidh, Dithreach, Fachan

The direach was an ATHACH, a type of FAIRY ANIMAL living in the Highlands of Scotland in Glen of Eiti near Ballachulish. This creature was described as having one eye, one leg, one hand, and an arm coming directly out of its chest; its head had random tufts of wiry hair.

Source: Briggs, *Encyclopedia of Fairies*, 102–3; Monaghan, *Encyclopedia of Celtic Mythology and Folklore*, 166; Rose, *Giants, Monsters and Dragon*, 99

Dismal Sauger

Originating in the lumberjack communities of the developing United States of America, the dismal sauger, one of the FEARSOME CRITTERS, was said to live in forest swamps; by nature, the creatures are silent but the constant drip-drip-drip of water droplets off of their bearded chin is enough to make a man go insane. It is said they are cousins to the HAPPY AUGER.

Source: Beath, *Febold Feboldson*, 83; Rose, *Giants, Monsters, and Dragons*, 119

Div, plural: divs (deo, deu, or dive)

Variations: Daivres, Devas

From the demonology of ancient Persia and in Zoroastrian mythology comes a species of demonic KHRAFSTRA known as the div; the word translates from ancient Iranian to mean "false god." Under the command of Aherman these demons prey upon animals, crops, man, and plants. Divs have the power of therianthropy enabling them to shapeshift into devils, GIANTs, OGREs, snakes, and other various forms. Female divs are known as perris; however, male divs are considered to be the more dangerous and evil of the two genders. All divs are subject to human frailties and weaknesses.

Divs live high up in the mountains in caves but can also be found wandering in the desert. Their capital city, Ahermanabad, is located on Mount Kaf. The god Mithra is their personal adversary.

Source: Spence, *Encyclopedia of Occultism*, 129; Turner, *Dictionary of Ancient Deties*, 147; Yadav, *Global Encyclopaedia of Education*, 513

Diwe

A group of anthropophagous KHRAFSTRA and monsters in Iranian folklore, the diwe were described as being gigantic and horned, and hunted and devoured any human who wandered into their territory.

Source: Lurker, *Dictionary of Gods and Goddesses, Devils and Demons*, 52; Rose, *Giants, Monsters, and Dragons*, 99; Zell-Ravenheart, *Wizard's Bestiary*, 35

Djieien

In the folklore of the Seneca people of the northeastern United States of America, Djieien ("spider") was a fierce spider as large as a man is tall; it attacked with reckless abandon because it could not suffer a fatal wound as it hid its heart in a secret place underground. The hero and warrior Othegwenhda, who was half human and half spirit, discovered the location of Djieien's heart and destroyed it.

Source: Curtin, *Seneca Fiction, Legends, and Myths*, 379–81; Maberry, *Vampire Universe*, 96–97; Rose, *Giants, Monsters, and Dragons*, 99; Zell-Ravenheart, *Wizard's Bestiary*, 35

Dobhar-chu

Variations: Anchu, Dhuraghoo, Dobarcu ("master otter"), Dorraghow, Dorraghowor, Doyarchu ("water dog"), King of all the Lakes, King Otter

A type of animal from Irish folklore, the vicious dobhar-chu ("water hound") was believed to have innate magical properties; for instance, a one-inch strip of its pelt was kept as a means to prevent a horse from injury, a man being injured by gunshot, and a ship from wrecking. The dobhar-chu, said to never sleep, are described as being much larger than other otters, gigantic by comparison, and completely white except for the tips of their ears and across their backs, both of which are jet black. It is interesting to note the dobhar-chu can only be killed by being shot with a silver bullet but also its assassin will then himself die within twenty-four hours. In folklore it has been said the dobhar-chu has killed people as well as horses and even to see one in the wild is enough to cause a person to die.

Source: Coleman, *Cryptozoology A to Z*, 79–81; Ho, *Mysteries Unwrapped*, 25; Shuker, *Beasts That Hide from Man*, 11–14; Zell-Ravenheart, *Wizard's Bestiary*, 35, 57

Dog Husband

A legend of the Quinault people of the Pacific Northwest coast tells the tale of the Dog Husband and the difference of ethnic cultures and races. A girl, the daughter of a chief, was not able to be happily married to any of the men in her village; while her father chastised her for this one day the family's white dog took her as its wife. When the girl became pregnant the father tied the dog up and took his daughter to an island where she could deliver the baby without anyone knowing. The girl gave birth to a litter of male puppies and her father would bring her and his grandchildren food. The dog never stopped looking for his wife and children but one day followed the grandfather and discovered where his family was. The grandfather became angry and killed the white dog. When the daughter discovered what had happened she instructed her children to kill their grandfather; as the boys were no longer pups but nearly grown dogs, they made quick work of their father's murderer. Over the years they hunted elk and fish and fed themselves and their mother. The boys could shape-shift into young men and the mother transformed into a dog. The boys took wives and had many children and when their little island became too populated they moved just across the water to the mainland where they built a village to live which is known now as Nash Harbor Village.

Source: Bastian, *Handbook of Native American Mythology*, 88–9; Zirkle, *Early History of the Idea of the Inheritance of Acquired Characters and of Pangenesis*, 267–68

Dog of Tobit

One of the ten animals allowed to enter into Paradise in Muslim mythology, the unnamed dog of Tobit was the only domestic dog mentioned in the Apocrypha scriptures. Of the ten animals admitted into Paradise, two of them are dogs; the other canine, KATMIR, is the dog of the Seven Sleepers.

Source: Brewer, *Dictionary of Phrase and Fable*, 205; Finch, *Gentleman's Magazine* Volume CCLXXIX, 528

Dogai

In the mythology of the people of the Torres Strait Islands, the dogai is said to be a female, witch-like creature of sub-human intelligence yet charming and shrewd. Living in stone, trees, or underground, the long-eared and sharp-featured dogai were always on the lookout for a human man to kidnap and keep as its husband. Most dogai were evil by nature and all of them had the ability to impersonate a living woman; their language was a gibberish version of the Islanders' native tongue.

Source: Monaghan, *New Book of Goddesses and Heroines*,

148–49; Ragan, *Fearless Girls, Wise Women, and Beloved Sisters*, 299

Dogs of Actæon

In classical Greek mythology, Actæon was raised by the CENTAUR CHEIRON to be a hunter and warrior but unfortunately in the prime of his youth came upon the virgin goddess Artemis (Diana) bathing in a pool on Mount Cithaeron. In her anger, either for having been seen in the nude or for his having bragged for having seen her in the nude, she transformed the young man into a stag. As Actæon fled, his pack of hunting dogs gave chase and when they caught him, ripped him apart.

The names of the dogs, some of which were named after other ancient Greek creatures, were: AELLO, AGRE, AGRIODUS, ALCE, ASBOLUS, CANACHE, CYPRIUS, DOORGA, DORCEUS, DROMAS, HARPALUS, HARPYES, HYLACTOR, HYLEUS, ICHNOBATES, LEBROS, LACHNE, LACON, LADON, LAELAPS, LEBROS, LELAPS, LEUCITE, LEUCON, LYCISCA, MELAMPUS, MELANCHETUS, MELANEUS, MOLOSSUS, NAPE, NEBROPHONOS, ORESITROPHUS, ORIBASUS, PACHYTOS, PAMPHAGUS, POEMENIS, PTERELAS, STICTE, STRICTO, THERON, THOUS, and TIGRIS.

Source: Leeming, *World of Myth*, 111; Murray, *Classical Manual*, 160

Dogs of Fo

Variations: Buddhist Dogs, Dogs of Buddha, Fo Dogs, Foo Dogs, Fu Dogs, Kara-Shiski, Koma-Inu ("Korean dogs"), Lions of Buddha

In Chinese mythology the dogs of Fo are chimerical canine guardians and protectors, having the body of a lion, the head of a dog, plumose tails, and wings. They are always depicted in art as a pair, the open mouthed female with a cub and the closed-mouth male with a carved globe. The appearance of a Fo dog was always taken as a good omen.

Source: Bates, *29 Chinese Mysteries*, 56, 58, 62; Rose, *Giants, Monsters, and Dragons*, 100; Zell-Ravenheart, *Wizard's Bestiary*, 40

Dokkaebi

A goblin-like monster from Korean mythology the red-faced dokkaebi with its bulging eyes is described as being covered with fur, having a horn or two atop its head, and carrying a magic wand in its hand. Seeing a dokkaebi is unlikely as it has the ability to shape-shift itself into anything it wants anytime it chooses. It also wears a magical cap which grants the power of invisibility. Additionally, the magic wand gives the ability to transform any item into any other item of its choosing. Although the dokkaebi seldom harassed good-hearted people, Korean folklore is full of stories of humans befriending one of these creatures; nevertheless they are easily annoyed and unpredictable. When they select a person to torment they do so relentlessly. Fortunately, dokkaebi are easily outsmarted.

Source: Cox, *Beyond the Grave*, 10; Suh, *Korean Patterns*, 212

Dongo

From Songhay folklore of West Africa the NATURE SPIRIT Dongo is said to be the one responsible for causing lightning bolts and thunder crashes. Associated with fertility, his symbol is the axe.

Source: Magnavita, *Crossroads / Carrefour Sahel*, 153; Rose, *Spirits, Fairies, Leprechauns, and Goblins, an Encyclopedia*, 90

Donn Cúailnge

Variations: Don Cooley, Donn Cuailnge, Donn Tarb

A great brown bull from Irish mythology, Donn Cúailnge ("brown bull of Cooley"), lived in Ulster in the fields of a minor king by the name of Daire; the animal was the mortal enemy of the great white bull, FINNBENNACH, which lived in the pastures of Ailill mac Mata, the consort of the provincial queen Medb. Donn Cúailnge was the reincarnated form of a swine herder named Friuch who was the enemy of a man named Rucht. In life the men argued over everything and time and again they were reincarnated in various forms—phantoms, ravens, stags, warriors, and worms—and always they continued on fighting. This is unique in Irish mythology because normally this is an ability given only to bards and gods.

According to the legend, Medb and Aililla argued over who owned more livestock; the queen, wanting to increase the size of her herds sent her warriors to the king with a vast sum asking to rent Donn Cúailnge for the year along with the promise of her own sexual favors. Before the king could agree and solidify the deal he overheard the queen's warriors bragging they intended to steal the bull no matter the king's decision. Enraged, the king refused the offer and as promised, the queen's men stole Donn Cúailnge. The brown bull was taken to Connacht but as soon as it and FINNBENNACH laid eyes upon their lives-long enemy, they charged and viciously attacked one another. The brown bull won, slaying the white and ending their eons-long feud; however, Donn Cúailnge was unable to recover from the wounds received in the battle and died a short while after.

Source: Haase, *Greenwood Encyclopedia of Folktales and Fairy Tales*, 173; Monaghan, *Encyclopedia of Celtic Mythology and Folklore*, 135; Sax, *Mythical Zoo*, 50

Doorga

A dog from ancient Greek mythology, Doorga was one of the DOGS OF ACTÆON, the unfortunate youth who was raised by the CENTAUR CHEIRON.

Source: Murray, *Classical Manual*, 160

Dorceus

Variations: Dorcaeus

A dog from ancient Greek mythology, Dorceus ("quick sight") was one of the DOGS OF ACTÆON, the unfortunate youth who was raised by the CENTAUR CHEIRON.

Source: Leeming, *World of Myth*, 111; Murray, *Classical Manual*, 160; Naso, *Fasti, Tristia*, 93–5

Dorotabo (DOH-roh TAH-boh)

Variations: Dorotabō

A YŌKAI from Japanese folklore, the dorotabo ("rice paddy man" or "mud man") first appeared in an eighteenth century book entitled *Konjaku Hyakki Shui* ("Tales of Monsters Then and Now") by Sekien Toriyama, an artist and scholar on Japanese folklore. As the dorotabo is more often heard than seen, the descriptions of this creature are vague and vary, but generally it's said to be made of the mud and marshy bog of the rice paddy it lives in, smelling like rich peat and possibly carrying the frogs, insects, and snakes which live in the paddies. Bipedal, and with only three fingers and a single eye in the center of its forehead, this creature never interacts with humans but rather spends the night crying out in torment until dawn. Because the creature is described as being moist, green, and composed of mud, it must be a seasonal being, existing only after the field is flooded but before the seedlings are planted, as none of the descriptions or original drawings of it show any rice shoots composing its body.

Stories of its creation vary but centralize around a poor but hardworking farmer who turned a useless bit of land into a prosperous rice paddy; some stories say he was cheated out of his land while others say after his death his family sold it for the money in order to indulge in personal vices.

Source: Yoda, *Yokai Attack*, 114–17

Dorylas

A CENTAUR from ancient Greek mythology, Dorylas was, according to Ovid's *Metamorphoses*, one of the CENTAURS who attended the wedding of Pirithous, became drunk on wine and following the lead of EURYTUS, who assaulted Hippodame, began to assault and rape any women they could grab. He was described as wearing a wolf-skin hat with curved horns he used as a savage weapon rather than a spear.

During the Centauromachy, a challenge was called out to Dorylas followed by a thrown spear. Unable to avoid the missile, he threw up his arms to protect his face; the spear pierced his arms and pinned them to his face. The hero Peleus then approached Dorylas and cut his stomach open; panicking, the CENTAUR pulled out his own intestines as he became entangled in them, and fell to the ground, dead.

Source: *Commentary, Mythological, Historical, and Geographical on Pope's Homer*, 55; Simpson, *Metamorphoses of Ovid*, 207

Dossenus

In the dramatic and literary traditions of ancient Rome, Dossenus ("ever-chomping"), a foolish braggart, was one of four standard stock characters; he was a hybrid of an animal and a human who was portrayed as eating its way through everything it encountered on the stage. It sometimes worked in tandem with Manducus ("jaws"), a foolish acting and clean shaven mime. The other characters were Bucco, a simpleton who lives to eat, depicted as having puffy cheeks and portrayed as always saying foolish things; and Pappus, an old farmer who takes advice from young cohorts who continuously mock him.

Source: Rose, *Giants, Monsters, and Dragons*, 100; Warner, *Monsters of our Own Making*, 25; Weiss, *Public Spectacles in Roman and Late Antique Palestine*, 127

Dracaenae

Variations: Drakaina ("she-serpent," plural: *Drakainai*), Drakonet

In Greek mythology a dracaenae is a classification of a type of monster; always female, these creatures have the head and torso of a woman and the lower body of a snake. ECHIDNA is one of the dracaenae.

Source: Garry, *Archetypes and Motifs in Folklore and Literature*, 74; Ogden, *Drakon*, 154, 388

Draco

Variations: LADON

In ancient Roman mythology, Draco was the DRAKON set to guard the Hesperian fruit. After it was slain by the demi-god and hero Hercules (Heracles) with his bow and arrow, the goddess Juno (Hera) took Draco up into the heavens and placed it in the northern night sky as a constellation between Ursa Major, the Big Dipper, and Ursa Minor, the Little Dipper.

Source: Andrews, *Seven Sisters of the Pleiades*, 341; Volney, *Ruins*, 227

Draconcopedes

In medieval European folklore the draconcopedes were a species of serpent said to have the body of a snake with the face and breasts of a woman; in art, the serpent from the Garden of Eden is often depicted as one of these creatures, tempting Eve with fruit from the Tree of Knowledge.

Source: Rose, *Giants, Monsters, and Dragons*, 103; Zell-Ravenheart, *Wizard's Bestiary*, 35

Draconia

According to the Cornish translator and author John Trevisa (1342–1402) the draconia was a species of flying DRAGON and the largest of all serpents; although it had venom, it was not poisonous, rather it killed its victims, elephants, with its powerful constricting tail and its saw-like teeth. Fearful of the panther, the draconia would flee from it.

Source: Metham, *Amoryus and Cleopes*, 118

Dragon, Occidental ("Western")

Variations: Drak (Slavic), DRAKON ("to watch"), Dreki, European Dragon, Iza, Lintver (Slavic), Lintvurm (Slavic), Lohikäärme, Louhikäärme, Orm, Ormr ("dragon," "serpent," or "worm"), Pozoj (Slavic), Premog (Slavic), Sárkánykígyó ("dragon snake," Hungarian), Verm, Viza (Slavic), Western Dragon, Worm, Wyrm, Zmaj (Slavic), Zmij (Slavic), Zmin (Slavic), Zomok (Hungarian)

Found in the myths of cultures from all over the world, the dragon is perhaps the best known and most easily recognized of all the mythological creatures. Man-made artifacts depicting the dragon date back as far as the fourth millennium, BC. The most ancient known traditions about vanquishing dragons go back to the Sumerian, Akkadian, and Egyptian mythologies of the first three millennia BC (see DRAGON, ORIENTAL).

Generally, the dragon is portrayed as an enormous creature with a scale covered crocodilian body, huge fangs filling its gaping maw, and lacertilian (lizard-like) legs ending in clawed feet; sometimes it is described as also having bat-like leathery wings enabling it to fly, a bony dorsal ridge extending down its spine, a serpentine and barbed tail. Wingless dragons from British and Scandinavian traditions are oftentimes called *worms* and usually have poisonous breath rather than breathe fire. Variations to the description include chimerical ad-ons, such as the head of a lion, a tail of a snake, or the wings of a bird. Additional attributes include the ability to breathe fire, poisonous breath, numerous heads, and the ability to cast magical spells, such as shapeshifting. The fourth century BC Greek playwright Euripides was perhaps the first classical author to write of a fire-breathing dragon although both Isaiah and Moses of the Old Testament speak of fire-breathing creatures capable of flight whose description could be taken as draconic. Visually, dragons have been described in virtually every color, including gradating from one color to another, iridescent, rabicano, and rainbow.

Typically dragons live in isolated locations, be it high up in a mountain or deep within a cave somewhere in uncharted wilderness. Castle ruins and swamps are also not uncommon. Typically the dragon will leave its home and travel out to its hunting grounds, preying on cattle, elephants, and humans. Stories of young maidens being sacrificed to appease the dragon's hunger and desire are common and typically involve a hero who must confront and defeat the dragon, saving not only the woman but the countryside as well. Occidental dragons hoard treasure and are exceedingly possessive of their stockpile. These treasure troves are frequently the reward of a hero's quest whose task it was to rid the land of the dragon.

From the earliest myths, such as with the Assyrians, Babylonians, and Sumerians, the dragon has been associated with water, originally as a cosmic being controlling its release into the world and having the power to cause droughts as well as floods. Although its strongest ties are to the element of water, it has ties to the elements of air, earth, and fire as well.

Beginning with ancient Greek mythology the *drakon* ("to look at" or "to watch") became the guardian of precious items or treasure. During this time the creature was depicted as a gigantic winged serpent which occasionally had the ability to breathe fire.

In the pre–Christian traditions of Western Europe the dragon had a largely ambivalent relationship with mankind as both a violent force of nature and a devoted guardian and protector. Stories for each abound. After the introduction of Christianity the dragon was demonized and became the symbol of evil and the Devil, as it was represented throughout the scriptures from the seducer of mankind in the Garden of Eden to the mount of the Whore of Babylon as the Beast of the Apocalypse.

As a symbol of evil the knights from the Middle Ages took it as a symbol to don on their coat of arms and brandish on their crests and shields; this was done to show their noble spirit and how they have vanquished the evil the dragon represented, not to elevate the creature. Tales of dragon slaying abounded and the creature was never quite able to regain the respect it once had.

The dragon of Arthurian folklore was described as having four legs, eagle talons, ribbed bat-like wings, a serpentine tail, and the underbelly of a crocodile.

The heraldic dragon was most often depicted on coats of arms much like the Arthurian dragon but lacking front legs; sometimes the beast would have a barbed tail and tongue, bat-like wings, the body of a serpent, eagle talons, and the head of a wolf.

The dragon of Hungarian folklore, the zomok, was described as being a flying serpentine creature; it was seen in the sky creating bad weather and storms. These creatures were caught and utilized as the mount of a type of magician known as a *garaboncias*.

In Russian folklore and legend dragons are a particularly popular subject; natural phenomena such as the eclipse of the moon or sun were attributed to them. Russian dragons tend not to be as intelligent as their more western counterparts, more animal-like in deed and thought.

Slavonic dragons are known as zmaj (masculine form of "snake"); they are usually three headed and have the ability to grow back a limb or head if ever one is cut off. They are almost always green and have the ability to breathe fire, similar to European dragons. In both Christian and pre–Christian tales they are oftentimes tricked into consuming some food or gift filled with sulphur which then kills them.

Source: De Kirk, *Dragonlore*, 37; Kropej, *Supernatural Beings from Slovenian Myth and Folktales*, 222; Leviton, *Hierophantic Landscapes*, 185; Matthews, *Element Encyclopedia of Magical Creatures*, 173–80; Norroena Society, *Asatrii Edda*, 380; Rose, *Giants, Monsters, and Dragons*, 104–05

Dragon, Oriental

Variations: Druk (Bhutanese), Long Wang, Long, Lung Meng, Lung, Na-Achia, NAGA

The DRAGON of oriental mythologies, although sharing some similarities of the DRAGON of western folklore, is decidedly different both in its physical description and relationship with humanity; they are held in high regard in Asian mythology held as a celestial being and associated with the elements of fire and water as well as the emperor.

The most ancient known traditions about vanquishing DRAGONS go back to the Sumerian, Akkadian, and Egyptian mythologies of the first three millennia BC. Baal of ancient Syrian mythology battles YAMM; Enil of ancient Sumeria defeats the DRAGON LABBU; Marduk vanquishes TIAMAT in the Akkadian epic of creation, *Enuma Elish*, of Babylon; Set of ancient Egyptian mythology defeats the DRAGON APOPHIS; and a weather god from the Hittite texts of Bogazkoy is confronted by the DRAGON ILLUYANKA.

Generally, the DRAGON is chimerical in appearance, described as having a long scaly, serpentine body and neck with short lacertilian (lizard-like) legs and eagle-like talons. Its head is camel-like and delicate, covered with a tufted beard and long whiskers. Depending on its age, gender, and species, it may have horns atop its head, either bovidae or as a rack of antlers. Most have a pearl, either in the mouth or just under the chin, which allows them to breathe fire, fly, or emit some sort of mist. Only in rare instances do they have wings, yet some still have the ability of wingless flight either by undulating their own body or riding waterspouts.

Although they can be quite fierce more often than not these DRAGONS are benevolent towards mankind. After the introduction of Buddhism, dragons began to take on a sinister attitude toward mankind and only the very ancient dragons were considered to be kindly. They love all jewelry but jade most of all; they despise centipedes and anything made of iron.

Buddhist mythology made a distinction between evil mountain dragons, which caused suffering for the people, and water dragons, which were considered beneficial and favorable.

Chinese dragons have a complex mythological status, deep symbology, and profound spiritual influence; they touch upon every aspect of life including the Zodiac. Living in elaborate palaces high in the sky or deep under the waves of the ocean, they are capable of becoming invisible at will and are skilled shape-shifters. Chinese dragons have many subdivisions: black dragons have dominion over mysterious lakes; blue dragons give compassion and are associated with courage; red dragons, said to live in the south, have dominion over fresh water lakes and are associated with the pleasures of summertime; white dragons, symbolic of virtue, are also harbingers of famine; yellow dragons, said to have invented writing, convey the prayers of man to the gods. In AD 200, the Shu Wen ("*Explaining and Analyzing Characters*") dictionary detailed three species of dragons: the scaly *chiao* were serpentine and lived in marshes and mountainous regions, the *li* lived in the oceans, and the *long* dominated the sky.

The ancient Chinese author Hwai nan Tsze attempted to prove all creatures are the progeny of the DRAGON. His writings explain: "All creatures, winged, hairy, scaly, and mailed find their origin in the dragon. The yu-kai produced the flying dragon, the flying dragon gave birth to the phoenixes and after them the lawn-niao and all birds, in general winged beings, were born successively. The mao-tuh ("hairy calf") produced the YING-LUNG and the ying ling gave birth to the KIEN-MA and afterwards the k'i-lin and all quadrupeds, in general the hairy beings were born successively. The KIAI-LIN then produced the *KIAO-LUNG* and gave birth to the kwun-keng and afterwards the KIEN-SIE and all fishes in general the scaly beings, were born successively. The KIAI-T'AN produced the sien-lung, and then gave birth to the yuen-yuen ("original tortoise") and afterwards the LING-KWEI ("divine power manifesting tortoise") and all tortoises in general the mailed beings were born successively."

Japanese dragons, often called *ryū*, are very similar to their Chinese cousins in physical appearance but rather than having four claws (or five if tied to the imperial house) they have only three claws or more than five. They are also similar to their Chinese cousins in appearance and growth, although, they are depicted as being more serpentine. Their relationship with man is ambivalent, as it is with the Occidental Dragon (see DRAGON, OCCIDENTAL), and there are many legends and stories to support this. The dragons of this country are associated with the will-o'-the-wisp (a floating ball of blue flame in the British folklore), called DRAGON lanterns, and rising up from the sea they fly to the mountains where they nest in trees. Japanese dragons are the natural born enemies of HULI JING and KITSUNE, (fox spirit).

In Korea there are three main species of dragons: the KYO live in the mountains, the YONG live in and are protectors of the sky, and the YO dwell in the ocean. All Korean dragons are a chimerical mix, having the belly of a frog, 81 scales on their back, the eyes of a rabbit, and four claws.

Vietnamese dragons are known as *ryo*; imperial dragons have five toes and "common" dragons have four; they all have the ability to breathe fire and have wings. They are depicted as having rounded bodies, long, sinuous, and serpentine as they slowly taper to the tail. The body is segmented into twelve sections, one for each month of the year. Its back has a ridge of small fins, and its hornless head has a beard, crested nose, long mane, long, thin tongue, and prominent eyes. Culturally important, the ryo brings rain and is symbolic of the King, representative of his power and the country's prosperity. According to Vietnamese creation mythology, all people are descended from a dragon.

The NAGA of India were most often portrayed as destructive, evil, and terrifying creatures living in the mountains. The guardians of great treasure hoards the NAGA were at constant war against the god-mount, GARUDA.

The dragons of Asia and the Middle East are depicted as coming in two varieties: in the first they have four legs, bat-like wings and are described as having a stocky build while in the second they are gigantic serpents with dragonesque heads.

Source: Bates, *All About Chinese Dragons*, 98–9; De Kirk, *Dragonlore* 30; De Visser, *Dragon in China and Japan*, 65; Kuehn, *Dragon in Medieval East Christian and Islamic Art*, 87; Matthews, *Element Encyclopedia of Magical Creatures*, 173–80; Roberts, *Chinese Mythology A to Z*, 29–31; Rose, *Giants, Monsters, and Dragons*, 279–89

Dragon-Carp

In Korean folklore the massive dragon-carp was the son of the DRAGON KING of the Sea and was capable of human speech; it was described as having the head of a DRAGON and the tail of a carp. The story of this creature says one day it was caught in the net of a fisherman and hauled up as his daily catch. The fisherman was very pleased with his haul but the dragon-carp spoke and begged to be released back into the water. Surprised by both its ability to speak and the eloquence of his voice, the fisherman gently lowered it back into the water. Pleased and grateful at this show of mercy, the dragon-carp thereafter made sure the fisherman had a fine catch in his nets.

Source: Matthews, *Element Encyclopedia of Magical Creatures*, 180; Rose, *Giants, Monsters, and Dragons*, 107

Dragon Horse

A messenger of the gods in Chinese mythology, the massive water-dwelling dragon horse was described as having the scaled body of a DRAGON and forequarters of a horse; it was believed to hold the vital essences of both Earth and Heaven. It revealed to the Yellow Emperor the symbol of the yin and yang, the perfectly balanced polarities of female and male energies, and how the cosmos is in a natural balance.

Source: De Kirk, *Dragonlore*, 25; Matthews, *Element Encyclopedia of Magical Creatures*, 180; Rose, *Giants, Monsters, and Dragons*, 107

The Dragon Kings

In ancient Chinese mythology there were said to be four DRAGON kings: AO CH'IN, AO JUN, AO KUANG, and AO SHUN; collectively known as LONG WANG, they controlled the rain and the waters of the sea; individually they each had their own domain but lived together on the bottom of the ocean within a thousand-feet-deep cave in a great palace made of crystal and pearl. The entrance to the palace was located in a deep mountain cave in the Eastern Sea. All the creatures of the sea were their servants. The DRAGON kings answer only to the Jade Emperor who tells them when and where to distribute the rain. The DRAGONS are described as being between three and five miles long, having shaggy legs and tails as well as a bearded muzzle, with the rest of their serpentine body being covered with golden scales. Whenever one of the four DRAGONs would breach the ocean's surface great waterspouts were created and when one took to the air, it caused typhoons. Only very special and exceptional individuals were ever allowed to meet with one of the DRAGON kings.

In sixteenth century Chinese literature the DRAGON kings played an important role, and additional kings were created: Lung Wang, the DRAGON king master of fire, and the uniquely white dragon, Pai Lung.

Source: De Kirk, *Dragonlore*, 25–6; Rose, *Giants, Monsters, and Dragons*, 21; Zell-Ravenheart, *Wizard's Bestiary*, 36

Dragon of the Lake

In African folklore there is a tale of the DRAGON of the lake which terrorized a lakeside community, as each year it demanded to be given a virgin as a sacrificial meal and in exchange it would allow them to draw water from its home, the lake, for one day a year. This made the people have to store all of their water and use it carefully. Eventually only Princess Fatouma remained so when the time for tribute came around, she had to be offered up to the DRAGON. A hero and prince named Hammadi was in the area and heard of the fate of the princess and the dangerous situation the town was in. The prince went to the lakeside, freed the princess and then confronted and slew the DRAGON.

Source: Knappert, *African Mythology*, 75; Monaghan, *New Book of Goddesses and Heroines*, 124

The Dragon Son of Ares

Variations: Aionian DRAGON, Drakon Aionia

According to classical Greek mythology, after consulting the oracle at Delphi, the hero Cadmus (Kadmos) was to go to the desert and follow a cow until it lay down and on that very spot found a city, naming it after himself, Cadeia; this was done and the city became the citadel of Thebes in the land of Boeotia ("land of the cow"). Wanting to make a blood sacrifice to the gods for the success of Cadeia, Cadmus ordered his men to find a source of pure water so it may be used to purify the offerings. The men came upon a spring which was jealously guarded by a fierce, unnamed DRAGON. Many of the men were killed in the resulting battle but eventually Cadmus was able to slay the beast; unfortunately it was actually one of the many sons of the god of war, Ares (Mars). In order to atone for the death, the hero was made to serve the god for "a long year" (eight months) to work off his blood-guilt. The goddess Athena (Minerva) appeared to Cadmus and ordered him to take the teeth of the DRAGON and in the adjacent land, sow a field and plant the teeth there as if they were seeds; no sooner was this done than armed men sprang up and fought one another to the death until only five remained. The survivors, CHTHONIOS, ECHION, HYPERENOR, OUDAIOS, and PELORS, were known collectively as the SPARTI ("sow-men"); they became future leaders of Thebes.

Source: Daly, *Greek and Roman Mythology, A to Z*, 29; Ogden, *Dragons, Serpents, and Slayers in the Classical and Early Christian Worlds*, 110; Seton-Williams, *Greek Legends and Stories*, 85

Dragon Turtle

Variations: Kwei, Longgui

In Chinese folklore the dragon turtle appeared after the world was destroyed so he may restore order and assume the responsibility of creating the earth and the heavens; this task took him 18,000 years to achieve.

According to the Qing dynasty scholar Hao Yixing dragon turtles were DRAGONS who had turtle-like bodies; one species of dragon turtle, the Jidiao, was said to have a snake's head and a turtle's body. The fat taken from these creatures was described as being finer than butter and would leak through a copper pot or pottery container; the only way to hold it was to put the substance in a chicken's egg shell.

Source: Strassberg, *Chinese Bestiary*, 126

Dragon Tygre

In the symbology of heraldry, a dragon tygre is a chimerical creature having the head of a tiger but the body of a DRAGON.

Source: Lower, *Curiosities of Heraldry*, 103; Rose, *Giants, Monsters, and Dragons*, 107; Zell-Ravenheart, *Wizard's Bestiary*, 36

Dragon Wolf

In the symbology of heraldry, a dragon wolf is a chimerical creature having the head of a wolf but the body of a DRAGON.

Source: Lower, *Curiosities of Heraldry*, 103; Rose, *Giants, Monsters, and Dragons*, 107; Zell-Ravenheart, *Wizard's Bestiary*, 36

Dragonet

A dragonet is a small DRAGON, about three feet long but every bit as hostile and territorial as its larger counterpart. Capable of breathing poisonous gas and having caustic blood which will damage anything it comes into contact with, dragonets are hostile toward humans. Most famous of the dragonets are the WILSER who live on Mount Pilate, Switzerland.

Source: De Kirk, *Dragonlore*, 41

Dragua, Plural dragonj

In northern Albanian mythology the dragua ("DRAGON") is a semi-human being born with the instinctual drive to seek out and slay KULSHEDRA. Born wearing a caul shirt, the dragonj have a set of two or four invisible wings under their armpits. As the arms and wings are the centralized location of their power dragonj must never hear the phrase "may your arms wither" as this will cause their immediate death. The mother of a dragua must hide the shirt-caul and not tell anyone what her child is, for doing so will also cause the infant to die. In the north of Albania it was said dragonj were born only to those couples whose ancestors had not committed adultery for three consecutive generations. When a dragua dies, if they are dissected it will be discovered their heart is a golden color and a jewel resides within it.

Even as a newborn infant dragonj have developed supernatural powers; for instance, during lightning and thunder storms dragonj magically assemble, crib in tow, in the dragua gathering place. Infant dragonj protect themselves from the attacks of a KULSHEDRA, hiding in their cribs or using it as a weapon. As the goal of a dragua's life is to combat and kill KULSHEDRA they spend their childhood developing the skills they need; especially important is to develop their ability to leap long distances quickly in order to avoid the KULSHEDRA's spraying attack of milk and urine, its main weapons.

When a dragua finally confronts its natural enemy it goes into a berserk rage, its soul leaving its body for the duration of the conflict. They can sense when a human is being attacked by a KULSHEDRA and will, by use of a magical felt hat, fly to their rescue and attack it with cudgels, thrown houses, lances, ploughs, stones, uprooted trees, and yokes; these attacks will look like lightning strike to the human.

Male animals can also be born as dragonj, particularly black roosters and black rams. In Korca and Pograde, Albania, the dragua can also be a beautiful and strong winged stallion bent of defending civilization. Billy-goats can never be born dragonj.

Source: Elsie, *Dictionary of Albanian Religion, Mythology, and Folk Culture*, 74–5

Drakaina

Variations: Draccena

In ancient Greek mythology a drakaina ("she DRAGON") is a female DRAGON or serpentine-like monster with feminine characteristics; these beings tend to prefer living in isolated areas in caves when possible. The goddess Hera (Juno) had her son, Typhoeus, nursed by the Delphic drakaina according to the *Homeric Hymn to Apollo*. The goddess Rhea assumed the form of a drakaina when her son Zeus (Jupiter) tried to rape her; he shape-shifted to a DRAKON (a male DRAGON) and eventually succeeded in his assault. Other examples of drakaina from ancient Greek mythology are CAMPE, DELPHYNE, ECHIDNA, LAMIA (or Sybaris), SCYLLA, POINE, and when represented as female, PYTHON.

Source: Ogden, *Drakon*, 42, 73, 80; Ogden, *Dragons, Serpents, and Slayers in the Classical and Early Christian Worlds*, 40–2

Drakon

Variations: Draco

In ancient Greek mythology a drakon ("DRAGON") is a male DRAGON or serpentine-like monster; these massive beings tend to live in isolated areas and were presented as the adversary and guardian for demi-gods and heroes to defeat. Ancient authors would often tie them to a particular region or landscape and compare them to the elemental forces of nature.

Source: Niles, *Dragons*, 37

Drakone

In classical Greek mythology, there was a classification of monster known as the drakone; they are similar to the AUTOCHTHON. Described as being gigantic, male, toothed serpents, sometimes these creatures had numerous heads, poisonous breath or venom, or wings. One such example of the drakone would be the HYDRA. The female of this species were known as the DRACAENAE.

Source: Garry, *Archetypes and Motifs in Folklore and Literature*, 74

The Drakones Aithiopes

Variations: Dracones Aethiopicum

A species of gigantic DRAGON-like, toothed serpent said to hunt elephants, the drakones aithiopes ("serpents of Ethiopia") were said to live in Ethiopia; according to the Roman author Claudius Aelianus, a teacher of rhetoric, they were the largest of all the DRAKONS, growing as long as one-hundred and eighty feet. He claimed they were also exceptionally long lived.

Source: Breverton, *Breverton's Phantasmagoria*, 163

The Drakones Indikoi

According to the Roman author Claudius Aelianus, the drakones Indikoi were a species of

DRAKON living in India which preyed upon their most deadly natural enemy, the Indian elephant. These gigantic, toothed, serpentine creatures would climb into the top branches of trees, allowing the lower portion of their body to remain hidden in the bushes; when the elephant would approach the tree to graze leaves from the branches the drakones Indikoi would gouge out its eyes and use its body to coil around the beast's neck, strangling it to death, eventually.

Source: Breverton, *Breverton's Phantasmagoria*, 163

Drakones Troiades

Variations: Drakones Trôiades

The drakones Troiades ("DRAGONS of Troy") were two massive SEA SERPENTs who were, according to Greek mythology, called up from the ocean by the goddess Athena (Minerva) to kill Laocoon, the Trojan hero and seer, as he attempted to warn his countrymen of the rouse of the gigantic wood horse outside the city's gates.

Source: Daly, *Greek and Roman Mythology, A to Z*, 84–5; Roman, *Encyclopedia of Greek and Roman Mythology*, 292

Drekavac

Variations: Drek, Drekalo

Description of the drekavac ("one that cries while yelling"), a NURSERY BOGIE from Serbian folklore, vary widely; however, what is consistent is the blood-curdling scream it emits which resounds throughout the forest.

Folklore says the drekavac is created when a child dies not having been baptized and may take on the appearance of a bird, child, dog, or werewolf-like creature.

Source: Maberry, *Cryptopedia*, 232; Zell-Ravenheart, *Wizard's Bestiary*, 36

Dromas

A dog from ancient Greek mythology, Dromas ("runner") was one of the DOGS OF ACTÆON, the unfortunate youth who was raised by the CENTAUR CHEIRON.

Source: Leeming, *World of Myth*, 111; Murray, *Classical Manual*, 160; Naso, *Fasti, Tristia*, 93–5

Drop Bear

Variations: Dropbear

A marsupial from Australian folklore, the drop bear has been described as a large and vicious koala-like creature which sits in the branches of the gum tree and waits for its prey, commonly a kangaroo, to pass beneath it; when this happens the drop bear dives off its perch and using its tusk-like lower teeth, rips out the throat of its prey. This creature is said to stand between three and five feet tall, covered in dense fur, and is extremely strong.

Source: Seal, *Great Australian Stories*, 136

Drösull

Variations: Drasill, Drosull

In Norse mythology, Snorri Sturlson (1179–1241), the Icelandic historian, poet, and politician, writes the horse Drösull ("dragger" or "roamer") was the preferred mount of Dellingr and was sometimes loaned to Dagr to pull his chariot and in order to give his own horses, GLADR and SKINFAXI, a rest in his translation of *Prose Edda*.

Source: Grimes, *Norse Myths*, 261; Thorpe, *Northern Mythology*, 154

Drudwyn

In Arthurian folklore, Drudwyn was one of the many hounds accompanying King Arthur on the quest to hunt down the boar TWRCH TRWYTH; however, it was only one of three dogs which were required to be present by a special condition placed by the GIANT Ysbaddaden as he was trying to make obtaining the object as difficult as possible for Cylhwch (see AETHLEM and ANED). Part of the provision required a special handler to be obtained for Drudwyn, Mabon ap Modron, who was to be assisted by Eli and Trachmyr. Additionally the hound was to be collared with the collar of Canhastry Hundred Hands, leased with the leash of Cors Hundred Claws, and the chain which held him had to be the chain of Cilydd Hundred Holds. Arthur himself obtained the dog and items on behalf of Culhwch.

Source: Bruce, *Arthurian Name Dictionary*, 153, 477; Ellis, *Celtic Myths and Legends*, 384, 385

Dryas

Variations: Dryalos ("he of the oaks"), Dryalus

A CENTAUR from ancient Greek mythology, Dryas was the brother of PERIMEDES; they were CENTAUR chieftains and born the sons of Peukeus ("fir-tree"). According to Ovid's *Metamorphoses*, he was one of the CENTAURS who attended the wedding of Pirithous, became drunk on wine and following the lead of EURYTUS, who assaulted Hippodame, began to assault and rape any women they could grab. He was described as being savage in battle.

During the Centauromachy, Dryas, along with CORYTHUS and EUAGRUS, was challenged by the hero, Rhoetus. As the hero charged the CENTAUR with a flaming torch, Dryas stabbed him in the neck with a wooden stake exactly where the neck meets the shoulders. He went on to slay AREAS, EURYNOMUS, IMBREUS, and IMBRIUS as they attempted to flee the battle.

Adding to the confusion of the battle, one of the Lapith soldiers was also named Dryas.

Source: Colvin, *Cornhill Magazine*, Volume XXXVIII, 296; *Commentary, Mythological, Historical, and Geographical on Pope's Homer*, 55; Simpson, *Metamorphoses of Ovid*, 205; Hesiod, *Works of Hesiod, Callimachus and Theognis*, 59

Dû Paikar

Variations: Do Patkar ("two figures")

In Persian mythology, dû paikar are a species of dual-faced KHRAFSTRA living in the China Sea; they are described as having anthropoid bodies.

Source: Mode, *Fabulous Beasts and Demons*, 267; Qazvīnī, *Zoological Section of the Nuzhatu-l-qulūb of amdullāh al-Mustaufī al-Qazwīnī*, 48

Dub Sainglend

Variations: Dubb Sainglenn, Dubh Saingleann, Saingliu

One of the two prized horses belonging to the hero Cúchulainn, Dub Sainglend ("black of Saingliu") and its equal LAITH MACHA pulled his chariot.

Source: Gerritsen, *Dictionary of Medieval Heroes*, 86; MacKillop, *Dictionary of Celtic Mythology*, 265

Dulcefal

Named in the legendary sage *Gaungu-Hrolfs*, Dulcefal was the sacred horse of Hreggwidur, king of Hilmgareariki. It was said Dulcefal was unequaled in size and strength and could accurately predict if defeat or victory awaited his master; the animal was further described as being "as active as a lion, swift as a bird, and as vicious as a wolf."

Source: Frances, *Notes and Queries*, 283; Webster, *Historic Magazine and Notes and Queries*, 582

Dund

Variations: Headless Horseman, the Truncated

In Hindu mythology and originating from the epic poem *Mahabharata*, the dund are supernatural beings; they have been described as headless or as nothing more than a torso, all their limbs having been severed. Appearing astride a horse in either form, its head tied to the pommel of the saddle, the dund travels through the village at night calling out the names of the head of a household. Anyone who answers the call of this psychopomp (death omen) will soon die.

Source: Crooke, *Introduction to the Popular Religion and Folklore of Northern India*, 159

Duneyr (DUN-ayr)

Variations: Duneyrr

Duneyr ("red ear") was one of the harts (a male Red Deer) or stags named in Thorgrimr's *Rhymes* and in Snorri Sturluson's (1179–1241) *Prose Edda*;

the other stags were DAIN, DURATHROR, and DVALIN. Duneyr was symbolic of strong winds. The stags all lived in the branches of the World Tree, Ygdrasil, eating its branches and leaves. It was from the antlers of these animals that honey-dew fell to the earth and supplied the water for all of the rivers of the world.

Source: Daly, *Norse Mythology A to Z*, 19; Guerber, *Hammer of Thor*, 9; Jennbert, *Animals and Humans*, 50

Dungavenhooter

Variations: Dungaven Hooter

A mouthless alligator-like creature from American folklore, the dungavenhooter was said to live in logging regions and have abnormally large nostrils. Lying in wait hidden in bushes, the dungavenhooter lashes out with its tail when an unsuspecting lumberjack passes by. The victim is beaten until it is pulverized into a gaseous form after which the dungavenhooter snorts up its meal.

Source: McKee, *Clan of the Flapdragon and Other Adventures in Etymology*, 112–13; Rose, *Giants, Monsters, and Dragons*, 119; Tryon, *Fearsome Critters*, 17

Dunlyrr

The hart (a male Red Deer) from Norse mythology which gnaws on the branches of the World Tree, Ygdrasil, Dunlyrr was one of the harts (male red deer) or stags named in the *Nafnaþulur*, a subsection of Snorri Sturluson's (1179–1241) *Prose Edda*. Oftentimes the characters listed in this section are omitted in other editions and translations.

Source: Lindow, *Norse Mythology*, 99

Dupo

In ancient Greek mythology, Dupo was one of the CENTAURS slain by the demi-god and cultural hero Hercules (Heracles) while visiting his friend, a CENTAUR named PHOLUS, between the conclusion of his third Labor and the onset of his fourth. When an old and particularly fragrant hogshead of wine was opened its aroma carried on the air and drove the local CENTAURS into a fury. Dupo, along with ARGEIUS, AMPHION, DAPHNIS, HIPPOTION, ISOPLES, MELANCHETES, OREUS, PHRIXUS, and THEREUS, was slain by Hercules (Heracles) as he defended himself from their violent and unwarranted assault.

Source: Barthell, *Gods and Goddesses of Ancient Greece*, 187; Diodorus, *Historical Library of Diodorus the Sicilian*, Volume 1, 229–30

Durathror (DUR-a-throhr)

Variations: Durathor, Duraþrór, Durabror

Durathror ("beast of slumber") was one of the harts (male Red Deer) or stags named in Thorgrimr's *Rhymes* and in Snorri Sturluson's (1179–1241) *Prose Edda*; the other stags were DAIN, DUNEYR, and DVALIN; he was symbolic of heavy winds. The stags all lived in the branches of the World Tree, Ygdrasil, eating its branches and leaves. It was from the antlers of these animals that honeydew fell to the earth and supplied the water for all of the rivers of the world.

Source: Daly, *Norse Mythology A to Z*, 19; Guerber, *Hammer of Thor*, 9; Jennbert, *Animals and Humans*, 50

Durinn's Kin

Variations: Durrinn's Folk

The collective name for the rock Jotnar (see JOTUN) from Norse mythology who were created by Durinn, and were said to have paid particular attention to his leadership; their names are ALFRIG, BERLING, BILDUR, BILLING, BRUNI, BURI, FJALARR, FRAGR, FRAR, GALARR, GLOINN, GRER, HAUR, HLAE-VANGR, JARI, LOFAR, LONI, SKAFIDR, and SVIARR.

Source: Grimes, *Norse Myths*, 7

Dvalar

Variations: DVALIN

Dvalar was one of the stags named in Thorgrimr's *Rhymes* and in Snorri Sturluson's (1179–1241) *Prose Edda*.

Source: Jennbert, *Animals and Humans*, 50; Lindow, *Norse Mythology*, 99

Dvalin (DVAL-in)

Variations: Dvalinn

Dvalin ("the dormant" or "unconscious one") was one of the harts (male Red Deer) or stags named in Thorgrimr's *Rhymes* and in Snorri Sturluson's (1179–1241) *Prose Edda*; the other stags were DAIN, DUNEYR, and DURATHROR. Dvalin was symbolic of the calm winds. The stags all lived in the branches of the World Tree, Ygdrasil, eating its branches and leaves. It was from the antlers of these animals that honey-dew fell to the earth and supplied the water for all of the rivers of the world.

Dvalin is also the name of a JOTUN in Norse mythology; he and his brother Durinn were created by Modsoghir at Odin's command. Dvalin had a devote group of Jotnar (see JOTUN) who were his followers; collectively they were known as DVALIN'S HOST and lived in Juravale's Marsh. Whenever he wished to visit his followers, Dvalin would ride his horse, MODNIR, there.

As a DWARF (DVERG), Dvalin, along with ALFRIG, BERLING, and GRER, were all skilled smiths who collectively were known as the four Brisingamen DWARFS, and constructed the golden necklace of the goddess Freyia.

Source: Daly, *Norse Mythology A to Z*, 19; Grimes, *Norse Myths*, 260; Guerber, *Hammer of Thor*, 9; Jennbert, *Animals and Humans*, 50; Thorpe, *Northern Mythology*, Volume 1, 32

Dwaallicht (Will-ict)

Variations: Corpse Candle

Dwaallicht is a Dutch word used to describe a being from the Netherlands which is essentially a corpse candle (a glowing, spectral ball of glowing light).

Source: Cordier, *T ung pao*, 43; Foundation, *Writing in Holland*, 5, 7; Mladen, *Dutch-English, English-Dutch Dictionary*, 209

Dwarf

Variations: Berg-Mänlein ("hill-mannikins"), Berg-Mänlein ("hill-mannikins"), Dorch, Drerge, Dverg, Dware, Dweeorg, Dwerger, Dwergugh, Dworh, Erd-Mänlein ("ground-mannikins"), Gotho, Härdmandle, Hel-kaplein, Hill TROLLS, Kleine Volk ("little people"), Moss People, Oennerbanske, Oennereeske, Stele Volk ("still people"), Tarn-kapppe, Tele Volk ("still people"), Timber, Torpek, Trold, TROLL, Unnerorske ("underground folks"), Wichtelweib, Wichtlein ("little Wights"), Wild, Zwerge, Zzwerg

The dwarf is a popular and staple figure in folklore. Generally these short but powerfully built beings are beneficent and will assist those who treat them with respect; however if injured or offended they will quickly vent their rage on cattle. They appear to be old, reach maturity at three years of age, and the males of the species have long, grey beards. Dwarfs who live underground do not involve themselves with humans if they can help it, as they would rather mine for their gold and precious gems. If they venture above ground, the dwarf will do so at night. They have the ability to become invisible and can walk through rocks and walls. The folklore varies as to why they do not venture out into the light; sometimes it is said they will turn to stone but other times it is said they spend their daylight hours in the guise of a frog. Because they are such isolationists they are said to be members of the Unseelie Court.

The fairies of England are the dwarfs of Germany and the lands to its north.

In Iceland dwarfs are said to wear red clothing. The fullest account of Icelandic dwarfs comes from the learned Bishop of Skalholt Finnus Johannaeus in his book *The Ecclesiastical History of Iceland*, but it makes almost no distinction between elves and dwarfs.

In Brenton dwarfs are called *korrigan*.

In Finland and Lapland it is believed dwarfs live

in a magnificent underground land and sometimes mortals are allowed to enter. While a guest, they are spectacularly entertained and given copious amounts of brandy and tobacco.

In Friesland, Netherlands, dwarfs are called oennereeske and tend to fall in love with mortal women and steal them away, keeping them for long periods of time. They also steal children and leave CHANGELINGS in their place. Oennereeske will also borrow and lend plates and pots as well as money, sometimes even charging interest. They will assist in the construction of churches and homes, help when a cart is stuck in the mud, and bring field workers pancakes and water.

In Switzerland dwarfs are called dverg ("spider") and are described as being generous, kind, and having a joyous nature. Fond of strolling throughout the land, they will randomly take part in random acts of kindness, such as driving sheep and leaving berries where poor children can find them. In Scandinavian folklore, the more common word used for the dwarf is TROLL or trold.

The fifteenth century German manuscript entitled The Heldenbuch (Book of Heroes) claims "God created the GIANTs that they might kill the wild beasts, and the great DRAGONS, that the dwarfs might be more secure."

Dwarfs in southern Germany live in large communal groups but tend to appear to man alone. They are described as being small, grey and old looking, hairy and covered in moss, standing as tall as a three year old child. Female dwarfs in southern Germany have a nicer disposition than their male counterparts; they wear green clothing trimmed in red and cocked hats upon their head. They live deep back in the woods and will give woodcutters good advice and assist in cooking and washing clothes. They most often appear where people are baking so they can use the fire. A bit of dough is left for them as an offering. The male dwarfs in southern Germany live in mines and dress like miners, carrying a hammer, lantern, and mallet. They enjoy throwing stones at miners but unless they have been offended, the assault is harmless.

In Lusatia, Germany, it is believed dwarfs are actually fallen angels.

In some German tales when a dwarf's hat is knocked off of their head it becomes visible. They can also bestow physical strength, curse a family to poverty, foresee future events, gift prosperity upon a family, and shape-shift into any form.

Interestingly, there are no dwarfs in Italian folklore.

Source: Bord, Fairies, 60; Briggs, Encyclopedia of Fairies, 115; Evans-Wentz, Fairy Faith in Celtic Countries, 374–75; Keightley, World Guide to Gnomes, Fairies, Elves, and Other Little People, 216–17, 229–30, 264, 281, 448; Lindow, Norse Mythology, 99–101

Each Uisce

Variations: AUGHISKY, Eač Uisge, Each Uisge

One of the many species of water horse, the each uisce ("water monster") of Scottish folklore is a fearsome creature, beautiful and sleek; it offers itself to be ridden. So long as the fairy horse never catches a glimpse of a body of salt water it will be a fine riding horse; however as soon as it does it will bound into the water, taking its rider with it. Once submerged the each uisce then turns and attacks its rider, devouring him if it is able, leaving only the liver behind. Untamed, unbridled each uisce will roam the countryside and consume cattle.

Similar to the AUGHISKY of Irish folklore, CEFFYL DWFR from Wales, and the SHOOPILTEE from the Shetlands, the each uisce differs from the KELPIE in that it lives in running water. Typically, it is sighted during the month of November, running down the sandy beaches.

Source: Briggs, Encyclopedia of Fairies, 115–16; Eberhart, Mysterious Creatures, 580; Illes, Encyclopedia of Spirits, 378; Rose, Spirits, Fairies, Leprechauns, and Goblins, 97

The Eale

Variations: Centicore, Jall, Yale ("mountain goat"), Yali

A species of chimerical and legendary antelope from southern India, the chimerical eale was described as being black or tawny brown in color, standing about as tall as a water-horse, and having an elephant-like tail, the jaws and tusks of a wild boar, and a set of moveable horns more than a cubit long atop its head (a cubit is the distance from a man's elbow to the tip of his middle finger). When the eale fights, much like the CENTICHORA, it lays one of its horns back and puts the other forward, utilizing only one at a time in battle. The eale is a popular creature in heraldry.

Source: Ashton, Curious Creatures in Zoology, 160; Druce, Archaeological Journal, Volume 68, 185; White, Book of Beasts, 55

Earth Spider

Variations: Tsuchi'gumo ("earth hider"), Tsuchi-gumo

A monstrous green spider from ancient Japanese folklore, the earth spider was depicted as having a catlike head, pointed ears, and whiskers; it also had white blood. Living inside the mysterious Mount Katsuragi, the floor of its lair was covered with the skeletal remains of its victims. Once when the hero

Yorimitsu cut off its head, 1,990 grew back in its place.

In the Noh play entitled *Tsuchi Gumo* which was based on the ancient text *Nihon Shoki* ("*The Chronicles of Japan*," AD 720), the earth spider has the supernatural ability to shape-shift into a Buddhist priest and an *oni* (OGRE).

Source: Bush, *Asian Horror Encyclopedia*, 43, 185; Mittman, *Ashgate Research Companion to Monsters and the Monstrous*, 140

Easg Saint

A pair of sacred fish from Celtic folklore, the easg saint ("holy fish") were said to live in a well located near a Christian church in the country of Ireland; red hazelnuts from a nearby tree fell into the well and were the sole source of food for these black-scaled, red speckled fish, imparting onto them magical qualities, one of which was the ability to speak. To kill or consume these fish which allegedly lived in the well for generations was believed to be a crime which the gods themselves would punish.

Source: Spence, *Magic Arts in Celtic Britain*, 96; Zell-Ravenheart, *Wizard's Bestiary*, 37

Ech Tened

The Irish pseudepigraph *Epistil Isu* ("*Sunday Letters*"), written by an anonymous author, describes five kinds of monsters which will descend upon those individuals and heathens who do not keep holy the Lord's Day, Sunday. The ech tened ("fiery horse") is the third of the creatures mentioned; anyone who in life rode a horse on a Sunday will be made to ride one of these creatures in death as a punishment for their transgression.

Source: Borsje, *From Chaos to Enemy*, 210; Olsen, *Monsters and the Monstrous in Medieval Northwest Europe*, 69–70

Echeneis

Variations: Mora, REMORA

Pliny the Elder, the Roman author, natural philosopher, naturalist, and army and naval commander, in his work *Natural History* (AD 77) described the echeneis ("ship-detaining") as a six-inch long SEA SERPENT who was responsible for Mark Antony losing the Battle of Actium. This creature would attach onto the hull of a ship with such a ferocious grip it would slow down the vessel if not stop it outright in the water altogether. Living in the polar seas, the echeneis also had the ability to freeze the water around it.

The natural enemy of the SALAMANDER, the elemental creature of fire, the echemeis was much sought after by physicians as it was instrumental in helping women during their pregnancy. These fish were commonly depicted in medieval bestiaries and found their way into the folklore of European fishermen, sailors, and travelers.

Source: Pliny the Elder, *Pliny's Natural History*, Volumes 1–3, 140; Rose, *Giants, Monsters, and Dragons*, 109; Zell-Ravenheart, *Wizard's Bestiary*, 37

Echidna

Variations: Chidna, Dracaena Scythia, Drakaina Skythia ("Scythian She-DRAGON"), Ekhidna, the "Mother of all Monsters," Scythian Dracaena, the Scythian Monster

Born the daughter of Gaea and Tartarus (or Ceto and Phorcys, ancient sources conflict), Echidna ("she viper") was a DRAKAINA, half-NYMPH and half-serpent, with a beautiful face and fearful black eyes who lived in a cave and consumed human flesh in classical Greek mythology.

Although Echidna has the moniker of being the Mother of all Monsters, she in fact only gave birth to about six. By Typhoeus, the largest and most grotesque of all creatures which have ever lived, she was the mother of numerous creatures, such as CERBERUS, the CHIMERA, and the HYDRA. By her own son, the two-headed dog ORTHOS, she was the mother of the Nemean Lion and the SPHINX. By the demi-god and hero Hercules(Heracles), she gave birth to four sons: Agathyrsus, Alcaeus, Gelonus, and Scythes, who went on to become king of the Scythians as he was the only one of the three who could use the bow and girdle his father left behind. Some versions of her story say she was also the mother of the CROMMYONIAN SOW, the DRAKON LADON which guarded the Golden Apples of Hesperos, the CAUCASUS EAGLE daily eating PROMETHEUS' liver, the GORGONS, and SCYLLA.

Echidna was killed one day while she slept by Argus Panoptes.

Source: Daly, *Greek and Roman Mythology, A to Z*, 48–49; Rosen, *Mythical Creatures Bible*, 91; Smith, *Dictionary of Greek and Roman Biography and Mythology*, 3

Eer-Moonan

In the legends of the Dreamtime from the mythology of the Australian native people, the eer-moonan is the collective name for chimerical, monstrous creatures described as having the bodies of dogs, the feet of human women, and the heads of spiny anteaters; they prey upon humans with their uncanny stealth.

Source: Reed, *Aboriginal Stories of Australia*, 108; Rose, *Giants, Monsters, and Dragons*, 110; Zell-Ravenheart, *Wizard's Bestiary*, 37

Egoir

Variations: Edgar, Edger, Egder ("wise beyond all knowing"), Egdir

A rusty-yellow-colored storm eagle from Norse mythology, Egoir ("eagle") will appear, it is told, at Ragnarok; until then it sits roosting on the topmost branch of Ygdrasil. The hawk VEDRFOLNIR blocks its view.

Source: Anderson, *Norse Mythology*, 443, 421; Grimes, *Norse Myths*, 263

Eight-Forked Serpent of Koshi

A massive serpent with eight heads and eight tails from Japanese folklore, Eight-Forked Serpent had glowing red eyes; it was so massive that when it moved, its furrows created mountains and valleys. Each year for seven years this gigantic HYDRA-like monster demanded one of the king's daughters as a sacrifice or else it would devour the rest of his population. In the eighth year as the king was about to offer up his final daughter, Princess Comb-Rice Field, a hero named Susa-No-O ("brave-swift-impetuous-male") devised a cunning plan to save her. He constructed a compound with eight tower gates and filled each one with rice beer. As soon as Eight-Forked Serpent appeared it smelled the beer rice and each head devoured the contents of one of the towers. Intoxicated it fell into a deep sleep allowing the hero to slice off each of its heads, flooding the area with its blood. In the tail of Eight-Forked Serpent the hero discovered an enchanted sword.

Source: De Bary, *Sources of Japanese Tradition*, 26–7; Rose, *Giants, Monsters, and Dragons*, 110

Eikthyrnir

Variations: Eikjjyrnir ("oak-stinger"), Eikthyrner, Eikthyrni, Eikthyrnir

In Norse mythology Eikthyrnir ("oak antlers" or "vigils horns") was one of the stags (male harts) named in Thorgrimr's *Rhymes* and in Snorri Sturluson's (1179–1241) *Prose Edda*. He was said to stand atop the shield-roof of Valhalla (Valaskialf) and as he did, water ran from his antlers creating the rivers which flowed into Midgard (earth), Eikin, Fimbulthul, Fjorm, Geirvimul, Gipul, Gomel, Gopul, Gunnthra, Sid, Sokin, Svol, and Vid.

Source: Grimes, *Norse Myths*, 263; Jennbert, *Animals and Humans*, 50; Norroena Society, *Asatrii Edda*, 343; Oehlenschläger, *Gods of the North*, xxxviii

Eingana

In the legends from the mythology of the Australian native people, Eingana was a RAINBOW SERPENT who had no means by which to give birth, her children constantly growing inside of her body. The god Barraiya took pity on her great pain and threw his spear at her, creating a wound by which all life flowed out. Eingana holds the umbilical cord of each of her children; when she breaks it, they die. According to the myth, it is said if ever she died, existence would end.

Source: Eason, *Fabulous Creatures, Mythical Monsters, and Animal Power Symbols*, 22; Monaghan, *New Book of Goddesses and Heroines*, 111

Ejderha

Variations: Evran, Evren ("DRAGON")

A serpentine DRAGON from Islamic Turkish literature of the eleventh century, ejderha ("serpent DRAGON") was described as being coiled around the wheel of an ecliptic and was responsible for the rotation of it, causing the progression of days into nights.

Source: Bacqué-Grammont, *Comité international d'études pré-ottomanes et ottomanes*, 5

Elatus

A CENTAUR from classical Greek mythology, Elatus was one of his kind who was present when the demi-god Hercules (Heracles) fought them in Arcadia. Having fled en masse to the cave of CHEIRON, they gathered around him for protection; Hercules shot an arrow into the group which passed through the arm of Elatus and struck the immortal CHEIRON in the knee.

Source: Apollodorus, *Gods and Heroes of the Greeks*, 94; Huber, *Mythematics*, 34

Die Elben

Variations: Alben

Benevolent female NATURE SPIRITS in German folklore, *die elben* enjoy dancing and music; in general they are friendly towards humans. Essentially, *elben* is the German word for Elves.

Source: Lurker, *Dictionary of Gods and Goddesses, Devils and Demons*, 56, 57

Elementary Spirits

The hermetic and neo-Platonic doctrine from which all medieval medicine and science was founded describes four Elemental spirits or classes of mortal, soulless beings: Air, Earth, Fire, and Water; accordingly the SYLPHS belong to the Air class, GNOMES to Earth, nereids (golden-haired sea nymphs) to Water, and SALAMANDERS to Fire.

Source: Briggs, *Encyclopedia of Fairies*, 192–3; Evans-Wentz, *Fairy Faith in Celtic Countries*, 241; Hall, *Secret Teachings of All Ages*, 317; Rose, *Spirits, Fairies, Leprechauns, and Goblins*, 304; Stepanich, *Faery Wicca*, Book One, 31

Elephant That Foretold the Birth of the Buddha

A white elephant with six tusks which appeared in a dream to Queen Maya, Elephant That Foretold the Birth of the Buddha came to foretell the birth of the Buddha. On the same night a *bodhisattva* (an enlightened being) descended from heaven in the form of a white elephant and entered the queen's womb on the right side.

Source: Borges, *El libro de los seres imaginarios*, 89; Dayal, *Bodhisattva Doctrine in Buddhist Sanskrit Literature*, 295

Elephant-Tiger

In the folklore of Thailand the jungle dwelling chimerical elephant-tiger was said to be huge; it was described as having the body of elephant with the head of a tiger. According to folklore, King Phan of Nakhon Pathom City sent out his best trackers to bring one back so he could improve the bloodline of the royal herd, hoping to add the creature's determined and ferocious attitude to his own. Successful, the trackers returned with an elephant-tiger and a new breed of war elephant was established.

Source: Knappert, *Pacific Mythology*, 72; Rose, *Giants, Monsters, and Dragons*, 110–11; Zell-Ravenheart, *Wizard's Bestiary*, 37

Elf

Variations: Elb, Elfin, Ellyll (plural Ellyllon), Ellyllon, Erl, Fary, Fay, Fée, Huldrafolk, Mannikin, Ouph, Wight

Elf is a generic word used world-wide to describe a wide array of FAIRY-folk, including DWARFS, GNOMES, and TROLLS; it is used interchangeably with the word *fairy*. They answer to their own royalty, having their own kings and queens, and greatly enjoy celebrating and feasting banquets and weddings. Descriptions of these creatures, from their appearance to their dress, vary widely, as does their disposition and personalities.

In England the elves are divided into two distinct classes: domestic and rural. Domestic elves are a type of household spirit (see HOUSE-SPIRIT) and live symbiotically with mankind on their farms and in their homes, such as the brownies and hobgoblins do. Rural elves live in the caverns, fields, mountains and wilderness. Trooping fairies are small, benevolent, and kind, freely helping humans whereas solitary fairies have a tendency to be injurious and if they choose to assist a person will set a price on their services. Generally speaking, each are skilled at spinning cloth and thread as well as making shoes.

As in British folklore, elves are divided into two classes in Scandinavia, the LIGHT ELVES of the Seelie Court and the DARK ELVES of the Unseelie Court. The voice of the elves in this part of the world is said to be soft and sweet, like the air. Children who are born on a Sunday have the natural ability to see elves and similar such beings.

In Scotland fairies are human size and are often called elves; their Fairyland was known as Elfame.

Common folklore in Wales claims the Ellyllon should be respected, as they are the souls of the ancient druids who are too good to be condemned to Hell but not good enough to be allowed to enter Heaven. The Ellyllon are assigned the punishment of wandering upon the earth among mankind until Judgment Day when they will be allowed to rise into a higher state of being.

In Africa elves are seasonal fairies and more akin to NATURE SPIRITS.

Teutonic and Norse folklore claims fairies (Huldrafolk) were once the spirits of the dead bringing fertility to the land. Later, they evolved into small, humanoid beings; the beautiful ones were considered to be elves of light while ugly ones were called black or DARK ELVES. Dutch elves (ellefolk) are beautiful creatures with hollow backs.

Source: Ashliman, *Fairy Lore*, 199; Bord, *Fairies*, 2; Illes, *Encyclopedia of Spirits*, 383; Keightley, *World Guide to Gnomes, Fairies, Elves, and Other Little People*, 57, 81; McCoy, *Witch's Guide to Faery*, 171; Stepanich, *Faery Wicca*, Book One, 270

Ellén Trechend

A three-headed monstrous vulture from Irish mythology, ellén trechend was said to have lived in the cave of Cruachan; it ravished the countryside until the hero Amergin and the poet Ulaid killed it.

Source: Best, *Book of Leinster*, 125–61; Joyce, *Smaller Social History of Ancient Ireland*, 112

Emela-Ntouka

Variations: Aseka-Moke, Chipekwe, Emeula Natuka, Emia-Ntouka, Forest Rhinoceros, Ngamba-Namae, Ngoulou, Nsanga, Nyama

Said to live in the lakes and rivers of the Likouala region of the Republic of the Congo, the large and hairless emela-ntouka ("killer of elephants") is a creature said to attack elephants and water buffaloes. Described as having grey or brown skin, a crocodile-like tail, a single ivory alicorn protruding from the center of its head, and heavy legs ending in three toes, the emela-ntouka is as large as an elephant and emits a low growl or rumble. Although this creature is an herbivore it is very violent.

Source: Coleman, *Cryptozoology A to Z*, 89; Eberhart, *Mysterious Creatures*, 163; Maberry, *They Bite*, 208

Empouse (Em-POO-say), plural: empousai

Variations: Démon du Midi ("mid-day demon"), Empusa, Empusae, Empusas, Empuse, Empusen, Mormo, Moromolykiai, "She who moves on one leg"

In Greek, the word *empouse* translates as "vampire," but technically, it was considered to be a demon by the ancient Greeks' own mythological standards of classification. They defined a demon as any creature born in another world but having the ability to appear in ours as a being of flesh. In spite of this, the word was *understood* to mean a vampire; therefore, the empouse is considered by some scholars to be the oldest recorded vampire myth.

In Greek mythology the empouse, or *empousai* as they are referred to collectively, are born the red-headed daughters of the witch goddess Hecate and act as her attendants. Their legs are mule-like and shod with bronze shoes. Along with its powers of illusion and shape-shifting, an empouse will also use its persuasive abilities to persuade a man to have sexual relations with it. However, during the act it will drain him of his life and, on occasion, make a meal of his flesh, much like a SUCCUBUS.

Avoiding an attack from an empouse is fairly easy, as long as one does not fall victim to its allurements. A thin-skinned and sensitive creature, it will shriek in pain and flee as quickly as it can if confronted for what it is with use of insults and profanities. Outrunning the vampire is also possible, as all references to it describe the empouse's fastest gait as being comically slow.

In Russian folklore, the empouse appears at harvest time as a widow. It breaks the arms and legs of every harvester it can lay hands on.

Source: Challice, *French Authors at Home*, Volume 2, 240; Curl, *Egyptian Revival*, 403; Oinas, *Essays on Russian Folklore and Mythology*, 117; Hicks, *Transformations*, 110

Enbarr

Variations: Enabarr ("foam" or "froth"), Enbarr of the Flowing Mane, Embarr

The horse of Niamh in Irish folklore, Enbarr ("imagination") had not only the ability to run across land and sea without touching either ground or water but also could not be slain by god or man; no one ever died while mounted upon her back. In some sources, Enbarr is also said to be the horse ridden by the god Manannán mac Lir.

Source: Brown, *Iwain*, 42; Rose, *Giants, Monsters, and Dragons*, 22

Encanto

Variations: Encantada, Enkanto, Ingkanto

A male diwata from Filipino mythology, encanto ("charm" or "enchantment") are believed to command some of the monstrous creatures in their mythology, such as the AMALANHIGS, ASWANG, BAL-BAL, MANANANGGALS, TIK TIKS, and the wak waks. Living in the sea, fishermen will make offerings to them in the hopes of having a good catch.

Source: Demetrio, *Myths and Symbols, Philippines*, 346; Olup na, *Beyond Primitivism*, 257–8

Encerrados

In the folklore from Chile, the monstrous grey-skinned and cannibalistic encerrados ("captive" or "recluse") are said to abduct children and give them to evil witches who would then sew up their orifices. Encerrados are in service to the INVUCHE and CHIVATO and in some cases may evolve to become one of these creatures.

Source: Meurger, *Lake Monster Traditions*, 282; Rose, *Giants, Monsters, and Dragons*, 112

Endrop

In Romanian folklore the endrop is a species of water horse (see FAIRY ANIMAL) similar to the KELPIE of Scottish folklore in that it would try to entice someone to ride upon its back. If successful the endrop would then run headlong into the water where it would drown its victim unless they could call out to the Lord Jesus to save them.

Source: Mode, *Fabulous Beasts and Demons*, 212; Rose, *Giants, Monsters, and Dragons*, 112

Enen-Ra (en-en RAH)

Variations: Enra-enra

In Japanese folklore the YŌKAI known as enen-ra appears as an amorphous cloud of smoke wherever there is a smoke generating fire; it does not have a physical form but only takes on the smoky form of animals, men, women, or whatever suits its need. Although they are completely harmless they are frightening and unsettling to see as they coalesce and disappear over and over again in the smoke. It is particularly disturbing when an enen-ra manifests during a last-rite immolation ceremony.

Source: Yoda, *Yokai Attack*, 178–82

Enfield

In heraldic symbology the chimerical enfield was depicted as having the head of a fox, chest of a greyhound, talons of an eagle, body of a lion, and hind legs and tail of a wolf. It occurs as the crest of most Irish families with the name of Kelly.

Source: Fearn, *Discovering Heraldry*, 32; Fox-Davies, *Complete Guide to Heraldry*, 231; Zell-Ravenheart, *Wizard's Bestiary*, 38

Enide's Dappled Palfrey

Presented to a heroine of Arthurian folklore, Enide, this unnamed dappled palfrey (an expensive and carefully bred riding horse during the middle ages) was described by her cousin who gave it to her as being calm enough for a child to ride, as gentle as a boat upon calm waters, and as swift as a bird; this horse was also said not to be balky, a biter, a fighter, a kicker, or skittish. It is possible this horse was a FAIRY ANIMAL or had fairy involvement in its origins. This splendid Norse mount was most likely the one she was riding when she was accompanying Erec on his adventures to prove his knightly prowess. Sadly, somewhere along the madcap journey, Enide lost her horse.

Source: de Troyes, *Erec and Enide*, 41; Karr, *King Arthur Companion*, 144

Enide's Sorrel Palfrey

This mount was presented to the heroine of Arthurian folklore, Enide, by Guivret the Little and his sister to replace the dappled one she lost while following Erec on his adventures (see ENIDE'S DAPPLED PALFREY). This palfrey (an expensive and carefully bred riding horse during the middle ages) had a tricolored head with one side of its head being white and the other side being black; there was a green line separating the two colors. This palfrey, like her dappled mount, may have had a supernatural origin or been a FAIRY ANIMAL.

Source: de Troyes, *Erec and Enide*, 41, 155; Karr, *King Arthur Companion*, 144–45

Enik

In Armenian mythology Enik was one of the winged horses said to assist in pulling the sun across the sky (see also BENIK, MENIK, and SENIK).

Source: Ananikian, *Armenian Mythology*, 51; Rose, *Giants, Monsters, and Dragons*, 178

Enkidu

In the *Epic of Gilgamesh*, the epic poem from ancient Mesopotamia dating back to 1800 BC, there is a character, a WEREWOLF and WILD MAN, by the name of Enkidu who was created by the god of the sky, Anu, to be an adversary to the hero Gilgamesh. Initially, the two are enemies but after Gilgamesh defeats Enkidu they become friends and have many adventures together. Enkidu learns culture and refinement from Gilgamesh and in turn teaches his friend humility and respect. The goddess Ishtar wanted to marry Gilgamesh who flatly and violently rejected her; hurt she begged her father to release the BULL OF HEAVEN to kill the hero; side by side the friends fought and eventually killed the creature.

The goddess Ishtar leapt to the wall of Uruk and began to utter a curse upon Gilgamesh but Enkidu ripped the right hind leg off of the BULL OF HEAVEN and waved it in her face, exclaiming how he wished he could do worse to her than he did to the Bull. For his hubris, Enkidu was haunted by horrific dreams and after twelve sleepless nights, died.

Source: Maberry, *They Bite*, 180; Sanders, *Epic of Gilgamesh*, 88

Eous

Variations: Eoös ("Orient"), Eoos, ERYTHREOS, Euos

According to the Roman poet Ovid (43 BC–AD 17), Eous, one of the HIPPOI ATHANATOI, along with AITHOPS, PHLEGON, and PYROIS, are the horses harnessed to the chariot which pulls the sun across the heavens. According to Apollodorus, Eous and AETHIOPS were stallions and the trace horses (the outside horse on a chariot team in which more than two horses are driven abreast). In ancient Greek mythology Eoos ("Orient") was one of the four winged horses of Aurora.

In the Latin narrative poem *Metamorphoses* (2.153) written by the Roman poet Ovid, the sun god and second generation Titan, Helios (Sol), had his golden chariot, Quadriga, pulled across the sky by the flying horses ACTHON (AETHON), ASTROPE, BRONTE, CHRONOS, Eous, LAMPON, PHAETHON, PHLEGON, and PYROIS. All of these horses are described as being pure white and having flaring nostrils which can breathe forth flame.

Source: Brewer, *Dictionary of Phrase and Fable*, 626; Hard, *Routledge Handbook of Greek Mythology*, 43; Hargreaves, *Hargreaves New Illustrated Bestiary*, 67; Rose, *Giants, Monsters, and Dragons*, 7, 178

Epidaurian Dragon

Variations: Epidaurian drakon

A golden-colored DRAKON from ancient Greek mythology, the benevolent Epidaurian DRAGON lived a peaceful co-existence with the humans in the region of Epidsurus.

Source: Pausanias, *Pausanias' Description of Greece*, Volume 1, 142; Rose, *Giants, Monsters, and Dragons*, 103

Equuleus

A species of small horses from ancient Greek mythology, Equuleus ("a foal") were said to be the offspring of the winged horse PEGASUS and an unnamed mare. It had been proposed by the Hellenistic period Greek astronomer, geographer, and mathematician Hipparchus of Nicaea that the vague myth of Equuleus was created simply so a constellation of it could be placed in the sky to fill the space between PEGASUS and DELPHINUS.

Source: Dixon-Kennedy, *Encyclopedia of Greco-Roman Mythology*, 124

Erensuge

A seven-headed anthropophagous (man-eating) snake from Basque mythology, Erensuge is said to live in the caves of Balzola (Dima) and Montecristo (Mondragon). The breath of this snake is sweet and lures humans toward it; once they are in striking range, Erensuge lashes out and devours them.

Source: Miguel de Barandiarán, *Selected Writings of José Miguel De Barandiarán*, 132

Erinnyes (EYE-reen-ees)

Variations: "The Angry Ones," Dirae ("the terrible"), Erinyes, Eumenides, the Fatal Sisters, FURIAE, FURIES, the Kindly Ones, the Solemn Ones

In ancient Greek and Roman mythology the erinnyes were demons of vengeance. Born from the blood of Uranus ("heaven") when he was castrated, they are described as winged, black-skinned female demons wearing black robes. They have fiery eyes, snakes in their hair, and doglike faces. There are three erinnyes in all: ALECTO, MEGAERA, and TISIPHONE.

The erinnyes, whose name translates from Greek to mean "a punisher," "punishing," or "to punish," would seek out those who have committed murder in order to enact justice upon them by causing the criminal to go insane. Usually victims of the erinnyes commit suicide. If they feel someone is about to escape from them, they can call upon the goddess of justice, Dike, for divine assistance. These demons are particularly devoted to their cause, especially when the crime is matricide. There is no amount of prayer or sacrifice which can be offered which will deter them from their relentless pursuit of unyielding justice.

The erinnyes live in the underworld. Some sources claim they dwell at the entrance to Tartarus while others say they live in Erbus, the darkest pit of the underworld. When home they torment those who have not yet atoned for their sins.

Source: Baynes, *Encyclopedia Britannica* Volume 17, 699, 730, 827–8; Bjerregaard, *Great Mother*, 268, 271; Keightley, *Mythology of Ancient Greece and Italy*, 38, 174–5, 302–3

Erymanthian Boar

Variations: Hus Erymanthios

In classical Greek mythology, the demi-god and hero Hercules (Heracles) was tasked by Eurystheus with the live capture of the Erymanthian boar and to return with it to court in Mycenae for his fourth Labor. Unwilling to confront the creature and use his brute strength in a physical confrontation for fear of accidentally killing it, Hercules (Heracles)

tracked the boar and chased it up Mount Erymanthus (or Mount Lampe, sources conflict). The boar ran directly towards the top of the mountain where it eventually encountered snow, an element it was completely unfamiliar with. With the boar trapped in a drift and exhausted from its attempts to escape, Hercules (Heracles) was able to walk directly up to the animal and pick it up, carrying it upside down and over his head all the way back to his cousin Eurystheus, who was so frightened of the beast, he hid in a bronze vase.

Source: Daly, *Greek and Roman Mythology, A to Z*, 69; Fiore, *Symbolic Mythology*, 177; Smith, *New Classical Dictionary of Greek and Roman Biography, Mythology and Geography*, 395

Erythreos (Erythre'os)

In ancient Greek mythology Erythreos ("red producer") was one of the horses which pulled the chariot of Sol. Erythreos, along with LAMPOS and PUROCIS, was considered to be the noontime horse and counted among the HIPPOI ATHANATOI.

Source: Brewer, *Dictionary of Phrase and Fable*, 419; Woodcock, *Short Dictionary of Mythology*, 53

Estas

In the mythology of the Carrier people of British Columbia, the estas was a benevolent bird which delivered, PROMETHEUS-like, to the freezing people of the world the gift of fire.

Source: Brinton, *Myths of the New World*, 239; Rose, *Giants, Monsters, and Dragons*, 115

Etasa

In Hindu mythology Etasa ("swift") was one of the winged horses said to assist in pulling the wheel of the sun across the sky.

Source: Macdonell, *Vedic Mythology*, 149–50; Rose, *Giants, Monsters, and Dragons*, 178

Ethiopian Dragon

According to medieval European legends and travelers' tales, the double-winged Ethiopian DRAGON was nearly thirty-five feet long and lived off of a diet of elephants. Legend says in years when the drought was too terrible for elephants to be found the DRAGONs would entwine themselves together and set to sea as a gigantic raft, floating over to the Arabian coast.

A precious stone known as a dtacontias was embedded in the brain of the Ethiopian dragon; this was a highly sought after prize for alchemists but the stone was difficult to obtain as it must be removed while the creature was alive.

Source: Matthews, *Element Encyclopedia of Magical Creatures*, 174; Rose, *Giants, Monsters, and Dragons*, 103

Ethon

In classical Greek mythology, Ethon ("fiery") was one of the horses of Hector (see GALATHE and PODARGE).

Source: Brewer, *Dictionary of Phrase and Fable*, 419; Webster, *Historic Magazine and Notes and Queries*, 581

Euryale (u-ri-a-le)

Variations: Euruale

One of the three GORGONS from classical Greek mythology, Euryale ("far howling," "far roaming," or "wide leaping") and her sister STHENO were each immortal but their sister MEDUSA was not. Born the daughters of Phorcys and Ceto, the once beautiful Euryale and her transformed sisters lived in Lybia; she is described as having brazen claws and serpents for hair. She and her sisters are so vile to look upon, anyone who sees them is transformed into stone.

After the hero Perseus slew MEDUSA the sisters gave chase, but as he was aided with the helmet of Hades (Dis) and could become invisible, he was able to evade them. It is said the goddess Athena (Minerva) invented flute-playing inspired by the wailing of the grieving cries of Euryale and STHENO.

Pherecydes of Syros (6th century BC), a Greek author and thinker, claimed in his writings Poseidon (Neptune) and Euryale were the parents of the god Apollo.

Source: Berens, *Myths and Legends of Ancient Greece and Rome*, 144; Dixon-Kennedy, *Encyclopedia of Greco-Roman Mythology*, 55, 141; Rose, *Handbook of Greek Mythology*, 22

Eurynomos

A daemon from the tradition at Delphi, Eurynomos is described as having black and blue colored skin similar to carrion eating flies; in art he is depicted as showing his teeth and sitting upon a vulture pelt. Living in Hades, Eurynomos devoured the flesh of the dead leaving behind only their bones.

Source: Fontenrose, *Python*, 231; Rice, *Source for the Study of Greek Religion*, 175

Eurynomus, Centaur

A CENTAUR from ancient Greek mythology, Eurynomus, one of the centaurs who attended the wedding of Pirithous, became drunk on wine and following the lead of EURYTUS, who assaulted Hippodame, began to assault and rape any women they could grab. During the ensuing Centauromachy, Eurynomus, along with AREOS, EURYNOMUS, IMBRIUS, and LYCIDAY, was slain by the Lapith soldier Dryas as they attempted to flee the battle.

Source: *Commentary, Mythological, Historical, and Geo-*

graphical on Pope's Homer, 55; Simpson, *Metamorphoses of Ovid*, 205

Eurytion

In Greek mythology Eurytion was one of the many named CENTAURS; driven from first Thessalia and then Arkadia he came to the city of Olenos which was ruled by the CENTAUR King DEXAMENUS. Eurytion met the king's daughter, Deianeira (Mnesimache), and asked to marry her but was refused because she was already promised to the godling and hero Hercules (Heracles). Enraged, Eurytion sued to marry the woman and her father, fearful of the ramifications, consented. On the day of the wedding Hercules (Heracles) returned and in his anger, slew Eurytion.

Source: Apollodorus, *Apollodorus: The Library*, Volume 1, 197; Grant, *Who's who in Classical Mythology*, 174; Smith, *Dictionary of Greek and Roman Biography and Mythology*, 995

Eurytus (u-ri-tus)

Variations: Eurytion

A CENTAUR from ancient Greek mythology, Eurytus ("rapids") was the most savage of his kind and, according to Ovid's *Metamorphoses*, one of the CENTAURS who attended the wedding of Pirithous. When he became drunk on wine celebrating the newlywed couple, he snatched up the bride, Hippodame, carried her off, and raped her. The other CENTAURS in attendance, and there were in excess of fifty of them, followed his lead and began to assault and rape any women they could grab.

Theseus was first to react and confronted the CENTAUR, demanding an answer to his actions; however, unable to respond, Eurytus began to punch him in the chest and face. Grabbing a wine bowl as large as him, Theseus crashed it down upon the rapist, smashing in his skull and spewing his brains out upon the sandy floor. A great Centauromachy then followed.

Source: *Commentary, Mythological, Historical, and Geographical on Pope's Homer*, 55; Simpson, *Metamorphoses of Ovid*, 204

Fad Felen

Variations: Y Fad Felen

Llywelyn Sion (1540–c.1615), a Welsh poet and professional manuscript copyist, wrote of the fad felen ("yellow fever") in one of his ancient manuscripts; he said the creature was seen through the keyhole of Rhos church by Maelgwn Gwynedd who subsequently died, presumably of yellow fever.

The Brythonic poet of Sub-Roman Britain Taliesin wrote of the fad felen in one of his poems, describing it as originating from the sea marsh and having eyes, hair, and teeth as yellow as gold and likening it to the yellow fever plague.

Source: Maclagan, *Scottish Myths*, 178; Sikes, *British Goblins*, 215

Fadda

Variations: DALDAH, Duldul

According to Islamic folklore, Fadda was the white mule of the prophet Mahomet; from its back he performed a great number of miracles including the profuse milking of a nearly dry goat and the expedient dropping of dates from a tree to sate Fadda's hunger. Fadda was described as having overly long ears and in some descriptions, pink speckles on its coat.

Source: Brewer, *Dictionary of Phrase and Fable*, 439, 869; Reading, *Complete Prophecies of Nostradamus*, 110; Renard, *Islam and the Heroic Image*, 209

Fafnir

Variations: Fáfnir, Frænir

Fafnir was one of the DRAGONS named in Thorgrimr's *Rhymes* and in Snorri Sturluson's (1179–1241) *Prose Edda*. According to the legend, Fafnir was born a DVERG (DWARF) (or JOTUN, sources vary) and one of the sons of Hreidmar the magician. He coveted his father's magical ring, Advarinaut, a wondrous magical item which had the ability to produce treasure. Over time Fafnir became corrupted by Advarinaut, and desirous to possess it, murdered his father and assumed control of the great hoard of accumulated treasure. In order to best protect his cache of wealth, Fafnir shape-shifted into a DRAGON; however, because of his corrupt nature he remained in the shape unable, or unwilling, to transform back.

Fafnir had a brother named Regin who also had wanted their father's treasure but was too slow to act on his impulses. Unwilling to allow his brother the DRAGON to keep it, Regin, foster father of the legendary hero Siegfried (Sigurd), solicited his assistance. Regin told Siegfried the DRAGON was covered with impenetrable scales and poison breath but he would repair and restore his father's sword, Nothung, if the hero would use it to kill the DRAGON, as there was no such protection on the beast's underbelly. Siegfried agreed and after the sword was restored he dug a pit on the trail Fafnir used each day; as the DRAGON passed overhead Siegfried stabbed into the DRAGON's gut with Nothung, delivering a fatal blow.

Source: Daly, *Norse Mythology A to Z*, 84; De Kirk, *Dragonlore*, 72–3; Jennbert, *Animals and Humans*, 50

Fairy Animal

Variations: Fairy Creature

Throughout the fairy folklore of the various cultures, there are those animals which have many of the magical or otherworldly qualities of the fay but lack the level of empathy, intelligence, and understanding associated with sentient beings. Oftentimes these fairy animals are kept by the fay for domestic use, such as with their cattle the CRODH MARA or their hunting hounds, as in the Hounds of Annwn (see ANNWN, HOUNDS OF), the ARKAN SONNEY, and the CU SITH.

When one of these otherworldly animals is not domesticated but rather runs wild throughout the countryside causing fear and wreaking havoc in the lives of mortals, it is considered to be a fairy creature, such as in the case of the BOOBRIE.

There are those fairies who are described as having animal physical characteristics but due to their behavior and obvious displays of intelligence, such as the ability to communicate by use of language, these beings would not be considered to be strictly a fairy animal but a species of fay.

Source: Briggs, *Encyclopedia of Fairies*, 1034; Campbell, *Superstitions of the Highlands and Islands of Scotland*, 141–3; Davis, *Myths and Legends of Japan*, 358–9; Howey, *Horse in Magic and Myth*, 146; Monaghan, *Encyclopedia of Celtic Mythology and Folklore*, 105

Fákr (FAHK-r)

Variations: Fakr

In Norse mythology, Snorri Sturlson (1179–1241), the Icelandic historian, poet, and politician, writes the horse Fákr ("jade") was the preferred mount of Haki, one of the twelve berserker sons of Arngrim and Eyfura, in his translation of *Prose Edda*.

Source: Grimes, *Norse Myths*, 264, 273; Sturluson, *Prose Edda*, 211

Falak

A monstrously vast serpent in Islamic mythology, Falak resides in Hell, located beneath the gigantic bull BAHAMUT, suffering and writhing amongst the flames.

Source: Borges, *Book of Imaginary Beings*, 26; Rose, *Giants, Monsters, and Dragons*, 37

Falcon-Fish

A chimerical creature from European heraldic symbology, the falcon-fish is depicted as having the body of a fish, the head and legs of a falcon, and the ears of a dog.

Source: Lower, *Curiosities of Heraldry*, 104; McCutcheon, *Wordsworth Word Finder*, 415; Rose, *Giants, Monsters, and Dragons*, 117

Falhofnir (FAL-hohv-nir)

Variations: Falhófnir, Falhofner ("hollow hoof")

Falhofnir ("Falf's Fetlocked," "hairy-hoof," or "shaggy fetlock") was one of the horses of the Aesir; it was named in both the *Grímnismál* and *Gylfaginning* as one of the mounts ridden each day to Ygdrasil where the gods would make their daily judgments although neither source assigned it a specific rider. Falhofnir was also listed as one of the many horses who would graze in the red-gilt-leafed Glasir Grove.

Source: Grimes, *Norse Myths*, 20; Rydberg, *Norroena*, Volume 3, 1018; Sturluson, *Prose Edda*, 28

Falm

An obscure monster of Scottish folklore, the falm is said to live upon a mountain in Glen Aven; it has been described as looking not like a creature of the natural world but rather an "occasional visitant" who is dangerous and evil by design. The falm has only ever been sighted near the top of his domain and then, just before sunrise; its head is twice as large as its body. Folklore says if a living creature walks over the tracks left behind by the falm before the sun shines upon them, certain death will follow.

Source: Hill, *Scottish Castles of the Sixteenth and Seventeenth Centuries*, 124; Spence, *Magic Arts in Celtic Britain*, 94

Familiar

Variations: Familiar Spirit, Owb ("mumble")

The phrase *familiar spirit* first appeared in the Old Testament; in 1 Samuel 28 the Witch of Endor is commissioned by Saul to utilize her familiar spirits in order to communicate with the ANCESTRAL SPIRIT of the deceased Samuel seeking military advice on how to defeat the Philistine army.

Christian demonology of the Middle Ages defined a familiar as a demonic spirit which acted as an attendant or assistant to a conjuror, demonologist, or witch both in domestic duties and in practicing their magical craft. It was given to them by the demon or devil they made the pact with soon after the contract was signed. This demonic being typically took on the guise of an animal companion but folklore claims it would usually have the ability to shape-shift into a human or DWARF.

Source: De Puy, *Encyclopædia Britannica* Volume 7, 63; Maggi, *In the Company of Demons*, 100–103; Russell, *Witchcraft in the Middle Ages*, 14, 55, 187

Faming

A PHOENIX-like bird from Chinese folklore, the faming is one of the five spirit avians of some power. Each of the birds are described as looking similar to the PHOENIX in size and plumage, sitting upon one of the four cardinal points, and in the center rests the PHOENIX itself. The faming is the protector of the East, JIAOMING the South, SUSHUANG the West, and YOUCHANG the North.

Source: Sterckx, *Animal and the Daemon in Early China*, 155

Fanany

Variations: Fananim-Pitoloha ("the fanany with the seven heads")

A creature from Malagasy folklore, the fanany is described as being a serpentine creature with seven heads, each with a horn; it is reminiscent of the HYDRA from ancient Greek mythology. Respected and venerated, the fanany is the embodiment of the Malagasy fear of snakes.

Source: Sibree, *Folk-lore Record*, Volume 2, 27; Tyson, *Madagascar*, 248

Fandrefiala

In Madagascan folklore the fandrefiala is a species of predatory snake which hunts from the treetops; according to folklore when an animal passes beneath it, the fandrefiala plunged down, in a spear-like fashion, tail first, into the animal. The body of this animal is yellow or brown but the tail portion red. It is believed moments before the fandrefiala strikes, either three or seven leaves will fall from the tree; this is done to check its trajectory.

Source: Breverton, *Breverton's Phantasmagoria*, n.pag.; Zell-Ravenheart, *Wizard's Bestiary*, 38

Farasi Bahari

Variations: Sabarifya

A species of emerald green horses living in the Indian Ocean; it is believed on certain nights of the year the stallions leave the water to graze upon an island off the African coast. At this time horse breeders will leave their mares upon the island in the hope matings will occur producing green foals with incredible endurance. It is believed the endurance is due to the animal's lack of lungs.

Source: Zell-Ravenheart, *Wizard's Bestiary*, 38

Farvann

Farvann was a green fairy dog from the folklore of Scotland (see FAIRY ANIMAL). According to legend, he was as large as a two year old heifer and was once set lose on Hugh MacLeod who had stolen a fairy chalice. The dog will bay three time when on the hunt, pausing between each sonorous howl; the sound of it could strike fear in a man's heart. The tail of Farvann was said to sometimes curl up over its back while other times it was braided in a long plait. The fairy dog was said to act as a guardian to the entryway of Fairyland and would accompany fairy women as they went out to fetch milk. Moving in perfect silence, Farvann's paw prints were as large as a man's hand.

Source: Briggs, *Encyclopedia of Fairies*, 165; Simpson, *Folk Lore in Lowland Scotland*, 108–9

Fastitocalon

Variations: ASPIDOCHELONE

Similar to the BEAST JASCONIUS from the story of Saint Brendan, the fastitocalon ("devil whale") described in Anglo-Saxon bestiaries was said to be a powerful whale whose body so much resembled a rock or sand barge sailors were fooled by it believing it to be an island; they would anchor their ship to it, make landing, and build a fire upon its back. Only as the fastitocalon began to submerge in pain would the mistake the seamen had made become apparent; anyone who had made camp would be dragged into the depths by the creature. It was also believed the fastitocalon had the ability to release from its mouth a sweet smelling perfume which muddled the mind causing sailors to break course and sail towards it.

Source: Magasich-Airola, *America Magica*, 162–3; Rose, *Giants, Monsters, and Dragons*, 118; Zell-Ravenheart, *Wizard's Bestiary*, 20

The Father of All Turtles

In Sumatran folklore the Father of all Turtles is a gigantic sea-turtle or a SEA SERPENT living in warm waters with many turtle-like features, such as large and prominent eyes, a scaled back, and a very wide mouth which when opened will seem to split its head in two.

Source: Coleman, *Cryptozoology A to Z*, 96–7; Zell-Ravenheart, *Wizard's Bestiary*, 38

Faun (fawns)

Variations: Faunus, Phaunos

A FAIRY ANIMAL from Roman mythology, the faun is often associated with Greek SATYRS and the Greek god Pan (Faunus). Described as a horned human from the waist up and a goat from the waist down, this NATURE SPIRIT would guide those who were lost in the woods or terrorize those who traveled through the woods—it depends on their whimsy. Fauns should not be confused with the Roman god Faunus nor the goddess Fauna.

Source: Dixon-Kennedy, *Encyclopedia of Greco-Roman Mythology*, 133; Euvino, *Complete Idiot's Guide to Italian History and Culture*, 274; McCoy, *Witch's Guide to Faery Folk*, 31; Roman, *Encyclopedia of Greek and Roman Mythology*, 171

Fe-Lian

Variations: Fei-Lain, Fung Po

In Chinese folklore the DRAGON god Fe-Lian was a rival to the DRAGON SHEN-YI. Fe-Lian, a renowned troublemaker, had dominion over the wind and carried it in a bag; he was closely watched by SHEN-YI who served to balance his behavior. Fe-Lian is depicted as a storm bird.

Source: De Kirk, *Dragonlore*, 26; Fontenrose, *Python*, 479

Fear Liath More

Variations: Am Fear Liath Mor ("big grey man"), Fear Liath Mór, Fer- Las Mhór, Ferla Mohr, Ferla Mór, Ferlie More, Fomor, Liath

Living on the summit cairn of Ben MacDhui, one of the great peaks of the Scottish Cairngorm Mountains fear liath more ("the grey man") has been physically attacking people for generations. Of the few times it has been seen this FAIRY ANIMAL has been described as standing over ten-feet tall, having olive toned skin, long arms, and broad shoulders. More commonly the fear liath more is said to be experienced as an icy feeling in the air or a cold brushing against the skin. It also will make unusual crunching noises and mimic the sound of echoing footsteps.

Source: Eberhart, *Mysterious Creatures*, 51; Townsend, *Scotland*, 283; Wilson, *Mammoth Encyclopedia of the Unsolved*, 168; Zell-Ravenheart, *Wizard's Bestiary*, 39

Fearsome Critter

Variations: Fearsome Creature

Originating in the frontiersmen and lumberjack communities of the developing United States of America, the fearsome critters were the folkloric and legendary creatures invented to explain the difficulties and fears experienced in the wilderness as well as a means of humorous entertainment in teasing those individuals who did not know the truth.

Fearsome critters came in all shapes and sizes, including chimerical animals, birds, fish, insects, and reptiles. Typically the name of the creature is enough of a descriptor as to the animal's appearance and disposition, such as with the AXEHANDLE HOUND and HOOP SNAKE. The fearsome critters are: ALBOTRITCH, ARGOPELTER, AXEHANDLE HOUND, BALL TAILED CAT, BED CAT, BILLDAD, BIM-BAM, CACTUS CAT, CAMP CHIPMUNK, CATTYWAM-PUS, CENTRAL AMERICAN WHINTOSSER, COLUMBIA RIVER SAND SQUINK, COME-AT-A-BODY, COUGAR FISH, CUBA, DEW MINK, DING BALL, DISMAL SAUGER, FLIBBERTIGIBBET, FUNERAL MOUNTAIN TERRASHOT, GALLIWAMPUS, GAZERIUM, GIDDY FISH, GILLYGALOO, GLAWACKUS, GOOFANG, GOOFUS BIRD, GUMBEROO, GUYASCUTUS, HANGDOWN, HAPPY AUGER, HICKLESNIFER, HIDEBEHIND, HODAG, HOOP SNAKE, HUGAG, HUMILITY, JAY HAWK, KANKAGEE, KICKLE SNIFTER, LOG GAR, LUFERLANF, MILAMO BIRD, MOSKITTO, PHILA-

MALOO BIRD, PINNACLE GROUSE, PROCK GWINTER, RACHET OWL, ROPERITE, RUBBERADO, RUMPTI-FUSEL, SANDHILL PERCH, SANTER, SHAGAMAW, SLIDE ROCK BOLTER, SILVER CAT, SNIPE, SNO-LIGOSTER, SNOW SNAKE, SNOW WASSET, SNYDAE, SPLINTER CAT, SQUONK, SWAMP AUGER, SWAMP-SWIVER, SWAMP-GAHOON, TEAKETTLE, TREE SQUEAK, TRIPODEROO, UPLAND TROUT, WAMPUS CAT, WHAPPERNOCKER, WHIRLIGIG FISH, WILL AM ALONE, and the WILLOPUS-WALLOPUS.

Source: Binney, *Nature's Ways*, 225; Cox, *Fearsome Creatures of the Lumberwoods*, 5; Rose, *Giants, Monsters, and Dragons*, 119

Feathered Serpent

In the pre-classical and classical periods of Mesoamerican mythology the feathered serpent was considered to be a powerful being, a shape-shifter, having the features of the quetzal bird and a rattlesnake, the combinations of each varying; sometimes it is a feather-covered snake while in other renditions it has wings attached. It was believed these creatures which helped create the cosmos were also involved in human events, thereby linking humanity's actions to cosmic events.

Throughout both periods the feathered serpent is depicted as both a creature as well as a deity, such as in Gukumatz, Kukulkan, and Quetzalcoatl. The duality of the feathered serpent symbolized the contradictory nature of these deities as both earth and sky, the physical link between humanity and heaven.

Typically appearing with jaguar figures in the pre-classical era (2000 BC–AD 200) the feathered serpent does not gain dominance until the classical era (AD 200–1000) when its image is shown next to elite and important individuals. Quetzalcoatl, perhaps the most well-known of the feathered serpents, becomes a title or rulership. As these beings joined cosmic and human events, it was believed the feathered serpent endowed leaders with special powers.

Source: Andrews, *Dictionary of Nature Myths*, 156; Bingham, *South and Meso-American Mythology A to Z*, 47; Read, *Mesoamerican Mythology*, 180–2

Fei Lian

Variations: Chi Po, Feng Bo ("wind lord")

A monstrous being in Chinese mythology Fei Lian controlled the winds which he kept in a bag he would open and close as he desired. Born the son of the ruler of Huang Di, Fei Lian conspired with the god of rain Chi Song-Zi to overthrow him but their undertaking was a complete disaster. Fei Lian was exiled to a cave high up in the mountains but even there he still released wild wind storms. Eventually the celestial archer Yi punctured the bag

with one of his arrows and then hamstrung Fei Lian, subjecting him to sweep the roads before the chariot of this father, the king.

Fei Lian is sometimes depicted as a DRAGON, but other times he is shown as a horrific chimerical being having the body and legs of a stag, the head of a sparrow topped with bull horns, the markings of a leopard, and the tail of a serpent.

Source: Roberts, *Chinese Mythology A to Z*, 39; Rose, *Giants, Monsters, and Dragons*, 119; Zell-Ravenheart, *Wizard's Bestiary*, 39

Feng

Variations: August Rooster, FENGHUANG, Feng-huang

The PHOENIX of China, feng ("wind") resembled a cinnabar-red colored rooster according to Daoist texts. It was symbolic of the southern direction, the direction in which the emperors and kings faced their palaces and thrones. In the Han dynasty (206 BC–AD 220) the feng was called the FENGHUANG.

Source: Manansala, *Quests of the Dragon and Bird Clan*, 280, 341

Fenghuang

Variations: Feng-Bird, Fêng-Huang, Feng-Huang, Feng Hwang, Fum Hwang, FUNG HWANG, Red Bird

In Chinese mythology the fenghuang was recorded as appearing as early as the Shang dynasty (1556 BC to 1046 BC) and in Zhou text as an omen of political harmony. The descriptions of the fenghuang have changed over the centuries, becoming more and more flamboyant, but originally it was depicted as a five colored bird resembling a rooster with glyphs on its body: duty on its wings, humaneness on its breast, ritual on its back, trust on its stomach, and virtue on its head. It was believed to have lived in the mountains of Cinnabar Caves (Tan-hsueh shan) located south of the Yueh kingdom, modern Zhejiand. Eating, dancing, drinking, and singing at will, it was said to see a fenghuang was an omen for world peace; it is essentially the Chinese version of a PHOENIX, although it does not die in a similar fashion.

Source: Manansala, *Quests of the Dragon and Bird Clan*, 280, 341; Roberts, *Chinese Mythology A to Z*, 39, 94; Strassberg, *Chinese Bestiary*, 193–4

Fenrir (Fen-reer) (FEHN-rir)

Variations: Fenrer, Fenrir, Fenris, Fenrisulfr ("fenris wolf"), Fenriswolf, Fenriswulf, Fenrisúlfr, Hrodvitnir ("the famous-wolf"), Úlfr Fenris, Vana-gandr, Vanargand ("afraid of the wolf of the marsh"), Vanargandr, Vanarganndr, Vanargand ("afraid of the wolf of the marsh")

Born one of the three children of Loki and his mistress, the JOTUN Angerboda, the malignant Fenrir ("bog dweller") was born in the likeness of a wolf whose eyes and nostrils projected fire. He and his siblings were prophesied to be the cause of a great calamity and while his brother and sister, the Midgard Serpent JORMUNGANDR, and the goddess Hel, had been cast out, Fenrir was raised among the Aesir. As the wolf matured his evil nature became more apparent and uncontrollable. He was so large his upper jaw could touch the heavens while his bottom jaw scraped along the earth.

The gods sought to eternally chain him but Fenrir was too powerful to remain captive for long. Ultimately Gleipnir, a magical and unbreakable chain forged of the beards of women, the breath of birds, the nerves of bears, the noise of cat feet, the roots of mountains, and the saliva of fish, was constructed to fetter the wolf. Fenrir was bound in Niffelheim at the gate of Helheim, the residence of Hel, where he is to remain until the battle of Ragnarok. When the time arrives, Fenrir will only then be able to break free and join the Jotnar (see JOTUN) in the war against the gods where he will devour Odin but will then be slain by Vidar.

Source: Daly, *Norse Mythology A to Z*, 28–9; Mortensen, *Handbook of Norse Mythology*, 34, 38; Oehlenschläger, *Gods of the North*, xxxvl

Fialar

Variations: Fiala, Fjalar ("all knowing"), Fjalarr ("hidder")

The purple or red colored rooster in Norse mythology, Fialar ("cock") lives in Gagalvid in Jotunheimr; it will crow at the start of Ragnarok summoning the Jotnar (see JOTUN) and the gods to battle. His counterpart is the rooster GULLINKAMBI.

Source: Daly, *Norse Mythology A to Z*, 29; Grimes, *Norse Myths*, 265; Oehlenschläger, *Gods of the North*, xxxl

Fideal

Variations: Fidealadh

The fideal is one of the FUATH, the collective name for the malicious and monstrous water fay in Scottish folklore; it is a personification of the ensnaring marsh grass and reeds. Singing a compelling and lovely song as it walks through the reedy edges of lakes, the voluptuous fideal will lure in her prey with a cold kiss and chilling embrace. It is said her victims die happily embraced in her arms.

Near Loch Maree Hotel is the isolated Loch na Fideil in Gairloch, Scotland, where a fideal was once said to haunt. The last encounter of this fairy was said to be in a fatal confrontation between it and a strong young man named Eoghainn. In their conflict, they killed one another.

Source: Briggs, *Encyclopedia of Fairies*, 175; Mackenzie, *Scottish Folk-Lore and Folk Life*, 234; Rose, *Spirits, Fairies, Leprechauns, and Goblins*, 121; Watson, *Place-Names of Ross and Cromarty*, 81, 281

Finnbennach

Variations: Findbennach, Finnbhennach, Fionn Bheannach

A splendid white-horned bull from Irish folklore, Finnbennach lived in the pastures of Ailill mac Mata, the consort of the provincial queen Medb. Finnbennach was once a swineherd named Rucht who would argue endlessly with another swineherd named Friuch. The bitterness between the two men was so great, when they died they would each reincarnate and begin their argument anew. As ravens they fought in the air and as stags they fought in the forest. When they were reborn as water worms they were in lakes separated by miles with no means by which they could continue their physical assaults so they each began planning for their next incarnation. Worm Rucht whispered to provincial queen Medb of Connacht to wed Ailill mac Mataa while Worm Friuch whispered to the king of Cuailnge to prepare for a war which will be fought over a bull. Each worm with their plan in place then positioned themselves to be drunk by a cow enabling them each to be reborn as a bull.

Rucht, now named Finnbennach, was the most magnificent bull in Connacht, but he resented being owned by a woman so he left to join the herd of Ailill. Whether it was his intention or not, in doing so Finnbennach upset the balance of power between the queen and her consort, so she set out to find a bull as magnificent as him and did so when the brown bull DONN CÚAILNGE was discovered in the fields of a minor Ulster king, Daire. Medb sent messengers to petition the rental of the bull for a year for a vast sum of money and her personal sexual favors, but before the king had the opportunity to accept the offer it was overheard that the queen's men planned on stealing DONN CÚAILNGE. Following the angry refusal of Daire, the cattle raid of Queen Medb became legendary; it brought together the eternal enemies in the guise of Finnbennach and DONN CÚAILNGE who upon sight of one another immediately began to engage in combat. Ultimately, Finnbennach was slain by his old adversary, but before he died he was able to gore DONN CÚAILNGE who died soon thereafter from the wound.

Source: Haase, *Greenwood Encyclopedia of Folktales and Fairy Tales*, 173; Monaghan, *Encyclopedia of Celtic Mythology and Folklore*, 188–9; Sax, *Mythical Zoo*, 50

Fire Drake

Variations: Firedrake

According to mediaeval folklore the fire drake was a species of fire-breathing DRAGON or gigantic serpent keeping guard over a treasure. In Celtic and Teutonic folklore the fire drake was also winged and capable of flight. Wherever it lived, be it in the wetlands or in a mountain cave, the fire drake was always a fearsome adversary.

Source: De Kirk, *Dragonlore*, 41; Hulme, *Myth-land*, 147; Rose, *Giants, Monsters, and Dragons*, 123; Zell-Ravenheart, *Wizard's Bestiary*, 40

Fire Drake of *Beowulf*

In the Old English poem *Beowulf*, written between the eighth and eleventh century, the tale of the epic's hero Beowulf battling the FIRE DRAKE, or DRAGON, is one of three major stories told.

At this point in the poem, Beowulf has inherited the kingdom from Heardred and has had a prosperous fifty year rule. One day one of his people discovers a DRAGON's treasure hoard which had been untouched by human hands for three-hundred years and while the creature is asleep he steals a golden cup. Although the thief gave the cup to Beowulf, the FIRE DRAKE awakes, enraged, and being an unintelligent creature which cannot be reasoned with, begins to assault the land and burn buildings, one of which is the king's great hall. Fearing this is divine punishment for some sin he has committed, Beowulf commits to battling the beast, discarding his wooden shield for a new one forged of iron. Guided by the thief, Beowulf and eleven of his retainers set out to confront the FIRE DRAKE. Unafraid and still seeking valor at his age, the king insists on attacking the beast alone. No sooner does he enter the cave calling out his challenge to the FIRE DRAKE than the conflict begins. The retainers flea in terror even when the king calls for them; only young Wiglaf remains and using his sword, a family heirloom, assists Beowulf. The FIRE DRAKE receives a blow to the head which causes it no injury but does shatter the king's sword; in the moment of shock which follows, the creature bites the king, envenoming him. Wiglaf strikes the beast, wounding it and buying the old hero time to free his arm, pull his dagger and deliver a death blow to the belly of the FIRE DRAKE. Although the creature is slain, the king cannot be saved, as the poison has ravished his body. The cursed treasure is buried with Beowulf and the remains of the FIRE DRAKE are deposited into the sea.

Source: Bloom, *Beowulf*, 22–6; De Kirk, *Dragonlore*, 66; Fulk, *Interpretations of Beowulf*, 23, 99–100

Firebird

Variations: Zhar-Ptitsa ("heat bird")

In Slavic folklore the firebird is usually described as being a large bird with beautiful orange, red, and yellow plumage which even when plucked, still glows with enough light to brighten a room. Some descriptions say the eyes are made of brilliant crystals, the feathers are made of solid gold, and the animal is in fact a celestial creature.

Originating in a land far away, the usual role of this bird, commonly a female, is to be the object of a quest; usually a king will send out a young hero to return with either a feather or the living firebird itself. The bird itself is highly coveted but hardship and misery always follow anyone who obtains one of its feathers or manages to capture it.

Source: Maisie, *Land of the Firebird*, 18–9; Rose, *Giants, Monsters, and Dragons*, 122; Zell-Ravenheart, *Wizard's Bestiary*, 40

Fish-Knight

Variations: Poisson Chevalier ("fish knight")

In the French Arthurian folklore the fish-knight was a monster which resembled an armored knight astride a charger; one such creature was slain by King Arthur in *Le Chevalier du Papegau* ("The Knight of the Parrot"), an anonymous French prose of the late fourteenth century. The fish-knight had been harassing the Lady of the Fair Hair of the Amorous City. After the fish-knight was vanquished, a violent storm at sea rose up.

Source: Bruce, *Arthurian Name Dictionary*, 185; Busby, *Comedy in Arthurian Literature*, 138

Fish-Man

Variations: Fish Man, el Hombre Pex

The legend of the fish-man originated in the 1700s from the village of Lierganes in northern Spain. There it is said a man by the name of Francisco de la Vega Casar went to Bilbao to work as a carpenter; one day he went down to the river to bathe and was never seen again. His family and friends had assumed he drowned. Nine years later some fishermen trolling in the Bay of Cadiz hauled up a scale-covered male humanoid they took back with them to town; there was webbing between his fingers and toes. There a Cantabrian recognized the odd catch as the lost Francisco de la Vega Casar by a birthmark. Although the creature did not have the ability to speak it was able to verify its identity. For the next nine years the fish-man was exploited as a curiosity, always chilly and damp. Although his care-givers never let him anywhere near the water again he was one day able to elude them and escape, never to be seen again.

Source: Facaros, *Northern Spain*, 189; McCarta, *Spain: North*, 90

Flibbertigibbet

Originating in the lumberjack communities of the developing United States of America, the flibbertigibbet is listed as one of the FEARSOME CRITTERS.

According to Bishop Harsnet, Flibbertigibbet was also the name of one of forty fiends who were cast out by Spanish Jesuits during the Spanish invasions.

In Shakespeare's *King Lear* he is described as the demon of mopping and mowing and possessing chambermaids and waiting women. He is said to walk the earth from dusk to dawn causing mildew on white wheat, harming the creatures of the earth, and causing harelips and squinting eyes (*King Lear*, III, 4 and IV, 1).

Source: Daniels, *Encyclopaedia of Superstitions, Folklore, and the Occult Sciences*, Volume 2, 1414; Rose, *Giants, Monsters, and Dragons*, 119

Flittericks

A species of flying squirrel said to frequent lumber camps, the flittericks are particularly dangerous because they fly so quickly they are virtually impossible to dodge. It is said a flitterick once struck an ox between the eyes and the impact of the collision was enough to kill both animals.

Source: Botkin, *American People*, 251; Gard, *Wisconsin Lore*, 72

Flying Heads

The Iroquois tribes of the northeastern United States of America have a vampiric creature in their folklore aptly named the flying heads. It is a large head with fiery red eyes, stringy hair, and rows of sharp teeth within a huge mouth that has locking jaws. It has wings where its ears should be. Flying heads glide through stormy skies, keeping aloft by the undulating of their hair while they look for prey. Once a suitable victim is found, the head dives down, biting into the person, its jaws locking into place.

Luring in a creature capable of flight so it can be close enough to kill would be a difficult thing to do in the best of circumstances; fortunately, flying heads are not exceedingly bright. The Iroquois would roast chestnuts over a fire made of many small coals. Then, they would eat them, making loud exclamations of how delicious the nuts tasted. The flying heads, wanting to eat something as wonderful tasting as the nuts, would swoop down and grab up a mouthful of the red-hot coals. Once the jaws locked shut, the coals would begin to burn, and soon, the flying heads would ignite and burst into flames.

Source: Beauchamp, *Iroquois Trail*, 95; Canfield, *Legends of the Iroquois*, 125–26; McLeish, *Myths and Legends*, 199; Rose, *Giants, Monsters and Dragons*, 124; Wonderley, *Oneida Iroquois Folklore*, 92

Folkvir (FAWLK-vir)

In Norse mythology, Snorri Sturlson (1179–1241), the Icelandic historian, poet, and politician, writes the horse Folkvir ("folk warrior") was the preferred mount of Haraldr in his translation of *Prose Edda*.

Source: Grimes, *Norse Myths*, 247; Norroena Society, *Asatrii Edda*, 346; Sturluson, *Prose Edda*, Volume 5, 212

Fox-Maiden

In the folklore from medieval Japan the fox maiden was a shape-shifting seductress, representing femininity and terrifying men with the secret knowledge they hold. They have the ability of therianthropy, enabling them to shape-shift between animal and human form at will; in most stories they are the wife or companion of a man who after a very long or short period of time die or mysteriously disappear. In some instances, children are produced from these unions. Normally the fox maiden is benign, although there are stories of them causing death, mischief, and suffering, but the stories of blatantly evil HUA YANG are a radical exception.

Source: Bush, *Asian Horror Encyclopedia*, 76–7; Sax, *Mythical Zoo*, 121; Seal, *Encyclopedia of Folk Heroes*, 150

Fox Serpent

Variations: Glyryvilu, Guirivilu, Neguruvilu, Vulpangue

A freshwater dwelling DRAGON or monstrous fish in the folklore of the people of Chile, the fox serpent was described by Juan-Ignacio Molina (1740–1829) in his *Essay on the Natural History of Chile* (1782) as being serpent-like with the head of a fox or as a vast and circular creature with its eyes around the edge. It also had a long tail with a double row of pointed nails and a claw at the tip. Living in a lake high up in the Andes Mountains the fox serpent was so vicious a creature the people who lived in its region could not be lured into entering the water; it would kill animals and people who entered into its realm by enveloping them with its body.

Source: Eberhart, *Mysterious Creatures*, 220; Meurger, *Lake Monster Traditions*, 275; Rose, *Giants, Monsters, and Dragons*, 145

Freke (FREHK-i)

Variations: Feke, Feki, Freki ("gluttony"), Gifr

In Norse mythology, Freke ("gobble up") was one

of the two wolves of the god Odin; the other was GERI. These wolves sat at his side and he fed them directly from his own table; they were the god's personal guardians. Freke was named in Thorgrimr's *Rhymes* and in Snorri Sturluson's (1179–1241) *Prose Edda*.

Source: Coulter, *Encyclopedia of Ancient Deities*, 181; Grimes, *Norse Myths*, 267; Jennbert, *Animals and Humans*, 50

Freybug

A monstrous BLACK DOG from the folklore of medieval England, Freybug was said to patrol country lanes in the night terrorizing anyone who would travel at night. It was mentioned in a manuscript dating back to 1555.

Source: Borges, *Book of Imaginary Beings*, n.pag.; Rose, *Giants, Monsters, and Dragons*, 125

Fu-T'sang Lung

Subterranean DRAGONs in Chinese mythology, the fu-t'sang lung ("treasure DRAGONs") are guardians of great wealth and treasure; they are similar to the ASDEEV.

Source: De Kirk, *Dragonlore*, 26

Fuath, plural Fuathan or Fauths

Variations: Arrachd, Fuath-Arrached

In Scottish folklore the fuath ("hate") is a generic term applied to any type of water spirit living in fresh or salt water, a loch, river, or sea. On occasion this title is given to a Highland or NATURE SPIRIT, but when this happens, the being is always maligned. Descriptions of fuaths vary widely, but generally speaking, they look like terribly deformed humans covered with long yellow fur or just have a mane running down their back. Typically dressed in green or having spikes, tails and webbed feet are also common features; however they are rarely seen because of the remote regions they live in. Susceptible to sunlight, the fuath are mindful of cold steel, as it will kill them instantly. Interestingly, they become restless when crossing a stream. Although the fuath are similar to the KELPIE or UISGES in Northern Ireland, they will intermarry with humans; their offspring will have the telltale sign of sporting a mane, tail, or webbed toes.

Source: Briggs, *Fairies and Traditions in Literature*, 52; Illes, *Encyclopedia of Spirits*, 420; Macleod, *Dictionary of the Gaelic Language*, 208; Rose, *Spirits, Fairies, Leprechauns, and Goblins*, 121

Fucanglong

A fiery underworld DRAGON from Chinese mythology Fucanglong ("DRAGON of the hidden treasures") is the guardian of lost treasure and pre-cious jewels. It is believed each time it burst forth from the earth a volcano erupts.

Source: Cox, *Spooky Spirits and Creepy Creatures*, 13; Rosen, *Mythical Creatures Bible*, 63

Fuku-Riu

A little-known DRAGON from Japanese mythology, the Fuku-Riu ("to be angry") is a venerated, three-toed luck DRAGON. The fuku-riu has the ability to fly although they only mature to the KIAO-LUNG phase of development.

Source: Bates, *All About Chinese Dragons*, 100; De Kirk, *Dragonlore*, 30; Forbes, *Illustrated Book of Dragons and Dragon Lore*, 18; Johnsgard, *Dragons and Unicorns*, 18, 155

Fulong

In Japanese mythology there are four species or types of DRAGONS: DILONG (earth DRAGONs), Fulong (underworld DRAGONs), SHENLONG (spiritual DRAGONs), and TIANLONG (celestial DRAGONS). The Fulong ("hidden DRAGON") guard the precious metals still buried within the earth. FUCANGLONG would be an example of one of the fulong.

Source: Giddens, *Chinese Mythology*, 48; Rosen, *Mythical Creatures Bible*, 63

Funeral Mountain Terrashot

Variations: Terrashot

Originating in the lumberjack communities of the developing United States of America, the Funeral Mountain terrashot, one of the FEARSOME CRITTERS, was first reported by Mormon emigrants and described as having a body shaped like a casket, stretching six to eight feet long, and having a shell covering the whole of its back. The terrashots, as they are sometimes called, have four long and unstable legs causing them to have an unsteady gait as they sway from side to side as they walk.

The terrashots live in herds in small meadows upon the mountains in the higher elevations; at some point they are apparently seized with an impulse to migrate and after struggling down the mountain begin to venture across the hot, open, sandy range. The creatures begin to distend with heat and eventually explode leaving a deep grave-like hole in the sand.

Source: Cox, *Fearsome Creatures of the Lumberwoods*, 19; Rose, *Giants, Monsters, and Dragons*, 119

Fung Hwang

Variations: Shui Ying bird

Called the PHOENIX of Chinese folklore the Fung Hwang was first mentioned in the '*Rh Ya*, which, known for its brevity, only commented the female of the species was called Hwang while the male was referred to as Fung; its commentator, Kwoh P'oh, added only it had a cock's head, a snake's neck, a swallow's beak, a tortoise's back, five colors, and a standing height of more than nine feet. Later editions (seventeenth century) combined the female and male names into one.

A small work devoted to ornithology written during the Tsing dynasty (AD 265–317) called the *Kin King* described the fung hwang as looking like a swan in the front but a Lin from behind; it also said the bird had several Chinese characters imprinted upon its body: its back, humanity; its foot, integrity; its head, virtue; its heart, sincerity; its poll, uprightness, and its wings, integrity (duplicate). The low notes of its call were described as sounding like a bell and its high notes like a drum; its body contains all five colors: black, red, azure (green, blue, or black), white, and yellow. The fung hwang will not peck at living grass and when it flies, flocks of birds follow in its wake.

Source: Gould, *Mythical Monsters*, 366, 368–9; Rose, *Giants, Monsters, and Dragons*, 126

Fur-Bearing Trout

Variations: Runt Beaver Trout

In the folklore near the lake along the Vermont-Quebec border the fur-bearing trout is said to have a fine covering of fur over its body in order to keep it warm during the harsh winter months; it is said to molt off in the spring. Some folklore claims it can only be caught by use of the ICE WORM, a creature so brittle and gelid it must first be warmed before it can be bent and placed on a hook, a process which then renders the worm invisible to the human eye. Unfortunately, no sooner is the fur-covered trout hooked and landed than exposure to the air nearly instantly evaporates the fur.

Source: Alexander, *Forgotten Tales of Vermont*, 47–6; Duffy, *Vermont Encyclopedia*, 132; Zell-Ravenheart, *Wizard's Bestiary*, 41

The Furies

Variations: Angry Ones, Dirae, Erinyes ("disturbers of the mind"), Errinys, Erynnes ("angry ones"), Eumenides ("kindly ones"), Furiae, Kindly Ones, Night Born Sisters, Strong Ones

The Furies of Greek mythology, three sisters named ALECTO ("envy" or "never ending"), MEGAERA ("envious anger" or "slaughter"), and TISIPHONE ("face of retaliation" or "rage"), are the opposite of the MUSES who were associated with upholding cosmic order and proper behavior; the Furies' primary concern was with the retribution for the killing of family members. Linked with darkness, death, night, and the Underworld, the furies drink human blood rather than wine. Born the daughters of Gia ("earth") and Uranus ("heaven") they find the practice of human sacrifice reprehensible and will lash out their anger on those who practice it. Described as having a ghastly physical appearance comparable to the GORGONS, the Furies wear black robes, their eyes ooze, and their breath reeks. In art the Furies are depicted as sucking the life-blood out of their victims, gnawing on flesh. Self-imposed outcasts of Olympia, the Furies are associated with death, pain, torture, and violence. Although the opposite of the clean and beautiful Olympians the Furies play an important role in Greek mythology, as without these unclean spirits mortals would have no fear of punishment and live in total anarchy. When the Furies punished someone with obvious compassion they were called the Eumenides ("mild").

Source: Illes, *Encyclopedia of Spirits*, 390; Keightley, *World Guide to Gnomes, Fairies, Elves, and Other Little People*, 495; Robbins, *Elements of Mythology*, 106–7; Roman, *Encyclopedia of Greek and Roman Mythology*, 173

Futa-Guichi Onna (FOO-tah-KOO che OHN-nah)

Variations: Futakuchi-Onna

A grotesque YŌKAI creature from Japanese mythology, the futa-guichi onna ("two-mouthed woman") is depicted as a woman who has a second mouth in the back of her head which is fed by her animated long hair. It is believed a woman can become one of these creatures after death if she does not properly feed her step-children during her life. Should a stepchild die of starvation the woman, even if alive, will transform into this YŌKAI forty-nine days after the death of the child. It is said the second mouth of the futa-guichi onna is unable to lie and will always speak the truth regardless of etiquette.

Source: Bush, *Asian Horror Encyclopedia*, 54; Yoda, *Yokai Attack*, 74–7

Fuwch Gyfeiliorn

Variations: The Cow, Stray Cow, LLYN BARFOG, Y Fuwch Frech ("speckled cow"), Y Fuwch Gyfeiliorn

In Welsh folklore Fuwch Gyfeiliorn was a FAIRY ANIMAL, one of the LLYN BARFOG. One day a farmer was fortunate enough to have one of the FAIRY ANIMALS fall in love with a bull from his herd; he named this fairy cow Fuwch Gyfeiliorn. The cow birthed the most amazing calves and gave the most delicious milk which was churned into the tastiest butter and cheese. The farmer grew rich off of the proceeds of his fairy cow but the time came when he felt it was too old to be of any further profit and began fattening it up for market. When the time of

Fuwch Gyfeiliorn's killing came, people from all over the region wanted to witness the event. The butcher's bludgeon hit the correct place on the cow's head but magically passed harmlessly through the cow, knocking over nine men who stood watching. From a crag which overlooked the lake the crowd saw a woman dressed in green and heard her call out "Come yellow anvil, stray horns, speckled one of the lake, and of the hornless Dodlin, arise and come home." Not only did Fuwch Gyfeiliorn begin to make her way into the lake in response to the call but all of her progeny going back four generations; only one cow remained behind and it turned raven black. The farmer, now financially ruined, drowned himself in the lake but the black cow became the progenitor of the Welsh black cattle.

Sources: Narváez, *Good People*, 163; Rhys, *Celtic Folklore Welsh and Manx*, Volume 1, 244–5; Thomas, *Welsh Fairy Book*, 79–80; Sikes, *British Goblins*, 39–40

Ga-Git (GAH-get)

From the mythology of the Haida Indians of the Queen Charlotte Islands off the west coast of North America comes a species of demonic creature known as the ga-git. It is said when a man survives a canoe wreck at sea and makes it back to shore, there is a chance, in a daze he may wander off into the woods where he will survive off berries, moss, and roots. Eventually he will discard his clothing and gain the power of flight and superhuman strength, shortly thereafter fully transforming into a ga-git. Should this creature intentionally breathe on a person's face, the transformation process will begin immediately and take only a few days to complete. Basically humanoid in appearance, its body is covered in heavy black fur with taloned hands and feet. The creature emits a deep continuous, rumbling growl; it smells of filth and rotting meat.

A nocturnal demon, it hunts by night, attacking anyone it happens upon. Ga-git are known to shake houses and uproot trees. Occasionally one will venture near a village and cast a magical spell causing a very deep sleep to fall over a house. Once this happens, it will slip inside and carry away its occupants. Ga-git also have the ability to change their shape at will. Although they have the ability to fly, only the very old and powerful ones can fly high enough to clear the top of a house; the rest can only rise up a few yards off the ground.

These creatures live in caves in the woods. If ever you are chased by a ga-git, immediately run to the nearest body of water, as they are phobic of it and will not follow.

Source: Harrison, *Ancient Warriors of the North Pacific*, 133–5; Jones, *Evil in Our Midst*, 19–22

Ga-Gorib

Variations: The Thrower Down

In Khoikhoi mythology of South Africa, the ga-gorib ("thrower down") was a murderous creature; it would sit upon the edge of a pit holding a stone against its forehead and wait for a person to wander by and then challenge them to take his stone and throw it as hard as they could at the place he indicated on his forehead. Anyone who accepted this challenge died, as the stone would always ricochet back and kill the opponent. Eventually the ga-gorib was slain by the legendary hero Heitsi-eibib; he distracted the creature and struck it behind its ears before pushing it into the very pit it perched upon. In another telling of the story, the hero chased the ga-gorib around the pit until the monster slipped and fell in. In a third rendition, Heitsi-eibib fell into the pit but was able to eventually climb out and wrestle the monster to death.

Source: Cotterell, *Dictionary of World Mythology*, 242; Coulter, *Encyclopedia of Ancient Deities*, 188; Lynch, *African Mythology, A to Z*, 47

Gaasyendietha

Variations: The Meteor DRAGON

In the mythology of the Seneca people of the New York region of North America, the fire-breathing DRAGON Gaasyendietha was said to have descended to earth in a meteor crash. Described as being gigantic and able to fly across the heavens on a trail of fire, it lived in lakes and rivers and was ill-tempered.

Source: De Kirk, *Dragonlore*, 48; Rose, *Giants, Monsters, and Dragons*, 129; Zell-Ravenheart, *Wizard's Bestiary*, 41

Gaborchend, plural, gaborchind

Variations: Goborchend

In Irish folklore, the gaborchind ("goat head") were the most primitive and possibly the original inhabitants of the island. These humanoids were described as having anthropomorphic bodies but the heads of dogs or goats.

Source: MacKillop, *Dictionary of Celtic Mythology*, 217; Rose, *Giants, Monsters, and Dragons*, 129

Gabriel Hound

Variations: Cron Annwn, Cwn Annwn, Dogs of Hell, Gabble Retchets, Gabriel Ratchets, Gabriel Ratchet's Hounds, Gobble-ratches, Gytrash, Heath Hounds, Hell Hounds, Sky Yelpers, WISH HOUNDS, Wisk, Yell Hounds, Yesk, Yell Hounds, Yeth Hounds

Similar to CWN ANNWFN (see ANNWN, HOUNDS OF) in Welsh fairy folklore, the Gabriel hounds are a pack of spectral hounds prowling Durham, Lancashire, North Devon, Staffordshire, and Yorkshire, England, led by the archangel Gabriel when the Wild Hunt is under way. Described as being overly large and having red ears and eyes, their bodies glow eerily green or white when they fly through the air; sometimes the hounds are said to have a human head. A Gabriel hound is believed to be created when an unbaptized baby dies. If seen hovering over a house, it is reputed these spectral hounds foretell death for one of its occupants, acting as a psychopomp (death omen).

Sometimes the cries and the wing beats of a species of geese known as Bean Goose (*Anser segetum*) flying at night are mistakenly misinterpreted as the sounding of the hounds.

Source: Allardice, *Myths, Gods, and Fantasy*, 88; Briggs, *Encyclopedia of Fairies*, 183; Chambers, *Book of Days*, 430; Wright, *English Dialect Dictionary*, 530

Gagana

In Russian folklore the gagana is a bird with copper claws and an iron beak said to live on Booyan Island, located in the eastern ocean near Paradise. The gagana is often invoked in incantations and spells.

Source: Berman, *Red Caps*, 41; Zell-Ravenheart, *Wizard's Bestiary*, 41

Gainjin

In Papuan mythology, the gainjin was the collective name of the animals which descended from Heaven in order to assist in the construction of the earth; they were described as being "larger than life." Afterwards only two gainjin remained: Bugal the snake and Warger the crocodile. The skin of Chel the python became the rainbow.

Source: Poignant, *Oceanic Mythology*, 88; Zell-Ravenheart, *Wizard's Bestiary*, 41

Gajasimha

In Sinhalese mythology the gajasimha ("elephant-trunk lion") is a hybrid creature, a monstrous and powerful lion with the head of an elephant. The gajasimha appears in the art of India as well.

Source: Malalasekera, *Encyclopaedia of Buddhism*, Volume 4, Issue 2, 304; Mode, *Fabulous Beasts and Demons*, 269

Galathe

In classical Greek mythology, Galathe ("cream colored") was one of the three horses of Hector (see ETHON and PODARGE).

Source: Brewer, *Dictionary of Phrase and Fable*, 419; Webster, *Historic Magazine and Notes and Queries*, 581

Galley-Trot

Variations: Churchyard Dog, Galleytrot, Gally-Trot, Gilitrutt, Hell Beast, Swooning Shadow

The galley-trot is a FAIRY ANIMAL from British folklore, typically said to roam in Bath-Slough and Woodbridge; it is very similar to the BARGUEST and the BLACK SHUCK but is described as looking like a shaggy, shadowy white dog (rather than black) about the size of a bullock. Fearsome to behold, its soulful and terrible howl is heard before it is ever seen, typically in graveyards or along the side of lonesome roads. Apparently harmless, the galley-trot is unable to actually catch anyone who it chases.

Source: Buckland, *Weiser Field Guide to Ghosts*, 25; Hartland, *Gloucestershire*, 85; Wright, *Rustic Speech and Folk-Folklore*, 194

Galliwampus

Originating in the lumberjack communities of the developing United States, the galliwampus was one of the FEARSOME CRITTERS. Unfortunately, there is no additional information on this creature other than its name, causing writers of the time, 1841–1861, to believe it had gone extinct.

Source: Mencken, *American Language Supplement 1*, 251

Gamayun

A prophetic bird of Russian folklore, the gamayun is symbolic of knowledge and wisdom and lives upon an island located near Paradise. In art, it is depicted as a large black feathered bird with a woman's head, similar to the SIRIN. Gamayun is a mournful creature and does not sing but rather flies from one end of the world to the other screaming out its despondent predictions. This bird never rests upon the celestial oak and her presence is dreaded by all as her visions only foretell disaster with no consolation, hope, or solution as to how to prevent the tragedy.

Source: Alexander, *Fairies*, 153; Sedia, *Secret History of Moscow*, 198; Zell-Ravenheart, *Wizard's Bestiary*, 41

Gandaberunda

In Hindu mythology the gandaberunda is a two-headed eagle, often used as the proud symbol of emperors and kings.

Source: Rao, *Brief Survey of Mystic Tradition in Religion and Art in Karnataka*, 176

Gandarəβa

Variations: Azi Sruuara

An aquatic KHRAFSTRA living in Lake Varukasha according to Zoroastrian mythology, Gandarəβa, the "yellow heeled monster of the sea," was said to be so large as to be able to devour twelve provinces at once (see SEA SERPENT). According to scripture, Gandarəβa will be slain by the hero, Kərəsāspa.

Source: Kuehn, *Dragon in Medieval East Christian and Islamic Art*, 192; Moazami, *Wrestling with the Demons of the Pahlavi Widēwdād*, 503

Gandareva

Variations: Gandarewa, Kundrav, Lord of the Abyss

A DRAGON from Sumerian mythology so immense its upper body reached the sky while its lower extremities sat upon the bottom of the ocean, the anthropophagous (man-eating) Gandareva fought many battles against the hero Keresapa; it cost the warrior fifteen horses and his eyesight, but he was eventually able to vanquish the creature.

Source: Coulter, *Encyclopedia of Ancient Deities*, 185; De Kirk, *Dragonlore*, 57; Rose, *Giants, Monsters, and Dragons*, 131–2

Gandarva

In Vedic mythology Gandarva was one of the winged horses said to assist in pulling the sun across the sky. It is believed its name is derived from the Sumerian DRAGON GANDAREVA.

Source: Rose, *Giants, Monsters, and Dragons*, 132

Gandharva

Masculine, celestial NATURE SPIRITS from Hindu mythology, the gandharva are collectively mated to the APSARAS. Highly skilled musicians who can play as beautifully as their mates can dance, the gandharva reside in the heaven of the god Indra, entertaining the gods. Gandharva by their very nature awaken sexual passion in human women, both with their god-like beauty and peerless musical talent. Like their mates, the APSARAS, the gandharva can be dangerous, as they can cause insanity; fortunately they are also healers and have a particular talent for the restoration of virility and are the guardians of soma, the elixir of immorality. The gandharva are also listed as being one of the eight classes of celestial beings in Hindu mythology.

Source: Benton, *God of Desire*, 137; De Visser, *Dragon in China and Japan*, xiii; Kramrisch, *Presence of Siva*, 27; Zell-Ravenheart, *Wizard's Bestiary*, 41

Ganiagwaihegowa

In the mythology of the Seneca people of New York, United States of America, the cannibalistic and nearly invulnerable monster Ganiagwaihegowa, described as looking like a furless bear, would terrorize communities and abduct to consume anyone who went alone into the wilderness. The heroes Hadentheni ("the speaker") and Hanigongendatha ("the interpreter") consulted with the Great Spirit and discovered the only vulnerable place on the creature's body was the soles of its feet. The two heroes traveled to its underworld home and there constructed the effigy of a man of brasswood to excite Ganiagwaihegowa's appetite and lure him out of his lodge. Their plan worked and in the ensuing battle they were able to shoot Ganiagwaihegowa in the soles of his feet and then cut them off. The limbs and the rest of his body were then destroyed with fire to prevent it from ever returning.

Source: Curtin, *Seneca Fiction, Legends, and Myths*, 259; Knudsen, *Fantastical Creatures and Magical Beasts*, 33; Rose, *Giants, Monsters, and Dragons*, 132

Ganj

A Persian species of DRAGON similar to the ASDEEV, the subterraneous ganj ("treasure"), one of the KHRAFSTRA, were described as being huge and having a gem embedded in their forehead. They were the guardians of treasure hoards of gems, gold, jewels, and silver.

Source: De Kirk, *Dragonlore*, 35; Gould, *Dragons, Unicorns, and Sea Serpents*, 211

Garafena

Variations: Garafina, Goruinich ("son of the Mountain")

In Russian folklore Garafena is a snake with magical abilities; it lives beneath the dripping oak where it guards the magical stone Alatyr on Booyan (Buyan) Island.

Source: Dole, *Young Folks History of Russia*, 51; Ralston, *Songs of the Russian People*, 375; Zell-Ravenheart, *Wizard's Bestiary*, 41

Garðrofa (GARTH-rawv-a)

Variations: Gardrofa, Garsrofa

In Norse mythology, the mare Garðrofa ("fence breaker") and the stallion HAMSKERPER were the parents who begot HÓFVARPNIR, the mount of the goddess Gna (Gnaa) and messenger to the god Frigga. Although the names of these horses appear in the *Prose Edda*, additional myths of them have disappeared.

Source: Lindow, *Norse Mythology*, 147; Rydberg, *Norroena*, Volume 3, 1021; Sturluson, *Prose Edda*, 47

Gargittios

A two-headed monstrous dog from classical Greek mythology, Gargittios and his companion hound ORTHOS (Orthros) were the two dogs utilized by the GIGANTE (a race of beings born from the goddess Gaea) Eurytion who guarded the herd of red oxen belonging to Geryon. The demi-god and hero Hercules (Heracles) was determined to have the herd and in the fight, slew all three of the guardians.

Source: Brewer, *Dictionary of Phrase and Fable*, 235; Daly, *Greek and Roman Mythology, A to Z*, 48–49; Rose, *Giants, Monsters, and Dragons*, 135

La Gargouille

Variations: Garguiem, Gargoyle, GUIVRE

A water DRAGON which once lived in the Seine River in Normandy, France, near Rouen, Gargouille ("gargler") emerged from a cave and began to cause flooding by projecting jets of water from its mouth; it would swim through the river and capsize boats, greedily eating the occupants as they fell into the water. Gargouille was described as having eyes which gleamed like moonstones, four membranous flippers, a long neck, a scaly head, a serpentine body, and a slender snout. Eventually the creature was confronted by the Archbishop of Rouen Saint Romain (Romanus) who subdued the DRAGON and led it into town where Gargouille was burned to death.

Source: De Kirk, *Dragonlore*, 42; Eberhart, *Mysterious Creatures*, 186; Shuker, *Dragons*, 18–9; Zell-Ravenheart, *Wizard's Bestiary*, 41–2

Garkain

From the folklore of the aboriginal people of the northern Australian territories comes a hominid-bat-like creature known as the garkain; hairy, man-sized with massive black wings and vicious canine teeth, it attacks travelers, consuming their flesh. The garkain hunts by roosting in a tree and waiting for someone to pass beneath it; many times its supernatural stench is enough to render its prey unconscious. Garkain are said to live in remote areas of the forest and swamp, in caves. Fortunately, folklore tells us this flesh-eating creature can be killed with mundane weaponry.

Source: Coulter, *Encyclopedia of Ancient Deities*, 187; Maberry, *Vampire Universe*, 133

Garm (GARM-r)

Variations: Garmr

Garm ("wolf hound") of Norse mythology was one of the dogs named in Thorgrimr's *Rhymes* and in Snorri Sturluson's (1179–1241) *Prose Edda*. A gigantic and ravenous hound, he is chained at the entryway to Gnipahellir (Gnypa) but when Ragnarok begins he will be set free and attack the god Tyr. In the ensuing battle, the two will slay one another.

Source: Jennbert, *Animals and Humans*, 49, 79; Oehlen-schläger, *Gods of the North*, xlii; Zell-Ravenheart, *Wizard's Bestiary*, 42

Garuda

Variations: Chirada, Gaganeshvara, Garuda Bird, Garuda, the Devourer, Garula, Garutman ("solar bird"), Kamayusha, Kashyapi, Khageshvara, Nagantaka, Pakshiraj ("lord of birds"), Sarparati ("enemy of serpents"), Sitanana, Sudhahara, Suparna ("beautiful wings"), Śyena ("eagle"), Tataswin ("swift one"), Tarkshya, Vainateya, Vishnuratha

In Buddhist and Hindu mythology Garuda ("winged") was a bird-like chimerical creature; it was described as having the head of a handsome young man, the body of an eagle, and a white ring about its neck. Garuda, hatched from an egg laid by his mother, Vinata (Diti), immediately took to the sky, his bright golden colored body blocking the light and the flap of his wings shaking the earth; the gods mistook the solar light his body radiated as originating from the god of fire, Angi. In the earliest versions of this mythology, Garuda was a gigantic bird and had no anthropomorphic qualities.

Garuda is the mount utilized by the god Vishnu; he was granted the boon of immortality and is bound to the god by an oath of obedience and servitude. He is the sworn enemy of NAGA and snakes.

As a species, the garudas are listed as one of the eight celestial beings in Hindu mythology; the others are: ASURAS, Devas, gandharvas, KINNARAS, MAHORAGAS, NAGAS, and the YAKSHAS.

Source: Beer, *Handbook of Tibetan Buddhist Symbols*, 73–4; Collin de Plancy, *Dictionnaire Infernal*, 297; De Visser, *Dragon in China and Japan*, xiii; Lurker, *Dictionary of Gods and Goddesses, Devils and Demons*, 66–7

Gashadokuro

Variations: Dokuro-No-Kai, O-Dokuro, Meku-rabe

A skeletal YŌKAI from Japanese folklore fifteen times taller than a person, the gashadokuro ("starving skeleton") bends over to attack its prey, humans, biting off their heads and letting the arterial spray cover as much of their body as it can. They prefer to hunt on cloudy and dark nights. Victims of the gashadokuro are said to hear ringing in their ears moments before the attack. Although these creatures cannot be destroyed, Shinto charms can ward them off and redirect their attention.

There are tales of these creatures dating back for a thousand years; at their most basic they are ravenous gigantic skeletons while some tales describe the being as a re-animated conglomerate of many skeletons. A nocturnal predator, if a gashadokuro is encountered it is advised to find a safe place to hide and wait out the sunrise; however this creature can virtually disassemble itself to squeeze into places one would not believe it to be able to fit into.

Source: Maberry, *Vampire Universe*, 133–34; Yoda, *Yokai Attack*, 54–7

Gavaevodata (gav-aēvō.dātā)

The primordial bull-cow of Zoroastrian mythology, Gavaevodata was one of Ahura Mazda's six material creations and the progenitor of all beneficent animal life on the planet. When Gavaevodata was slain, its marrow, organs, seed, and soul were used to populate the world with animal life.

Source: Boyce, *History of Zoroastrianism*, volume. 1, 138–9

Gazerium

Originating in the lumberjack communities of the developing United States of America, the gazerium, one of the FEARSOME CRITTERS, was only found in the Kennebec River, Maine. Described as looking like a shrimp but with two legs in the front and only one in the rear, the gazerium was said to have been a wonderful delicacy enjoyed by the local Indians and settlers; it tasted like French fried potatoes with a hint of tartar sauce, a unique flavor given to the gazerium from its only source of food, the SNYDAE, a microscopic form of marine life. Ironically, the SNYDAE only fed upon the eggs of the gazerium. Because of their unique diet, these two creatures soon drove one another to extinction.

Source: Mencken, *American Language*, 251; Rose, *Giants, Monsters, and Dragons*, 119

Geirdnir

Geirdnir was one of the goats named in Thorgrimr's *Rhymes* and in Snorri Sturluson's (1179–1241) *Prose Edda*.

Source: Jennbert, *Animals and Humans*, 49

Genbu

Variations: Chin Ming, Xuan Wu ("military black warrior," "mysterious warrior")

In Chinese folklore when a capital city is constructed, it was believed it should be designed to the Four God principle: on each side of the city, representation of each one is present in the form of their respective creatures. In the east is SEIRYU the blue DRAGON, dominant in spring time; to the north is Genbu, a snake and turtle hybrid dominant in the winter; in the south is SUZAKU, depicted as a red PHOENIX-like bird, and in the west, BYAKKO, a white tiger.

Source: Bates, *29 Chinese Mysteries*, 133; Brown, *Genius of Japanese Carpentry*, n.pag.; Grafetstätter, *Islands and Cities in Medieval Myth, Literature, and History*, 119

Gengen Wer

Variations: Negeg ("cackler")

In ancient Egyptian mythology Gengen Wer ("Great Honker") is the cosmic goose which laid the egg from which all living things hatched; it is a powerful force of creative energy.

Source: Hart, *Routledge Dictionary of Egyptian Gods and Goddesses*, 60; Zell-Ravenheart, *Wizard's Bestiary*, 42

Genko

A black HULI JING (fox spirit) from Japanese mythology, the genko is said to be a good-luck omen if seen; generally, it is benign to humans.

Source: Maberry, *Vampire Universe*, 177; Picken, *Essentials of Shinto*, 124

Geraher

A species of sea-bird mentioned in medieval bestiaries, the geraher was said to lay eggs so enormous it would cause the female of the species incredible pain. After the egg was laid, she would then take the egg to the bottom of the ocean in order to protect it from predatory species. When the eggs hatched the mother geraher would then lead her offspring to the surface and then the land to feed.

Source: Zell-Ravenheart, *Wizard's Bestiary*, 42

Geri (GER-i)

Variations: Gjere ("hungry"), Gere ("greedy guts"), Gerr

Geri ("greedy") of Norse mythology was one of the wolves named in Thorgrimr's *Rhymes* and in Snorri Sturluson's (1179–1241) *Prose Edda*; he was one of the two wolves of the Norse god Odin, the other being FREKE. These wolves sat at his side and he fed them directly from his own table; they were the god's personal guardians.

Source: Anderson, *Norse Mythology*, 446; Grimes, *Norse Myths*, 269; Jennbert, *Animals and Humans*, 50

Gering

Gering ("gleaming") was one of the horses utilized by the Aesir in Norse mythology; its specific owner or rider is not mentioned. Gering was also listed as one of the many horses who would graze in the red-gilt leafed Glasir Grove.

Source: Grimes, *Norse Myths*, 20, 269

Gerjis

Variations: Gergasi

A ferocious and gigantic anthropophagous (man-eating) tiger-like monster from west Malaysian folklore, the gerjis preyed upon every living thing in the forest; nothing could safely traverse its territory. According to the legend, the animals of the forest conspired to kill the gerjis and elected Kanchil the mousedeer to the task. A pit was dug and by use of cunning and persuasion Kanchil convinced the gerjis the sky was about to fall but safety could be found in the bottom of a special pit. When the gerjis jumped in, the earth was pushed back into the pit and an elephant took up a tree and smacked down the dirt, crushing the gerjis' skull.

Source: Knappert, *Pacific Mythology*, 88; Rose, *Giants, Monsters, and Dragons*, 135

Geush Urvan

Variations: Gosh, Gosh Goshuurun, Goshuuruan, Goshuurvan

A cosmic cow of Zoroastrian mythology, Geush Urvan was said to contain all the seeds of every animal and plant within her body. It was believed for three-thousand years she grazed upon the barren earth until she was slain by Mithra. From her body came a pair of cattle, two-hundred and eighty-two pairs of various species of animals, and sixty-five types of vegetation. In some tellings, this animal is a bull and was slain by the great evil being Ahriman.

Source: Rose, *Giants, Monsters, and Dragons*, 150; Zell-Ravenheart, *Wizard's Bestiary*, 42

Ghul (Gool)

In Muslim folklore there is a female vampiric demon known as a ghul which eats only the flesh of the dead. It breaks into the graves of those properly buried and feeds off their corpses. If it cannot find an easy meal in a graveyard, it shape-shifts into a beautiful woman in order to trick male travelers into thinking it is a prostitute. Then, once alone with a man, she kills him.

Source: Delcourt, *Oedipe*, 108–9; Gibb, *Shorter Encyclopaedia of Islam*, 114, 159; Stetkevych, *Mute Immortals Speak*, 95-99; Villeneuve, *Le Musée des Vampires*, 368

Gian Ben Gian

Variations: Gnan, Gyan, Gyan-ben-Gian, Jnana

In ancient Persian mythology, Gian Ben Gian ("occult wisdom" or "true wisdom"), the Chieftain of the female *peris* (see DIV), was said to have been the Governor of the world for the two thousand years after the creation of Adam. She carries a shield impervious to all forms of black or evil magic. Her personal adversary is Eblis, against whom her shield is useless.

Source: Blavatsky, *Secret Doctrine: The Synthesis of Science, Religion, and Philosophy*, Volume 2, 394; Brewer, *Dictionary of Phrase and Fable*, 339

Giant

Variations: GIGANTES, Ispolini, Iöunn, Jättar (Swedish), Jättiläiset (Finnish), Jotnar (see JOTUN), OGREs

Giants are common to most of the world's mythologies. They are universally described as being larger and taller than a human, be it by a few or several hundred feet; there the similarity ends. Depending on the culture, religion, and reason for having a giant in a tale, these beings come in a wide variety of characteristics, descriptions, and personalities. Giants have been wizened war chiefs capable of leading armies while others of their species are barely intelligent enough to talk and walk at the same time, easily outwitted by the Simple Jacks of folklore. Some have been said to be gods and the creators of the universe and the progenitors of the great noble families, while others yet are more animal-like, living in caves, barely clothed in furs, wielding a misshapen club, and robbing the countryside of its goats and sheep.

Having great strength is common among giants as well, but this is typically in proportion to their size and not otherwise remarkable. Traditionally, they represent an obstacle a cultural hero must overcome and defeat on a quest. Many tales have characters in them who are described as being a half-giant, where one of its parents was a human.

Giants are good or evil depending on their motivation; for instance, Paul Bunyan from American folklore is a giant who is helpful to humans, assisting in taming the west and bringing civilization to mankind. Many natural landmarks are named after them, for giants are often accredited with having created islands, mountains, rivers, and standing stones.

It appears whenever a giant is particularly bloodthirsty, cruel, and preys on humans to consume for their flesh it is called an OGRE; this would be incorrect, for although an OGRE can be gigantic in size, not all are; most are in fact human size but monstrous in appearance due to their physical deformities.

Giants play a particularly important role in Greek and Norse mythology, representing the force of nature and violent natural phenomena.

Source: Briggs, *Encyclopedia of Fairies*, 186–90; Daniels, *Encyclopedia of Superstitions, Folklore, and the Occult Sciences of the World*, 1375–8; Keightley, *World Guide to Gnomes, Fairies, Elves, and Other Little People*, 321; Leeming, *Oxford Companion to World Mythology*, 149; Rose, *Giants, Monsters, and Dragons*, 136–9

Giant Dingo

A monstrous and gigantic anthropophagous (man-eating) creature from the Dreamtime mythology of the Native Australian people of Western Australia, the Giant Dingo had been on an unchecked killing spree, butchering and consuming so many people those who remained were too afraid to light a fire for cooking or warmth. The hero Jitta-Jitta hunted down and killed Giant Dingo.

Source: Rose, *Giants, Monsters, and Dragons*, 139–40

Giddy Fish

Originating in the lumberjack communities of the developing United States of America, the giddy fish, one of the FEARSOME CRITTERS, were a species of elastic-like small fish caught during the winter months. To catch one, first a single giddy fish must be spotted and successfully struck on the head with a paddle. Bouncing like a rubber ball, the giddy fish's motion would attract the attention of others of its kind, causing them to bounce as well. After a few moments, several giddy fish would have landed themselves and could easily be gathered up.

Source: Binney, *Nature's Ways*, 225; Botkin, *American People*, 254–55; Rose, *Giants, Monsters, and Dragons*, 119

Gigante

Variations: GIANT

In Greek mythology the gigante were a race of beings born from Gaea, the earth, when the blood of Uranus ("heaven") fell upon her. They were enormous humanoids, sometimes described as having serpents for feet. Wanting revenge for the death of Uranus, Gaea made the gigante invincible by the use of a special herb to protect them from the Olympian gods, and then she sent her children to battle against them in the Gigantomachy. The only way the gigantes could be destroyed was if the Olympians gained the assistance of a mortal; in most renditions of this myth, the individual was the demi-god and cultural hero Hercules (Heracles).

Source: Hansen, *Handbook of Classical Mythology*, 177; Lurker, *Dictionary of Gods and Goddesses, Devils and Demons*, 69; Smith, *Complete Idiot's Guide to World Mythology*, 238

Gigelorum

Variations: Giol-daoram

According to Scottish folklore the gigelorum is the smallest of all the creatures; it made its nest in the ear of a mite and therefore is too small to be seen with the human eye.

Source: Campbell, *Superstitions of the Highlands and Islands of Scotland*, 220; Spence, *Magic Arts in Celtic Britain*, 95

Gillygaloo

One of the FEARSOME CRITTERS from the lumberjack folklore of the United States of America, the gillygaloo was a species of bird which made its nest on the Pyramid Forty, a mountain with a forty-acre base, which was said to have been cleared of its lumber by the folkloric hero and GIANT Paul Bunyan. The eggs of the gillygaloo were cube-shaped and much prized by lumberjacks who would take the eggs, hard-boil them, and use them as dice.

Source: Binney, *Nature's Ways*, 225; Cavendish, *Man, Myth and Magic*, Volume 5, 2101; Gard, *Wisconsin Lore*, 77; Rose, *Giants, Monsters, and Dragons*, 143

Girp

In the Swedish fairy tale *The Bird Girp* it was said the FAIRY ANIMAL, a bird by the name of Girp, had the ability to restore sight to the blind with its song. This bird was kept in a cage by a king and was guarded as his greatest treasure.

Source: Lang, *Pink Fairy Book*, 132–42

Girtablullu

Variations: Girtabilli, Girtablilu

The girtablullu ("scorpion man") of Akkadian, Babylonian, and Mesopotamian mythology is, along with the BASMU, KUSARIKKU, and MUSHHUSH, a creature of TIAMAT; however the girtablullu later became an attendant of the god of the sun, Shamash (Utu), protecting it and the Mountain of Mashu where the sun rises in the east. This chimerical creature is described as having the head of a bearded man, the hindquarters of a scorpion, and a snake-headed penis; on occasion it also has wings. In art the girtablullu is occasionally depicted wearing the horned cap, a sign of divinity.

Source: Black, *Concise Dictionary of Akkadian*, 93; Ford, *Maskim Hul*, 152–3; Wiggermann, *Mesopotamian Protective Spirits*, 174; Zell-Ravenheart, *Wizard's Bestiary*, 43

Gisl (GEES-l)

Gisl ("beam," "ray," or "sunbeam") was one of the horses of the Aesir in Norse mythology. Gisl is mentioned in the poems *Grímnismál* and *Gylfaginning* as being one of the mounts ridden by the gods each day as they travel to Ygdrasil, however, neither poem says which god is Gisl's rider. Gisl was also listed as one of the many horses who would graze in the red-gilt leafed Glasir Grove.

Source: Anderson, *Norse Mythology*, 189; Grimes, *Norse Myths*, 270; Sturluson, *Prose Edda*, 28

Gladr (GLATH-r)

Variations: Glad

Gladr ("bright" or "glad") was one of the horses of the Aesir mentioned in both *Grímnismál* and *Gylfaginning* as one of the mounts ridden each day to Ygdrasil where the gods would make their daily judgments; neither source assigned it a specific rider.

Source: Anderson, *Norse Mythology*, 189; Norroena Society, *Asatrii Edda*, 351; Sturluson, *Prose Edda*, 28

Glær (GLAIR)

Variations: Glaer, Glener, Glenr, Glen

Glær ("glassy" or "gleam") of Norse mythology was one of the horses of the Aesir; it was mentioned in both *Grímnismál* and *Gylfaginning* as one of the mounts ridden each day to Ygdrasil where the gods would make their daily judgments. Neither source assigned it a specific rider. Glær was also listed as one of the many horses which would graze in the red-gilt leafed Glasir Grove.

Source: Anderson, *Norse Mythology*, 189; Grimes, *Norse Myths*, 20, 271; Lindow, *Norse Mythology*, 145

Glamr (Glahm-r)

A creature from Nordic folklore whose story is told in the epic poem *Grettis Saga*, the monster

Glamr ("gleaming") haunts a particular farmstead; each year on Christmas Eve he savagely attacks and kills the shepherds. The story begins describing Glamr as once having been a shepherd himself who worked the very farm he now haunts as a *draugr* (a type of vampiric REVENANT). When he was human, Glamr was described as being large, powerful and not to everyone's taste. A person who had other-worldliness about him, Glamr was vocally Pagan, had an aversion to church and church music, and flaunted his lack of faith.

The hero Grettir upon hearing the news of a farmstead under assault from a draugr, decides to confront the monster in spite of his uncle's warnings. Lying down in his clothes Grettir pretends to be asleep until Glamr enters the hall and attacks. The battle between the two is fierce and almost razes the hall. Near death and defeat Glamr places a curse upon the hero promising him to live the life of an outlaw whose strength will never increase and deeds turn to ill luck. When Glamr has spoken his last words, Grettir beheads him.

Source: Norroena Society, *Asatrii Edda*, 25; Orchard, *Pride and Prodigies*, 153; Williamson, *"Beowulf" and Other Old English Poems*, 224

Glas Ghailbhleann

In Welsh folklore Glas Ghailbhleann was a fairy cow renowned for giving copious amounts of milk. The FAIRY ANIMAL would, each day, make its rounds from farm to farm to be milked until one day a greedy woman tried to take more than her fair share. Once the woman was finished milking Glas Ghailbhleann, like the GLASGAVLEN of Irish folklore, walked off and was never seen again.

Source: Monaghan, *Encyclopedia of Celtic Mythology and Folklore*, 233

Glasgavlen

Variations: Dun Cow, Dun Cow of Kirkham, Dun Cow of Mac Brandy's Thicket, Glas Gaivlen

A fairy cow from Irish folklore, the glasgavlen would present itself to every household in the anticipation of being milked. Described as being milk-white and studded with bright green spots it was said this FAIRY ANIMAL regularly made the rounds until one day a greedy woman was determined to obtain more than her daily pail and milked the glasgavlen into a sieve, running it dry and causing the cow to leave Ireland forever. There are various versions of this folklore told all over Wales and Ireland, but the basic premise of a generous cow being used up by an avaricious or evil person, such as a witch, remains consistent. It is said wherever the glasgaven walks the grass grows greener, the hay is reaped in greater abundance, and the potatoes grow larger.

Source: Briggs, *Encyclopedia of Fairies*, 113, 191; Wood-Martin, *Traces of the Elder Faiths of Ireland*, 127–8

Glashtyn

Variations: GLASHTIN, Glaistyn, Glashan, Glastyn

A FAIRY ANIMAL from the Isle of Man, the glashtyn is a water horse similar to the Irish AUGHISKY and the Scottish EACH UISCE. In its human guise this fairy is described as looking like a handsome, curly, dark haired youth; his horse ears are hidden well beneath his hair. Typically, the glashtyn keeps his equine shape and lingers along the banks of lochs and rivers enticing people to mount up on its back. As soon as it has a rider this water horse takes its prey into the water and devours it.

Source: Briggs, *Encyclopedia of Fairies*, 191–2; Rose, *Giants, Monsters and Dragons*, 144; Spence, *Fairy Tradition in Britain*, 84; Varner, *Creatures in the Mist*, 23

Glaumr (GLOUM-r)

In Norse mythology, Snorri Sturlson (1179–1241), the Icelandic historian, poet, and politician, writes the horse Glaumr ("noisy") was the preferred mount of Atli, son of Budli, in his translation of *Prose Edda*.

Source: Norroena Society, *Asatrii Edda*, 25; Sturluson, *Stories of the Kings of Norway Called the Round World*, 505; Sturluson, *Prose Edda*, Volume 5, 212

Glawackus

Variations: Granby Panther, Injun Devil

Originating in the lumberjack communities of the developing United States of America, the glawackus, one of the FEARSOME CRITTERS, was alleged to have been heard quite frequently in the winter of 1939 outside the northern Connecticut community of Glastonbury. While its tracks were said to resemble a mountain lion's the creature itself was described as looking like a large cat or dog standing about two feet tall and being twice as long; in addition to having a bushy long tail, the glawackus emitted a blood-curdling cry.

Source: Eberhart, *Mysterious Creatures*, 208; Rose, *Giants, Monsters, and Dragons*, 119

Gler (GLEHR)

Gler ("glassy" or "shining") was one of the horses utilized by the Aesir in Norse mythology; its specific owner or rider is not mentioned. Gler was also listed as one of the many horses who would graze in the red-gilt leafed Glasir Grove.

Source: Anderson, *Norse Mythology*, 447; Grimes, *Norse Myths*, 20, 271; Puryear, *Nature of Asatru*, 199

Gloso

In Swiss Christmas folklore the sow Gloso ("glow-sow") expected to have offerings of wheat stalks left for her in the field at harvest time as well as fish heads and a bowl of porridge set out for her consumption on Christmas Eve. If these offerings were not left she would haunt the darkness beneath the table throughout the Twelve Nights of Christmas. The eyes of Gloso were said to burn like twin coals and could be seen from some distance off; the bristles upon her back would also give off sparks as she walked.

Source: Raedisch, *Old Magic of Christmas*, 142

Gnome

Variations: Álfur, Djendoes, Djude, Domovoi Djedoe ("earth fairy"), Domovoi, Dudje, Duende, Dvergur, Erdmanlein, Erd-Mänlein, Erdmanleins, Foddenskkmaend, Follet, Gartenzwerg ("garden gnome"), Gnom, Gommes, Gnomiko, Gnomo, Gnomos, goblin, Ground Manikins, Hammerlinge, Heinzemannchens, Hill manikins, HOB, Hustomte, Kabauter, Kabouter, Kaukis, Kepec, Klabauter, Kleinmanneken, Krasnoludek, Maahinen, Mano, Manó, Menninkäinen, Nains, Nanu, Nisse, Nissen, Patuljak, Polutan, Škriatok, SKRITEK, Skřítek, Skrzat, Småtomte, Tomte, Tomtenisse, Tomte Gubbe, Tontti, VÆTTIR, Wichtel, Гном (gnom), Патуљак (patuljak), Полушан (polušan)

The hermetic and neo-Platonic doctrine from which all medieval medicine and science was founded describes four Elemental classes: Air, Earth, Fire, and Water; accordingly the Gnomes belong to the Earth class, nereids (golden-haired sea nymphs) to Water, SALAMANDERS to Fire, and sylphs to Air.

In the earliest mythology, gnomes lived underground and moved through it as easily as a fish moves through water. They acted as the protectors of the treasures of the earth. Paracelsus describes them as standing two spans high (a *span* is the distance from the tip of an adult's thumb to the tip of his pinky finger, fingers spread), and inclined to silence.

Gnomes are traditionally a part of fairy folklore but in truth have no folkloric stories or legends of their own; they have little in common with the DWARFS they are likened to except by physical appearance. In the late middle ages German folklore said the gnomes had a king named Number-nip or Rübezahl, but it was not until very modern times the gnome was fleshed out and fully described, reimagined into a kindly, forest dwelling being with a highly developed culture.

Source: Briggs, *Encyclopedia of Fairies*, 192–3; McCoy, *Witch's Guide to Faery Folk*, 219; Monaghan, *Encyclopedia of Celtic Mythology and Folklore*, 218; Patrick, *Chambers's Encyclopædia*, Volume 4, 174

Gnyan

Variations: Gnyab

In Tibetan folklore the gnyan ("demon god" but literally "wild sheep") are a species of NATURE SPIRIT dwelling within mountains, rocks, trees, and valleys. Related to the mountain gods, the gnyan are easily annoyed and disrupted by human activity and to punish this transgression send out death in the form of disease and plague.

Source: Ferrari, *Health and Religious Rituals in South Asia*, 83; Knapp, *Women, Myth, and the Feminine Principle*, 5

Goayr Heddagh

A FAIRY ANIMAL in Manx folklore, the goayr heddagh is a large and terrifying looking goat which is said to prey upon travelers who journey down lonely roads at night; it is similar to the BLACK DOG of the British Isles.

Source: Monaghan, *Encyclopedia of Celtic Mythology and Folklore*, 498; Rose, *Giants, Monsters, and Dragons*, 145; Zell-Ravenheart, *Wizard's Bestiary*, 44

Goblin Scarecrow

In the folklore from Pennsylvania, United States of America, the goblin scarecrow is found in rural areas and farms; it is described as a grinning jack-o-lantern dressed in raggedy clothes, speaking as it moves. Screaming, it chases people, trying to bite them.

Source: Maberry, *Vampire Universe*, 133–34

Goborchinu

The goborchinu from Irish folklore were described as being horse-headed monstrous humanoids.

Source: Hargreaves, *Hargreaves New Illustrated Bestiary*, 63; Rose, *Giants, Monsters, and Dragons*, 145

Goin (GOH-in)

Variations: Góin, Goinn, Góinn

Goin ("living deep within the earth") was one of the dark-spotted serpents or Ormar (see ORMR) named in Thorgrimr's *Rhymes* and in Snorri Sturluson's (1179–1241) *Prose Edda*; it was said to live beneath the tree Ygdrasil at the Hvergelmir Well where it spent its days gnawing upon its Niflheimr root. The siblings of Goin were MÓINN, GRÁBAKR, GRAFVÖLLUDR, OFNIR, and SVAFNIR.

Source: Grimes, *Norse Myths*, 14, 271; Jennbert, *Animals and Humans*, 50; Norroena Society, *Asatrii Edda*, 352; Puryear, *Nature of Asatru*, 199

Gold-Digging Ant

Variations: Myrmekes Indikoi

In medieval Bestiaries the dog-sized gold-digging ants of Ceylon purify gold and separate it out in piles of pure and impure on the surface. These ants were first reported by the ancient Greek historian Herodotus (484–425 BC) who said the insects will not tolerate the presence of humans but are amiable to other creatures. In very hot weather the ants seek shelter from the sun beneath ground and it is during this time men rush to the fields and collect the daily gold harvest. In other times when it is not so hot men will use mares which have recently had a foal as their conveyance. Penning up the foal they tie baskets to each side of the mare and lead it out to the field where the ants leave the processed gold. Compelled to fill an empty container the gold-digging ants will fill the basket on the mare. In the evening, the foal is released and immediately cries for its mother, who quickly comes in from the ants' depository field, its baskets laden down with gold.

Source: Mandeville, *Travels of Sir John Mandeville*, 183; Royal Anthropological Institute of Great Britain and Ireland, *Indian Antiquary*, Volume 4, 225

Goldfax (GUL-vaks-i)

Variations: Gullfaxi ("golden mane")

In Norse mythology Goldfax ("gold-mane") was the horse which belonged to the JOTUN Hrungnir, chief of the FROST GIANTS; it was said to be able to run as fast across water as it could on land, although for all its speed it was still not as fast as SLEIPNIR, Odin's horse. After Hrungnir was slain by the god Thor, the god gave Goldfax to his youngest son, Mangi, for the role he played in defeating the JOTUN.

Source: Anderson, *Norse Mythology*, 305; Pratt-Chadwick, *Legends of Norseland*, 122–5; Puryear, *Nature of Asatru*, 200

Golem

In Kabbalistic folklore the myth of the golem ("form" or "humanoid"), a man made out of clay and brought to life by the use of the powers of the letters of the Hebrew alphabet, are numerous and said to trace back to the *Sefer Yetzirah* ("Book of Creation"), one of the earliest kabalistic texts. Although there are variations to the story, the Kabbalist creates a clay image of a man from unploughed mountain earth, living water, and writes a word on its forehead; typically it is the word *emet* ("truth") and when the first letter of the word is erased, the *aleph*, it leaves behind the word *met* ("death") thereby destroying the creature. It is then animated by means of *tzeruf*, combining the *Terragrammaton* with a series of 221 (or 231) permutations of the Hebrew alphabet as described in the *Sefer Yetzirah*. It is not clear if the permutations must be spoken or written upon the limbs. The golem seems to have neither free will nor the ability to speak, although there are a few tales of it uttering words of warning from heaven.

The earliest Talmudic tale of the golem involves Rabbi Zera attempting to speak to a man who will not respond. The Rabbi realizes the golem for what it is and returns it to dust. The most popular tale of the golem is that of Rabbi Loew of Prague who creates one to protect his people from anti–Semitic violence; like many golem tales the creature inevitably becomes too powerful and unpredictable and needs to be destroyed by its creator thereby teaching the Rabbi a lesson in humility.

Source: Dennis, *Encyclopedia of Jewish Myth, Magic and Mysticism*, 110–11; McCoy, *Witch's Guide to Faery Folk*, 236; Schwartz, *Tree of Souls*, 251, 279–80

Gong-Gong

Variations: Kung Kung

In Chinese mythology Gong-Gong was a gigantic and terrible black DRAGON and god who once had almost destroyed the heavens and the earth with the horn upon its head; he was hideously ugly, having the body of a snake and a human head covered with a mass of long red hair. He was born the son of Zhu Rong, the god of fire and ruler of the southern hemisphere. In his hatred of the celestial emperor Yeo and his great desire to upset the balance of the cosmos, first Gong-Gong tore asunder Imperfect Mountain, one of the pillars holding up the sky which also held back a world flooding deluge; then he ripped open a gash in the sky causing the light of the moon and sun to wither. Gong-Gong has a companion named XIANG YAO; together the two of them foul lakes with their excrement.

Source: Roberts, *Chinese Mythology A to Z*, 26, 49; Rosen, *Mythical Creatures Bible*, 362; Zell-Ravenheart, *Wizard's Bestiary*, 129

Gonibilla

A NURSERY BOGIE from Sinhalese folklore, the gonibilla ("sack kidnapper") uses a sack to carry off unruly children; unlike other bogeymen, the gonibilla can make away with a child day or night.

Source: Roberts, *Sinhala-ness and Sinhala Nationalism*, 20

Goofang

Originating in the lumberjack communities of the developing United States of America, the goofang, one of the FEARSOME CRITTERS, was described as being "about the size of a sun fish, but much bigger" and swam backwards its entire life to keep water out of its eyes.

Source: Botkin, *American People*, 255; Rose, *Giants, Monsters, and Dragons*, 119

Goofus Bird

Originating in the lumberjack communities of the developing United States of America, the goofus bird, one of the FEARSOME CRITTERS, was said to not only build its nest upside-down but also fly backwards because it only wants to know where it has been.

Source: Binney, *Nature's Ways*, 225; Leeming, *Myths, Legends, and Folktales of America*, 80–1; Rose, *Giants, Monsters, and Dragons*, 119

Gorgo, plural GORGONS

Variations: Gorgo the MEDUSA

In *The Odyssey*, the epic Greek poem attributed to Homer, the greatest of Greek epic poets, only one gorgo ("fear") is mentioned; she appears in the poem as one-eyed, rising up from a lake with a head full of hissing snakes for hair. The Greek poet Hesiod (ca. 750–650 BC) claimed there were three GORGONS, two of which were immortal—EURYALE ("far howling") and STHENO ("strong")—whereas the third, MEDUSA ("mad"), was not. An image of MEDUSA the Gorgo appears on the shield of the hero Agamenmon.

Source: Anthon, *Classical Dictionary*, 559; Brann, *Homeric Moments*, 73; Forlong, *Encyclopedia of Religions*, Volume 2, 160

Gorgoniy

A creature from Russian folklore, the gorgoniy is said to protect Paradise against those mortals who would dare to invade it.

Source: Zell-Ravenheart, *Wizard's Bestiary*, 44

Gorgons (Gore-guns)

Variations: The Phorcydes

The Gorgons ("the grim ones") were three demonic creatures from ancient Greek mythology; their names were EURYALE ("the far howler"), MEDUSA ("the queen"), and STHENO ("the mighty"). These sisters were born the daughters of the god of the sea Phorcys (also one of the Titans) and Ceto and were priestesses in the temple of Athena (Minerva). MEDUSA had sexual relations with the god Poseidon (Neptune) in the Athenian temple and in a fit of rage the goddess transformed the three sisters into the monstrous Gorgons. They were cursed with boar-like tusks; bronze claws; long, razor-sharp teeth; pockmarked faces; snakes for hair; and leathery wings. The Gorgons were so hideously ugly

if a mortal were to look directly at them the fearful sight would turn a man to stone.

Source: Fontenrose, *Python*, 283–6, 288–9, Illes, *Encyclopedia of Spirits*, 488–9

Gorri Txiki

Small red NATURE SPIRITS from Basque mythology, the gorri txiki ("red small") are said to be found in the Aya and Orio regions; they are described as being half ELF and half forest elemental.

Source: Callejo, *Elves: Volume 1 of Guide magical beings of Spain*, 113

Gorynytch

Variations: Zmei Gorynytch

A three-headed DRAGON with seven tails from Russian folklore, Gorynytch, a fire-breather with iron claws, was well known for being both very insidious and powerful; he was confronted by the gallant warrior and hero Dobrynya Nikititch who made it his personal crusade to protect Russia's boarders, defeat her enemies, and slay her monsters. Nikititch confronted Gorynytch in the middle of a river and although was victorious, the DRAGON begged for its life. Nikititch conceded and let the monster live but the evil Gorynytch immediately took flight to Kiev, Ukraine, where it kidnapped Zabava, the niece of Prince Vladimir.

Determined to correct his mistake Nikititch set out on a quest to find the DRAGON's lair; a journey taking him to the Underworld. There, Nikititch not only rescued Zabava but also slew Gorynytch and its mate.

Source: Seal, *Encyclopedia of Folk Heroes*, 186; Sherman, *Storytelling*, 118

Goti (GAWT-i)

In Norse mythology, Snorri Sturlson (1179–1241), the Icelandic historian, poet, and politician, writes the horse Goti ("the Goth" or "man") was the preferred mount of Gunnarr in his translation of *Prose Edda*. Goti refused to pass through the wall of flame surrounding Brunhilde.

Source: Norroena Society, *Asatrii Edda*, 353; Sturluson, *Prose Edda*, Volume 5, 212

Gou Mang

Two of China's cosmic DRAGONS, Gou Mang and ROU SHOU, are also messengers to the gods. Gou Mang is a TI-EN LUNG DRAGON and brings with it good fortune as it is also the herald for the coming of spring and is associated with the east. Gou Mang is said to be a giver of the gift of immortality.

Source: De Kirk, *Dragonlore*, 26; Lurker, *Dictionary of Gods and Goddesses, Devils and Demons*, 70, 218; Rose, *Giants, Monsters, and Dragons*, 150

Gowrow

Variations: Fillyfoo, Golligog, Gollygog, Moogie

In Arkansas, United States of America, in the Ozark Native American mythology the gowrow was a subterranean DRAGON-like creature described as being more than twenty feet long and having gigantic tusks protruding from its mouth. According to local folklore a gowrow lived in the vertical cave known as the Devil's Hole, Arkansas. Local legend says some men once tied a boulder to rope and lowered it into the cave; after a few minutes they heard horrible hissing and pulled up the rope only to discover several bites had been taken out of the boulder.

Source: De Kirk, *Dragonlore*, 49; Rife, *America's Nightmare Monsters*, 70–1; Zell-Ravenheart, *Wizard's Bestiary*, 39

Grábakr (GRAH-bak-r)

Variations: Graabak, Grabak, Grabakr

Grábakr ("grey-back") was one of the dark-spotted serpents or Ormar (see ORMR) named in Thorgrimr's *Rhymes* and in Snorri Sturluson's (1179–1241) *Prose Edda*; it was said to live beneath the tree Ygdrasil at the Hvergelmir Well where it spent its days gnawing upon its Niflheimr root. The siblings of GRÁBAKR were GOIN, MÓINN, GRÁBAKR, GRAFVÖLLUDR, OFNIR, and SVAFNIR.

Source: Anderson, *Norse Mythology*, 190–1; Grimes, *Norse Myths*, 14; Jennbert, *Animals and Humans*, 50; Puryear, *Nature of Asatru*, 199

Grabofc

Variations: Grabovac

A monstrous two-head serpent from Albanian mythology, Grabofc hunts for humans in a most particular way. Concealing its second head, Grabofc lies out in the open where it will be noticed by someone; upon approach, it pretends to be weeping, letting tears escape its eyes. When the person approaches to comfort the pitiful creature the head which had been hidden lashes out and strikes the unsuspecting prey.

Source: Elsie, *Dictionary of Albanian Religion, Mythology, and Folk Culture*, 104

Graeae

Variations: The Deion ("terrible ones"), Graes, Graiai

In Greek mythology the Graeae ("gray ones" or "old ones") was the collective name of the three sisters, Dino ("alarm"), Enyo ("dread"), and Pemphredo ("horror"), who were born looking like old hags having grey hair, wrinkled skin, and a single eye and tooth between them. The Graeae were the sisters of the GORGONS and living in the far west upon Mount

Atlas played a significant role in the story of the hero Perseus on his quest to kill MEDUSA.

Source: Dixon-Kennedy, *Encyclopedia of Greco-Roman Mythology*, 141; Leeming, *Oxford Companion to World Mythology*, 159

Grafvitnir (GRAV-vit-nir)

Variations: Grafvitner, Graftner, Grafvitnit

According to Norse mythology Grafvitnir ("grave wolf") was the sire of the dark-spotted serpents named in Thorgrimr's *Rhymes* and in Snorri Sturluson's (1179–1241) *Prose Edda* said to live beneath the tree Ygdrasil at the Hvergelmir Well where they spent their days gnawing upon its Niflheimr root. The names of his offspring are GOIN, GRÁBAKR, MÓINN, GRÁBAKR, GRAFVÖLLUDR, OFNIR, and SVAFNIR.

Source: Anderson, *Norse Mythology*, 190–1; Grimes, *Norse Myths*, 14; Jennbert, *Animals and Humans*, 50; Puryear, *Nature of Asatru*, 200

Grafvölludr (GRAV-vuhl-uth-r)

Variations: Grafvollud, Grafvollund, Grafvolludr

Grafvölludr ("grave burrower") was one of the dark-spotted serpents or Ormar (see ORMR) named in Thorgrimr's *Rhymes* and in Snorri Sturluson's (1179–1241) *Prose Edda*; it was said to live beneath the tree Ygdrasil at the Hvergelmir Well where it spent its days gnawing upon its Niflheimr root. The siblings of Grafvölludr were GOIN, MÓINN, GRÁBAKR, OFNIR, and SVAFNIR.

Source: Anderson, *Norse Mythology*, 190–1; Grimes, *Norse Myths*, 14; Jennbert, *Animals and Humans*, 50; Puryear, *Nature of Asatru*, 200

Grane

Variations: Grani ("hairy"), Granni, Greyfell

The horse of the shield-maiden and Valkyrie (a NYMPH of battle) Brunhilde from German mythology, Grane slept beside her in the ring of flames until she was awakened by the hero Siegfried. Brunhilde gave her beloved grey Grane, known for his swiftness, to the hero. After Siegfried's death, Brunhilde mounts Grane and the two of them jump into the funeral pyre to join the hero in the Halls of Valhalla.

In Norse mythology, Snorri Sturlson (1179–1241), the Icelandic historian, poet, and politician, writes the horse Grani ("hairy lip" or "shining lip") was the preferred mount of Sigurdr (Sigurd Fafnisbane, the Siegfried of the *Nibdungenlied*) in his translation of *Prose Edda*. Grani is the son of SLEIPNIR, the eight-legged mount of the god Odin. According to Sturlson, Sigurdr was trying to choose a horse and followed the advice of an old man who suggested driving the herd down and into the

Busiltjörn River. All of the horses but one swam to shore and the old man, the god Odin in disguise, said the large grey horse was "one of SLEIPNIR kin" and if well cared for "will be the best of all horses."

Source: Brewer, *Dictionary of Phrase and Fable*, 626; Eliade, *Woman Who Pretended to Be Who She Was*, 54, 57; Sturluson, *Prose Edda*, Volume 5, 212

Great Cackler

Variations: Kenken-Ur

A sacred goose from Egyptian creation mythology, the Great Cackler was believed to have laid the primordial egg from which the earth was hatched among the sycamores.

Source: Budge, *Gods of the Egyptians*, 96, 108; Mercatante, *Who's Who in Egyptian Mythology*, 50; Remler, *Egyptian Mythology, A to Z*, 72

Grendel (Gren-del)

Grendel, the monster from the legendary epic saga *Beowulf*, is often overlooked in vampiric folklore, but in truth it is a vampiric creature. In the saga, Grendel is said to be a descendant of Cain; a gigantic monster, half man and half water TROLL. At night he would leave his watery cave, located in Dark Lake, and attack the men of King Hrot's court and all who served him. Grendel would rip them apart with his bare hands, drinking their blood and eating their flesh. A vicious warrior already, he was rendered impervious to swords by a spell cast upon him by his mother, a witch. His only pleasure was killing. Beowulf was asked by the king to slay the beast, which the hero does, by ripping off one of his arms in a wrestling match.

The story of Beowulf and his encounter with Grendel is similar to many ancient Norse stories regarding the vampiric REVENANTS known as *drauge* and *draugr* (types of vampiric REVENANTS). Both of these creatures are described as large and exceptionally strong, as Grendel was. Both were said to be able to kill a man in a single swipe, as Grendel did. The draugr was created by magic, and Grendel was protected by the witchcraft his mother placed on him. The draugr was re-imagined when Christianity was introduced; the story of Beowulf was written during the time when the old religion was giving way to the new. Draugr wanted what they had in life—warmth, food, and family; and since they couldn't have it, they gleaned what pleasure they could through death and destruction. Grendel, who also had none of those things, only found pleasure in killing as well. Neither a draugr nor Grendel could be harmed by mere weapons. A draugr could only be defeated by a hero in a wrestling match, which was exactly how Grendel was defeated.

Source: Hoops, *Kommentar zum Beowulf*, 163; Olsen, *Monsters and the Monstrous*, 79; Perkowski, *Vampires of the Slavs*; Robinson, *Tomb of Beowulf*, 185–218; Tolkien, *Beowulf*, 278

Griffin

Variations: Epimacus, Griffon, Gryph, Gryphus, Grype, Gryp, Gryps ("curved"), Gryphon

A chimerical creature appearing in several different mythologies, the griffin ("to seize") combines the features of a hawk, lion, and snake. In Egyptian mythology the god Horus sometimes assumed this form. Like DRAGONS, griffins hoard treasure and were fierce protectors of it. They were also the symbol of regal courage, such as when they appeared on heraldic coat-of-arms. Often pictured in bestiaries, the griffin became symbolic of Christ, as it was both a creature of the earth and of the air, paralleling His divine and human aspects.

Source: Farrow, *Farrow's Military Encyclopedia*, 786; Pinch, *Handbook of Egyptian Mythology*, 120; Rosen, *Mythical Creatures Bible*, 118–19; Zell-Ravenheart, *Wizard's Bestiary*, 45

Grim

Variations: Bloody Man, Church Grim, Kirk Grim, Kirkegrim, Kirkigrim

In the folklore of Yorkshire, England, the grim is a tutelary or guardian spirit usually described as having the appearance of a large black dog. It would patrol the building and the property but on stormy nights would go "maraud about." In some stories it would let loose with a mournful BANSHEE-like death-knell when someone in the parish passed away; it may also be seen in the window of the church watching the funeral procession, the expression on its face telling if the person was saved or damned to Hell.

In classical English literature, there is a GIANT by the name of Grim (also called Blood Man) who had the terrible reputation of attacking and consuming pilgrims on their way to the holy land. According to John Bunyon's work *Pilgrim's Progress* (1682), the allegorical Grim, in the company of a pride of lions, was the first of three GIANTS to be confronted by a group of pilgrims; their guide, Greatheart, stepped forward to protect his charges and savagely slew the cannibalistic GIANT. As it happened, the lions were chained and unable to attack, allowing the pilgrims to pass by safely.

Source: Daniels, *Encyclopedia of Superstitions, Folklore, and the Occult Sciences of the World*, 1377; Rose, *Giants, Monsters, and Dragons*, 154; Simpson, *Dictionary of English Folklore*, n.pag.

Grine

In Moroccan folklore there is a species of djinn (a race of demons) known as a grine. It is said each time a human is born, a duplicate of them is born as a grine in an adjacent world. The actions of one inevitably influence the actions of the other.

Source: Legey, *Folklore of Morocco*, 155

Gringolet

Variations: Gringalet, Gringolet with the Red Ears, Grinquljete, Kincaled, Winwalite

In Arthurian folklore, Gringolet ("handsome-hardy" or "white-hardy") was the sturdy charger with extreme dexterity and strength belonging to Sir Gawain; a horse of sterling qualities, it was well known for its combat prowess. Gringolet first appeared in Chrétien de Troyes' *Erec and Enide* where even he was not able to save Sir Cai (Kay) from losing the match against Erec. In the Lancelot-Grail Cycle Gawain won the horse from a Saxon king named Clarion; in another version Gringolet bears the brand of the Grail Castle and was owned originally by Lybbeals of Prienlascors. In yet another telling of the acquisition of the horse Gawain was said to have been gifted the horse by the fairy Eselarmonde. In the Welsh telling of Arthurian folklore, Gawain's counterpart, Gwalchmei, called his horse Kincaled. Gringolet carried Gawain throughout his quest for the Bleeding Lance and made the famous leap over Perilous Gorge.

Source: Bruce, *Arthurian Name Dictionary*, 239; Karr, *Arthurian Companion*, 212

Groot Slang

Variations: Kayman, Khoisan, Ki-man, Nama

A large, monstrous creature from the folklore and legends of the Dahomey of West Africa, the groot slang was reported by European travelers as being as large as an elephant and having a serpent's tail. The groot slang was said to live in the caves in the swamp along the west coast.

Source: Eberhart, *Mysterious Creatures*, 217; Rose, *Giants, Monsters, and Dragons*, 156

Grugyn Gwrych Ereint

In Arthurian folklore, Grugyn Gwrych Ereint ("silver-bristle") was one of the seven piglets acting as part of the warrior entourage for the boar TWRCH TRWYTH. For many days and nights King Arthur and his men fought the boar and piglets in the valley Dyffryn Amanw; although some of the men died, all of the piglets were eventually slain. Grugyn Gwrych Ereint and LLWYDAWG GOVYNNYAD were the first to kill, taking the lives of Arthur's first group of hunters and scouts.

Source: Bruce, *Arthurian Name Dictionary*, 240, 477; Kibler, *Medieval Arthurian Epic and Romance*, 96

Grylio

An evil SALAMANDER from medieval bestiaries, the grylio was said to climb up into fruit trees and poison the ripe fruit with venom so toxic that it not only would kill whoever ate the fruit but would also poison any water or patch of earth onto which the infected fruit fell.

Source: Rose, *Giants, Monsters, and Dragons*, 156; Zell-Ravenheart, *Wizard's Bestiary*, 45

Gryllus, plural: Grylli

Variations: Grillus, plural grilli; Stomach Faces

A humanoid hybrid creature appearing in the margins of medieval manuscripts, such as the *Book of Hours*, the gryllus ("cricket," "grunting pig," or "pig") is depicted as having a head where its genitalia should be. It was symbolic for the folly and vice of man.

In eastern Mediterranean countries it was said to have another head in place of a stomach; images of these beings were popular on jewelry in the Greco-Roman period. Although the meaning is now lost, the image of the gryllus made for a powerful amulet.

Plutarch, the Greek historian and philosopher, mentions them in a version of Odysseus' encounter with the sorceress Circe. When his men were being restored to their original form, one gave an eloquent speech as to why he should retain his form.

Source: Minissale, *Framing Consciousness in Art*, 81; Rose, *Giants, Monsters, and Dragons*, 156–7; Zell-Ravenheart, *Wizard's Bestiary*, 45

Gryneus

Gryneus was a CENTAUR from ancient Greek mythology; he may have been one of the centaurs who attended the wedding of Pirithous, became drunk on wine, and following the lead of EURYTUS, who assaulted Hippodame, began to assault and rape any women they could grab. A great Centauromachy then followed.

Source: *Commentary, Mythological, Historical, and Geographical on Pope's Homer*, 55; Lemprière, *Classical Dictionary*, 264

Guardian Angel

A guardian angel is an angelic being with the ability to intervene in human affairs in order to assist and help; although they are said to have the ability to ignite the imaginations and influence people's senses they cannot affect their will. Some religious beliefs claim each individual has a guardian angel assigned to them at the moment of conception and it stays with them throughout their life and will even remain at their side in Heaven; others believe these ANGELS move about assisting people as the need arises and do not necessarily tend to one but many people. According to ancient and pre–Christian Roman belief, it was said these beings were assigned at birth, a Genius would tend to a Roman male child while a Juno would assist a Roman female. The ancient Greeks had their daemons, the Japanese have the KAMI, and the Zoroastrians call these beings FRAVASHIS. The idea of a church, city, individual, and nation having a guardian angel is a very old concept. The bible is filled with stories of ANGELS assisting individuals; in the New Testament Jesus confirmed their existence in Matthew 18:10.

The Talmud says each Jew has eleven thousand guardian angels watching over him. Muslim folklore said each follower has four guardian angels, known as the *hafaza*; two guards by day and two by night. They write down all of the good and bad a person does in a book they will be confronted with on Judgment Day.

Sadly, guardian angels are capable of being corrupted. According to legend there was once a collection of seventy guardian angels each of whom looked after one nation; they were known collectively as the Ethnarchs. With the exception of Michael, the guardian of Israel, they each fell to corruption and became fallen angels.

Source: Beliefnet, *Big Book of Angels*, 17; Oliver, *Angels A to Z*, 167–70; Webster, *Encyclopedia of Angels*, 70–1

Gudanna

Variations: BULL OF HEAVEN, Gugalana

A monstrous bull from ancient Sumer, Gudanna ("an attacker") was described as being gigantic and having breath so poisonous it could kill two hundred warriors at a time. The goddess Ishtar requested such a creature be created to assault the hero Gilgamesh who had spurned her advances; the god Anu fulfilled the need. Gudanna was slain and dismembered by the hero and his companion Enkidu; the death of the bull so enraged Ishtar she slew Gilgamesh's faithful companion.

Source: De Lafayette, *Sumerian English Dictionary, Volume 2*, 126; Rose, *Giants, Monsters, and Dragons*, 158

Guhin

A species of TENGU from Japanese mythology, the guhin ("dog guests") are more canine-like in their appearance than other species of TENGU. The guhin are akin to NATURE SPIRITs and are particularly vigilant in their protection of certain forests and woodlands.

Source: Pauley, *Pauley's Guide*, 32

Gui Xian

Variations: Xuanwu

A species of demonic creature in Chinese mythology, the gui xian are said to be the souls of people who committed suicide or drowned and are ineligible for reincarnation. Unable to move on, the gui xian haunt this world.

Source: Kelly, *Who in Hell*, 102; Lurker, *Dictionary of Gods and Goddesses, Devils and Demons*, 71; Zell-Ravenheart, *Wizard's Bestiary*, 45

Guirivulu

Variations: Fox-Snake

A chimerical creature from the folklore of Chile, South America, the guirivulu is described as having the body of a puma with the head of a fox and a massive claw at the end of its tail. Living in the deepest pools and rivers the guirivulu will fearlessly attack animals and humans, pulling them into its enormous mouth and swallowing its prey whole; its body expands to accommodate its meal similarly to the way a snake's body expands to take in its food whole. The guirivulu also has the ability of therianthropy, enabling it to shape-shift into a gigantic snake.

Source: Conway, *Mysterious, Magical Cat*, 98; Cooper, *Symbolic and Mythological Animals*, 49; Rose, *Giants, Monsters, and Dragons*, 159

Guivre

Originally a monster from French folklore, the chimerical guivre was described in bestiaries as having the body of a serpent and the head of a HORNED DRAGON. Said to live in forests, pools, woodlands, and damp places, the predatory and vicious guivre would hunt and kill humans. It is depicted in French heraldry.

Source: Rose, *Giants, Monsters, and Dragons*, 159; Zell-Ravenheart, *Wizard's Bestiary*, 45

Gulgun (gul-GOON)

The roan-colored stallion belonging to the Persian king Khosrau Parvez, Gulgun ("rose-hued") was said to be the world's second fastest horse; his stablemate, SHABDIZ, was the fastest.

Source: Renard, *Islam and the Heroic Image*, 208, 143; Shakespeare, *Dictionary Hindustani and English*, LVIII

Gullinborsti (GUL-in-burst-i)

Variations: Grinbulsti, Gullinborst, Gullinborste, Gullinburste, Gullinbursti, Gullin-Bursti, Gullinbusti, Gyllenbuste, Gyllinborste, Hilde-svine, Hildisvini ("battle swine"), Slidrugtanni ("razortooth"), Sliorugtanni ("fearful tusk")

In Norse mythology Gullinborsti ("golden-bristle") is the golden-red boar of the god Freyr; typically he would use it to pull his chariot but on occasion the god would ride upon it, as the animal was faster than any horse. Gullinborsti also had a glow about its body, so there was never a night so dark it could not be ridden. Gullinborsti was constructed by Sindri in order to help his brother win a bet against Loki; it was later given to Freyr as a gift.

Source: Conway, *Norse Magic*, 143–4; Grimes, *Norse Myths*, 272; Lindow, *Handbook of Norse Mythology*, 153; Oehlenschläger, *Gods of the North*, xlvi

Gullinkambi (GUL-in-kam-bi)

Variations: Gollinkambi, Gullinkambe, Gullin-kam'bi, Gullin-kambi, Gyllenkambe, Salgofni, Salgofnir ("the one crowing in the hall"), Vidofner, Víðófnir, Víðópnir, Vithafnir

In Norse mythology Gullinkambi ("goldcomb") is a bright red rooster which crows alerting the *einherjar* (spirits of those brave Norse warriors who died in battle), gods, and heroes as Ragnarok begins. Gullinkambi perches atop the upper branches of the tree Ygdrasil where it crows each morning to awaken the gods. His counterpart is the rooster FIALAR.

Source: Barber, *Dictionary of Fabulous Beasts*, 151; Coulter, *Encyclopedia of Ancient Deities*, 198; Daly, *Norse Mythology A to Z*, 43; Grimes, *Norse Myths*, 273

Gulltoppr (GUL-tawp-r)

Variations: Golltoppr, Gulltop, Gulltopp, Gultopr

In Norse mythology Gulltoppr ("gold top") was the golden-maned horse of the god Heimdal; he rode it each day, back and forth across the bridge Bifrost, heralding in the new day.

Source: Anderson, *Norrœna*, 1023; Grimes, *Norse Myths*, 16, 273; Sturluson, *Prose Edda*, 28

Gulon

Variations: Gulo, Jerff, Rossamaka, Vielfras

Described by the Swedish Catholic ecclesiastic and writer Olaus Magnus in his *History of the Northern People* (1555), the gulon was said to be comparable in size to a large dog but had the face of a cat, long brown fur, sharp claws, and a short tail. Living in the northern snowfields of Sweden, the gulon lived off the carcasses left behind by other predators. According to the creature's description as soon as it came upon a carcass it would consume as much of it as possible, stretching out its stomach until it was as tight as a drum. Then, the gulon would seek out two trees growing close to one another and would squeeze itself between the trunks, presumably to aid in its digestion. Once this was completed, it would return to the carcass and begin the process anew. Because of its odd eating

habit the gulon appeared in many bestiaries as the symbol of gluttony.

Source: Ashton, *Curious Creatures in Zoology*, 100–02; Rose, *Giants, Monsters, and Dragons*, 159–60; Rosen, *Mythical Creatures Bible*, 104; Zell-Ravenheart, *Wizard's Bestiary*, 45

Gumberoo

One of the FEARSOME CRITTERS from the lumberjack folklore of the United States of America, the ferocious gumberoo was a gigantic creature, larger than a bear and able to kill a man with a swipe of its paw. The gumberoo was said to resemble a walking football; its leathery hide was particularly resilient and could withstand attacks from arrows, axes, and bullets. The only means by which to kill a gumberoo was to set it on fire and wait until it exploded.

Source: Botkin, *American People*, 251; Godfrey, *Monsters of Wisconsin*, 131; Rose, *Giants, Monsters, and Dragons*, 119

Gumiho

According to Korean folklore a gumiho ("nine tailed fox") is a fox with nine tails. These creatures having achieved a level of enlightenment then developed the ability to shape-shift into the form of a beautiful woman. In their human guise the gumiho will seduce a man, kill him, and then consume his liver.

Source: Tudor, *Korea*, n.pag.; Wallen, *Fox*, 166

Gurangatch

Gurangatch was one of the creatures from the Dreamtime folklore of the Australian aboriginals; it was described as being half fish and half lizard covered with beautiful, shimmering scales of gold, green, and purple. Living in a deep waterhole, his eyes shone up through the water like two bright stars. At mid-day Gurangatch would bask in the shallows and at night he would retreat into the water's depths. He is said to have created the Wollondilly and Wingeecaribee rivers and many of the underwater caverns in New South Wales by carving an escape route when he was being hunted.

Source: Rose, *Giants, Monsters, and Dragons*, 160; Thomas, *Some Myths and Legends of the Australian Aborigines*, n.pag.; Zell-Ravenheart, *Wizard's Bestiary*, 46

Gurula (goo-roo-luh)

Variations: GARUDA

In Sinhalese Hindu mythology Gurula is an eagle hybrid, half human and half avian, which pulls the god Vishnu across the sky.

Source: Mahanama-sthavira, *Mahavamsa*, 400

Guyascutus (gay-as-cut-as)

Variations: Gyascutus

Originating in the lumberjack communities of the developing United States of America, the guyascutus, one of the FEARSOME CRITTERS, was originally described as being a gigantic DRAGON but in later tales was reduced in size and shape to something akin to a chimerical ten-foot-long alligator covered with an armadillo-like hide and having a ridge of horns running the length of his spine. As time passed the description of the chimerical guyascutus changed again, this time to a creature more like a white-tailed deer with a mouth full of vicious fangs and rabbit-like ears atop its head. No matter the appearance of the chimerical guyascutus what remained consistent was the legs on one side of its body were shorter than the others but had the ability to telescope to a desired length; by use of these unique legs and its prehensile tail the guyascutus was said to be able to maneuver about the steeply sloped mountains with ease.

Source: Botkin, *American People*, 251; Godfrey, *Monsters of Wisconsin*, 131; Hendrickson, *Facts on File Dictionary of American Regionalisms*, 235

Gwartheg Y Llyn

In Welsh folklore the gwartheg y llyn ("kine of the lake") are the fairy cows (see FAIRY ANIMAL) belonging to the Gwragedd Annwn (a species of water fairy); they are similar to the CRODH MARA of the Scottish Highlands. Described as being milk-white with the occasional one having red ears, these fairy bovines were capable of interbreeding with mortal cattle producing a hybrid cow which would yield a prodigious amount of milk. Interestingly, in Ireland and Scotland the gwartheg y llyn are said to be red bodied and have white ears. FUWCH GYFEIL-IORN and GLAS GHAILBHLEANN are each specific famous gwartheg y llyn.

Source: Briggs, *Encyclopedia of Fairies*, 209–10; Monaghan, *Encyclopedia of Celtic Mythology and Folklore*, 233

Gwiber

Variations: Gwydir

A white DRAGON and the Welsh symbol for England, the Gwiber is, according to an eighth century legend, fated to engage Y DDRAIG GOCH in combat and lose to it; this battle is symbolic of a war to be fought between Britain and Wales in which Wales will win and have its independence restored.

Source: Breverton, *Wales*, n.pag.; Rose, *Giants, Monsters, and Dragons*, 307

Gwyllgi

Variations: Black Bog of Hergest, Cŵn Annwfn ("dog of the Underworld"), Cŵn annwn, Cŵn bendith y manau ("fairy dog"), Cŵn Cyrff ("corpse dog"), Cŵn Toili, Cŵn Wybr ("sky dog"), Gwyllgi the Dog of Darkness

A BLACK DOG from Welsh folklore, gwyllgi ("dog of darkness") are said to haunt the fields where the sheep of Yspaddaden Pencawr castle graze; these creatures are described as looking like shaggy mastiffs as large as "a steed nine winters old," with fiery eyes, terrible breath, and an unearthly howl. Their coat color has been given as black, red-grey, and white and there are even reports of them running in packs. All of the dead bushes and trees in the area are said to have died as a direct result of a gwyllgi having breathed upon them.

Source: Eberhart, *Mysterious Creatures*, 222; Sikes, *British Goblins*, 169

Gwys

In Arthurian folklore, Gwys was one of the seven piglets acting as the warrior entourage for the boar TWRCH TRWYTH. For many days and nights King Arthur and his men fought the boar and piglets in the valley Dyffryn Amanw; although some of the men died, all of the piglets were slain. Gwys was slain at the battle in Mynydd Amanw.

Source: Bruce, *Arthurian Name Dictionary*, 255, 477; Kibler, *Medieval Arthurian Epic and Romance*, 96

Gyller

Variations: Gyllir

Gyller ("glider" or golden") was one of the twelve horses utilized by the Aesir in Norse mythology; its specific owner or rider is not mentioned. Gyller was also listed as one of the many horses who would graze in the red-gilt leafed Glasir Grove.

Source: Anderson, *Norse Mythology*, 189; Grimes, *Norse Myths*, 20, 273; Norroena Society, *Asatrii Edda*, 356

Gyllir (GEL-er)

Variations: Gyllinger

Gyllir ("golden" or "yellow") was one of the horses utilized by the Aesir in Norse mythology; its specific owner or rider is not mentioned.

Source: Sturluson, *Prose Edda*, 28; Puryear, *Nature of Asatru*, 201

Gypsum

In ancient Sumerian mythology, Gypsum was one of the many monsters slain by the warrior god Ninurta. Little is known of this creature other than Gudea, a ruler of Lagash (ca. 2100 BC), referred to it, and the other monsters vanquished by Ninurta, as the SLAIN HEROES; he elevated them all to the status of god and made a place of worship for them in the temple.

Source: Ataç, *Mythology of Kingship in Neo-Assyrian Art*, 185

Gytrash

Variations: Brash, Guytrash, PADFOOT, Shagfoal, Shriker, Skriker, TRASH

Gytrash was a large black and white fairy-hound in Horton, England; it had the ability to take the shape of a cow, horse, or mule (see FAIRY ANIMAL); it took its onomatopoeian name from the sound its feet makes, similar to that of heavy boots on a mired road. It has also been seen in Lincolnshire and Yorkshire. Sometimes Gytrash was said to roam the roads with chains dragging behind it and other times not. This fairy-hound was said to be malevolent, chasing travelers or leading them astray, but there are no stories of it actually hurting anyone. Its presence was said to foretell disaster.

Source: Briggs, *Encyclopedia of Fairies*, 209; Campbell, *Strange World of the Brontës*, 115, 116; Peacock, *Folklore Journal*, Volume 12, 266–7; Wright, *English Dialect Dictionary*, 226

Ha-puu

In Hawaiian mythology Ha-puu ("to be many") is a DRAGON goddess, a descendant of the primordial DRAGON goddess MO-O-INANEA.

Source: Monaghan, *Encyclopedia of Goddesses and Heroines*, 155

Haakapainizi

A gigantic anthropophagous (man-eating) grasshopper from the Native American Kawaiisu mythology, haakapainizi hunted throughout Southern California, United States of America. Carrying a basket, it would hunt human children, capture them, and carry them back to its lair in the basket to consume later. Eventually the hero Mouse tricked the haakapainizi into swallowing a red-hot coal which transformed the insect into stone from the inside out.

Source: Rose, *Giants, Monsters, and Dragons*, 165; Zigmond, *Kawaiisu Mythology*, 159

Habergeiss (HABBER-gies)

Variations: Schrattl, Ziegenmelker

A vampiric demonic creature from Serbia, the habergeiss looks like a THREE-LEGGED BIRD. Using its therianthropy ability it shape-shifts to appear like various types of animals; it utilizes its disguised form to attack cattle during the night, feeding off their blood. The cry of the habergeiss is considered to be a psychopomp (death omen).

Source: Folkard, *Plant Lore*, 84; Friend, *Flowers and Flower Lore*, Volume 1, 64; Hillman, *Pan and the Nightmare*, 127; Jones, *On the Nightmare*, 108

Habrok

Variations: Hábrók

Habrok ("high pants") was one of the birds named in Thorgrimr's *Rhymes* and in Snorri Sturluson's (1179–1241) *Prose Edda*. This hawk from Norse mythology was, according to *Grímnismál*, described as being the "best of hawks" on a list of "the best" things.

Source: Jennbert, *Animals and Humans*, 50; Lindow, *Norse Mythology*, 365

Hadhayosh

Variations: Hadhayaosh, Sarsaok

The primordial ox from Zoroastrian mythology, Hadhayosh carried the first humans across the primordial ocean Vourukasha. For the resurrection of the righteous, Hadhayosh will offer up its body fat which will be mixed with white haoma herbs to create the Draft of Immortality.

Source: Boyce, *A History of Zoroastrianism*, 89; Iyer, *Faith and Philosophy of Zoroastrianism*, 146; Rose, *Giants, Monsters, and Dragons*, 165

Háfeti

Variations: Hafeti

In Norse mythology, Snorri Sturlson (1179–1241), the Icelandic historian, poet, and politician, writes the horse Háfeti ("high-heels") was the preferred mount of Hjalmther in his translation of *Prose Edda*. Háfeti was also listed as one of the many horses who would graze in the red-gilt leafed Glasir Grove.

Source: Grimes, *Norse Myths*, 20, 273; Young, *The Prose Edda*, 211, 252

Hāhau-Whenua

In Maori tradition Hāhau-Whenua ("search for land") was the name of the gigantic fish caught by Māui; its body became the North Island of New Zealand.

Source: White, *Ancient History of the Maori*, Volume II, 116–17

Hai Ho Shang

A species of MERMAN from Chinese mythology, the highly aggressive hai ho shang ("sea Buddhist priest") haunts the south sea; it is described as having the body of a large fish but the shaved head of a Buddhist monk. The hai ho shang is an exceptionally strong creature, powerful enough to take hold of a fishing vessel and pull it beneath the waves, drowning the entire crew. The hai ho shang may be repelled, in a pinch, by burning feathers, but a more effective method is for someone on the crew to perform a set ritual dance which will drive the creature off. At one time it was common for someone on board to know this dance and be responsible for its execution in addition to their other duties.

Source: Conway, *Magickal Mermaids and Water Creatures*, 61; Rose, *Giants, Monsters, and Dragons*, 166; Zell-Ravenheart, *Wizard's Bestiary*, 46

Hai Riyo

Variations: Schachi Hoko, Tobi Tatsu

The chimerical hai riyo from Japanese mythology are considered to be among the most evolved of all various species of DRAGONS. Described as having the body, talons, and wings of a bird, the rest of it is dragonesque.

Source: Eberhart, *Mysterious Creatures*, 148; Hargreaves, *Hargreaves New Illustrated Bestiary*, 59; Rose, *Giants, Monsters, and Dragons*, 166

Hai-Uri

Variations: Adroa, Hai-Uru, Tikdoshe

Folktale of the Khoikhoi people of South Africa tell of the hai-uri ("dimensional being"), a dangerous male creature; it is described as having only one half of a human body—one arm and leg and one half of a head with one eye and half a nose and mouth. The hai-uri is a cannibal and hunts for its prey by jumping and leaping with its extremely powerful leg, moving as fast as a gazelle. It uses a club to subdue its prey but it will also throw punches, as it is strong enough to break bones with a single blow. This monster consumes nearly every bit of its prey, leaving almost nothing behind. The female version of this creature is called the BI-BLOUK.

Source: Cotterell, *Dictionary of World Mythology*, 241–2; Knudsen, *Fantastical Creatures and Magical Beasts*, 28; Maberry, *Vampire Universe*, 147–48

Haietlik

Variations: Heitlik, Lightning Serpent, Sisiutl, WASGO

A serpentine DRAGON from the folklore of the Clayoqut and the Nootka Native Americans of the Pacific Northwest of North America, the chimerical haietlik is described as having a long serpentine body, horse's head, powerful jaw like an alligator, and many teeth in its mouth. Living in lakes and waterways, this creature related to the THUNDERBIRD was seldom seen.

Source: De Kirk, *Dragonlore*, 49, 52; Dixon-Kennedy, *Native American Myth and Legend*, 104; Meurger, *Lake Monster Traditions*, 168; Sierra, *Gruesome Guide to World Monsters*, 17

Haizum (hä' züm)

In Muslim folklore and named in the Koran, Haizum was the name of the mare ridden by the archangel Gabriel.

Source: Brewer, *Dictionary of Phrase and Fable*, 626; Rose, *Giants, Monsters, and Dragons*, 167; Tozer, *Horse in History*, 87

Hakulaq

A gigantic, amphibious, female, shape-shifting creature, the hakulaq is from the folklore of the Tsimshian Native American coastal peoples of the Northwest United States of America. The hakulaq makes its own offspring assume the form of an infant or small child and has it splash about in the water between two islands where it will be heard calling out for help. Once the young hakulaq is upon land its mother, in the guise of an irate human, appears and accuses the would-be rescuers of attempting to abduct her child. Finally, in a fit of anger the hakulaq raises up a mighty storm, the waves of which wash upon the shore and drown everyone involved in the rescue attempt.

Source: Locher, *Serpent in Kwakiutl Religion*, 79; Rose, *Giants, Monsters, and Dragons*, 167; Zell-Ravenheart, *Wizard's Bestiary*, 47

Hākuturi

NATURE SPIRITS in Maori mythology, the hākuturi guard, protect, and avenge any desecration done to them. According to the folklore, the bird-like hākuturi are considered to be the children of Tāne, the god of the forests and the ancestor of all birds.

Source: Orbell, *Concise Encyclopedia of Māori Myth and Legend*, 23–24; Tregear, *Maori-Polynesian Comparative Dictionary*, 43; *Ancient History of the Maori, 7 Volumes*, Volume 2, 2

Hala

Variations: Ala

In Bulgarian folklore the hala ("hail") is the personification of bad weather, often described as a DRAGON with the ability to shape-shift into a dense fog; it is believed to have the ability to cause eclipses and pour tainted water from its tail in order to destroy crops.

Source: Kmietowicz, *Slavic Mythical Beliefs*, 207; Turner, *Dictionary of ancient Deities*, 201

Halulu

In Hawaiian folklore the halulu are a species of anthropophagous (man-eating) birds with the ability to shape shift into human form; they are described as having feathers made of water from the sun. One of these birds was dispatched by the god Kane to the four directions of chaos to announce he was about to construct the world.

Source: Beckwith, *Hawaiian Mythology*, n.pag.; Zell-Ravenheart, *Wizard's Bestiary*, 47

Hameh (Hay-ma)

A vampiric bird with beautiful green or purple feathers from the mythology of Arabia, the hameh is created from the blood of a murder victim. The hameh has a monotonous cry, *"iskoonee,"* which translates to mean "give me blood." It will also cry out if it sees a murder about to happen. The hameh will tirelessly seek out its own murderer, never stopping until it has drunk its fill of his blood. Once the creature has tracked down its killer, it will fly off to the land of spirits and gladly announce its murder has been avenged.

Source: Hulme, *Myth-land*, 140–41; Lane, *Selections from the Kur-án*, 35; Muir, *Songs and Other Fancies*, 157–59; Reddall, *Fact, Fancy, and Fable*, 250

Hamingja (HAM-ing-ya), plural Hamingjur

Variations: Fylgukona

In Icelandic and Norse mythology the hamingjur ("luck") are feminine, invisible beings who attach themselves to a man and act as an advisor to him, directing, if they can, his course of action similar to the GUARDIAN ANGEL of Christian folklore. The hamingjur are very similar to the FYLGIA and are related to the goddesses known as the NORNS. These supernatural beings would on occasion take the form of an animal or a woman in order to guide their charge.

Source: Cleasby, *Icelandic-English Dictionary*, 236; Coulter, *Encyclopedia of Ancient Deities*, 183; Puryear, *Nature of Asatru*, 203

Hamou Ukaiou

Hamou Ukaiou is the husband to the djinn (a race of demons) AICHA KANDIDA in Moroccan folklore. A nocturnal demon, he preys upon women who travel alone at night, stalking up and then devouring them. Sharpening a knife on the ground in his presence will prevent his attack.

Source: Illes, *Encyclopedia of Spirits*, 145; Rose, *Giants, Monsters, and Dragons*, 20

Hamsa

The hamsa ("swan") of Buddhist and Hindu mythology is a sacred bird described as being the vehicle of the Asvins, the divine twin horsemen; it is often represented in art as being the *vahana* ("mount" or "vehicle") of Visnu.

Source: Hopkins, *Epic Mythology*, 19; Mishra, *Studies in Hindu and Buddhist Art*, 73, 74

Hamshamtsus

A cannibalistic monster from the mythology of the Kwakiutla people of Canada, North America, Hamshamtsus is one of the attendants of the horrific and monstrous Bakbakwakanooksiewae, a cannibalistic bird-spirit; he is said to be less violent than the others.

Source: Hawthorn, *Art of the Kwakiutl Indians and Other Northwest Coast Tribes*, 51; Werness, *Continuum Encyclopedia of Native Art*, 127

Hamskerper (HAM-skerp-ir)

Variations: Hamskerpir ("thin loined")

In Norse mythology, Hamskerper ("hide-hardener") and GARÐROFA were the two horses who sired HÓFVARPNIR, the mount of the goddess Gna (Gnaa) and messenger to the god Frigga. Although the names of these horses appear in the *Prose Edda*, additional myths of them have disappeared.

Source: Anderson, *Norræna*, Volume 5, 1024; Lindow, *Norse Mythology*, 147; Rydberg, *Norroena*, Volume 3, 1021; Sturluson, *Prose Edda*, 47, 128

Han-Riu

Variations: Han-Ryu

A multi-colored species of DRAGON from Japanese mythology, the han-riu, similar to the CH'I-LUNG of Chinese mythology, is described as being more than forty feet long and is striped with nine different colors; unfortunately, according to the folklore, no matter how hard it tries, it will never be able to reach the heavens.

Source: Bates, *All About Chinese Dragons*, 99; De Kirk, *Dragonlore* 30; Ingersoll, *Dragons and Dragon Lore*, 103; Jones, *Instinct for Dragons*, 161

Hanadaka Tengu (HAH-nah-dah-kah TEN-goo)

A species of demonic creature from Japanese mythology, the hanadaka tengu ("long nose tengu") are famed for their obsession with discipline and spiritual training; although they rarely engage in acts of malicious or unnecessary violence they will play tricks in order to teach a willful soul a much needed lesson. Victims of these hard-learned lessons may discover they have been spirited away to a distant location. The hanadaka tengu are also well known for their vanity and revel in being able to show-off their vast martial-arts knowledge; with proper approach, these creatures have been known to accept human students, teaching them martial skills. They are particularly renowned for their swordsmanship.

In Tengu society the hanadaka are regarded as leaders of the clans, the most powerful of them being called O-Tengu ("great tengu"); in fact, they are often described as minor gods. All hanadaka are considered to be superior to the KARASU-TENGU ("raven tengu") on the hierarchy of tengu society.

They are described as being barefoot or wearing single-toothed "geta" clogs and having bright red skin, an enormous and especially long nose, massive plumose wings, and a muscular humanoid body. They have the ability to communicate without moving their mouths, fly as fast as a jet, generate strong winds using leaf like fans, use mimicry, and shape-shift.

Source: Yoda, *Yokai Attack*, 22–25

Hangdown

Originating in the lumberjack communities of the developing United States of America, the hangdown, one of the FEARSOME CRITTERS, was described as a sloth-like creature as it would hang from tree branches by either its front or rear legs, and "walk" through the forest in this fashion. Legend says the hide of the hangdown brought a high price; they were hunted at night with axes.

Source: Botkin, *American People*, 251; Rose, *Giants, Monsters, and Dragons*, 119

Hannya (Han-ya)

Variations: Akeru, Hannya-Shin-Kyo ("emptiness of forms")

A vampiric, demonic type of creature from Japanese mythology, *hannya* ("empty") are said to feed exclusively off truly beautiful women and infants. They are described as having large chins, long fangs, horns, green scales, serpentine forked tongues, and eyes burning like twin flames.

Normally, hannya live near the sea or in wells, but they are never too far from humans, as they can sneak unseen into any house containing a potential victim (a sleeping woman). Just before it attacks, the hannya lets loose with a horrible shriek. While the woman is startled, the creature possesses her, slowly driving her insane and physically altering her body into a hideous monster. Eventually, it drives her to attack a child, drink its blood, and eat its flesh.

There is no known potential weakness to exploit, but there is a Buddhist sutra which renders humans invisible to spirits and demons. In No dramas, young men are depicted as the favorite victims of an especially vicious and vindictive hannya.

Source: Frédéric, *Japan Encyclopedia*, 287–88; Pollack, *Reading Against Culture*, 50; Toki, *Japanese Nō Plays*, 40

Happy Auger

Variations: Schnellgeiste ("quick spirit"), Snallygaster, Snollygoster

Originating in the lumberjack communities of the developing United States of America, the happy auger, one of the FEARSOME CRITTERS, was described as being kangaroo-like in appearance, as it stood on its hind legs and had a long, thick, and heavy tail curled like a corkscrew. When the happy auger would sit upon the ground and spin on its tail it would become rooted to the spot.

As the snallygaster, this is a deadly chimerical creature of avian and reptile combinations, having a metallic beak and razor-like claws. It was said to fly out of the sun and sweep up people, draining them dry of their blood.

Source: Beath, *Febold Feboldson*, 100–01; Rose, *Giants, Monsters, and Dragons*, 119; Zell-Ravenheart, *Wizard's Bestiary*, 91

Harpagos

Variations: Xanthos

One of the two horses owned by the Dioskouroi twins from classical Greek mythology, Castor and Pollux, Harpagos ("one that carries off rapidly") and his stablemate CYLLAROS were said to be immortal white stallions; they were each HIPPOI ATHANATOI.

Source: Brewer, *Dictionary of Phrase and Fable*, 626; Ruthven, *Shaman Pathways*, n.pag.

Harpalus

A dog from ancient Greek mythology, Harpalus ("snap" as in "to snatch") was one of the DOGS OF ACTÆON, the unfortunate youth who was raised by the CENTAUR CHEIRON. Harpalus is noted for having a white spot in the middle of his black forehead.

Source: Leeming, *World of Myth*, 111; Murray, *Classical Manual*, 160; Naso, *Fasti, Tristia*, 93–5

Harpy, plural Harpies ("swift robbers")

Variations: Harpyia, Harpyiai, Hounds of Zeus

Originally the harpies of ancient Greek mythology were born the daughters of the sea NYMPH Electra and an ancient god of the sea and Titan called Thaumus. Some authors said they were the daughters of Oceanus and Terra while Gaius Valerius Flaccus, a Roman poet of the Silver Age, believed them to be the daughters of Typhoeus.

Stories of harpies described them as beautiful winged women who would appear suddenly, snatch up an object or person, and vanish without being seen; any sudden disappearance was credited to them. The harpies of this era were under the dominion of the god Zeus (Jupiter); he would send them out in thunder storms to do his bidding; for this they became the personifications of storm winds and whirlwinds.

The Greek poet Hesiod (ca. 750–650 BC) named two harpies in his writings, AELLO and Ocypete. Homer, the greatest of ancient Greek epic poets, added a third harpy to the list, Pordage ("fleetfoot"); this creature, he wrote, was married to the western wind Zephyrus, and by her husband gave birth to the two great horses of Achilles, BALIOS and XANTHOS.

In the stories of Jason and the Argonauts harpies were described as vicious, rank smelling chimerical creatures with bodies like vultures, ears like bears, faces like women, and the feet and hands hooked like talons carrying off food and treasure in their razor-sharp claws.

In Roman mythology harpies were, according to Virgil's *Aeneid*, said to have attacked Aeneas and his Trojan crew; here the name of another harpy appears, Celaeno.

Source: Daly, *Greek and Roman Mythology, A to Z*, 63; *London Encyclopaedia*, Volume 11, 53

Harpyes

Variations: Harpyia

A dog from ancient Greek mythology, Harpyes ("ravener") was one of the DOGS OF ACTÆON, the unfortunate youth who was raised by the CENTAUR CHEIRON. Harpyes ran in the pack with her two pups in tow.

Source: Leeming, *World of Myth*, 111; Murray, *Classical Manual*, 160; Naso, *Fasti, Tristia*, 93–5

Harun

A water-dwelling NATURE SPIRIT from Moroccan mythology, Harun assumes the form of a snake; it is placated by throwing bits of bread or cous-cous into the river. Harun's mate is named Haruna.

Source: Lurker, *Dictionary of Gods and Goddesses, Devils and Demons*, 75

Hashi Hime (HAH-she HEE-may)

A YŌKAI from Japanese folklore, the hashi hime ("bridge princess") appears as a topless human woman with her long black hair parted and rolled into seven loops; atop her head is a crown with lit candles. In very rare occasions, the hashi hime may manifest as a male.

A powerful NATURE SPIRIT, this singular being was created by the sheer force of the power of her jealousy and desire for revenge against her philandering husband. After seven days of prayers for divine justice a priest was sent a message in a dread as to how she could enact her revenge: first she was to don all red clothing and cover her face and body with poisonous cinnabar.

Then she was to do up her hair in seven loops, place a brazier alit with candles atop her head, and carry a rod of pure iron to the Uji River where she was to remain for twenty-one days. If she was still there she would be transformed into a being which would enable her have the vengeance she sought. Since her vengeance was carried out the hashi hime now attacks travelers as they attempt to cross bridges, in particular happy couples.

Source: Ashkenazi, *Handbook of Japanese Mythology*, 257; Yoda, *Yokai Attack*, 162–6

Hati

Variations: Gamr, Garm, Garm the Watchdog of the Dead, Garme, Hati Hrodvitnisson, Hati Hrodvitnirsson, MAANEGARM, Mana-garm, Manigarm ("moon hound"), Mara-garme, Moongarm

Hati ("hateful") was one of the gigantic wolves named in Thorgrimr's *Rhymes* and in Snorri Sturluson's (1179–1241) *Prose Edda*; he chased the moon across the sky whereas his brother, SKOLL, chased the sun; collectively they were known as the Vars (Varns). His father was HRODVITNER and his mother, JARNVIDS.

As Garm, Hati was said to be the guardian at the gates to the domain of the goddess Hel. In some versions of the mythology the god FENRIR and the ASYNJR GULVEIG are the parents of the Vars.

Source: Coulter, *Encyclopedia of Ancient Deities*, 206; Jennbert, *Animals and Humans*, 50

Hatif

In being heard but never seen from Arabic writings, the hatif ("invisible speaker" or "one who cries out harshly") typically appears as the giver of some needed advice, direction, warning, or wisdom to a character in a story through poetic verse. This is also a method by which a djinn (a race of demons) may choose to manifest and let its presence be known.

Source: Burton, *Plain and Literal Translation of the Arabian Nights' Entertainments*, Volume 13, 519; Houtsma, *E.J. Brill's First Encyclopaedia of Islam*, Volume 2, 289

Hatuibwari

Melanesian mythology tells of the half demonic and half divine DRAGON or serpentine-like being known as Hatuibwari. The upper body is female with four eyes and four breasts; the lower half is a huge serpent with a pair of wings. Hatuibwari is said to be the progenitor of the human race: she used her breasts to give nourishment to everything.

Source: Riesenfeld, *Megalithic Culture of Melanesia*, 151–3; Rose, *Giants, Monsters, and Dragons*, 169; Turner, *Dictionary of Ancient Deities*, 206

Hau

A monstrous serpent from ancient Egyptian mythology, Hau would grapple with Osiris as he made his way through the third section of Tuat, the Underworld. In *The Text of Unas* there is a magical spell which when performed will cause the destruction of monstrous beasts and serpents alike; Hau would be affected by this spell.

Source: Coulter, *Encyclopedia of Ancient Deities*, 32; Spence, *Myths and Legends of Ancient Egypt*, 117

Havhest

The havhest ("sea horse") of Scandinavian folklore is a hybrid SEA SERPENT described as either having the body of a fish and the head of a horse or as having a serpentine-like body, a vast torso, and the head of a horse with a double row of fanged teeth, yellow eyes, and the ability to breathe fire.

Source: Eberhart, *Mysterious Creatures*, 232; Meurger, *Lake Monster Traditions*, 225; Rose, *Giants, Monsters, and Dragons*, 169

Hea-bani

Variations: Heabani

The ancient Roman poet and philosopher Titus Lucretius Carus (99 BC–55 BC) described Hea-bani in his work *De rerum natura* as a FAUN- or SATYR-like being, having very prominent ears and the feet, horns, and tail of an ox. Hea-bani, something of a sage and interpreter or dreams, lived in a cave with wild animals preferring their company to humans. By day Hea-bani would graze with cattle and at night he would graze with gazelles. He was eventually slain by Lion- or Scorpion men.

Source: Ashton, *Curious Creatures in Zoology*, 79–80; Forlong, *Rivers of Life*, 51, 52

Headless Mule

Originating in twelfth century Iberian folklore the story of the headless mule spread to Portugal, Spain, and eventually to Brazil by colonials. At this time the creature was a female species of *lobisomen* (WEREWOLF) dwelling specifically in towns where the houses were built encircling the church. In spite of its common point of origin, it should be noted the Portuguese and Spanish *lobisomen* is a different creature from the Brazilian *lobisomen*.

In Brazilian folklore it is believed when a woman takes a priest as her lover she will inevitably be transformed into the fire-breathing headless mule ("mula sem cabeca").

Source: Atala-Atala, *Lunch with God*, 38; Linger, *Anthropology Through a Double Lens*, 205

Heavenly Cock

Variations: Bird of Dawn, Celestial Cock, Chu-Ya ("he who enlightens the night"), THREE-LEGGED BIRD, Tsin-Ssi ("the golden cock")

Perched upon the branches of a willow tree the golden-plumed heavenly cock of Chinese mythology sings its song at sunrise; like the tree it roosts on, it is symbolic of the sun. The three-legged heavenly cock belongs to a class of animals from Chinese mythology protecting mankind from the evil influences of demons.

Source: Ashman, *Fabulous Beasts*, 117; Laufer, *American Anthropologist*, Volume 2, 302

Hedammu

Hedammu is a demonic creature from Hurrian (ancient Anatolia) mythology which is described in Kumarbi Cycle's *Song of the Sea*. An aqueous devil, it was born the reptilian child of Kumarbi and the daughter of a sea-god. Serpentine in its appearance and raging with its insatiable appetite, it attacked anything which came into its territory. According to the tale, the creature was lured to the shore with music, beautiful dancing women, and offerings of blood tainted with a sleeping elixir. Once ashore, he consumed the blood offerings and was then possibly slain by Sausga, sister of Tessub, or by Ishtar, but it will remain a mystery, as the original source is incomplete.

Source: Cotterell, *Encyclopedia of World Mythology*, 26, 29; Foley, *Companion to Ancient Epic*, 261; Rose, *Giants, Monsters, and Dragons*, 170

Heidrun (HAYTH-roon)

Variations: Heidrún

Heidrun ("clear stream") was one of the goats named in Thorgrimr's *Rhymes* and in Snorri Sturluson's (1179–1241) *Prose Edda*. Standing atop the roof of Valaskialf, it is said her teats provide a constant supply of hydromel to the guests of Valhalla as she chews on the leaves of Ygdrasil.

Source: Jennbert, *Animals and Humans*, 49; Norroena Society, *Asatrii Edda*, 357; Oehlenschläger, *Gods of the North*, xlvii

Hekret

Variations: AKENEH, Hek, Hekau, Hyk

A feared serpent from ancient Egyptian mythology, Hekret was said to consume the bodies and drink the blood of people who made their way through the Underworld. In *The Text of Unas* there is a magical spell which when performed will cause the destruction of monstrous beasts and serpents alike; Hekret would be affected by this spell.

Source: Budge, *Gods of the Egyptians*, 23; Coulter, *Encyclopedia of Ancient Deities*, 32, 209

Helhest

In Danish folklore a helhest ("Hel's horse") is a three-legged horse; it is associated with death and has made its way into a number of colloquial sayings, such as "he walks like Hel's horse," meaning the person blunders about noisily. Hel, daughter of the JOTUN god Loki, has dominion over a realm bearing her name, located in Niflheim, according to Norse mythology.

Source: Grimm, *Teutonic Mythology*, 844

Helimus

A CENTAUR from ancient Greek mythology, Helimus was one of the centaurs who attended the wedding of Pirithous, became drunk on wine, and following the lead of EURYTUS, who assaulted Hippodame, began to assault and rape any women they could grab. A great Centauromachy then followed.

Source: *Commentary, Mythological, Historical, and Geographical on Pope's Homer*, 55; Lemprière, *Classical Dictionary*, 15

Heliodromos

In medieval Europe the heliodromos ("courier of the sun") was said to be a hybrid creature, a cross between a GRIFFIN and a vulture.

Source: Gilman, *New International Encyclopædia*, Volume 13, 632; Rose, *Giants, Monsters, and Dragons*, 170

Hellhound

Variations: Bakgest, Bargeist, Bargest, Bargheist, Barghest, Bargtjest, BARGUEST, Barguist, BLACK ANGUS, Black Dog of Hergest, BLACK DOG, BLACK SHUCK, Black Shug, Bo-guest, CAPELTHWAITE, Choin Dubh ("muckle black tyke"), Cu Sith ("fairy dog"), Cwn Annw, Cŵn Annwfn ("dog of the Underworld"), Cŵn Annwn, Cŵn bendith y manau ("fairy dog"), Cŵn Cyrff ("corpse dog"), Cŵn Toili, Cŵn Wybr ("sky dog"), Devil Dog, Devil's Dandy Dog, Doom Dog, Gabriel Hound, Galleytrot, Gurt Dog, Gwyllgi the Dog of Darkness, GWYLLGI, Gytrash, Hounds of Annwn, Mauthe Dhoog, MODDEY DHOO of Norfolk, Morphing Shuck, Night Hound, Old Shock, Old Shuck, PADFOOT, Pooka, Shuck, Shucky Dog, SKRIKER, Suicide Shuck, Tchian du Bouolay, Trash, Wish Hounds, Yeth Hounds

Cultures from all over the world have in their folklores and mythologies gigantic black dogs with fiery eyes and scorching hot breath prowling the roads at night, running down travelers, and carrying their souls back to Hell with them. Typically these creatures are referred to by their regional name. In most versions of this folklore the person must somehow manage to evade the creature until the first crow of the morning cock in order to save their soul.

Source: Maberry, *Vampire Universe*, 152; Steiger, *Real Monsters, Gruesome Critters, and Beasts from the Darkside*, 41

Helops

A CENTAUR from ancient Greek mythology, Helops was, according to Ovid's *Metamorphoses*, one of the CENTAURS who attended the wedding of Pirithous, became drunk on wine and following the lead of EURYTUS who assaulted Hippodame, began

to assault and rape any women they could grab. He was described as being savage in battle.

During the Centauromachy, Helops, along with CHROMIS, DICTYS, and LYCUS, was slain by the hero Pirithous. Helops had a javelin stabbed into his right ear with such might it passed straight through his head and came out of his left ear.

Source: *Commentary, Mythological, Historical, and Geographical on Pope's Homer*, 55; Simpson, *Metamorphoses of Ovid*, 206

Hemetch

A serpent-like demonic creature from the mythology of ancient Egypt, Hemetch was mentioned in a magical formula written by King Unas of the sixth dynasty (2290–2155 BC, Old Kingdom). The newly deceased en route to Osiris's paradise would have to make their way past this creature by using various incantations and spells, many of which were to be provided for them by mortuary cults.

Source: Bunson, *Encyclopedia of Ancient Egypt*, 148, 165; Mercatante, *Who's Who in Egyptian Mythology*, 56

Hemth

A feared serpent from ancient Egyptian mythology, Hemth was said to consume the bodies and drink the blood of people who made their way through the Underworld. In *The Text of Unas* there is a magical spell which when performed will cause the destruction of monstrous beasts and serpents alike; Hemth would be affected by this spell.

Source: Budge, *Gods of the Egyptians*, 23; Coulter, *Encyclopedia of Ancient Deities*, 32, 211

Hen Wen

Variations: Henwen, Hen-Wen, the sow of Dallweir Dallpenn

In Welsh folklore Coll ap Collfrewy was one of the three powerful swine herders on the Isle of Britain; he kept the fairy swine of Dallwyr Dallben in the valley of Dallwyr in Cornwall (see FAIRY ANIMAL). One of the swine under Coll ap Collfrewy's protection was named Hen Wen. It had been prophesied when this pig gave birth it would bring evil to the land. King Arthur assembles a troop of men to seek out the animal and destroy it. Hen Wen, about to give birth, became frightened and ran but her herder caught her by the bristles; unfortunately he was not strong enough to stop her charge. The man held on as Hen Wen ran across the country and swam through the sea, delivering its offspring as it went: in Arvon she delivered a grain of rye, in Dyved she delivered a grain of barley and a piglet, in Gwent she delivered three grains of wheat and three bees, in Maen Du she delivered a kitten, and in Rhiwgyverthwch she delivered an eagle and wolf cub. It is believed by scholars the story is a device used to explain how food and animals not native to the island arrived there.

Source: Morgan, *Notes on Wentwood, Castle Troggy, and Llanvair Castle*, 13; Schreiber, *The Mabinogion*, 330–2

Henham Dragon

Variations: Essex Serpent, Henham Serpent

A DRAGON from British folklore, this creature named after the town it was said to have been seen flying over, was said to have been seen several times in 1668 throughout the month of May; according to the anonymously written pamphlet recording the event, "*A True Relation of a Monstrous Serpent Seen at Henham on the Mount in Saffron Walden*," the DRAGON was described as being eight or nine feet in length, as "round as a man's leg," and having fierce fangs, large eyes, and a set of tiny wings no longer than a foot each upon its back. It was also said to have eaten several cattle, sheep, and townsfolk.

Source: Gilmore, *Monsters*, 66–7; Simpson, *Green Men and White Swans*, 92–3

Hercinia

A bird with brightly glowing feathers from medieval folklore, the hercinia was said to have lived in the ancient and vast woodland known as the Hercynian Forest, Germany. The feathers of this bird shone so brightly in the night travelers said it acted like a beacon, lighting the path for them through the woods. The hercinia was recorded by both Saint Isidore of Seville (AD 560–636), the "last scholar of the ancient world," and Pliny the Elder.

Source: Breverton, *Breverton's Phantasmagoria*, 172; Pliny the Elder, *Pliny's Natural History*, 235

Hercynian Stag

Variations: The Great Black Stag of the Hercynian Forest, Unicorn Stag

A creature alleged to have lived in the ancient and vast woodland known as the Hercynian Forest, Germany, the Hercynian stag was described as having the body of a stag but a long alicorn (a single horn) growing from its brow, between its ears. Although gentle with other animals, this creature with a dissonant call was well known to fight others of its kind.

Source: Carlyle, *Fraser's Magazine*, Volume 56, 89; Nigg, *Book of Fabulous Beasts*, 51; Zell-Ravenheart, *Wizard's Bestiary*, 48

Herok'a

A species of NATURE SPIRIT from the mythology of the Algonkian, Chippewa, Cree, and Nascopie tribes of North America, the herok'a ("those with-out horns") were considered to be benevolent to mankind. Red Horn, the chief of the herok'a, appears in many stories.

Source: Coulter, *Encyclopedia of Ancient Deities*, 214; Lankford, *Reachable Stars*, 84, 122

Hert-Nemmat-Set

According to ancient Egyptian mythology Hert-Nemmat-Set was a female fiend living in the fourth pit of the fourth section, or hour, of Tuat, the Underworld; there she punished the heads and shadows of the damned. There is a fiendish woman by the name of HERT-SEFU-S who also lives in this *hour*, performing the same job as Hert-Nemmat-Set. In the eleventh hour there is an underworld city in Sebuit-Nebt-Uaa-Khesfet-Sebau-Em-Pert-F that contains many pits, some named and others not; one of the unnamed pits is guarded by Hert-Nemmat-Set.

Source: Coulter, *Encyclopedia of Ancient Deities*, 215, 417; Mercatante, *Who's Who in Egyptian Mythology*, 57

Hert-Sefu-S

According to ancient Egyptian mythology Hert-Sefu-S was a female fiend living in the fifth pit of the eleventh section, or hour, of Tuat, the Underworld; there she punished the heads and shadows of the damned. She assisted HERT-NEMMAT-SET in guarding the unnamed pit located in the eleventh hour of Sebuit-Nebt-Uaa-Khesfet-Sebau-Em-Pert-F.

Source: Coulter, *Encyclopedia of Ancient Deities*, 215, 417, Mercatante, *Who's Who in Egyptian Mythology*, 57

Hetch-Nau

According to the mythology of the ancient Egyptians, Hetch-Nau was a monstrous serpent with two heads, one at each end of its body; it and NEHE-BKAU were the guardians of Osiris while the god was in his form known as Osiris the Seeker.

Source: Coulter, *Encyclopedia of Ancient Deities*, 418; Mercatante, *Who's Who in Egyptian Mythology*, 58

Hiai Chai

As described in the work *Yuen Kien Lei Han*, the Chinese hiai chai was similar to the KAI-TSI from Japanese mythology as it had the ability to distinguish between right and wrong, guilt and innocence. Described as being a deer and UNICORN hybrid, whenever a hiai chai sees an evil person it attacks, goring the individual with its alicorn.

Source: Ball, *Proceedings of the Society of Biblical Archaeology*, Volume 12, 418; Gould, *Mythical Monsters*, 348, 357–8

Hicklesnifer

Originating in the lumberjack communities of the developing United States of America, the hicklesnifer was one of the FEARSOME CRITTERS. Unfortunately, there is no additional information on this creature other than its name, causing writers of the time, 1841–1861, to believe it had gone extinct.

Source: Mencken, *American Language Supplement 1*, 251

Hide

A creature living in Lake Lacar, Argentina, the hide has been described as having a body flat and flexible like a manta ray but round like a turtles; the personification of destructive forces and evil, to see the hide is a portent of disaster. Villagers say the folkloric monster's existence is proven by the copious amounts of animal carcasses found along the shore of the lake.

Source: Dixon-Kennedy, *Native American Myth and Legend*, 109; Maberry, *Vampire Universe*, 152

Hidebehind

Originating in the lumberjack communities of the developing United States of America, the hidebehind, one of the FEARSOME CRITTERS, was a brutish and dangerous monster of the woods responsible for the disappearance of many woodsmen. Generally it would, as its name suggests, hide behind a tree trunk, but any large object would do, and from its ambush position, waylay its unsuspecting prey, dragging them kicking and screaming into the depths of the woods never to be seen again. Even if a lumberjack suspected he was being stalked or watched, no matter how quickly he would spin to confront his aggressor, the hidebehind was always faster and able to retreat to its ambush position.

Source: Botkin, *American People*, 251; Gard, *Wisconsin Lore*, 73; Rose, *Giants, Monsters, and Dragons*, 119; Theitic, *Witches' Almanac, Issue 34*, 16

Hieracosphinx

Variations: Hieraco-Sphinx, Hierocosphinxex

In ancient Egyptian mythology there were three types of Sphinxes, the ANDROSPHINX, the CRIOSPHINX, and the hieracosphinx. Each of these variations represented the king as well as a token of respect to the god whose head they most resembled. The hieracosphinx had the head of a hawk and the body of a lion and therefore was associated with the god Re.

Source: Wilkinson, *Manners and Customs of the Ancient Egyptians*, Volume 5, 200–01

Hili (Hil-ee)

Variations: TIKOLOSHE, Tokoloshe

The Xhosa people of Lesotho, Africa, tell of a vampiric bird called a hili. Large and skull-headed, it drips bile and fecal matter from its body as it flies. If so much as a single drop lands on a person, they will contract a disease so powerful only the strongest magic can cure it. To keep the illness from spreading throughout the community, the infected person must be driven out. As the victim grows sicker and sicker, the hili returns to be near so it may be the first animal on the scene when the person dies.

Source: Broster, *Amagqirha*, 60; Bud-M'Belle, *Kafir Scholar's Companion*, 82; Doyle, *Francis Carey Slater*, 38, 121; Theal, *Faffir*, 149–50

Himefaxi

Variations: Hrimefath, Hrímfaxe, Hrimfaxi, Hrímfaxi, Hrymfaxe, Rimefax ("rime-mane"), Rimfakse, Rimfaxi

The horse of Nott (Night) in Norse mythology, Hemifaxi ("frost mane") pulls the chariot across the sky; the saliva from its bit forms the morning dew on Midgard.

Source: Anderson, *Norse Mythology*, 450; Bennett, *Gods and Religions of Ancient and Modern Times*, Volume 1, 390; Grimes, *Norse Myths*, 279

Himinbrjoter

Variations: Heaven Bellower, Heaven Breaker, Himinbrioter, Himinhriot, Himinhrjodr ("heaven bellowing" or "heaven springer"), Himinhrjot ("sky-bellower")

A gigantic black ox belonging to the JOTUN Hymir, Himinbrjoter ("Heaven-breaker" or "sky cleaver") was the largest in his herd. Thor, impatient with the JOTUN, seized the animal, ripped off its head, and used it as bait for a fishing exposition to catch JORMUNGANDR, the Midgard Serpent.

Source: Anderson, *Norse Mythology*, 449; Jennbert, *Animals and Humans*, 49; Rydberg, *Norroena, the History and Romance of Northern Europe*, Volume 3, 1025; Sturluson, *Prose Edda*, Volume 5, 213

Hinqumemen

Variations: Engulfer

A literal lake monster from the mythology of the Coeur d'Alene Native American people of British Columbia, Canada, Hinqumemen is a living and sentient lake. If anyone were ever to take water from it and carry it back to the village or camp, Hinqumemen would move, following them back to wherever they were headed as an amorphous form. Having arrived, it would then engulf the individual with its watery body and return with its victim back to its last location. Once it has returned, Hinqumemen will then drown its captive. Naturally, this living lake is avoided.

Source: Dixon-Kennedy, *Native American Myth and Legend*, 110; Meurger, *Lake Monster Traditions*, 317; Rose, *Giants, Monsters, and Dragons*, 173

Hinthar

A mythical duck from Burmese mythology, Hinthar was said to reside in Hantharwaddy ("land of Hinthar").

Source: Mann, *International Glossary of Place Name Elements*, 73; Rajshekhar. *Myanmar's Nationalist Movement (1906–1948) and India*, 107

Hiphinous

A CENTAUR from ancient Greek mythology, Hiphinous was one of the centaurs who attended the wedding of Pirithous, became drunk on wine, and following the lead of EURYTUS, who assaulted Hippodame, began to assault and rape any women they could grab. A great Centauromachy then followed.

Source: *Commentary, Mythological, Historical, and Geographical on Pope's Homer*, 55; Lemprière, *Classical Dictionary*, 15

Hippalektryon

Variations: Cock Horse, Hippalectryon

A rarely seen creature from ancient Greek mythology, the hippalektryon ("horse cock"), one of the HIPPOI ATHANATOI, first appeared in early vase paintings in the first half of the sixth century and was used until the middle of the fifth century, BC. These creatures were shown being ridden by a hero, although no story involving one has survived. The hippalektryon is depicted as having the forequarters of a horse but the hind legs, tail, and wings of a rooster. According to some authors, the hippalektryon has become the personification of ridiculous pomposity, particularly in the plumed helmets of military leaders.

Source: Crowley, *Psychology of the Athenian Hoplite*, 29; Eaverly, *Archaic Greek Equestrian Sculpture*, 94; Zell-Ravenheart, *Wizard's Bestiary*, 48

Hippason

A CENTAUR from ancient Greek mythology, Hippason was one of the centaurs who attended the wedding of Pirithous, became drunk on wine, and following the lead of EURYTUS, who assaulted Hippodame, began to assault and rape any women they could grab. A great Centauromachy then followed.

Source: *Commentary, Mythological, Historical, and Geographical on Pope's Homer*, 55

Hippocamp, plural hippocampi or hippocamps

Variations: Hippocambus, Hippocampe, Hippocampes, Hippocampos, Hippocampus, Hippocampus, Hippokampoi, Neptune's Horse, Sea Horse, Sea-Horse, Steed of Neptune

Appearing in Etruscan, Greek, and Phoenician mythologies, the hybrid creature known as the hippocamp ("horse monster") is depicted as a hybrid between a horse and a fish, the former being the front part of the creature and the latter making up its hindquarters; it lived in both fresh and salt water. The ancients believed the sea horse was the infant stage of these creatures, the nereids (golden-haired sea nymphs) rode upon them, and a team of such creatures pulled the chariot of Poseidon (Neptune) throughout the ocean.

In ancient Greek mythology the hippocampos was depicted in art and described as having the forebody of a horse and the hindquarters of a dolphin or fish; these "brazen-hoofed" creatures were said to pull the chariot of Poseidon (Neptune), a concept later adopted by the ancient Romans for their god of the sea Neptune. The carousing TRITONS are often depicted as riding them in art.

Source: Breverton, *Breverton's Phantasmagoria*, 202; Brewer, *Dictionary of Phrase and Fable*, 626; Conway, *Magickal Mermaids and Water Creatures*, 69; Hansen, *Handbook of Classical Mythology*, 320; Hard, *Routledge Handbook of Greek Mythology*, 99; Howey, *Horse in Magic and Myth*, 133–4

Hippocerf

Variations: Hippocervus ("deer horse")

A hybrid creature from medieval folklore and making its way into the heraldic repertoire, the hippocerf was said to have the forequarters of a stag or deer and the hindquarters of a horse; it was the personification of the fainthearted who act without considering the consequences and become victims of their own device.

Source: Mollett, *Illustrated Dictionary of Words Used in Art and Archaeology*, 170; Rose, *Giants, Monsters, and Dragons*, 174; Zell-Ravenheart, *Wizard's Bestiary*, 48

Hippogriff

Variations: Hippogtyph, ("horse GRIFFIN"), SEEMURG, Semurv, Simoorgh, Simurgh

A chimerical creature originating in medieval European folklore, the hippogriff was said to be a cross between a GRIFFIN and a horse, its favorite food source; it was depicted as having the head, claws, and wings of the GRIFFIN and the hindquarters of a horse. Making for an excellent mount, as it is reputed to fly as fast as lightning, a hippogriff was featured in the poem *Orlando Furioso* (1516) by the Italian author and poet Ludovico Ariosto. In the poem the hippogriff served as the mount for the wizard Atlante as he adventured saving various maidens in need of rescuing.

Source: Fox-Davies, *Complete Guide to Heraldry*, 232; Rosen, *Mythical Creatures Bible*, 119; Zell-Ravenheart, *Wizard's Bestiary*, 48

Hippoi Athanatoi

Variations: Hippoi Troiades ("horses of Troy")

Hippoi Athanatoi is the collective name for the immortal horses of the Greek gods. Many but not all of these horses are said to be the offspring of one of the wind gods, usually NOTOS, and were assigned to pull Zeus's chariot. Included amongst the Hippoi Athanatoi are ABRAXAS, AITHON, AITHOPS, AMETHA, AREION, ASTROPE, BALIOS, BAYARD, BOREAS, BRONTE, CHRONOS, CONABOS, CYLLAROS, EOUS, ERYTHREOS, EUROS, HARPAGOS, HIPPALEK-TRYON, HIPPOKAMPOI (a breed of fish-tailed aquatic horses), KONABOS, LAMPOON, LAMPOS, NOTOS, PEGASOI (a breed of immortal winged horses), PEGASUS, PHAETHON, PHAITHON, PHLEGON, PHLO-GEOS, PHLOGIOS, PHOBOS, PODARKES, PUROCIS, PYROIS, STEROPE, THERBEEO, TROJAN HIPPOI (the collective name for the twelve immortal horses owned by King Erikhthonios), XANTHOS, and ZEPHYROS.

Source: Glover, *1000 Famous Horses Fact and Fictional Throughout the Ages*, 269; Gemondo, *Animal Totems*, 60; Hardy, *Ancient Ethics*, 208

Hippoi Monokerata

Variations: Monokerata, UNICORN, "Unicorn of the East"

The UNICORN of the East, the hippoi monokerata were described as a species of equine having a magnificently white hide, being agile and fast, and having a long, lone, brightly-colored alicorn growing out of the middle of their forehead. In India these creatures were said to be larger than the free-roaming wild asses and horses, having blue eyes, dark red heads, and white bodies; their horns growing to more than a cubit in length (a *cubit* is the distance from a man's elbow to the tip of his middle finger). The part of the horn nearest the body was white, the middle section black, and the top most part very bright red. The hippoi monokerata are excellent long distance runners; at first they do not move so quickly, but the longer they run, the faster they excel. If one is able to be shot down its meat is too bitter to consume but a cup made out of its horn will cure a person of convulsions, epilepsy, and poisonings so long as they immediately consume some water or wine out of the cup.

Source: Breverton, *Breverton's Phantasmagoria*, 368

Hippotion

In classical Greek mythology, Hippotion was one of the CENTAURS slain by the demi-god and cultural hero Hercules (Heracles) while visiting his friend, a CENTAUR named PHOLUS, between the conclusion of his third Labor and the onset of his fourth. When an old and particularly fragrant hogshead of wine was opened its aroma carried on the air and drove the local CENTAURS into a fury. Hippotion, ARGEIUS, AMPHION, DAPHNIS, DUPO, ISOPLES, MELANCHETES, OREUS, PHRIXUS, and THEREUS were slain by Hercules (Heracles) as he defended himself from their violent and unwarranted assault.

Source: Barthell, *Gods and Goddesses of Ancient Greece*, 187; Diodorus, *Historical Library of Diodorus the Sicilian*, Volume 1, 229–30

Hircocervus

Variations: Goat Stag, Horse Stag, Tragelaph

A legendary creature described as being a stag and goat hybrid, the hircocervus ("he-goat stag") is said to have appeared in medieval bestiaries but there are no specific legends about them.

Source: Merriam-Webster, Inc., *Merriam-Webster's Encyclopedia of Literature*, 548

Hitotsume-Kozō (hee-TOH-tsoo-may ko-ZOH)

In Japanese folklore the cyclopean YŌKAI known as hitotsume-kozō ("one-eyed boy") appears as a seven-year old boy dressed in traditional clothing with either a bald or a closely shaven head and an extremely long tongue; in the middle of his forehead is an oversized eye. On occasion he is said to carry objects of the Buddhist faith. Generally tales involving this being take place in the mountains but can occur any place where people live. Basically harmless, the hitotsume-kozō hides someplace outdoors and waits for the opportunity to jump out and surprise a person, razzing its overly long tongue before running off. It is rare for a sighting to occur indoors but when they do the hitotsume-kozō will cause trouble by kicking on walls, moving decorations out of place, and the like.

Source: Foster, *Book of Yokai*, 201–4; Yoda, *Yokai Attack*, 170–4

Hiyakudori

A two-headed bird from Japanese folklore, the hiyakudori is used symbolically in stories to represent two lovers.

Source: Zell-Ravenheart, *Wizard's Bestiary*, 48

Hizri

An initially benevolent being from Albanian mythology, the hizri travels from village to village and door to door begging and claiming it has been sent by God to test the giving nature of the family. If the hizri is not treated with kindness and generosity as well as food and money it will become angry and place a spell upon the home.

Source: Elsie, *Dictionary of Albanian Religion, Mythology, and Folk Culture*, 114

Hjalmther

Hjalmther was one of the horses utilized by the Aesir in Norse mythology; its specific owner or rider is not mentioned. Hjalmther was also listed as one of the many horses who would graze in the red-gilt leafed Glasir Grove.

Source: Grimes, *Norse Myths*, 20

Hlid

Hlid was one of the oxen named in Thorgrimr's *Rhymes* and in Snorri Sturluson's (1179–1241) *Prose Edda*.

Source: Jennbert, *Animals and Humans*, 49; Sturluson, *Prose Edda*, Volume 5, 240

Hnikur

Variations: Nickur, Nikar, Ninner, Nok

In the folklore of the Faroe Islands and Iceland the hnikur appears as a fine apple-grey horse with reversed hooves; it stands on the seashore awaiting someone foolish enough to climb up on its back. Should ever this FAIRY ANIMAL get a rider it would charge off into the sea.

Source: Keightley, *World Guide to Gnomes, Fairies, Elves, and Other Little People*, 162; Thorpe, *Northern Mythology*, Volume 1, 22

Hō-ō

A good-luck PHOENIX from Chinese folklore, the hō-ō, one of the classical beasts of good omens, is a chimerical creature, described as having the back of a turtle, the beak of a chicken, the breast of a giraffe, the forehead of a swallow, the haunches of a deer, the head of a snake, and the tail of a fish. The hō-ō is attracted to Paulownia trees and for this reason they are often planted in gardens with the intention of luring one of these creatures to roost upon it.

Source: Dalby, *East Wind Melts the Ice*, 50

Ho-Oo

Variations: Hoo-oo, Hou-ou

A hermaphroditic PHOENIX from Japanese folklore the appearance of the ho-oo ("male-female") heralds the dawn of a new era; while present, it will do good deeds for people in need and eventually return to its heavenly bode. Just as the Chinese royal family has adopted the FENGHUANG as its symbol, the Japanese royal family has made the ho-oo its symbol, as it is representative of a good and wise government, justice, obedience, and the sun.

Source: Lehner, *Big Book of Dragons, Monsters, and Other Mythical Creatures*, 148; Zell-Ravenheart, *Companion for the Apprentice Wizard*, 178

Hochigan

In the beginning, according to Bushman Creations legends, animals were capable of speech; Hochigan, a Bushman who hated all animals, stole their gift and disappeared one day, never to return.

Source: Borges, *Book of Imaginary Beings*, 106; Skyes, *Who's Who in Non-Classical Mythology*, 87

Hodag

Variations: Black Hodag

Originating in the lumberjack communities of the developing United States of America, the hodag, one of the FEARSOME CRITTERS, was said to live in the swamps of West Virginia and Wisconsin; it was described as having horns and spikes on its body and wielding a maniacal grin. Other sources say it was more MINOTAUR-like with a bull's head but a man's face, short stout legs, claws for feet, and a serpentine tail ending in a sharpened arrowhead. Native American folklore describes it as being a chimerical hybrid of a frog, lizard, and a Mammoth. No matter its description this creature feeds on indigenous wildlife and the occasional human; it was said to have a stench so powerful it could cause an adult man to faint.

Source: Botkin, *American People*, 255; Maberry, *Vampire Universe*, 152; Rose, *Giants, Monsters, and Dragons*, 119

Hoefir

Hoefir ("meat") was one of the four oxen named in Thorgrimr's *Rhymes* and in Snorri Sturluson's (1179–1241) *Prose Edda* belonging to Gefjun; in truth they were her sons by an unnamed JOTUN. The siblings of Hoefir were HYRR, RAUDR, and REKINNI.

Source: Grimes, *Norse Myths*, 278; Sturluson, *Prose Edda*, Volume 5, 213

Hófvarpnir (HOHV-varp-nir)

Variations: Hofvarpnir, Hofvarpner, Hofvarpur

The horse of the goddess of fullness Gnaa, Hófvarpner ("he who throws his hoofs about," "hoof-flourisher" or "hoof-thrower") was born the colt of the mare GARÐROFA and the stallion HAMSKERPER; he could run equally well through both air and water. Hófvarpnir and SLEIPNIR are often cited as being examples of unequalled horses in Norse mythology.

Source: Grimes, *Norse Myths*, 279; Norroena Society, *Asatrii Edda*, 362; Oehlenschläger, *Gods of the North*, l; Rydberg, *Norroena*, Volume 3, 1021

Hokhokw

Variations: Hoxhogwaxtewae, Hoxhok-of-the-Sky, Huxwhukw

A long beaked monstrous bird from the mythology of the Kwakiutla people of Canada, North America, Hokhokw is one of the attendants of the even more horrific and monstrous Bakbakwakanooksiewae cannibalistic bird-spirit. Hokhokw used his long, narrow, square-tipped beak to pop open the human skull and then drink out the brains.

Source: Shearar, *Understanding Northwest Coast Art*, 58–9; Werness, *Continuum Encyclopedia of Native Art*, 127

Holkvir (HUHLK-vir)

Variations: Holvir

The name of a horse mentioned in Snorri Sturluson's *Edda*, Holkvir ("winner") was the mount Hogni (Högni) rode when Gunnar attempted to marry Sigurd.

Source: Jennbert, *Animals and Humans*, 49; Magnússon, *Völsunga Saga*, 97; Norroena Society, *Asatrii Edda*, 361; Sturluson, *Prose Edda*, Volume 5, 212

Homa

Variations: Homa Bird, Karv, Roc, SEEMURG, Simurgh

A GRIFFIN of Assyrian and Persian mythology, the homa was considered to be a divine guardian of sacred places and treasure hoards as well as a protector against evil in general.

Source: Ananda. *Comparative Study of Religion*, 8; Bentorah, *Hebrew Word Study*, 9

El Hombre Caiman

Variations: Hombre Caimán

A hybrid creature living in the Magdalena River, Colombia, the hombre caiman ("alligator man") is described as being a humanoid alligator; it appears each year on Saint Sebastian's Day, December 18, to hunt for human prey. According to the folklore of Colombia, Magdalena, and Plato, the hombre caiman was once a lecherous fisherman who had been tricked and punished by a river spirit.

Source: Budd, *Weiser Field Guide to Cryptozoology*, 75; Cooper, *Social Work Man*, 10

Hombre Del Saco

A NURSERY BOGIE from the folklore of Latin America, the hombre del saco ("sack man") is described as looking like a hobo carrying a sack; in truth this creature is on the prowl for disobedient children to kidnap.

Source: Krensky, *Bogeyman*, 43

Homocane

Variations: Minocane

A creature from the symbology of heraldry, the homocane is depicted as the composite of a child and a spaniel dog.

Source: Barber, *Dictionary of Fabulous Beasts*, 106; Dickens, *Household Words: A Weekly Journal*, Volumes 17–18, 300; Lower, *Curiosities of Heraldry*, 103

Homunculus, plural: homunculi

An artificial human being created through the use of alchemy, the homunculus ("little human being") was said to be the greatest goal obtainable for an alchemist to achieve as it was representative of achieving the dream of "nature through art."

To create a homunculus the alchemist would place an amount of human semen into a flask, seal it, and gently heat it over a flame for forty days when it will begin to move and resemble a human being in form. The creature is then fed a special prepared chemical diet consisting largely of human blood for forty weeks after which it will be a fully formed homunculus. Although it will look like a human child the creation will have innate knowledge and powers, such as knowing all of the arts required to create itself. It will also have other deep and great knowledge as it was not created with the taint of the female element. It was said if the same experiment was done using menstrual blood rather than semen the result would produce a BASILISK.

Source: Draaisma, *Metaphors of Memory*, 212; Principe, *Secrets of Alchemy*, 131–32

Hongaek

Variations: Hoengaek ("sudden disaster")

In Korean folklore the hongaek ("red disaster") is a malevolent red mass or cloud of misfortune capable of engulfing people and intensifying any calamity or illness they would have naturally encountered. People who are naturally unlucky are particularly susceptible to the hongaek and are advised not to attend funerals or visit the sick. Wherever there has been an accident or some sort of terrible misfortune trace amounts of hongaek gather at the site; the more often a tragedy occurs in the area, the larger the hongaek becomes.

For instance, it is believed in patches of road where there are many car accidents, a massive hongaek has developed; if driving through the area tossing a handful of mullet seed as you pass by may disrupt the mass long enough to ensure your personal safety.

Source: Kendall, *Shamans, Housewives, and Other Restless Spirits*, 102, 192; Rose, *Spirits, Fairies, Leprechauns, and Goblins, an Encyclopedia*, 154

Honoyeta

In Papua New Guinean mythology, Honoyeta is an enormous snake (demon or god, sources conflict) who was responsible for bringing mortality into the world. According to the legend, he had two wives who would have sexual intercourse with him in his snake guise. Each day his wives would set off to work and Honoyeta would shape-shift into an attractive human man by shedding his snake skin and enjoy intercourse with any attractive woman he would find. One day, his wives found his snake skin, discovered his infidelity, and burned it. Angered as he was now condemned to spend eternity in human guise, he inflicted death onto humanity.

Source: Leeming, *Oxford Companion to World Mythology*, 188–89; Stookey, *Thematic Guide to World Mythology*, 87

Hoop Snake

Originating in the lumberjack communities of the developing United States of America, the hoop snake, one of the FEARSOME CRITTERS, was typically found in the southwest desert living off of the small animals it could catch; however, states all along the east coast from Maryland to North Carolina also have folklore containing these creatures. When stretched out the hoop snake was about ten to fifteen feet long and resembled an ordinary black snake common to these areas; however, it had a unique means of locomotion. When pursuing its prey the hoop snake would take its tail into its mouth and stiffening its body, roll across the desert like a bicycle tire. The venom of the hoop snake is highly toxic and almost fatal; it is advised if ever one is being chased by such a creature to acrobatically leap through the center of its hoop; this will likely confuse the hoop snake long enough to make an escape.

Source: McQuillan, *Narrative Reader*, 18–9; Rose, *Giants, Monsters, and Dragons*, 119

Horned Alligator

Variations: Zemo'hgu-ani

A lake monster of extraordinary size from Kiowa mythology, the horns of the horned alligator were greatly sought after as they contained magical properties assisting practitioners in healing, hunting, poisoning, and war (see SEA SERPENT). These creatures were said to live in deep holes along the bottom of streams.

Source: Gatschet, *Journal of American Folk-lore*, Volume 7, 259; Rose, *Giants, Monsters, and Dragons*, 175–76

Horned Dragon

Variations: Lung

A species of DRAGON from Chinese folklore, the horned dragon ("*qiu lung*") is one of the major types of DRAGON. They are very powerful, as they can control the clouds and produce rain; however they are completely deaf. It is not until this species is around two thousand years old that they begin to grow their horns. This species of DRAGON both acts and looks wiser than their younger counterparts. These DRAGONs have five claws on their feet and usually eighty-one scales running down the length of their spine. In art they are depicted with their head facing south and their tail pointing north; they are also associated with the east and the sun.

Source: De Kirk, *Dragonlore*, 27; Johnsgard, *Dragons and Unicorns*, 15

Horned Serpent

Variations: Great Horned Snake, Water Monster

Common to North America, the horned serpent is a species of huge serpentine DRAGON having either one or two horns upon their head. Having gills and living in the water they also have the ability to breathe air. Horned serpents are the mortal and natural born enemy of THUNDERBIRDS. The horned serpent is the personification of the power inherent in life itself.

Source: De Kirk, *Dragonlore*, 47; Versluis, *Sacred Earth*, 62

Horomatangi

Variations: Horo-Matangi, Ihu-Maataotao

One of the TANIWHA, Horomatangi was a huge and hideous creature resembling a gigantic lizard; interestingly, unlike most other creatures in its class, although Horomatangi did harass the Maori when they hunted and fished, it never sought to consume them. There are several tales of Horomatangi helping out humans in need, as well as its creating the Karapiti blowhole. In spite of the fact Horomatangi did not eat humans it nevertheless did claim many lives, as, according to modern folklore, it still overturns canoes and motorboats alike. Horomatangi had a FAMILIAR, a human by the name of Ati-a-muri; it is said his servant can be seen paddling across the lake at dusk looking for unsuspecting strangers to bring to his master's attention.

Source: Gudegeon, *Journal of the Polynesian Society*, Volume 14, 189; Rose, *Giants, Monsters, and Dragons*, 177; Zell-Ravenheart, *Wizard's Bestiary*, 93

Hoto-Puku

One of the TANIWHA from Maori folklore Hoto-Puku was described as a gigantic anthropophagous (man-eating) lizard who once lived in the area between Rotorua and Taupo. People kept disappearing from the region and began to blame various tribes until it was discovered the DRAGON-like

Hoto-Puku was responsible. A cruel and horrid creature, it had the appearance and the ability to move mountains; its spiny back had numerous protuberances. A local hero by the name of Pitaka organized a hunting party and using himself as bait tricked the creature into placing its head into a noose. After Hoto-Puku was strangled to death, his body was cut open, revealing many of the missing people. In the monster's lair was a great treasure hoard of items it had stockpiled after taking them from its victims containing cloaks, clubs, cooking utensils, darts, garments, jars of domestic animal fat, and ornamental feathers.

In life, Hoto-Puku's greatest rival was the TANI-WHA TAWAKE-TARA.

Source: De Kirk, *Dragonlore*, 60, 104–5; Gilmore, *Monsters*, 148; Gudegeon, *Journal of the Polynesian Society*, Volume 14, 191; Zell-Ravenheart, *Wizard's Bestiary*, 93

Hrid

Variations: Hríð

Hrid ("snow storm") was one of the oxen named in Thorgrimr's *Rhymes* and in Snorri Sturluson's (1179–1241) *Prose Edda*. Hrid is also the name of the eleven rivers flowing out of Hvergelmar.

Source: Daly, *Norse Mythology A to Z*, 24; Jennbert, *Animals and Humans*, 49

Hrimfaxi (REEM-vaks-i)

Variations: Hrimfax ("frost bringer"), Hrímfaxe, Hrimfaxi ("moon"), Hrímfaxi, Hrymfaxe, Rimefax, Rimfakse, Rimfaxi ("frost-mane")

As the goddess Nott drove her chariot through the night sky, her lead horse Hrimfaxi ("frosty mane" or "rime-mane") would froth at the bit, and as the substance fell to earth it would become the morning dew. During the day when at rest, Hrimfaxi would graze upon the grass of Jormungrund and the leaves of Ygdrasil, each saturated with sacred mead. Hrimfaxi is also listed by some scholars as being one of the many winged horses said to assist in pulling the sun across the sky (see also AARVAK, AVAK, ALSVID, and SKINFAXI); the chariot was driven by Dagr the son of Dellingr and Natt.

Source: Brewer, *Dictionary of Phrase and Fable*, 626; Daly, *Norse Mythology A to Z*, 51; Norroena Society, *Asatrii Edda*, 362; Oehlenschläger, *Gods of the North*, l; Rose, *Giants, Monsters, and Dragons*, 178

Hrodvitner

Variations: Hritvitnir, Hrothvitnir

Hrodvitner ("mighty wolf") was one of the wolves named in Thorgrimr's *Rhymes* and in Snorri Sturluson's (1179–1241) *Prose Edda*. According to Norse mythology, Hrodvitner was the father of the wolf HATI.

Source: Grimes, *Norse Myths*, 280; Jennbert, *Animals and Humans*, 49; Sturluson, *Prose Edda*, 129

Hsiao

A chimerical creature from Chinese folklore, the hsiao is described as an owl-like humanoid, having an ape's body, a dog's tail, and a man's face. Its presence foretells of an upcoming prolonged drought.

Source: Borges, *El Libro de los Seres Imaginarios*, 103

Hsieh-Chai

Variations: Haetae

A creature from ancient Chinese folklore, the hsieh-chai was described as being caprine (goatlike) in appearance but having an alicorn; however, some sources say it was leonine. Most interesting about this creature was its ability to discern the difference between good and evil, right and wrong, and justice from injustice. It was said the famous minister Kao Yao would keep a hsieh-chai for cases where he was unable to tell who the guilty party was; he would order the animal to butt the guilty person. In Korea this animal is known as the haetae.

Source: Bodde, *Essays on Chinese Civilization*, 194; Ch'oe, *Law and Justice in Korea: South and North*, 35, 78; Zell-Ravenheart, *Wizard's Bestiary*, 46

Hsigo

Variations: HSIAO

In Chinese folklore the chimerical hsigo are described as having the face of a human, wings like a bat, and the body of a monkey.

Source: Cooper, *Symbolic and Mythological Animals*, 133; Zell-Ravenheart, *Companion for the Apprentice Wizard*, 50, 178

Hsing-T'ien

In Chinese mythology the hsing-t'ien is a creature which once rose up and confronted the gods; it was decapitated for its effort and being immortal, remained headless ever since. The eyes of the hsing-t'ien are located in its chest and its mouth in its navel, similar to the ACEPHALI from the mythology of ancient Greece. It carries an axe with it as it moves through the countryside.

Source: Borges, *Book of Imaginary Beings*, 81

Hu Hsien

In China the hu hsien ("a fox fairy") is a species of a malicious fox-fairy; they are powerful shapeshifters. Hu hsien are believed to be the guardians of the seal of high officials. A nine-tailed fox from Chinese folklore is known as a *jinwei hu*.

Source: Moorey, *Fairy Bible*, 388; Rose, *Spirits, Fairies, Gnomes, and Goblins*, 155; Sullivan, *Introduction to Chinese Art*, 202; Wallen, *Fox*, 69

Hua-Fish

Variations: Huayu

A fish from Chinese folklore, the hua-fish has two very different descriptions. The first claims the hua-fish lives in Lord Millit Lake which is fed by the Peach River. The lake contains a great quantity of white jade as well. Here this species of fish is said to have a serpentine body and four legs; they prey on other fish.

The second description of the hua-fish claims they live in Lake Excess and except for having bird wings otherwise look like any other fish. The hua-fish in this version of the folklore are described as emanating a brilliant white light as they leave and re-enter the water, making a quaking sound distinctly similar to the mandarin duck. If a hua-fish is seen, it is an omen of an impending, world-wide drought.

Source: Asian Folklore Institute, *Asian Folklore Studies*, Volume 39, 61; Strassberg, *Chinese Bestiary*, 108, 142–3

Hua-Hu-Tiao

A gigantic white elephant from Chinese Buddhism, Hua-Hu-Tiao was a wild and carnivorous creature with a set of wings upon its shoulders; in some versions of the tale it is a white rat with the ability to shape-shift into a winged elephant. This being, no matter its true form, is under the command of the god Mo-Li Ch'ing. Periodically it would break free of its confinement, a panther-skin bag, and go on a murderous feeding frenzy, consuming as many humans as possible before it was recaptured. Eventually it was slain by the hero Yang Ching who allowed himself to be swallowed so he could hack away at its heart from within.

Source: Werner, *Myths and Legends of China*, 121; Zell-Ravenheart, *Wizard's Bestiary*, 50

Hua Yang

Variations: Lady Kayo, Pao Shis, Pau-Su

A magical white FOX MAIDEN from India, Hua Yang was more than malicious; according to folklore she bewitched King Ran Tsu and convinced him to kill for her pleasure over one thousand innocent people because she supposed it might amuse her. Thereafter, she then managed to convince some of the Indian princes she was an actual goddess. Hua Yang came to China in the tenth century and assumed the name Pao Shis when she joined the court of the twelfth emperor of the Chou Dynasty, Emperor Yu. Over time she maneuvered into position where she was able to become queen and using her powers of memorization had Yu perform horrific acts of torture on innocent subjects. Because of her terrible abuse of power, the Chou Dynasty fell.

Source: Bush, *Asian Horror Encyclopedia*, 76–7; Stevenson, *Yoshitoshi's Strange Tales*, 61–2

Huallepen

Variations: Gullipen, Hui

A monstrous hybrid from the folklore of the Araucanian (Mapuchen) people of Chile, the hullepen has the head of a calf but the body of a sheep. It is believed if an expecting mother dreamt of these creatures for three nights in a row her child would be born with deformities. Living in isolated ponds and water causeways, the huallepen will seek out a mate with either a cow or a ewe; the offspring of such couplings always has twisted feet and muzzles.

Source: Bingham, *South and Meso-American Mythology A to Z*, 53; Rose, *Giants, Monsters, and Dragons*, 180

Huang Long

Variations: Huanglong

In Chinese mythology Huang Long ("yellow DRAGON") is well known for its scholarly knowledge; it was this DRAGON who taught the first emperor the art of writing.

Source: Rosen, *Mythical Creatures Bible*, 63

Hugag

Originating in the lumberjack communities of the developing United States of America, the hugag, one of the FEARSOME CRITTERS, was a prehistoric looking species living mostly in the lake states region. About the size and shape of a moose, the hugag has an overly long and rather cumbersome upper lip which prevents it from grazing; it also has no ankle or knee joints, four-toed feet, a long bushy tail, a bushy coat, and ragged, uneven, floppy ears. It is devoid of hair on its leathery head and neck. Constantly on the move, hobbling its way through the wilderness, the hugag eats leaves and tree bark as it wanders. At night it leans against trees to stabilize itself as it sleeps.

Source: Cox; *Fearsome Creatures of the Lumberwoods*, 9; Rose, *Giants, Monsters, and Dragons*, 119

Huginn (HUG-in)

Variations: Hugin, Hunin

One of the two ravens utilized by the god Odin in Norse mythology, Huginn ("thought") and his counterpart MUNIN would descend to Earth and bring back news of events they whisper in his ear during dinner at Valhalla. When not engaged, the two birds perch upon the god's shoulder.

Source: Grimes, *Norse Myths*, 281; Norroena Society, *Asatrii Edda*, 364; Oehlenschläger, *Gods of the North*, li

Hui

A hybrid-looking creature in Chinese folklore, the hui is described as being a gigantic human-headed dog capable of leaping over any obstacle and an extremely fast runner. Its presence is an omen of an impending typhoon; it is fearless of humans.

Source: Rose, *Giants, Monsters, and Dragons*, 180; Zell-Ravenheart, *Wizard's Bestiary*, 50

Huma

Variations: Ustukhwan Kh'ur, the Ossifrage

Essentially a PHOENIX from Persian folklore, the huma ("auspicious") was described as being a benevolent and peaceful bird; its touch was able to bring good fortune. The huma only feeds on carrion and is said to be the embodiment of both female and male nature; it never lands upon the earth and every couple of centuries or so, like the PHOENIX, the huma bird allows itself to be consumed in flames so it may be born anew.

Source: Eastwick, *Gulistan*, 43; Warhol, *Birdwatcher's Daily Companion*, 71; Zell-Ravenheart, *Wizard's Bestiary*, 50

Human Snakes

In the mythology of the Seminole people of Florida and Oklahoma, human snakes are a species of powerful humanoid monsters known for spreading evil about the community. One story related how a medicine man was able to rid his village of their influence. Once it had been discovered they were the cause of a young man growing more ill each day, he placed the ashes of menstrual blood inside a medicine bag made of deerskin and took it along with a menstruating woman to the cave where the human snakes were living. Upon arrival the woman, under the direction of the medicine man, lowered the medicine bag into the cave; this caused the creatures to transform into their true forms, horrific looking half-human and half snake creatures. The human snakes writhed in agony until they all died.

Source: Rose, *Giants, Monsters, and Dragons*, 180

Humility

Variations: Humility Bird

Originating in the lumberjack communities of the developing United States of America, the humility, one of the FEARSOME CRITTERS, was first described by Reverend Samuel Peters in his 1781 *General History of Connecticut*. The humility was onomatopoeically named because the bird could speak this singular word. Peters said the humility never lighted upon a branch but rather was only ever seen in flight or walking along the ground; it

also never flew too high. Its body, about the size of a blackbird, was exceedingly lean; its eyes more piercing than a falcon's; its legs long enough to out-run a dog for a short while. Plumed with blue, black, red, and white feathers, the bird was swift as an eagle; its wings were long and narrow. Living off of spawn, tadpoles, and worms, a humility was nearly impossible to shoot, as it was so aerobatic it could dodge bullets.

Source: Peters, *General History of Connecticut*, 256–7; Rose, *Giants, Monsters, and Dragons*, 119, 181

Hundred-Heads

Variations: Fish with One Hundred Heads

Kapila, a Buddhist monk from Chinese folklore, was of the habit of insulting his fellow monks by calling them "as stupid as a dog," "as stupid as a donkey," "as stupid as a swine," and so forth. When he was reborn, the karma of his insults caused him to come back as a gigantic fish with one-hundred heads, one for each species of animal he insulted his fellow monks with during his previous life.

Source: van Oort, *Iconography of Chinese Buddhism in Traditional China*, 25

Huri

Variations: Furi

A species of large bird from Ainu folklore the huri were said to live in caves and consume human beings; they were said to have a large and voracious appetite.

Source: Munro, *Ainu Creed and Cult*, n.pag.; Philippi, *Songs of Gods*, 165

Huru-Kareao

Variations: Hurukareao, Huru Kareao

A TANIWHA from the mythology of the Maori people, Huru-Kareao is said to reside in a submerged cave at the bottom of Lake Rotoaria. Extraordinarily large, even for a TANIWHA, the lacertilian (lizard-like) Huru-Kareao would harass the Maori whenever they would attempt to hunt or fish; there was also a sacred log which floated in this lake and the creature would look after its wellbeing. According to folklore, when two women from a near-by village were being treated cruelly by a neighboring village, Huru-Kareao stirred up the water of Lake Roroaria so much it swelled and flooded out the offending village. In spite of its protective nature on that singular occasion, it is said whenever a small boat or canoe passes over its cave, Huru-Kareao creates a whirlpool to sink it.

Source: Gordon, *Hot Lakes, Volcanoes, and Geysers of New Zealand, with Legends*, 33–34; Rose, *Giants, Monsters, and Dragons*, 181; Zell-Ravenheart, *Wizard's Bestiary*, 93

Huspalim

A monster from Ethiopian folklore, the huspalim was first described by European traveler and physician Ambroise Paré (1517–1590) in the late Middle Ages as a creature looking much like a gigantic marmot with an enormous round head, red-spotted skin, round paws, tiny ears, and a simian (monkeylike) face. The flesh of the huspalim was not at all digestible unless it was thoroughly beaten with sticks first.

Source: Rose, *Giants, Monsters, and Dragons*, 182; Zell-Ravenheart, *Wizard's Bestiary*, 50

Hvcko Capko

A monstrous being from the mythology of the Seminole people of Florida, United States of America, the hvcko capko ("long ears") was described as having enormous ears, grey body, horse tail, wolflike head, and emitting a most horrid and wretched stench. Living in desolated rocky places, the hvcko capko is not a predator but does carry a number of diseases; fortunately its smell alerts people in time to avoid a chance encounter.

Source: Rose, *Giants, Monsters, and Dragons*, 182

Hwa Yih

In Chinese folklore there is a species of bird, the LWAN, said to look like a beautiful, large, and graceful pheasant; these birds have the ability to change their color; each color the bird can assume is given a different name. The hwa yih is the white form. The additional forms are: FUNG, TO FU, YU SIANG, and the YIN CHU.

Source: Gould, *Mythical Monsters*, 370; Rose, *Giants, Monsters, and Dragons*, 182–3

Hydra (hi-drah)

Variations: Exedra, Hydra of Lerna, Hydra Lernaia, Hydra of Lernaea, Lernaean Hydra

A multi-headed DRAGON from ancient Greek mythology, the hydra ("water snake") lived in the marshes of Lernean in Argolis in a bottomless lake connected to the Underworld. The hydra was described as having seven or nine heads, the middle of which was immortal. In some tales it was given fifty or one hundred heads, but seldom in art was it ever depicted with so many. In some depictions and descriptions it was given feet or wings or said to have had a serpentine body. Other versions claimed it had the body of a gigantic dog; what is essential is each time one of its heads was cut off, a new one (or two, depending on the version of the tale) would quickly grow back in its place. It also had breath so toxic it could kill any man who inhaled it. Its blood was also poisonous and capable of killing a man instantly.

The hydra was born the child of ECHIDNA and Typhoeus; it was the sibling of CERBERUS, the CHIMERA, the NEMEAN LION, ORTHOS, and the SPHINX.

In the second of Hercules' (Heracles) twelve labors he was sent to slay the hydra which had been reared by the goddess Hera (Juno) specifically to be a mortal enemy of the heroic demi-god. During the battle, each time Hercules (Heracles) cut off one of its heads, a new one, or two, would grow back in its place. Hera (Juno), wanting to ensure victory, sent the crab-monster CARCINUS to interfere in the battle but it was quickly dispatched by the hero. Hercules felt if Hera (Juno) could send in allies to the fray he was perfectly within his rights to call for assistance from his companion Iolaols. As Hercules cut off a head, his companion, using a hot iron, would quickly cauterize the wound, preventing the regeneration. The final and immortal head, once decapitated, was buried beneath a gigantic boulder. The body remained where it fell and legend says the foul stench given off by the river Elis is because the body of the monster is still decaying. Hercules dipped the tips of his arrows in the blood of the hydra before departing and later used them to slay the Titan Geryon. It was also with one of these arrows Hercules accidentally shot his friend the CENTAUR CHEIRON.

The African hydra is a water monster with seven heads and the ability to control the level of water in the river it lives in; it was not uncommon for people to make offerings to the creature to ensure the flow of the river. In one popular tale a couple offers their daughter as a wife to the hydra in return for a constant supply of water. The child, named Jinde, begged the creature to let her return home to visit her parents; the hydra agreed but swore if she did not return after one day it would come after her. Jinde's parents refused to help her escape her situation for fear of the hydra so the girl sought the assistance of her lover. When she did not return the hydra kept its word and came to retrieve his bride, but her lover met it and in combat was able to decapitate each of its seven heads.

Source: De Kirk, *Dragonlore*, 42, Hard, *Routledge Handbook of Greek Mythology*, 62, 63, 255, 258; Rose, *Handbook of Greek Mythology*, 23, 174; Yolen, *Fish Prince and Other Stories*, 114–5

Hydrippus

In medieval folklore the hydrippus, similar to the HIPPOCAMP, was a hybrid creature, having the forequarters of a horse and the hindquarters of a golden fish. Symbolic of Moses, the hydrippus is the leader of all fish as in the "eastern part" of the world there resides a golden scaled fish who is their king. The fish of the sea will gather together and seek out the hydrippus and upon finding it will follow it to where the golden fish dwells. Upon arrival all the fish, the hydrippus included, regard the golden fish as their king.

Source: Barber, *Dictionary of Fabulous Beasts*, 89; Godfrey, *Mythical Creatures*, 120; Loxton, *Abominable Science*, 119

Hydrus

Variations: Hydros, Ichneumon, Idrus

In medieval Judeo-Christian folklore the hydrus, an animal appearing in bestiaries of the era, was a species of winged serpentine creatures said to live in the Nile River, Egypt. The hydrus despised the crocodiles above all other animals and whenever it would see the opportunity to kill one, it would. The method of assassination was depicted in a British made bestiary from 1230. First the hydrus would roll its body in the mud to become more slippery and then seek out a crocodile asleep on the bank with its mouth agape. The creature would dive into its mouth aiming for the back of the throat and startle the animal awake; the croc would inadvertently gulp down the hydrus. Now within its enemy the hydrus would burst forth from the side of the crocodile, killing it with the created fatal wound. This process, the text explains, is symbolic of Christ defeating death and his visit to hell in order to rescue Adam and Eve.

Source: Bovey, *Monsters and Grotesques in Medieval Manuscripts*, 22; Rose, *Giants, Monsters, and Dragons*, 188; Zell-Ravenheart, *Wizard's Bestiary*, 50–1

Hylactor

A dog from ancient Greek mythology, Hylactor ("babbler") was one of the DOGS OF ACTÆON, the unfortunate youth who was raised by the CENTAUR CHEIRON. Hylactor was noted for his shrill bark.

Source: Leeming, *World of Myth*, 111; Murray, *Classical Manual*, 160; Naso, *Fasti, Tristia*, 93–5

Hylaios

Variations: Hylaeus

In ancient Greek mythology Hylaios ("he of the woods") was the name of a CENTAUR huntsman. He and fellow CENTAUR ROIKOS became drunk one evening and were aroused by the beauty of Atalanta and attempted to rape her; Melanion attempted to intervene but was beaten with a club by Hylaios. Before any harm could befall her, Atalanta slew her would-be attackers with her bow and arrows.

Source: Colvin, *Cornhill Magazine*, Volume XXXVIII,

296; *Commentary, Mythological, Historical, and Geographical on Pope's Homer*, 55; Fontenrose, *Orion*, 178–9; Hard, *Routledge Handbook of Greek Mythology*, 545

Hyles

Variations: Hyle

A CENTAUR from ancient Greek mythology, Hyles was, according to Ovid's *Metamorphoses*, one of the centaurs who attended the wedding of Pirithous, became drunk on wine and following the lead of EURYTUS, who assaulted Hippodame, began to assault and rape any women they could grab. Hyles was slain at a distance by Peleus, as was fellow CENTAUR PHLEGRAEOS during the great Centauromachy which followed.

Source: *Commentary, Mythological, Historical, and Geographical on Pope's Homer*, 55; Simpson, *Metamorphoses of Ovid*, 207

Hyleus

Variations: Hylaeus

A dog from ancient Greek mythology, Hyleus ("wood-ranger") was one of the DOGS OF ACTÆON, the unfortunate youth who was raised by the CENTAUR CHEIRON.

Before the death of his master, Hyleus had been in a recent hunting accident where he had been wounded, gored by a wild boar.

Source: Leeming, *World of Myth*, 111; Murray, *Classical Manual*, 160; Naso, *Fasti, Tristia*, 93–5

Hylonome

According to Ovid's *Metamorphoses*, CYLLARUS and Hylonome was a young CENTAUR couple who were deeply in love; she is described as the loveliest of the CENTAURIDES (female CENTAUR), a truly enchanting beauty who spends some amount of her time grooming to make herself as beautiful as possible. She is described as wearing flowers in her hair and clothing made of high-quality animal skins.

During the Centauromachy which takes place after the wedding of Pirithous to Hippodame, CYLLARUS and Hylonome fought bravely side-by-side to one another. During the fray, a spear lands directly in CYLLARUS' chest, and although it is a small wound, it pierces his heart. As he lies dying Hylonome rushes to his side and presses her lips against the wound to keep his soul from escaping his body, but sadly, she is too late. After muttering something unheard by anyone and therefore unrecorded, she uses the spear to kill herself, collapsing into his arms.

Source: *Commentary, Mythological, Historical, and Geographical on Pope's Homer*, 55; Simpson, *Metamorphoses of Ovid*, 206

Hyman Topodes

A creature from Libyan folklore, the hyman topodes was documented by Gaius Julius Solinus the Latin grammarian and compiler (early third century) in his work *Wonders of the Worlds*; there he described it as being a pathetic caprine (goatlike) animal with legs so bowed it could not walk but rather had to drag itself along in a shuffle.

Source: Zell-Ravenheart, *Wizard's Bestiary*, 51

Hyosube

Variations: Hyosubo, Hyosue, Hyosunbe, Hyousunbo

A species of KAPPA from Japanese folklore, the hyosube is a dangerous YŌKAI said to be completely covered with thick fur or hair.

Source: Curran, *Dark Fairies*, n.pag.

Hypnalis

According to medieval bestiaries, the hypnalis was a species of asp known to kill its victim in their sleep. Supposedly, this was the sort of snake used by Cleopatra to commit suicide, as its bite induces a sleep the victim never awakens from.

Source: Clark, *Medieval Book of Beasts*, 198; Grant, *Early Christians and Animals*, 139; Zell-Ravenheart, *Wizard's Bestiary*, 51

Hyrr

Variations: Hýrr

Hyrr ("gentle") was one of the oxen named in Thorgrimr's *Rhymes* and in Snorri Sturluson's (1179–1241) *Prose Edda* belonging to Gefjun; in truth they were her sons by an unnamed JOTUN. The siblings of Hyrr were named HOEFIR, RAUDR, and REKINNI.

Source: Grimes, *Norse Myths*, 278; Sturluson, *Prose Edda*, Volume 5, 213

Iaculi

Variations: Jaculus, Javelin Snake

Believed to live in cemeteries and in tombs, the species of pseudo-DRAGON known as iaculi ("javelin") were written of in medieval bestiaries as interacting with mankind since the days of the ancient pharaohs as theses winged snakes were said to keep watch over the spirits of the dead. As a sort of guardian and intermediary between the deceased and the living, these creatures had access to the wisdom of generations and were able to dispense it to the young and see to their moral development.

When on the hunt or having to defend its territory the iaculi lies still nestled in the branches of trees and when the time is right springs forward upon its prey, biting, envenoming, and easily killing the target.

Source: Clark, *Medieval Book of Beasts*, 42; MacKenzie, *Dragon Keeper's Handbook*, 42; Zell-Ravenheart, *Wizard's Bestiary*, 52

Ice Worm

In the folklore near the lake along the Vermont-Quebec border the ice worm is said to be a creature so brittle and gelid it must first be warmed before it can be bent and placed on a hook, a process which then renders the worm invisible to the human eye.

In extremely cold weather they will emerge from the ice en masse to bask in the frigid weather. The ice worm is the preferred lure utilized to catch the FUR-BEARING TROUT.

Source: Alexander, *Forgotten Tales of Vermont*, 47–6; Zell-Ravenheart, *Wizard's Bestiary*, 51

Ichchadhari Nag

A shape-shifting and highly venomous snake from Indian folklore, the ichchadhari nag, or nagin if female, could take the form of any living thing it wished but was said to prefer assuming a human guise.

Source: Berninger, *Comics as a Nexus of Cultures*, 180

Ichnobates

A dog from ancient Greek mythology, Ichnobates ("tracker") was one of the DOGS OF ACTÆON, the unfortunate youth who was raised by the CENTAUR CHEIRON. Ichnobates of the Creatan (Gnossian) breed, along with MELAMPUS were the first two hounds to give chase.

Source: Leeming, *World of Myth*, 111; Murray, *Classical Manual*, 160; Naso, *Fasti, Tristia*, 93–5

Ichthyocentaur, plural: Ichthyocentauri

Variations: Centauro Tritons, Ikhthyokentauroi

The ichthyocentauri ("fish CENTAUR") of Greek mythology were a classification of CENTAUR described by an unknown author in the second or third century AD in the *Physiologus*. The work described the chimerical being as having the head and torso of a man, the forequarters of a horse, or on occasion a lion, and the hindquarters of a dolphin. Identified with the TRITONS, the sea-dwelling ichthyocentauri were often depicted in art.

Source: Borges, *Book of Imaginary Beings*, 111; Rose, *Giants, Monsters, and Dragons*, 187; Zell-Ravenheart, *Wizard's Bestiary*, 51

Iele (Ee-lays)

Variations: "Those without"

In Romania and throughout Eastern Europe there exists a species of vampiric, bipedal cat known as an iele. Standing about four feet tall with a rather lithe and thin build, they travel in small groups numbering from three to seven, looking for prey near crossroads, fields, village fountains, woods, or any place where they may find a person alone in a fairly isolated area. Although iele feed mostly on human and sheep blood, they will also entice children into dancing with them, and as they do, drain away their life-energy.

Fond of music and dancing, an iele occasionally falls in love with a beautiful young person, taking one as its lover and placing itself completely under the person's control. Shepherds who play their pipes exceptionally well are placed under the protection of the iele, whether they know it or not. The iele have their own musical abilities and are known to join in and play along with the shepherds. Iele are also known to set fields on fire and can cause insanity and paralysis in people.

Source: Ankarloo, *Early Modern European Witchcraft*, 211, 213; McNally, *In Search of Dracula*, 68; Senn, *Were-wolf and Vampire in Romania*, 24, 41; Stratilesco, *From Carpathian to Pindus*, 185–86

Iemisch (yem-ish)

Variations: Chimchimen, Erefil U, Guarifil U, Hymche, Jemechim, Jemisch, Nerrefil u, Nervelu, Ngurüvil u, Niribil u, Nirribil u, Nürüfil u, Tehuel Che chon, Tigre de Agua ("water-tiger"), Vulpangue ("fox serpent"), Yem'chen, Yemische, Zorro-vibora ("fox viper")

In Patagonian folklore in South America the iemisch is a nocturnal species of foxlike creature having a serpentine body and a prehensile tail. Usually descriptions of the creature say it has smooth scales but sometimes these stories claim it has short brown fur. The iemisch, about the size of a puma, kills its prey by ensnaring it in the coils of its body and constricting in the same fashion as a boa constrictor or python while submerging into the river.

Source: De Kirk, *Dragonlore*, 55; Eberhart, *Mysterious Creatures*, 243; Shuker, *Beasts That Hide from Man*, 261; Zell-Ravenheart, *Wizard's Bestiary*, 51

Ihuaivulu

A gigantic seven-headed DRAGON from the folklore of the Araucanian (Mapuchen) people of Argentina and Chile, Ihuaivulu is described as having a long, slinky, and serpentine body covered with burnished copper and red colored scales. Living in a volcano, the Ihuaivulu also has the ability to breathe fire.

Source: De Kirk, *Dragonlore*, 55; Rose, *Giants, Monsters, and Dragons*, 188

Ikalu Nappa

A species of MERMAID from the Inuit people of the Arctic regions, the ocean dwelling ikalu nappa has the upper body and face of a woman and the lower body of a fish.

Source: Rose, *Giants, Monsters, and Dragons*, 188; Zell-Ravenheart, *Wizard's Bestiary*, 51

Ikaroa

Variations: Ika, Ika-o-te-rangi, Ika-Roa, Mangōroa ("long shark"), Mangōroa i ata ("long shark in the early dawn"), Te Ikaroa

According to Maori mythology the long fish Ikaroa ("the Milky Way") was married to Kohu ("mist") and gave birth to Nga Whetu ("the stars").

Source: Shortland, *Maori Religion and Mythology*, 17; Tregear, *Maori-Polynesian Comparative Dictionary*, 103

Iko-Turso

Variations: Iki-Tursas, Iku-Tursas, *Meritursas* ("octopus"), Turisas, Tursas ("giant")

A SEA SERPENT named in Finnish folklore, Iko-Turso ("eternal Turso") was described as being "wicked" and living on the depths of the sea. In the tale of *The Capture of Sampo*, Iko-Turso was summoned by Louhi to sink the ship of Wainamoinen, consume its crew, and return with the vessel *Sampo*.

Source: Eivind, R, *Finnish Legends for English Children* 184; Johnson, *Kalevala*, 271

Ikugan

In Filipino folklore there are a group of simian-like, long tailed creatures living in the branches of the jungles of Eastern Mindanao, Philippines, known as ikugan ("long tail"); they are described as having large hands and feet, a long tail, and a soft, fur covered body. These fierce creatures hang by their tails waiting for human prey to pass beneath; when it does, they will snatch the person up, kill, and consume them.

Source: Ramos, *Creatures of Midnight*, 62; Paraiso, *Balete Book*, 52

Ikuutayuuq

A murderous humanoid creature from the folklore of the Inuit people of Hudson Bay, Canada, Ikuutayuuq ("one who drills") and his brother would patrol their territory for invading humans. Anyone they found they would track, capture, and torture by holding them down on their back, and drill holes into their body. When the person finally died the brothers would cover them with *inuksuut*, a pile of rocks. Eventually Ikuutayuuq and his brother were confronted by one of the *tuniiit* or "original people" who slayed Ikuutayuuq; the remaining brother ran off, never to be seen again.

Source: Rose, *Giants, Monsters, and Dragons*, 188–9

Illuyanka

Variations: Illujanka

A gigantic DRAGON from Hittite mythology, Illuyanka ("serpent") fought against the storm god Tarhunna (Tarhunta); there are two versions to this tale; in both tellings Illuyanka initially defeats Tarhunna. In the first variation Tarhunna enlists the aid of the goddess Inara who seduces Illuyanka and his children out of their lair, invites them to a lavish banquet and ensures they become quite inebriated. In exchange for sexual favors from the goddess the mortal hero Hupasiya ties up Illuyanka so Tarhunna can safely slay him with his lightning bolts.

In the second variant, after Illuyanka defeats the god he steals his heart and eyes. Tarhunna some years later has a son who grows up to marry one of the daughters of Illuyanka who betrays her father and returns the organs to her father-in-law. Restored, Tarhunna confronts Illuyanka again, this time not only defeating him, but also slaying his own son in the process.

Source: Kuehn, *Dragon in Medieval East Christian and Islamic Art*, 87; Ogden, *Drakon*, 12–3; Ogden, *Dragons, Serpents, and Slayers in the Classical and Early Christian Worlds*, 260–1

Ilomba

A vampiric snake created by a sorcerer to be his FAMILIAR, the ilomba looks like a snake but its head resembles its owner's, even copying any ornamentation which is worn. To create this magical creature the sorcerer takes blood from his back, chest, and forehead and mixes it with fingernail clippings and a concoction of magical roots collected from the forest. All ingredients are mixed together in a Chamba pan. This process is repeated several days in a row until the snake begins to form. The creature is born without teeth and cannot be used to kill for five years, the length of time it will take to generate fangs. Unlike other types of FAMILIAR the bond between the ilomba and its owner is so close that to kill one will also destroy the other.

Source: Reynolds, *Magic, Divination, and Witchcraft Among the Barotse of Northern Rhodesia*, 36; Zell-Ravenheart, *Wizard's Bestiary*, 52

Imap Umassoursa

A gigantic sea creature in Inuit folklore of the people of Greenland, Imap Umassoursa was so large it was oftentimes mistaken for an island (see SEA SERPENT). The creature would doze just beneath the surface of the water and as boats would pass overhead it would rise up and tip the vessel, plunging the fishermen into the water where they would very often quickly die from the freezing temperature of the ocean.

Source: Rose, *Giants, Monsters, and Dragons*, 189; Zell-Ravenheart, *Wizard's Bestiary*, 52

Imbrius

Variations: Imbreus, Imbros

A CENTAUR from ancient Greek mythology, Imbrius ("rain storm") attended the wedding of Pirithous, became drunk on wine and following the lead of EURYTUS, who assaulted Hippodame, began to assault and rape any women they could grab. During the ensuing Centauromachy, Imbrius, along with AREOS, EURYNOMUS, and LYCIDAY, was slain by the Lapith soldier DRYAS as they attempted to flee the battle.

Source: *Commentary, Mythological, Historical, and Geographical on Pope's Homer*, 55; Simpson, *Metamorphoses of Ovid*, 205

Impundulu (Im-pon-do-lou) plural: iimpumdulu

Variations: Inyoni Yezulu, Ishologu, Izulu, Thekwane

From the Cape region of South Africa comes the impundulu ("lightning bird"). A vampiric creature only about three inches tall in its true form, it uses its therianthropy and usually stays in its shapeshifted form—a bird with a red bill, legs, and tail. In addition to its shape-shifting ability, it can also spread "the wasting disease" (tuberculosis), cause infertility in cattle and men, and cause near instant death in a person through a sudden pain in their chest. In its natural form, the impundulu flies in a small flying machine powered by human blood.

At night it attacks both cattle and humans, drinking their blood and consuming their flesh. It has been said a lone impundulu can kill an entire herd of cattle in a single evening, as its hunger is insatiable. Additionally, it enjoys the pain and torment it causes.

An impundulu makes an excellent FAMILIAR for a witch, as it is loyal by nature, cannot be destroyed, and can be passed down from mother to daughter, even if the child is not a witch herself. However, if a nonwitch comes to own one of these prized FAMILIARS, it must be used or it will turn and kill its master. When bound as a FAMILIAR, it will only show itself to its master in its bird form. The impundulu must be fed every night or at least allowed to hunt for itself, or it will turn on the witch and kill her. Obligated to protect the witch as well as her family line, the impundulu can only be passed on to the next master at the time of the witch's death. If not so transferred, the impundulu is freed from its obligations and is now referred to as an *ishologu* and will do as it pleases.

Source: Hodgson, *God of the Xhosa*, 32, 47–48; Laubscher, *Pagan Soul*, 128, 131, 151, 153; Marwick, *Witchcraft and Sorcery*, 371, 427

Imugo

Variations: Imoogi

A species of DRAGON or proto-dragon from Korean folklore, the imugo is a large python-like creature living in caves in water. Benevolent, gigantic, and hornless, some folklore says the imugo must live to be one-thousand years old and then capture a *yeouija* as it falls from Heaven before they can fully develop into a DRAGON. On occasion the *yeouija* is represented as a young virgin and if she offers herself as its bride the imugo will become an honorable DRAGON. Other folklore claims they have been cursed as a species and will never see their potential realized. To see an imugo is considered to be an omen of good fortune.

Source: Bates, *All About Chinese Dragons*, 97; Niles, *Dragons*, 75

Imy-Hemef

According to ancient Egyptian mythology Imy-Hemef ("dweller in his flames") lived atop Bakhau, the mountain of the sunrise; this gigantic serpent was said to be about fifty feet long.

Source: Coulter, *Encyclopedia of Ancient Deities*, 209; Mercatante, *Who's Who in Egyptian Mythology*, 72

In Bao A Qou

Variations: Abang Aku, A Bao A Qu, Á Bao A Qu

In Chitor, India, an ageless being known as the In Bao A Qou lives in the very spot where the *Vijay Stambh* ("Tower of Victory") was constructed in 1440 by Rana Kumbha to commemorate his victory over Mahmud Khilji of Malwa.

The In Bao A Qou remains invisible until someone interesting touches the first of the 157 narrow steps of the tower. Then, it manifests as a being made of translucent skin. As the person ascends the spiral stairs, In Bao A Qou, always staying to their right side and feeding off their courage, becomes more and more vibrant and solid. If an individual can reach the top of the stairs and has previously achieved nirvana, he will cast no shadow and In Bao A Qou will completely physically manifest.

If someone should make it to the top of the stairs and has not achieved nirvana or casts a shadow, In Bao A Qou will moan in horrible pain and disappear. Nevertheless, the person will still be rewarded

with a view of one of the most beautiful landscapes in the world. Legend has it only once has anyone made it all the way to the top of the stairs, although there is no report as to what, if anything, happened or who the person was.

Source: Borges, *Book of Imaginary Beings*, 15–16; Leee, *Tanah Tujuh*, 49–51; Manguel, *Dictionary of Imaginary Places*, 689; Zell-Ravenheart, *Wizard's Bestiary*, 14

Incubus (In-cue-bus), plural: incubi

Variations: Ag Rog ("old hag"), Agumangia, ALP, Aufhöcker, Barychnas ("the heavy breather"), Buhlgeist, Cauchmar ("trampling OGRE"), Da Chor, Dab ("nightmare"), Ducci, Duendes, Ephélés, Haegte, Haegtesse, Haehtisse, Hagge, Hegge, Hexendrücken, Hmong, Ka wi Nulita ("scissors pressed"), Kanashibara ("to tie with iron rope"), Kikimora, Kokma, Mab, Maere, Mair, Mar, Mara, Mare-Hag, Molong, More, Morúsi, Móry, Muera, Ngarat, Nightmare, Phi Kau ("ghost possessed"), Phi Um ("ghost covered"), Pnigalion ("the choker"), Preyts, Raukshehs, Tsog ("evil spirit"), Tsog Tsuam ("evil spirit who smothers"), Ukomiarik, Urum, Védomec, Zmora

Cultures from all over the world and from all time periods have reports of a type of vampiric demonic creature feeding off the sexual energy of humans. The incubus is generally described by its female victims as "feeling" male. At night it assaults a woman while she is asleep, stealing her sexual energy from her. She seldom awakes during the attack but rather will experience the event as if it were an erotic dream.

Once an incubus has locked on to a woman (it prefers nuns), it can be very difficult to drive away, although there are many recommendations the Church offers in order to ward it off, such as performing an exorcism, relocating, repeatedly making the sign of the cross, or, as a last resort, performing an excommunication on the woman being assaulted. Traditional folklore says to hang garlic and a druid stone (a stone with a natural hole through it) next to your bed will keep an incubus away.

Incubi can father children with their female victims; these offspring are known as CAMBIONS. There is a report of a man from Bologna, Italy, who staffed his entire brothel with incubi and the female equivalent, succubi (see SUCCUBUS).

Source: Cohn, *Europe's Inner Demons*, 235; Doniger, *Britannica Encyclopedia of World Religions*, 503; Jones, *On the Nightmare*, n.pag.; Robbins, *Encyclopedia of Witchcraft and Demonology*, 28, 125

Indacinga

A gigantic monstrous creature from the folklore of the Ponca people of the Great Plains, United

States of America, the indacinga are a NURSERY BOGIE used by parents to frighten their children into good behavior. Described as being immensely strong, these creatures, living in the deep woods, are said to be responsible for uprooting trees; they are even strong enough to lift a house off of its foundation and toss it about like a handful of twigs.

Source: Rose, *Giants, Monsters, and Dragons*, 189

Indrik the Beast

Variations: Indrik

A UNICORN-like creature from Russian folklore, Indrik the Beast was said to be the Lord of Animals, living alone on the holy and sacred Saint Mountain where no other is allowed; he had dominion over the water as well and utilized the crocodiles and snakes to this end. Described as having two horns; the earth trembles when he becomes agitated.

Source: Gilmore, *Monsters*, 65; Pickeral, *Encyclopedia of Horses and Ponies*, 149; Zell-Ravenheart, *Wizard's Bestiary*, 52

Inet

Variations: Ant

In ancient Egyptian mythology Inet and ABDU were the two fish swimming on either side of the boat of the sun god Ra; their duty was to chase away any evil being approaching the vessel.

Source: Avant, *Mythological Reference*, 144; Coulter, *Encyclopedia of Ancient Deities*, 9; Mercatante, *Who's Who in Egyptian Mythology*, 2

Inguma

Variations: Caucavielha, Chauchevieille

A nocturnal simian-like (monkey-like) creature from Basque folklore, the inguma ("butterfly") is said to slip into people's home at night and while they sleep, cause them to have nightmares or choke and throttle them. To prevent the inguma from its assault, appeals can be made to the household spirit (see HOUSE-SPIRIT) known as GAUARGI.

Source: Aulestia, *Basque-English Dictionary*, 304; Lurker, *Dictionary of Gods and Goddesses, Devils and Demons*, 88; Miguel de Barandiarán, *Selected Writings of José Miguel De Barandiarán*, 87

Inkanyamba

Sometimes considered to be a creature while other times it is spoken of as a god, Inkanyamba is in either case accredited for the creation of tornadoes and waterspouts. An enormous serpentine creature, Inkanyamba was said to grow larger and larger as he left his pool and reduced in size as he would withdraw back into it.

Source: Andrews, *Dictionary of Nature Myths*, 96; Varner, *Creatures in the Mist*, 123

Inkhomi

In the folklore of the people of central Africa the inkhomi ("the killer") is typically described as looking like a very large, more than twenty-feet long, crested cobra but there are also stories where it is said to be more like a serpentine BASILISK-like DRAGON. The inkhomi is exceptionally poisonous and had a cult following; its skin and crest were considered to be prized possessions by its worshipers while other body parts were allegedly used in charms and medicines created by traditional herbalists.

Source: Jones, *Instinct for Dragons*, 15; Shuker, *Extraordinary Animals Worldwide*, 32

Intulo (in-TOOL-oh)

In the rural South African province of Kwalulu Nata the native Zulu people believe in a creature they call Intulo. Described as walking upright in a human fashion it appears to be a hybrid of a man and a lizard or alligator. Intulo is a psychopomp (death omen), a messenger of death sent by the Great One to claim those whose time it is to die.

Source: Maberry, *Vampire Universe*, 161–62; Teachers' Curriculum Institute. *Ancient World History Activity Sampler*, 26; Zell-Ravenheart, *Wizard's Bestiary*, 52

Intxixu

Variations: Inntxixu, Inttxixu, Intxix, Intxixa, Intxixua, Intxixue, Intxixui, Intxixuo, Intxoxu, Intxxiu, Inxtixu, Itnxixu, Mairu

In Basque mythology an intxixu is a type of small half human and half *betizu*, a breed of wild cow found in the Basque region of Spain. Mischievous yet shy, this hybrid will occasionally offer to help humans. They live in deserted mines and are said to build megalithic monuments on the Aiako Harria Mountain, Spain.

Source: Aulestia, *Basque-English, English-Basque Dictionary*, 274; Miguel de Barandiarán, *Selected Writings of José Miguel de Barandiarán*, 88; Whitmore, *Trials of the Moon*, 73

Inuragullit

A type of monster from Inuit folklore, the inuragullit ("DWARF") are recognized for having humanoid behavior and motivations and therefore were not consider to be animals such as one would hunt, but a type of "other," or creature.

Source: Halpin, *Manlike Monsters on Trial*, 205

Invunche (Een-iwn-che)

Variations: Incunche

Of all the vampiric beings, creations, and creatures, the invunche ("master of the hide") is perhaps the most pitiable. It is said in Chile a witch will kidnap a firstborn male child while it is an infant and take it back to her cave, a place accessible only through an underground lake entrance. Once the baby is in her lair, the witch first breaks one of its legs and twists it over the baby's back. The other leg, arms, hands, and feet are broken and disjointed and twisted into unnatural positions. A hole is cut under the right shoulder blade and then the right arm is inserted through it so the arm will look as if it's growing off the child's back. The baby's head is gradually bent and shaped over time as well so it will be misshapen. After the procedure is completed, the witch then rubs a magical ointment over the mangled infant, causing it to grow thick hair all over its body. Finally, its tongue is cut down the center so it resembles a snake's forked tongue. A baby no longer, the invunche is from then on fed a diet of human flesh, completing the transformation.

The creature is never able to leave the witch's cave lair, as it does not have the physical capability of swimming due to the imposed deformities of its body, unless the witch chooses to use her magic to fly it out. Otherwise its primary duty is to act as a guardian of her cave, killing anyone who enters it, unless they know the secret to entering the cave without violence—kissing it on its posterior. The creature can emit a blood-curdling scream, a talent it gained in lieu of the ability to speak. The sound is enough to freeze a man with fear, permanently.

The invunche has control over a lesser being, a TRELQUEHUECUVE. The invunche uses it to lure young girls to the water, abduct them, and bring them back to him so it can then drain them dry of their blood. It is believed only a hero can kill a TRELQUEHUECUVE and an invunche.

Source: Beech, *Chile and Easter Island*, 324; Minnis, *Chile*, 276–77; Roraff, *Chile*, 98; Rose, *Giants, Monsters, and Dragons*, 190

Iorek

Iorek was one of the bears named in Thorgrimr's *Rhymes* and in Snorri Sturluson's (1179–1241) *Prose Edda*.

Source: Jennbert, *Animals and Humans*, 50

Iormuni

Iormuni was one of the cattle named in Thorgrimr's *Rhymes* and in Snorri Sturluson's (1179–1241) *Prose Edda*.

Source: Jennbert, *Animals and Humans*, 49

Iphinous

A CENTAUR from ancient Greek mythology, Iphinous was, according to Ovid's *Metamorphoses*, one of the centaurs who attended the wedding of Pirit-

hous, became drunk on wine and following the lead of EURYTUS, who assaulted Hippodame, began to assault and rape any women they could grab. Iphinous was slain, just as CLANIS was, in up-close, personal combat by Peleus in the ensuing Centauromachy.

Source: *Commentary, Mythological, Historical, and Geographical on Pope's Homer*, 55; Simpson, *Metamorphoses of Ovid*, 207

Ipopodes

A species of CENTAUR from classical Greek and Roman mythology, the ipopodes were described as having the body of a human but the legs and hooves of a horse; they were believed to live in Scythia.

Source: Ashman, *Fabulous Beasts*, 54; Hargreaves, *Hargreaves New Illustrated Bestiary*, 27; Rose, *Giants, Monsters, and Dragons*, 190

Ipotane

Variations: Hippotaynes

Described by Sir John de Mandeville in his travel journals which were printed by Wynken de Worde in 1499, ipotanes, a hybrid creature between a horse and a man, lived part of its life in water and part of it on land; they were also noted as being cannibals.

Source: Vinycomb, *Fictitious and Symbolic Creatures in art with Special Reference to their use in British Heraldry*, 144

Iqalu-Nappa

Variations: Qilalugak-Nappa

A type of sea creature from Inuit folklore, the iqalu-nappa ("half-fish") is basically a species of MERMAN, larger in size than a human, whose humanoid body transforms at the waist into the lower body of a fish.

Source: Halpin, *Manlike Monsters on Trial*, 199, 205

Iriz Ima

A large, monstrous creature from the folklore and legends of the West African people, the iriz ima, nearly identical to descriptions of the GROOT SLANG, was reported by European travelers as being as large as an elephant and having a serpent's tail. The iriz ima was said to live in the caves in the swamp along the west coast.

Source: Rose, *Giants, Monsters, and Dragons*, 190

Iromunrek

Iromunrek was one of the oxen named in Thorgrimr's *Rhymes* and in Snorri Sturluson's (1179–1241) *Prose Edda*.

Source: Jennbert, *Animals and Humans*, 49

Isa Bere

A DRAGON from the folklore of Africa, Isa Bere was said to live upon the mountains of Futa Jallon, Africa; it once drank all of the water from the Niger River creating a great drought. The king, Samba, and his bard Tarafe went off to confront and slay the creature. The battle lasted eight years and used more than eight hundred spears. In the end, the king was victorious, piercing Isa Bere through its heart with a long sword; this blow along with killing the DRAGON released all of the water back into the Niger.

Source: Knappert, *African Mythology*, 96

Isiququmadevu

Variations: Isikqukqumadevu

In Zulu folklore Isiququmadevu was a semi-aquatic female monster as large as a mountain living in the Ilulange; it was described as being bloated, bearded, and squat. It was believed whoever went into the river would never return for Isiququmadevu with her voracious appetite would consume them. In folktales, the monster is antagonized into an eating frenzy by a chief's daughter; after consuming her, Isiququmadevu moved inland to the village and there consumed everything she could, including cattle and dogs. The story has varied endings; sometimes Isiququmadevu is slain by a father bereaved at the loss of his twin sons, sometimes by a woman looking to prevent the death of her infant she hid. Nevertheless, after the monster is slain and its stomach opened, those who were not killed during the initial attack are able to crawl out to safety.

Source: Callaway, *Nursery Tales, Traditions, and Histories of the Zulus*, 84–89; Westermann, *Africa*, 208

Isitoq

A TORNAK from Inuit mythology, the Isitoq ("giant eye") is a NATURE SPIRIT covered in coarse, thick hair. Each eye is divided by a large mouth containing one long tooth flanked on either side by a shorter one. Isitoq is beseeched when it is necessary to find or locate a person who has broken a taboo.

Source: Dixon-Kennedy, *Native American Myth and Legend*, 126

Isitwalangcengce

Variations: Basket Monster

The Bantu mythology the Isitwalangcengce ("basket bearer") is a flesh-eating creature from Zululand appearing whenever an ox is slaughtered. Traditionally, the women who are invited to the slaughter party show up with a basket as they will each receive a slice of the meat. Isitwalangcengce is described as looking humanoid but has a broad basket for a head and a pair of ears which stick out like handles. When the women travel back home the creature snatches one up, drops her in its basket and makes for the nearest cliff; there it will throw its victim off and make its way down to lap up the brains.

Source: Knappert, *Bantu Myths and Other Tales*, 171–2; Mack, *Field Guide to Demons, Vampires, Fallen Angels and Other Subversive Spirits*, 207; Zell-Ravenheart, *Wizard's Bestiary*, 22

Isonade

A gigantic shark-like monster from Japanese fishing folklore, the isonade ("beach stroker") is said to capsize boats and catch fishermen with the barbs on its huge tail; it is also said to have the ability to cause strong winds.

Source: Helfman, *Fishes*, 131

Isoples

In ancient Greek mythology, Isoples was one of the CENTAURS slain by the demi-god and cultural hero Hercules (Heracles) while visiting his friend, a CENTAUR named PHOLUS, between the conclusion of his third Labor and the onset of his fourth. When an old and particularly fragrant hogshead of wine was opened its aroma carried on the air and drove the local CENTAURS into a fury. Isoples, ARGEIUS, AMPHION, DAPHNIS, DUPO, Hippotion, MELANCHETES, OREUS, PHRIXUS, and THEREUS were slain by Hercules (Heracles) as he defended himself from their violent and unwarranted assault.

Source: Barthell, *Gods and Goddesses of Ancient Greece*, 187; *Commentary, Mythological, Historical, and Geographical on Pope's Homer*, 55; Diodorus, *Historical Library of Diodorus the Sicilian*, Volume 1, 229–30

Itcuintlipotzotli

Variations: Itzcuintlipotzotli

In Mexican folklore the itcuintlipotzotli ("hunch-backed dog") was first described and illustrated by a Jesuit priest in 1780; it is depicted as being hairless but black skinned with brown and white spots, the size of a terrier dog, having a hump running the length of its back, a short neck and tail, and a wolf-like head.

Source: Eberhart, *Mysterious Creatures*, 252; Zell-Ravenheart, *Wizard's Bestiary*, 52

Ittan-Momen

A harmless looking YŌKAI from Japanese folklore, the ittan-momen, a class of TSUKOMOGAMI, appears as a very long strip of cloth; some descriptions say it is over thirty feet in length. It flies in the night sky until it finds prey and then sweeps down, wrapping itself about the victim's head, crushing the skull while smothering them to death. Folklore says if a person can gain the trust of one of the ittan-momen, it enjoys being worn as a turban.

Source: Frater, *Com's Ultimate Book of Bizarre Lists*, 533; Joly, *Scary Monsters and Super Creeps*, n.pag.

Iwakoshinpuk

A creature from Ani folklore, the mischievous mountain dwelling iwakoshinpuk ("mountain ELF") has the ability to shape-shift into any form it wishes.

Source: Batchelor, *Ainu and Their Folk-Lore*, 591

Iwanci

Variations: Iwanei

A demonic DRAGON living in the Ecuadoran Amazon river basin, Iwanci is a shape-shifter who, using therianthropy, can assume two different forms. The first is called *macanci*, a water snake; the other form is *pani*, the anaconda. Iwanci also has the ability to enter into the trees of the forest.

Source: De Kirk, *Dragonlore*, 56; Rose, *Spirits, Fairies, Leprechauns, and Goblins, an Encyclopedia*, 164; Zell-Ravenheart, *Wizard's Bestiary*, 52–3

Iya

In Lakota folklore the iya ("to speak") is said to be a formless, large, and terrible monster having fetid breath and an appetite for human flesh.

Source: Buechel, *Lakota Dictionary*, 135; Palmer, *Dakota Peoples*, 22

Jackalope

Variations: Antelabbit, Aunt Benny, Horny Bunny, Jack-a-Lope, Jack-pine Jackelope, Stag Bunny

The jackalope of the Great Plains and Rocky Mountains area of southwestern United States of America is described as having a jackrabbit's body and a proportional rack of spiked deer antlers or antelope horns atop its head. In Nebraska and South Dakota the jackalopes are reported as having pheasant wings and tail as well. An extremely shy animal, the jackalope will avoid trouble at all cost, but when it is finally forced into action it will charge its opponent at speeds in excess of sixty-five miles an hour, and gore its aggressor with its horns. It is told when the animal becomes this enraged the only thing which can stop the assault is to take it down with a buffalo gun. The jackalope is also said to have the ability to mimic the human voice and will sing, in a noted French accent, the songs night-herding cowboys sing; these animals are particularly vocal during thunderstorms. Jackalopes only mate during the flashes of lightning and the milk from does is said to host a wide array of ailments.

Source: Brunvand, *American Folklore*, 831; Eberhart, *Mysterious Creatures*, 238; Rosen, *Mythical Creatures Bible*, 116; Zell-Ravenheart, *Wizard's Bestiary*, 52

Jaguar-Man

Variations: Jaguareté Avá, Jaguarete Ova

A WERE-CREATURE in Paraguayan folklore, jaguar-men are by day completely indistinguishable from any other person; however, at night and by use of sorcery, they are able to temporarily transform themselves into a jaguar. In this guise, it is not uncommon for a jaguar-man to stalk, kill, and consume a human being.

Source: Rose, *Giants, Monsters, and Dragons*, 193

Jala-Turga

In Hindu mythology the jala-turga is a predatory water-horse living in lonely stretches of water; it is one of the KRAVYAD.

Source: Knappert, *Indian Mythology*, 128; Rose, *Giants, Monsters, and Dragons*, 193

Jan

Variations: Jan the Sun

According to Burmese folklore, the jan are one of the four different species of the nats (the generic name for the indigenous NATURE SPIRITS of the air, cultivated fields, earth, forest, hills, households, rain, rivers, sky, streams, wind, and the like) of the Air; generally the jan are considered to be beneficial towards mankind. Once a year they are worshiped by the village chief; sacrifices are not required.

Source: Hastings, *Encyclopedia of Religion and Ethics*, Part 5, 22; Porteous, *Forest in Folklore and Mythology*, 125; Scott, *Burman: His Life and Notions*, Volume 1, 286

Jaracas (Ja-rock-ka)

Variations: Jaracaca

In Brazil there is a vampiric demonic creature known as a jaracas. It assumes the form of a snake when it is time to feed, slithers up to a mother while she is asleep, and attaches itself to her breast, draining her breast milk. During the attack, the jaracas slips the end of its tail into the baby's mouth to prevent it from crying and waking its mother. When it attacks a sleeping man, it will bite him in his upper arm, taking a survivable amount of blood. Victims will eventually begin to grow weaker as the attacks continue, and will never be able to fully recover until the jaracas has moved on to other prey. Mothers will discover their milk has dried up.

A jaracas can only be driven off if one hopes to save its victims, as it cannot be destroyed. Catholic prayers to the saints are said to work, as will the blessing of a Catholic priest. There are also several ancient and traditional incantations, spells, and talismans which can be purchased or created to ward it off.

Source: Masters, *Natural History of the Vampire*, 51; Volta, *The Vampire*, 85

Jarita

In Hindu mythology Jarita ("old) was the name of the female SARNGIKA bird who became the mate of Manda-pala when he returned from Hell and assumed a SARNGIKA form. Jarita bore him four sons: Drona, Jaritari, Sarisrikta, and Stamba-mitra; after the birth of the last, Manda-pala promptly abandoned her. Jarita was a devoted mother to her sons and during the great burning of the Khandava forest her devotion moved Manda-pala to have the gods intervene and save her and the children.

Source: Dowson, *Classical Dictionary of Hindu Mythology and Religion, Geography, History, and Literature*. 134; Gandhi, *Penguin Book of Hindu Names*, 171

Jatayu (Ja-TA-yu)

A gigantic eagle or vulture from Hindu mythology, Jatayu is the king of his kind; while the *Ramayana* says he is the son of Aruna and Shyeni, other texts say he is a son of the god GARUDA.

According to the *Ramamyana*, he was the only animal in the jungle not too frightened of the ten-headed demon king Ravana to give chase as the demon kidnapped Sita, the beloved wife of Prince Rama. Swooping in to attack Ravana with its razor sharp beak and talons, the demon slashed off Jatayu's wings with his sword and left the bird to die on the forest floor. With its dying breath Jatayu was able to describe the kidnapper to Rama, informing the Prince of who had taken his wife. Rama blessed the bird and praying over it revealed himself to be the god Vishnu. Jatayu died contented and ascended into heaven in a chariot of fire.

Source: Chatterjee, *Elephant-headed God and Other Hindu Tales*, 1–2; Dalal, *Hinduism*, 178

Jay Hawk

Variations: Jay-Hawk

Originating in the lumberjack communities of the developing United States of America, the jay hawk, one of the FEARSOME CRITTERS, was a ferocious type of bird noted for its aggressive nature, as it would kill other birds for sport.

Source: Rose, *Giants, Monsters, and Dragons*, 119; Walsh, *Handy-Book of Literary Curiosities*, 570

Jersey Devil

A monstrous creature from the folklore of Leeds Point, New Jersey, United States of America, the Jersey Devil is surrounded with mystery beginning with its origin, dating back from the eighteenth century. Some tales claim it was born the thirteenth child of a couple, Daniel and Jane Leeds, while others say it was the result of an illicit affair between a Colonial girl and British soldier. Another version says an unconventional woman, possibly a witch, named Jenny Leeds discovered to her dismay she was pregnant with her thirteenth child. She is said to have begged God to have her baby born as a devil. After a normal delivery, the child quickly underwent a transformation into a horrid and violent beast; killing the midwife, it fled into the nearby Pine Barrens where it lives to this day.

This DRAGON–like chimerical creature is said to be about nine feet long from tip of its elongated snout to end of its long, serpentine tail, having bat wings, caprine (goatlike) legs, hairy hide, a horned horse head, a human torso, oversized paws on powerful arms, and talon claws.

Source: Brunvand, *American Folklore*, 850; Maberry, *Vampire Universe*, 162–64; Watts, *Encyclopedia of American Folklore*, 227–8

Jiaolong

A species of scaled DRAGON from Chinese mythology, the jiaolong ("HORNED DRAGON") are said to live in the sea and have the ability to control floods; additionally they have the ability of therianthropy and can shape-shift into many forms including fish and people.

Source: Cox, *Spooky Spirits and Creepy Creatures*, 13; Rosen, *Mythical Creatures Bible*, 63

Jiaoming

A PHOENIX-like bird from Chinese folklore, the jiaoming is one of the five spirit avians of some power. Each of the birds is described as looking similar to the PHOENIX in size and plumage and sitting upon one of the four cardinal points while in the center rests the PHOENIX itself. The jiaoming is the protector of the South, FAMING the East, SUSHUANG the West, and YOUCHANG the North.

Source: Sterckx, *Animal and the Daemon in Early China*, 155

Jingwei

A bird from Chinese folktales, the onomatopoeically named Jingwei bird is at best an ambiguous character, representing either a lone heroic individual or someone engaged in an effort in futility. According to the story, Nu Wa, the daughter of Emperor Yan Di, while playing on the beach was carried out into the Eastern Sea where she drowned; Nu Wa was reborn as a little bird whose call went *"Jingwei! Jingwei!"* Although reborn as a bird she remembered her death and hated the ocean; Nu Wa swore she would fill it to avenge her death. Each day the little bird would fly to the Western Hills for pebbles and twigs to drop into the sea. For years she carried out her mission until one day one of the twigs pierced her beak and she died.

Source: An, *Handbook of Chinese Mythology*, 55; Zalon, *Jingwei Bird*, 46

Jinmenju (JIN-men-joo)

A YŌKAI tree from Chinese folklore which made its way into Japanese tales, the jinmenju ("human faced tree," "tree with human fruit") is described as looking like a bread fruit tree but its branches are laden with fruit which appear to be human heads. In some tellings of the tale, the fruit are capable of speech, either in groups or individually but more often than not the fruit just hang from the branch giggling. If the fruit ends up laughing too much, it will fall off the branch and crash into the earth. According to the stories the fruit of the jinmenju tree is edible; it is described as having a tangy-sweet citrus taste.

Source: Mittman, *Ashgate Research Companion to Monsters and the Monstrous*, 146; Yoda, *Yokai Attack*, 118–21

Jinshin-Mushi

Variations: The Earthquake Beetle

In Japanese folklore the gigantic DRAGON-headed beetle and KAMI, jinshin-mushi ("earthquake beetle"), is responsible for causing earthquakes with its subterranean movements as it burrows. It is said to be covered with scales and have ten hairy legs ending in claws.

Source: Rose, *Giants, Monsters, and Dragons*, 196; Rosen, *Mythical Creatures Bible*, 15, 370; Zell-Ravenheart, *Wizard's Bestiary*, 54

Jinshin Namazu

A KAMI from Japanese folklore, jinshin namazu is in all ways identical to JINSHIN UWO except for the fact it is a gigantic catfish rather than an eel.

Source: Rosen, *Mythical Creatures Bible*, 370

Jinshin Uwo

A KAMI from Japanese folklore, jinshin uwo is a gigantic eel so large the islands of Japan rest upon its back; the city of Kyoto is located above its head and Aomori rests atop its tail some seven-hundred miles away. Whenever this creature rolls over or flicks its tail, an earthquake or tsunami is created. In order to keep the island from slipping off of jinshin uwo's back a rivet called *kaname ishi* ("keystone") is driven through a stone located within a Shinto temple in Kashima.

Source: Barber, *Dictionary of Fabulous Beasts*, 91; Borges, *Book of Imaginary Beings*, 114; Rose, *Giants, Monsters, and Dragons*, 196; Rosen, *Mythical Creatures Bible*, 370

Jiu Tou Niao

Variations: Jiufeng, Nine-Headed Bird

An ill omen from Chinese mythology, the jiu tou niao ("nine-headed bird") is a demonic creature popular in many fairy tales with the reoccurring theme of a male hero facing an arch-nemesis, namely the jiu tou niao. Typically these stories begin with the jiu tou niao terrorizing a region by kidnapping its young maidens and carrying them back to its lair where he watches them eventually die of starvation. The hero appears and manages to slay the jiu tou niao with the assistance of the most recently kidnapped victim, a beautiful princess.

In the easternmost part of central China, in the province of Hubei ("north of the lake"), *jiu tou niao* is considered to be a derogatory word implying a person is of a combative and dishonest character.

Source: Bates, *10,000 Chinese Numbers*, 210

Joint Snake

Variation: Glass Snake

A creature from American folklore and wivestales, the joint snake has the very unique ability to reassemble its dismembered body. If a joint snake is discovered and beaten with a stick and its body cut into six or seven pieces, according to the folklore, it will if left alone begin to wriggle about the piece which would connect to the head, making its way there and reconnecting. Following suit, each severed segment will then rejoin the main body of the creature until it is fully restored; once this occurs, it will quickly dart off. If one of the middle segments is removed before it can rejoin with its body, the process of the joint snake's restoration will cease and the creature will not be able to recover. Early descriptions of this creature claim it had a horn at the end of its tail "as long as a needle and twice as sharp."

Source: Clark, *Unexplained*, n.pag.; Theitic, *Witches' Almanac*, Issue 34, 17; Traquair, *Transactions of the Edinburgh Field Naturalists' and Microscopical Society*, Volume 3, 171–2

Jór (YOHR)

Variations: Jor

Jór ("horse") was one of the horses utilized by the Aesir in Norse mythology; its specific owner or rider is not mentioned. Jor was also listed as one of the many horses who would graze in the red-gilt leafed Glasir Grove.

Source: Grimes, *Norse Myths*, 20, 283; Source: Norroena Society, *Asatrii Edda*, 367

Jormungandr (YUHR-mun-gand-r)

Variations: Iormungandr, Iörmungandr, Iormungandur, Jormindgand, Jormindgand, Jörmungand, Jormun-gander, Jörmungandr ("earth monster"), Jormungandur, Jormungard ("earth mouth enclosure"), Midgard Serpent, Midgardrsormr, Miðgarðrsormr, Miðgarðsorm, Midgard-sormr, Miðgarðsormr, Mithgarthsorm, Mithgarth-Worm

A gigantic poison-spitting SEA SERPENT from Norse mythology, Jormungandr, perhaps better known as the Midgard Serpent, was born the child of the god Loki and his mistress, the ASYNJR, Angerboda. Jormindgand was born so large and terrible to behold the gods decided he could not remain in their world and hurled him down into the ocean which surrounds Midgard where he will remain until the time of Ragnarok when he will engage Thor in battle. He grew non-stop until he was so large he could encircle the land and place his tail in his mouth. According to the legend, Jormindgand will be slain by his long time enemy, Thor, but the god will soon thereafter succumb to the effects of the venomous bites he will receive in the battle.

Source: De Kirk, *Dragonlore*, 44; Grimes, *Norse Myths*, 283, 287; Jennbert, *Animals and Humans*, 50; Oehlenschläger, *Gods of the North*, lii; Zell-Ravenheart, *Wizard's Bestiary*, 54

Jotun (Yoo-tun), plural: Jotnar

Variations: Eoten, Etin ("eater"), Hrym, Jetunn, Jöttin, Jotnar, Jötunn (plural, Jötnar), Jute, Iotunn, Thurse

Born of the body of YMIR and living in Jotunheimr, the Jotnar came in many shapes and sizes; for instance, some had multiple hands and heads; there were the *bergrisar* (hill and rock jotun), fire jotnar also called the *eldjotnar*, and frost jotnar known as *hrimpursar*.

The first Jotnar were created while YMIR was exploring Ginnungagap; as he slept near Muspelheimr its heat cause him to sweat; the moisture from beneath his left arm formed two jotnar, one male and the other female. Additionally, his left foot then begot a son born with six heads who was named Thrudgelmir.

Powerful and wise to be on par with the gods, the jotnar are oftentimes thought of as gigantic beings, but not of all them were so large; some were even the size of humans. Also, not all the Jotnar were the enemy of the Aesir; there are stories of them not only being neutral to the gods but some are even considered to be devoted friends; there are also instances of them having relationships together, such as Freyr's wife Gerd, which resulted in the birth of children. One would be hard pressed to find one of the Aesir who did not have some Jotun blood in their veins.

In Norse mythology are many named Jotnar of whom nothing else is known beyond a name: Aepir ("to bellow," "to cry," or "roarer"), AETI ("eaten"), Alfarinn ("fire- ELF" or "well-traveled"), Amr ("darkness"), Alsvartr ("all black" or "coal black"), Ari ("eagle" or "fast one"), Aurgrimnir ("mud-grimnir"), Baugi ("ring"), Beinvidr ("big-bone," "wide-bone"), Beitr ("the caustic"), Beli ("the bellower," "the howler"), Bergrisar ("mountain-giants"), Berlingr ("builder"), Bjorgolfr ("mountain-wolf"), Blappvari ("chattering-weapon"), Eimgeitr ("fire-goat"), Eimnir ("reeking with blood"), Eldr ("fire"), Etin ("eater"), Eyrgjafa ("she who gives sandbanks"), Fangbodi ("challenger"), Farbanti ("anger striker" or "the one inflicting harm"), Fenja ("swampy" or "water-maiden"), Fiorgwyn, Fjolvarr ("glutton"), Fjolverkr ("pain filled" or "worker"), Fornjotr ("destroyer"), Frekr ("greedy"), Frosti ("frosty" "frozen"), Fyrnir ("the ancient"), Ganglati ("lazy," "lazy-goer," "slow moving," "walk slacker," "tardy"), Ganglot ("slow"), Gangr ("traveler"), Geitir ("goat"), Gestur, Gjolp ("boastful," "braggart"), Glaumvor ("the praised"), Gor ("slaughterer"), Grimlingr ("mask-wearer"), Grimliongr ("mask-wearer"), Grimnir ("the masked one"), Gusir ("gusty" or "outpouring"), Gylfi ("king"), Gyllingr ("the loud grating"), Gyllir ("golden"), Haki ("hook"), Hardgreipr ("hard grip"), Hardverkr ("hard-worker"), Haustigi ("autumn"), Helblindi ("he who blinds with death"), Helreginn ("death-reginn," "death-smith" or "Ruler over Hel"), Hengjankjoptr ("Hanging-Chin"), Herkir ("boorish"), Hlebardr ("protecting beard"), Hloi ("the bellowing"), Hraudnir ("destroyer"), Hraudungr ("the hasty"), Hrimgrimnir ("rime-grimnir"), Hrimr ("frost," "rime"), Hringvolnir ("round-pole bearer"), Hripstodi ("spotted"), Hroarr ("spear-famous"), Hrodr ("famous" or "glory"), Hrokkvir ("the stooping" or "whipper"), Hrosspjoft ("horse thief"), Hrungnir ("the noisy"), Hrymr ("decrepit"), Hundolfr ("hound ELF" or "wolf hound"), Hvalr ("whale"), Imr ("the dark"), Isungr ("iceling," "child of the Ice"), Jari ("The Disputing"), Jokull ("Glacier"), Kaldgrani ("cold-mouth"), Köll ("cold"), Kottr ("the catlike"), Kyrmir ("screamer"), Leidi ("the sorrowful"), Leili ("deserter"), Liitr ("the disgraceful"), Lodinn ("hairy" or "shaggy"), Midi ("the average"), Mornir ("agonizing"), Nati ("nettle"), Nor ("sailor"), Oflugbardi ("strong-beard"), Ogladnir ("the unhappy"), Ondudr ("the opponent"), Ornir ("the quick"), Osgriii ("ash-heap"), Oskrudr ("screamer"), Rangbein ("the bowlegged"), Saekarlsmuli ("sea-man's mouth"), Salfang ("hall-robber"), Samendill ("the familiar foe"), Skalli ("bald-headed"), Skerkir ("the noisy"), Skramr ("the frightening"), Skrati ("troll"), Skrimnir ("the frightening"), Skroggr ("the wolf"), Skserir ("dusk," "twilight"), Snaer ("snow"), Sprettingr ("the springing"), Stigandi ("the leading"), Storverkr ("strong-worker"), Stumi ("pitch-dark"), Sumarr ("summer"), Svarangr ("the hard," "the bad"), Svartr ("the swarthy"), Svasudr ("the delightful"), Thistilbardi ("thistle-beard"), Thorri ("black-frost"), Thrigeitir ("three-goats"), Vetr ("winter"), Vidblindi ("forest-blind"), Viddi ("wide"), Vidgymnir ("wide-sea"), Vidolfr ("forest-wolf"), Vilmeidr ("soothsayer"), Vindr ("wind"), Vingrip ("friendly-hold," "friendly-grip"), Vipar ("the trifling"), Vornir ("the cautious"), Ymsi ("the loud").

Source: Anderson, *Norse Mythology*, 38–40; Daniels, *Encyclopedia of Superstitions, Folklore, and the Occult Sciences of the World*, 1377; Grimes, *Norse Myths*, 286; Norroena Society, *Asatrii Edda*, 336–401; Vigfússonn *Court Poetry*: Volume 2, 424–5

Jujak

A type of PHOENIX from Korean folklore, the jujak was said to only eat bamboo fruit and roost only upon Chinese parasol trees. This bird embodied the five virtues of a nobleman: benevolence, propriety, righteousness, sincerity, and wisdom.

Source: Pak, *From Prehistory to the Joseon Period*, 35

Julenisse

Variations: Christmas Nisse

Originating in twentieth century Swedish folklore, the julenisse is described as being smaller than the Norwegian nisse (a species of fairy) from which it seems to have evolved. In the later part of the nineteenth century the Julemand (Santa Claus) became associated with the nisse and the two folktales merged, creating the bearded, grey clothed, red-hat wearing, and small julenisse.

According to the folklore, on Christmas Eve the julenisse would knock upon the front door and ask "Do any good children live here?" If the answer was in the affirmative, it would leave the parents a bag of presents to distribute to the children of the home.

Source: Baker, *Discovering Christmas Customs and Folklore*, 69; Kissinger, *Christmas Past*, 73, 90

Jumar

Variations: Juma

A chimerical creature described in the sixteenth-century English writer John Baptist Porta's work entitled *Natural Magick*, the jumar was said to be a hybrid of an ass and a bull living in the grassy saline plains or in the salt wastes. The animal with acute hearing and sense of smell is alleged to be about the size of a mule but swift, timid, and untamable; its ears and tail are like those of a zebra, its hooves like an ass, and its legs like a horse.

Source: Harris, *Natural History of the Bible*, 30; Rose, *Giants, Monsters, and Dragons*, 198; Zell-Ravenheart, *Wizard's Bestiary*, 54

Jumbies

Variations: Heg, Jhumbies, Jumbee, Jumbi, Jumby, SOUCAYANT

In Caribbean island folklore, the word *jumbies* refers collectively to any and all vampiric creatures of the night. They are described as looking like a corpse candle (a glowing, spectral ball of glowing light) flying through the night sky as they seek out those who travel alone in the dark or children to drain dry of their blood. Apart from their desire to drink blood, jumbies also "ride" a person, much the way an ALP or INCUBUS does, draining the victim of their life, sexual energy, and sperm.

Jumbies can be good or evil and have been seen in populated downtown areas where the streetlights happen not to reach. Oftentimes they will hover just outside a window, peeking in as they hunt for prey. Because of this hunting technique, it is said never to throw water out a window because a wet jumbie is a special kind of dangerous and vengeful creature.

Jumbies move by their ability to fly, but they can do so only over continuous ground; they cannot fly across water, fly off a cliff, or over a hole. What they can do that other vampires of their type cannot, such as the corpse candle (a glowing, spectral ball of glowing light), is steal the voice of a child in order to have a means by which they may speak.

It is said the jumbie by day wears a faux human skin and can pass as a person, but at night the skin is removed and the corpse candle (a glowing, spectral ball of glowing light) is free to go hunting. If the skin can be found and rubbed with salt, it will shrivel up. When the jumbie returns just before daybreak, it will find its skin does not fit and the creature will perish when exposed to the light of day.

Source: Abrahams, *Man-of-Words*, 45, 179; Allsopp, *Dictionary of Caribbean English Usage*, 317; Bell, *Obeah*, 121–26, 144, 158; Philpott, *West Indian Migration*, 49, 154, 158

Jurik

A DRAGON from Indonesian folklore, Jurik was said to be seen flying in fiery profile against the night sky.

Source: Knappert, *Pacific Mythology*, 61; Rose, *Giants, Monsters, and Dragons*, 199

Ka-Riu

A species of DRAGON from Japanese mythology, the fiery-red ka-riu were said to be small, only about six or seven feet long, but were exceptionally powerful. Ka-Riu is also the name of one of the four DRAGON KINGS of Japan, HAN RIU, RI RIU, and SUI RIU being the other three.

Source: Bates, *All About Chinese Dragons*, 100; Ingersoll, *Dragons and Dragon Lore*, 104; Johnsgard, *Dragons and Unicorns*, 18

Ka Ryu

Variations: Ka-Ryu

A small red DRAGON from Japanese folklore only about the length of a horse, the Ka Ryu is said by some sources to be made up entirely of flames. The smallest of all the Japanese DRAGONS, the ka ryu stops growing during the KIAO-LUNG phase.

Source: Bates, *All About Chinese Dragons*, 100; De Kirk, *Dragonlore*, 30

Kaaguy Pori

From the folklore of the Guaraní Indians of Paraguay, the kaaguy pori is a mass of tentacles, one acting as its body, another for its leg, one coming off the tip of its nose, and many more for its arms.

Source: O'Rourke, *Give War a Chance*, 49

Kabandha

Variations: Visvavasu

An evil and monstrous gigantic creature slain by Rama, Kabandha ("headless torso") was born a son of the goddess Sriand. According to the Rama myth cycle, unaware of his boon of immortality for having performed a *tapas* (penance) given to him to Brahma, Visvavasu, as he was originally called, attacked Indra who, using his divine discus, compressed Visvavasu's body into a new form during the battle. After the battle, he was now called Kabandha ("headless torso") as his head and neck were pushed into his chest, a mouth with oversized teeth was located in the middle of his chest, and a single eye appeared in his breast. Indra then gave the GIANT two long hands saying only when Rama cut off his hands would he gain back his original form. Eventually Kabandha happened upon Rama and his companion Lakshmana as they were in the forest looking for Sita. Kabandha grabbed up each one making a fist around their body and began to squeeze; the men pulled their weapons and each cut off one of the GIANT's hands. Pleased, Kabandha told them his story before passing away; he also advised they visit the monkey king Surgiva to learn more of Sita's abduction. Rama burned Kabandha's body in a pyre and he was reborn once again as Visvavasu.

Source: Parmeshwaranand, *Encyclopaedic Dictionary of Puranas*, Volume 1, 711; Williams, *Handbook of Hindu Mythology*, 166–7

Kadimakara

Variations: Kadimurka

The collective name for the gigantic prehistoric creatures of Aboriginal folklore, the sky-dwelling Kadimakara one day fell to earth. They lived here for a long time until the sun burned them so badly only their bones remained.

Source: Eberhart, *Mysterious Creatures*, 263; Zell-Ravenheart, *Wizard's Bestiary*, 54

Kai Kai

A large serpentine DRAGON from Chilean folklore of the Araucanian (Mapuchen) people, Kai Kai was described as having the head of an ox, three arms which were trees, and a tail rooted into the ground; he lived in a lake located upon TREN TREN. When Kai Kai, the symbol of water, was awake, it looked as if his eyes were closed and when he was asleep, it appeared as if his eyes were open.

There are two stories in the folklore which mention Kai Kai. In one he is an evil DRAGON or seabird which sought to destroy the people of the world by creating a global flood; although TREN TREN saved most of the population those who drowned, human and animal alike, are transformed by Kai Kai into fish, sea lions, MERMAIDS, and whales.

In the other tale the creature simply enjoyed being at peace, resting upon the shore of his lake. In the latter tale the people would climb up the mountain and strike his tail with a stick, and although it did not harm him, it did startle him awake. One day, Kai Kai had enough of their foolish behavior and as Chief of all the Animals, summoned them to him. By use of his great innate power he marched them all up and into the sky, leaving with them, never to return. Although no one knows where Kai Kai and the animals went to, the spirits of those animals returned to the region as PILLIAN who look after the well-being of all animals.

Source: Faron, *Hawks of the Sun*, 76–7; Walter, *Shamanism*, Volume 1, 419

Kai-Tsi

Variations: Kai Tsu, Sin You ("divine sheep")

A creature from Japanese mythology, the kai-tsi is said to be a creature originally from a foreign country; it was described as resembling a lion with a long alicorn growing out of the top of its head. Interestingly the kai-tsi had the remarkable ability to distinguish the difference between right and wrong just as the CHIAI TUNG could. One such creature was in the employ of a judge named Kau You who, when in doubt, would let the kai-tsi make the determination; the animal would dispense justice by assaulting and mauling the guilty party.

Source: Gould, *Mythical Monsters*, 357; Rose, *Giants, Monsters, and Dragons*, 201

Kaibyou (Ki-be-you)

In Japanese folklore there is a vampiric cat with two tails known as the kaibyou ("cat"); it is capable of slowly draining its victims of their life-energy, causing them to have bad dreams, although, on occasion, the creature will simply strangle its victims to death. This highly intelligent creature has the gift of therianthropy and can shape-shift into the forms of its victims, but even in doing so, it is not enough to mask the sense of uneasiness its presence emits. It also has the capability to put large numbers of people to sleep at one time.

Source: Copper, *Vampire in Legend*, 49–50; Davis, *Myths and Legends of Japan*, 265; Howey, *Cat in Magic*, 176

Kajjutajuk

A type of monster from Inuit folklore the Kajjutajuk ("hammer head") are recognized for having humanoid behavior and motivations and therefore were not considered to be animals such as one would hunt, but a type of "other," or creature.

Source: Halpin, *Manlike Monsters on Trial*, 205

Kakamora

In the province of the Solomon Islands, upon the island of Makira, there is said to be living in the inaccessible inland caves or within the fruit and nut trees a tiny race of people or NATURE-SPIRITS known as the Kakamora. Although generally benign toward humans they will attack with their long, sharp nails and tiny teeth if provoked. They are described as having a dark complexion, although some have been said to be fair skinned; their long straight hair comes down to their knees and they wear no clothes. The kakamora are exceedingly strong, stand about three feet tall, and stoop over as they run.

Sources: Barber, *Dictionary of Fabulous Beasts*, 91; Forth, *Images of the Wildman in Southeast Asia*, 243; Stanley, *South Pacific Handbook*, 920

Kakli Besar

A demonic creature from Malaysian folklore, the kakli besar was said to have been created by demonic forces for the sole purpose of harassing and hunting mankind. Described as looking like a hairy WILD MAN, the evil and nine-foot-tall kakli besar uses its nearly two-foot-long claws to slash humans and cattle. Although they are completely

without fear regarding man, they can be repelled by fire, smoke, and the sound of clanging metal.

Source: Maberry, *Vampire Universe*, 165–66

Kakua Kambuzi

A NATURE SPIRIT similar to a dryad (a nymph of the forests and trees, particularly oak trees in Greek mythology), the kakua kambuzi is part of the belief of the Basoga people of Uganda, central Africa, and is said to protect the tall spreading incense tree. According to custom, if a man is found having improper relations with a virgin the couple is tied to the incense tree; in the morning they are released and allowed to make a home together beneath its shade and protection.

Source: Frazer, *Golden Bough: A Study in Magic and Religion*, Volume 2, 112; Porteous, *Lore of the Forest*, 135–6

Kalakeyas

Variations: Kalakanjas

In Vedic mythology the Kalakeyas are a race of cruel, ferocious, and powerful danavas (a race of ASURAS) born to a woman by the name of Puloma; they had been granted a boon by Brahma—no Deva would be able to kill them. The Kalakeyas, under the leadership of the Virtra, oppressed the gods but after their leader was slain they hid in the ocean and would make nighttime raids upon the world killing many Brahmins. The gods were fearful of the Kalakeyas but knew they could not be reached unless the ocean was drained in order to expose them; this was a task only Agastya could perform and did so gladly. Once exposed, they were easily slain by the gods.

Source: Nath, *Dictionary of Vedanta*, 97; Parmeshwaranand, *Encyclopaedic Dictionary of Puranas*, Volume 1, 7

Kaliya

Variations: Kaliyanaga

A HYDRA from Indian mythology, the bejeweled Kaliya was once the King of the Serpents; born of Kasyapa the progenitor, he was described as having five heads (although some texts say it was one-thousand), two less than his successor, DHRANA. While other NAGA were susceptible to the attacks of the sun eagle GARDUA, Kaliya was granted a boon; so long as he and his lineage remained in the Kalindi river they would be spared. Kaliya's poison was so powerful it quickly contaminated the entire river; even the trees along the banks died. One day a cow herder drank from the river and died; this enraged Krishna so deeply he attacked Kaliya and beat him into submission. Kaliya, his wives, and their children retreated, with the blessings of Lord Krishna, to Ramanaka Island where they were promised to remain under the protection the boon, safeguarding them from GARUDA.

Source: De Kirk, *Dragonlore*, 35; Williams, *Handbook of Hindu Mythology*, 175

Kaluk

A species of nats (the generic name for the indigenous NATURE SPIRITS of the air, cultivated fields, earth, forest, hills, households, rain, rivers, sky, streams, wind, and the like) from Burmese folklore, the dryad-like (a *dryad* is a nymph of the forests and trees, particularly oak trees in Greek mythology) kaluk inhabit the trees of the forest and violently protect the ones they live in. If ever a tree were to be cut down without first offering up prayers, a man would die. The people of the region claim to know when the kaluk are about, as the leaves of the trees are moving without any other visible cause. It is said there are thirty-seven different varieties of kaluk but they are all under the leadership of their king, Min-Magayi.

Source: Porteous, *Lore of the Forest*, 124–5; Scott, *The Burman*, 235

Kamadhenu

Variations: Nandini, Surabhi

The mother of all cattle, Kamadhenu is on occasion referred to as a goddess, as she has marvelous attainments and powers. Although all the cattle of the world are her descendants, there were several cows with this name through the mythology each owned by a different Devas. One Kamadhenu came into being during the time the ASURAS and the Devas were churning the ocean of milk; along with many other splendid items, Kamadhenu was born. Another was born when Amrta, tricked into swallowing more than his limit, vomited forth Kamadhenu. It is also believed the progenitor Kamadhenu lives in a realm known as Rasatala and has four Kamadhenu around her, one on each side. At one time one of the Kamadhenu was going to be abducted by Visvamitra but rather it transformed into a terrible monster; from the different parts of her body emerged fierce warriors who clashed with Visvamitra's followers.

Source: Parmeshwaranand, *Encyclopaedic Dictionary of Puranas*, Volume 1, 733–4

Kamaitachi

A wind or NATURE SPIRIT from Japanese folklore, the kamaitachi ("sickle weasel") is a swamp dwelling YŌKAI manifesting in the form of three weasels. A vicious creature, it knocks a person down, severely cuts their face with the tiny sickles they carry and then before more than a few drops of blood can be spilt, heals the horrid wounds it just created before scurrying away.

Source: Barber, *Dictionary of Fabulous Beasts*, 92; Bush, *Asian Horror Encyclopedia*, 92; Maberry, *Vampire Universe*, 167–8

Kami

In Japanese folklore and mythology a kami ("spirit") is a species of NATURE SPIRIT traditionally held responsible for causing earthquakes. Depicted as a *namazu* (catfish) it remains fixed to the earth by a sword thrust through its head by the god of Deer Island. Whenever the island quakes it is said the god grasps the granite sword hilt which is protruding from the ground, and stills the earth.

Source: Andrews, *Dictionary of Nature Myths*, 106; Rosen, *Mythical Creatures Bible*, 370; Zell-Ravenheart, *Wizard's Bestiary*, 55

Kamikiri

Variations: Kami-kiri

The kamikiri ("hair cutter"), a little-known YŌKAI of Japanese folklore, slips into homes during the night and cuts the hair of sleeping young women. Some stories tell of the kamikiri appearing the night before a man is about to unknowingly marry a ghost, a spirit in disguise, or a YŌKAI; the hair cutting in this instance is to show the perversion of the act about to be committed as the would-be bride would now be less attractive and have the hair-style of a nun.

Source: Meyer, *Night Parade of One Hundred Demons*, 204; Tabori, *Humor and Technology of Sex*, 385

Kammapa

Variations: Karnmapa, Khodumodumo, Khodumodurno, Kholomodumo

In the mythology of the Sotho people of Lesotho, South Africa, the kammapa was a gigantic beast which one day devoured all of humanity except for one pregnant woman who had managed to hide from it. Some moments after his birth, her son, the hero Ditaolane, was fully matured and in possession of three spears and a string of divining stones. Without hesitation, he killed the monster; cutting open its belly, he freed all of the animals and people the kammapa had consumed.

Source: Lynch, *African Mythology, A to Z*, 85; Werner, *Myths and Legends of the Bantu*, 208

Kanae

In Maori folklore the kanae ("salmon") were a species of evil NATURE SPIRITS who, along with the PONATURI, a species of evil goblin, left the water to live on land. When the PONATURI were slain to the last by Tawhaki in retaliation for the death of his father, the kanae escaped by making tremendous leaps, returning to the water.

Source: Bailey, *Wright Brothers' Glider*, 13; Craig, *Dictionary of Polynesian Mythology*, 99

Kane-Kua-Ana

A DRAGON from Hawaiian mythology, Kane-kua-ana was said to have lived in Ewa Lagoon, better known in modern times as Pearl Harbor, and was the one who introduced *pipi* (oysters) to the area; she was worshiped by those who gathered shellfish and gathered pearls. She was also responsible for warding off sickness. In 1850 when the pipi began to disappear the natives claimed it was because Kane-kua-ana had become angry with them and was moving the shellfish to a far-away land.

Source: Craig, *Dictionary of Polynesian Mythology*, 104; Westervelt, *Legends of Gods and Ghosts*, 258

Kaneakeluh

A gigantic bird from the Kwakiutl people of British Columbia, Canada, the kaneakeluh is credited for having gifted humanity with fire from Heaven and thereby saving them from freezing to death.

Source: Brinton, *Myths of the New World*, 239; Rose, *Giants, Monsters, and Dragons*, 203

Kankagee

Originating in the lumberjack communities of the developing United States of America, the kankagee, one of the FEARSOME CRITTERS, was said to have been from Maine. Unfortunately, there is no additional information on this creature other than its name, causing writers of the time, 1841–1861, to believe it had gone extinct.

Source: American Dialect Society, *Dialect Notes*, Volume 5, 188; Mencken, *American Language Supplement 1*, 251; Rose, *Giants, Monsters, and Dragons*, 119

Kappa (KAY-pah)

Variations: Fuchi-zaru ("deep water monkey"), Kawako, Kawa-zaru ("river-monkey")

In Japan there is a vampiric creature living in ponds called a *kappa* ("river child"). It looks like a green child with a long nose, round eyes, tortoise shell on its back, and webbed fingers and toes, and smells like fish. However, its most interesting physical feature is a dent in the top of its head deep enough to hold water. The water sitting in the dent is representative of its power. Should a kappa attempt to attack you, quickly bow to it. As it is a stickler for courteousness and ritual, the kappa will pause to return the bow. When it does so, the water in the dent will spill out, rendering the creature powerless.

The kappa hunts from its home in the water. It waits until a cow or horse comes to drink and then it pulls the animal down into the water. As the animal drowns, the kappa bites into the animal's anus to drain it of its blood. The only time a kappa will leave its watery home is to steal cucumbers and melons, rape women, and to rip the liver out of people.

The kappa is incredibly strong and a highly skilled sumo wrestler. It is also a skilled teacher in the art of bone setting and medical skills.

It may well be the kappa is the only vampire which has a cucumber fetish. No matter what may be happening all around it, a kappa will stop whatever it is doing to steal away with one should the opportunity arise. By writing one's family name on a cucumber and giving it to a kappa, the entire family will be temporarily protected from its attacks.

Kappas can be surprisingly courteous, honorable, and trustworthy beings. They are highly respectful of ritual and tradition, even going so far as to challenge one of its would-be victims to a wrestling match. A kappa can even be bargained with, willing to enter into contractual agreements not to attack certain people.

Source: Davis, *Myths and Legends of Japan*, 350–52; Hyatt, *Book of Demons*, 30; Mack, *Field Guide to Demons, Fairies, Fallen Angels, and Other Subversive Spirits*, 17–18

Kapre (ka'-pre)

Variations: Xue-rén

A large dark skinned hominid from Tagalog folklore, the kapre wanders the woods or sits atop Balete trees smoking cigars and imitating bird calls. Something of a NURSERY BOGIE, the kapre will frighten any children it sees wandering in the woods at night. Usually this creature is described as standing over eight feet tall, having eyes as large as plates and legs as big around as the Acacia tree, but the kapre has the ability not only to change its height but also by therianthropy shape-shifts into other forms. If it can, it will trick a person into losing their way as they travel through the forest; should this occur the person must remove their shirt and wear it inside out if they want to find their way again.

Source: Eberhart, *Mysterious Creatures*, 266; Ramos, *Creatures of Philippine Lower Mythology*, 29; Zell-Ravenheart, *Wizard's Bestiary*, 55

Kara Fish

Variations: Kar-Fish

The kara fish of ancient Iranian folklore was said to live in the Vourukasa sea, particularly in the region where the Tree of all Seeds grew. The kara fish with its eyesight so keen it could detect a ripple as fine as a hair would relentlessly patrol the area of the Tree to ward off KHRAFSTRA, especially frogs as they are always ready to gnaw the roots of the life giving tree.

Source: Barber, *Dictionary of Fabulous Beasts*, 92; Boyce, *A History of Zoroastrianism*, 89; Darmesteter, *Zend-Avesta*, 266; Zell-Ravenheart, *Wizard's Bestiary*, 55

Kara-Shishi

Variations: Chinese Lion, Dog Foo, Shishi Dog, SHISHI

Guardian creatures from Japanese mythology, the kara-shishi, a female canine and lion hybrid, protects sacred places and are symbolic of divine protection. Seen in pairs, the male (KOMA-INU) is always placed on the left and female is always placed on the right; each is often colored, one blue and one green; the horned male's mouth is open, roaring, while the female's is closed. The female, hornless and silent, is cradling a club.

Source: Allen, *Japanese Art Motives*, 53; Ball, *Animal Motifs in Asian Art*, 59

Karakasa (KAH-rah KAH-sah)

Variations: Kara Kasa, Karakasa Kozo, Karakasa Obake, Kara-Kasa, Kasa-Bake, Kasa-Obake ("umbrella ghost"), Kozo

A class of YŌKAI known as TSUKOMOGAMI, the karakasa ("paper umbrella") is a paper parasol animated and mimicking life; it is described as having a single hairy male leg in place of a handle and a lolling tongue. Basically harmless, the karakasa will, out of boredom from disuse, rise into the air and fly away. Occasionally, it will appear out of a darkened corner to scare a person.

Source: Bush, *Asian Horror Encyclopedia*, 95; Drazen, *Gathering of Spirits*, 74; Joly, *Scary Monsters and Super Creeps*, n.pag.

Karasu Tengu (Ka-rah-shoe Ten-goo)

Variations: Demonic Crow Tengu, Kotengu, Minor Tengu

Originally, there were two types of *tengu* ("sky dog") demons in Japan: the karasu tengu ("raven tengu") and the yamabushi tengu. However, as time passed the two species of tengu demons became intertwined and developed into a singular entity.

The karasu tengu is a demon in the truest sense of the word in that it was never a human; it was always an immortal being. It looks rather like a small humanoid with a green face but has the beak, claws, and wings of a crow. It lives in the mountains and is malicious and fiercely territorial, attacking anyone who enters; it is particularly fond of the flesh of children, stealing them to get it if it must.

Able to shape-shift into the forms of a man, woman, or child, it is often seen carrying a ring-tipped staff called a *shakujos* which aids it in exorcisms and protects it from magic. Known for its unusual sense of humor, the karasu tengu can possess people and speak through them. Fortunately, an offering of bean paste and rice can appease it.

Source: Davis, *Myths and Legends of Japan*, 170; Louis-Frédéric, *Japan Encyclopedia*, 958; McNally, *Clutch of Vampires*; Yoda, *Yokai Attack*, 18–21

Karawatoniga

In Melanesian folklore creatures called karawatoniga are believed to live among the rocks near the seashore or in the bush where they spend their time walking about attracted to the wailing of mourners. Normally they can only be seen on special occasions, but they have been described as wearing their long hair in *doione* (long ringlets worn during mourning) and while having all their facial features—eyes, nose, and a mouth full of teeth—they are indistinguishable or under developed.

Source: Renner, *Primitive Religion in the Tropical Forests*, 84; Rose, *Spirits, Fairies, Leprechauns, and Goblins, an Encyclopedia*, 363; Seligman, *Melanesians of British New Guinea*, 647–8

Kargas

A gigantic bird from Turkish mythology, the kargas is similar to other large, mythical birds such as the ANQA and ROK; some sources describe it as looking more like a GRIFFIN.

Source: Crooke, *Popular Religion and Folk-Lore of Northern India*, Volume 2, 158; Zell-Ravenheart, *Wizard's Bestiary*, 55

Karina

Variations: Kuntiak

A female, demonic creature from Islamic folklore, the karina has the ability to cast the evil eye upon crops, livestock, and people; described as looking similar to an owl it may also assume the shape of a dog, snake, or woman.

Source: Rose, *Spirits, Fairies, Leprechauns, and Goblins*, 176; Zell-Ravenheart, *Wizard's Bestiary*, 55

Karkadan

Variations: Carcazonon, Cartazoon, Karg, Karkadann, Karkadanno, Karkedden, Karkend, Karmadan, Kartajan ("lord of the desert"), Kezkezan

In the folklore of India and Persia the aggressive and predatory karkadan was described by European travelers as having a very large rust-colored body set upon the legs and cloven hooves of a deer; its hindquarters being thicker and hairier than the front. Its equine head is resting on a short, maneless neck. In some descriptions it had an alicorn (a single horn) upon its head like a UNICORN, which it used to kill and carry off its prey; this item was desired by merchants as a means by which to detect poison. The swift karkadan could never be captured and taken alive; it would kill itself first.

Source: Lane, *Arab Society in the Time of the Thousand and One Nights*, 454; Rose, *Giants, Monsters, and Dragons*, 204; Zell-Ravenheart, *Companion for the Apprentice Wizard*, 178

Karkanxhol

Variations: Kallukanxhe, Shenendre ("Saint Andrew")

A WEREWOLF-like being from Albanian mythology, the Karkanxhol ("black bogey" or "black WEREWOLF") is described as looking like a small man bearing clothes made of iron or as the corpse of a Gypsy appearing during Twelfth Night, rattling chains; its breath is lethal.

Source: Elsie, *Dictionary of Albanian Religion, Mythology, and Folk Culture*, 150

Karkotaka

Karkotaka was a NAGA who once cheated the most powerful sage, Narada, at a game of chance. Angered, Narada used his magic to curse Karkotaka both with immortality and the inability to leave his forest; the only means by which the curse could be broken was if a monarch named Nala came to his aid. Unknown to Karkotaka there was such a king, a youthful, handsome man with a good heart and a loving wife; unfortunately he was unskilled in being king. As his kingdom began to dwindle, sadness overtook Nala allowing the goddess Kali to possess him. She caused him to lose his land to his brother in a game of dice. Disgraced and humiliated Nala fled into the forest. As it happened, a great fire erupted in the woods burning it all to ashes. As Nala was leaving he heard a cry for help; unwilling to not lend aid he returned to the inferno and came upon Karkotaka. As he lifted the NAGA and broke the curse, they were able to flee safely. The two became great friends so the god Indra warned Karkotaka that Kali still lingered in the king. The NAGA lashed out and envenomed Nala; his poison caused the man's body to shrivel and deform, no longer recognizable as the handsome youth he was. Karkotaka told his friend it was not a betrayal but rather so, in perfect disguise, he could go to another land and study leadership under a king and gain enlightenment; once enlightened, Kali would leave of her own free will. Karkotaka then gave him a magical cloak and told Nala, once enlightenment is achieved, to don the cloak as it will restore him to his true form. Nala followed his friend's advice, returned home, reunited with his wife and reclaimed his kingdom.

Source: Niles, *Dragons*, 99–100; Parmeshwaranand, *Encyclopaedic Dictionary of Puranas*, Volume 1, 1113; Vogel, *Indian Serpent-lore*, 80–1

Karshipta

Variations: Karsiptar ("black winged")

In Persian folklore there is a bird named Karshipta dwelling in Heaven because if it lived upon the earth it would be the King of the Birds; he recited the *Avesta* in the language of the birds. It was also sent to spread the faith of Ahura Mazda among the men who had gathered together in order to protect themselves from the harsh winter sent to destroy mankind.

Source: Blavatsky, *Secret Doctrine*, 292; Boyce, *A History of Zoroastrianism*, 90; Darmesteter, *Zend-Avesta*, 20–1

Karura

In Japanese mythology, GARUDA is known as Karura, the mount of Naraen-ten; described as having golden wings and holding a flute, Karura is depicted as hybrid, having a bird's head on a yellow, human body, sometimes with four or eight arms. Karura was the king of the birds and ate NAGAS.

Source: Bakshi, *Hindu Divinities in Japanese Buddhist Pantheon*, 136–8; Thakur, *India and Japan, a Study in Interaction During 5th Cent.-14th Cent. A.D.*, 32, 39–40

Kashchei

Variations: Kashchei the Deathless, Kashchey, Koschei, Kościej, Koshchey, Koshchei, Koshchiy, Kostěj

A serpentine DRAGON from Russian folklore, Kashchei had managed to make itself nearly immortal by removing its soul and placing it in an egg which it carefully hid; no matter the attack or the amount of damage its body received, its soul was safely hidden and protected. The hero Bulat learned of Kaschei's secret and was able to discover the location of the egg; when the DRAGON was not near, Bulat took the egg and smashed it, instantly killing Kashchei. Although Kashchei is described as being a DRAGON with two arms and legs, in some versions of the story he is said to be a human magician.

Source: De Kirk, *Dragonlore*, 42; Haase, *Greenwood Encyclopedia of Folktales and Fairy Tales: Q-Z*, 874, 880; Rose, *Giants, Monsters, and Dragons*, 204

Kashehotapolo

In the folklore of the Choctaw people of the southeastern United States of America the kashehotapolo ("woman call") is a creature said to live in the marshes and swampy woodlands. Described as a humanoid monster with an undersized head, and the feet and legs of a deer, whenever the kashehotapolo sees a hunter in its area it will release an ear-piercing shriek and immediately flee. Sometimes the kashehotapolo is mistaken by hunters to be the NALUSA FALAYA.

Source: Bastian, *Handbook of Native American Mythology*, 136; Rose, *Giants, Monsters, and Dragons*, 204

Al Kaswa

The favorite camel of the Muslim prophet Mahomet was named al Kaswa ("crop-eared"); the location where it knelt down was taken as a sign for God and, according to legend, the mosque at Koba now covers the location. It was one of the ten animals allowed to enter into Paradise in Muslim mythology. Al Kaswa was also the mount Mahomet rode into several battles as well as on his last pilgrimage to Mecca.

Source: Brewer, *Dictionary of Phrase and Fable*, 205; Holland, *Mohammed*, 84, 90

Kataore

A TANIWHA from the folklore of New Zealand, the DRAGON Kataore was the would-be pet of a chief named Tangaroa-mihi near the Rotorua region; unfortunately the creature was not tame and soon began attacking people. When not marauding, he lived in a cave overlooking a route well used by travelers, a perfect location for his ambush tactics. One day, according to the story, he attacked and consumed a high born maiden by the name of Tuhikarapapa; her husband-to-be, Reretoi, was so angered by his beloved's death he organized a hunting party, including local *tohunga* ("wizards") to drain the creature's strength, in order to slay the murderous Kataore. A DRAGON slayer and hero, Pitaka happened to be in the area and joined in with the hunting party. By use of cunning and stealth he slipped unseen and unheard into the DRAGON'S lair as it slept and carefully placed several nooses about its neck. When he gave the signal, the men outside began to pull the DRAGON out of its cave. Kataore's own wild thrashing caused the beast to strangle itself to death. The TANIWHA was roasted and a great feast was held.

Source: De Kirk, *Dragonlore*, 61, 105; Reed, *Reed Book of Māori Mythology*, 265–8

Katmir

Variations: Ketmir, Kratim, al Raqim, Qatmir

A donkey-sized collie from Moslem folklore, Katmir was a dog said to belong to one of the Seven Youths who were walled up in a cavern and went to sleep to avoid capture from Emperor Decius' men. Said to possess the divine ability of human speech, the dog said to his human companions, "I love those who are dear unto God; go to sleep, therefore, and

I will guard you"; the faithful Katmir did so for three-hundred and nine years. It is a popular belief carrying a scrap of paper with his name written upon it will act as a charm of protection while traveling. Upon his death, Katmir was given entrance into Heaven, a rare privilege.

Source: Brewer, *Dictionary of Phrase and Fable*, 205; Choron, *Planet Dog*, 10, 179; Finch, *Gentleman's Magazine* Volume CCLXXIX, 528

Katoblepon

The Roman author and rhetoric teacher Aelianus described the katoblepon ("down looker") of Libya as being a heavy hoofed species of animal, about the size of a bull, which grazes upon poisonous roots, and has a grim expression upon their face. The katoblepon are said to walk with their head hung low. The face of the animal sports oxen-like eyes but are bloodshot and narrow, set beneath high-arching bushy eyebrows. Katoblepon have a pungent and rank smelling breath so foul it lingers in the air about them; its stench is so powerful any animal which gets within the noxious air will lose their voice and fall over, convulsing until they die.

Source: Irby-Massie, *Greek Science of the Hellenistic Era*, 272; McNamee, *Desert Bestiary*, 22

Katraresh, plural: katraveshi

A type of cannibalistic monster, the katraresh ("the four-eared one") appears in southern Albanian folklore; the word is also used to refer to a filthy or unwashed person.

Source: Elsie, *Dictionary of Albanian Religion, Mythology, and Folk Culture*, 151

Katsura-otoko

Japanese tradition claims to look too long upon the moon is to invite danger as a being known as Katsura-otoko would call to people; those unlucky enough to see him would die soon thereafter.

Source: Japan Society of London, *Transactions and Proceedings*, Volume 9, 25

Katytayuuq

A type of monster from Inuit folklore, the katytayuuq of the Hudson Bay region in Canada are said to be humanoid in appearance but have small, tattooed heads; their breasts are located above their mouths on their cheeks and their genitalia are located beneath their mouth. They and their male counterparts known as the TUNNITUAQRUK scavenge behind humans on the trail searching out scraps.

Source: Rose, *Giants, Monsters, and Dragons*, 204

Kaukas

In Lithuanian folklore the kaukas is a species of household spirit (see HOUSE-SPIRIT) said to bring good luck. However, in the Baltic, the kaukas is said to be a flying DRAGON with a fiery tail well known to be the guardian of hidden treasure.

Source: Dixon-Kennedy, *Encyclopedia of Russian and Slavic Myth and Legend*, 148; Lurker, *Dictionary of Gods and Goddesses, Devils and Demons*, 101

Kauravya

A NAGA from Hindu mythology, Kauravya was the king of the NAGA of Manipur; his daughter ULUPI married a Pandavan prince named Arjuna; to this day the royal family of Manipur claim to be descendants of the NAGA.

Source: Garg, *Encyclopaedia of the Hindu World*, Volume 3, 615; Vogel, *Indian Serpent-Lore*, 191

Keelut

Variations: Ke'lets

In the beliefs of the Inuit people of Alaska, United States of America and Canadian arctic regions, the keelut is a malevolent, massive, hairless dog. Similar to the BLACK DOG of British folklore the keelut was a nocturnal predator, following and eventually attacking travelers.

Source: Fanthorpe, *Satanism and Demonology*, 29; Rose, *Giants, Monsters, and Dragons*, 204; Zell-Ravenheart, *Wizard's Bestiary*, 56

Kelpie, the

Variations: Afanc, ANTHROPOPHAGI, AUGHISKY, BÄCKAHÄSTEN ("brook horse"), Each Uisge, Eisges, ENDROP, FUATH, Goborchinu, HNIKUR, NECK, Nekke, Nick, Nicker, Nickur, Nikyr, Nix, Nuggies, SHOOPILTEE, Shoney, Sjofn, Uisges, Water-Spirit

Originating in Scottish folklore and spreading into Cornish, Icelandic, Irish, German, Orkney, and Shetland fairy folklore, the kelpie is a species of cannibalistic, foul-tempered, and malicious FAIRY ANIMAL. Rarely seen, when fairies or humans are not available to consume the kelpie will kill deer which wander too near its watery home.

In Ireland the kelpie is known as the AUGHISKY or the EACH UISCE and are described as looking like web-footed women with the mane and tail of a horse; however, in Scotland the kelpie is said to look like a horse wandering along the seashore; it first allows humans to ride upon it before taking them off into the ocean and drowning them. Scottish kelpies also have the ability to shape-shift and can appear as a hairy man.

There are several names the kelpie is known by in Iceland, such as the HNIKUR, NECK, Nickur, Nin-

ner, and Water-Spirit to name a few. There, this FAIRY ANIMAL appears as an apple-grey horse with reversed hooves hunting along the seashore.

Interestingly, there are no kelpies in the Avon, the Thames, or any other English streams.

There is also the belief it is possible to capture and tame a kelpie by managing to get a bridle over its head; however, this is a difficult and dangerous task as the kelpie is physically powerful and strong and has a singularly willful nature. If a kelpie is bridled it will serve its new master well and make for a wonderful and versatile horse.

Source: Briggs, *Encyclopedia of Fairies*, 246; Froud, *Faeries*, 109; Keightley, *World Guide to Gnomes, Fairies, Elves, and Other Little People*, 162, 360, 370, 385; McCoy, *Witch's Guide to Faery Folk*, 253–4

Kergrim

Variations: Grim

In British folklore a kergrim is said to be a churchyard demon or GHOUL. Believed to be creatures of evil, the kergrim fortunately cannot travel too far beyond the borders of the churchyard where their body is buried.

Source: Harries, *Ghost Hunter's Road Book*, 86; Rose, *Spirits, Fairies, Leprechauns, and Goblins, an Encyclopedia*, 178

Kerkes

Variations: Anka

A PHOENIX from Turkish folklore, the kerkes would, according to the oldest traditions, live for one thousand years, after which it would beat its wings to make an all-consuming fire to engulf its body. Once the kerkes has been completely consumed and nothing remains but its ashes it is believed Almighty God then restores the ashes to life. This process can be repeated up to seven times, for then is the arrival of the Day of Judgment.

Source: Blavatsky, *Anthropogenesis*, 617; Van den Broek, *Myth of the Phoenix*, 205, 213; Zell-Ravenheart, *Wizard's Bestiary*, 56

Kertr

In Norse mythology, Snorri Sturlson (1179–1241), the Icelandic historian, poet, and politician, writes the horse Kertr ("candle") was the preferred mount of Bjarr in his translation of *Prose Edda*.

Source: Grimes, *Norse Myths*, 283; Sturluson, *Prose Edda*, Volume 5, 212

Keshi

Variations: Keshin

A demonic, gigantic, lustful, and savage horse from Hindu mythology, Keshi ("long-haired"), married to the submissive minor goddess Daityasena, was one of the main assassins sent by Mathura the demon king to slay his nephew, the child-god Krishna. Krishna, easily fending off the attacks of the brutal and fierce Keshi, was able to shove both of his arms into the creature's mouth, suffocating it to death; this earned the child god the name of Keshimanthana ("destroyer of Keshi").

Source: Lochtefeld, *Illustrated Encyclopedia of Hinduism: A-M*, 364–5; Williams, *Handbook of Hindu Mythology*, 114

Kesprap Kamui

A benevolent bird from Ainu folklore, the kesprap kamui was said to have the most beautiful plumage and a pitying heart.

Source: Munro, *Ainu Creed and Cult*, n.pag.

Khalkotauroi

In Greek mythology the khalkotauroi were the pair of bronze-hoofed bulls the hero Jason needed to wrestle into submission in order to yoke them to a plough. The bulls, fierce, fire-breathing beasts, grazed upon the Range of Ares (Mars). Jason needed the bulls to pull the plough in order to sow the teeth of a DRAGON in order to raise up the SPARTI and defeat them. If these tasks are completed the King will give him the Golden Fleece.

Source: Apollonius, Argonautica, 116; Hunter, *Argonautica of Apollonius*, 16

Khara

Variations: Three-Legged Ass

A gigantic three-legged ass from ancient Persian mythology, Khara was said to stand in the middle of the cosmic ocean Vourukasha, where he, by the use of his sharp eyes, overcomes evil and assists in ordering the world. Khara is described as having an immense white body as large as a mountain, an alicorn (a single horn) atop his head like a UNICORN, nine mouths, and six eyes—two in the typical position, an additional set on the top of its head, and another pair on its hump. This creature consumes spiritual food and defecates amber. Its horn enables it to purify the sea of all uncleanliness.

Source: Coulter, *Encyclopedia of Ancient Deities*, 268; Hopkins, *History of Religions*, 387; Warner, *World of Myths*: Volume Two, 98; Zell-Ravenheart, *Wizard's Bestiary*, 94

Kheglen

In Siberian mythology Kheglen was the cosmic elk (or moose) who would steal the sun, causing winter; she was then relentlessly pursued across the sky by Main Mangi the great bogatyr (or bear), who eventually catches and kills her, releasing the sun and causing the onset of spring.

Source: Blazer, *Shamanic Worlds*, 188; Walter, *Shamanism*, 550; Zell-Ravenheart, *Wizard's Bestiary*, 56

Khepra

Variations: He Who Is Coming Into Being, Kheper, Khepere, Khepri

In ancient Egyptian mythology Khepra was the cosmic scarab beetle who created the sun and pushes it across the sky each day just as the dung beetle pushes its ball of dung; it also created the earth from one of its dirt balls as well as itself. Khepra, the controller of celestial motion, is only occasionally depicted as an anthropomorphic god; it is symbolic of the land of Egypt and the sun at dawn.

Source: Bunson, *Encyclopedia of Ancient Egypt*, 201; Hart, *Routledge Dictionary of Egyptian Gods and Goddesses*, 84–5; Zell-Ravenheart, *Wizard's Bestiary*, 56

Kheti

According to ancient Egyptian mythology Kheti ("worm") was a monstrous serpent found in the eighth section, or hour, of Tuat, the Underworld. Ordered by the god Horus, Kheti breathed fire upon those who went against the rights connected with the god Osiris, destroying both their bodies as well as their souls. Upon the back of Kheti stand seven gods. In *The Text of Unas* there is a magical spell which when performed will cause the destruction of monstrous beasts and serpents alike; Kheti would be affected by this spell.

Source: Budge, *Gods of the Egyptians*, 192; Coulter, *Encyclopedia of Ancient Deities*, 32; Mercatante, *Who's Who in Egyptian Mythology*, 84

Kholkian Drakon

Variations: Colchis DRAGON

The DRAKON from ancient Greek mythology which guarded the Golden Fleece while it was a holding of King Ares of Colchis, the Kholkian Drakon was described as being as long and wide as a ship, having endless enormous coils, its sinuous armored body completely covered with hard and dry scales. The DRAKON lived in a sacred grove where hanging from a sacred tree was the Golden Fleece; the DRAKON also lounged in the branches of the same tree. According to the story, Medea by use of her magic and potions put the sleepless DRAKON in a deep slumber so Jason or she could slay it. In some versions of the story, the DRAKON first swallowed Jason whole and then soon disgorged him, presumably because of the ointment Medea had the foresight to cover the hero's body in.

Source: Garry, *Archetypes and Motifs in Folklore and Literature*, 75; Ogden, *Dragons, Serpents, and Slayers in the Classical and Early Christian Worlds*, 126–7

Khrafstra

In Persian and Zoroastrian folklore a khrafstra ("predator" or "wild beast") is a generic term for any sort of injurious creature harmful to crops, domestic animals, and mankind. Usually the khrafstra were horrid, monstrous terrestrial creatures which were ultimately slain by the hero of the tale. To kill one is an act of merit since it reduces the amount of evil in the world. Such creatures include all the beasts of prey, DRAGONS, insects, monsters, rodents and serpents as well as AZI, cats, frogs, lions, lizards, mice, spiders, tigers, and tortoises. Birds, dogs, and hedgehogs would never fall into this category.

Source: Boyce, *A History of Zoroastrianism*, 90–1; De Jong, *Traditions of the Magi*, 338, 340

Khyung

Variations: Khyungpo

In Tibetan folklore Khyung was the cosmic eagle; it was hatched from its egg fully grown and was symbolic of latent potential and true enlightenment. Khyung was the mount of the gods and the patron spirit of lamas and mediums. In art it is depicted as having horns on its head, a humanoid body, four arms, and outstretched wings. Khyung is similar to GARUDA from Buddhist and Hindu mythology.

Source: Kværne, *Tibet Bon Religion* 18, 33; Zell-Ravenheart, *Wizard's Bestiary*, 56

K'i-Lin

Variations: KI-LIN, KIRIN

The ancient Chinese author Hwai nan Tsze attempted to prove all creatures are the progeny of the DRAGON. He claimed the k'i-lin, born of the KIEN-MA, gave birth to all quadrupeds and hairy beasts. The chimerical k'i-lin is described as standing twelve feet tall and having the body of a young deer, the hooves of a horse, and the tail of an ox; its body is a bluish-yellow and a single antler or alicorn with a fleshy tip grows from the center of its forehead. Its voice harmonizes with bells and chimes. K'i-lin walk at a regular pace and once they set out in a direction they do not stop and rest until they are certain it is safe. They will not walk upon a living creature nor will they harm growing herbage or be found in the company of other animals. It is an impossible animal to catch as it never falls in a pit trap and cannot be caught in a net. K'i-lin are not born but rather spontaneously generate. They are exceedingly rare and only appear when the reign of royalty is prosperous; DRAGONS are sighted more often than the k'i-lin.

Source: De Visser, *Dragon in China and Japan*, 65; Eastlake, *Transactions*, Volumes 13–14, 217

Ki-Lin (chee-lin)

Variations: Chai Tung, Ch'i-Lin Lin, Hai Chiai, Kilin, Ky-Lin, Lin-Che-Chi, Lu, Man Chw'en, Qilin, Tso'po (Tibetan)

One of the species of UNICORN described in Chinese folklore, the ki-lin is the most popular and well-known of them; it is also one of the four animals said to live in the heavens, the other three being the DRAGON, the PHOENIX, and the tortoise. The ki-lin was first mentioned in the Bamboo Books, and then, only in passing: a notation states that during the rule of Hwanf Ti (2697 BC) ki-lin were seen in the parks. Their appearance was generally accepted to be a sign of a benevolent monarch in power as they only left their heavenly abode to herald the birth of a wise person, (as one did for the birth of Confucius) or to intervene in human affairs, such as when a ki-lin taught Emperor Fu His the secrets of the written language. Of the three hundred and sixty kinds of hairy animals documented, the ki-lin was said to be the chief of them all; it was believed if one of its kind could be tamed, all other beasts would lose their fear and not show terror; this seems unlikely, as the ki-lin is incapable of being captured.

Source: Dudley, *Unicorns*, 13–4; Gould, *Mythical Monsters*, 348, 349, 351, 352, 362; Johnsgard, *Dragons and Unicorns*, 85, 159; Zell-Ravenheart, *Companion for the Apprentice Wizard*, 178

Kiai-Lin

The ancient Chinese author Hwai nan Tsze, in his attempt to prove how all creatures are the progeny of the DRAGON, shows the Piscean kiai-lin as the progenitor of the KIAO-LUNG.

Source: De Visser, *Dragon in China and Japan*, 65, 72

Kiai-T'an

The ancient Chinese author Hwai nan Tsze, in his attempt to prove how all creatures are the progeny of the DRAGON, shows the kiai-t'an as the progenitor of the SIEN-LUNG.

Source: De Visser, *Dragon in China and Japan*, 65, 72

Kiao

Variations: DRAGON-CARP, Gyoryu, Horse Lasso

According to the sixth century author Jen Fang who wrote the *Shus I ki*, the kiao ("carp DRAGON") is one stage of a DRAGON's development. Fang writes the earliest stage of development is that of a water snake, and after five hundred years it transforms into a kiao; after another one thousand years it transforms into a LUNG, and after another five hundred years transforms again, this time into a KIOH-LUNG; finally after one thousand more years it transforms into its final stage of development, the YING-YING.

Numerous books, such as the *Kia-Yu* ("Family Discourse"), *P'i-Ya*, *Shan Hai King*, *Shuh-I-Ki*, *Siang Shu* ("Book of Physiognomy"), and the *Yueh-*

kiu ("*Divisions of Seasons*") offer a line or two of information; although individually they do not say much, collectively they add the Kiao is created when a fish reaches the age of three thousand six hundred years old; it transforms into this species of hornless DRAGON. It is described as being five cubits wide (a *cubit* is the distance from a man's elbow to the tip of his middle finger), having the body of a serpentine DRAGON, a small head set upon a delicate neck covered with white ornamentation, eye-brows uniting over its eyes, and a mouth large enough to swallow a man. By use of its flexible body and the fleshy rings of its tail it constricts around its prey before ripping off the head. It is said to have green bones and lays eggs with a capacity of three catties. The Kiao will not live in a pond with another of its kind already occupying it and autumn is an unlucky time for it.

Source: De Visser, *Dragon in China and Japan*, 72; Gould, *Dragons, Unicorns, and Sea Serpents*, 407

Kiao-Lung

Variations: HORNED DRAGON

According to the sixth century author Jen Fang who wrote the *Shus I ki*, the kiao-lung ("crossed reptile") is one stage of a DRAGON's development. Fang writes the earliest stage of development is of a water snake, and after five hundred years it transforms into a KIAO; after another one thousand years it transforms into a LUNG, and after another five hundred years it transforms into a kioh-lung; finally after one thousand more years it transforms into its final stage of development, the YING-YING.

However, Hwai nan Tsze, in his attempt to prove the lineage of all creatures descends from the DRAGON, shows the kiao-lung as being the progeny of the kiai-lin, a type of fish.

In addition to having horns at this stage the kiao-lung whose transformation takes place in the deepest water also has scales; if there is a school of three hundred and sixty fishes, it will dominate them and take control, flying away with the school. These DRAGONS prefer to live in rivers but will not inhabit any marshes where people maintain the water level in order to raise fish.

Source: De Kirk, *Dragonlore*, 24; De Visser, *Dragon in China and Japan*, 65, 72, 73, 76, 77; Gould, *Dragons, Unicorns, and Sea Serpents*, 394;

Kiau

Variations: Chiao

A classification of DRAGON from Chinese mythology, the kiau tend to live in marshes but on occasion will take up residency in a den in the mountains.

Source: Barber, *Dictionary of Fabulous Beasts*, 92; Forbes, *Illustrated Book of Dragons and Dragon Lore*, n.pag.; Johnsgard, *Dragons and Unicorns*, 155

Kibuka

Variations: Kibuuka

In Gandan mythology Kibuka is the BALUBAALE of War; it is one of some fifty different NATURE SPIRITS under the dominion of the god Katonda. Kibuka, deified in some African regions, was contacted by people for advice and inspiration on defense and warfare.

Source: Cotterell, *Dictionary of World Mythology*, 246; Coulter, *Encyclopedia of Ancient Deities*, 271; Lynch, *African Mythology, A to Z*, 58

Kickle Snifter

Variations: Hickle Snifter, Kicklesnifter

Originating in the lumberjack communities of the developing United States of America, the thumb-sized kickle snifter, one of the FEARSOME CRITTERS, was especially well-known in the Minnesota and Wisconsin regions. They were said to live in the beards of men as well as in circular lakes. The ones living in the beard were always moving about, as the facial hair tickled the men, causing them to continuously scratch and pull at their beard.

Source: Colombo, *Colombo's Book of Marvels*, 93; Rose, *Giants, Monsters, and Dragons*, 119, 208

Kien-Ma

The ancient Chinese author Hwai nan Tsze, in his attempt to prove how all creatures are the progeny of the DRAGON, shows the kien-ma as being the progeny of the YING LING and the progenitor of the K'I-LIN.

Source: De Visser, *Dragon in China and Japan*, 65

Kien-Sie

The ancient Chinese author Hwai nan Tsze, in his attempt to prove how all creatures are the progeny of the DRAGON, shows the kien-sie as being the progeny of the KWUN-KENG and the progenitor of all scaled fishes.

Source: De Visser, *Dragon in China and Japan*, 65

Kigatilik

In Inuit mythology Kigatilik are a species of vicious and violent fanged demons or monsters preying upon shamans eating their hearts and organs. These creatures, described as powerfully built beasts covered with thick white fur and sporting long claws and teeth, are similar to a tribe of spirits known as Claw People. The Kigatilik will also work to corrupt a person, turning them from their religious beliefs by shape-shifting into a pleasing form in order to trick a person into committing adultery and speaking out against the faith. These creatures live in icy water.

Source: Grimal, *Larousse World Mythology*, 447; Maberry, *Vampire Universe*, 175; Turner, *Dictionary of Ancient Deties*, 271

Kihawahine

In Hawaiian mythology Kihawahine is the primary DRAGON goddess possessing miraculous powers; she was a descendant of the primordial DRAGON goddess MO-O-INANEA. Kihawahine would sit upon a rock called Lauoho Rock located in the middle of Haneo'o fishpond where she would comb out her long hair.

Source: Craig, *Dictionary of Polynesian Mythology*, 50, 114; Monaghan, *Encyclopedia of Goddesses and Heroines*, 155; Westervelt, *Legends of Gods and Ghosts*, 258

Kikituk (kee-KEE-tuk)

Variations: Qivittoq, Tupilak, Tupilaq, Tupilat

From the demonology of the Inuit of Alaska, North America, comes the demonic creature known as the kikituk. Using animal flesh and bones, cloth, and human flesh and bones, a sorcerer makes a *peat* doll. Then a magical charm is sung over it and as the doll becomes a living being and grows larger, it must be suckled on the sorcerer's sexual organs. Each kikituk looks different, as the sorcerer makes its creature to suit his needs or fancy. These demons are usually sent to kill the enemies of the sorcerer who made it; however, if made by a shaman, it will seek out the demon of illness which is attacking his people. Only a truly evil or utterly reckless sorcerer would set a kikituk free by releasing it into a body of water in order to cause random terror to those who walk along the shore.

This demonic creature is very similar to the TUPILAK of the Inuit of Greenland.

Source: Jones, *Evil in Our Midst*, 26–31; Kleivan, *Eskimos, Greenland and Canada*, 21–2; Lyon, *Encyclopedia of Native American Healing*, 17, 135

Kiko

A type of KITSUNE (fox spirit) from Japanese mythology, the kiko ("ghost fox") is used by Yamabushi ("one who lies in the mountains"), ascetic mountain hermits, in divinations; generally, it is benign to humans.

Source: Maberry, *Vampire Universe*, 177; Picken, *Essentials of Shinto*, 124

Kiko Myojin

A KAMI fox from Japanese folklore and mythology, Kiko Myojin ("venerable fox god") was a gracious and venerable messenger of Inari, the god of

commercial success. CHOKO, the King of all Foxes, is a descendant of his.

Source: Picken, *Essentials of Shinto*, 124

Kilyakai

Described as being a hybrid of demons, NATURE SPIRITS, and Neanderthals, the Kilyakai of Papua New Guinea are a tribe of small and incredibly evil humanoids living in the dense jungle. These maligned beings are said to sneak into a town and steal children and pigs when not hiding in bushes and shooting people with darts infected with malaria. The Kilyakai kidnap children in order to imbue their own demonic nature into them in order to populate their race.

Source: Lawrence, *Gods, Ghosts and Men in Melanesia*, 153; Maberry, *Vampire Universe*, 175

Kin Ryu

A golden DRAGON from Japanese folklore, Kin Ryu is considered to be of less importance than other DRAGONS.

Source: Bates, *All About Chinese Dragons*, 100

Kinabalu

A shimmering blue-scaled DRAGON from the island of Borneo folklore, Kinabalu, who lived on Mount Kinabalu, Borneo, was said to be in possession of a great pearl of wisdom which was greatly coveted by the emperor of China. Sending his two sons to retrieve it, Wee Ping and Wee San, only the latter came up with a plan to steal it. Waiting for Kinabalu to leave his lair in search of food, Wee Sans used a kite to fly to the mountain top entrance and replaced the pearl with a counterfeit. As he fled back to his ship, the DRAGON discovered the truth and gave chase. Wee San ordered his men to preheat a cannonball and then to fire it at the creature. Believing it was his pearl being sent back to him, Kinabalu intercepted the cannon ball in mid flight, swallowed it, and died from massive internal injuries. Wee Ping took the pearl from his brother and told his father it was he who retrieved it; Wee Sans, not wanting to cause trouble with his brother, left China and eventually became the ruler of Brunei in Borneo.

Source: De Kirk, *Dragonlore*, 35

Kingmingoarkulluk

A species of NATURE SPIRITS (or a singular being, sources conflict) from Inuit mythology, the tiny kingmingoarkulluk were said to sing whenever approached by a human.

Source: Coulter, *Encyclopedia of Ancient Deities*, 271; Guirand, *New Larousse Encyclopedia of Mythology*, 426

Kingu

Variations: Kingugu

A DRAGON and the consort of the DRAGON and goddess TIAMAT from Babylonian mythology, Kingu was given charge of the Tablets of Destiny by his queen. Kingu was born of TIAMAT as her youngest son while she was enraged over the death of her husband Apsu; she married him, making Kingu her consort, and then appointed him as her Supreme Commander of War. Kingu was then the father to TIAMAT's newest generation of monstrous offspring, such as DRAGON, Man Scorpion, Mad Dog, and Worm. As the general of this terrifying army, Kingu leads his brood to war against the gods. TIAMAT's eldest son Marduk steps forward, offering to take command of the gods' army if he is appointed the first king of Babylon. No sooner than he is crowned, Marduk is on the battlefield; he manages to kill TIAMAT, capture Kingu, and win the war. To restore Order to the world, Kingu is sacrificed; his arteries are sliced opened and his blood creates humanity to serve as the servants of the gods.

Source: Coulter, *Encyclopedia of Ancient Deities*, 272; Eason, *Fabulous Creatures, Mythical Monsters, and Animal Power Symbols*, 45; Smith, *Complete Idiot's Guide to World Mythology*, 31–2

Kinie Ger

A ruthless and murderous beast from Australian Aborigine mythology, Kinie Ger did little else but commit acts of ruthless murder. Described as having the body, ears, head, and mouth of a cat with human arms and legs, Kinie Ger did not have the mental capacity of rational thought or reason nor did he have empathy, love, or pity. The only pleasure Kinie Ger took in life was killing; he delighted in watching the life-blood leave a gaping wound, as eyes no longer focused on the world but stared vacantly ahead, and the body shuddered with its last breath.

Seeking to avenge the deaths of their children, Crow and Owl conspired together to kill Kinie Ger; they laid a trap for him at the water hole and waited patiently for him to arrive. With all of their strength, they threw their spears at him and each hit a vital spot, killing him before he even had the opportunity to drink. Wanting to be sure the famously cruel Kinie Ger was dead, they removed their spears and hacked his body to bits before setting it ablaze and scattering the ashes.

Source: Reed, *Aboriginal Stories of Australia*, 115–117; Smith, *Myths and Legends of the Australian Aborigines*, 101–04

Kinnaras

Variations: Kimpurushas

Celestial musicians to the god of wealth Kuvera of Hindu mythology, the kinnaras are demi-gods created from the limbs of Brahma and are described as having human bodies but the heads of horses, almost the opposite of the Greek CENTAUR. Kinnaras are listed as being one of the eight classes of celestial beings in Hindu mythology.

Source: De Visser, *Dragon in China and Japan*, xiii; Garrett, *Classical Dictionary of India*, 335; Hargreaves, *Hargreaves New Illustrated Bestiary*, 67

Kioh-Lung

In Chinese folklore the kioh-lung ("HORNED DRAGON") is the fourth of the five stages of a DRAGON's development; it is achieved after two thousand years of growth and development. According to the folklore, the cycle begins when the creature is born as a water snake; after five hundred years it develops into a KIAO (see KIOH-LUNG), a Piscean DRAGON. Then after one thousand years has passed it transforms into a lung ("DRAGON"). Once another five hundred years has passed the lung develops into a kioh lung and finally after one thousand years more it reaches its full potential as a ying lung ("winged DRAGON").

Source: De Visser, *Dragon in China and Japan*, 72; Picart, *Speaking of Monsters*, 55

Kioh Twan

One of the species of UNICORN described in Chinese folklore, the kioh twan was described in the classic *Yuen Kien Lei Hau* as having the appearance of a greenish deer with the tail of a horse, and an alicorn growing above its nose; this creature was said to be able to cover eighteen thousand *li* in a single day, approximately 5,592 miles (8,046 meters).

Source: Gould, *Mythical Monsters*, 348, 359; Rose, *Giants, Monsters, and Dragons*, 376; South, *Mythical and Fabulous Creatures*, 12

Kirata

A race of hybrid beings said to live in the central Himalayas, the Kirata were described in the *Ramayana* as literally being half human and half tiger; their upper body is of a tiger and their lower half human. The Kirata were foresters and mountaineers who ate a diet of raw fish and were said to live in the water. The females of the species were described as being "gold-colored and pleasant to behold" even with the sharply pointed hair knots they wore.

Source: Dowson, *Classical Dictionary of Hindu Mythology and Religion*, 158; Vālmīki, *Ramayana of Valmiki*, 142, 300; Zell-Ravenheart, *Wizard's Bestiary*, 57

Kirin

Variations: Ki-Rin, Kirien, Qilin

A type of gentle and proud species of chimerical UNICORN from Japanese folklore, the kirin is described as being covered with multi-colored scales, having the body of a deer, the hooves of a horse, the tail of an ox, and a single, short alicorn atop its DRAGON head. On occasion, it was described as looking like a lion with an alicorn upon its head. Able to determine a person's guilt or innocence, it was said judges would, when able, use a kirin to assist them in making a decision in a difficult case. The kirin would know who the guilty party was and using its horn, kill them.

Source: Dudley, *Unicorns*, 14–15; Garry, *Archetypes and Motifs in Folklore and Literature*, 68; Gould, *Dragons, Unicorns, and Sea Serpents*, 357, 372

Kirmira

A RAKASHASA from Hindu mythology, the monstrous ASURAS Kirmira threatened to consume Bhima if he and his party attempted to enter into the Kamyaka forest. A terrific battle ensued with Kirmira and the prince, as they hurled uprooted trees at one another. Eventually the son of the god of the wind strangled Kirmira and broke all the bones in his body.

Source: Dowson, *Classical Dictionary of Hindu Mythology and Religion, Geography, History, and Literature*, 50, 159

Kirni

The kirni was a GRIFFIN-like bird from Japanese mythology.

Source: Barber, *Dictionary of Fabulous Beasts*, 74, 93; Rose, *Giants, Monsters, and Dragons*, 210

Kirtimukha

A demonic and terrible creature of Hindu mythology, Kirtimukha ("mask of glory") was created by Shiva, the god of asceticism and flesh eaters, to fight Rahu who at one time opposed him. According to the story, when Rahu saw the horrific leonine Kirtimukha he begged for mercy; Shiva granted it but the KRAVYAD's demand for a meal needed to be fulfilled. Shiva offered up his feet in sacrifice but Kirtimukha did not stop there; rather it consumed his entire body leaving only the god's head behind. The image of Kirtimukha is often used as the main decorative element on a temple tower.

Source: Lochtefeld, *Illustrated Encyclopedia of Hinduism: A-M*, 368; Seth, *Gods and Goddesses of India*, 44; Zell-Ravenheart, *Wizard's Bestiary*, 57

Kishi, plural: makishi

A species of malevolent monster from Angolan folklore, the hill-dwelling kishi has two faces, one of a handsome man and the other of a ravenous hyena it hides by growing its hair long or by wearing a headdress. Alluring and charming, the kishi enters into a village, courts the most attractive woman it can and lures her off to a secluded location where it reveals its true face, that of the hyena. The kishi will terrorize its victim before killing and consuming her as it needs to feed off of the fear of the person as much as it needs to eat the flesh. Brave, crafty, cunning, and strong, the kishi has extremely powerful lockable jaws which guarantee its first bite is always fatal. Fortunately the kishi can be warded off with fire and magic need not be employed in its destruction, as ordinary weapons can kill it; however, it is very unlikely it could ever be killed in one-on-one combat. According to the Ambundu tribe of Angola, it was a kishi which killed the cultural hero Kimanaueze.

Source: Lynch, *African Mythology, A to Z*, 86; Maberry, *Vampire Universe*, 175–77

Kitsune (KIT-soon-nay)

Variations: Huli jing, Ki-Tsune

The kitsune ("come always"), a type of lewd and wanton species of demon from Japanese demonology, is rarely seen in its true form, a fox or humanoid fox, as it usually appears as a beautiful woman in order to better prey upon men. This demonic creature commits terrible acts of mischief, such as cutting off women's hair and shaving men's heads while they sleep. It lures travelers astray and possesses humans. If, while in human form, a kitsune drinks too much wine, it will revert to its true form.

These beings have the ability to cast magic and cause rain during bright and sunny days. It can shape-shift into human form if it twitches its tail, places a skull on its head, and bows to the moon. If the skull does not fall off, it becomes a bewitchingly beautiful woman. Once transformed, it will seduce a man and drain his energy from him.

An annual festival called *Kitsune-okuri* ("fox-expelling") is held in the Totomi province of Japan each January 14th to prevent their attacks for the coming year. Priests lead a procession of villagers carrying straw foxes which are taken outside of town and buried.

Source: Bathgate, *Fox's Craft in Japanese Religion and Folklore*, 18–20, 34; Mack, *Field Guide to Demons, Fairies, Fallen Angels, and Other Subversive Spirits*, 128–30; Rosen, *Mythical Creatures Bible*, 255, 370

Kiwahkw

Variations: Ice Giants

In the mythology of the Maliseet-Passamaquoddy people, the kiwahkw ("cannibal ice GIANTS") was a race of fearsome and strong anthropophagous (man-eating) and cannibalistic creatures; the females of the species were said to be more deadly than their male counterparts. It was believed among the Maliseet-Passamaquoddy when a *metewelen* (a person who has a spirit helper or FAMILIAR; a witch) was killed by another *metewelen* their body did not decompose but rather remained intact and capable of catching and consuming anyone who ventured too close to it. When the fallen *metewelen* consumed three people it transformed into a kiwahkw. The strength of each kiwahkw was in direct proportion to the size of the ice heart within its body.

Source: Rose, *Giants, Monsters, and Dragons*, 187; Sturtevant, *Handbook of North American Indians*, 132

Kiyo

Variations: Kiyohime

A symbol of power and vengeance, the DRAGON Kiyo of Japanese Buddhist folklore was once a woman who fell in love with a traveling priest; they met when he visited the tea house where she worked. Although the priest returned her love, he refused to break his vows. Angered at being spurned the woman learned how to transform herself into a fire-breathing DRAGON at the temple of Kompira so she might seek her revenge. As she flew to the monastery the priest tried to hide himself under a bell, but Kiyo was not fooled and breathed down upon the bell, melting it, and killing the priest.

Source: De Kirk, *Dragonlore*, 31; Roberts, *Japanese Mythology A to Z*, 68

Knight Fish

Variations: Sea Knight

In medieval bestiaries a knight fish was said to have been caught in 1305; it was described as being covered in a complete suit of armor. After three weeks of being held in captivity, it died.

Source: Bassett, *Legends and Superstitions of the Sea and Of Sailors in All Lands and At All Times*, 207

Knucker

Variations: Lyminster, Lyminster Nicor ("water monster"), Lyminister Nucker

A DRAGON from Sussex folklore, Knucker lived in a well named Knucker Hole located in Lyminster; the creature was problematic as it preyed upon livestock and the occasional farmer. Although the DRAGON was eventually slain, there are a number of variations as to how the events unfolded.

In one version the King of Sussex offered his daughter's hand in marriage to the man who killed the beast, an offer accepted and completed by a wandering knight. Another variation tells the tale of a local farm boy by the name of Jim Pulk who outwitted Knucker by baking poison laced pies and leaving them for the DRAGON to find and eat. Although Knucker died, so too did Jim, as during the victory celebration he fell over dead. In yet another telling of the tale, a man by name of Jim Puttock of Wick answers the call to slay Knucker offered by the Mayor of Arundel. Puttock also uses poison but does not die; rather he collects the reward offered. In one final variation, a man named Jim made a gigantic poisonous pie to feed Knucker but did not use enough to kill the monster; fortunately it did make Knucker very sluggish and sleepy and after staggering for an hour, the beast finally collapsed in exhaustion. Taking the opportunity, Jim used his axe to behead the defenseless beast. Jim managed to drag the head back to town as proof of his accomplishments but because he was not of noble blood was not granted the hand of the king's daughter in marriage; rather he was hailed as a hero and offered a tidy sum of money enabling him to live in luxury for the rest of his life. A great feast was held in his honor. When Jim died he was buried at the Church of Saint Mary Magdalene under an impressive gravestone the locals to this day call Slayer's Stone.

Source: De Kirk, *Dragonlore*, 43; Niles, *Dragons*, 133–5; Whitlock, *In Search of Lost Gods*, 24–7

Kogukhpuk

A type of subterranean monstrous being from the folklore of the Inuit people in the area of the Bearing Sea, Alaska, the kogukhpuk ("earth moles") are said to live nearly their entire life below ground, burrowing and tunneling through the earth in search of food, as they are highly photophobic; the sunlight is lethal to them. Only one night a year in the middle of winter do they ever dare to come to the surface.

Source: Rose, *Giants, Monsters, and Dragons*, 211; Zell-Ravenheart, *Wizard's Bestiary*, 58

Kolivilor, plural kolivilori

In Albanian mythology, a kolivilor ("WEREWOLF") is a type of filthy and licentious demon; typically male, these demonic creatures appear during the Twelve Nights of Christmas (December 25 to January 6) to drive herds apart and molest women. Kolivilor can be kept at bay by use of fire, as they are afraid of it.

Source: Elsie, *Dictionary of Albanian Religion, Mythology, and Folk Culture*, 152

Kolowisi

Variations: Palulukong (Hopi)

In Zuni mythology, Kolowisi was described as being an enormous serpentine DRAGON having Piscean fins rather than legs and a pair of horns upon it head; it was considered to be the guardian of freshwater springs.

Source: De Kirk, *Dragonlore*, 50; Tyler, *Pueblo Gods and Myths*, 245

Koma-Inu

Variations: Chinese Lion, Dog Foo, Shishi Dog

Guardian creatures from Japanese mythology, the koma-Inu, a male canine and lion hybrid, protects sacred places and are symbolic of divine protection. Seen in pairs, the male is always situated on the left and female (KARA-SHISHI) always on the right; each is often colored, one blue and one green; the male's mouth is open while the female's is closed. The male's open mouth is saying "*aum*" a word inviting all good things; it also has an alicorn (a single horn) atop its head and its left foot resting upon a highly decorated *chu*. The female, hornless and silent, is cradling a club.

Source: Allen, *Japanese Art Motives*, 53; Ball, *Animal Motifs in Asian Art*, 59

Konaki-Jijii (KOH-nah-kee JEE-jee)

A particularly malicious YŌKAI from Japanese folklore, the konaki-jijii ("old man crying like a baby") preys on Good Samaritans. A shape-shifter, the konaki-jijii assumes the form of an infant or an old man and lies just off the side of the road in remote mountain areas crying; when someone stops to help, the creature increases its density and crushes the person who tried to pick it up and help. Then, assuming the form of a flesh-eating demon, it drastically increases its weight, crushing its victim, and then it makes a meal of its prey. However, if the person somehow manages to survive the crushing attacks of the konaki-jijii they will be rewarded with magical gifts. The konaki-jijii is similar to the OBARIYON.

Source: Frater, *Com's Ultimate Book of Bizarre Lists*, 533; Maberry, *Vampire Universe*, 178; Yoda, *Yokai Attack*, 62–5

Konoha-Tengu

In Japanese mythology the Konoha-Tengu ("small leaf tengu"), a species of TENGU, looks like a man with a long beaklike nose and a red face; they are also said to have wings but are able to conceal them with their supernatural powers.

Source: Rose, *Giants, Monsters, and Dragons*, 356; Smith, *Complete Idiot's Guide to World Mythology*, 219

El Kookooee

Variations: Kukui

A NURSERY BOGIE from Chicano folklore. Parents will warn their children of el kookooee, a mas-

culine BOGEYMAN who preys on children who partake in sexual experimentation.

Source: Castro, *Chicano Folklore*, 74, 136; Leen, *International Perspectives on Chicana/o Studies*, 72

Kore

A child eating demonic creature from Northern Albanian mythology, Kore is used as a NURSERY BOGIE by the people of the Kelmendi tribe. On Easter Sunday lit torches were tossed into the river to symbolically rid the village of his influence.

Source: Elsie, *Dictionary of Albanian Religion, Mythology, and Folk Culture*, 152; Pausanias, *Commentary on Books II-V*, 203

Koresck

In Persian folklore goats are divided into five groups of which sheep and goats form the second class; the group is further divided in five subgroups and the second of them is where the koresck resides. This creature is a mixture of caprine (goatlike) and equine characteristics, noted for its cloven hoofs. It is described as having a large alicorn (a single horn), living apart from other animals, and staying near the tops of hills.

Source: Rose, *Giants, Monsters, and Dragons*, 212; Shepard, *Lore of the Unicorn*, 239; Zell-Ravenheart, *Wizard's Bestiary*, 58

Kornwolf

A species of WEREWOLF from the folklore of Estonia, France, Germany, Hungary, Latvia, Poland, and Russia, the exceptionally cunning and intelligent kornwolf preys on farmers and their families while they work the corn fields. Fortunately, this creature can be destroyed with ordinary weapons, such as a bow and arrow.

Source: Maberry, *Vampire Universe*, 180

Koryo

A fox spirit (KITSUNE) from Japanese mythology, the koryo ("haunting fox") has the ability to bewitch people.

Source: Maberry, *Vampire Universe*, 177; Source: Picken, *Essentials of Shinto*, 124

Kosmatushko

In Russian folklore Kosmatushko ("shaggy horse") was often the name given to a shaggy horse utilized by a *bogatyr* (hero); typically these horses would have some sort of magical or supernatural property. Ultimately the Kosmatushko is essential for the *bogatyr* to complete his task.

Source: Bailey, *Anthology of Russian Folk Epics*, 255, 397

Kosode-no-te (Koh-SOH-day noteh)

A female YŌKAI from Japanese mythology, the kosode-no-te ("haunted kimono robe") is described as an animated short-sleeved kimono; apart from being able to move of its own accord it is not known to do anything more than give people a quality scare.

Source: Yoda, *Yokai Attack*, 182–5

Kotai

According to Shinto mythology a kotai is a regiment of KITSUNE, fox spirits, appearing as human soldiers.

Source: Picken, *Essentials of Shinto*, 124

Koto-Furunushi (KOH-toh FOO-ROO-new-shee)

One of the YŌKAI of Japanese folklore, the koto-furunushi ("old master floor harp") is a sub-species of the TSUKOMOGAMI, as it is an old musical instrument which has taken on a humanoid form. Originating in the second century AD, the story claims after the emperor had a patch of land cleared for an outdoor banquet he was so pleased he left a *koto* (floor harp) as an offering. Instantly the harp transformed into a fully grown camphor tree. Even years after the tree died of natural causes, it was claimed one could still hear the faint plucking of harp strings in the area. On occasion the spirit of the tree rises up, possesses a harp, and transforms into the koto-furunushi. In art the koto-furunushi is typically shown with the BIWA-BOKUBBOKU and the SHAMISEN-CHORO. If encountered these beings are willing to have a musician play them, but if not, they are more than willing to play themselves.

Source: Meyer, *Night Parade of One Hundred Demons*, 212; Yoda, *Yokai Attack*, 106–10

Koyemshi

Variations: Mudheads

In Zuni mythology, the koyemshi were created by the union between a brother and sister; the ten resulting children were born with bulbous lumps on their heads and minimal cranial development, and were impotent. The behavior of the koyemshi is always socially unacceptable. In spite of their conduct, the Zuni revered the koyemshi because they have the ability to bring about the rain and if not properly worshiped, could bring about violent weather.

Source: Bonvillain, *Zuni*, 24–5; Lynch, *Native American Mythology A to Z*, 24

Kraken (crock-en)

Variations: Hafgufe, Krabben, Krabbern, Kraxen, Polyp, Sciu-Crak, Sol Draulen ("sea mischief"), Skykraken

Described by Pliny the elder, the Roman author, natural philosopher, naturalist, and army and naval commander in his work *Natural History* (AD 77), the kraken, which he referred to as a polyp, had a jelly-like body, long tentacles, and a sharp parrot-like beak. It was a fearful and gigantic creature feared by sailors who claimed it to be several miles long and appearing usually out of a calm sea on hot days.

An octopus or squid-like creature about the size of an island, the kraken from Scandinavian mythology was said to rise up from the depths of the ocean and wrap its many tentacles about a ship before pulling it and all hands beneath the waves. When not destroying ships in so obvious a fashion this gigantic SEA SERPENT would create large and dangerous whirlpools also capable of sinking ships.

Source: Barber, *Dictionary of Fabulous Beasts*, 93; Nigg, *Sea Monsters*, 146; Rappoport, *Superstitions of Sailors*, 141–5; Rosen, *Mythical Creatures Bible*, 144; Zell-Ravenheart, *Wizard's Bestiary*, 58

Krampus

Variations: Bartel, Bartelor the Wild Bear, Bellzebub, Belzeniggl, Belznickel, Black Peterm, Black Pit, Buzebergt, Drapp, Fertility Diables, Gumphinkel, Gumphinkel, Hans Muff, Hanstrapp, Knecht Ruprecht, Kneckt Ruprecht, Krampuss, Krampusz, Le Père Fouettard, Pelzebock, Pelznickel, Pelznickel, Rumpelklas, Ruprecht, Schmutzli, Stoppklos

Krampus ("claw") is a dark skinned, demonic looking, goat-faced humanoid in Austrian, Bavarian, Hungarian, and Swiss Christmas traditions which accompanies Saint Nicholas (or Father Christmas, Père Fouettard, Santa Claus, etc.) on his tasks. Described in more modern times as a traditional Christian devil standing seven feet tall, sporting horns atop his head, hairy, with a long tail and lolling tongue, Krampus roams the street dragging chains and sporting a birch switch he threatens to use on naughty children. Following Saint Nicholas' orders Krampus will hand out presents to "good" children and beat with his switch and send bad dreams to the "naughty" ones.

In Austria he is said to be the evil twin of Saint Nicholas arriving there on the fifth of December and leaving birch brooms at the houses of children who did not behave adequately the previous year. In a Dutch myth, Krampus, acting as Saint Nicholas' darker side, once used a birch switch bundle to nearly beat to death a local bishop who had forbidden the singing of yule songs praising the Saint.

Source: Helterbran, *Why Rattlesnakes Rattle*, 115; Moore, *Sacred to Santa*, 159; Scott, *Upside-Down Christmas Tree*, 129–30

Kravyad (CRAV-yad)

In India the word *kravyad* ("flesh eater") refers to anything which consumes flesh, including animals, cannibals, and funeral pyres. There is also a type of vampiric spirit called a kravyad because it feeds off human flesh. It is said to be a hideously ugly thing with teeth made of iron.

Source: Dowson, *Classical Dictionary of Hindu Mythology and Religion, Geography, History, and Literature*, 160; Feller, *Sanskrit Epics' Representation of Vedic Myths*, 91, 117; Macdonell, *Vedic Mythology*, 164; Singh, *Vedic Mythology*, 34–5, 117; Turner, *Dictionary of Ancient Deities*, 26, 275

Kravyada

Dwelling in the Hindu hell known as Maharaurava there is a class of RURŪ known as the kravyada ("eater of flesh"); these carnivorous creatures consume the flesh of men who lived a selfish life and indulged in feeding only their own body.

Source: Bhattacharji, *Fatalism in Ancient India*, 143; Venkatesananda, *Concise Srimad Bhagavatam*, 142

Krenaios

In ancient Greek mythology Krenaios ("water spring") was the name of a CENTAUR.

Source: Colvin, *Cornhill Magazine*, Volume XXXVIII, 296

Kreutzet

Variations: Biaolozar

In the folklore from northwest Russia the kreutzet was a gigantic bird similar to the ROC of Arabic legends. Comparable to an eagle in appearance if not size, it terrorized other birds.

Source: Barber, *Dictionary of Fabulous Beasts*, 95; Rose, *Giants, Monsters, and Dragons*, 213

Krodha

Variations: Krodha-Vasa, Krodhaa, Krodhavasha

In Hindu mythology Krodha ("anger") was one of the many daughters of the rishi Daksha and one of the sister-wives of Kasyapa, a Vedic sage. Krodha was said to be the mother of all KRAVYAD, "sharp-toothed monsters, whether on the earth, amongst the birds, or in the waters, that were devourers of flesh"; this included the Bhutas ("spirits") and the *pishacha*. The collective name for her brood is Krodhavasa.

Source: Dalal, *Hinduism*, 212; Dowson, *Classical Dictionary of Hindu Mythology and Religion, Geography, History, and Literature*, 69; Wilson, *Vishnu Purana*, 74

Kuchisake Onna (KOO-chee SAH-kay OHN-na)

A YŌKAI of Japanese folklore, kuchisake onna ("slit-mouth woman") appeared in urban legends in the 1970s; according to the folktale, there was once a beautiful and vain woman married to (or the concubine of, sources conflict) a jealous warrior. The warrior suspected his lover was cheating on him so he used his sword to slit her mouth open from ear to ear, asking her if others would still find her attractive. Now, Kuchisake Onna wanders the streets with her head partially covered with a veil and asks people "Am I beautiful?" as she reveals her mutilated face. Should the victim panic and run she will give chase wielding a bladed weapon. According to the folklore, she will not be able to rest in peace until someone can honestly answer "yes" to her desperate plea.

Source: Foster, *Pandemonium and Parade*, 160, 190; Yoda, *Yokai Attack*, 150–4

Kuda-Gitsune

Variations: Kanko, KWANKO

A miniature KITSUNE (fox spirit) from Japanese folklore, the kuda-gitsune ("pipe fox") is used by a *yamabushi* (a mystical hermit who lives in the mountains) for divination; the creatures are said to be inserted into pipes for this purpose.

Source: Nozaki, *Kitsuné*, 170; Picken, *Essentials of Shinto*, 124

Kudan

In Japanese folklore a kudan is a creature, typically born of a cow, with the face of a man and the body of a bull; it is an omen "something" is going to happen. The kudan, having the ability to speak, always tells the truth.

Source: Barber, *Dictionary of Fabulous Beasts*, 95; Daniels, *Encyclopaedia of Superstitions, Folklore, and the Occult Sciences of the World*, Volume 2 1361; Hearn, *Glimpses of Unfamiliar Japan*, 567

K'uh-Lung

According to Chinese mythology, k'uh-lung DRAGONS are not born of calcium carbonate type eggs but rather jeweled eggs; they are created from seaweed. Similar to many other types of DRAGONS the k'uh-lung remains in the KIAO-LUNG stage throughout their life. They have webbed feet, more flipper-like than clawed paws. The k'uh-lung are entirely aquatic beings and cannot fly.

Source: De Kirk, *Dragonlore*, 27

Kui

Variations: Kui Yi Zu ("one Kui will be enough"), Yi Zu ("one is enough")

In Chinese mythology the Kui was a divine beast said to live upon Mount Kiubo ("flowing wave") which was killed by Huang Di so he could use its hide to make a drum to defeat Chiyou. The descriptions of the Kui vary greatly in ancient writings but generally it is described as being a grey, hornless, ox-like animal with one leg, jumping slowly to get to where it needs to be. Whenever the kui would come out of or go into the water a storm would follow. The drum made from its hide could be heard for 500 miles.

Source: An, *Handbook of Chinese Mythology*, 33–34; Hung, *Going to the People: Chinese Intellectuals and Folk Literature*, 170

Kujata

In Islamic mythology Kujata is a gigantic bull of nearly unimaginable size and scope. It is described as having four thousand ears, eyes, feet, mouths, noses, and tongues; each of these organs is a five hundred year journey from one to the next. Kujata is forever standing upon the back of an even larger fish called BAHAMUT. Upon the back of Kujata is a solid ruby and upon it stands an ANGEL who is supporting the entire planet earth.

Source: Hargreaves, *Hargreaves New Illustrated Bestiary*, 75; Skyes, *Who's Who in Non-Classical Mythology*, 111; Zell-Ravenheart, *Wizard's Bestiary*, 58

Kuko

An air KITSUNE (fox spirit) from Japanese mythology, the kuko is virtually identical to the TENGU and is extremely malevolent.

Source: Maberry, *Vampire Universe*, 177; Picken, *Essentials of Shinto*, 124

Kuli-Ana

In ancient Sumerian mythology, Kuli-Ana was one of the many monsters slain by the warrior god Ninurta. Little is known of this creature other than Gudea, a ruler of Lagash (ca. 2100 BC), referred to it, and the other monsters vanquished by Ninurta, as the SLAIN HEROES; he elevated them all to the status of god and made a place of worship for them in the temple.

Source: Ataç, *Mythology of Kingship in Neo-Assyrian Art*, 185; Salem, *Near East, the Cradle of Western Civilization*, 102–3

Kulika

One of the serpent kings or NAGARAJA of Hindu mythology, the NAGA Kulika ("of good family") was described as being dusky-brown in color and having a mark of a half-moon on his head.

Source: Chandra, *Encyclopaedia of Hindu Gods and Goddesses*, 193; Dowson, *Classical Dictionary of Hindu Mythology and Religion, Geography, History, and Literature*, 170

Kulili, Sumerian

Variations: Kilili, Kililu, Kulilu

A monster created by TIAMAT, Kulili ("dragon-fly" or "flying DRAGON") was likely the DRAGON of Chaos conquered by Marduk in the Sumerian cre-ation myth. Not to be confused, there is also a goddess by the name of Kulili associated with Ishtar.

The kulili are also a type of freshwater MERMAID from Assyrian folklore; the kulili and their male counterparts, the kulullu, were generally hostile toward humans. Living in lakes, pools, and wells, they were said to stir up the water and pollute it so that it was not usable or fit to drink. Fortunately it was believed the kulili could be appeased with music and having a *paean* (a song of praise) sung to them; it would assure a lifetime of friendship.

Source: Barber, *Dictionary of Fabulous Beasts*, 95; Gray, *Mythology of All Races*, Volume 5, 86; Sandars, *Poems of Heaven and Hell from Ancient Mesopotamia*, 171; Zell-Ravenheart, *Wizard's Bestiary*, 58

Kulshedra

Variations: Bolla, Bullar, Kucedre

Kulshedra is a demonic DRAGON with faceted silver eyes, four legs, a long, serpentine body, and small wings. When it is 12 years old it grows horns and nine tongues, its wings increase in size, and it gains the ability to breathe fire. Occasionally it is described as an enormous woman covered with hair and having very large breasts. Human sacrifices were once made to this creature to prevent it from attacking.

This demon of drought from Albanian mythology sleeps all year, waking only on Saint George's Day (April 23) to kill the first human it sees and then it returns to sleep. Of note, Saint George's Day marks the beginning of summer and the New Year in ancient Albania. In more modern times it is celebrated on May 6.

Source: Elsie, *Dictionary of Albanian Religion, Mythology, and Folk Culture*, 154–6; Lurker, *Dictionary of Gods and Goddesses, Devils and Demons*, 106; Rose, *Spirits, Fairies, Gnomes, and Goblins*, 188, 244

Kumakatok

In Filipino folklore it is believed a visit from the trio known collectively as the kumakatok is a psychopomp (death omen); the figures are described as being one pretty, young girl and two elderly men, all of which are wearing hooded robes. There are no stories of who they are or how this group came together but it is believed if there is a knock on the door in the middle of the night from them someone in the immediate family will soon die; there is nothing known to ward them off or spell of protection to revert the tragedy of their visit.

Source: Frater, *Listverse. Com's Ultimate Book of Bizarre Lists*, 530

Kumbhakarna

An ASURA from Hindu mythology, Kumbhakarna, brother of Ravana, was under a curse from Brahma causing him to sleep for six months for each day he remained awake. Upon awaking, he was ravenously hungry and in spite of his normally good nature would devour anything he could consume including humans. Kumbhakarna was gigantic in size and devoted to his brother; a fierce warrior with a fearful battle cry he remained loyal to his brother and helped defend him knowing the abduction of Sita was wrong. In battle defending his beloved brother, Kumbhakarna was gruesomely slain by Rama, having each hand and leg severed before he was finally decapitated.

Source: Sehgal, *Encyclopaedia of Hinduism*, 1542–4; Williams, *Handbook of Hindu Mythology*, 192

Kumiho

Variations: GUMIHO

A species of vampiric fox spirit (KITSUNE) from Korean folktales, the kumiho feeds off of people's energy, be it their life force or sexual energy; usually meeting with one of these creatures is fatal. Preferring to assume seductive human forms the kumiho enjoy luring their victim into their own demise. The malevolent and predatory kumiho has nine tails and the ability to live for a thousand years.

Source: Maberry, *Vampire Universe*, 187; Wallen, *Fox*, 69; Zell-Ravenheart, *Wizard's Bestiary*, 58

Kumo

In Japanese folklore, the kumo ("cloud" or "spider") is a gigantic spider whose stomach is said to contain 1,900 human skulls.

Source: Bush, *Asian Horror Encyclopedia*, 104

Kumuda

A NAGA or NAGARAJA from Hindu mythology, Kumuda ("a lotus") is the brother of Kumudvati.

Kumuda is also the name of one the DIG-GAJAS which protect the eight compass points; he guards the southwest and his mate is named Anupama. Symbols of protection, stability, and strength, they were born of the halves of the cosmic golden egg Hiranyagarbha, which hatched the sun.

Source: Dowson, *Classical Dictionary of Hindu Mythology and Religion, Geography, History, and Literature*, 92, 171, 180; Gupta, *Elephant in Indian Art and Mythology*, 7

Kun

Variations: K'un, Kw'en, Peng

In Chinese folklore Kun was a gigantic fish from the North Ocean which transformed into a gigantic bird known as PENG; the wings of this creature are said to be a thousand leagues long and when it puffs out its chest it fills the sky with clouds.

Source: Birrell, *Chinese Mythology*, 191–2, 304; Roberts, *Chinese Mythology A to Z*, 67; Sterckx, *Animal and the Daemon in Early China*, 169

Kunapipi

Variations: Guanapipi

A monstrous creature from Aboriginal folklore, the kunapipi lives in streams and attacks young boys who are fishing. According to folklore, it was eventually persuaded by an eagle owl to regulate its killing.

Source: Zell-Ravenheart, *Wizard's Bestiary*, 59

Kuniya (Coo-nee-ah)

In the Australian Dreamtime the Kuniya were a race of snake people or an individual female, the story varies, similar to the NAGA, as they were part human and part python. According to the folklore Kuniya traveled to a place known as Uluru to lay her eggs; while there she came upon the place where the LIRU, a race of snake people (or an individual brown snake as the story varies), had killed her nephew. The LIRU mocked Kuniya for her sadness, enticing her anger and vengeance; she performed a powerful dance and spat poison into the sand sending it deep into the ground. Now in a full rage, Kuniya hefted up her axe and killed the first LIRU warrior she saw "at first gently, then fatally." Today, the terrain is said to bear the battle scars, as there are fig and gum trees growing which are poisonous and deep grooves from the axe and snake tracks carved into the stones.

Source: Farfor, *Northern Territory*, 272; Kng, *Tracing the Way*, 11–2

Kuon Khryseos

Variations: Cyon Chryseus, Golden Hound

A golden dog from ancient Greek mythology, Kuon Khryseos was created by the god Hephaistos (Vulcan) for the Titan Rhea to be the guardian of the goat AMALTHEA as it nursed the infant god Zeus (Jupiter). After the Titanomachy, Zeus assigned the canine protector to watch over his sanctuary in Crete. Kuon Khryseos was then stolen by Pandareos and taken to Mount Sipylos to be held in safe keeping by Tantalos. When Zeus (Jupiter) discovered the theft he found the two collaborators together; Pandareos was transformed into a pillar of stone where he stood and Mount Sipylos was picked up and brought crashing down atop Tantalos's head.

Source: Graves, *Green Myths*, 26; Smith, *New Classical Dictionary of Greek and Roman Biography, Mythology and Geography*, 853; Trzaskoma, *Anthology of Classical Myth*, 14–5

Kupua (KOO-poo-ah)

In Hawaiian mythology kupua is a classification for a being somewhere between demi-god and trickster; these shape-shifters are usually born in some non-human form, such as an egg, plant, or a bit of rope, and are not recognized for what they truly are except by a maternal grandparent who raises them. As a general rule kupua are gifted in some magical or special aspect, have a heightened intelligence, and a voracious appetite. Typical stories involving a kupua begin with their being offered the chief's daughter as a wife if they can overcome some terror preying on the land or people.

Source: Coulter, *Encyclopedia of Ancient Deities*, 260; Thompson, *Hawaiian Myths of Earth, Sea, and Sky*, 82

Kur

A DRAGON from Sumerian mythology, Kur ("land," "mountain") lived in the underworld, just above the cosmic waters, similar to TIAMAT of Babylonian mythology. Kur had once incurred the wrath of the gods by abducting Ereshkigal, the earth goddess, and bringing her forcibly to the Underworld. In another tale Sharur, the weapon of Ninurta, convinces the warrior god to set out and destroy Kur; the reason as to why is unknown as that portion of the ancient text is lost. Eventually after a back-and-forth struggle Ninurta gains the upper hand and slays Kur; however in doing so, he has killed the only thing holding back the primal waters. The world is flooded with tainted water; Ninurta then leads the surviving people to the Tigris River to rebuild society.

Source: De Kirk, *Dragonlore*, 58; Kramer, *Sumerian Mythology*, 76, 79–80

Kurits

The first of four deadly monsters in the Moro tradition, Kurits was described as looking much like a crocodile but much larger and having skin so tough it was unable to be penetrated by any weapon wielded by man. Kurits was equally fast on land and in the water; like the PHOENIX he had the ability to rise from the dead, literally climbing out of the pool of his own life-blood. He lived on Mount Kalaban.

Source: Hurley, *Swish of the Kris*, 259, 263–4

Kurrea

Variations: Kurria

A gigantic crocodile-like monster from the Australian Dreamtime mythology, Kurrea lived in a fetid swamp where, for a long time, he lived off of the wildlife there. One day, according to the story, he tired of his usual fare and began to consume humans; he ate so many only a scant few were left hiding in a cave behind a waterfall. Toolalla, a hero and brave warrior, went into the swamp to confront the monster, but even after throwing every one of his spears Kurrea was still alive, unhurt, and coming after the hero. Apart from this monster the only other thing in the world he feared was his mother-in-law, the bumble tree, so Toolalla ran straight towards her as Kurrea was quickly gaining ground as it gave chase. Toolalla scrambled up into her branches as quickly as he could but Kurrea stopped dead in its tracks and spinning in a circle, created a deep hole in the earth before fleeing in the other direction out of fear of the bumble tree. Kurrea retreated into the swamp, never again to eat a person, and the hole left in its wake is a refreshing watering hole in the wet season.

Source: Buchler, *Rainbow Serpent*, 60; Rose, *Giants, Monsters, and Dragons*, 215; Zell-Ravenheart, *Wizard's Bestiary*, 59

Kusarikku

The kusarikku ("bison-man" or "bull man") of Mesopotamian mythology is, along with the BASMU, GIRTABLULLU, and MUSHHUSH, one of the creatures of TIAMAT. Depicted as having the body of a monstrously strong bull standing upright with the bearded head of a double horned man, the kusarikku is often featured on battle maces dedicated to the sun god.

Source: Ford, *Maskim Hul*, 154; Wiggermann, *Mesopotamian Protective Spirits*, 174

Kutkinnaku

Variations: Acicenaqn ("big grandfather"), Quikirnaqu ("big raven"), Raven-Big-Quikil, Tenantomwan ("creator")

Sometimes cited as being a raven god of the Koryak as opposed to a NATURE SPIRIT, Kutkinnaku is in either case benevolent, as he is the one who taught mankind how to create fire, fish, hunt, negotiate with nature, and the shamanistic use of the drum to alter consciousness during ritual.

Source: Drew, *God/Goddess*, 113, 210; National Museum of Canada, *Bulletin*, Issue 119, 337

Kuvalayapida

A gigantic and fierce elephant from Hindu mythology, Kuvalayapida was owned by Kamsa and intended to be used by him, along with his two best wrestlers, to kill Krishna and his brother Balarama. The assassination failed and Krishna killed Kuvalayapida.

Source: Dallapiccola, *Hindu Myths*, 39; Venkatesananda, *Concise Srimad Bhagavatam*, 279

Kwakwakalanooksiwae

A cannibalistic raven from the mythology of the Kwakiutla people of Canada, North America,

Kwakwakalanooksiwae is one of the attendants of the horrific and monstrous Bakbakwakanooksiewae, cannibalistic bird-spirit. Kwakwakalanooksiwae was described as a gigantic creature, so large it could swallow a man in one bite; when it flew its wings would shake the sky.

Source: Maberry, *Vampire Universe*, 188; Werness, *Continuum Encyclopedia of Native Art*, 127

Kwanko

Variations: KUDA-GITSUNE, Osaki Gitsune ("osaki fox")

A small fox or foxlike creature from Shinto mythology, the kwanko ("pipe fox") is used by the mountain hermits known as *Yamabushi* ("one who lies in the mountains"); these creatures are inserted into small pipes to use in their divinations. The kwanko is said to be as small as a mouse and to look like a fox, but has a tail resembling a pipe cut in two. Once tame these creatures are inseparable from their owners, living in their pocket or shirt sleeve. The kwanko are said to scamper about, exploring as much as they can, and then report their findings to their owner; the information gathered allows the person to correctly surmise the past and predict the future.

Source: Asiatic Society of Japan, *Transactions of the Asiatic Society of Japan*, 123–4; Picken, *Essentials of Shinto*, 124

Kwun-Keng

The ancient Chinese author Hwai nan Tsze attempted to prove all creatures are the progeny of the DRAGON. He claimed the Kwun-Keng were the progeny of the *KIAO-LUNG*.

Source: De Visser, *Dragon in China and Japan*, 65

Kye-Ryong

Variations: Kyeryong

A COCKATRICE from Korean folklore, the kye-ryong ("chicken DRAGON") are sometimes seen in art pulling the chariot of an important person or the parents of a legendary hero; they are depicted as a two-legged DRAGON with a rooster's head.

Source: Bates, *All About Chinese Dragons*, 98; Niles, *Dragons*, 76; Zell-Ravenheart, *Wizard's Bestiary*, 59

Kyo

One of the three main species of DRAGON from Korean folklore, the kyo are said to live in the mountains. They, like all Korean DRAGONS, are chimerical, having the belly of a frog, eighty-one scales on their back, the eyes of a rabbit, and four claws.

Source: Mooney, *Dragons*, 46

Kyr

Kyr was one of the oxen named in Thorgrimr's *Rhymes* and in Snorri Sturluson's (1179–1241) *Prose Edda*.

Source: Jennbert, *Animals and Humans*, 49

Kyubi no Kitsune

In Shinto mythology the kyubi no kitsune ("nine-tailed fox") is said to be a divine fox with nine tails; to see one is a sign of good fortune. They are described as having a red or white body and the voice of an infant.

Source: Asiatic Society of Japan, *Transactions of the Asiatic Society of Japan*, 13; Picken, *Essentials of Shinto*, 124

Labbu

Variations: ASAG, BASMU, Labu, MUSHUSSU

A DRAGON from Sumerian mythology, Labbu ("lion") is confronted and ultimately defeated by the god Enil. The Akkadian *Story of the Slaying of Labbu* recounts the battle of the god Tishpak over not just Labbu but also BASMU and MUSHUSSU.

Labbu was described in ancient texts as being a gigantic sea DRAGON some 50 to 60 *biru* (approximately 325 to 390 miles) long and one *biru* tall (six or seven miles). Another text claimed his head alone was 30 *biru* tall (20 miles). No matter his size, Labbu was gigantic; he raided the cities, seas, and wilderness eating man and beast alike; all things living trembled before him. Although described as being "from the sea" the texts claim he, as many DRAGONS did, lived in the mountains; this is attributed to the fact ancient man considered the mountains to be a barren stony waste, a place of chaos. Another contradictory aspect to Labbu, adding to his ties of chaos, is although he was a serpentine-like creature his name translated to mean lion, indicating he was a hybrid, a leonine DRAGON. Had Labbu a set of wings he could pass for ZU, a GRIFFIN-like storm bird.

Because of his merciless appetite the god Sin called upon Tishpak to kill Labbu, promising him once the task was complete he would make him king; Tishpak refused. There is a break in the text and when the story resumes the god Ea has already sent Marduk to kill Labbu. As the great DRAGON dies, his body bleeds out for three years, three months, a day and a night.

Source: Fontenrose, *Python*, 146–7, 152, 219; Kuehn, *Dragon in Medieval East Christian and Islamic Art*, 79, 87, 170

Lachne

A dog from ancient Greek mythology, Lachne ("stickle") was one of the DOGS OF ACTÆON, the unfortunate youth who was raised by the CENTAUR CHEIRON. Lachne was noted for being particularly shaggy.

Source: Leeming, *World of Myth*, 111; Murray, *Classical Manual*, 160; Naso, *Fasti, Tristia*, 93–5

Lacon

A dog from ancient Greek mythology, Lacon was one of the DOGS OF ACTÆON, the unfortunate youth who was raised by the CENTAUR CHEIRON. Lacon was noted for having incredible strength and named after the country of his breeding.

Source: Leeming, *World of Myth*, 111; Murray, *Classical Manual*, 160; Naso, *Fasti, Tristia*, 93–5

Ladon (LAY-don) or (luh-DAHN)

Variations: The Hesperidean DRAGON, the Hesperidean Snake Ladôn, Ladwn, Ogygian

A DRAKON from ancient Greek mythology, Ladon had several possible alternatives as to its parentage; Hesiod proposed Ceto and Phorcys and Ptolemy offered the idea of Gaea but it was Hyginus' suggestion of Typhoeus and ECHIDNA which is most commonly accepted. Just as its lineage is uncertain so too are the number of heads Ladon had; some sources say it was two while others claim it had one hundred, and others only remaining nebulous saying it was "many."

Even in antiquity, scholars had set forward the idea Ladon was not in fact the guardian of the Golden Apples of Hesperos but a flock of golden sheep from where the Golden Fleece originated, the homonym (both apple and sheep in ancient Greek are *mêlon*) slightly altering and confusing the story.

There are also several versions of the story regarding Ladon's fate. Sometimes as the guardian of the Golden Apples he was slain by the hero and demi-god Hercules (Heracles) in combat; other times he was shot by an arrow. Ladon was also said to have been killed by Medea after she put it to sleep with a magical philter while the hero Jason stole the Golden Fleece.

Source: Daly, *Greek and Roman Mythology, A to Z*, 69, 84; Fontenrose, *Python*, 346, 370; Ogden, *Drakon*, 60,-2; Roman, *Encyclopedia of Greek and Roman Mythology*, 211

Ladon, dog

Variations: Ladom

A dog from ancient Greek mythology, Ladon (named for the river Ladon in Sicyon) was one of the DOGS OF ACTÆON, the unfortunate youth who was raised by the CENTAUR CHEIRON. Ladon was a Sicyon breed and was noted for having slender flanks.

Source: Leeming, *World of Myth*, 111; Murray, *Classical Manual*, 160; Naso, *Fasti, Tristia*, 93–5

Lady of the Land

Variations: Lady of Largo

Folklore from the Greek isle of Largo and recorded by Sir John de Mandeville in his work, *The Travels of Sir John Mandeville*, is the story of a DRAGON known as Lady of the Land. According to the local folklore the island was once ruled by a king named Ypocras; for an unmentioned reason the goddess Diana transformed one of his daughters into a DRAGON a hundred fathoms in length. So cursed, the maiden was to remain in that form until such a time as a brave warrior would approach her and kiss her upon the mouth. Although the spell would then be broken and restore the girl to her true form she would then die shortly thereafter. Until then, Lady of the Land lives in a cave in an abandoned castle only leaving her lair two or three times a year. The creature has never ravaged the land or caused any harm to anyone who has not tried to cause her harm first.

Source: Mandeville, *Travels of Sir John Mandeville*, 53–4; Meier, *Healing Dream and Ritual*, 16–7

Laelaps

Variations: Canis, Lailaps, Lalaps, LELAPS, DOG

A hunting dog from ancient Greek mythology, Laelaps ("tempest"), created by the god Hephaistos (Vulcan) out of bronze, had the remarkable ability to catch everything it was sent after as it could outrun any prey. Zeus (Jupiter) gave the animal to Europa to be her guardian. The goddess Artemis (Diana) would take the dog hunting with her and one day gave it to Procris along with a magical javelin which never missed its mark; Procris in turn gave the gifts to her husband Cephalus. Around this time the god Bacchus (Dionysos) sent the TEUMESSIAN FOX to plague the people of Theban and although they tried to capture or kill the creature, it outran every dog. Cephalus took his javelin and Laelaps to hunt the creature, creating an impossible situation. Zeus (Jupiter), not wanting to confront the paradox, turned both the fox and Laelaps into stone.

Source: Smith, *New Classical Dictionary of Biography, Mythology, and Geography*, 363; Westmoreland, *Ancient Greek Beliefs*, 90, 753

Laelaps, dog

A dog from ancient Greek mythology, Laelaps ("tempest") was one of the DOGS OF ACTÆON, the unfortunate youth who was raised by the CENTAUR CHEIRON. Laelaps was noted for being particularly fierce, powerful, and swift, like a whirlwind.

Source: Leeming, *World of Myth*, 111; Murray, *Classical Manual*, 160; Naso, *Fasti, Tristia*, 93–5

Lahamu (la-ah-mu)

Variations: Lakhamu

The first born daughter of the DRAGON Goddess TIAMAT, Lahamu is depicted as a gigantic serpent as well as a woman with six long curls of hair, symbolic for massive quantities of hair and a chaotic nature. She was the goddess of primordial clay, mud, or ocean silt.

Lahamu has a brother, the primordial god and first born creature and son of TIAMAT, LAHMU. Together they were the parents of the gods Anshar and Kishar. LAHMU and Lahamu are never mentioned separately.

Source: De Lafayette, *New de Lafayette Mega Encyclopedia of Anunnaki*. Volume 5, 1329; Ford, *Maskim Hul*, 147; Jordan, *Dictionary of Gods and Goddesses*, 170

Lahmu Ippiru

A NUTUM from Babylonian mythology, the chimerical lahmu ippiru is a form sometimes assumed by the god Ea; it is described in incomplete detail, as text is missing from the ancient source, as having a bird claw for a right foot, ears of an ox, (*incomplete*) of a lion, body of a naked *kissugu* (possibly a swordfish but scholars are uncertain), and face and fist of a man; it wears a headband and a doublet upon its chest.

Source: Ford, *Maskim Hul: Babylonian Magick*, 161; Thompson, *Devils and Evil Spirits of Babylonia*, Volume 15, 155

Laibolos

Variations: Asbolos the Diviner

In Greek mythology Laibolos ("stone hurler") was the name of a CENTAUR who attended the wedding of Pirithous, became drunk on wine, and following the lead of EURYTUS, who assaulted Hippodame, began to assault and rape any women they could grab. A great Centauromachy then followed.

Source: Colvin, *Cornhill Magazine*, Volume XXXVIII, 296; D'Angour, *Greeks and the New*, 76

Lalomena

A creature from Malagasy folklore, the lalomena is said to be an ox-like beast with bright red horns; it lives in the water.

Source: Sibree, *Folk-lore Record*, Volume 2, 27; Tyson, *Madagascar*, 247

Laman Lupa

In the folklore of the Bagobo, Marinduque, Mindoro, and Tagalog people of the Philippines the laman lupa ("earth's substance") are described as invisible, small NATURE SPIRITS living in the fields and hills. Highly territorial, the laman lupa live in communities and only allow certain people to work their land and only then on the provision they are made offerings before planting and after the harvest is reaped. The blood of a red rooster must also be sprinkled on the rice paddies during the growing season. If these conditions are not met the laman lupa will work as one to destroy the crop. They are said to abhor salt and all spices.

Source: Paraiso, *Balete Book*, 77

Lamassu

Variations: Ach-Chazu, Alu, Dimmea, Dimme-Kur, Gallu, Labashu, Lama, Lamastu, Lammassu, LAMMASU, Mula, Mulla

From Acadian, Babylonian, and Mesopotamian demonology comes the protective deity, demon, or creature known as Lamassu. In Acadia she was described as a bare-chested woman suckling a dog or a pig who inflicted infants with diseases and fevers.

In Babylon she was chimerical, having a bull's body, eagle wings, and a human head; she was considered to be a protective being. In Mesopotamia, however, Lamassu was considered a chimerical creature with eagle wings, a lion's body, and a human man's head; it guarded temples and attacked anyone who was not either of the purest good or of the purest evil.

Lamassu's name is possibly Sumerian in origin. Her male counterpart is called Alad (Šêdu in Acadian).

Source: Jastrow, *Religion of Babylonia and Assyria*, 260; Lenormant, *Chaldean Magic*, 24; Zell-Ravenheart, *Wizard's Bestiary*, 59

Lamb Tree

Variations: Barbary Lamb, Barmotez, Jeduah, Lycopodium Barometz, Tartary Lamb, Vegetable Lamb of Tartary

The lamb tree is a unique zoophyle (animal-plant hybrid), a tree or large shrub from which a living animal grows like a fruit. There were two distinct species of lamb trees. The first was delineated by the seventeenth century German author Joannes Zahn who had written in his work the plant existed many centuries ago. He described it as being more akin to a large shrub from which a long and flexible stalk extended outward enabling the lamb to graze freely. The creature was a lamb in every sense of the word, having flesh, blood, bones, and wool as well as the temperament of its more free-roaming relations. If ever the stalk connecting the animal to the plant was severed, the lamb would die. Wolves were particularly fond of the flesh of the lamb and were proposed by Zahn as being the source for the plant's rarity if not extinction.

The second version of the lamb tree comes from an account given by Sir John de Mandeville in his work, *The Travels of Sir John Mandeville*. Therein, he claims if ever a person is traveling from Cathay to India they will pass through a kingdom known as Cadissen; this is where the lamb tree grows. He describes the tree as growing large gourds or melons which when ripened are cut in half to reveal a small lamb. Apart from the animal, the remaining fruit of the gourd was also said to be rather delicious.

Source: Ashton, *Curious Creatures in Zoology*, 165–6, 169–70; Mandeville, *Travels of Sir John Mandeville*, 20, 165

Lambton Wyrm

Variations: Lambton DRAGON, Lambton Worm, Lambton Wurm

A black scaled DRAGON or worm from the folklore of Durham, England, the story of the Lambton wyrm dates back to the twelfth century and the time of the Crusades. According to the folklore, the beast once lived in the Wear River as a small eel but was caught on a hook and line one day when John Lambton was fishing. Repulsed at the sight of the horrid looking creature with its dragonesque head, he tossed it into a well and forgot about it. Not too long afterwards, he decided to travel to the Holy Land and repent for the sins of his youth.

While the Lord of Lambton was gone the wyrm grew so large it could wrap itself around the nearby hill nine times; it began attacking the town and taking livestock. Although the locals tried to kill the beast they were never successful. By the time Lord Lambton returned the wyrm was quite the monster; and realizing he was the one responsible for it, he decided to take action. After consulting a witch he had constructed a suit of armor covered with spikes and learned he not only had to slay the wyrm near the river where he first captured it but then had to slay the very first living thing he saw immediately afterwards or his family line would be cursed for nine generations.

Lord Lambton returned to the lake and confronted the wyrm; it wound its body around him, piercing itself on the armor and enabling the Lord to chop it easily into bits. With the creature slain he returned to his home to fulfil the second part of his obligation expecting his dog to meet him at the gate; rather he was met by his father. Refusing to kill his own father, he attempted to defer the curse by slaying the dog, but it did not work and the curse befell the Lambton family.

Source: Briggs, *Fairies in Tradition and Literature*, 81–2; Jones, *Instinct for Dragons*, 143–4; Maberry, *Vampire Universe*, 191–92

Lamiae

According to the *Malleus Maleficarum* ("Hammer of the Witches"), a treatise on witches written by Inquisitors Heinrich Kramer and Jacob Sprenger in 1486, the lamiae ("render") were a species of evil fairy or a FAIRY ANIMAL described as having a human face but a bestial body. Sent by a witch, the lamiae would sneak into a home, tear an infant to pieces, and then restore it to life.

Source: Briggs, *Encyclopedia of Fairies*, 260–61; Broedel, *Malleus Maleficarum and the Construction of Witchcraft*, 104–5; Latham, *Elizabethan Fairies*, 52–3

Lamies

In African folklore the lamies were a species of creature described as having the head of a woman and the body and tail of a serpent; they are similar in description to the DRACAENAE of ancient Greek mythology.

Source: Brewer, *Dictionary of Phrase and Fable*, 441; Daniels, *Encyclopedia of Superstitions, Folklore, and the Occult Sciences of the World*, 1416

Lammasu

Variations: Lama, LAMASSU, Lamma, SHEDU

In Mesopotamian mythology, lammasu were a chimerical species of creature having the body of a lion, the face of a man and the wings of an eagle, similar in appearance to the SPHINX of ancient Egypt, although sometimes they were depicted as a winged bull with a human face. The lammasu were utilized as temple guardians and would attack anyone who was not of the purest evil or the purest good. Males of the species are sometimes referred to as SHEDU.

Source: Bertman, *Handbook to Life in Ancient Mesopotamia*, 121; Leick, *Dictionary of Ancient Near Eastern Mythology*, 109

Lampalugua

A predatory DRAGON from Chilean folklore, the lacertilian (lizard-like) lampalugua has coppery reddish scales and large claws; it is said to prey upon cattle and humans.

Source: De Kirk, *Dragonlore*, 56; Zell-Ravenheart, *Wizard's Bestiary*, 60

Lampon

In classical Greek mythology, Lampon ("bright eyes" or "the shining") was one of the four MARES OF DIOMEDES, King of Aetolia and son of the god Ares (Mars) (see DINOS, PHOLGIOS, and XANTHOS). Although the horses are mares, the Latin author Hyginus (64 BC–AD 17), the only author who ever named them, gave them all masculine names. In his eighth labor the demi-god Hercules (Heracles) was charged with the capture and return of these savage mares which pulled the chariot of the king and were fed a diet of human flesh.

In the Latin narrative poem *Metamorphoses* (2.153) written by the Roman poet Ovid (43 BC– AD 17), the sun god and Titan Helios (Sol) had his golden chariot, Quadriga, pulled across the sky by the flying horses, AETHON, ASTROPE, BRONTE, CHRONOS, EOUS, Lampon, PHAETHON, PHLEGON, and PYROIS. All of these horses are described as being pure white and having flaring nostrils which can breathe forth flame.

Source: Breese, *God's Steed*, 86; Hard, *Routledge Handbook of Greek Mythology* 262; Rose, *Giants, Monsters, and Dragons*, 178; Webster, *Historic Magazine and Notes and Queries*, 581

Lampong

A species of DWARF from Filipino folklore, the lampong at first appears to be a one-eyed white deer, and as it approaches, it seems to become at least two feet taller. The bright-eyed and long bearded lampongs wear a tall, black two-peaked cap upon their head; they consider themselves to be guardians of the animals of the forests and will tempt a man to shoot at them knowing their magic will cause the hunter's first five shots to always miss. If the hunter is persistent and manages to strike an animal or the lampong itself, it will transform into a *duende* (a type of species of vampiric fairy) and have its revenge.

Source: Ramos, *Creatures of Philippine Lower Mythology*, 9; Wilson, *Ilongot Life and Legends*, 8–8

Lampos (LAM-pos)

In classical Greek and Roman mythology Lampos ("glitter" or "shine") was one of the many winged horses said to assist in pulling the sun across the sky; it was one of the HIPPOI ATHANATOI. In the ancient Greek epic poem the *Iliad* ("Song of Ilion") (1240 BC) attributed to Homer, Lampos was the name of the horse ridden by the eminent Trojan warrior and son of King Priam, Hector.

Source: Brewer, *Dictionary of Phrase and Fable*, 626; Contemporary Review, Volume 27, 809; Rose, *Giants, Monsters, and Dragons*, 178

Lamya

A creature from the symbology of heraldry, the lamya is depicted as the hybrid composite of a dog, DRAGON, goat, horse, lion, and a woman.

Source: Lower, *Curiosities of Heraldry*, 103

Laohu

In Chinese folklore the term laohu ("old fox") is applied to any fox old enough to have gained the ability to shape-shift; these foxes were not considered to be good or evil and had no specific moral connotation.

Source: Kang, *Cult of the Fox*, n.pag.; Wallen, 60, 60

Latawiec (La-ta-vec)

Variations: Potercuk

In Poland and the Ukraine there is a vampiric creature, a huge bird with a child's face, called a latawiec. The word *latawiec* translates to mean "vampire falcon." It flies down from the sky and with a blood-freezing shriek grabs up children, livestock, and women; it carries its prey back to its roost to consume.

Source: Bonnerjea, *Dictionary of Superstitions and Mythology*, 148; Jobes, *Dictionary of Mythology*, 975; Lecouteux, *History of the Vampire*

Latreus

A CENTAUR from ancient Greek mythology, Latreus was, according to Ovid's *Metamorphoses*, one of the CENTAURS who attended the wedding of Pirithous, became drunk on wine and following the lead of EURYTUS who assaulted Hippodame, began to assault and rape any women they could grab. He was said to be the largest of his kind, having huge arms and legs. Although he was middle-aged and greying at the temples, he was still as strong as a man half his age.

During the Centauromachy, Latreus stripped the armor of the fallen heroes he had slain, also taking up Halesus' shield and Macedonia's sword. At a full gallop he called out vicious taunts to Caeneus accusing him of being a woman. Caeneus struck him with his spear exactly where his horse body met with his human spine. Even wounded Latreus struck his opponent a half dozen times but the youth was invulnerable to his attacks. When Caeneus delivered a death blow to Latreus, all remaining CENTAURs attacked him, but with similar results. MONYCHUS, enraged and embarrassed neither he nor any of his race could put down a single youth, demanded they pile earth, stones, and trees atop the undefeatable warrior.

Source: Commentary, *Mythological, Historical, and Geographical on Pope's Homer*, 55; Simpson, *Metamorphoses of Ovid*, 208–09

Laura

Variations: Laure

In Albanian mythology, particularly in the Tirana region, the laura is described as being an ugly hag with the ability to transform herself into amphibious animals. Her raucous voice can be heard near ponds, rivers, and roadsides but when approached she will disappear; dogs will chase her.

Source: Elsie, *Dictionary of Albanian Religion, Mythology, and Folk Culture*, 158

Lavellan

A species of creature from the Scottish highlands, the lavellanis are a type of gigantic water rat with the ability to harm cattle at a distance of up to forty yards. Farmers are said to catch these creatures and skin them, keeping the pelt as a component for use in the remedy for their affected herd. Water which has been stirred with the pelts is then given to the cattle to cure them.

Source: Barber, *Dictionary of Fabulous Beasts*, 98; Campbell, *Superstitions of the Highlands and Islands of Scotland*, 220–1; Zell-Ravenheart, *Wizard's Bestiary*, 60

Lebros

Variations: Labros

A dog from ancient Greek mythology, Lebros ("worrier") was one of the DOGS OF ACTÆON, the unfortunate youth who was raised by the CENTAUR CHEIRON. Lebros was noted for being cross bred of a Cretan mother and a Spartan father, just like fellow pack member AGRIODUS.

Source: Leeming, *World of Myth*, 111; Murray, *Classical Manual*, 160; Naso, *Fasti, Tristia*, 93–5

Lei Chen-Tzu

Variations: Lei Zhe Zi

A winged DRAGON from Chinese mythology, Lei Chen-Tzu is described as having a boar-like tusked green face. Sometimes in art he is depicted with a monkey head and three eyes.

According to the legend, he was born human from an egg created after a huge clap of thunder created by his birth father, Lei, the god of thunder. Lei Chen-Tzu was sent to live with Wen Wang and after he was adopted was sent off to live with Taoist hermits. Once Wen Wang was kidnapped; Lei Chen-Tzu set out to find a means to rescue him. He came upon two magical apricots, ate them, and was transformed into a DRAGON. Using his new form, he was able to save Wen Wang. Lei Chen-Tzu is the symbol of heroism and righteousness.

Source: De Kirk, *Dragonlore*, 27; Roberts, *Chinese Mythology A to Z*, 71

Lelaps

A dog from ancient Greek mythology, Lelaps was one of the DOGS OF ACTÆON, the unfortunate youth who was raised by the CENTAUR CHEIRON.

Source: Leeming, *World of Myth*, 111; Murray, *Classical Manual*, 160

Lenapizka

A lake monster from the mythology of the Peoria people of Illinois, the lenapizka ("true tiger") was a venerated amphibious creature.

Source: Meurger, *Lake Monster Traditions*, 161; Rose, *Giants, Monsters, and Dragons*, 222; Zell-Ravenheart, *Wizard's Bestiary*, 60

Leokampoi

Variations: Leokampos

The hybrid known as the leokampoi was a creature from the mythology of the ancient Etruscans; it was described as having the forequarters of a lion and the hind-section of a fish.

Source: Breverton, *Breverton's Phantasmagoria*, n.pag.

Leongalli

A DRAGON from Mongolian folklore, leongalli was described as having a serpentine body with the head and forequarters of a lion; it was similar in appearance to the TATZELWURM.

Source: De Kirk, *Dragonlore*, 35; Jones, *Instinct for Dragons*, 9; Zell-Ravenheart, *Wizard's Bestiary*, 60

Leontophone

Variations: Leopard's Bane

A creature from medieval bestiaries, the leontophone ("lion killers") is the natural born enemy of the lion in spite of its size. According to Pliny the Elder, the Roman author and natural philosopher, the leontophone only lives in those places where lions dwell; its very flesh is exceptionally poisonous to the great cat, so much so when the body is burned the ashes can then be used as a poison to specifically kill lions. Naturally, lions are abhorrent to the leontophone and they must master how to kill one without inflicting a bite. When combating a lion the leontophone will urinate on the lion, as this fluid is also highly toxic.

Source: Ashton, *Curious Creatures in Zoology*, 157; Barber, *Dictionary of Fabulous Beasts*, 98; Breverton, *Breverton's Phantasmagoria*, n.pag.; Clark, *Medieval Book of Beasts*, 122, Zell-Ravenheart, *Wizard's Bestiary*, 60

Leshy, plural: lechies

Variations: Lešak, Leshak, Leshii, Leshiy, Lesiy, Lesní mužík, Lesnik, Lesný mužík ("forest man"), Lesny mužik/ded, Lesovij, Lesovik, Lesovy, Lesun, Lešy, Leszi, Leszy

Originally a god or NATURE SPIRIT of the forest in Slavonic mythology, a leshy ("forest") was named as a type of terrestrial devil in Colin de Plancy's *Dictionaire Infernale* (1818, 1863); the male of the species was known as leshouikha. SATYR-like humans from the waist up with notable beards, ears, and the horns of a she-goat, these NATURE SPIRITs used their ability to imitate voices as a way to lure people back to their caves. Once the victim was inside, they would be tickled to death. Lechies, as they are called in numbers, have a banshee-like cry and the ability to shrink down to the height of grass when marching through fields. They can also grow as tall as a tree when running through the forest where they live.

Source: Johnson, *Slavic Sorcery*, 8, 88; Mack, *Field Guide to Demons, Fairies, Fallen Angels, and Other Subversive Spirits*, 111–13; Varner, *Mythic Forest*, 30–1

Léttfeti (LEET-veht-i)

Variations: Letfet, Letfeti, Letteti, Lettfeti ("light stepper")

Léttfeti ("light foot" or "light stepper") was one of the horses utilized by the Aesir in Norse mythology; its specific owner or rider is not mentioned. Léttfeti was also listed as one of the many horses who would graze in the red-gilt leafed Glasir Grove.

Source: Anderson, *Norse Mythology*, 189; Grimes, *Norse Myths*, 20; Sturluson, *Prose Edda*, 28, 30, 131, 285

Leucite

A dog from ancient Greek mythology, Leucite was one of the DOGS OF ACTÆON, the unfortunate youth who was raised by the CENTAUR CHEIRON.

Source: Leeming, *World of Myth*, 111; Murray, *Classical Manual*, 160

Leucon

A dog from ancient Greek mythology, Leucon ("white") was one of the DOGS OF ACTÆON, the unfortunate youth who was raised by the CENTAUR CHEIRON. Leucon was noted for having a white coat.

Source: Leeming, *World of Myth*, 111; Murray, *Classical Manual*, 160; Naso, *Fasti, Tristia*, 93–5

Leucrocotta

Variations: CROCOTTA, Leucrota, Leukrokotai

Described by Pliny the Elder, the Roman author, natural philosopher, naturalist, and army and naval commander in his work *Natural History* (AD 77), the offspring of a CROCOTTA and a lion was a chimerical beast known as a leucrocotta ("white dog wolf") and is described as having the body of a lion, cloven hooves, the head of a badger, its mouth slit up as far as its ears, the height of a donkey, and one continuous bone instead of individual teeth.

Source: Ashton, *Curious Creatures in Zoology*, 160; Barber, *Dictionary of Fabulous Beasts*, 96; Druce, *Archaeological Journal*, Volume 68, 185; Zell-Ravenheart, *Wizard's Bestiary*, 60

Leviathan (Lev-ya-TAN)

Variations: Behemah ("beast"), Livyatan, Liwyāṭān ("twisted coil"), Levitan, Lotan, Taninim

Originating in ancient Hebrew folklore and popularized in medieval demonology, Leviathan, the demon of envy and faith, was an aquatic, arch she-demon; she was also said to be a fallen angel of the Order of Seraphim. Her name in Hebrew means "the crooked (or piercing) serpent (or DRAGON)" or "whale."

Created by God on the fifth day of Creation, the leviathan is described as a monstrous, female sea creature three hundred miles long with eyes glowing as brightly as twin suns. It is the symbol of chaos. Using its supernatural strength it hunted and ate a whale a day. Its breath was so foul to breathe it in was enough to kill. It could send a wave of intense heat from its mouth which could boil water instantly.

Especially mean-natured, even for a demon, the leviathan was fearful of a species of sea-worm called a *kilbit*, as it clings to the gills. It was said to have lived in the Mediterranean Sea, but God slew the female leviathan, salted it, and fed it to His people so it could not reproduce with its mate. The hide of the beast was used to make the tent the feast was held under. The male species of this demon is known as Behemoth.

Source: Aikin, *General Biography*, 493; Barton, *Journal of Biblical Literature*, Volumes 30–31, 165; Hayatt, *Book of Demons*, 43, 45; Bayle, *Historical and Critical Dictionary*, 262; Melton, *Encyclopedia of Occultism and Parapsychology*, 315; Voltaire, *Works of M. de Voltaire*, 193

Li

Variations: Chi

Mature, hornless DRAGONS from Chinese mythology, *li* is a classification of DRAGON; the *chi* are also hornless DRAGONS, but they are young and still immature, not having reached their full potential. Beginning in the Ming dynasty there was a definitive difference between the *chi* and the *li* but in more modern times the words are used interchangeably. Li tend to live in the sea, but this is not always the case.

Source: Bates, *All About Chinese Dragons*, 4; Forbes, *Illustrated Book of Dragons and Dragon Lore*, n.pag.

Li-Lung

Variations: Li Long

In Chinese mythology the benevolent li-lung ("hornless DRAGON") are DRAGONS of the earth, water, and wind. As they ascend into the heavens they assume the form of a typhoon or a waterspout. Li-lung are said to be the ones to carve out the courses of rivers and are the rulers of the oceans. They are chimerical, described as being yellow, having a lion's body, a human face, and a hornless DRAGON's head. Usually the li-lung live beneath the surface of the earth and their movements are the cause of earthquakes and landslides.

Source: De Kirk, *Dragonlore*, 27; Ingersoll, *Dragons and Dragon Lore*, 84

Liath Macha

One of the two prized horses belonging to the hero Cúchulainn, Liath Macha ("the grey of Macha") and its equal, DUB SAINGLEND ("the black of Saingliu"), pulled his chariot. The favorite of the two animals, Liath Macha arose from a lake, a gift to the hero from the goddess Macha. In his final battle, when Cúchulainn receives his death blow, the hero ties himself to a boundary stone so he can literally die on his feet; Liath Macha stood over the hero while he still lived in order to protect him.

Source: Gerritsen, *Dictionary of Medieval Heroes*, 89; MacKillop, *Dictionary of Celtic Mythology*, 265; Monaghan, *Encyclopedia of Celtic Mythology and Folklore*, 288

Lidérc (Lied-ric)

Variations: Lüdérc

In Hungarian folklore there is a vampiric creature very similar to the INCUBUS and SUCCUBUS in that it drains off the blood and life energies of a person through sexual intercourse. Called a lidérc, it is created in the most interesting way—by placing the first egg laid by a black hen under one's armpit and keeping it there until it hatches. The lidérc also acts as something of a FAMILIAR, as it is known for its ability to find treasure. It can shape-shift into a chicken or into a person who has one foot which is a chicken's foot. The lidérc will ask to do odd jobs for the person who hatched it. It is always asking for more to do, never satisfied with its given task and wanting to move on to the next one as quickly as possible. Keeping a lidérc out of your home so it cannot assault you during the night as you sleep is as easy as hanging garlic on your bedroom doorknob. Killing a lidérc is also easy, if you know how. Simply give it an impossible task to complete, such as cutting an odd length of rope or dehydrating water into a powder. The little creature will try its hardest, but eventually it will become so frustrated it will suffer a stroke and die.

Source: Dömötör, *Hungarian Folk Beliefs*, 83

Lightning Monsters

In the traditional stories of Zambia of southern Africa the lightning monsters were a type of creature said to live in the heavens but during storms would descend to the earth on flexible threads; when the thread was taut it would snap the monster back up into the sky, creating a bolt of lightning. These creatures are described as having the fore-quarters of a goat and the hindquarters of a crocodile. If ever the string connected to the lightning monster broke and released it upon the earth, hunters would have to be dispatched to hunt it down and kill it; otherwise the monster would destroy the land.

Source: Hargreaves, *Hargreaves New Illustrated Bestiary*, 81; Knudsen, *Fantastical Creatures and Magical Beasts*, 10; Zell-Ravenheart, *Wizard's Bestiary*, 61

Lightning Serpent

Variations: Lightning Snake

In the mythology of the Native Australian people lightning serpents were a type of gigantic snake that lived in the heavens but descended to earth during storms, creating lighting as they traveled and rain as they touched the ground.

Many of the Native American tribes also have a lightning serpent in their mythology; the Algonquins believed it was vomited forth by the creator god Manito and the Pawnee claimed the rumble of thunder was its hissing, to cite two such examples.

Source: Hargreaves, *Hargreaves New Illustrated Bestiary*, 81; Rose, *Giants, Monsters, and Dragons*, 224; Spence, *Brief Guide to Native American Myths and Legends*, n.pag.

Lik

Variations: Mast of the Water

In South American folklore from Gran Chaco, Bolivia, the lik is said to be an ancient and gigantic water snake living in the river; it is so large it has palm trees growing on its moss covered back. Lik is believed to be the guardian of the fish living in the lakes and rivers.

Source: Rose, *Giants, Monsters, and Dragons*, 224; Zell-Ravenheart, *Wizard's Bestiary*, 61

Likho

Variations: Licho, Liho, One-Eyed Likho

The very embodiment of an evil Fate and misfortune in Slavic folklore, the one-eyed likho ("excessive," "too much") is said to look like an old hag dressed in black or as a male goblin (a general term for any of the grotesque, small but friendly beings among the fay) when living in the forests. Generally speaking, stories involving Likho run a similar course and teach a moral lesson: in one variant, someone cheats Likho and runs off with the hag in pursuit; while escaping they see some object they think will help so they grab it but the item sticks fast and eventually they end up amputating their own appendage. In another, Likho cheats a person and rides on their back; the victim, trying to drown the hag, wades into the river only to drown themselves.

Source: Dixon-Kennedy, *Encyclopedia of Russian and Slavic*

Myth and Legend, 167–8; Ralston, *Russian Folk-Tales*, 186–9

Lindorm

Variations: Drage, Drake, Lindorm Snake, Lindworm, Lind-Wurm, Lindwurm ("DRAGON"), Vassorm

A legless, bat-winged wormlike DRAGON from Norse mythology, the lindorm ("flexible body serpent") was said to be covered with gold or greenish scales; these creatures were believed to be the guardians of hidden treasure. In the travel journals of Marco Polo lindorms were fast and strong enough to take down a galloping horse. The German hero Siegfried, in his legends, combated a lindorm near Worms, Germany. According to some folklore lindorms prefer to live in the wastelands but will on occasion come into civilized areas and take up residence in a church tower. By day it grazes on wooden crosses and new shoots; by night it lies before the door of the church so no one may enter the building. In one such tale the locals placed ordnance near where the creature roosted and managed to kill it but also destroyed part of their church tower. Its body was so large it took many men three days to remove the corpse.

Source: Craigie, *Scandinavian Folk-lore*, 258–9; De Kirk, *Dragonlore*, 42; Eberhart, *Mysterious Creatures*, 294–5; Lehner, *Big Book of Dragons, Monsters, and Other Mythical Creatures*, 30

Ling-Kwei

The ancient Chinese author Hwai nan Tsze, in his attempt to prove how all creatures are the progeny of the DRAGON, shows the ling-kwei ("divine power manifesting tortoise") as being the progeny of the YUEN-YUEN and the progenitor of all tortoises and mailed (armor-skinned) creatures.

Source: De Visser, *Dragon in China and Japan*, 65

Linton Worm

A DRAGON from the medieval folklore of Roxburghshire, Scotland, the legless Linton worm was said to have one day slithered out of the River Tweed and taken up residence on Linton Hill from where it staged raids on nearby livestock, asphyxiating them with poisonous breath to consume at its leisure before enjoying a sunbath up in the hills. Because of its voracious appetite farmers established a large reward for anyone who would slay the beast. According to the tale in 1174 the Laird of Lariston, a man described as having "reckless bravery," answered the call. Using a method first set forth by the Biblical hero David, the laird applied peat dipped in red-hot sulphur and pitch to the end of his lance, a venture which proved successful.

Source: Henderson, *Notes on the Folk-Lore of the Northern Counties of England and the Borders*, 295–6; Monaghan, *Encyclopedia of Celtic Mythology and Folklore*, 137; Shuker, *Beasts That Hide from Man*, 206

Lintrache

Variations: Lint-Drache, Lintwurm ("DRAGON" or "large snake")

In the *Nibelungenlied*, the Lintrache ("lithe-DRAGON") was a DRAGON slain by the hero Siegfried; it, like nearly all German DRAGONS of this era, was a guardian of not only treasure but carefully guarded knowledge. The city of Worms, Germany, is said to have taken its name from this creature which appears on its coat of arms.

Source: Grimm, *Teutonic Mythology*, 979; McConnell, *Nibelungen Tradition*, 161

Liosalfar

Variations: Liosálfar, Lios-Alfar, Ljosalfar

In Scandinavian and Teutonic mythology the liosalfar ("LIGHT ELVES") are light bringers; they are a species of ELF described as being tall, exceedingly beautiful, and having skin paler than the sun. They live in Alfhime, a place located between Earth and the Heavens.

Source: Grimm, *Teutonic mythology*, Volume 2, 446; Illes, *Encyclopedia of Spirits*, 17; Keightley, *World Guide to Gnomes, Fairies, Elves, and Other Little People*, 64

Liru

In the Australian Dreamtime the Liru were a race of poisonous snake-people warriors (or an individual brown snake as the story varies) who had killed the nephew of KUNIYA and then mocked her grief. The ensuing battle which took place between KUNIYA and Liru altered the landscape of southwest Uluru, Australia, where evidence, it is said, is still apparent in the deeply scarred rocks.

Source: Farfor, *Northern Territory*, 272; Kng, *Tracing the Way*, 11–2

Lit

Lit was one of the oxen named in Thorgrimr's *Rhymes* and in Snorri Sturluson's (1179–1241) *Prose Edda*.

Source: Daly, *Norse Mythology A to Z*, 22; Jennbert, *Animals and Humans*, 49

Litanu

Variations: The Fleeing Serpent, Lotan, the Twisting Serpent

The personification of Chaos from Semitic Ugaritic folklore, the DRAGON Litanu ("twisted one") was described as having seven heads; it was likely an early predecessor of LEVIATHAN. It is uncertain in the folklore if the god of storms, Baal, killed Litanu or not.

Source: Angel, *Chaos and the Son of Man*, 4; Leviton, *Encyclopedia of Earth Myths*, n.pag.

Llamhigyn Y Dwr

In Welsh folklore a FAIRY ANIMAL called the llamhigyn y dwr ("the water leaper") was described as looking like a toad but having a tail, teeth, and a set of leathery wings, and being as large as a market hog. Living in lakes and remote streams, it was said to be a highly territorial creature that would break fishing lines and come ashore to eat sheep.

Source: Eberhart, *Mysterious Creatures*, 299; Maberry, *Vampire Universe*, 200–201; Monaghan, *Encyclopedia of Celtic Mythology and Folklore*, 469; Rhys, *Celtic folklore: Welsh and Manx*, Volume 1, 95–6.

Llamrei

Variations: Lamri

In Arthurian folklore, Llamrei ("the curveter" or "one that prances or frolics") was one of King Arthur's mares; this was the mount he rode in the tale "How Culhwch Won Olwen" from *The Mabinogion*. Arthur was also upon Llamrei during the great boar hunt of YSGITHYRWYN where his dog CABAL kills the swine. Later in this story, some of the king's men are injured and put upon the mare to be carried to safety as it was strong enough to carry four men at once. Caw of Scotland, also according to *The Mabinogion*, was astride Llamrei when he fought TWRCH TRWYTH with CABAL.

Source: Brewer, *Dictionary of Phrase and Fable*, 626; Bruce, *Arthurian Name Dictionary*, 321; Reno, *Arthurian Figures of History and Legend*, 63, 172; Rubin, *Writer's Companion*, 869; Tozer, *Horse in History*, 82.

Llwydawg Govynnyad

Variations: Llwydawg the Killer

In Arthurian folklore, Llwydawg Govynnyad ("the hewer") was one of the seven piglets acting as part of the warrior entourage for the boar TWRCH TRWYTH. For many days and nights King Arthur and his men fought the boar and piglets in the valley Dyffryn Amanw; although some of the men died, all of the piglets were slain. GRUGYN GWRYCH EREINT and Llwydawg Govynnyad were the first to kill in the battle at Ystral, taking the lives of Arthur's first group of hunters and scouts. Llwydawg Govynnyad killed Gwrfoddw, Llgadrudd Emys, and Peissawg the Tall.

Source: Bruce, *Arthurian Name Dictionary*, 323, 477; Kibler, *Medieval Arthurian Epic and Romance*, 96.

Llyn Barfog

Variations: Elfin Cow

The llyn barfog were the Welsh black cattle born from the droves owned by the plant annwn (Welsh fairies) and tended to by their women, the gwragedd annwn (a species of water fairy). According to legend, a band of green clad gwragedd annwn would emerge from a lake located near Aberdover near dusk, driving their cows, the GWARTHEG Y LLYN.

Source: Avant, *Mythological Reference*, 68; Eberhart, *Mysterious Creatures*, 5; Sikes, *British Goblins*, 39–40.

Loathly Worm

Variations: Laidly Worm, Laidly Worm of Bamborough, Loathsome DRAGON

A gigantic and hideous species of DRAGON from British folklore, loathly worms are described as being gigantic, wingless, and having two feet on the front part of their serpentine bodies.

There is also a folktale of a specific loathly worm from the area of Spindleston Heugh as told in a ballad written by Robert Lamb in the eighteenth century entitled "The Laidley Worm of Spindleston Heugh"; Lamb claimed the tale originated from an old mountain bard named Duncan Frasier who lived in Cheviot in 1270. In the tale a princess named Margaret was transformed into a loathly worm by her evil step-mother, the queen, and was banished to live in the Spindleston Hills, west of Bamburgh. The breath of this creature was so toxic for miles around nothing would grow, causing the local population to fear the countryside would be turned into a wasteland. Margaret's brother, the prince, just having returned from adventuring abroad and surviving assassination attempts made against him by the evil queen, promised to slay the DRAGON, unaware it was his own sister. He approached the cave and challenged the beast; it came out and begged the prince not to kill it but rather to kiss it three times and it would surrender. The prince obliged and the princess was restored. Hand-in-hand the reunited siblings went home to Bamburg Castle where the king, their father, rejoiced. The wicked queen was revealed for her treachery and was herself transformed into a loathly worm. To this day and until the end of time she will forever remain on the beach spitting poison at maidens who pass her by.

Source: Jacobs, *English Fairy Tales*, 249; Rose, *Spirits, Fairies, Leprechauns, and Goblins*, 226; Kingshill, *Fabled Coast*, n.pag.; Zell-Ravenheart, *Wizard's Bestiary*, 62.

Lobis-Homem

Variations: Lobishomen

Originating in ancient Portuguese folklore there was a species of WEREWOLF known as the lobishomem ("wolf-man"); it is described only as having a short, yellow tail. Those individuals who are lobis-homem are so either because they were one of the *fado* (fated to do so), or they were placed under an evil *sina* (spell).

In the southern providence the lobis-homem is a different species of WEREWOLF than it is in the north; it even has a completely different way of thinking and method of transformation. Those who are lobis-homem here would travel to a crossroads at night and there would spin in a circle five times very quickly, then fall to the ground groveling and howling only to arise as a WEREWOLF. If by chance some other animal had lain in the very spot the person fell upon, the lobis-homem would rise up in animal form. The most obvious difference between the northern and southern WEREWOLVES is the southern lobis-homem has no desire to harm anyone or anything; it actually avoids human contact.

Source: Summers, *Werewolf in Lore and Legend*, 167; Vaz da Silva, *Metamorphosis*, 57

Lobishomen (Low-biz-show-men)

Variations: Lobishumen, Loberia (feminine)

In Brazil there is a vampiric creature called a lobishomen, which is created through the use of witchcraft or is born through an incestuous relationship. It is one of the smallest types of vampires, standing only two inches tall. It has black teeth, bloodless lips, a hunched back, yellowish skin, a white beard, and the overall appearance of a monkey. It prefers to feed off sleeping women and will have a group of several it will rotate through. It seldom kills its victims, taking a survivable amount of blood from each and letting enough time pass between feedings so she can fully recuperate. Eventually, over-use will cause the women to become nymphomaniacs.

The lobishomen has the ability of therianthropy and can shape-shift into small animals, but it should not be confused with the LOBIS-HOMEM of Portugal, which is a species of WEREWOLF.

Source: Critchfield, *Villages*, 348; Folklore Society, *Folklore Record*, Volume 3, 143–44; Knowles, *Nineteenth Century and After*, 78; Woodward, *Werewolf Delusion*

Lobison

Variations: Lobizon, LUISON

In Argentinean folklore the lobison, a WERE-WOLF, is only a concern during the full moon; these creatures prey upon cattle but it is believed anyone who is bitten by one in its wolf form will become a lobison also. It is said when a seventh son is born, he is fated to be a lobison.

Source: Link, *Argentina*, 46; Maberry, *Vampire Universe*, 202; Rose, *Giants, Monsters, and Dragons*, 226

Locuste

The Irish pseudepigraph *Epistil Isu* ("*Sunday Letters*"), written by an anonymous author, describes five kinds of monsters which will descend upon those individuals and heathens who do not keep holy the Lord's Day, Sunday. The locuste ("locusts"), the second of the tormentors mentioned, are described as coming from the East, just as the BRUCHA do, and have wings of iron which they press against anything which gets in their way. The locuste get into the wheat fields and cut the ears off of the plants.

Source: Olsen, *Monsters and the Monstrous in Medieval Northwest Europe*, 69–70

Lofjerskor

Variations: Lof Jerskor

A species of ELF from Swedish folklore or the collective name for the RADANDE, the lofjerskor were the protectors of the sacred groves used by ancient people to worship within, similar to a dryad (a nymph of the forests and trees, particularly oak trees in Greek mythology). If a tree within the grove was larger and healthier than the others it was said to be inhabited by one of the lofjerskor who invisibly lived within its shadow. In exchange for residency this NATURE SPIRIT blessed the tree with health and prosperity and protected it, with violence if need be, against any who would do it harm.

Source: Porteous, *Forest in Folklore and Mythology*, 189; Thorpe, *Northern Mythology*, Volume 2, 71, 73

Log Gar

Originating in the lumberjack communities of the developing United States of America, the log gar, one of the FEARSOME CRITTERS, had teeth like a saw; it was said this fish could slice through a log easily in order to get to an arm and sever it from a person in an instant. A voracious creature, the log gar would cut through nearly anything in its path to get to a person who had fallen into the water.

Source: Godfrey, *Monsters of Wisconsin*, 132; Rose, *Giants, Monsters, and Dragons*, 119

Loha-Mukha

A race of monstrous GIANTS from Hindu mythology, the loha-mukha ("iron faced"), one of the KRAVYAD, have faces made of iron and only one leg and foot. In spite of what would seem to be a handicap, these humanoid cannibals are cunning hunters living exclusively off of humans who wander into their territory.

Source: Coulter, *Encyclopedia of Ancient Deities*, 293; Rose, *Giants, Monsters, and Dragons*, 227

Long Ma (loong ma)

Variations: Long-Mâ

Similar to the DRAGON HORSE and QILIN of Chinese mythology, the long ma of Vietnamese mythology was a DRAGON-horse hybrid; its scales are described as being Piscean.

Source: Eberhart, *Mysterious Creatures*, 142; Jones, *Instinct for Dragons*, 166

Long Wang

Variations: Longwang

A chimerical DRAGON from Chinese mythology, the Long Wang, having a human body but a DRAGON's head, is said to live in the sea where he keeps guard over his great treasure hoard he has amassed from the junks he has sunk over the years. Within his hoard are two priceless gems resembling the eyes of a large fish. Local folklore of the Juanch'eng district claims whenever a dead fish washes ashore without its eyes, Long Wang has added them to his hoard.

In Taoist Chinese mythology the four DRAGON KINGS, AO CH'IN, AO JU, AO KUANG, and AO SHUN, are collectively known as Long Wang.

Source: Forbes, *Illustrated Book of Dragons and Dragon Lore*, n.pag.; Rosen, *Mythical Creatures Bible*, 63; Smith, *Complete Idiot's Guide to World Mythology*, 230

Lord Samanana

In ancient Sumerian mythology, Lord Samanana was one of the many monsters slain by the warrior god Ninurta. Little is known of this creature other than Gudea, a ruler of Lagash (c.a. 2100 BC), referred to it, and the other monsters vanquished by Ninurta, as the SLAIN HEROES; he elevated them all to the status of god and made a place of worship for them in the temple.

Source: Ataç, *Mythology of Kingship in Neo-Assyrian Art*, 185; Salem, *Near East, the Cradle of Western Civilization*, 102–3; Sherman, *Storytelling*, 332

Lotan

Variations: The Fleeting Serpent, LTN, Potentate with Seven Heads, Twisty Serpent

A seven-headed aquatic DRAGON in Canaanite mythology, Lotan sided with the gods Yam ("sea") and Mot ("death") in the attempt to overthrow the fertility god Baal in the battle to restore Chaos (see SEA SERPENT). In scriptures it was described as being a "tortuous serpent"; Lotan was likely the inspiration for the LEVIATHAN of the Hebrew Bible (Old Testament). Ultimately, Baal defeated Mot and delivered a fatal blow to Lotan, as only a god held the power to destroy him.

Source: Anderson, *Out of the Depths*, 27; Isaacs, *Animals in Jewish Thought and Tradition*, 180

Lou Carcolh

In French folklore the lou carcolh was a gigantic chimerical monster, a combination of a mollusk, snail, and serpent, slimy, having long hairy tentacles, and a shell upon its back. The lou carcolh was said to live in a cave beneath the town of Hastingue in southwest France; its viscous slime trail could be seen long before the creature itself, so it was said, but no one would ever dare to follow it, as its tentacles could reach further than could be seen and would snatch up an unsuspecting person to be tossed into the creature's vast mouth.

Source: Covey, *Beasts!*, 61; Rose, *Giants, Monsters, and Dragons*, 229; Zell-Ravenheart, *Wizard's Bestiary*, 63

Loup Carou (Lou Ca-roo)

Variations: Letiche ("carnivorous, aquatic humanoid")

In the Honey Island Swamp in Louisiana, United States of America, there is a bipedal, hairy vampiric creature known as the loup carou. Said to stand over seven feet tall and thought to weigh in excess of 400 pounds, it smells of death and has piercing, sickly yellow eyes set wide apart on its head. It is said the loup carou was once a child who was either lost in the swamp or abandoned there, but in either event was saved and rescued by a mother alligator and raised as one of its own. The loup carou lives in an area only accessible by boat, but routinely finds its way to civilization where it feeds on humans and livestock.

Source: Dickinson, *Haunted City*, 184–87; Holyfield, *Encounters with the Honey Island Swamp Monster*, 10–15; Nickell, *Mystery Chronicles*, 165–75; Summers, *The Werewolf*, 12

Loup Garou

Variations: Bleiz-Garo, Bleiz-Garou, Den-Vleiz, Grek-Vleiz, Lagahoo, Lugarhoo, Rougarou, Rugaru, Rou Garou, Warou

A WEREWOLF originating in French folklore, the loup garou ("a man who turns into a wolf") of Caribbean island folklore appears as a great humanwolf hybrid with a chain about its neck, walking on its hind legs. Some islanders believe a sure sign to identify a loup garou by day is to examine their palms and knees for bruises, as the Devil rides them at night. Another method to reveal the identity of one of these beings is more drastic and would take a person of great commitment; to spill the blood of a loup garou while it is transformed will cause it to instantly revert back to its human guise but the curse will spread to the attacker and last for one hundred and one days; so long as the attacker tells no one what has occurred, the curse will be lifted once it has run its course. However if they tell what happened to them, the curse will become permanent. Perhaps the least aggressive method to detect a loup garou is to take some *yampee* (mucus) from a dog's eye and rub in into your own; then look through a keyhole at midnight to see who becomes apparent as a loup garou.

Source: Grimm, *Teutonic Mythology*, Volume 3, 1094, 1193; Leid, *Myths and Maxims*, n.pag.

Lu Dja Lako

Variations: Lû' Dja Låko

A gigantic bull turtle from the folktale of the Southeastern Indians, the lu dja lako lives in a lake. Although not initially dangerous to humans, if they were to ride upon its back they would discover by the time he reached the water's edge they would be stuck to its shell. No matter how hard they plead or yell or pull at their limbs to make an escape, they will stay fastened to the shell as the creature slips into the water and submerges.

Source: Swanton, *Myths and Tales of the Southeastern Indians*, 36

Luath Luchar

In Irish mythology Luath Luchar was a FAIRY ANIMAL, one of the many hunting dogs of the cultural hero Finn Mac Cumhaill; his other dogs were ADHUNALL, BRAN, SCEOLAN, and SEAR DUGH.

Source: Gregory, *Gods and Fighting Men*, 238, 398; Monaghan, *Encyclopedia of Celtic Mythology and Folklore*, 3

Lubina

In the country of Grenada it is a popular custom to name one's dog CUBILON, LUBINA, or MELAMPO after one of the three dogs who, according to folkloric belief, accompanied the shepherds to look upon the newborn Christ child at Bethlehem. Tradition claims any dog having one of these names will never go mad.

Source: Bates, *Outlook*, Volume 120, 100; Finch, *Gentleman's Magazine* Volume CCLXXIX, 528

Luduan

A type of UNICORN from Chinese folklore, the luduan is similar to the CHIAI TUNG with the ability to detect the truth. A highly auspicious creature, the luduan could travel great distances in a very short amount of time and also had the ability to speak all the varied tongues of the tribes along the borders of ancient China.

Source: Guan, *Behind the veil of the Forbidden City*, 84

Luferlang

Variations: Lufferlang

Originating in the lumberjack communities of the developing United States of America, the luferlang, one of the FEARSOME CRITTERS, was an especially dangerous creature as it would attack without any provocation. Although it only bites once a year, it is always a fatal assault. It was described as having a dark blue stripe along the length of its back and a tail in the middle of its spine. It also had the ability to run backward or forward equally fast without having to turn and face the direction it needed to travel because of its triple jointed legs.

Source: Barber, *Dictionary of Fabulous Beasts*, 98; Rose, *Giants, Monsters, and Dragons*, 119; Tryon, *Fearsome Critters*, 31

Luideag

The luideag ("little shaggy woman" or "the rag") was a type of ATHACH, a FAIRY ANIMAL haunting Loch nam Breacan Dubha ("loch of the black trout") in Skye, Scotland. Said to be evil and injurious by nature, it was described as looking squalid with a mop of shaggy hair atop its head.

Source: Briggs, *Encyclopedia of Fairies*, 272–3; Monaghan, *Encyclopedia of Celtic Mythology and Folklore*, 299; Thompson, *Supernatural Highlands*, 152

Luison

A WEREWOLF-like being from Paraguayan folklore, a luison is created when a person is born the seventh son of an uninterrupted line of boys. The transformation takes place on a Friday night; the person cannot force the change sooner nor can they prevent it from occurring. The luison must roll about on the ground in ashes or sand and will transform into a dog; at dawn he reverts back into his human form.

Once in canine form the luison will go to the cemetery where it will feed upon human corpses and attempt to bite anyone who tries to stop it, passing along a bit of its evil in its saliva, but not the curse. The human form of a luison is easy to spot, as these people have a pronounced pallor and are generally ill-looking and weak. Their social behavior and habits are aberrant; they do not work, and have no desire for any sort of sexual relationship. The luison may attempt to break his curse by being baptized by the Church and having the President of the Republic stand in as his godfather. Some of the police are said to carry specially blessed bullets intended to kill a luison.

Source: MacDonald, *Traditional Storytelling Today*, 492

Lumerpa (loo-MER-pa)

Variations: Lucidius

A bird of Asian folklore, the lumerpa was said to glow so brightly it absorbed its own shadow. It was believed even after the lumerpa died it continued to radiate; however, if any of its feathers were plucked, the lone feather would cease to shine.

Source: Barber, *Dictionary of Fabulous Beasts*, 98; Paul, *Literary Works of Leonardo Da Vinci*, 322

Lung

According to the sixth century author Jen Fang who wrote the *Shus I ki*, the lung ("DRAGON") is one stage of a DRAGON's development. Fang writes the earliest stage of development is that of a water snake, and after five hundred years it transforms into a KIAO; after another one thousand years it transforms into a lung, and after another five hundred years transforms again, this time into a KIOH-LUNG; finally after one thousand more years it transforms into its final stage of development, the YING-YING. Lung dragons tend to live in the sky, but this is not always the case.

In Chinese mythology the lung is also a species of DRAGON said to be the most powerful of dragonkind even though they are completely deaf. Lungs have the ability to control the clouds and make it rain. In art, lungs are depicted with their head facing south and their tail pointing to the north; they are associated with the east and the sun.

Source: De Kirk, *Dragonlore*, 27; De Visser, *Dragon in China and Japan*, 72; Forbes, *Illustrated Book of Dragons and Dragon Lore*, n.pag.

Lung Wang

In the mythology of the ancient Chinese there were said to be four DRAGON KINGS: AO CH'IN, AO JU, AO KUANG, and AO SHUN; however, in sixteenth century Chinese literature the DRAGON KINGS played an important role and two additional kings were created: Lung Wang ("DRAGON KING"), the master of fire, and the uniquely white DRAGON, PAI LUNG. Lung Wang was chimerical, having the body of a human and the head of a DRAGON; he remained tightly coiled up on the bottom of the sea during droughts and in the rainy season would fly through the sky. On occasion, the term Lung Wang is used as the collective name for the DRAGON KINGS.

Source: Andrews, *Dictionary of Nature Myths*, 57; Barber, *Dictionary of Fabulous Beasts*, 98; De Kirk, *Dragonlore*, 25–6, 28

Lungr

Lungr ("the quick") was one of the horses utilized by the Aesir in Norse mythology; its specific owner or rider is not mentioned. Lungr was also listed as one of the many horses who would graze in the red-gilt leafed Glasir Grove.

Source: Grimes, *Norse Myths*, 20; Norroena Society, *Asatrii Edda*, 372

Lupo Mannaro

Variations: Lupo Manaro ("wolf-man")

A WEREWOLF from Italian folklore dating back to ancient Roman times, the lupo mannaro is believed to be a man who transforms into a wolf and is equated with a *bandito* ("he who is banned" and now lives outside of the community). The lupo mannaro savages its prey anywhere on the body, as it needs no specific orifice or particular location on the body in order to kill or rape. As both a man and an animal it is welcomed neither in the countryside nor in human settlements.

Source: Jewell, *Monsters in the Italian Literary Imagination*, 74, 271; Maberry, *Vampire Universe*, 205

Lusca

Variations: Gigant Scuttle, Him of the Hairy Hands, Luska

A gigantic sea creature living in the blue holes off of Andros Island, Bahamas, Lusca, as she is referred to, has been described as being a hybrid, having the jaws of a shark and tentacles like an octopus; she is said to wreck ships and to have the ability to change color, and snatch people off of the deck with her long reach (see SEA SERPENT).

Source: Budd, *Weiser Field Guide to Cryptozoology*, 53–4; Coleman, *Cryptozoology A to Z*, 146; Ho, *Mysteries Unwrapped*, 54; Zell-Ravenheart, *Wizard's Bestiary*, 63

Lutr

Variations: Lut, Lút, Lútr

In Norse mythology, Lutr ("bent" or "stooping") was one of the sons of the hrymthursars (Frost Giants) Thrael and Thir.

Source: Grimes, *Norse Myths*, 27, 286

Lwan

Variations: The Felicitous Yen, Luan, Lwan Shui

Similar to the PHOENIX, the lwan of Chinese mythology looks upon hatching like a common pheasant but when it reaches maturity it gains its full plumage of colors; sometimes it is said to have five different colors but other times it is described as having feathers whose colors change to one of five colors; each color the bird assumes changes the name by which it is called: Fung when red, Hwa Yih when white, To Fu when yellow, Yu Chu when black, or Yu Siang when blue.

The lwan is a divine creature and the very embodiment of beauty and in possession of every grace. When a lwan takes to the sky, one hundred birds follow suit and when one of the lwan dies, one-hundred birds gather around it and peck at the ground in order to bury it.

Source: Gould, *Dragons, Unicorns, and Sea Serpents*, 369–

70; Rose, *Giants, Monsters, and Dragons*, 230; Zell-Ravenheart, *Wizard's Bestiary*, 63

Lycabas

A CENTAUR from ancient Greek mythology,
Lycabas attended the wedding of Pirithous, where
drunken EURYTUS who assaulted the bride, Hippodame, led the way for other inebriated Centaurs to
assault and rape any women they could grab. During the ensuing battle, Lycabas, along with MER-
MEROS ORNEUS, PISENOR, and THAUMAS, was slain
by spear-wielding Lapith soldier Dryas.

Source: *Commentary, Mythological, Historical, and Geographical on Pope's Homer*, 55; Simpson, *Metamorphoses of
Ovid*, 205

Lycetus

A CENTAUR from ancient Greek mythology, Lycetus was one of the many who fought against the
demi-god and hero Hercules (Heracles) during the
Battle of Arcadia.

Source: *Commentary, Mythological, Historical, and Geographical on Pope's Homer*, 55; Murray, *Classical Manual*, 55

Lyciday

A CENTAUR from ancient Greek mythology, Lyciday, one of the centaurs who attended the wedding
of Pirithous, became drunk on wine and following
the lead of EURYTUS who assaulted Hippodame,
began to assault and rape any women they could
grab.

During the ensuing Centauromachy, Lyciday,
along with AREOS, IMBRIUS, and EURYNOMUS, was
slain by the the Lapith soldier Dryas as they
attempted to flee the battle.

Source: *Commentary, Mythological, Historical, and Geographical on Pope's Homer*, 55; Simpson, *Metamorphoses of
Ovid*, 205

Lycides

Variations: Lycidas

A CENTAUR from ancient Greek mythology,
Lycides was one of the many who fought against
the demi-god and hero Hercules (Heracles) during
the Battle of Arcadia.

Source: *Commentary, Mythological, Historical, and Geographical on Pope's Homer*, 55; Lemprière, *Bibliotheca Classica*,
694

Lycisca

Variations: Lycisce

A dog from ancient Greek mythology, Lycisca
("wolf") was one of the DOGS OF ACTÆON, the
unfortunate youth who was raised by the CENTAUR
CHEIRON. Lycisca, a female, was the sister of fellow
pack member CYPRIUS.

Source: Leeming, *World of Myth*, 111; Murray, *Classical
Manual*, 160; Naso, *Fasti, Tristia*, 93–5

Lycus

A CENTAUR from ancient Greek mythology,
Lycus was, according to Ovid's *Metamorphoses*, one
of the guests at the wedding of Pirithous, who
became drunk on wine and following the lead of
EURYTUS who assaulted Hippodame, began to
assault and rape any women they could grab. In the
ensuing Centauromachy, he and CROMIS were slain
by Pirithous.

Source: *Commentary, Mythological, Historical, and Geographical on Pope's Homer*, 55; Simpson, *Metamorphoses of
Ovid*, 206

Lyon-Poisson

A very rare creature from the symbology of heraldry, the lyon-poisson is depicted as a fish with the
body and head of lion.

Source: Lower, *Curiosities of Heraldry*, 99; Millington, *Heraldry in History, Poetry, and Romance*, 290; Zell-Ravenheart,
Wizard's Bestiary, 63

Ma Yüan-shuai

A three-eyed monster from Chinese folklore, Ma
Yüan-shuai had been known for his excessive cruelty in the methods he employed in destroying evil
spirits; for his actions he was condemned by Ju Lai
to reincarnate. Reborn, at the age of just a few days
old, he was already capable of fighting and had
killed the DRAGON KING of the Eastern Sea, AO
KUANG.

Source: Werner, *Myths and Legends of China*, 114

Maanegarm (MAHN-a-garm-r)

Variations: Maana-Garm, Mana-Garm, Mána-
garm, Mánagarm, Mána-Garm, Managarma, Managarmr, Mánagarmr, Managarmr, Mána-Garmr,
Manigarm, Moongarm, Moongarm

A wolf born the son of Angroboda and FENRIR,
Maanegarm ("moon hound," "moon swallower" or
or "moon wolf") lives in the Jarnvidr Forest and endlessly pursues the moon with the intent to consume
it; according to folklore, he will at the time of Ragnarok.

Source: Anderson, *Norse Mythology*, 452; Grimes, *Norse
Myths*, 286; Jennbert, *Animals and Humans*, 50; Norroena
Society, *Asatrii Edda*, 373; Oehlenschläger, *Gods of the North*,
liv

Macan Gadongan

Variations: Gadungan, Macan Gadungan

A were-tiger from Javanese folklore, the macan
gadongan ("tiger disguised" or "tiger false") is
described as a mad or rabid tiger with the soul of a
sleeping man. It is also believed a person may trans-

form themselves into a macan gadonga by participating in a magical ritual known as the *ngelmu gadungan*. In this instance, a tell-tale sign of a person who has undergone the ceremony is they will not have a philtrum.

Source: Newman, *Tracking the Weretiger*, 102

Mada

A fearsome and gigantic monster, Mada ("drunkenness, frenzy; insanity, lust, madness") was created by the sage Chyavana; it was divided into four parts—drinking, hunting, gambling, and women—the four vices. When the sage and god Indra quarreled over admission into the Soma Offering ceremony Indra hurled a mountain and thunderbolts at the sage who retaliated by creating Mada, a frightening open-mouthed monster created from the substance of the oblation; it was described as having grinders and fangs of significant length and jaws so large its upper set could sink into the heavens while the lower set pierced the earth. The gods were fearful of being consumed by Mada and Indra conceded to Chyavana, thereby allowing the Ashvins to become soma drinkers. Once they settled their differences, the sage then slew Mada, chopping its body into many pieces.

Source: Monier-Williams, *Sanskrit-English Dictionary*, 734; Muir, *Original Sanskrit Texts on the Origin and History of the People of India*, 471; Zell-Ravenheart, *Wizard's Bestiary*, 64

Maera

In ancient Greek mythology Maera was the faithful dog of Erigone and her father, Icarius. The god Bacchus (Dionysos) paid the small family a visit and was so impressed with their hospitality he taught them the secret of winemaking and took the enthralled and enamored Erigone as his lover. One day Icarius came upon some shepherds from another village and gave them a sample of his wine, warning them to be sure to dilute it first. The shepherds did not follow the warning and when they managed to awaken the next day believed Icarius tried to poison them; in an act of what they believed to be revenge they found and killed Icarius, leaving his body beneath a pine tree. Erigone could not find her father but Maera was able to track his scent and they made the gruesome discovery. The daughter was beyond grief over the loss of her father and as inconsolable as she was, hung herself from the tree shading her father's corpse. Maera, faithful to his owners, refused to leave them and remained with their bodies until he too died, succumbing to starvation. When Bacchus (Dionysos) discovered what had occurred he caused all of the women from the village where the shepherds lived to hang themselves. For his devotion Maera was taken into the night sky and became *Canis Minor*, the constellation of the Lesser Dog-Star.

Source: Smith, *Dictionary of Greek and Roman Biography and Mythology*, 558; Westmoreland, *Ancient Greek Beliefs*, 53, 65

Maero

Variations: Maeroero, Mairoero, Mohoao, Mohowao, Te-aitanga-a-Hine-mate-roe

A type of WILD MAN from Maori folklore, the maero ("WILD MAN of the woods") live in the forested mountains of New Zealand. Naked, as their bodies are covered with very long and thick yellow hair, and weaponless, they hunt using nothing more than their brute strength and their long and sharp fingernails, harpooning birds with them and disemboweling and consuming them on the spot. They are said to be tall and have tusks pointing downwards from the corners of their mouth and their nocturnal cry of *"makona!"* is frightening enough to shock a man to death. Both cunning and mischievous the maero are known to kidnap young adults and maidens from time to time but there are tales of escapes occurring. Maero have the ability of speech and laugh a great deal when pleased with themselves. In one story, a severed head of a maero continues to live on holding conversations with his wife; in another tale, a hunter's bullet dodges around the Maero afraid to hit it.

Source: Forth, *Images of the Wildman in Southeast Asia*, 248; Tregear, *Maori Race*, 572

Mafedet

Variations: Sta

In ancient Egyptian mythology the mafedet was a hybrid creature having the body of a lion but the neck and head of a snake, similar to the MUSHUSSU of Akkadian, Babylonian, and Mesopotamian mythology.

Source: Hargreaves, *Hargreaves New Illustrated Bestiary*, 84; Rose, *Giants, Monsters, and Dragons*, 233; Zell-Ravenheart, *Wizard's Bestiary*, 91

Magtitima

A species of NATURE SPIRIT from Filipino folklore, the invisible magtitimas are said to live in balete trees; unless these beings are given an offering of white chickens they will cause a serious illness to befall anyone who cuts down one of their trees.

Source: Ramos, *Creatures of Philippine Lower Mythology*, 62

Maha-Pudma

In Hindu mythology, CHUKWA is the gigantic tortoise which the great elephant Maha-Pudma stands upon which in turn supports the world we live upon. Maha-Pudma was one of the four mountainous elephants who supported the weight of the world upon their heads; he was the guardian of the South. BHARDRA guarded the North, SAUMANASA guarded the West, and VIRUPAKSHA guarded the East. Maha-Pudma, as he and his companions support the earth from below, is not one of the DIG-GAJAS.

Source: Brewer, *Wordsworth Dictionary of Phrase and Fable*, 1086; Dalal, *Hinduism*, 43; Vālmīki, *Ramayana: Book 1*, 223

Mahoragas

One of the eight classes of celestial beings in Hindu mythology, the mahoragas ("moving on a great belly") are described as having a human body but snake heads.

Source: De Visser, *Dragon in China and Japan*, xiii; Hsing Yun, *Universal Gate*, 7, 132

Maiangara

The RAINBOW SERPENT of Karadjeri mythology of Australia, Maiangara ("rainbow death adder") is associated with the mythical water snake PULANG.

Source: Buchler, *Rainbow Serpent*, 4, 102

Maide

In Basque mythology the maide are nocturnal NATURE SPIRITS living in the mountainous regions; they are the builders of the *cromlechs* (ancient structures of single stones encircling a mound); the female counterpart is known as LAMINAK. In the night the maide leave their mountain home and descend into town, entering into the homes of those who have left offerings for them by use of the chimney.

Source: Gimbutas, *Living Goddesses*, 174; Miguel de Barandiarán, *Selected Writings of José Miguel De Barandiarán*, 88

Maighdean Uaine

One of the FUATH of Scottish folklore, maighdean uaine ("green maiden") was always described as being beautiful, even when taking on the form of a goat, a half goat and half woman, or as a woman. Sitting by the side of a brook, river, or stream, she waited for someone to come along so she may ask for assistance in crossing. Those who agreed were found with their throats cut.

There was also the belief the maighdean uaine was a species of psychopomp (death omen). Attached to a family it would do chores around the house while the family slept and would wail out like a banshee (an Irish ancestral spirit) when one of her chosen family died.

Sources: Rose, *Giants, Monsters, and Dragons*, 234; Swire, *Skye*, 197

Mairi

In Basque mythology the mairi are the NATURE SPIRITS believed to have built the dolmens and the megalithic structures consisting of two upright stones and a capstone.

Source: Gimbutas, *Living Goddesses*, 174; Miguel de Barandiarán, *Selected Writings of José Miguel De Barandiarán*, 88

Maka

A crocodile in ancient Egyptian mythology, Maka, a son of the god Set, attacks Ra the sun god as he makes his daily journey across the sky; Maka also is said to have devoured the arms of the god Osiris.

Source: Renouf, *Lectures on the Origin and Growth of Religion*, 115; Zell-Ravenheart, *Wizard's Bestiary*, 64

Makara

Variations: Fish-lion

A chimerical species of water-dwelling DRAGON from Vedic mythology, the makara ("crocodile," "a monster") are described as having the forequarters of an antelope, cat, or elephant and the hindquarters of a fish. Having the ability of therianthropy, enabling them to shape-shift, they can assume many different forms but seemed to favor a hybrid-looking creature with the forequarters of a crocodile and the hindquarters of a snake. A makara is the mount of the god Varuna. Creatures with similar appearance appear in the folklore and mythology of Indonesia, Indo-China, Kashmire, Nepal, and Tibet.

Source: Debroy, *Mahabharata: Volume 3*, 247; De Kirk, *Dragonlore*, 36; Ingersoll, *Dragons and Dragon Lore*, 46, 48–9; Jones, *Instinct for Dragons*, 9

Maliades

Variations: Maliadus, Meliades

The maliades were, in classical Greek mythology, the hamadryads (the nymphs of oak trees) of fruit trees or sheep flocks, as the Greek word for apple and sheep is the same.

Source: Coulter, *Encyclopedia of Ancient Deities*, 202; Keightley, *Mythology of Ancient Greece and Italy*, 209

Mama Dlo (MAH-mah D'low)

Variations: Mama Dglo, Mama Glow, Mama D'leau, Maman de l' eau

In the mythology of the people from the Republic of Trinidad and Tobago, the aquatic creature or devil called Mama Dlo ("mother of the water") is described as having the appearance of a DRAKAINA, the head and shoulders of a beautiful woman with long hair and the body of a snake. This demon uses her beauty to lure men off to their deaths by crushing their bodies during her lovemaking, restoring them back to life and killing them anew, for all time her sex slaves. Although she will prey upon any man she can get, Mama Dlo particularly hunts out those who destroy the natural swamp habitat where she lives.

Telltale signs of Mama Dlo's presence in an area are reports of men on work crews disappearing. Survivors also say they heard a loud cracking sound, which is said to be the noise she makes with her tail as she slaps it on the surface of a mountain pool or a still lagoon. Should this demon ever be encountered, remove your left shoe and place it upside-down on the path before you, then walking backwards, quickly return to your home.

Source: Jones, *Evil in Our Midst*, 126–9; Lewis, *Guinea's Other Suns*, 179; Philpott, *Trinidad and Tobago*, 53, 89

Mameleu

In Filipino folklore, the mameleu is said to be a gigantic white-horned serpentine DRAGON, capable of breathing fire and having glowing and evil looking red eyes. Preying on fishermen, it hunts the waters of Laguna Bay on nights of the full moon (see SEA SERPENT). The MARCUPO is said to be its land-based cousin.

Source: Ramos, *Creatures of Midnight*, 23; Redfern, *Most Mysterious Places on Earth*, 112

Mamlambo

Variations: Brain Sucker

In African witchcraft the serpentine mamlambo ("mother of the river") is sometimes kept as a FAMILIAR and utilized as a lover. The witch creates one of these creatures by placing a root, twig, or "something like a fish" in a bottle. In due time, the object will come to life, as can be told by its nocturnal glow, and eventually will transform into a large hairy snake with oversized fangs and eyes which twinkle like diamonds. By day the mamlambo is hidden in the river but by night it takes on a human form appearing as a white man or white woman with silver hair to become the witch's lover.

The mamlambo are exceptionally demanding and possessive creatures; they will not tolerate the witch having a traditional relationship with a human nor allow them to marry or have children. The mamlambo will make regular offerings of money to its witch and some of these people become wealthy because of it; however the FAMILIAR expects regular sacrifices of beef, chicken, or human blood. If the mamlambo's demands are not met, it will kill the witch. The mamlambo is the personification of greed.

Source: Ashforth, *Witchcraft, Violence, and Democracy in South Africa*, 41; Kiernan, *Power of the Occult in Modern Africa*, 93–4; Zell-Ravenheart, *Wizard's Bestiary*, 64

Manaul

In the Visayan creation legend there were only three things in the world: the air, the sea, and a bird by the name of Manaul. Ever on the search for a place to land and rest, Manaul was unsuccessful; one day he cried out to the gods for help. Kaptan and the god of the sea created tidal waves to beat the sky while Magauayan, god of the air, created whirlwinds to beat back the waves with rocks and soil; their battle created dry land. This process lasted for several thousand years until Manaul, wanting desperately to rest, carried some stones from the top of a mountain and dropped them on the heads of the dueling gods. This not only ended their battle but also created the Philippine islands. Alighting on a branch of bamboo Manaul then heard a faint cry for help coming from within the bamboo. Pecking at it until it split open, out came the first man, Si-Kalac, and the first woman, Si-Kavay.

Source: Halili, *Philippine History*, 16

Manetuwi-Rusi-Pissi

A venerated lake monster in Shawnee folklore, Manetuwi-Rusi-Pissi ("water tiger") is similar to the LENAPIZKA of the Peoria people of Illinois; it is the guardian of the fish and the lakes.

Source: Meurger, *Lake Monster Traditions*, 161; Zell-Ravenheart, *Wizard's Bestiary*, 65

Mang

A species of DRAGON from Korean folklore, the mang ("four-clawed DRAGON") are similar in appearance to the KIOH-LUNG; they are the symbol of the power held by lesser nobles and officials.

Source: De Kirk, *Dragonlore*, 36; Eberhart, *Mysterious Creatures*, 142; Jung, *Feel of Korea*, 142

Mangarsahoc

Variations: Mangarisaoka

In Madagascan folklore the mangarsahoc ("whose ears hide its chin") is described as being a large creature having ears so lengthy they fall over its eyes whenever it walks downhill, tripping over them with its equine hooves. The mangarsahoc, the very sight of which is said to bring bad luck, brays like a wild ass.

Source: Heuvelmans, *On The Track of Unknown Animals*, 299; Zell-Ravenheart, *Wizard's Bestiary*, 65

Mangmangkit

A species of hamadryads (the nymphs of oak trees in Greek mythology) from Filipino folklore, the mangmangkit live within the trees; to avoid their vengeance, prayers are said to these NATURE SPIRITS before felling a tree.

Source: Ramos, *Creatures of Philippine Lower Mythology*, 63

Mantahungal

In the demonology of the Tagbanua people of the Philippines the mantahungal is a demonic creature living in the forests on top of high mountains. Described as being a hornless, shaggy cow with a monstrous mouth and tusk-like incisors, it rips humans apart with its tusks.

Source: Ramos, *Creatures of Philippine Lower Mythology*, 344

Manticora

Variations: Leucrocuta, Lympago, Mantegre, Mantichora, Manticore, Manticory, Manticoras, Man-Tiger, Man-Tigeris, Mantikhoras, Mantiserra, Mancomorion, Mantygre, Mard-Khor ("man-eater"), Maricomorion, Martikhorai, Martiora, Memecoleous, Montegre, Satyral

Originating in Persian literature as a creature of Indian mythology, the chimerical manticora ("to eat man") is described as having the head of a grey-eyed man, the blood-red body of a lion, a tail with a scorpion stinger, and three rows of fangs in its mouth; it is one of the KHRAFSTRA. Ancient writers claimed its voice as being a low hiss while others said it's high-pitched. Later authors added to the original description of the creature bovine udders, eagle or GRIFFIN talons, horns upon the head, wings, and a tail covered with spikes which could be thrown great distances. It has been compared to the CROCOTTA.

Extremely agile and sure footed, the manticora had powerful and strong legs, capable of leaping over or out of any ditch or obstacle established to capture it. In spite of its human head, the manticora had an insatiable and voracious appetite for human flesh.

Source: Allaby, *Animals*, 83–4; Fox-Davies, *Complete Guide to Heraldry*, 232; Lehner, *Big Book of Dragons, Monsters, and Other Mythical Creatures*, 71; White, *Book of Beasts*, 52

Mantindane (Man-tin-dane)

Variations: Chitauli, TIKOLOSHE

The people of Kenya tell of a vampiric creature standing two or three feet tall called a *mantindane* ("fairy man" or "star monkey"). Its very wide body is covered with brown-orange fur. It has a narrow head, pointed ears, and dark, slitted eyes. Because it never wears any clothes, we also know it has a long, serpentine penis.

Often bound to a witch and used as her FAMILIAR, the mantindane is well suited for this purpose. It knows how to use magic, as well as the secret to brewing its own type of poison. Often asked to kill the witch's enemies, the mantindane will make a batch of its special poison and sneak into a person's home completely undetected, as it also knows how to turn invisible. Its poison is carried through the air and soon will kill everyone inside. Just a few drops of the toxin in the local water supply will kill anyone who drinks from it.

Mantindanes drink the blood they need to survive from cattle mostly. They have a compulsion to drink milk directly from the animal, so when they look for a cave near water to live in, preferably along the riverbank, they like to be sure cows frequent the area. Otherwise, if opportunity presents itself and there is no danger or risk in doing so, the mantindane will feed off a sleeping child or woman. Fortunately, for cows and humans alike, it can easily be warded off with iron.

Mantindane are often blamed for spreading a mysterious sickness in a community, and because of this, a witch doctor is often employed to make a magical trap to capture the vampire, paralyze it, and remove all of its powers. However, never point at one of these traps and say "Look, it's captured!" or something similar, as doing so will break the spell, free the mantindane, and restore its powers.

It is advised women sleep in an elevated bed so as not to attract the attention of a mantindane, should one sneak into the home invisibly and wander around looking for some mischief to cause. There is a growing belief the mantindane is not a species of vampiric creature, but rather an alien trying to use the women of Africa to perpetuate its own species.

Source: Curran, *Vampires*, 177–8; Jacobs, *UFOs and Abductions*, 225

Mao-Tuh

The ancient Chinese author Hwai nan Tsze, in his attempt to prove how all creatures are the progeny of the DRAGON, shows the quadruped mao-tuh ("hairy calf") as being the progenitor of the YING-LUNG.

Source: De Visser, *Dragon in China and Japan*, 65, 72

Marakihan

A SEA SERPENT living off of the coast of New Zealand, the marakihan is described as having the head of a man but the body of a fish. Using its long tubular tongue the creature draws canoes and other small water craft into its mouth, consuming them.

Source: Kubesh, *Mythological Creatures Around the World*, 17; Zell-Ravenheart, *Wizard's Bestiary*, 66

Marcupo

Variations: Macupo

In the folklore from the Philippines, the marcupo is a type of gigantic snake said to live near the mountain peaks. In addition to its unusual size, the marcupo is noted for its forked tail, red-crested head, sharp tusks, and thorn-like hairs covering its forked tongue. It has the ability to breathe out a blast of virulent poison, an ingredient much sought after by those who make potions. On quiet days it is said the marcupo can be heard singing sonorously.

Source: Ramos, *Creatures of Philippine Lower Mythology*, 36; Redfern, *Most Mysterious Places on Earth*, 112

Mareikura

Variations: Apa-Mareikura

A species of supernatural female beings from Polynesian mythology, the mareikura, along with their male counterparts the Whatukura, live in the upper world as the attendants of the god Io. Acting as his attendants and couriers they have control over the beings, creatures, and denizens of the lower worlds. They had the ability to move freely among the twelve worlds. The mareikura utilized their own species of servitors known as the APA; they were said to resemble whirlwinds.

Source: Reed, *Reed Book of Māori Mythology*, 43–4, 88; Whatahoro, *Lore of the Whare-wānanga*, xv

Mares of Diomedes

Variations: Mares of Thrace

In ancient Greek mythology the eighth Labor of the demi-god and hero Hercules (Heracles) involved taming the Mares of Diomedes, four anthropophagous (man-eating) wild and uncontrollable creatures belonging to King Diomedes of Aetolia or the GIGANTE Diomedes (sources conflict); no matter who the owner, he was only just able to contain them as they had been driven insane, raised on a diet of human flesh. Some tellings described fire shooting from their nostrils.

There are many versions of the tale and of how the demi-god completed this task; most all of them involve him having to kill Diomedes and then feeding his body to the horses, which cures them of their insanity enabling him to then take the horses to King Eurystheus. Once the horses arrive the story again splinters into different endings: they were dedicated to Hera (Juno); set free to roam Argos; taken to Olympus and sacrificed to Zeus (Jupiter); slain by bears, lions, and wolves at Zeus's command.

Although the horses are mares, the Latin author Hyginus (64 BC–AD 17), the only author who ever named them, gave them all masculine names: DINOS, LAMPON, PHOLGIOS, and XANTHOS. Alexander the Great claimed his horse Bucephalus (Bucephalas) to be descended from these mares.

Source: Daly, *Greek and Roman Mythology, A to Z*, 70; Dixon-Kennedy, *Encyclopedia of Greco-Roman Mythology*, 1, 156; Roman, *Encyclopedia of Greek and Roman Mythology*, 210

Marine Lion

The French barber surgeon for kings Henry II, Francis II, Charles IX and Henry III, Ambroise Paré (1517–1590) said of the marine lion in his book *On Monsters and Marvels* that it was a creature like a lion but its body was covered entirely with scales rather than fur. Alleged to have been caught in the Tyrrhenian Sea in or around 1540, the marine lion was presented to the bishop of Castre, but it expired soon after. The marine lion was said to have a voice similar sounding to a human's.

Source: Evlin, *Elvin's Dictionary of Heraldry*, 84; Pare, *On Monsters and Marvels*, 109–10; Rose, *Giants, Monsters, and Dragons*, 236–7

Marine Sow

A SEA SERPENT or monster alleged to have been once caught off the Isle of Thylen in Scandinavian waters, the marine sow was described in great detail by traveler Olaus Magnus in 1538. Said to have been seventy-two feet long, fourteen feet wide and seven feet from eye to eye on its porcine (piglike) head, the marine sow had an additional six eyes, three pairs running down each side of is long scaly body. Its liver was said to have been so large it filled the entirety of five wine caskets.

Source: Pare, *On Monsters and Marvels*, 114; Rose, *Giants, Monsters, and Dragons*, 237

Marool

The marool is an extremely malevolent FAIRY ANIMAL from Scotland. This creature was described as looking like a large fish with a crest of flame running down its back and many sets of eyes covering its head. Appearing when the sea-foam was phosphorescent, the marool was especially active during storms, calling out with a wild triumphant song.

Source: Briggs, *Encyclopedia of Fairies*, 281; Saxby, *Shetland Traditional Lore*, 140

Marrock

Variations: Marrocke, Marrok the Good Knight, Marrok, Merrak, Mewreke

A WEREWOLF from Arthurian folklore told by Malory, Marrock, a knight of the Round Table, could not assume human form unless he was in possession of his clothes. One day his wife, wishing to spend time with her lover, hid them, forcing him to live in the hills like an animal for seven years. King Arthur encountered the animal and was soon able to discern it was under an enchantment; he took the wolf back to court with him where it came face to face with his wife. Rather than attacking her, Sir Marrock was exceedingly friendly; so moved, she returned the clothes, restoring her husband to his human form. Marrock was slain in battle by Modred.

Source: Ackerman, *Index of the Arthurian Names in Middle English*, Volume 10, 161; Bruce, *Arthurian Name Dictionary*, 348; Monaghan, *Encyclopedia of Celtic Mythology and Folklore*, 315

Marsok

Appearing on the Hereford map is a chimerical creature scholars call the marsok, a wild quadrupedal animal with the ability to change shape; it is depicted on the map in a most curious manner. The marsok's feet are each of a different class of animal; its forefeet are a mammalian paw and a bird's webbed foot while its back feet are shown to be a hoof and a five-toed human foot. More than a shape-shifter, the marsok, most interestingly placed near the Tower of Babel, had the ability to move between predator and prey, animal and human.

Source: Harvey, *Hereford World Map*, 159; Mittman, *Maps and Monsters in Medieval England*, 54–5

Marsyas

A SATYR from ancient Greek mythology, Marsyas of Phrygia was once a skilled flautist who was proud of his skill. One day he came upon an *auios* (double flute) shortly after the goddess Athena (Minerva) had invented it. Impressed with how wonderfully he could instantly play the newly constructed instrument he challenged the god Apollo to a contest, the prize being that the loser had to do whatever the winner said. In some versions of the tale, Apollo had set out from the beginning to teach the proud SATYR a lesson and was the one who had challenged him to a contest, already having a cunning plan in the works. The MUSES acted as the judges. As each contestant played equally well, Apollo then inverted his lyre and asked Marsyas do the same; when he was unable to comply as a woodwind instrument cannot be played in such as fashion, the MUSES declared Apollo the winner. To punish Marsyas for his boastful pride, thinking he could beat a god, Apollo hung the SATYR from a tree and had him flayed alive. The Marsyas River was created from a combination of the SATYR'S blood and the tears wept from the local NYMPHS, SATYRS, and shepherds.

Source: Apollodorus, *Library of Greek Mythology*, 32; Hard, *Routledge Handbook of Greek Mythology*, 157

Martlet

Variations: Mercula, Merle, Merlette

In the heraldic symbology the beakless and feetless martlet is symbolic of the fourth-born son. The bird was said to be unable to take flight again if it ever landed upon the ground as it had no legs to launch from and its wings too long to catch air under. For this reason the martlet would make their perch and nest only in high places where they could dive off before opening up their wings and maintaining flight.

Source: Dennys, *Heraldic Imagination*, 182; Porny, *Elements of Heraldry*, 336; Zell-Ravenheart, *Wizard's Bestiary*, 66

Massaru Tami

Variations: The Muddy Ones

Massaru Tami ("guardians of the sea") is the collective name for the first children born of the DRAGON goddess TIAMAT, LAHAMU and Lahmu. The siblings are considered to be primordial because they were born before the other gods banished their mother to the darkness.

Source: Ford, *Maskim Hul*, 147

Master Stoorworm

Variations: Mester Stoorworm, Stoorworm ("great serpent")

A gigantic SEA SERPENT from Celtic folklore, Master Stoorworm would come inland daily to raid the farmlands of any stock and unfortunate people he could snatch up to devour. A young man by the name of Jamie (or Assipattle) was said to have slain the horrid creature; its teeth became the foundation upon which the Faroe, Orkney, and Shetland Islands rest and its body became Iceland.

Source: De Kirk, *Dragonlore*, 43–44; Zell-Ravenheart, *Wizard's Bestiary*, 91

Mata

A sea-turtle once said to live in the Valley of the Mata, Ireland, and there so named, Mata ("monster") was said to be so large it could consume a man in full armor in a single bite; it was described as having one hundred forty legs and four heads. The monument to commemorate the location of its death is known as the Stone of Benn.

Source: Gregory, *Gods and Fighting Men*, 78; Madden, *Shrines and Sepulchres of the Old and New World*, Volume 1, 391

Matlose

A hobgoblin from the folklore of the Nuu-chah-nulth people of the Pacific Northwest Canadian coast, Matlose is described as having the semblance of a humanoid head, monstrous teeth, bristly black fur, and ursine (bearlike) claws. It is said whoever hears its voice will fall into a trance and walk right up to it; then Matlose will kill them with a single swipe of his claws.

Source: Dorman, *Origin of Primitive Superstitions and Their Development*, 89; Eberhart, *Mysterious Creatures*, 322

Matruculan

A type of creature or INCUBUS from Filipino folklore, the matruculan is particularly malevolent; first it stalks a virgin, rapes her, impregnates her, and then at some point during the pregnancy returns to kill the mother and consume the unborn fetus. In order to protect the mother and child the husband of the woman must swing a balisong (butterfly or fan knife) over the mother's belly while she is in labor.

Source: Frater, *Listverse*, n.pag.

Mau-Ola

In Hawaiian mythology Mau-ola is a DRAGON goddess, a descendant of the primordial DRAGON goddess MO-O-INANEA.

Source: Monaghan, *Encyclopedia of Goddesses and Heroines*, 155

Mauari

Variations: Spirits of the Water

NATURE SPIRITS in Venezuelan folklore, the mauari are the benign counterpart to the evil sarauna; collectively they are referred to as the two *gamihas*.

Source: Porteous, *Lore of the Forest*, 146; Rose, *Spirits, Fairies, Leprechauns, and Goblins, an Encyclopedia*, 124; Tylor, *Primitive Culture*, 249

Mbōn

The mbōn are NATURE SPIRITS or nats (the generic name for the indigenous NATURE SPIRITS of the air, cultivated fields, earth, forest, hills, households, rain, rivers, sky, streams, wind, and the like) from Burmese folklore, specifically of the wind. Worshiped only during the national harvest, the mbōn are credited with bringing the fertilizing rains.

Source: Hastings, *Encyclopedia of Religion and Ethics*, Part 5, 22; Porteous, *Forest in Folklore and Mythology*, 125; Scott, *The Burman: His Life and Notions*, Volume 1, 286

Mbumba Luangu

Variations: Mbumba, Rainbow Snake

In the mythology of the people living along the Congo-Gabon boarder, Mbumba Luangu is a gigantic snake living in the water; when it tires of the rain falling, it climbs up a tree and its reflection creates a rainbow. It is said a secret society called the Bakimba worship it. Local folklore warns against standing where the mbumba luangu is likely to rise up or looking into the mist which accompanies its appearance because to do so will ruin your eyesight.

Source: Savil, *Pears Encyclopedia of Myths and Legends*, 157; Werner, *Myths and Legends of the Bantu*, n.pag.

Mebeddel

In Moroccan folklore a mebeddel is a species of CHANGELING, a creature left behind by one of the djinn (a race of demons) when it kidnaps a human child shortly after its birth. This creature, no matter how well it is cared for, will become thin and grow wizened and ugly. The human infant may be returned to its natural mother if the parent notices the switch quickly enough. To regain her child she must take the mebeddel to a graveyard and place it in an open tomb with offerings to the djinn. The mother must then walk away and remain unseen until she hears the baby cry; then she must quickly take up the child and lay claim to it, returning home to bathe it in holy water.

Source: Legey, *Folklore of Morocco*, 154; Rose, *Spirits, Fairies, Leprechauns, and Goblins*, 216

Medon

A CENTAUR from ancient Greek mythology, Medon was the younger brother of PHOLUS; he once stole a human baby from a settlement determined to raise it as his foster son, as his own mate Hipponoe was deceased. PHOLUS agrees to assist in rearing the boy, determined to make him into a fierce warrior who will one day avenge their death should they need it.

Medon attended the wedding of Pirithous, where drunken EURYTUS who assaulted the bride, Hippodame, led the way for other inebriated CENTAURS to assault and rape any women they could grab. During the ensuing Centauromachy, he, along with LYCABAS, ORNEUS, PISENOR, and THAUMAS, was slain by spear-wielding Lapith soldier Dryas.

Source: *Commentary, Mythological, Historical, and Geographical on Pope's Homer*, 55; Lemprière, *Bibliotheca Classica*, 694

Medusa

The best known of the three GORGONS from ancient Greek mythology, Medusa ("the mad" and "the queen") and her sisters, EURYALE and STHENO, were born the daughters of Phorcys and Ceto. Medusa was a beautiful, golden-haired maiden and a sworn virgin priestess of the goddess Athena (Minerva). Her beauty drew the attention of the god of the sea, Poseidon (Neptune); the two fell in love and consummated their affection for one another in the temple of the goddess she served. Athena (Minerva) punished not only Medusa but her sisters as well, transforming them all into GORGONS: each curly lock of hair became a venomous snake, their gentle eyes were now furious blood-shot orbs, their milk-white skin took on a green tint and developed scales; boar teeth protruded from their mouths, and their hands became brass claws.

Medusa wandered the world hated and shunned as the sight of her could frighten a man to death or turn him to stone. As she walked over Africa, infant snakes hatched and fell from her head, delivering poisonous vipers to the land. She led a life of lonesome misery until she was slain by the hero Perseus, as Medusa was the only mortal GORGON. The blood from her beheading birthed Chrysaor and the winged horse PEGASUS. Blood taken from the right side of a GORGON could bring the dead back to life, while blood from the left was an instantly fatal poison.

The remaining GORGONS, EURYALE and STHENO, are said to live in the Underworld as the servants of the god Hades (Dis) or on a mysterious and remote island far out to sea, beyond even the sacred stream of OCEANUS.

Source: Apollodorus, *Library of Greek Mythology*, 66, 211; Berens, *Myths and Legends of Ancient Greece and Rome*, 144–5; Daly, *Greek and Roman Mythology, A to Z*, 90

Megaera

Variations: Megaira

One of the three FURIES from classical Greek mythology, Megaera ("envious anger" or "slaughter") was the sister who specialized in jealousy. She like her sisters, ALECTO ("envy" or "never ending") and TISIPHONE ("face of retaliation" or "rage"), was described as looking like an old hag with bat wings, bloodshot eyes, and snakes in her hair; sometimes they were confused as being a GORGON. The ancient Greek tragedian Aeschylus (525 BC–456 BC) claimed the sisters were the daughters of Night while the tragedian Sophocles (497 BC–406 BC) said they were the daughter of Skotos, the personification of darkness, and the earth.

Source: Drury, *Dictionary of the Esoteric*, 93; Hard, *Routledge Handbook of Greek Mythology*, 39

Mehen

According to ancient Egyptian mythology Mehen was a gigantic serpent which surrounded the sun god, Ra, in order to protect him from the monstrous serpent APOPHIS while the god was in his boat. When depicted in art as crossing the heavens Ra appears as a ram-headed man wearing a solar disk; around the god is a cabin and the serpent Mehen is tightly coiled around the cabin. Sometimes Mehen is depicted as having a head at each end of his body in order to better protect his charge.

Source: Bunson, *Encyclopedia of Ancient Egypt*, 234; Mercatante, *Who's Who in Egyptian Mythology*, 93

Mei (My)

The *mei* ("to bewitch men with feminine charms") is said to be a species of vampiric creature from Chinese folklore; they feed off the souls of humans.

Source: Kang, *Cult of the Fox*, 76; Nan Nü, *Men, Women, and Gender in Early and Imperial China*, 86

Melampo

In the country of Grenada it is a popular custom to name one's dog CUBILON, LUBINA, or MELAMPO after one of the three dogs who, according to folkloric belief, accompanied the shepherds to look upon the newborn Christ child at Bethlehem. Tradition claims any dog having one of these names will never go mad.

Source: Bates, *Outlook*, Volume 120, 100; Finch, *Gentleman's Magazine* Volume CCLXXIX, 528

Melampus

A dog and wolf hybrid from ancient Greek mythology, Melampus ("black foot") was one of the DOGS OF ACTÆON, the unfortunate youth who was raised by the CENTAUR CHEIRON. Melampus of the Spartan breed, along with ICHNOBATES, were the first to give chase.

Source: Leeming, *World of Myth*, 111; Murray, *Classical Manual*, 160; Naso, *Fasti, Tristia*, 93–5

Melanchetes

In ancient Greek mythology, Melanchetes was one of the CENTAURS slain by the demi-god and cultural hero Hercules (Heracles) while visiting his friend, a CENTAUR named PHOLUS, between the conclusion of his third Labor and the onset of his fourth.

When an old and particularly fragrant hogshead of wine was opened its aroma carried on the air and drove the local CENTAURS into a fury. Melanchetes, along with ARGEIUS, AMPHION, DAPHNIS, DUPO, Hippotion, ISOPLES, OREUS, PHRIXUS, and THEREUS, was slain by Hercules (Heracles) as he defended himself from their violent and unwarranted assault.

Source: Barthell, *Gods and Goddesses of Ancient Greece*, 187; Diodorus, *Historical Library of Diodorus the Sicilian*, Volume 1, 229–30

Melanchetus

Variations: Melanchaetes

A dog from ancient Greek mythology, Melanchetus ("black hair") was one of the DOGS OF ACTÆON, the unfortunate youth who was raised by the CENTAUR CHEIRON.

This was the first dog to reach its master after he had been transformed, and took a bite into his flesh.

Source: Leeming, *World of Myth*, 111; Murray, *Classical Manual*, 160; Naso, *Fasti, Tristia*, 93–5

Melaneus

In ancient Greek mythology, Melaneus may have been one of the CENTAURS who attended the wedding of Pirithous, became drunk on wine, and following the lead of EURYTUS, who assaulted Hippodame, began to assault and rape any women they could grab. A great Centauromachy then followed.

Source: *Commentary, Mythological, Historical, and Geographical on Pope's Homer*, 55; Lemprière, *Classical Dictionary*, 361

Melaneus, dog

A dog from ancient Greek mythology, Melaneus ("black coat") was one of the DOGS OF ACTÆON, the unfortunate youth who was raised by the CENTAUR CHEIRON.

Source: Leeming, *World of Myth*, 111; Murray, *Classical Manual*, 160; Naso, *Fasti, Tristia*, 93–5

Melnir (MEEL-nir)

In Norse mythology, Melnir ("bit bearer" or "bridle-wearer") was a horse named in the *Poetic Edda*; it and MYLNIR were to be ridden to Myrkwood as per Hothbrodd's orders.

Source: Bellows, *Poetic Edda*, 54, 360; Norroena Society, *Asatrii Edda*, 373

Meneleus

A CENTAUR from ancient Greek mythology, Meneleus, not to be confused with the Spartan king whose wife Helen sparked off the Trojan War, was one of the centaurs who attended the wedding of Pirithous, became drunk on wine, and following the lead of EURYTUS, who assaulted Hippodame, began to assault and rape any women they could grab. A great Centauromachy then followed.

Source: Berens, *Myths and Legends of Ancient Greece and Rome*, 285; *Commentary, Mythological, Historical, and Geographical on Pope's Homer*, 55

Menik

In Armenian mythology Menik was one of the winged horses said to assist in pulling the sun across the sky (see also BENIK, ENIK, and SENIK).

Source: Ananikian, *Armenian Mythology*, 51; Rose, *Giants, Monsters, and Dragons*, 178

Menmenu

According to ancient Egyptian mythology Menmenu lived in the fourth section, or hour, of Tuat, the Underworld, where it lived off of whatever it could find. This monstrous creature was described as having disks on its back and three heads, each with fourteen stars and fourteen human heads; he, along with HETCH-NAU, was the guardian of Osiris while the god was in his form known as Osiris the Seeker.

Source: Coulter, *Encyclopedia of Ancient Deities*, 418; Mercatante, *Who's Who in Egyptian Mythology*, 94

Merlion

A hybrid creature from the folklore of Singapore, the merlion is said to have the forequarters of a lion and the hindquarters of a fish. According to legend a Sumatran prince once took shelter from a storm on the island and while there encountered the merlion. After he defeated the Temasek, the inhabitants of the island's only settlement, the prince renamed the island Singa Pura ("lion city) in honor of the merlion. Later versions of the founding tale claim there are only five truly mythic creatures inhabiting the earth; the merlion choosing Singapore as its home provides evidence of the island's "sacred mission."

Source: Rose, *Giants, Monsters, and Dragons*, 232; Tarulevicz, *Eating Her Curries and Kway*, 104

Mermaid

Variations: Ben-Varrey, Gorgone, Haffrii, Halfway People, Ocean Men, Maighdean-Mara, Mary Morgan, Morgens, Morrough, Moruach ("sea maid"), Moruadh, Muir-Gheilt, Murdhuch'a, Moruadh, Nereis, Samhghubh'a, SIREN, Sirena, Suire

Mermaids ("sea maidens"), beings half fish and half women, have permeated the folklore of the ocean since ancient times. Described as beautiful enchantresses, destructive and seductive as the ocean itself, the mermaid also personifies the dangers of rocky coastlines and treacherous waters.

The physical appearance of the mermaid likely dates back to the ancient Babylonian god of the sea, Oannes, and his companions, the Atargatis (Derketo). These companions were in their earliest times depicted as wearing cloaks but over time the cloaks evolved into fish tails. Oannes, an early adaptation of the Sumerian fish-god, Ea, was worshiped as the beneficial aspects of the ocean and a sun god; conversely the Atargatis came to be worshiped as moon-goddesses and represented the ocean's more destructive aspects.

The physical description of the mermaid has not changed much since its early inception. Typically described as having flowing and long hair either sea-green or sun-ray yellow, they hold mirrors in their hands, symbolic of the moon, as they sit upon the rocks grooming. There are some folklores where the mermaid is not attractive, said to have green teeth, a porcine (piglike) nose, and red eyes. The domain of the mermaid is said to be on the bottom of the sea, made of priceless pearls and coral.

These FAIRY ANIMALS possess a natural fear of man and will quickly flee as soon as they realize they have been seen by mortal eyes. Both mermaids and mermen (see MERMAN) alike long to have a mortal's soul and according to the legend any one of the merfolk can acquire one if a human falls in love with it. In tales involving the romance of a mermaid and a mortal, the creature will use its singing to lure the sailor in. In the tragic versions of the tales the ship is dashed along the rocky coast or the mermaid takes her would-be love down to the depths where she inadvertently drowns him. In the less romanticized tales, mermaids are vicious and cause the ships to wreck, drowning the survivors at will.

The mermaid of ancient Greece did not have any Piscean attributes but rather looked exactly like a human. Greek mermaids can, however, change their form at will. Usually benevolent, merfolk in Greek folklore can become malevolent and unpredictable.

In European folklore the mermaids wore a cap upon their heads called a *cohuleen druith*; this magical garment granted them some degree of protection. Should a mermaid be taken as a wife this cap needed to be stolen and kept by the husband, as it would prevent her from returning to the ocean; this is similar to the folklore of the SEAL WOMEN's coat and SWAN MAIDEN's cloak.

Source: Andrews, *Dictionary of Nature Myths*, 118–19; Briggs, *Encyclopedia of Fairies*, 287–89; Dixon-Kennedy, *Encyclopedia of Greco-Roman Mythology*, 205; Matson, *Celtic Mythology A to Z*, 82–3; Monaghan, *Encyclopedia of Celtic Mythology and Folklore*, 325–7

Merman, plural mermen

Variations: Blue Men, Dinny-Mara, Dooinney Marrey, Dunya Mara, Havmand, Ocean Men

Mermen are the male counterpart of the MERMAID. In the folklore of ancient Greece, mermen were traditionally offspring of a sea god, such as Poseidon (Neptune), but could also be identified with the conch shell dwelling Tritons.

In Irish and Scottish folklore the merman is rarely attractive, described as having piggy eyes, breath stinking of rotting fish, and a nose blushed red from having consumed too much brandy from the ships it wrecked.

As the Scandinavian havmand, the merman is rather handsome and has a black or green beard and hair. Living on the bottom of the sea or in the caves in the cliffs along the shore this version of the merman is considered to be a benign creature.

Source: Briggs, *Encyclopedia of Fairies*, 290; Dixon-Kennedy, *Encyclopedia of Greco-Roman Mythology*, 205; Knightly, *Fairy Mythology*, 152; Monaghan, *Encyclopedia of Celtic Mythology and Folklore*, 327

Mermeros

A CENTAUR from ancient Greek mythology, Mermeros was noted for being a fast runner; he attended the wedding of Pirithous, where drunken EURYTUS who assaulted the bride, Hippodame, led the way for other inebriated Centaurs to assault and rape any women they could grab. During the ensuing Centauromachy, Mermeros, along with LYCABAS, ORNEUS, PISENOR, and THAUMAS, was slain by spear-wielding the Lapith soldier Dryas.

Source: *Commentary, Mythological, Historical, and Geographical on Pope's Homer*, 55; Lemprière, *Bibliotheca Classica*, 694; Simpson, *Metamorphoses of Ovid*, 205

Meshekenabec

A monstrous aquatic serpent from Algonquin folklore, Meshekenabec was described as having glowing eyes, iridescent scales, a red head, and an overall terrifying aspect; it lived in numerous lakes with its entourage of snake attendants. Eventually it was slain by the cultural hero Manabozho.

Source: Barber, *Dictionary of Fabulous Beasts*, 104; Rose, *Giants, Monsters, and Dragons*, 244–6

Meshkenabec

Variations: Kinepeikwa

A gigantic SEA SERPENT of the Shawnee myth, Meshkenabec is a singular creature; it began its life resembling a fawn with one red and one blue alicorn (a single horn) atop its head. Over the course of many, many years, it shed its skin and metamorphosed into a new form until eventually it became a SEA SERPENT of gigantic proportions; plate sized ruby-red scales covered its body. Meshkenabec was slain by the hero Manabozho.

Source: De Kirk, *Dragonlore*, 50

Mi-Ni-Wa-Tu

In the Teton Sioux mythology, Mi-Ni-Wa-Tu is a nocturnal river monster living in the Missouri River. Described as having the body of a buffalo, one eye, red hair all over its body, and an alicorn (a single horn) in the middle of its forehead, its backbone looked like a cross-cut saw, flat and notched. Anyone who saw Mi-Ni-Wa-Tu during the day would, at best, suffer from insanity for a day; typically people would go mad at the sight of it and begin to writhe in pain until they died. In the springtime, Mi-Ni-Wa-Tu would break the ice which formed over the river.

Source: Dorsey, *Journal of American* Folklore, Volume 7, 135; Meurger, *Lake Monster Traditions*, 235; Zell-Ravenheart, *Wizard's Bestiary*, 68

Michipichi

Variations: Matchi-Manitou ("evil one"), Michipichik, Michi-Pichi, Michi-Pichoux, Mitchipichi

Described by French priest Father Louis Nicholas in his book *Histoire Naturelle* (1675), the michipichi of Cree folklore lived along the estuary of the Saint Lawrence River preying on humans, particularly children who wandered along the river's banks. The chimerical creature was said to have a tiger-like body some eighteen feet long, a beaver-like tail, clawed feet, and an oversized head with fangs nearly two feet long.

Source: Godfrey, *Lake and Sea Monsters*, 109; Rose, *Giants, Monsters, and Dragons*, 246; Zell-Ravenheart, *Wizard's Bestiary*, 68

Migas

A river monster living in the Congo, migas is said to be a gigantic, fleshy, flat bodied creature with long tentacles; anything or anyone who came too near it was snatched by its tentacles and pulled beneath the surface and into its watery lair before being consumed (see SEA SERPENT).

Source: Meurger, *Lake Monster Traditions*, 96; Rose, *Giants, Monsters, and Dragons*, 247; Zell-Ravenheart, *Wizard's Bestiary*, 68

Mikonawa

In the folklore from the Philippines, Mikonawa is described as being a massive bird-like monster covered with feathers as long and sharp as swords and having a beak and talons of the purest and strongest steel. In order to prevent it from devouring the moon, folklore says to leave a bowl of hot and delicious food outside your front door at night or to sing to it a pleasant local lullaby.

Source: Redfern, *Most Mysterious Places on Earth*, 113; Simbulan, *Time for Dragons*, 118

Milamo Bird

Originating in the lumberjack communities of the developing United States of America, the milamo bird, one of the FEARSOME CRITTERS, was a species of bird said to be larger than a crane but smaller than an ostrich living off of foot-long earthworms. Using its long auger-like beak the milamo would drill down into the earth and then walk around in a circle until its neck was twisted like a corkscrew. Then when it had a worm in its beak it would sharply pull it out, the action causing the worm to pop the milamo in the eye. Apparently unhurt, the bird would find tremendous humor in its situation and let loose with a hearty laugh, a sound which was said to be heard for miles off.

Source: Barber, *Dictionary of Fabulous Beasts*, 105; Blakely, *More Wild Camp Tales*, 154–5; Rose, *Giants, Monsters, and Dragons*, 119

Milcham

Variations: Hol, PHOENIX

A PHOENIX from Rabbinical folklore, the milcham was the only creature who did not eat the Forbidden Fruit from the Garden of Eden. According to the story, after being exiled from the Garden of Eden, Eve became increasingly jealous of the animals remaining behind, as they still had immortality; eventually she returned to the Garden and tempted each one of them to also eat the fruit, causing them to share in her fate; only the milcham bird did not comply. The Lord rewarded the bird for its devotion and obedience; He forbade the Angel of Death to ever lay claim to it. Then God constructed a walled city for the milcham to peacefully dwell within, safely hidden away from the horrors of the world and where they will never know sin. Because the birds do not die, every thousand years they are consumed by fire and within their own ash is an egg from which they are reborn. Some interpretations say the birds lose their feathers and shrink to the size of an egg from which they are then reborn.

Source: Abrahams, *Jewish Quarterly Review*, Volume 6, 343–4; Sax, *Imaginary Animals*, 191; Zell-Ravenheart, *Wizard's Bestiary*, 68

Milk-White Milch Cow

A FAIRY ANIMAL of Welsh folklore, Milk-White Milch Cow (y fuwh laethwen lefrith) had the ability to give just enough milk every day to everyone who wanted it, no matter how many households milked her. It was said to drink her milk would cure nearly any illness, make a foolish man wise, and a miserable person happy. Milk-White Milch Cow was owned by no one and wandered the land as she pleased, leaving calves in her wake. One of her calves was a long-horned ox called Ychen Bannog; it killed a monstrous KELPIE. According to legend the residents of the Vale of Towy tried to capture her with the intent of slaughtering her to eat but the elfin cow literally disappeared from their grasp and was never seen again.

Source: Monaghan, *Encyclopedia of Celtic Mythology and Folklore*, 141; Sikes, *British Goblins*, 41

Mimas

Variations: Melanchaites

A black-maned CENTAUR from ancient Greek mythology, Mimas ("mocker") was one of the CEN-

TAURS who attended the wedding of Pirithous, became drunk on wine, and following the lead of EURYTUS, who assaulted Hippodame, began to assault and rape any women they could grab. The hero Theseus, along with Caeneus, Dryas, Exadius, Hopleus, Mopsus, Phalerus, Pirithous, and Prolochusm, confronted the CENTAURS. The men, armed with spears, were met by the CENTAURS who ripped up fir trees and used them as weapons, swatting at them with the trunks.

Source: D'Angour, *Greeks and the New*, 76; Hesiod, *Works of Hesiod, Callimachus and Theognis*, 59; Westmoreland, *Ancient Greek Beliefs*, 202

Mimi

Variations: Mini

In Australian Aboriginal mythology the Mimi were a race of mischievous NATURE SPIRITS living in the crags of rocks and in caves; they were so tall and thin a wind gust could sweep them off their feet, breaking bones or carrying them far away. They are described as being tall and exceedingly thin with gaping mouths, long arms and necks, and small heads. Mimis helped the early Aboriginal people, teaching them how to hunt and paint. In some tales the mimis would lure people into a cave and hold them hostage.

Source: Finley, *Aboriginal Art of Australia*, 20

Mimick Dog

Variations: Canis Lucernarius, Getulian Dogge, Mimike Dog

According to the 1607 bestiary *The History of Foure-Footed Beasts* written by Edward Topsell the mimick dog originated in the Libyan province of Getulia; described as being a canine-simian hybrid, it had a simian-like (monkey-like) body, a back like a hedgehog, dense fur, long limbs, shaggy hair, a short tail, and a slender muzzle. Mimick dogs had the unique ability to imitate anything they saw and from their youth could be trained to learn admirable and strange feats, such as dancing to music or waiting on tables. One such creature is recorded as having performed for King Ptolemy and another source says one performed for Emperor Vespasian.

Source: Ashton, *Curious Creatures in Zoology*, 150–2; Barber, *Dictionary of Fabulous Beasts*, 105; Shuker, *Beasts That Hide from Man*, 231–4; Zell-Ravenheart, *Wizard's Bestiary*, 68

Minhocão

A species of gigantic, amphibian earthworm from Brazilian folklore, the minhocão ("giant earthworm") burrows out from marshes and riverbeds, knocking over trees as it moves beneath the near-surface of the earth. Described as being about one hundred fifty feet long and nearly twenty feet wide, its body is covered in armored plates; upon its head are two flexible antennae, feelers, or horns. After a particularly rainy period the minhocão leaves its lair and burrows out, making a wide arch before eventually returning. Any mysterious burrow, furrow, or trench in the landscape as well as sinkholes and the sudden collapse of bridges and roadways is said to be because of the passing of a minhocão.

Source: Coleman, *Cryptozoology A to Z*, 160; Maberry, *They Bite*, 224; Newton, *Hidden Animals*, 170–1; Zell-Ravenheart, *Wizard's Bestiary*, 68

Minokawa

A gigantic bird from Filipino mythology, Minokawa preys upon the moon, always conspiring to consume it. The moon, according to the legend, has made for itself eight holes in the eastern sky as well as eight holes in the western sky so Minokawa will never know which entrance or exit it will be using on any given day. Every once in a long while, however, Minokawa is able to catch the moon and the people of earth experience an eclipse. During this time they must make as much noise as possible so as to entice Minokawa to poke his head down into the sky to see what is happening; when he does, he opens his mouth and the moon is able to escape. If ever this does not happen and Minokawa swallows the moon he will then begin to hunt the sun. When the day finally comes he has devoured it as well, he will then sweep down to earth and begin to consume all of humanity.

Said to be as large as the island of Bohol or Negros, Minokawa lives outside of the sky near the eastern horizon, his favorite place to hunt the moon. He is said to have a beak and claws of steel, eyes like mirrors, and feathers made of swords.

Source: Benedict, *Journal of American Folklore*, Volume 26, 19; Eugenio, *Philippine Folk Literature*, 267

Minotaur (MIHN-oh-tor)

Variations: Asterion ("starry"), Asterios

In ancient Greek mythology Asterion, better known as the Minotaur ("bull of Minos"), was born the son of Queen Pasiphae, a daughter of the sun god and second generation Titan Helios (Sol), and a divine bull; however the story itself is said by a few scholars to have Egyptian origins.

King Minos and the queen had four sons of their own, Androgeos, Deukalion, Glaukos, and Katreus, but the king had many illegitimate children with various NYMPHS. To prove his legitimacy to the throne, for he had to battle his brother to gain it, Minos prayed to the god of the sea Poseidon (Neptune) to send him up a bull which he would then sacrifice to honor the god (or mix it in with his herds and each year sacrifice the best of the new bulls; sources conflict). Poseidon (Neptune) fulfilled the request but Minos did not sacrifice the animal as he was so taken with the creature's exceptional beauty and magnificence. The broken promise angered the god so deeply he caused the animal to become feral and made the queen develop an unnatural and uncontrollable passion for it. The resulting child of her union with the bull created a hybrid born with the head and tail of its father but the body of a human. Although the bastard prince of Crete was named Asterion he became known as the Minotaur.

The king hired the inventor Daidalos to construct a gigantic enclosed labyrinth to be the hybrid's home and prison. The Minotaur, exceedingly fierce and strong, was fed a diet of youths and maidens; these individuals were supplied by the city of Athens as tribute for being responsible for the death of Crete's Prince Androgeos. Each year (or every nine years; sources conflict) Athens had to send seven youths and seven maidens to be its food for as long as the monster lived. The tribute continued until Theseus, son of Aigeus, was one of the youths sent; with the assistance of one of the daughters of the king, he was able to kill the Minotaur with a sword and escape with her back to Athens. Although the oral story claims he used a sword to slay the beast, when the story is depicted on vases, he is shown using a spear.

Source: Bulfinch, *Bulfinch's Greek and Roman Mythology*, 122–3; Dowden, *Companion to Greek Mythology*, 466–7; Evslin, *Gods, Demigods and Demons*, n.pag.; Hard, *Routledge Handbook of Greek Mythology*, 337–41, 347

Miqqiayuuq

In the folklore of the Intuits of the eastern Hudson Bay region in Canada the malicious miqqiayuuq is a faceless, gigantic, fur-covered being living in the depths of frozen freshwater. Coming to the edge of the water it waits for buckets to be lowered so it can tangle them up and prevent water from being drawn.

Source: Rose, *Giants, Monsters, and Dragons*, 250; Zell-Ravenheart, *Wizard's Bestiary*, 69

Mirag

A creature appearing in many medieval bestiaries, the mirag was described as being a species of horned hare living upon an unnamed island.

Source: Flaubert, *Temptation of St. Anthony*, 255

Al Mi'raj

Variations: Mi'Raj, Mir'aj, Miraj

In Islamic mythology the al mi'raj was said to be a species of large yellow hare with a single, great black alicorn (a single horn) atop its head living in North Africa and throughout the Middle East and on the island of Jezîrat al-Tennyn in the Indian Ocean; it allegedly had the properties of a UNICORN. The al mi'raj is a territorial predator from Islamic folklore.

Source: Hargreaves, *Hargreaves New Illustrated Bestiary*, 61; Rose, *Giants, Monsters, and Dragons*, 250; Zell-Ravenheart, *Wizard's Bestiary*, 69

Mishipeshu

Variations: Water Lynx, Mishipissy, Mishipizhiw ("master of fishes"), Miskena

A chimerical creature living in the Great Lakes, United States of America, from the Ojibew and Menominee mythology, the mishipeshu is described as being a horned serpentine aquatic feline (see Horned Snake and SEA SERPENT); its body is covered in scales, has a DRAGON-like tail, and its clawed paws enable it to swim very quickly through the water. Feared and respected the mishipeshu can be either benevolent or malicious, depending on the circumstances in which one meets this creature in the stories. Using its tail, this protector of Lake Superior can create storms and pull both boats and planes (in modern retellings of the myths) down into the lake's icy depths.

Source: Colombo, *Mysteries of Ontario*, 99; Godfrey, *Mythical Creatures*, 63–4; Zell-Ravenheart, *Wizard's Bestiary*, 69

Miskena

Called Chief of the Fishes by the Native American people of Winnipeg, Canada and the United States of America, Miskena is the fish-snake hybrid living in Lake Winnipeg; it is described as being a gigantic serpent with the head and forequarters of a sturgeon (see SEA SERPENT).

Source: Meurger, *Lake Monster Traditions*, 308, 312, 316; Rose, *Giants, Monsters, and Dragons*, 251

Missipissy

Variations: Master of the Fishes

A fish-serpent hybrid from the mythology of the Native Americans living in the Great Lakes regions of Canada and the United States of America, the missipissy was strikingly similar to the MISKENA (see SEA SERPENT). Missipissy was considered to be the guardian of the sturgeon living in the lakes; during the winter months it was said to hibernate along the lake bottom.

Source: Meurger, *Lake Monster Traditions*, 317; Rose, *Giants, Monsters, and Dragons*, 251

Mizuchi

Originally a water god in Japanese mythology Mizuchi was reduced in status to aquatic DRAGON or serpent after the introduction of Buddhism. Records dating back to the year 379 described a *mizuchi* ("water elder") dwelling in the Kahashima River, Kibi Province, harassing and killing people with its poison as they passed by. Many people had been killed by this mizuchi; ultimately the district warden had to order the creature hunted down and destroyed (see SEA SERPENT).

Source: Daigaku, *Asian Folklore Studies*, Volume 57, 2; van Gulik, *Irezumi*, 117

Mlokowy Smij

A good-natured DRAGON from German folklore, the mlokowy smij ("milk DRAGON") is known to bring milk to the dairy barn it favors; it has been described as a fiery blaze streaking across the sky.

Source: Grimm, *Teutonic Mythology*, 1019; MacKenzie, *Dragons for Beginners*, 91

Mmoatia

Variations: Aboatia

A species of NATURE SPIRIT from Ashanti mythology, the mmoatia ("little animals") is said to stand about a foot tall, converse by whistling, and have long hair on its face, head, and pubic regions as well as backward pointing feet. Mmoatia are said to come in three varieties: black, red, and white. While the black ones are generally innocuous, red and white ones create all manner of mischief and trouble such as stealing palm wine and left-over food. The white mmoatia can create *suman* (a dish prepared with glutinous rice boiled in coconut milk and spices) which they occasionally barter to mortals by means of "the silent trade."

Source: Coulter, *Encyclopedia of Ancient Deities*, 326; Herskovits, *Myth of the Negro Past*, 256

Mo-O-Inanea

In Hawaiian mythology Mo-O-Inanea ("self-reliant DRAGON") was a DRAGON goddess who, along with her brothers, migrated from the Hidden Land of Kane to the visible world; she was considered to be extremely powerful and all DRAGONS and spirits were under her domain. When the number of DRAGONs became too great she sent some of them to wander the world while others she had to relocate throughout the other Hawaiian islands; she took up residence in wet mud of the clay pits; flowers and prayers were offered to her at these locations. The favorite clay pit of Mo-O-Inanea, laupalolo ("pit of sticky clay"), was declared taboo by the last traditional queen of Hawaii, Kaahumanu; having the ability to shape-shift into the form of a human woman she lived her life easily shifting between the two. Other DRAGON goddesses who

are her descendants are ALA-MUKI, Ha-puu, Kihawahine, and Mau-ola.

Source: Monaghan, *Encyclopedia of Goddesses and Heroines*, 155; Westervelt, *Legends of Gods and Ghosts*, 256–7

Moddey Dhoo

Variations: Moddey Dohe, Mauthe Dog, Mauthe Doog

The nocturnal BARGUEST of Peel Castle on the Isle of Man, the Moddey Dhoo ("black dog") was a singular entity; it was described as looking like a large black spaniel standing as big as a calf with curly black hair and glowing red eyes. Although it was seen in every room of the castle at one time or another, Moddey Dhoo frequented the guard chambers most often; as soon as the candles were lit there, this FAIRY ANIMAL would appear and lay down before the fireplace. Those guards who claimed to have seen it said they feared it would harm them should they use profanity in its presence; the guards also walked the castle in pairs whenever Moddey Dhoo was apparent as it created a presence of dread.

Source: Cumming, *Guide to the Isle of Man*, 119–20; Eberhart, *Mysterious Creatures*, 344; Evans-Wentz, *Fairy Faith in Celtic Countries*, 129; Glover, *Glover's Illustrated Guide and Visitors' Companion*, 86–7

Modnir (MOHTH-nir)

Variations: Módnir

In Norse mythology, Snorri Sturlson (1179–1241), the Icelandic historian, poet, and politician, writes the horse Modnir ("the courageous" or "spirited") was the horse of the DWARF DVALIN.

Source: Grimes, *Norse Myths*, 260; Norroena Society, *Asatrii Edda*, 375

Móinn (MOH-in)

Variations: Moinn

In Norse mythology Móinn ("moor-beast") was one of the dark-spotted serpents or Ormar (see ORMR) named in Thorgrimr's *Rhymes* and in Snorri Sturluson's (1179–1241) *Prose Edda*; it was said to live beneath the tree Ygdrasil at the Hvergelmir Well where it spent its days gnawing upon its Niflheimr root. The siblings of Móinn were GOIN, GRÁBAKR, GRAFVÖLLUDR, OFNIR, and SVAFNIR.

Source: Grimes, *Norse Myths*, 14, Jennbert, *Animals and Humans*, 50; Norroena Society, *Asatrii Edda*, 346

Molossus

A dog from ancient Greek mythology, Molossus was one of the DOGS OF ACTÆON, the unfortunate youth who was raised by the CENTAUR CHEIRON.

Source: Leeming, *World of Myth*, 111; Murray, *Classical Manual*, 160

Momonjii

Variations: Momonjaa

A NURSERY BOGIE from Japanese folklore, the momonjii ("boar meat") was a creature said to be so hairy it had only one other feature, an incredibly large eye or mouth; it was used to frighten children into behaving and going to sleep at night.

Source: Gill, *Woman Without a Hole*, 56–7

Monk Fish

Variations: Angel Fish

Anatomist, botanist, naturalist, and zoologist Guillaume Rondelet (1507–1566) described the monk fish as having a man's face as it looked "rude and ungrateful," a bald head, and a monk's hood of scales; rather than arms or fins it had long winglets and its body eventually tapered out into a tail.

Source: Bassett, *Legends and Superstitions of the Sea and Of Sailors*, 207; Godfrey, *Mythical Creatures*, 69; Hargreaves, *Hargreaves New Illustrated Bestiary*, 86, 94

Mono-No-Ke

A specific type of rarely occurring phenomenon described in the Heian period (AD 794–1185), the mono-no-ke originally applied to all manner of frightening and mysterious experiences, such as the sudden appearance of a ripple on what one believed to be a solid surface, such as a wall. By the Kamakura period (1185–1133) and thereafter the mono-no-ke became synonymous with the TSUKUMOGAMO, common household objects having reached the age of one hundred years old, developing arms and legs and taking on a life of their own.

Source: Foster, *Pandemonium and Parade*, 6–7; Roberts, *Japanese Mythology A to Z*, 24

Monoceros Marinus

Believed to be living in the murky depths of Lake Darmsee, the monoceros marinus of medieval German folklore was depicted as being a gigantic Piscean creature with an oversized horn protruding out of the center of its head (see SEA SERPENT).

Source: Rose, *Giants, Monsters, and Dragons*, 253

Monocerus

Variations: Carcazonon, Karkadann, Monocerotem

First appearing in *Historia Naturalis* (AD 77), written by Pliny the Elder (AD 23–79), the Roman author and natural philosopher, the monocerus ("one horn") was described as a chimerical creature, having the body of a horse, the feet of an elephant, the head of a deer, and the tail of a boar; in the middle of its horsehead was an enormous, straight, black alicorn reaching a length of about four feet. Said to have the most horrible sounding bray, this creature was feared, as its horn was as sought after as a UNICORN'S alicorn but the monocerus was a man-killer. Although the creature could be slain, there are no tales of any ever being taken alive. By the Middle Ages the monocerus appeared regularly in bestiaries.

Source: Magasich-Airola, *America Magica*, 154; Rose, *Giants, Monsters, and Dragons*, 252–3

Monokerata

Variations: Onoi Monokerata ("one horned asses")

A species of UNICORN from the folklore of India, the monokerata were described as being swift-footed and beautiful white horses having a single brightly colored horn growing from the center of their forehead. These animals were much prized for the alleged magical properties their alicorn (a single horn) held.

Source: Breverton, *Breverton's Phantasmagoria*, n.pag.

Monychus

A CENTAUR from ancient Greek mythology, Monychus was, according to Ovid's *Metamorphoses*, one of the CENTAURS who attended the wedding of Pirithous, became drunk on wine and following the lead of EURYTUS, who assaulted Hippodame, began to assault and rape any women they could grab. A great Centauromachy then followed.

Source: *Commentary, Mythological, Historical, and Geographical on Pope's Homer*, 55; Simpson, *Metamorphoses of Ovid*, 208–09

Moogie

A monster described in the folklore of the Ozark Mountains, the moogie is said to be lacertilian (lizard-like) in appearance.

Source: Rose, *Giants, Monsters, and Dragons*, 255

Moon Rabbit

Variations: Beloved Hare, Jade Moon Rabbit, Jade Rabbit, Tsukino Usagi

In Chinese, Japanese, and Korean folklore moon rabbit is said to live on the moon beneath a cassia tree; there he sits eternally with a mortar and pestle pounding gold, jade, and jewels into the Pill of Immortality (Elixir of Jade) which confers everlasting life and has many of the same properties as the Philosophers' Stone. He is described as having very short front legs, exceedingly long back legs, and a fluffy white tail curled over like a feather.

Source: Barber, *Dictionary of Fabulous Beasts*, 108; Bredon, *Moon Year*, 409; Newman, *Food Culture in China*, 165

Mor (MOHR)

Variations: Mór

In Norse mythology, Snorri Sturlson (1179–

1241), the Icelandic historian, poet, and politician, writes the horse Mor ("the brown") was the preferred mount of Meinthjofr in his translation of *Prose Edda*.

Source: Norroena Society, *Asatrii Edda*, 375; Sturluson, *Prose Edda*, 257

Mora

Variations: Kikimora (Russian), Mara ("demon," Polish), Zmora

In Slavic folklore the mora ("nightmare") is a species of vampiric creature similar to the hag, a being causing nightmares and stealing vital life energy from its victims, similar to a vampire. Typically female, if a mora falls in love with her victim she will drink his blood. If the mora is a male they are described as having bushy black eyebrows which meet over the bridge of the nose. Sometimes the folklore will claim the mora is a living human being who has these vampiric abilities and can be either a man or a woman. In this instance, when the person is asleep their soul leaves their body and, assuming any number of forms, travels to the home of its victim where it will attempt to suffocate their sleeping prey while sending them nightmares and drinking their blood.

Similar to the Slavic folklore, the mora of the Kashub people of Ontario, Canada, also has vampiric tendencies. Here, the mora is said to be the wandering unsettled spirit or the soul of a sleeping girl who has not been properly baptized. In either event, the mora will attempt to suffocate its prey. Should the victim awaken, the being will instantly transform into an apple, a ball of wool, or a massive hair ball before it disappears. To prevent the mora from attacking simple precautions can be taken, such as filling your unused keyholes with wax and pointing your shoes away from the bed at night.

Source: Guiley, *Encyclopedia of Vampires, Werewolves, and Other Monsters*, 206; Melton, *Vampire Book*, 369; Monaghan, *Encyclopedia of Goddesses and Heroines*, 305

Mormo (More-moe)

In ancient Greece, there was a species of monstrous vampiric creatures known as the *mormo* ("terrible one"), or, when gathered in numbers, they were referred to as *mormolykeia* ("terrible wolves"). In their true form, they were covered in their own blood and blisters, though not as ugly as the EMPOUSE.

The mormo have the ability to shape-shift into a beautiful young lady and will use this form to lure handsome young men into a fatal indiscretion, draining them of their blood, and consuming their flesh. When no suitable men were available, they settled on consuming the elderly and young children. It was believed the mormo by use of theri-

anthropy can shape-shift into over 1,000 hideous forms.

Montague Summers, in his book *Vampire: His Kith and Kin* mentions only by name some vampires whose names are similar to the mormo: mormolikeion, mormoliki, mormolix, and moromolukiai. Perhaps these were regional variations of the mormo, in either singular or plural form.

Over the years the vampiric mormo became something more akin to a common NURSERY BOGIE, as children are told if they misbehave during the day, at night the mormo will sneak into their room and bite them.

Source: Buxton, *Imaginary Greece*, 18; Fontenrose, *Python*, 116; Summers, *Vampire: His Kith and Kin*; n.pag.; Suter, *Lament*, 214–15

Moselantja

In African mythology the Moselantja is believed to be a river monster, a (likely) singular being with a humanoid body covered with scales sporting cruel and fierce eyes, a pair of keen ears, a mouth full of sharp teeth, and wielding an extremely long tail (see SEA SERPENT). Approaching anyone who is walking alone along the riverbank, Moselantja would sneak up from behind and begin to whisper lies into the person's ear; should they spin around and see him, Moselantja would demand clothing, favors, food, jewelry, and other objects or he would ravage them with violence and devour them completely, leaving nothing behind for anyone to find. Moselantja uses his long tail to fish for crabs, his favorite food.

Source: Knappert, *Myths and Legends of Botswana, Lesotho, and Swaziland*, 144–8; Lynch, *African Mythology, A to Z*, 86

Moshiriikkwechep

Variations: Mohiriikkwechep

A gigantic fish from Japanese mythology, Moshiriikkwechep ("world backbone trout") is said to have been one of the first beings created and supports the world upon its back; whenever it writhes, the shockwaves it makes create earthquakes and tsunamis. Because of its inability to remain perfectly still for all time it was secured beneath the mud of the ocean by the two gods but on occasion it manages a spasm whose shockwaves ripple up to the surface.

Source: Godfrey, *Mythical Creatures*, 70, 122; Rose, *Giants, Monsters, and Dragons*, 256–7; Zell-Ravenheart, *Wizard's Bestiary*, 70

Moskitto

Variations: Miskitto

Originating in the lumberjack communities of the developing United States of America, the moskitto, one of the FEARSOME CRITTERS, was said to be a gigantic version of the common mosquito so oversized it could arch its body over the width of a stream and drain a log steering crew dry of their blood. Escape from a moskitto was dangerous, for if a lumberjack dove into the water he faced the danger of confronting a COUGAR FISH or a LOG GAR.

Source: Godfrey, *Monsters of Wisconsin*, 131; Rose, *Giants, Monsters, and Dragons*, 119, 257

Mu

The mu are NATURE SPIRITS or nats (the generic name for the indigenous NATURE SPIRITS of the air, cultivated fields, earth, forest, hills, households, rain, rivers, sky, streams, wind, and the like) from Burmese folklore; they are sky nats controlling the people's overall prosperity and wealth. The core mu nat are a collection of seven, eight, or nine brothers and although there is little argument over what their names are, there is a great deal of uncertainty over the order of their birth. Names commonly appearing on lists of the brothers include Hkringwan, Jan, Madai, Mu-Iam, Musheng, and Sinlap. It has been established the chief of mu nats is La N'Roi Madai; he is also the youngest of the brothers.

Source: Leach, *Essential Edmund Leach*, Volumes 1–2, 21–2; Porteous, *Forest in Folklore and Mythology*, 125; Scott, *The Burman: His Life and Notions*, Volume 1, 286

Mucalinda

Variations: Mahamucilinda, Mucilinda

A great, seven-headed NAGARAJA from Buddhist mythology, Mucalinda ruled over an impressive realm beneath a large lake. According to the story, after the Buddha attained enlightenment he traveled at a very leisurely pace through a great forest and rested beneath a Bodhi tree to meditate. Because he was so deep in thought the Buddha did not notice the approaching storm but Mucalinda did; leaving his realm, the great NAGA coiled himself around the tree and, rising up, spread his hoods to protect the meditating Buddha from the ravages of the storm. The tempest lasted seven days and in all that time Mucalinda did not move; once it had passed, he assumed his human form so he could bow before the Buddha. Then, with a heart filled with joy, Mucalinda assumed his NAGA form and returned to his kingdom.

Source: De Visser, *Dragon in China and Japan*, 3, 29; Niles, *Dragons*, 104

Muirdris

Variations: Muidris, Sinach Sinach ("monster"), Smirdris

A gigantic lake monster from Irish folklore, Muirdris was described as having spikes covering its greenish-blue scaled body, numerous teats on its belly, and the ability to swell up its body like a puffer-fish (see SEA SERPENT). According to legend it dwelt in Loch Rudrainge in Devon County in the kingdom of Fergus mac Leti. Although a *geis* prohibits Fergus from entering the water, he does so in order to confront the dangerous creature. Although breaking his *geis* ends his kingship he confronts the monster nevertheless, slaying it violently but not before Muirdris leaves a slash across his face which heavily scars when it heals.

Source: De Kirk, *Dragonlore*, 44; Brownlow, *Moth*, Volume LXIX, 238; Mittman, *Ashgate Research Companion to Monsters and the Monstrous*, 63–5; Zell-Ravenheart, *Wizard's Bestiary*, 70–1

Mujina

A small, furry animal in its true form, the mujina of Japanese folklore is little more than a cruel trickster. According to legend, after sunset along the Akasaka Road in Tokyo there is a section of road known as the Kii-no-kuni-zaka ("slope of the province of Kii"). To one side of the road is a vast field but the other has a deep pond. After sunset the shape-shifting mujina would walk the road looking for people to frighten. In one story it pretended to be a woman weeping and about to jump into the pond and drown herself; when a man came to help her it showed him a face having no eyes or mouth. The man ran off in fear and came upon a buckwheat seller and told him the story; unfortunately this was either the same or another mujuna for after it heard the story it said "Did it look like this?" and removed all the features of its face and caused the lights in his shop to instantly extinguish.

Source: Hearn, *Kwaidan*, 51–2; Joly, *Scary Monsters and Super Creeps*, n.pag.

Mukunga M'bura

In the folklore of the Kikuyu people of Kenya, Mukunga M'bura, the rainbow, was said to be a predatory nocturnal monster living in the water; at night it would come out and steal and eat cattle.

Source: Lynch, *African Mythology, A to Z*, 85, 109

Mulassa

Variations: Guita ("kicking mule"), Mula Fera, Mula Guita

In Catalonian folklore the mulassa was said to be a ferocious and large green DRAGON or mule-like creature in a constant state of anger always on the lookout for an opportunity to hurt or pursue onlookers. It was the personification of irresponsibility and recklessness; it was linked to the Farriers' guild in the Middle Ages.

Source: Hernandez, *Forms of Tradition in Contemporary Spain*, 94; Zell-Ravenheart, *Wizard's Bestiary*, 45

Muldarpe

An evil shape-shifter from Australian Aborigine mythology, the muldarpe ("devil") has the ability of therianthropy and uses it to assume the form of a kangaroo, lizard, or wombat.

Source: Smith, *Myths and Legends of the Australian Aborigines*, 349

Muldjewangk

In Aboriginal Australian mythology Muldjewangk was said to be a gigantic and malicious MERMAN–like creature from the Dreamtime living in the Murray River in South Australia; the folklore has never been clear if this is an individual entity or a species. According to one tale it once wrapped its oversized arms around a riverboat and threatened to pull it down into the murky depths. As the captain of the ship was about to open fire some Aboriginal elders who were on board warned him against harming the creature but the captain gave the order to shoot. Although Muldjewangk was driven off, the captain soon fell ill and his body was covered in blisters; he died in agony six months later. In more modern time the Muldjewangk is considered to be a NURSERY BOGIE, a monster which will pull in children who walk too near the river's edge.

Source: Cox, *Wicked Waters*, 15; le Roux, *Myth of 'Roo*, 102

Munin (MUN-in)

Variations: Muninn

Munin ("memory") was one of the ravens named in Thorgrimr's *Rhymes* and in Snorri Sturluson's (1179–1241) *Prose Edda*. According to Norse mythology, the two ravens of Odin, HUGINN and Munin, were used as his messengers, sent to the netherworld to bring him back news. When not being employed to carry messages, they remained perched on his shoulder.

Source: Jennbert, *Animals and Humans*, 50; Norroena Society, *Asatrii Edda*, 375; Oehlenschläger, *Gods of the North*, li

Murghi-I-Adami

The name shared by this pair of birds of Islamic folklore, the murghi-i-adami were said to be beautiful, resembling peacocks but having human faces and the ability of human speech. Stories of these birds were brought to Europe by medieval era travelers. It was said if one happened upon the two birds talking to one another and listened carefully to their conversation they would be discussing matters which would greatly interest the listener.

Source: Hargreaves, *Hargreaves New Illustrated Bestiary*, 140; Rose, *Giants, Monsters, and Dragons*, 259; Zell-Ravenheart, *Wizard's Bestiary*, 71

Murrisk

Variations: Muiriasc, Rosualt

A creature of Irish folklore, the deadly murrisk was said to live along the coast of Croagh Patrick; it was so poisonous should it ever disgorge the contents of its stomach all the fish for miles around would die. The breath of the murrisk was so wretched its fumes would cause birds to fall dead from the sky as they passed overhead.

Source: Barber, *Dictionary of Fabulous Beasts*, 108; Rose, *Giants, Monsters, and Dragons*, 259–60; Zell-Ravenheart, *Wizard's Bestiary*, 71

Muscaliet

A chimerical creature from the bestiary of Pierre de Beauvais, the muscaliet ("query squirrel") is described as having a body like a rabbit, ears of a weasel, hair like a pig, legs and tail like a squirrel, snout like a mole, and teeth like a boar. Able to climb trees, it jumps from branch to branch by springing off of its tail. The muscaliet is not good for any tree it comes into contact with as it devastates the fruit and leaves it touches with its extreme body heat. This creature makes a nest for itself in the hollows beneath a tree but because of its natural body temperature it eventually causes the tree to dry up and die.

In medieval bestiaries the muscaliet is symbolic of human pride which destroys the soul.

Source: Architectural and Archaeological Society of the County of Lincoln, *Reports and Papers of the Architectural and Archaeological Societies of the Counties of Lincoln and Northampton*, Volume 20, 202; Breverton, *Breverton's Phantasmagoria*, n.pag.; Zell-Ravenheart, *Wizard's Bestiary*, 71

Mushussu

Variations: Mušḫuššu, Musrussu DRAGON, Mušḫuššu, Sirrušu, Sirrush

A chimerical DRAGON from Akkadian, Babylonian, and Mesopotamian mythology, Mushussu ("the furious snake") is described as having a serpentine body, the forelegs of a lion, the rear legs and talons of an eagle, the neck and mane of a bull, and the head of a snake. A minion of the great DRAGON of Chaos TIAMAT, Mushussu fought alongside of her against the god Marduk; after TIAMAT was defeated he was allowed to live on as a shrine guardian. In the Story of the Slaying of Labbu, the god Tishpak defeated the DRAGONs BASMU, LABBU, and Mushussu, minions of TIAMAT.

Source: Kuehn, *Dragon in Medieval East Christian and Islamic Art*, 170; Wiggermann, *Mesopotamian Protective Spirits*, 174; Zell-Ravenheart, *Wizard's Bestiary*, 89

Musical Serpent

The musical serpent is described as having a

snake's head and four wings; it makes a sound similar to the musical stone.

Source: Borges, *Book of Imaginary Beings*, 81

Musilindi

A species of DRAGON or a race of NAGA from the Indian mythology, the Musilindi are described as having serpentine bodies, humanoid heads, two arms, and wings. These beings have the gift of therianthropy and can shape-shift into a human or a snake.

Source: De Kirk, *Dragonlore*, 36

Musimon

Variations: Musimu, Tityron, Tityrus

A chimerical creature from the symbology of heraldry, the musimon is depicted as having the body of a goat and the head of a ram sporting four horns, two of which are the straight horns of the goat while the other two are the curved horns of the ram. Although the musimon appears in many books of heraldry the creature itself does not appear on any coat of arms.

Source: Fox-Davies, *Complete Guide to Heraldry*, 231; Parker, *Glossary of Terms Used in Heraldry*, 421; Zell-Ravenheart, *Wizard's Bestiary*, 71; Zieber, *Heraldry in America*, 374

Mylnir (MEEL-nir)

In Norse mythology, Mylnir ("biter" or "the haltered") was a horse named in the *Poetic Edda*; it and MELNIR were to be ridden to Myrkwood as per Hothbrodd's orders.

Source: Bellows, *Poetic Edda*, 54, 360; Norroena Society, *Asatrii Edda*, 375

Myobu

Variations: Myōbu

A species of fox spirit (KITSUNE) from Japanese folklore, the myobu were revered upon Mount Inari, Japan.

Source: Picken, *Essentials of Shinto*, 124

Nabeshima, Cat of (Nob-bay-she-ma)

The nabeshima, as it has come to be called, is a vampiric cat from the folklore of ancient Japan. It looks like a common cat except for having two tails. The creature can shape-shift into a specific person and uses this tactic to get close to its intended prey. It chokes a person unconscious and then drains them of their blood. It will also engage in sexual activity with its victim and drain their life-energy as well. The last report of a nabeshima attack was made on July 14, 1929, in the Japanese newspaper *Sunday Express*. The article claimed the vampire cat of Nabeshima was harassing the wives of the descendants of a samurai.

There is an ancient Japanese tale of this vampire taking place in Hizen, an old province which no longer exists. The prince, an honorable member of the Nabeshima family, was in love with a concubine named O-Toyo. After a lover's walk in the garden one night, O-Toyo was followed to her quarters by the nabeshima who killed her and buried her body beneath a veranda. Then, assuming the guise of the prince's beloved concubine, the nabeshima visited him each night, draining him of his blood and life, much like a SUCCUBUS does. All methods to restore his health failed and it was finally determined something supernatural had to be the cause of his failing health. Each night all the guards stationed around the prince's room would fall asleep, but one solider from the guard, a man named Ito Soda, offered to sit up with the prince; eventually permission was granted. He stabbed a knife deep into his leg so the pain would keep him alert and awake. At the time when the other guards all mysteriously fell asleep, the nabeshima in the guise of O-Toyo entered the prince's chambers. The nabeshima felt the presence of another in the room, and made uncomfortable by it, was not able to drain the prince. For two consecutive nights Ito Soda stood on watch and each night the nabeshima was unable to draw life from him. As time passed, the prince showed signs of recovery, Ito Soda kept his vigil, and the guards were now able to stay awake. Ito Soda knew now O-Toyo was responsible and tried to kill her one night, but the nabeshima dropped its guise and fled into the mountains. It harassed locals until the prince was recovered enough to lead a hunting exposition to hunt it down. He was able to do so and avenged the death of his beloved.

Source: Dale-Green, *Archetypal Cat*, 106; Davis, *Myths and Legends of Japan*, 264–68; Howey, *Cat in Magic*, 173

Naga (NA-ga)

Variations: Nāga, Nagis

In Hindu mythology the nagas are demonic beings, members of a demonic race born of the union between the sage Kasyapa and Kadru, the daughter of Daksha, according to *The Mahabharata*, one of the two major Sanskrit epics of Ancient India. The females of the species are called NAGINI. Their name translates from Sanskrit to mean "a hooded snake" or "those who do not walk, who creep."

The nagas are described as being human with the lower body of a snake. Sometimes they are said to have as many as seven heads. A precious gem is embedded into their head or throat, granting them magical powers. Typically they only attack humans when they have been mistreated, but they are known to prey upon wealthy individuals, singling them out, attacking with their venom, and then stealing the victims' wealth. Especially greedy, nagas hoard jewels, treasure, and precious metals in their underwater homes. They have the ability to shapeshift into a cobra or DRAGON, and they possess an array of undefined magical abilities from the gem embedded in their head.

The homeland of the naga is called Patala and is located on the bottom of the ocean. The personal adversary of the naga is their cousin GARUDA. The nagas are also listed as being one of the eight classes of celestial beings in Hindu mythology.

The most famous of the Nagas, as named in the *Mahabharata*, are mentioned only in passing or simply named; beyond this, there is little to no other information on them as individuals: AIRAVAT, Amahatha ("wanting a house"), Andha, Aparajita, Apta, Apurana, ARYAKA, Ashvatara, Badhira, Bahyakunda, Bilvapatra, Citraka ("painted"), Dadhimukha ("milk face"), Dadhimukha, DHANANJAYA ("fire"), Dharana, DHRITARASHTRA, DILIPA, Elapatra, Entilaka ("marked"), Halimaka ("poison spewing"), Haranyabahu ("golden armed"), Haridraka ("timid snake"), Hastibhadra ("hood as wide as a palm"), Jaya ("victory"), Jyotiratha ("chariot of light"), Jyotishka, Kailasaka, Kalasha, KALIYA, Kambala, Karavira, Karotaka, Kashyapa, Khaga, Kotanaka, Kouravya, Kukuna, Kukura, Kumara, KUMUDA, Kushaka, Mahahanu ("large jawed"), Mahanila ("dark blue sapphire"), Mahasankha ("great conch"), Mahavikrama ("very valorous"), Malyapindaka, Mangalya ("sandalwood"), Manicuda ("jewel crested"), Manimat ("adorned with jewels"), Maninaga, Mucilinda, Mudgaraparnaka, Mukhara, Mushikada, Nahusha, NANDA, Nandakam, Nishthurika, Nisthurika ("roar"), Padmas, Pala ("guardian"), Pindara, Pinjaraka, Pitharaka, Potaka, PUNDARIKA, Pushpa, Sabala ("spotted"), Samvritta, Sankhacuda ("crested with conch shells"), Sanku ("arrow"), Sarabha, Sarana ("protecting"), Shankha, Shankhashirsa, Shikhi, Shirishaka, Subahu, Sumanomukha ("nice face and heart"), Sumanomukha, Surasa, Susena ("wanting a missile"), Susenda ("wanting a good missile"), Svasana ("hissing"), Takshaka, Tittiri, Ulmka ("tip of a needle"), Upanandaka, Valisikha ("crest of hair"), VAMANA, Vasara ("day"), Vasuki, Vikunda, Viraja, Viranaka ("made of kitus grass"), Virasa, Virohama ("causing to heal"), and Vritta.

Source: Allardice, *Myths, Gods, and Fantasy*, 1990; Dange, *Myths from the Mahābhārata*, 26, 41, 126; De Visser, *Dragon in China and Japan*, xiii; De Kirk, *Dragonlore*, 59; Gandhi, *Penguin Book of Hindu Names for Boys*, 22, 46, 118, 493, 564; Hyatt, *Book of Demons*, 19, 24; Turner, *Dictionary of Ancient Dieties*, 498; Zell-Ravenheart, *Wizard's Bestiary*, 72

Nagaraja

Variations: Naga Raja

In Indian folklore the honorific title of nagaraja ("king of snakes") is given to those NAGAS acting as guardians of lake, rivers, swamps, and the like. Typically when described or depicted in art a nagaraja will have a minimum of five hoods; oftentimes they are shown as anthropomorphic, having the upper body of a man and the lower body of a great snake, sitting in repose next to their *agramahishi* (chief consort) who is attending to them with a fly-whisk. In Buddhist accounts all of the nagaraja are also converts to Buddhism.

The names of some of the nagaraja are listed here, taken for the most part from Brahmanical catalogues and the *Mahavyutpatti* which simply list names en masse; no additional information is available for many of these NAGAS: Ambarisha, Amratirtha, Anavatapta, Andha ("blind"), Apelala, Apta ("apt"), Aruna ("ruddy"), Aryaka, Asvatara ("mule"), Badhira ("deaf"), Badhira ("deaf"), Bilvapatha ("yellow sandal tree"), Buhumulaka, Champeya, Chitra ("uariegated"), Dhananjaya, Dhritarashtra, Dilipa, Elapatra, Girika, Haridraka ("curcumalonga"), Janamejaya, Kala, Kalika, Kalmasha ("black spotted"), Kapila ("brown, reddish"), Karavira ("oleander"), Kardama ("poisonous turnip"), Karkara ("hard"), Karkotaka, KAURAVYA, Khaga ("bird"), Krisaka ("thin"), Krishna ("black"), Kukura ("dog"), KULIKA, Kumuda ("lotus"), Kunjara ("elephant"), Kushmanda ("pumpkin"), Lohita ("red"), Mahapadama ("lotus"), Manasvin, Manikantha, Nanda, Nandopananda, Nila ("dark blue"), Nishthurika ("hard"), Nishthurika ("hard"), Padma ("lotus"), Pandara, Pindaraka ("aegle marmelos"), Pingala ("tawny"), Pinjaraka ("reddish brown"), Prithusravas, Pundarika ("lotus"), Raghava, Sabala ("brindled"), Sagara, Sagara, Sankhapala, Sirishaka ("acacia sirissa"), Sumana ("kind"), Sveta ("white"), Takshaka, Tittiri ("partridge"), Udayana, Ugraka ("terrible"), Upananda, Utpala, Utpalaka ("lotus"), Varuna, Vasuki, Vidyujjvala, Vilvaka ("aegle marmelos"), Vritta ("round").

Source: Ogden, *Drakon*, 244; Vogel, *Indian Serpent-lore*, 39, 44, 101, 191

Nagini

Variations: Nāgī, Nāginī

In Hindu mythology the nagini are female NAGAS; they were the powerful guardians of great treasures of books, secret knowledge, and wealth. Dispensing their treasures to those who were deemed worthy, they also protected the secret to eternal life. Described as DRAKAIAN in appearance, they have the upper body of a woman and the lower body of a great snake. Nagini are the personification of terrestrial water and as such are in charge of directing lakes, oceans, ponds, and rivers.

Source: Wittke-Rüdiger, *Translation of Cultures*, 150; Zimmer, *Myths and Symbols in Indian Art and Civilization*, 59

Nai

A feared serpent from ancient Egyptian mythology, Nai was said to consume the bodies and drink the blood of people who made their way through the Underworld. In *The Text of Unas* there is a magical spell which when performed will cause the destruction of monstrous beasts and serpents alike; Nai would be affected by this spell.

Source: Budge, *Gods of the Egyptians*, 23; Coulter, *Encyclopedia of Ancient Deities*, 32, 419

Nak

In Egyptian mythology and named in the *Book of the Overthrowing of Apophis* the serpent-fiend Nak and his assistant SEBAU were the monstrous helpers of APOPHIS. All three suffered a brutal demise, being gashed, slashed, their arms severed, and finally set ablaze while still alive.

Source: Budge, *Gods of the Egyptians*, 335, 339; Mercatante, *Who's Who in Egyptian Mythology*, 13–14

Namahage

Similar to the AMAMEHAGI, the namahage ("blister-peeler") is a fierce looking YŌKAI from Japanese folklore, having bright red (male) or bright blue-green (female) skin, a demonic face, horns upon its head, and a *mino* ("straw") coat; they carried a knife or machete. Some scholars say they are a form of ONI. The namahage despise lazy and spoiled children and are utilized by parents as a NURSERY BOGIE. According to folklore, in the dead of winter they would burst into a home and demand to see the children; lazy children who sat near the fire all day would have heat-blisters upon their feet and the namahage would punish their sloth by breaking the blisters and removing the skin. In spite of their violence, the namahage are considered to be harbingers of good fortune and luck.

Source: Bocking, *Popular Dictionary of Shinto*, 98; Yoda, *Yokai Attack*, 122–5

Namazu

A gigantic catfish from Japanese mythology, Namazu usually appears in a semi-human form. He is said to be the cause of earthquakes but also the bringer of wealth. During the Edo periods (1603 and 1868) economic conditions were extremely polarized and the poor were literally on the brink of death. When Namazu caused an earthquake, the disaster would, along with great destruction, bring about the opportunity for change. The poor had the opportunity to get assistance and better themselves while the rich, who had a great deal more to lose, were forced to spend money in the region repairing what they lost; this opportunity of growth and potential prosperity, called *yo-naoshi* (the renewal of the world) was how Namazu delivered wealth to the people.

Namazu lives in the bowels of the earth and it is his movements which cause earthquakes to happen. According to the folklore Takemikazuchi-no-miko drove a great stone called kaname-ishi through the earth to pin the catfish to one place. The stone is still visible and is located at the kashima shrine in Hitachi.

Source: Ashkenazi, *Handbook of Japanese Mythology*, 220–1; Piccardi, *Myth and Geology*, 78–9, 83

Namorodo (Nem-road-dough)

The Aboriginal people of West Arnhem Land, Australia, have in their mythology a species of vampiric demonic creature called a namorodo. It is said to be a skeletal humanoid held together by ligaments and has long, razor-sharp finger bones. Inactive by day, at night it flies through the sky seeking prey. The namorodo enters a home and when it finds a sleeping person, attacks and drains them of their blood. If so inclined, it has the ability to create more of its own kind. The namorodo are associated with shooting stars and sorcery.

Source: McLeish, *Myth*, 407; Rose, *Giants, Monsters, and Dragons*, 263; Tresidder, *Complete Dictionary of Symbols*, 335

Nanda

Variations: Nan-t'o (Chinese)

The chief of the DRAGON KINGS or a NAGARAJA in Indian mythology, Nanda was said to have four heads and six arms; upon one of his heads he wore a crown and in two of his hands he held a serpent while two others were shooting an arrow from a bow. Fierce, Nanda lived in the mountains and was far more reasonable than other DRAGONS who dwelt there and were generally evil by nature; he was described as being the most exalted of the DRAGONS of this world but WEI-TE-LUN-KAI was the most exalted of all the DRAGONS of the universe.

Source: Eitel, *China Review, Or, Notes and Queries on the Far East*, Volume 10, 385, 405; Roberts, *Chinese Mythology, A to Z*, 31;

Nandi

A bull or calf from Hindu mythology, Nandi ("he who grants joy") is the *vahan* ("vehicle") or mount of the god Siva as well as his single greatest devotee. In ancient times Shiva was worshiped as a fertility deity and was represented as a bull. Nandi, bull or calf, is always white, symbolic of justice, purity and righteousness.

Source: Barber, *Dictionary of Fabulous Beasts*, 109; Balfour, *Cyclopædia of India and of Eastern and Southern Asia*, Volume 1, 681; Gauding, *Signs and Symbols Bible*, 123

Nanes Bakbakwalanooksiwae

A cannibalistic grizzly bear from the mythology of the Kwakiutla people of Canada, North America, Nanes Bakbakwalanooksiwae ("Grizzly Bear at the Door") is one of the attendants of the horrific and monstrous Bakbakwakanooksiewae, cannibalistic bird-spirit.

Source: Shearar, *Understanding Northwest Coast Art*, 19; Werness, *Continuum Encyclopedia of Native Art*, 127

Nanggu Moksin

Variations: Moksin Tongbop

A species of particularly malicious NATURE SPIRIT from Korean folklore, the nanggu moksin will try to enter into a person's home for the singular purpose of causing perpetual illness to befall the family. As it cannot cross the threshold of its own volition and needs to be taken into the home it will attempt to do so by hiding within newly purchased wooden objects. On an inauspicious day the nanggu moksin can enter the home by hiding in firewood as it is taken indoors.

According to the folklore the nanggu moksin must have its attention drawn to a victim; activities such as bringing firewood into the home, building houses, or cutting down a tree on an inauspicious day will attract it.

Source: Kendall, *Shamans, Housewives, and Other Restless Spirits*, 90–1; Rose, *Spirits, Fairies, Leprechauns, and Goblins, an Encyclopedia*, 231

Nape

A dog and wolf hybrid from classical Greek mythology, Nape ("forester") was one of the DOGS OF ACTÆON, the unfortunate youth who was raised by the CENTAUR CHEIRON.

Source: Leeming, *World of Myth*, 111; Murray, *Classical Manual*, 160; Naso, *Fasti, Tristia*, 93–5

Naras

Similar to the KINNARAS of Hindu mythology, the naras are described as having the body of a human but the limbs of a horse, reminiscent of the CENTAURS of Greek mythology. The naras were created by the god Brahma at the same time he created the KINNARAS and the RAKSHASAS.

Source: Blavatsky, *Secret Doctrine*, Volume 1, 65; Garrett, *Classical Dictionary of India*, 418

Nargun

A creature from Australian folklore, the Nargun is said to be a singular being but there are many caverns said to be the residence of this cave-dweller, all of which are known as the Den of Nargun. Consistently it is described as being female and evil; sometimes it is said to be covered in scales while other times Nargun is said to be made of living stone except for her arms, breasts, and hands, which are flesh. As a NURSERY BOGIE Nargun is said to snatch up children who wander off unattended. In other tales it will drag anyone who comes too near its home into the bowels of her cave, never to be seen again. Nargun cannot be harmed by the boomerang or by the spear.

Source: Clark, *Historical Geography of Tourism in Victoria, Australia*, 91, 94, 100; Smyth, *Aborigines of Victoria*, Volume 1, 456–7

Nasnas

Variations: Nashas, Nesnas

A lower form of djinn (a race of demons), the nasnas ("twice people") of Islamic mythology were believed to live all over the world, but particularly thrived in the country of China. Those nasnas who live more localized to the Ismalic people, like the GHOUL and SHIQQ, preferred to keep far away from developed and urban areas.

Nasnas are a hybrid creature, said to be something between animal and human, an archaic, abnormal, enigmatic, and weak oddity; there are tales of people hunting them and the nasnas fleeing in terror at the sight of humans; there are however, a few tales of the nasnas being aggressive and preying on humans, frightening them and carrying them off. They are described as having demonic features, standing tall and upright and having wide fingernails.

In very old Arabic folklore the nasnas were a tribe who turned their back on the prophet and were punished by God, transformed in creatures. In this myth, they are said to hop like birds and graze like an animal.

Other folklore claims the nasnas are the offspring of a *shiqq* (a species of djinn) and a human being. In this instance the creature is found living in Yemen and is said to have only half a body, one arm, one leg, and half a head, moving itself by hopping from place to place as it is extremely agile.

Like all evil beings the nasnas has the free will and the choice to turn their back on their malicious lives, convert, and become Muslim.

Source: El-Zein, *Islam, Arabs, and the Intelligent World of the Jinn*, 142–3; Hughes, *Dictionary of Islam*, 137; Zell-Ravenheart, *Wizard's Bestiary*, 72

Nathraig Luamning

The Irish pseudepigraph *Epistil Isu* (*"Sunday Letters"*), written by an anonymous author, describes five kinds of monsters which will descend upon those individuals and heathens who do not keep holy the Lord's Day, Sunday. The nathraig luamning are the fourth of the tormentors mentioned. If the Sabbath is not observed, these flying serpents arrive with heavy storms, bringing with them fiery lightning and breathing down sulfurous fire which will burn out families and nations alike. The arrival of the nathraig luamning is a precursor to the coming of non-Christian invaders who will take locals hostage and sacrifice them to foreign gods.

Source: Olsen, *Monsters and the Monstrous in Medieval Northwest Europe*, 69–70

Nature Spirit

Variations: Elemental, KAMI, Nature Deities, Sylvan

Nature spirits are common in many of the world's folklores, mythologies, religions, and spiritual beliefs; they have appeared in Aborigine, African, ancient Greek and Roman, Hawaiian, Japanese, Native American, Norse, Polynesian, and Shinto to name but a scant few. These beings are perhaps best described as being the energy of the animals and plants of nature. Nature spirits are also described as being the spirits or returned souls of deceased ancestors. In most cases nature spirits have the ability to shape-shift, taking on an unlimited array of animal forms; these can be female, male, or genderless. As beings of nature, they are neither good nor evil but are labeled as such by human perceptions. When they are described as wearing clothing they are usually said to dress in green.

Source: Barstow, *Elementally Speaking*, 16–17; Bord, *Fairies*, 111–12; Keightley, *World Guide to Gnomes, Fairies, Elves, and Other Little People*, 34; McCoy, *Witch's Guide to Faery Folk*, 32–34

Nau

Variations: Bull of the Gods, Nen

According to ancient Egyptian mythology Nau was a monstrous serpent having "seven serpents on his seven necks"; it lived in Tuat, the Underworld. Little is known of this creature. In *The Text of Unas* there is a magical spell which when performed will cause the destruction of monstrous beasts and serpents alike; Nau would be affected by this spell.

Source: Coulter, *Encyclopedia of Ancient Deities*, 32, 338; Mercatante, *Who's Who in Egyptian Mythology*, 101

Nau-Shesma

Variations: Nau, Naut

A monstrous serpent in ancient Egyptian mythology having seven heads, Nau-Shesma had authority over seven archers in Tuat, the underworld of the ancient Egyptians, where it dwelled. In *The Text of Unas* there is a magical spell which when performed will cause the destruction of monstrous beasts and serpents alike; Nau-Shesma would be affected by this spell.

Source: Coulter, *Encyclopedia of Ancient Deities*, 32, 338; Mercatante, *Who's Who in Egyptian Mythology*, 101

Ndogbojusui

The collective name for the NATURE SPIRITS of West African folklore; living in the mountains by day, the ndogbojusui wander the bush at night looking for hunters and lone travelers to harass. Described as looking like very hairy men or men with exceptionally long beards, the ndogbojusui will, by use of deception, lure their prey deeper and deeper into the jungle until they die of exhaustion.

Source: Brown, *African-Atlantie Cultures and the South Carolina Lowcountry*, 136

Ndzoodzoo

In the folklore of the Makua people of Southeast Africa the ndzoodzoo is a species of UNICORN said to be about the size of a horse, exceedingly fast and strong, and having an alicorn (a single horn) about two and half feet long protruding from its forehead. These animals are extremely fierce and will attack a man without provocation. When asleep the horn is said to be rather flexible and curls up upon their head, sometimes even remaining in position while the animal is awake and calm; however when enraged or threatened, the horn becomes hard and a most formidable weapon. The female ndzoodzoo does not have an alicorn.

Source: Gould, *Mythical Monsters*, 347; Lavers, *Natural History of Unicorns*, 164; Zell-Ravenheart, *Wizard's Bestiary*, 72

Neade

According to ancient Greek historians the neade was a creature believed to have lived when the "origin of life was recent" and the mountains were still forming. Having found a large fossil bed the Greeks recognized the bones as animals no longer living upon the world and believed they died en masse before humans populated the land. Calling these creatures *neades*, naturalists of the time, such as Claudius Aelian (AD 175–235) and Euphorion of Chalcis (circa 275 BC), surmised that the animals were among the original inhabitants of the island of Samos and their roar was powerful enough to rip the ground open; they were associated with earthquakes. The legend of the neades is fragmentary at best although there are mentions of neade bones on display in various temples.

Source: Debus, *Prehistoric Monsters*, 14; Mayor, *First Fossil Hunters*, 58, 60, 204, 261

Nebrophonos

Variations: Nebrophonus

A dog from ancient Greek mythology, Nebrophonos ("kill-buck") was one of the DOGS OF ACTÆON, the unfortunate youth who was raised by the CENTAUR CHEIRON. Nebrophonos was noted for being particularly fierce.

Source: Leeming, *World of Myth*, 111; Murray, *Classical Manual*, 160; Naso, *Fasti, Tristia*, 93–5

Nedymnus

A CENTAUR from ancient Greek mythology, Nedymnus was, according to Ovid's *Metamorphoses*, one of the CENTAURS who attended the wedding of Pirithous, became drunk on wine and following the lead of EURYTUS, who assaulted Hippodame, began to assault and rape any women they could grab.

During the battle, Nedymnus and the spear thrower LYCOPES were clubbed to death by the hero Theseus.

Source: *Commentary, Mythological, Historical, and Geographical on Pope's Homer*, 55; Simpson, *Metamorphoses of Ovid*, 206

Neha-Hra

According to ancient Egyptian mythology Neha-Hra, an enemy of the sun god Ra, was described as being a monstrous serpent, attempting to prevent him from completing his journey East. Neha-Hra was slain daily along with NAK, SEBAU, and the other offspring, shadows and spirits of APOPHIS, pinned to the ground with six knives.

Source: Budge, *Gods of the Egyptians: Or, Studies in Egyptian Mythology*, Volume 1, 232, 246; Mercatante, *Who's Who in Egyptian Mythology*, 104

Nehebkau

Variations: Neheb Ka, Nehebu-Kau

A DRAGON-like creature from Egyptian mythology, Nehebkau is depicted as having a long serpentine body with human hands and legs; tamed by the sun god, Ra, it accompanies him on his journey east in the sun boat.

Immune to fire, water, and various other magics, Nehebkau has an infamous temper and is well known to be dangerous to humans. Nehebkau and HETCH-NAU were the guardians of Osiris while the god was in his form known as Osiris the Seeker. His image was often used on talismans to protect against scorpion poison.

Source: Coulter, *Encyclopedia of Ancient Deities*, 418; De Kirk, *Dragonlore*, 58; Pinch, *Handbook of Egyptian Mythology*, 169

Nekomata (NEH-koh MAH-ta)

Variations: Neko-Mata

A type of YŌKAI from Japanese folklore, the nekomata ("forked cat") appears as an exceptionally large house cat but has twin tails. In addition to possessing the ability to create fireballs, shape-shift into human form, speak, and walk on their hind legs, they also have the ability to control the dead. The nekomata are able to assume human form by consuming the corpse of the person they wish to impersonate and reanimate a corpse by jumping over the head of the deceased. Interestingly, the nekomata has a preference for the consumption of lamp oil.

Source: Kohen, *World History and Myths of Cats*, 49–51; Yoda, *Yokai Attack*, 38–41

Nemean Lion

Variations: CITHAERONIAN, Nemeian Lion, Leon Nemeios

In ancient Greek mythology the Nemean lion was born one of the children of ECHIDNA and Typhoeus; it was the sibling of CERBERUS, the CHIMERA, the HYDRA, ORTHOS, and the SPHINX. Hesiod, the ancient Greek poet, claimed in his stories the lion was the offspring of ECHIDNA and the two-headed, serpent tailed dog, ORTHRUS.

The demi-god and hero Hercules (Heracles) is tasked by his cousin, King Eurystheus of Mycenae, as his first of twelve Labors to confront and slay the golden-coated Nemean lion. The creature was said to have a hide impervious to all weapons; in order to defeat it, Hercules was forced to physically attack the animal using his own brute strength against it. Ultimately Hercules was able to wrestle the lion and strangle it to death. An interesting and little known variation to the story is told by the first century ancient Greek author Alexander of Myndus; in his version of the events Hercules had a pet DRAKON reared from birth and it accompanied him on this Labor, assisting in the battle to defeat the lion.

Source: Ogden, *Drakon*, 58, 195; Stookey, *Thematic Guide to World Mythology*, 136

Nependis

In European heraldic symbology the nependis is a hybrid creature, part ape and part boar, although in some versions the boar is replaced with a dog; it embodies the worst qualities of the animals it represents.

Source: Barber, *Dictionary of Fabulous Beasts*, 109; Cooper, *Symbolic and Mythological Animals*, 166; Lower, *Curiosities of Heraldry*, 103; Rose, *Giants, Monsters, and Dragons*, 264

Nessus

Variations: Nessos

One of the CENTAURS from ancient Greek mythology, Nessus worked as a ferryman on a river carrying people across on his back. According to the legend, when Hercules (Heracles), newly wed to his second wife, Deianira, needed to cross he employed the CENTAUR to carry them; unable to take them both at the same time Nessus took Deianira first, but about halfway across the river his lust for her became too much to control. Hercules pulled from his quiver the arrow he had dipped in the poisonous blood of the HYDRA and shot Nessus; however, before the vengeful CENTAUR died he managed to convince Deianira to collect some of the blood from his wound and use it as a love potion should her husband ever stray. Years later Hercules decided to have his lover, Iole, move into the family home. Fearful she would completely lose her husband to his mistress, Deianira coated a robe with Nessus' blood and gave it to Hercules as a gift, inadvertently poisoning him. Unable to live with the guilt of what she had done, Deianira committed suicide. Hercules, being a demi-god, was unable to die from the effects of the poison and suffered in great agony until he finally took his own life in a funeral pyre made for him by his son Hyllus upon Mount Oeta.

Source: Daly, *Greek and Roman Mythology, A to Z*, 70; Roman, *Encyclopedia of Greek and Roman Mythology*, 339, 494; Rose, *Giants, Monsters, and Dragons*, 266

Ngani-Vatu

Variations: Ngutu-Lei

A gigantic anthropophagous (man-eating) bird from Fijian mythology, the ngani-vatu is similar to the POUA-KAI of Maori folklore and the ROC of the popular Arabic tale, *One-Thousand and One Arabian Nights*. It was so large its body blocked out the sun as it flew overhead and the flapping of its wings would create storms. According to the story ngani-vatu took the wife of the hero Okiva. Unable to rescue her in time he did manage to track down the creature to its nightly resting place and returned with his brother-in-law, Kokoua. Together they managed to kill ngani-vatu and roll its body into the ocean, creating a tidal wave which threatened many far off islands.

Source: Rose, *Giants, Monsters, and Dragons*, 265; Skyes, *Who's Who in Non-Classical Mythology*, 139; Zell-Ravenheart, *Wizard's Bestiary*, 72

Ngorieru

In Polynesian mythology Ngorieru is the chief of the ADARO, a species of malevolent sea creatures; he is said to live off of the coast of San Christobal in the Galapagos archipelago. When paddling past this area in their canoes people are said to do so quietly and speak in hushed tones lest they disturb malicious Ngorieru or attract his attention.

Source: Andrews, *Dictionary of Nature Myths*, 4; Rosen, *Mythical Creatures Bible*, 138

Nguruvilu

Variations: FOX SERPENT, Guirivilo, Guruvilu, Neguruvilu, Ñirivilo o Nirivilo, Ñirivilu, Ñivivilu, Ñuruvilu

A species of water-snake in Araucanian (Mapuchen) folklore, the nguruvilu ("fox snake") are said to be catlike in appearance, living in the river. Preying on both animals and humans, the nguruvilu snatch up their prey with their claw-tipped tail and drag them to the bottom of the lake, drowning them, and consuming the remains.

Source: Alexander, *Mythology of All Races*-Volume XI Latin-American, 328; Bingham, *South and Meso-American Mythology A to Z*, 54

Nian, the Beast

Variations: Nien

A creature of Chinese folklore, Nian ("year") was said to live deep in the thickly forested mountains. It was said to be a terrifying creature, having fiery red eyes, horns, and a vicious maw full of teeth; it was so horrific people would pale at the very mention of its name. Nian consumed any living thing he came upon from the smallest of insects to humans. It was discovered every three hundred sixty-five days Nian would descend upon a human settlement and begin killing, his onslaught lasting until the cock crowed the coming of morning. Knowing when the monster would attack was nerve-racking as no one knew where it would strike; so on that night before its assault, each family would have an early but sumptuous meal together, as it might be their last as a family. Then they would clean the house, light a fire, lock up the animals, and remain huddled together inside the home. All night the family remained awake, telling stories and reminiscing together, thus creating the tradition of staying up all night long on New Year's Eve. The only things capable of frightening the Nian are the lion and very loud noises, such as the pounding of drums and the report of firecrackers.

Source: Perkins, *Encyclopedia of China*, 354; Wei, *Chinese Festivals*, 18–9

Nicor, plural Niceras

In Scandinavian mythology the chimerical nicor was a species of SEA SERPENT or monster famed for eating sailors. Described as being three fathoms long they had the body of a bison, the beard of a man, the head of a cat, and tusks an ell (forty-five inches) long. The cultural hero Beowulf makes mention of these creatures many times in his storytelling.

Source: Brewer, *Dictionary of Phrase and Fable*, 888; Thorpe, *Northern Mythology*, Volume 1, 82

Nidfollr (NITH-vuhl-r)

In Norse mythology Nidfollr ("pale black") was said to be the eagle who tears into the corpses at the battle of Ragnarok; beyond a name, there is nothing else known.

Source: Norroena Society, *Asatrii Edda*, 376

Nidhogg (NEETH-huhg-r)

Variations: Hidhaegg, Nidhhogg, Nidhhoggr, Nidhøg, Nidhögg, Nídhögg, Níðhögg, Nidhoggr ("corpse eater"), Nidhöggr, Niðhoggr, Nídhöggr, Níðhoggr, Niðhöggur, Níðhöggur, Nidhoggur, Nidhug, Nithhogg, Nithhoggr, Nithhöggr, Niðhöggr

Nidhogg ("abuse blower," "one full of hatred" or "malice striker") was one of the DRAGONS named in Thorgrimr's *Rhymes* and in Snorri Sturluson's (1179–1241) *Prose Edda*. Known as the DRAGON of Death, Nidhogg would drink the blood of the dead before eating their corpses. Living in Nastrond he would forage under the tree Ygdrasil to chew upon its roots, and according to legend, will survive the destruction of the world and live on to see the next world created where he will thereafter reside once it is complete.

Source: Jennbert, *Animals and Humans*, 50; Matthews, *Element Encyclopedia of Magical Creatures*, 179; Norroena Society, *Asatrii Edda*, 376; Oehlenschläger, *Gods of the North*, xxxviii

Nihniknoovi

A gigantic bird-like, predatory creature from the folklore of the Native American people known as the Kawaissu Tubatulabal, the nihniknoovi is described as having enormous talon tipped feet it uses to snatch up humans. It takes its prey off to a particular waterhole where it drains the blood of its prey into the water before consuming the corpse.

Source: Rose, *Giants, Monsters, and Dragons*, 267–8

Ningyo

First recorded in AD 619 during the twenty-seventh year of the reign of Empress Suiko, the ningyo ("human fish") is a species of FAIRY ANIMAL from Japanese folklore; its name is typically translated as MERMAID, but it is in fact neither human or MERMAID-like in appearance.

Originally the ningyo were described as having a crest of thick fur atop their head; humanoid, webbed fingers; a simian (monkey-like) mouth; small Piscean teeth; and golden scales. Like the SIREN, these beings had a hauntingly beautiful voice, similar to a flute or skylark; their song did not consist of words but was nevertheless hypnotic.

In their underwater domain, the ningyo lived in a highly intricate society; they were believed to be highly skilled in the art of healing and magic. If a fisherman caught one, it was considered to bring about misfortune and storms so these beings were usually thrown back. If a ningyo was willing to offer up a bit of itself, anyone who consumed any amount of its flesh would be granted immortality. The blood of the ningyo was said to have the ability to heal any wound. However, to take these elements from the creature without its permission was to be the victim of dire consequences.

In the modern telling of the mythology the ningyo is described as looking like a traditional MERMAID, having long black hair rather than the golden or green of Celtic folklore. Elusive and avoiding human contact, it is believed the sighting of a ningyo brings good luck. It is also believed when they cry, their tears are precious pearls of considerable value.

Source: Loar, *Goddesses for Every Day*, 72; Rosen, *Mythical Creatures Bible*, 132; Yamaguchi, *We Japanese*, 318; Zell-Ravenheart, *Wizard's Bestiary*, 73

Ninki Nanka

Variations: Ningiri, Nini-Ganne, Rainseou

A ravenously hungry fresh-water river monster from the folklore of West Africa, the Ninki Nanka is said to have a crocodile-like body, equine head on a long neck, and three horns upon its head (see SEA SERPENT). Living in the mangroves, this nocturnal river monster is said to have the ability to take the form of a gigantic snake, perhaps some thirty feet in length.

Source: Eberhart, *Mysterious Creatures*, 388; Oldale, *World of Curiosities*, n.pag.

Nirgalli (NER-gal-le)

According to ancient Assyrian demonology, the nirgalli ("winged lions") were a species of demonic guardians stationed at the entranceways to the royal palace. Always appearing in pairs, these hybrid lion-headed humans with the legs of eagles fight one another with clubs and daggers. Magical incantations mention the nirgalli saying "the evil demons should get out; they should mutually kill one another."

Source: Carus, *History of the Devil and the Idea of Evil*, 39–40; Cheyne, *Prophecies of Isaiah*, 299; Methodist Book Concern, *Methodist Review*, Volume 35, 118

Nobiagari (NOH-bee AH-gah-ree)

A YŌKAI from Japanese mythology, nobiagari ("shadow specter" or "stretching specter") is a singular entity appearing and attacking its prey from behind, suddenly and seemingly out of nowhere, and then growing to a massive size with alarming speed. Its physical appearance varies from region to region; some say it is a living shadow while others claim it to be a hybrid creature of a human and some unknown monster which assumes the appearance of a Buddhist monk. Other versions of the tale say it does not have the actual ability to increase its size but rather only the ability of fooling people into thinking it does.

No matter what it looks like the nobiagari stalks travelers who utilize trails and walkways near lakes and rivers. It is more active in the winter months and seldom does it cause any true or lasting physical harm. To avoid being assaulted by the nobiagari it is said one should turn and face the creature, keeping one's gaze towards the ground, and shout "*Mioroshita!*" ("I look down upon you!") as this will cause it to disappear. Another method is to kick the air about a foot off the ground in the hope it will cause the nobiagari to lose its balance, fall over, and disappear.

Source: Yoda, *Yokai Attack*, 190–3

Nobusuma

In Japanese folklore it is believed when a bat manages to live for a very long time it will become a vampiric creature called a *nobusuma* ("most ancient"). This species of energy vampire flies through the night sky looking for a sleeping person to assault. When it finds suitable prey, the nobusuma lands on their chest and begins to tap on the sleeping person's chest, making them cough. When this happens, the nobusuma takes in the escaping breath, leaching off some of the person's life. Over the course of the next three days, unless the nobusuma is stopped, the victim will die, their life energy drained away. To prevent this from happening, someone needs to be present to witness the assault, as their presence will then drive the nobusuma off, never to return. The victim will instantly recover to full vigor and go on to live a long and healthy life.

Source: Iinkai, *Japan*, 794; Japan Society of London, *Transactions and Proceedings*, Volume 9, 27–28; Poulton, *Spirits of Another Sort*, 64

Nocnitsa

Variations: Gorska Makna, Krisky ("scream"), Night Hag, Plaksy ("snivel")

A NURSERY BOGIE in Slavic folklore, the nocturnal hag Nocnitsa harasses children with nightmares; to protect their offspring parents would place a knife under their cradle or draw a circle of protection around it.

Source: Hastings, *Encyclopedia of Religion and Ethics*, Part 8, 625; Khanam, *Demonology*, 256; Sherman, *Storytelling*, 330

Nocny Forman

The nocny forman was a nocturnal *carman* (coach driver) from Slavic folklore.

Source: Wolff, *Odd Bits of History*, 152

Nocny Hanik

Variations: Nocny Murava

The nocny hanik was a nocturnal huntsman from Slavic folklore.

Source: Wolff, *Odd Bits of History*, 152

Nogitsune

A species of KITSUNE (fox spirit) from Japanese mythology, nogitsune ("wild fox") were messengers to the goddess of rice, Inari; they were known to be malicious pranksters who oftentimes caused harm. Preferring to deceive by means of enchantment, the nogitsune favored possessing wizards in spite of having the ability to make themselves invisible and shape-shift into any form.

Dogs can see the nogitsune for what they truly are no matter the form these creatures may assume. Regardless of its form, should a nogitsune's shadow fall upon the water it will reflect the shadow of a fox. Although the nogitsune may be slain by any method, to do so is a risky endeavor as the assailant runs the risk of being cursed by the creature's family or the ghost of the nogitsune itself. Should the slayer of a nogitsune consume the flesh of the creature before the curse can be placed, it will render them immune to the effects. If a nogitsune manages to live for one hundred years it will grow a pure white coat and be referred to as an Inari fox.

Source: Hearn, *Glimpses of an Unfamiliar Japan*, 282; Maberry, *Vampire Universe*, 177

Nokken

A NURSERY BOGIE from Norwegian folklore, the nokken ("water horse"), a lake monster, preys upon children who do not come when their parents call them; however throughout Scandinavia the nokken is a malicious shape-shifting FAIRY ANIMAL in the guise of a beautiful horse. Letting itself be seen unattended, the nokken waits for someone to mount upon its back, then it takes off running, heading straight for a pond or river. Diving in with its unfortunate rider, the person is never seen again, presumably drowned and possibly consumed but possibly taken to serve in the nokken's underwater home.

Source: Frater, *Listverse*, 580; Steward, *Trolls*, 42

Nomos

Variations: Nonios, Nonius

One of the four black horses of the god of the Underworld, Hades (Dis), from ancient Greek mythology, Nomos and his stable mates, ABASTER, ABATOS, and AETON, pulled the god's chariot.

Source: Brewer, *Dictionary of Phrase and Fable*, 626; Rubin, *Writer's Companion*, 868; Ruthven, *Shaman Pathways*, n.pag.

Noolmahl

Variations: The Fool Dancer

A cannibalistic monster from the mythology of the Kwakiutla people of Canada, North America, Noolmahl is one of the attendants of the horrific and monstrous Bakbakwakanooksiewae, cannibalistic bird-spirit.

Source: Werness, *Continuum Encyclopedia of Native Art*, 127

Nopperabo (NOH-peh-rah BOW)

Variations: Mujina, Noppera-bō, Noppera-Bo, Nopperabō, Zunbera-bō

In Japanese demonology nopperabo ("blank face," "faceless ones," "no face") demons typically appear as women with a perfectly featureless and smooth face; however in more modern times adult male appearances of this YŌKAI are becoming more frequent. Sometimes one will impersonate someone familiar to the victim before revealing itself for what it truly is. Exceptionally frightening to experience, nopperabo are otherwise harmless.

As the nopperabo ages, its facial features become more rudimentary and eventually a pair of working eyes will appear on the palms of its hands. It is possible an aged nopperabo is also a type of YŌKAI known as TE-NO-ME.

It should be noted there is a type of creature called the mujina, which are small, furry, shape-shifting beings frequently taking on the guise of nopperabo to frighten people.

Source: Bush, *Asian Horror Encyclopedia*, 136; Frédéric, *Japan Encyclopedia*, 727; Hearn, *Kwaidan*, 42; Yoda, *Yokai Attack*, 134, 166–8

Nora (Nor-ah)

Variations: Nore

From Hungarian folklore comes a species of vampiric creature known as a nora. Humanoid, bald, and invisible, it moves about on all fours, attacking amoral and disrespectful women, drinking blood and breast milk from them. It is said smearing garlic paste over one's breasts will offer some protection from a nora attack, but the surest way to ensure one's safety is never to become a prostitute. It has been speculated the nora was an attempt to explain sexually transmitted diseases and other such ailments.

Source: Dömötör, *Hungarian Folk Beliefs*, 116; Keyworth, *Troublesome Corpses*, 60, 111

Notos

In ancient Greek mythology Notos was born of the goddess Eos ("dawn") and her official consort Astraios ("starry") and was sometimes referred to as the god of the south wind. Having the ability to shape-shift into the form of a horse, he was employed to pull the chariot of the god Zeus (Jupiter). While in his equine form he became the foundation stallion of the HIPPOI ATHANATOI, the collective name for the immortal horses of the Greek gods.

Source: Glover, *1000 Famous Horses Fact and Fictional Throughout the Ages*, 269; Hansen, *Handbook of Classical Mythology*, 321; Hard, *Routledge Handbook of Greek Mythology*, 48

Nue (NU-ay)

Variations: Japanese CHIMERA

A nocturnal chimerical creature from Japanese folklore, the nue is described as having the body of a raccoon-dog, head of a monkey, legs of a tiger, tail of a snake, and voice of a bird; because it has the natural ability to shape-shift into a black cloud and would fly about causing illness and nightmares it is often considered to be an ill omen. The nue was first mentioned in a twelfth century tale entitled *Tale of the Heike*. Because the nue is an extremely elusive creature it is impossible to determine if this is a singular entity or a rare species. It is unknown if the nue intends to do harm, for if it did, the creature most certainly could attack with its fangs, poisonous bite, and vicious claws rather than spreading illness from a distance.

Source: Rosen, *Mythical Creatures Bible*, 107; Yoda, *Yokai Attack*, 42–5; Zell-Ravenheart, *Wizard's Bestiary*, 74

Nuggie

Variations: Neugle, Noggle, Nogle, NUGGLE, Nygel

A species of water FAIRY ANIMAL from the folklore of Scalloway, Scotland, the nuggie was believed to live in the Njugals Water. Described as looking like a horse with a wheel-like tail arching up and over its back, the nuggie, like the EACH UISGE, would appear as a bridled and saddled horse; when a rider would climb up on its back, the nuggie would dash off into the water and attempt to drown its victim. Fond of mills and water wheels, nuggies would take great pleasure in making the wheel stop spinning by backing up into it.

In the folklore of Cornwall, England, there was a species of fairy also called a nuggie said to live in tin-mines.

Source: Briggs, *Encyclopedia of Fairies*, 255; Rose, *Spirits, Fairies, Leprechauns, and Goblins*, 235; Wright, *English Dialect Dictionary*, 309

Nuggle

Variations: Noggle, Nygel, Nyuggle

A species of FAIRY ANIMAL from the Shetland Islands, the nuggle is similar to the other species of water horses, such as the KELPIE; it will use its shape-shifting abilities to take the form of a magnificent grey Shetland pony and entice weary travelers to ride it. As soon as the nuggle is mounted, it will bolt, delivering a wild ride to its passenger; the ordeal only begins to end when the creature crashes into a lake or river, attempting to drown its prey.

Never seen far from water, nuggles will also torment mill owners; this most frequently happens when corn is being ground. Using its back, the FAIRY ANIMAL will back up against the water wheel and prevent it from spinning, no matter how much water is rushing over the top of the wheel. The only method to prevent the creature from this action is to drop a fire brand as close to it as possible, as they are terrified of fire.

Source: Briggs, *Encyclopedia of Fairies*, 277; Littell, *Living Age*, Volume 150, 811–12; Monaghan, *Encyclopedia of Celtic Mythology and Folklore*, 362–63

Nukekubi

A disembodied head from Japanese folklore, the nukekubi ("creeper," "prowler," or "sulker") detaches itself from its host body and flies off screaming into the night in search of prey; it screams to increase the victim's fear. By day, the nukekubi looks like a normal human being except for having red rings around its neck, presumably from where the creature detaches.

Source: Hearn, *Lafcadio Hearn*, 64; Rose, *Mythical Creatures Bible*, 219

Nuku-mai-tore

A species of NATURE SPIRIT from Maori folklore, the nuku-mai-tore are the ones who taught Whiro the art of cooking, the uses of fire, natural childbirth, and the ceremonies to perform during childbirth.

Source: Beckwith, *Hawaiian Mythology*, 502; White, *Ancient History of the Maori*, Volume 6, 17–9

Nuli'rahak

A NATURE SPIRIT from Inuit folklore, the Nuli'rahak ("big woman") is said to live on the bottom of the ocean and has dominion over all of the sea crea-tures; she feeds herself on the bodies of those drowned at sea.

Source: Bogoraz, *Chukchee*, 318; Jordan, *Dictionary of Gods and Goddesses*, 227

Nun

According to the Koran, Nun the fish and with BALAM THE OX will provide themselves to be the food consumed in Paradise; the lobes of the livers of BALAM and Nun will feed 70,000 saints.

Source: Brewer, *Reader's Handbook of Famous Names in Fiction, Allusions, References, Proverbs, Plots, Stories, and Poems*, 764; Sale, *Koran*, 72

Nunda

Variations: The Eater of People, the Swallowing Monster

A creature from the Swahili-speaking Africans, the nunda appears in the story of Sultan Majnun; in it, the nunda begins life as an ordinary cat, catching and consuming chickens. Each year it grows in ferocity and size until it is gigantic, as large as an elephant, devouring everything it happens upon. Eventually it is slain by the youngest son of the Sultan by bringing it a series of creatures, each one larger than the next, ending with an elephant.

Source: Werner, *Myths and Legends of the Bantu*, n.pag.

Nuno Sa Punso

Variations: Nuno

The secretive and shy nuno sa punso ("grandparent of the anthill") from Filipino folklore are very similar to the GNOME of British folklore; they live in earthen mounds or abandoned ant hills and appear as wizened old men with long flowing beards and reddish skin. Although they seldom have anything to do with humans, the nuno sa punso are quick to enact revenge if their ant-hill is disrupted by placing a curse upon the perpetrator; the spell causes the face and hands to swell, hair to begin growing all over the body, and the offender's urine to turn black.

Source: Demetrio, *Encyclopedia of Philippine Folk Beliefs and Customs*, Volume 2, 403; Redfern, *Most Mysterious Places on Earth*, 112

Nunyenunc

A gigantic ROC-like predatory bird from Native American folklore of the Bannocks, Gosiute, Paiutes, and the Shoshone, the nunyenunc, five times the size of an eagle, feeds nearly exclusively on humans, sweeping down and snatching up unwary hunters and travelers. When people are not to be found the nunyenunc eats antelope, deer, and mountain sheep. It takes all its prey to its mountain top roost where it consumes them.

Source: Barber, *Dictionary of Fabulous Beasts*, 110; Hall, *Thunderbirds*, 60; Rose, *Giants, Monsters, and Dragons*, 271

Nuppeppo (NEW-pep-poh)

Variations: Nuppebbo, Nuppefuhō, Nupperabo, Nuhehho

In Japanese folklore the YŌKAI known as a nuppeppo ("blobby") is said to be an animated, genderless lump of human flesh; some facial features and fingers and toes are sometimes said to be seen in the many folds of its body. Shambling, it is most often sighted in deserted temples and graveyards around the midnight hour; it is accompanied by the distinct odor of rotting flesh but folklore claims whoever consumes some of it will be granted eternal youth and immortality.

Source: Frater, *Listverse. Com's Ultimate Book of Bizarre Lists*, n.pag.; Yoda, *Yokai Attack*, 194–8; Zell-Ravenheart, *Wizard's Bestiary*, 74

Nure-Onna (NOO-ray OHN-nah)

Variations: Nure Onna

An evil YŌKAI from Japanese folklore, the nure-onna ("wet woman") is said to be a flying, reptilian creature with the face of a long haired woman but froglike legs and an extremely elongated tongue; it is the personification of evil. If ever this singular creature is encountered it will attempt to capture by means of its paralyzing stare and then consume anyone it meets by constricting them within its coils. The nure-onna is said to dwell in coves, harbors, shallow ocean inlets, and the occasional river.

Source: Foster, *Pandemonium and Parade*, 59; Gilmore, *Monsters*, 134; Yoda, *Yokai Attack*, 146–9

Nurikabe (NEW-ree KAH-bay)

A YŌKAI from Japanese folklore, the nurikabe ("the wall" and "plastered wall"), typically choosing to remain invisible, presents itself as an anthropomorphic obstacle, usually a wall, appearing anywhere, be it inside a home or in a remote field. No matter how hard the person tries to go around, over, under, or through the nurikabe, all attempts will prove futile; although its presence is highly frustrating, encounters almost never fatal.

Source: Foster, *Pandemonium and Parade*, 168; Yoda, *Yokai Attack*, 138–41

Nursery Bogie

Variations: Frightening Figures

A nursery bogie is any FAIRY ANIMAL or being used by parents to frighten their children into good behavior; they appear in many cultures from all around the world and all along the time-line. Generally, these beings not only have a frightening physical appearance but also extremely harsh, if not deadly, means by which they deal with mortals. Nursery bogies are not only used to urge children into proper social behavior but also to protect crops and keep children away from dangerous environments and situations.

Source: Briggs, *Encyclopedia of Fairies*, 313; Rose, *Spirits, Fairies, Leprechauns, and Goblins*, 241; Wright, *Rustic Speech and Folk-Lore*, 198

Nutum

In Babylonian mythology a nutum is a classification of a chimerical or hybrid creature of both earth and the heavens, such as with the LAHMU IPPIRU.

Source: Ford, *Maskim Hul: Babylonian Magick*, 161; Thompson, *Devils and Evil Spirits of Babylonia*, 155

Nyam Nyam (Nam Nam or Yum Yum)

Variations: Niam-Niam

Vampiric creatures from African folklore, the nyam nyam are members of a mythical tribe of dwarflike people with short tails. During the period of slavery, the word came to be used as a racial slur to describe the Azande people and their allied tribes. It could have been a mispronunciation of the word *nimyam*, which means "cannibal."

Source: Battuta, *Travels in Asia and Africa*, 379; Hasluck, *Letters on Religion and Folklore*, 38; Petrinovich, *Cannibal Within*, 121; Volta, *The Vampire*, 116

Nykr (Neeck-ore)

Variations: Kumbur, Nicor, Nennir, Nixie, Vatna-Hestur

In Icelandic folklore the nykr is a type of FAIRY ANIMAL appearing like a magnificent looking grey horse, or on the rare occasion black, but its hooves and fetlocks are always turned backwards. It has the ability to shape-shift into any form it likes; whenever the opportunity presents itself it will try to procreate with a horse to add to its numbers. It is said horses who dash into water or wallow in it are descendants of a nykr.

One of the favorite cruel tricks the dangerous and deceitfully friendly nykr plays is to lure someone, preferably a shepherd girl, to climb upon its back and attempt to ride it; once this happens the rider will soon discover they are stuck to the creature and will not have the chance or ability to dismount. Old folklore claims if the person is able to yell out the word *andskoti* ("fiend") they will be released and able to escape as this is the creature's true name and has a power over them. Another malicious act the nykr will commit is to come up on herds of cows and neigh at them, as the sound it produces maddens the animals and causes them to run into the nearest body of water.

Source: Árnason, *Icelandic Legends Collected by Jón Árnason*, lvii-lx

O Goncho

Variations: O-gon-cho

An enormous white, winged DRAGON from Japanese folklore, O Goncho is said to live in a pool called Ukisima, Kyoto. Every fifty years it would transform into a bird with golden plumage; its cry sounded like the howl of a wolf. To see the bird form of O Goncho or to hear the bird call was an indicator of some great impending disaster, such as famine.

Source: Barber, *Dictionary of Fabulous Beasts*, 112; Bates, *All About Chinese Dragons*, 100; Rose, *Giants, Monsters, and Dragons*, 273; Zell-Ravenheart, *Wizard's Bestiary*, 74

Obariyon (oh-BAH-ree-on)

Variations: Onbu-Obake ("back monster")

A ghost, humanoid creature, or YŌKAI from Japanese folklore, the nocturnal obariyon lives in forests and thickets from where it can ambush its prey, lone travelers utilizing heavily canopied trails. Descriptions of the being vary widely but based on its behavior it is speculated it has the ability to gain mass. Although experiencing an obariyon is frightening and exhausting, it is never harmful. It is similar to the far more lethal KONAKI-JIJII.

It waits patiently for its prey to walk down the path and then leaps from behind them crying out "*Obusaritei!*" ("I want a piggyback ride!") as it lands on their shoulders. Clinging tightly to its prey, the obariyon begins to increase it mass until it is heavier than the person can bear, causing them to fall to the ground. If the person is unable to wrestle the obariyon off, if they wait patiently, it will eventually become bored and leave of its own volition.

Source: Yoda, *Yokai Attack*, 174–6

Ocasta

In the Yamasee Cherokee folklore of southern United States of America the Ocasta ("stone coat") is said to be a gigantic anthropoid whose entire body is covered with flint, rendering it impervious to all types of weaponry; however, he is repelled by the sight of "moon sick" (menstruating) women. Originally he was sent by the divine to earth to help mankind but he had too much evil in his heart and was soon corrupted. Having only one innate magical ability—the power to turn invisible at will—he could only use it if no one was looking at him. Ocasta created evil spirits and witches and cast them out into the world.

Using the walking stick it carries, Ocasta throws it across a chasm creating a temporary bridge which disappears as soon as it has walked across. The staff also guides Ocasta to its favorite food—human livers.

Source: Lankford, *Native American Legends of the Southeast*, 131–2; Sierra, *Gruesome Guide to World Monsters*, 16

Odites

Variations: Oditus

A CENTAUR from ancient Greek mythology, Odites was born the son of Ixion and Nephele. During the great Centauromachy occurring at the wedding of Pirithous, Odites was slain by Mopsus who threw darts; one pinned his tongue to his chin and another pinned his chin to his throat.

Source: *Commentary, Mythological, Historical, and Geographical on Pope's Homer*, 55; Lemprière, *Classical Dictionary*, 512; Ovid, *Metamorphoses of Ovid*, 430

Odontotyrannos

A species of gigantic, horned, black-scaled DRAGON said to live long the Ganges River, an odontotyrannos ("toothy king") once attacked the army of Alexander the Great and the Macedonian army; it was described as being horse-like in appearance, having three horns upon its black head, and stronger than an elephant. When the army happened upon the odontotyrannos it was drinking water; suddenly, it charged, killing twenty-six men and trampling another fifty-two. Eventually the soldiers were able to gain the upper hand and slay it.

Source: Barber, *Dictionary of Fabulous Beasts*, 111; De Kirk, *Dragonlore*, 36; Leo, *History of Alexander's Battles*, 82; Zell-Ravenheart, *Wizard's Bestiary*, 74

Oeclus

A CENTAUR from ancient Greek mythology, Oeclus was slain in the Centauromachy occurring at the wedding feast of Pirithous; he was run through by the warrior Ampyx with a pointless spear made from a cornel tree.

Source: *Commentary, Mythological, Historical, and Geographical on Pope's Homer*, 55; Ovid, *Metamorphoses of Ovid*, 195

Ofnir (OH V-nir)

Variations: Ofner

Ofnir ("the entangler") was one of the dark-spotted serpents or Ormar (see ORMR) named in Thorgrimr's *Rhymes* and in Snorri Sturluson's (1179–1241) *Prose Edda*; it was said to live beneath the tree Ygdrasil at the Hvergelmir Well where it spent its days gnawing upon its Niflheimr root. The siblings of OFNIR were GOIN, MÓINN, GRÁBAKR, GRAFVÖLLUDR, and SVAFNIR.

Source: Anderson, *Norse Mythology*, 190–1; Grimes, *Norse Myths*, 14; Jennbert, *Animals and Humans*, 50

Ogre

Variations: Ogro, Orculli, Norrgens

All throughout fairy folklore the ogre, a cannibal-istic humanoid with an extremely malicious tem-perament, exists. Described as larger and more broad than a man but not quite the size and strength of a GIANT, the ogre is variously defined as being hairy, carrying a club, and having an overly large head. The female of the species is called an *ogress*.

It has been suggested the word *ogre* originated in the pre–Christian folklore of the Scandinavian Vikings. The Norse term *yggr* ("lord of death") was a title of the god Odin to whom human sacrifices were made. As the stories of Odin spread to the British Isles and were retold over the years the god eventually evolved into a GIANT, living in the clouds and consuming human flesh; the word *yggr* trans-formed into the word *ogre*. Some sources claim *ogre* was a French word originally created by author Charles Perrault (1628–1703) for his book *His-toires ou Contes du temps Passé* (1697) while other sources say it was first used by his contemporary Marie-Catherine Jumelle de Berneville, Comtesse d' Aulnoy (1650–1705).

The fairy mythology of Yorkshire, England, has more GIANT and ogre folklore than any other loca-tion in the world. In Scandinavian folklore the words ogre and TROLL are oftentimes used interchangeably.

Some famous ogres from folklore, literature and mythology are Allewyn, Babau, Babou, Balardeu, Croque-mitaine (Croquemitaine), Dents Rouge, Fine Oreille, Galaffre, Grand Colin, Huorco, L'Homme Rouge, Orch, Orlo, Pacolet, Père Fouet-tard, Père Lustucru, Pier Jan Claes, Raminagrobis, Saalah, and Tartaro.

Source: Hamilton, *Ogres and Giants*, 16–18; McCoy, *Witch's Guide to Faery Folk*, 29, 230–31; Perrault, *Histoires ou Contes du temps Passé*, 60–2, 112–18

Ohaguro-Bettari

A species of NOPPERABO from Japanese demonology, an ohaguro-bettari ("nothing but blackened teeth") is a frightening but otherwise harmless type of YŌKAI. From behind this creature looks like a beautiful woman wearing a kimono and may be found standing outside of a temple near twi-light. When a man, curious about her presence, approaches it will spin around revealing its face: a hideous, featureless surface covered in layers of makeup save for a gaping maw filled with black teeth. As the victim stands there in shock the ohaguro-bettari releases a blood chilling cackle sending the man screaming away. Sometimes this event can occur in a man's home; he will think he is looking at his wife's back but will eventually fall prey to the ohaguro-bettari.

Source: Meyer, *Night Parade of One Hundred Demons*, 122

Ollipeist

A green-scaled DRAGON from Irish folklore, Ollipeist was said to have created the Shannon Val-ley. According to the story, when Saint Patrick was ridding the island of snakes and improvising the DRAGONS, Ollipeist attempted to escape, and in doing so dug a deep furrow in the earth, creating the Shannon Valley.

Source: De Kirk, *Dragonlore*, 44

Onachus

Variations: Bonacho, Onacho

According to medieval French folklore Onachus was the sire of the chimerical DRAGON known as TARASCONUS; it was said to have been born of the LEVIATHAN. Onachus lived in the region of Galatia and had the ability to project its dung like darts as far as an acre, about two hundred feet; wherever it landed, it scorched the earth and set fire to it.

Source: Jacobus, *Golden Legend*, 183–4; Ogden, *Dragons, Serpents, and Slayers in the Classical and Early Christian Worlds*, 254; Zell-Ravenheart, *Wizard's Bestiary*, 75

Onibaba (OH-nee BAH-bah)

Variations: Goblin of Adachigahara, Kurozuka

A YŌKAI from Japanese mythology, the onibaba ("demon HAG") appears as a disheveled elderly woman with an oversized mouth, a maniacal look in her eye, and wielding a kitchen knife. This sin-gular being lives in caves and mountain passes but leaves its territory in search of its favorite food: the livers of unborn children. According to the folklore Onibaba was once a wealthy woman who gave birth to a little girl. Although the child never wanted for anything by the age of five she still had not uttered a single word. Desperate for any help they took the advice of a fortune-teller who advised feeding the child the liver of an unborn infant. The nanny set out in search of a woman who would willingly give up her child; before she left, the nanny gave her own daughter an *o-mamori* (an amulet of luck). It was many years later and the old nanny was taking refuge in a cave when she came upon a pregnant woman traveling alone. Without hesitation she set upon the woman and killed her, removing the child, and then the liver. It was only after the gruesome crime was committed that she saw the necklace of her victim, and recognized it as the very one she gave her own daughter. Driven insane, the nanny now attacks anyone she happens upon.

Source: Yoda, *Yokai Attack*, 78–82

Onocentaur

Variations: Monocentaur, Monocentaurus, Ono-kentauroi, Onoscentaurus

A creature from ancient Greek mythology and appearing in medieval bestiaries, the onocentaur is a hybrid described as having the head and torso of a man but the body of an ass. The onocentaur is the personification of hypocrisy; its upper body is rational while its lower body is untamed and wild, and it speaks of doing good but commits evil acts.

Source: Barber, *Dictionary of Fabulous Beasts*, 114; Breverton, *Breverton's Phantasmagoria*, 85; Rose, *Giants, Monsters, and Dragons*, 252; Zell-Ravenheart, *Wizard's Bestiary*, 74

Onoscèles

The onoscèles is a vampiric creature from the Greek islands described as looking like a beautiful woman with one leg ending in a mule-like hoof. It is said to lure men into secluded places so it can attack them and consume their blood, flesh, and sperm. It lives near the water and has the ability to shape-shift into water. The onoscèles is repelled by the root of a plant whose name has been lost to history.

Source: Cunningham, *Synagoge*, 355

Onyx Monoceros

The Greek historian and physician Ctesias of the fifth century BC described the onyx monoceros as having piercing blue eyes, a mule-shaped purple head, a white coated body, and an alicorn (a single horn) in the middle of its forehead which was red at its tip, black in the middle, and white at its base. Essentially a UNICORN, the onyx monoceros lived in the untamed areas of Persia.

Source: Hargreaves, *Hargreaves New Illustrated Bestiary*, 126; Rose, *Giants, Monsters, and Dragons*, 278; Zell-Ravenheart, *Wizard's Bestiary*, 75

Oozlum Bird

Variations: Ooer, Ouzelum

In Australian and British folktales the oozlum bird was said to take off and fly about in ever decreasing circles whenever it was startled; ultimately the circle becomes so small the bird disappears in a puff of smoke, thereby making it very rare.

Source: Green, *Cassell's Dictionary of Slang*, 1048; Partridge, *Dictionary of Slang and Unconventional English*, 833

Oph (OPH-el)

A gigantic, sacred, horned snake from Egyptian mythology, Oph ("serpent"), the genius who governed all things, was symbolic for the element of Earth and was depicted as having two horns upon its head and lying prone. In Delphi and Fane, Oph was worshiped as a god. In the Book of Deuteronomy (18:10–11) *oph* is the word used for a FAMILIAR spirit.

Source: Deane, *Worship of the Serpent Traced Throughout the World*, 86, 128, 259; Garnier, *Worship of the Dead*, 131, 240

Ophies Pteretos

Variations: Ophies Amphipterotoi ("serpents with two pairs of wings")

Described by the ancient Greek historian Herodotus (484–425 BC), the ophies pteretos, a species of feathered serpents, lived in the trees of Arabia where myrrh was extracted; these serpents act as guardians of the trees making the collection of oil very difficult. Small and numerous, they will not abandon their post unless they are forcibly smoked out by burning storax.

Ophies pteretos are said to have a brutal mating ritual; after the male has performed, the female bites down on his neck, just below the head, until she manages to decapitate him. As the unborn snakes develop inside of the female they begin to eat away at her insides until they consume their way out.

Source: Breverton, *Breverton's Phantasmagoria*, n.pag.

Opinicus

Variations: Epimachus, Epimacus

In the symbology of heraldry, the chimerical opinicus has the body and forelegs of a lion, the head, neck, and wings of an eagle, and the tail of a camel; sometimes the wings are omitted. Although it is seldom seen on armor, when this occurs it is depicted as a winged GRIFFIN with lion legs and a short tail.

Source: Barber, *Dictionary of Fabulous Beasts*, 113; Fox-Davies, *Complete Guide to Heraldry*, 231; Rose, *Giants, Monsters, and Dragons*, 279; Zell-Ravenheart, *Wizard's Bestiary*, 75

Orc

Variations: Orch, Ork, Orke

According to Pliny the Elder an orc was a huge SEA SERPENT "armed with teeth." In the Gaelic language the word orc means "a small sort of whale," like the orcas living in pods all around the Orkney Islands. Michael Drayton (1563–1631) described the orcs as being man eating sea-monsters. In John Milton's *Paradise Lost* (1667) he writes of "seals, orcs, and sea-mews (gulls)" living in the ocean. The idea of the orc as a large barbaric, brutish, uncivilized humanoid first appeared in J.R.R. Tolkien's fantasy novel *Lord of the Rings* (1954).

Source: Dasent, *Orkneyingers Saga*, 10; Manser, *Facts on File Dictionary of Allusions*, 349; Milton, *Paradise Lost*, 641

Oreios

Variations: OREUS, Oureios, Orobios

Oreios was the name of a CENTAUR in Greek mythology who attended the wedding of Pirithous, became drunk on wine, and following the lead of EURYTUS, who assaulted Hippodame, began to assault and rape any women they could grab. A great Centauromachy then followed.

Source: Colvin, *Cornhill Magazine*, Volume XXXVIII, 296; Lemprière, *Classical Dictionary*, 36

Oresitrophus

A dog and wolf hybrid from ancient Greek mythology Oresitrophus ("rover") was one of the DOGS OF ACTÆON, the unfortunate youth who was raised by the CENTAUR CHEIRON. This was the third dog to reach its master after he had been transformed, and took a bite into his flesh; Oresitrophus bit deeply into the shoulder.

Source: Leeming, *World of Myth*, 111; Murray, *Classical Manual*, 160; Naso, *Fasti, Tristia*, 93–5

Oreus

In classical Greek mythology, Oreus was one of the CENTAURS slain by the demi-god and cultural hero Hercules (Heracles) while visiting his friend, a CENTAUR named PHOLUS, between the conclusion of his third Labor and the onset of his fourth. When an old and particularly fragrant hogshead of wine was opened its aroma carried on the air and drove the local CENTAURS into a fury. Oreus, along with ARGEIUS, AMPHION, DAPHNIS, DUPO, Hippotion, ISOPLES, MELANCHETES, PHRIXUS, and THEREUS, was slain by Hercules (Heracles) as he defended himself from their violent and unwarranted assault.

Source: Barthell, *Gods and Goddesses of Ancient Greece*, 187; D'Angour, *Greeks and the New*, 76; Diodorus, *Historical Library of Diodorus the Sicilian*, Volume 1, 229–30

Oribasus

A dog from ancient Greek mythology, Oribasus ("ranger") was one of the DOGS OF ACTÆON, the unfortunate youth who was raised by the CENTAUR CHEIRON. Oribasus was said to be Arcadian bred, strong, and swifter than the wind.

Source: Leeming, *World of Myth*, 111; Murray, *Classical Manual*, 160; Naso, *Fasti, Tristia*, 93–5

Ork

Variations: Hymir, Il Orco, Lorge, Norge, Norglein, Norkele, Orco, Orge

In South Tyrolean folklore, Ork is a good natured DWARF or HOUSE-SPIRIT but in very old tales he was described as being an anthropophagous (man-eating) devil; it is possible Ork may have at one time been the Roman god of the underworld Orcus.

Source: Wagenwoorf, *Studies in Roman Literature, Culture and Religion*, 103

Ormr (AWRM-r), plural Ormar (AWRM-ar)

Variations: Orm, Verm, Worm, Wyrm

In Norse mythology an ormr ("DRAGON," "serpent," or "worm") is a serpent but is also used to describe a DRAGON when the ormr is gigantic in size. For example, in the *Prose Edda*, NIDHOGG was never referred to as an ormr but only ever as a *dreki*, a DRAGON. The earliest known image of an ormr is on a wooden panel dated 1100; it shows the ormr having its jaws opened and full of teeth in the process of presumably consuming (rather than disgorging) a human male. It has almond-shaped eyes, curved nose, laid-back ears, a long neck in two coils, a long snout, a recurved horn, and the evidence of a rider upon its back.

Source: Acker, *Revisiting the Poetic Edda*, 55, 67; Norroena Society, *Asatrii Edda*, 380

Orneus

A CENTAUR from ancient Greek mythology, Orneus attended the wedding of Pirithous, where drunken EURYTUS who assaulted the bride, Hippodame, led the way for other inebriated Centaurs to assault and rape any women they could grab. During the ensuing battle, Orneus along with LYCABAS, MERMEROS, PISENOR, and THAUMAS were slain by the spear-wielding Lapith soldier Dryas.

Source: *Commentary, Mythological, Historical, and Geographical on Pope's Homer*, 55; Simpson, *Metamorphoses of Ovid*, 205

Orobon

According to medieval folklore the orobon was an amphibious creature living in the Red Sea in the Mount Mazovan region; it was about nine or ten feet in length and covered in thick, crocodile-like scales. Using its long tail it would snatch up people from the banks and in constrictor-like fashion crush them to death as they were pulled into the water where they were swallowed whole.

Source: Pare, *On Monsters and Marvels*, 114–5; Zell-Ravenheart, *Wizard's Bestiary*, 76

Oroboros

Variations: Oroborus, Oureboros, Ouroboros, Uroboros, Uroborus

Originating in Egyptian mythology and borrowed by first the Phoenicians and then the ancient

Greeks, the oroboros ("tail eater") is depicted as a gigantic winged serpentine DRAGON with clawed feet, holding its tail in its mouth, making it the symbol of eternity. JORMUNGANDR of Norse mythology is a later interpretation of the oroboros, as it lies along the ocean floor biting its own tail awaiting Ragnarok.

In Alchemic symbology the oroboros is a purifier and keeps the cosmic waters under control.

Source: De Kirk, *Dragonlore*, 44; Jones, *An Instinct for Dragons*, 6; Zell-Ravenheart, *Wizard's Bestiary*, 76

Orochi

Variations: Yamata-no-Orochi ("Orochi of Yamata"), Yamata

A HYDRA-like serpentine DRAGON from Japanese Shinto mythology, the eight-headed Orochi was completely evil and compelled by his cruel nature; there is not a single tale of his ever having done anything for the benefit of mankind, a nearly unique feature for a Japanese DRAGON. As soon as Orochi conquered the Izumo region, he terrorized the landscape and people, demanding virgins to be sacrificed to him on a regular schedule. Unfortunately there were only eight virgins in the region and all from ruling families. The trickster god and hero Susanowo was moved by the sorrow of the families and prepared eight jugs of *sake* he disguised to look like the women. In his arrogant haste to consume the offering, Orochi did not notice what he had eaten and was soon too drunk to defend himself. Susanowo, using his katana, quickly severed all eight of Orochi's heads, saving the virgins, restoring peace to the region, and marrying Kushiinada-Hime, the most beautiful of the women to be sacrificed.

Source: De Kirk, *Dragonlore*, 32; De Visser, *Dragon in China and Japan*, 197–8; Smith, *Complete Idiot's Guide to World Mythology*, 232–3

Orphan Bird

A species of bird from medieval bestiaries, the orphan bird was said to originate in India and was described as having the beak of an eagle, body of a crane; crest and neck of a peacock, feet of a swan, and black, red, and white wings. It was said to lay its eggs in the water in order to determine which ones would hatch, as worthy chicks would float to the surface while the rest would sink to the bottom of the lake, hatch, and live out their existence in darkness.

Source: Taylor, *Encyclopedia of Religion and Nature*, 171

Orthos

Variations: Orthros, Orthrus, Orthus

A two-headed monstrous dog from classical Greek mythology, Orthos and his companion hound GARGITTIOS were the two dogs utilized by the GIGANTE (a race of beings born from the goddess Gaea) Eurytion who guarded the herd of red oxen belonging to Geryon. The more vicious of the two dogs, Orthos also had a serpent for a tail. The demi-god and hero Hercules (Heracles) was determined to have the herd and in the fight, slew all three of the guardians.

Source: Brewer, *Dictionary of Phrase and Fable*, 235; Daly, *Greek and Roman Mythology A to Z*, 48–49; Rose, *Giants, Monsters, and Dragons*, 135; Zell-Ravenheart, *Wizard's Bestiary*, 76

Orusula (Or-OO-sue-la)

In Costa Rican demonology Orusula is a demonic giantic pig; the froth from its mouth causes a rash which can kill. Living in lagoons and muddy swamps, Orusula cuts off the heads of people.

Source: Ashley, *Complete Book of Devils and Demons*, 101; Stone, *Talamancan Tribes of Costa Rica*, 52

Oschaert

A type of malicious BLACK DOG from Belgian folklore, specifically in and around the town of Hamme, Belgium, the oschaert would wander along the road seeking to attack and otherwise terrorize travelers; it was especially fond of singling out individuals with an uneasy conscience. Unlike a BARGUEST, Oschaert has no set form and has been sighted in the shape of a dog, donkey, horse, and rabbit. Like the KLUDDE it would play pranks on lost travelers, but the oschaert being far more vicious would jump on people's backs, pin them to the ground, and increasing its body mass, crush them beneath its weight. The only means by which to escape an attacking oschaert would be to stand in a crossroads or present it with a picture of the Virgin Mary.

Source: Henderson, *Notes on the Folk-Lore of the Northern Counties of England and the Borders*, 273; Rose, *Giants, Monsters, and Dragons*, 282

Otoroshi

Variations: Ke-Ippai, Odoroshi, Odoro-Odoro, Osoroshii ("scarry")

Hairy, tutelary creatures from Japanese mythology, the otoroshi ("to cause great fear") are said to perch atop anyplace which separated the physical world from the realm of the gods, such as the roofs of shrines and temples and tori archways. They are described as being four-legged, hunched beasts with fierce claws and tusks. Normally these creatures eat the animals which live on the temple grounds, such as pigeons, rats, and sparrows, but on occasion they will attach to a human as they keep watch to ensure only those worthy of entering the sacred space make it within; if ever an impious or truly evil person were to attempt entering the shrine or temple the otoroshi leap from its perch, letting loose with a terrifying cry, landing on their prey, and then tear apart the intruder.

Source: Meyer, *Night Parade of One Hundred Demons*, 148; Takagi, *Collection of Japanese Legends*, 105

Ovda

An aggressive and murderous species of NATURE SPIRIT from Finnish folklore, the ovda wandered the woods appearing to be a naked man or woman with backward-facing feet. When it came upon a woodsman it would attempt to convince the person to dance or wrestle it; if successful the ovda would then dance or tickle the person to death. In Finnish Russian folklore Ovda was a singular forest entity who also wandered the woods naked with backward-facing feet; when annoyed with humans it would pick them up in whirlwinds and spin them to death. It was believed there was a small hole under her left arm which, when prodded, would cause her to seize up in a state of paralysis.

Source: Barber, *Dictionary of Fabulous Beasts*, 113; Cotterell, *Dictionary of World Mythology*, 167; Monaghan, *Encyclopedia of Goddesses and Heroines*, 217

Pa Snake

A species of gigantic serpentine DRAGONS from Chinese mythology, pa snakes have neither limbs nor wings. Pa snakes prefer to consume elephants and spit out the bones after one to three years of digestion. It was once believed consuming the flesh of a pa snake, an expensive medicine only afforded to the wealthy, would cure a person of consumption (Tuberculosis).

Source: De Kirk, *Dragonlore*, 28; Gould, *Mythical Monsters*, n.pag.; Zell-Ravenheart, *Wizard's Bestiary*, 77

Pachytos

A dog and wolf hybrid from ancient Greek mythology, Pachytos was one of the DOGS OF ACTÆON, the unfortunate youth who was raised by the CENTAUR CHEIRON.

Source: Leeming, *World of Myth*, 111; Murray, *Classical Manual*, 160

Padfoot

Variations: Padfooit

A monstrously large BLACK DOG from the folklore of Leeds, England, Padfoot was a sheep-sized creature. Like the KLUDDE and OSCHAERT of the Kingdom of Belgium, Padfoot was normally invisible but it could shape-shift; most often it would take the form of a bear; a gigantic black or white dog walking on two or three legs; a demonic-looking sheep with burning eyes; a calf; or an enormous black donkey. Its eyes were said to be as large as tea-plates. No matter the form this FAIRY ANIMAL assumes it would always be accompanied by the sound of dragging chains. To see Padfoot was a psychopomp (death omen); sometimes to see it would cause a person to die of fright. Any attempt to fend off the creature would guarantee it will maul its victim.

Source: Cole, *Glossary of Words Used in South-West Lincolnshire*, 96; Henderson, *Notes on the Folk-Lore of the Northern Counties of England and the Borders*, 274; Rose, *Giants, Monsters, and Dragons*, 285

Padmavati

A NAGA queen, Padmavati and her companion Dharanendra are, according to Hindu mythology, the attendants of Parshvantha and particularly powerful intercessors on the behalf of his worshipers. Padmavati is worshiped as a goddess by some.

Source: Cort, *Framing the Jina*, 186; Vogel, *Indian Serpentlore*, 33

Pah

The third of four monsters was a great bird called Pah, so large when he came between the sun and the earth darkness fell upon the land for a distance of a day's journey. Pah lived on Mount Bita, Philippines, and was eventually slain by Raja Sulayman.

Source: Hurley, *Swish of the Kris*, 264; Saleeby, *Studies in Moro History, Law, and Religion*, 18

Pai Lung

In the mythology of the ancient Chinese there were said to be four DRAGON KINGS: AO CH'IN, AO JU, AO KUANG, and AO SHUN; however, in sixteenth century Chinese literature the DRAGON KINGS played an important role, and additional kings were created: the uniquely white DRAGON, Pai Lung ("white DRAGON"), and LUNG WANG, the DRAGON KING, master of fire. Pai Lung was not just white, but his scales were remarkably dazzling and brilliantly white. He was said to be born from a human mother who was a virgin.

Source: De Kirk, *Dragonlore*, 25–6, 28; Savill, *Pears Encyclopaedia of Myths and Legends*, Book 3, 231

Pairika

In Zoroastrian folklore the pairika are said to be a hybrid between animals and demons which appear in various forms and live in abandoned places; they are numerous in their forms and functions. For instance, one of the pairika called

Duzyairya blights crops; Mus ("rat") appears as a ratlike creature; Khnathaiti assumed a beautiful and desirable human form and became the companion of the hero Keresaspa—she was eventually his undoing. Another unnamed pairika lived as a wild dog and was sought by the Kayanian hero Srit when he wished to die. Each time the pairika charged at him, he used his sword and cut the beast in two, but each half then reformed the missing part of its respective body. He continued to slice and attack until there were thousands of dogs and he was eventually overrun and killed.

Source: Ananikean, *Armenian Mythology*, 95; Boyce, *History of Zoroastrianism*, 86

Paiste

Variations: Lag-na-Paiste

An ancient DRAGON from Irish folklore, Paiste was said to be eleven feet long and had ebony scales as big as dinner plates, long fangs, ram horns, and venom; it terrorized the inhabitants of Roe Valley. The people sought the assistance of Saint Murrough. After nine days of prayer, he approached the DRAGON and offered him a deal: if he could place three rods upon its back he would freely offer himself up to be consumed. Paiste agreed to the terms. No sooner had the third bar been placed upon its back than they grew and extended down into the ground, pinning it. Saint Murrough then banished Paiste to the bottom of Loch Foyle until Judgment Day.

Source: De Kirk, *Dragonlore*, 44; McCullough, *Dragonslayers*, 50–1

Paiyuk

In Ute folklore the paiyuk are said to be a species of evil natured water-dwelling, flesh eating elk. Preying upon humans, shamans believe these creatures have supernatural powers.

Source: Rose, *Giants, Monsters, and Dragons*, 285–6; Zell-Ravenheart, *Wizard's Bestiary*, 77

Pal-Rai-Yuk

Variations: Palraiyuk, Tizheruk, Yuk

In the Inuit mythology of the King Island region of Alaska, United States of America, there is said to live a species of serpentine DRAGON-like creatures called pal-rai-yuk. According to folklore and based on their depictions in art, the creatures have a crocodile-like or serpentine head, a long tongue, short horns, a tail with a flipper on its end, thick fur covering its body, three dorsal fins, and three pairs of legs. Carnivorous man-eaters, pal-rai-yuk are said to attack and consume those who kayak in the bay. They are attracted to the sound of knocking

on the bottom of boats and the wooden piers and are said to be repelled by their image painted on the bottom of boats, kayaks, and *umiaks*.

Source: De Kirk, *Dragonlore*, 50; Eberhart, *Mysterious Creatures*, 415; Rose, *Giants, Monsters, and Dragons*, 286

Palasik

A species of vampiric creature from the folklore of the Minangkabau people of the Island of Sumatra, the palasik are said to prey upon children and infants. Able to pass as an ordinary looking person, they are able to detach their head from their body in order to fly out into the night to look for prey. Children who have been attacked by a palasik will have diarrhea, an enlarged stomach, and watery eyes; their fontanelle (membrane-covered "soft spot" on their skull) will smell; and they will suffer from thiness. To protect children, their mothers need to commission a set of amulets called *tangka palasik* from a specialist known as a *dukun tangka palasik*; the mother and child each must wear them.

Source: Sanday, *Women at the Center*, 111, 258

Palm-Tree-King

Variations: Palm Tree King

In ancient Sumerian mythology, Palm-Tree-King was one of the many monsters slain by the warrior god Ninurta. Little is known of this creature other than Gudea, a ruler of Lagash (c.a. 2100 BC), referred to it, and the other monsters vanquished by Ninurta, as the Slain Heroes; he elevated them all to the status of god and made a place of worship for them in the temple.

Source: Ataç, *Mythology of Kingship in Neo-Assyrian Art*, 185; Salem, *Near East, the Cradle of Western Civilization*, 102–3; Sherman, *Storytelling*, 332

Palulukon

A species of plumed water serpent from Hopi Native American mythology, the palulukon is the oldest variation of Quetzalcoatl, the feathered DRAGON of Mesoamerican beliefs. Neither evil nor good, the palulukon are the bringers of rain; it was believed the cosmic ocean rested upon the backs of two of these creatures. If the palulukon were not shown proper respect or mistreated they were said to cause earthquakes, dry up rivers, wells, and watering holes, and prevent rainfall.

Source: Coulter, *Encyclopedia of Ancient Deities*, 273, 371; De Kirk, *Dragonlore*, 47, 51–52; Zell-Ravenheart, *Wizard's Bestiary*, 77

Pamba

A gigantic lake monster in Tanzanian folklore, particularly in the Lake Tanganyika region, the pamba is described as being so large it can devour a fishing canoe and all its crew in one swallow; as it swims, the water around it turns red.

Source: Meurger, *Lake Monster Traditions*, 252; Rose, *Giants, Monsters, and Dragons*, 286; Zell-Ravenheart, *Wizard's Bestiary*, 77

Pamphagus

A dog from ancient Greek mythology, Pamphagus ("glutton") was one of the DOGS OF ACTÆON, the unfortunate youth who was raised by the CENTAUR CHEIRON. Pamphagus was said to be Arcadian bred, strong, and swifter than the wind.

Source: Leeming, *World of Myth*, 111; Murray, *Classical Manual*, 160; Naso, *Fasti, Tristia*, 93–5

Pan

Variations: FAUN, Paniskoi ("little Pans"), Satyr

A species of goat and human hybrids, the panes of ancient Greek mythology were said to be the descendants of the god Pan (Faunus); their ancient Roman counterparts would have been Fauns (or Fauni), descendants of the NATURE SPIRIT and god Faunus and his wife, Fauna. Panes would assist Pan (Faunus) in tending his flocks of cattle and swine; generally, when left to amuse themselves, they were mischievous at their worst, leading travelers astray.

Source: Hard, *Routledge Handbook of Greek Mythology*, 215; Society for the Diffusion of Useful Knowledge, *Penny Cyclopaedia*, Volume 10, 208

P'an-Lung

Variations: P'an-Long, Pan Long, Panlong

In Chinese mythology the p'an-lung ("coiling DRAGON") are a species of water DRAGON; they remain in the KIAO-LUNG stage throughout their entire life, have no wings, and are incapable of flight because they lack both *chi'ih-muh* and *po-shan*, the elements necessary for flight. P'an-lung hibernate in the depths of watery marshes.

Source: De Kirk, *Dragonlore*, 28; De Visser, *Dragon in China and Japan*, 73; Forbes, *Illustrated Book of Dragons and Dragon Lore*, n.pag.; Rosen, *Mythical Creatures Bible*, 63

Pannagas

Variations: NAGA

The Pannagas of Hindu mythology are a subspecies of NAGA, and as such are counted among the divine races; however, apart from this knowledge there is little distinction between NAGA, Pannagas, and the URAGAS, the words often being used synonymously. On the occasion when a distinction is attempted, the Pannagas are said to be the children of Kadru and the NAGA descendants of the Surasa.

In the *Ramayana*, when Sagara appeared before Rama, he did so accompanied by seven flaming Pannagas; they were described as having seven faces, seven flaming tongues, and seven hoods.

Source: Coulter, *Encyclopedia of Ancient Deities*, 332; Sharma, *Socio-political Study of the Vālmīki Rāmāyaṇa*, 205–6, 216

Panthera

Variations: Panther

According to medieval folklore, the panthera was a creature friendly to all animals, attracting them by the sweetness of its exhaled breath; DRAGONS were the only creature immune to this effect. The panthera roamed the land between India and Paradise. In *Reynard the Fox*, Reynard sends the queen a comb made from the bone of a panthera; it was described as being a natural charm against illness, more colorful than a rainbow, smelling more wonderful than any perfume, and a universal panacea.

Source: Brewer, *Wordsworth Dictionary of Phrase and Fable*, 819; De Sanctis, *Reynard the Fox*, 137

Papillon

The courteous, skilled, and wise horse of the hero Ogier the Dane, Papillon ("butterfly") would kneel so his rider would be able to mount and dismount with ease; he had the ability to breathe fire and ran incredibly fast, even over difficult and treacherous terrain. A FAIRY ANIMAL, long-maned Papillion was the most beautiful horse Ogier had ever seen and was a member of the Court of Morgan la Fay.

Source: Baldwin, *Horse Fair*, 15; Bulfinch, *Bulfinch's Mythology: The Age of Fable; The Age of Chivalry; Legends of Charlemagne*, 868, 869, 871; Keightley, *World Guide to Gnomes, Fairies, Elves, and Other Little People*, 47

Papstesel

A chimerical creature symbolic of papal corruption during the sixteenth century, the papstesel ("pope ass") had the body of a woman covered in scales, the head of an ass, the image of a bearded man upon its back, one arm being the trunk of an elephant, one foot being an eagle claw and the other a cow hoof, and a cock-headed tail ending in an AMPHISBAENA. According to folklore, a papstesel was pulled from the Tiber River, Italy, during the flood of 1496.

Source: Rose, *Giants, Monsters, and Dragons*, 287; Zell-Ravenheart, *Wizard's Bestiary*, 77

Parandrus

Variations: Parander, Parandus

A hybrid between a bear and an ibex, the parandrus of Ethiopia was described in medieval bestiaries as being as large as an ox and having branching horns, cloven hooves, deer legs, large horns, a shaggy bear pelt, a stag-like head, and the chameleon-like ability to blend into any environment.

Source: Clark, *Medieval Book of Beasts*, 141; Wiener, *Contributions Toward a History of Arabico-Gothic Culture*, Volume 4, 50, 54

Parata

Variations: Te Parata

A sea creature and one of the TANIWHA from the folklore of the Maori of New Zealand, the parata is one of the TANIWHA, a type of tutelary FAIRY ANIMAL (see SEA SERPENT). The parata, living in either the deepest part of the ocean or at the edge of the sky, was described as being immensely large and having a mouth so deep and wide it was in a constant state of taking in and sending out all the water of the ocean, thereby creating the waves of the ocean.

Source: Orbell, *Concise Encyclopedia of Māori Myth and Legend*, 170; Rose, *Giants, Monsters, and Dragons*, 287; Zell-Ravenheart, *Wizard's Bestiary*, 93

Paravataksha

A NAGARAJA from Hindu mythology, Paravataksha lived in the northern quadrant of the Vindhya forest in a lake shaded by a holy acoka tree; he was described as clothed in dense clouds, having fiery eyes, and a roar like thunder. Paravataksha carried a sword which had the ability to cause earthquakes given to him by the ASURAS and the gods.

Source: Coulter, *Encyclopedia of Ancient Deities*, 333; De Visser, *Dragon in China and Japan*, 17–18

Pard

Variations: Pantheon, Pardal, Pardus

According to medieval bestiaries the pard is a species of big cat, very fast, spotted, and driven by its lust for blood. The male pards are said to willfully seek out sexual liaisons with lionesses solely for the purposes of creating the species of big cat known as the leopard ("lion pard"). Pliny the Elder, the Roman author and natural philosopher, writes in his work *Natural History*, when the coupling between a lion and a pard occurs, no matter which great cat is the sire, the offspring are degenerate and incapable of reproducing. In the late medieval era the pard was symbolic of the anti–Christ, said to be "spotted with crimes and wrong-doings."

Source: Clark, *Medieval Book of Beasts*, 123; Coss, *Heraldry, Pageantry and Social Display in Medieval England*, 73; Zell-Ravenheart, *Wizard's Bestiary*, 77

Pardalo

A FAIRY ANIMAL from Spanish folklore, Pardalo was the horse belonging to the rock NYMPH of Biscay; it ran "without a rider" wild and free in the mountains. When Iniguez sought her assistance to rescue his father, she called Pardalo and bridled him with a bit of gold and reins of silk. The fairy then instructed the hero to not feed or water, unbridle or unsaddle or shoe Pardalo's feet and the horse would carry him to Toledo so quickly he would be there in a single day, a distance of three hundred miles.

Source: Keightley, *World Guide to Gnomes, Fairies, Elves, and Other Little People*, 461; Charnock, *Legendary Rhymes, and Other Poems*, 33–4, 216

Pardalokampoi

Variations: Pardalocampoi

A hybrid species, the pardalokampoi was from the mythology of the ancient Etruscans; they were described as having the forequarters of a panther and the hind-section of a fish.

Source: Borges, *Book of Imaginary Beings*, 27; Breverton, *Breverton's Phantasmagoria*, n.pag.

Pashu Gaung Phyat

The pashu gaung phyat ("headhunter") is a NURSERY BOGIE from the folklore of Burma and Myanmar used by parents to coerce their children into acceptable behavior.

Source: Gatehouse, *Demons and Elementals #2*, 20

Passé Brewell

Variations: Passe Brewell, Passetroill

The fine charger of Sir Tristram, Passé Brewell was his horse for many years. When Tristram was lost in madness the animal was kept for him by Sir Fergus.

Source: Brewer, *Dictionary of Phrase and Fable*, 626; Ruthven, *Shaman Pathways*, n.pag.; Wright, *Morte D'Arthure*, Volume 2, 132

Pastinaca

A gigantic weasel-like creature from Greek folklore appearing in many medieval bestiaries, the pastinaca was larger than an elephant and had a scent so repugnant it could kill trees.

Source: Flaubert, *Temptation of St. Anthony*, 255; Gilmore, *Monsters*, 40

Patasola

A species of female vampiric NATURE SPIRIT from South American folklore, the patasola ("one-foot") are said to appear to men who are out hunting in the jungle and let their minds wander to thoughts of women. Appearing as a beautiful and seductive woman, the patasola will lure the man off and when in a secluded place reveal her true form, a hideous one-legged creature which will then kill its prey, consuming its flesh and drinking its blood. Protective of the prestige forest it lives in, the patasola single out animal herders, hunters, loggers, millers, and miners as often as possible.

Source: Hellman, *Vampire Legends and Myths*, 24–5; Sloan, *Runaway Daughters*, 80

Pedasos

In the ancient Greek epic poem the *Iliad* ("*Song of Ilion*") (1240 BC), attributed to Homer, Pedasos was the trace horse (the outside horse on a chariot team in which more than two horses are driven abreast) first utilized by Eerion and then taken as a war-prize by the heroic and semi-divine Achilles the Myrmidon leader during his sack of Thebes. Pedasos was not only a symbol of the hero's accomplishments but also a psychopomp (death omen) as it foreshadowed his death. A mortal creature, Pedasos was slain by a spear thrown by Sarpedon; it landed directly behind his shoulder, pierced his lung, and killed the animal before it fell to the ground.

Source: Cook, *Iliad*, 275, 457; *Contemporary Review*, Volume 27, 810

Pegasies

A hybrid species of bird from Ethiopian folklore and recorded by Pliny, the pegasi were described as being very large and having the head of a horse (see PEGASUS).

Source: Barber, *Dictionary of Fabulous Beasts*, 116; Zell-Ravenheart, *Companion for the Apprentice Wizard*, 178

Pegasoi Aithiopes

A species of winged horse, the pegasoi aithiopes were said to also have an alicorn (a single horn) growing out of the middle of their forehead (see PEGASUS).

Source: Breverton, *Breverton's Phantasmagoria*, 177

Pegasus, plural Pegasies

Variations: Pegasis, Pegasos, Pégasos

A winged, white stallion from ancient Greek mythology, Pegasus ("born near the *pege*, the source of the ocean"), one of the HIPPOI ATHANATOI, was the name of the individual creature as well as the name of the species it has come to represent. There are several versions to the origin of this creature. The one claims the GORGON MEDUSA and the god of the sea, Poseidon (Neptune), had sexual relations which resulted in impregnating her; before she gave birth, the hero Perseus beheaded the GORGON, and the blood which poured forth birthed the first pegasus and his brother Chrysaor. Another version says the golden winged stallion was birthed from the blood spilt when MEDUSA was beheaded by Perseus.

One final explanation simply states Pegasus was one of the children of Poseidon (Neptune) who assumed the form of a horse and lived his life as such.

No matter its origin, shortly after its birth Pegasus was quickly tamed by the hero Perseus; together they saved the princess Andromeda from CETUS. After the heroics, the creature was freed and it wandered Mount Helicon; Pegasus struck the ground with his hoof and created a sacred spring the Muses named Hippocrene ("horse's spring").

Bellerophon, a hero of Greek mythology, tamed Pegasus and used the creature as his mount; together they slew the CHIMERA. Ultimately Bellerophon became arrogant and attempted to use Pegasus to fly up and into Mount Olympus. Zeus (Jupiter) sent a gadfly to bite the animal which bucked and threw its rider. Bellerophon landed blind and lame and Pegasus never accepted another rider again; however, it did collect lightning bolts and bring them to Zeus (Jupiter).

Source: Brewer, *Dictionary of Phrase and Fable*, 626; Daly, *Greek and Roman Mythology A to Z*, 111–12; Dixon-Kennedy, *Encyclopedia of Greco-Roman Mythology*, 239; Lehner, *Big Book of Dragons, Monsters, and Other Mythical Creatures*, 144

Peist

Variations: Ollphiest, Piast

In Irish folklore a peist ("beast," "monster," or "worm") is any serpentine, water-dwelling species of DRAGON. According to ancient tales, peist were the traditional adversary to regional heroes, attempting to prevent them from rescuing a maiden; over the course of three consecutive days the hero battles and eventually defeats the monster and wins the love of the maiden. The peist were also said to have attempted to prevent Saint Patrick from journeying across Ireland but were driven out when he cleansed the land of all poisonous reptiles. Only the most powerful of the peist were able to remain, but they retreated to the depths of their watery domains.

Source: Barber, *Dictionary of Fabulous Beasts*, 116; Curtin, *Myths and Folk-Lore of Ireland*, 272; Mahon, *Ireland's Fairy Lore*, 186–7

Peke-Haua

A TANIWHA from Maori mythology, Peke-Haua was a lacertilian (lizard-like) DRAGON said to have lived in a difficult to reach and exceedingly deep water-hole known as Te Waro-uri; like HOTO-PUKU, he was slain by the hero Pitaka. With his death there was much rejoicing; Peke-Haua was cut open and inside his body was found an uncountable number of bodies with their garments, implements, weapons, and other items on their person at the time of their death. The body of the beast was roasted and broiled and consumed by the people; some of it was made into preserves in calabashes filled with its own fat.

Source: Gilmore, *Monsters*, 148–9; Gudegeon, *Journal of the Polynesian Society*, Volume 14, 205

Peluda

Variations: La Velue ("shaggy beast"), the Shaggy Beast of La Ferte-Bernard, Peallaidh, Pehuda

A gigantic fire-breathing DRAGON from medieval French folklore, Peluda was said to have lived in the Huisne River near the village of La Ferte-Bernard. Although it had been invited onto Noah's ark, it declined the offer and somehow managed to survive the Flood. Peluda was described as having four stubby legs, needle-sharp quills along its back, scales upon its tail, shaggy green fur covering its body, and turtle-like claws; it was so large, each time it entered into the river it caused the water level to rise and flood the farms for miles around.

Peluda eventually developed a taste for young maidens and one day consumed the fiancé of a young man who then sought a wise woman's advice on how to enact his vengeance. She revealed to him its one weakness—its tail. Armed and armored, the hero sought out Peluda and in single combat, eventually defeated it by chopping off its tail.

Source: Barber, *Dictionary of Fabulous Beasts*, 116; Hargreaves, *Hargreaves New Illustrated Bestiary*, 101; Jones, *Instinct for Dragons*, 144–5; Rose, *Giants, Monsters, and Dragons*, 217; Zell-Ravenheart, *Wizard's Bestiary*, 60

Penangglan (Pen-non-gwen)

Variation: Pananggaln, Penangglan, Pênangal, Penanggalan, Pennanggalan, PONTIANAK

In Malaysian folklore there is a type of female vampiric creature called a penangglan. Usually it is created when a woman dies in childbirth, but there is another circumstance which can happen to cause a penangglan to come into being: if a woman in the process of performing religious penance is so surprised by a man she literally dies of the shock.

A penangglan can pass as a normal woman by day, but at night it can detach its head from its body and fly off, dangling all of its soft tissue organs beneath it, everything from the esophagus to its rectum. As it hunts, it drips bile so toxic if it should touch human skin it will cause the person to break out with open sores. It flies out looking for its prey: children and women in labor. It despises children bitterly and takes great delight in killing them. The penangglan cries out "*Mangilai!*" when one is born. Only if its usual prey is not available and it is hungry enough will it settle for the blood of a man. When it returns to its home, its intestines will be bloated

with the blood from its victims, so it dips them into a vat of vinegar to shrivel them up to fit back into its body.

To prevent the penangglan from flying near your home, place the thorny branches of the jeruju plant on the roof, as the thorns will snag on the dangling organs, trapping the creature There is no known way to destroy a penangglan, but if someone manages to figure out who in the village the penangglan is, wait for it to detach from its body and leave. While it is gone, sneak into its home and destroy its vat of vinegar as well as its body. When the penangglan returns from its hunt, it will not be able to continue its ruse as its body is no more and its vinegar is not available to shrink up its organs.

Source: Laderman, *Wives and Midwives*, 126–27; Skeat, *Malay Magic*, 325–28; Wright, *Vampires and Vampirism*

Penezny Smij

A species of DRAGON from Lithuanian folklore, the penezny smij ("penny DRAGON") is said to bring wealth. According to the folklore they will leave a three-penny coin out in the open to be found; when it is picked up, the next day there will be a six-penny piece, and if the coin is taken, a dollar coin will then be found the next day. If the dollar is taken the penezny smij will think you greedy and move into your home, assuming the position of a HOUSE-SPIRIT and demanding to be treated with respect; if ever it is neglected, it will burn down the house. The only way to be rid of the penezny smij after it moves in is to sell the dollar to someone for less than it is worth; if the dollar is given away, it will manage to make its way back.

Source: Grimm, *Teutonic Mythology*, 1019–20; MacKenzie, *Dragons for Beginners*, 91

Peng

Variations: P'eng

According to a fourth century Chinese text entitled *Chuang Tzu*, the peng is a gigantic bird, similar to the ROC. Beginning its life as a K'UN FISH, the peng is described as having a back countless thousands of leagues wide; it flies so high up in the sky it cannot tell if the sky below is blue, the waves of the sea roll to the rhythm of its flapping wings in flight. The Peng lives in a place called North Gloom and migrates to South Gloom creating whirlwinds and tsunamis as it travels.

Source: Birrell, *Chinese Mythology*, 191–2, 308

P'eng-Niao

Rare in Chinese mythology, the p'eng-niao are a species of bird-like DRAGONs, having the head of a DRAGON and the wings and lower body of a bird;

sometimes they are depicted as having wings and bird-like feet while their serpentine bodies are covered with plumose scales.

Source: De Kirk, *Dragonlore*, 28; Lehner, *Big Book of Dragons, Monsters, and Other Mythical Creatures*, 99; Zell-Ravenheart, *Wizard's Bestiary*, 78

Pénghoú

Variations: Count P'eng, Penghou, P'eng-hou

A type of hamadryad (the nymphs of oak trees in Greek mythology) from Chinese folklore, the pénghoú were associated with the camphor tree. Described as having the body of a black dog with no tail and the face of a man, these NATURE SPIRITS were said to taste quite good when properly steamed. In Japan this same being is called a *hōkō*.

Source: Gan, *In Search of the Supernatural*, 215; White, *Myths of the Dog-Man*, 282, 285

Perimedes (per-i-mé-déz)

A CENTAUR from ancient Greek mythology, Perimedes attended the wedding of Prince Pirithous to Hippodame. The epic Greek poem *The Shield of Heracles*, written by the Greek poet Hesiod, records the Centauromachy between the Lapith soldiers and the CENTAURS which took place when fellow CENTAUR EURYTUS became drunk and attempted to rape the bride during the reception. He and his brother, DRYAS, CENTAUR chieftains, were the sons of Peukeus.

Source: D'Angour, *Greeks and the New*, 76; Hesiod, *Works of Hesiod, Callimachus and Theognis*, 59; Lawson, *Modern Greek Folklore and Ancient Greek Religion*, 242

Peryton

A species of hybrid creature from ancient Greek folklore, the peryton of the island of Atlantis were described as having the body, plumage, and wings of a bird with the head and legs of a deer.

Source: Breverton, *Breverton's Phantasmagoria*, n.pag.; Fox-Davies, *Complete Guide to Heraldry*, 641; Hargreaves, *Hargreaves New Illustrated Bestiary*, 102; Zell-Ravenheart, *Wizard's Bestiary*, 78

Pesanta

In Catalonian mythology the pesanta is a species of ALP; assuming the form of a gigantic black cat or dog it sits upon a person's chest at night while they sleep, causing nightmares while it crushes their chest, making breathing extremely difficult.

Source: Magyar Tudományos Akadémia. *Acta Ethnographica Hungarica*, Volume 53, 394

Petraeus

Variations: Petreus, Petraios

A CENTAUR from ancient Greek mythology, huge Petraeus ("rocky") attended the wedding of Prince Pirithous to Hippodame. The epic Greek poem *The Shield of Heracles*, written by the Greek poet Hesiod, records the Centauromachy between the Lapith soldiers and the CENTAURS which took place when fellow CENTAUR EURYTUS became drunk and attempted to rape the bride during the reception. Upon the surface of the intricately worked shield are representatives of each army; on one side are the Lapith soldiers Prince Caeneus, Dryas, Exadius, Hopleus, Phalerus, King Pirithous, and Prolochusc and rushing at them are the CENTAURS ARCTUS, ASBOLUS, black-maned MIMAS, and UREUS. The men, armed with spears, were met by the CENTAURS who ripped up fir trees and used them as weapons, swatting at them with the trunks.

Source: D'Angour, *Greeks and the New*, 76; Hesiod, *Works of Hesiod, Callimachus and Theognis*, 59; Westmoreland, *Ancient Greek Beliefs*, 202

Peuchen

Variations: Piguchen, Pihuchen, Pihuichen, Pihuychen, Piuchen, Piwuchen

In Chilote and Mapuche mythology the peuchen is a species of shape-shifting vampiric creature; although they can assume the form of any animal, they are said to prefer the form of a gigantic bat-winged, flying snake. Using their hypnotic stare, they paralyze their prey and then drain them dry of their blood. It is believed only a *machi* (medicine woman) has the ability and power to destroy these creatures. Some scholars suggest the peuchen is an ancient ancestor, mythologically speaking, of the CHUPACABRA.

Source: Hellman, *Vampire Legends and Myths*, 125; Ninness, *Macabre Rising*, 140

Phaethon

Variations: Sheen-Mane, Shining-Mane

In the Latin narrative poem *Metamorphoses* (2.153) written by the Roman poet Ovid (43 BC–AD 17), the sun god and second generation Titan, Helios (Sol), had his golden chariot, Quadriga, pulled across the sky by the flying horses AETHON, ASTROPE, BRONTE, CHRONOS, EOUS, LAMPON, Phaethon ("shining one"), PHLEGON, and PYROIS. All of these horses are described as being pure white and having flaring nostrils which can breathe forth flame.

Source: Breese, *God's Steed*, 86; Brewer, *Dictionary of Phrase and Fable*, 626; *Contemporary Review*, Volume 27, 809; Rose, *Giants, Monsters, and Dragons*, 178

Phaeton (FAE-ton)

Variations: Phaithon

In classical Greek and Roman mythology Phaeton was one of the HIPPOI ATHANATOI; along with LAMPOS, they pulled the purple chariot of Eos, the goddess of the dawn.

Source: Bechtel, *Dictionary of Mythology*, 122, 171; Breese, *God's Steed*, 92

Phalmant

Variations: Copard Phalmant

A species of leopard appearing in many medieval bestiaries, the phalmant was said to inadvertently split open its stomach while roaring.

Source: Flaubert, *Temptation of St. Anthony*, 175, 255

Phareus

A CENTAUR from ancient Greek mythology, Phareus was one of the CENTAURS slain by the demi-god and cultural hero Hercules (Heracles) while visiting his friend, a CENTAUR named PHOLUS, between the conclusion of his third Labor and the onset of his fourth.

Source: *Commentary, Mythological, Historical, and Geographical on Pope's Homer*, 55

Pheng

A gigantic bird from Chinese mythology and described in a work entitled *San thsai thou hoei*, the pheng lived in an island country known as Kuen Lun, located in the south-west of China's mainland. The pheng was described as being so large it could swallow a camel in a single bite, its body could eclipse the sun, and its quills were made of water-tuns; it was similar to the ROC of Arabian mythology.

Source: Barber, *Dictionary of Fabulous Beasts*, 116; Poole, *Thousand and One Nights*, 446; Zell-Ravenheart, *Companion for the Apprentice Wizard*, 179

Pheocomes

A CENTAUR from ancient Greek mythology, Pheocomes was one of the CENTAURS slain by the demi-god and cultural hero Hercules (Heracles) while visiting his friend, a CENTAUR named PHOLUS, between the conclusion of his third Labor and the onset of his fourth.

Source: *Commentary, Mythological, Historical, and Geographical on Pope's Homer*, 55

Phii Krasue

Variations: Phi Krasue

A type of vampiric phi from Thailand, the phii krasue is described as a flying head with dangling entrails, a long tongue, and sharp teeth. The phii krasue uses its tongue to drain a person of their blood by inserting it into its victim's anus. As it drains the blood, the vampire chews on the body, taking out bite-sized chunks of flesh.

Source: Ĕchĭas˝ksã, *Asian Review*, Volume 2, 116; Phongphit, *Thai Village Life*, 54, 70; Sotesiri, *Study of Puan Community*, 44

Philamaloo Bird

Originating in the lumberjack communities of the developing United States of America, the Philamaloo bird is one of the FEARSOME CRITTERS; beyond a name there is nothing else known.

Source: Rose, *Giants, Monsters, and Dragons*, 119

Phillyloo Bird

A bird of American folklore, the phillyloo was described as having a storklike beak and legs and a body covered with numerous feathers; in addition to flying upside down in order to keep warm and stave off rheumatism in its long limbs, it laid grade D eggs. Unfortunately, there is no additional information on this creature other than its name, causing writers of the time, 1841–1861, to believe it had gone extinct.

Source: Barber, *Dictionary of Fabulous Beasts*, 116; Botkin, *American People*, 254; Mencken, *American Language Supplement 1*, 251

The Philyrides

The Philyrides were the specific breed of CENTAURS from ancient Greek mythology born of the union between Cronos and Philyra. Perhaps the best known of the Philyrides was the CENTAUR scholar CHEIRON.

Source: Dixon-Kennedy, *Encyclopedia of Greco-Roman Mythology*, 85; Hard, *Routledge Handbook of Greek Mythology*, 73; Rose, *Handbook of Greek Mythology*, 38

Phlegon

In the Latin narrative poem *Metamorphoses* (2.153) written by the Roman poet Ovid (43 BC–AD 17), the sun god and second generation Titan, Helios (Sol), had his golden chariot, Quadriga, pulled across the sky by the flying horses AETHON, ASTROPE, BRONTE, CHRONOS, EOUS, LAMPON, PHAETHON, Phlegon ("flaming"), and PYROIS. All of these horses are described as being pure white and having flaring nostrils which can breathe forth flame and are HIPPOI ATHANATOI.

Source: Breese, *God's Steed*, 86; Brewer, *Dictionary of Phrase and Fable*, 626; Hargreaves, *Hargreaves New Illustrated Bestiary*, 67; Rose, *Giants, Monsters, and Dragons*, 7

Phlegraeos

Variations: Hyle

A CENTAUR from ancient Greek mythology, Phlegraeos was, according to Ovid's *Metamorphoses*, one of the centaurs who attended the wedding of Pirithous, became drunk on wine and following the lead of EURYTUS, who assaulted Hippodame, began to assault and rape any women they could grab. Phlegraeos was slain at a distance by Peleus as was fellow CENTAUR HYLES.

Source: *Commentary, Mythological, Historical, and Geographical on Pope's Homer*, 55; Simpson, *Metamorphoses of Ovid*, 207

Phlogios

One of the fire-breathing horses from the mythology of the ancient Romans, Phlogios, one of the HIPPOI ATHANATOI, belonged to Ares (Mars), the god of war; his stable mates were AITHON ("fire"), CONABOS ("flame"), and PHOBOS ("terror"). Phlogios was also said to have at one time been one of the two horses owned by the Dioskouroi twins, Castor and Polydeuces (Pollux).

Source: Coulter, *Encyclopedia of Ancient Deities*, dccxv; Gemondo, *Animal Totems*, 60

Phobos

One of the fire-breathing horses from the mythology of the ancient Romans, Phobos ("terror"), one of the HIPPOI ATHANATOI, belonged to Ares (Mars), the god of war; his stable mates were AITHON ("fire"), CONABOS ("tumult") and PHLOGIOS ("flame").

Source: Coulter, *Encyclopedia of Ancient Deities*, dccxv; Gemondo, *Animal Totems*, 60

Phoenix

Variations: Fenis, Fenix, Phénix, Po-Ni-Ke, Qoqnos, Qoqnus, ZIZ

The phoenix, a bird said to die and then become reborn of its own ashes, exists in the myths and folklore of many cultures including Arabic, Chinese, Early Christian, Egyptian, Japanese, Jewish, and the folklore of the Middle Ages. No matter where the phoenix appears its mythology is consistent in its having an extremely long life span and having to die in order to be reborn. It is likely the myth of the phoenix originated in ancient Egypt as the BENNU and traveled to Asia by means of Mesopotamia; what scholars consider certain is that the main myth did not develop in ancient Greece.

There are essentially two versions of the phoenix's rebirth. In the first and lesser known of the myths the bird creates a nest of aromatic plants and wills itself to die there, its body decomposing into the nest, and from the mulch becomes a worm which eventually matures into a young bird. When mature enough the bird takes flight carrying with it as much of its previous remains as it can all the way to Heliopolis, Egypt, where it deposits its old body in a temple to the sun god Ra. In the better known version of its regeneration, the phoenix creates a nest of aromatics and there, ignited by the light of the sun, is consumed in flames; emerging from the ashes of the pyre is a new phoenix, either

as a developed bird or an egg which hatches quickly thereafter. The rejuvenation of the bird happened at varying intervals, depending on the myth or story being told; sometimes it was a daily event while other times it occurred only once a millennium. For instance the ancient Greek poet Hesiod cites the lifespan of a phoenix as being nine hundred and seventy-two generations of thirty-three and one half years each, a total of 32,400 years.

The phoenix is virtually always referenced as interacting in the world of man as opposed to the animal kingdom; ironically, only a few authors have written of it with a slant towards natural history. In all of its various cultures the phoenix has been symbolic for aspects of Christian life, Christ, concentration, human existence, life in the heavenly Paradise, Mary, metempsychosis, renewal in general, resurrection, the empire, the exceptional man, the sun, time, and virginity.

Source: Isaacs, *Animals in Jewish Thought and Tradition*, 181; Van den Broek, *Myth of the Phoenix*, 9, 10, 146, 399–401

Pholgios

Variations: Podargos ("the fast")

In classical Greek mythology, Pholgios was one of the four MARES OF DIOMEDES, King of Aetolia and son of the god Ares (Mars) (see DINOS, LAMPON, and XANTHOS). Although the horses are female, the Latin author Hyginus (64 BC–AD 17), the only author who ever named them, gave them all masculine names. In his eighth labor the demi-god Hercules (Heracles) was charged with the capture and return of these savage mares which pulled the chariot of the king and were fed a diet of human flesh. Pholgios was given to him by the god Hermes.

Source: Brewer, *Dictionary of Phrase and Fable*, 419; Hard, *Routledge Handbook of Greek Mythology* 262; Webster, *Historic Magazine and Notes and Queries*, 581

Pholus

Variations: Pholos

A CENTAUR from ancient Greek mythology, Pholus lived upon Mount Pholoe, a mountain named after him. While entertaining the demi-god and cultural hero Hercules (Heracles), Pholus removed a hogshead of wine he had buried in the earth a long time ago, given to him by the god Bacchus (Dionysos), and served it to his guest. When the wine was opened it was so aromatic and strong its aroma carried on the air and intoxicated the nearby CENTAURS, driving them into a fit of drunken madness. The creatures assailed Hercules with fir-trees and boulders but in spite of their great strength and the violent rainstorm their mother, Nephele, sent, Hercules was able to defend himself and kill many of them. While Pholus was collecting the dead, he accidentally cut himself with a dart and died. Hercules buried Pholus at the base of the mountain named after him with a lavish funeral ceremony.

Source: *Commentary, Mythological, Historical, and Geographical on Pope's Homer,* 55; Diodorus, *Historical Library of Diodorus the Sicilian,* Volume 1, 229–30; Lemprière, *Bibliotheca Classica,* 694

Phooka

Variations: Bookhas, Bwcas, Dgèrnésiais, GLASHTYN, Gruagach, Kornbockes, Phouka, Pooka, Pouka, Pouke, Pouque, Púca, Púka, Pwca

In Irish folklore the malicious phooka is the bane of the countryside. It is said when it rains while the sun is shining the phooka will be out that night.

A shape-shifting trickster which takes great delight in tormenting travelers, the phooka will assume the form of a wild colt dragging chains, enticing a weary traveler to mount up upon its back. As soon as it has a rider the phooka takes its victim on a violent ride, kicking and bucking hard enough to break human bones; ultimately it dumps its prey off in a ditch. In the guise of an eagle it will snatch up a man and fly him toward the moon. As a black goat with an impressive set of horns the phooka will jump upon a person's back and claw at him with its hooves until the victim is dead or has managed to bless himself three times. It is also known to take on the form of a demonic horse, black, huge, and well muscled, breathing blue flames from its nostrils and smelling like sulfur.

When blackberries begin to go to seed and rot on the vine children are told not to eat them because the phooka "dirtied" them. When the berries are killed by a frost it is said the phooka spit upon them. After the first of November it is tradition not to eat blackberries as the phooka has defecated or urinated over the remaining crop.

According to legend only one man, the High King of Ireland, Brian Boru, was ever able to successfully ride upon a phooka. By use of a magical bridle containing three hairs from the creature's own tail he managed to stay mounted on it until the FAIRY ANIMAL was too exhausted to move and surrendered to the King. Boru solicited two promises from the phooka—first, it would no longer torment Christians or ruin their land; second, it would never again attack an Irishman unless he was drunk or intended to harm another.

Source: Froud, *Faeries,* 93; Keightley, *World Guide to Gnomes, Fairies, Elves, and Other Little People,* 371; McCoy, *Witch's Guide to Faery Folk,* 293–4; Monaghan, *Encyclopedia of Celtic Mythology and Folklore,* 384–85; Wallace, *Folk-lore of Ireland,* 91

Phrixus

In ancient Greek mythology, Phrixus was one of the CENTAURS slain by the demi-god and cultural hero Hercules (Heracles) while visiting his friend, a CENTAUR named PHOLUS, between the conclusion of his third Labor and the onset of his fourth. When an old and particularly fragrant hogshead of wine was opened its aroma carried on the air and drove the local CENTAURS into a fury. Phrixus, along with ARGEIUS, AMPHION, DAPHNIS, DUPO, Hippotion, ISOPLES, MELANCHETES, Oreus, and THEREUS, was slain by Hercules (Heracles) as he defended himself from their violent and unwarranted assault.

Source: BARTHELL, *Gods and Goddesses of Ancient Greece,* 187; Diodorus, *Historical Library of Diodorus the Sicilian,* Volume 1, 229–30

Pi-Hsi

Variations: Lord of the River

A hybrid DRAGON from Chinese lore, the pi-hsi is depicted as having the armored shell of a tortoise and the feet, head, and tail of a DRAGON.

Source: De Kirk, *Dragonlore,* 28; Lehner, *Big Book of Dragons, Monsters, and Other Mythical Creatures,* 39; Zell-Ravenheart, *Wizard's Bestiary,* 79

Pi Yao

A species of chimerical DRAGON from Chinese folklore, the pi-yao are depicted as having an alicorn (a single horn) upon a leonine head, doglike features, hooves, and wings; these creatures are said to protect people from evil spirits and have the power to counteract bad luck.

Source: Too, *Total Feng Shui,* 266

Piasa (PIE-a-saw)

A large chimerical DRAGON from Algonquin folklore, the anthropophagous (man-eating) piasa ("bird that devours men," "destroyer," "stormbringer" or "thunderer") was depicted as having bat wings, bear legs, eagle claws, elk horns, fish scales covering its fifty-foot long body, forked tail, head of a bear with humanoid features, large teeth, and a mane covering its head and shoulders. Strong enough to sweep down, snatch a deer, and return to the sky, the piasa was said to have been slain by chief Ouatoga of the Illini tribe with the assistance of twenty of his warriors in Illinois, United States of America. A petroglyph was created to commemorate the event and was carved into a rock face and painted black, blue, and red. Still visible in 1673, the petroglyph was completely destroyed by 1867 and no reliable sketches of what the petroglyph may have looked like now remain.

Source: De Kirk, *Dragonlore,* 51; Eberhart, *Mysterious*

Creatures, 432–3; Zell-Ravenheart, *Companion for the Apprentice Wizard*, 179

Piast

Variations: Biast, Bestia, DRAGON of the Apocalypse

A gigantic lake-dwelling monster from Irish folklore, the piast was a hybrid creature, part salmon and part serpent. One of the ATHACH, the piast was believed to be able to breathe fire. It was one of the lake monsters banished by Saint Patrick to remain in its watery home until Judgment Day (see SEA SERPENT).

Source: Eberhart, *Mysterious Creatures*, 426; Flaubert, *Temptation of St. Anthony*, 175

Pictish Beast

Variations: Pictish DRAGON, Swimming Elephant

Carved onto a standing stone by the ancient Picts in the Scottish Highlands, the pictish beast, as historians have come to call it, is depicted as having four flippers rather than legs and a long, narrow head, similar in appearance to a DRAGON or seahorse. While some scholars believe it is nothing more than a symbolic image others allege it to be an early image of the cryptid known as the Loch Ness Monster. Images of this creature appear on over sixty standing stones across the country.

Source: Scales, *Poseidon's Steed*, n.pag.; Woods, *Seven Natural Wonders of Europe*, 10

Pihuechenyi

In Chilean folklore of the Araucanian (Mapuchen) people the pihuechenyi are considered to be a species of large winged, nocturnal, blood drinking, vampiric snakes.

Source: Graves, *Larousse Encyclopedia of Mythology*, 453; Rose, *Giants, Monsters, and Dragons*, 293; Zell-Ravenheart, *Wizard's Bestiary*, 79

Pinari

A species of NATURE SPIRIT from the mythology from the people of the Solomon Islands, the pinari are described as having hairy, humanoid bodies and long legs.

Source: Rose, *Spirits, Fairies, Leprechauns, and Goblins, an Encyclopedia*, 261

Ping Feng

A monstrous creature from Chinese folklore, the ping feng is described as being a black boar with a human (or boar) head on each end of its body, similar to the CH'OU-T'I. Said to live in the Land of Magic Water, it first appeared in a work entitled *T'ai P'ing Kuang Chi* ("Great Records Made in the

Period of Peace and Prosperity") which was published in AD 981.

Source: Barber, *Dictionary of Fabulous Beasts*, 121; Borges, *Book of Imaginary Beings*, 82; Rose, *Giants, Monsters, and Dragons*, 293

Pingala

One of the NAGARAJA of Hindu mythology, the NAGA Pingala ("tawny colored") was sometimes identified as the great authority on the Chhandas.

Source: Dowson, *Classical Dictionary of Hindu Mythology and Religion, Geography, History, and Literature*, 234; Monier-Williams, *Sanskrit-English Dictionary*, 572

Pinnacle Grouse

Originating in the lumberjack communities of the developing United States of America, particularly in the Minnesota and Wisconsin regions, the pinnacle grouse, one of the FEARSOME CRITTERS, was described as having only one wing and therefore only able to fly in continuous circles of the conical side of the mountain upon which it made its nest.

Source: Leary, *Wisconsin Folklore*, 146; Mencken, *American Language Supplement 1*, 250; Rose, *Giants, Monsters, and Dragons*, 119, 293

Piranu

In Argentinean folklore the aggressive and territorial piranu is a species of monstrous fish described as having a black Piscean body but the head of a horse with large eyes. Living in deep fresh-water rivers, these malicious creatures will ram any boat which ventures into their region of the river.

Source: Eberhart, *Mysterious Creatures*, 437; Rose, *Giants, Monsters, and Dragons*, 293

Pirobolus plural: Piroboli

A species of rock, according to medieval folklore, found only in the East, the piroboli come in both feminine and masculine genders. It was believed at the times as long at the stones were kept apart from one another they would not burn; however, if they were placed next to one another, they would combust and consume everything in their surroundings.

Source: Curley, *Physiologus*, 6

Pisenor

A CENTAUR from ancient Greek mythology, Pisenor was, according to Ovid's *Metamorphoses*, one of the CENTAURS who attended the wedding of Pirithous, became drunk on wine, and following the lead of EURYTUS, who assaulted Hippodame, began to assault and rape any women they could grab. During the battle, Pisenor attempted to flee but along with LYCABAS, MEDON, ORNEUS, and THAU-

MAS was slain by the spear-wielding Lapith soldier DRYAS.

Source: *Commentary, Mythological, Historical, and Geographical on Pope's Homer*, 55; Lemprière, *Bibliotheca Classica*, 694; Simpson, *Metamorphoses of Ovid*, 205

Pistris

Variations: Pistrix, Pristis, Pistris vel Pistrix, Pristrix

A chimerical SEA SERPENT from ancient Greek mythology sent to consume Andromeda, Pistris is depicted in art as having the body and tail of a fish, fins for forelegs, and the head and neck of a DRAGON. In Christian art, the pistris was commonly used to represent the whale sent by God to swallow Jonah.

Source: Brewer, *Dictionary of Phrase and Fable*, 690; Ogden, *Dragons, Serpents, and Slayers in the Classical and Early Christian Worlds*, 160

Pita-Skog

In Abenaki folklore the pita-skog ("great snake") was described as being a gigantic horned serpent, similar to the LINDORM of Norse mythology.

Source: Hallenbeck, *Monsters of New York*, 5

Pixiu

Variations: Mengshou ("fierce beast"), Pi Xiu

A species of creature originating in ancient Chinese folklore, the fierce pixiu ("male/female leopard") is often utilized as a guardian for buildings of importance, such as temples, in a manner similar to the DOGS OF FO. In ancient times the word *pixiu* was synonymous for *army*. First described in a text entitled *The Book of Han* and in another tome called *The Accounts of the Western Region*, they were said to live mainly in the country of Wu Ge Shan Li and were compared to lions both in appearance and ferocity.

According to the most common legend of the pixiu's origin, originally it was not a species of creature but rather the ninth son of the DRAGON KING, his favorite child, and as such, horribly spoiled. One day Pixiu was being particularly mischievous and while rampaging about on his father's royal desk shattered the seal of the office of the DRAGON KING and the symbol of his power. Enraged, the King used magic to punish his son, transforming him into an animal with a sealed rectum, forcing him to live a life in constant constipation. Additionally Pixiu could only consume items associated with wealth, such as gold and jewelry, but because he was unable to excrete, everything remained within his body.

A variation of this legend tells of Pixiu sucking the blood or life essence out of demons and con-

verting it into items of wealth, all of which remain within his body.

Source: Bates, *29 Chinese Mysteries*, 47–52

Plakavac

A vampiric creature from Slavic folklore in the region of Herzegovina, a plakavac is said to be about the size of a frog and is created when a mother strangles her child to death. Crawling about, the plakavac curses its mother who first gave it life and then cruelly took it.

The word plakavac is also used to refer to a child who dies unbaptized or when a mother kills her own illegitimate child; if the latter is the case, it is folkloric belief the village will suffer a hailstorm which will destroy their crops.

Source: Filipović, *Among the People*, 176

Plata Yryguy

The plata yryguy is a headless dog from the folklore of Paraguay.

Source: O'Rourke, *Give War a Chance*, 49

Plon

A creature from Wend folklore, the plon ("DRAGON") is described as a terrifying ball of light with a long tail flying through the air, but was known to bring people treasure.

Source: Institut für Sorbische Volksforschung, *Lětopis*, Volumes 53–54, 65; Wolff, *Odd Bits of History*, 152

Podarge

Variations: Podarce ("fleet-footed"), PODARGUS

In classical Greek mythology, Podarge ("swift-foot") was one of the horses of Hector (see ETHON and GALATHE); occasionally added to this list were AETHON, Lampus (LAMPOS), and Xanthus (XANTHOS).

Source: Brewer, *Dictionary of Phrase and Fable*, 419; Murray, *Classical Manual*, 196; Webster, *Historic Magazine and Notes and Queries*, 581

Podargos

Variations: Podargus

In the ancient Greek epic poem the *Iliad* ("Song of Ilion") (1240 BC) attributed to Homer, Podargos is the name given as the horse of King Menelaus of Mycenae, brother of Agamemnon, and the husband of Helen of Troy.

Source: *Contemporary Review*, Volume 27, 810; Murray, *Classical Manual*, 259

Podarkes (po-DAR-seez)

Variations: Podarces, Podarkês, Podarkês ("swift-footed")

One of the HIPPOI ATHANATOI from ancient

Greek mythology, the mare Podarkes was one of a pair of immortal horses given to the king of Athens, Erekhtheus, as the bride-price for marrying Oreithyia, the daughter of the north wind, Boreas; the other horse given to him was XANTHOS (BAYARD).

Podarkes was also the name of the chariot horse belonging to Thoas, son of Jason the Argonaut.

Source: Atsma, *Hippoi Erekhtheioi*, n.pag.; Papinius, *Togail Na Tebe*, 153

Poemenis

A dog from ancient Greek mythology, Poemenis ("shepherdess") was one of the DOGS OF ACTÆON, the unfortunate youth who was raised by the CENTAUR CHEIRON. Poemenis was noted for being a shepherd dog.

Source: Leeming, *World of Myth*, 111; Murray, *Classical Manual*, 160; Naso, *Fasti, Tristia*, 93–5

Poh

One of the species of UNICORN described in Chinese folklore, the vicious poh were described by the Shan Hai king as living on the Mongolian plains and looking similar to a white horse, having a black tail, claws and fangs like a tiger, a roar like a rolling drum, and an alicorn (a single horn) protruding from the forehead. The poh were believed to use their horn as a weapon when hunting leopards and tigers upon which they fed. There is a story of a herd of six poh once entering a town and slaughtering nearly half of the population.

Source: Gould, *Mythical Monsters*, 348, 359; Shepard, *Lore of the Unicorn*, n.pag.; South, *Mythical and Fabulous Creatures*, 12

Polar Worms

Similar to the DRAGONS of Europe, the polar worms from Inuit mythology were said to be long, serpentine creatures having dragonesque heads and vicious tempers.

Source: De Kirk, *Dragonlore*, 52

Polevik, plural: polewiki

Variations: Mittagsfrau ("Lady Midday"), Polednice, Polevoi, Poludnica, Południca, Poludnitsa, Přezpołdnica, Připołdnica, Pschesponiza, Pscipolnitsa, Roggenmuhme ("lady of the rye")

A species of Polish NATURE SPIRIT, the polewiki are said to live in cultivated fields and murder workers who fall asleep after drinking on the job; they are especially active around noon. Described as dressing all in white, having a dwarflike appearance, mis-matched colored eyes, and grass rather than hair, the polewiki may be appeased from their murderous tendencies by leaving them an offering

of a crow, a rooster, a toad, and two eggs in a ditch when no one is watching. Polewiki are also said to spread disease and lead people astray in the field.

Source: Coulter, *Encyclopedia of Ancient Deities*, 386; Franklin, *Working with Fairies*, 124; Graves, *Larousse Encyclopedia of Mythology*, 300–01

Pollo Maligno

A malicious type of creature from Colombian folklore, the pollo maligno ("evil chicken") is a harbinger of misfortune. Usually this creature will appear whenever two or more horseback riders congregate; the creature will follow them when they eventually ride off, clucking the whole while; the intensity of its call is in proportion to the tragedy about to happen. It is also possible someone walking along the road may be followed by a pollo maligno; in this instance, its clucking is maddening and will eventually cause the traveler to return to their home. It is believed the only way to ward-off one of these creatures is to pray a novena to the archangel Michael.

Source: Potts, *Chicken*, 90–1

Polong (Poe-long)

In Malaysia witches can create a vampiric FAMILIAR known as a polong out of the blood of a murdered man. Taking the blood and placing it in a bottle, a magical ceremony is performed; this spell may take as long as two weeks to perform. During the ceremony, a bond develops between the witch and the developing FAMILIAR. Finally, when the sound of chirping is heard coming from within the bottle, the spell is complete and the vampiric FAMILIAR known as a polong has finally been created. Before the creature is released from the bottle, the witch must let the polong bite her finger and drink her blood to permanently seal the bond between them. It will continue to feed from her daily. When not in use by the witch, the FAMILIAR will stay inside its bottle home.

The polong looks like a one-inch-tall woman and is a natural liar and trickster. Witches who have a polong oftentimes have another FAMILIAR, a type of vampire called a PELESIT. Together the two familiars will attack whomever the witch sends them after. The PELESIT will cut a hole with its sharp tail in the victim and the polong will crawl inside, causing sickness and insanity in the person. A person who is believed to be ill because of a polong will have many unexplained bruises on their body as well as blood around their mouth.

A polong is resistant to the magic of other people, unless it is completely overwhelmed. It can be captured and with the use of powerful magic be forced to tell the name of its witch. Charms can also be made to neutralize and destroy a captured polong.

Source: Endicott, *Analysis of Malay Magic*, 57–59; Folklore Society of Great Britain, *Folklore*, Volume 13, 150–51, 157; Kadir, *Hikayat Abdullah*, 113–17; Masters, *Natural History of the Vampire*, 62

Pombero

A species of NATURE SPIRIT from Guaraní mythology, the pombero are described as appearing as black skinned, long-armed, hairy, small beings with a simian (monkey-like) face who, when seen, appear at night; when not seen their presence can be detected by the whistling sound they make. Generally the pombero do have a set opinion of mankind but their favor can be purchased by offerings of alcohol, honey, and tobacco; in exchange the creature will lend it assistance and protection in hunting expeditions. Likewise, the pombero can be made an enemy of by insulting it and will retaliate by inflicting physical and psychological harm upon the offender's livestock. Occasionally a pombero will have a sexual encounter with a woman and leave her pregnant; typically the woman has no memory of the event and seldom realizes she is pregnant until she is obviously showing. Children born of these unions are recognized as having a pombero as a father. It is believed the pombero may be warded away by Roman Catholic prayers, making the sign of the Cross, or by receiving the Sacrament of Baptism.

Source: Leddon, *Child's Eye View of Fair Folk*, 58; MacDonald, *Traditional Storytelling Today*, 491

Ponaturi

A species of evil, nocturnal goblins from Maori folklore, the ponaturi are the catalyst for the stories of Tawhaki and his grandson Rata. In the first tale, Tawhaki and his brother Karihi set out to avenge the abduction of their mother and murder of their father by the ponaturi. The brothers were able to learn the creatures were highly susceptible to sunlight so when they discovered the location of their lair they covered all the holes and openings. In the morning, the ponaturi overslept and when they finally arose flung open the front doors believing it to still be night, sunlight flooded the lair and killed many of the ponaturi.

Rata also set out to slay the ponaturi to avenge the death of his father, Wahiero; when he came upon them, the creatures were praying to their god and using the bones of Wahiero in a ceremony known as the Tikikura. Rata listened to the chant, memorized the words, then leapt into the middle

of them, slaying their priest. He grabbed up his father's bones and ran back to his fortress. The ponaturi gave chase and were met by Rata's men; a fierce battle took place but Rata was able to restore life to his men by use of a magical spell. Thousands of ponaturi were slain.

Source: Andersen, *Myths and Legends of the Polynesians*, n.pag.; Craig, *Dictionary of Polynesian Mythology*, 213

Pongo

In medieval Sicilian legends Pongo was the name of a gigantic and horrific SEA SERPENT described as being a hybrid between a "land-tiger and sea-shark"; it devoured at least five hundred Sicilians and attempted to render the island uninhabitable, maintaining a twenty mile perimeter. Eventually, Pogo was slain by the three sons of Saint George.

Source: Bassett, *Legends and Superstitions of the Sea and of Sailors in all Lands and at all Times*, 212; Rose, *Giants, Monsters, and Dragons*, 296

Ponik

Variations: Pohenegamook

According to regional folklore Ponik is the name of a lake monster said to reside in Lake Pohenegamook near the towns of Saint Eleuthere, Saint Estcourt, Scully, in Quebec, Canada; it is described as looking like a forty-foot long overturned canoe with the head of an earless horse and having saw-toothed protrusions running the length of its dorsal ridge (see SEA SERPENT). Although considered to be a non-predatory creature, the arrival of Ponik is always preceded by frothing waters. In some of the stories of Ponik, it is able to come upon land and is described as being amphibious.

Source: Meurger, *Lake Monster Traditions*, 43, 46; Rose, *Giants, Monsters, and Dragons*, 296

Pontarf

A monstrous fish from medieval folklore, the pontarf was a NURSERY BOGIE said to live in the seas off the European coast; it was so large it could stretch its body to snatch up children who had wandered away from their parents, no matter how far inland they were (see SEA SERPENT).

Source: Barber, *Dictionary of Fabulous Beasts*, 121; Rose, *Giants, Monsters, and Dragons*, 296

Pontianak (Pont-ah-nook)

Variation: Buo, Kuntilanak, Mati-anak, Pontipinnak

In Indonesia and Malaya folklore there is a vampiric demon known as a pontianak. It is believed when a woman dies in childbirth, or as a virgin, or is the victim of a pontianak attack, she will then transform into this type of creature unless specific burial rites are followed. Glass beads must be placed in the corpse's mouth, an egg in each armpit, and needles driven into the palms and soles of the feet.

A pontianak can pass as a human woman except for two tell-tale signs: a hole in the back of its neck and a smell exactly like the tropically sweet frangipani flower. These creatures will also announce their presence with a call which sounds like a crying baby.

At night, the pontianak leaves its banana tree home and shape-shifts into a bird; then the creature flies out looking for prey. Although any person will suffice, these creatures have a preference for the blood of infants and pregnant women as they hate themselves for never having been a mother to their own child. When a pontianak finds a suitable target, it then reverts into its human guise and detaches its head from its body, dangling its intestines and organs as it flies back to where it saw its prey. If it can, the creature will rip the unborn child right out of the mother's body, eating it on the spot.

As a species, the pontianak have a unique fear among vampire kind: they will flee in terror from anyone who manages to pull a hair out of their head. It is also believed if a nail can be placed into the hole in the back of their neck, they will change into a beautiful woman and thus remain until someone pulls the nail back out. It is fortunate to know the pontianak has these weaknesses, because there is no known method for destroying them.

Source: Laderman, *Wives and Midwives*, 126–27; McHugh, *Hantu Hantu*, 74; Skeat, *Malay Magic*, 326–28

Poua-Kai

Variations: Pouakai, Poukai, Pouki

A species of gigantic anthropophagous (man-eating) bird from Maori folklore, the poua-kai ("aged eating" or "aged glutton") are similar to the NGANI-VATU of Fijian mythology and the ROC of the popular Arabic folktale *One-Thousand and One Arabian Nights*. In one story of a poua-kai, one of these creatures had taken up residence near a village and although its wings made ample noise as it flew overhead, it did so at such great speed that no man, woman, or child was able to escape its accurate talons. A wandering hero by the name of Te-hau-o-tawera ("the sacred power of Tawera") came upon the fearful settlement and led an expedition to slay the monster. Utilizing a water pit trap and fifty men, he was able to lure the poua-kai into chasing him where it fell into the pit filled with water. Once submerged, fifty men with spears attacked the beast until it was dead.

Source: Skyes, *Who's Who in Non-Classical Mythology*, 158;

White, *Ancient History of the Maori*, 194–5; Zell-Ravenheart, *Wizard's Bestiary*, 79

Presteros

A creature appearing in many medieval bestiaries, the presteros was said to have the ability to make anyone who touched it an imbecile.

Source: Flaubert, *Temptation of St. Anthony*, 255; Nigg, *Book of Fabulous Beasts*, 330

Pricolic

In Romania, in addition to the vampiric REVENANT called a pricolic, there is a vampiric creature by the same name, but it is born of an incestuous relationship and has a tail. This person has the ability to shape-shift into a dog, although whether this is a given talent or something gifted to the pricolic by the Devil remains to be answered. While in his dog form, the pricolic mingles in the company of wolves. The person will find it begins to spend more and more time in its other form, until eventually, one day, it shape-shifts into a wolf and, giving in to its wanderlust, joins a pack. To prevent it from attacking family and livestock, the pricolic can be kept at bay by leaving offerings of food for it to eat.

Source: Melton, *Vampire Book*

Priculics (Pray-cue-lics)

Variations: Priccolitsch, Prikolotsch, Varcolaci

In the geographic and historic region of Romania once known as Wallachia, there is the folklore of a vampiric WERE-CREATURE called a *priculics* ("wolf coat"). By day it passes as a handsome young man, but at night it has the ability to shape-shift into a large and shaggy black dog. In its animal form it will attack anyone it encounters, draining them of their blood.

Source: Baskin, *Sorcerer's Handbook*, 88; Leland, *Gypsy Sorcery and Fortune Telling*, 65; Masters, *Natural History of the Vampire*, 93; Perkowski, *The Darkling*, 40

Prithusravas

A NAGARAJA from Hindu mythology, Prithusravas was one of the many NAGA mentioned only by name in Vedic mythology.

Source: Vogel, *Indian Serpent-Lore*, 191

Prock Gwinter

Variations: Cute-Cuss, Cutter-Cuss, Guiaskuitas, Guyanosa, Guyanousa, Guyascuttus, Guyastacuttus, Gyascuttus, Lunkus, Perockius Oregoniensis, Rickaboo Racker, Side Hill Dodger, Sidehill Badger, Sidehill Dodger, Sidehill Gouger, Sidehill Sauger, Sidewinder, Stone-Eater

Originating in the lumberjack communities of

the developing United States of America, the prock gwinter, one of the FEARSOME CRITTERS, was originally written about in *Knickerbocker Magazine* in 1846; initially called a guyanousa, this creature was described as being as tall as the highest poplar tree. Traveling side shows were said to sell tickets to see it but as soon as the tent was near full capacity, an employee would run through yelling for everyone to flee, as the creature had broken loose and was on a rampage. The money-swindling show traveled widely and the name of the creature changed often. Later descriptions of the creature included the ability to dislocate its shoulders at will so it could graze with ease along steep hills and mountainsides.

As the gyascutus, it was said to be a harmless rodent-like creature about three feet tall and nine feet long with powerful forelegs and sharp claws which it used to dig for the roots of the wild hyacinth, its primary food source. The back of the animal was covered with plates or shield-like scales and the rest of its body had a thick, pachydermatous hide. A pair of short and slightly recurved horns extended over its shoulders toward its rear legs.

Source: Cavendish, *Man, Myth and Magic*, Volume 5, 2101; Mencken, *American Language*, 245–7; Rose, *Giants, Monsters, and Dragons*, 119, 299; Theitic, *Witches' Almanac, Issue 34*, 17–8

Psoglav

Psoglav ("doghead") is a demonic creature from Slavic folklore described as looking like a man with horse legs, a dog's head, a mouth filled with teeth of iron, and one eye on its forehead. An opportunity hunter, it excavates graves and consumes the dead. It is said to live in gemstone caves throughout Bosnia and Montenegro.

Source: Doirievich, *Srpski etnografski zbornik 66*, 106–7; Kulišić; *Српски митолошки речник*, 249

Pterelas

A dog from ancient Greek mythology, Pterelas ("to drive onward" or "wing") was one of the DOGS OF ACTÆON, the unfortunate youth who was raised by the CENTAUR CHEIRON. Pterelas was noted for being a swift runner.

Source: Leeming, *World of Myth*, 111; Murray, *Classical Manual*, 160; Naso, *Fasti, Tristia*, 93–5

Ptitsy-Siriny

A species of humanoid creatures from Russian folklore, the ptitsy-siriny are described as having the body of a bird with the torso and head of a young woman, similar to the HARPY and associated with the FIREBIRD. In the oldest versions of the folklore the ptitsy-siriny are a classification of primitive

fertility and hunting deities known as *bereginy* ("the place where land and water meet").

Source: Dixon-Kennedy, *Encyclopedia of Russian and Slavic Myth and Legend*, 38, 228; Hubbs, *Mother Russia*, 15; Rose, *Giants, Monsters, and Dragons*, 300

Ptoophagos

Variations: Ptoophagus

In the mythology of the ancient Greeks, ARCTOPHONOS and Ptoophagos ("the glutton of Ptoon") were the two hunting dogs of the GIGANTE Orion.

Source: Brewer, *Character Sketches of Romance, Fiction and the Drama*, Volume 3, 131; Rose, *Giants, Monsters, and Dragons*, 25

Pukwudgie

In Abenaki, Algonquin, Ojibwe, Mochican, Wampanoag tribal folklore the pukwudgie ("person of the wilderness") were a species of NATURE SPIRIT dangerous only to those individuals who did not show them respect. Typically the pukwudgie played harmless pranks which may turn deadly; only on rare occasion did they kidnap a child. Described as standing no taller than a few feet and emitting a sweet fragrance, they were associated with flowers. The pukwudgie also had the ability to magically become invisible, confuse the thoughts of a person's mind, and shape-shift into a cougar.

In one legend of the pukwudgie they were jealous of the love the Wampanoag people showed to the creator of Cape Cod, Maushop, and began to torment him by acting out in a mischievous fashion. Maushop and his wife, Granny Squanit, grabbed up many of them, shook them violently, and threw them over the land. Although many died, those who lived regrouped, returned, and began burning down entire villages, kidnapping children, and murdering the Wampanoag. Maushop sent his five sons to handle the pukwudgie situation but they surrounded the sons and shot them all dead with magical arrows. Enraged and filled with grief Maushop attacked the pukwudgie, crushing and killing as many as he could find. Some versions of the story claim he was slain by the NATURE SPIRITS while others say his anger eventually ran its course and in his profound grief, wandered off into the woods; no matter the ending of the tale, Maushop disappears from legend.

Source: Coleman, *Monsters of Massachusetts*, 65; Hallenbeck, *Monsters of New York*, 84

Pugot

Variations: Cafre, Child-Snatcher, Kafar, Mánguang Anak, Numputol, Pugut

A headless, and occasionally armless, black-skinned humanoid from Filipino folklore, the pugot ("dark" or "headless") has a strong smell about it, and can be found living in abandoned buildings, deserted places, and inside trees. Terrifying in appearance, with blood gushing from its severed stumps, the pugot may snatch up a person and carry them off some distance, but is otherwise harmless; however, encounters with these creatures have been known to cause insanity in some individuals. Consuming centipedes and snakes and enjoying smoking over-sized cigars, these creatures also have the ability to shape-shift into various animal forms, all of which have the ability to breathe fire out of their mouths. Some descriptions of the pugot say they are as large as a bull and have tusks protruding from their mouth; moving very quickly through the jungle, they are said to hunt and consume humans.

Source: Eugenio, *Philippine Folk Literature*, 434; Maberry, *Vampire Universe*, 60; Ramos, *Creatures of Midnight*, 13; Rose, *Giants, Monsters, and Dragons*, 300

Pugwis

Variations: Man of the Sea

In Kwakwaka'wakw folklore of the native people of British Columbia, Pugwis is the name of an anthropoid NATURE SPIRIT living beneath the water; it is described as having a Piscean face, gills, prominent but rounded facial features, round eyes, two large beaver-like front teeth, and well defined eye sockets.

Source: Shearar, *Understanding Northwest Coast Art*, 85; Zell-Ravenheart, *Wizard's Bestiary*, 80

Puk

Variations: Puck, Pukje, Pukys, Puuk

A species of small, four-footed household DRAGON from Frisian folklore, the serpentine puk are oftentimes utilized as a FAMILIAR and tasked with the responsibility of stealing food for their master and guarding their possessions. Older descriptions of the puk say they have wings and can fly through the air, streaming behind them a fiery tail; on the ground, they more closely resemble a cat.

Source: Hargreaves, *Hargreaves New Illustrated Bestiary*, 38; Lurker, *Dictionary of Gods and Goddesses, Devils and Demons*, 156; Rose, *Giants, Monsters, and Dragons*, 300

Pumpot

A curious species of BARGUEST, the pumpot of Slavic folklore is as likely to play a mischievous prank on a person as it is to assist them and do a good deed.

Source: Wolff, *Odd Bits of History*, 152

Pundarika

Variations: Vamana

One of the DIG-GAJAS from Hindu mythology and post–Vedic legend, Pundarika is one of the eight elephant protectors of the eight compass points; he and his mate Kapila protect and uphold the southeast edge. All of these elephants are symbols of protection, stability, and strength and were born of the halves of the cosmic golden egg Hiranyagarbha, which hatched the sun.

Pundarika is also the name of one of the many Nagas mentioned in the *Mahabharata* of whom, beyond a name, little else is known.

Source: Dowson, *Classical Dictionary of Hindu Mythology and Religion, Geography, History, and Literature*, 180; Gupta, *Elephant in Indian Art and Mythology*, 7

Punyaiama (Pom-ah-ya-ma)

Variations: VETALA

In the Bihar and Orissa regions of India there is the belief in a type of vampiric creature called a punyaiama ("pure race"); they are described as looking like an old woman with black skin, poisonous fingernails, and slit eyes. Usually they are covered in the funeral pyre ashes, as this is where they sleep during the day. At night, the punyaiama attacks lone travelers as they walk down quiet roads. These vampires will also climb up to the roofs of houses and feed a magical string down into the home's chimney. The thread they use is enchanted to find sleeping women or women who are passed out drunk, insert itself into their skin, and feed blood back up to the waiting punyaiama. These vampires also have the ability to possess a corpse, and when they do so, the corpse's feet distort and bend backward.

Source: Kosambi, *Introduction to the Study of Indian History*, 35–45; Saletore, *Indian Witchcraft*, 83; Volta, *The Vampire*, 151

Purocis

Variations: Puroeis

In classical Greek and Roman mythology Purocis ("fiery hot") was one of the many winged horses said to assist in pulling the sun chariot Quadriga belonging to the second generation Titan Helios (Sol) across the sky. Purocis, LAMPOS and PHLEGON were considered to be the noontime horses and counted among the HIPPOI ATHANATOI.

Source: Brewer, *Wordsworth Dictionary of Phrase and Fable*, 565; Rose, *Giants, Monsters, and Dragons*, 178

Pushpa-Danta

Variations: Puspadanta

One of the DIG-GAJAS from Hindu mythology, Pushpa-Danta is one of the eight elephant protectors of the eight compass points; he guards the northwest and his female Subha-Danti. Symbols of protection, stability, and strength, they were born of the halves of the cosmic golden egg Hiranyagarbha, which hatched the sun.

Source: Dowson, *Classical Dictionary of Hindu Mythology and Religion, Geography, History, and Literature*, 180; Gupta, *Elephant in Indian Art and Mythology*, 7

Pyinsa Rupa

A chimerical creature from the folklore of Yangon, Burma, the pyinsa rupa ("five beauties") is made up of five different animals, the bullock, carp, elephant, horse, and the TOENAYAR (DRAGON) although other times it is described as consisting of elements from buffalo, carp, elephant, hinthar (a duck-like bird), and the lion.

Source: Edwards, *Jane's Airline Recognition Guide*, 267; Oa, *Aspects of Myanmar Culture*, 28

Pyong

The pyong is a species of gigantic, ROC-like bird in Chinese folklore and legend.

Source: Cooper, *Symbolic and Mythological Animals*, 185; Rose, *Giants, Monsters, and Dragons*, 301

Pyralli

Variations: Pyrotocone, Pyrotokon ("firebred"), Pyrausta

Described by Pliny the Elder, the Roman author and natural philosopher, in his work entitled *Inventorum Natura*, the pyralli were a species of fly-sized PHOENIX with armored insect-like wings from the island of Pyrallis; they fed exclusively on fire.

Source: Pliny the Elder, *Storie Naturali*, 505

Pyrassoupi

A species of UNICORN from Arabic folklore, the pyrassoupi is described by Ambroise Paré (1517–1590) in his work *On Monsters and Marvels* as being about the shape and size of a mule, having cloven hooves, a shaggy yellow ursine coat, and two twisted horns protruding from its forehead. It was believed the horns, when soaked in water, would be given to snake-bite victims to drink in order to neutralize the poison.

Source: Paré, *On Monsters and Marvels*, 165–6; Rose, *Giants, Monsters, and Dragons*, 302

Pyrois

Variations: Pyroeis

According to the Roman poet Ovid (43 BC–AD 17) Pyrois ("fiery"), and the other HIPPOI ATHANATOI, ACTHON (AETHON), ASTROPE, BRONTE, CHRONOS, EOUS, LAMPON, PHAETHON, and PHLEGON, pull the golden chariot Quadriga belonging to the second generation Titan Helios (Sol) across the sky. All of these horses are described as being pure white and having flaring nostrils which can breathe forth flame.

Source: Breese, *God's Steed*, 86; Hargreaves, *Hargreaves New Illustrated Bestiary*, 67; Rose, *Giants, Monsters, and Dragons*, 7, 178

Pytho

Variations: Delphyne, Pythia, Pythios, Python

Greek mythology's Pytho, the DRAGON of Delphi, was the chthonic enemy of the god Apollo. According to the earliest collected versions of the myth no details of the combat or the lineage of the creature are given; later versions dwell on the creature's death-throes and Apollo's victory speech. The gender of the creature varied between male and female, depending on the time period the story was being told in. In Hyginus' version, when the goddess and second generation Titan Leto was ready to deliver a set of twins—Apollo and Artemis (Diana)—fathered by Zeus (Jupiter), his wife, Hera (Juno) sent Pytho to chase the soon-to-be-mother so she would not be able to deliver any place the sun could reach. As soon as Apollo was born, the infant sought out the DRAGON confronting it in its home on Mount Parnassus; there he killed it with his arrows near the place where the oracle would sit to deliver her divinations. Thereafter the priestess became known as Pythia.

Source: Fontenrose, *Python*, 15–16, 21; van der Toorn, *Dictionary of Deities and Demons in the Bible*, 670

Qaxdascidi

A gigantic and malicious lake monster from Tanaina folklore, qaxdascidi is seldom seen as it lives in the depths of the frozen Alaskan waters; however its angry roars are said to be heard often (see SEA SERPENT).

Source: Rose, *Giants, Monsters, and Dragons*, 303; Sturtevant, *Handbook of North American Indians: Subarctic*, 635

Qianlima

Variations: Qianli Ma

A type of horse from Chinese folklore, a qianlima was said to be a stallion able to run one thousand *li* in a single day (approximately three hundred fourteen miles) without the need to drink or eat. Described as having a broad chest, level spine, protruding eyes, and the skull of a DRAGON, the qianlima are sometimes in art depicted as having wings.

Source: Fragner, *Horses in Asia*, 188; McNeilly, *Sun Tzu and the Art of Modern Warfare*, 230

Qilaluga-Nappa

A type of monster from Inuit folklore, the qilaluga-nappa ("half white whale") is basically a species of MERMAN, much larger in size than a human, whose humanoid body transforms at the waist into the lower body of a white whale.

Source: Manlin, *Manlike Monsters on Trial*, 199, 205

Qilin (chee-lin)

Variations: Kilin, KI-LIN, Kylin

A species of UNICORN from Chinese folklore, the qilin is a bulky creature said to only appear at the onset of a wise and virtuous leader; this animal has perfect benevolence, gentleness, and goodwill toward all creatures. It has the ability not only to walk on water but to also be so gentle as to not bend a blade of grass it treads upon; it will not step upon insects and never eats carrion food.

Originally the qilin had only an alicorn (one horn) but during the Ming dynasty it suddenly manifested as a two horned creature and with the influence of Buddhism and Confucianism it lost all of its aggressive nature to become a wholly auspicious creature.

Physical descriptions of the qilin are inconsistent; some sources say it has the body of an ox while others say its frame is more like a bear, deer, or goat. Cloven hooves and a DRAGON- or camel-like head are common descriptors, as well as a bushy tail, DRAGON scales, and a ridge down its back. Its alicorn (a single horn) is too short and rounded to be a useful weapon, further drawing attention to its gentle nature.

Source: Bates, *29 Chinese Mysteries*, 76–90; Sax, *Imaginary Animals*, 86

Qiqion

Variations: Qiqirn

In the Inuit folklore from the region of Baffin Island, Hudson Bay, the qiqion is described as looking like a gigantic hairless dog with only tufts of fur on and near its ears, feet, mouth, and tail. Other than causing convulsions in humans who look upon it, the qiqion is harmless towards mankind, preferring to leave the area when people approach.

Source: Barber, *Dictionary of Fabulous Beasts*, 122; Maberry, *Vampire Universe*, 253; Rose, *Giants, Monsters, and Dragons*, 303

Quanekelak

A cosmic whale in the folklore of the Bela Bela Indians of northwest Canada, Quanekelak is described as being an anthropid hybrid, having the body of a man but the head of an orca ("killer whale").

Source: Zell-Ravenheart, *Wizard's Bestiary*, 80

Questing Beast

Variations: Beast Glatisant ("barking beast"), Glatisaunt

According to Arthurian legend the chimerical questing beast was described as having the body of a leopard, feet of a stag, head and neck of a serpent, and the hindquarters of a lion; it received its name not because it was a creature knights would hunt out on a quest but rather after the sound of its roar, a call like forty hounds on the hunt. In the stories, Merlin reveals to King Arthur the creature came into being having been born of an incestuous relationship between a brother and sister; in this way, the questing beast is a psychopomp (death omen).

In the stories, Sir Palamedes spent his life hunting the creature and fought with the many other knights who sought to find and slay it first including Sir Bors, Sir Galahad, Sir Gawain, Sir Hector, Sir Lancelot, Sir Pellinore, Sir Perceval, and Sir Yvain the Bastard. Pellinore claimed only he or his bloodline was capable of killing the questing beast but in spite of the fact Merlin prophesied it would be Perceval who would ultimately destroy it, Palamedes achieved his life-long goal. The body of the questing beast was then tossed into what would come to be called the Lake of the Beast; as its body sank beneath the surface, the water boiled.

Source: Barber, *Dictionary of Fabulous Beasts*, 122; Brewer, *Reader's Handbook of Allusions, References, Plots and Stories*, 808; Bruce, *Arthurian Name Dictionary*, 414–5; Rosen, *Mythical Creatures Bible*, 120

Quinotaur

A chimerical sea creature, the quinotaur ("bull with five horns") is described in French folklore as being part bull, DRAGON, and fish (see SEA SERPENT). The quinotaur is said to have been the progenitor of the Merovingian bloodline; officially the father of Frankish King Merovee (448–57) was Clodion the Long-haired but there were persistent rumors his mother had been raped by this creature while she had been out on a swim.

Source: Bitel, *Women in Early Medieval Europe*, 51; Fanthrope, *Unsolved Mysteries of the Sea*, 44, 210

Rabicano

Variations: Rabican

Astolpho's horse in Ludovico Ariosto's epic poem *Orlando Furioso* (*Frenzy of Orlando*, 1532), Rabicano was sired by a hurricane and said to be born of fire; it fed upon the air and had a gait so light it never left a mark upon the ground. When Rabicano ran at full speed, it could outrace any arrow.

Source: Ariosto, *Orlando Furioso*, Volume 1, 230; Barber, *Dictionary of Fabulous Beasts*, 123; Brewer, *Wordsworth Dictionary of Phrase and Fable*, 899

Rachaders

Variations: Rach'aders

The Rachaders were the second tribe of GIANTS or evil djinn (a race of demons) in Hindu mythology which made the earth subject to their rule; ultimately they were punished by the gods Shiva and Vishnu.

Source: Brewer, *Dictionary of Phrase and Fable*, 1033; Ruoff, *Standard Dictionary of Facts*, 340; Southey, *Southey's Commonplace Book*, Volume 4, 253

Rachet Owl

Originating in the lumberjack communities of the developing United States of America, the rachet owl, one of the FEARSOME CRITTERS, was said to be photophobic and always faced west when perched.

Source: Davidson, *Rocky Mountain Tales*, 284; Rose, *Giants, Monsters, and Dragons*, 119

Racumon

A gigantic serpent in Carib folklore, the racumon was believed to be responsible for the creation of hurricanes and wind; it was said to live deep in the valley and had on its head a shiny stone, possibly a carbuncle, which was covered with a skin flap similar to an eyelid.

Source: Brinton, *Myths of the New World*, 138; Rose, *Giants, Monsters, and Dragons*, 305; Zell-Ravenheart, *Wizard's Bestiary*, 81

Radande

Variations: Ra

In Swedish folklore it was believed if a particular tree was growing faster than the others in its proximity this was because the tree was occupied by a type of NATURE SPIRIT known as a radande ("to be able"); their generic or collective name was LOFJERSKOR. Similar to the dryad (a nymph of the forests and trees, particularly oak trees) and hamadryads (the nymphs of oak trees) of Greek mythology, the invisible radande lived in the tree and tended to its health and prosperity; it was especially fond of lime trees. The radande would punish anyone who caused any harm to a tree under its protection but the fairy could not travel beyond the shadow of the tree. In Westmanland there was once a pine tree growing out from a boulder said to be under the protection of a MERMAID who acted as its radande.

Source: Hastings, *Encyclopedia of Religion and Ethics*, Part 1, 23; Porteous, *Forest in Folklore and Mythology*, 189; Rose, *Spirits, Fairies, Leprechauns, and Goblins, an Encyclopedia*, 273; Thorpe, *Northern Mythology*, Volume 2, 71

Raghava

A NAGARAJA from Hindu mythology, Raghava was one of the many NAGA mentioned only by name in Vedic mythology.

Source: Vogel, *Indian Serpent-Lore*, 191

Rahab

Variations: Rager

A SEA SERPENT mentioned in the Judaic and Christian bible, Rahab was described as being a gigantic and powerful force of primordial chaos. He was defeated when God dried up the waters of the Great Abyss and dealt the creature a fatal blow; then the body of Rahab was hacked into pieces.

Source: Ogden, *Drakon*, 14; Zell-Ravenheart, *Wizard's Bestiary*, 81

Raicho

A THUNDERBIRD from Japanese mythology, pine-dwelling Raicho ("thunder bird") is the companion animal to god of thunder, Raiden. Described as resembling a rook, it also has spurs of flesh which when they grind together, make a terrible sound. It is said it is often sighted flying through the sky during storms.

Source: Andrews, *Dictionary of Nature Myths*, 230; Rose, *Giants, Monsters, and Dragons*, 305; Skyes, *Who's Who in Non-Classical Mythology*, 163

Raiju

Companion of Raijin, Shinto god of lightning, the raiju ("thunder animal" or "thunder beast") is a demonic creature in Japanese demonology. A demon of lightning, a raiju is described as looking like a cat, badger, ball of fire, ball of lightning, monkey, TANUKI (Japanese raccoon dog), weasel, a white and blue wolf, and a wolf wrapped in lightning (its body is made of lightning and its cry sounds like thunder).

Attacking only during thunderstorms, the raiju is normally calm and harmless, but if it falls asleep in its favorite place, inside a person's navel, Raiden, god of thunder and lightning, will shoot bolts at it to wake it up, usually killing the person. These creatures become extremely agitated during thunderstorms, jumping from tree to tree. Lightning strikes on trees and houses are said to be the claw marks of the raiju.

Source: Ashkenazi, *Handbook of Japanese Mythology*, 276; Chopra, *Academic Dictionary of Mythology*, 243; Hearn, *Glimpses of Unfamiliar Japan*, 116; Littleton, *Gods, Goddesses, and Mythology*, Volume 1, 406; Smith, *Complete Idiot's Guide to World Mythology*, 280

Rain Bird

Variations: Rainbird, Shang Yang, Shang Yung

In Chinese folklore the rain bird is said to be a gigantic one legged bird which draws water up from the river with its long and thin beak and then blows it out as the rain; it is still a common custom for farmers to call upon it to water their fields.

Source: Rosen, *Mythical Creatures Bible*, 164–5; Werner, *Myths and Legends of China*, n.pag.; Zell-Ravenheart, *Wizard's Bestiary*, 987–8

Rainbow Crow

In Lenape mythology the crow was once a magnificently colored bird with a beautiful voice; when the Snow Spirit appeared in the world all the animals and people began to freeze to death, unprepared and unable to survive in the new element. Crow was chosen to speak for everyone and to go ask Kijilamuh Ka'ong ("the creator who creates by thinking what will be") to make it warm again. For three days Crow flew upward and when he finally came upon the god, eloquently delivered the request. Kijilamuh Ka'ong said he was unable to return the world to the warm and pleasant place it once was, as he had already thought of the cold and could not undo his creation, but he did imagine and create fire. He placed it on a stick and told Crow to quickly return to the earth with it, as it burned and would only last so long as there was stick left to consume. Crow flew as quickly as he could to save the world; the flames permanently blackened his feathers and the flames and heat scorched his throat, but he was successful and delivered fire to the people. Although he was disfigured, Crow was considered a hero and shown respect.

Source: Hitakonanulaxk, *Grandfathers Speak*, 73–4; Hurst, *Once Upon A Time*, 172–3

Rainbow Serpent

Variations: Aido Hwedo, Bobi-Bobi, Bolung, Bulanj, Degei, Dhakhan of the Kabi, Galeru, Kaleru, Kunmanngur, Jarapiri, Julunggul, Karia, Kunmanngurr, Langal, Maiangara, Mindi, Muti, Ngalbjod, Pulang, Pullangi, Pullanj, Purlanj, Purling, Rainbow Monster, Rainbow Snake, Taipan, Ungur, Wanambi, Woinunggur, Wollunquain, Wondzad, Worombi, Wulungen, Wulungu, Yero, Yulunggu

The snake is associated with rainbows in a supernatural fashion in many different cultures, particularly in Australia, the Congo, Dahomey (Benin), Haiti, Melanesia, and Papua New Guinea; of all these, it is most prevalent in the Dreamtime mythology of the Australian Aboriginal people.

Generally described as a gigantic, python-like snake, the Rainbow Serpent, sometimes considered to be an ANCESTOR SPIRIT, is associated with freshwater billabongs, lakes, and pools. They sleep in the deep mud during the dry season and when awake

create channels, gullies, and riverbeds as they crawl along the surface. Unless their rest during the dry season is disturbed they are generally benign toward humans; if disturbed they will consume the offender and possibly cause great flooding when the rains come. Rainbow Serpents hate blood but are fascinated by anything iridescent, such as pearls.

In the Australian myths, the male rainbow serpent is called Ngalyod and is the transformer of the land while the female is named Yingarna and is considered to be the mother of all life—animals, humans, and plants. Droughts, floods, and storms are sent by the pair as a means of punishment.

Source: Buchler, *Rainbow Serpent*, 4, 102; Eason, *Fabulous Creatures, Mythical Monsters, and Animal Power Symbols*, 22; Rose, *Giants, Monsters, and Dragons*, 305; Zell-Ravenheart, *Wizard's Bestiary*, 81

Raja Naga

The largest of the water serpents of Hindu mythology, the Raja Naga ("king of the serpents") is said to be the largest of the DRAGONS of the sea; he resides in a magnificent palace beneath the waves called Pusat Tasik.

Source: Jones, *Instinct for Dragons*, 166; Ogden, *Drakon*, 244; Rose, *Giants, Monsters, and Dragons*, 306

Rakhsh

The blue-eyed, rose-colored, lightly dappled mare belonging to the hero Roostem (Rustam), Rakhsh was said to have vision so keen and sharp it could see an ant's footprint upon a black cloak two leagues away. Only Roostem was able to ride Rakhsh as only she was strong and large enough to carry his size and weight; she and the intelligent animal were close companions and shared many adventures together. The price he had to pay for her purchase was to restore justice to Iran.

Source: Johns, *Horses*, 80; Renard, *Islam and the Heroic Image*, 208

Rakshasas

Variations: Ramayana, Reksoso

In the branch of Hinduism practiced in India there is a vampiric race of demonic KRAVYAD known as the rakshasas; they were created by Brahma to protect the ocean from those who sought to steal the secret Elixir of Immortality. These demons are part human and part animal, but the human-to-animal ratio varies widely depending on the source being cited. Most often the animal hybrids are said to be tiger. The *Vedas*, a Hindu religious text, describes the beings as having five legs and a body completely covered in blood. Modern descriptions of rakshasas add they have fangs and the ability to use magic.

When not protecting the Elixir of Immortality, the rakshasas are said to live in the treetops; however, they will often wander in cemeteries where they will disrupt services and religious incantations. When hunting for humans to feed upon, the male of the species will stay up in the treetops and wait for its favorite prey to pass underneath: infants or pregnant women. Then, the rakshasas will vomit down onto them, killing them. Female rakshasas, called rakshasis, have the ability to shape-shift into beautiful women, and in such a guise will lure men off to a discreet location in order to attack them, draining them of their blood.

There is a belief if a child can be persuaded to eat human brains, it will transform into this vampiric creature. A type of sorcerer is said to exist which follows the rakshasas' activities closely, as they will consume the uneaten remains of a rakshasa's kill. This act is called *yatu-dhana*.

Rakshasas can be killed if an exorcism is performed on them, but prolonged exposure to sunlight and burning them to ash work as well.

Source: Crooke, *Introduction to the Popular Religion*, 124, 154–58, 234, 320; Curran, *Vampires*, 137; Hyatt, *Book of Demons*, 15, 20, 22; Knapp, *Machine, Metaphor, and the Writer*, 161–62, 171; Walker, *Hindu World*, 277, 280, 292

Rataosk (Rat-at-awsk)

Variations: Ratatosk

Rataosk ("boar tooth" or "swift tusked") of Norse mythology lived in the ash-tree Ygdrasil and spent his days running the length of its trunk carrying hateful gossip and inciting words between EGOIR the eagle in the upper branches and the DRAGON of Death, NIDHOGG, who lived among its roots below. Traveling easily between the two worlds, Rataosk is said to be the personification of the destroying and life-giving elements.

Source: Bellows, *Poetic Edda*, 97; Jennbert, *Animals and Humans*, 50; Lindow, *Norse Mythology*, 259; Oehlenschläger, *Gods of the North*, lx

Raudr

Raudr ("red") was one of the oxen named in Thorgrimr's *Rhymes* and in Snorri Sturluson's (1179–1241) *Prose Edda* belonging to Gefjun; in truth they were her sons by an unnamed JOTUN. The siblings of Raudr were named HOEFIR, HYRR, and REKINNI.

Source: Grimes, *Norse Myths*, 278; Sturluson, *Prose Edda*, Volume 5, 213

Rawhead

Variations: Tommy Rawhead

From the folklore of England and the United States of America, Rawhead and his companion, BLOODY-BONES, were often used as NURSERY BOGIES by parents to trick children into good behavior or for avoiding a certain activity or area, whichever was appropriate. Rawhead was said to dwell in bogs and ponds as well as in little used cabinets and under stairs. Exceedingly ugly and with a continuous flow of blood drooling from his mouth, Rawhead sits atop a pile of bones waiting for his next prey.

Source: Brewer, *Reader's Handbook of Famous Names in Fiction*, 129; Monaghan, *Encyclopedia of Celtic Mythology and Folklore*, 450; Wright, *Rustic Speech and Folk-Lore*, 198

Redjal el Marja

In Moroccan folklore the djinn (a race of demons) known collectively as the redjal el marja ("men of the marshes") originally were said to inhabit the marshland outside the city of Marrakech; however, when the marshes were drained the djinn moved into the canals and fountains supplying the city with water. To ensure the redjal el marja do not contaminate the water supply or taint it in any way they are shown respect by the lighting of votive candles called *saait redjal el marja*.

Source: Legey, *Folklore of Morocco*, 73–4; Rose, *Spirits, Fairies, Leprechauns, and Goblins, an Encyclopedia*, 275

Re'em

Variations: Karakadan, Reem, Urus

In the Septuagint, a Greek translation of the Torah commissioned by Ptolemy Philadelphus (283–47 BC), the phrase *"he has fought the to'afos of a re'em"* had been translated to *"he has fought the glory of a monokeros,"* an animal with an alicorn (a single horn), which some scholars interpret to mean a re'em is a species of UNICORN. Since this original translation, the words have become entangled and appear in many translations as UNICORN. Traditionally the re'em is said to be a gigantic creature, once mistaken for a mountain by a young King David when he was a shepherd boy. Psalms 22:22 recounts the story of how he escaped both a lion and a re'em.

The species of these gigantic beasts consists of only one male and one female each living on opposite ends of the world; every seventy years the two unite in order to mate. During copulation the female gives the male an infectious bite, killing it. After twelve years of pregnancy, the stomach of the female bursts open, killing it and birthing a set of twins, one male and one female, who immediately set off to wander opposite ends of the earth.

Source: Isaacs, *Animals in Jewish Thought and Tradition*, 181; Schwartz, *Tree of Souls*, 148; Slifkin, *Sacred Monsters*, 45–5; Zell-Ravenheart, *Wizard's Bestiary*, 81

Regenmöhme

A NURSERY BOGIE from German folklore, the Regenmöhme ("with her heat") from the historic region of Altmark is said to abduct noisy children with her long, black, and hot arms.

Source: Grimm, *Grimms Sagen*, 102

Reiko

In Japanese folklore a reiko ("ghost fox") is a powerful fox spirit (KITSUNE); as it can cause hauntings and possessions, it is sometimes referred to as a demonic creature.

Source: Maberry, *Vampire Universe*, 177, 178; Picken, *Essentials of Shinto*, 124

Rekinni

Variations: Rekinn

Rekinni ("driven") was one of the oxen named in Thorgrimr's *Rhymes* and in Snorri Sturluson's (1179–1241) *Prose Edda* belonging to Gefjun; in truth they were her sons by an unnamed JOTUN. The siblings of Rekinni were named HOEFIR, HYRR, and RAUDR.

Source: Grimes, *Norse Myths*, 278; Sturluson, *Prose Edda*, Volume 5, 213

Reksh

In Persian folklore, Reksh was the brave and strong horse of the cultural hero Roostem (Rustam); out of fifty thousand horses, only Reksh was capable of carrying the weight of Roostem and was given as much acclaim as his noble rider. In one story, as Roostem slept in a meadow Reksh was sent to graze. A lion approached and attacked the horse thinking it an easy meal but the horse fought the lion blow for blow and struck it in the head with its forelegs and grabbed it up by its throat with its teeth, slaying the lion. Roostem chided the animal for not awaking him and attacking the lion on his own. Later when a gigantic serpent crept up on Roostem one night Reksh, remembering his master's words, neighed loudly to wake the hero with enough time for him to arise, arm and armor himself, and then easily slay the creature; however the snake ran off leaving a very annoyed Roostem thinking his horse woke him to be spiteful. When the serpent returned Reksh, fearful his master would kill him if again aroused, attacked the creature. The ensuing battle awoke Reksh who quickly joined the fray and slew the gigantic serpent.

Source: Brewer, *Wordsworth Dictionary of Phrase and Fable*, 567; Keightley, *World Guide to Gnomes, Fairies, Elves, and Other Little People*, 18; Malcolm, *Sketches of Persia*, Volume 1, 154, 157–8

Remora

According to Pliny the Elder, the Roman author and natural philosopher, the remora ("delay") was a species of small fish which had the ability to command the wind; by use of its ability, it was powerful enough to cause a ship to stop moving. Physical descriptions of these creatures vary widely; the one said to have delayed the fleet of Caligula was described as being rather like a large slug and a psychopomp (death omen) while other travelers say it was more Piscean and had a wide, flat tail. In ancient Greece its image was used on amulets to prevent premature deliveries as well as to facilitate childbirth.

Source: Barber, *Dictionary of Fabulous Beasts*, 124; Finger, *Shocking History of Electric Fishes*, 40; Kingshill, *Fabled Coast*, n.pag.

Rerek

According to ancient Egyptian mythology Rerek was the monstrous serpent form taken by the god of evil and darkness, Set, in order to oppose the sun god Ra. Daily, as Rerek, Set would attempt to oppose Ra from appearing in the east. Rerek, seven cubits long and capable of breathing fire, was identified with the great serpent APOPHIS (a cubit is the distance from a man's elbow to the tip of his middle finger).

Source: Mercatante, *Who's Who in Egyptian Mythology*, 132; Von Dassow, *Egyptian Book of the Dead*, 122

Revenant (Rev-a-nint)

The word *revenant*, a variation of the French word *revenir* ("to return"), simply means "one who has returned after death or a long absence." It is used in vampiric folklore to describe any being or creature which has died, risen up from its grave, and returned to a kind of "unlife" or undeath as it is more popularly called, among the living. Not all revenants are vampires, although many types of vampires are revenants.

Source: Ashley, *Complete Book of Vampires*; Barber, *Vampires, Burial, and Death*, 85; Day, *Vampires*, 194

Rhoetus, CENTAUR

Variations: Rhoecus

In Greek mythology Rhoetus was the name of one of the CENTAURS who, according to Ovid's *Metamorphoses*, attended the wedding of Pirithous, became drunk on wine and following the lead of EURYTUS, who assaulted Hippodame, began to assault and rape any women they could grab. During the ensuing Centauromachy, Rhoetus was the second fiercest combatant of the battle; only EURYTUS fought more savagely. Rhoetus was wounded by the hero and the Lapith soldier Dryas with a burning post stabbed between his neck and shoulders; as Rhoetus fell in combat the other CENTAURS were so stunned Dryas was able to press the attack and kill five more in rapid succession as they stood nearly helpless in their bewilderment.

Source: Lemprière, *Bibliotheca Classica*, 694; Rose, *Giants, Monsters, and Dragons*, 311; Schwab, *Gods and Heroes of Ancient Greece*, 220

Rhoetus, GIANTE

Variations: Eurytus

In Greek mythology Rhoetus was a GIANTE who during the Gigantomachy attempted to climb up Mount Olympus; he was thwarted by the god Bacchus (Dionysos) who shape-shifted into a lion and tore out his throat.

Source: Anthon, *Classical Dictionary*, 250; Coulter, *Encyclopedia of Ancient Deities*, 469; Rose, *Giants, Monsters, and Dragons*, 311

Ri Riu

Variations: Ri-Ryu

A species of DRAGON from Japanese mythology, ri riu were said to be able to see for more than one hundred miles with perfect clarity; they are well known for their exceptional sight. The ri-ryu also have wings and the ability to fly when they reach full maturity.

Ri Riu is also the name of one of the four DRAGON KINGS, HAN RIU, KA-RIU, and SUI RIU being the other three.

Source: Bates, *All About Chinese Dragons*, 100; De Kirk, *Dragonlore*, 31; Ingersoll, *Dragons and Dragon Lore*, 104; Johnsgard, *Dragons and Unicorns*, 18

The Righteous Ass

The white-coated Righteous Ass from Zoroastrian mythology was described as being as large as a mountain, having a golden alicorn (single horn) protruding from the center of its forehead, nine mouths, six eyes, and treelike legs each foot of which was large enough to cover an area which could hold one thousand sheep. Standing in the middle of the Vourukasha sea, it destroyed all harmful sea creatures and protected the Tree of All Seeds.

Source: Hopkins, *History of Religions*, 387; Warner, *World of Myths*: Volume Two, 98

Rigi

In Nauruan mythology Rigi the caterpillar (or eel, grub, or worm) happened along the primordial spider AREOP ENAP who had been caught in a clam shell; using his magic AREOP ENAP gave Rigi the temporary ability to be incredibly strong so he could force the clam to open. During the process, Rigi sweated so much salty water the clam was forced to open up or die. Unfortunately Rigi died from exhaustion immediately following the rescue; AREOP ENAP wrapped up the body of his savior and hung it from the sky, creating the Milky Way.

Source: Bartlett, *Mythology Bible*, 176; Coulter, *Encyclopedia of Ancient Deities*, 404; Dixion, *Oceanic*, 250; Zell-Ravenheart, *Wizard's Bestiary*, 81

Rimau Jadi-Jadian

Variations: Harimau Jadi-Jadian ("made-up tiger")

A type of were-tiger from the Malay Peninsula, the rimau jadi-jadian ("tiger imitation") can transform only on clear nights beneath the light of the moon. It is believed these were-tigers spend much of their time buried in a grave, and when they are ready to emerge, burst forth in the form of a wild boar. It is believed those who are descendants of tigers or are were-tigers have a distinguishing mark on their toenails or are lacking a philtrum.

Source: Newman, *Tracking the Weretiger*, 102; Skeat, *Malay Magic*, 188–9

Riphens

A CENTAUR from ancient Greek mythology, Riphens was one of his kind who attended the wedding of Pirithous, became drunk on wine, and following the lead of EURYTUS, who assaulted Hippodame, began to assault and rape any women they could grab. A great Centauromachy then followed and Riphens was slain by Theseus.

Source: *Commentary, Mythological, Historical, and Geographical on Pope's Homer*, 55; Lemprière, *Classical Dictionary*, 532

Roc

Variations: Anka, Akra, Anqa, Anqua, Bird of Immortality, Pyong, Rok, Ruc, Rucke, Rukh, Rukhkh, Samru, Sinurgh

A gigantic predatory bird from Persian folklore, the roc, one of the KHRAFSTRA, was popularized by its appearance in the tale translated by Richard Burton (1829–1890) *One-Thousand and One Arabian Nights*; in the tale, Sinbad the Sailor was taken by one back to its nest, but was able to escape. Similar to the ANQA, NGANI-VATU, and the POUA-KAI, the roc is described as looking much like an eagle or vulture, being bulky, horns upon its head, and having overly wide wings so broad they can block out the sun as it passes overhead; sometimes it is also said the roc is part lion or has leonine features. The roc is large enough it can easily swoop down and snatch up an adult elephant to bring back to its nest to feed to its young. The Venetian merchant traveler Marco Polo (1254–1324) claimed to have personally seen a feather from this creature while staying at the court of Kublai Khan; he believed the roc to be a native animal of the island of Madagascar.

Source: Rose, *Giants, Monsters, and Dragons*, 312; Skyes, *Who's Who in Non-Classical Mythology*, 166

Rogo-Tumu-Here

Rogo-Tumu-Here is a demonic creature from Hawaiian mythology. While Turi-a-faumea and his wife, Hina-arau-riki, were surfing, Rogo-Tumu-Here grabbed Hina and fled to the bottom of the ocean (see SEA SERPENT). Tangaroa, a Polynesian god, built Turi a canoe, which they used to sail out over Rogo's home. Baiting a hook with sacred red feathers, they caught the demon and pulled him on the boat, cutting off his tentacles one at a time, until Tangaroa beheaded him, releasing Hina in a font of slime.

Source: Beckwith, *Hawaiian Mythology*, 268; Turner, *Dictionary of Ancient Deities*, 178

Roikos

Variations: Rhoecus, Rhoikos

In Greek mythology Roikos and fellow CENTAUR HYLAIOS became drunk one evening and were aroused by the beauty of Atalanta; they attempted to rape her but she noticed the light of their torches as they approached, and slew them both with her bow and arrows.

Source: Colvin, *Cornhill Magazine*, Volume XXXVIII, 296; *Commentary, Mythological, Historical, and Geographical on Pope's Homer*, 55; Fontenrose, *Orion*, 178–9; Hard, *Routledge Handbook of Greek Mythology*, 545

Rokuro-Kubi (ROH-koo-roh koo-bee)

Variations: Rokurokubi

Rokuro-kubi ("flying head woman," "long necked woman," and "snake-necked woman") are a species of demonic creatures in Japanese demonology. Thought to have once been humans, through an act of karma they were transformed for their transgressions into this species of YŌKAI. Usually appearing as human females by day, at night their faces become horrific and their necks stretch to great lengths or, in some cases, detach from their bodies. Who a rokuro-kubi preys upon varies upon the individual creature's preference; some attack those who broke a particular Buddhist doctrine while others only attack men. At night, the rokuro-kubi's neck elongates or detaches from the body, allowing it to spy on its prey before attacking. As it flies it makes the traditional ghost laughing sound of *kèta-kèta!*

Tricksters by nature, they are compelled to frighten and spy on humans; these demons feed off life energy and drink lamp oil. Some rokuro-kubi

live as humans, keeping their demonic nature a secret. Some revel in their nature, and others are not even aware they are anything other than human.

Source: Hearn, *Kwaidan*, 81–100; Hearn, *Oriental Ghost Stories*, 63–72; Hearn, *Romance of the Milky Way*, 36–7; Japan Society of London, *Transactions and Proceedings of the Japan Society, London*, Volume 9, 33–4; Yoda, *Yokai Attack*, 142–6

Rolling Calf

In Jamaican folklore a rolling calf is a species of DUPPY said to haunt hillsides and lonely, out-of-the-way locales in order to terrorize travelers. Described as looking like a bovine calf with fiery eyes and accompanied by the sound of rattling chains, the rolling calf will chase its prey and if caught, the person will be killed and transformed into a rolling calf themselves. Typically, however, a rolling calf is created when a man dies who is too good for Hell but not fit for Heaven; he is transformed into this type of creature. The only way to escape one of their attacks should it chase you is to run uphill, as they are unable to follow; rolling calves are also afraid of the moon.

Source: American Folklore Society, in *Journal of American Folklore*, Volume 7, 296–7; Spinner, *Living Age*, Volume 206, 161

Rompo

In the folklore of Africa and India lives a species of creature known as the rompo ("man eater"); a scavenger by nature, it lives largely off of the bodies of deceased humans, digging its meal up from a grave if it must. When it happens upon a corpse, the forest-dwelling rompo will not rush in to consume it but rather circle it several times as if it is fearful to approach. The rompo is a chimerical creature, described as being about three feet long, not including the tail, and having badger-like forelegs, ursine (bearlike) hindquarters, head and mouth like a hare, human ears, and a horse's mane.

Source: Barber, *Dictionary of Fabulous Beasts*, 126; Drury, *Dictionary of the Esoteric*, 270; Hulme, *Myth-land*, 12

Rồng

Variations: Long, Ryong

A species of DRAGON in Vietnamese folklore, the chimerical rồng is said to have the features of a bird, crocodile, lizard, and snake; it is an important and sacred symbol as well as representative of the king, reflective of his power and the prosperity of the nation. As an imperial DRAGON, it has five toes. Similar to Chinese DRAGONS, the rồng are able to bring the rain and like all species of Vietnamese DRAGONS the rồng can breathe fire and has wings.

Source: Bates, *All About Chinese Dragons*, 98

Roperite

Originating in the lumberjack communities of the developing United States of America, the roperite, one of the species of FEARSOME CRITTERS, was described as being about the size of a horse but having a long, prehensile muzzle it used like a lariat in order to lasso its usual prey, rabbits, although there are some tales of it catching the occasional lumberjack and running off, dragging its prey behind through thorny chaparral until they are dead. There is no animal fast enough to outrun a roperite and no obstacle it cannot go around, over, or through. Some stories of these creatures also describe rattles growing in their tail, making a sound very much like a rattlesnake. When the roperite is on the hunt, it makes its tail rattle.

Source: Barber, *Dictionary of Fabulous Beasts*, 126; Cox, *Fearsome Creatures of the Lumberwoods*, 13; Rose, *Giants, Monsters, and Dragons*, 313

Roshwalr

Variations: Cetus Dentatus, Horse-Whale, Ruszor

A SEA SERPENT from Norwegian folklore, the roshwalr is described as having the smooth and vast body of a whale with the head of a huge horse. The severed head of one of these creatures was supposedly given to Pope Leo X in 1520; it eventually made its way to naturalist Ambroise Paré (1510–1590), the author of *On Monsters and Marvels*.

Source: Meurger, *Lake Monster Traditions*, 307, 318; Rose, *Giants, Monsters, and Dragons*, 313

Rou Shou

Variations: Ru Shou

Two of China's cosmic DRAGONS, GOU MANG and Rou Shou, are also messengers to the gods. Rou Shou is a TI-EN LUNG DRAGON and brings with it bad luck as it is also the herald for the coming of Fall and is associated with the west.

Source: De Kirk, *Dragonlore* 26; Lurker, *Dictionary of Gods and Goddesses, Devils and Demons*, 70; Rose, *Giants, Monsters, and Dragons*, 150

Rubberado

Originating in the lumberjack communities of the developing United States of America, the rubberado, one of the FEARSOME CRITTERS, was a species of porcupine with rubber-like quills covering its body; it bounced around the countryside. The flesh of the rubberado was also rubber-like and once cooked it was uneatable, as teeth could not bear down into it to take a bite.

Source: Rose, *Giants, Monsters, and Dragons*, 314

Rumptifusel

Originating in the lumberjack communities of the developing United States of America, the rumptifusel, one of the FEARSOME CRITTERS, was described as having a long, thin body covered with dense fur. These creatures were in the habit of winding their body around the base of a tree when going to sleep; when a woodsman would happen upon one, unless he knew better, he would mistake the rumptifusel for a mink coat, pick it up and attempt to put it on. Naturally, when this occurred the animal would viciously attack the person.

Source: Binney, *Nature's Ways*, 225; Godfrey, *Monsters of Wisconsin*, 131; Mencken, *American Language Supplement 1*, 250; Rose, *Giants, Monsters, and Dragons*, 315

Rurū

In Hindu mythology there is a class of beings known as the rurū who dwell in the various hells where they punish people according to their sins; for instance in the hell known as Rungnir the rurū are in the form of snakes and punish those who in life committed violent acts driven by envy. In the hell known as Maharaurava the rurū are carnivorous, black deer called KRAVYADA and torment those who in life maintained themselves by causing bodily harm to others.

Source: Knapp, *Secret Teachings of The Vedas*, n.pag.; Venkatesananda, *Concise Srimad Bhagavatam*, 142

Ryo-Wo

A DRAGON KING from Japanese mythology, Ryo-wo has dominion over the Tidal Jewels, said to control the tides of the world. Ryo-Wo is also said to have been the one who gave the jellyfish its shape; his palace, called Ryugu ("DRAGON palace"), is located beneath the sea.

Source: De Kirk, *Dragonlore*, 31; De Visser, *Dragon in China and Japan*, 142

Ryujin

Variations: Rinjin, Ryujin the DRAGON God

One of the DRAGON KINGS from Japanese mythology, Ryujin was a gigantic being; his mouth could open wide enough to swallow large ships and whales whole and when it did open, it created whirlpools on the ocean's surface. His claws, horns, scales, and tongue were all a beautiful shade of deep blue. It was believed no human could look upon Ryunin in his full majesty and survive the experience. In addition to having magical jewels which allowed him to control the weather, he, like most DRAGONS, had the ability to shape-shift into human form (see DRAGON, ORIENTAL). In his human guise Ryujin was able to mate with human women and fathered many children; one of his daughters was the mother of Japan's first emperor.

Living in a magnificent bejeweled palace made of red coral located on the bottom of the sea, Ryujin's home had four great halls, each one devoted to one of the four seasons. The autumn hall was the color of maple leaves, spring was lined with blooming cherry blossom trees in full bloom, summer had the melodic sound of chirping crickets, and winter was decked out in all white. Time moved differently in the palace; one hundred years would pass on the surface for each day spent within it.

Source: Andrews, *Dictionary of Nature Myths*, 165; Barber, *Dictionary of Fabulous Beasts*, 125; Niles, *Dragons*, 77–8; Rose, *Giants, Monsters, and Dragons*, 312

Sa-Yin

Variations: Master of the Fishes

A lake monster from Bolivian folklore, the sa-yin is said to live in the waters in the region of Gran Chaco, Cordillera, Bolivia (see SEA SERPENT). Its description varies; sometimes it is said to look like a man with long black hair riding a horse through the water, or a knight in armor astride a charger riding through the water, and on occasion it has even been described as being a CENTAUR.

Source: Meurger, *Lake Monster Traditions*, 132; Rose, *Giants, Monsters, and Dragons*, 322

Saa-Set

According to ancient Egyptian mythology Saa-Set was depicted as a gigantic serpent standing upon its tail; it was a guardian in the first section of Tuat, the Underworld. In *The Text of Unas* there is a magical spell which when performed will cause the destruction of monstrous beasts and serpents alike; Saa-Set would be affected by this spell.

Source: Coulter, *Encyclopedia of Ancient Deities*, 32, 408; Mercatante, *Who's Who in Egyptian Mythology*, 135

Saapin

From East Indian folklore, the saapin spends much of the year living among humans in society in the guise of a human with a tattoo of a cobra down its back or thigh. Over the course of its life, it will have up to seven different lovers. During certain times of the year, and only when the moon is properly aligned and full, the tattoo will come alive and transform into a NAGA-like or DRACAENAE-like creature, having the upper body of a human and the lower body of a snake. It uses the opportunity to bite its current lover while they are asleep and thereby marking it for death. Some days later, the lover will die in an accident in such a way suspicion will not be cast on the saapin.

Source: Leid, *Myths and Maxims*, n.pag.

Sadhuzag

Depicted in medieval bestiaries, the sadhuzag is a hybrid creature, having the body of a deer or stag and the head of a goat. Atop its head and over its body are seventy-four flutelike horns which can create either a melodious call when it faces into the south wind or a fearsome bellow dreadful enough to strike fear in the heart of man when it faces the north wind.

Source: Flaubert, *Temptation of Saint Anthony*, 244; Rose, *Giants, Monsters, and Dragons*, 317; Zell-Ravenheart, *Wizard's Bestiary*, 83

Saehrimnir (SAI-reem-nir)

Variations: Saehrímnir, Saehrimner

Saehrimnir ("sooty black sea beast") was one of the boars or pigs named in Thorgrimr's *Rhymes* and in Snorri Sturluson's (1179–1241) *Prose Edda*. According to Norse mythology Saehrimnir was slain each morning so its flesh could provide the daily food for the *Einherjar* of Valhalla; then at night, it would reform and revive.

Source: Barber, *Dictionary of Fabulous Beasts*, 126; Jennbert, *Animals and Humans*, 49; Norroena Society, *Asatru Edda*, 382; Oehlenschläger, *Gods of the North*, lx

Saena

Variations: SEEMURG, Sena Meregha, Senamurv, Simurgh

In Persian folklore the saena is a gigantic falcon which perched upon the Tree of All Seeds growing in the middle of the Vourukasa sea; the weight of the creature and the flapping of its wings caused the branches to break and shake as well as the seeds to fall and catch in the wind. This bird, able to suckle its young, found, adopted, and raised the hero Zal, who had been abandoned in his infancy, as one of its own.

Source: Boyce, *History of Zoroastrianism*, 89; Warner, *World of Myths: Volume Two*, 95

Safat

A species of DRAGON from medieval bestiary folklore, the safats were described as having serpentine bodies and wings, but a draconian head; living in the upper heavens, located above the clouds, the safat were rarely seen on the ground.

Source: Hargreaves, *Hargreaves New Illustrated Bestiary*, 38; McCutcheon, *Wordsworth Word Finder*, 416; Rose, *Giants, Monsters, and Dragons*, 317

Sahab

First described in the sixteenth century by Catholic ecclesiastic and Swedish writer Olaus Magnus, the sahab was a sea creature living off of the Norwegian coast in the North Sea (see SEA SER-

PENT). Proposed to be amphibious in nature as it seemed able to breathe both above and below water, it had a blow hole and a huge body. Its most interesting features were its feet, as three of its legs were like those of a cow but the fourth was overly long and used to feed itself.

Source: Barber, *Dictionary of Fabulous Beasts*, 127; Rose, *Giants, Monsters, and Dragons*, 317; Zell-Ravenheart, *Wizard's Bestiary*, 83

Saint Attracta's Monster

A SEA SERPENT from Irish folklore, Saint Attracta's Monster was described as being a chimerical creature, having boar tusks, fiery eyes, horse mane, iron claws, ram ears, the roar of a lion, a single eye in its forehead, and the tail of a whale. It lived on the island of Inis Cathaig (Scattery Island) in the Shannon river estuary and would make fires by scraping its claws along the rocks. The creature was banished in the sixth century by a bishop who had established a monastery upon the island but the monster was named for Saint Attracta who had founded a local safe house for travelers.

Source: Rose, *Giants, Monsters, and Dragons*, 318; Zell-Ravenheart, *Wizard's Bestiary*, 83

Sak

Appearing in the seventeenth dynasty, the sak of ancient Egyptian mythology was depicted as a chimerical creature combining the head of a hawk, the body of a lion, hindquarters of a horse, numerous triangular *mamelles*, and the tail as a fully bloomed lotus. The sak was always female and had the ability to produce new monsters as horrid as itself, a trait most unusual in hybrids.

Source: Bonwick, *Egyptian Belief and Modern Thought*, 235; Wilkinson, *Manners and Customs of the Ancient Egyptians*, Volume 3, 312

Salamander

Variations: Dea, Salamandra, Stellio

The hermetic and neo-Platonic doctrine from which all medieval medicine and science were founded describes four Elemental classes, Air, Earth, Fire, and Water; accordingly the Salamanders belong to the Fire class, GNOMES to Earth, nereids (golden-haired sea nymphs) to Water, and slyphs to Air. Salamanders look exactly like the amphibians they are named after and were believed to be powerful beings; they were well aware of their own value to magicians and are considered to be supreme in the elemental hierarchies.

Source: Briggs, *Encyclopedia of Fairies*, 192–3; McCoy, *Witch's Guide to Faery Folk*, 304; Rose, *Spirits, Fairies, Leprechauns, and Goblins*, 282; Stepanich, *Faery Wicca*, Book One, 31

Samebito

A fierce, black skinned, green-eyed monster from Japanese folklore, Samebito ("shark man") had been so evil he was banished from the ocean by the sea king. Weak and homeless, Samebito wandered aimlessly and eventually came to a bridge where he met the hero Totaro. Rather than fighting the hero, as he would have been prone to do in the past, Samebito begged Totaro for food. Taking great pity on the creature, the hero allowed Samebito to follow him back to his palace and permitted him to live in a lake on his property. Samebito was very content with his new fortune and eventually grew healthy again. One day he learned the news Totaro had fallen ill because he so much wanted to marry a beautiful princess but her father demanded 10,000 precious gems, far too high a bride price for anyone to pay, especially Totaro. Samebito went to see his master and began to weep bloody tears when he realized his savior was dying. As each tear fell upon the bedchamber floor it turned into a precious ruby. Discovering he would soon be able to collect the jewels, Totaro's health instantly began to recover and after thanking his friend, collected up the gems to have delivered to the father of his soon-to-be bride.

Source: Davis, *Myths and Legends of Japan*, 376–8; Roberts, *Japanese Mythology A to Z*, 100–101; Rose, *Giants, Monsters, and Dragons*, 318; Zell-Ravenheart, *Wizard's Bestiary*, 83

Samjogo

In Korean folklore Samjogo ("crow") is the name of its three-legged bird; its image is considered to be a symbol of power, superior to even the DRAGON and the PHOENIX.

Source: Rosen, *Mythical Creatures Bible*, 164

Sampaati

Variations: Sampati

One of the two sons of the god GARUDA from Hindu mythology, Sampaati and his brother, JATAYU, were a pair of gigantic vultures; other texts say they were the sons of Aruna and Shyeni.

In his youth, Sampaati, a vulture of unparalleled strength, had lost his wings. One day he and his brother JATAYU set out to confront and defeat Indra. After their success, the two brothers flew too high in the sky and neared the sun; JATAYU began to feel faint so Sampaati flew higher and spread his wings wide to give his brother shade. Although this saved his brother, Sampaati's wings caught fire and he fell, plummeting to earth and landing in the Vidhya mountains. There he met and was nursed back to reasonable health by the sage Nishakara who prophesied on the day Rama and the vanaras came to earth in search of Sita, the wings would grow back. Many years had passed, but eventually, Sampaati and his son Suparshva saw Ravana flying through the sky. Shortly thereafter they met Rama and the vanaras as predicted. Sampaati learned of his brother's death at the hands of Ravana and was eager to enact revenge. His wings grew back and having inherited his father's ability to see clearly for thousands of miles, he flew into the sky and scanned the earth for his brother's murderer. He saw Sita in Lanka and informed Rama of this.

Source: Dalal, *Hinduism*, 357; Wilkins, *Hindu Mythology, Vedic and Purānic*, 159, 382

Samvarta

A gigantic mare from Hindu mythology, Samvarta lives in the ocean and has within her body a great fire raging; in some versions of the myth, there are seven mares, each one living in one of the world's seven oceans. No matter the telling, Samvarta (and possibly the others of her kind) will rise up from the water and bring about the end of the world, spreading their fire globally, consuming everything. Samvarta is one of the KRAVYAD.

Source: Rose, *Giants, Monsters, and Dragons*, 319; Zell-Ravenheart, *Wizard's Bestiary*, 83

Sandhill Perch

Originating in the lumberjack communities of the developing United States of America, the Sandhill perch, one of the FEARSOME CRITTERS, was a species of fish said to reside in waterless areas, such as in dustbowls; in addition to swimming through the air it does so backwards in order to keep the dust and dirt from getting into its eyes.

Source: American Folklore Society, *Journal of American Folk-lore*, Volumes 54–55, 27; Rose, *Giants, Monsters, and Dragons*, 119

Santelmo

Variations: Saint Elmo's fire, Santo Elmo

In Filipino folklore the santelmo is considered by some, especially those living in the Sierra Madre Mountain region, to be a supernatural phenomenon occurring in the night sky. Described as looking like balls of fire, the santelmo are said to be SALAMANDERS in their fiery form; there are also reports of the santelmo being seen flying down seldom used dirt roads and zipping through the dense jungle.

Source: Eugenio, *Philippine Folk Literature*, 407; Licauco, *Dwarves and Other Nature Spirits*, 6

Santer

Originating in the lumberjack communities of the developing United States of America, the santer,

one of the FEARSOME CRITTERS, was most often seen in North Carolina, described as looking like a large cat about the size of a shepherd dog and having a grey coat striped from head to toe.

Source: Eberhart, *Mysterious Creatures*, 472; Rose, *Giants, Monsters, and Dragons*, 119; Zell-Ravenheart, *Wizard's Bestiary*, 306

Sarabha

An extremely fierce creature from Hindu folklore, the sarabha is described as having between one and three horns and either six or eight legs; its body is covered with arrow-like spikes and sometimes it is said to have wings and a second head. The sarabha is so powerful and violent it can easily overcome an elephant or a lion in combat; the only thing this KRAVYAD fears is the clap of thunder.

Source: Brown, *Story of Kālaka*, 82; Garg, *Encyclopaedia of the Hindu World*, 483

Sarama

Variations: The Messenger of Indra, Sarava, Sharama

A female brindle coated dog belonging to the Hindu god Indra, Sarama ("she who walks, runs, or flows") was both the messenger of the god and the protector of his great treasure hidden within a mountain containing cows, horses, and a wide array of various riches. Sarama also sat with Sita while she was being held captive, before her rescue. Sarama was capable of traversing the heavens, swimming through the rivers of Hell, and delighted in hunting and taking down her prey.

Sarama is passionately fond of her two male offspring, Sarameya ("the courser") and Svanau ("the hound"), collectively known as the SARAMEYAS; they share her characteristics and are appointed as guardians of the gates of Hell.

Source: De Gubernatis, *Zoological Mythology*, 19–23; Forlong, *Encyclopedia of Religions*, Volume 3, 251; Zell-Ravenheart, *Wizard's Bestiary*, 88

The Sarameyas

Variations: Sharameyas

In Hindu mythology the Sarameyas, Sarameya ("the courser") and Svanau ("the hound"), are the two sons of SARAMA; these dogs, like their mother, are devoted to the god Indra and were appointed as the guardians of the gates of Hell, ensuring monsters did not escape. Only barking at robbers and thieves, they were silent as the followers of Yama passed them on the road. The brothers were described as having a fierce temperament, four eyes, large lungs, spotted luminous coat (brindle), reddish teeth which shone like spears, vast nostrils, and great strength.

Source: De Gubernatis, *Zoological Mythology*, 19–23; For-long, *Encyclopedia of Religions*, Volume 3, 251; Knappert, *Indian Mythology*, 222

Sarangay

In Ibanag folklore the sarangay is a creature said to resemble a dark and tall anthropoid with a jewel or wooden rings attached to its ear. Coarse, black, thick hair covers its large body; the sarangay lows like a bull as it chases after children.

Source: Ramos, *Creatures of Midnight*, 15

Sardula

Variations: Saravha

In Hindu symbology the sardula is a species of horned leonine; the lion and tiger are interchange-able in art and are the foremost among the animals. Considered to be stronger than a lion, sometimes it is depicted as having eight legs. If the sardula has the head of a lion it is referred to as a *simpha-virala*; if the head is of a man, it is called a *nara-virala*; and if the head is of an elephant it is called a *gaja-virala*. This creature is one of the KRAVYAD.

Source: Garg, *Encyclopaedia of the Hindu World*, 483; Kramrisch, *Hindu Temple*, Volume 2, 333

Sargon

A species of amphibious, horned fish said to lust after nanny goats whenever it goes ashore, it was caught by fishermen who would cover themselves in goat skins. The sargon is the personification of adultery.

Source: Barber, *Dictionary of Fabulous Beasts*, 128;

Sarimanok

In *Filipino* folklore the sarimanok bird is sym-bolic of courage, freedom, and love; there are many stories of it appearing to a person, usually royalty like a young prince or beautiful princess, and then disappearing with them, never to be seen again. In art it is always depicted brightly colored and with a fantastic tail; sometimes it has a fish in its beak.

Source: Halili, *Philippine History*, 55; Rodell, *Culture and Customs of the Philippines*, 218

Sárkánykígyó

Variations: Zomok

A serpentine DRAGON in Hungarian folklore, Sárkánykígyó ("DRAGON") was a gate guardian to an entrance into Fairyland. The folk hero Jancsi (János Vitéz, John the Valiant) slew Sárkánykígyó by jumping into its mouth, traveling down its throat and piercing its heart with his sword.

Source: Cornis-Pope, *History of the Literary Cultures of East-Central Europe*, 45

Sarngika

A species of bird in Hindu folklore, the sarngika was the form assumed by the childless Manda-Pala; as a sarngika he found a mate, a female of the species named JARITA by whom he had four sons: Drona, Jaritari, Sarisrikta, and Stamba-mitra; after the birth of the last, Manda-Pala promptly abandoned his family.

Source: Dowson, *Classical Dictionary of Hindu Mythology and Religion, Geography, History, and Literature*. 197; Gandhi, *Penguin Book of Hindu Names*, 171

Sarva-Bhauma

Variations: Himapandara, Sarvabhavma

One of the DIG-GAJAS from Hindu mythology, Sarva-Bhauma is one of the eight elephant protec-tors of the eight compass points; he guards the north and his mate's name is Tamrakarna.

Source: Dowson, *Classical Dictionary of Hindu Mythology and Religion, Geography, History, and Literature*, 180; Gupta, *Elephant in Indian Art and Mythology*, 7

Sasabonsam (Sa-so-bun-sum)

Variations: Kongamato

In Ashanti folklore there is a vampiric creature called sasabonsam. This bearded man-faced crea-ture stands about five feet tall, has a mouth full of fanged teeth, a row of scaly ridges over its bloodshot eyes, and a small horn which protrudes from the top of its head. Its very long arms are like gigantic bat wings which have a twenty-foot wingspan, its torso is skeletally thin, its legs are permanently bent, and there are three toes on each of its feet. The sasabonsam's body is covered with black and white spots, adding to its camouflage as it sits in the cot-ton tree, dangling its stringy legs below. When a person walks underneath, if the legs are brushed against, it snatches up the person, pulling them into the tree and biting off their head, then drinking up the blood. The belief the sasabonsam lives in cotton trees is prevailing, as can be proven by the great height these trees grow to—everyone is afraid to cut them down.

Sasabonsam are said to be able to cause sickness in a person just by looking at them and are often-times used as a servant by an OBAYIFO.

There is an article which was written in 1939 for *The West African Review* reporting a sasabonsam had been successfully hunted down and killed.

Source: Jahoda, *Psychology of Superstition*, 12; Rattray, *Ashanti Proverbs*, 48; Shuker, *Beasts That Hide from Man*, 103–5; Williams, *Psychic Phenomena of Jamaica*, 16–18

Satyr

Variations: Satry

In Greek mythology, satyrs are a type of NATURE SPIRIT; living in the mountains and woods they were described as having the upper half of a man and the lower half of a goat, curly hair, flat noses, full beards, pointed ears, a long thick tail, and short goat horns atop their head. In art the satyrs were often depicted wearing a wreath of ivy on their heads and carrying a *thyrsus* (the rod of Bacchus [Dionysos] tipped with a pine cone) in their hand.

There are many origin stories for the creation of satyrs but according to the Greek oral poet, Hesiod, the satyrs were born of the five OREAD granddaughters of Phoroneus; satyrs were described by the poet as being "worthless and unsuitable for work." The satyrs' fondness for uninhibited carousing made them perfect companions for the gods Bacchus (Dionysos) and Pan (Faunus). As Dionysiac creatures they are natural born lovers of boys, women, and wine; they play bagpipes, cymbals, castanets, and pipes and love to dance with NYMPHS, their fellow ageless immortals. Older satyrs were referred to as *sileni* and younger ones were called *satyrisci*.

Source: Conner, *Everything Classical Mythology Book*, 191–92; Hansen, *Classical Mythology: A Guide to the Mythical World of the Greeks and Romans*, 279–80; Littleton, *Gods, Goddesses, and Mythology*, Volume 11, 1256

Satyre-Fish

Variations: Sea SATYR

A creature from heraldic symbology, the chimerical satyre-fish is said to have the body of a fish, the head of a SATYR, and wings.

Source: McCutcheon, *Wordsworth Word Finder*, 416; Zell-Ravenheart, *Wizard's Bestiary*, 84

Saumanasa

Variations: Anjana

In Hindu mythology, according to the Ramayana, Saumanasa was one of the four mountainous elephants who supported the weight of the world upon their heads; he was the guardian of the West. BHARDRA guarded the North, MAHA-PUDMA guarded the South, and VIRUPAKSHA guarded the East. Saumanasa, as he and his companions support the earth from below, is not counted among the DIG-GAJAS.

Source: Coulter, *Encyclopedia of Ancient Deities*, 293; Dalal, *Hinduism*, 43; Vālmīki, *Ramayana: Book 1*, 223

Sazae-Oni

In modern Japanese folklore and urban legend the sazae-oni is a turban snail with the ability to shape-shift into a beautiful woman.

Source: Joly, *Scary Monsters and Super Creeps*, n.pag.

Sburator (Sue-but-or)

Variations: Zburãtor, ZBURATOR

In Romanian folklore there is a vampiric creature called a *sburator* ("flying man"), which is essentially a variation of an INCUBUS. Described as being an extremely handsome man, the sburator is virtually custom made for the victim, making it the perfect lover. Once every seven years, at night, it attacks the woman, slipping into her home through an open window. While she is asleep, it kisses her so gently she may not even wake up. The next day, the woman awakes feeling drained of energy, her body throbbing with pain, and she is easily agitated. Once a woman has had an encounter with a sburator, she is not interested in other men.

Source: Florescu, *The Complete Dracula*, 374; Senn, *Werewolf and Vampire in Romania*, 44; Stratilesco, *From Carpathian to Pindus*, 175

Sceadugenga

A creature mentioned in the Old English epic poem *Beowulf*, sceadugenga ("shadow-goer" or "wanderer in the darkness") may have been a reference to the story's antagonist, GRENDEL; it has come to reference NATURE SPIRITS who, with the ability to shape-shift, are neither wholly alive nor deceased.

Source: Amodio, *Anglo Saxon Literature Handbook*, 304; Sedgefield, *Beowulf*, 23, 223

Sceolan

Variations: Sceolang, Sgeolaind

In British folklore Sceolan was one of the hounds of the cultural hero Finn Mac Cumhaill. This FAIRY ANIMAL was bound to its master by a secret blood-tie, for it was born while its mother, Uirne, Finn's aunt, had been bewitched and transformed into a hound. Had Uirne been in human form when she gave birth her twin sons Bran and Secolan would have been born human. Both hounds were excellent hunters, fighters, and sentinels. Other dogs belonging to Finn Mac Cumhaill were ADHUNALL, BRAN, LUATH LUCHAR, and SEAR DUGH.

Source: Briggs, *Encyclopedia of Fairies*, 347; Gregory, *Gods and Fighting Men*, 238, 398; Monaghan, *Encyclopedia of Celtic Mythology and Folklore*, 410

Schechirion

Schechirion is a monstrous black-colored demonic creature. It is a chimerical mix of insect, reptile, and shellfish; it has a demonic face.

Source: Ford, *Bible of the Adversary*, 121; Mathers, *Sorcerer and his Apprentice*, 26

Der Schwarze

Variations: Der Schwarze Mann ("the black man")

A BOGEYMAN or NURSERY BOGIE from German folklore, der schwarze ("the black") lives in dark places such as beneath beds, inside closets, under the stairs, and within the forest. Like all of its kind, the threat of der schwarze "getting" children has been used by parents to coerce their children into good behavior.

Source: Breverton, *Breverton's Phantasmagoria*, n.pag.; Krensky, *Bogeyman*, 13

Scitalis

A monster named in many medieval bestiaries, the slow moving scitalis was described as being a species of winged DRAGON, having the head and tail of a serpent but only its two front legs. Most remarkable about the scitalis was its multicolored skin said to be so beautiful anyone or anything who looked upon it would become transfixed. While the prey stood there, unaware of its surroundings, the scitalis took advantage of the opportunity to kill its prey. According to twelfth century Latin bestiaries the scitalis glowed with so much heat even in the most severe frosts it would still venture outside to shed it skin.

Source: Clark, *Medieval Book of Beasts*, 198; Breverton, *Breverton's Phantasmagoria*, n.pag.; Rose, *Giants, Monsters, and Dragons*, 323

Scolopendra

Variations: Skolopendra ("centipede")

A chimerical, gigantic, and monstrous SEA SERPENT, the scolopendra of medieval European legends was described as having a shark-like body with numerous webbed appendages protruding from its underside lining its flanks, a flayed Piscean tail, hair spilling out from its nostrils, and a whale's blowhole. It was believed whenever this beast was caught with a fishing hook, it would vomit up its own stomach, release the hook, and then consume its stomach again.

Source: Barber, *Dictionary of Fabulous Beasts*, 129–30; Rose, *Giants, Monsters, and Dragons*, 323; Zell-Ravenheart, *Companion for the Apprentice Wizard*, 179

Scylla

Variations: Skylla

One of two monsters from ancient Greek mythology believed to live in the Straits of Messina located between the island of Sicily and the mainland of Italy, Scylla was described as having the body of a woman but from her waist grew six long necks each having the head of a dog; each of these heads had three rows of teeth and released ferocious barks, bays, and growls.

Scylla was once a beautiful sea NYMPH who had the great misfortune to have fallen in love with the same man as the witch Circe. Wanting to remove her rival, Circe poured a magical poison into the tidal pool Scylla used for bathing. When the NYMPH entered the water up to her waist, the poison took effect and caused the lower half of her body to sprout long necked vicious dogs. Horrified with her hideous transformation, Scylla threw herself into the treacherous rocky area of the Straits of Messina. From that day forth, whenever a ship passed too close to the location the dogs of her waist would attack the vessel.

Although the witch Circe had warned the hero Odysseus of the dangers of the Strait because of the monsters who lived there, Scylla was still able to devour six of his crewmen.

The monster who resided on the other side of the Straits of Messina was CHARYBDIS.

Source: Andrews, *Dictionary of Nature Myths*, 171; Daly, *Greek and Roman Mythology A to Z*, 116–17

Scyphius

In Greek mythology Scyphius, the first horse, was created in Thessaly by the god of the sea, Poseidon (Neptune), with a wave of his trident.

Source: Maro, *Ecolgues and Georgics of Virgil translated by J.B. Rose*, 141; Virgil, *P. Vergili Maronis opera*, 160

Sea-Dog

Variations: Sea Wolf

In heraldic symbology the chimerical sea-dog is depicted like a Talbot (an old breed of hunting dog) but having a beaver's tail, fish-scaled body, scalloped fins along its spine, and webbed feet.

Source: Fox-Davies, *Complete Guide to Heraldry*, 205; Vinycomb, *Fictitious and Symbolic Creatures in Art with Special Reference to their use in British Heraldry*, n.pag.

Sea Goat

Variations: Goat Fish, Suhur-Mas ("ram fish")

The mount of the god Ea (Marduk) from Sumerian mythology, the sea goat ("suhur-mash-ha") had the ability to traverse both land and sea while the god stood upon its back. The front part of its body was a goat (or antelope or gazelle) while the back half of its body was a fish. Often used as a symbol to represent the god Ea, it was associated with floods and full moons. The Sumerian sea goat was the likely progenitor of the Greek CAPRICORN and the Etruscan AIGKAMPOI; in Chinese this creature was known as the *mo-ki* ("goat fish").

Source: Ingersoll, *Dragons and Dragon Lore*, 24, 46, 48, 84; Rose, *Giants, Monsters, and Dragons*, 145; Shadick, *Skywatcher's Companion*, n.pag.

Sea-Gryphon

Caspar Plautius was a Benedictine abbot who

sailed with Christopher Columbus on his second voyage to the Indies; he documented the trip in a book published under his pseudonym Honorius Philoponus in 1621 entitled *Nova typis transacta navigatio novi orbis Indiæ occidentalis*. In the work, replete with illustrations, is a description of Columbus meeting five West Indians who came to meet him mounted upon a single sea-gryphon. The animal is described and depicted as being large with four large paws sporting three fingers each, a fringed collar, a hog's head, a lashing tail, a scaled back, and tremendous wings, as well as a set of fins.

Source: Plautius, *Nova typis transacta navigatio novi orbis Indiae Occidentalis*, xxxiv; Zell-Ravenheart, *Wizard's Bestiary*, 85

Sea Hog

Variations: Marine Boar, Marine Sow, Wonderful Pig of the Ocean

Originating in European sailor tales from the 1500s, the sea hog was said to have the front legs, head, and tusks of a hog, reptilian forelegs, but the tail of a fish. Eventually the word sea hog came to be used for a dolphin which was caught and used for food onboard the ship. A heraldic version of the sea hog is represented with DRAGON feet, eyes on the side of its belly, a fish tail, and a quarter moon behind its horned head.

Source: Godfrey, *Mythical Creatures*, 68; Zell-Ravenheart, *Wizard's Bestiary*, 85

Sea Monk

Variations: BISHOP FISH, Jenny Haniver, Monachus Marinus, Monkfish, Sea Bishop

A fish from medieval bestiaries, the sea monk was said to have a human head, a monk's tonsure, and a scarlet colored and speckled body, the upper part of which was covered by a cape; rather than arms, it had two long tentacles.

Source: Eberhart, *Mysterious Creatures*, 477; Godfrey, *Mythical Creatures*, 68; Nigg, *Sea Monsters*, 26

Sea-Satyr

A species of MERMAN, the sea-satyr is depicted as having arms which end in pincers, the head of a horned animal, and short webbed feet.

Source: White, *Book of Beasts*, 266; Zell-Ravenheart, *Wizard's Bestiary*, 86

Sea Serpent

Variations: Bledmall, Bledmail, Beisht Kione, Cirein Croin ("grey crest"), Great Sea Serpent, Great Unknown of the Seas, Kampos, Ketos, Lake Monster, Mester Stoorworm, Physeter ("the blower"), Sea Creature, Sea Monster, Sjo-Orm ("sea worm") Tennin

Appearing in nearly every culture's mythology over the course of human history, the sea serpent is most often described as being a gigantic, serpentine water-dwelling creature living near enough to man to make fishing or seagoing travel dangerous; they have been reported living in fjords, lakes, rivers, and the ocean alike. Although descriptions vary widely, they typically have dragonesque heads; horns and flippers are common traits.

The heroes who battled these monsters were typically sun gods or their offspring, or have solar characteristics at the very least. In ancient tales, sea serpents were representative of the clouds, as they would rise up and block out the light of the sun just as they would attempt to consume the hero.

Source: Andrews, *Dictionary of Nature Myths*, 173–4; Barber, *Dictionary of Fabulous Beasts*, 130; De Kirk, *Dragonlore*, 45; Eberhart, *Mysterious Creatures*, 478; Zell-Ravenheart, *Wizard's Bestiary*, 86

Sea-Stag

A creature from heraldic symbology, the sea-stag is depicted as having the antlers, forequarters, and head of a stag but the hindquarters of a fish.

Source: Fox-Davies, *A Complete Guide to Heraldry*, 210; Woodward, *Treatise on Heraldry, British and Foreign*, 299; Zell-Ravenheart, *Wizard's Bestiary*, 86

Sea Wolf

Variations: SEA-DOG, Tirichik

An aggressive aquatic creature from British Columbian folklore, the sea wolf is described as having a canine-like head, a long neck, and occasionally tails; some descriptions give it tusks or wings. Although some authors and researchers freely interchange the sea wolf and the SEA-DOG they are considered to be two distinctly different creatures.

Source: Godfrey, *Mythical Creatures*, 66–7; Vinycomb, *Fictitious and Symbolic Creatures in art with Special Reference to their use in British Heraldry*, 144–5

Sea-Wyvern

A creature from heraldic symbology, the sea-wyvern has the forebody of a WYVERN and hindpart of a fish; one such creature appears on the coat of arms for the West Dorset District Council.

Source: Cox, *Spooky Spirits and Creepy Creatures*, 19; Friar, *Basic Heraldry*, 12; Fox-Davies, *Complete Guide to Heraldry*, 226–7

Sealah (SHE-la)

Variations: Djinn, Saaláh, Sealáh

A sealah is a demonic species of creature in Arabic folklore. It is a type of djinn (a race of demons) born the offspring of a human and a djinn which consumed human flesh. Absolutely hideous in its appearance, the sealah prey upon men, hunting and capturing them, forcing them to dance, torturing them, and using them to practice their hunting techniques.

Sealah live in the forests and ancient Arabic geographers have marked an island off the coast of China named "the island of the sealah," believing it is populated by these demons.

Hated by wolves, when attacked by one, the sealah will cry out "*Come to my help, for the wolf devoureth me!*" or "*Who will liberate me? I have a hundred deenars, and he shall receive them!*" But be forewarned, and do not answer its call for help. The wolf will destroy the demon and consume its body.

Source: Campbell, *Popular Tales of the West Highlands*, 297; *Chambers's Encyclopaedia: A Dictionary of Universal Knowledge*, 749; Poole, *The Thousand and One Nights*, 32–3

Sear Dugh

In Irish mythology Sear Dugh was a FAIRY ANIMAL, one of the many hunting dogs of the cultural hero Finn Mac Cumhaill; his other dogs were ADHUNALL, BRAN, LUATH LUCHAR, and SCEOLAN.

Source: Gregory, *Gods and Fighting Men*, 238, 398; Monaghan, *Encyclopedia of Celtic Mythology and Folklore*, 3

Seatco

In the folklore of the Indians living in the Pacific northwest the Seatco, neither animal nor man, are said to live around and in the beautiful lake located at the base of Loo-wit Mountain (Mount Saint Helens), United States of America. These beings were the spirits of people from many different tribes who had been cast out for their evil tendencies; now, having banded together, they called themselves the Seatco, after their leader, and did little but commit acts of evil and wrongdoing.

The Seatco not only caused storms to ravish up and down the coast, throwing dead fish upon the beach, tipping over canoes, and drowning their occupants. They were also great impersonators, having the ability to mimic the sound of animals, birds, and the wind passing through the trees; furthermore they could make these sounds appear to be either very near or far off. Whenever an Indian killed one of the Seatco, the tribe would retaliate and kill twelve people from the tribe where the offender came from.

The leader of these spirits, Seatco, was a GIANT terrible to behold as his face was animalistic, he was taller than the tallest fir tree and had a voice which roared louder than the ocean. Seatco was also immensely strong, able to destroy an entire forest, pulling it up by the roots, create a mountain range by stacking boulders, cause earthquakes, and change the course of a river by blowing hard with his breath.

Source: Clark, *Indian Legends of the Pacific Northwest*, 46, 63, 125; Washington State, *Report of the Governor of Washington Territory*, 59

Sebau

In Egyptian mythology and named in the *Book of the Overthrowing of Apophis*, the serpent-fiend NAK and his assistant Sebau were the monstrous helpers of APOPHIS. All three suffered a brutal demise, being gashed, slashed, their arms severed, and finally set ablaze while still alive.

Source: Budge, *Gods of the Egyptians*, 324; Mercatante, *Who's Who in Egyptian Mythology*, 13–14

Sebi

According to ancient Egyptian mythology Sebi was a monstrous serpent guardian to the twelfth section, or hour, of Tuat, the Underworld, as the sun god, Ra, passes by it in his boat. In *The Text of Unas* there is a magical spell which when performed will cause the destruction of monstrous beasts and serpents alike; Sebi would be affected by this spell.

Source: Budge, *Gods of the Egyptians*, 32, 324; Mercatante, *Who's Who in Egyptian Mythology*, 139

Seemurg

Variations: Farmanvawa, Shah-I Mur Ghan, Seemurgh, Senmurv, Senmurw, Simargl, Simurgh, Simorq, Simyr, Sinam

A fantastic bird in Persian folklore, Seemurg ("thirty birds") was so old it was said to have seen the destruction and creation of the universe three times; it was described as looking like a peacock with the claws of a lion; it is large enough to swoop down, snatch up an elephant or whale, and fly away. The Seemurg, one of the KHRAFSTRA, is able to speak all languages and has all knowledge of past, present, and future events.

In Iranian folklore there are two separate Seemurg birds. The first was the guardian of Roostem (Rustam) and Zal and lived on Mount Albur. Its nest, called *kakh*, was made of columns of aloe wood, ebony, and sandal-wood. As it flew overhead, darkness fell across the land, as it was large enough to block the rays of the sun. The other Seemurg was seen as a monstrous creature which was eventually slain by the hero Isfandiyar in one of his seven adventures. This Seemurg also lived atop a mountain and resembled a black cloud or a black mountain as it flew overhead. Its claws enabled it to pluck up crocodiles, elephants, and panthers with ease.

Source: Houtsma, *E.J. Brill's First Encyclopaedia of Islam*, 427; Keightley, *World Guide to Gnomes, Fairies, Elves, and Other Little People*, 17; Rosen, *Mythical Creatures Bible*, 152; Zell-Ravenheart, *Wizard's Bestiary*, 86

Seesha

Variations: Ananta ("endless"), Sesha ("eternal"), Sesha-Naga, Shesha, Vasuki

A multi-headed NAGA from Hindu mythology, Seesha is the king of the infernal region known as Patala; the number of heads it is said to have varies between seven and one thousand; said to have encircled the body of Vishnu and acting as his couch, Seesha uses its head and open hoods known as *manidwipa* ("island of the jewels"), creating a canopy to protect him as he sleeps. Whenever this gigantic Naga yawns, it causes an earthquake; at the end of every *kalpa* it spits forth fire and destroys all of creation. In the *Samudra Manthana* ("Churning of the Ocean") tale, Seesha's body was used as the rope to pull the churn. In some tales it is said Seesha is supporting the weight of the world and in others they claim it is acting as a support pillar for the hells. The wife of Seesha is named Ananta-Sirsha and they live in his home named Mani-Bhitti ("jewel walled").

Source: Barber, *Dictionary of Fabulous Beasts*, 133; Chatterjee, *Sacred Hindu Symbols*, 28; Dowson, *Classical Dictionary of Hindu Mythology and Religion*, 291–2; Vogel, *Indian Serpent-Lore*, 83

Sefer

According to ancient Egyptian mythology Sefer was described as a fantastical animal, having the winged body of a lion and the head of an eagle or hawk.

Source: Coulter, *Encyclopedia of Ancient Deities*, 418; Mercatante, *Who's Who in Egyptian Mythology*, 140; Wilkinson, *Manners and Customs of the Ancient Egyptians*, 310

Segben (Seg-bin)

Variations: SIGBIN

In the Philippines there is a vampiric creature whose description varies from case to case, but generally it is said to be a dark-colored, hornless, large, smelly goat called a segben. During the day, it is invisible.

The segben attacks its prey only at night. Although it can kill a person simply by looking at them or by biting their shadow, its mere presence will drain off the life of a dying person, consuming it for its own. Any child which falls prey to the segben will have their heart made into a magical amulet. It usually does not eat the flesh and blood of those it kills; it prefers to gorge itself on charcoal, corpses, and pumpkins. If seen while in its goat form, it will only be pretending to eat grass.

The segben uses its supernatural speed to prevent capture, but it has a number of forms which it can shape-shift into: a frog with extraordinary long legs, a goat with exceptionally floppy ears whose hips are higher than its shoulders, and a locust. In all of its forms, it has a horrible smell.

The smell and sight of thick smoke is enough to keep a segben away, as will the scent of spices and the clang of knives.

Source: Ateneo de Davao University, *Kinaadman*, 50; Paraiso, *The Balete Book*, 15; Ramos, *Creatures of Philippine*, 70; Ramos, *Creatures of Midnight*, 53, 95

Seilenoi

Variations: Seilenos

The collective name for the lustful NATURE SPIRITS of Greek mythology who were a part of the retinue of the god Bacchus (Dionysos), the seilenoi were relentless in their music, pursuit of NYMPHS, and wine-drinking. Seilenoi are easily mistaken for SATYRS in art, as they are depicted as anthropoids with bestial features who are always male and visibly aroused; in early art, however, SATYRS were shown with horse ears, legs, and tails but in the Hellenistic period they took on more of the semblance of a goat having horn-stubs and cloven hooves.

Seilenoi first appear in text as the lovers of the mountain NYMPHS in *Homeric Hymn to Aphrodite* (Venus). Devoted to their merry-making, drinking, and carousing, seilenoi are utter cowards and will flee confrontation except on the occasion when they are in a Dionysiac frenzy.

The leader of the species is named Seilenos and was said to have been a philosopher, preacher, scholar, and tutor to a young Bacchus (Dionysos).

Source: Coulter, *Encyclopedia of Ancient Deities*, 431; Hard, *Routledge Handbook of Greek Mythology*, 212–13; Rose, *Handbook of Greek Mythology*, 128

Seiryu

Variations: Azure DRAGON, Green DRAGON, Seryu

In Chinese folklore when a capital city is constructed, it was believed it should be designed to the Four God principle; on each side of the city, representation of each one is present in the form of their respective creatures. In the east is Seiryu the blue DRAGON; to the north is GENBU, a snake and turtle hybrid; in the south SUZAKU, depicted as a red PHOENIX-like bird; and in the west, BYAKKO, a white tiger.

Source: Brown, *Genius of Japanese Carpentry*, n.pag.; Grafetstätter, *Islands and Cities in Medieval Myth, Literature, and History*, 119

Seker

According to ancient Egyptian mythology Seker was a hawk-headed creature and one of the guardians of Osiris while the god was in his form known as Osiris the Seeker.

Source: Coulter, *Encyclopedia of Ancient Deities*, 418; Mercatante, *Who's Who in Egyptian Mythology*, 187

Selkie

Variations: Roane, Seal fairy, Seal-Faeries, Seal People, Selchies, Selkie Folk, Silkie, Water KELPIE

Living in the seas around the Orkney and Shetland Islands, the shape-shifting selkies ("seal") often take the form of grey seals or great seals as they travel through the ocean. There is the regional belief the selkies are fallen angels who were not so evil; they partook in the war against heaven but were condemned to earth to live as they do for some far less trivial sin.

When a selkie comes upon land it removes its seal-skin covering and appears in all ways to be a human; however sometimes the folklore will say, like the merrow (a species of merfolk), selkies have wide palms or webbing between their fingers and toes. It will hide the skin or guard it carefully, as it cannot return back to the ocean without it. Male selkies not only have the ability to raise storms and capsize boats but are also very willing to avenge the indiscriminate slaughter of seals.

Occasionally a selkie will make contact with a human and on rare occasions will take one as a mate, but those relationships never last. If the selkie is female she will eventually return to the sea; if the selkie is male it will after seven years offer its mate a fee for rearing the child, wanting to return to the ocean with it.

Unlike the MERMAID, selkies always appear in groups and do not reside in a magical underwater kingdom decked out beautifully; rather selkies are considered to be a completely different species of fairy which prefer to live in their own company on an outlying skerry.

Source: Briggs, *Dictionary of British Folk-Tales in the English Language*, Volumes 1–2, 226–28; Froud, *Faeries*, 119; McCoy, *Witch's Guide to Faery Folk*, 307–08; Stevenson, *Scottish Antiquary, or, Northern Notes and Queries*, Volume 7–8, 172–73

Semargl

Variations: Simargl, Semargl-Pereplut

A creature from Slavic folklore but of Persian origins, the semargl is described as being chimerical, having attributes of a bird, dog, GRIFFIN, and a lion; sitting upon the tree from which all seeds originate, when it would shake its wings, the seeds would disperse, much like the CHAMROSH of ancient Mesopotamia and Persian mythology and SAENA of Persian folklore.

Source: Rose, *Giants, Monsters, and Dragons*, 334; Warner, *Russian Myths*, 17; Zell-Ravenheart, *Wizard's Bestiary*, 88

Semi

According to ancient Egyptian mythology Semi was a fantastical animal, described as a winged uraeus and standing upon its tail. Semi dwells in the tenth section, or hour, of Tuat, the Underworld.

Source: Coulter, *Encyclopedia of Ancient Deities*, 419; Mercatante, *Who's Who in Egyptian Mythology*, 142

Senad

A creature appearing in many medieval bestiaries, the senad was described as being a triple-headed bear which would tear her cubs while licking them with her rough tongue.

Source: Flaubert, *Temptation of St. Anthony*, 255;

Senenahemthet

According to ancient Egyptian mythology Senenahemthet was a demonic creature described as being serpent-like in appearance; it was mentioned in a magical formula written by King Unas of the fifth dynasty (BC 2450–2290, Old Kingdom). He was known for attacking the deceased in their tombs.

Source: Coulter, *Encyclopedia of Ancient Deities*, 419; Mercatante, *Who's Who in Egyptian Mythology*, 142

Senik

In Armenian mythology Senik was one of the winged horses said to assist in pulling the sun across the sky (see also BENIK, ENIK, and MENIK).

Source: Ananikian, *Armenian Mythology*, 51; Rose, *Giants, Monsters, and Dragons*, 178

Senmurv

Variations: Cynogriffin, SEEMURG, Senmurw, Simargl

A chimerical creature from early Persian folklore, the senmurv ("dog bird") was described as having the body of a lion, the head of a dog, and the talons and wings of an eagle; other descriptions say it had the features of a bat, bird, dog, and musk-ox; another source claims it was a hybrid between a peacock, DRAGON, and a dog. Living within the branches of the Tree of All Seeds, each time it would alight, the movement of its body and wings caused the tree to shake and disperse its seeds; in later legends it lost its canine features and became more bird-like in its appearance. The senmurv is very similar to the SAENA and SEEMURG.

Source: Rose, *Giants, Monsters, and Dragons*, 327; Lurker, *Dictionary of Gods and Goddesses, Devils and Demons*, 170; Shuker, *Beasts That Hide from Man*, 203–4; Zell-Ravenheart, *Companion for the Apprentice Wizard*, 179

Senrima

A species of PEGASUS-like horse from Korean folklore, a senrima is said to be able to run for one thousand *ri* without stopping; although the measure of a *ri* has varied over the centuries, this is a distance of approximately three hundred and ten miles.

Source: Goodman, *Endless Punchers*, 442

Seps

Described by the short lived but remarkable Roman poet Lucan (Marcus Annaeus Lucanus, AD 39–65), the seps is a small snake whose venom is powerful enough to not only corrode away flesh but dissolve bone as well.

Source: Clark, *Medieval Book of Beasts*, 200; Zell-Ravenheart, *Companion for the Apprentice Wizard*, 87

Serou

Variations: Tsopo

The serou is a species of UNICORN native to Tibet and named in the Tibetian-Mongolian dictionary *Minghi Ghiamtso*; it has been described as being very aggressive and having an alicorn (single horn).

Source: *Asiatic Journal and Monthly Register for British India and Its Dependencies*, Volume 2, 94; Gould, *Dragons, Unicorns, and Sea Serpents*, 346; Zell-Ravenheart, *Wizard's Bestiary*, 97

Serpent of Isa

Variations: The "Flying Serpent" of Isa

According to medieval Christian folklore, the serpent of Isa was a monstrous creature hatched from the egg of a COCKATRICE. Travelers who passed through the desert of Ethiopia claimed it was the most dangerous of all serpents as it not only was highly poisonous but was capable of flight; this, they claimed, made it more dangerous than the COCKATRICE it hailed from.

Source: Rose, *Giants, Monsters, and Dragons*, 329; Zell-Ravenheart, *Wizard's Bestiary*, 40

Serpopard

Variations: Setcha

In Egyptian mythology the serpopard is a hybrid creature crossing the body of a leopard and the head and neck of a serpent; it was symbolic for the chaos thriving beyond the borders of Egypt which the Pharaoh must defeat or tame. In some depictions the serpopard was more chimerical, having the addition of a falcon head and wings. However in Mesopotamian art, the serpopard was always depicted in pairs in symmetrical, organized compositions.

Source: Godfrey, *Mythical Creatures*, 20; Mercatante, *Who's Who in Egyptian Mythology*, 145; Ross, *From the Banks of the Euphrates*, 174, 177

Serra

Variations: Flying Fish, Sarce, Sarre, Sawfish, Scie, Serre

A winged SEA SERPENT with a serrated back in maritime folklore, the serra is said to be captivated by sailing ships; when it sees them it will rush to the surface and, unfurling its wings, try to race alongside or even pass the vessel. After three or four miles, the creature tires and falls back, returning to the depths. It was symbolic in writings for the person who attempts a task and once tiring, quits.

Source: Clark, *Medieval Book of Beasts*, 206; Mittman, *Ashgate Research Companion to Monsters and the Monstrous*, 418; Zell-Ravenheart, *Wizard's Bestiary*, 87

Set-Hra

According to ancient Egyptian mythology Set-Hra was a monstrous serpent standing as a guardian to the entrance into the eighth section, or hour, to Tuat, the Underworld, as the sun god, Ra, passed by in his boat. In *The Text of Unas* there is a magical spell which when performed will cause the destruction of monstrous beasts and serpents alike; Set-Hra would be inadvertently affected by this spell.

Source: Coulter, *Encyclopedia of Ancient Deities*, 32, 421, 477; Mercatante, *Who's Who in Egyptian Mythology*, 145

Set-Qesu

A demonic creature from the mythology of the ancient Egyptians, Set-Qesu ("crusher of bones") is mentioned in the ceremonial chant "The Negative Confession" recited by the dead while they stand in the Hall of Judgment.

Source: Coulter, *Encyclopedia of Ancient Deities*, 421; Mercatante, *Who's Who in Egyptian Mythology*, 153

Setcheh

According to ancient Egyptian mythology Setcheh was a demonic creature described as being serpent-like in appearance; it was mentioned in a magical formula written by King Unas of the fifth dynasty (BC 2450–2290, Old Kingdom). He was known for attacking the deceased in their tombs. In *The Text of Unas* there is a magical spell which when performed will cause the destruction of monstrous beasts and serpents alike; Setcheh would be affected by this spell.

Source: Coulter, *Encyclopedia of Ancient Deities*, 32, 421; Mercatante, *Who's Who in Egyptian Mythology*, 145

Sethu

According to ancient Egyptian mythology Sethu was a monstrous serpent guarding the entrance into the tenth section, or hour, to Tuat, the Underworld, as the sun god, Ra, passed by in his boat. In *The Text of Unas* there is a magical spell which when performed will cause the destruction of monstrous beasts and serpents alike; Sethu would be inadvertently affected by this spell.

Source: Coulter, *Encyclopedia of Ancient Deities*, 32, 421; Mercatante, *Who's Who in Egyptian Mythology*, 145

Setotaishō (SHE-toh TIE-show)

Variations: Seto Taisho, Teapot Samurai

A YŌKAI from Japanese folklore, Setotaishō ("General Seto" or "the crockery general") is a singular being standing less than two feet tall whose entire body is made up from discarded bowls, dishes, and other kitchenware. Having a *tokkuri* (gourd-shaped saki bottle) for a head and a tea-pot for its main body, Setotaishō comes into being through an unknown process but once alive it consumes items made of iron and attacks anyone in its vicinity using a wooden spoon as a spear. Because of its size and frailty, it is not a sturdy opponent but makes up in ferocity what it lacks in size and strength.

Source: Meyer, *Night Parade of One Hundred Demons*, 206; Yoda, *Yokai Attack*, 94–7

Seven-Colored Horse

In Spanish folklore the seven-colored horse is a FAIRY ANIMAL; it looks like a small pony whose coat is always changing between seven different colors. In folklore this animal also has the ability to speak, fly, and grant wishes to anyone who can capture it, typically the hero of the story who needs the seven-colored horse in order to win his bride.

Source: Zell-Ravenheart, *Wizard's Bestiary*, 147

Seven-Headed Snake

Variations: Musmahhu

In ancient Sumerian mythology, Seven-Headed Snake was one of the many monsters slain by the warrior and champion of the gods Ninurta (Ningirsu). Little is known of this creature other than Gudea, a ruler of Lagash (ca. 2100 BC), referred to it, and the other monsters vanquished by the warrior Ninurta, as the SLAIN HEROES; he elevated them all to the status of god and made a place of worship for them in the temple. The only written description of Seven-Headed Snake reads as follows: "*a weapon when he runs, death when he passes.*"

Source: Ataç, *Mythology of Kingship in Neo-Assyrian Art*, 185; Salem, *Near East, the Cradle of Western Civilization*, 102–3; Wiggerman, *Mesopotamian Protective Spirits*, 153, 217

Sevienda

A species of PHOENIX from Hindu folklore, the sevienda when in need of renewal is consumed by flames and emerges from the ash as a caterpillar or small worm. As a mature bird, its beak is described as having many holes in it.

Source: Barber, *Dictionary of Fabulous Beasts*, 133; Zell-Ravenheart, *Wizard's Bestiary*, 87, 174

Shabdiz

The beloved black stallion belonging to the Persian king Khosrau Parvez (Parwiz) Shabdiz ("midnight") was said to be beautiful, intelligent and the "world's fastest horse," so quick not even a storm could keep pace with it; his stablemate GULGUN was the second fastest. Shabdiz was employed to carry Shirin after she saw a portrait of Parvez and agreed to marry him. Parvez so loved his horse he swore he would kill the man who would inevitably one day bring him the news of the creature's death.

Source: Browne, *Literary History of Persia*, Volume 1, 17–8; Renard, *Islam and the Heroic Image*, 208; Warner, *World of Myths*: Volume Two, 142

Shabrang

The horse of the Persian hero Bizhan, Shabrang ("color of night") was described as being a matchless black charger and a peerless mount; his horseshoes alone weighed one hundred and twenty *maunds* (at different times a single maund's weight varied; at its lowest it was twenty-five pounds and at its height, one hundred and sixty). Shabrang was also the name of a horse belonging to Bahram Gur.

Source: Lakhnavī, *Adventures of Amir Hamza*, 388; Renard, *Islam and the Heroic Image*, 208

Shachihoko

Variations: Shachi

In Chinese and Japanese folklore the shachihoko is believed to be a carp with the head of a tiger (on rare occasions, it will have the head of a DRAGON); its body is covered with poisonous scales. When the shachihoko finds it must leave the water and walk upon the land it shape-shifts into a tiger. Statues of these creatures are placed on buildings to protect them against fires as it is believed the shachihoko also has the ability to make it rain.

Source: Garcia, *Geek in Japan*, 52

Shadhahvar

Variations: Shadavar

A carnivorous UNICORN-like species from Persian folklore, the shadhahvar had a hollow, branched alicorn (a single horn) growing out of its forehead. As the wind blew, the alicorn would create such beautiful music other animals would draw near to listen and when opportunity presented itself, the shadhahvar would strike and kill its prey.

Source: Suckling, *Unicorns*, 37; Zell-Ravenheart, *Wizard's Bestiary*, 87

Shag-Foal

Variations: Shagfoal, Tatter-Foal, Tatterfoal, Tatter Foal

In Lincolnshire, England, there is a shape-shifting BRAG known as a shag-foal; it travels the roads in the guise of a shaggy donkey or horse with fiery eyes. Frightening in appearance, this FAIRY ANIMAL will chase a person but there are no tales of it actually catching or hurting anyone. Picktree Brag is the name of a well-known shag-foal.

Source: Briggs, *Encyclopedia of Fairies*, 360; Rose, *Spirits, Fairies, Gnomes, and Goblins*, 289; Westwood, *Lore of the Land*, 560–61

Shagamaw

Variations: Tote Road Shagamaw

Originating in the lumberjack communities of the developing United States of America, the shagamaw of Maine was one of the species of FEARSOME CRITTERS; described as having the front legs of a bear and the hind quarters of a moose these creatures walk very deliberately on tote roads where their tracks will be easily seen leaving prints behind precisely placed at one yard increments. At quarter-mile intervals, the shagamaws change their footing, first walking on their front legs then switching to only walk on their back. They were well known to sneak into camps at night and consume any plaid shirts which were left outside to dry overnight.

Source: Barber, *Dictionary of Fabulous Beasts*, 133; Cox, *Fearsome Creatures of the Lumberwoods*, 23; Mencken, *American Language*, 250; Rose, *Giants, Monsters, and Dragons*, 119

Shakko

A red KITSUNE (fox spirit) from Japanese mythology, the shakko ("ghost fox") is said to be an omen of good fortune; generally, it is benign to humans.

Source: Maberry, *Vampire Universe*, 177, 178; Picken, *Essentials of Shinto*, 124

Shamir

According to Hebrew folklore the shamir was created on the twilight of the very first Sabbath; possessing amazing strength, these small creatures, no bigger than a grain of barley, can bore through the hardest diamonds without leaving behind a single grain of dust. In legend, it was said one of these worms was used to engrave the breastplate of the *kohen gadol* ("high priest"; the chief of the Kohanim who alone may enter into the Holy of Holies) as well as to have carved the text on the stone slabs creating the Ten Commandments Moses took down from atop Mount Saini; in another story these worms were used to cuts the stones for the Temple commissioned by King Solomon as it was forbidden to use metal tools in its construction.

Source: Isaacs, *Animals in Jewish Thought and Tradition*, 181; Zell-Ravenheart, *Wizard's Bestiary*, 87

Shamisen-Choro (SHAH-me-sen CHO-roh)

One of the a YŌKAI of Japanese folklore, the shamisen-choro ("elder Shamisen," "old man Shamisen") is a sub-species of the TSUKOMOGAMI, as it is an old musical instrument (a three-string guitar-like instrument) which has taken on an animal form. Some sources claim the shamisen-choro is the spirit of a famed shamisen master who so loved his instrument he would not be parted with it even in death; other sources claim this YŌKAI is wordplay of the saying *shami kara choro ni wa nareun* ("a monk in training can't quickly become a master"). In art the shamisen-choro is typically shown with the BIWA-BOKUBBOKU and the KOTO-FURUNUSHI. If encountered these beings are willing to have a musician play them, but otherwise they are more than willing to play themselves.

Source: Meyer, *Night Parade of One Hundred Demons*, 212; Yoda, *Yokai Attack*, 106–10

Shan Kiao

A KIAO species of DRAGON, the shan kiao are described as having eyebrows which have grown together, horns, a red mane, and a serpentine body with projecting scales. These creatures have a unique ability called "mark of the sea" where they draw in breath and exhale clouds in the shape of carriages, city walls, horses engaged in activities, imperial palaces, people, and towers.

Sources: Gould, *Dragons, Unicorns, and Sea Serpents*, 407; Gould, *Mythical Monsters*, 406

Shed plural: shed and Shedim

Variations: Shaddim, SHEDU

Originally a class of storm-demons from Chaldean mythology, the shed were absorbed into Jewish demonology where they were said to be the descendants of Adam and Lilith or the descendants of serpents. Another Hebrew legend says God created them but had to stop when the Sabbath came and never finished making them. The word translates to mean "demon" or "destroyer."

Typically shedim, as they are called in numbers, are described as having the legs and feet of a rooster and are often depicted as bulls or as having bull horns. They have the ability to possess inanimate objects such as statues. To determine if shedim are in the area, spread ashes on the ground; if they are present, their tracks will become visible. They follow the dead and linger near graves.

There is a belief in which sinners in an attempt to purify themselves would sacrifice their daughters to the shedim, but it is uncertain if this was a blood, life, sexuality, or some other kind of sacrifice. It should be noted at one time benevolent shedim were used in kabalistic ceremonies.

Source: Jastrow, *Religion of Babylonia and Assyria*, 260; Rogers, *Religion of Babylonia and Assyria*, 147; Zell-Ravenheart, *Wizard's Bestiary*, 88

Shellycoat

Variations: Shellicoat, Shelly Coat

The shellycoats are one of the FUATH, the collective name for the malicious and monstrous water fairies and BOGIES in Scottish folklore. Found in freshwater streams and wearing a coat of shells which rattles when it moves, the shellycoats take great pleasure in leading travelers astray. There are many tales of these fairies and their little tricks but they never do any harm nor do they lead the person into a dangerous area, just out of their way.

Source: Briggs, *Encyclopedia of Fairies*, 362; McCoy, *Witch's Guide to Faery Folk*, 310; Rose, *Spirits, Fairies, Leprechauns, and Goblins*, 290

Shemti

According to ancient Egyptian mythology Shemti was a monstrous serpent found in the ninth section, or hour, of Tuat, the Underworld; it was described as having four heads at each end of its body. In *The Text of Unas* there is a magical spell which when performed will cause the destruction of monstrous beasts and serpents alike; Shemti would be inadvertently affected by this spell.

Source: Coulter, *Encyclopedia of Ancient Deities*, 4, 32, 64; Mercatante, *Who's Who in Egyptian Mythology*, 154

Shen-Yi

Variations: The Anchor

In Chinese folklore the DRAGON god Shen-Yi was a rival to the DRAGON FE-LIAN; Shen-Yi was ever watchful of his rival who was a renowned troublemaker and would counter his actions to restore balance. He is described as having the body of a stag, head of a horned bird, tail of a snake, and the wings of a DRAGON.

Source: De Kirk, *Dragonlore*, 26; Fontenrose, *Python*, 478

Shetu

Variations: Shethu

A serpentine tortoise-like creature from ancient Egyptian mythology, Shetu dwelled in the eleventh section, or hour, of Tuat, the Underworld, and was represented by the constellation of the tortoise. When addressed by the sun god, Ra, Shetu would appear in human form; its duty was to "emit life to Ra every day." When the god ceased speaking to it, Shetu would disappear into its own body.

Source: Budge, *Gods of the Egyptians*, 254; Mercatante, *Who's Who in Egyptian Mythology*, 155

Shibaten

In Japanese folklore, in the area of Shikoku, there is a belief that the enko-kappa ("monkey kappa"), a species of kappa, has among its kind a subspecies known as the shibaten. Typically, these creatures live in the mountains as monkeys but on the sixth day of the sixth moon they descend from their home and enter into the rivers, becoming KAPPAS. The folklore assumes after the rice harvest, the shibaten leave the river, reassume their monkey form, and return to the mountains.

Source: Asiatic Society of Japan. *Transactions of the Asiatic Society of Japan*, 1962, 186

Shikk (SHEEK)

Variations: Shiq, Shiqq

The shikk ("the half" or "one sided") is a demonic creature from Arabic folklore. Its body is literally divided longitudinally, one half human, the other half demon. The offspring of a shikk and of a human being is called a NESNAS. The shikk preys on travelers.

Source: Burton, *Arabian Nights, in 16 Volumes*, 354; Forbes, *Dictionary, Hindustani and English*, 504; Knowles, *Nineteenth century*, Volume 31, 449; Poole, *Thousand and One Nights*, 33

Shikome

Variations: Gogome, Gogo-Me, Hisame, Hisa-Me, Shikome ("terrible woman"), Shiko-Me, Yomo-tsu-shiko-me ("ugly female of the world of the dead"), Yomotsu-Shiko-Me, Yomotsu-Shikome

A species of barbaric and sadistic NATURE SPIRIT (storm Hag) from Japanese folklore, the savage shikome ("terrible woman") are described as having bloodshot eyes and sharp, jagged teeth. Bands of these vile creatures roam the mountains, attacking unwary travelers. Some accounts of the shikome claim they are female devils who reside in Yomi, the Underworld, and the predecessors of the ONI. When Izanami was driven out of Yomi with his entourage of eight attendants and fifteen hundred assistant devils, it was done by a mob of shikome.

Source: Bush, *Asian Horror Encyclopedia*, 164; Coulter, *Encyclopedia of Ancient Deities*, 426; Mittman, *Ashgate Research Companion to Monsters and the Monstrous*, 175

Shinseen

In Chinese folklore the diminutive shinseen live in a state of blissful ease, exempt from the cares of human life; however, they hold an influence over mortal affairs. These NATURE SPIRITS are believed to live in the mountains and woods. They have appeared as both old men with long beards and young maidens.

Source: Keightley, *Fairy Mythology Illustrative of the Romance and Superstition of Vairous Countries*, 511; Penwyche, *World of Fairies*, 108; Porteous, *Forest Folklore*, 127

Shirime

Variations: Shiri-me

A disturbing creature from Japanese folklore, all the information of the shirime ("anus eye") originates from a tale told and illustrated by artist and poet Yosa Buson of Kyoto. According to the story, a samurai was traveling down a road when he heard someone call out his name; turning, he saw a man standing in the middle of the road undressing. Once nude, the man then turned around, bent over and pointed to his buttocks; where an anus should have been was an eyeball. Horrified, the samurai ran screaming and the creature was never seen again.

Source: Frater, *Com's Ultimate Book of Bizarre Lists*, 533; Haustein, *Mythologien der Welt: Japan, Ainu, Korea*, 44; Yoda, *Yokai Attack*, 137

Shirouneri

Variations: Shiro-uneri ("white winder")

A shirouneri ("white undulation") is a species of YŌKAI from Japanese folklore; born of a dish towel or rag which has been used for too many years, the item animates and takes on the appearance of a fierce but small cloth DRAGON. Flying through the air the shirouneri will chase kitchen staff and servants alike, attacking them by wrapping its old, mildewed, slimy, and smelly body around their heads causing them to pass out from its stench. On occasion, a person has died during these attacks, but the shirouneri is not murderous but rather a malicious being; any death which occurred was accidental.

Source: Meyer, *Night Parade of One Hundred Demons*, 206;

Shisa

A dog and lion hybrid from Japanese folklore, the shisa are powerful guardians, usually working in pairs; in statuary art they are depicted with one of them having its mouth closed and the other having its mouth open, barking.

Source: Maberry, *Cryptopedia*, 230

Shishi

A species of lion originating in Chinese folklore and then imported into Japanese folklore, the shishi are well known for their protective nature and are often utilized as a guardian for a child as they are equally playful and seemingly nonthreatening. Described as having bulging eyes, bushy curly tails and a pleasant temperament, these creatures are impervious to magic. Although known for being fantastic guardians and devoted parents to their own young, the shishi will throw their cubs off of a cliff to test them for their toughness and vitality, only raising the ones who survive the plunge. A shishi was the mount of the Buddhist god of wisdom, education, and calligraphy, Monju-bosatsu.

Source: Ashkenazi, *Handbook of Japanese Mythology*, 119

Shishiga, plural: shishigi

A species of female, malicious NATURE SPIRITS in Russian folklore and mythology, the shishigi live in the forests usually away from people; however what makes them especially dangerous is unlike most every other type of NATURE SPIRIT, they work in cooperative unison, collectively singling out a victim to destroy. Having no leader among them, all it takes is for one shishiga to choose a man, their most common prey, to victimize; then it calls together the rest of the race and informs them of the target. Any and all who wish to follow the sudden and impetus hunt-master will obey her orders flawlessly and without question. Once the shishigi sense fear in their prey, there is no way to be rid of them until they have achieved their goal, be it death, ruin, or a terrible fright. The only way not to have an experience with them is to show bravery from the moment one is sighted; they are described as being pale skinned nudes with wild hair.

Source: Inavits, *Russian Folk Belief*, 63; Mozhaev, '*Lively*' *and Other Stories*, 427

Shíta

A gigantic, cannibalistic creature from Hopi mythology, the shíta was said to have terrorized the village of Oraibi, capturing and consuming any children it could lay hands upon; when the children were too well protected, it would then grab up anyone it chose and, rending their body apart, consume them on the spot. The villagers asked for the assistance of the two magical heroes Pookonghoy and his younger brother Balongahoy. They had the villagers construct for them two magical arrows utilizing the wing feathers of a blue bird on the shaft; then they sought out the shíta, allowed the monster to consume them whole; from within, they shot it in the heart with the arrows, killing it.

Source: Maberry, *They Bite*, 233–4; Voth, *Traditions of the Hopi*, Volume 8, 82, 285

Shitta

According to Burmese folklore, the shitta ("the moon") are one of the four different species of the nats (the generic name for the indigenous NATURE SPIRITS of the air, cultivated fields, earth, forest, hills, households, rain, rivers, sky, streams, wind, and the like) of the Air; generally they are considered to be beneficial towards mankind. Once a year they are worshiped by the village chief; sacrifices are not required.

Source: Hastings, *Encyclopedia of Religion and Ethics*, Part 5, 22; Porteous, *Forest in Folklore and Mythology*, 125; Scott, *The Burman: His Life and Notions*, Volume 1, 286

Shojo

Variations: Shōjō

A NATURE SPIRIT in Japanese folklore, the shojo is also sometimes described as being a WILD MAN in appearance, humanoid but with pink or red skin, red hair, and wearing seaweed for clothing. Living in the ocean seabed, these amphibious creatures are said to be masters of the herbal and medical arts; the shojo also manufacture a type of saki which when consumed by a "good" person tastes like sweet nectar but when drunk by a wicked person tastes and acts like poison.

Source: Davis, *Myths and Legends of Japan*, 426; Rose, *Giants, Monsters, and Dragons*, 332

Shokera

A roof-top dwelling YŌKAI from Japanese folklore, the shokera ("roof devil"), more insidious than an ONI, uses its perch to carefully spy on the family within a home, gathering intelligence so it can create the most mischief possible. Described as being both hairy and slime covered, the shokera eventually enters into the home and creeps up on someone in order to catch them by surprise and scare them; they are so sinister and stealthy the fright they cause has been known to literally scare a person to death.

Source: Gilmore, *Monsters*, 136; Weinstock, *Ashgate Encyclopedia of Literary and Cinematic Monsters*, 449

Shoopiltee

Variations: CABYLL-USHTEY, Shoopiltie

In the Shetland and Ornkey Islands, shoopiltee are playful little water horses; they are said to be friendly to humans they encounter along the shoreline as well as sailors they encounter at sea. It has been over one hundred years since a shoopiltee has been sighted, but at one time they were said to be numerous in the North Sea.

Source: Briggs, *Encyclopedia of Fairies*, 363; Keightley, *World Guide to Gnomes, Fairies, Elves, and Other Little People*, 171; McCoy, *Witch's Guide to Faery Folk*, 311

Shudala Madan

A species of demonic GHOUL from Tamil folklore, the shudala madan ("graveyard fiend") are said to live in graveyards and linger about in locations where crimes, executions, and murders have been committed. These creatures are said to be made of half fire and half water and when not dwelling in one of these elements is in the other. Through a boon from the god Siva, they have the ability to assume any form they choose and to transform one thing into another.

Source: Blavatsky, *Isis Unveiled: Science, Volume 2*, 227

Shug Monkey

Shug Monkey is a FAIRY ANIMAL from Dutch folklore. Described as looking like an ape and black mastiff hybrid, it is very similar to the BARGUEST, the BLACK SHUCK, and the GALLEY-TROT.

Sources: Buckland, *Weiser Field Guide to Ghosts*, 113; Westwood, *Lore of the Land*, 70

Shurale

In the Russian folklore of the Volga Tartars, the shurale is a BOGEYMAN or NATURE SPIRIT haunting the forests at night; it would kill its victims by tickling them to death with its exceedingly large nipples.

Source: Krensky, *Bogeyman*, 43; *Medical Aspects of Human Sexuality*, Volume 3, 50

Shuryo

In Japanese folklore the KITSUNE (fox spirit) are divided into three ranks: the shuryo, YORIKATA, and the YAKO. The shuryo are highest of the three ranks; they are the chiefs of their kind, governing the activities of the YORIKATA and YAKO beneath them; they have no sway over KITSUNE which are not within their chain of command. Shuryo are numerous and when one tries to assume the command of a fox in the clan of another, its shuryo becomes very angry and never forgets who it was who tried to undermine him.

Source: De Visser, *Transactions of the Asiatic Society of Japan*, 82; Picken, *Essentials of Shinto*, 124

Sianach

In Scottish oral folklore the sianach ("monster") was a particularly aggressive species of deer, large and ugly. These creatures were so predatory when a hunter happened upon one, he would leave it alone and try to steal away, unseen.

Source: Rose, *Giants, Monsters, and Dragons*, 333; Zell-Ravenheart, *Wizard's Bestiary*, 88

Sien-Lung

The ancient Chinese author Hwai nan Tsze, in his attempt to prove how all creatures are the progeny of the DRAGON, shows the sien-lung having been born of the KIAI-T'AN and as being the progenitor of the YUEN-YUEN. Aquatic DRAGONs, the sien-lung live in and are only found in pools.

Source: De Visser, *Dragon in China and Japan*, 65, 72; Gould, *Mythical Monsters*, 400

Sigbin (SEAG-been)

The sigbin is a demonic creature from Philippine Visayan folklore. It is said to be a companion animal to the aswang vampire. Although descriptions of this demon vary because it has the ability to shape-shift, it is usually said to be a doglike creature with long back legs, similar to a rabbit or kangaroo; as having the body of a crow but with grasshopper legs; or as a gigantic bat with sharp teeth and long floppy ears.

A nocturnal demon, the sigbin bites the shadow of its victim, usually children, in the neck area to mystically drink their blood. Should a victim survive their attack, he must be treated with a special herbal rub. Sigbin also eat charcoal. These demons cause illness and can kill with their bite or by the smell of their flatulence. If it has large ears, it can clap them together like gigantic hands. Should its aswang master have a child, the sigbin will have an offspring itself for the aswang child.

Having the power to become invisible, the sigbin is most visible during the last phases of the moon; however, applying the tears of a dog to your eyes will let you see a sigbin for what it is. Although a sigbin cannot be drowned, once it has been slain it must be burned down to the very last hair or its aswang witch will be able to call it back to life.

Source: Icon, *Victims*, 492; Lieban, *Cebuano Sorcery*, 68

Si'lat, plural: sa'ali

Variations: Si'la

A si'lat is an invisible, demonic creature or djinn (a race of demons) from Arabic folklore. Sa'ali, as they are called in numbers, are shape-shifters who commonly choose to appear as women. These demons capture men and force them to dance for their pleasure. Sa'ali are hated by wolves and when attacked they will cry out for help, even going so far as to offer vast sums of money to anyone who would rescue them. It is said the Arabic clan 'Amr b.Yarbu are descended from a si'lat.

Source: Hastings, *Encyclopedia of Religion and Ethics*, Part 2, 670; Hughes, *Dictionary of Islam*, 137; Thompson, *Semitic Magic*, 70; Zwemer, *Influence of Animism on Islam*, 126

Silenus

Variations: Sileni, Silenoi

In ancient Greek mythology Silenus was the oldest and the wisest of the SATYRS. An attendant of the god Bacchus (Dionysos), Silenus was often depicted as a comical, drunken, obese, old man riding upon a mule. If a person was able to capture Silenus and tie him up, he would reveal his captor's destiny, as Silenus possessed the ability to see both the future and the past. In some myths Silenus was said to be born the son of the god Pan (Faunus) while others said he was born the son of the god Hermes (Mercury) and the goddess Gaea. Silenus was the father of three sons, two SATYRS named Astraeus and Maron, and a CENTAUR named PHOLUS.

In later myths aged SATYRS were all named Silenus and had the lower body of a horse; the younger ones had goat legs.

Source: Graves, *Larousse Encyclopedia of Mythology*, 161; Littleton, *Gods, Goddesses, and Mythology*, Volume 11, 1305–06; Rose, *Spirits, Fairies, Leprechauns, and Goblins*, 293

Silfrintoppr

Variations: Silfrintop, Silfrintopp, Silfrtoppr

Silfrintoppr ("silver forelock" or "silver top") was one of the horses utilized by the Aesir in Norse mythology; its specific owner or rider is not mentioned. Silfrintoppr was also listed as one of the many horses who would graze in the red-gilt leafed Glasir Grove.

Source: Anderson, *Norse Mythology*, 189; Grimes, *Norse Myths*, 20, 296; Norroena Society, *Asatrii Edda*, 384; Sturluson, *Prose Edda*, 28

Simmurgh

The King of the Birds in Arabic folklore, the simmurg, related to the PHOENIX and ROC, is believed to live for either one thousand seven hundred years or two thousand years, or perhaps is immortal. Making its nest in the Tree of Knowledge the simmurgh is so large it can carry an elephant in each talon.

Source: Zell-Ravenheart, *Companion for the Apprentice Wizard*, 179

Simorgh

Variations: Rahshi, Siorgh, Simarghu, Simug, Simurgh, Sina Mru, Sumargh

A gigantic creature, the simorgh is described as being chimerical, having the features of a winged GRIFFIN, a lion, and PHOENIX. Possessing legendary oracular powers, it acted as the guardian of the ancient Persian Mysteries. Tahmurath, the Persian equivalent of the Biblical Adam, had one of these creatures as his personal mount.

Source: Barber, *Dictionary of Fabulous Beasts*, 140; Blavatsky, *Theosophical Glossary*, 299, 317; Zell-Ravenheart, *Wizard's Bestiary*, 88

Sinaa

A hybrid monstrosity from Brazilian folklore, Sinna was born of the union between a woman and a gigantic jaguar; described as being humanoid in appearance, he was born with "an ancient appearance," meaning his eyes were set in the back of his head. He is sometimes considered to be the ancestral progenitor of the Juruna people who live along the Xingu River. Sinna has the ability to rejuvenate himself when he removes his skin by pulling it off over the top of his head. There is a prophecy claiming the end of the world will occur when Sinna removes the pole which separates the heavens from the earth.

Source: Cotterell, *Dictionary of World Mythology*, 288; Rose, *Giants, Monsters, and Dragons*, 335

Siner (SIN-ir)

Variations: Sinir

In Norse mythology, Siner ("strong of sinew") was one of the named mounts of the twelve Norse gods; each day he was ridden to the daily gathering and is noted for being the seventh best horse of the herd.

Source: Anderson, *Norse Mythology*, 189; Daly, *Norse Mythology A to Z*, 51; Norroena Society, *Asatrii Edda*, 384

Singa

In Batak folklore the singa ("lion") is a creature with unsettled and undefined appearance; features range from anthropomorphic to buffalo-like to leonine. Generally they are given large bulging eyes and a long face but almost always they have a set of eyebrows so prominent as to look like a rack of antlers. Sometimes it has an alicorn (a single horn) growing out of the center of its forehead. The image of the singa is used as a protective symbol.

Source: Maberry, *Vampire Universe*, 263; Zell-Ravenheart, *Wizard's Bestiary*, 89

Sinhika

A female DRAGON from Hindu mythology, Sinhika ("lioness") was the enemy of the ape-god Hanuman. She was the mother of gigantic *daitya* (a race of hostile giants from Hindu mythology) Rahu. In her final confrontation, Hanuman dove into her mouth and allowed her to swallow him whole; then from within, he stabbed at her and she died.

Source: Fontenrose, *Python*, 207; Gilman, *New International Encyclopædia*, Volume 16, 654; Rose, *Giants, Monsters, and Dragons*, 335

Sinlap

According to Burmese folklore, the sinlap, the givers of wisdom, were a species of the nats (the generic name for the indigenous NATURE SPIRITS of the air, cultivated fields, earth, forest, hills, households, rain, rivers, sky, streams, wind, and the like); generally they were considered to be beneficial towards mankind. Once a year they are worshiped by the village chief; sacrifices are not required.

Source: Hastings, *Encyclopedia of Religion and Ethics*, Part 5, 22; Porteous, *Forest in Folklore and Mythology*, 125; Scott, *Burman*, Volume 1, 286

Sint Holo

A species of HORNED SERPENT or NATURE SPIRIT from Chickasaw folklore, the sint holo ("sacred snake") were said to harm neither cattle nor man and lived peaceably in large creeks or in caves. Not everyone had the ability to see these creatures but on occasion one would allow a person to catch a glimpse and in doing so would invest them with wisdom. Whenever the snakes needed to move from one water source to another, they would make it rain so they could leave their hiding places in secret and unseen. The sint holo are noted for making a sound very much like the crack of thunder.

Source: Eberhart, *Mysterious Creatures*, 500; Swanton, *Chickasaw Society and Religion*, 79

Siren Serpent

In Persian folklore the siren serpents, one of the KHRAFSTRA, were said to be a species of winged snake so poisonous a person would die before the pain of the bite could be comprehended. These creatures were fearful of horses and would flee their presence.

Source: Clark, *Medieval Book of Beasts*, 200; Hassig, *Mark of the Beast*, 194

Sirin

Variations: Ptitsa Sirin ("sirin bird")

A creature of Russian folklore which likely originated in Persian folklore, the sirin was described as having the face (and sometimes the breasts) of a beautiful maiden but the body of a bird; unlike the SIREN of Greek folklore using its voice to lure sailors to their death, the sirin used its enchanting voice as a reward gifted upon the virtuous. In art the sirin was depicted as having a long peacock tail with distinctive eyes patterned upon it and wearing a crown upon its head. Flying down from heaven, it would sing its song to the fortunate few; but it would be the last thing they ever heard, as anyone who has ever listened to its song would instantly forget everything and then, die. The sirin is considered to be a heavenly bird of happiness; her counterpart is the ALKONOST, the bird of sorrow.

Source: Alexander, *Fairies*, 153; Dixon-Kennedy, *Encyclopedia of Russian and Slavic Myth and Legend*, 258

Sirius

Variations: T'ein Kou

In Greek mythology Sirius ("brightness and heat"), the dog of Orion, was said to have followed his master when he became a constellation; there are many versions of how this came to be. In one telling Orion was accidentally shot with an arrow by the goddess Artemis by the instigation of her brother, Apollo. In another version Artemis slew Orion because he had bragged too much about having hunted and killed all the wild beasts in Crete. And in yet another telling, Orion, after having attempted and failing to rape the goddess, Artemis created a scorpion from the earth and set it to kill him; the monster killed both Orion and his faithful dog, Sirius.

The earliest reference to this constellation comes from Homer. There are no independent stories of Sirius apart from its connection to the constellation.

Source: Baker, *Enigmas of History*, n.pag.; Barber, *Dictionary of Fabulous Beasts*, 143; Olcott, *Star Lore of All Ages*, 67

Sivko Burko

In Russian folklore Sivko Burko ("black steed") was the magical horse of the hero Ivan the Fool. A renowned warhorse with the ability to see the future, when Sivko Burko ran, sparks flew from his eyes and hooves, a pillar of steam pumped from his nostrils, and the earth shook. The horse could make such long and incredible leaps, it was as if it were flying. Whenever Ivan the Fool would climb into the horse's right ear, he would emerge from its left as a handsome young man, expensively and nicely dressed.

Source: Haney, *Complete Russian Folktale*, 77–9; Propp, *Russian Folktale by Vladimir Yakovlevich Propp*, 40, 173–4

Six-Headed Wild Ram

In ancient Sumerian mythology, Six-Headed Wild Ram was one of the many monsters slain by the warrior god Ninurta. Little is known of this creature other than Gudea, a ruler of Lagash (c.a. 2100 BC), referred to it, and the other monsters vanquished by Ninurta, as the SLAIN HEROES; he elevated them all to the status of god and made a place of worship for them in the temple.

Source: Ataç, *Mythology of Kingship in Neo-Assyrian Art*, 185; Salem, *Near East, the Cradle of Western Civilization*, 102–3; Sherman, *Storytelling*, 332

Siyokoy (sho-koy)

A species of MERMEN from Filipino folklore, the siyokoy, counterpart to the female sirena (see MERMAID), has the upper body of a man and the lower body of a fish or, in some stories, is an anthropoid whose body is covered in glistening brown or green fish scales and webbed feet. Some descriptions also give them long, green tentacles and gill slits. Siyokoy drown fishermen and consume them for food.

Source: de Las Casas, *Tales from the 7,000 Isles*, xvi; Newton, *Hidden Animals*, 167

Sjörå

Variations: Havsfru

A freshwater NATURE SPIRIT from German folklore, the sjörå was said to be helpful by pointing out good fishing spots and warning of storms if it was given offerings or left alone. When angered these creatures would cause death by drowning. Although the sjörå are almost always female, there are a few stories where one has been said to be male. A sjörå can be magically "bound" to its location by encircling its pond or lake with consecrated soil. Desperate to escape she will make offerings of fish in exchange for her freedom.

Source: Leddon, *Child's Eye View of Fair Folk*, 53; Monaghan, *Encyclopedia of Goddesses and Heroines*, 292

Skaevadr (SKAI-vath-r)

Variations: Skævadr

In Norse mythology, Snorri Sturlson (1179–1241), the Icelandic historian, poet, and politician, writes the horse Skaevadr ("the hurrying") was the preferred mount of the Ruler of Haddings, Haddingr, in his translation of *Prose Edda*. Skaevadr was also listed as one of the many horses who would graze in the red-gilt leafed Glasir Grove.

Source: Grimes, *Norse Myths*, 20; Norroena Society, *Asatrii Edda*, 385; Young, *Prose Edda*, 211

Skeidbrimir (SKAYTH-brim-ir)

Skeidbrimir ("fast galloper") was one of the horses utilized by the Aesir in Norse mythology; its specific owner or rider is not mentioned. Skeidbrimir was also listed as one of the many horses who would graze in the red-gilt leafed Glasir Grove.

Source: Grimes, *Norse Myths*, 20; Norroena Society, *Asatrii Edda*, 385; Sturluson, *Prose Edda*, 28

Skelkingr

A king of the TROLLS in Norse mythology, Skelkingr ("mockery" or "scary") ruled his people from his land of Dumbshfr ("misty sea") in the Arctic Ocean, north of Norway.

Source: Grimm, *Teutonic Mythology*, Volume 3, 1043; Lindow, *Trolls*, n.pag.

Skinfaxi (SKIN-vaks-i)

Variations: Skinfax

In Norse mythology Skinfaxi ("shining-mane") was one of the many winged horses said to assist in pulling the sun across the sky (see also AARVAK,

AVAK, ALSVID, and HRIMFAXI); the chariot was driven by Dagr, the son of Dellingr and Natt. Skinfaxi was considered to be the most beautiful as well as the best of these horses.

Source: Daly, *Norse Mythology A to Z*; Oehlenschläger, *Gods of the North*, lxii; Norroena Society, *Asatrii Edda*, xxx; Rose, *Giants, Monsters, and Dragons*, 178

Skoedbrimir (SKURTH-brim-ir)

In Norse mythology Skoedbrimir ("fire shoes" or "shoe brimir") was one of the many named horses of the Aesir who, beyond a name, there is nothing else known.

Source: Norroena Society, *Asatrii Edda*, 385

Skoffin

Variations: Scoffin

The skoffin of Icelandic myth is similar to the BASILISK in appearance (a bird with DRAGON-like qualities) and behavior. The only thing which could kill a skoffin was the deadly stare of another skoffin. In later versions of the myth, it was said in order to rid the island of these deadly creatures the people had to shoot each one with a silver button upon which the Cross had been engraved.

Source: Barber, *Dictionary of Fabulous Beasts*, 136; Conway, *Magickal, Mystical Creatures*, 185; Zell-Ravenheart, *Wizard's Bestiary*, 89

Skrat

Variations: Scrat, Scrato, Skraethins

In Teutonic, German, folklore there is a FAIRY ANIMAL called a skrat similar to the British bogart (an injurious species of fairy) and the Irish cluricaunes (a sub-species of bogart); it is described as looking like a chicken caught out in the rain; its wingtips and tail dragging along the ground. Reported to live in beech trees or caves, the skrat has the ability to shape-shift into a cat, dog, goose, or a hair-covered man. Any family the skrat lived with soon became rich; however in Saxon folklore the skrat were reputed to attack women.

Source: Knight, *Sexual Symbolism*, 163; Forlong, *Faiths of Man*, 317

Skratt

Variations: Skrati ("guffawing"), Skratte, Skratten

An undefined NATURE SPIRIT from Old Norse traditions, the skratt is described in a chimerical fashion, said to have the properties of a Devil, GIANT, ghost, hobgoblin, TROLL, Wizard, and woodland sprite.

Source: Grimm, *Teutonic Mythology*, 1004; Philological Society (Great Britain), *Publications of the Philological Society*, Volume 1, 160

Skriker

Originating from Yorkshire folklore, Skriker is a FAIRY ANIMAL appearing as a BLACK DOG or BARGUEST; it also has the ability to become invisible. This creature received its name for the horrific scream it makes while invisible. It has been said Skriker is a psychopomp (death omen) appearing to someone who will soon have a death in their family; it also splashes in ponds creating a disturbance, and stalks behind travelers as they walk down lonely roads at night. Those who have attacked the skriker have never been able to deliver any sort of damage to it, as there has never been a successful solid blow hitting it; it is likely weapons are passing right through the creature.

Source: Briggs, *Fairies in Tradition and Literature*, 279; Eberhart, *Mysterious Creatures*, 555; Turner, *Yorkshire Notes and Queries*, Volumes 1–2, 203

Skrimsl

Variations: Haf-Skrimsl, Haf-Strambr, Skirimsl

A FAIRY ANIMAL and wormlike SEA SERPENT from Icelandic folklore, the skrimsl is said to live in lakes and along the coastline of Lagafljot. Malevolent and malicious, they were especially unfriendly towards humans, sinking fishing vessels which sail along the Thorska-fjord. The skrimsl are described as looking like an overturned ship between 180 and 240 feet (54 to 73 meters) long, bobbing along the surface of the water; they have a hump on their back and a blow-hole which sprays up water like jets, similar to a whale. Violent and predatory, they were rendered harmless and bound by Saint Gudmund to remain that way until doomsday.

Source: Baring-Gould, *Iceland*, 345–46, 348; Rose, *Spirits, Fairies, Leprechauns, and Goblins*, 296; Zell-Ravenheart, *Wizard's Bestiary*, 91

Sky Women

Variations: Sky Maidens

In Polish folklore the sky women were said to be a species of RUSALKA, who would in warm weather months rise from water, such as ponds and wells, in the form of small whirlwinds or tiny tornadoes and ascend up into the clouds. With them the sky women would carry water to seed the clouds with so it would rain and replenish the earth.

Source: Pellowski, *Polish Folktales and Folklore*, 192; Larrington, *Woman's Companion to Mythology*, 107

Skyphios

Variations: Skeironiles

In Thessalian legends, Poseidon (Neptune) was said to be the progenitor of equines as one day he was lying asleep upon the shore in a location called

Petraios ("he of the rock," so named to honor the event) where he had inadvertently released some semen upon the rocky ground and caused the creation of the first horse, Skyphis ("ship of the plains"). Some accounts say it was at this time AREION was also created. Later accounts say the god struck the earth with his trident creating the first horse. The city of Athens boasted the event of the creation of the first horse there when Poseidon (Neptune), fertilizing the land at Kolonos, created the first horse they called Skeironites.

Source: Baldwin, *Horse Fair*, 131; Hard, *Routledge Handbook of Greek Mythology*, 102; Ogden, *Companion to Greek Religion*, 276

The Slain Heroes

In ancient Sumerian mythology, the Slain Heroes was the collective name given by the ruler of Lagash, Gudea (ca. 2100 BC), to the monsters slain by the warrior god Ninurta; Gudea elevated them all to the status of god and created a place of worship for them in the temple. The names of the Slain Heroes are ANZU, ASAG the DRAGON, BISON BULL, GYPSUM, KULI-ANA, LORD SAMAN-ANA, MAGILLUM-BOAT, PTKINS, SEVEN-HEADED SNAKE, SIX-HEADED WILD RAM, and STRONG COPPER.

Source: Ataç, *Mythology of Kingship in Neo-Assyrian Art*, 185; Salem, *Near East, the Cradle of Western Civilization*, 102–3

Sleipnir (SLAYP-nir)

Variations: Sleipne ("tie slipper"), Slipener

One of the chargers belonging to Odin from Norse mythology, Sleipnir ("the runner" or "the slipper") was described as having eight legs, one for each of the cardinal points. Born of a union between the stallion SVADILFARE and the god Loki who assumed the form of a mare in order to distract the horse from its work constructing the walls of Asguard, Sleipnir was gifted to Oden in order for the Trickster to regain his brother's good graces. Sleipner had a long body and reminded Odin of standard bearers carrying a coffin; he also ran at incredible speeds, had runes of wisdom carved upon his teeth, was an excellent high-jumper, and knew the journey between Valhalla and Helheimr.

Source: Brewer, *Dictionary of Phrase and Fable*, 627; Norroena Society, *Asatrii Edda*, 386; Oehlenschläger, *Gods of the North*, lxii; Sturluson, *Prose Edda*, 28; Zell-Ravenheart, *Wizard's Bestiary*, 91

Slide Rock Bolter

Originating in the lumberjack communities of the developing United States of America, the frightful slide rock bolter of Colorado is counted among the FEARSOME CRITTERS. Living in the areas of the mountains were the land is at least sloped at a forty-five degree angle, it was described as having an overly large head, tiny eyes, a sculpin-like mouth reaching back almost to its ears, and a tail which was like twin flippers with hooks at the end and which it would use to anchor itself to rock faces where it would hang for days waiting for a hiking tourist to pass nearby. When this would finally happen, it would drool down a stream of greasy saliva, release its tail, and like a flesh landslide, skid at its prey, snatching it up in its mouth as it rocketed by heading to the next slope. Then using its tail it would latch onto something and halt.

Source: Cox, *Fearsome Creatures of the Lumberwoods*, 21; Rose, *Giants, Monsters, and Dragons*, 119

Slidrugtanni

Variations: Sliorugtanni

Slidrugtanni ("fearful tusk") was one of the boars or pigs named in Thorgrimr's *Rhymes* and in Snorri Sturluson's (1179–1241) *Prose Edda*. Although many sources list Slidrugtanni as an alternate name for GULLINBORSTI, the boar of the god Freyr, some scholars claim he owned two animals.

Source: Jennbert, *Animals and Humans*, 49; Rydberg, *Teutonic Mythology: Gods and Goddesses of the Northland*, Volume 3, 876

Sliver Cat

Originating in the lumberjack communities of the developing United States of America, sliver cat, one of the FEARSOME CRITTERS, was native to the Wisconsin area. Described as being gigantic, having feathery long fur tufts at the tips of its ears, vertical red-slit eyes, and an extremely lethal tail: one side of it was hard and flat and used for slapping its prey in the head, the other side had a huge spike which the sliver cat used to slay its stunned opponent.

Source: Gard, *Wisconsin Lore*, 73; Godfrey, *Monsters of Wisconsin*, 132; Rose, *Giants, Monsters, and Dragons*, 119

Slöngvir

Variations: Slongvir, Slungnir ("the hurling")

In Norse mythology, Snorri Sturlson (1179–1241), the Icelandic historian, poet, and politician, writes the horse Slöngvir ("slinger") was the preferred mount of King Adils as it was the fastest of all the steeds, in his translation of *Prose Edda*.

Source: Grimes, *Norse Myths*, 299; Norroena Society, *Asatrii Edda*, 387; Sturluson, *Prose Edda*, Volume 5, 212

The Small Man

A NURSERY BOGIE from the Bahamas folklore, the small man is utilized by parents whose children will not come indoors after sundown. Touring the town in his small cart, the small man is in constant search for children; if he finds them, he will capture them and toss them in the back of his cart where they will be condemned to ride forever.

Source: Frater, *Listverse*, 579

Smerkava

In Wend mythology the smerkava ("dusk woman") is a being or creature said to be fatal to children.

Source: Wolff, *Odd Bits of History*, 152

Snake Griffin

Usually depicted with scales covering its body, the snake griffin is considered by some scholars such as Heinz Adolf Mode (August 15, 1913–July 6, 1992), a former professor of Oriental archaeology at University of Halle, as being a variant of the DRAGON while others, like H. Prinz, see it as being its own unique mythological species along with the bird griffin and the lion griffin. The snake griffin was said to have the body of a lion covered with scales and the neck and head of a snake.

Source: Mode, *Fabulous Beasts and Demons*, 128; South, *Mythical and Fabulous Creatures*, 87; Zell-Ravenheart, *Wizard's Bestiary*, 91

Snavidka

Variations: Snavidhka, Srvara

A fearsome and monstrous DRAGON from Zoroastrian mythology, Snavidka was poisonous, horned, with hands of stone, and a man-eater; he was described as having yellow scales covering his humanoid body. From an early age, Snavidka boasted proudly upon reaching adulthood he would summon the spirits of Good and Evil and harness them to his chariot, making them pull him around the earth. It was realized if his power was not contained he would become the threat he promised, so Snavidka was killed at an early age by the hero Keresaspa of the Sama family.

Source: Boyce, *History of Zoroastrianism*, 91; Cohn, *Cosmos, Chaos, and the World to Come*, 108

Snawfus

A magical white deer in Ozark folklore, United States of America, the snawfus was not considered to be dangerous and had the ability to make incredible leaps from the ground up into the treetops; in some descriptions, it was said to have wings.

Source: Cavendish, *Man, Myth and Magic*, Volume 5, 2101; Rose, *Giants, Monsters, and Dragons*, 343

Snee-Nee-Iq

A NURSERY BOGIE from the Kwakiutl folklore of the Canadian province of British Columbia, the boney-legged and tall Snee-Nee-Iq is said to capture and consume children who wandered too far away from their parents. Living high up in the mountains,

she secretly sneaks down to snatch up children, tosses them in her pannier, and carries them back up to her mountain top home where she smokes them over a fire as if they were salmon before she eats them.

Source: Rose, *Giants, Monsters, and Dragons*, 343; Sierra, *Gruesome Guide to World Monsters*, 9

Snipe

Originating in the lumberjack communities of the developing United States of America, the snipe, perhaps the best known of the FEARSOME CRITTERS, is said to be a common nocturnal bird (or small breed mammal) which has been seen on occasion but never captured. It is told the only way to capture one is for a group of individuals to venture out into the woods at night leaving one person in an isolated area to be the catcher while the others walk off so they can drive the snipe into the net of the waiting catcher.

Source: Leary, *Wisconsin Folklore*, 375; Rose, *Giants, Monsters, and Dragons*, 119; Watts, *Encyclopedia of American Folklore*, 206

Snoligoster

Originating in the lumberjack communities of the developing United States of America, the snoligoster of the cypress swamps of Florida is listed as being one of the FEARSOME CRITTERS. This creature is gigantic in size and has a voracious appetite which can only be temporarily quenched by consuming humans in its particularly gruesome way. The snoligoster is said to look like a legless crocodile whose body is covered with short, slick fur. The tail of the creature ends with three bony plates affixed to its body in such a way they are utilized exactly like a boat propeller, the method by which this creature is then able to swim through the water. Upon its back is a tall spike. The snoligoster cruises through the water seeking out unsuspecting people to prey upon; when it comes upon them, it snatches them up and flings them high into the air giving itself time to maneuver its body so the person lands on the spike, impaling them. After the snoligoster has collected several people in this fashion it now uses its tail to dig a deep hole in the mud where it then works the bodies off its back and into the hole. Finally, it lowers its tail into the pit and grinds the bodies up into a soupy human batter which the creature then greedily consumes.

Source: Cox, *Fearsome Creatures of the Lumberwoods*, 15; Rose, *Giants, Monsters, and Dragons*, 119; Zell-Ravenheart, *Wizard's Bestiary*, 226

Snow Snake

Originating in the lumberjack communities of the developing United States of America, the snow snake, one of the FEARSOME CRITTERS, was said to be a white scaled serpent with flashing red eyes, active mostly during the winter months. All but invisible in the snow, the snow snakes, native of North Asia and imported here with immigrants relocating, were able to slide up on their prey and attack from near complete stealth without their prey ever knowing they were there until they felt the bite of their fangs.

Source: Brown, *Wisconsin Folklore Publications: 1947–1948*, 89, 95; Rose, *Giants, Monsters, and Dragons*, 343

Snow Wasset

Originating in the lumberjack communities of the developing United States of America, the snow wasset of Canadian folklore, one of the FEARSOME CRITTERS, was one of the few migratory animals lumberjacks had to contend with. Spending winter months in the Great Lakes region near the Hudson Bay and their summers in Labrador and the Barren Grounds regions, the snow wassets only hibernated in the warmest parts of the year when their fur would turn green and curl and their bodies would sprout small rudimentary legs; they would make their burrows in cranberry bogs. Immediately after the first snow fall they shed their legs and, swimming porpoise-like in the snow, they hunt in corporative packs for grouse, rabbits, and in hard winters, even wolves. Having a voracious appetite, the snow wasset is said to be four times as active, large, and hungry as the wolverine.

Source: Cox, *Fearsome Creatures of the Lumberwoods*, 39; Rose, *Giants, Monsters, and Dragons*, 119; Zell-Ravenheart, *Wizard's Bestiary*, 226

Snydae

Originating in the lumberjack communities of the developing United States of America, the snydae, one of the FEARSOME CRITTERS, were a microscopic form of marine life which only lived in the Kennebec River of Maine. The minute snydae only ate the eggs of another creature which thrived in the same river, the GAZERIUM. Interestingly the GAZERIUM only feed on snydae. Because of this gruesome symbiotic relationship between the two, both the GAZERIUM and the snydae went extinct.

Source: Mencken, *American Language*, 251; Rose, *Giants, Monsters, and Dragons*, 119

Sojobo

Variations: Dai Tengu (DAITENGU), Dai Tengu Sojobo

In Japanese legend, Sojobo was said to be the king of the TENGU; he was said to have given sword-fighting lessons to Minamoto no Yoshitsune on Mount Kurama. In art, Sojobo was depicted as having a long crow's beak, a long white beard which reached his belt, and wings; his mount was a boar.

Source: Ashkenazi, *Handbook of Japanese Mythology*, 97; Ball, *Animal Motifs in Asian Art*, 127; Frédéric, *Japan Encyclopedia*, 899, 958

Solaris

The Greek didactic text *Physiologus* written by an unknown author and dated to the second century AD describes the solaris as a fish which when caught is happy to be on land, as it so loves the sunlight. It was said to grow quite large, have black slippery eel-like skin, a large head, and a wide mouth, and when cooked, was rather tasty.

Source: Zell-Ravenheart, *Wizard's Bestiary*, 91

Songomby

A carnivorous creature from Malagasy folklore, the songomby ("ox with upper lip turned upward") is described as being about the size of an ox but moves with the swiftness of a horse and is addicted to human flesh. Living in caves, these nocturnal creatures are utilized as a NURSERY BOGIE, as to capture one requires placing a child in a pot with ample breathing holes and a locking lid. The bait is then suspended outside the creature's cave and the terrified crying of the child will lure the songomby out of its lair.

Source: Littell, *The Living Age*, Volume 200, 563; Sibree, *Folk-lore Record*, Volume 2, 27; Tyson, *Madagascar*, 247

Sóti (SOHT-i)

Variations: Soti

Sóti ("soot colored") was one of the horses utilized by the Aesir in Norse mythology; its specific owner or rider is not mentioned. Sóti was also listed as one of the many horses who would graze in the red-gilt leafed Glasir Grove.

Source: Grimes, *Norse Myths*, 20, 299; Norroena Society, *Asatrii Edda*, 387

Soucayant (Soo-koo-yah)

Variations: Heg, Ol' Higue, Soucouyant, Soucouyen, Soukoyan

On the island of Trinidad there is a vampiric creature called a soucayant which looks like an old woman who sleeps all day. However, at night, it removes its skin and emerges as a ball of light, resembling a corpse candle (a glowing, spectral ball of glowing light), and flies out looking for sleeping people to attack in order to drink their blood. Victims of the attack will have two small bite marks side by side someplace on the body.

If the soucayant is seen before it attacks, the vampire can be driven off by beating it with a stick. The next day search the community for an old woman who is covered in bruises. When you find her, you have found the soucayant. Like many of the vampires who can remove their skin and turn into a ball of light, such as the asema and the aswang mannanang-gal, if you can find its shed skin and rub it with salt, its hide will shrivel up. When the soucayant returns, it will not be able to fit back into its skin and will die when the sun rises. Also, like the asema and the ch'ing shih, the soucayant is compelled to count seeds it comes across. The easiest way to kill a soucayant is to toss a handful of poppy seeds down at the crossroads, as the vampire will be compelled to count them all, a feat which will take all night. The light from the rising sun will then destroy it.

Source: Besson, *Folklore and Legends of Trinidad and Tobago*, 31–33; Liverpool, *Rituals of Power and Rebellion*, 202, 210, 237; Russell, *Legends of the Bocas*, 49–51; University College of the West Indies, *Caribbean Quarterly*, Volume 45, 72

Sphinx, Egyptian

A chimerical creature from ancient Egyptian mythology, the sphinx is described as having the head of a hawk, king, queen, or ram and the body of a lion. Often employed as a guardian to a temple or tomb, the sphinx is the embodiment of the power and duty of Pharaoh to defend Egypt.

There were three types of sphinxes: the ANDROSPHINX, the CRIOSPHINX, and the HIERA-COSPHINX. Each of these variations represented the king as well as being a token of respect to the god whose head they most resembled. As a symbol of the king of Egypt, the idea of this creature being female came much later on in their history. The ANDROSPHINX had the head of a man and the body of a lion; it represented the union of intellectual and physical power; it therefore was associated with the human-headed gods Amon, Khem, Pthah, and Osiris. The CRIOSPHINX had the head of a ram and the body of a lion and therefore was associated with the god Neph. The HIERACOSPHINX had the head of a hawk and the body of a lion and therefore was associated with the god Re.

When depicted standing, the Egyptian sphinx is most often shown trampling the enemies of Egypt beneath its feet. The female sphinx is sometimes shown as being winged and may have influenced the appearance of the Greek sphinx. The aker is a double headed sphinx; it is the guardian of the two horizons, the sunrise and sunset, the entrance and exit to Tuat, the Egyptian Underworld.

Source: Budge, *Gods of the Egyptians*, 60; Mercatante, *Who's Who in Egyptian Mythology*, 169; Pinch, *Handbook of Egyptian Mythology*, 206–7; Remler, *Egyptian Mythology, A to Z*, 182–3; Wilkinson, *Manners and Customs of the Ancient Egyptians*, Volume 5, 200–01

Spider Hengeyokai

In Japanese folklore spider hengeyokai are creatures described as having burning red eyes and sharp teeth; they have the ability to shape-shift into the form of beautiful women.

Source: Bush, *Asian Horror Encyclopedia*, 172

Splinter Cat

Variations: Splintercat

Originating in the lumberjack communities of the developing United States of America, the frightfully destructive splinter cat, one of the FEARSOME CRITTERS, was found between the Great Lakes to the Gulf and east to the Atlantic, but not in the Rocky Mountains. Surviving exclusively on honey and raccoon flesh, it would hunt for its food only on dark, stormy, and windy nights. At random, the splinter cat would select a tree it hoped contained either a honeycomb or a nest of raccoons and then climb up a nearby tree. From the topmost branches it would then leap across to its intended tree and using its face, slam into the trunk, creating a path of destruction as it slid down, leaving the tree broken and splintered in its wake.

Source: Botkin, *American People*, 257; Cox, *Fearsome Creatures of the Lumberwoods*, 37; Rose, *Giants, Monsters, and Dragons*, 119; Theitic, *Witches' Almanac, Issue 34*, 17

Spornvitnir (SPAWR-vit-nir)

Variations: Sporvitnir ("wolf-trampler")

In Norse mythology, Spornvitnir ("spur-wolf") was a horse named in the *Poetic Edda*; it was to be ridden to Sparinsheith as per Hothbrodd's orders.

Source: Bellows, *Poetic Edda*, 306; Norroena Society, *Asatrii Edda*, 387

Spumador

Variations: The Foamy Steed

In Arthurian folklore the fierce Spumador ("foam gilded" or "the foaming one") was the name of one of the horses of King Arthur. In battle, Spumador was described as running down and trampling the enemy like weeds beneath his hooves and having a lineage tracing back to the heavenly divine horses given to Tros by his grandfather, the Greek god Zeus (Jupiter).

Source: Brewer, *Dictionary of Phrase and Fable*, 627; Hamilton, *Spenser*, 264, 290; Tozer, *Horse in History*, 82

Squonk

Originating in the lumberjack communities of the developing United States of America, the squonk, one of the FEARSOME CRITTERS, was seldom seen outside of its native Pennsylvania where it lives in the hemlock forests. Described as having ill-fitting skin covered in moles and warts, the squonk travels little but when it must, does so only during dusk and twilight. Heavily depressed over their appearance, all squonks are constantly weeping over their wretchedness; they shed so many tears hunters are able to track them in this way. When cornered, frightened, surprised, or in a situation where escape seems impossible, the squonk may erupt into gigantic tears and dissolve away.

Source: Barber, *Dictionary of Fabulous Beasts*, 139; Cox, *Fearsome Creatures of the Lumberwoods*, 31; Rose, *Giants, Monsters, and Dragons*, 119; Theitic, *Witches' Almanac, Issue 34*, 16

Sri (SHREE)

Variations: Srin

Originating in the Bon religion of Tibet is the sri, a species of demonic subterranean vampiric beings. As corpse eaters, they are especially fond of consuming children, chasing them down, and when catching them, devouring them. Sri live underground and linger in places where corpses have been laid out. They have the ability to possess a person, after which a sri-pressing exorcism must be performed to force the demon to return to the underworld until it has received "the Bodhisattiva mind."

Source: Jäschke, *Tibetan-English Dictionary*, 581; Kloppenborg, *Female Stereotypes in Religious Traditions*, 182, 192; Lurker, *Dictionary of Gods and Goddesses, Devils and Demons*, 176; Mumford, *Himalayan Dialogue*, 148

Stefiu

The Stefiu are a collection of four beings from ancient Egyptian mythology who reside in the tenth section, or hour, of Tuat, the Underworld; there they hold the arch-serpent, APOPHIS, on a chain, keeping him as their prisoner.

Source: Budge, *Gods of the Egyptians*, 198; Mercatante, *Who's Who in Egyptian Mythology*, 169

Sterope

In classical Greek and Roman mythology Sterope ("lightning"), one of the HIPPOI ATHANATOI, was one of the many winged horses said to assist in pulling the sun across the sky. Sterope was said to be faster than lightning; she and BRONTE were said to be mares and the yoke horses of the team.

Source: Apollodorus, *Apollodorus' Library and Hyginus' Fabulae*, 158; Rose, *Giants, Monsters, and Dragons*, 178

Sthenius

In classical Greek mythology, Sthenius ("powerful," "strengthening") was the name of one of the horses of the god of the sea, Poseidon (Neptune); beyond a name, little else is known.

Source: Smith, *Dictionary of Greek and Roman Biography and Mythology: Oarses-Zygia*, 911

Stheno

Variations: Sthenno, Sthenusa

One of the three GORGONS from classical Greek mythology, Stheno ("forceful" or "mighty one") and her sister EURYALE were each immortal but their sister MEDUSA was not. Born the daughters of Phorcys and Ceto the once beautiful Stheno and her transformed sisters lived in Lybia; she is described as having brazen claws and serpents for hair. She and her sisters are so vile to look upon that anyone who sees them is transformed into stone.

After the hero Perseus slew MEDUSA the sisters gave chase, but as he was aided by the helmet of Hades (Dis) and could become invisible, he was able to evade them. It is said the goddess Athena (Minerva) invented flute-playing after being inspired by the grieving cries of EURYALE and Stheno.

Source: Berens, *Myths and Legends of Ancient Greece and Rome*, 144; Dixon-Kennedy, *Encyclopedia of Greco-Roman Mythology*, 284; Rose, *Handbook of Greek Mythology*, 22

Sticte

A dog from ancient Greek mythology, Sticte ("spot") was one of the DOGS OF ACTÆON, the unfortunate youth who was raised by the CENTAUR CHEIRON. Sticte, a female, was noted and named for her coat which offered a variety of colors and a diverse arrangement of spots.

Source: Leeming, *World of Myth*, 111; Murray, *Classical Manual*, 160; Naso, *Fasti, Tristia*, 93–5

Stihi

The stihi is a demonic creature from southern Italo-Albanian demonology. This female, fire-breathing DRAGON greedily guards her treasure trove.

Source: Elsie, *Dictionary of Albanian Religion, Mythology, and Folk Culture*, 241; Lurker, *Routledg Dictionary of Gods and Goddesses, Devils and Demons*, 330; Maberry, *Vampire Universe*, 272; Rose, *Giants, Monsters, and Dragons*, 345

Stiifr (STOOV-r)

Variations: Stufr

In Norse mythology Stiifr ("the kicking") was the horse Vifill rode in the Battle on the Lake of Ice, as recorded in the poem *Kalfsvisa*.

Source: Norroena Society, *Asatrii Edda*, 388; Young, *Prose Edda*, 211

Stikini (Sta-key-nee)

The Seminole people of Oklahoma in the United States of America have a vampiric creature in their mythology called *stikini* ("man owl"). By day, it looks like a human, but at night it vomits up all its internal organs so it can shape-shift into a great horned owl to fly out in search of a sleeping person to prey upon. It removes their still-beating heart from their body by pulling it out of their mouth, then it takes the heart back to its home. There, it cooks the heart in an enchanted pot and eats it in secret. Before dawn, it returns to where it hid its organs and swallows them back down before changing into its human guise.

The only way to destroy this vampire is to find its intestines while it is out hunting. Then, using magical herbs and owl feathers, construct an arrow. When the stikini returns to consume its organs, fire upon it then with the magic arrow, as this is the only time the creature is vulnerable.

Source: Gill, *Dictionary of Native American Mythology*, 288; Hitchcock, *Traveler in Indian Territory*, 139–40; Howard, *Oklahoma Seminoles Medicines*, 97; Martin, *Sacred Revolt*, 26; Rose, *Giants, Monsters, and Dragons*, 346

Stiphilus

A CENTAUR from ancient Greek mythology, Stiphilus was one of the CENTAURS slain by the demi-god and cultural hero Hercules (Heracles) while visiting his friend, a CENTAUR named PHOLUS, between the conclusion of his third Labor and the onset of his fourth.

Source: *Commentary, Mythological, Historical, and Geographical on Pope's Homer*, 55

Stollenwurm

Variations: Bergstutzen ("mountain stump"), Dazzelwurm, Praatzelwurm, Springwurm ("jumping worm"), TATZELWURM

A terrifying DRAGON from Swiss folklore, the stollenwurm ("tunnel worm") is a chimerical creature having the face of a cat, the head of a lizard, a DRAGON'S scaled body covered with bristles, red veins, and warts, and an exceedingly long tail. This creature would rise up upon its hind legs, towering over people it encountered, terrifying them. Said to live in the Alpine Pass between Austria and France, the stollenwurm is known to the locals as the TATZELWURM.

Source: Cox, *Spooky Spirits and Creepy Creatures*, 27; Rose, *Giants, Monsters, and Dragons*, 346

Stricto

A dog from ancient Greek mythology, Stricto was one of the DOGS OF ACTÆON, the unfortunate youth who was raised by the CENTAUR CHEIRON.

Source: Leeming, *World of Myth*, 111; Murray, *Classical Manual*, 160

Strigae (Stree-gay)

Variations: Striglais

In ancient Roman folklore there was a deformed and vicious species of vampiric owl-like creature described as having the face of a woman; they were known as the strigae. At night these creatures flew out into the sky to attack children and drain them of their blood. By day, they would shape-shift into the form of an old woman. The strigae fell under the domain of Hecate, the goddess of the three paths and witchcraft; she was also the guardian of the household and the protector of all new-born life. Offerings of honey-cakes and chicken hearts as well as puppies and black lambs would keep the strigae at bay. King Stephen the First of Hungary (969–1038) made it against the law for strigae to leave their home at night or to do harm to anyone.

Source: Burns, *Witch Hunts in Europe*, 96–97, 195; Levack, *The Witch-Hunt in Early Modern Europe*, 46; Russell, *Witchcraft in the Middle Ages*, 68–70, 132; Talasi, *Acta Ethnographica*, 129–69

Strix

Variations: Sheerree, Shre

The strix originated in ancient Roman mythology, even being catalogued by Pliny in his *Natural History*, who commented they must be imaginary creatures since the bat is the only "bird" which breast-feeds its young. The strix did not become a demonic creature linked to Satan until the medieval times. The word *strix* translates as "owl" in Greek, but it has come to mean "witch" in Italian.

The strixes of medieval demonology, as described in Saint Isidore of Seville's *Etymologiae*, are demonic subterranean creatures under the command of Satan. A strix is created when a person turns to Satan and renounces their humanity; they are then transformed into this unnatural creature, a bird-like monster with huge talons and human breasts.

Working to bring about the downfall of mankind, these spiteful, nocturnal demons live in caves and prey upon nursing babies. They are susceptible to garlic and hawthorn. When one is killed, during its dissection, its entrails can be read to discern who it was in life. After the dissection, the body of the strix must then be cremated.

Source: De Gubernatis, *Zoological Mythology*, 202; Maggi, *In the Company of Demons*, 34; McDonough, *Transactions of the American Philological Association*, 315–44; Oliphant, *Transactions and Proceedings of the American Philological Association*, Volume 44, 133–49

Strong Copper

In ancient Sumerian mythology, Strong Copper was one of the many monsters slain by the warrior god Ninurta. Little is known of this creature other than Gudea, a ruler of Lagash (ca. 2100 BC), referred to it, and the other monsters vanquished by Ninurta, as the SLAIN HEROES; he elevated them all to the status of god and made a place of worship for them in the temple.

Source: Ataç, *Mythology of Kingship in Neo-Assyrian Art*, 185; Salem, *Near East, the Cradle of Western Civilization*, 102–3; Sherman, *Storytelling*, 332

Strong Toad

A species of toad from Chilean folklore, the strong toads are described as having a tortoise shell upon their back. These toads glow like a firefly and have the ability to attract or to repel anything they can cast their glare upon. The strong toads are so difficult to kill the only way to destroy one is to completely reduce its body to ashes.

Source: Henderson, *Book of Barely Imagined Beings*, x

Strymon

Named for the river Strymon in Trace, Strymon was the white horse immolated in sacrifice by Xerxes before he invaded Greece; the invader had hoped the offering would appease the gods and lessen the number of losses he knew he would take. Strymon was chosen to be the sacrifice because it was believed he had been bred in the region.

Source: Brewer, *Dictionary of Phrase and Fable*, 627; Ruthven, *Shaman Pathways*, n.pag.; Tozer, *Horse in History*, 50

Stúfr

In Norse mythology, Snorri Sturlson, the Icelandic historian, poet, and politician, writes the horse Stúfr was one of the mounts of Vifill in his translation of *Prose Edda*.

Source: Norroena Society, *Asatrii Edda*, 16

Stvkwvnaya

Variations: Tire Snake

A huge serpentine aquatic DRAGON from Seminole folklore, the stvkwvnaya was described as having an alicorn (a single horn) atop its head. The stvkwvnaya, like the UNICORN, was hunted for its horn, as it was believed when made into a powder it was a powerful aphrodisiac. The creature was summoned from its watery home by singing to it along the banks. When the stvkwvnaya emerged, its alicorn was quickly pared off.

Source: De Kirk, *Dragonlore*, 52; Zell-Ravenheart, *Wizard's Bestiary*, 91

The Stymphalian Birds

In Greek mythology, the cultural hero and demigod Hercules (Heracles), for his sixth (or fifth, sources conflict) Labor was tasked with driving the carnivorous and anthropophagous (man-eating) birds from their home in the swamps around Lake Stymphalus in Arcadia; these birds were sacred to the god Ares (Mars). The birds, not given a name by species, were described as being about the size of a crane and having brass beaks, metallic feathers they could project like arrows, razor talons, and bronze wings; native to the Arabian desert where they preyed upon lions and panthers, they had been badly frightened by the wolves along the Orchomen Road and sought refuge in the swamp. Because they were so violent and vicious their numbers had greatly increased and they were so numerous when the flock took flight, they blotted out the sun. By using a rattle (or castanets, sources conflict) the goddess Athena (Minerva) helped him to construct, Hercules made a horrifying and frightful noise with it, scaring the flock so badly they took flight and never returned (or he shot them down with his arrows to the last; sources conflict).

Source: Barber, *Dictionary of Fabulous Beasts*, 140; Daly, *Greek and Roman Mythology, A to Z*, 69; Graves, *Greek Myths*, n.pag.; Roman, *Encyclopedia of Greek and Roman Mythology*, 169, 210

Su

Variations: Succarath

An untamable creature, the su from Patagonian folklore is said to have an extremely warm coat for which it is hunted; not an easy task as it is said to be blood-thirsty, cruel, fierce, impatient, ravaging, strong, violent, and believes itself to be more intelligent and witty than man. Carrying her young upon her back and covering them with her tail, the mother su is ever mindful of hunters, aware they will kill her for her warm coat and take her cubs to domesticate and raise for their own. Vindictive as well, the su will kill its own offspring if it suspects there is a chance a hunter will take them.

Source: Ashton, *Curious Creatures in Zoology*, 163–5; Topsell, *History of Four Footed Beasts*, 511; Zell-Ravenheart, *Wizard's Bestiary*, 91–2

Su-Pratika

Variations: Supratika

One of the DIG-GAJAS from Hindu mythology, Su-Pratika is one of the eight elephant protectors of the eight compass points; he guards the northeast and his mate is named Anjanavati. Symbols of protection, stability, and strength, they were born of the halves of the cosmic golden egg, Hiranyagarbha, which hatched the sun.

Source: Dowson, *Classical Dictionary of Hindu Mythology and Religion, Geography, History, and Literature*, 180; Gupta, *Elephant in Indian Art and Mythology*, 7

Succubus (SUC-you-bus), plural: succubi

Variations: ALUGA, Alukah, Aulak, Belili, Buhlgeist, COMPUSAE, Daitja, Ephélés, Hyphialtes,

Kiel-Gelal, Lilin, Lilit, Pishauchees, RUSALKA, Succuba, Succumbus, Unterliegerinnen

Men have been assaulted by the vampiric female demon known as the *succubus* ("spirit bride" or "to lie under") as far back as ancient Akkadia, Sumeria, and Greece, where it was clearly defined and described. The male counterpart to the succubus is known as an INCUBUS, and according to medieval folklore, the incubi outnumber the succubi by a ratio of nine to one. A human and succubus hybrid is a half demonic being known as a CAMBION. The Princess of all the succubi is Nahemah.

At night succubi, as they are collectively called, appear as beautiful women and can be very alluring and persuasive. They seek out sleeping men to have sexual intercourse with and, according to medieval folklore, are particularly fond of monks. During the sex act, the succubi are said to drain off a number of vital essences and fluids, such as blood, breath, life-energy, and semen to the point of their victim's death. A succubus need not even be physically in the room for the assault to take place, as it can visit a man in his dreams, causing his body to fall into a state of sleep paralysis. Succubi are specifically interested in semen, taking it and implanting it into unsuspecting and innocent women.

If a man wanted an encounter with a succubus, he need not wait in hopeful anticipation for one to show, as it is a demonic being and can be summoned to appear by use of magical incantations. Likewise, if a man is desirous of ridding himself of its assaults, he must seek help through the church.

Source: Bullough, *Human Sexuality*, 298–99; Cavendish, *The Powers of Evil in Western Religion, Magic and Folk Belief*, 103–5; Doniger, *Britannica Encyclopedia of World Religions*, 503, 1035; Jones, *On the Nightmare*, 125, 243, 320

Sucoyan (Sue-coin)

Variations: Ligaroo (masculine), Sukuyan

In the West Indies there is a vampiric creature called a sucoyan. Looking like an old woman by day, at night it removes its skin and hides it in the hollow of a tree. Then, it shape-shifts into a corpse candle (a glowing, spectral ball of glowing light) and flies out in search of its prey—a sleeping person it will drain dry of their blood. Like many vampires with the ability to remove their skin, such as the asema (a vampiric witch) and the LOOGAROO, finding its skin and rubbing it with salt so it shrinks will ultimately destroy the sucoyan, as it will die if exposed to direct sunlight.

Source: Allsopp, *Dictionary of Caribbean English Usage*, 161; David, *Folklore of Carriacoum*, 29–30

Sughmaire

An aquatic monster from Irish folklore, the sughmaire ("sea sucker") was imported into the country by the hero Fionn MacCumhail to drain a lake. The creature had the ability to gulp down vast quantities of waters. According to the folklore, there are only nine such creatures in existence and they are scattered about the world where they are in a constant state of drinking in and sending back out water, creating the tides of the world's seas.

Source: Zell-Ravenheart, *Wizard's Bestiary*, 92

Sui Riu

Variation: SUI-RYU

A species of DRAGON from Japanese mythology, sui riu is said to create a reddish rain when it is suffering.

Source: Bates, *All About Chinese Dragons*, 99; Ingersoll, *Dragons and Dragon Lore*, 103; Johnsgard, *Dragons and Unicorns*, 18

Sui-Ryu

Variations: Rain King

A Japanese DRAGON KING, Sui-Ryu has obtained full growth maturity and has dominion over the rain. When it is in pain, the sui-ryu causes the rain to turn red, colored by its blood.

Source: Bates, *All About Chinese Dragons*, 99; De Kirk, *Dragonlore*, 31

Suileach

In Irish folklore it is believed the multi-eyed suileach once lived in Lough Swilly in Donegal County terrorizing the countryside until it was killed by Saint Colum Cille in the sixth century.

Source: Eberhart, *Mysterious Creatures*, 666; Zell-Ravenheart, *Wizard's Bestiary*, 92

Sulanuth

In the Hebrew Book of Jasher (80:2–51), the Lord sends a series of fifteen plagues against the Egyptians in an attempt to convince Pharaoh to allow Moses to lead the Hebrews out of Egypt; many of the plagues are repeated in Exodus, but one of those which is not is the Plague of Sulanuth. Described as an aquatic female creature, it was summoned by God and sent to Egypt. There, the Egyptians were hiding in their houses behind locked and shuttered doors and windows because of the plagues of fleas, flies, frogs, gnats, hornets, lice, mice, reptiles, scorpions, serpents, toads, weasels, and winged animals besieging them. The sulanuth was ordered to use its arms, ten cubits long each, and from the rooftops of their homes, rip up the rafting, stretch out her arms, and unlock the doors and windows from within, throwing them open so the other plagues may enter.

Source: Anonymous, *Book of Jasher Referred to in Joshua and Second Samuel*, 6; Jasher, *Book of Jasher*

Sumukha

A NAGARAJA from Hindu folklore, Sumukha was described as being beautiful, handsome, and radiant, full of energy and fortitude. Born of Airavata's lineage, Sumukha was the grandson of Aryaka on his father's side and of VAMANA on his mother's.

Source: Debroy, *Mahabharata*, 426; Vogel, *Indian Serpent-Lore*, 83

Sunakake-Baba

Variations: Suna-Kake-Baba

A relatively obscure YŌKAI from Japanese folklore, the sunakake-baba ("sand throwing granny") is usually said to be lurking in various locations throughout Nara Prefecture, Japan. Although she has never been seen and no eye-witness can verify the creature is either a female or old, the sunakake-baba sprinkles sand over people as they pass through the shadows cast by shrines in lonely forest locations.

Source: Bush, *Asian Horror Encyclopedia*, 175; Foster, *Pandemonium and Parade*, 168

Sundal Bolong (Sun-dil Bal-long)

Variations: Sundelbolong, Sundel Bolong

In Java, there is a type of vampiric REVENANT known as a *sundal bolong* ("hollowed bitch"). It is created when a woman commits suicide or when a child who was conceived by rape dies. It appears to its prey, mostly travelers and foreigners, as a beautiful woman with unkempt hair wearing her burial shroud. Using its beauty, this vengeful and angry creature will lure a man to a quiet place with the promise of an indiscretion but instead will turn and attack him, draining him of his blood.

Source: Bunson, *Vampire Encyclopedia*, 250; Geertz, *Religion of Java*, 18; Koentjaraningrat, *Javanese Culture*, 342

Surabhi

Variations: The Calf of Kamadhenu, Cow of Plenty

In Hindu mythology Surabhi was the first of the fourteen creations which sprung up from the *Samudra Manthana* ("Churning of the Ocean"). Described as being "god-shaped," the boon-granting Surabhi was said to be an eternal fountain of milk; she and all of her descendants are revered by all classes of Hindus.

Source: Balfour, *Cyclopædia of India and of Eastern and Southern Asia*, Volume 3, 773; Chatterjee, *Sacred Hindu Symbols*, 60; Krishna, *Sacred Animals of India*, n.pag.

Surma

A HELLHOUND from Finnish mythology, Surma, like CERBERUS from ancient Greek mythology, was an Underworld guardian. Wandering in the Finnish Underworld known as Tuonela, the carnivorous and flesh-eating Surma hunted and consumed any souls he could find, as he was the guardian of the Gates of Decay, the only entrance or exit into the realm. Only the children of Tuoni and Tuonetar, the lord and lady of the Underworld, were allowed to come and go through the gates.

Source: Bartlett, *Mythology Bible*, 139; Wilkinson, *Myths and Legends*, 103; Zell-Ravenheart, *A Wizard's Bestiary*, 92

Sushuang

Variations: Su Shuang

A PHOENIX-like bird from Chinese folklore, the sushuang is one of the five spirit avians of some power. Each of the birds are described as looking similar to the PHOENIX in size and plumage, sitting upon one of the four cardinal points, and in the center rests the PHOENIX itself. The sushuang is the protector of the West. The FAMING guards the East, JIAOMING the South, and YOUCHANG the North.

Source: Sterckx, *Animal and the Daemon in Early China*, 155

Suzaku

Variations: Meng Chang PHOENIX, Su-Zaku

In Chinese folklore when a capital city is constructed, it was believed it should be designed to the Four God principle; on each side of the city, representation of a god is present in the form of an associated creature. In the east is SEIRYU the blue DRAGON; to the north is GENBU, a snake and turtle hybrid; in the south is Suzaku ("VERMILION BIRD"), depicted as a red PHOENIX-like bird and is dominant in the summertime, and in the west, BYAKKO, a white tiger, is dominant in autumn.

Source: Bates, *10,000 Chinese Numbers*, 108; Brown, *Genius of Japanese Carpentry*, n.pag.; Grafetstätter, *Islands and Cities in Medieval Myth, Literature, and History*, 119

Svadilfari (SVATH-il-var-i)

Variations: Svaðifoeri, Svadilfare, Svaðilfari, Svadilföri, Svathrlfari

The stallion Svadilfari ("traveling misfortune") of Norse mythology was the sire of SLEIPNIR, the eight-legged horse of Odin. Svadilfari, a clever and exceedingly strong animal, was owned by the disguised and unnamed Hrimthursars who constructed the walls of Asgard. Loki assumed the form of a white mare and lured Svadilfari from the construction site so the masons would not be able to finish the work on time and therefore being in breach of contract, would not have to be paid. Loki, in the form of a mare, had succeeded in luring off Svadilfari and conceived SLEIPNIR in the process. The next morning, Svadilfari had heard his master had accidentally let himself become exposed to the ray of sun and died, so the horse galloped off, never to be seen again.

Source: Grimes, *Norse Myths*, 300; Norroena Society, *Asatrii Edda*, 388

Svarnir (SVAHV-nir)

Variations: Svafner

In Norse mythology Svarnir ("sleep-inducer") was one of the dark-spotted serpents or Ormar (see ORMR) named in Thorgrimr's *Rhymes* and in Snorri Sturluson's (1179–1241) *Prose Edda*; it was said to live beneath the tree Ygdrasil at the Hvergelmir Well where it spent its days gnawing upon its Niflheimr root. The siblings of Svarnir were GOIN, MÓINN, GRÁBAKR, GRAFVÖLLUDR, and OFNIR.

Source: Anderson, *Norse Mythology*, 190–1; Grimes, *Norse Myths*, 14; Jennbert, *Animals and Humans*, 50

Svuvara

A fearsome anthropophagous (man-eating) DRAGON from Zoroastrian mythology, the yellow scaled Svuvara was so poisonous had he not been slain, he would have destroyed the entire universe.

Source: Cohn, *Cosmos, Chaos, and the World to Come*, 108

Swamfisk

A predatory fish from Norwegian folklore, the swamfisk was said to secrete a layer of putrid slime over its body and then, looking and smelling as if it were dead, float along the current until it was noticed by another fish as an easy meal. As soon as any fish came near enough, the swamfisk would snatch it up and consume it whole.

Source: Barber, *Dictionary of Fabulous Beasts*, 141; Rose, *Giants, Monsters, and Dragons*, 349; Zell-Ravenheart, *A Wizard's Bestiary*, 92

Swamp Auger

Originating in the lumberjack communities of the developing United States of America, the swamp auger, one of the FEARSOME CRITTERS, was said to be a mole-like creature living in and near lakes. Having an extremely long elephantine snout which was curved like a corkscrew, it would swim beneath boats and drill holes in their hulls until the vessel was no longer sea-worthy, and sank.

Source: Leary, *Wisconsin Folklore*, 99; Rose, *Giants, Monsters, and Dragons*, 119; Tryon, *Fearsome Critters*, 50

Swamp-Gahoon

Originating in the lumberjack communities of the developing United States of America, the swamp-gahoon, one of the FEARSOME CRITTERS, was said to leave tracks which look exactly like the ones created by snow shoes. Unfortunately, there is no additional information on this creature other than its name, causing writers of the time, 1841–1861, to believe it had gone extinct.

Source: American Dialect Society. *Dialect Notes*, Volume 5, 188; Mencken, *American Language Supplement 1*, 251

Swamp-Swiver

Originating in the lumberjack communities of the developing United States of America, the swamp-swiver was listed as one of the FEARSOME CRITTERS. Unfortunately, there is no additional information on this creature other than its name, causing writers of the time, 1841–1861, to believe it had gone extinct.

Source: Mencken, *American Language Supplement 1*, 251

Swan of Tuonela

In Finnish mythology the beautiful swan of Tuonela is the personification of the black waters of the Underworld, Tounela.

Sources: Werness, *Continuum Encyclopedia of Animal Symbolism in Art*, 396; Wilkinson, *Myths and Legends*, 103

Sylph

Variations: Aurae, Windsingers

The hermetic and neo-Platonic doctrine from which all medieval medicine and science was founded describes four Elemental classes, Air, Earth, Fire, and Water; accordingly the Sylphs belong to the Air class, GNOMES to Earth, nereids (golden-haired sea nymphs) to Water, and SALAMANDERS to Fire.

In ancient Greek folklore a sylph ("butterfly") was said to be a beautiful, long-lived, small fairy with the ability to shape-shift into human guise. These fairies lived atop mountains and were inclined to grant wishes involving the air. Female sylphs were called sylphids; the leader of the sylphs is named Paralda.

Source: Briggs, *Encyclopedia of Fairies*, 192–3; Evans-Wentz, *Fairy Faith in Celtic Countries*, 241; Hall, *Secret Teachings of All Ages*, 317; Rose, *Spirits, Fairies, Leprechauns, and Goblins*, 304; Stepanich, *Faery Wicca, Book One*, 31

Syqenez

A female, humanoid creature from Albanian mythology, a syqenez ("one with the eyes of a bitch") is described as being hag-like in appearance and having four eyes, two in the front and two in the back of her head which she keeps hidden by her scarf. The syqenez will lure young maidens into her home, roast them alive in her oven, and then eat them.

Source: Elsie, *Dictionary of Albanian Religion, Mythology, and Folk Culture*, 69, 247–8

Syren

Variations: Sirena

Described in medieval bestiaries, the syren was said to be a gigantic winged serpent of Arabia which could slither along the ground faster than a horse could gallop; it could fly even faster. The bite of this creature was so poisonous the victim would be dead before the body could touch the ground.

Source: Rose, *Giants, Monsters, and Dragons*, 350; Zell-Ravenheart, *Wizard's Bestiary*, 92

Sz

Variations: Sword Ox

A species of UNICORN from Malaysian folklore, the sz ("sword ox") is described as looking like an emaciated water buffalo with a single sharp-edged alicorn (horn).

Source: Gould, *Dragons, Unicorns, and Sea Serpents*, 361; Zell-Ravenheart, *Companion for the Apprentice Wizard*, 179

Tachash

A mysterious creature from Hebrew mythology and folklore, no one is sure what the tachash were, exactly, but there is, according to some scholars and rabbis, strong evidence it was a species of kosher UNICORN living wild in the wilderness while others believe it to be some non-kosher animal. In a few English translations the word tachash was exchanged for "badger." The only thing certain about these animals is its skin, along with ram hide and acacia wood, was used as part of the cover for the holy Tabernacle. The Midrash describes the tachash as having a glistening coat of six colors and an alicorn (a single horn) protruding from its head. Its hide was taken and made into tapestries.

Source: Slifkin, *Sacred Monsters*, 55–60; Smith, *Dictionary of the Bible*, xxi, 1135

Tagamaling

Variations: The Good BUSO

In Filipino mythology the tagamaling were a species of BUSO, in existence long before the word was made; after the creation of the planet and mankind the tagamaling were considered to be a desirable alternative to the BUSO, as they were not compelled to harm man and were not beings of pure evil driven by maliciousness. These creatures were only full BUSO when they ate human flesh, so they did so only every other month. During the time they consumed human flesh they were evil, but in the off-months were more like the gods.

Tagamaling live in hardwood trees with low, broad hanging branches; their houses although invisible are said to shimmer like gold and are called *palimbing*.

Source: Kroeber, *History of Philippine Civilization as Reflected in Religious Nomenclature*, Volume 19, 40; Neff, *Journal of American Folk-lore*, Volume XXV, 50–1

Takshaka

One of the most cunning and powerful NAGA from Hindu mythology, Takshaka was the ancient enemy of the god of thunder, Indra. According to the *Mahābhārata*, he was a NAGA-RAJA and ruled a city called Takshasila. According to the story Takshaka shape-shifted into the form of a worm and hid in an apple King Parikshit of Hastinapura was about to eat. Just as the king discovered the worm, Takshaka revealed himself, assumed his true form, bit the king, set his body ablaze, and destroyed the palace in fire. Janamejaya, the late king's son, was determined to avenge his father's brutal murder and discovered a ceremony called *Sarpa-sattra* ("serpent sacrifice"); when performed, it compelled snakes to gather and throw themselves into a prepared pit of fire. The ceremony was planned and once it began, snakes from all over the world were called in; they came in all shapes, sizes, and colors, one after another going into the pit of fire and being consumed by the flames. Millions died. Just as Takshake was about to fall into the pit and die, Astika, a youth who had the affection of the prince, asked for the ceremony to be stopped, and the prince complied.

Source: De Kirk, *Dragonlore*, 36; Ogden, *Dragons, Serpents, and Slayers in the Classical and Early Christian Worlds*, 272

Takujui

A chimerical creature from Japanese folklore, the takujui was similar to the KUDAN; it was described as having the body of a bull, a man's head, three eyes on each of its flanks, and a ridge of horns running down the length of its back. An auspicious creature, the takujui appeared only to virtuous mortals. It was further believed when a virtuous sovereign assumed the throne the takujui then had the gift of human speech.

Source: Cooper, *Symbolic and Mythological Animals*, 224; Hope, *Temple and Shrines of Nikko, Japan*, 30; Zell-Ravenheart, *Wizard's Bestiary*, 93

Talas

In Albanian mythology, Talas ("foaming wave") was the personification of the sea wind.

Source: Elsie, *Dictionary of Albanian Religion, Mythology, and Folk Culture*, 249

Talasam (Ta-lah-SUMM)

Variations: Tolosum

In Bulgarian and Macedonian folklore there is a demonic creature, usually assuming the appearance of a large snake with an overly large head, known as a talasam ("dead man"); it is the guardian of a great treasure. Once a year on a Church holiday it will appear at midnight as a fire. It is said if you want the talasam's treasure you must throw an article of your clothing into the flames. In the morning, if there is a set of footprints it will lead you to the treasure, but before the treasure can be taken, a human sacrifice must be made. If this offering is not made and the treasure is taken, great misfortune and death will befall anyone who touches it. If there are no visible tracks, it may be there is a scent trail to follow in order to reach the treasure; if this is the case, an animal sacrifice must be made in order to take the treasure.

Source: Klaniczay, *Christian Demonology and Popular Mythology*, 217

Tangie

A water creature from Scottish folklore, the tangie ("sea-weedy"), a FAIRY ANIMAL similar to the NUGGLE, was covered in sea-weed; it would appear as either a horse or a man in both fresh and salt-water in and around the Orkney Islands.

Source: Eberhart, *Mysterious Creatures*, 580; Keightley, *World Guide to Gnomes, Fairies, Elves, and Other Little People*, 173; Monaghan, *Encyclopedia of Celtic Mythology and Folklore*, 440

Taniwha

Variation: Tanihwa

In Maori mythology, the taniwha are a species of tutelary FAIRY ANIMAL living in dark caves, deep pools, or in the sea; they are particularly fond of living in places where the current is dangerous; each tribal group is believed to have its own taniwha. In some traditions the taniwha are seen less as guardians and more as dangerous, predatory serpentine SEA SERPENTs kidnapping women to keep as wives.

Source: De Kirk, *Dragonlore*, 105; Rosen, *Mythical Creatures Bible*, 67

Tanngiost

Tanngiost was one of the goats named in Thorgrimr's *Rhymes* and in Snorri Sturluson's (1179–1241) *Prose Edda*. Beyond its name, there is nothing else known of this creature.

Source: Jennbert, *Animals and Humans*, 49

Tanngnjostr (TAN-nyohst-r)

Variations: Tanngnjost, Tanngnistr, Tanngnost, Tanngniostr

In Norse mythology Tanngnjostr ("tooth cracker," "tooth gnasher") and TANNGRISNIR were the two male goats who pulled the thunder chariot of the god Thor; they were bridled with silver reins. Should either of these goats ever be killed, they could be resurrected if their bones were reconstructed.

Source: Grimes, *Norse Myths*, 301; Norroena Society, *Asatrii Edda*, 390; Rydberg, *Teutonic Mythology*, Volume 3, 853

Tanngrisnir (TAN-gris-nir)

Variations: Tanngrisne, Tanngrisner, Tanngrisni, Tanngrisnr

In Norse mythology Tanngrisnir ("gap tooth," "tooth gnasher") and TANNGNJOSTR were the two male goats who pulled the thunder chariot of the god Thor; they were bridled with silver reins. Should either of these goats ever be killed, they could be resurrected if their bones were reconstructed.

Source: Grimes, *Norse Myths*, 301; Norroena Society, *Asatrii Edda*, 390; Jennbert, *Animals and Humans*, 49; Rydberg, *Teutonic Mythology*, Volume 3, 853

Tanuki (TAH-new-key)

Variations: Ana-gumi ("raccoon dogs"), Mujina, Tanooki

A shape-shifter from Japanese folklore, the tanuki ("raccoon dog") are a type of ambiguous supernatural trickster, mischievous but not necessarily murderous; some authors and scholars liken them to a *bakemone* ("monster") or YŌKAI. Bumbling, pot-bellied, sake drinking pranksters, the tanuki will often use their shape-shifting abilities to appear as a Buddhist monk. A symbol of fertility, the appearance of one of these creatures is a good omen.

In folklore these creatures are well known for leading people astray by use of mimicking animal sounds, either to frighten or to lure. Traditionally the tanuki were nearly always seen as being comical and fun-loving rather than having a monstrous aspect.

In literature tales of the tanuki were originally almost interchangeable with those of the KITSUNE but gradually they became more comical and eventually dying by the story's end.

Source: Lang, *Crimson Fairy Book*, 306–09; Weinstock, *Ashgate Encyclopedia of Literary and Cinematic Monsters*, 526–8; Yoda, *Yokai Attack*, 126–9; Zell-Ravenheart, *Wizard's Bestiary*, 93

Tao Tie

Variations: T'AO-T'IEH, Thao-Thieh ("glutton"), Taotie

A DRAGON-like face found only on food vessels,

the tao tie is believed to be the fifth (or seventh, sources conflict) son of a DRAGON, had a wolfish appearance, is symbolic of gluttony, and acts as a reminder not to be greedy or have insatiable appetites.

Source: Bates, *All About Chinese Dragons*, 60; Skiff, *Land of the Dragon*, 105

T'ao t'ieh

This six legged DRAGON is one of the oldest from Chinese mythology; the t'ao t'ieh ("glutton") has one head but two bodies, each with its own tail and hind legs. The t'ao t'ieh represents gluttony and is a common motif on dishware to act as a subtle reminder not to be greedy. Other descriptions of these creatures say they are nothing more than monstrous heads seeking to consume as much as they can, their bodies having been long ago destroyed.

Source: Campbell, *Mythic Image*, 121, 126; De Kirk, *Dragonlore*, 29

Taranaki

Variations: Egmont

In Maori legend Taranaki was a NATURE SPIRIT embodied as a volcano; he fought fellow NATURE SPIRIT Ruapehu for the love of another volcano named Tongariro. Ruapehu bit off the top of his own mountain, chewed it up, melted it, and spat it at Taranaki forcing him to flee into the sea. The path of Taranaki's retreat carved out the Wanganui River. It is said Taranaki is still brooding off the coast to this day.

Source: Andrews, *Dictionary of Nature Myths*, 219; Grattan, *Natural Disasters and Cultural Change*, 149

Tarandrus

A species of animal originating in ancient Roman folklore and continuing on into medieval bestiaries, the tarandrus ("reindeer") was described as being ox-like in appearance with a long grey coat, but what made it remarkable was its ability to change colors. If ever the tarandrus was startled by a hunter or predatory animal, it had the ability to change the color of its coat and take on the hue of surrounding vegetation, effectively camouflaging itself.

Source: Barber, *Dictionary of Fabulous Beasts*, 141; Rose, *Giants, Monsters, and Dragons*, 353; Zell-Ravenheart, *Wizard's Bestiary*, 93

Tarasconus

Variations: The Offspring of LEVIATHAN, Taras, Tarasque, Tauriskos

According to medieval French folklore there was said to live a chimerical DRAGON or river dwelling SEA SERPENT named Tarasconus; it was described as being amphibious and chimerical, living in the forest along a stretch of Rhone River between Arles and Avignon. Described as being larger than an ox, it also had bear paws, a leonine (lion-like) head, impenetrable scales covering its body, a long serpentine tail ending in a sharp barb, six legs, and a hard shell upon its back covered in spikes. Unbelievably savage, with a mouth filled with sharp, sword-like teeth, Tarasconus sank ships and killed anyone who tried to pass down river. People of the region believed it was born the offspring of LEVIATHAN and another creature called Onachus. Tarasconus arrived in Arles having swum there from the place of its birth in Galati, Asia.

Christian folklore claims when Saint Martha arrived in the town of Tarascon the locals beseeched her to do something about Tarasconus. She set off into the wood and came upon the creature in the process of devouring a man. She threw Holy Water on it and presented the Cross to it; instantly Tarasconus was defeated and under her control. Saint Martha led it meekly back to town where the people, using spears and stones, eventually killed it.

Source: De Kirk, *Dragonlore*, 46; Jacobus, *Golden Legend*, 183–4; Ogden, *Dragons, Serpents, and Slayers in the Classical and Early Christian Worlds*, 254; Zell-Ravenheart, *Wizard's Bestiary*, 93, 179

Tarbh Uisge

Variations: Cablyy-Ushtey, Tairbh Uisge, Tairbh-Uisge, Taroo Ushtey, Theroo Usha

Living in Lochan, near the Tarmachans Mountains in Scotland, the tarbh uisge ("water bull") is a FAIRY ANIMAL; unlike the EACH UISGE and the KELPIE, it is not prone to assaulting those who happen upon it. Described as being all black, having no ears, and with a soft and velvety appearance, the nocturnal tarbh uisge makes a sound similar to the call of a rooster. Calves born with short ears are said to be the offspring of a tarbh uisge; these animals were often killed in order to prevent the bad luck they could bring.

Source: Eberhart, *Mysterious Creatures*, 580; Rose, *Giants, Monsters, and Dragons*, 353; Zell-Ravenheart, *Wizard's Bestiary*, 93–4

Tarroo-Ushtey

Variations: Tarbh Eithre

Exclusive to the Isle of Man, the tarroo-ushtey is a water bull which although far less dangerous than the EACH UISGE is still risky to encounter. Living in pools and swamps it is described as looking like an ordinary bull but with glittering eyes and rounder ears. This FAIRY ANIMAL will mingle with mundane cattle and occasionally produce offspring with very short ears. The tarroo-ushtey cannot be captured or domesticated, and although there are no stories of one ever having hurt a human there are numerous stories of it having done a great deal of damage ripping up fencing.

Source: Conway, *Magickal Mermaids and Water Creatures*, 72; Moore, *Folk-Lore of the Isle of Man*, 59–60; Rhys, *Celtic folklore: Welsh and Manx*, Volume 1, 284

Tartaruchus, plural Tartaruchi

In the non-canonical Christian *Apocalypse of Paul*, the tartaruchus ("to shiver with cold") was said to be a species of demonic anthropoid beings who were the keepers of Tartarus (Hell); the work describes them as using one hand to choke the damned souls and the other using an "iron of three hooks." The only named tartaruchus is called Temeluchus ("far away fighter") and is described as being an ANGEL without mercy, consumed with fire.

Source: Botha, *Demonology*, n.pag.; Bunson, *Angels A to Z*, 273

Tatsu

Variations: LUNG, Ryo, Ryu

The common word for DRAGON in Japanese, the tatsu are all said to be descended from a primitive species of three-toed Chinese DRAGON. Tatsu are more often associated with the sea than the rain in Japan as the country is more prone to devastating droughts. These DRAGONs were said to live in rivers and seas and would bestow proper amounts of rain upon their worshipers when suitably appeased; otherwise they would cause drought and whirlwinds.

Source: Barber, *Dictionary of Fabulous Beasts*, 142; De Kirk, *Dragonlore*, 30; De Visser, *Dragon in China and Japan*, 142, 154, 225

Tatzelwurm

Variations: Holedewelling, Spring Worm, STOL-LENWURM, Bergstutzen ("mountain stump"), Dazzelwurm, Praatzelwurm, Springwurm ("jumping worm")

Said to live in the Austrian, Bavarian, and Swiss Alps, the tatzelwurm ("worm with claws," "worm with feet") is a creature described as being whitish in color, lacertilian (lizard-like) in appearance, with clawed feet, but not scaly, and only about eight feet long. Sometimes it was said to have hind-legs, but not always. Its skin was so tough a sword was unable to penetrate it; however if it ever was wounded, it would bleed green blood. The head of the creature is shaped like a cat and it has a poisonous bite it will inflict on its prey when it pounces on them.

Source: Cox, *Spooky Spirits and Creepy Creatures*, 27; De Kirk, *Dragonlore*, 46–7

Tauri Silvestres

Variations: Aurochs, Urus

A species of bull said to be native to Ethiopia, the tauri silvestres ("forest bulls") were larger than other species of bulls and faster as well; they had blue eyes, horns which could pivot, tawny colored coats, and a hide as hard as flint, repelling weapon attacks. The tauri silvestres hunted a wide array of prey but to kill one, a deep pit trap needed to be employed.

Source: Barber, *Dictionary of Fabulous Beasts*, 149; Nigg, *Book of Fabulous Beasts*, 62; Pliny the Elder, *Natural History of Pliny*, Volume 3, 55

Tauroi Aithiopes

Variations: Bronze Bulls, Tauroi Aithiopikoi, Tauros Aithiopikos, Tauri Aethiopicum Sylvestres

A species of bull said to be native to Ethiopia, the wild and untamable tauroi aithiopes (Ethiopian Forest Bulls) were described as being twice as large as their domestic counterparts with red colored hides so tough they could not be harmed by any weapon. These animals were vicious and were well known to run down and consume humans.

Source: Maberry, *Cryptopedia*, 221; Nigg, *Book of Fabulous Beasts*, 62; Pliny the Elder, *Natural History of Pliny*, Volume 3, 55

Taurokampoi

Variations: Taurokampos

The hybrid known as the taurokampoi was a creature from the mythology of the ancient Etruscans; it was described as having the forequarters of a bull and the hind-section of a fish.

Source: Breverton, *Breverton's Phantasmagoria*, n.pag.

Tawake-tara

One of the TANIWHA from Maori folklore, Tawake-tara controls the shadows on the west side of Pirongia Mountain, an area which held the only road used to travel between Alexandra and Kawhia. Tawake-tara was an eater of human flesh and when people from the region disappear along the trail, it is attributed to him; however, a person of rank or status has never been taken by him.

Source: Gudegeon, *Journal of the Polynesian Society*, Volume 14, 191

Taxim

The taxim ("walking dead") is a type of vampiric REVENANT feared throughout Eastern Europe. Described as being a decomposing, rotting, and shambling corpse, the taxim maintain their mobility purely by sheer force of desire and will. These wretched creatures are doomed to roam the earth, spreading disease as they wander until they are able to achieve a goal they did not in life or enact revenge for their death.

Source: Bunson, *Vampire Encyclopedia*, 252

Tcheser-Tep

A serpent-like monstrous creature from ancient Egyptian mythology, Tcheser-Tep was mentioned in a magical formula written by King Unas of the fifth dynasty (BC 2450–2299, Old Kingdom). He was known for attacking the deceased in their tombs. In *The Text of Unas* there is a magical spell which when performed will cause the destruction of monstrous beasts and serpents alike; Tcheser-Tep would be affected by this spell.

Source: Coulter, *Encyclopedia of Ancient Deities*, 32; Mercatante, *Who's Who in Egyptian Mythology*, 184

Tchet

A winged monstrous serpent from ancient Egyptian mythology, Tchet dwelled in the eleventh section, or hour, of Tuat, the Underworld. In *The Text of Unas* there is a magical spell which when performed will cause the destruction of monstrous beasts and serpents alike; Tchet would be affected by this spell.

Source: Coulter, *Encyclopedia of Ancient Deities*, 32, 456; Mercatante, *Who's Who in Egyptian Mythology*, 184

Tchetbi

A monstrous serpent from ancient Egyptian mythology, Tchetbi guarded the entranceway to the fourth section, or hour, of Tuat, the Underworld, as the sun god, Ra, passed by in his boat. In *The Text of Unas* there is a magical spell which when performed will cause the destruction of monstrous beasts and serpents alike; Tchet would be affected by this spell.

Source: Coulter, *Encyclopedia of Ancient Deities*, 32, 477; Mercatante, *Who's Who in Egyptian Mythology*, 184

Tcinto-Saktco

A species of gigantic serpent in Cree folklore, the tcinto-saktco ("long horned snake") are all described as having a rack of antlers upon their head and the ability to make it rain; each of the creatures are distinguished from one another by their coloration, be it blue, red, white, or yellow.

Source: Meurger, *Lake Monster Traditions*, 162, 318; Rose, *Giants, Monsters, and Dragons*, 355

Te-No-Me (TEH-no-meh)

In Japanese mythology the te-no-me ("eyes for hands") is likely a singular YŌKAI rather than a species; sightings of this creature are mostly in rural areas where people live, as opposed to isolated loca-tions. Said to look like a typical average sized man dressed in traditional robes, this YŌKAI walks about with his eyes tightly squeezed closed and if it were not for the eyes on the palms of its hand would pass for a human carefully making its way down the hall-way, or road, or wherever the encounter is taking place. Because the te-no-me blends into society so well, it is able to get extremely close to its intended victim before it reveals itself for what it is. The te-no-me always catches its victim by surprise and frightens them; however, there are no stories or reports of any of them ever touching let alone cap-turing a person; apparently its sole purpose is to frighten.

Source: Yoda, *Yokai Attack*, 134–7

Te Tuna

A monstrous eel from Polynesian folklore Te Tuna ("the penis") was the first husband of Hina, the archetypal faithless wife, who left him for being an inadequate lover. After she was rejected by sev-eral tribes who feared the retribution of Te Tuna, the folk hero and trickster Maui took Hina as his own wife. Several years passed before Te Tuna was informed of where his wife was; at first he was not interested but eventually the thought gnawed at him and he raced off in a rage to kill his rival. Approach-ing Maui's island from the sea, Te Tuna rose up from the water, exposing his penis and creating a tidal wave with it; Maui exposed himself and using his own member blocked the wave, saved the island, and used it to beat to death Te Tuna's entourage of monstrous creatures. Impressed with one another Te Tuna and Maui decided a polygamous relation-ship between the three of them was the answer. This worked for some years but eventually the males decided they needed to fight for the exclusive right to Hima. In the end, Maui decapitated Te Tuna and buried his head; from it grew up the first coconut tree.

Source: Cotterell, *Dictionary of World Mythology*, 282; Leeming, *Oxford Companion to World Mythology*, 253

Te Wheke-a-Muturangi

A gigantic octopus from Polynesian folklore, Te Wheke-a-Muturangi once lived off of the coast of an island named Aotearoa ("long white cloud"); when the land was discovered by the first great chief, Kupe, he slew the monster in order to inhabit the land as it kept removing the bait from his hooks. Kupe chased the creature in his canoe from Hawaii, across the Pacific Ocean, to New Zealand where, after a series of dangerous encounters, Kupe finally managed to club and spear Te Wheke-a-Muturangi to death.

Source: Anderson, *Tangata Whenua*, 54; Craig, *Dictionary of Polynesian Mythology*, 24

Teakettler

Originating in the lumberjack communities of the developing United States of America, the teakettler, one of the FEARSOME CRITTERS, was said to be a small vermin which made a sound very similar to the sound of a whistling teakettle. These shy creatures are rarely seen but often heard in the backwoods; they are described as looking like a small dog with cat ears and stumpy legs; if spotted, it will back away issuing forth a spray of steam from its mouth as it releases its shrill cry.

Source: Binney, *Nature's Ways*, 225; Rose, *Giants, Monsters, and Dragons*, 355; Theitic, *Witches' Almanac, Issue 34*, 16; Zell-Ravenheart, *Wizard's Bestiary*, 226

Tearai Oni (TEY-ah-rye OH-nee)

Variations: Dendenbome

One of the YŌKAI from Japanese folklore, the tearai oni ("hand washing demon") is as large as a mountain and is likely also one of the Daidarabochi (a species of GIANT); as apart from its compulsion to bend over backward and wash its hands in deep canyon rivers, it is otherwise indistinguishable. Rarely encountered or otherwise observed, it is unknown if a tearai oni has ever harmed a human.

Source: Yoda, *Yokai Attack*, 70–4

Tecumbalam

According to the Quiche people's creation myth recorded in the *Popol Vuh*, the Mayans' sacred book, Tecumbalam was one of four birds which played a significant role in the destruction of the first race of people created by the god of the wind, Hurakan. The creation myth says after the gods made the animals, earth, moon, sky, and sun they created a race of people made of wood who were meant to appreciate the gods and see to the well-being of the animals. This first attempt of humanity was a failure as the wooden people insulted the gods and abused the animals. Hurakan sent a great flood to drown the wooden people; he also sent Tecumbalam who broke their bones and sinews, and then ground their bodies into powder. CAMULATZ bit off the heads of the drowning; CATZBALAM pecked away their flesh and XECOTCOVACH tore out their eyes.

Source: Bingham, *South and Meso-American Mythology A to Z*, 121; Spence, *Arcane Secrets and Occult Lore of Mexico and Mayan Central America*, 241

Teehooltsoodi

Variations: Tieholysodi, Tieholtsali

A gigantic smooth-furred otter or lake monster from Navajo folklore, Teehooltsoodi ("king of the ocean") was described as being very powerful and having buffalo horns upon its head. In one tale involving Teehooltsoodi, his son is kidnapped and in his grief, his tears cause a great flood.

Source: De Kirk, *Dragonlore*, 52; Rose, *Giants, Monsters, and Dragons*, 355; Zell-Ravenheart, *Wizard's Bestiary*, 95, 118

Teelget

In the folklore of the Navajo people of the United States of America, Teelget was one of the ANAYE, a type of gigantic and monstrous supernatural being causing fear, misery, and wickedness throughout the world. Described as being a quadruped and having a rack of antlers atop its head, Teelget was extremely predatory. The cultural hero Nayenezgani used a gopher to dig a tunnel into the monster's body and then once he located its heart, shot it with an arrow forged of chain lightning. Teelget was racked with anger and pain; it ripped apart its own body to get Nayenezgani out, killing itself in the process.

Source: Cotterell, *Dictionary of World Mythology*, 220; Rose, *Giants, Monsters, and Dragons*, 356

Teka-Hra

A monstrous serpent from ancient Egyptian mythology, Teka-Hra stood guard at the entranceway to the fifth section, or hour, of Tuat, the Underworld, as the sun god, Ra, passed by in his boat. In *The Text of Unas* there is a magical spell which when performed will cause the destruction of monstrous beasts and serpents alike; Teka-Hra would be affected by this spell.

Source: Coulter, *Encyclopedia of Ancient Deities*, 32, 457, 477; Mercatante, *Who's Who in Egyptian Mythology*, 184

Tengu

Variations: Ten-Gu, Tien-Kou

Originating in eighth-century Japanese chronicles, tengu ("celestial dogs") are psychopomps (death omens) and omens of catastrophes and war. In medieval times it was believed haughty insincere Buddhist monks were reborn as these beings. Tengu are typically described looking like a crow, a crow with a long beak and claws, or a man with a crow's beak. In human form they have a large nose and red face. It is said the larger the beak or nose, the more powerful the tengu. They speak through telepathy.

Tengu do not have a definite preference for any specific evil, but they are very imaginative and will exploit any situation; they are particularly fond of harassing children and monks who retired to the mountains to meditate. They struggle with feelings of compassion and vengeance.

These demons cause rock slides, collapse buildings, fell trees, and set forest fires. They are very quick, have the ability to bewitch humans and to become invisible, wield magical powers, and are renowned martial artists and storytellers.

Tengu live in the mountains and to hear the sound of falling timber or to see bird droppings on mats indicates the tengu are near. With proper gifts and offerings a tengu may lend its powers to a human, aiding him with a magical amulet or spell, knowledge of the mountain, a mantra to render someone invisible, stamina, or swordsmanship. A tengu can only be slain by a power greater than its own or by a superior martial combatant.

Source: Ashkenazi, *Handbook of Japanese Mythology*, 271; Bonnefoy, *Asian Mythologies*, 285–7; Hyatt, *Book of Demons*, 31; Mack, *Field Guide to Demons, Fairies, Fallen Angels, and Other Subversive Spirits*, 58–60

Tenjōname

Variations: Tenjō-name

A YŌKAI of Japanese folklore, the tenjōname ("ceiling licker") are said to be boney, tall creatures with exceedingly long tongues they use to lick wooden ceilings as they float, seeming suspended in the air; they are partial to tall ceilings where it is dark and cold. When one of these creatures is present, it is said the person will feel a chill in their dreams. Older descriptions of this creature claim it causes stains and leaves behind a layer of filth as it licks; because of this aspect of its behavior, some sources list it among the BAKEMONO.

Source: Foster, *Pandemonium and Parade*, 171–6

Tenko

Variations: Red Fox

Possibly a species of TENGU from Japanese folklore, the tenko ("celestial fox") is described as having golden colored fur and nine tails; these creatures are all at least one thousand years old and very evil.

Source: Maberry, *Vampire Universe*, 178; Source: Picken, *Essentials of Shinto*, 124

Tepan

A monstrous serpent from ancient Egyptian mythology, Tepan dwelled in the fifth section, or hour, of Tuat, the Underworld; he carried the offerings made by the living to the hawk-headed god, Seker. ANKH-AAPAU and Tepan are watched over by two SPHINXES. In *The Text of Unas* there is a magical spell which when performed will cause the destruction of monstrous beasts and serpents alike; Tepan would be affected by this spell.

Source: Budge, *Gods of the Egyptians*, 222; Coulter, *Encyclopedia of Ancient Deities*, 32; Mercatante, *Who's Who in Egyptian Mythology*, 187

Tepi

A monstrous serpent from ancient Egyptian mythology, Tepi was described as having four human heads, four breasts, and four pairs of human arms and legs; it dwelled in the ninth section, or hour, of Tuat, the Underworld. In *The Text of Unas* there is a magical spell which when performed will cause the destruction of monstrous beasts and serpents alike; Tepi would be affected by this spell.

Source: Coulter, *Encyclopedia of Ancient Deities*, 4, 5, 32; Mercatante, *Who's Who in Egyptian Mythology*, 187

Ter

A two-headed monstrous serpent from ancient Egyptian mythology, Ter dwelled in the fifth section, or hour, of Tuat, the Underworld; he was the guardian to the Night Chamber, preventing anyone who threatened to disturb or destroy the Gem of Life from entering. In *The Text of Unas* there is a magical spell which when performed will cause the destruction of monstrous beasts and serpents alike; Ter would be affected by this spell.

Source: Coulter, *Encyclopedia of Ancient Deities*, 32, 459; Mercatante, *Who's Who in Egyptian Mythology*, 187–88

Tesso (TEH-soh)

One of the YŌKAI of Japanese folklore, Tesso ("iron rat") is an anthropoid with a rat-like body and iron teeth; once a Buddhist monk named Raigo, he had been ordered to pray for the birth of a son for the emperor and if the prayers were answered, his temple would be expanded. Although Raigo was successful and a son was born, his promised reward was never given; enraged, he committed to a hunger strike which eventually caused his death. Reborn as Tesso, a human rodent hybrid with iron teeth, he had the ability to summon and control hordes of rats, up to eighty thousand at a time. He led his rats on a rampage destroying temple libraries and uncountable numbers of Buddhist effigies, holy sutras, and other relics. Eventually Tesso's reign of terror was stopped when he and his rat army were buried alive in a gigantic pit; other legends claim Tesso's rage eventually ran its course, he disbanded his army, and remains at large.

Source: Yoda, *Yokai Attack*, 66–8

Tetramorph

Described by the Hebrew prophet Ezekiel while in exile in Babylonia, the tetramorph ("fourfold form") was said to have four faces, one of an eagle, lion, man, and an ox; each had four wings as well as wheels which "turned not when they went."

Christianity utilizes the tetramorph as the symbol of the four holy evangelists, John, Luke, Mark, and Matthew, each of these animals being representative of one of the authors: eagle (John), lion (Mark), ox (Luke), and man (Matthew). Christian iconography often shows Christ enthroned and surrounded by four tetramorphs. The Apocalypse of Saint John describes four of these beings living near the throne of God. In the Eastern Church the tetramorph was symbolic of the four doctors: Anthanasius, Basil, Gregory of Nazianzus, and John Chrysoston; in the Western Church it symbolized their four doctors: Ambrose, Augustine, Gregory the Great, and Jerome.

Western mysticism has adopted the tetramorph for the symbol of the four cardinal points, the four elements (air, earth, fire, and water), and the four faces of man. It is also representative of the four horizontal Directions of Space, the four animals destined for service, and the four fixed constellations of the zodiac—Aquarius, Leo, Scorpio, and Taurus.

Source: Channing, *Chemical Serpents*, 44; Cirolt, *Dictionary of Symbols*, 75–6; Lanzi, *Saints and Their Symbols*, 29

Teumessian Fox

Variations: Alopekos Teumesios, Cadmean Vixen

In the mythology of ancient Greece, this gigantic fox was sent to torment the citizens of Thebes for a national crime which they committed; each month the creature demanded a child be sacrificed to its appetites. The ruling regent, Kreon, asked the hero Amphitryon (Cephalus) to catch and destroy an animal ordained by the gods to be uncatchable and save his people. Amphitryon enlisted the assistance of LAELAPS (Lailaps), a hunting dog blessed by the goddess Hera (Juno) to have the ability to catch any game it was sent after. The god Zeus (Jupiter) recognized the paradox and transformed both the fox and the hound into a pair of standing stones.

Source: Fontenrose, *Orion*, 99–101, 109; Smith, *New Classical Dictionary of Biography, Mythology, and Geography*, 363; Westmoreland, *Ancient Greek Beliefs*, 90

Teurst

In Morlaix, France, there is said to be a species of FAIRY ANIMAL known as a teurst; these fearsome creatures appear as a large black version of various domestic animals.

Source: Croker, *Fairy Legends and Traditions of the South of Ireland*, Volumes 1–3, 149; Spence, *Legends and Romances of Brittany*, 71

Teyu Yagua

In Gauranían mythology Teyu Yagua was a large jaguar-lizard hybrid creature which guarded Paititi, the land of gold located near Lake Cuni-Cuni and

ruled by El Gran Moxo; his hide was covered with gold and precious gems from having rolled around in the treasure.

Source: Coleman, *Dictionary of Mythology* 1003; Dixon-Kennedy, *Native American Myth and Legend*, 185; Savill, *Pears Encyclopaedia of Myths and Legends: Chapter 7*, 211

Thabet Tase (Thab-it Say)

In Burma there is a type of SUCCUBUS called a thabet tase. Created when a woman dies in childbirth, the thabet tase returns to its community and preys on the men there each night.

Source: Hastings, *Encyclopedia of Religion and Ethics*, 25; Leach, *Funk and Wagnalls Standard Dictionary of Folklore*, 1104; Scott, *Gazetteer of Upper Burma*, 28

Thanacth

The thanacth was a creature said to have originated in India and was exported en masse to the Middle East as a food source according to French folklore; it was described as looking like a large black, tailless tiger with a human head, kinky hair, and a gentle nature.

Source: Pare, *On Monsters and Marvels*, 146–7; Rose, *Giants, Monsters, and Dragons*, 356; Zell-Ravenheart, *Wizard's Bestiary*, 94

Thaumas

A CENTAUR from ancient Greek mythology, Thaumas attended the wedding of Pirithous, where drunken EURYTUS who assaulted the bride, Hippodame, led the way for other inebriated CENTAURS to assault and rape any women they could grab. During the ensuing battle, Thaumas, along with LYCABAS, MERMEROS ORNEUS, and PISENOR, was slain by the spear-wielding Lapith soldier Dryas.

Source: *Commentary, Mythological, Historical, and Geographical on Pope's Homer*, 55; Simpson, *Metamorphoses of Ovid*, 205

Thaye Tase (They Say)

In Burma there is a vampiric REVENANT called a thaye tase. It is created when a person has died a violent death; when it returns it does so as an ugly GIANT, causing cholera and smallpox outbreaks wherever it goes. It takes great pleasure in going to the deathbed of those dying and visible only to them, laughs and revels in their misery.

Source: Bryant, *Handbook of Death and Dying*, 99; Hastings, *Encyclopedia of Religion and Ethics*, 25; Jobes, *Dictionary of Mythology, Folklore and Symbols*, 1537

Thelgeth

In the folklore of the Navajo people of the United States of America, the headless thelgeth was one of the ANAYE, a type of gigantic and monstrous supernatural being causing fear, misery, and wickedness throughout the world; they are related to the limbless BINAYE AHANI and the feathered TSANAHALE.

Source: Cotterell, *Dictionary of World Mythology*, 220; Rose, *Giants, Monsters, and Dragons*, 18, 49

Thereus

In ancient Greek mythology, Thereus was one of the CENTAURS slain by the demi-god and cultural hero Hercules (Heracles) while visiting his friend, a CENTAUR named PHOLUS, between the conclusion of his third Labor and the onset of his fourth. When an old and particularly fragrant hogshead of wine was opened its aroma carried on the air and drove the local CENTAURS into a fury. Thereus, along with ARGEIUS, AMPHION, DAPHNIS, DUPO, Hippotion, ISOPLES, MELANCHETES, OREUS, and PHRIXUS, was slain by Hercules (Heracles) as he defended himself from their violent and unwarranted assault.

Source: Barthell, *Gods and Goddesses of Ancient Greece*, 187; Diodorus, *Historical Library of Diodorus the Sicilian*, Volume 1, 229–30

Theridamas

A dog from ancient Greek mythology, Theridamas ("kilham" or "subdue") was one of the DOGS OF ACTÆON, the unfortunate youth who was raised by the CENTAUR CHEIRON. This was the second dog to reach its master after he had been transformed, and took a bite into his flesh.

Source: Naso, *Fasti, Tristia*, 93–5; Ruthven, *Shaman Pathways–Aubry's Dog*, n.pag.

Theron

A dog from ancient Greek mythology, Theron ("hunter") was one of the DOGS OF ACTÆON, the unfortunate youth who was raised by the CENTAUR CHEIRON. Theron was said to be especially fierce.

Source: Leeming, *World of Myth*, 111; Murray, *Classical Manual*, 160; Naso, *Fasti, Tristia*, 93–5

Thes-Hrau

A monstrous serpent from ancient Egyptian mythology, Thes-Hrau was described as having a head at each end of its body; it dwelled in the tenth section, or hour, of Tuat, the Underworld. Thes-Hrau was depicted as wearing the white crown of Egypt on one of its heads and the red crown on the other; it was further described as having two pairs of human legs, one set turned to the right and the other turned to the left. In *The Text of Unas* there is a magical spell which when performed will cause the destruction of monstrous beasts and serpents alike; Thes-Hrau would be affected by this spell.

Source: Budge, *Gods of the Egyptians*, 246; Coulter, *Ency-*

clopedia of Ancient Deities, 32; Mercatante, *Who's Who in Egyptian Mythology*, 189

Thethu

A demonic serpent from ancient Egyptian mythology, Thethu was mentioned in a magical formula written by King Unas of the fifth dynasty (BC 2500–2290, Old Kingdom). He was known for attacking the deceased in their tombs.

In *The Text of Unas* there is a magical spell which when performed will cause the destruction of monstrous beasts and serpents alike; Thethu would be inadvertently affected by this spell.

Source: Coulter, *Encyclopedia of Ancient Deities*, 32; Mercatante, *Who's Who in Egyptian Mythology*, 189

Thonius

A CENTAUR from ancient Greek mythology, Thonius was one of the CENTAURS slain by the demigod and cultural hero Hercules (Heracles) while visiting his friend, a CENTAUR named PHOLUS, between the conclusion of his third Labor and the onset of his fourth.

Source: *Commentary, Mythological, Historical, and Geographical on Pope's Homer*, 55

Thous

A dog and wolf hybrid from ancient Greek mythology, Thous ("swift") was one of the DOGS OF ACTÆON, the unfortunate youth who was raised by the CENTAUR CHEIRON.

Source: Leeming, *World of Myth*, 111; Murray, *Classical Manual*, 160; Naso, *Fasti, Tristia*, 93–5

Three-Legged Bird

The three-legged-bird is a creature which appears in the mythologies of China, Japan, and Korea where it is believed to live near and represent the sun.

In China the three-legged bird is called the HEAVENLY COCK, represented as a three-legged rooster perched in the branches of a tree hundreds of miles tall where it sings its song each dawn in order to awaken mankind.

In Japanese mythology the three-legged bird is depicted as a raven named YATAGARASU; it is representative of the sun goddess Amaterasu from the Shinto religion.

In Korea SAMJOGO is the name of its three-legged bird, its image is considered to be a symbol of power, superior to even the DRAGON and the PHOENIX.

Source: Ashman, *Fabulous Beasts*, 117; Bates, *10,000 Chinese Numbers*, 21; Rosen, *Mythical Creatures Bible*, 164

Three-Legged Toad

Variations: Chan Chu

The three-legged toad of Chinese folklore lives upon the moon with MOON RABBIT where they guard the Pill of Immortality (Elixir of Jade); it is believed the number of legs corresponds to the three lunar phases and it also represents heaven, earth, and the opportunity for prosperity as it is associated with the god of prosperity, Liu Hai. During a lunar eclipse, it is believed the three-legged toad swallows the moon.

Source: Bates, *10,000 Chinese Numbers*, 21; Eason, *Fabulous Creatures, Mythical Monsters, and Animal Power Symbols*, 132

Thrumpin

In old Scottish folklore there is a belief in a species of sprite known as a thrumpin; each person was said to have one of these vengeful creatures assigned to them. Thrumpin had the ability to take a person's life but only on nights when a series of specific natural events occurred during the midnight hour, such as the moon being in its latter half, owl chicklets restless in their nests, and hawks flying in the night sky to name but a few. On these rare nights, the thrumpin are able to take life and leave the person's body in such a way as for it to be an unsightly carcass.

Source: Briggs, *British Folktales*, 121; Henderson, *Notes on the Folk-Lore of the Northern Counties of England and the Borders*, 262

Thu'ban (thuw-BAN)

Variations: Thuban, Tinnin

A DRAGON from Persian folklore, Thu'ban ("serpent") was described as having numerous fire-breathing heads, by some accounts one hundred, and a serpentine body; it was one of the KHRAFS-TRA.

Source: Hargreaves, *Hargreaves New Illustrated Bestiary*, 38; Rose, *Giants, Monsters, and Dragons*, 359; Simpson, *Guidebook to the Constellations*, 26

Thunderbird

Variations: Tinmiukpuk, Wakinyan, Wakinyan Tanka, Waukheon

Throughout Native American mythology the thunderbirds were gigantic birds, feared for the violent storms and tempests they created; beating their wings produced thunder, flashing their eyes created streaks of lightning, and shaking their plumage released rain; wherever one alighted upon the ground, it caused a wild brushfire. Arrows of lightning were shot from the tips of their wings or beaks.

Perceived as creatures of destruction, thunderbirds appear in the stories of each individual tribe;

sometimes they are seen as a god. In some descriptions the thunderbird is a singular being with the face of a human (Sioux) or a human face on its midsection (Haida). The Algonquian thunderbirds use their claws to strike trees looking for grubs while in the Haida tradition thunderbirds sweep down and fish for whales as eagles would for salmon; the Yukons say they eat deer and humans as well as whales. The Algonquian say the thunderbirds are at constant war with the water serpents, reminiscent of GARUDA's eternal war against the NAGA. The Lakota Sioux had four different types of thunderbirds in their folklore they called the wakinyan: black with a long beak, blue with no ears or eyes, scarlet, and yellow with no beak. They traveled the west wind and protected people from the north winds. People who dreamed of the wakinyan became *contraries*, people who acted and spoke in backward ways.

Source: Andrews, *Dictionary of Nature Myths*, 203; Lynch, *Native American Mythology A to Z*, 42–3; Porteous, *Forest in Folklore and Mythology*, 161, 195; Rose, *Giants, Monsters, and Dragons*, 359; Zell-Ravenheart, *Wizard's Bestiary*, 94

Ti-En Lung

Variations: Ti'en-Lung, Tien-Long

A classification of DRAGON from Japanese mythology, the ti-en lung are the guardians of celestial palaces of the gods.

Source: De Kirk, *Dragonlore* 29; Zell-Ravenheart, *Wizard's Bestiary*, 129

Ti-Lung

A species of Celestial Water DRAGON from Chinese folklore, Ti-Lung ("river DRAGON") are said to control the water in lakes, rivers and streams; they spend the autumn in the heavens and the spring time in the sea and the rest of the time beneath the earth.

Source: Bates, *10,000 Chinese Numbers*, 207; Niles, *Dragons*, 65; Rose, *Giants, Monsters, and Dragons*, 360

Tiamat (TEA-ah-mat)

Variations: Tiamet

Tiamat ("the ocean"), a winged cosmic serpent-DRAGON, is a demonic goddess from the Babylonian creation epic. She is the demon of the sea, the personification of chaos and saltwater; described as able to cast magic, having four ears, four eyes, four wings, she has a hide of scales that weapons cannot penetrate, horns, poison, tail, and two faces.

Tiamat gave birth to all the bull-men, demons, fish-men, gods, HORNED SERPENTs, and monsters. Apsu was her consort, and he was the personification of freshwater. She commanded this alliance of monsters, the elements of Chaos and Night, and the rebel gods.

She was slain by her great-great grandson, the solar god Marduk; in order to defeat her, he needed to employ a talisman of red clay, an *abubu* (a "storm flood" mace), bows and arrows, a coat of mail, a four horse chariot, herbs to counteract her poison, his body filled with flames, a net, seven terrible winds, thunderbolts, and a vast array of other "storm flood" weapons. He then used her slain body to create the heavens and the earth, clouds, fog, mountains, rain, and rivers.

Source: Fontenrose, *Python*, 153–4, 158, 239; Mack, *Field Guide to Demons, Fairies, Fallen Angels, and Other Subversive Spirits*, 7–9; Zell-Ravenheart, *Companion for the Apprentice Wizard*, 95

Tiangou

Variations: Celestial Dog, Tain Gou, TENGU, T'ien Kuo

In Chinese folklore there is a species of creature known as tiangou ("heavenly dog") which lives in the region of Fanplant Lake near Muddy Bath River and Dark Mountain. These creatures are said to be small, wildcat-like in appearance, and have a white head; other times they are described as being more like a raccoon, having a white neck, and making catlike sounds. The tiangou have the natural ability to repel evil and can assist a ruler in such a fashion if eaten but is more useful if its pelt is worn as a talisman.

Source: Li, *Ambiguous Bodies*, 299; Smith, *Complete Idiot's Guide to World Mythology*, 219; Strassberg, *Chinese Bestiary*, 111

Tianlong

Variations: Tian Long

A species of Celestial DRAGON from Chinese folklore, the Tianlong ("heaven DRAGON") are described as being sky colored and having control over the clouds; these are the creatures utilized by the gods as praetorian guards, both to pull their chariots and to protect their palaces.

Source: Bates, *All About Chinese Dragons*, 2, 31, 54; Cox, *Spooky Spirits and Creepy Creatures*, 13; Rosen, *Mythical Creatures Bible*, 63

Tianma

Variations: Tian Ma

In Chinese folklore, living upon Horse-Success Mountains is a creature known as the tianma ("celestial horse"); it is described as looking like a white dog with a black head and when it sees people it takes to the air and flies away. Although not resembling a horse in the least, it is named onomatopoeically after the sound of its cry. In the Western Han dynasty celestial horses were the horses the rulers obtained from Central Asia which were important for military purposes.

Source: Strassberg, *Chinese Bestiary*, 130

Tiansi

Variations: T'ien-shih

In Chinese folklore Tiansi ("heavenly master") was the earliest ancestral horse; it was sired by a lake DRAGON and a wild mare living in the Pamir Mountains. In its earliest descriptions, Tiansi sweats a red resin which resembles blood; possibly the substance is cinnabar.

Source: Zell-Ravenheart, *Wizard's Bestiary*, 147

Ticholtsodi

An aquatic monster in Apache, Navajo, and Papago folklore, the ticholtsodi were described as looking similar to buffalo calves but covered in spots; the god To'nenile ("water sprinkler") saved the people from them.

Source: Coulter, *Encyclopedia of Ancient Deities*, 466, 472; Muskett, *Identity, H'ozh'o, Change, and Land*, 231

Tien-Schu

Variations: Tyn-Schu, Yn-Schu

A species of ox-sized mouse from Chinese lore, the tien-schu ("the mouse that hides itself") was said to live its entire life in subterranean caverns living off of roots beneath the forest; they had no tail, a dark colored coat, short neck, small eyes, and was immensely strong. It was also believed the tien-schu would die as soon as the ray of the moon or the sun touched its body. The tien-schu are similar to the KOGUHPUKS.

Source: Figuier, *World Before the Deluge*, 343; Zell-Ravenheart, *Wizard's Bestiary*, 95

Tigbanua

A species of cadaver-eating, malicious BUSO from Malaysian folklore, the tigbanua crave human flesh; they will cause accidents to kill a person so they can eat his corpse. Living in small groups in the large forests they dwell in balitit, liwaan, magbo, and pananag-trees. As a species, they are frightened by dogs; the larger the canine, the more fearful of it they become.

Source: Coleman, *Dictionary of Mythology*, 1018; Ramos, *Creatures of Philippine Lower Mythology*, 112

Tigris

A dog and wolf hybrid from ancient Greek mythology, Tigris was one of the DOGS OF ACTÆON, the unfortunate youth who was raised by the CENTAUR CHEIRON.

Source: Leeming, *World of Myth*, 111; Murray, *Classical Manual*, 160

Tik-Tik

This species of onomatopoeically named ASWANG from the Philippines gets its name from the small owl which accompanies it. The owl will make a cry of alarm sounding like "tik-tik," alerting a potential sleeping victim of the monster's presence.

The tik-tik ASWANG only hunts at night when it shape-shifts from its human guise into a bird. It flies to the house of its intended victim, usually a child, and perches on the roof directly over the spot where its prey lies sleeping. Then it sends its long, thin, tube-like tongue into the house. Using a barb on the end of its tongue, it pierces a small hole in the flesh and sips up its meal. When the vampire has finished eating, the breasts of its bird form will be large and swollen with blood. It then flies back to its home where it breastfeeds its own children. In some versions of the myth, it is said rather than shape-shifting into a bird, the tik-tik maintains its human appearance while hunting and feeding. Rather than looking like a bird with plump breasts, it looks like a pregnant woman.

It is believed if the tik-tik licks the shadow of a person, they will die.

Source: Curran, *Vampires*, 37; Ramo, *Creatures of Philippine*, 28, 66, 118; Roces, *Culture Shock*, 214; Serag, *Remnants of the Great Ilonggo*, 60

Tikbalang

Variations: Binangunan (Negrito), Tigbalan, Tigbalang, Tikbalan, Tulung, Tuwung

A species of demonic creature from the Philippines, the tikbalang are created whenever a fetus is aborted; they are described as looking like a tall man with a horse head. Typically, they are black-skinned but there are very rare instances of them being white. White tikbalang have greater magical properties. They have thick manes with spines, clawed feet, an enlarged penis, a large mouth full of teeth, and long hair. Their legs are so long, when they sit, their knees are over their head. Nocturnal, the tikbalang kidnap women and hold them captive in bamboo cages until they murder them. They also lead travelers astray.

The tikbalang spread death, misfortune, and sickness. They can assume any form or size they wish. They can also bewilder, blind, and cause insanity; disappear in a dusty cloud and falling stones; cause fevers and invisibility; shape-shift into a human; and steal rosary beads from Christians.

Tikbalang live atop balete and kalumpang trees; in balete, banana, and bamboo groves; and in the pitcher plant (*Sterculia foetida*). They are also found beneath bridges, near hot springs, or in any sparsely populated, foliage-overgrown area.

The call of the tikbalang can be heard when one is near: "*Tik-Tik*." To prevent being attacked by these demons, when passing through the territory of one, first ask for permission by saying "*by your leave*" or by wearing your shirt inside out. Using a specially prepared rope, a person may jump onto its back and hang on while the tikbalang tries to throw him off; when it is completely exhausted it will admit defeat. Then, pluck three of the thickest spines in its mane as they can be made into a talisman to make the tikbalang into your servant. These creatures have a magic jewel which is the source of its power. It will give up if captured in exchange for its freedom.

Source: Ramos, *Creatures of Midnight*, 17; Rosen, *Mythical Creatures Bible*, 103; Zell-Ravenheart, *Wizard's Bestiary*, 95

Tikoloshe

Variations: Gilikango, HILI, Thokolosi, Tikaloshe, Tokolosh, Tokoloshe, Tokoloshi

The Xhosa people of Lesotho, Africa, have in their folklore a vampiric creature known as a tikoloshe. It is an excellent FAMILIAR for a witch and many do not mind the high price which must be paid for its summoning spell to work—a family member of the witch will die within a year's time of the spell being cast. Accepting this, a tikoloshe is created by removing the eyes and tongue from a corpse, piercing the skull with a red-hot iron poker, and then blowing a magical powder, whose ingredients are a well-guarded secret, into its mouth. The powder will animate and transform the corpse into an obedient and much-prized FAMILIAR.

Always male, a tikoloshe is a short, hairy, baboon-like creature with a tall forehead and a receding hairline. It has a single buttock and a penis so long it keeps it slung over its shoulder. Able to use magic, the tikoloshe will create for itself a magical stone allowing it to become invisible. It keeps the stone hidden in its mouth at all times. Although it can shape-shift into any form it wishes, there will always be a simian (monkey-like) characteristic to its form. Should it need to fly, it shape-shifts into the form of a HILI, a species of vampiric bird also a part of the Xhosa people's mythology.

In exchange for being the witch's FAMILIAR, the tikoloshe will demand a daily supply of cow's milk, food, lodgings, and the right to have sex with the witch whenever it wants (or a woman at his disposal to fulfill his sexual needs should the tikoloshe's witch be a man). In exchange for all of this, the tikoloshe will otherwise be completely at its witch's disposal, day or night.

Very quick and as strong as a man, the tikoloshe's greatest weakness is its voracious sexual appetite even its witch cannot control. A serial rapist, the tikoloshe will have a collection of women it will return to assault over and over, traveling hundreds of miles if it must. It feeds off their sexual energy, leaving victims physically battered and emotionally drained. Eventually its repeated assaults will kill the women.

Source: Broster, *Amagqirha*, 60; Knappert, *Bantu Myths and Other Tales*, 173–74; Mack, *Field Guide to Demons*, 35; Scobie, *Murder for Magic*, 80–82; St. John, *Through Malan's Africa*, 152–53

Timingila

Variations: Samudraru, Tinnin ("SEA SERPENT"), Timin, Timin-Gila ("swallower of the Timin")

A gigantic SEA SERPENT from Hindu mythology mentioned in both the *Mahabharata* and *Ramayan*, the timingila ("whale swallower") was said to be so huge it could swallow a whale whole. There are said to be two even larger creatures, the timi-timin-gila ("swallower of the timingila") and the timin-gila-gila.

Source: Debroy, *Mahabharata*: Volume 3, 247; Dowson, *Classical Dictionary of Hindu Mythology and Religion, Geography, History, and Literature*, 319

Tingoi

Variations: Dyinyinga

Originating in the Mende tribe of Sierra Leone, the tingoi are beautiful, MERMAID-like demonic creatures with white skin but smelling of rotting fish. Living in deep rivers, the ocean, and deep ponds, they sit on rocks combing out their long hair with golden combs. If a comb is stolen, the tingoi to which it belonged will beg desperately and pathetically for it to be returned; however, if it is, the thief will suffer poverty for the rest of his life. The only way to break the curse is for the comb to be burned and its ashes spread over cooking stones. If tingoi are approached at exactly the right time and in the proper way, they will be pleasant and polite and will give their guest a present.

Source: Rose, *Spirits, Fairies, Leprechauns, and Goblins*, 96, 309; Schön, *Vocabulary of the Mende Language*, 139

Tinmiukpuk

A species of THUNDERBIRD living in the Yukon, the tinmiukpuk was said to be very large; it not only carried off humans and reindeer, but whales as well.

Source: Leviton, *Encyclopedia of Earth Myths*, n.pag.; Lynch, *Native American Mythology A to Z*, 43

Tipaka

A beautiful and magical horse from Thai folklore, Tipaka was said to have belonged to King Sison; it was said this horse was so fast he could arrive at his destination even as it began the journey.

Source: Coleman, *Dictionary of Mythology*, 1020; Zell-Ravenheart, *Wizard's Bestiary*, 147

Tipua

Shape-shifting NATURE SPIRITS from Maori folklore, the tipua are said to live within trees, similar to dryad (a nymph of the forests and trees, particularly oak trees in Greek mythology) or nats (the generic name for the indigenous NATURE SPIRITS of the air, cultivated fields, earth, forest, hills, households, rain, rivers, sky, streams, wind, and the like); often the word *tipua* is translated to mean "demon," however in truth refers to anything which possess supernatural or weird powers. Tipua can in fact occupy any natural object, be it a log or a boulder; once within the object it will then establish its powers and parameters. For instance a particular log near a pond may have a tipua within it which prevents eels from coming too near the bank.

Source: Coleman, *Dictionary of Mythology*, 1020; Royal Society of New Zealand, *Transactions*, Volume 40, 191

Tirisuk

A massive DRAGON of Inuit folklore, Tirisuk had leathery feelers and a gigantic set of jaws which could bite through anything; typically stories involving this creature were of its consuming Inuit braves and hunting parties.

Source: Blackman, *Field Guide to North American Monsters*, 157; Zell-Ravenheart, *Wizard's Bestiary*, 96

Tisiphone

One of the three FURIES from classical Greek mythology, Tisiphone ("face of retaliation" or "rage") was the sister who specialized in avenging acts of evil. As a guardian of the gates of Tartaros, Tisiphone wears a bloody robe and whips the wicked dead who had been locked up in a steel cage. She like her sisters, ALECTO ("envy" or "never ending") and MEGAERA ("envious anger" or "slaughter"), was described as looking like an old hag with bat wings, bloodshot eyes, and snakes in her hair; sometimes they were confused as being a gorgon. The ancient Greek tragedian Aeschylus (525 BC–456 BC) claimed the sisters were the daughters of Night while the tragedian Sophocles (497 BC–406 BC) said they were the daughters of Skotos, the personification of darkness and the earth.

Source: Chopra, *Academic Dictionary of Mythology*, 112, 284; Drury, *Dictionary of the Esoteric*, 93; Hard, *Routledge Handbook of Greek Mythology*, 39, 124

Tjaldari (TYAL-dar-i)

Tjaldari ("racer," "trotting") was one of the horses utilized by the Aesir in Norse mythology; its specific owner or rider is not mentioned. Tjaldari was also listed as one of the many horses who would graze in the red-gilt leafed Glasir Grove.

Source: Grimes, *Norse Myths*, 20, 304; Norroena Society, *Asatrii Edda*, 393

Tlateculhtli

A gigantic crocodile-like creature from Mexican Aztec mythology, Tlateculhtli was depicted as having a large fanged mouth which was also the entrance into the Underworld and the Land of the Dead. According to the myth, after the fourth age when everything was submerged in water, Tlateculhtli swam through the cosmic water looking for human flesh to devour; Quetzalcoatl and Tezcatlipoca captured her and cut her in two. The upper portion of her body was used to make the earth and the lower portion, the heavens and stars. The other gods transformed her eyes into caves, springs, and well; her hair into grass and trees; her mouth into rivers and caves; her nose into mountains; her skin into flowers. Still in pain from the ordeal and bleeding, Tlateculhtli cries out in pain, demanding human flesh

Source: Bingham, *South and Meso-American Mythology A to Z*, 126; Zell-Ravenheart, *Wizard's Bestiary*, 96

To Fu

In Chinese folklore there is a species of bird, the LWAN, said to look like a beautiful, large, and graceful pheasant; these birds have the ability to change its color; each color the bird can assume is given a different name. The to fu is the white form and is described as looking like a beautiful, graceful and large pheasant. The additional forms are: FUNG, HWA YIH, YU SIANG, and the YIN CHU.

Source: Gould, *Mythical Monsters*, 370; Rose, *Giants, Monsters, and Dragons*, 362

To Kas

A species of white-horned SEA SERPENTS in Klamath folklore, the to kas are gigantic, terrifying, and especially aggressive towards mankind, consuming them at every opportunity as soon as one enters into their territory.

Source: Meurger, *Lake Monster Traditions*, 175; Rose, *Giants, Monsters, and Dragons*, 362

Toad Woman

A NURSERY BOGIE from Algonquin folklore, the Toad Woman was said to sneak into villages, seduce men, and steal children out of profound sorrow for having lost her own; her story is strikingly similar to LA LLORONA from Hispanic folklore. Toad woman will also kill children by staying just outside of the village and singing beautifully, enticing a child to come to her as she hides in the nearby swamp. Once the child is within her grasp, she snatches it

and drowns it in the water. A cowardly being, she will only attack when no one is able to stop her or witness her crime.

Source: Bruchac, *When the Chenoo Howls*, xii, 131; Bunson, *Vampire Encyclopedia*, 254

Tobi-Tatsu

Variations: Hai-ryu, Sachi Hoko, Ying Lung

A serpentine DRAGON from Japanese folklore, the tobi-tatsu ("to start and fly, or flee away") is described as having the head of a DRAGON, feathered wings, and the lower body of a bird; they are related to the P'ENG-NIAO from Chinese mythology. The tobi-tatsu are rarely depicted as decorations.

Source: De Kirk, *Dragonlore*, 31; Hepburn, *Japanese-English and English-Japanese Dictionary*, 280; Ingersoll, *Dragons and Dragon Lore*, n.pag.

Toenayar

Variations: Nayar

A species of chimerical DRAGON or UNICORN from Burmese folklore, the horned toenayar is described as having four legs and aspects of buffalo, carp, elephant, and a horse.

Source: Bazino, *Zawgyi, l'alchimiste de Birmanie*, 178

Tōfu-Kozō (TOH-foo KOH-zoh)

Variations: Tofu-Kozo

A species of YŌKAI from Japanese folklore first reported in the eighteen hundreds, the tōfu-kozō ("tofu boy") is described as looking like a small boy wearing traditional clothing including a straw conical hat, straw sandals, and kimono, carrying a tray with a single block of gelatinous tofu. Encounters with these creatures vary only slightly, but in general, an unsuspecting person who is walking at night will see the small form approaching them, a boy in traditional clothing carrying a plate with a delicious cube of tofu upon it, bearing a *momiji* (maple) leaf insignia. Accepting the tofu triggers a reaction. In some accounts once the food is eaten, a virulent fungus begins to grow inside the person, draining away their life force; in other versions, nothing perceivable or associated to the event occurred.

Source: Yoda, *Yokai Attack*, 80–5

Tokan-dia

Variations: Tokandia, Tokan-Tongotra, Tokantongotra

A creature from Malagasy folklore, the tokan-dia ("the single-footed") is described as having only one foreleg and one rear leg but is still able to run faster than any other animal. A nocturnal predator, the tokan-dia will also kill and consume a person if the opportunity presents itself.

Source: Littell, *The Living Age*, Volume 200, 563; Sibree, *Folk-lore Record*, Volume 2, 27; Tyson, *Madagascar*, 247

Toko

Variations: Inari

A species of KAMI from Japanese folklore, the toka ("rice carrying") are said to be found in the mountains and are associated with Inari, the god of commercial success.

Source: Picken, *Essentials of Shinto*, 124

Tome

A species of KITSUNE (fox spirit) in Inari folklore from Japan, the tome ("fox" and "old woman") were shown reverence in the Byakko region.

Source: Asiatic Society of Japan. *Transactions of the Asiatic Society of Japan*, 55, 56; Picken, *Essentials of Shinto*, 124

Tompondrano

A SEA SERPENT from Madagascan folklore, the tompondrano ("lord of the sea") is described as looking like a gigantic snake or worm which causes mysterious floating light to appear beneath the surface of the Indian Ocean; to see the creature or the light was an omen of an upcoming storm.

Source: Clarke, *Britain's X-traordinary Files*, 152–3; Eberhart, *Mysterious Creatures*, 553; Zell-Ravenheart, *Wizard's Bestiary*, 96

Tonton Macoute

Variations: Uncle Gunnysack

A NURSERY BOGIE from Haitian folklore, Tonton Macoute was described as being a scarecrow with human flesh covering its body; it preyed upon children who did not respect their elders, snatching them up and taking them away in his gunnysack.

Source: Davies, *Encyclopedia of the African Diaspora*, 890; Rotberg, *Haiti Renewed*, 150

Too Jon Sheu

Variations: Too Jun, Too Jun Shen, Too Jor Shen

One of the species of UNICORN described in Chinese folklore, the too jon sheu was said to have a leonine body and head, cloven hooves, and a short and blunt alicorn (single horn) growing from the center of its forehead. It, like other species of Chinese UNICORNS, was said to appear when an upright monarch assumed power. A solitary creature, the too jon sheu cannot be captured, no matter the cunning, the plan, or the method implemented against it.

Source: Gould, *Mythical Monsters*, 348, 362; Shepard, *Lore of the Unicorn*, n.pag.; Zell-Ravenheart, *Wizard's Bestiary*, 96, 218

Torbalan

A NURSERY BOGIE from Bulgarian folklore, the torbalan is utilized by parents whose children will not behave; the torbalan will snatch up naughty children, toss them in his sack, and run off with them, presumably to consume.

Source: Frater, *Listverse*, 579

Tork

Variations: Tork Angegh

A DEV, GIANT, or OGRE from Armenian folklore, Tork was once an angry and raging individual who eventually came to master his temper and became a hero, after a fashion. In most of his stories, it is his reputation for his propensity for violence which enables him to overcome obstacles. He was described as being gigantic and having eyes as blue as heaven, eyebrows as black as pitch, a hooked nose, a veritable hump, teeth like hatchets, fingernails like knives, and being thick chested like a mountain with a waist resembling a rocky vale.

Tork was also immensely strong; as a child he could crumble up boulders into pebbles with his hands. Although a skilled architect and mason, Tork was by trade a shepherd; as lions and tigers feared him, these creatures would protect his flocks. If he should accidentally destroy a town or in a fit of anger raze it to the ground, he was quick to rebuild it. Meek and modest, he was not vengeful nor was he a glutton, as his favorite foods were honey, milk, and yogurt.

Source: Hacikyan, *Heritage of Armenian Literature*, 388–9

Tragelaphus

A hybrid creature appearing in many medieval bestiaries, the tragelaphus was described as being half deer and half ox (or goat). It was symbolic of the goddess Diana.

Source: Cassin, *Dictionary of Untranslatables*, 1253; Whitney, *Century Dictionary and Cyclopedia*, Volume 8, 6419

Tragopan

Variations: Goteface

According to Pliny the Elder, the Roman author and natural philosopher, the tragopan was a species of bird larger than an eagle, whose purple head was topped with ram horns; the rest of its body had brown feathers.

Source: Barber, *Dictionary of Fabulous Beasts*, 143–4

Tree Squeak

Variations: Treesqueak

Originating in the lumberjack communities of the developing United States of America, the tree squeak of the woods of Maine is listed among the FEARSOME CRITTERS; its cry is said to sound exactly like the noise tree branches make when they rub together when moved by the wind.

Source: Hendrickson, *Facts on File Dictionary of American Regionalisms*, 313; Rose, *Giants, Monsters, and Dragons*, 119

Trelquehuecuve

Variations: Trequehuecuve

In Araucanin mythology the trelquehuecuve is a creature which is employed by witches to be their servants; they are placed under the command of her INVUNCHE. The primary task of the trelquehuecuve is to capture young girls while they are drawing water and then feed them to the CHIVITO. Described as looking like a large octopus, its ears are covered in eyes, it has the power of dilation, and its tentacles end in claws. It is believed only a hero can kill a trelquehuecuve; the best time to attempt this is when it is sunning itself upon the beach.

Source: Alexander, *Mythology of All Races*-Volume XI, 328; Rose, *Giants, Monsters, and Dragons*, 80

Tripoderoo

Originating in the lumberjack communities of the developing United States of America, the tripoderoo of California was one of the FEARSOME CRITTERS; a small creature with a prehensile snout, it also had telescopic legs it would use to sneak silently through the forest to close in on its prey. Once within striking distance, it would shoot a clay or mud bullet out of its snout.

Source: Barber, *Dictionary of Fabulous Beasts*, 144; Rose, *Giants, Monsters, and Dragons*, 365; Zell-Ravenheart, *Wizard's Bestiary*, 226

The Tritons

A race of aquatic GIANTES from ancient Greek mythology, the Tritons were a part of the entourage of the god of the sea, Poseidon (Neptune); they had the upper body of a human and the lower body of a fish. Sporting with the nereids (golden-haired sea nymphs), the tritons were seen as NATURE SPIRITS of low status among the pantheon but were a favorite theme of artists, especially when families of these creatures were the subject.

Triton, an individual being of Greek mythology, was depicted as a MERMAN and was considered by some to be the god of Lake Tritonis in Libya. In one myth he was wrestled by the cultural hero Hercules (Heracles), and in losing, was forced to give the route to the Hesperides. His descendants, in some accounts, were called the Tritons and were depicted as having scaled bodies, gills beneath their ears, and fingernails which were in fact small seashells.

Source: Andrews, *Dictionary of Nature Myths*, 211; Barber, *Dictionary of Fabulous Beasts*, 144; Hard, *Routledge Handbook of Greek Mythology*, 106; Zell-Ravenheart, *Wizard's Bestiary*, 96

Troll

Variations: Berg People, Foddenskkmaend, Guild Neighbors, Guild-folk, Hill Men, Hill-People, Holder-Folk, Hollow-Men, Jutul, Orcs, Rise, Trolds, Trows, Trulli, Tusse, Underground-People

In Scandinavian myth, trolls are one of the four species of fairies and are generally described as being the enemies of mankind; they also appear as such in the folklore of Finland, Germany, Russia, and Siberia. Larger and stronger than humans, these cannibalistic beings came to be approximately the size of humans over time. Usually trolls have a hunchback and a long, bent nose, and dress in grey coats and wear red hats. By use of a magical hat, trolls can walk about invisibly; they also have the ability to bestow bodily strength on anyone, foresee the future, shape-shift into any form, and perform an array of superhuman feats as needed in folklore. Only in ballads do the trolls have a king ruling over them; they do not in folklore or mythology.

On the Faroe Islands trolls are called *foddenskkmaend*, *holder-folk*, *hollow-men*, and *underground-people*. There it is believed trolls carry humans into their underground lairs and detain them there.

Trolls who dwell on the land are called *guild-folk*; they live beneath the green hills. The walls of their homes are said to be lined with gold and silver. Those trolls who live in the woods are called *skovtrolde*; these trolls constantly seek to injure and torment mankind. Hill trolls ("*bjerg-trolde*") are the trolls living in the hills, sometimes alone or with their family.

It is said because of a racial memory from the time when the god of thunder, Thor, used to throw his hammer at them, trolls disdain loud noises. Trolls are believed to be virtually indestructible due to their hard skin and size; however, if they are exposed to sunlight they will retreat into the shadows or they will turn into stone.

Source: Keightley, *World Guide to Gnomes, Fairies, Elves, and Other Little People*, 63, 95–6, 162, 164; McCoy, *Witch's Guide to Faery Folk*, 322–23; Rose, *Spirits, Fairies, Leprechauns, and Goblins*, 316

Tsanahale

In the folklore of the Navajo people of the United States of America, the feathered tsanahale was one of the ANAYE, a type of gigantic and monstrous supernatural being causing fear, misery, and wickedness throughout the world; they are related to the limbless BINAYE AHANI and the headless THELGETH.

Source: Cotterell, *Dictionary of World Mythology*, 220; Rose, *Giants, Monsters, and Dragons*, 18, 49

Tsemaus

Variations: The Snag, Ts'um'a'ks

A SEA SERPENT from the Native American folklore of British Columbia, Canada, the tsemaus was described as being a gigantic, monstrous fish with a tall dorsal fin so sharply edged it could cut a swimmer clean in half.

Source: Barbeau, *Tsimsyan Myths*, Issue 174, 89; Rose, *Giants, Monsters, and Dragons*, 367; Zell-Ravenheart, *Wizard's Bestiary*, 97

Tsenahale

In the folklore of the Navajo people of the United States of America, the tsenahale was one of the ANAYE, a type of gigantic and monstrous supernatural being causing fear, misery, and wickedness throughout the world. Tsenahale was a gigantic eagle-like monster with vicious claws which nearly killed the cultural hero Nayanezgani ("slayer of alien gods"). By use of his magical arrows, the hero was able to destroy the ANAYE. Once the monster was slain, its feathers were plucked and transformed into small birds, such as warblers and wrens. The young offspring of the tsenahale transformed into eagles and later generations of men used their feathers for headdresses.

Source: Cotterell, *Dictionary of World Mythology*, 220; Rose, *Giants, Monsters, and Dragons*, 18; Zell-Ravenheart, *Wizard's Bestiary*, 97

Tsiatko

Variations: Sheahah, Snanaik, Steh-tathl, Timber Giants

A race of mountain-dwelling anthropoids appearing throughout Native American Indian folklore, descriptions of the tsiatko vary widely. To one tribe the tsiatko are described as being extremely large; their feet, ursine (bearlike) in appearance, are eighteen inches long. They say although the tsiatko do not wear clothes their bodies are covered with doglike hair and they carry a noticeable and pungent smell. Making their homes in the caves deep in the mountains, the tsiatko usually only leave during the fishing season in order to carry off young girls, smother babies, and steal salmon. Another tribe may say these creatures are the size of a typical man but are noted for their constant gibbering to one another in an unintelligible language, making enough noise any two of them could pass as a party of a dozen or more. The Nisqually tribe says the tsiatko have the voice of an owl and use it to entrance people; anyone who hears them speaking will fall down in a swoon.

Source: *Oregon Historical Quarterly*, Volumes 56–57, 313–4; Penz, *Cryptid*, n.pag.; Varner, *Creatures in the Mist*, 75

Tsuchigumo (TSOO-chee GOO-moh)

Variations: Dirt Spider, EARTH SPIDER, Ground Spider, Spider-Woman, Tsuchi-Gumo, Yatsukahagi ("long-legged one")

An evil gigantic, grotesque white spider in Japanese legends, the spider woman Tsuchigumo ("earth hider"), one of the YŌKAI, was said to have lived in a mountain lair near some ruins. According to the folklore, one night the hero Raiko and his faithful and heroic retainer Tsuna were traveling and came upon the sight; there they saw a skull fly into the cave. Deciding to follow it in, the pair came upon a beautiful woman who immediately began to encase Raiko with webbing. Drawing his sword, he lashed out, cut himself free and broke his sword off in the woman's midsection. After Tsuna removed the last of the webbing from his master the two set off in search of the woman; they came upon her in her true form—a monstrous spider—dying from her wound. The two finished her off; from her belly rolled out the skulls of her victims followed by an egg sack spilling out her offspring. Raiko and Tsuna killed the last of them, thereby ridding the region of gigantic spiders.

Source: Barber, *Dictionary of Fabulous Beasts*, 145; Rose, *Giants, Monsters, and Dragons*, 344; Rosen, *Mythical Creatures Bible*, 170; Zell-Ravenheart, *Wizard's Bestiary*, 97

Tsuchinoko

Variations: Bachi-Hebi, Gigi-Hebi, Koro, Koro-Hebi, Nozuchi, Tsuchikorobi

A plump serpentine creature from Japanese folklore, the tsuchinoko ("child of the earth," "mallet child," or "small mallet") is said to have a fondness for alcohol and the ability to jump up to three feet into the air. This creature has been described as having a distinctive catlike triangular head, narrow neck, a short skinny tail, and a flat triangular body.

Source: Foster, *Book of Yokai*, 199; Zell-Ravenheart, *Wizard's Bestiary*, 97

Tsukomogami (TSU-koo-moh GAH-mee)

Variations: Artifact Spirits, Thing-Wraiths, Tsukumogami, Tsukumo-Gami, Tsukumogamo

The YŌKAI of Japanese folklore are collectively known as the tsukomogami ("ninety-nine year gods"); these beings were once household items. If intact enough after one hundred years of use (or abandonment) they may develop a soul and consciousness and become animate out of a sense of disattachment and misery, acting of their own accord. There are many different types of household items which may develop into YŌKAI and each one is different; in general, the tsukomogami do enjoy playing pranks or terrorizing humans for all of their years of abandonment, abuse, or usage.

Source: Bathgate, *Fox's Craft in Japanese Religion and Folklore*, 20; Foster, *Pandemonium and Parade*, 7–8; Li, *Ambiguous Bodies*, 142, 166; Meyer, *Night Parade of One Hundred Demons*, 206

Tsurube-Otoshi

Described as being the gigantic disembodied head of a human, ONI, or TENGU, the tsurube-otoshi ("to drop quickly, like a bucket into a well") species of YŌKAI from Japanese folklore is an ambush predator, living high up in the branches of conifer, kayan, and pine trees growing along paths deep in the forests. Spending most of their lives in the treetops, these nocturnal hunters wait until an animal or unsuspecting traveler passes beneath them on the trail; then leaping from its branch, wildly laughing as it plummets to earth, the tsurube-otoshi attempts to land on its prey, crushing them. If successful, it will consume its meal and then ascend into the tree branches once again roaring out a challenge for others to try and make their way down the trail. When not hungry, the tsurube-otoshi will laugh as it drops stones or even water buckets down on travelers on the path below; obviously it has a sense of humor. Solitary creatures, the tsurube-otoshi range in size from about the size of a human head to more than 6 feet across (two meters); it should be noted, however, in the region of Tohoku the tsurube-otoshi hunt in packs but remain small in size.

Source: Meyer, *Night Parade of One Hundred Demons*, 74

Tuba

Variations: Toom Ahr, Tubae

In Mongolian folklore the tuba are said to be yard-long snail-like creatures living within their coiled shells; their horned heads are like a mountain goat's and although they crawl through the mountain caves of the Khangay and Altai mountains they occupy, tuba also have the ability to climb walls by their secretions of a sticky mucus. This mucus also protects it from predators. Tuba live entirely off of mold but there are a handful of stories in which they have consumed tiny invertebrates. It is considered a sign of good fortune to come upon one of these creatures so long as no harm comes to it.

Source: Zell-Ravenheart, *Wizard's Bestiary*, 97

Tuchulcha

A daemon from ancient Etruscan mythology, Tuchulcha was said to have lived in Aita, the underworld. The only known depiction of Tuchulcha is in the Tomb of Orcus II, located in Tarquinia, Italy; there it is shown as having anthropoid features and qualities of both genders. It is shown having a beard, breasts, the beak of a vulture, pale pink skin, pointed ears, snakes for hair, and wearing a woman's or unisex gown.

Source: Bonfante, *Etruscan Myths*, 230; de Grummond, *Etruscan Myth, Sacred History and Legend*, 299–30

Tugarin Zmey

A DRAGON from Russian mythology, Tugarin Zmey was the personification of cruelty and evil. A plague upon Kiev, Ukraine, this fire-breathing, snake-headed menace was gigantic in size with wings large enough to carry him into the sky; however, they were as fragile, pale, and thin as paper. Tugarin Zmey would raid the countryside, burning buildings, stealing livestock, and killing anyone who confronted him either with his brute force or his magical abilities. This creature was eventually slain by the cultural folk hero Alyosha Popovich, the youngest of three brothers in an adventuring family who had studied to be a priest, as he was not as brawny as his brothers. There are many versions of the battle between the DRAGON and the hero but generally after Tugarin Zmey breathes fire, creates thick clouds of blinding smoke, spews forth showers of sparks, and tosses smoldering charred logs at the hero he finally rises up into the air for his final assault. Unable to penetrate the DRAGON's hide with his sword the hero readies himself for death but before the creature can descend and end the fight, a thunderstorm occurs, the rain ripping his frail wings asunder. Tugarin Zmey falls helplessly to earth, and dies. Before the monster's magic can restore it, the hero chops the body into pieces and spreads them over the countryside.

Source: Dixon-Kennedy, *Encyclopedia of Russian and Slavic Myth and Legend*, 283; Niles, *Dragons*, 148–50; Seal, *Encyclopedia of Folk Heroes*, 203–4

Tulpar

In Turkish mythology a tulpar is a winged horse sired by a sea-stud utilized by a cultural hero in a story; in appearance they are similar to PEGASUS. When a tulpar is not the mount of a hero the word is translated to mean *charger* or *warhorse*. As a colt, the tulpar tends to be unattractive if not outright ugly, skinny because of poor fodder; it takes the special inner-sight to truly see and recognize the animal for its special qualities. Tulpars are typically grey or red in color, a distinctive trait taken from their sire's lineage.

Source: Hainsworth, *Traditions of Heroic and Epic Poetry*, 102; Kappler, *Intercultural Aspects in and Around Turkic Literatures*, 180

Tumu-Ra'i-Fuena

A gigantic spotted octopus from Tahitian folklore, Tumu-Ra'i-Fuena uses his many tentacles to pervade and hold together the earth and the heavens; his grip is so profound when the god Rua tried to use his chanting and magic to make Tumu-Ra'i-Fuena release his hold, the attempt failed.

Source: Rose, *Giants, Monsters, and Dragons*, 368; Zell-Ravenheart, *Wizard's Bestiary*, 97

La Tunda

A species of female, vampiric NATURE SPIRITS from Colombian folklore, the la tunda are well known and feared for their voracious appetites; they lure unsuspecting people into the forest and when in a secured location will turn on them and drain them dry of their blood. Although shape-shifters, these creatures are unable to transform perfectly, as one leg will always become a *molinillo* (wooden whisk used in making hot chocolate). Cunning and well-practiced at hiding their defect, la tunda are nevertheless merciless predators.

Source: Hellman, *Vampire Legends and Myths*, 123–4

Tunnituaqruk

A type of anthropoid monster from Inuit folklore, the tunnituaqruk ("tattooed ones") of the Hudson Bay region in Canada are said to be humanoid in appearance but have an enormous head covered with tattoos. The tunnituaqruk and their female counterparts known as the KATYTAYUUQ scavenge behind humans on the trail searching out scraps. These creatures hide whereever they can and will terrify anyone who happens upon one or surprises it.

Source: Halpin, *Manlike Monsters on Trial*, 198, 205; Rose, *Giants, Monsters, and Dragons*, 368

Turul

Variations: Togrul, Turgul

A gigantic bird symbolic of nobility, power, and strength, the turul ("peregrine falcon") was a divine messenger; it would sit atop the Tree of Life with the souls of unborn children. According to the mythic origins of the Magyars of Hungary, Emesse, the mother of Almos, founder of the Hungarians, had a dream in which a turul impregnated her and foretold the child to be the founder of a great nation. The turul appear in many of the country's foundation tales and myths.

Source: Warhol, *Birdwatcher's Daily Companion*, 158; Zell-Ravenheart, *Wizard's Bestiary*, 97

Tutara-Kauika

A TANIWHA from the folklore of the native people of New Zealand, the Tutara-Kauika was a FAIRY ANIMAL, a sperm whale said to accompany the hero Takitimu in his voyage to the island Aotearoa. Tutara-Kauika was the chief of all the whales in the ocean and commanded a large army of them.

Sources: Cowan, *Tales of the Maori*, 33–4; Orbell, *Concise Encyclopedia of Māori Myth and Legend*, 195

Twrch Trwyth

Variations: Orc Treith, Terit, Troit, Troynt

In Arthurian folklore, Twrch Trwyth ("the boar Trwyth") was the enchanted boar which King Arthur and his cadre pursued, following the lead of the hunting dog, CABAL.

According to the legend, the boar was originally an Irish king, born the son of Taredd, who had been transformed as punishment for his sins. Culhwch, as one of his tasks, needed to retrieve a comb, razor, and scissors from Twrch Trwyth, as the GIANT Ysbaddaden demanded them for his personal grooming. A provision was added to the hunt; first, the dogs AETHLEM, ANED, and DRUDWYN—who who had to be held with a special leash, collar, and chain—must take part in the event. The other provision was the services of King Arthur, Bwlch, Cyfwlch, Cynedyr, Garselid, Gwilenhin, Gwynn, Mmabon, and Syfwlch needed to be employed.

Twrch Trwyth was found in Ireland with an entourage of seven piglets acting as its warriors. The legend only names six of them: BANW, BENNWIG (Benwig), GRUGYN GWRYCH EREINT ("silver-bristle"), GWYS, LLWYDAWG GOVYNNYAD ("the hewer"), and TWRCH LLLAWIN.

After the items were retrieved Arthur and the remaining warriors drove Twrch Trwyth into the sea where it disappeared beneath the waves and was never seen again.

Source: Barber, *Dictionary of Fabulous Beasts*, 145; Bruce, *Arthurian Name Dictionary*, 156, 477; Rhys, *Celtic Folklore: Welsh and Manx*, Volume 1, n.pag.

Tyger

In heraldic symbology the tyger was a chimerical creature, depicted as having the body of a wolf, the mane and tail of a lion, pointed snout, and tusks protruding from the lower jaw; interestingly, it was without stripes. The female of the species was said to be particularly fierce especially when protecting her cubs; however the females were also easily hypnotized by their own reflection.

Source: Elvin, *Dictionary of Heraldry*, 128; Friar, *Basic Heraldry*, 166; Zell-Ravenheart, *Wizard's Bestiary*, 97–8

Uchaishravas

Variations: Uchchaih-Srauas, Uchchaihshravas

A seven-headed flying horse from Hindu mythology, Uchaishravas ("sharp-ears") was created during the Churning of the Ocean; it was mighty, powerful, and snow white in color (although black snakes were once entwined around its tail to give the impression it was black). The leader of the ASURAS, Bali, originally took possession of the animal but it eventually became the personal mount of the king of the gods, Indra.

Source: Chinmayananda, *Holy Geeta*, 714; Dowson, *Classical Dictionary of Hindu Mythology and Religion*, 127; Niles, *Dragons*, 95

Udayana

A NAGARAJA from early Buddhist and Hindu mythology, Udayana had been subdued by the deity Vajrppani.

Source: Donaldson, *Iconography of the Buddhist Sculpture of Orissa*, 214; Vogel, *Indian Serpent-Lore*, 191

Ufa

A demonic serpent from ancient Egyptian mythology, Ufa was mentioned in a magical formula written by King Unas of the fifth dynasty (2500–2290 BC, Old Kingdom). In *The Text of Unas* there is a magical spell which when performed will cause the destruction of monstrous beasts and serpents alike; Ufa would be inadvertently affected by this spell.

Source: Coulter, *Encyclopedia of Ancient Deities*, 32; Mercatante, *Who's Who in Egyptian Mythology*, 205

Ugjuknarpak

A gigantic predatory mouse from Inuit folklore, the ugjuknarpak was said to swim underwater and maneuver beneath kayaks, then using its prehensile tail, grab up the hunter, pulling him beneath the surface. Having excellent hearing and being extremely fast, the ugjuknarpak was fairly brazen as its hide is also impervious to all weapons.

Source: Zell-Ravenheart, *Wizard's Bestiary*, 98

Uilebheist

Variations: Draygan

A creature from Orkney and Shetland Islands folklore, the uilebheist ("monster") is a multi-headed SEA SERPENT said to protect coastal inlets and the rocky coastline of the Orkney and Shetland Islands.

Source: Barber, *Dictionary of Fabulous Beasts*, 146; Eberhart, *Mysterious Creatures*, 426; McCoy, *Witch's Guide to Faery Folk*, 147, 327–28; Spence, *Minor Traditions of British Mythology*, 136

Ukasima

A gigantic white-scaled DRAGON from Japanese mythology, Ukasima lives in Lake Ukasima, located near Kyoyo. According to legend, every fifty years Ukasima ascends from the water and takes the form of an *o-goa-cho*, a golden song bird. The song of the creature brings misery and sadness to the land and is described as sounding like the mournful cries of a wolf. To hear the song of Ukasima is a portent of a pending great disaster, ill-fortune, and severe drought.

Source: De Kirk, *Dragonlore*, 31; Zell-Ravenheart, *Wizard's Bestiary*, 129

Uktena

A winged and HORNED SERPENT from North Carolina and Tennessee folklore in the United States of America, the water-dwelling uktena, similar to a NURSERY BOGIE, feeds upon children—and fisherman—who venture too near to its home. Within its skull is said to be a magical stone which has the ability to cure all diseases; not only is this crystal dangerous to acquire, as first the vicious uktena must be defeated and its poisons and toxic breath avoided, but to maintain the power of healing the stone must be fed human blood daily.

Source: Sierra, *Gruesome Guide to World Monsters*, 8; Zell-Ravenheart, *Wizard's Bestiary*, 98

Ulupi

Variations: Uloopi

A NAGA from Hindu mythology, Ulupi was the daughter of the NAGARAJA of Manipur; she married Pandavan Prince Arjuna; to this day the royal family of Manipur claim to be descendants of the NAGA. In the Mahabharata, Ulupi is aggressive and very forward in her approach to the Prince as once while he was bathing she demanded he give her a child. Arjuna refused but she called upon the law of fertility of the god Indra, who proclaimed any woman when in her fertile cycle could demand a child from a man of her choosing. The prince then relented and remained with Ulupi until he gave her a son.

Source: Garg, *Encyclopaedia of the Hindu World*, Volume 3, 615; Pattanaik, *Goddess in India*, 50; Vogel, *Indian Serpent-Lore*, 191

Uma Na-Iru

Variation: Lion-DRAGON

A variation of the GRIFFIN, an uma na-iru ("roaring weather beast") of Akkadian and Mesopotamian mythology was the chimerical mount of the god of storms, Adad (Ishkur, in Akkadia). These creatures were described as having the forebody of a lion and the back, tail, and wings of an eagle; the uma na-iru could produce rain from their mouth; rainclouds were known as "Adad's bull-calves."

Source: Wiggermann, *Mesopotamian Protective Spirits*, 171; Zell-Ravenheart, *Wizard's Bestiary*, 98

Umm Naush

In Persian folklore the umm naush, one of the KHRAFSTRA, was an invisible, vampiric, nocturnal predator which fed upon the life force of newborn babies.

Source: Maher, *Anthropology of Breast-Feeding*, 57

Umu Dabrutu

The collective name for the hordes of demons and monsters created by TIAMAT, the umu dabrutu ("violent storms") do not have any set or specific form, as there is no mention of these beings of chaos in either ancient Babylonian art or text; however, they have been referenced, as in "Anzu bared his teeth like the umu dabrutu" before his battle with Ninurta. The umu dabrutu are also referenced as being "aggressive," "Leonine monsters," and "weather beasts."

Source: Ford, *Maskim Hul*, 137; McBeath, *Tiamat's Brood*, 87

Underwater Panther

Variations: Copper Cat, "Fabulous Night Panther," Gichi-anami'e-bizhiw, Great Underwater Wildcat, Michi-Pichoux ("great lynx"), Mishibizhiw, Mishipeshu, Ukena, Underwater Cat, Wi Katca

A species of feline NATURE SPIRITS from Native American folklore, the underwater panthers were powerful chimerical beings, having the body and tail of a mountain lion, feathers of a bird, horns of a bison or deer and scales of a snake, with regional variations for each of the tribes in the Great Lakes region. Said to live in the deepest parts of lakes and rivers, the underwater panthers could be helpful and protective but were more often malevolent monsters bringing death and misfortune when they arrived. They jealously guarded the copper mines all along the rivers. It was believed whenever a body washed ashore with white sand in its mouth, the underwater panther was the culprit.

Source: Godfrey, *American Monsters*, n.pag.; Zell-Ravenheart, *Wizard's Bestiary*, 98, 166

Unhcegila

In the mythology of the Lakota, Unhcegila is a DRAGON-like, female monster whose body is covered with scales made of flint; her heart is a crystal, and her eyes can project flames. Although she lives in the ocean, several times a year she swims along the shore, causes tidal waves, and turns the water brackish and unfit for human use. Only one place on her body is vulnerable to attack—the seventh point beneath her head. Two brothers learned of this and armed with arrows and magic to slow her reactions, set off to slay her. While one brother chanted out the magical incantations the other shot his arrow into the vulnerable place on her head, killing her. Taking her crystal heart they gained the gift of prophecy.

Source: Rose, *Giants, Monsters, and Dragons*, 374; Walker, *Lakota Belief and Ritual*, 122

Unicorn

Variations: ABADA (Congo, Africa), Alicorno (Italian), Cartazonon (India), Eenhoorn (Dutch), Einhorn (German), Enhjoning (Norwegian), Hippoceros, Jednorozec (Polish), Karkadann (Arabian), Koresk (Persian), Licorne (French), Monoceros (Greek), Ndzoodzoo (South Africa), PYRASSOUPI (Arabian Peninsula), Re'em (Judeo-Christian), Unicornio (Spanish), Unicornus (Latin), Unicünio (Portuguese), Unukornulo (Esperanto), Vienaragis (Lithuanian), Yedinorog (Russian), Yksisarvinen (Finnish)

Tales of the unicorn date throughout the centuries; the first recorded images have been found in China dating back to 2,500 BC and ancient Mesopotamia in the Indus Valley dating back to approximately 4,000 BC. Across the world, in the many different countries, cultures, and time periods, the descriptions of the unicorn varied creating numerous "species" and variations but in general it was described as a cloven hoofed animal with an alicorn (a single horn), straight or spiraled, growing from the center of its forehead. The general form and shape of the animal's body was in the earliest traditions usually based upon the antelope, bull, deer, goat, and ram; it was much later the horse was added to this list. Always, the animal was rarely seen and sightings of it were always significant. (See UNICORN, OCCIDENTAL and UNICORN, ORIENTAL below.)

Source: Barber, *Dictionary of Fabulous Beasts*, 146–9; Isaacs, *Animals in Jewish Thought and Tradition*, 181–2; Rose, *Giants, Monsters, and Dragons*, 374–77; Zell-Ravenheart, *Wizard's Bestiary*, 98

Unicorn, Occidental

Variations: ABADA (Congo, Africa), Alicorno (Italian), Cartazonon (India), Eenhoorn (Dutch), Einhorn (German), Enhjoning (Norwegian), Hipposeros, Jednorozec (Polish), Karkadann (Arabian), Koresk (Persian), Licorne (French), Monoceros (Greek), Ndzoodzoo (South Africa), Pyrassoupi (Arabian Peninsula), Re'em (Judeo-Christian), Unicornio (Spanish), Unicornus (Latin), Unicünio (Portuguese), Unukornulo (Esperanto), Vienaragis (Lithuanian), Yedinorog (Russian), Yksisarvinen (Finnish)

The occidental unicorn as described by ancient Greek historians was said to have blue eyes; the body of a horse; feet of an elephant; head of a deer (with a single long black horn); alicorn of black, red, and white; purple head; tail like a boar.

In ancient India the CARTAZONON was described as a reddish-yellow horse with a black horn and long mane. This aggressive animal attacked lions and lived in the deserts and mountain wastes. Although it could be killed as any animal may, it was never able to be taken alive.

The biblical unicorn of Judeo-Christian mythology, the re'em, has three noted characteristics, all of which are gleaned from the Book of Job (39:9–12), which gives the longest description of the animal: its inability to be tamed, its strength, and that it cannot be trusted. However, in the later Christian tradition the unicorn was added to the list of emblematic beasts; it was able to kill an elephant with its alicorn. It was in the twelfth century when the stratagem of using a virgin to entrap a unicorn came into being, as it was believed to be attracted to her purity and once resting upon her lap would not notice the hunters surrounding it, moving in for the kill. As the unicorn was a symbol of Christ, this method of hunting the animal became symbolic for His betrayal.

The Persian species, the koresk, was aggressive and appeared in many traveler tales including those of Marco Polo; it was revered as a royal animal.

The Russian unicorn, the yedinorog, also aggressive, had a fork prong on the end of its horn.

Source: Isaacs, *Animals in Jewish Thought and Tradition*, 181–2; Rose, *Giants, Monsters, and Dragons*, 374–77; Zell-Ravenheart, *Wizard's Bestiary*, 98

Unicorn, Oriental

Variations: Ch'I Lin (China), CHIAI TUNG (Chinese), Hai Chai, Kere (Mongolia, Tibet), KI-LIN (China), KIOH TWAN (China), Kio-Touan, ("the straight horn," Chinese), KIRIN (Japan), Lu, POH (Mongolia), SEROU (Tibet), SZ (Malaysian), Tou-Kio-Cheou ("one-horned animal," Chinese)

The UNICORN of the East has many different traits when compared to its western counterpart. To begin, the animal is believed to have both female and male aspects but is spoken of as a singular unit. Its body is deer-like or equine and multicolored— black, blue, red, white, yellow; it has a finely shaped head; the hooves of a horse; an alicorn (a singular horn); a tail like a water buffalo; and a height of twelve feet. A celestial creature on par with the DRAGON, its appearance was auspicious and its presence was considered to be an honor.

Source: Isaacs, *Animals in Jewish Thought and Tradition*, 181–2; Rose, *Giants, Monsters, and Dragons*, 374–77; Zell-Ravenheart, *Wizard's Bestiary*, 98

Unktehi

Variations: Unktehila, Unktexi

A serpentine DRAGON from Lakota folklore, Unktehi was a gigantic, scale covered snake with a huge horn protruding from the tip of her nose and the end of her tail; her feet sported vicious talons. Living in the Missouri River, she stretched the length of it from end to end, about 2,341 miles. All of the water monsters living in the smaller streams and lakes were her children. Neither she nor her offspring had any love for the humans of the world so they conceived a plan to destroy them all. Puffing up their bodies they each flooded their respective water source and began to flood the world; many humans were killed and only those fast enough to climb to the top of the tallest mountains managed to survive. The THUNDERBIRDS were not pleased, as the humans revered them and so taking up their cause waged war on Unktehi. It was a long and desperate battle fought between the two species; Unktehi had the advantage from the beginning and was winning the war but the Thunderbirds pulled together, flew up into the sky and simultaneously released all the lightning they could produce. The collective blast caused the water to boil so fast and hot it not only evaporated back to its true levels but killed Unktehi and all of her children, their charred bones becoming the scattered boulders across all the countryside. The humans who had taken refuge atop the stone capped mountains thanked their ally and returned to the ground to spread out and repopulate the world.

Source: Erodes, *American Indian Myths and Legends*, 220–1; Lynch, *Native American Mythology A to Z*, 10, 49; Zell-Ravenheart, *Wizard's Bestiary*, 98

Unnati

Variations: Vinayaka

In Buddhist and Hindu mythology Unnati is the bird-headed woman who is the wife of GARUDA; together the couple have a son named Sampati.

Source: Barber, *Dictionary of Fabulous Beasts*, 149; Dowson, *Classical Dictionary of Hindu Mythology and Religion, Geography, History, and Literature*, 109

L'uomo Nero

Variations: Babau

A NURSERY BOGIE from Italian folklore, the l'uomo nero ("the black man") is utilized by parents to entice their children to eat their food. Knocking loudly under the table, the parent pretends the sound came from the door and announces "It must be l'uomo nero, he knows you won't eat your dinner! Hurry up and eat or he will get you." This particular NURSERY BOGIE does not kidnap and consume children but rather whisks them off to a mysterious land, a literal nightmarish landscape filled with frightening terrain and creatures. L'uomo nero is described as looking like a tall man wearing a black heavy coat and a black hood to conceal his face.

Source: Breverton, *Breverton's Phantasmagoria*, n.pag.; Frater, *Listverse*, 580; Krensky, *Bogeyman*, Page 43

Upaka

The upaka are NATURE SPIRITS or nats (the generic name for the indigenous NATURE SPIRITS of the air, cultivated fields, earth, forest, hills, households, rain, rivers, sky, streams, wind, and the like) from Burmese folklore, specifically of the air; they fly about through the clouds and sky on the hunt for men they can swoop down and snatch up.

Source: Porteous, *Forest in Folklore and Mythology*, 125; Scott, *The Burman: His Life and Notions*, Volume 1, 286

Upland Trout

Originating in the lumberjack communities of the developing United States of America, the upland trout, one of the FEARSOME CRITTERS, was said to be a species of flying fish; afraid of water, they would build their nest high up in the tree branches. When caught, the upland trout was said to be delicious.

Source: Barber, *Dictionary of Fabulous Beasts*, 149; Botkin, *American People*, 255; Rose, *Giants, Monsters, and Dragons*, 119, Zell-Ravenheart, *Wizard's Bestiary*, 226

Uragas

The Uragas ("breast going") of Hindu mythology are a sub-species of NAGA, and as such are counted among the divine races; however, apart from this knowledge there is little distinction between NAGA, PANNAGAS, and the Uragas; the words are inevitably used synonymously. When a distinction is attempted the Uragas seem to be idealized heroes who are chariot warriors.

Source: Hopkins, *Epic Mythology*, 28; Sharma, *Socio-political Study of the Vālmīki Rāmāyaṇa*, 205–6

Ureus

Variations: Urius

A CENTAUR from ancient Greek mythology, Ureus attended the wedding of the prince of Pirithous to Hippodame. The epic Greek poem *The Shield of Heracles* written by the Greek poet Hesiod records the Centauromachy between the Lapith soldiers and the CENTAURS which took place when fellow CENTAUR EURYTUS became drunk and attempted to rape the bride during the reception. Upon the surface of the intricately worked shield are representatives of each army; on one side are the Lapith soldiers Prince Caeneus, Dryas, Exadius, Hopleus,

Phalerus, King Pirithous, and Prolochusc and rushing at them are the CENTAURS ARCTUS, ASBOLUS, black-maned MIMAS, and PETRAEUS. The men, armed with spears, were met by the CENTAURS who ripped up fir trees and used them as weapons, swatting at them with the trunks.

Source: Hesiod, *Works of Hesiod, Callimachus and Theognis*, 59; Westmoreland, *Ancient Greek Beliefs*, 202

Uridimmu

Variation: Ugallu

One of the creations of the DRAGON TIAMAT, Uridimmu ("dog/lion-howling," "raging mad") of Babylonian mythology was depicted as having the upper body of a bearded man with a leonine aspect, wearing the horned cap of divinity upon his head and holding a crescent moon staff; his lower body was a bull. Uridimmu was associated with rabid dogs and may have been a servant of Marduk.

Source: Ford, *Maskim Hul*, 151; McBeath, *Tiamat's Brood*, 82; Wiggermann, *Mesopotamian Protective Spirits*, 138, 162; Zell-Ravenheart, *Wizard's Bestiary*, 99

Urisk

Variations: Ùruisg ("water man")

The urisk is one of the FUATH, a collective name for the malicious and monstrous water fay in Scottish folklore. A solitary fairy from Scottish lore, the urisk is described as looking half-goat and half-human with flowing yellow hair and wearing a broad, blue bonnet. Associated with waterfalls and said to live in remote pools and rivers, the friendly urisk is desperately lonely because of its hideously ugly appearance. His physical appearance will frighten away, if not frighten to death, any mortal who sees it.

Source: Bord, *Fairies*, 2; Briggs, *Encyclopedia of Fairies*, 420; McCoy, *Witch's Guide to Faery Folk*, 330; Rose, *Spirits, Fairies, Leprechauns, and Goblins*, 323; Zell-Ravenheart, *Wizard's Bestiary*, 98

Urmahlullu

A fierce CENTAUR and lion hybrid from Babylonian mythology, the winged Urmahlullu ("untamed lion man") was depicted as holding a club and wearing a cap of divinity upon his head. Urmahlullu was a guardian and utilized against the winged death demon Mukil-res-lemutti, the upholder of evil.

Source: Ford, *Maskim Hul*, 155; Wiggermann, *Mesopotamian Protective Spirits*, 149

Uroo

A water snake from Australian Aboriginal mythology, Uroo was the greatest of all the reptiles but because his skin had no means to protect itself against the rays of the sun, he burrowed down into the earth. It is believed he still lives there in a subterranean creek a mile long.

Source: Smith, *Myths and Legends of the Australian Aborigines*, 181

Uwabami

Variations: Uwibami

A gigantic winged serpent from Japanese folklore, Uwabami would fly through the air hunting humans relentlessly, taking them up in its large jaws, and consuming them whole; even armed and armored knights mounted on horseback were no match for it. Eventually the hero Yegara-no-Heida was able to slay it.

Source: De Kirk, *Dragonlore*, 3; Rose, *Giants, Monsters, and Dragons*, 379; Zell-Ravenheart, *Wizard's Bestiary*, 99, 222

Vakr (VAK-r)

In Norse mythology, Snorri Sturlson, the Icelandic historian, poet, and politician, writes the horse Vakr ("alert," "wakeful" or "waking") was the preferred mount of Morn (Morginn) in his translation of *Prose Edda*; he was said to be a much prized ambling palfrey (a horse which moves its legs on each side together). Vakr was also one of the names Odin used when he traveled in disguise.

Source: Cleasby, *Icelandic-English Dictionary*, 674; Norroena Society, *Asatrii Edda*, 395

Valr (VAL-r)

In Norse mythology, Snorri Sturlson, the Icelandic historian, poet, and politician, writes the horse Valr ("the dragging" or "the tearing") was the preferred mount of Vesteinn in his translation of *Prose Edda*. Valr was also the horse ridden by Vesteinn to the Battle on the Lake of Ice, as recorded in the poem *Kalfsvisa*.

Source: Norroena Society, *Asatrii Edda*, 395; Young, *Prose Edda*, 211

Valravn

In Danish folklore the valravn ("raven of the slain") are a species of raven with supernatural powers, the descendants of the ravens who consumed the flesh of the dead from battlefields. These birds, once they have eaten the heart of a child, will gain the ability to shape-shift into the guise of a knight and a hybrid raven and wolf creature. Ravens who consume the flesh of a deceased king become known as *valravne* and those who eat of his heart are gifted with human knowledge, the ability to perform miracles, and an assortment of supernatural powers they would use to lead people astray; they were considered to be "terrible animals."

Source: Grimm, *Deutsche Mythologie*, Volume 2, 949

Vamana

One of the DIG-GAJAS from Hindu mythology, Vamana is one of the eight elephant protectors of the eight compass points; he protected the south and his mate was Pingala. Symbols of protection, stability, and strength, they were born of the halves of the cosmic golden egg, Hiranyagarbha, which hatched the sun.

Source: Dowson, *Classical Dictionary of Hindu Mythology and Religion, Geography, History, and Literature*, 180; Gupta, *Elephant in Indian Art and Mythology*, 7

Vanadevatas

In the Vedic mythology of India, the vanadevatas were considered to be benign NATURE SPIRITS not so different from the hamadryads (the nymphs of oak trees in Greek mythology) of ancient Greek mythology; these beings were intent on doing good and were typically friendly to those who looked after the tree they lived in but were especially vengeful to anyone who felled one. Easily frightened, the vanadevatas would flee an area where a god or monster appeared.

Source: Begde, *Living Sculpture*, 2; Hopkins, *Epic Mythology*, 57; Rose, *Spirits, Fairies, Leprechauns, and Goblins*, 325

Vanara

In Hindu mythology the vanara ("forest dweller") are simian (monkey-like) humanoids who inhabit the forests; as a species they are adventurous, brave, inquisitive, kind, and loyal. The vanara are described as being anthropoids, shorter than humans, having a long monkey's tail and a simian face. The avatar of the god Shiya, Hanuman, is one of the vanara.

The *Mahabharata* describes the vanara as a tribe of brave forest dwelling people whose totem was the monkey.

Source: Keishna, *Sacred Animals of India*, n.pag.; Rosen, *Mythical Creatures Bible*, 344

Vanir

Variations: Vaner, Vanr Van

A species of powerful fertility NATURE SPIRITS in Norse mythology, the Vanir were godlike in their ability and power; wielders of witchcraft, they used a type of battle magic called *vigspa* which gave them foreknowledge of the battle when they fought as they did not believe in engaging in physical combat or in the glory of battle. The Vanir lived in a land high up in the branches of Ygdrasil called Vanaheimr (also known as Upland and Upphiminn). Described as being bright and shiny, they were born out of the air and existed before the Aesir. The leader of the Vanir is a powerful individual called Njordr.

Source: Daly, *Norse Mythology A to Z*, 106; Grimes, *Norse Myths*, 33, 306; Lindow, *Norse Mythology*, 311

Varengan

In Iranian myths the varengan was a species of magical raven, the fastest of all the birds; its feathers were said to be used as a charm against curses and spells.

Source: Barber, *Dictionary of Fabulous Beasts*, 150; Coulter, *Encyclopedia of Ancient Deities*, 495

Vasi Pancasadvara

In Persian folklore the vasi pancasadvara was a species of LEVIATHAN living in the sea of Vourukasa. This creature was said to be so large that if it were to swim as quickly as it was able from sunrise to sunset it would not have covered a distance equal to the length of its own body. The vasi pancasadvara has dominion over the denizens of the water.

Source: Boyce, *History of Zoroastrianism*, 89

Vasuki

A thousand-headed NAGARAJA from Hindu mythology, Vasuki, associated with the god Siva, assisted the gods in recovering the Elixir of Immortality from the Churning of the Ocean by allowing himself to be used as a cord to be wrapped around Mount Mandara. Vasuki also worked out a sort of truce with GARUDA in one tale by offering him the sacrifice of one NAGA a day to be consumed as food. According to the folktale of the Iron Pillar of Delhi, the monument rested upon the head of Vasuki who ensured the stability of the kingdom; however, one king decided to have the monument dug up and it was discovered the base of it was covered with blood. Shortly thereafter, Delhi was conquered by the Muslims. It is said cobras with bright blue pearls in their hoods are descendants of Vasuki.

Source: Balfour, *Cyclopædia of India and of Eastern and Southern Asia*, Volume 1, 96; Vogel, *Indian Serpent-lore*, 191

Vasunemi

A NAGA from the Hindu fairy tale *Kathasaritsagara*, Vasunemi ("felly of the gods") was the owner of a wonderful lute; the item was said to produce sweet sounds as its strings were divided up according to the divisions of the quarter tones and betel leaf. Out of gratitude Vasunemi gifted his prized possession to the human king Udayana as a reward for saving him from the clutches of a snake charmer.

Source: Gandhi, *Penguin Book of Hindu Names for Boys*, 665; Vogel, *Indian Serpent-lore*, 191

Vedrfolnir (VEHTH-r-vuhl-nir)

In Norse mythology Vedrfolnir ("storm pale," "weather-bleached," "wind-witherer") was the hawk sitting upon the brow of the unnamed eagle perched in the uppermost branches of Ygdrasil. The eagles, said to be very knowledgeable, may be the god Odin in disguise. Vedrfolnir only appears in Snorri Sturluson's (1179–1241) *Prose Edda*.

Source: Jennbert, *Animals and Humans*, 50; Norroena Society, *Asatrii Edda*, 397; Orchard, *Cassell's Dictionary of Norse Myth and Legend*, 174

Vermilion Bird

Variations: Ling Guang, Ling K'uang, SUZAKU, Zhū Què

A creature represented in Chinese constellations, the vermilion bird, representative of the south, is an elegant and noble bird, both in its appearance and in its behavior; its feathers are every shade of red and orange. The vermilion bird is said to be very particular about what it eats and where it perches; it is also often confused with the FENGHUANG, the sovereign of birds. After Daoism became popular, the vermilion bird was given the human name of Ling Guang.

Source: Bates, *29 Chinese Mysteries*, 16, 133; Bates, *10,000 Chinese Numbers*, 108

La Víbria

In Catalonian folklore the víbria ("poisonous serpent" or "viper") is said to have been the poisonous female DRAGON which fought Saint George. It is said to live in the cave systems throughout France, Italy, and Spain. Depicted as having exposed female breasts, a long and fiery tongue protruding from an eagle-beak, scale covered body, a serpentine tail and wings, the víbria has become the personification of evil and temptation.

Source: Gatehouse, *Demons and Elementals #2*, 128; Hernandez, *Forms of Tradition in Contemporary Spain*, 94

Vigg (VIG)

Variations: Viggr ("toothy")

Vigg ("carrier") was one of the horses utilized by the Aesir in Norse mythology; its specific owner or rider is not mentioned. Vigg was also listed as one of the many horses who would graze in the red-gilt leafed Glasir Grove.

Source: Grimes, *Norse Myths*, 20, 308; Norroena Society, *Asatrii Edda*, 398

Vingskornir (VING-skawrn-ir)

In Norse mythology Vingskornir ("mighty in battle," "victory bringer"), the white horse with a fiery mane and tail, was the mount of the Valkyrie (a NYMPH of battle) Hildr. In the *Poetic Edda* Vingskornir is said to be the horse of Brunhilde.

Source: Anderson, *Norrœna*, Volume 12, 179; Norroena Society, *Asatrii Edda*, 399

Vircolac

A wolf-like creature from traditional Romanian folklore, the vircolac was believed to devour the moon and sun; when the moon had a reddish cast it was said the blood of the vircolac was washed over it. In the sixteenth century the word *vircolac* began to be used to refer to vampires.

Source: Melton, *Vampire Book*, 584–5, 685; Rose, *Giants, Monsters, and Dragons*, 384

Virupaksha

In Hindu mythology, Virupaksha was one of the four mountainous elephants who supported the weight of the world upon their heads; he was the guardian of the East. When he shook his head to relieve his weariness, it caused earthquakes. BHARDRA guarded the North, MAHA-PUDMA guarded the South, and SAUMANASA guarded the West. Virupaksha and his companions who support the earth from below are not counted among the DIG-GAJAS.

Source: Dalal, *Hinduism*, 43; Vālmīki, *Ramayana: Book 1*, 223

Vis

A species of vampiric beings from Lakalai folklore, the vis of New Britain, Melanesia, are nocturnal predators, flying through the sky in search of prey. When they attack, they do so using their long shiny talons to rip out the victim's eyes before consuming their flesh and drinking their blood.

Source: Moon, *Encyclopedia of Archetypal Symbolism*, 173; Rose, *Giants, Monsters and Dragons*, 384

Vitore

A type of benign and helpful HOUSE-SPIRIT from Albanian folklore, the vitore is described as looking like a golden snake with horns although in Permet it is said to look like a bird (see horned snake); in southern Cameria it is more likened to a fate, present three days after the birth of child to determine the course it will take in life. Living inside the walls of a home, whenever this FAIRY ANIMAL hisses aloud an important family event is about to occur.

Source: Elsie, *Dictionary of Albanian Religion*, 260

Vitra

Variations: The Archfiend Vitra, the Shoulderless, Vritra, Vrtra

A gigantic serpentine DRAGON from Vedic mythology, Vitra was the personification of chaos, darkness, fanaticism, ignorance, intolerance, and superstition; it held in its body all the water of the heavens and refused to release any of it. Indra, the god of light, nature, and warriors, knew if it did not rain the earth would perish and after beseeching the DRAGON many times realized the only way to release the water was to kill Vitra. The two engaged in a mighty battle and just as Indra was about to lose Vitra blinked, allowing the god enough time to strike it with one of his thunderbolt arrows, slaying Vitra "like a tree trunk split asunder with an axe."

Source: De Kirk, *Dragonlore*, 37, 93; Meletinskiĭ, *Poetics of Myth*, 234; Schouler, *Everything Hinduism Book*, 44, 46

Voivre

Variations: Vouivre, Vuire, Wouivre, Wivre, Wyvre

A WYVERN from French folklore, the Voivre was said to have had the upper body of a voluptuous woman; embedded in her forehead was a garnet or ruby which enabled her to navigate through the Underworld. Living in the mountains and castle ruins, Voivre guards her hoard of treasure but will only attack a clothed intruder; to strip naked and enter her domain will cause her to flee.

Source: De Kirk, *Dragonlore*, 47; Zell-Ravenheart, *Wizard's Bestiary*, 100

Vough

The vough ("hatred") is one of the FUATH, a collective name for the malicious and monstrous water fay in Scottish folklore. This female KELPIE-like creature is one of the most fearful and terrifying beings in the Highlands. Described being dressed in green, having a noseless face, and webbed feet, they prefer to live a nocturnal life but would come out during the day if the occasion called for it. The vough are said to enjoy the intellectual and sexual companionship of humans and some Scottish families, such as the Munroes, claim to have vough blood in their family line.

Source: Briggs, *Encyclopedia of Fairies*, 43; Monaghan, *Encyclopedia of Celtic Mythology and Folklore*, 466; Rose, *Spirits, Fairies, Leprechauns, and Goblins*, 329

Vrikshakas

In Hindu mythology the vrikshakas are a benign species of NATURE SPIRIT similar to the hamadryads (the nymphs of oak trees) of ancient Greek mythology. Like the dryad (a nymph of the forests and trees, particularly oak trees in Greek mythology) the vrikshakas can be attached to either a singular specific tree or an entire forest. These beings are described as looking like voluptuous women and in art are representative of fertility.

Source: Begde, *Living Sculpture*, 160; Rose, *Spirits, Fairies, Leprechauns, and Goblins*, 329

Vucub Caquix (wookob-kahkeesh)

Variations: Seven Macaw

In ancient Mayan mythology Vucub Caquix ("seven macaw") was a gigantic and vain bird living on the earth after the great flood; he proclaimed himself to be brighter than the moon, more glorious than the sun, and the ruler of the world. Vucub Caquix was only interested in dominating others and exalting himself; he had a wife by the name of Chimalmat and by her had two sons, Cabracan and Zipacna, who were both every bit as arrogant as their father. Vucub Caquix and his sons were slain by the gods and brothers Hunahpu and Xbalanque for their pride and haughtiness, as this aspect of the creatures annoyed them greatly.

Source: Recinos, *Popol Vuh*, xlv, 17–32; Wilkinson, *Myths and Legends*, 294–5

Vuokho

A species of THUNDERBIRD from Finnish folklore, the vuokho was believed to have had enormous wings which made a thunderous sound as they flapped. A malicious and predatory creature, the vuokho took great pleasure in causing pain to mankind particularly by spreading the plague and calling up swarms of mosquitoes.

Source: Barber, *Dictionary of Fabulous Beasts*, 151; Hall, *Thunderbirds*, 148; Rose, *Giants, Monsters, and Dragons*, 386

Wahwee (WA-wee)

An amphibious demonic creature from Australian Aboriginal folklore, the wahwee is described as being about thirty feet long with a froglike head, long tail, and three legs on each side of its body; it is an ambush predator hunting and consuming kangaroos, wallabies, wombats, and the occasional human. According to the folklore, after everyone in camp is asleep, the wahwee with its insatiable appetite creeps in and consumes its victim whole. Living in deep water holes, this demon creates droughts, floods, and rains.

Source: Anthropological Institute of Great Britain and Ireland, *Journal of the Royal Anthropological Institute of Great Britain and Ireland*, Volume 25, 301; Folklore Society, *Folklore*, Volume 9, 314; Mack, *Field Guide to Demons, Fairies, Fallen Angels, and Other Subversive Spirits*, 24–5

Waillepen

In Araucanian (Mapuchen) mythology the waillepen is an evil, fierce, powerful, shape-shifting REVENANT which preys on the Mapuche Indians of South America; among the forms it can assume are animal, human, and horrific spontaneous chimerical conglomerates. The disease spreading waillepen are a species of vampire; they have the ability to consume flesh and drink blood but they also enjoy feeding off of the fear and terror they instill in their prey by mercilessly chasing them for hours. Only a *machi* (a female shaman) of great power and her FAMILIAR can hope to confront one of these terrible creatures; she will wear charms of protection but they will only shield her as she does not have the ability to destroy them. Prayers to the god of the Mapuchen deities, Nenechen, are the only chance a community has against one of these creatures, as no weapon or spell can kill it. If the *machi* is successful, she will convince the god to intervene and he will abduct the waillepen and drag it back to the land of the dead.

Source: Maberry, *Vampire Universe*, 296; Pratt, *Encyclopedia of Shamanism*, Volume 1, 285

Wakandagi

Variations: Si Wakandage, Wakndagi Pezi

A species of gigantic aquatic DRAGON from Mohawk and Omaha folklore, the Wakandagi ("water monster") is described as having a serpentine body, a rack of antlers upon its head, and four deer-like legs and hooves. Some stories also say they have seven heads and in one story the creature could spit balls of fire. Living in bluffs along the Missouri River these creatures are highly territorial and will attack anyone they come upon both by brute force and spitting spheres of water. Seldom seen, and then only through the fog and mist, the wakandagi will also overturn boats and canoes, drowning and consuming the passengers.

Source: Powell, *Congressional Serial Set*, 336, 386; Rose, *Giants, Monsters, and Dragons*, 387; Zell-Ravenheart, *Wizard's Bestiary*, 100

Waldgeister

Variations: Waldgeist

A type of NATURE SPIRIT in German and Scandinavian folklore, the waldgeister, similar to the hamadryads (the nymphs of oak trees) from Greek folklore, live within the trees of the more ancient forests. While some waldgeister are benign, others are malicious, but they all hold the knowledge of the healing herbs of the forest. Frau Holle ("mother spirit"), a onetime goddess reduced to the status of fairy or NATURE SPIRIT, lives in the elder trees or on the bottom of ponds, and is counted among the waldgeister.

Source: Porteous, *Forest in Folklore and Mythology*, 90; Rose, *Spirits, Fairies, Leprechauns, and Goblins*, 331

Walichu

A malicious NATURE SPIRIT from Patagones folklore, the walichu were known to send "bad and evil things" to the people if they were not appeased, such as disease or any sort of misfortune. Offerings of animals were made before the walichus' sacred trees and left in the trunks of their trees or scattered around the base. In cases of great calamity, performances of mock battles between the villagers and the walichu were performed in an attempt to drive them out of the village.

Source: Rose, *Spirits, Fairies, Leprechauns, and Goblins, an Encyclopedia*, 331; Steward, *Handbook of South American Indians, Comparative Ethnology*, 586

Walutahanga

A SEA SERPENT from the mythology of the Solomon Islands, Walutahanga ("eight fathoms") was born of a human mother as a snake. The mother, fearing how the father would react, hid the infant in the woods but when he discovered the truth cut the snake into eight pieces. After eight days of rain the body reformed and now enraged Walutahanga sought her revenge among the people, tormenting them. Eventually she was captured and slain; her body was taken and boiled into a stew which everyone consumed save for a mother and her daughter. The remnants of the stew and the bones were tossed into the ocean. Again it rained for eight days and the bones of Walutahanga reformed from the depths of the ocean and sent eight tidal waves to destroy everyone, saving only the mother and child who did not consume her previous body. To the survivors Walutahanga gave many gifts including the coconut tree and clean drinking water. In some traditions or tellings of the tale Walutahanga is worshiped as a goddess while in others she is regarded strictly as a creature of the sea.

Source: Coulter, *Encyclopedia of Ancient Deities*, 178; Monaghan, *Encyclopedia of Goddesses and Heroines*, 159–60; Rose, *Giants, Monsters, and Dragons*, 387–8

Wampus Cat

Originating in Cherokee folklore and spreading into the lumberjack communities of the developing United States of America, the wampus cat found itself counted among the FEARSOME CRITTERS. According to the legend, a Cherokee woman did not trust her husband when he went out on hunting expeditions and as it was forbidden for women to accompany men on such journeys, she decided to don the pelt of a mountain lion and follow behind unseen. When the men encamped they shared their magic and stories; the woman, fascinated by all she learned and saw, crept too close and was caught. As punishment she was transformed into the wampus cat, a creature half mountain lion and half woman. It is said this hybrid monster still roams the hills and mountains of Kentucky, Tennessee, and Virginia to this day. It is most active on the nights of the full moon.

Source: Rose, *Giants, Monsters, and Dragons*, 119; Rosen, *Mythical Creatures Bible*, 116

Wanagemeswak

Variations: Wana-Games-Ak

A species of dangerous NATURE SPIRIT, the river dwelling wanagemeswak are from Penobscot folklore. Described as being small they are most notably unimaginably thin, so much so the wanagemeswak cannot be seen in profile. The wanagemeswak have an angular shape to their head, similar to a hatchet, and use it as a weapon to attack swimmers. On occasion they will make small clay effigies and leave them on the riverbanks to dry. If found these items are said to be good luck charms.

Source: Rose, *Spirits, Fairies, Leprechauns, and Goblins, an Encyclopedia*, 332; Sierra, *Gruesome Guide to World Monsters*, 8

Wani

In Japanese folklore the wani are a species of crocodilian creatures living in the rivers and the sea. In traditional art the wani are represented as a DRAGON and linked to the king of the sea, making them royalty and even the NAGARAJA of India; however in modern times the word is used to mean crocodile.

Source: De Visser, *Dragon in China and Japan*, 140

Wappentier

A rare bird in Hebrew folklore, the wappentier is said to be the only surviving offspring of the ZIZ. Never having had the opportunity to know any of its kind, the wappentier is a sad creature, choosing never to preen its dark colored feathers or speak. It is described as having a wingspan wide enough to reach each end of the horizon but there is not enough room in the sky for it to fly; it sits forever atop a desolate crag. The wappentier, possessing both genders, hunts and eats; each time it consumes food it lays an egg which will never hatch.

Source: Berman, *Red Caps*, 41

Wasgo

Variations: Wasco

A species of SEA SERPENT in British Columbian folklore, the wasgo ("sea wolf") are described as having finned forelegs, large dorsal fin, prominent teeth, wide black eyes, and a wolf-like tail; they are believed to be a hybrid between an orca and a wolf. The wasgo typically preys upon black whales, carrying them on their back behind their ears or in the curl of their tail, but there are stories of them hunting and consuming humans.

Source: Hill, *Indian Petroglyphs of the Pacific Northwest*, 274; Ruddell, *Raven's Village*, 38

Water Babies

Water babies are a species of nocturnal, demonic creatures from Washo folklore. Described as being small, hideous, humanoid creatures with the "body of an old man and long hair like a girl," they are said to live in the lakes, springs, and large bodies of water throughout Nevada. At night they make a crying or whimpering sound to lure people to the shoreline or out into the water. Once the prey has fallen for the trick, the water baby grabs them and, pulling them into the water, drowns them there. To prevent these demonic creatures from attacking, a shaman must communicate with the water babies and explain to them why his tribe needs to use their water. To speak of them is taboo as they are considered to be a psychopomp (death omen). Offerings of baskets filled with cord and pine nuts are weighted, sealed, and thrown into the lake.

Source: Downs, *Two Worlds of the Washo*, 62; Jones, *Evil in Our Midst*, 6–4; Oesterle, *Weird Las Vegas and Nevada*, 44; Roth, *American Elves*, 66, 128

Water-Elephant

In Burmese folklore the water-elephant is a rare species of small, tusked creature no larger than a mouse but strong enough to attack elephants and consume their brains; they live in the muddy and brackish water high up in the mountains and make a roaring sound similar to the elephants they hunt. It is believed anyone who carries a tusk from a water-elephant will never be harmed should they find themselves in the path of a charging elephant. Among the Kammu people it is traditional to never go near bodies of water between 8 a.m. and 11 a.m. (approximately) as this is when the water-elephants can be found sunbathing along the shore. The spirits of water-elephants are considered to be a form of ANCESTRAL SPIRIT. Shamans will utilize a specific form of magical formula to keep these spirits at bay as they can be malicious.

Source: Eberhart, *Mysterious Creatures*, 446; Tayanin, *Being Kammu*, 4, 19, 60

Water Leaper

Variations: LLAMHIGYN Y DWR

Living in the sea off the Welsh coast, the water leapers are a species of vicious water fairy preying on fishermen by luring their ships into rocks where they will wreck and drown or by tricking them into falling overboard and into the water. These FAIRY ANIMALS have been described as being winged toad-like creatures with long, barbed tails. When these fay cannot successfully hunt fishermen they have been known to eat sheep.

Source: Eberhart, *Mysterious Creatures*, 299; McCoy, *Witch's Guide to Faery Folk*, 33–34; Rose, *Giants, Monsters, and Dragons*, 225

Wati-Kutjara

In Australian Dreamtime mythology wati-kutjara ("men iguana") was the collective name for the twins Kurukadi ("white iguana") and Mumba ("black iguana") who lived beneath the earth in a deep sleep. One day they awoke and walked the earth creating animals, plants, rocks, and waterholes as they traveled.

Source: Bartlette, *Mythology Bible*, 244; Jobes, *Dictionary of Mythology, Folklore and Symbols*, 1669

Wei-Te-Lun-Kai

According to Chinese folklore, the DRAGON KING Wei-Te-Lun-Kai is the most exalted of all the DRAGONS of the universe.

Source: Eitel, *China Review, Or, Notes and Queries on the Far East*, Volume 10, 405

Were-Creature

Variations: Anjing Ajak (Java), Azeman (Surinam), Bleiz-Garv (Brittany), Den-Bleiz (Brittany), Jaguar-Man (Paraguay), Legarou (Haiti), Lobison (Brazil), Loup-Garou (France), Macan Gadungan (Java), Sukuyan (Trinidad and Tobago), Therianthrop, Tigre Capiango (Argentina), Upir (Russia), Vilkatas (Lithuania), Vilkolakis (Lithuania), Vseslav (Belorussia), Were-Being, Zmag Ognjeni Vuk (Bosnia and Serbia)

Although WEREWOLVES are perhaps the most well-known of the species of were-creatures (man-creatures), there are numerous other *weres* which originate from cultures all over the world. A were-creature is most of the time a human being who for some reason—be it a curse, the willful application of a magical item or spell, or an innate ability—has the ability to shape-shift into an animal form or an anthromorphic hybrid of the animal; at some point, the individual reverts back to their original human form. The driving compulsions of the were-creature depend on the nature of the animal, the culture of origin, and the intent of the tale, as not all of them are murderous, violent, and driven to destruction as is the WEREWOLF. Such creatures include, but are hardly limited to, were-bear (United States of America), were-boar (Greece and Tur-key), were-cat, were-crocodile (Africa), were-cow (*Boanthropy*, ancient Greece), were-dog (*Kuanthropy*, ancient Greece), were-fox (China and Japan), were-hyena (Africa), were-jackal (Africa), were-jaguar (South America), were-leopard (Africa), and the were-mountain lion (United States of America).

Therianthropy ("wild animal man") is the ability of a human being able to shape-shift their body into the form of an animal; typically a person has the ability to change into one specific species of animal but what the animal may be is limited only to the range of known animals. All WEREWOLVES are by definition therianthrops, and more specifically lycanthropes; individuals who shape-shift into a dog are Kuanthrops.

Traditionally, were-creatures are at best tricksters or content to hunt for woodland prey but they can be as horrific and violent as legend can imagine; additionally they are immune to most forms of damage inflicted upon them, unless it is delivered by a traditional hero, is magical, or comes from another were-creature.

Not all were-creatures are dangerous, evil, or malevolent. In many religions and traditions shamans have the ability to shape-shift into an animal form, either physical or in a dream state, doing so for the benefit of their community in order to perform certain tasks; this sort of transformation is known as spiritual therianthropy. Among the Vikings, *berserkers* ("bear skin") would, at least on a psychological level, mentally shape-shift into a bear before going into combat.

Source: Rose, *Giants, Monsters, and Dragons*, 391–3; Sax, *Imaginary Animals*, 223; Smith, *Complete Idiot's Guide to World Mythology*, 248

Werewolf

Variations: Bisclaveret (Brittany), Lob Ombre (Spain), Lob Omem (Portugal), Lobombre (Spain), Loup Garpou (France), Louweerou (France), Lupo Manaro (Italy), Lycanthrope (Greece), Slovalia, Versipellis ("turnskin," Ancient Greek and Roman), Vircolak (various Balkan states), Vlkodlaks ("wolf hair," Slovakia), Vookodlaks (Slovakia), Vulkodlak (Russia), Wawkalak (Byelorus), Werewolf (Germany), Wer-wold (Germany)

A werewolf ("man wolf") is person with the ability to transform into a wolf or a wolf-human anthromorphic hybrid; this folklore is present in many cultures worldwide and dates back to man's earliest day. The ability to transform may be innate, a curse placed on the individual, or by magical means, be it an item or a spell. The first recorded story of a *lycanthrope* (the ability to transform into a wolf) was the Greek tale of Lycaon written by Ovid in his tale *Metamorphoses*; although older unrecorded oral traditions date back even further in Icelandic, Norse, Scandinavian, and Teutonic traditions.

In many cultures, there are physical manifestations present in the person's visage when not trans-formed which give them away for their ability no matter how they came about it; such tell-tale signs are eyebrows which have grown together; fanglike incisors; hirsute skin; the "Mark of Cain," a ruddy birthmark of no specific or set description; eyes of mis-matched color; and short fingers with claw-like nails.

Werewolves are feared no matter how they came into being because of their proclivity for violence, ravenous appetite, and wanton destruction; there are many tales of a single werewolf slaughtering an entire herd of cattle or sheep in a single night; crashing into people's homes, snatching up the children, and fleeing off into the night. In both instances the creature destroys anything and anyone who gets in its way. Typically, while transformed, the creature is nearly indestructible and immune to most weapons. The means by which to prevent their attack or damage these creatures vary by culture, from region to region, and the time period from which the story originates; they are too numerous to list.

The idea of *therianthropy* ("wild animal man," were-creatures, see WERE-CREATURE) also exists and is prevalent throughout the world and all along the time-line; popular were-creatures are the were-bear (United States of America), were-boar (Greece and Turkey), were-cat, were-crocodile (Africa), were-cow (*Boanthropy*, ancient Greece), were-dog (*Kuanthropy*, ancient Greece), were-fox (China and Japan), were-hyena (Africa), were-jackal (Africa), were-jaguar (South America) were-leopard (Africa) and the were-mountain lion (United States of America).

Source: Baring-Gould, *Book of Were-Wolves*, 4–9; Guiley, *Encyclopedia of Vampires, Werewolves, and Other Monsters*, 316–8; Rose, *Giants, Monsters, and Dragons*, 391–3

Whappernocker

Originating in the lumberjack communities of the developing United States of America, the whappernocker, one of the FEARSOME CRITTERS, was said to be larger than a weasel and had a beautiful brown-red coat consisting of silky, fine hairs. These nocturnal animals were said to live off of birds and worms and were so wild they could not be tamed. Because their coat was so luxurious, they were hunted and trapped for it.

Source: Kippis, *New Annual Register*, 120; Rose, *Giants, Monsters, and Dragons*, 119, 393

Whatukura

Variations: Apa-Whatu-Kura

A species of supernatural male beings from Polynesian mythology, the whatukura, along with their female counterparts the MAREIKURA, live in the upper world as the attendants of the god Io. Acting as his attendants and couriers, they have control over the beings, creatures, and denizens of the lower worlds. They had the ability to move freely between the twelve worlds. The whatukura utilized their own species of servitors known as the APA; they were said to resemble whirlwinds.

Source: Reed, *Reed Book of Māori Mythology*, 43–4, 88; Whatahoro, *Lore of the Whare-wānanga*, xv

Whirligig Fish

Originating in the lumberjack communities of the developing United States of America, the whirligig fish, one of the FEARSOME CRITTERS, was said to be related to the GIDDY FISH, as they both swam in circles and were fished for in the winter months when the water had frozen over. Loggers would cut a hole in the ice and lather the edges in bacon grease; soon the fish, smelling the bait, would swim up and around the greased ledge, circling faster and faster until it spun itself up and out of the water.

Source: Botkin, *American People*, 255; Godfrey, *Monsters of Wisconsin*, 131; Rose, *Giants, Monsters, and Dragons*, 119

White Merle

In ancient Basque folklore the white merle is a FAIRY ANIMAL, a bird whose singing could restore sight to the blind.

Source: Brewer, *Wordsworth Dictionary of Phrase and Fable*, 1137; Daniels, *Encyclopedia of Superstitions, Folklore, and the Occult Sciences of the World*, 1417

Whowie

In Australian Aborigine mythology, the six-legged whowie was described as looking like a goanna lizard with a dog shaped head, but a great deal larger; in spite of its extra legs it was not fast but rather slow. In order to catch and consume people, the whowie would use its incredible stealth and sneak into a camp while everyone slept; carefully it would eat up one person after another, up to sixty people a night. A treacherous creature, the whowie was said to live in the caves along the banks of the Murray River. Eventually this horrible creature was nearly slain and left dying; although it is still dying, and its cries of pain can be heard, it will, in NURSERY BOGIE fashion, snatch up children who wander too far away from their parents.

Source: Eliot, *Universal Myths*, 137–8; Smith, *Myths and Legends of the Australian Aborigines*, 147–51; Zell-Ravenheart, *Wizard's Bestiary*, 101

Wi-Lu-Gho-Yuk (WEE-Loo-Go-Yuk)

Wi-lu-gho-yuk are a *tunerak*, a type of demonic creature from the demonology of the Inuit of Alaska, United States of America. Looking like

small mouse-like creatures, they are attracted to their prey by movement. Making their way through the ice, they gnaw a hole into a person's shoe, scamper over their body, burrow into their chest, and then consume their heart. A mortal man cannot withstand the attacks of a *tunerak*; however, if the victim sees the wi-lu-gho-yuk before it attacks and stands perfectly still, it will ignore him and the victim will instead become a successful hunter, and his first new kill will be this demon. These creatures can be slain by any attack which would kill a small animal.

Source: Jones, *Evil in Our Midst*, 32–4; Sproul, *Primal Myths*, 226

Wihwin

A species of amphibious creature from Caraibes folklore, the wihwin is described as looking like a large, fanged horse; during the dry and hot seasons they leave the sea and stalk the hills, hunting humans to consume. When the rainy season comes, the wihwin return to the water.

Source: Porteous, *Lore of the Forest*, 146; Rose, *Giants, Monsters, and Dragons*, 394; Zell-Ravenheart, *Wizard's Bestiary*, 101

Wikatcha

Variations: Wi Katcha

A species of underwater-dwelling feline from Creek folklore, the wikatcha was a type of aquatic monster living in the water near the town of Coosa which had an affair with a human woman. The people of the town were intent on killing the resulting child upon its birth but the creature was determined to protect its family; it created a great flood which destroyed everything in the area. The few people who managed to survive the devastation founded the town of Tulsa. Although the woman and child survived, they were never seen or heard of again.

Source: Rose, *Giants, Monsters, and Dragons*, 394; Zell-Ravenheart, *Wizard's Bestiary*, 101–2

Will Am Alone

Originating in the lumberjack communities of the developing United States of America, the will am alone, one of the FEARSOME CRITTERS of Maine, was said to be a small squirrel-like creature which albeit playful is extremely vicious. The will am alone will gather up balls of poisonous fungi and drop them into the ears and eyes of sleeping woodsmen; this will cause them to have strange dreams. The will am alone is fond of alcohol and wild hunting parties with large quantities of it.

Source: Cox, *Fearsome Creatures of the Lumberwoods*, x; Rose, *Giants, Monsters, and Dragons*, 119

Willopus-Wallopus

Originating in the lumberjack communities of the developing United States of America, the willopus-wallopus is one of the FEARSOME CRITTERS. Unfortunately, there is no additional information on this creature other than its name, causing writers of the time, 1841–1861, to believe it had gone extinct.

Source: Mencken, *American Language Supplement 1*, 251

Wilser Dragon

In Swiss folklore the Wilser Dragon was a DRAGONET, a species of small but highly aggressive and extremely territorial DRAGON which lived upon Mount Pilate in Switzerland; it had the ability to breathe a poisonous cloud and its blood was caustic. According to the folklore, a man named Winckelriedt had been banished from the town of Wilser for committing the crime of manslaughter; however, he was told he would be pardoned if he slew the DRAGON with a sword. Wanting to return home, Winckelriedt took up the challenge and was successful in his task, but as he raised the sword in victory, the acidic blood of the creature ran down the sword, killing him.

Source: De Kirk, *Dragonlore*, 41

Wirwir

A flesh-eating creature from Filipino folklore, the wirwir exhumes graves and consumes the bodies laid to rest therein; there is no physical description of these creatures except to say they are relentless and tireless in their pursuit of human flesh.

Source: Paraiso, *Balete Book*, 66; Ramos, *Creatures of Philippine Lower Mythology*, 71

Wish Hound

Variations: Wisked Hound, Yell-Hound, Yeth-Hound

In British folklore, the headless wish hounds are said to be seen walking along the oldest roads and across the moors during the midnight hours; it is believed if mortal dogs hear the baying call of these FAIRY ANIMALS, they will die. Wish hounds have a headless pack master who follows them; described as being dressed all in black, this spectral huntsman is believed to lead the Wild Hunt in the Devonshire region.

Source: Briggs, *Encyclopedia of Fairies*, 440; Hardwick, *Traditions, Superstitions, and Folklore*, 153, 192; Hunt, *Popular Romances of the West of England*, 29, 145

Wishpooshi

A gigantic beaver from Nez Perce folklore, the clawed wishpooshi lives in the lakes of Washington, United States of America. According to the folklore, the wishpooshi did not want anyone or anything catching the fish in his lake so he drove off what he did not kill. The people asked the trickster god, Coyote, to intervene on their behalf. A violent and devastating battle took place between the two, churning the water, creating channels and gorges, and eventually draining the lake. The wishpooshi finally managed to swallow Coyote but it was a fatal mistake, as the trickster, now unopposed, stabbed the creature in his heart. From the wishpooshi carcass the Chinook Klickitat and Yakima people were created.

Source: Rose, *Giants, Monsters, and Dragons*, 396; Zell-Ravenheart, *Wizard's Bestiary*, 102

Wiwilemekw

Variations: Weewilmekq, Wiwilemekq

A horned SEA SERPENT in Maliseet-Passamaquoddy folklore, the wilwilemekw is described as being crocodilian in appearance but with a rack of horns, the focus-point of its power. It was believed anyone who was brave enough to acquire a scraping of antler off of a live wilwilemekw would gain power and strength. The wilwilemekw is said to be found in rushing water, such as in rapids, waterfalls, and whirlpools.

Source: Rose, *Giants, Monsters, and Dragons*, 397; Zell-Ravenheart, *Wizard's Bestiary*, 101

Wolpertinger

Variations: Elwedritsche, JACKALOPE, Rasselbock, Skvader (Swedish), Wolperdinger

A chimerical creature from Bavarian folklore, the wolpertinger is described as having bird feet, boar tusks, a coxcomb in the forehead, deer antlers, hawk wings, rabbit ears, rabbit hindquarters, and a rabbit-, squirrel-, or weasel-like body. It is believed the saliva of this creature stimulates hair growth; to cure impotence, nectar is sipped through one of its shank bones and then the person is to urinate across the current of a stream.

Source: Brunvand, *American Folklore*, 831; Zell-Ravenheart, *Wizard's Bestiary*, 102

Wuchowsen

Variations: The Great Wind Bird, Wochowsen

A gigantic white bird or eagle from Passamaquoddy folklore, Wuchowsen ("wind blower") was believed to sit upon a rock located at the Northern-most end of the world; each time this massive bird moved its wings, it would cause the wind to blow. This immortal creature is said to be as ancient as time, born in the earliest moments of creation.

Source: Leland, *Algonquin Legends of New England*, n.pag.; Nichols, *Birds of Algonquin Legend*, 138; Rose, *Giants, Monsters, and Dragons*, 398

Wulver

A human and wolf hybrid from Scottish folklore, the wulver was something of a WILD MAN, living alone in the wilderness in caves and having as little to do with mankind as possible; however, in some tales these creatures would leave a gift of food on the doorstep of a needy person. Wulvers are described as anthropoids covered in short brown fur and having a wolf-like head.

Source: Monaghan, *Encyclopedia of Celtic Mythology and Folklore*, 475; Zell-Ravenheart, *Wizard's Bestiary*, 102

Wyvern

Variations: Wivern

A species of chimerical DRAGON from European folklore, the two-legged wyvern ("life viper") was originally seen as a bringer of life and a protector of the land, but after the introduction of Christianity it was maligned, said to be a vicious predator associated with envy, pestilence, and war. It has avian legs, a barbed tail, the body of a serpent, feet tipped with eagle talons, head of a DRAGON, wings of a bat, and occasionally a set of horns upon its head. In heraldic symbology the wyvern is traditionally green with a red belly, chest, and underwings.

Source: De Kirk, *Dragonlore*, 46–7; Rose, *Giants, Monsters, and Dragons*, 399; Zell-Ravenheart, *Wizard's Bestiary*, 103

Xan (SHAHN)

A mosquito-like creature in ancient Mayan mythology, xan was described as having a stinger large enough to kill a man; after stinging, it would drain the person of their blood.

Source: Goetz, *Popol Vuh*, xlv, 68, 75; Recinos, *Popol Vuh*, 135; Zell-Ravenheart, *Wizard's Bestiary*, 103

Xanthos

Variations: Xanthus

According to Greek mythology Xanthos ("blond," "bright eyes," or "dun"), one of the HIPPOI ATHANATOI, was an immortal horse; he and his brother, the stallion BALIOS, were the offspring of the god of the wind, Zephyros, and the HARPY PODARGE. In the ancient Greek epic poem the *Iliad* ("*Song of Ilion*") (1240 BC) attributed to Homer, BALIOS was the horse ridden by heroic cultural hero and semi-divine Achilles the Myrmidon leader as well as being the horse who drew his chariot during the Trojan War. Both horses are described as having manes long enough to touch the ground but Xanthos was said to be capable of human speech.

Another horse by the name of Xanthos was one of the four MARES OF DIOMEDES, King of Aetolia and son of the god Ares (Mars) (see DINOS, PHOLGIOS, and LAMPON). Although the horses are female, the Latin author Hyginus (64 BC–AD 17), the only author who ever named them, gave them all masculine names. In his eighth Labor the demigod Hercules (Heracles) was charged with the capture and return of these savage mares which pulled the chariot of the king and were fed a diet of human flesh.

Source: Brewer, *Character Sketches of Romance, Fiction and the Drama*, Volumes 8, 266; *Contemporary Review*, Volume 27, 810; Hard, *Routledge Handbook of Greek Mythology* 262; Markman, *Horse in Greek Art*, 5

Xecotcovach

According to the Quiche people's creation myth recorded in the *Popol Vuh*, the Mayans' sacred book, Xecotcovach was one of four birds which played a significant role in the destruction of the first race of people created by the god of the wind, Hurakan. The creation myth says after the gods made the animals, earth, moon, sky, and sun they created a race of people made of wood who were meant to appreciate the gods and see to the well-being of the animals. This first attempt of humanity was a failure as the wooden people insulted the gods and abused the animals. Hurakan sent a great flood to drown the wooden people; he also sent Xecotcovach who tore out their eyes. CAMULATZ bit off the heads of the drowning; CATZBALAM pecked away their flesh; and TECUMBALAM broke their bones and sinews, and then ground their bodies into powder.

Source: Bingham, *South and Meso-American Mythology A to Z*, 142; Spence, *Arcane Secrets and Occult Lore of Mexico and Mayan Central America*, 241

Xexeu

A species of gigantic birds in South American folklore, the xexeu, similar to THUNDERBIRDS, are believed to be the creators of the large, black, billowing clouds which gather together just before violent storms erupt.

Source: Rose, *Giants, Monsters, and Dragons*, 401; Zell-Ravenheart, *Wizard's Bestiary*, 103, 271

Xiang Yao

In Chinese folklore Xiang Yao is a disgusting and hideous monster said to have a serpentine body with nine human heads; it is the companion to the black DRAGON and god GONG-GONG; together the two of them foul lakes and rivers with their excrement causing them to transform into fetid swamps.

Source: Rose, *Giants, Monsters, and Dragons*, 401; Zell-Ravenheart, *Wizard's Bestiary*, 103

Xiao

Variations: Shanxiao

In Chinese folklore the xiao are a species of
NATURE SPIRIT dwelling in the mountains;
described by Qing Dynasty author Pu Songling
(1640–1715) as being trouble-makers with a "puck-
like humor." Single-footed and looking like hybrid
birdmen, the xiao have the ability to shape-shift and
the reputation for being arsonists, setting ablaze
houses and huts.

Source: Songling, *Strange Tales from Liaozhai*, Volume1,
29; Unschuld, *Chinese Traditional Healing*, 2349

Xiezhi

Variations: Xie Chai, Xie Zhi

In Chinese folklore the xiezhi was a UNICORN-
like chimerical creature described as having a bear's
tail, the body of a lion, the head of a DRAGON, a
lion's mane and paws, and an alicorn (single horn)
emerging from the top of its head. The xiezhi was
noted for its ability to discern the truth from lies
and would instantly use its horn to pierce the chest
of anyone who lied in its presence; this trait made
it a fitting symbol for the emblem of the office of
the Censoriate. The xiezhi is very similar to the
CHIAI TUNG.

Source: Bates, *29 Chinese Mysteries*, 79; Welch, *Chinese
Art*, 131, 147

Xiuhcoatl, plural: xiubhcocab

A flaming serpent from Aztec mythology which
could withstand even the most scorching of heat,
Xiuhcoatl ("flaming serpent") was associated with
turquoise and was the personification of extreme
drought. The supreme god Huitzilopochtli used
Xiuhcoatl as the implement to behead his sister
Coyolxauhqui after she earnestly threatened to kill
their mother, the earth goddess, Coatlicue. In art
Xiuhcoatl is depicted as having a head at each end
of its serpentine body and a snout like a hog-nose
snake; he is often depicted next to the god of fire,
Xiuhtecuhtli. Because of his two heads, Xiuhcoatl
is sometimes referred to in the plural as Xiubhcocab.

Source: Aguilar-Moreno, *Handbook to Life in the Aztec
World*, 195; Bingham, *South and Meso-American Mythology
A to Z*, 142–3; De Kirk, *Dragonlore*, 55, 103

Xolotl

In ancient Aztec mythology Xolotl was a *nahualli*
(disguise) of the god Quetzalcoatl as well as his twin;
he would accompany him on trips to the underworld
in order to collect human bones. Xolotl is depicted
in art as having physical deformities—backward
turned feet and hands, ears pointing off in random

directions—and is associated with dwarves and
hunchbacks. Each evening he would chase the sun
across the sky, catch it, and take it into the underworld where he kept it until morning. Although he
is credited with having given humans fire, his ambiva-
lence to them suggests it was more likely the result
of a disaster or misfortune he caused. In order to
avoid death he underwent many transformations
until he became the larval amphibian Axolotl.

Source: Aguilar-Moreno, *Handbook to Life in the Aztec
World*, 152; Rose, *Giants, Monsters, and Dragons*, 401; Zell-
Ravenheart, *Wizard's Bestiary*, 103

Y Ddraig Goch

Variations: Red DRAGON of Wales

A fiery red DRAGON and the symbol of Wales, Y
Ddraig Goch ("the red DRAGON") was the protector
of the Welsh people. An eighth century legend foretells of a battle between GWIBER, the white
DRAGON, symbolic of Britain, and Y Ddraig Goch
who would be victorious and return the country
back to its people.

Source: Breverton, *Wales*, n.pag.; Rose, *Giants, Monsters,
and Dragons*, 307

Y Wrach

Variations: Yr hen Wrach

In British folklore the y wrach ("old hag") is a hag
of disease said to spread the mysterious *fad felen*
("yellow death"); she is described as having yellow
eyes, hair, and teeth and living in a marsh. The y
wrach spreads this illness by fixing her baleful gaze
intently upon a selected victim.

Source: Rhys, *Celtic Britain*, 68; Spurrell, *Dictionary of the
Welsh Language*, 88

Yagarua

A creature from New Guinea folklore, the
yagarua are a species said to consist entirely of males
and are described as being anthropoids, only slightly
larger than a human, and having a head full of tan
gled locks of hair. Each one of the yagarua haunts
a specific location and is generally harmless, as the
worst of them is said to occasionally pelt unsuspecting victims with rocks.

Source: Seligman, *Melanesians of British New Guinea*, 649

Yagim

Variations: Iak Im

A malevolent and malicious SEA SERPENT from
Kwakiutl folklore, the yagim is described as looking
like a large shark; responsible for all manner of
mishaps occurring on the water, the yagim is most
feared for its attacks on boats, capsizing them and
devouring the occupants. When it was feeling particularly vindictive, the yagim would create violent

storms and send huge waves crashing inland, attempting to destroy entire villages.

Source: Rose, *Giants, Monsters, and Dragons*, 403; Zimmerman, *Exploring the Life, Myth, and Art of Native Americans*, 75; Zell-Ravenheart, *Wizard's Bestiary*, 51

Yagis

A SEA SERPENT from Kwakiutl folklore, the yagis, similar to the YAGIM, is said to prey on boats off of the coast of Vancouver Island. Described as an aquatic fire-breathing snake, a gigantic snake, and a carnivorous turtle, the yagis capsizes boats either with its body or by causing waves which will flip the boat; no matter how the sailors end up in the water the creature will then move in and devour each one.

Source: Maberry, *Vampire Universe*, 304

Yakan

Variations: Shikkara

According to twelfth century Japanese folklore, the most powerful of the fox spirits (KITSUNE) was the yakan; when gods visited the earth, it was the form they preferred; its bark is similar to a wolf. In Buddhist sutras, the yakan is the most haunting, harm-doing, and worst of all the fox spirits.

Source: Asiatic Society of Japan. *Transactions of the Asiatic Society of Japan* 1965, 20, 57–8; Picken, *Essentials of Shinto*, 124

Yako

In Japanese folklore the KITSUNE (fox spirit) are divided into three ranks, the SHURYO, YORIKATA, and the Yako. The lowest of the three ranks, the yako are field foxes and the ones most likely to do harm to mankind.

Source: De Visser, *Transactions of the Asiatic Society of Japan*, 82; Picken, *Essentials of Shinto*, 124

Yala

A species of large chimerical black bovines with the jowls of a boar and the tail of an elephant, the yala are said to have a pair of preposterously long horns set atop their head which the creature can move forward and backwards at will.

Source: Zell-Ravenheart, *Companion for the Apprentice Wizard*, 179

Yali

Variations: Yalaka

A chimerical creature from Hindu mythology, the yali is described as having the body of a lion with the trunk and tusks of an elephant; it acts as a guardian, protecting a person physically as well as spiritually. It is believed this creature has complete supremacy over the animal world and is completely fearless of them. Symbolic of man's struggle over the elemental forces of nature, the yali is said to be *vyala* ("vicious").

Source: Garg, *Encyclopaedia of the Hindu World*, 483; Zell-Ravenheart, *Wizard's Bestiary*, 103

Yama-Uba

Variations: Yamauba

A mountain dwelling YŌKAI from Japanese folklore, the yama-uba ("mountain grandmother"), also one of the BAKEMONO, is an ancient being, having long white hair, a thin face, and a withered body. She will present herself to travelers using her shape-shifting abilities to appear as a beautiful young woman. Once she has lured a person off, she will capture, kill, and consume her victim.

Source: Lee, *Encyclopedia of Asian American Folklore and Folklife*, Volume 1, 576; Monaghan, *Goddesses in World Culture*, Volume 1, 164; Roberts, *Japanese Mythology A to Z*, 24

Yama-Waro

A species of WILD MAN from Japanese folklore, the mountain dwelling yama-waro are described as looking like a large black-haired anthropoid with incredible strength. Although these creatures will steal food from the villages they are also quick to assist woodcutters in the transportation of their goods in exchange for a ball of rice. If ever an attempt is made to capture one of the yama-waro, a sudden calamity will befall the would-be captor, such as contracting the plague, suddenly becoming insane, or otherwise dying unexpectedly.

Source: Brinklye, *Japan, Its History, Arts and Literature*, Volume 5, 215

Yamabito

In Japanese folklore the yamabito ("mountain people") are a species of ONI, descended from earth deities; these hairy anthropoid creatures live in the mountains.

Source: Li, *Ambiguous Bodies*, 121; Iinkai, *Japan*, 989

Yamata

Variations: Koshi DRAGON, OROCHI

A HYDRA-like DRAGON from Japanese mythology, Yamata was described as having eight heads and eight tails; it would kidnap people who walked along the Koshi Road and consume them. Ultimately, Yamata was defeated by Susawona, the Shinto god of sea and storms.

Source: De Kirk, *Dragonlore*, 32

Yamm

In the mythology of the ancient Syrians the DRAGON-like monster YAMM ("sea") was overcome by the god Baal. According to the story, Yamm sends his messenger to the chief of the gods of the Ugaritic pantheon, El, requesting Baal, the god of storms, and all of his possessions to be turned over to him. El agrees and an enraged Baal threatens the life of the messenger. Kothar-wa-Hassis then takes Baal aside and gives to him two weapons which can destroy Yamm, a pair of clubs. Baal, now properly armed, confronts Yamm, thoroughly defeats him, and declares himself king.

Source: Angel, *Chaos and the Son of Man*, 3–4; Kuehn, *Dragon in Medieval East Christian and Islamic Art*, 87, 90

Yamo

Yamo ("wind") are a species of demonic creatures commonly used as messengers by Tipu in the demonology of the Lango people of Uganda. Usually they are seen as being an elflike or rat-like creature between six and eighteen inches tall. Yamo prey upon those who have thwarted the will of their master, Tipu; they are numerous and unpredictable demons of all things negative. The yamo can cause illness, possess people, and shape-shift into any form a person can imagine. Anyone who has contracted a disease from one of these demons must perform a *mako yamo* ("catching the wind") ceremony to save themselves. The yamo live in human-like communities on hilltops or near rocks, springs, and streams. Motivated by their greed, they are extremely desirous of clothing, food, and money.

Source: Curley, *Elders, Shades, and Women*, 160–1, 178; Jones, *Evil in Our Midst*, 141–3

Yannig

Variations: Yannig an Od

An aquatic monster from Breton folklore, the yannig spends the daylight hours in the water but at night comes up on land to hunt. Making a call similar to the sound of an owl it waits for a person to answer the call; when this happens they give away their position and the yannig instantly hones in on their location. Moving in from behind, it takes them by surprise, and devours them instantly.

Source: Rose, *Giants, Monsters, and Dragons*, 403; Zell-Ravenheart, *Wizard's Bestiary*, 103

Yaquaru

Variations: Yaquaruigh ("water-tiger")

An aquatic monster from Argentinean folklore, the yaquaru is said to live in freshwater rivers; it is described as looking very much like an otter but nearly the size of a bull and has long shaggy hair, sharp talons, strong tusks, a tapering tail, and thick but short legs. The yaquaru is especially fond of cattle and consumes great numbers of them in the seasonal crossing of the rivers. The attack is described

as being quite savage; the cow is one moment swimming and the next is quickly and violently pulled beneath the water, and moments later its intestines and lungs appear on the surface.

Source: Heuvelmans, *On the Track of Unknown Animals*, n.pag.; Rose, *Giants, Monsters, and Dragons*, 403

Yasha

Variations: Yakkha, Yaksa, Yashi

The yasha is a vampiric creature from Japanese folklore. Looking like a vampire bat, it is in fact the reincarnated form of a woman who was filled with anger in her past life.

Source: Bush, *Asian Horror Encyclopedia*, 207; Chopra, *Dictionary of Mythology*, 310; Smith, *Ancient Tales and Folklore*, 217

Yata Garasu

Variations: Yatagarasu

In Japanese folklore Yata Garasu is a gigantic bird resembling a crow but having three red legs (symbolic of its masculinity); it is employed by the gods to act as their messenger but is under the dominion of the goddess of the sun, Amaterasu. It often descends to the earth so it may feed upon the plant of immortality.

Source: Bates, *10,000 Chinese Numbers*, 21; Coulter, *Encyclopedia of Ancient Deities*, 514; Rosen, *Mythical Creatures Bible*, 164; Zell-Ravenheart, *Wizard's Bestiary*, 104, 271

Yato-No-Kami

Variations: Yato No Kami, Yatso No Kami

A species of NATURE SPIRITS manifesting as a HORNED SERPENT from Japanese folklore, the yato-no-kami were said to have lived in a marshy valley. According to the eighth century story, when the local lord wished to expand his rice paddy field he sent his warrior Matachi to rid the area of the creatures. Matachi drove them from the valley and into the foothills of the mountain; there he planted a stick and declared everything to one side of it belonged to man while the land on the other side belonged to the gods. To ensure the yato-no-kami would not bear a grudge against him, his warlord, or future generations, he also announced he would become their first priest and construct a temple there so he could worship them.

Source: Breen, *Shinto in History*, 35–6

Yech

Variations: Yach

In Indian folklore the yech is a humorous, powerful FAIRY ANIMAL described as looking like a dark civet cat with a small white hat on its head. If someone manages to gain possession of the creature's hat, the yech will then become the devoted servant;

wearing the hat will make a person invisible. Making catlike noises, and having the ability to shapeshift into any form, the yech has such small fee that they are mistaken for being invisible.

Sources: Crooke, *Popular Religion and Folk-Lore of Northern India*, Volume 2, 80; Spence, *Encyclopedia of Occultism and Parapsychology*, 1005; Zell-Ravenheart, *Wizard's Bestiary*, 104

Yeitso

Variations: Ye'iitsho La'I Naaghaii ("GIANT Ye'ii" or "One Walking Giant")

In the folklore of the Navajo people of the United States of America, Yeitso ("great genius" or "great God") was one of the ANAYE, a type of gigantic and monstrous supernatural beings causing fear, misery, and wickedness throughout the world. The chief of his kind and born of the union between a wicked woman and a stone, scaly Yeitso lived by a lake; he was slain by the cultural heroes Nayanezgani ("slayer of alien gods") and Thobadzistshini ("child born of water") and with the assistance of Tsohanoai, was scalped.

Source: Cotterell, *Dictionary of World Mythology*, 220; Leviton, *Encyclopedia of Earth Myths*, n.pag.

Yelapahi

In the folklore of the Navajo people of the United States of America, Yelapahi ("brown GIANT") was one of the ANAYE, a type of gigantic and monstrous supernatural being causing fear, misery, and wickedness throughout the world. Said to be both cruel and evil, Yelapahi was described as being half as tall as the tallest pine tree.

Source: Coulter, *Encyclopedia of Ancient Deities*, 51; Leviton, *Encyclopedia of Earth Myths*, n.pag.; Rose, *Giants, Monsters, and Dragons*, 18

Yin Chu

In Chinese folklore there is a species of bird, the LWAN, said to look like a beautiful, large, and graceful pheasant; these birds have the ability to change color; each color the bird can assume is given a different name. The yin chu is the black form of the LWAN. The additional forms are: FUNG, HWA YIH, TO FU, and the YU SIANG.

Source: Gould, *Mythical Monsters*, 370; Rose, *Giants, Monsters, and Dragons*, 405

Ying-Long

Variations: Yonglong

A unique species of DRAGON in Chinese mythology, the ying-long has fur rather than scales covering its body; usually its wings are covered in feathers. The ying long are one of the few species of Chinese DRAGONS to have actual wings which they use to fly. Other DRAGONS capable of flight have a lump

on their head known as a *chi mu* which enables flight. The number of claws on these DRAGONS is usually three but it is not uncommon to see five clawed ying-long.

The ying long was said to be a powerful servant of the Chinese emperor Huang di; according to legend, it stopped the Yellow River from flooding by carving out channels with its tail.

Source: Bates, *All About Chinese Dragons*, 5, 23, 28; De Kirk, *Dragonlore* 29; Rosen, *Mythical Creatures Bible*, 63

Ying-Lung

Variations: Proper Conduct DRAGON

The ancient Chinese author Hwai nan Tsze attempted to prove all creatures are the progeny of the DRAGON. He claimed the ying-lung were the offspring of the MAO-TUH and were themselves the progenitors of the KIEN-MA. According to Chinese folklore the ying-lung were plumose winged, had bird claws, and lived beneath the earth or in lakes and pools; they were associated with clouds and were said to be the guardians of the earth and water.

Source: De Visser, *Dragon in China and Japan*, 65; Gould, *Mythical Monsters*, 238, 255, 400; Rose, *Giants, Monsters, and Dragons*, 405; Zell-Ravenheart, *Wizard's Bestiary*, 104

Ying-Ying

According to the sixth century author Jen Fang who wrote the *Shus I ki*, the ying-ying is one stage of a DRAGON's development. Fang writes the earliest stage of development is a water snake, and after five hundred years it transforms into a KIAO; after another one thousand years it transforms into a LUNG, and after another five hundred years transforms again, this time into a KIOH-LUNG; finally after one thousand more years it transforms into its final stage of development, the ying-ying.

Source: De Visser, *Dragon in China and Japan*, 72

Yo

One of the three main species of DRAGON from Korean folklore, the hornless yo are said to live in the ocean. They, like all Korean DRAGONs, are chimerical, having the belly of a frog, eighty-one scales on their back, the eyes of a rabbit, and four claws.

Source: Mooney, *Dragons*, 46

Yofune-Nushi

A particularly vicious DRAGON and SEA SERPENT from Japanese mythology, Yofune-nushi demanded a human sacrifice each June 13 in order to placate its raging fury and prevent the devastating flooding and storms it could create. According to the legend, one year a young woman named Tokyo appeared and offered to be the sacrifice; as Yofune-nushi neared Tokyo quickly drew her knife and slashed the beast across its eyes. As the DRAGON reeled back in pain and surprise, Tokyo stepped forward and slew it.

Source: De Kirk, *Dragonlore*, 32; Roberts, *Japanese Mythology A to Z*, 126–7; Rose, *Giants, Monsters, and Dragons*, 405

Yoh Shoh

Variations: Yohshoh

In Chinese folklore yoh shoh is the collective name for the chicks of the FENGHUANG bird.

Source: Gould, *Legendary Creatures*, n.pag.; Rose, *Giants, Monsters, and Dragons*, 406

Yōkai (YOU-ki)

Variations: Yamamba, Yamanba, Yamauba

The collective name for an assorted myriad creature of Japanese folklore, the yōkai have no set form or purpose as they can manifest as anthropoids with more or less animal or human characteristics, inanimate objects which became sentient, or the physical personification of a natural phenomenon or linguistic pun. Yōkai are also morally ambiguous; they can have a frightening appearance and be helpful or physically attractive and murderous. Some do not even have a physical form but make their presence known by sending out feelings, impressions, or making unexplainable noises. The scientific cataloging, debunking reports of, and study of the yōkai is known as *yokaigaku*.

According to Japanese folklore, once a household item reaches an advanced age, about one hundred years, it may develop a soul and become a living and self-aware being known as yōkai ("APPARITIONs," "demons," or "spirits"); items particularly susceptible to this transformation, should they survive so long, are clocks, cloth draped from folding screens, clothing, lutes, mirrors, mosquito netting or dust cloths, old jars, paper lanterns, paper walls, sake containers, scrolls and paper, straw sandals, tea kettles, temple gongs, tools, and umbrellas.

Generally these beings have both animal and human features, the ability to shape-shift, and an array of supernatural powers. Yōkai is a broad term and includes virtually all fantastical creatures and supernatural beings. Collectively these beings are known as TSUKOMOGAMI.

Source: Bathgate, *Fox's Craft in Japanese Religion and Folklore*, 20; Li, *Ambiguous Bodies*, 142, 166; Meyer, *Night Parade of One Hundred Demons*, 206; Yoda, *Yokai Attack*, 7–8

Yonagorri

Variations: Yona Gorri

A fiery colored NATURE SPIRIT in Pyrenees folklore, the yonagorri is greatly feared by the residents of the area as it vents its rage by savaging the countryside with terrific thunderstorm. Although it is most often seen in its red flame form it has the ability to appear in any number of hues; the yonagorri is believed to live in a cave near the summit of Mount Anie near Luz.

Source: Miguel de Barandiarán, *Selected Writings of José Miguel De Barandiarán*, 102; Weld, *Pyrenees, West and East*, 141

Yong

One of the three main species of DRAGON from Korean folklore, the yong are said to live in and to be the protectors of the sky. They, like all Korean DRAGONS, are chimerical, having the belly of a frog, eighty-one scales on their back, the eyes of a rabbit, and four claws.

Source: Grayson, *Korea*, 224; Mooney, *Dragons*, 46

Yong-Wang

Variations: Hae-Wang ("king of the sea")

In Korean folklore the Yong-Wang ("DRAGON KING") is said to be the most beautiful and grand of all the DRAGONS; he is the ruler of the sea and of everything which lives and moves within it. In times of drought people will make offerings to him in the hope he will let it rain. Fishermen will often say a prayer to him before setting out to sea. Many fishing villages will also have a shrine dedicated to him.

Source: Grayson, *Korea*, 224

Yorikata

In Japanese folklore the KITSUNE (fox spirit) are divided into three ranks, the SHURYO, Yorikata, and the YAKO. The yorikata are the second rank of the fox, beneath the SHURYO and above the YAKO; they are essentially assistants.

Source: De Visser, *Transactions of the Asiatic Society of Japan*, 82; Picken, *Essentials of Shinto*, 124

Youchang

A PHOENIX-like bird from Chinese folklore, the youchang is one of the five spirit avians of some power. Each of the birds, described as looking similar to the PHOENIX in size and plumage, sits upon one of the four cardinal points and in the center rests the PHOENIX itself. The youchang is the protector of the North, FAMING the East, JIAOMING the South, and SUSHUANG the West.

Source: Sterckx, *Animal and the Daemon in Early China*, 155

Ypotryll

In heraldic symbology the ypotryll is a chimerical creature having the body of a camel or dromedary with glowing red eyes; the face, head, and tusks of a boar; a gigantic penis, the legs and hooves of a goat or an ox, and the tail of a snake. It first appeared in coat of arms in the fifteenth century.

Source: Cooper, *Symbolic and Mythological Animals*, 255; Dennys, *Heraldic Imagination*, 51; Zell-Ravenheart, *Wizard's Bestiary*, 105

Ysgithyrwyn

In Arthurian folklore, Ysgithyrwyn ("white tusk") was the great boar killed by CABAL the dog of King Arthur in the tale *"How Culhwch Won Olwen"* from *The Mabinogion*. According to the story the GIANT Ysbaddaden would only allow his daughter Olwen to marry if the warrior Culhwch performed thirty-nine *anoethur* ("things hard to come by"); one of these tasks required the construction of a razor made from the tusk of Ysgithyrwyn on the promise the tusk would be pulled by Odgar, son of Aedd, while the creature was alive. Then the tusk was to be delivered to King Caw who would then shave the head of the GIANT with it. In the story, once the tusk of Ysgithyrwyn was pulled, the hunt continued; CABAL and Caw killed it.

Source: Bruce, *Arthurian Name Dictionary*, 321, 501; Reno, *Arthurian Figures of History and Legend*, 63, 172

Yu

Variations: Golden DRAGON Yu

According to Chinese legend the Yellow Emperor was displeased with the evil nature of man and wanting to wipe him off the face of the earth, ordered it to begin to rain so a great flood would cover the world. Kun, the grandson of the Yellow Emperor, begged for the rain to stop but his pleas went unanswered. Kun then broke into the treasury and stole a jar of magical mud; wherever it was thrown, an island was created. The Yellow Emperor was displeased and sent a fire god to assassinate Kun and leave the body where it fell. Soon thereafter a new life began to grow from the remains and Yu, a beautiful gold-scaled DRAGON, emerged complete with a resplendent mane and five claws upon each savage paw. Yu was determined to finish his father's work and visited his great-grandfather, beseeching him to end the flood rains. The Yellow Emperor finally relented and named Yu a god of rain. Yu immediately stopped the rain and finished the creation of the islands. Yu went on to become the first emperor of China and now his image is symbolic of the emperor of China and of rebirth.

Source: De Kirk, *Dragonlore*, 26, 87–9; Forbes, *Illustrated Book of Dragons and Dragon Lore*, n.pag.; Ingersoll, *Dragons and Dragon Lore*, n.pag.

Yu-Kia

The ancient Chinese author Hwai nan Tsze attempted to prove all creatures are the progeny of the DRAGON; according to his genealogy the yu-kia were the progenitors of flying DRAGONS (see DRAGON, ORIENTAL for the complete genealogy).

Source: De Visser, *Dragon in China and Japan*, 65

Yu-Lung

Variations: DRAGON-CARP, KIAO

A species of DRAGON from Chinese mythology, the yu-lung ("fish DRAGON") has the body and fins of a fish and a DRAGON-like head; to see the yu-lung is considered to be a very lucky omen. The yu-lung are symbolic of high aspirations and success in examinations; they are similar to the CHIAO.

Source: De Kirk, *Dragonlore* 29; Zell-Ravenheart, *Wizard's Bestiary*, 105

Yu Siang

In Chinese folklore there is a species of bird, the LWAN, said to look like a beautiful, large, and graceful pheasant. These birds have the ability to change color; each color the bird can assume is given a different name. The yu siang is the blue form. The additional forms are: FUNG, HWA YIH, TO FU, and the YIN CHU.

Source: Gould, *Mythical Monsters*, 370;

Yuen-Yuen

The ancient Chinese author Hwai nan Tsze attempted to prove all creatures are the progeny of the DRAGON. He claimed the yuen-yuen ("original tortoise") were born the progeny of the SIEN-LUNG and were themselves the progenitor of the LING-KWEI.

Source: De Visser, *Dragon in China and Japan*, 65

Yurupari

In the folklore of the Tupiian people of Brazil the word yurupari has several meanings; some say it is a generic term for all demons and spirits while others claim Yurupari is a malicious individual being but are uncertain if he is a god, OGRE of the forest, or a NATURE SPIRIT.

Source: Coulter, *Encyclopedia of Ancient Deities*, 520; Graves, *Larousse Encyclopedia of Mythology*, 447

Zagh

In Islamic mythology the zagh is a human-faced speaking crow; it sometimes identifies with the ROC. The zagh is said to have the ability to not only speak but understand all human language.

Source: Hargreaves, *Hargreaves New Illustrated Bestiary*, 67; Zell-Ravenheart, *Wizard's Bestiary*, 105, 271

Zahhak

Variations: Azi Dahaka, Aži Dahāka ("DRAGON Man"), Bēvar-Asp ("[he who has] 10,000 horses"), Dahāg ("having ten sins"), Dahak, Zahhāk, Zahhāk-e Tāzi ("the Arabian Zahhāk"), Zohak, Zohhāk

Originally described as a monstrous DRAGON with six eyes, three heads (one of which is human), and three mouths, Zahhak was a demonic DRAGON from ancient Persian folklore and Zoroastrian mythology, one of the KHRAFSTRA; the personification of evil, he was in the service of Angra Mainyu. Born the child of an Arab ruler named Merdas and a woman named Wadag (or Ōdag) who was a great sinner, Zahhak went on to take his mother as his lover.

Later, texts describe him as appearing as a human with a snake growing off each shoulder. Zahhak is cunning and capable of committing all possible sins. He controls disease and storms, is exceptionally strong, and when cut, bleeds scorpions, snakes, and other venomous creatures.

Zahhak lives in an inaccessible fortress of Kuuirinta in Babylon. He was defeated by Oraetaona, son of Aθβiya, who chained and imprisoned him on the mythical Mount Damāvand. At the end of the world Zahhak will break his bonds and consume one in three humans and livestock. The hero Az ī Srūwar (also known as Feridun and Thraetaona) will come back to life to slay him.

Source: Russell, *The Devil*, 116; Turner, *Dictionary of Ancient Deities*, 524; Yamamoto, *Oral Background of Persian Epics*, 115, 129

Zashiki-Warashi (ZAH-she-key WAH-rah-she)

A YŌKAI from Japanese folklore, zashiki-warashi ("child in the room," "floor mat child"), also one of the BAKEMONO, is depicted as a six-year-old child with black hair cut in a bob, and a red face; he prefers to haunt houses which are well cared for and will bring good fortune to the occupants to the home so long as he is not mistreated and, more importantly, the home it occupies is well maintained. If the zashiki-warashi leaves the home, he will take the good-fortune with him, leaving the family to suffer bankruptcy, domestic strife, and possible property damage. Basically harmless, the pranks this YŌKAI will play are along the lines of climbing on top of sleeping individuals during the night, causing music to be heard coming from unoccupied rooms, flipping over pillows, re-arranging small household items, unmaking the beds, and showing signs of his presence.

Source: Lee, *Encyclopedia of Asian American Folklore and Folklife*, Volume 1, 576–7; Roberts, *Japanese Mythology A to Z*, 24; Yoda, *Yokai Attack*, 30–3

Zburator (ZOO-bah-rat-or)

The *zburator* ("the flying thing") is a vampiric creature from Romanian folklore, similar to an INCUBUS. Described as a winged and handsome young man with black eyes and hair, it is said to look like a shooting star as it flies across the sky. At night, the zburator visits young girls and women, has sexual intercourse with them, and drains off some of their life-energy with each visit, leaving them ill, pale, and thin. It is easily repelled by leaving a clove of garlic on the window sill.

Source: Lecouteux, *History of Vampires*; Mackenzie, *Dracula Country*, 92; Magyar Tudományos Akadémia, *Acta Ethnographica Hungarica*, 322

Zhar-Ptitsa

Variations: Fire-Bird, Ptak Ohnivak

A beautiful and magical bird from Russian folklore, the zhar-ptitsa ("glow bird") is described as having feathers so beautiful as to make a person weep; they glow with a rich golden or silvery light; its eyes are like two brightly lit crystals. In nearly every story, it lives in a gold cage under the protection of a king or powerful ruler. By day the zharptitsa sleeps so soundly it appears to be dead but as the sun sets it rouses and appears to come alive. After awakening, it flies off into a beautiful garden, either adjacent or in the land of a far-off ruler; there its presence illuminates the garden as if a thousand torches were ablaze.

A single tail feather glows brightly enough to light up an entire room. Once in the garden the bird will eat its fill of magical apples or grasses from which it gains its powers. The zhar-ptitsa has numerous magical abilities, which vary from story to story, but consistently it can bestow youth and beauty on a person, carry the weight of a person safely upon its back as it flies, induce a deep sleep on a person, and resuscitate the dead by use of the "dead" and "living" water it keeps stored in its beak. Additionally its song can heal the gravely ill and restore sight to the blind as pearls fall from its beak.

Source: Ralston, *Russian Folk-Tales*, 242, 289–92; Rosen, *Mythical Creatures Bible*, 152

Zhu

Variations: Crimsonowl, Zhu Bird

A bird from Chinese folklore, the onomatopoeically named zhu ("torch") was said to live upon Willow Mountain and looked similar to an owl but rather than feet had human hands. It was believed sighting a zhu was an omen of a comet to cross the sky, the death of a whale, and the exile of the local district officials by the ruler.

Source: Strassberg, *Chinese Bestiary*, 91; Warner, *World of Myths*: Volume Two, 206

Zhulong

Variations: Candle DRAGON, Pig-DRAGON, Zhu Long, the Torch DRAGON, Torch Darkness

In Chinese mythology Zhulong ("torch DRAGON") was the divine DRAGON who created the concept of day and night, the seasons, and the wind. According to a seventeenth century drawing Zhulong had a gigantic red serpentine body more than three hundred miles long with a human head, but with only one eye in the middle of its forehead, similar to a CYCLOPS of Greek mythology. In a later slight variation, he had two eyes but they were stacked vertically on his face; it was day when they were open and night when they were closed. He neither ate nor drank but rather swallowed the wind and rain.

Later still he was given additional powers; when he blew his breath it became cold and brought forth the winter and when he exhaled heavily, it became warm and was the summer. Although he did not breathe, when he chose to do so, it created the winds. Different periods also have his home in different locations; originally Zhulong was said to live upon Mount Zhangwei but later myths say he lived on Mount Bell.

Source: An, *Handbook of Chinese Mythology*, 246–7; Strassberg, *Chinese Bestiary*, 223

Zig

A gigantic bird from the Babylonish Talmud, Zig was said to stand upon the earth but its head touched the heavens; when it spread its wings, it blotted out the light of the sun and caused an eclipse. It was said the sound of Zig's crowing pleased the Lord.

Source: Brewer, *Dictionary of Phrase and Fable*, 1323; Irving, *Life of Mahomet*, 70

Zilant

A DRAGON from Russian mythology and the brother of TUGARIN ZMEY, Zilant was employed by a powerful heroine Princess (unnamed in the story) to act as the final line of defense against her castle. He slept in a nest made of iron which was suspended above the ground by twelve chains tethered to twelve strong oak trees. Zilant had a terrifying roar and could fly faster than a loosed arrow. When he encountered the *muzhik* ("peasant") knight Gol Voyansky (Gol the Naked, Gol the Needy) he became suspicious of his poor attire and, letting his guard down so he might inspect the ill-clad human,

was overcome by Gol and his ax. The hero chopped the body of Zilant up in small bits.

Source: Falkayn, *Russian Fairy Tales*, 12–14

Zin

In West African folklore the zin are said to be a species of NATURE SPIRITS who are said to reside in mountains, rocks, trees, and water; the Songhay people of the region liken them to djinn (a race of demons).

Source: Parker, *Mythology*, 312; Skyes, *Who's Who in Non-Classical Mythology*, 221

Zitny Smij

A good-natured DRAGON from Lithuanian folklore, the zitny smij ("corn DRAGON") is known to bring corn to the threshing room floor of its favorite people; it has been described as a fiery blaze streaking across the sky.

Source: Grimm, *Teutonic Mythology*, 1019; MacKenzie, *Dragons for Beginners*, 91

Ziz

A gigantic bird from Hebrew folklore and described in the Book of Psalms, the ziz was described as being more than five hundred miles tall with wings wide enough to darken the entire skyline when spread, creating an eclipse; in this way it is similar to the ROC. A female ziz once dropped one of her eggs, causing the destruction of three hundred cedar trees and flooding three cities. The ziz was, according to the folklore, originally created to protect a smaller species of bird, but the other species has long since died out. Like the demon Behemoth and the aquatic LEVIATHAN, the ziz are destined to have their flesh consumed by the righteous people of the world as a reward for their having abstained from consuming forbidden species of fowl.

Source: Isaacs, *Animals in Jewish Thought and Tradition*, 182; Zell-Ravenheart, *Companion for the Apprentice Wizard*, 179

Zlatorog

Variations: Goldhorn, Goldenhorn

In Slovenian folklore Zlatorog ("goldenhorn") was a white chamois buck or steinbock (Alpine ibex, Capra ibex) with a rack of golden antlers living in his realm atop Mount Triglav; he was the possessor and guardian of a great treasure hoard. In some tales a multi-headed DRAGON assisted him in keeping the treasure safe. Many of the tales of Zlatorog involve him performing an amazing feat of animal athleticism which had a profound impact on the landscape or terrains; an example is the tale in which he created an area of tumbled boulders now known as the Triglav Lakes Valley.

According to legend, the region was once a beautiful and lush garden maintained by the White Ladies, a collection of NATURE SPIRITS or fairies who kept the land rich and assisted the occasional human in need. Meanwhile, a rich suitor presented a local girl with many gifts and in order to appease her parents, her love, a young hunter, was told he must bring back either the treasures of Zlatorog in order to marry her or a bouquet of red roses to at least prove his fidelity; this was in the middle of winter. The hunter set out, eventually found Zlatorog and shot him. The animal's blood melted the snow and a red rose of Triglav sprang up, instantly in bloom. Zlatorog ate a few petals which healed his wound and sprang off. In the place he landed a rose sprouted up. The hunter followed the animal higher and higher into the mountains but lost his footing and fell into a deep gorge. Enraged a human would treat him so badly, Zlatorog destroyed the area, ripping it up with his horns; then he left the region in the care of the White Ladies, never to return.

Source: Dixon-Kennedy, *Encyclopedia of Russian and Slavic Myth and Legend*, 321; Fallon, *Slovenia*, 126; Kropej, *Supernatural Beings from Slovenian Myth and Folktales*, 58

Zmag Ognjeni Vuk

A fire-breathing WEREWOLF from Bosnian folklore, the Zmag Ognjeni Vuk ("fiery DRAGON wolf") was born into nobility in the fifteenth century as Lord Despot Vuk, the son of a DRAGON; he was described as having fiery red eyes, a red birthmark, and tufts of red hair growing on his forearms. Maturing very quickly, the lord developed into a mighty warrior and was destined to slay the regional DRAGON, his father. However, it was believed during the night and on overcast days he had the ability of therianthropy and would transform into a WEREWOLF, terrorizing the countryside.

Source: Dixon-Kennedy, *Encyclopedia of Russian and Slavic Myth and Legend*, 318; Rose, *Giants, Monsters, and Dragons*, 410

Zmey Gorenetch

Variations: Zmej Goronech

A gigantic serpent or DRAGON, Zmey Gorenetch ("serpent (or DRAGON) of the mountain") was a popular figure in Russian folklore; he was the sinister obstacle the hero of the story needed to vanquish in order to achieve his goal. Another popular character, Zarevna Militrissa, was oftentimes in danger of being consumed by Zmey Gorenetch.

Source: Blavatsky, *Isis Unveiled: Science, Volume 2*, 550

Zorigami

The zorigami, a YŌKAI of Japanese folklore, is one of the TSUKOMOGAMI; it is an animated clock.

Source: Joly, *Scary Monsters and Super Creeps*, n.pag.

Bibliography

Abrahams, Israel, and Claude Goldsmid Montefiore. *The Jewish Quarterly Review*, Volume 6. London: David Nutt, 1894.

Abrahams, Roger D. *The Man-Of-Words in the West Indies: Performance and the Emergence of Creole Culture*. Baltimore: Johns Hopkins University Press, 1983.

Acker, Paul, and Carolyne Larrington. *Revisiting the Poetic Edda: Essays on Old Norse Heroic Legend*. New York: Routledge, 2013.

Ackerman, Robert William. *An Index of the Arthurian Names in Middle English*, Volume 10. Stanford: Stanford University Press, 1952.

Adams, William Henry Davenport. *The Amazon and Its Wonders: With Illustrations of Animal and Vegetable Life in the Amazonian Forest*. London: Thomas Nelson and Sons, 1884.

Aguilar-Moreno, Manuel. *Handbook to Life in the Aztec World*. New York: Oxford University Press, 2007.

Aikin, John, and William Enfield. *General Biography; Or, Lives, Critical and Historical, of the Most Eminent Persons of All Ages, Countries, Conditions and Professions, Chiefly Composed by J. Aikin and W. Enfield*; Volume IV. London: Robinson, 1803.

Akehurst, F. R. P., and Stephanie Cain Van D'Elden. *The Stranger in Medieval Society*. Minneapolis: University of Minnesota Press, 1997.

Albertus Magnus, Saint. *Man and the Beasts (De Animalibus, Books 22–26)*. Binghamton: Medieval and Renaissance Texts and Studies, Center for Medieval and Early Renaissance Studies, 1987.

Aldrich, Thomas Bailey. *The Young Folks' Library: The Child's Own Book*. Boston: Hall and Locke, 1901.

Alexander, Hartley Burr. *Latin-American [Mythology]* Volume 11. Boston: Marshall Jones Company, 1920.

Alexander, Hartley Burr. *The Mythology of All Races*, Volume XI Latin-American. Boston: Marshal Jones and Company: 1920.

Alexander, Skye. *Fairies: The Myths, Legends, and Lore*. Avon: F+W Media, Incorporated, 2014.

Alexander, William M. *Forgotten Tales of Vermont*. Charleston: The History Press, 2008.

Alip, Eufronio Melo. *Political and Cultural History of the Philippines*. Alip, 1954.

Allaby, Michael. *Animals: From Mythology to Zoology*. New York: Infobase Publishing, 2010.

Allardice, Pamela. *Myths, Gods, and Fantasy: A Sourcebook*. Garden City Park: Avery Publishing Group, Incorporated, 1990.

Allen, Herbert J. "Chinese Antiquity." *Journal of the Royal Asiatic Society of Great Britain and Ireland*, Volume 22 (1908), pp. 511–525.

Allen, Maude Rex. *Japanese Art Motives*. Chicago: A. C. McClurg and Company, 1917.

Allsopp, Richard. *Dictionary of Caribbean English Usage*. Kingston, Jamaica: University of the West Indies Press, 2003.

American Dialect Society. *Dialect Notes*, Volume 5. New Haven: American Dialect Society, 1918.

American Folklore Society. *Journal of American Folklore*, Volumes 30, 54–55, 1917, 1941.

American Folklore Society. "Record of Negro Folk-Lore," in *Journal of American Folklore*, Volume 7 of *Bibliographical and Special Series of the American Folklore Society*, edited by the American Folklore Society, pp. 296–7. Boston: American Folk-lore Society, 1904.

Amodio, Mark C. *The Anglo Saxon Literature Handbook*. Sussex: John Wiley and Sons, 2013.

Amor, Anne Clark. *Beasts and Bawdy*. New York: Taplinger Publishing Company, 1975.

An, Deming. *Handbook of Chinese Mythology*. Santa Barbara: ABC-CLIO, 2005.

Ananda. *A Comparative Study of Religion: A Sufi and a Sanatani, Ramakrishna*. Delhi: Ajanta Publications, 1993.

Ananikean, Martiros Harootioon. *Armenian Mythology: Stories of Armenian Gods and Goddesses, Heroes and Heroines, Hells and Heavens, Folklore and Fairy Tales*. Los Angeles: Indo-European Publishing, 2010.

Andersen, Johannes Carl. *Myths and Legends of the Polynesians*. New York: Courier Dover Publications, 1928.

Anderson, Atholl, Judith Binney, and Aroha Harris. *Tangata Whenua: An Illustrated History*. Auckland: Bridget Williams Books, 2014.

Anderson, Bernhard W., and Steven Bishop. *Out of the Depths: The Psalms Speak for Us Today*. Louisville: Westminster John Knox Press, 2000.

Anderson, Rasmus Björn. *Norræna: The History and Romance of Northern Europe*, Volume 5. London: Norræna Society, 1906.

Anderson, Rasmus Björn. *Norræna: The History and Romance of Northern Europe*, Volume 12. London: Norræna Society, 1906.

Anderson, Rasmus Björn. *Norse Mythology*. Chicago: S.C. Griggs, 1884.

Andrews, Munya. *The Seven Sisters of the Pleiades: Stories from Around the World*. Melbourne: Spinifex Press, 2004.

Andrews, Tamra. *Dictionary of Nature Myths: Legends of

the Earth, Sea, and Sky. New York: Oxford University Press, 2000.

Angel, Andrew. *Chaos and the Son of Man: The Hebrew Chaoskampf Tradition in the Period 515 BCE to 200 CE T and T Clark Library of Biblical Studies.* New York: A and C Black, 2006.

Anima, Nid. *Witchcraft, Filipino-Style.* Quezon City, Philippines: Omar Publications, 1978.

Ankarloo, Bengt, and Gustav Henningsen. *Early Modern European Witchcraft: Centres and Peripheries.* Ventnor: Clarendon Press, 1990.

Anthon, Charles. *A Classical Dictionary, Containing an Account of the Principal Proper Names Mentioned in Ancient Authors and Intended to Elucidate All the Important Points Connected with the Geography, Bibliography, Mythology, and Fine Arts of the Greeks and Romans.* New York: Harper and Brothers, 1872.

Anthropological Institute of Great Britain and Ireland, JSTOR. *Journal of the Royal Anthropological Institute of Great Britain and Ireland,* Volume 25. London: Kegan Paul, Trench, Trübner and Company, 1896.

Antoninus, Francis Celoria. *The Metamorphoses of Antoninus Liberalis: A Translation with Commentary.* London: Psychology Press, 1992.

Antropov, Vladimir Andreevich. *Fairy Tales,* Volume 4874 of *Skazki: Kniga DliĀ ChteniiĀ Na Angliĭskom IĀzyke DliĀ VII Klassa.* Moscow: Uchpedgiz, 1963.

Apollodorus, edited and translated by Sir James George Frazer. *Apollodorus: The Library,* Volume 1. London: W. Heinemann, 1921.

Apollodorus, edited and translated by Sir James George Frazer. *Apollodorus: The Library,* Volume 2. London: W. Heinemann, 1921.

Apollonius (Rhodius), translated by Edward Philip Coleridge. "The Argonautica," of *Apollonius Rhodius.* London: George Bell, 1889.

Apollodorus, translated by Michael Simpson. *Gods and Heroes of the Greeks: The Library of Apollodorus.* Amherst: University of Massachusetts Press, 1976.

Apollodorus, translated by Robin Hard. *The Library of Greek Mythology.* New York: Oxford University Press, 1997.

Apollodorus and Hyginus, R. Scott Smith, and Stephen M. Trzaskoma. *Apollodorus' Library and Hyginus' Fabulae.* Indianapolis: Hackett Publishing, 2007.

Architectural and Archaeological Society of the County of Lincoln, Northamptonshire Architectural and Archaeological Society, Yorkshire Architectural and York Archaeological Society, Worcestershire Archaeological Society. *Reports and Papers of the Architectural and Archaeological Societies of the Counties of Lincoln and Northampton,* Volume 20. Yorkshire: Architectural and Archaeological Society, 1889.

Ariosto, Lodovico, translated by William Stewart Rose. *The Orlando Furioso,* Volume 1. London: John Murray, 1823.

Armstrong, Robert Archibald. *A Gaelic Dictionary in Two Parts, to Which Is Prefixed a New Gaelic Grammar.* London: Duncan, 1825.

Árnason, Jón. *Icelandic Legends Collected by Jón Árnason.* Longmans, Green, and Company,1866.

Arnott, W. Geoffrey. *Birds in the Ancient World from A to Z.* New York: Routledge, 2007.

Asante, Molefi Kete, and Ama Mazama. *Encyclopedia of African Religion,* Volume 1. Thousand Oaks: SAGE, 2009.

Ashforth, Adam. *Witchcraft, Violence, and Democracy in South Africa.* Chicago: University of Chicago Press, 2005.

Ashkenazi, Michael. *Handbook of Japanese Mythology.* Santa Barbara: ABC-CLIO, 2003.

Ashley, Leonard R. N. *The Complete Book of Devils and Demons.* Fort Lee: Barricade Books, 1996.

Ashley, Leonard, R. N. *The Complete Book of Vampires.* New York: Barricade Books, 1998.

Ashliman, D. L. *Fairy Lore: A Handbook.* Westport: Greenwood Publishing Group, 2005.

Ashman, Malcolm, and Beryl Joyce Hargreaves. *Fabulous Beasts.* New York: Overlook Press, 1997.

Ashton, John. *Curious Creatures in Zoology: With 130 Illus. Throughout the Text.* London: John C. Nimmo, 1890.

Asian Folklore Institute, Society for Asian Folklore, Nanzan Daigaku. Jinruigaku Kenkyūjo, and Nanzan Shūkyō Bunka Kenkyūjo. *Asian Folklore Studies,* Volume 39. Nagoya: Nanzan University Institute of Anthropology, 1980.

The Asiatic Journal and Monthly Register for British India and Its Dependencies, Volume 2. London: Black, Parbury, and Allen, 1830.

Asiatic Society of Japan. *Transactions of the Asiatic Society of Japan.* Yokohama: Asiatic Society of Japan, 1965.

Ataç, Mehmet-Ali. *The Mythology of Kingship in Neo-Assyrian Art.* Cambridge: Cambridge University Press, 2010.

Atala-Atala. *Lunch with God.* Bloomington: AuthorHouse, 2008.

Ateneo de Davao University, Ateneo de Zamboanga University, and Xavier University. *Kinaadman,* vol. 19–20. Cincinnati, Ohio: Xavier University, 1997.

The Atlantic Monthly, Volume 49. Boston: Atlantic Monthly Company, 1882.

Atsma, Aaron J. "Hippoi Erekhtheioi," theoi.com. http://www.theoi.com/Ther/HippoiErekhtheioi.html (retrieved November 21, 2014).

Audsley, William James, and George Ashdown Audsley. *Popular Dictionary of Architecture and the Allied Arts,* Volume 1. New York: G. P. Putnam's Son, 1881.

Aulestia, Gorka. *Basque-English Dictionary.* Reno: University of Nevada Press, 1989.

Austin, Alfredo López. *Tamoanchan, Tlalocan: Places of Mist.* Niwot: University Press of Colorado, 1997.

Avant, G. Rodney. *A Mythological Reference.* Bloomington, AuthorHouse, 2005.

Aylesworth, Thomas G. *Servants of the Devil.* Reading: Addison-Wesley, 1970.

Bacqué-Grammont, Jean-Louis, and E. J. van Donzel, editors. *Comité International D'études Pré-Ottomanes Et Ottomanes, Vith Symposium, Cambridge, 1rst–4th July 1984: Proceedings,* Volume 6. Istanbul: Divit Press, 1987.

Bahr, Lauren S., and Bernard Johnston. *Collier's Encyclopedia: With Bibliography and Index,* Volume 16. New York: P. F. Collier, 1993.

Bailey, Gerry, and Karen Foster. *The Wright Brothers' Glider.* New York: Crabtree Publishing Company, 2008.

Bailey, James, and Tatyana Ivanova. *An Anthology of Russian Folk Epics.* Armonk: M.E. Sharpe, 1999.

Baker, Alan. *The Enigmas of History: Myths, Mysteries and Madness from Around the World.* New York: Random House, 2012.

Baker, Margaret. *Discovering Christmas Customs and Folklore: A Guide to Seasonal Rites.* London: Osprey Publishing, 1992.

Baker, W. Buck. *Celtic Mythological Influences on American Theatre, 1750–1875*. Lanham: University Press of America, 1994.

Bakshi, Dwijendra Nath. *Hindu Divinities in Japanese Buddhist Pantheon: A Comparative Study*. Calcutta: Benten Publishers, 1979.

Baldwin, James. *The Horse Fair*. New York: Century Company, 1904.

Baldwin, James. *The Story of Roland*. New York: Charles Scribner's Sons, 1919.

Balfour, Edward. *Cyclopædia of India and of Eastern and Southern Asia, Commercial, Industrial and Scientific: Products of the Mineral, Vegetable and Animal Kingdoms, Useful Arts and Manufactures*, Volume 1. Madras: Scottish and Adelphi Presses, 1871.

Balfour, Edward. *Cyclopædia of India and of Eastern and Southern Asia, Commercial, Industrial and Scientific: Products of the Mineral, Vegetable and Animal Kingdoms, Useful Arts and Manufactures*, Volume 2. Madras: Scottish and Adelphi Presses, 1871.

Balfour, Edward. *Cyclopædia of India and of Eastern and Southern Asia: Commercial, Industrial and Scientific, Products of the Mineral, Vegetable, and Animal Kingdoms, Useful Arts and Manufactures*, Volume 3. London: B. Quaritch, 1885.

Ball, Reverend C. J., and the Society of Biblical Archæology (London, England). "The New Accadian," in *Proceedings of the Society of Biblical Archaeology*, Volume 12, 394–418. Bloomsbury: The Society, 1890.

Ball, Katherine M. *Animal Motifs in Asian Art: An Illustrated Guide to Their Meanings and Aesthetics*. Mineola: Courier Dover Publications, 2011.

Balzer, Marjorie Mandelstam. *Shamanic Worlds: Rituals and Lore of Siberia and Central Asia*. Armonk: M.E. Sharpe, 1997.

Bancroft, Hubert Howe. *The Native Races of the Pacific States: The Works of Hubert Howe Bancroft*, Volume 5. San Francisco: A. L. Bancroft, 1882.

Banis, V. J. *Charms, Spells, and Curses for the Millions*. Holicong: Wildside Press LLC, 2007.

Barbeau, Marius. *Tsimsyan Myths*, Issue 174. Ottawa: Department of Northern Affairs and National Resources, 1961.

Barber, Paul. *Vampires, Burial, and Death: Folklore and Reality*. New Haven, Conn.: Yale University Press, 1988.

Barber, Richard. *Bestiary: Being an English Version of the Bodleian Library, Oxford M.S. Bodley 764 with All the Original Miniatures Reproduced in Facsimile*. Woodbridge: Boydell Press, 2006.

Barber, Richard W., and Anne Riches. *A Dictionary of Fabulous Beasts*. Sussex: Boydell and Brewer, Incorporated, 1996.

Baring-Gould, Sabine. *The Book of Werewolves*. New York: Cosimo, Incorporated, 2008.

Baring-Gould, Sabine, and Alfred Newton. *Iceland: Its Scenes and Sagas*. London: Smith, Elder and Company, 1863.

Barstow, Cheri, and Trafford Publishing. *Elementally Speaking: The Nature Spirits' Guide to Their World*. Bloomington: Trafford Publishing, 2006.

Barthell, Edward E. *Gods and Goddesses of Ancient Greece*. Miami: University of Miami Press, 1971.

Bartlett, Harley Harris. "Malayan Words in English," in *Quarterly Review: A Journal of University Perspectives*, Volume 60, Autumn 1953, edited by Frank E. Robbins,-40–55. Ann Arbor: University of Michigan. Alumni Association and the University of Michigan Libraries, 1953.

Bartlett, Sarah. *The Mythology Bible: The Definitive Guide to Legendary Tales*. New York: Sterling Publishing Company, Incorporated, 2009.

Barton, George A., the Society of Biblical Literature, and the Society of Biblical Literature and Exegesis (U.S.). "The Origin of the Names of Angels and Demons in the Extra-Canonical Apocalyptic Literature," *Journal of Biblical Literature*, Volumes 30–31. New York: G. E. Stechert and Company, 1911.

Baskin, Wade. *The Sorcerer's Handbook*. New York: Philosophical Library, 1974.

Bassett, Fletcher S. *Legends and Superstitions of the Sea and of Sailors in All Lands and at All Times*. Chicago: Belford, Clarke, 1885.

Bastian, Dawn Elaine, and Judy K. Mitchell. *Handbook of Native American Mythology*. Santa Barbara: ABC-CLIO, 2004.

Batchelor, John. *The Ainu and Their Folk-Lore*. London: Forgotten Books, 2013.

Bates, Katharine Lee. *The Outlook*, Volume 120. New York: Outlook Company, 1918.

Bates, Roy. *All About Chinese Dragons*. Raleigh: Lulu.com, 2007.

Bates, Roy. *10,000 Chinese Numbers*. Beijing: China History Press, 2007.

Bates, Roy. *29 Chinese Mysteries*. Raleigh: Lulu.com, 2008.

Bathgate, Michael. *The Fox's Craft in Japanese Religion and Folklore: Shapeshifters, Transformations, and Duplicities*. New York: Psychology Press, 2004.

Battuta, Ibn, and Hamilton Alexander Rosskeen Gibb, translator. *Travels in Asia and Africa, 1325–1354*. London: Routledge, 2004.

Bauckham, Richard, editor. *The Epistle to the Hebrews and Christian Theology*. Cambridge: William. B. Eerdmans Publishing, 2009.

Baudler, Seigneur Michael. *A Collection of Voyages and Travels, Consisting of Authentic Writers in Our Own Tongue,... And Continued with Others of Note, That Have Published Histories, Voyages, Relating to Any Part of the Continent of Asia, Africa, America, Europe, and with a Great Variety of Cuts, Prospects, Ruins, Maps, and Charts. Compiled from the Curious and Valuable Library of the Late Earl of Oxford*, Volume 2. London: Thomas Osborne of Gray's-Inn, 1745.

Baughman, Ernest W. *Type and Motif-Index of the Folktales of England and North America*. Bloomington: Walter de Gruyter, 1966.

Bayle, Pierre. *An Historical and Critical Dictionary, Selected and Abridged, Volume 3*. London: Hunt and Clarke, 1826.

Baynes, Thomas Spencer. *The Encyclopædia Britannica: A Dictionary of Arts, Sciences and General Literature*, Volume 17. New York: Henry G. Allen, 1890.

Bazino, Jak. *Zawgyi, L'alchimiste De Birmanie*. Paris: Mon Petit Éditeur, 2012.

Beath, Paul R. *Febold Feboldson: Tall Tales from the Great Plains*. Lincoln: University of Nebraska Press, 1962.

Beauchamp, William Martin, and David Cusick. *The Iroquois Trail: Or Foot-Prints of the Six Nations, in Customs, Traditions, and History*. Fayetteville: H. C. Beauchamp Recording Office, 1892.

Bechtel, John Hendricks. *A Dictionary of Mythology*. Philadelphia: The Penn Publishing Company, 1905.

Beckwith, Martha. *Hawaiian Mythology*. Honolulu: University of Hawaii Press, 1970.

Beech, Charlotte, Jolyon Attwooll, Jean-Bernard Carillet, and Thomas Kohnstamm. *Chile and Easter Island*. Victoria: Lonely Planet, 2006.

Beer, Robert. *The Handbook of Tibetan Buddhist Symbols*. Chicago: Serindia Publications, Incorporated, 2003.

Begde, Prabhakar V. *Living Sculpture: Classical Indian Culture as Depicted in Sculpture and Literature*. New Delhi: Sagar Publications, 1996.

Belanger, Michelle. *Sacred Hunger: The Vampire in Myth and Reality*. Fort Wayne: Dark Moon Press, 2005.

Beliefnet (Firm). *The Big Book of Angels: Angelic Encounters, Expert Answers, Listening to and Working with Your Guardian Angel*. Emmaus: Rodale, 2002.

Bell, Henry Hesketh Joudou. *Obeah: Witchcraft in the West Indies*. London: S. Low, Marston and Company Limited, 1893.

Bell, John E. *Bell's New Pantheon; or Historical Dictionary of the Gods, Demi-Gods, Heroes and Fabulous Personages of Antiquity*. London: John Bell, 1790.

Bell, John E. *Place Names in Classical Mythology: Greece*. Santa Barbara: Clio Press, 1989.

Bellows, Henry Adams. *The Poetic Edda: The Mythological Poems*. Mineola: Courier Dover Publications, 2012.

Benedict, Laura Watson. "Bagobo Myths," in *Journal of American Folklore*, Volume 26 edited by the American Folklore Society, pages 13–63. Lancaster: American Folk-lore Society, 1913.

Benjamins, Herman Daniël, and Johannes François Snelleman. *Encyclopaedie Van Nederlandsch West-Indië*. Dordrecht: M. Nijhoff, 1917.

Bennett, De Robigne Mortimer. *The Gods and Religions of Ancient and Modern Times*, Volume 1. New York: D. M. Bennett, 1881.

Bennett, De Robigne Mortimer. *The Gods and Religions of Ancient and Modern Times*, Volume 2. New York: D. M. Bennett, 1881.

Bennett, Randall H. *The White Mountains: Alps of New England*. Charleston: Arcadia Publishing, 2003.

Benton, Catherine. *God of Desire: Tales of Kamadeva in Sanskrit Story Literature*. Albany: State University New York Press, 2006.

Bentorah, Chaim. *Hebrew Word Study: A Hebrew Teacher Explores the Heart of God*. Bloomington: WestBow Press, 2013.

Beolens, Bo, Michael Watkins, and Michael Grayson. *The Eponym Dictionary of Mammals*. Baltimore: Johns Hopkins University Press, 2009.

Beorh, Skadi Meic. *Pirate Lingo*. Rockville: Wildside Press LLC, 2009.

Berens, E M. *The Myths and Legends of Ancient Greece and Rome: Being a Popular Account of Greek and Roman Mythology*. London: Blackie and Son, 1880.

Berman, Steve. *Red Caps: New Fairy Tales for Out of the Ordinary Readers*. Maple Shade: Lethe Press, 2013.

Berninger, Mark, Jochen Ecke, and Gideon Haberkorn, eds. *Comics as a Nexus of Cultures: Essays on the Interplay of Media, Disciplines and International Perspectives*. Jefferson, NC: McFarland, 2010.

Bertman, Stephen. *Handbook to Life in Ancient Mesopotamia*. New York: Infobase Publishing, 2003.

Besson, Gérard A., Stuart Hahn, and Avril Turner. *Folklore and Legends of Trinidad and Tobago*. Paria Bay: Paria, 1989.

Best, Richard Irvine, and M. A. O'Brien. *The Book of Leinster: Formerly Lebar Na Núachongbála*, Volume 5. Dublin: Dublin Institute for Advanced Studies, 1967.

Bettini, Maurizio. *Women and Weasels: Mythologies of Birth in Ancient Greece and Rome*. Chicago: University of Chicago Press, 2013.

Bharati, Agrhananda, editor. *Agents and Audiences*, Volume 1 of *Bharati, Agehanada: The Realm of the Extra-Human World Anthropology*. Chicago: Walter de Gruyter, 1976.

Bhattacharji, Sukumari. *Fatalism in Ancient India*. New Delhi: Baulmon Prakashan, 1995.

Bienkowski, Piotr, and Alan Ralph Millard. *Dictionary of the Ancient Near East*. Philadelphia: University of Pennsylvania Press, 2000.

Bilby, Julian W. *Among Unknown Eskimo: An Account of Twelve Years Intimate Relations with the Primitive Eskimo of Ice-Bound Baffin Land: With a Description of Their Ways of Living, Hunting Customs and Beliefs*. Philadelphia: J.B. Lippincott, 1923.

Bingham, Ann, and Jeremy Roberts. *South and Meso-American Mythology A to Z*. New York: Infobase Publishing, 2010.

Binney, Ruth. *Nature's Ways: Lore, Legend, Fact and Fiction*. Cincinnati: David and Charles, 2006.

Birrell, Anne. *Chinese Mythology: An Introduction*. Baltimore: Johns Hopkins University Press, 1999.

Bitel, Lisa M. *Women in Early Medieval Europe, 400–1100*. Cambridge: Cambridge University Press, 2002.

Bjerregaard, Carl Henrik Andreas, Eugénie R. Eliscu, William Frank Fraetas, and Grace Gallatin Seton. *The Great Mother, a Gospel of the Eternally-Feminine: Occult and Scientific Studies and Experiences in the Sacred and Secret Life*. New York: Innerlife Publishing Company, 1913.

Black, Jeremy A., Andrew George, and J. N. Postgate. *A Concise Dictionary of Akkadian*. Wisebaden: Otto Harrassowitz Verlag, 2000.

Black, Jeremy A., and Anthony Green. *Gods, Demons and Symbols of Ancient Mesopotamia: An Illustrated Dictionary*. Austin: University of Texas Press, 1992.

Blackman, W. Haden. *Field Guide to North American Monsters: Everything You Need to Know About Encountering Over 100 Terrifying Creatures in the Wild*. New York: Three Rivers Press, 1998.

Blakely, Mike. *More Wild Camp Tales*. Plano: Taylor Trade Publishing, 1996.

Blavatsky, Helena Petrovna. *Isis Unveiled: Science*, Volume 1 of *Isis Unveiled: A Master-Key to the Mysteries of Ancient and Modern Science and Theology*. New York: J.W. Bouton, 1877.

Blavatsky, Helena Petrovna. *Isis Unveiled: Science*, Volume 2 of *Isis Unveiled: A Master-Key to the Mysteries of Ancient and Modern Science and Theology*. New York: J.W. Bouton, 1877.

Blavatsky, Helena Petrovna. *The Secret Doctrine: Anthropogenesis*. London: Theosophical Publishing Company, 1888.

Blavatsky, Helena Petrovna. *The Secret Doctrine: The Synthesis of Science, Religion, and Philosophy*, Volume 1. Charleston: Forgotten Books, 1893.

Blavatsky, Helena Petrovna. *The Secret Doctrine: The Synthesis of Science, Religion, and Philosophy*, Volume 2. Charleston: Forgotten Books, 1893.

Blavatsky, Helena Petrovna. *The Theosophical Glossary*. London: Theosophical Publishing Society, 1892.

Bloom, Harold. *Beowulf*. New York: Infobase Publishing, 2009

Boas, Franz, and Henry W. Tate. *Tsimshian Mythology*. Washington D.C: Government Printing Office, 1916.

Bocking, Brian. *a Popular Dictionary of Shinto*. New York: Psychology Press, 1997.

Bodde, Derk. *Essays on Chinese Civilization*. Princeton: Princeton University Press, 2014.

Bogoraz, Vladimir Germanovič, and Waldemar Bogoras. *The Chukchee: Jessup North Pacific Expedition, Publications*, Number 7. New York: Ams Press Incorporated, 1975.

Boĭkova, Elena Vladimirovna, and R. B. Rybakov, editors. *Kinship in the Altaic World: Proceedings of the 48th Permanent International Altaistic Conference, Moscow 10–15 July 2005*. Wiesbaden: Otto Harrassowitz Verlag, 2006.

Bois, G. J. C. *Jersey Folklore and Superstitions Volume Two: A Comparative Study with the Traditions of the Gulf of St. Malo (The Channel Islands, Normandy and Brittany) with Reference to World Mythologies*. Central Milton Keynes: AuthorHouse, 2010.

Bolle, Kees W. *The Freedom of Man in Myth*. Nashville, Tenn.: Vanderbilt University Press, 1968.

Bone, J. H. "The Mediaeval Naturalist," in *The Atlantic Monthly*, Volume 33 edited by the Cairns Collection of American Women Writers, 269–275. Boston: H. O. Houghton and Company, 1874.

Bonfante, Larissa, and Judith Swaddling. *Etruscan Myths*. Austin: University of Texas Press, 2006.

Bonnefoy, Yves, and Wendy Doniger. *Asian Mythologies*. Chicago: University of Chicago Press, 1993.

Bonnefoy, Yves, Wendy Doniger, and Gerald Honigsblum. *American, African, and Old European Mythologies*. Chicago: University of Chicago Press, 1993.

Bonnerjea, Biren. *The Allborough New Age Guide: Biren Bonnerjea's a Dictionary of Superstition and Mythology*. London: Allborough Publishing, 1992.

Bonnerjea, Biren. *A Dictionary of Superstitions and Mythology*. Auburn: Singing Tree Press, 1969.

Bonvillain, Nancy. *The Zuni*. New York: Infobase Publishing, 2009.

Bonwick, James. *Egyptian Belief and Modern Thought*. London: C. Keagan Paul and Company, 1878.

The Book of Jasher Referred to in Joshua and Second Samuel. n.pag.: Library of Alexandria, N.d.

Bord, Janet. *Fairies: Real Encounters with Little People*. New York: Carroll and Graf, 1997.

Boreman, Thomas. *A Description of Three Hundred Animals,: Viz. Beasts, Birds, Fishes, Serpents, and Insects. with a Particular Account of the Manner of Their Catching of Whales in Greenland. Extracted from the Best Authors, and Adapted to the Use of All Capacities*. London: H. Woodfall, J. Rivington, R. Baldwin, Hawes, Clarke and Collins, S. Crowder, T. Caslon, and Robinson and Roberts, 1769.

Borges, Jorge Luis, and Margarita Guerrero. *El Libro De Los Seres Imaginarios*. New York: Dutton, 1969.

Borges, Jorge Luis, Norman Thomas Di Giovanni, and Margarita Guerrero. *The Book of Imaginary Beings*. New York: Penguin, 1974.

Borsje, Jacqueline. *From Chaos to Enemy: Encounters with Monsters in Early Irish Texts: An Investigation Related to the Process of Christianization and the Concept of Evil*. Turnhout: Brepols, 1996.

Bossieu. "The Ocean of the Chaldean Traditions," *The Academy, Issue 14*. London: Robert Scott Walker, 1878.

Botha, Dr. Phillip. *Demonology: Demons and Devils: Spiritual Warfare*. Raleigh: Lulu.com, 2011.

Botkin, B. A. *The American People: Stories, Legends, Tales, Traditions, and Songs*. New Brunswick: Transaction Publishers, 1946.

Boulay, R. A. *Flying Serpents and Dragons: The Story of Mankind's Reptilian Past*. Palo Alta: Book Tree, 1999.

Bovey, Alixe. *Monsters and Grotesques in Medieval Manuscripts*. Toronto: University of Toronto Press, 2002.

Boyce, Mary. *A History of Zoroastrianism: The Early Period*. Leiden: Brill, 1989.

Brann, Eva. *Homeric Moments: Clues to Delight in Reading the Odyssey and the Iliad*. Philadelphia: Paul Dry Books, 2002.

Bredon, Juliet, and Igor Mitrophanow. *The Moon Year: A Record of Chinese Customs and Festivals*. New York: Routledge, 2005.

Breen, John, and Mark Teeuwen, editors. *Shinto in History: Ways of the Kami*. New York: Routledge, 2013.

Breese, Daryl, and Gerald D'Aoust. *God's Steed-Key to World Peace*. Raleigh: Lulu.com, 2011.

Breverton, Terry. *Breverton's Phantasmagoria: A Compendium of Monsters, Myths and Legends* London: Quercus, 2011.

Breverton, Terry. *Wales: A Historical Companion*. Gloucestershire: Amberley Publishing Limited, 2012.

Brewer. *Dictionary of Phrase and Fable*, 1033.

Brewer, Ebenezer Cobham. *Character Sketches of Romance, Fiction and the Drama*, Volumes 1–2. New York: Selmar Hess, 1902.

Brewer, Ebenezer Cobham. *Character Sketches of Romance, Fiction and the Drama*, Volume 3. New York: Selmar Hess, 1902.

Brewer, Ebenezer Cobham. *Character Sketches of Romance, Fiction and the Drama*, Volumes 5–6. New York: Selmar Hess, 1902.

Brewer, Ebenezer Cobham. *Character Sketches of Romance, Fiction and the Drama*, Volumes 7–8. New York: Selmar Hess, 1902.

Brewer, Ebenezer Cobham. *Dictionary of Phrase and Fable: Giving the Derivation, Source, or Origin of Common Phrases, Allusions, and Words That Have a Tale to Tell*. Philadelphia: Henry Altemus Company, 1898.

Brewer, Ebenezer Cobham. *The Reader's Handbook of Allusions, References, Plots and Stories: With Two Appendices*. Philadelphia: Lippincott, 1880.

Brewer, Ebenezer Cobham. *The Reader's Handbook of Famous Names in Fiction, Allusions, References, Proverbs, Plots, Stories, and Poems*. London: Chatto and Windus, 1902.

Brewer, Ebenezer Cobham. *The Wordsworth Dictionary of Phrase and Fable*. Hertfordshire: Wordsworth Editions, 2001.

Briggs, Katharine Mary. *Dictionary of British Folk-Tales in the English Language*, Volumes 1–2. London: Routledge, 1991.

Briggs, Katharine Mary. *An Encyclopedia of Fairies: Hobgoblins, Brownies, Bogies, and Other Supernatural Creatures, Volume 1976*. New York: Pantheon Books, 1976.

Briggs, Katharine Mary. *The Fairies in Tradition and Literature*. London: Psychology Press, 2002.

Briggs, Katharine Mary, editor. *British Folktales*. New York: Dorset Press, 1988.

Brinkley, Frank. *Japan, Its History, Arts and Literature*, Volume 5. Boston: J. B. Millet Company, 1902.

Brinton, Daniel Garrison. *The Myths of the New World:*

A Treatise on the Symbolism and Mythology of the Red Race of America. Philadelphia: David McKay, 1896.

Broedel, Hans Peter. *The Malleus Maleficarum and the Construction of Witchcraft: Theology and Popular Belief*. Manchester: Manchester University Press, 2003.

Broster, Joan A., and Herbert Bourn. *Amaggirha: Religion, Magic and Medicine in Transkei*. Cape Town, Africa: Via Afrika Limited, 1982.

Brown, Arthur C. L. *Iwain: A Study in the Origins of Arthurian Romance*. New York: Haskell House Publishers, Limited, 1968.

Brown, Azby. *The Genius of Japanese Carpentry: Secrets of an Ancient Craft*. North Clarendon: Tuttle Publishing, 2014.

Brown, Dorothy Moulding. *Wisconsin Folklore Publications: 1947–1948*. N.p., n.d.

Brown, Nathan. *The Complete Idiot's Guide to the Paranormal*. New York: Penguin, 2010.

Brown, Nathan. *The Complete Idiot's Guide to Zombies*. New York: Penguin, 2010.

Brown, Ras Michael. *African-Atlantic Cultures and the South Carolina Lowcountry*. New York: Cambridge University Press, 2012.

Brown, William Norman, editor. *The Story of Kālaka: Texts, History, Legends, and Miniature Paintings of the Śvetāmbara Jain Hagiographical Work, the Kālakācāryakathā*. Washington: Lord Baltimore Press, 1933.

Browne, Edward Granville. *A Literary History of Persia*, Volume 1. New York: Charles Scribner's Sons, 1902.

Brownlow, Canon, Reverend. "Slavery and Serfdom in the British Isles," in *The Month: An Illustrated Magazine of Literature, Science and Art*, Volume LXIX, edited by The Moth, pages 236–45. London: Burns and Oats, The Month, 1890.

Bruce, Christopher W. *The Arthurian Name Dictionary*. New York: Routledge, 2013.

Bruchac, James, and Joseph Bruchac. *When the Chenoo Howls: Native American Tales of Terror*. New York: Bloomsbury Publishing USA, 2009.

Brunvand, Jan Harold. *American Folklore: An Encyclopedia*. New York: Routledge, 1998.

Bryant, Clifton D. *Handbook of Death and Dying*. Thousand Oaks: Sage, 2003.

Buchler, Ira R., and Kenneth Maddock. *The Rainbow Serpent: A Chromatic Piece*. Chicago: Walter de Gruyter, 1978.

Buckland, Raymond. *The Weiser Field Guide to Ghosts: Apparitions, Spirits, Spectral Lights and Other Hauntings of History and Legend*. Boston: Weiser, 2009.

Budd, Deena West. *The Weiser Field Guide to Cryptozoology: Werewolves, Dragons, Skyfish, Lizard Men, and Other Fascinating Creatures Real and Mysterious*. San Francisco: Weiser Books, 2010.

Budge, Sir Ernest Alfred Wallis. *The Gods of the Egyptians: Or, Studies in Egyptian Mythology*, Volume 1. North Chemsford: Courier Dover Publications, 1969.

Bud-M'Belle, I. *Kafir Scholar's Companion*. Cape Town, Africa: Lovedale Missionary Press, 1903.

Buechel, Eugene, and Paul Manhart. *Lakota Dictionary: Lakota-English/English-Lakota*. Lincoln: University of Nebraska Press, 2002.

Buenconsejo, José Semblante. *Songs and Gifts at the Frontier: Person and Exchange in the Agusan Manobo Possession Ritual, Philippines*. London: Routledge, 2002.

Buitenen, Johannes Adrianus Bernardus. *The Mahabharata, Volume 2: Book 2: The Book of Assembly*; Book 3: *The Book of the Forest*. Chicago: University of Chicago Press, 1981.

Bulfinch, Thomas. *Bulfinch's Greek and Roman Mythology: The Age of Fable*. Mineola: Courier Dover Publications, 2012.

Bulfinch, Thomas. *Bulfinch's Mythology: The Age of Fable; the Age of Chivalry; Legends of Charlemagne*. New York: Thomas Y. Crowell Company, 1913.

Bullough, Vern L., and Bonnie Bullough. *Human Sexuality: An Encyclopedia*. Oxfordshire: Taylor and Francis, 1994.

Bunson, Margaret. *Encyclopedia of Ancient Egypt*. New York: Infobase Publishing, 2009.

Bunson, Matthew. *Angels A to Z: A Who's Who of the Heavenly Host*. New York: Crown Publishing Group, 1996.

Bunson, Matthew. *The Vampire Encyclopedia*. New York: Gramercy Books, 2000.

Burnett, Thom. *Conspiracy Encyclopedia: The Encyclopedia of Conspiracy Theories*. London: Collins and Brown, 2005.

Burns, William E. *Witch Hunts in Europe and America: An Encyclopedia*. Westport, Conn.: Greenwood Publishing Group, 2003.

Burton, Richard F. *Arabian Nights, in 16 Volumes*. New York: Cosimo, Incorporated, 2008.

Burton, Sir Richard Francis. *A Plain and Literal Translation of the Arabian Nights' Entertainments, Now Entituled the Book of the Thousand Nights and a Night: With Introduction, Explanatory Notes on the Manners and Customs of Moslem Men, and a Terminal Essay Upon the History of the Nights*, Volume 13. Denver: Burton Society, 1900.

Burton, Richard Francis, Isabel Burton, and Ernest Henry Griset. *Vikram and the Vampire: Or, Tales of Hindu Devilry*. London: Tylston and Edwards, 1893.

Busby, Keith, and Roger Dalrymple, editors. *Comedy in Arthurian Literature*. Rochester: Boydell and Brewer Ltd, 2003.

Bush, Laurence C. *Asian Horror Encyclopedia: Asian Horror Culture in Literature, Manga and Folklore*. San Jose: Writers Club Press, 2001.

Buxton, Richard. *Imaginary Greece: The Contexts of Mythology*. Cambridge, England: Cambridge University Press, 1994.

Caduto, Michael J., and Joseph Bruchac. *Keepers of the Animals: Native American Stories and Wildlife Activities for Children*. Golden: Fulcrum Publishing, 1991.

California Folklore Society. *Western Folklore*, Volumes 27–28. Berkeley: California Folklore Society, 1968.

Callaway, Henry Canon. *Nursery Tales, Traditions, and Histories of the Zulus: In Their Own Words*. London: Trubner and Company, 1868.

Callejo, Jesus, translated by Ricardo Sánchez. *Elves: Volume 1 of Guide Magical Beings of Spain*. N.p : Edaf Editorial, 1994.

Campbell, John Francis. *Popular Tales of the West Highlands: Orally Collected*, Volume 3. Edinburgh: Edmonston and Douglas, 1862.

Campbell, John Francis. *Popular Tales of the West Highlands: Orally Collected*, Volume 4. Paisley: Alexander Gardner, 1893.

Campbell, John Gregorson. *Superstitions of the Highlands and Islands of Scotland: Collected Entirely from Oral Sources*. Glasgow: James Maclehose and Sons, 1900.

Campbell, John Gregorson, translator. *Witchcraft and Second Sight in the Highlands and Islands of Scotland: Tales and Traditions Collected Entirely from Oral Sources*. London: J. MacLehose and Sons, 1902.

Campbell, Joseph, and M. J. Abadie. *The Mythic Image*. Princeton: Princeton University Press, 1981.

Campbell, Marie. *Strange World of the Brontës*. Wilmslow: Sigma Leisure, 2001.

Candelaria, Cordelia, and Peter J. García. *Encyclopedia of Latino Popular Culture*. Westport, Conn.: Greenwood Publishing Group, 2004.

Canfield, William Walker, and Cornplanter. *The Legends of the Iroquois*. New York: A. Wessels Company, 1904.

Cannell, Fenella. *Power and Intimacy in the Christian Philippines*. Cambridge, England: Cambridge University Press, 1999.

Carlyle, Thomas. "Landseer's Pictures of Deer. Part II," in *Fraser's Magazine*, Volume 56 edited by James Anthony Froude and John Tulloch, July 1857, 72–89. London: J. Fraser, 1857.

Carlyon, Richard. *A Guide to the Gods*. London: Heinemann/Quixote, 1981.

Carus, Paul. *The History of the Devil and the Idea of Evil: From the Earliest Times to the Present Day*. Chicago: Open Court, 1899.

Casey, John. *After Lives: A Guide to Heaven, Hell, and Purgatory*. Oxford: Oxford University Press, 2009.

Cassin, Barbara, Emily Apter, Jacques Lezra, and Michael Wood, editors. *Dictionary of Untranslatables: A Philosophical Lexicon*. Princeton: Princeton University Press, 2014.

Castro, Rafaela. *Chicano Folklore: A Guide to the Folktales, Traditions, Rituals and Religious Practices of Mexican Americans*. Oxford: Oxford University Press, 2000.

Cavendish, Richard. *Man, Myth and Magic: An Illustrated Encyclopedia of the Supernatural*, Volume 5. London: Purnell, 1971.

Cavendish, Richard. *The Powers of Evil in Western Religion, Magic and Folk Belief*. London: Routledge, 1975.

Chahin, Mack. *The Kingdom of Armenia: New Edition*. Oxon: Routledge, 2013.

Challice, Annie Emma Armstrong. *French Authors at Home: Episodes in the Lives and Works of Balzac—Madame De Girardin—George Sand—Lamartine—Léon Gozlan—Lamennais—Victor Hugo, Etc*, Volume 2. London: L. Booth, 1864.

Chambers, Robert, editor. *The Book of Days: A Miscellany of Popular Antiquities in Connection with the Calendar, Including Anecdote, Biography and History, Curiosities of Literature, and Oddities of Human Life and Character*, Volume 2. London: W. and R. Chambers, 1888.

Chambers's Encyclopaedia: A Dictionary of Universal Knowledge, Volume 10. London: Lippincott, 1912.

Chandra, Suresh. *Encyclopaedia of Hindu Gods and Goddesses*. New Delhi: Sarup and Sons, 1998.

Channing, Anton. *Chemical Serpents—Silver Edition*. Raleigh: Lulu.com, 2011.

Charnock, Mary Anna E. *Legendary Rhymes, and Other Poems*. London: Longman, Brows Green, and Longmans, 1843.

Chatterjee, Debjani. *The Elephant-Headed God and Other Hindu Tales*. Cambridge: James Clarke and Company, 1989.

Chatterjee, Gautam, and Sanjay Chatterjee. *Sacred Hindu Symbols*. New Delhi: Abhinav Publications, 2001.

Chaucer, Geoffrey, translated by David Wright. *The Canterbury Tales*. Oxford: Oxford University Press, 2011.

Cherry, John F. *Mythical Beasts*. London: Published for the Trustees of the British Museum by British Museum Press, 1995.

Cheyne, Thomas Kelly. *The Prophecies of Isaiah: A New Translation with Commentary and Appendices*, Volume 2. London: Kegan, Paul, Trench, and Company, 1889.

Ching, Julia, and R. W. L. Guisso. *Sages and Filial Sons: Mythology and Archaeology in Ancient China*. Shatin: Chinese University Press, 1991.

Chinmayananda, Swami. *The Holy Geeta*. Langhorne: Chinmaya Mission, 1992.

Chisholm, Hugh, editor. *The Encyclopædia Britannica: A Dictionary of Arts, Sciences, Literature and General Information*, Volume 3. Cambridge: University Press, 1910.

Ch'oe, Chong-go. *Law and Justice in Korea: South and North*. Seoul: Seoul National University Press:, 2005.

Chopra, Ramesh. *Academic Dictionary of Mythology*. New Delhi: Gyan Books, 2005.

Choron, Sandra, and Harry Choron. *Planet Dog: A Doglopedia*. New York: Houghton Mifflin Harcourt, 2005.

Cirlot, J. C. *Dictionary of Symbols*. New York: Routledge, 2006.

Clark, Ella Elizabeth. *Indian Legends of the Pacific Northwest*. London: University of California Press, 2003.

Clark, Ian D. *An Historical Geography of Tourism in Victoria, Australia: Case Studies*. Victoria: De Gruyter Open, 2014.

Clark, Jerome. *Unexplained!: Strange Sightings, Incredible Occurrences, and Puzzling Physical Phenomena*. Canton: Visible Ink Press, 2012.

Clark, Willene B. *A Medieval Book of Beasts: The Second-Family Bestiary: Commentary, Art, Text and Translation*. Rochester: Boydell Press, 2006.

Clarke, David. *Britain's X-Traordinary Files*. London: Bloomsbury Publishing, 2014.

Cleasby, Richard, and Guðbrandur Vigfússon. *An Icelandic-English Dictionary: Chiefly Founded on the Collections Made from Prose Works of the 12th–14th Centuries*. Oxford: Clareon Press, 1869.

Clifford, Sir Hugh Charles, and Sir Frank Athelstane Swettenham. *A Dictionary of the Malay Language: Malay-English, Parts 1–4*. Taiping: Government Printing Office, 1894.

Cohn, Norman. *Cosmos, Chaos, and the World to Come: The Ancient Roots of Apocalyptic Faith*. Yale: Yale University Press, 2001.

Cohn, Norman. *Europe's Inner Demons: The Demonization of Christians in Medieval Christendom*. Chicago: University of Chicago Press, 1993.

Cole, Robert Eden George. *A Glossary of Words Used in South-West Lincolnshire: (Wapentake of Graffoe)*. London: Trübner and Company, 1886.

Coleman, J. A. *The Dictionary of Mythology: An A-Z of Themes, Legends and Heroes*. London: Arcturus Publishing, 2007.

Coleman, Loren. *Monsters of Massachusetts: Mysterious Creatures in the Bay State*. Mechanicsburg: Stackpole Books, 2013.

Coleman, Loren, and Jerome Clark. *Cryptozoology a to Z: The Encyclopedia of Loch Monsters, Sasquatch, Chupacabras, and Other Authentic Mysteries of Nature*. New York: Simon & Schuster, 1999.

Collin de Plancy, Jacques Albin Simon. *Dictionnaire Infernal: Répertoire Universel Des Êtres, Des Personnages Des Livres Qui Tiennent Aux Esprits, Aux Démons, Aux Sorciers*. Paris: Plon, 1863.

Colombo, John Robert. *Colombo's Book of Marvels*. Chapel Hill: University of North Carolina Press, 1979.

Colombo, John Robert. *Mysteries of Ontario*. Tonawanda: Dundurn, 1999.

Colvin, S. "The Centaurs," in *Cornhill Magazine*, Volume XXXVIII, edited by the staff, pages 284–96. London: Smith, Elder, and Company, 1878.

Comay, Joan. *Who's Who in the Old Testament: Together with the Apocrypha*. London: Psychology Press, 2002.

Combe, Taylor. *A Description of the Collection of Ancient Marbles in the British Museum; With Engravings*, Volume 4. London: Bulmer, 1820.

A Commentary, Mythological, Historical, and Geographical on Pope's Homer, and Dryden's Aeneid of Virgil: With a Copious Index. London: John Murray, 1829.

Condos, Theony. *Star Myths of the Greeks and Romans: A Sourcebook Containing the Constellations of Pseudo-Eratosthenes and the Poetic Astronomy of Hyginus*. Grand Rapids: Red Wheel/Weiser, 1997.

Conner, Nancy. *The Everything Classical Mythology Book: From the Heights of Mount Olympus to the Depths of the Underworld—All You Need to Know About the Classical Myths*. Avaon: Everything Books, 2010.

The Contemporary Review, Volume 27. London: A. Strahan, 1876.

Conway, Deanna J. *Magickal Mermaids and Water Creatures: Invoke the Magick of the Waters*. Franklin Lakes: Career Press, 2005.

Conway, Deanna J. *Magickal, Mystical Creatures: Invite Their Powers into Your Life*. St. Paul: Llewellyn Worldwide, 2001.

Conway, Deanna J. *The Mysterious, Magickal Cat*. St. Paul: Llewellyn Publications, 1998.

Conway, Moncure Daniel. *Barons of the Potomack and the Rappahannock*. New York: Grolier Club, 1892.

Cook, A. B. *Zeus: A Study in Ancient Religion*, Volume 2, Part 2. New York: Cambridge University Press, 2010.

Cook, Arthur Bernard. *Zeus: God of the Dark Sky (Thunder and Lightning)*. New York: Cambridge University Press Archive, 1925.

Cook, Erwin. "Introduction." In *The Iliad* (transl. Edward McCrorie). Baltimore: Johns Hopkins University Press, 2012.

Cooper, J. C. *Symbolic and Mythological Animals*. New York: Aquarian/Thorsons, 1992.

Cooper, Philip. *Social Work Man*. Leicester: Troubador Publishing Ltd, 2013.

Copper, Basil. *The Vampire in Legend, Art and Fact*. Secaucus: Carol Publishing Group, 1989.

Cordier, Henri, Edouard Chavannes, Paul Demiéville, Jan Julius Lodewijk Duyvendak, Paul Pelliot, and Gustaaf Schlegel. *T'Ung Pao: T'Oung Pao*. Haiti: E. J. Brill, 1902.

Cornis-Pope, Marcel, and John Neubauer. *History of the Literary Cultures of East-Central Europe: Types and Stereotypes*. Philadelphia: John Benjamins, 2010.

Cort, John. *Framing the Jina: Narratives of Icons and Idols in Jain History*. Oxford: Oxford University Press, 2009.

Coss, Peter R., and Maurice Hugh Keen. *Heraldry, Pageantry and Social Display in Medieval England*. Rochester: Boydell Press, 2002.

Cotterell, Arthur. *A Dictionary of World Mythology*, New York, G. P. Putnam's Sons, 1980.

Coulter, Charles Russell, and Patricia Turner. *Encyclopedia of Ancient Deities*. Oxon: Routledge, 2013.

Covey, Jacob. *Beasts!* Seattle: Fantagraphics Books, 2007.

Cowan, James. *Tales of the Maori*. Auckland: Reed, 1982.

Cox, Barbara, and Scott Forbes. *Beyond the Grave*. New York: The Rosen Publishing Group, 2013.

Cox, Barbara, and Scott Forbes. *Spooky Spirits and Creepy Creatures*. New York: The Rosen Publishing Group, 2013.

Cox, Barbara, and Scott Forbes. *Wicked Waters*. New York: The Rosen Publishing Group, 2013.

Cox, William Thomas. *Fearsome Creatures of the Lumberwoods: With a Few Desert and Mountain Beasts*. Washington, D.C.: Press of Judd and Detweiler, Incorporated, 1910.

Craig, Robert D. *Dictionary of Polynesian Mythology*. Westport: Greenwood Publishing Group, 1989.

Craigie, Sir William Alexander, translator. *Scandinavian Folk-Lore: Illustrations of the Traditional Beliefs of the Northern Peoplest*. London: Alexander Gardner, 1896.

Critchfield, Richard. *Villages*. Garden City, New York: Doubleday, 1981.

Croker, Thomas Crofton. *Fairy Legends and Traditions of the South of Ireland*, Volumes 1–3. London: John Murray, 1828.

Cronin, Vincent. *The Last Migration*. New York: Dutton, 1957.

Crooke, William. *An Introduction to the Popular Religion and Folklore of Northern India*. Allahabad: Printed at the government Press, North-Western Provinces and Oudh, 1894.

Crooke, William. *The Popular Religion and Folk-Lore of Northern India*, Volume 1. London: A. Constable and Company, 1896.

Crooke, William. *The Popular Religion and Folk-Lore of Northern India*, Volume 2. Westminster: Archibald Constable and Company, 1896.

Crowley, Jason. *The Psychology of the Athenian Hoplite: The Culture of Combat in Classical Athens*. Cambridge: Cambridge University Press, 2012.

Cumming, Joseph George. *A Guide to the Isle of Man*. London: Edward Stanford and Sons, 1861.

Cunningham, Graham. *Deliver Me from Evil: Mesopotamian Incantations, 2500–1500 BC*. Rome: Biblical Institute, 1997.

Cunningham, Ian Campbell. *Synagoge*. Berlin: Walter de Gruyter, 2003.

Curl, James Stevens. *The Egyptian Revival: Ancient Egypt as the Inspiration for Design Motifs in the West*. New York: Routledge, 2013.

Curley, Michael J., translator. *Physiologus: A Medieval Book of Nature Lore*. Chicago: University of Chicago Press, 2009.

Curley, Richard T. *Elders, Shades, and Women: Ceremonial Change in Lango, Uganda*. Berkeley: University of California Press, 1973.

Curran, Bob. *Dark Fairies*. New York: Open Road Media, 2012.

Curtin, Jeremiah. *Myths and Folk-Lore of Ireland*. London: Abela Publishing Ltd, 2009.

Curtin, Jeremiah. *Seneca Fiction, Legends, and Myths*. Washington, D.C.: Government Printing Office, 1918.

Daigaku, Nanzan, Jinruigaku Kenkyūjo, Nanzan Shūkyō Bunka Kenkyūjo, and the Asian Folklore Institute, Society for Asian Folklore. *Asian Folklore Studies*, Volume 57. Madras: Asian Folklore Institute, 1998.

Dalal, Roshen. *Hinduism: An Alphabetical Guide*. London: Penguin UK, 2014.

Dalby, Liza Crihfield. *East Wind Melts the Ice: A Memoir*

Through the Seasons. Berkeley: University of California Press, 2007.

Dale-Green, Patricia. *The Archetypal Cat.* Dallas: Spring Publications, 1983.

Dallapiccola, A. L. *Hindu Myths.* Austin: University of Texas Press, 2003.

Dalton, David. *The Rough Guide to the Philippines.* New York: Penguin, 2007.

Daly, Kathleen N. *Norse Mythology A to Z.* New York: Facts on File, 2009.

Daly, Kathleen N., and Marian Rengel. *Greek and Roman Mythology, A to Z.* New York: Infobase Publishing, 2009.

Dange, Sadashiv Ambadas. *Myths from the Mahābhārata: Quest for Immortality.* New Delhi: Aryan Books International, 1997.

D'Angour, Armand. *The Greeks and the New: Novelty in Ancient Greek Imagination and Experience.* Cambridge: Cambridge University Press, 2011.

Daniélou, Alain. *The Myths and Gods of India: The Classic Work on Hindu Polytheism from the Princeton Bollingen Series.* Rochester: Inner Traditions/Bear and Company, 1991.

Daniels, Cora Linn (Morrison), and Charles McClellan Stevans. *Encyclopedia of Superstitions, Folklore, and the Occult Sciences of the World: A Comprehensive Library of Human Belief and Practice in the Mysteries of Life.* Chicago: J. H. Yewdale and Sons Company, 1903.

Daniels, Cora Linn (Morrison), and Charles McClellan Stevans. *Encyclopaedia of Superstitions, Folklore, and the Occult Sciences of the World: A Comprehensive Library of Human Belief and Practice in the Mysteries of Life,* Volume 2. Chicago: J. H. Yewdale and Sons Company, 1903.

Darmesteter, James, and Lawrence Heyworth Mills. *The Zend-Avesta: The Sîrôzahs, Yasts, and Nyâyis, Translated by James Darmesteter.* Oxford: The Clarendon Press, 1883.

Dasent, George Webbe. *The Orkneyingers Saga: And Other Historical Documents Relating to the Settlements and Descents of the Northmen on the British Isles.* Charleston: Forgotten Books, 2008

David, Christine. *Folklore of Carriacou.* Wildey: Coles Printery Limited, 1985.

Davidson, Levette Jay, and Forrester Blake. *Rocky Mountain Tales.* Norman: University of Oklahoma Press, 1947.

Davies, Carole Boyce. *Encyclopedia of the African Diaspora: Origins, Experiences, and Culture.* Santa Barbara: ABC-CLIO, 2007.

Davis, Charles Henry Stanley, editor. *The Egyptian Book of the Dead: The Most Ancient and the Most Important of the Extant Religious Texts of Ancient Egypt.* New York: G.P. Putnam's Sons, 1895.

Davis, Frederick Hadland, and Evelyn Paul. *Myths and Legends of Japan.* New York: Farrar and Rinehart, 1932.

Davis, Mike. *Ecology of Fear: Los Angeles and the Imagination of Disaster.* New York: Vintage Books, 1999.

Day, Peter. *Vampires: Myths and Metaphors of Enduring Evil.* New York: Rodopi, 2006.

Dayal, Har. *The Bodhisattva Doctrine in Buddhist Sanskrit Literature.* Delhi: Motilal Banarsidass Publ., 1999.

Deane, John Bathurst. *The Worship of the Serpent Traced Throughout the World: Attesting the Temptation and Fall of Man by the Instrumentality of a Serpent Tempter.* London: J. G. and F. Rivington, 1833.

De Bary, William Theodore. *Sources of Japanese Tradition: From Earliest Times to 1600.* Columbia: Columbia University Press, 2001.

Debroy, Bibek, translator. *The Mahabharata.* New Delhi: Penguin Books India, 2012.

Debus, Allen A. *Prehistoric Monsters: The Real and Imagined Creatures of the Past That We Love to Fear.* Jefferson, NC: McFarland, 2009.

de Grummond, Nancy. *Etruscan Myth, Sacred History and Legend.* Philadelphia: University of Philadelphia Museum, 2006.

De Gubernatis, Angelo. *Zoological Mythology: Or, the Legends of Animals.* London: Trübner, 1872.

De Jong, Albert. *Traditions of the Magi: Zoroastrianism in Greek and Latin Literature.* Leiden: Brill, 1997.

Dekirk, Ash. *Dragonlore: From the Archives of the Grey School of Wizardry.* Franklin Lakes: Career Press, 2006.

De Lafayette, Maximillien. *The New De Lafayette Mega Encyclopedia Of Anunnaki.* Volume 5. Raleigh: Lulu. com, 2010.

De Lafayette, Maximillien. *Sumerian English Dictionary, Volume 2: Vocabulary and Conversation.* Raleigh: Lulu. com, 2011.

de Las Casas, Dianne, and Zarah C. Gagatiga. *Tales from the 7,000 Isles: Filipino Folk Stories: Filipino Folk Stories.* Santa Barbara: ABC-CLIO, 2011.

Delcourt, Marie. *Oedipe: Ou La Légende Du Conquérant.* Paris: Belles Lettres, 1944.

DeLoach, Charles. *Giants: A Reference Guide from History, the Bible, and Recorded Legend.* Lanham: Scarecrow Press, 1995.

Demetrio, Francisco R. *Encyclopedia of Philippine Folk Beliefs and Customs,* Volume 2. Cincinnati: Xavier University, 1991.

Demetrio, Francisco R. *Myths and Symbols, Philippines.* Manila: National Book Store, 1981.

Demetrio, Francisco R. *Towards a Survey of Philippine Folklore and Mythology.* Manila: Ateneo de Manila University Press, 1968.

Dempster, Charlotte Louisa Hawkins. "Dragons and Dragonslayers, Part 1," in *Essays,* 181–194. London: Smith, Elder and Company, 1872.

Dennis, Geoffrey W. *The Encyclopedia of Jewish Myth, Magic and Mysticism.* Woodbury: Llewellyn Worldwide, 2007.

Dennys, Rodney. *The Heraldic Imagination.* New York: C. N. Potter, 1976.

DePorte, Anton W. *Lithuania in the Last 30 Years.* New Haven: Human Relations Area Files, 1955.

De Puy, William Harrison. *The Encyclopædia Britannica: A Dictionary of Arts, Sciences, and General Literature; the R.S. Peale Reprint, with New Maps and Original American Articles, Volume 7.* Chicago: Werner Company, 1893.

De Sanctis, translator. *Reynard the Fox.* London: W. S. Sonnenschein and Company, 1885.

de Troyes, Chrétien, translated by Ruth Harwood Cline. *Erec and Enide.* Athens: University of Georgia Press, 2011.

De Visser, M. W. *The Dragon in China and Japan.* New York: Cosimo, Incorporated, 2008.

De Visser, Dr. M. W., and the Asiatic Society of Japan. "The Fox and the Badger in Japanese Folklore," in *Transactions of the Asiatic Society of Japan,* pages 1–159. Yokohama: Asiatic Society of Japan, 1965.

Dexter, Miriam Robbins, and Edgar C. Polomé. *Varia on*

the Indo-European Past: Papers in Memory of Marija Gimbutas, Issue 19 of Journal of Indo-European Studies: Monograph. Washington, D.C.: Institute for the Study of Man, 1997.

Dickens, Charles. Household Words: A Weekly Journal, Volumes 17–18. London: Bradbury and Evans, 1858.

Dickinson, Joy. Haunted City: An Unauthorized Guide to the Magical, Magnificent New Orleans of Anne Rice. Secaucus: Carol Publishing Group, 1995.

Diodorus (Siculus.), translated by George Booth. The Historical Library of Diodorus the Sicilian: In Fifteen Books. To Which Are Added the Fragments of Diodorus, and Those Published by H. Valesius, I. Rhodomannus, and F. Ursinus, Volume 1. London: W. M'Dowall, 1814.

Dixon, Roland Burrage. Oceanic [Mythology] Volume 9 of Mythology of All Races. Boston: Marshall Jones, 1916.

Dixon-Kennedy, Mike. Encyclopedia of Greco-Roman Mythology. Santa Barbara: ABC-CLIO, 1998.

Dixon-Kennedy, Mike. Encyclopedia of Russian and Slavic Myth and Legend. Santa Barbara: ABC-CLIO, 1998.

Dixon-Kennedy, Mike. Native American Myth and Legend: An A-Z of People and Places. London: Brockhampton Press, 1998.

Doirievich, Tihomir R. "Doghead in Our People's Beliefs," Srpski Etnografski Zbornik 66: 106–107, 1959.

Dole, Nathan Haskell. Young Folks History of Russia. Chicago: The Werner Company, 1895.

Dominicis, María Canteli, and John J. Reynolds. Repase Y Escriba: Curso Avanzado De Gramática Y Composición. Hoboken: John Wiley and Sons, 2002.

Dömötör, Tekla. Hungarian Folk Beliefs. Bloomington: Indiana University Press, 1982.

Donaldson, Thomas E. Iconography of the Buddhist Sculpture of Orissa: Text. New Delhi: Abhinav Publications, 2001.

Doniger, Wendy. Britannica Encyclopedia of World Religions. Chicago: Encyclopaedia Britannica, 2006.

Doniger, Wendy. Merriam-Webster's Encyclopedia of World Religions. Springfield: Merriam-Webster, 1999.

Doran, Dr. John. Miscellaneous Works, Volume 2. New York: Redfield, 1857.

Dorman, Rushton M. The Origin of Primitive Superstitions and Their Development into the Worship of Spirits and the Doctrine of Spiritual Agency Among the Aborigines of America. Philadelphia: J.B. Lippincott and Company, 1881.

Dorsey, F. Owen. "Tenton Folk-Lore Notes," in Journal of American Folklore, Volume 7 of Bibliographical and Special Series of the American Folklore Society edited by American Folklore Society, pages 135–9. Boston: American Folk-lore Society, 1888.

Dorson, Richard Mercer. Man and Beast in American Comic Legend. Bloomington: Indiana University Press, 1982.

Dotan, Yossi. Watercraft on World Coins: America and Asia, 1800–2008. Eastbourne: Sussex Academic Press, 2010.

Dowden, Ken, and Niall Livingstone. A Companion to Greek Mythology. West Sussex: John Wiley and Sons, 2011.

Downs, James F. The Two Worlds of the Washo: An Indian Tribe of California and Nevada. New York: Holt, Rinehart and Winston, 1966.

Dowson, John. A Classical Dictionary of Hindu Mythology and Religion, Geography, History, and Literature. London: Trübner and Company, 1870.

Doyle, John Robert. Francis Carey Slater. New York: Twayne, 1971.

Draaisma, D. Metaphors of Memory: A History of Ideas About the Mind. Cambridge: Cambridge University Press, 2000.

Drazen, Patrick. A Gathering of Spirits: Japan's Ghost Story Tradition from Folklore and Kabuki to Anime and Manga. Bloomington: iUniverse, 2011.

Drew, A. J. A Wiccan Bible: Exploring the Mysteries of the Craft from Birth to Summerland. Franklin Lakes: Career Press, 2003.

Drew, A. J., and Patricia Telesco. God/Goddess: Exploring and Celebrating the Two Sides of Wiccan Deity. Pompton Plains: Career Press, 2003.

Druce, George C. "Notes on the History of the Heraldic Jall or Yale," in The Archaeological Journal, Volume 68, edited by the British Archaeological Association, Royal Archaeological Institute of Great Britain and Ireland, pages 173–199. London: Royal Archaeological Institute. 1911.

Drury, Nevill. The Dictionary of the Esoteric: 3000 Entries on the Mystical and Occult Traditions. Delhi: Motilal Banarsidass, 2004.

DuBois, Page. Centaurs and Amazons: Women and the Pre-History of the Great Chain of Being. Ann Arbor: University of Michigan Press, 1991.

Dudley, William. Unicorns. San Diego: Capstone, 2008.

Duffy, John J., Samuel B. Hand, and Ralph H. Orth. The Vermont Encyclopedia. Lebanon, University Press of New England, 2003.

Dumont, Jean-Paul. Visayan Vignettes: Ethnographic Traces of a Philippine Island. Chicago: University of Chicago Press, 1992.

Dutt, William Alfred. Highways and Byways in East Anglia. London: Macmillian and Company, Limited, 1901.

Dymock, John. Bibliotheca Classica, or a Classical Dictionary, on a Plan Entirely New. London: Longman, Reese, Orme, Brown, Green, and Longman, 1833.

Eason, Cassandra. A Complete Guide to Faeries and Magical Beings: Explore the Mystical Realm of the Little People. Boston: Weiser Books, 2002.

Eason, Cassandra. Fabulous Creatures, Mythical Monsters, and Animal Power Symbols: A Handbook. Westport: Greenwood Publishing Group, 2008.

Eastlake, F. Warrington. "The Kirin," in Transactions, Volumes 13–14, edited by the Asiatic Society of Japan, 211–224. Yokohama: Asiatic Society of Japan, 1885.

Eastwick, Edward B, editor. The Gulistan; or Rose-Garden or Shekh Muslihu'D-Din Sadi of Shiraz. London: Trubner and Company, 1880.

Eaverly, Mary Ann. Archaic Greek Equestrian Sculpture. Ann Arbor: University of Michigan Press, 1995.

Eberhart, George M. Mysterious Creatures: A Guide to Cryptozoology, Volume 1. Santa Barbara: ABC-CLIO, 2002.

Ēchīasˊksā, Čhulālongkǫnmahāwitthayālai. "Sathāban.," Asian Review, Volume 2. Bangkok: Institute of Asian Studies, Chulalongkorn University, 2003.

Edmonds, Radcliffe G. III. Redefining Ancient Orphism: A Study in Greek Religion. Cambridge: Cambridge University Press, 2013.

Edwards, Agustín. My Native Land: Panorama, Reminiscences, Writers and Folklore. London: E. Benn Limited, 1928.

Edwards, Graham, Gunter Endres, and the Smithsonian

Institution. *Jane's Airline Recognition Guide*. New York: Collins, 2006.

Edwards, Iorwerth Eiddon Stephen, editor. *The Cambridge Ancient History*, Volumes 1–4. Cambridge: Cambridge University Press, 1973.

Eilperin, Juliet. *Demon Fish: Travels Through the Hidden World of Sharks*. New York: Random House LLC, 2012.

Eitel, Ernest John, Nicholas Belfield Dennys, and James Dyer Ball. *The China Review, Or, Notes and Queries on the Far East*, Volume 10. Hong King: National Library Press, 1882.

Eivind, R. *Finnish Legends for English Children*. London: T.F. Unwin, 1893.

Eliade, Wendy Doniger Mircea. *The Woman Who Pretended to Be Who She Was: Myths of Self-Imitation: Myths of Self-Imitation*. Oxford: Oxford University Press, 2004.

Eliot, Alexander. *The Universal Myths: Heroes, Gods, Tricksters, and Others*. New York: New American Library, 1990.

Ellis, George. *Saxon Romances: Guy of Warwick. Sir Bevis of Hamptoun. Anglo-Norman Romance: Richard Coeur De Lion. Romances Relating to Charlemagne: Roland and Ferragus. Sir Otuel. Sir Ferumbras*. London: Longman, Hurst, Rees, and Orme, 1805.

Ellis, Peter Berresford. *Celtic Myths and Legends*. New York: Running Press, 1999.

Ellis, Peter Berresford. *The Chronicles of the Celts: New Tellings of Their Myths and Legends*. London: Robinson, 1999.

Ellwood, Robert S., and Gregory D. Alles, editors. *The Encyclopedia of World Religions*. New York: Infobase Publishing, 2009.

Elsie, Robert. *A Dictionary of Albanian Religion, Mythology, and Folk Culture*. New York: New York University Press, 2001.

Elvin, Charles Norton. *Elvin's Dictionary of Heraldry*. Baltimore: Genealogical Publishing Company, 2009.

El-Zein, Amira. *Islam, Arabs, and the Intelligent World of the Jinn*. Syracuse: Syracuse University Press, 2009.

Endicott, Kirk Michael. *An Analysis of Malay Magic*. Ventnor, Isle of Wight: Clarendon Press, 1970.

Epstein, Marc Michael. *The Medieval Haggadah: Art, Narrative, and Religious Imagination*. New Haven: Yale University Press, 2011.

Erdoes, Richard, and Alfonso Ortiz. *American Indian Myths and Legends*. New York: Knopf Doubleday Publishing Group, 2013.

Espinosa, José Manuel, and the American Folklore Society. *Spanish Folk-Tales from New Mexico, Number 30*. New York: Kraus Reprint, 1969.

Eugenio, Damiana L. *Philippine Folk Literature: The Myths*. Diliman: University of the Philippines Press, 2001.

Euvino, Gabrielle, and Michael San Filippo. *The Complete Idiot's Guide to Italian History and Culture*. New York: Penguin, 2001.

Evans, Kirsti. *Epic Narratives in the Hoysaḷa Temples: The Rāmāyaṇa, Mahābhārata, and Bhāgavata Purāṇa in Haḷebīd, Belūr, and Amṛtapura*. Leiden: BRILL, 1997.

Evans, Thomas Christopher. *History of Llangynwyd Parish*. Llanelly: Llanelly and County Guardian Office, 1887.

Evans-Wentz, Walter Yeeling. *The Fairy Faith in Celtic Countries: The Classic Study of Leprechauns, Pixies, and Other Fairy Spirits*. New York: Citadel Press, 1994.

Evslin, Bernard. *Gods, Demigods and Demons: An Encyclopedia of Greek Mythology*. New York: Open Road Media, 2012.

Facaros, Dana, and Michael Pauls. *Northern Spain*. London: New Holland Publishers, 2009.

Falkayn, David, editor. *Russian Fairy Tales*. Doral: The Minerva Group, Incorporated, 2004.

Fallon, Steve. *Slovenia*. Victoria: Lonely Planet, 2010.

Falola, Toyin, and Ann Genova. *Historical Dictionary of Nigeria*. Lanham: Scarecrow Press, 2009.

Fansler, Dean Spruill, editor. *Filipino Popular Tales*, Volume 12. Lancaster: American Folk-lore Society, 1921.

Fanthorpe, Lionel, and Patricia Fanthorpe. *Satanism and Demonology*. Tonawanda: Dundurn, 2011.

Fanthorpe, Lionel, and Patricia Fanthorpe. *Unsolved Mysteries of the Sea*. Tonawanda: Dundurn, 2004.

Farfor, Susannah. *Northern Territory*. Victoria: Lonely Planet, 2003.

Faron, Louis C. *Hawks of the Sun: Mapuche Morality and Its Ritual Attributes*. Pittsburgh: University of Pittsburgh Press, 1964.

Faron, Louis C. *The Mapuche Indians of Chile*. New York: Holt, Rinehart, and Winston, 1968.

Farrar, Janet, and Virginia Russell. *The Magical History of the Horse*. London: Robert Hale, 1992.

Farrow, Edward Samuel. *Farrow's Military Encyclopedia: A Dictionary of Military Knowledge*. West Point: Military-Naval Publishing Company, 1895.

Faulkner, Harry Charles. *A Handy Classical and Mythological Dictionary for Popular Use*. New York: A. L. Burt, 1884.

Fearn, Jacqueline. *Discovering Heraldry*. Buckinghamshire: Osprey Publishing, 2006.

Feller, Danielle. *The Sanskrit Epics' Representation of Vedic Myths*. Delhi: Motilal Banarsidass, 2004.

Ferrari, Fabrizio. *Health and Religious Rituals in South Asia: Disease, Possession and Healing*. New York: Taylor and Francis, 2011.

Figuier, Louis, and Henry William Bristow. *The World Before the Deluge*. London: Cassell, Peter, and Galpin, 1867.

Filipović, Milenko S. *Among the People, Native Yugoslav Ethnography: Selected Writing of Milenko S. Filipović*. Ann Arbor: Michigan Slavic Publications, Dept. of Slavic Languages and Literatures, 1982.

Finch, Barbara Clay. "Dogs," in *Gentleman's Magazine* Volume CCLXXIX edited by Sylvanus Urban, 526–34. London: Chatto and Windus, 1895.

Findlater, Doctor Andrew. *Chambers's Encyclopædia*, Volume 1, *A Dictionary of Universal Knowledge*. London and Edinburgh: William and Robert Chambers, 1897.

Finger, Stanley, and Marco Piccolino. *The Shocking History of Electric Fishes: From Ancient Epochs to the Birth of Modern Neurophysiology*. Oxford: Oxford University Press, 2011.

Finley, Carol. *Aboriginal Art of Australia: Exploring Cultural Traditions*. Minneapolis: Lerner Publications, 1999.

Fiore, John. *Symbolic Mythology: Interpretations of the Myths of Ancient Greece and Rome*. Lincoln: iUniverse, 2001.

Florescu, Radu, and Raymond T. McNally. *The Complete Dracula*. Acton, Mass.: Napc/Copley Custom Textbooks, 1992.

Foley, John Miles. *A Companion to Ancient Epic*. London: Wiley-Blackwell, 2005.

Folkard, Richard. *Plant Lore, Legends and Lyrics: Embracing the Myths, Traditions, Susperstitions, and Folk-Lore of the Plant Kingdom*. London: Sampson Low, Marston, Searle, and Rivington, 1884.

Folklore Society (Great Britain). *Folk-Lore Journal*, Volume 9. London: Elliot Stock, London, 1898.

Folklore Society of Great Britain. *Folklore*, Volume 13. Folk-lore Society, 1902.

Folklore Society of Great Britain. *The Folk-Lore Record*, Volume 3. Folk-lore Society, 1880.

Fontenrose, Joseph Eddy. *Orion: The Myth of the Hunter and the Huntress*. Berkeley: University of California Press, 1981.

Fontenrose, Joseph Eddy. *Python: A Study of Delphic Myth and Its Origins*. Berkeley: University of California Press, 1980.

Forbes, Alexander Robert. *Gaelic Names of Beasts (Mammalia), Birds, Fishes, Insects, Reptiles, Etc: In Two Parts: I. Gaelic-English.—II. English-Gaelic. Part I. Contains Gaelic Names or Terms for Each of the Above, with English Meanings. Part II. Contains All the English Names for Which Gaelic Is Given in Part I., with Gaelic, Other English Names, Etymology, Celtic Lore, Prose, Poetry, and Proverbs Referring to Each, Thereto Attached All Now Brought Together for the First Time*. Edinburgh: Oliver and Boyd, 1905.

Forbes, Andrew, Daniel Henley, and David Henley. *The Illustrated Book of Dragons and Dragon Lore*. Chiang Mai: Cognoscenti Books, 2006.

Forbes, *Dictionary, Hindustani and English*, 504; Knowles, Nineteenth Century, Volume 31, 449;

Ford, Michael. *The Bible of the Adversary*. Raleigh: Lulu, 2008.

Ford, Michael. *Luciferian Witchcraft*. Raleigh: Lulu, 2005.

Ford, Michael. *Maskim Hul: Babylonian Magick*. Raleigh: Lulu.com, 2011.

Forlong, James George Roche. *Faiths of Man: A Cyclopædia of Religions*. London: Benard Quaritch, 1906.

Forlong, James George Roche. *Rivers of Life*. Moscow: Ripol Classic Publishing House, 2002.

Forlong, John G. R. *Encyclopedia of Religions*, Volume 2. New York: Cosimo, Incorporated, 2008.

Forlong, John G. R. *Encyclopedia of Religions*, Volume 3. New York: Cosimo, Incorporated, 2008.

Forth, Gregory. *Images of the Wildman in Southeast Asia: An Anthropological Perspective*. New York: Taylor and Francis, 2008.

Foster, Michael Dylan. *The Book of Yokai: Mysterious Creatures of Japanese Folklore*. Oakland: University of California Press, 2015.

Foster, Michael Dylan. *Pandemonium and Parade: Japanese Monsters and the Culture of Yokai*. Berkeley: University of California Press, 2008.

Foundation for the Promotion of the Translation of Dutch Literary Works. *Writing in Holland and Flanders*. Amsterdam: Foundation for the Promotion of the Translation of Dutch Literary Works, 1960.

Fox, William Sherwood. *Greek and Roman [Mythology]*. Boston: Marshall Jones Company, 1916.

Fox-Davies, Arthur Charles. *A Complete Guide to Heraldry*. New York: Skyhorse Publishing Incorporated, 2007.

Fragner, Bert G. *Horses in Asia*. Vienna: Austrian Academy of Sciences Press, 2009.

Frances, John. *Notes and Queries*. London: Strand, 1877.

Franklin, Anna. *Working with Fairies: Magick, Spells, Potions and Recipes to Attract and See Them*. Franklin Lakes: Career Press, 2005.

Franklyn, Julian. *Shield and Crest: An Account of the Art and Science of Heraldry*. London: Geneal Pub. MacGibbin and Kee, 1967.

Frater, Jamie. *Listverse.com's Ultimate Book of Bizarre Lists: Fascinating Facts and Shocking Trivia on Movies, Music, Crime, Celebrities, History, and More*. Berkeley: Ulysses Press, 2010.

Frazer, Sir James George. *The Golden Bough: A Study in Magic and Religion*, Volume 2. London: Macmillan, 1966.

Frédéric, Louis. *Japan Encyclopedia*. Cambridge: Harvard University Press, 2005.

Freeman, Richard Austin. *Travels and Life in Ashanti and Jaman*. New York: Frederick A. Stokes Company, 1898.

Friar, Stephen. *Basic Heraldry*. New York: W. W. Norton and Company, 1993.

Friend, Hilderic. *Flowers and Flower Lore*, Volume 1. London: W. S. Sonnenschein and Company, 1884.

Froud, Brian, and Alan Lee. *Faeries*. New York: Harry N. Abrams, Incorporated, 1978.

Fulk, Robert Dennis. *Interpretations of Beowulf: A Critical Anthology*. Bloomington: Indiana University Press, 1991.

Gan, Bao; Kenneth J. DeWoskin, and J. I. Crump, Jr., translators. *In Search of the Supernatural: The Written Record*. Palo Alto: Stanford University Press, 1996.

Gandhi, Menka. *Penguin Book of Hindu Names for Boys*. London: Penguin UK, 2004.

Garcia, Hector. *A Geek in Japan: Discovering the Land of Manga, Anime, Zen, and the Tea Ceremony*. North Clarendon: Tuttle Publishing, 2013.

Garcia, J. Neil C. *Philippine Gay Culture: The Last Thirty Years: Binabae to Bakla, Silahis to MSM*. Diliman: University of the Philippines Press, 1996.

Gard, Robert Edward, and L. G. Sorden. *Wisconsin Lore*. Ashland: Heartland Press, 1987.

Garg, Gaṅgā Rām. *Encyclopaedia of the Hindu World*. Delhi: Concept Publishing Company, 1992.

Garlock, J.M. *The Tao of the Alligator and the Crocodile*. Bloomington: Booktango, 2013.

Garnier, J. *The Worship of the Dead or the Origin and Nature of Pagan Idolatry and Its Bearing Upon the Early History of Egypt and Babylonia*. Moscow: Ripol Klassik, 1997.

Garrett, John. *A Classical Dictionary of India: Illustrative of the Mythology, Philosophy, Literature, Antiquities, Arts, Manners, Customs, Etc., of the Hindus*. Madras: Higginbotham and Company, 1871.

Garry, Jane, and Hasan El-Shamy. *Archetypes and Motifs in Folklore and Literature*. Edmonds: M.E. Sharpe, 2005.

Garza, Xavier. *Creepy Creatures and Other Cucuys*. Huston: Arte Publico Press, 2004.

Gaster, Theodor Herzl, and Sir James George Frazer. *Myth, Legend, and Custom in the Old Testament: A Comparative Study with Chapters from Sir James G. Frazer's Folklore in the Old Testament*. New York: Harper and Row, 1969.

Gatschet, Albert S. "Water Monsters of the American Aborigines," in *The Journal of American Folk-Lore*, Volume 7 edited by the American Folklore Society, 255–60. Boston: American Folk-lore Society, 1898.

Gatschet, Albert S., and the American Folklore Society.

The Journal of American Folk-Lore, Volume 4, Parts 1– 2. Boston: Houghton, Mifflin, and Company for the American Folk-lore Society, 1891.

Gauding, Madonna. *The Signs and Symbols Bible: The Definitive Guide to Mysterious Markings*. New York: Sterling Publishing Company, Incorporated, 2009.

Geertz, Clifford. *The Religion of Java*. Chicago: University of Chicago Press, 1976.

Gemondo, Millie, and Trish MacGregor. *Animal Totems: The Power and Prophecy of Your Animal Guides*. Gloucester: Fair Winds, 2004.

Gerritsen, Willem Pieter, and Anthony G. Van Melle. *A Dictionary of Medieval Heroes: Characters in Medieval Narrative Traditions and Their Afterlife in Literature, Theatre and the Visual Arts*. Woodbridge: Boydell and Brewer, 2000.

Gettings, Fred. *Dictionary of Demons: A Guide to Demons and Demonologists in Occult Lore*. North Pomfret: Trafalgar Square Publishing, 1988.

Gibb, Hamilton Alexander Rosskeen, Koninklijke Nederlandse Akademie van Wetenschappen, and Johannes Hendrik Kramers. *Shorter Encyclopaedia of Islam*. Ithaca: Cornell University Press, 1953.

Giddens, Owen, and Sandra Giddens. *Chinese Mythology*. New York: The Rosen Publishing Group, 2005.

Gilhus, Ingvild Saelid. *Animals, Gods and Humans: Changing Attitudes to Animals in Greek, Roman and Early Christian Thought*. New York: Routledge, 2006.

Gill, Robin D. *The Woman Without a Hole—And Other Risky Themes from Old Japanese Poems*. New York: Paraverse Press, 2007.

Gill, Sam D., and Irene F. Sullivan. *Dictionary of Native American Mythology*. New York: Oxford University Press, 1994.

Gilman, Daniel Coit, Frank Moore Colby, and Harry Thurston Peck. *The New International Encyclopædia*, Volume 13. New York: Dodd, Mead, and Company, 1911.

Gilman, Daniel Coit, Frank Moore Colby, and Harry Thurston Peck. *The New International Encyclopædia*, Volume 16. New York: Dodd, Mead, and Company, 1911.

Gilmore, David D. *Monsters: Evil Beings, Mythical Beasts, and All Manner of Imaginary Terrors*. Philadelphia: University of Pennsylvania Press, 2003.

Gimbutas, Marija. *The Living Goddesses*. Berkeley: University of California Press, 2001.

Gimlette, John Desmond. *Malay Poisons and Charm Cures*. New York: Oxford University Press, 1971.

Glover, FJH. *1000 Famous Horses Fact and Fictional Throughout the Ages (Not Race Horses and Not Show Jumping Horses)*. Philadelphia: Xlibris Corporation, 2011.

Glover, Matthew. *Glover's Illustrated Guide and Visitors' Companion Through the Isle of Man: With Sea and Trout Fishing*. London: Matthew Glover, 1873.

Godfrey, Linda S. *American Monsters: A History of Monster Lore, Legends, and Sightings in America*. New York: Penguin, 2014.

Godfrey, Linda S. *Lake and Sea Monsters*. New York: Infobase Publishing, 2009.

Godfrey, Linda S. *Monsters of Wisconsin: Mysterious Creatures in the Badger State*. Mechanicsburg: Stackpole Books, 2011.

Godfrey, Linda S., and Rosemary Ellen Guiley. *Mythical Creatures*. New York: Infobase Publishing, 2009.

Goetz, Delia, and Sylvanus Griswold Morley. *Popol Vuh: The Book of the Ancient Maya*. Mineola: Courier Corporation, 2003.

Goodman, Loren Seth. *Endless Punchers: Body, Narrative, and Performance in the World of Japanese Boxing*. Ann Arbor: ProQuest, 2006.

Goodwin, Grenville. *Myths and Tales of the White Mountain Apache*. Tucson: University of Arizona Press, 1994.

Gordon, Terence. *Hot Lakes, Volcanoes, and Geysers of New Zealand, with Legends*. Hawke's Bay: Dinwiddie, Walker and Company, Limited, 1888.

Gould, Charles. *Dragons, Unicorns, and Sea Serpents: A Classic Study of the Evidence for Their Existence*. Mineola: Courier Dover Publications, 2002.

Gould, Charles. *Mythical Monsters*. London: W. H. Allen and Company, 1886.

Gould, Charles, Odell Shepard, and Ernest Ingersoll. *Legendary Creatures*. N.p.: Publish This, LLC, 2011.

Grafetstätter, Andrea, Sieglinde Hartmann, and James Michael Ogier, editors. *Islands and Cities in Medieval Myth, Literature, and History: Papers Delivered at the International Medieval Congress, University of Leeds, in 2005, 2006, and 2007*. Leeds: Peter Lang, 2011.

Grant, Michael, and John Hazel. *Who's Who in Classical Mythology*. New York: Psychology Press, 2002.

Grant, Robert M. *Early Christians and Animals*. New York: Routledge, 2002.

Grattan, John, and Robin Torrence. *Natural Disasters and Cultural Change*. New York: Routledge, 2003.

Graves, Robert. *The Greek Myths: Classics Deluxe Edition*. New York: Penguin, 2012.

Graves, Robert. *The Larousse Encyclopedia of Mythology*. New York: Barnes and Noble, Incorporated, 1994.

Gray, Louis Herbert. *The Mythology of All Races*, Volume 5. Boston: Marshal Jones Company, 1931.

Gray, Louis Herbert, George Foot Moore, and John Arnott MacCulloch, editors. *The Mythology of All Races*, Volume 11. Boston: Marshall Jones Company, 1920.

Gray, Louis Herbert, and John Arnott MacCulloch. *The Mythology of All Races: Armenian, M. H. Ananikian. African*, Volume 7. New York: Cooper Square Publishers, 1964.

Grayson, James H. *Korea—A Religious History*. New York: Routledge, 2013.

Green, Jonathon. *Cassell's Dictionary of Slang*. London: Sterling Publishing Company, Incorporated, 2005.

Green, Miranda. *Animals in Celtic Life and Myth*. New York: Routledge, 1998.

Gregory, Lady Augusta. *Gods and Fighting Men: The Story of the Tuatha De Danaan and of the Fianna of Ireland*. London: J. Murray, 1905.

Grimal, Pierre, *Larousse World Mythology*, Secaucus, New Jersey, Chartwell Books, 1965.

Grimes, Heilan Yvette. *The Norse Myths*. Boston: Hollow Earth Pubishing, 2010.

Grimm, Jacob, and Elard Hugo Meyer. *Deutsche Mythologie*, Volume 2. Gottingen: Dieterichsche Buchhandlung, 1854.

Grimm, Jacob, and Wilhelm Grimm. *Grimms Sagen: Vollständige Und Illustrierte Ausgabe*. Erschienen: Null Papier Verlag, 2014.

Grimm, Jacob Ludwig C. *Teutonic Mythology*, Volume 2. London: George Bell, 1888.

Grimm, Jacob Ludwig C. *Teutonic Mythology*, Volume 3. London: George Bell, 1883.

Grimm, Jacob Ludwig C., translated by James Steven Stallybrass. *Teutonic Mythology, Translated by J.S. Stallybrass.* London: George Bell and Son, 1883.

Grimm, Wilhelm, and Donald Ward. *The German Legends of the Brothers Grimm.* Philadelphia: Institute for the Study of Human Issues, 1981.

Guan, Yuehua, and Liangbi Zhong. *Behind the Veil of the Forbidden City.* Beijing: Chinese Literature Press, 1996.

Gudegeon, Lieutenant Colonel W. E. "Maori Superstitions," in *The Journal of the Polynesian Society,* Volume 14 edited by the Polynesian Society (N.Z.), 167–192. Wellington: Polynesian Society, 1967.

Guerber, H. A. *Hammer of Thor—Norse Mythology and Legends—Special Edition.* N.p.: El Paso Norte, 2010.

Guiley, Rosemary. *The Encyclopedia of Vampires, Werewolves, and Other Monsters.* New York: Infobase Publishing, 2004.

Guiley, Rosemary, and J. B. Macabre. *The Complete Vampire Companion.* New York: Macmillan, 1994.

Guiley, Rosemary, and John Zaffis. *The Encyclopedia of Demons and Demonology.* New York: Infobase Publishing, 2009.

Guiley, Rosemary Ellen. *The Encyclopedia of Witches, Witchcraft and Wicca.* New York: Infobase Publishing, 2008.

Guirand, Félix. *Larousse Encyclopedia of Mythology.* Lancaster: Prometheus Press, 1959.

Guirand, Félix, and Robert Graves. *New Larousse Encyclopedia of Mythology.* London: Hamlyn, 1968.

Guppy, Shusha. *The Blindfold Horse: Memories of a Persian Childhood.* London: Tauris Parke Paperbacks, 2004.

Gupta, S. K. *Elephant in Indian Art and Mythology.* New Delhi: Abhinav Publications, 1983.

Haase, Donald. *The Greenwood Encyclopedia of Folktales and Fairy Tales.* Westport: Greenwood Publishing Group, 2007.

Hacikyan, Agop Jack, Gabriel Basmajian, Edward S. Franchuk, and Nourhan Ouzounian. *The Heritage of Armenian Literature: From the Eighteenth Century to Modern Times.* Detroit: Wayne State University Press, 2005.

Hainsworth, John Bryan, and Arthur Thomas Hatto. *Traditions of Heroic and Epic Poetry: Characteristics and Techniques.* London: Modern Humanities Research Associations, 1989.

Haksteen, John Jacob. *Searching for Power.* Bloomington: AuthorHouse, 2012.

Halili, Christine N. *Philippine History.* Manila: Rex Bookstore, Incorporated, 2004.

Hall, Manly P. *The Secret Teachings of All Ages: An Encyclopedic Outline of Masonic, Hermetic, Qabbalistic, and Rosicrucian Symbolical Philosophy.* Charleston: Forgotten Books, 1928.

Hall, Mark A., and Mark Lee Rollins. *Thunderbirds: America's Living Legends of Giant Birds.* New York: Cosimo, Incorporated, 2008.

Hallenbeck, Bruce G. *Monsters of New York: Mysterious Creatures in the Empire State.* Mechanicsburg: Stackpole Books, 2013.

Halpin, Marjorie M., and Michael M. Ames, editors. *Manlike Monsters on Trial: Early Records and Modern Evidence.* Vancouver: University of British Columbia Press, 1980.

Hamilton, A. C. *Spenser: the Faerie Queene.* New York: Routledge, 2014.

Hamilton, John. *Ogres and Giants.* Edina: ABDO, 2004.

Haney, Jack V. *The Complete Russian Folktale: Russian Animal Tales.* Armonk: M.E. Sharpe, 1999.

Hansen, William, and William F. Hansen. *Classical Mythology: A Guide to the Mythical World of the Greeks and Romans.* Oxford: Oxford University Press, 2005.

Hansen, William F. *Handbook of Classical Mythology.* Santa Barbara: ABC-CLIO, 2004.

Hard, Robin. *The Routledge Handbook of Greek Mythology: Based on H.J. Rose's "Handbook of Greek Mythology.".* London: Psychology Press, 2004.

Hardy, Jörg, and George Rudebusch. *Ancient Ethics.* Vandenhoeck and Ruprecht, 2014.

Haren, Michael, and Yolande de Pontfarcy, editors. *The Medieval Pilgrimage to St Patrick's Purgatory: Lough Derg and the European Tradition.* Enniskillen: Clogher Historical Society, 1988.

Hargreaves, Joyce. *Hargreaves New Illustrated Bestiary.* Glastonbury: Gothic Image, 1990.

Harries, John. *The Ghost Hunter's Road Book.* London: Muller, 1968.

Harris, Thaddeus Mason. *The Natural History of the Bible: Or, a Description of All the Birds, Fishes, Reptiles and Insects, Trees, Plants, Precious Stones, Mentioned in the Sacred Scriptures. Collected from the Best Authorities, and Alphabetically Arranged.* Boston: Wells and Lilly, 1820.

Harrison, Charles. *Ancient Warriors of the North Pacific: The Haidas, Their Laws, Customs and Legends, with Some Historical Account of the Queen Charlotte Islands.* London: H. F. and G. Witherby, 1925.

Hart, Derek. *Secret of the Dragon's Eye.* Lincoln: Robert Lenthart, 2007.

Hart, George. *The Routledge Dictionary of Egyptian Gods and Goddesses.* New York: Routledge, 2005.

Hartland, Edwin Sidney, editor. *Gloucestershire.* London: David Nutt, 1895.

Hartston, Willam. *Encyclopedia of Useless Information.* Naperville: Sourcebooks, Incorporated, 2007.

Harvey, P. D. A. *The Hereford World Map: Medieval World Maps and Their Context.* London: British Library, 2006.

Hasluck, Frederick William, Richard McGillivray Dawkins, and Margaret Masson Hardie Hasluck. *Letters on Religion and Folklore.* London: Luzac and Company, 1926.

Hassig, Debra. *The Mark of the Beast: The Medieval Bestiary in Art, Life, and Literature.* New York: Routledge, 2013.

Hastings, James. *Encyclopedia of Religion and Ethics,* Part 5. Whitefish: Kessinger Publishing, 2003.

Hastings, James. *Encyclopedia of Religion and Ethics,* Part 8. Whitefish: Kessinger Publishing, 2003.

Hastings, James. *Encyclopedia of Religion and Ethics,* Part 24. Whitefish: Kessinger Publishing, 2003.

Hastings, James, and John A. Selbie. *Encyclopedia of Religion and Ethics* Part 2. Whitefish: Kessinger Publishing, 2003.

Hastings, James, John Alexander Selbie, and Louis Herbert Gray. *Encyclopaedia of Religion and Ethics,* Volume 3–4. New York: Scribner, 1928.

Hastings, James, Louis Herbert Gray, and John Alexander Selbie. *Encyclopaedia of Religion and Ethics,* Volume. 13. Edinburgh: T. and T. Clark, 1922.

Hausman, Gerald, and Loretta Hausman. *The Mythology of Horses: Horse Legend and Lore Throughout the Ages.* New York: Random House Digital, Incorporated, 2003.

Haustein, Michaela. *Mythologien Der Welt: Japan, Ainu, Korea*. Berlin: epubli, 2011.

Hawthorn, Audrey. *Art of the Kwakiutl Indians and Other Northwest Coast Tribes*. Vancouver: University of British Columbia, 1967.

Hearn, Lafcadio. *Glimpses of an Unfamiliar Japan: First Series*. Auckland: The Floating Press, 2012.

Hearn, Lafcadio. *Kwaidan: Ghost Stories and Strange Tales of Old Japan*. Mineola: Courier Dover Publications, 2012.

Hearn, Lafcadio. *Kwaidan: Stories and Studies of Strange Things*. Charleston: Forgotten Books, 1930.

Hearn, Lafcadio. *Lafcadio Hearn: Japan's Great Interpreter: A New Anthology of His Writings, 1894–1904*. Kent: Japan Library, Limited, 1992.

Hearn, Lafcadio. *The Romance of the Milky Way and Other Stories*. Teddington: Echo Library, 2006.

Helfman, Gene, and Bruce Collette. *Fishes: The Animal Answer Guide*. Baltimore: Johns Hopkins University Press, 2011.

Hellman, Roxanne, and Derek Hall. *Vampire Legends and Myths*. New York: Rosen Group, 2012.

Helterbran, Valeri R. *Why Rattlesnakes Rattle: …And 250 Other Things You Should Know*. Lanham: Taylor Trade Publications, 2012.

Henderson, Caspar. *The Book of Barely Imagined Beings: A 21st Century Bestiary*. Chicago: University of Chicago Press, 2013.

Henderson, William. *Notes on the Folk-Lore of the Northern Counties of England and the Borders*. London: Folklore Society by W. Satchell, Peyton, 1879.

Hendrickson, Robert. *The Facts on File Dictionary of American Regionalisms*. New York: Infobase Publishing, 2000.

Henriksen, Georg. *I Dreamed the Animals: Kaneuketat: The Life of an Innu Hunter*. New York: Berghahn Books, 2009.

Hepburn, James Curtis. *Japanese-English and English-Japanese Dictionary by J. C. Hepburn*. New York: A.D.F Randolph, 1873.

Herbert, Agnes. *The Isle of Man*. London: John Lane, 1909.

Herdt, Gilbert H. *Ritualized Homosexuality in Melanesia*. Berkeley: University of California Press, 1993.

Hernandez, Jo Farb. *Forms of Tradition in Contemporary Spain*. Jackson: University Press of Mississippi, 2005.

Herrera-Sobek, María. *Celebrating Latino Folklore: An Encyclopedia of Cultural Traditions*, Volume 1. Santa Barbara: ABC-CLIO, 2012.

Herrera-Sobek, María. *Chicano Folklore: A Handbook*. Westport: Greenwood Publishing Group, 2006.

Herskovits, Melville Jean. *The Myth of the Negro Past*. Boston: Beacon Press, 1990.

Hesiod, Callimachus, Theognis, James Davies, Sir Charles Abraham Elton, Henry William Tytler, and John Hookham Frere. *The Works of Hesiod, Callimachus, and Theognis*. London: Henry G. Bohn, 1856.

Hesiod, translated by Hugh Gerard Evelyn-White. *Hesiod, the Homeric Hymns, and Homerica*. London: Harvard University Press, 1914.

Heuvelmans, Bernard. *The Kraken and the Colossal Octopus: In the Wake of Sea-Monsters*. London: Kegan Paul International, 2003.

Heuvelmans, Bernard. *On the Track of Unknown Animals*. New York: Routledge, 2014.

Hewitt, John Napoleon Brinton. *Seneca Fiction, Legends, and Myths*. Washington, D.C.: United States Government Printing Office, 1918.

Hicks, Jim, and Time-Life Books. *Transformations: Mysteries of the Unknown*. New York: Time-Life Books, 1989.

Hill, Beth, and Ray Hill. *Indian Petroglyphs of the Pacific Northwest*. Saanichton: Hancock House Publishers, 1974.

Hill, Oliver. *Scottish Castles of the Sixteenth and Seventeenth Centuries*. London: Country Life, 1953.

Hillman, James, and Wilhelm Heinrich Roscher. *Pan and the Nightmare*. Dallas: Spring Publications, 2000.

Hìtakonanulaxk. *The Grandfathers Speak: Native American Folk Tales of the Lenapé People*. Northampton: Interlink Books, 1994.

Hitchcock, Ethan Allen. *A Traveler in Indian Territory: The Journal of Ethan Allen Hitchcock, Late Major-General in the United States Army*. Norman, Okla.: University of Oklahoma Press, 1996.

Hlobil, Karel. *Before You*. Ontario: Insomniac Press, 2009.

Ho, Oliver. *Mysteries Unwrapped: Mutants and Monsters*. New York: Sterling Publishing Company, Incorporated, 2008.

Hobart, Angela, Albert Leemann, and Urs Ramseyer. *The People of Bali*. New York: Wiley-Blackwell, 2001.

Hodgson, Janet. *The God of the Xhosa: A Study of the Origins and Development of the Traditional Concepts of the Supreme Being*. New York: Oxford University Press, 1982.

Holland, Edith. *Mohammed*. New York: Frederick A. Stokes Company, 1914.

Hollenbaugh, Henry. *Nessus the Centaur*. Huston: Alondra Press, 2009.

Holmen, Marianne. *Danish-English, English-Danish Dictionary*. New York: Hippocrene Books, 1990.

Holton, David, Peter Mackridge, and Irene Philippaki-Warburton. *Greek: An Essential Grammar of the Modern Language*. New York: Psychology Press, 2004.

Holyfield, Dana. *Encounters with the Honey Island Swamp Monster*. Pearl River, La.: Honey Island Swamp Books, 1999.

Homer, Bernadotte Perrin, and Thomas Day Seymour. *Eight Books of Homer's Odyssey*. Boston: Ginn and Company, 1897.

Homer, translated by Edgar Alfred Tibbetts. *The Iliad of Homer: To Which Is Added an Appendix Containing Poems Selected from Twenty-Six Languages*. Boston: Richard G. Badger, 1907.

Homer, translated by Robert Fitzgerald. *The Odyssey: The Fitzgerald Translation*. New York: Macmillan, 1998.

Hoops, Johannes. *Kommentar Zum Beowulf*. Heidelberg, Germany: Carl Winter, 1932.

Hope, Robert Charles. *The Temple and Shrines of Nikko, Japan*. Yokohama: Kelly and Walsh, 1896.

Hopkins, Edward Washburn. *Epic Mythology*. New York: Biblo and Tannen Publishers, 1968.

Hopkins, Edward Washburn. *The History of Religions*. New York: Macmillan, 1918.

Houtsma, Martijn Theodoor. *E.J. Brill's First Encyclopaedia of Islam, 1913–1936, Volume 2*. Leiden: Brill, 1987.

Howard, James H., and Willie Lena. *Oklahoma Seminoles Medicines, Magic and Religion*. Norman: University of Oklahoma Press, 1990.

Howey, M. Oldfield. *The Cat in Magic and Myth*. North Chemsford: Courier Dover Publications, 2003.

Howey, M. Oldfield. *The Horse in Magic and Myth*. Mineola: Courier Dover Publications, 2002.

Hsing Yun, Xingyun, translated by Robert Smitheram. *The Universal Gate: A Commentary on Avalokitesvara's Universal Gate Sutra*. Hacienda Heights: Buddha's Light Publishing, 2011.

Hubbs, Joanna. *Mother Russia: The Feminine Myth in Russian Culture*. Bloomington: Indiana University Press, 1993.

Huber, Michael. *Mythematics: Solving the Twelve Labors of Hercules*. Princeton: Princeton University Press, 2009.

Hufford, David J. *The Terror That Comes in the Night: An Experience-Centered Study of Supernatural Assault Traditions*. Philadelphia: University of Pennsylvania Press, 1989.

Hughes, Thomas Patrick. *A Dictionary of Islam: Being a Cyclopaedia of the Doctrines, Rites, Ceremonies, and Customs, Together with the Technical and Theological Terms, of the Muhammadan Religion*. London: W. H. Allen, 1885.

Hugo, Victor. *The Toilers of the Sea*, Volume 1. London: George Routledge and Sons, Limited, 1896.

Hulme, Frederick Edward. *Myth-Land*. London: Sampson Low, Marston, Searle, and Rivington, 1886.

Hung, Chang-tai. *Going to the People: Chinese Intellectuals and Folk Literature, 1918–1937*. London: Harvard University Asia Center, 1985.

Hunt, Robert, editor. *Popular Romances of the West of England: Or, the Drolls, Traditions, and Superstitions of Old Cornwall*. London: John Camden Hotten, 1865.

Hunter, R. L. *The Argonautica of Apollonius*. Cambridge: Cambridge University Press, 2005.

Hurley, Vic. *Swish of the Kris, the Story of the Moros, Authorized and Enhanced Edition*. Salem: Cerberus Books, 2010.

Hurst, Carol Otis. *Once Upon a Time—: An Encyclopedia for Successfully Using Literature with Young Children*. Allen: DLM, 1990.

Hurst, Peter W. "The Encyclopedic Tradition, the Cosmological Epic, and the Validation of the Medieval Romance," in *Comparative Criticism*: Volume 1, *The Literary Canon: A Yearbook*, edited by Elinor Shaffer, 53–73. Cambridge: Cambridge University Press, 1979.

Hyatt, Victoria, and Joseph W. Charles. *The Book of Demons*. New York: Simon & Schuster, 1974.

Hyde, Douglas. *Beside the Fire: A Collection of Irish Gaelic Folk Storie*. Charleston: Forgotten Books, 1973.

Icon Group International, Incorporated. *Demons: Webster's Quotations, Facts and Phrases*. San Diego: ICON Group International, Incorporated, 2008.

Icon Group International, Incorporated. *Hanging: Webster's Quotations, Facts and Phrases*. San Diego: ICON Group International, Incorporated, 2008.

Icon Group International, Incorporated. *Victims: Webster's Quotations, Facts and Phrases*. San Diego: ICON Group International, Incorporated, 2008.

Ignasher, Jim. *Forgotten Tales of Rhode Island*. Charleston: The History Press, 2008.

Iinkai, Nihon Yunesuko Kokunai. *Japan: Its Land, People and Culture*. Tokyo: Bureau, Ministry of Finance, 1958.

Illes, Judika. *Encyclopedia of Spirits: The Ultimate Guide to the Magic of Fairies, Genies, Demons, Ghosts, Gods and Goddesses*. New York: HarperCollins, 2009.

Inavits, *Russian Folk Belief*, 63;

Ingpen, Robert R., and Molly Perham. *Ghouls and Monsters*. New York: Chelsea House Publishers, 1996.

Institut für Sorbische Volksforschung in Bautzen, Sorbisches Institut (Bautzen, Germany). *Lětopis*, Volumes 53–54. Bautzen: Sorbisches Institut, 2006.

Irby-Massie, Georgia L., and Paul T. Keyser. *Greek Science of the Hellenistic Era: A Sourcebook*. New York: Routledge, 2013.

Irving, Washington. *Life of Mahomet*. London: Henry G. Bohn, 1850.

Irving, Washington. *Mahomet and His Successors*. New York: Pollard and Moss, 1882.

Irwin, Harvey J., and Caroline A. Watt. *An Introduction to Parapsychology, 5th Edition*. Jefferson, NC: McFarland, 2007.

Isaacs, Ronald H. *Animals in Jewish Thought and Tradition*. Northvale: Jason Aronson, 2000.

Iyer, Meena. *Faith and Philosophy of Zoroastrianism*. Delhi: Gyan Publishing House, 2009.

Jackson, Nigel Aldcroft. *The Compleat Vampyre: The Vampire Shaman, Werewolves, Witchery and the Dark Mythology of the Undead*. Somerset: Capall Bann Publishing, 1995.

Jacobs, David Michael. *UFO and Abductions: Challenging the Borders of Knowledge*. Lawrence, Kan, 2000.

Jacobs, Joseph, and Donald Haase, editors. *English Fairy Tales: And, More English Fairy Tales*. Santa Barbara: ABC-CLIO, 1890.

Jacobus, edited by Christopher Stace. *The Golden Legend: Selections*. New York: Penguin, 1998.

Jahoda, Gustav. *The Psychology of Superstition*. New York: Penguin, 1970.

Japan Society of London. *Transactions and Proceedings of the Japan Society*, London, Volume 9. London: Kegan Paul, Trench, Trübner and Company, 1912.

Jarymowycz, Roman Johann. *Cavalry from Hoof to Track*. Westport: Greenwood Publishing Group, 2008.

Jäschke, H. A. *a Tibetan-English Dictionary: With Special Reference to the Prevailing Dialects, to Which Is Added an English-Tibetan Vocabulary*. London: Routledge, 1881.

Jasher. *The Book of Jasher*. Lanham: Start Classics, 2014.

Jastrow, Morris. *The Religion of Babylonia and Assyria*. Boston: Ginn and Company, 1898.

Jennbert, Kristina. *Animals and Humans: Recurrent Symbiosis in Archaeology and Old Norse Religion*. Lund: Nordic Academic Press, 2011.

Jennison, George. *Animals for Show and Pleasure in Ancient Rome*. Manchester: Manchester University Press, 1937.

Jewell, Keala Jane. *Monsters in the Italian Literary Imagination*. Detroit: Wayne State University Press, 2001.

Jobes, Gertrude. *Dictionary of Mythology, Folklore and Symbols*. Lanham: Scarecrow Press, 1961.

Jocano, F. Landa. *Folk Medicine: In a Philippine Municipality*. Manila, Philippines: National Museum Publication, 1973.

Jocano, F. Landa. *Growing Up in a Philippine Barrio*. New York: Holt, Rinehart, and Winston, 1969.

Johns, Catherine. *Horses: History, Myth, Art*. Cambridge: Harvard University Press, 2006.

Johnsgard, Paul. *Dragons and Unicorns: A Natural History*. London: Macmillan, 1992.

Johnson, Aili Kolehmainen. *Kalevala: A Prose Translation from the Finnish*. Hancock: Printed by the Book Concern, 1950.

Johnson, Kenneth. *Slavic Sorcery: Shamanic Journey of Initiation*. Woodbury: Llewellyn Publications, 1998.

Johnson, Severance. *The Dictator and the Devil*. New York: Ecnareves Press, 1943.

Joly, Dom. *Scary Monsters and Super Creeps: In Search of the World's Most Hideous Beasts*. London: Simon & Schuster, 2012.

Jonáš, Karel. *Bohemian and English Dictionary*. Chicago: Nakl. Ceského ústředního knihkupectví, 1890.

Jones, David E. *Evil in Our Midst: A Chilling Glimpse of Our Most Feared and Frightening Demons*. Garden City Park: Square One Publishers, Incorporated, 2001.

Jones, David E. *An Instinct for Dragons*. New York: Psychology Press, 2002.

Jones, Ernest. *On the Nightmare*. London: Hogarth Press, 1949.

Jones, Marie D. *Modern Science and the Paranormal*. New York: The Rosen Publishing Group, 2009.

Jones, William Lewis. *King Arthur in History and Legend*. Cambridge: University Press, 1914.

Jordan, Michael. *Dictionary of Gods and Goddesses*. New York: Infobase Publishing, 2009.

Jordan, Michael, *Encyclopedia of Gods*. New York, Facts on File, Incorporated, 1993.

Journal of Near Eastern Studies V. "Sumerian Mythology: A Review Article," Chicago: Journal of Near Eastern Studies, 1946.

Joyce, Judith. *The Weiser Field Guide to the Paranormal: Abductions, Apparitions, ESP, Synchronicity, and More Unexplained Phenomena from Other Realms*. San Francisco: Weiser Books, 2011.

Joyce, Patrick Weston. *A Smaller Social History of Ancient Ireland: Treating of the Government, Military System and Law, Religion, Learning and Art, Trades, Industries and Commerce, Manners, Customs and Domestic Life of the Ancient Irish People*. New York: Longmans, Green and Company, 1908.

Jung, In-hah. *The Feel of Korea: A Symposium of American Comment*. Seoul: Hollym Corp., 1966.

Kadir, Abdullah bin Adbul, and Abdullah, A. H. Hill. *The Hikayat Abdullah*. New York: Oxford University Press, 1970.

Kang, Xiaofei. *The Cult of the Fox: Power, Gender, and Popular Religion in Late Imperial and Modern China*. Irvington, New York: Columbia University Press, 2006.

Kappler, Matthias. *Intercultural Aspects in and Around Turkic Literatures: Proceedings of the International Conference Held on October 11th–12th, 2003 in Nicosia*. Wiesbader: Otto Harrassowitz Verlag, 2006.

Karr, Phyllis Ann. *The Arthurian Companion: The Legendary World of Camelot and the Round Table*. Oakland: Chaosium Books, 1997.

Karr, Phyllis Ann. *The King Arthur Companion: The Legendary World of Camelot and the Round Table as Revealed by the Tales Themselves*. Reston: Reston Publishing Company, 1983.

Kaylan, Muammer. *The Kemalists: Islamic Revival and the Fate of Secular Turkey*. Amherst: Prometheus Books, 2005.

Keightley, Thomas. *The Fairy Mythology: Illustrative of the Romance and Superstition of Various Countries*. London: George Bell and Sons, 1905.

Keightley, Thomas. *The Mythology of Ancient Greece and Italy*. London: Whittaker and Company, 1854.

Keightley, Thomas. *World Guide to Gnomes, Fairies, Elves, and Other Little People*, New York: Random House Value Publishing, 1878.

Kelly, Douglas. *Medieval Imagination: Rhetoric and the Poetry of Courtly Love*. Madison: University of Wisconsin Press, 1978.

Kelly, Sean, and Rosemary Rogers. *Who in Hell: A Guide to the Whole Damned Bunch*. New York: Villard, 1996.

Kendall, Laurel. *Shamans, Housewives, and Other Restless Spirits: Women in Korean Ritual Life*. Honolulu: University of Hawaii Press, 1987.

Keyworth, David. *Troublesome Corpses: Vampires and Revenants, from Antiquity to the Present*. Essex, England: Desert Island Books, 2007.

Khanam, R. *Demonology: Socio-Religious Belief of Witchcraft*. New Deli: Global Vision Publishing House, 2003.

Kibler, R. William W., and Barton Palmer, editors. *Medieval Arthurian Epic and Romance: Eight New Translations*. Jefferson, NC: McFarland, 2014.

Kiernan, James. *The Power of the Occult in Modern Africa: Continuity and Innovation in the Renewal of African Cosmologies*. Berlin: LIT Verlag Münster, 2006.

Kingshill, Sophia, and the Estate of Jennifer Westwood. *The Fabled Coast: Legends and Traditions from Around the Shores of Britain and Ireland*. London: Random House, 2012.

Kipfer, Barbara Ann. *The Order of Things*. New York: Workman Publishing, 2008.

Kippis, Andrew. *The New Annual Register, Or, General Repository of History, Politics, and Literature for the Year 1781*.London: G.G.J. and J. Robinson, 1782.

Kissinger, Barbara Hallman. *Christmas Past*. Gretna: Pelican Publishing, 2005.

Klaniczay, Gábor, and Éva Pócs. *Christian Demonology and Popular Mythology*. Budapest: Central European University Press, 2006.

Kleivan, Inge, and Birgitte Sonne. *Eskimos, Greenland and Canada*. Leiden: Brill, 1985.

Kloppenborg, Ria, and Wouter J. Hanegraaff. *Female Stereotypes in Religious Traditions*. Leiden: Brill, 1995.

Kmietowicz, Frank A. *Slavic Mythical Beliefs*. Windsor: F. Kmietowicz, 1982.

Knapp, Bettina Liebowitz. *Machine, Metaphor, and the Writer: A Jungian View*. University Park: Penn State Press, 1989.

Knapp, Bettina Liebowitz. *Women, Myth, and the Feminine Principle*. Albany: State University New York Press, 1998.

Knapp, Stephen. *The Secret Teachings of the Vedas*. Mumbai: Jaico Publishing House, 1993.

Knappert, Jan. *African Mythology: An Encyclopedia of Myth and Legend*. Berkeley: Diamond Books, 1995.

Knappert, Jan. *Bantu Myths and Other Tales*. Leiden: Brill Archive, 1977.

Knappert, Jan. *Indian Mythology: An Encyclopedia of Myth and Legend*. Wellingborough: Aquarian Press, 1991.

Knappert, Jan. *Myths and Legends of Botswana, Lesotho, and Swaziland*. Leiden: Brill Archive, 1985.

Knappert, Jan. *Myths and Legends of the Congo*. London: Heinemann Educational Books, 1971.

Knappert, Jan. *Pacific Mythology: An Encyclopedia of Myth and Legend*. Wellingborough: Aquarian Press, 1992.

Kng, Hans. *Tracing the Way: Spiritual Dimensions of the World Religions*. New York: A and C Black, 2006.

Knight, Brenda. *Goth Magick: An Enchanted Grimoire*. New York: Citadel Press, 2006.

Knight, Richard Payne, and Thomas Wright. *Sexual Symbolism: A History of Phallic Worship*. Mineola: Courier Dover Publications, 2006.

Knight, Sirona. *Celtic Traditions: Druids, Faeries, and Wiccan Rituals.* New York: Citadel Press, 2000.

Knudsen, Shannon. *Fantastical Creatures and Magical Beasts.* Minneapolis: Lerner Publications, 2009.

Koch, John T., editor. *Celtic Culture: A Historical Encyclopedia.* Volume 1 and Volume 2. Santa Barbara: ABC-CLIO, 2006

Koentjaraningrat and Southeast Asian Studies Program. *Javanese Culture.* New York: Oxford University Press, 1985.

Kohen, Elli. *World History and Myths of Cats.* Lewiston: Edwin Mellen Press, 2003.

Kölbing, Eugen, Johannes Hoops, Arthur Kölbing, and Albert Wagner, editors. *Englische Studien,* Volume 5. Heilbronn: Verlag von Gebr. Henninger, 1882.

Komar, Kathleen L. *Reclaiming Klytemnestra: Revenge or Reconciliation.* Champaign: University of Illinois Press, 2003.

Kosambi, D. D. *An Introduction to the Study of Indian History.* Maharashtra, India: Popular Prakashan, 1996.

Kramer, Samuel Noah. *Sumerian Mythology: A Study of Spiritual and Literary Achievement in the Third Millennium B.C.* Philadelphia: University of Pennsylvania Press, 1972.

Kramrisch, Stella. *The Hindu Temple,* Volume 2. Delhi: Motilal Banarsidass Publ., 1976.

Kramrisch, Stella. *The Presence of Siva.* Princeton: Princeton University Press, 1994.

Krensky, Stephen. *The Bogeyman.* Minneapolis: Lerner-Classroom, 2007.

Krishna, Nanditha. *Sacred Animals of India.* London: Penguin UK, 2014.

Kroeber, A.L. *History of Philippine Civilization as Reflected in Religious Nomenclature,* Volume 19. New York: The Trustees, 1918.

Kroll, Jennifer L. *Wings and Tales: Learning About Birds Through Folklore, Facts, and Fun Activities: Learning About Birds Through Folklore, Facts, and Fun Activities.* Santa Barbara: ABC-CLIO, 2011.

Kropej, Monika. *Supernatural Beings from Slovenian Myth and Folktales.* Ljubljana: Založba ZRC, 2012.

Kruger, John, R. *Uralic and Altaic Series,* Volume 111. Bloomington: Taylor and Francis, 1975.

Kubesh, Kati, Kimm Bellotto, and Niki McNeil. *Mythological Creatures Around the World.* Colma: In the Hands of a Child, 2007.

Kuehn, Sara. *The Dragon in Medieval East Christian and Islamic Art: With a Foreword by Robert Hillenbrand.* Leiden: Brill, 2011.

Kulišić; P. Ž. Petrović, N. Pantelić. "Псоглав," (in Serbian). *Српски Митолошки Речник,* .p. p. 249. Belgrade: Nolit.

Kurnitzky, Horst. *Chollima Korea: A Visit in the Year 23.* Raleigh: Lulu Incorporated, 2006.

Kværne, Per. *Tibet Bon Religion: A Death Ritual of the Tibetan Bonpos.* Leiden: Brill, 1985.

Laderman, Carol. *Wives and Midwives: Childbirth and Nutrition in Rural Malaysia.* Berkeley: University of California Press, 1987.

Lakhnavī, Ghālib, and Abdullah Husain Bilgrami. *The Adventures of Amir Hamza.* New York: Random House Publishing Group, 2012.

Landy, David, and the University of Puerto Rico (Río Piedras Campus). Social Science Research Center. *Tropical Childhood: Cultural Transmission and Learning in a Rural Puerto Rican Village.* New York: Harper and Row, 1959.

Lane, Edward William, editor. *Selections from the Kur-Án, Commonly Known in England as the Koran, with an Interwoven Commentary Translated from the Arabic, Methodically Arranged and Illustrated with Notes Chiefly from Sale's Edition: To Which Is Prefixed an Introduction, Taken from Sale's Preliminary Discourse, with Corrections and Additions: By Edward William Lane.* London: James Madden and Company, 1843.

Lane, Edward William, and Stanley Lane-Poole. *Arab Society in the Time of the Thousand and One Nights.* North Chemsford: Courier Dover Publications, 2004.

Lang, Andrew. *The Crimson Fairy Book.* New York: Longmans, Green, and Company, 1903.

Lang, Andrew. *The Pink Fairy Book.* New York: Dover Publications, Incorporated, 1967.

Lankford, George E. *Native American Legends of the Southeast: Tales from the Natchez, Caddo, Biloxi, Chickasaw, and Other Nations.* Tuscaloosa: University of Alabama Press, 2011.

Lankford, George E. *Reachable Stars: Patterns in the Ethnoastronomy of Eastern North America.* Tuscaloosa: University of Alabama Press, 2007.

Lanzi, Fernando, and Gioia Lanzi. *Saints and Their Symbols: Recognizing Saints in Art and in Popular Images.* Collegeville: Liturgical Press, 2004.

Large, Mark. *Tree Ferns,* Portland: Timber Press, Incorporated, 2009.

Larrington, Carolyne. *King Arthur's Enchantresses: Morgan and Her Sisters in Arthurian Tradition.* New York: I.B.Tauris, 2006.

Larrington, Carolyne. *The Woman's Companion to Mythology.* N.p.: Pandora, 1992.

Larson, Gerald James, C. Scott Littleton, and Jaan Puhvel. *Myth in Indo-European Antiquity.* Berkeley: University of California Press, 1974.

Latham, Minor White. *The Elizabethan Fairies: The Fairies of Folklore and the Fairies of Shakespeare.* Ely: Octagon Books, 1972.

Laubscher, Barend Jacob Frederick. *The Pagan Soul.* Cape Town, Africa: H. Timmins, 1975.

Laufer, Berthold. "Preliminary Notes on Explorations Among the Amoor Tribes," in *American Anthropologist,* Volume 2 edited by the Board of Editorial Board of American Anthropologist, 297–338. New York: George Putman and Son, 1900.

Lavers, Chris. *The Natural History of Unicorns.* London: Granta, 2009.

Lavine, Sigmund A. *The Ghosts the Indians Feared.* New York: Dodd, Mead, 1975.

Lawrence, Bruce B. *Shahrastani on the Indian Religions.* Chicago: Walter de Gruyter, 1976.

Lawrence, Peter, and Mervyn J. Meggitt. *Gods, Ghosts and Men in Melanesia: Some Religions of Australian New Guinea and the New Hebrides.* Oxford: Oxford University Press, 1965.

Lawson, John Cuthbert. *Modern Greek Folklore and Ancient Greek Religion: A Study in Survivals.* Whitefish: Kessinger Publishing, 2003.

Leach, Edmund, Stephen Hugh-Jones, and James Laidlaw. *The Essential Edmund Leach,* Volumes 1–2. New Haven: Yale University Press, 2001.

Leach, María. *Funk and Wagnalls Standard Dictionary of Folklore, Mythology, and Legend.* New York: Funk and Wagnalls, 1972.

Leary, James P. *Wisconsin Folklore*. Madison: University of Wisconsin Press, 1999.

Lecouteux, Claude. *The History of the Vampire*. Paris: Éditions Imago, 1999.

Leddon, Alan. *A Child's Eye View of Fair Folk*. Madison: Spero Publishing, 2011.

Lee, Jonathan H. X., and Kathleen M. Nadeau. *Encyclopedia of Asian American Folklore and Folklife*, Volume 1. Santa Barbara: ABC-CLIO, 2011.

Lee, S. L. *The English Charlemagne Romances: The Boke of Duke Huon of Burdeux, Done into English by Sir John Bourchier, Lord Berners and Printed by Winknnde Ward About 1534 A. D. Edited from the Unique Copy of the First Edition Now in the Possession of Crawford and Balcarres, with an Introduction by S. L. Lee*. London: Trubner and Company, 1887.

Leee, Kit Antares, and Charles Spaegel. *Tanah Tujuh: Close Encounters with the Temuan Mythos*. Kuala Lumpur, Malaysia: Silverfish Books, 2007.

Leeming, David Adams. *A Dictionary of Asian Mythology*. New York: Oxford University Press, 2001.

Leeming, David Adams. *A Dictionary of Creation Myths*. Oxford: Oxford University Press, 1994.

Leeming, David Adams. *The Oxford Companion to World Mythology*. Oxford: Oxford University Press, 2005.

Leeming, David Adams. *The World of Myth: An Anthology*. Oxford: Oxford University Press, 1991.

Leeming, David Adams, and Jake Page. *Myths, Legends, and Folktales of America: An Anthology*. Oxford: Oxford University Press, 1999.

Leen, Catherine, and Niamh Thornton. *International Perspectives on Chicana/O Studies: "This World Is My Place."*, New York: Routledge, 2013.

Legey, Françoise, translated by Lucy Hotz. *The Folklore of Morocco*. London: G. Allen and Unwin, Limited, 1935.

Lehner, Ernst, and Johanna Lehner. *Big Book of Dragons, Monsters, and Other Mythical Creatures*. Mineola: Courier Dover Publications, 2004.

Leick, Gwendolyn. *A Dictionary of Ancient Near Eastern Mythology*. London: Routledge, 2002.

Leid, Josanne. *Myths and Maxims: A Catalog of Superstitions, Spirits and Sayings of Trinidad and Tobago, and the Caribbean*. N.p.: Josanne, 2014.

Leland, Charles Godfrey. *The Algonquin Legends of New England (Extended Annotated Edition)*. Altenmunster: Jazzybee Verlag, 2012.

Leland, Charles Godfrey. *Gypsy Sorcery and Fortune Telling: Illustrated by Incantations, Specimens of Medical Magic, Anecdotes, and Tales*. New York: Charles Scribbner and Sons, 1891.

Lemprière, John. *Bibliotheca Classica: Or, a Dictionary of All the Principal Names and Terms Relating to the Geography, Topography, History, Literature, and Mythology of Antiquity and of the Ancients: With a Chronological Table*. New York: William E. Dean, 1853.

Lemprière, John. *A Classical Dictionary, Containing a Copious Account of All the Proper Names Mentioned in Ancient Authors with the Value of Coins, Weights, and Measures Used Among the Greeks and Romans*. London: T. Cadell, 1839.

Lenormant, François. *Chaldean Magic: Its Origin and Development*. Whitefish: Kessinger Publishing, 1994.

Leo (Archipresbyter), edited by Roger Telfryn Pritchard. *The History of Alexander's Battles: Historia De Preliis, the J1 Version*. Toronto: Pontifical Institute of Mediaeval Studies, 1992.

le Roux, Deon. *The Myth of 'Roo*. Raleigh: Lulu.com, 2011.

Levack, Brian P. *The Witch-Hunt in Early Modern Europe*. Essex, England: Pearson Longman, 2006.

Leviton, Richard. *Encyclopedia of Earth Myths: An Insider's A-Z Guide to Mythic People, Places, Objects, and Events Central to the Earth's Visionary Geography*. Norfolk: Hampton Roads Publishing, 2005.

Leviton, Richard. *Hierophantic Landscapes: Lighting Up Chalice Well, Lake Tahoe, Yosemite, the Rondanes, and Oaxaca*. Bloomington: iUniverse, 2011.

Lewis, D. Geraint. *Gomer's Dictionary for Young People*. Llandysul: Gwasg Gomer, 1994.

Lewis, James R. *The Astrology Book: The Encyclopedia of Heavenly Influences*. Michigan: Visible Ink Press, 2003.

Lewis, Maureen Warner. *Guinea's Other Suns: The African Dynamic in Trinidad Culture*. Dover: The Majority Press, 1991.

Li, Michelle Ilene Osterfeld. *Ambiguous Bodies: Reading the Grotesque in Japanese Setsuwa Tales*. Stanford: Stanford University Press, 2009.

Licauco, Jaime T. *Dwarves and Other Nature Spirits: Their Importance to Man*. Quezon City: Rex Bookstore, Incorporated, 2005.

Lieban, Richard Warren. *Cebuano Sorcery: Malign Magic in the Philippines*. Berkeley: University of California Press, 1977.

Lim, David C. L. *The Infinite Longing for Home: Desire and the Nation in Selected Writings of Ben Okri and K.S. Maniam*. Amsterdam: Rodopi, 2005.

Lindahl, Carl, John McNamara, and John Lindow. *Medieval Folklore: A Guide to Myths, Legends, Tales, Beliefs, and Customs*. Oxford: Oxford University Press, 2000.

Lindow, John. *Handbook of Norse Mythology*. Santa Barbara: ABC-CLIO, 2001.

Linger, Daniel Touro. *Anthropology Through a Double Lens: Public and Personal Worlds in Human Theory*. Philadelphia: University of Pennsylvania Press, 2011.

Link, Theodore, and Rose McCarthy. *Argentina: A Primary Source Cultural Guide*. New York: The Rosen Publishing Group, 2004.

Littell, Eliakim. "A Malagasy Forest," in *The Living Age*, Volume 200 edited by Eliakim Littell and Robert S. Littell, 161–169. Boston: Living Age Company Incorporated, 1894.

Littell, Eliakim, Robert S. Littell, and the Making of America Project., "Scottish, Shetlandic, and Germanic Water Tales," in *The Living Age*, Volume 150, pages 809–17. Boston: The Living Age Company, Incorporated, 1881.

Littleton, C. Scott, and Marshall Cavendish Corporation. *Gods, Goddesses, and Mythology*, Volume 1. Tarrytown: Marshall Cavendish, 2005.

Littleton, C. Scott, and the Marshall Cavendish Corporation. *Gods, Goddesses, and Mythology*, Volume 11. Tarrytown: Marshall Cavendish, 2005.

Liverpool, Hollis. *Rituals of Power and Rebellion: The Carnival Tradition in Trinidad and Tobago, 1763–1962*. Chicago: Research Associates School Times, 2001.

Loar, Julie. *Goddesses for Every Day: Exploring the Wisdom and Power of the Divine Feminine Around the World*. Novato: New World Library, 2010.

Locher, Gottfried Wilhelm. *The Serpent in Kwakiutl Religion: A Study in Primitive Culture*. Leiden: E. J. Brill Limited, 1932.

Lochtefeld, James G. *The Illustrated Encyclopedia of Hinduism: A-M.* New York: The Rosen Publishing Group, 2002.

Lomas, Adriano García. *Mitología Y Supersticiones De Cantabria.* Santander: Ediciones Librería Estudio, 2000.

The London Encyclopaedia: Or Universal Dictionary of Science, Art, Literature, and Practical Mechanics, Comprising a Popular View of the Present State of Knowledge, Volume 11. Minneapolis: Thomas Tegg and the University of Minnesota, 1829.

Lopatin, Ivan Alexis. *The Cult of the Dead Among the Natives of the Amur Basin.* Paris: Mouton, 1960.

Lopez, Mellie Leandicho. *A Handbook of Philippine Festivals.* Honolulu: University of Hawaii Press, 2003.

Lower, Mark Antony. *The Curiosities of Heraldry.* London: John Russell Smith, 1845.

Loxton, Daniel, and Donald R. Prothero. *Abominable Science: Origins of the Yeti, Nessie, and Other Famous Cryptids.* New York: Columbia University Press, 2013.

Loy, David. *The World Is Made of Stories.* Somerville: Wisdom Publications Incorporated, 2010.

Lurker, Manfred. *Dictionary of Gods and Goddesses, Devils and Demons.* London: Routledge Kegan and Paul, 1987.

Lynch, Patricia Ann, and Jeremy Roberts. *African Mythology, A to Z.* New York: Infobase Publishing, 2010.

Lynch, Patricia Ann, and Jeremy Roberts. *Native American Mythology A to Z.* New York: Infobase Publishing, 2010.

Lyon, William S. *Encyclopedia of Native American Healing.* New York: W. W. Norton and Company, 1996.

Maberry, Johathan. *Vampire Universe: The Dark World of the Supernatural Beings That Haunt Us, Hunt Us, and Hunger for Us.* Secacus: Citadel; Press, 1996.

Maberry, Jonathan, and David F. Kramer. *The Cryptopedia: A Dictionary of the Weird, Strange, and Downright Bizarre.* New York: Citadel Press, 2007.

Maberry, Jonathan, and David F. Kramer. *They Bite: Endless Cravings of Supernatural Predators.* New York: Citadel Press, 2009.

Maberry, Jonathan, and Janice Gable Bashman. *Wanted Undead or Alive: Vampire Hunters and Other Kick-Ass Enemies of Evil.* New York: Citadel Press, 2010.

Mabie, Hamilton Wright, editor. *Young Folks' Treasury: Childhood's Favorites and Fairy Stories.* New York: University society, Incorporated, 1909.

MacCulloch, John Arnott, Jan Máchal, and Louis Herbert Gray. *Celtic Mythology,* Volume 3. Boston: Marshall Jones Company, 1918.

MacDonald, Margaret Read. *Traditional Storytelling Today: An International Sourcebook.* London: Routledge, 2013.

Macdonell, Arthur Anthony. *Vedic Mythology.* Strassburg: K. J. Trübner, 1897.

Mack, Carol K., and Dinah Mack. *A Field Guide to Demons, Fairies, Fallen Angels, and Other Subversive Spirits.* New York: Henry Holt and Company, 1998.

Mackenzie, Andrew. *Dracula Country: Travels and Folk Beliefs in Romania.* London: Barker, 1977.

Mackenzie, Donald Alexander. *Scottish Folk-Lore and Folk Life: Studies in Race, Culture and Tradition.* Glasgow: Blackie and Sons, Limited, 1935.

MacKenzie, Shawn. *The Dragon Keeper's Handbook.* Woodbury: Llewellyn Worldwide, 2011.

MacKenzie, Shawn. *Dragons for Beginners: Ancient Creatures in a Modern World.* Woodbury: Llewellyn Worldwide, 2012.

Mackerle, Ivan "In Search of the Killer Worm of Mongolia," in *Far Out Adventures: The Best of World Explorer Magazine* edited by David Hatcher Childress. 198–201. Kempton: Adventures Unlimited Press, 2001.

MacKillop, James. *Dictionary of Celtic Mythology.* New York: Oxford University Press, 1998.

Mackley, Jude S. *The Legend of St. Brendan: A Comparative Study of the Latin and Anglo-Norman Versions.* Leiden: Brill, 2008.

Maclagan, Robert Craig. *Scottish Myths: Notes on Scottish History and ˙Tradition.* Edinburgh: Maclachlan and Stewart, 1882.

Macleod, Norman. *a Dictionary of the Gaelic Language, in Two Parts: I. Gaelic and English.—II. English and Gaeli.* Edinburgh: W. R. M'Phun, 1853.

Madden, Richard Robert. *The Shrines and Sepulchres of the Old and New World: Records of Pilgrimages in Many Lands and Researches Connected with the History of Places Remarkable for Memorials of the Dead, or Monuments of a Sacred Character; Including Notices of the Funeral Customs of the Principal Nations Ancient and Modern,* Volume 1. London: T. C. Newby, 1851.

Magasich-Airola, Jorge, and Jean-Marc de Beer. *America Magica (2nd Edition): When Renaissance Europe Thought It Had Conquered Paradise.* London: Anthem Press, 2007.

Maggi, Armando. *In the Company of Demons: Unnatural Beings, Love, and Identity in the Italian Renaissance.* Chicago: University of Chicago Press, 2006.

Magnanini, Suzanne. *Fairy-Tale Science: Monstrous Generation in the Tales of Straparola and Basile.* Toronto: University of Toronto Press, 2008.

Magnavita, Sonja, Lassina Koté, Peter Breunig, and Oumarou A. Idé. *Crossroads / Carrefour Sahel: Cultural and Technological Developments in First Millennium BC/AD West Africa.* Frankfurt: Africa Magna Verlag, 2009.

Magnússon, Eiríkr, and William Morris, translators. *Völsunga Saga: The Story of the Volsungs and Niblungs, with Certain Songs from the Elder Edda.* London: F. S. Ellis, 1870.

Magyar Tudományos Akadémia. *Acta Ethnographica Hungarica,* Volume 53, Issue 2. Budapest: Akadémiai Kiadó, 2008.

Mahaffy, John Pentland, and Archibald Henry Sayce. *A History of Classical Greek Literature.* London: Longmans, Green, 1883.

Mahanama-sthavira, Thera. *Mahavamsa: The Great Chronicle of Sri Lanka.* Fremont: Jain Publishing Company, 1999.

Maher, Vanessa. *Anthropology of Breast-Feeding: Natural Law or Social Construct.* London: Berg Publishers, 1992.

Mahon, Michael Patrick. *Ireland's Fairy Lore.* Boston: Thomas J. Flynn, and Company, 1919.

Maisie, Suzanne. *Land of the Firebird.* New York: Simon & Schuster: 1980.

Malalasekera, Gunapala Piyasena, editor. *Encyclopaedia of Buddhism,* Volume 4, Issue 2. Ceylon: Government of Ceylon, 1984.

Malcolm, Sir John. *Sketches of Persia,* Volume 1. New York: Cassell, limited, 1888.

Malinowski, Sharon. *The Gale Encyclopedia of Native American Tribes: Northeast, Southeast, Caribbean.* Detroit: Gale, 1998.

Manansala, Paul Kekai. *Quests of the Dragon and Bird Clan.* Raleigh: Lulu.com, 2006.

Mandeville, Sir John. *The Travels of Sir John Mandeville*. New York: Penguin, 1983.

Manguel, Alberto, Eric Beddows, James Cook, Graham Greenfield, and Gianni Guadalupi. *The Dictionary of Imaginary Places*. Boston: Houghton Mifflin Harcourt, 2000.

Mann, Joel F. *An International Glossary of Place Name Elements*. Lanham: Scarecrow Press, 2005.

Manser, Martin H. *The Facts on File Dictionary of Allusions*. New York: Infobase Publishing, 2008.

Markham, Sir Clements Robert. *The Voyages of Sir James Caldwell to the East Indies, Works Issued by the Hakluyt Society*, Volume 56. London: Hakluyt Society, 1877.

Markman, Sidney David. *The Horse in Greek Art*. New York: Biblo and Tannen Publishers, 1969.

Maro, Publius Vergilius, translated by John Benson Rose. *The Eclogues and Georgics of Virgil Translated by J.B. Rose*. London: Dorrell and Sons, 1866.

Martin, Joel W. *Sacred Revolt: The Muskogees' Struggle for a New World*. Boston: Beacon Press, 1993.

Marwick, Max. *Witchcraft and Sorcery: Selected Readings*. New York: Penguin Books, 1982.

Masters, Anthony. *The Natural History of the Vampire*. London: Hart-Davis, 1972.

Masters, Robert E. L. *Eros and Evil: The Sexual Psychopathology of Witchcraft, Contains the Complete Text of Sinistrari's Demoniality*. New York: Viking Press, 1974.

Mathers, Samuel Liddell MacGregor, and J. W. Brodie-Innes. *The Sorcerer and His Apprentice: Unknown Hermetic Writings of S.L. MacGregor Mathers and J.W. Brodie-Innes*. Wellingborough: Aquarian, 1983.

Matson, Gienna, and Jeremy Roberts. *Celtic Mythology A to Z*. New York: Infobase Publishing, 2010.

Matthews, John, and Caitlin Matthews. *The Element Encyclopedia of Magical Creatures: The Ultimate A-Z of Fantastic Beings from Myth and Magic*. New York: Barnes and Nobel, 2005.

Matthews, John, and Caitlin Matthews. *The Encyclopaedia of Celtic Myth and Legend: A Definitive Sourcebook of Magic, Vision, and Lore*. London: Globe Pequot, 2004.

Mayer, Fanny Hagin, editor. *The Yanagita Kunio Guide to the Japanese Folk Tale*. Bloomington: Indiana University Press, 1986.

Mayor, Adrienne. *The First Fossil Hunters: Dinosaurs, Mammoths, and Myth in Greek and Roman Times*. Princeton: Princeton University Press, 2011.

McAndrew, John P. *People of Power: A Philippine Worldview of Spirit Encounters*. Quezon City, Philippines: Atenco de Manila University Press, 2001.

McBeath, Alastair. *Tiamat's Brood: An Investigation into the Dragons of Ancient Mesopotamia*. London: Dragon's Head, 1999.

McCall, Gerrie. *Dragons: Fearsome Monsters from Myth and Fiction*. New York: Tangerine Press, 2007.

McCarta, Robertson, and Nelles Verlag. *Spain: North*. London: Robertson McCarta, 1991.

McClintock, John, and James Strong. *Cyclopaedia of Biblical, Theological, and Ecclesiastical Literature*, Volume 1. New York: Harper and Brothers, 1891.

McConnell, Winder, Werner Wunderlich, Frank Gentry, and Ulrich Mueller. *The Nibelungen Tradition: An Encyclopedia*. London: Routledge, 2013.

McCoy, Edain. *Celtic Myth and Magick: Harness the Power of the Gods and Goddesses*. St. Paul: Llewellyn Worldwide, 1995.

McCoy, Edain. *A Witch's Guide to Faery Folk: Reclaiming Our Working Relationship with Invisible Helpers*. St. Paul: Llewellyn Publications, 1995.

McCullough, Joseph, and Peter Dennis. *Dragonslayers: From Beowulf to St. George*. London: Osprey Publishing, 2013.

McCutcheon, Marc. *The Wordsworth Word Finder*. Hertfordshire: Wordsworth, 1999.

McDonough, Christopher Michael. "Carna, Proca and the Strix on the Kalends of June," *Transactions of the American Philological Association*, Volume 127. 1997.

McHugh, James Noel. *Hantu Hantu: An Account of Ghost Belief in Modern Malaya*. Singapore: Donald Moore for Eastern Universities Press, 1959.

McKee, Richard. *The Clan of the Flapdragon and Other Adventures in Etymology*. Tuscaloosa: University of Alabama Press, 1997.

McLeish, Kenneth. *Myth: Myths and Legends of the World Explored*. New York: Facts on File, 1996.

McNally, Raymond T. *In Search of Dracula: The History of Dracula and Vampires*. Boston: Houghton Mifflin Harcourt, 1994.

McNamee, Gregory. *A Desert Bestiary: Folklore, Literature, and Ecological Thought from the World's Dry Places*. Boulder: Big Earth Publishing, 1996.

McNeilly, Mark R. *Sun Tzu and the Art of Modern Warfare: Updated Edition*. Oxford: Oxford University Press, 2014.

McQuillan, Martin. *The Narrative Reader*. New York: Psychology Press, 2000.

Medical Aspects of Human Sexuality, Volume 3. Boston: Cahners Publishing Company, 1969.

Meier, C. A. *Healing Dream and Ritual: Ancient Incubation and Modern Psychotherapy*. Einsiedeln: Daimon, 2003.

Meletinskiĭ, Eleazar Moiseevich, translated by Guy Lanoue. *The Poetics of Myth, Volume 1944 of Garland Reference Library of the Humanities*. New York: Taylor and Francis Group, 1998.

Melton, J. Gordon. *Encyclopedia of Occultism*. Detroit: Gale Research Incorporated, 1996.

Melton, J. Gordon. *The Vampire Book: The Encyclopedia of the Undead*. Michigan: Visible Ink Press, 1999.

Mencken, Henry L. *American Language Supplement 1*. New York: Knopf Doubleday Publishing Group, 2012.

Menon, Ramesh. *The Mahabharata: A Modern Rendering*, Volume 1. Bloomington: iUniverse, 2006.

Mercatante, Anthony S. *Who's Who in Egyptian Mythology*. New York: Barnes and Noble Books, 1998.

Merriam-Webster's Encyclopedia of Literature. Springfield: Merriam-Webster, 1995.

Metham, John, and Stephen F. Page. *Amoryus and Cleopes*. Kalamazoo: Published for TEAMS by Medieval Institute Publications, 1999.

Methodist Book Concern. *The Methodist Review*, Volume 35. New York: The Methodist Book Concern, 1883.

Meurger, Michel, and Claude Gagnon. *Lake Monster Traditions: A Cross-Cultural Analysis*. London: Fortean Tomes, 1988.

Meyer, Elard Hugo. *Mythologie Der Germanen*. Strazburg, Germany: Karl J. Trübner, 1903.

Meyer, Matthew. *The Night Parade of One Hundred Demons: A Field Guide to Japanese Yokai*. N.p.: Matthew Meyer, 2012.

Miguel de Barandiarán, José, and Jesús Altuna. *Selected Writings of José Miguel De Barandiarán: Basque Prehistory and Ethnography*. Reno: Center for Basque Studies, University of Nevada, 2009.

Millington, Ellen J. *Heraldry in History, Poetry, and Romance.* London: Chapman and Hall, 1858.

Milton, John, and Alastair Fowler. *Paradise Lost.* London: Longman, 1998.

Minissale, Gregory. *Framing Consciousness in Art: Transcultural Perspectives.* Amsterdam: Rodopi, 2009.

Mishra, P. K. *Studies in Hindu and Buddhist Art.* New Delhi: Abhinav Publications, 1999.

Mitchell, Laurence. *Slow Norfolk and Suffolk.* Bristol: Bradt Travel Guides, 2010.

Mittman, Asa. *Maps and Monsters in Medieval England.* London: Routledge, 2013.

Mittman, Asa Simon, and Peter J. Dendle, editors. *The Ashgate Research Companion to Monsters and the Monstrous.* Burlington: Ashgate Publishing, Limited, 2012.

Mizuki, Shigeru. *Mujara 5: Tōhoku, Kyūshū-Hen.* Japan: Soft Garage, 2005.

Mladen, Davidovic. *Dutch-English, English-Dutch Dictionary: With a Brief Introduction to Dutch Grammar.* New York: Hippocrene Books, 1990.

Moazami, Mahnaz. *Wrestling with the Demons of the Pahlavi Widēwdād: Transcription, Translation, and Commentary.* Leiden: Brill, 2014.

Mode, Heinz Adolf. *Fabulous Beasts and Demons.* New York: Penguin Group (USA) Incorporated, 1975.

Mollett, John William. *An Illustrated Dictionary of Words Used in Art and Archaeology: Explaining Terms Frequently Used in Works on Architecture, Arms, Bronzes, Christian Art, Colour, Costume, Decoration, Devices, Emblems, Heraldry, Lace, Personal Ornaments, Pottery, Painting, Sculpture, Etc., with Their Derivations.* London: Sampson Low, Marston, Searle, and Rivington, 1883.

Monaghan, Patricia. *The Encyclopedia of Celtic Mythology and Folklore.* New York: Infobase Publishing, 2004.

Monaghan, Patricia. *Encyclopedia of Goddesses and Heroines: Revised.* Novato: New World Library, 2014.

Monaghan, Patricia. *Goddesses in World Culture,* Volume 1. Santa Barbara: ABC-CLIO, 2010.

Monaghan, Patricia. *New Book of Goddesses and Heroines.* St. Paul: Llewellyn Publications, 1997.

Monaghan, Patricia. *Women in Myth and Legend.* London: Junction Books, 1981.

Monier-Williams, Monier. *A Sanskrit-English Dictionary.* London: Clarendon, 1872.

Monier-Williams, *Sanskrit-English Dictionary,* 572

Moon, Beverly Ann, and George Elder. *Encyclopedia of Archetypal Symbolism.* Boston: Shambhala, 1991.

Mooney, Carla. *Dragons.* San Diego: Capstone, 2011.

Moore, Arthur William. *The Folk-Lore of the Isle of Man: Being an Account of Its Myths, Legends, Superstitions, Customs, and Proverbs, Collected from Many Sources; with a General Introduction; and with Explanatory Notes to Each Chapter.* London: David Nutt, 1891.

Moore, Tara. *Christmas: The Sacred to Santa.* London: Reaktion Books, 2014.

Moorey, Teresa. *The Fairy Bible: The Definitive Guide to the World of Fairies.* New York: Sterling Publishing Company, 2008.

Morgan, Octavius, and Thomas Wakeman. *Notes on Wentwood, Castle Troggy, and Llanvair Castle.* Newport: Monmouthshire and Caerleon Antiquarian Association, by H. Mullock, 1863.

Mortensen, Karl. *A Handbook of Norse Mythology.* Mineola: Courier Dover Publications, 2003.

Mountain, Harry. *The Celtic Encyclopedia,* Volume 3. Aveiro: Universal-Publishers, 1998.

Mountain, Harry. *The Celtic Encyclopedia,* Volume 5. Aveiro: Universal-Publishers, 1998.

Mozhaev, Boris A., and Alexander I. Solzhenitsyn. *'Lively' and Other Stories.* Surry: Hodgson Press, 2007.

Muir, Henry Dupee. *Songs and Other Fancies.* Chicago: Henry Dupee Muir, 1901.

Muir, John. *Original Sanskrit Texts on the Origin and History of the People of India, Their Religions and Institutions.* London: Trübner and Company, 1868.

Müller, Friedrich Max. *Vedic Hymns: Hymns to the Maruts, Rudra, Vâyu, and Vâta.* Oxford: Clarendon Press, 1891.

Müller, Wilhelm Max, and Sir James George Scott. *Egyptian [Mythology].* Boston: Marshall Jones Company, 1918.

Mumford, Stan. *Himalayan Dialogue: Tibetan Lamas and Gurung Shamans in Nepal.* Madison: University of Wisconsin Press, 1989.

Munro, Alice. *Ainu Creed and Cult.* New York: Routledge, 1996.

Murakami, Kenji. *Yōkai Jiten.* Tokyo: Mainichi Shimbun Press, 2000.

Murray, Alexander Stuart. *Manual of Mythology: Greek and Roman, Norse and Old German, Hindoo and Egyptian Mythology.* New York: Scribner, Armstrong, and Company, 1876.

Murray, J. *A Classical Manual, Being a Mythological, Historical, and Geographical Commentary on Pope's Homer, and Dryden's Aeneid of Virgil: With a Copious Index.* London: J. Murray, 1833.

Muskett, Milford B. *Identity, H'Ozh'O, Change, and Land: Navajo Environmental Perspectives.* Madison: University of Wisconsin, 2003.

Nan Nü. *Men, Women, and Gender in Early and Imperial China.* Boston: Brill, 1999.

Narváez, Peter. *The Good People: New Fairylore Essays.* Lexington: University Press of Kentucky, 1997.

Naso, Publius Ovidius, and translated by Henry Thomas Riley. *The Fasti, Tristia, Pontic Epistles, the Metamorphoses. the Heroides ... the Amours ... and Minor Works of Ovid, Literally Translated into English Prose, with Copious Notes and Explanations.* London: G. H. Bohn, 1851.

Nath, Samir. *Dictionary of Vedanta.* New Delhi: Sarup and Sons, 2002.

National Museum of Canada, Geological Survey of Canada. *Bulletin,* Issue 119. Ottawa: F.A. Acland, 1950.

Neff, Mary L. "Pima and Papago Legends," in *The Journal of American Folk-Lore,* Volume XXV, edited by the American Folklore Society, pages 51–65. Lancaster: American Folk-lore Society, 1913.

Nelson, Edward William. "The Eskimo About Bering Straits," in *Annual Reports,* Volume 18, Part 1, edited by the United States American Ethnology Bureau, 452–464. Washington D. C.: Washington Printing Office, 1899.

Newman, Jacqueline M. *Food Culture in China.* Westport: Greenwood Publishing Group, 2004.

Newman, Patrick. *Tracking the Weretiger: Supernatural Man-Eaters of India, China and Southeast Asia.* Jefferson, NC: McFarland, 2012.

Newton, Michael. *Encyclopedia of Cryptozoology: A Global Guide to Hidden Animals and Their Pursuers.* Jefferson, NC: McFarland, 2005.

Newton, Michael. *Hidden Animals: A Field Guide to Bat-squatch, Chupacabra, and Other Elusive Creatures*. Santa Barbara: ABC-CLIO, 2009.

Nichols, Robert E. *Birds of Algonquin Legend*. Ann Arbor: University of Michigan Press, 1995.

Nickell, Joe. *The Mystery Chronicles: More Real-Life X-Files*. Lexington: University Press of Kentucky, 2004.

Nigg, Joe. *The Book of Fabulous Beasts: A Treasury of Writings from Ancient Times to the Present*. Oxford: Oxford University Press, 1999.

Nigg, Joseph. *Sea Monsters: A Voyage Around the World's Most Beguiling Map*. Chicago: University of Chicago Press, 2014.

Niles, Doug. *Dragons: The Myths, Legends, and Lore*. Avon: F+W Media, 2013.

The Nineteenth Century and After: A Monthly Review, vol. 63, Jan.-June. London: Spottiswoode and Company, 1908.

Ninness, James. *Macabre Rising: Tales of Man, Myth and Monster*. N.p.: James Ninness, 2012.

Norroena Society. *The Asatrii Edda: Sacred Lore of the North*. Bloomington: iUniverse, Incorporated, 2009.

Nozaki, Kiyoshi. *Kitsuné: Japan's Fox of Mystery, Romance and Humor*. Tokyo: Hokuseido Press, 1961.

Nozedar, Adele. *The Secret Language of Birds: A Treasury of Myths, Folklore and Inspirational True Stories*. London: HarperElement, 2006.

Nuzum, Eric. *The Dead Travel Fast: Stalking Vampires from Nosferatu to Count Chocula*. New York: Macmillan, 2007.

Oa, Tin Mg. *Aspects of Myanmar Culture*. Yangon: Cho-Tay-Than Publishing House, 2003.

Oehlenschläger, Adam Gottlob, and William Edward Frye, translator. *The Gods of the North: An Epic Poem*. London: W. Pickering, 1845.

Oesterle, Joe, Tim Cridland, and Mark Moran. *Weird Las Vegas and Nevada: Your Alternative Travel Guide to Sin City and the Silver State*. New York: Sterling Publishing Company, 2007.

Ogden, Daniel. *A Companion to Greek Religion*. West Sussex: John Wiley and Sons, 2010.

Ogden, Daniel. *Dragons, Serpents, and Slayers in the Classical and Early Christian Worlds: A Sourcebook*. New York: Oxford University Press, 2013.

Ogden, Daniel. *Drakon: Dragon Myth and Serpent Cult in the Greek and Roman Worlds*. Oxford: Oxford University Press, 2013.

Oinas, Felix J. *Essays on Russian Folklore and Mythology*. Bloomington: Slavica Publishers, 1985.

Olcott, William Tyler. *Star Lore of All Ages: A Collection of Myths, Legends, and Facts Concerning the Constellations of the Northern Hemisphere*. New York: George P. Putnam's Sons, 1911.

Oldale, John. *A World of Curiosities: Surprising, Interesting, and Downright Unbelievable Facts from Every Nation on the Planet*. New York: Penguin, 2012.

Oliphant, Samuel Grant. "The Story of the Strix: Ancient," *Transactions and Proceedings of the American Philological Association,'* Vol. 44. 1913.

Oliver, Douglas L. *Oceania: The Native Cultures of Australia and the Pacific Islands*, Volume 1. Honolulu: University of Hawaii Press, 1989.

Oliver, Evelyn Dorothy, and James R. Lewis. *Angels A to Z*. Michigan: Visible Ink Press, 2008.

Olrik, Axel. *The Heroic Legends of Denmark*. New York: American-Scandinavian Foundation, 1919.

Olsen, Karin E., and L. A. J. R. Houwen. *Monsters and the Monstrous in Medieval Northwest Europe*. Sterling: Peeters Publishers, 2001.

Olupǫna, Jacob Obafẹmi Kẹhinde. *Beyond Primitivism: Indigenous Religious Traditions and Modernity*. London: Psychology Press, 2004.

Opler, Edward Morris. *Myths and Tales of the Jicarilla Apache Indians*. Mineola: Courier Dover Publications, 2012.

Orbell, Margaret Rose. *A Concise Encyclopedia of Māori Myth and Legend*. Christchurch: Canterbury University Press, 1998.

Orchard, Andy. *Cassell's Dictionary of Norse Myth and Legend*. London: Cassell, 2002.

Orchard, Andy. *Pride and Prodigies: Studies in the Monsters of the Beowulf-Manuscript*. Toronto: University of Toronto Press, 2003.

Oregon Historical Quarterly, Volumes 56–57. N.p.: W.H. Leeds, State Printer, 1955.

Ornan, Tallay. *Orbis Biblicus Et Orientalis / Bd.213*. Paulusrerlag Fribourg: Saint-Paul, 2005.

O'Rourke, P. J. *Give War a Chance: Eyewitness Accounts of Mankind's Struggle Against Tyranny, Injustice and Alcohol-Free Beer*. New York: Grove Press, 2007.

Ovid, translated by Henry Thomas Riley. *The Metamorphoses of Ovid*. London: H.G. Bohn, 1858.

Ovid and Stanley Lombardo. *Metamorphoses*. Indianapolis: Hackett Publishing, 2010.

Page, Michael F., and Robert R. Ingpen. *Encyclopedia of Things That Never Were: Creatures, Places, and People*. New York: Viking Press, 1987.

Paine, Lauran. *The Hierarchy of Hell*. New York: Hippocrene Books, 1972.

Pak, Yŏng-dae. *From Prehistory to the Joseon Period: Essential Korean Art*. Seoul, Hyeonamsa, 2004.

Palmer, Abram Smythe. *Folk-Etymology: A Dictionary of Verbal Corruptions or Words Perverted in Form or Meaning, by False Derivation or Mistaken Analogy*. London: Johnson Reprint, 1882.

Palmer, Jessica Dawn. *The Dakota Peoples: A History of the Dakota, Lakota and Nakota Through 1863*. Jefferson, NC: McFarland, 2011.

Palmer, Robin. *Dragons, Unicorns, and Other Magical Beasts: A Dictionary of Fabulous Creatures with Old Tales and Verses About Them*. New York: H. Z. Walck, 1966.

Pálsson, Hermann. *The Book of Settlements: Landnámabók*. Manitoba: University of Manitoba Press, 2007.

Papinius, Publius Statius, and George Calder. *Togail Na Tebe, the Thebaid of Statius: The Irish Text*. Cambridge: Cambridge University Press Archive, 1922.

Parada, Carlos. *Genealogical Guide to Greek Mythology*. Lund C. Bloms Boktryckeri, 1993.

Paraiso, Salvador, and Jose Juan Paraiso. *The Balete Book: A Collection of Demons, Monsters, Elves and Dwarfs from the Philippine Lower Mythology*. Quezon City, Philippines: Giraffe Books, 2003.

Paré, Ambroise. *On Monsters and Marvels*. Chicago: University of Chicago Press, 1995.

Parker, James, and Henry Gough. *A Glossary of Terms Used in Heraldry*. Oxford: C. E. Tuttle Company, 1970.

Parker, Janet, Alice Mills, and Julie Stanton. *Mythology: Myths, Legends and Fantasies*. Cape Town: Struik, 2007.

Parmeshwaranand, Swami. *Encyclopaedic Dictionary of Puranas*, Volume 1. New Delhi: Sarup and Sons, 2001.

Parratt, John. *Papuan Belief and Ritual*. New York: Vantage Press, 1976.

Partridge, Eric. *A Dictionary of Slang and Unconventional English*. London: Routledge, 2006.

Paschalis, Michael. *Virgil's Aeneid: Semantic Relations and Proper Names*. New York: Oxford University Press, 1997.

Pattanaik, Devdutt. *The Goddess in India: The Five Faces of the Eternal Feminine*. Rochester: Inner Traditions / Bear and Company, 2000.

Paul, Jean. *The Literary Works of Leonardo Da Vinci, Compiled and Edited from the Original Manuscripts*. London: Sampson Low, Marston, Searle, and Rivington, 1883.

Pauley, Daniel C. *Pauley's Guide: A Dictionary of Japanese Martial Arts and Culture*. Dolores: Samantha Pauley, 2009.

Paulus, Aegineta. *The Seven Books of Paulus Aegineta: Translated from the Greek, with a Commentary Embracing a Complete View of the Knowledge Possessed by the Greeks, Romans, and Arabians on All Subjects Connected with Medicine and Surgery by Francis Adams. II.* London: Sydenham Society, 1846.

Pausanias, translated by Arthur Richard Shilleto. *Pausanias' Description of Greece*, Volume 1. New York: George Bell and Sons, 1900.

Pausanias, translated by Sir James George Frazer. *Commentary on Books II-V: Corinth, Laconia, Messenia, Elis*. New York: Macmillan, 1898.

Pavlidis, Stephen J. *On and Off the Beaten Path: The Central and Southern Bahamas Guide: From South Florida to the Turks and Caicos*. N.p.: Seaworthy Publications, 2002.

Peacock, Mable. "The Folklore of Lincolnshire," in *Folklore*, Volume 12, edited by Joseph Jacobs, Alfred Trübner Nutt, Arthur Robinson Wright, William Crooke, 161–256. London: David Nutt, 1901.

Pedrini, Lura, and Guilio T. Pedrini. *Serpent Imagery and Symbolism*. New Haven: Rowman and Littlefield, 1966.

Pellowski, Anne. *Polish Folktales and Folklore*. Englewood: Libraries Unlimited, 2009.

Penard, A. P., and T. G. Penard. "Surinam Folk-Tales," in *The Journal of American Folk-Lore*, Volume 7 of *Bibliographical and Special Series of the American Folklore Society* edited by the American Folklore Society, 239–251. Lancaster: American Folk-lore Society, 1917.

Penwyche, Gossamer. *The World of Fairies*. New York: Sterling Publishing, 2001.

Penz, Eric. *Cryptid: The Lost Legacy of Lewis and Clark*. Bloomington: Booktango, 2013.

Perkins, Dorothy. *Encyclopedia of China: History and Culture*. London: Routledge, 2013.

Perkowski, Jan Louis. *The Darkling: A Treatise on Slavic Vampirism*. Columbus: Slavica Publishers, 1989.

Perkowski, Jan Louis. *Vampires of the Slavs*. Columbus, Ohio: Slavica Publishers, 1976.

Perrault, Charles. *Histoires Ou Contes Du Temps Passé Avec Des Moralités*. Montpezat-en-Provence: AURORÆ LIBRI, Éditeur, 1982.

Perry, Thomas Sergeant. *A History of Greek Literature*. New York: Henry Holt, 1890.

Peters, Samuel. *A General History of Connecticut: From Its First Settlement Under George Fenwick, Esq. to Its Latest Period of Amity with Great Britain; Including a Description of the Country, and Many Curious and Interesting Anecdotes. To Which Is Added, an Appendix, Wherein New and the True Sources of the Present Rebellion of America Are Pointed Out; Together with the Particular Part Taken by the People of Connecticut in Its Promotion*. London: J. Bew, 1782.

Petrinovich, Lewis F. *The Cannibal Within*. New Brunswick: Aldine Transaction, 2000.

Petzoldt, Ruth, and Paul Neubauer. *Demons: Mediators Between This World and the Other—Essays on Demonic Beings from the Middle Ages to the Present*. New York: Peter Lang Publishing Group, 1998.

Philippi, Donald. *Songs of Gods, Songs of Humans: The Epic Traditions of the Ainu*. Princeton: Princeton University Press, 1979.

Phillips, Kendall. *Projected Fears: Horror Films and American Culture*. Santa Barbara: ABC-CLIO, 2005.

Philological Society (Great Britain). *Publications of the Philological Society*, Volume 1. London: Philological Society, 1913.

Philpott, Don, and Hunter Publishing. *Trinidad and Tobago*. Madison: Hunter Publishing, Inc, 2002.

Philpott, Stuart B. *West Indian Migration: The Montserrat Case*. London: Athlone Press, 1973.

Phongphit, Sērī, and Kevin Hewison. *Thai Village Life: Culture and Transition in the Northeast*. Bangkok: Mūnnithī Mūbān, 1990.

Picart, Caroline Joan S., and John Edgar Browning. *Speaking of Monsters: A Teratological Anthology*. London: Palgrave Macmillan, 2012.

Piccardi, Luigi, and W. Bruce Masse. *Myth and Geology*. London: Geological Society of London, 2007.

Pick, Daniel, and Lyndal Roper. *Dreams and History: The Interpretation of Dreams from Ancient Greece to Modern Psychoanalysis*. New York: Psychology Press, 2004.

Picken, Stuart D. B. *Essentials of Shinto: An Analytical Guide to Principal Teachings*. Westport: Greenwood Publishing Group, 1994.

Pickeral, Tamsin. *Encyclopedia of Horses and Ponies*. Bath: Parragon, 2003.

Pinch, Geraldine. *Handbook of Egyptian Mythology*. Santa Barbara: ABC-CLIO, 2002.

Planché, James Robinson. *The Pursiuvant of Arms, or Heraldry Founded Upon Facts*. London: Robert Hardwicke, 1859.

Plaut, Hermann. *Japanese Conversation-Grammar with Numerous Reading Lessons and Dialogues*. London: David Nutt, 1905.

Plautius, Caspar. *Nova Typis Transacta Navigatio Novi Orbis Indiae Occidentalis... Nunc Primum E Varijs Scriptoribus in Vnum Collecta... Authore... Honorio Philopono... [I. E. C. Plautio].* n.p.: Ordinis S. Benedicti Monacho, 1621.

Pliny the Elder, John Bostock, and Henry Thomas Riley. *The Natural History of Pliny*, Volume 2. London: Henry G. Bohn, 1855.

Pliny the Elder, John Bostock, and Henry Thomas Riley. *The Natural History of Pliny*, Volume 3. London: Henry G. Bohn, 1855.

Pliny the Elder, translated by Francesco Maspero. *Storie Naturali* (VIII-XI). Milan: Bur, 2003.

Pliny the Elder, translated by John Bostock and Henry Thomas Riley. *The Natural History of Pliny*, Volume 6. London: Henry G. Bohn, 1857.

Pliny the Elder, translated by Philemon Holland. *Pliny's Natural History. in Thirty-Seven Books*, Volumes 1–3. London: Wernerian Club, 1848.

Plutarch and John Dryden, edited by Arthur Hugh Clough. *Plutarch's Lives of Illustrious Men*, Volume 1. Philadelphia: John C. Winston Company, 1908.

Plutschow, Herbert. *Matsuri: The Festivals of Japan: With a Selection from P.G. O'Neill's Photographic Archive of Matsuri.* London: Routledge, 2013.

Poignant, Roslyn. *Oceanic Mythology: The Myths of Polynesia, Micronesia, Melanesia, Australia.* London: Hamlyn, 1967.

Pollack, David. *Reading Against Culture: Ideology and Narrative in the Japanese Novel.* New York: Cornell University Press, 1992.

Poole, Edward Stanley. *The Thousand and One Nights: Commonly Called the Arabian Nights Entertainments, a New Translation from the Arabic, with Copious Notes by Edward William Lane … Edited by His Nephew Edward Stanley Poole, with a Preface by Stanley Lane-Poole, Introduction by William Allan Neilson, Edward Stanley Poole.* New York: Hearst's International Library Company, 1914.

Porny, M.A. *The Elements of Heraldry.* London: Thomas Carnan, 1787.

Porteous, Alexander. *Forest Folklore: Mythology and Romance.* Whitefish: Kessinger Publishing, 2006.

Porteous, Alexander. *The Forest in Folklore and Mythology.* Mineola: Courier Dover Publications, 2001.

Porteous, Alexander. *The Lore of the Forest.* New York: Cosimo, Incorporated, 2005.

Porter, Darwin, and Danforth Prince. *Frommer's Bahamas.* Hoboken: John Wiley and Sons, 2012.

Porter, Joshua Roy, and William Moy Stratton Russell, editors. *Animals in Folklore.* Cambridge: D. S. Brewer, 1978.

Porterfield, Jason, and Corona Brezina. *Chile: A Primary Source Cultural Guide.* New York: The Rosen Publishing Group, 2003.

Potts, Annie. *Chicken.* London: Reaktion Books, 2012.

Poulton, M. Cody. *Spirits of Another Sort: The Plays of Izumi Kyōka.* Ann Arbor, Mich.: The University of Michigan, 2001.

Powell, J. W., director, and the United States. Government Printing Office. *Congressional Serial Set. 11th Annual Report of the Bureau of Ethnology to the Secretary of the Smithsonian Institution, 1889–90.* Washington, D.C.: U.S. Government Printing Office, 1895.

Pratt, Christina. *An Encyclopedia of Shamanism, Volume 1.* New York: The Rosen Publishing Group, 2007.

Pratt-Chadwick, Mara Louise. *Legends of Norseland.* Boston: Educational Publishing Company, 1894.

Preston, Richard J. *Cree Narrative: Expressing the Personal Meanings of Events.* Quebec City: McGill-Queen's Press—MQUP, 2002.

Principe, Lawrence. *The Secrets of Alchemy.* Chicago: University of Chicago Press, 2013.

Prioreschi, Plinio. *Medieval Medicine.* Omaha: Horatius Press, 2003.

Propp, Vladimir Yakovlevich. *The Russian Folktale by Vladimir Yakovlevich Propp.* Detroit: Wayne State University Press, 2012.

Pughe, William Owen. *A Dictionary of the Welsh Language, Explained in English: With Numerous Illustrations, from the Literary Remains and from the Living Speech of the Cymry, Volume 1.* London: Williams, 1803.

Puryear, Mark. *The Nature of Asatru: An Overview of the Ideals and Philosophy of the Indigenous Religion of Northern Europe.* Lincoln: iUniverse, 2006.

Qazvīnī, Ḥamd Allāh Mustawfī. *The Zoological Section of the Nuzhatu-L-Qulūb of Ḥamdullāh Al-Mustaufī Al-Qazwīnī.* London: The Royal Asiatic Society, 1928.

Radford, Ken. *Tales of South Wales.* London: Skilton and Shaw, 1979.

Raedisch, Linda. *The Old Magic of Christmas: Yuletide Traditions for the Darkest Days of the Year.* Woodbury: Llewellyn Worldwide, 2013.

Ragan, Kathleen. *Fearless Girls, Wise Women, and Beloved Sisters: Heroines in Folktales from Around the World.* London: W. W. Norton and Company, 1998.

Raheem, M. R. M. Abdur. *Muhammad the Prophet.* Singapore: Pustaka Nasional Pte Ltd, 1988.

Rahner, Karl. *Encyclopedia of Theology: A Concise Sacramentum Mundi.* New Delhi: Continuum International Publishing Group, 1975.

Rajshekhar. *Myanmar's Nationalist Movement (1906–1948) and India.* Delhi: South Asian Publishers, 2006.

Ralston, William, and Shedden Ralston. *Russian Folk-Tales.* New York: R. Worthington, 1880.

Ralston, William, and Shedden Ralston. *The Songs of the Russian People: As Illustrative of Slavonic Mythology and Russian Social Life.* London: Ellis and Green, 1872.

Ramos, Maximo D. *The Aswang Syncrasy in Philippine Folklore: With Illustrative Accounts in Vernacular Texts and Translations.* Quezon City, Philippines: Philippine Folklore Society, 1971.

Ramos, Maximo D. *The Creatures of Midnight: Faded Deities of Luzon, the Visayas and Mindanao.* Quezon City: Island Publishers, 1967.

Ramos, Maximo D. *Creatures of Philippine Lower Mythology.* Diliman: University of the Philippines Press, 1971.

Ranade, R. D. *Mysticism in India: The Poet-Saints of Maharashtra.* Albany: State University New York Press, 1983.

Rao and Shanta Rameshwar. *The Mahabharata.* New Delhi: Orient Blackswan, 1985.

Rao, M. V. Krishna. *A Brief Survey of Mystic Tradition in Religion and Art in Karnataka.* Mardas: Wardha Publishing House, 1959.

Rappoport, Angelo S. *Superstitions of Sailors.* Mineola: Courier Dover Publications, 2012.

Rattray, Robert Sutherland, and Johann Gottlieb Christaller. *Ashanti Proverbs: The Primitive Ethics of a Savage People.* Ventnor, Isle of Wight: Clarendon Press, 1916.

Read, Kay Almere, and Jason J. Gonzalez. *Mesoamerican Mythology: A Guide to the Gods, Heroes, Rituals, and Beliefs of Mexico and Central America.* Oxford: Oxford University Press, 2002.

Reade, W. Winwood. *Savage Africa: Being the Narrative of a Tour in Equatorial, Southwestern, and Northwestern.* New York: Johnson reprint Corporation, 1864.

Reading, Mario. *The Complete Prophecies of Nostradamus.* New York: Sterling Publishing Company, Incorporated, 2009.

Recinos, Adrián, translated by Delia Goetz, Adrián Recinos, and Sylvanus Griswold Morley. *Popol Vuh: The Sacred Book of the Ancient Quicche Maya.* Norman: University of Oklahoma Press, 1950.

Reddall, Henry Frederic. *Fact, Fancy, and Fable: A New Handbook for Ready Reference on Subjects Commonly Omitted from Cyclopaedias; Comprising Personal Sobriquets, Familiar Phrases, Popular Appellations, Geographical Nicknames, Literary Pseudonyms, Mythological Characters, Red-Letter Days, Political Slang, Contractions and Abbreviations, Technical Terms Foreign Words and Phrases, and Americanisms.* Chicago: A. C. McClurg, 1892.

Redfern, Nick. *The Most Mysterious Places on Earth.* New York: The Rosen Publishing Group, 2013.

Reed, Alexander Wyclif. *Aboriginal Stories of Australia.* London: Reed, 1980.

Reed, Alexander Wyclif. *Reed Book of Māori Mythology.* London: Reed, 2004.

Remler, Pat. *Egyptian Mythology, A to Z.* New York: Infobase Publishing, 2010.

Renard, John. *Islam and the Heroic Image: Themes in Literature and the Visual Arts.* Macon: Mercer University Press, 1999.

Renner, George Thomas. *Primitive Religion in the Tropical Forests: A Study in Social Geography.* New York: Columbia University, 1927.

Reno, Frank D. *Arthurian Figures of History and Legend: A Biographical Dictionary.* Jefferson, NC: McFarland, 2010.

Renouf, Peter Le Page. *Lectures on the Origin and Growth of Religion as Illustrated by the Religion of Ancient Egypt: Delivered in May and June, 1879.* London: Williams and Norgate, 1893.

Reynolds, Barrie. *Magic, Divination, and Witchcraft Among the Barotse of Northern Rhodesia.* Berkeley: University of California Press, 1963.

Rhys, Sir John. *Celtic Britain.* London: Society for Promoting Christian Knowledge, 1908.

Rhys, Sir John. *Celtic Folklore: Welsh and Manx*, Volume 1. Charleston: Forgotten Books, 1983.

Riccardo, Martin V. *Liquid Dreams of Vampires.* Woodbury: Llewellyn Publications, 1996.

Rice, David G., and John E Stambaugh. *Source for the Study of Greek Religion: Corrected Edition.* Atlanta: Society of Biblical Literature, 2009.

Richardson, John. *A Dissertation on the Languages, Literature, and Manners of Eastern Nations.* Oxford: Claredon Press, 1777.

Richardson, John, and Charles Wilkins. *A Dictionary, Persian, Arabic and English*, Volume 1. London: William Bulmer and Company, 1806.

Riesenfeld, Alphonse. *The Megalithic Culture of Melanesia.* Leiden: Brill, 1950.

Rife, Philip L. *America's Nightmare Monsters.* Lincoln: iUniverse, 2001.

Robbins, Eliza. *Elements of Mythology, Or, Classical Fables of the Greeks and Romans: To Which Are Added Some Notices of Syrian, Hindu, and Scandinavian Superstitions : Together with Those of the American Nations : The Whole Comparing Polytheism with True Religion : For the Use of Schools.* Philadelphia: Hogan and Thompson, 1849.

Robbins, Rossell Hope. *The Encyclopedia of Witchcraft and Demonology.* New York: Crown Publishers, 1959.

Roberts, Jeremy. *Chinese Mythology A to Z: [A Young Reader's Companion].* New York: Infobase Publishing, 2004.

Roberts, Jeremy. *Japanese Mythology A to Z.* New York: Infobase Publishing, 2009.

Roberts, Michael. *Sinhala-Ness and Sinhala Nationalism.* Colombo: Marga Institute, 2001.

Robertson, John M. *Christianity and Mythology.* London: Watts and Company, 1900.

Robinson, Fred C. *The Tomb of Beowulf and Other Essays on Old English.* Cambridge, Mass.: Blackwell, 1993.

Roces, Alfredo, and Grace Roces. *Culture Shock! Philippines.* New York: Times Books International, 1986.

Rodell, Paul A. *Culture and Customs of the Philippines.* Westport: Greenwood Publishing Group, 2002.

Rogers, Robert William. *The Religion of Babylonia and Assyria, Especially in Its Relations to Israel: Five Lectures Delivered at Harvard University.* New York: Eaton and Mains, 1908.

Roman, Luke, and Mónica Román. *Encyclopedia of Greek and Roman Mythology.* New York: Infobase Publishing, 2010.

Room, Adrian. *The Naming of Animals: An Appellative Reference to Domestic, Work, and Show Animals, Real and Fictional.* Jefferson, NC: McFarland, 1993.

Roque, Mela Ma. *Tales from Our Malay Past.* Manila: Filipinas Foundation, 1979.

Roraff, Susan, and Laura Comacho. *Chile.* Portland: Publisher Graphic Arts Center Publishing Company, 2001.

Rose, Carol. *Giants, Monsters, and Dragons: An Encyclopedia of Folklore, Legend, and Myth (In English).* New York: W. W. Norton and Company Incorporated, 2001.

Rose, Carol. *Spirits, Fairies, Leprechauns, and Goblins: An Encyclopedia.* New York: W. W. Norton and Company, 1996.

Rosen, Brenda. *The Mythical Creatures Bible: The Definitive Guide to Legendary Beings.* New York: Sterling Publishing Company, Incorporated, 2009.

Ross, Anne. *Folklore of Wales.* Gloucestershire: Tempus Pub Limited, 2001.

Ross, Micah. *From the Banks of the Euphrates: Studies in Honor of Alice Louise Slotsky.* Winona Lake: Eisenbrauns, 2008.

Rotberg, Robert I. *Haiti Renewed: Political and Economic Prospects.* Washington, D.C.: Brookings Institution Press, 2001.

Roth, John E. *American Elves: An Encyclopedia of Little People from the Lore of 380 Ethnic Groups of the Western Hemisphere.* Jefferson, NC: McFarland, 1997.

Roth, Walter E. "An Inquiry into the Animism and Folk Lore of the Guiana Indians," in *Annual Report of the Bureau of American Ethnology to the Secretary of the Smithsonian Institution* edited by W. H. Holmes, pages 103–386. Washington, D.C.: U.S. Government Printing Office, 1915.

Royal Anthropological Institute of Great Britain and Ireland. *Indian Antiquary*, Volume 4, 225

Royal Asiatic Society of Great Britain and Ireland. *Journal of the Royal Asiatic Society of Great Britain and Ireland*, Volume 21, 291;

Royal Society of New Zealand. *Transactions*, Volume 40. Wellington: New Zealand Institute, 1908.

Rubin, Louis Decimus, and Jerry Leath Mills, editors. *A Writer's Companion.* Baton Rouge: LSU Press, 1995.

Rubino, Carl R. Galvez. *Ilocano: Ilocano-English, English-Ilocano: Dictionary and Phrasebook.* New York: Hippocrene Books, 1998.

Ruddell, Nancy J., and the Canadian Museum of Civilization. *Raven's Village: The Myths, Arts and Traditions of Native People from the Pacific Northwest Coast: Guide to the Grand Hall, Canadian Museum of Civilization.* N.p.: Canadian Museum of Civilization, 1995.

Ruoff, Henry Woldmar. *The Standard Dictionary of Facts: History, Language, Literature, Biography, Geography, Travel, Art, Government, Politics, Industry, Invention, Commerce, Science, Education, Natural History, Statistics and Miscellany.* Buffalo: The Frontier Press Company, 1908.

Russell, Alexander David. *Legends of the Bocas, Trinidad.* London: C. Palmer, 1922.

Russell, Jeffrey Burton. *The Devil: Perceptions of Evil from Antiquity to Primitive Christianity.* Ithaca: Cornell University Press, 1987.

Russell, Jeffrey Burton. *Witchcraft in the Middle Ages.* Ithica: Cornell University Press, 1972.

Ruthven, Suzanne. *Shaman Pathways—Aubry's Dog: Power Animals in Traditional Witchcraft.* Washington, D.C.: John Hunt Publishing, 2013.

Ruthven, Suzanne, and Melusine Draco. *Shaman Pathways—Black Horse, White Horse.* Washington, D.C.: John Hunt Publishing, 2013.

Rydberg, Viktor. *Norroena, the History and Romance of Northern Europe: A Library of Supreme Classics Printed in Complete Form,* Volume 3. London: Norroena Society, 1906.

Rydberg, Viktor, Rasmus Björn Anderson, James William Buel. *Teutonic Mythology: Gods and Goddesses of the Northland,* Volume 3. London: Norrœna Society, 1905.

St. John, Robert. *Through Malan's Africa.* Garden City, New York: Doubleday, 1954.

Sale, George. *The Koran: Commonly Called the Alcoran of Mohammed; Translated into English Immediately from the Original Arabic, with Explanatory Notes, Taken from the Most Approved Commentators: To Which Is Prefixed a Preliminary Discourse.* London: Thomas Tegg, 1844.

Saleeby, Najeeb Mitry. *Studies in Moro History, Law, and Religion.* Manila: Bureau of Public Printing, 1905.

Salem, Sema'an I., and Lynda A. Salem. *The Near East, the Cradle of Western Civilization.* Lincoln: iUniverse, 2000.

Saletore, Rajaram Narayan. *Indian Witchcraft.* New Delhi, India: Abhinav Publications, 1981.

Sandars, N., editor and translator. *The Epic of Gilgamesh.* London: Penguin UK, 1973.

Sandars, Nancy K. *Poems of Heaven and Hell from Ancient Mesopotamia.* New York: Penguin, 1971.

Sanday, Peggy Reeves. *Women at the Center: Life in a Modern Matriarchy.* New York: Cornell University Press, 2003.

Sanders, Robert H. *Revealing the Heart of the Galaxy.* New York: Cambridge University Press, 2013.

Sanderson, Ivan T. *Abominable Snowmen, Legend Come to Life.* New York: Cosimo, Incorporated, 2007.

Sarianidi, Viktor Ivanovich. *Margiana and Protozoroastrism.* Athens: Kapon Editions, 1998.

Savil, Sheila. *Pears Encyclopedia of Myths and Legends.* "Western and Northern Europe, Central and Southern Africa.," London. Pelham Books Limited, 1977.

Savill, Sheila, Christopher Cook, Edward Geoffrey Parrinder, L. Mary Barker. *Pears Encyclopaedia of Myths and Legends: The Orient, Book 3.* London: Pelham Books, Limited, 1977.

Sax, Boria. *Imaginary Animals: The Monstrous, the Wondrous and the Human.* London: Reaktion Books, 2013.

Sax, Boria. *The Mythical Zoo: An Encyclopedia of Animals in World Myth, Legend, and Literature.* Santa Barbara: ABC-CLIO, 2001.

Saxby, Jessie Margaret Edmondston. *Shetland Traditional Lore.* Norwood: Norwood Editions, 1932.

Scales, Helen. *Poseidon's Steed: The Story of Seahorses, from Myth to Reality.* New York: Penguin, 2009.

Schön, James Frederick. *Vocabulary of the Mende Language.* London: The Society for Promoting Christian Knowledge, 1884.

Schouler, Kenneth, and Susai Anthony. *The Everything*

Hinduism Book: Learn the Traditions and Rituals of the "Religion of Peace.," Avon: Everything Books, 2009.

Schreiber, Charlotte. *The Mabinogion: From the Llyfr. Cocho Hergest, and Other Ancient Welsh Manuscripts. Part 3, Containing Geraint the Son of Erbin,* Volume 2. London: Longman, Brown, Green, and Longmans, 1849.

Schwab, Gustav. *Gods and Heroes of Ancient Greece.* New York: Knopf Doubleday Publishing Group, 2011.

Schwartz, Howard. *Tree of Souls: The Mythology of Judaism: The Mythology of Judaism.* Oxford: Oxford University Press, 2004.

Scobie, Alastair. *Murder for Magic: Witchcraft in Africa.* London: Cassell, 1965.

Scott, Delilah, and Emma Troy. *The Upside-Down Christmas Tree: And Other Bizarre Yuletide Tales.* Guildford: Globe Pequot, 2009.

Scott, James George. *The Burman: His Life and Notions,* Volume 1. London: Macmillan and Company, 1882.

Seal, Graham. *Encyclopedia of Folk Heroes.* Santa Barbara: ABC-CLIO, 2001.

Seal, Graham. *Great Australian Stories: Legends, Yarns and Tall Tales.* Crows Nest NSW: ReadHowYouWant.com, 2010.

Sedgefield, Walter John, editor. *Beowulf.* Manchester: Manchester University Press, 1918.

Sedia, Ekaterina. *The Secret History of Moscow.* Rockville: Wildside Press LLC, 2007.

Segal, Charles. *Singers, Heroes, and Gods in the Odyssey.* New York: Cornell University Press, 2001.

Sehgal, Sunil. *Encyclopaedia of Hinduism: (H—Q), Volume 3.* New Delhi: Sarup and Sons, 1999.

Selbie, John Alexander, and Louis Herbert Gray. *Encyclopædia of Religion and Ethics,* Volume 1. Edinburgh: T. and T. Clark, 1917.

Seligman, Charles G. *The Melanesians of British New Guinea.* Cambridge: CUP Archive, 1975.

Senn, Harry A. *Were-Wolf and Vampire in Romania.* Boulder: East European Monographs, 1982.

Serag, Sebastian Sta. Cruz. *The Remnants of the Great Ilonggo Nation.* Quezon City, Philippines: Rex Bookstore, Incorporated, 1997.

Seth, Kailash Nath, and B. K. Chaturvedi. *Gods and Goddesses of India.* New Delhi: Diamond Pocket Books (P) Limited, 2000.

Seton-Williams, Marjory Veronica. *Greek Legends and Stories.* New York: Barnes and Noble Publishing, 2000.

Shadick, Stan. *Skywatcher's Companion: Constellations and Their Mythology.* Toronto: Heritage House Publishing Company, 2011.

Shakespear, John. *A Dictionary Hindustani and English.* London: Parbury, Allen and Company, 1834.

Sharma, Ramashraya. *A Socio-Political Study of the Vālmīki Rāmāyaṇa.* Delhi: Motilal Banarsidass Publ., 1986.

Shearar, Cheryl. *Understanding Northwest Coast Art: A Guide to Crests, Beings and Symbols.* Vancouver: Douglas and McIntyre, 2000.

Shepard, Leslie, Nandor Fodor, and Lewis Spence. *Encyclopedia of Occultism and Parapsychology.* Detroit: Gale Research Company, 1985.

Shepard, Odell. *The Lore of the Unicorn.* Mineola: Courier Dover Publications, 1930.

Sherman, Josepha. *Storytelling: An Encyclopedia of Mythology and Folklore.* Armonk: M. E. Sharpe Reference Incorporated, 2008.

Shortland, Edward. *Maori Religion and Mythology.* Longmans: London, 1882.

Shryock, John Knight. *The Temples of Anking and Their Cults: A Study of Modern Chinese Religion*. Philadelphia: University of Pennsylvania, 1931.

Shuker, Karl. *The Beasts That Hide from Man: Seeking the World's Last Undiscovered Animals*. New York: Cosimo, Incorporated, 2003.

Shuker, Karl. *Dragons: A Natural History*. London: Taschen Benedikt Verlag Gmbh., 2006.

Shuker, Karl. *Extraordinary Animals Worldwide*. London: R. Hale, 1991.

Shuker, Karl. *From Flying Toads to Snakes with Wings*. St. Paul: Llewellyn, 1997.

Sibree, James. "Malagasy Folklore and Popular Superstitions," in *The Folk-Lore Record*, Volume 2 edited by the Folklore Society (Great Britain), 19–46. London: Folklore Society, 1879.

Sierra, Judy. *The Gruesome Guide to World Monsters*. Cambridge: Candlewick Press, 2005.

Sikes, Wirt. *British Goblins: Welsh Folk Lore, Fairy Mythology, Legends and Traditions*. Boston: James R. Osgood and Company, 1881.

Simbulan, Vincent Michael. *A Time for Dragons: An Anthology of Philippine Draconic Fiction*. Pasig City: Anvil Pub., 2009.

Simons, Geoffrey Leslie. *The Witchcraft World*. London: Abelard-Schuman, 1974.

Simpson, Evelyn Blantyre. *Folk Lore in Lowland Scotland*. London: J.M. Dent and Company, 1908.

Simpson, Jacqueline. *British Dragons*. London: Batsford, 1980.

Simpson, Jacqueline. *Green Men and White Swans: The Folklore of British Pub Names*. London: Random House, 2010.

Simpson, Jacqueline, and Stephen Roud. *A Dictionary of English Folklore*. Oxford: Oxford University Press, 2000.

Simpson, Michael. *The Metamorphoses of Ovid*. Amherst: University of Massachusetts Press, 2003.

Simpson, Phil. *Guidebook to the Constellations: Telescopic Sights, Tales, and Myths*. Cloudcroft: Springer Science and Business Media, 2012.

Singh, Nagendra Kr. *Vedic Mythology*. Delhi: APH Publishing, 1997.

Skeat, Walter William, and Charles Otto Blagden. *Malay Magic: Being an Introduction to the Folklore and Popular Religion of the Malay Peninsula*. London: Macmillan and Company, Limited, 1900.

Skidmore, Monique. *Karaoke Fascism: Burma and the Politics of Fear*. Philadelphia: University of Pennsylvania Press, 2011.

Skiff, Carl. *The Land of the Dragon*. Pittsburgh: Dorrance Publishing, 2014.

Skyes, Edgerton, and Alan Kendall. *Who's Who in Non-Classical Mythology*. London: Routledge, 2002.

Slifkin, Nosson. *Sacred Monsters: Mysterious and Mythical Creatures of Scripture, Talmud and Midrash*. Brooklyn: Zoo Torah, 2007.

Sloan, Kathryn A. *Runaway Daughters: Seduction, Elopement, and Honor in Nineteenth-Century Mexico*. Albuquerque: University of New Mexico Press, 2008.

Sloane-Evans, William Sloane. *A Grammar of British Heraldry: Consisting of Blazon and Marshalling with an Introduction on the Rise and Progress of Symbols and Ensigns*. London: John Russell Smith, 1854.

Smith, Evans Lansing, and Nathan Robert Brown. *The Complete Idiot's Guide to World Mythology*. New York: Penguin, 2008.

Smith, Nigel J. H. *The Enchanted Amazon Rain Forest: Stories from a Vanishing World*. Gainesville: University Press of Florida, 1996.

Smith, Peter Alderson. *W.B. Yeats and the Tribes of Danu: Three Views of Ireland's Fairies*. Dublin: Smythe, 1987.

Smith, Richard Gordon, and Mo-No-Yuk. *Ancient Tales and Folklore of Japan: By Richard Gordon Smith*. London: A. and C. Black, 1908.

Smith, W. Ramsay. *Myths and Legends of the Australian Aborigines*. Mineola: Courier Dover Publications, 2003.

Smith, William. *Dictionary of Greek and Roman Biography and Mythology*, Volume 3: Oarses-Zygia. London: J. Walton, 1849.

Smith, Sir William. *A Dictionary of the Bible, Edited by W. Smith. [With] Appendix*, Volume 3. London: John Murray, 1863.

Smith, Sir William. *New Classical Dictionary of Biography, Mythology, and Geography*. London: John Murray, 1850.

Smith, Sir William, and Charles Anthon. *A New Classical Dictionary of Greek and Roman Biography, Mythology and Geography: Partly Based Upon the Dictionary of Greek and Roman Biography and Mythology*. New York: Harper and Brothers, 1862.

Smith, William, William George Smith, Henry Wace, editors. *A Dictionary of Christian Biography, Literature, Sects and Doctrines: Being a Continuation of "The Dictionary of the Bible."* London: John Murray, 1877.

Smollett, Tobias, and Robert Anderson. *The Miscellaneous Works of Tobias Smollett, M.D.: The Adventures of Sir Launcelot Greaves. Travels Through France and Italy*. Edinburgh: Stirling and Slade, 1820.

Smyth, Robert Brough. *The Aborigines of Victoria*, Volume 1. Melbourne: J. Ferres, Government Printer, 1878.

Snow, Edward Rowe. *Incredible Mysteries and Legends of the Sea*. New York: Dodd, Mead, 1967.

Society for the Diffusion of Useful Knowledge. *The Penny Cyclopaedia of the Society for the Diffusion of Useful Knowledge: Ernesti-Frustum*, Volume 10. London: Charles Knight, 1838.

Songling, Pu, translated by Sidney L. Sondergard. *Strange Tales from Liaozhai*, Volume 1. Fremont: Jain Publishing Company, 2008.

Sorensen, Eric. *Possession and Exorcism in the New Testament and Early Christianity*. Tubingen: Mohr Siebeck, 2002.

Sotesiri, Roj. *The Study of Puan Community, Pho Si Village, Tambon Bang Pla Ma, Suphan Buri*. Bangkok: Office of the National Culture Commission, Ministry of Education, 1982.

South, Malcolm. *Mythical and Fabulous Creatures: A Source Book and Research Guide*. Westport: Greenwood Press, 1987.

Southey, Robert. *Southey's Common-Place Book*, Volume 4. London: Longman, Brown, Green and Longmans, 1851.

Spence, Lewis. *Arcane Secrets and Occult Lore of Mexico and Mayan Central America: A Treasury of Magic, Astrology, Witchcraft, Demonology, and Symbolism*. Detroit: B. Ethridge Books, 1973.

Spence, Lewis. *A Brief Guide to Native American Myths and Legends: With a New Introduction and Commentary by Jon E. Lewis*. Philadelphia: Constable and Robinson, 2013.

Spence, Lewis. *An Encyclopædia of Occultism: A Compendium of Information on the Occult Sciences, Occult*

Personalities, Psychic Science, Magic, Demonology, Spiritism and Mysticism. New York: Dodd, Meade, and Company, 1920.

Spence, Lewis. *Fairy Tradition in Britain.* London: Rider, 1948.

Spence, Lewis. *Legends and Romances of Brittany.* Charleston: Forgotten Books.

Spence, Lewis. *The Magic Arts in Celtic Britain.* New York: Dover Publications, 1999.

Spence, Lewis. *The Minor Traditions of British Mythology.* London: Rider and Company, 1948.

Spence, Lewis. *Myths and Legends of Ancient Egypt.* Rockville: Wildside Press LLC, 2008.

Spencer, George John Spencer (second earl), George John Spencer Spencer (Earl), Thomas Frognall Dibdin, Luigi? Serra (duca di Cassano.), and John Rylands Library. *Bibliotheca Spenceriana: Or, a Descriptive Catalogue of the Books Printed in the Fifteenth Century and Many Valuable First Editions in the Library of George John, Earl Spencer.* London: Shakespeare Press, 1815.

Spinner, Alice. "Concerning Duppies," in *The Living Age,* Volume 206 edited by Eliakim Littell and Robert S. Littell, 161–169. Boston: Living Age Company Incorporated, 1895.

Sprague de Camp, L. and Willy Ley. *Lands Beyond.* New York: Barnes and Noble Books, 1993.

Sproul, Barbara C. *Primal Myths: Creation Myths Around the World.* San Francisco: HarperCollins, 1979.

Spurrell, William. *A Dictionary of the Welsh Language: With English Synonymes and Explanations.* Carmarthen: Spurrell, 1853.

Stanley, David. *South Pacific Handbook.* Emeryville: David Stanley, 1999.

Steiger, Brad. *Real Monsters, Gruesome Critters, and Beasts from the Darkside.* Canton: Visible Ink Press, 2010.

Stepanich, Kisma K. *Faery Wicca,* Book One. St. Paul: Llewellyn Worldwide, 1997.

Sterckx, Roel. *The Animal and the Daemon in Early China.* Albany: State University New York Press, 2012.

Stetkevych, Suzanne Pinckney. *The Mute Immortals Speak: Pre-Islamic Poetry and the Poetics of Ritual.* Ithaca: Cornell University Press, 1993.

Stevenson, J. H., editor. *The Scottish Antiquary, Or, Northern Notes and Queries,* Volume 7–8. Edinburgh: Lorimer and Gillies, 1900.

Stevenson, John. *Yoshitoshi's Strange Tales.* Amsterdam: Hotei Pub., 2005.

Steward, Julian Haynes, editor. *Handbook of South American Indians: The Comparative Ethnology of South American Indians.* New York: Cooper Square Publishers, 1963.

Stewart, William. *Dictionary of Images and Symbols in Counselling.* London: Jessica Kingsley Publishers, 1998.

Stokes, Whitley. *Acallamh Na Seanórach Acallamh Na Senórach,* Volume 4. Leipzig: Hirzel, 1900.

Stone, Doris. *The Talamancan Tribes of Costa Rica.* Kraus Reprint Company, 1973.

Stookey, Lorena Laura. *Thematic Guide to World Mythology.* Westport: Greenwood Publishing Group, 2004.

Strassberg, Richard E. *A Chinese Bestiary: Strange Creatures from the Guideways Through Mountains and Seas.* Berkeley: University of California Press, 2002.

Stratilesco, Tereza. *From Carpathian to Pindus: Pictures of Roumanian Country Life.* Boston: John W. Luce, 1907.

Sturluson, Snorri, translated by Arthur Gilchrist Brodeur.

The Prose Edda, Volume 5. New York: General Books, 2003.

Sturluson, Snorri. *The Prose Edda: Norse Mythology.* Mineola: Dover, 2004.

Sturluson, Stories of the Kings of Norway: Called the Round of the World. Translated by William Morris and Eiríkr Magnússon. London: Bernard Quaritch, 1905.

Sturtevant, William C., editor. *Handbook of North American Indians.* Washington, D.C.: Government Printing Office, 1978.

Suckling, Nigel. *Unicorns.* London: AAPPL, 2007.

Suh, Jai-sik. *Korean Patterns.* Seoul: Hollym International Company, 2007.

Sullivan, Michael. *An Introduction to Chinese Art.* Berkley: University of California Press, 1961.

Summers, Montague. *Werewolf.* Whitefish: Kessinger Publishing, LLC, 2003.

Summers, Montague. *The Werewolf in Lore and Legend.* Mineola: Courier Dover Publications, 2012.

Summers, Montague. *Witchcraft and Black Magic.* North Chemsford: Courier Dover Publications, 2000.

Summers, Montague. *Vampire: His Kith and Kin.* Whitefish: Kessinger Publishing, 2003.

Suter, Ann. *Lament: Studies in the Ancient Mediterranean and Beyond.* New York: Oxford University Press, 2008.

Swanton, John Reed. *Chickasaw Society and Religion.* Lincoln: University of Nebraska Press, 1928.

Swanton, John Reed. *Myths and Tales of the Southeastern Indians.* Norman: University of Oklahoma Press, 1929.

Swire, Otta F., and Ronald Black. *Skye: The Island and Its Legends.* Edinburgh: Birlinn, 2006.

Szabo, Vicki Ellen. *Monstrous Fishes and the Mead-Dark Sea: Whaling in the Medieval North Atlantic.* Leiden: Brill Academic Pub, 2008.

Szasz, Ferenc Morton. *Larger than Life: New Mexico in the Twentieth Century.* Albuquerque: University of New Mexico Press, 2006.

Tabori, Paul. *The Humor and Technology of Sex.* New York: Julian Press, 1970.

Tada, Katsumi. *Edo Yōkai Karuta.* Tokyo: Kokushokan Kōkai, 1998.

Takagi, Toshio. *A Collection of Japanese Legends.* Winchester: Huntingtower, 1999.

Talasi, Vajda I., and L. Vajda Talasi. "Hexe, Hexendruck.," *Acta Ethnographica* 4 (1950): 129–69. Budapest: Akademiai Kiado, 1950.

Tarulevicz, Nicole. *Eating Her Curries and Kway: A Cultural History of Food in Singapore.* Champaign: University of Illinois Press, 2013.

Tayanin, Damrong. *Being Kammu: My Village, My Life.* Ithica: Southeast Asia Publications, 1994.

Taylor, Bron. *Encyclopedia of Religion and Nature.* London: A. and C. Black, 2008.

Teachers' Curriculum Institute. *Ancient World History Activity Sampler.* Palo Alto: Teachers' Curriculum Institute, 1999.

Temple, Charles R. *Traditional Themes in Japanese Art.* Berkeley: Regent Press, 2008.

Thakur, Upendra. *India and Japan, a Study in Interaction During 5th Cent.-14th Cent. A.D.* New Delhi: Abhinav Publications, 1992.

Theal, Georg Mc Call. *Faffir (Xhosa) Folk-Lore: A Selection from the Traditional Tales.* Charleston: Forgotten Books, 2007.

Theitic, editor. "Lumberjack Folklore: Squonks and Other Odd Critters," in *The Witches' Almanac, Issue 34,*

Spring 2015-Spring 2016: Fire: The Transformer, edited by Theitic, pages 16–8. Grand Rapids: Red Wheel/Weiser, 2014.

Thomas, W. J. *Some Myths and Legends of the Australian Aborigines*. Sugar Land: Netlancers Inc, 2014.

Thomas, William Jenkyn. *The Welsh Fairy Book*. Charleston: Forgotten Books, 1979.

Thompson, Francis. *The Supernatural Highlands*. London: R. Hale, 1976.

Thompson, Reginald Campbell. *The Devils and Evil Spirits of Babylonia, Being Babylonian and Assyrian Incantations Against the Demons, Ghouls, Vampires, Hobgoblins, Ghosts, and Kindred Evil Spirits, Which Attack Mankind*. London: Luzac, 1903–1904.

Thompson, Reginald Campbell. *Semitic Magic, Its Origins and Development*. London: Luzac and Company, 1908.

Thompson, Susan Conklin, Keith Steven Thompson, and Lidia López de López. *Cuentos Folklóricos Mayas*. Westport: Libraries Unlimited, 2007.

Thompson, Vivian Laubach. *Hawaiian Myths of Earth, Sea, and Sky*. Honolulu: University of Hawaii Press, 1966.

Thoreau, Henry David, edited by Jeffrey S. Cramer. *The Maine Woods: A Fully Annotated Edition*. New Haven: Yale University Press, 2009.

Thorpe, Benjamin. *Northern Mythology, Comprising the Principal Popular Traditions and Superstitions of Scandinavia, North Germany and the Netherlands: Compiled from Original and Other Sources. in Three Volumes. Scandinavian Popular Traditions and Superstitions*, Volume 1. London: Edward Lumley, 1851.

Thorpe, Benjamin. *Northern Mythology, Comprising the Principal Popular Traditions and Superstitions of Scandinavia, North Germany and the Netherlands: Compiled from Original and Other Sources. in Three Volumes. Scandinavian Popular Traditions and Superstitions*, Volume 2. London: Edward Lumley, 1851.

Timmins, Steve. *French Fun: The Real Spoken Language of Québec*. Sussex: John Wiley, 1995.

Toki, Zenmaro. *Japanese Nō Plays*. Tokyo: Japan Travel Bureau, 1954.

Tolkien, John Ronald Reuel. *Beowulf: The Monster and the Critics*. New York: HarperCollins Publishers, 1997.

Tomlinson, Sally, and the University of North Carolina at Chapel Hill. *Demons, Druids and Brigands on Irish High Crosses: Rethinking the Images Identified as "The Temptation of Saint Anthony."* Chapel Hill: ProQuest, 2007.

Too, Lillian. *Total Feng Shui: Bring Health, Wealth, and Happiness into Your Life*. San Francisco: Chronicle Books, 2004.

Topsell, Edward. *History of Four Footed Beasts*. London: Routledge, 2013.

Torrance, Robert M. *Encompassing Nature: A Sourcebook*. Washington, D.C.: Counterpoint Press, 1999.

Townsend, Chris. *Scotland*. Milnthorpe, Cicerone Press Limited, 2011.

Tozer, Basil. *The Horse in History*. New York: Charles Scribner, 1908.

Trachtenberg, Joshua. *Jewish Magic and Superstition: A Study in Folk Religion*. Charleston: Forgotten Books, 2008.

Traquair, R. H. "Popular Delusions in Natural History," in *Transactions of the Edinburgh Field Naturalists' and Microscopical Society*, Volume 3 edited by the Edinburgh Field Naturalists' and Microscopical Society. Edinburgh: The Club, 1895.

Tregear, Edward R. *Maori-Polynesian Comparative Dictionary*. Wellington: Lyon and Blair, Lambton Quay, 1891.

Tregear, Edward. *The Maori Race*. Wanganoi: A.D. Willis, 1904.

Tresidder, Jack, editor. *The Complete Dictionary of Symbols*. San Francisco: Chronicle Books, 2005.

Trevelyan, Marie. *Folk-Lore and Folk-Stories of Wales*. Whitefish: Kessinger Publishing, 1973.

Tryon, Henry Harrington. *Fearsome Critters*. New York: The Idlewild Press, 1939.

Trzaskoma, Stephen M., R. Scott Smith, Stephen Brunet, and Thomas G. Palaima. *Anthology of Classical Myth: Primary Sources in Translation*. Indianapolis: Hackett Publishing, 2004.

Tudor, Daniel. *Korea: The Impossible Country: The Impossible Country*. North Clarendon: Tuttle Publishing, 2013.

Turner, Joseph Horsfall. *Yorkshire Notes and Queries*, Volumes 1–2. Bingley: T. Harrison, 1888.

Turner, Patricia, and Charles Russell Coulter. *Dictionary of Ancient Deities*. New York: Oxford University Press, 2001.

Tyler, Hamilton A. *Pueblo Gods and Myths*. Norman: University of Oklahoma Press, 1964.

Tylor, Sir Edward Burnett. *Primitive Culture: Researches into the Development of Mythology, Philosophy, Religion, Art, and Custom*, Volume 2. London: John Murray, 1871.

Tyson, Peter. *Madagascar—The Eighth Continent: Life, Death and Discovery in a Lost World*. London: Bradt Travel Guides, 2013.

University College of the West Indies. *Caribbean Quarterly*, vol. 45. Mona, Jamaica: University College of the West Indies, 1999.

University of San Carlos. *Philippine Quarterly of Culture and Society*, vol. 10–11. Cebu City: University of San Carlos, 1981.

University of the Philippines. *Asian Studies*, vol. 8–9. Quezon City, Philippines: Philippine Center for Advanced Studies, 1970.

Unschuld, Paul Ulrich, and Jinsheng Zheng. *Chinese Traditional Healing: The Berlin Collections of Manuscript Volumes from the 16th Through the Early 20th Century (3 Volume Set)*. Leiden: Brill, 2012.

Vālmīki, edited by Robert P. Goldman. *Ramayana: Book 1: Boyhood, Book 1*. New York: New York University Press, 2005.

Vālmīki, edited by Rosalind Lefeber and Robert P. Goldman. *The Ramayana of Valmiki: An Epic of Ancient India-Kiskindhakanda*. Princeton: Princeton University Press, 1994.

van den Broek, Roelof. *The Myth of the Phoenix: According to Classical and Early Christian Traditions*. Leiden: Brill Archive, 1972.

van der Toorn, K., Bob Becking, and Pieter Willem van der Horst. *Dictionary of Deities and Demons in the Bible DDD*. Grand Rapids: Wm. B. Eerdmans Publishing, 1999.

van Gulik, Willem R. *Irezumi*. Leiden: Brill Archive, 1982.

van Oort, H. A. *The Iconography of Chinese Buddhism in Traditional China: Han to Liao*. Leiden: Brill, 1986.

van Scott, Miriam. *The Encyclopedia of Hell*. New York: Macmillan, 1999.

Varner, Gary R. *Creatures in the Mist: Little People, Wild Men and Spirit Beings Around the World: A Study in*

Comparative Mythology. New York: Algora Publishing, 2007.

Varner, Gary R. *The Mythic Forest, the Green Man and the Spirit of Nature: The Re-Emergence of the Spirit of Nature from Ancient Times into Modern Society*. New York: Algora Publishing, 2006.

Vaz da Silva, Francisco. *Metamorphosis: The Dynamics of Symbolism in European Fairy Tales*. New York: Peter Lang, 2002.

Venkatesananda, Swami. *The Concise Srimad Bhagavatam*. Albany: State University New York Press, 1989.

Versluis, Arthur. *Sacred Earth: The Spiritual Landscape of Native America*. Rochester; Inner Traditions / Bear and Company, 1992.

Vigfússon, Guðbrandur, and Frederick York Powell, editors. *Court Poetry*: Volume 2 of *Corpus Poeticvm Boreale: The Poetry of the Old Northern Tongue, from the Earliest Times to the Thirteenth Century*, Guðbrandur Vigfússon.

Villeneuve, Roland, and Jean-Louis Degaudenzi. *Le Musée Des Vampires*. Paris: Henri Veyrier, 1976.

Vinycomb, John. *Fictitious and Symbolic Creatures in Art with Special Reference to Their Use in British Heraldry*. London: Chapman and Hall, 1906.

Virgil and Henry Nettleship. *P. Vergili Maronis Opera: The Eclogues and Georgics*. London: Whittaker, 1881.

Virgil and Richard F. Thomas, editor. *Georgics*, Volume 2. Cambridge: Cambridge University Press, 1988.

Vogel, Jean Philippe. *Indian Serpent-Lore: Or, the Nāgas in Hindu Legend and Art*. New Delhi: Asian Educational Services, 1926.

Volney, Constantin-François. *The Ruins; Or, Meditation on the Revolutions of Empires: And the Law of Nature*. New York: Peter Eckler Publishing Company, 1890.

Volta, Ornella. *The Vampire*. London: Tandem Books, 1963.

Voltaire, Tobias George Smollett, and Thomas Francklin. *The Works of M. De Voltaire: The Ancient and Modern History*. London: J. Newbery, R. Baldwin, W. Johnston, S. Crowder, T. Davies, J. Coote, G. Kearsley, and B. Collins, at Salisbury, 1761.

von Dassow, Eva, editor. *The Egyptian Book of the Dead: The Book of Going Forth by Day—The Complete Papyrus of Ani Featuring Integrated Text and Full-Color Images*. San Francisco: Chronicle Books, 2008.

Voth, Henry R. *The Traditions of the Hopi*, Volume 8. Chicago: Field Columbian Museum, 1905.

Wagenwoorf, H. *Studies in Roman Literature, Culture and Religion*. Leiden: Brill Archive, 1956.

Wakeman, Mary K. *God's Battle with the Monster: A Study in Biblical Imagery*. Leiden: Brill Archive, 1973.

Walford, Edward, John Charles Cox, and George Latimer Apperson, editors. *The Antiquary*, Volume 38. London: Elliot Stock, 1902.

Walker, Benjamin. *The Hindu World: An Encyclopedic Survey of Hinduism*, Volume 2. Westport: Praeger, 1968.

Walker, James R. *Lakota Belief and Ritual*. Lincoln: University of Nebraska Press, 1980.

Walker, John. *A Selection of Curious Articles from the Gentleman's Magazine*, Volume 1. London: Longman, Hurst, Rees, Orme, and Brown, 1814.

Wall, Otto, A. "Demons of Disease," in *Meyer Brothers Druggist*, Volume 31, edited by H. M. whelpley, page 141. Saint Louis: C.F.G. Meyer, 1910.

Wallace, Kathryn. *Folk-Lore of Ireland: Legends, Myths and Fairy Tales*. Chicago: J.S. Hyland, 1910.

Wallen, Martin. *Fox*. London: Reaktion Books, 2006.

Walravens, Hartmut, editor. *Der Fuchs in Kultur, Religion Und Folklore Zentral- Und Ostasiens, Part 1*. Gottingen: Otto Harrassowitz Verlag, 2001.

Walsh, E. H. "The Coinage of Nepal," in *Journal of the Royal Asiatic Society of Great Britain and Ireland*, 64–669. London: Royal Asiatic Society of Great Britain and Ireland, 1908.

Walsh, William Shepard. *Handy-Book of Literary Curiosities*. Philadelphia: J.B. Lippincott, 1892.

Walter, Mariko Namba, and Eva Jane Neumann Fridman. *Shamanism: An Encyclopedia of World Beliefs, Practices, and Culture*, Volume 1. Santa Barbara: ABC-CLIO, 2004.

Ward, William Hayes. *The Seal Cylinders of Western Asia*. Washington, D.C.: Carnegie Institution of Washington, 1910.

Warhol, Tom, and Marcus Schneck. *Birdwatcher's Daily Companion: 365 Days of Advice, Insight, and Information for Enthusiastic Birders*. Schneck: Quarry Books, 2010.

Warner, Elizabeth. *Russian Myths*. Austin: University of Texas Press, 2002.

Warner, Marina. *Monsters of Our Own Making: The Peculiar Pleasures of Fear*. Lexington: University Press of Kentucky, 1999.

Warner, Marina, and Felipe Fernández-Armesto. *World of Myths: Volume Two*. Austin: University of Texas Press, 2004.

Washington State. *Report of the Governor of Washington Territory*. Washington: U.S. Government Printing Office, 1884.

Watkins, Calvert. *How to Kill a Dragon: Aspects of Indo-European Poetics: Aspects of Indo-European Poetics*. New York: Oxford University Press, 1995.

Watson, William John. *Place-Names of Ross and Cromarty*. Edinburgh: The Northern Counties Printing and Publishing Company, Limited, 1904.

Watt, James C. Y., Prudence Oliver Harper, and the Metropolitan Museum of Art. *China: Dawn of a Golden Age, 200–750 AD*. New York: Metropolitan Museum of Art, 2004.

Watts, Donald. *Dictionary of Plant Lore*. Burlington: Academic Press, 2007.

Watts, Linda S. *Encyclopedia of American Folklore*. New York: Infobase Publishing, 2006.

Webster, N.B., editor. *Historic Magazine and Notes and Queries: A Monthly of History, Folk-Lore, Mathematics, Literature, Art, Arcane Societies, Etc*. Manchester: S.C. and L.M. Gould, 1882.

Webster, Richard. *Encyclopedia of Angels*. Woodbury: Llewellyn Worldwide, 2009.

Wei, Liming. *Chinese Festivals*. Cambridge: Cambridge University Press, 2011.

Weinstock, Jeffrey. *The Ashgate Encyclopedia of Literary and Cinematic Monsters*. Burlington: Ashgate Publishing, Limited, 2014.

Weiss, Zeev. *Public Spectacles in Roman and Late Antique Palestine*. Cambridge: Harvard University Press, 2014.

Welch, Patricia Bjaaland. *Chinese Art: A Guide to Motifs and Visual Imagery*. North Claredon: Tuttle Publishing, 2008.

Weld, Charles Richard. *The Pyrenees, West and East*. London: Longman, Brown, Green, Longmans, and Roberts, 1859.

Werner, Alice. *Myths and Legends of the Bantu*. N.p.: Senate, 1933.

Werner, Edward Theodore Chalmers. *Myths and Legends of China*. Lawrence: Digireads.com Publishing, 2011.

Werness, Hope B. *The Continuum Encyclopedia of Animal Symbolism in Art*. New York: A and C Black, 2004.

Werness, Hope B. *Continuum Encyclopedia of Native Art: Worldview, Symbolism, and Culture in Africa, Oceania, and North America*. New York: Continuum International, 2003.

Westermann, Diedrich, Edwin William Smith, and Cyril Daryll Forde. *Africa*. Oxford: Oxford University Press, 1992.

Westervelt, William Drake. *Legends of Gods and Ghosts*. London: Constable and Company,1915.

Westmoreland, Perry L. *Ancient Greek Beliefs*. San Ysidro: Lee and Vance Publishing Company, 2007.

Westropp, Thomas Johnson, and Gearóid Ó Crualaoich. *Folklore of Clare: A Folklore Survey of County Clare and County Clare Folk-Tales and Myths*. Clare: Clasp Press, 2000.

Westwood, Jennifer, and Jacqueline Simpson. *The Lore of the Land: A Guide to England's Legends, from Spring-Heeled Jack to the Witches of Warboys*. New York: Penguin, 2005.

Whatahoro, H. T. *Lore of the Whare-Wānanga: Or Teachings of the Maori College on Religion, Cosmogony, and History*. Cambridge: Cambridge University Press, 2011.

White, David Gordon. *Myths of the Dog-Man*. Chicago: University of Chicago Press, 1991.

White, J. *The Ancient History of the Maori*, 7 Volumes, Volume 2. Wellington: Government Printer, 1887–1891.

White, J. *The Ancient History of the Maori*, 7 Volumes, Volume 6. Wellington: Government Printer, 1887–1891.

White, John. *The Ancient History of the Maori: His Mythology and Traditions*: Volume 3. London: G. Didsbury, 1889.

White, Terence Hanbury. *The Book of Beasts: Being a Translation from a Latin Bestiary of the Twelfth Century*. Mineola: Courier Dover Publications, 1954.

Whitlock, Ralph. *In Search of Lost Gods: A Guide to British Folklore*. London: Phaidon, 1979.

Whitmore, Ben. *Trials of the Moon: Reopening the Case for Historical Witchcraft. a Critique of Ronald Hutton's the Triumph of the Moon: A History of Modern Pagan Witchcraft*. Auckland: Briar Books, 2010.

Whitney, William Dwight. *The Century Dictionary and Cyclopedia: Dictionary, a Work of Universal Reference in All Departments of Knowledge, with a New Atlas of the World*, Volume 1 of the Century Dictionary. New York: Century Company, 1906.

Whitney, William Dwight, and Benjamin Eli Smith, editors. *The Century Dictionary and Cyclopedia: A Work of Universal Reference in All Departments of Knowledge, with a New Atlas of the World*, Volume 8. New York: Century Company, 1895.

Wiener, Leo. *Contributions Toward a History of Arabico-Gothic Culture*, Volume 4. Philadelphia: Innes and Sons, 1921.

Wiggermann, F. A. M. *Mesopotamian Protective Spirits: The Ritual Texts*. Leiden: Brill, 1992.

Wildridge, Thomas Tindall. *The Grotesque in Church Art*. London: William Andrews and company, 1899.

Wilkins, William Joseph. *Hindu Mythology, Vedic and Purānic*. Calcutta: Thacker, Spink and Company, 1882.

Wilkinson, Sir John Gardner. *Manners and Customs of the Ancient Egyptians: Including Their Private Life, Government, Laws, Arts, Manufactures, Religion, and Early History: Derived from a Comparison of the Paintings, Sculptures, and Monuments Still Existing, with the Accounts of Ancient Authors*, Volumes 3 and 5. London: Murray, 1847, 1878.

Wilkinson, Sir John Gardner. *A Second Series of the Manners and Customs of the Ancient Egyptians*. London: John Murry, 1841.

Wilkinson, Philip. *Myths and Legends: An Illustrated Guide to Their Origins and Meanings*. New York: Penguin, 2009.

Williams, G. J. "The History of the Parish of Llanbrynmair," in *Collections Historical and Archaeological Relating to Montgomeryshire*, Volume 22 edited by the Powys-land Club, 314–28. London: The Club, 1888.

Williams, George M. *Handbook of Hindu Mythology*. Oxford: Oxford University Press, 2008.

Williams, Joseph J. *Psychic Phenomena of Jamaica*. New York: Dial Press, 1934.

Williamson, Craig. *"Beowulf," and Other Old English Poems*. Philadelphia: University of Pennsylvania Press, 2011.

Williston, Teresa Peirce, and the Oliver Wendell Holmes Library Collection. *Japanese Fairy Tales, Illustrated by Sanchi Ogawa*. Chicago: Rand McNally and Company, 1904.

Willoughby-Meade, Gerald. *Chinese Ghouls and Goblins*. London: Constable and Company Limited, 1928.

Wilson, Amelia. *The Devil*. N.p. : Barrons Educational Series Incorporated, 2002.

Wilson, Colin, and Damon Wilson. *The Mammoth Encyclopedia of the Unsolved*. New York: Carroll and Graf, 2000.

Wilson, Horace Hayman. *The Vishnu Purana: A System of Hindu Mythology and Tradition*. London: Trubner and Company, 1865.

Wilson, Laurence Lee. *Ilongot Life and Legends*. New York: Southeast Asia Institute, 1947.

Winstedt, Richard. *The Malay Magician: Being Shaman, Saiva and Sufi*. Oxfordshire, England: Taylor and Francis, 1982.

Wittke-Rüdiger, Petra, Petra Rüdiger, and Konrad Gross. *Translation of Cultures*. Amsterdam: Rodopi, 2009.

Wolff, Henry William. *Odd Bits of History: Being Short Chapters Intended to Fill Some Blanks*. London: Longmanns, Green, and Company, 1894.

Wonderley, Anthony Wayne, and Hope Emily Allen. *Oneida Iroquois Folklore, Myth, and History: New York Oral Narrative from the Notes of H. E. Allen and Others*. Syracuse: Syracuse University Press, 2004.

Woodcock, Percival George. *Short Dictionary of Mythology*. Rockville: Wildside Press LLC, 2009.

Woodgate, Fred. *Kamilaroi and Assimilation*. Canberra: National Library of Australia, 1995.

Wood-Martin, William Gregory. *Traces of the Elder Faiths of Ireland: A Folklore Sketch; a Handbook of Irish Pre-Christian Traditions*, Volume 1. New York: Longmans, Green, and Company, 1902.

Woods, Damon L. *The Philippines: A Global Studies Handbook*. Oxford, England: ABC-CLIO, 2006.

Woods, Michael, and Mary B. Woods. *Seven Natural Wonders of Europe*. Minneapolis: Twenty-First Century Books, 2009.

Woodward, Ian. *The Werewolf Delusion*. New York: Paddington Press, 1979.

Woodward, John, and George Burnett. *A Treatise on Heraldry, British and Foreign: With English and French Glossaries*, Volume 1. Edinburgh: W. and A.K. Johnston, 1896.

Worcester, Dean C. *The Philippine Islands and Their People*. New York: Macmillan, 1899.

Wright, Dudley. *Vampires and Vampirism*. London: W. Rider and Son, Limited, 1914.

Wright, Elizabeth Mary. *Rustic Speech and Folk-Lore*. London: Humphrey Milford, 1913.

Wright, Joseph. *The English Dialect Dictionary, Being the Complete Vocabulary of All Dialect Words Still in Use, or Known to Have Been in Use During the Last Two Hundred Years*. London: Henry Frowde, 1900.

Wright, Thomas, editor. *La Morte D'Arthure: The History of King Arthur and of the Knights of the Round Table*, Volume 2. London: Reeves and Turner, 1889.

Wurmser, Léon, and Heidrun Jarass. *Jealousy and Envy: New Views About Two Powerful Emotions*. Mahwah: Lawrence Erlbaum Associates, 2007.

Wyman, Walker Demarquis. *Wisconsin Folklore*, Volume 3. Madison: University of Wisconsin, Extension, Dept. of Arts Development, 1979.

Yadav, Rama Sankar, and B.N. Mandal. *Global Encyclopaedia of Education*. New Delhi: Global Vision Publishing House, 2007.

Yamaguchi, Kenkichi, Frederic De Garis, Atsuharu Sakai, and Fujiya Hoteru. *We Japanese: Being Descriptions of Many of the Customs, Manners, Ceremonies, Festivals, Arts and Crafts of the Japanese, Besides Numerous Other Subjects*. Japan: Fujiya Hotel, 1964.

Yamamoto, Kumiko. *The Oral Background of Persian Epics: Storytelling and Poetry*. Leiden: Brill, 2003.

Yardley, Edward. *The Supernatural in Romantic Fiction*. London: Longmans, Green, and Company, 1880.

Yar-Shater, Ehsan. *Encyclopaedia Iranica*, Volume 2, Issues 1–4. London: Routledge and Kegan Paul, 1990.

Yar-Shater, Ehsan. *Encyclopaedia Iranica*, Volume 4, Issues 5–8. London: Routledge and Kegan Paul, 1990.

Yoda, Hiroko, and Matt Alt. *Yokai Attack!: The Japanese Monster Survival Guide*. North Claredon: Tuttle Publishing, 2013.

Yolen, Jane, Paul Hoffman, and Shulamith Levey Oppenheim. *The Fish Prince and Other Stories: Mermen Folk Tales*. New York: Interlink Books, 2001.

Young, Dr. Jean. *The Prose Edda: Tales from Norse Mythology*. Berkley: University of California Press, 2001.

Yuan, Ke, Kim Echlin, and Nie Zhixiong. *Dragons and Dynasties: An Introduction to Chinese Mythology*. New York: Penguin Books, 1993.

Zalon, Rick. *The Jingwei Bird*. Bozeman: Christopher Matthews Publishing, 2014.

Zell-Ravenheart, Oberon. *A Wizard's Bestiary*. Franklin Lakes: Career Press, 2007.

Zell-Ravenheart, Oberon, and the Faculty of the Grey School of Wizardry. *Companion for the Apprentice Wizard*. Franklin Lakes: Career Press, 2006.

Zieber, Eugene, and the Bailey, Banks and Biddle Company of Philadelphia, Dept. of Heraldry. *Heraldry in America*. Philadelphia: Department of Heraldry of the Bailey, Banks and Biddle Company, 1895.

Zigmond, Maurice L. *Kawaiisu Mythology: An Oral Tradition of South-Central California*. Menlo Park: Ballena Press, 1980.

Zimmer, Heinrich. *Myths and Symbols in Indian Art and Civilization*. Delhi: Motilal Banarsidass Publishe, 1990.

Zimmerman, Larry J. *Exploring the Life, Myth, and Art of Native Americans*. New York: The Rosen Publishing Group, 2010.

Zirkle, Conway. *Early History of the Idea of the Inheritance of Acquired Characters and of Pangenesis: Transactions of the APS*. Philadelphia: American Philosophical Society, 2007.

Zwemer, Samuel Marinus. *The Influence of Animism on Islam: An Account of Popular Superstitions*. New York: Macmillan Company, 1920.

Index

A Bao A Qu 170
Aaapef 36
Aarak 11
Aarvak 11, 25, 47, 162, 294
Aavak 11, 47
Ab-Esh-Imy-Duat 11, 20
Ab-She 11, 20
Ab-Ta 11
Ababil 11
Abac 12
Abada 11, 326
Äbädä 11, 326
Abaddon 31
Abaia 11
Abakur 12
Abang Aku 170
Abas 12
Abaster 12, 16, 242
Abath 12
Abatos 12, 16, 242
Abchanchu 12
Abdu 12, 171
Abele 12
Abenaki folklore 261
Abenaki mythology 264
Abenaki people 48
Aberdover 209
Abere 12
Abhac 12, 13
Abhramu 18, 43, 101
Abiku 13
Aboatia 228
Abonsam 13, 279
Aboriginal folklore 50, 179, 198, 332
Aboulomri 13
Abraham 66
Abraxas 14, 158
Abtu 12
abuelo 93
Abuk 12
the Abyss 14, 42, 133, 269
Abyss, Lord of the 133
Abyssinia mythology, ancient 69
Abzu 14, 42
Acadia 202
Accounts of the Western Region 261
Acdestis 16
Ach-Chazu 202

Achilles 53, 84, 151, 254, 338
Achlis 14
Acicenaqn 199
Acipenser 14
Acmon 82
acoka tree 253
Actæon 14
Actaeon 8, 14, 84
acten 46
Acthon 14, 119, 267
Acusilaus of Argos 92
Adad 325
Adam and Eve 166
Adam and Lilith 288
Adanc 12
adar llwch gwin 14
Adaro 14–5, 239
Addanc 12
Addane 12
aderyn y corph 15
al Adha 15
Adhunall 15, 67, 212, 280, 283
Adils, King 296
Adissechen 15
Adis'sechen 15
Adlivun 32
Adrastia 77
Adrastus of Argos, King 40
Adrestos 39
Adro Onzi 15
Adro 15
adroa 149
The Adroanzi 15
adultery, personification of 279
Advarinaut 122
Aedd 344
Aeetes, King 40
Aegipan 99
Aegipanes 15
aegis of Zeus (Jupiter) 25
Aelianus 27, 110
Aello 15–6, 104, 151
Ællo 15
Aeneas 152
Aeneid 16, 152
Aeolus 84
Aepir 177
Aeschylus 22, 222, 318

the Aesir 126, 135, 137, 138, 147, 159, 176, 177, 206, 213, 292, 294, 295, 298, 318, 329, 330
Aeternae 16
Aethenoth 16
Aethiops 16, 119
Aethlem 16, 30, 72, 111, 324
Aethon 14, 16, 44, 68, 119, 202, 256, 257, 261, 267
Æthon 16
Aetolia, King 103, 203, 258, 338
Aetolian boar 74
Ætolian boar 74
Aeton 12, 16, 242
Æton 16
Aëton 19
Aetos Kaukasios 78
afanc 12, 189
Afghanistan 21
Afra-Sia-Ab 16
Afrasiab 16
Africa 7, 28, 29, 58, 77, 78, 104, 117, 131, 144, 149, 156, 169, 171, 131, 144, 149, 156, 169, 171, 173, 180, 181, 189, 203, 207, 218, 222, 227, 237, 240, 270, 274, 309, 317, 326, 334, 335
African coast 13, 26, 123
African Congo 11
African folklore 28, 107, 203, 237, 244, 346
African mythology 59, 230
African witchcraft 217
Afrosiyob 16
ag rog 170
Agamemnon 19, 39, 261
Agastya 180
Agathyrsus 115
Agdistis 16–7
Agha the Asura 17
Agha 17
Aghasura 17
Agloolik 17
Agouti 28
agramahishi 234
Agre 17, 104
Agriodus 17, 104, 205

agriogourouno 17
agumangia 170
ahani 29, 60
Aherman 102
Ahermanabad 103
Ahermanabâd 41
Ahi 17, 48
ahool 17
Ahriman 41, 97, 136
Ahuitazotl 17–8
Ahuitzotl 17
Ahura Mazda 134, 184
ai tojon 18
äi 18
Aiako Harria Mountain, Spain 171
Aiatar 18
Aicha Kandida 18, 150
Aido Hwedo 270
Aigeus 227
Aigicampoi 18
aigikampoi 18
Aigokeros 18
Ailill mac Mata 104, 126
Ailill 104
Aillen Trechenn 18
Ainu folklore 164, 187
Aionian Dragon 109
Airapadam 18
Aïrapadam 18
Airavana 18
Airavat 18–9, 43, 101, 234
Airavata 18, 43, 304
Airavati 18
Airitech 19
Aisakos 80
Aita 323
Aithe 19
Aithiopia, Africa 309
Aithon 19, 91, 158, 258
Aithops 19, 119, 158
aitvaras 19
Aja Akapad 19
Aja Ekapad 19
Ajatar 18
Ajattarais 18
Ajattaro 18
Ak-Baba 13
Ak-Kula 19–20
akabo 92
Akadian Hind 38
Akaname 20

Akandoji 20, 22
Akasaka Road,Tokyo 231
Aken 11
Akeneh 20, 153
Akerbeltz 20
Akeru 151
Akhekh 20
akhekhu 20
Akhen 20
Akhlut 20
Akkadia 106, 108, 200, 303, 325
Akkadian, Babylonian and Mesopotamian mythology 137, 215, 232
Akkadian folklore 34
Akkadian mythology 37, 56
Akkorokamui 21
akra 273
Aksar 21
Akupara 21, 101
Al-Buraaq 66
Al 21
Ala-muki 21, 228
Ala 21, 149
Alad 202
aladlammu 37
alan 21
Alarabi 21
Alaska, USA 30, 59, 186, 190, 193, 251, 336
Alatyr 133
Alazbo 92
Alb 23
Albania 69, 110, 197
Albanian folklore 65, 71, 100, 185, 331
Albanian-Italian mythology 33
Albanian mythology 54, 110, 142, 158, 184, 193, 194, 197, 204, 305, 306
alben 116
Albert the Great 66
albotritch 21, 124
Alcaeus 115
Alcathous 89
Alce, dog 22, 104
Alce 22
alchemic symbology 249
alchemist 30, 59, 193
alchemy 160
Alcida 22
alcohol 263, 322, 336
Alecto 22, 120, 222, 318
Aleiron 22
Alekto 22
Alerion 22
Alexander of Myndus 238
Alexander the Great 16, 69, 75, 219, 245
Alexandra 309
Alf 23
Alfarinn 177
Alfemoe 23
Alfhime 208
álfur 139
Algonquian 315

Algonquin folklore 224, 259, 319
Alicanto 22
Alicha 22
alicorn 12, 42, 44, 58, 69, 74, 75, 77, 85, 86, 117, 155, 158, 162, 179, 183, 187, 188, 191, 192, 194, 224, 227, 229, 237, 247, 254, 259, 262, 268, 271, 273, 286, 287, 293, 302, 306, 320, 326, 327, 339
Alien Gods 29, 322, 342
Alklha 22
Alkonost 22–3, 293
Alkuntane 23
All Saints' Day 95
All Strong 25
All-Strong 25
All Swift 25
All-Swift 25
Allecto 22
allergorhai horhai 98
Allerion 22
Allewyn 246
Allghoi Khorkhoi 23, 98
Allicanto 23
alligator-like 112
alligator 147, 149, 160, 161, 171, 211
allocamelus 23
alloes 23
almond tree 17
Almos 324
alopekos Teumesios 313
Alouqâ 25
Alouque 25
Alp Er Tonga 16
alp-luachra 25
Alp 23–5, 37, 52, 170, 178, 256
Alpdaemon 23
alpdrücke 24
Alpen 23
Alpes 23
alphyn 25
Alpine Pass 301
Alpmann 23
Alsean folklore 43
Alsvartr 177
Alsvid 11, 25, 47, 162, 295
Alsvider 25
Alsvidr 25
Alsvidur 25
Alsvin 25
Alsvinnr 25
Alsvith 25
Alswid 25
Alswider 25
Altai mountains 323
Altaic Buryat mythology 48
Altmark, Germany 272
Altviksas 19
Alu 202
aluga 25, 302
alukah 25, 302
Aluqa 25
Alyosha Popovich 323
am fear liath mor 124

Am-Mit 26, 33
Amahage 26
Amahatha 234
Amairgin 18
Amalthea 25, 77, 198
Amaltheia 25
amamehagi 26, 235
Amamet the Devourer 33
Amamet 26, 33
Aman 26, 49
Amanojaku 26
Amarok 26
Amarum 26
Amaterasu 314, 341
Ambarisha 234
Ambergris 42
Ambize 26
Ambrose 313
Ambundu tribe 192
amefurashi 26
Amemait 26
Amemet 26
Amen 26
Amergin 117
American folklore 60, 72, 74, 112, 136, 159, 176, 207, 243, 253, 257, 322, 326, 338
Amermait 26
Amesha Spentas 99
Amethea 26
Amfivena 27
Amhuluk 26–7, 29, 34
amikiri 27
Amit the Devourer 26
Amit 26
Ammet 26
Ammit 26
Ammut the Eater of the Dead 49
Ammut 26, 49
Amon 30, 299
Amphimedon 27
Amphion 27, 39, 98, 112, 158, 173, 222, 248, 259, 314
amphiptere 27, 28
amphisbaena 27, 252
amphisbaina 27
amphisbainai 27
amphisbene 27
amphisboena 27
amphisbona 27
amphisien-cockatrice 28
amphisien 28
amphista 28
amphiteres 28
Amphithemis 80
Amphitrite 99
Amphitryon (Cephalus) 313
amphivena 27
Ampyx 245
Amr b.Yarbu 292
Amr 277
Amratirtha 234
amrita 41
Amrta 181
amulet 12, 144, 246, 284, 312

Amunet 26
Amycus 28
ana-gumi 307
anaconda 174
analopos 28
Ananmese folklore 90
Ananse-Sem 28
Ananse 28
Anansi-Tori 28
Anansi 28
Ananta Boga 28–9, 44
Ananta Sesha 28
Ananta Shisha 28
Ananta-Sirsha 284
Ananta 284
Anantaboga 28
Anaon 33
anaskelades 29
Anavatapta 234
anaye 29, 60, 311, 313, 321, 322, 342
ancestral spirit 13, 29, 54, 123, 216, 334
Ancho 34
the Anchor 289
anchu 103
Ancient One 29
Ancient Spider 39
Ancud 86
andandara 29
andandara 29
Andaokut 30
Andes Mountains 128
Andha 234
André de Thevet 23
andro-sphinx 30
Androgeos 226, 227
Androgeos, Prince 227
Andromeda 82, 254, 261
Andros Island, Bahamas 213
Androsphinx 30, 92, 156, 299
andura 30
Aned 16, 30, 72, 111, 324
angel 30–1, 44, 51, 66, 144, 145, 150, 309
angel fish 229
Angel of Death 225
Angel of the Bottomless Pit 31
Angel of the Sea 31
angelic being 144
Angerboda 177
Angi 134
Angina 43
angka 31
Anglo-Saxon bestiaries 124
Angola 192
Angolan folklore 192
Angont 32
Angra Mainya 49
Angra Mainyu 99, 345
Angroboda 214
angry ones 120, 130
angula 26
angulo 26
Anguta 32
Ani folklore 174
animal-like 35

animal-man hybrid 34
animal-plant creature 55
animal sacrifice 307
animalitos 32
aniukha 32
aniwye 32
Anja 32
Anjanā 101
Anjana 32, 43, 101, 280
Anjanavati 32, 43, 101, 302
anjing ajak 33, 334
anka 186, 273
Ankh-Aapau 33, 312
Ankhi 33
Ankou 33
anksymen 27
anmalfrosh 33
Annamese folklore 91
annes de la mer 55
Annwn, Hounds of 33, 41,
   62, 93, 94, 122, 131
Annwn 33, 41, 62, 93, 94,
   122, 131, 147, 154, 209
anoethur 344
anphine 27
anphivena 27
anqa 33–4, 183, 273
anqä 33
anqu mughrib 33
anqua 273
Anshar 202
Ansi, China 80
ant-lion 34
ant 34, 48, 140, 171, 243
Antaf 34
antelabbit 174
antelope 20, 28, 51, 74, 99,
   114, 174, 216, 243, 281,
   326
antelopes with six legs 34
anthalops 22
Anthanasius 313
antholops 34
anthromorphic hybrid
   334, 335
anthropoid 41, 112, 245,
   266, 279, 309, 312, 323,
   324, 340
anthropophagous 49, 69,
   73, 81, 99, 103, 120, 133,
   135, 136, 148, 149, 161,
   192, 219, 239, 248, 259,
   264, 302, 305
anti–Christ, symbolic of
   253
antidote 11, 12
Antimachus 39
antlers 38, 71, 81, 86, 97,
   108, 112, 113, 116, 174,
   282, 293, 310, 311, 332,
   337, 346
antlion 34
antukai 34
Antxo 34
Anu 70, 119, 145
Anupama 43, 101, 198
Anxo 34
Anzu Bird 34
Anzu 34, 296, 326
ao ao 35

Ao Bing 35
Ao Chin 35
Ao Ch'in 35, 108
Ao Ghun 35
Ao Guang 35
Ao Ji 35
Ao Jun 35
Ao Kuang 35, 108, 211,
   213, 214, 250
Ao Ming 35
Ao Ping 35
Ao Qin 35
Ao Shun 35, 108, 211, 213,
   250
aobōzu 35
Aomori, Japan 176
Aonbarr 35
Aonbharr 35
Aosagibi 35
aosaginohi 35
Aotearoa 310, 324
apa atua 35–6
apa-mareikura 219
apa-whatu-kura 335
apa 35–6, 219, 336
Apache mythology 60
Apache 60, 316
Apala 36
Apalala 36
Apam Napat 75
Aparajita 234
Apelala 234
Apep 36
Aper Calydonius 74
Aphareus 36
Aphidas 36
Aphophis 36
Aphrodisiac 12, 302
Apli 36
Apocalypse of Paul 309
Apocrypha scriptures 103
Apollo 84, 95, 99, 110,
   121, 220, 267, 294
Apollodorus 16, 79, 99,
   119
Apophis 36, 107, 222, 235,
   238, 272, 283, 300
apotamkin 36
apotharni 36–7
apparition 31, 37, 48
apree 37
apres 37
après 37
apsaras 23, 37, 133
apsasu 37
Apsû 14
Apsu 14, 161, 315
Apta 234
aptaleon 28, 74
Apurana 234
aqrabuamelu 37
Aquarius 313
aquatic devil 37
aqueous devil 153
Aqueous 37
Aquila 38
Ara the beautiful 38
Arabia 88, 149, 247, 306
Arabian Peninsula 326
Arabic folklore 31, 99, 100,

236, 264, 267, 282, 289,
   292
Arabic tale 239
Arachne 38
aralez 38
aranda 5, 38
arassas 38
arasses 38
Araucanian (Mapuchen)
   folklore 239
Araucanian (Mapuchen)
   mythology 74, 332
Araucanian (Mapuchen)
   people 86, 87, 90, 163,
   168, 179, 260
Araucanin mythology 321
Arawker 11
Arawn, Lord of Annwn 33
Arcadia 38, 84, 116, 214,
   302
Arcadian Hind 38
archangel 132, 149, 262
Archbishop of Rouen 134
Archfiend Vitra 331
Arctic Ocean 294
Arctophonos 38, 265
Arctus 39, 42, 256, 328
Ardha-Matanga 18
Areion of the Black Mane
   39
Areion 39, 158, 296
Areop Enap 39, 273
Areos 39, 121, 169, 198,
   214
Ares (Mars) 19, 19, 98,
   109, 187, 203, 258, 302,
   338
Ares of Colchis, King 187
Aretophonus 38
Arf 39
Arfr 39
Arfuni 39
Argeius 27, 39, 98, 112,
   158, 173, 222, 248, 259,
   314
Argentina 35, 101, 153,
   168, 210, 334
Argentinean folklore 83,
   210, 260, 341
Arges 95
Argolis 38, 165
Argopelter 39, 124
Argos 40, 68, 82, 92, 219
Argos, king of 82
argus fish 40
Argus Panoptes 40, 115
Ari 177
ariels 40
Aries 40
Arion 39, 40, 99
Arioso, Ludovico 157
Arius 40
Arizona, USA 72
Arjuna 186, 325
Arkadia 121
Arkan Sonney 41, 122
Arkansas, Unites States of
   America 142
Arkasodara 18
Arktos 41

Arles, France 308
Arlez 38
armadillo-like 147
Armenia 99, 320
Armenian folklore 38
Armenian mythology 119,
   223, 285
Armenian, Libyan, and Persian folklore 21
Armorus City 127
Arneus 41
arngnasiutik 41
Arngrim 122
arrachd 129
arrow 27, 30, 38, 54, 74,
   88, 105, 116, 194, 201,
   234, 235, 239, 268, 278,
   294, 301, 311, 326, 346
Artemis (Diana) 74, 84,
   104, 201
Arthur, King 14, 16, 30,
   53, 54, 72, 75, 76, 78,
   111, 119, 127, 144, 147,
   154, 209, 219, 268, 299,
   324, 344
Arthurian folklore 30, 53,
   68, 72, 76, 107, 111, 119,
   127, 144, 209, 219, 299,
   324, 344
Arthurian legend 268
artifact spirits 322
Aruna 175, 234, 277
Arundel 41
Arusha 41
Arushi 41
Arvak 11
Árvak 11
Arvaka 11
Arvakr 11
Árvakr 11
Arvon 154
Arwakr 11
Aryaka 41, 234, 3004
Arzshenk 41
Asag 42, 200, 296
Asakku 42
Asavan 42
Asban 48
Asbolos the Diviner 202
Asbolus, dog 42
Asbolus 39, 42, 104, 256,
   328
asbsar 42
Asclepios 84
Asclepius 95
Asdeev 42, 129, 133
aseka-moke 177
asema 299, 303
Asena 42
Ash-Hrau 43
Ashanti folklore 279
ashiarai yashiki 43
Ashmog 43
Ashtadiggajas 43, 44, 101
Ashtadikkaranis 43
Ashvatara 234
Asian folklore 212
Asian mythology 108
asin 43
Asipatra 43

askefruer 43
aso zusta 44
Asootee 44
asp turtle 44
asp 167
aspido-tortoise 44
aspidochelon 44
aspidochelone 44, 124
aspidodelone 44
ass-bittern 44
ass camel 23
ass of Balaam 15, 44
ass with three legs 44
Assipattle 220
Assyrian folklore 240
Asterion 44, 92, 226, 227
Asterios 226
Asterius 44
Astika 306
Astraeus 292
Astraios 242
Astrope 16, 44, 68, 119, 158, 204, 256, 257, 267
Astyle 44
Asvatara 234
aswang mandurugo 45
aswang mannananggal 45, 299
aswang shape-shifter 45
aswang tik-tik 45, 46
aswang tiyanak 45, 46
aswang witch 45, 46, 292
aswang 45–6, 118, 292, 316
Atacama Desert 22
Atalanta (Atalante) 74
atanukans 46
Atar 49
Atargatis 99, 223
atce'n 46
Atfalati 27
athach 46, 58, 102, 212, 260
Athamas, King 40
Athena (Minerva) 38, 109, 111, 220, 221, 300, 302
Athens 47, 57, 92, 227, 262, 296
Athens, king of 47, 57, 92, 262
athsheniss 46
Atlante 157
Atlantis 256
Atli 138
atoosh 46
atraoimen 46
atshen 46, 47
Attica, king of 79
atunkai 34
Audhumbla 47
Audhumla 47
Audumbla 47
Audumla 47
aufhöcker 47
aufhocker 47, 170
aughisky 47, 114, 138, 186
August rooster 125
Augustine 313
Aulak 25, 302
Aunt Benny 174
Aunt Nancy 28

aunyaina 47
aurae 305
Aurgrimnir 177
aurochs 309
Aurora 119
Aurva 50
Australia 29, 38, 50, 64, 70, 100, 111, 115, 116, 134, 136, 146, 191, 198, 199, 207, 208, 216, 226, 232, 235, 236, 247, 270, 328, 332, 334, 336
Australian Aboriginal mythology 226
Australian and British folktales 247
Australian folklore 111, 236
Australian myths 270
Austria 38, 195, 301, 309
Austrian, Bavarian, and Swiss Alps 309
autochthon 47, 79, 110
avagrah 47
Avak 11, 25, 47, 162, 295
avanc 12
avatar 329
Avelerion 22
Avesta 44, 97, 183, 184
Avignon, France 308
Avon River 186
ax-handle hound 48
axe-handle hound 48
axehandle hound 48, 124
axex 48
axhandle hound 48
Axolotl 339
Aya 141
ayakashi 48
Az Dahak 48
Az ī Srūwar 345
az-i-wa'-giimki-mukh'tt 48
az-i-wu-gum-ki-mukh-ti 48
Azaban 48
Azande people 29, 244
Azban 48
Azcatl 48
Azdahak 48
Azeban 48
azéman 48
azeman 48, 334
Azhdak 48
Azhi Dahaka 48, 49
Azhi Dahaki 49
Azhi 48
Azi-Dahak 49
Aži Dahāka 349
Azi Dahaka 48, 349
Azi Sruuara 132
Azi Sruvara 49
Aži Višāpa 49
Aži Zairita 49
azi 48, 188
Azidahaka 48
Aztec folklore 17, 75
Aztec mythology 48, 88, 319, 399
azuki arai 49
azuki-koshi 49

azuki-toge 49
azuki-togi 49
azukiarai 49
azukitogi 49
azure dragon 284

ba she 49
ba-snake 49
Baal 107, 209, 211, 340, 341
Baba Yaga 87
Babai 49
babalawo 13
babau 246, 327
babayka 50
Babi 49
baboon-like 317
Babou 246
Babylon 30, 82, 99, 107, 108, 137, 191, 199, 202, 215, 223, 232, 244, 312, 315, 326, 328, 345, 346
Babylonian creation epic 14, 315
Babylonian mythology 30, 191, 199, 202, 244, 328
Bacchis 50
Bacchus (Dionysos) 80, 201, 215, 258, 273, 280, 284, 292
bachi-hebi 322
Bacis 50
bäckahästen 50, 186
Baconaua 50
baconawa 56
Badabada 50
badger 20, 68, 206, 264, 269, 274, 306
Badhava 50
Badhira 234
badigui 50
Baffin Island, Hudson Bay 268
bagat 50
baginis 50–1
Bagobo 202
Bagrada River 77
bagwyn 51
Bahamas 85, 213, 296
Bahamut 51, 122, 197
bahasa kapor 61
Bahram Gur 287
bahri 51
Bahyakunda 234
bai ze 51
Bai Ze Tu 51
baital 51
baitala 51
baitel 51
baitol 51
bâjang 51–2
bajang 52
baka 52
baka-asura 52
Bakbakwakanooksiewae 150, 200, 236, 242
bake-chochin 70
bakemone 307
bakemono 52, 312, 340, 345

bakeneko 52
bakezori 52
bakgest 62, 154
Bakhau 170
bakhtak 52
Bakimba 221
baklava 82
Bakonaua 50
Bakonawa 50
Bakunawa 50
bal-bal 52, 118
Bala Bhardra 53
Baladeva 53
Balaam 44
Balaam's ass 44
Baladeva 53
Balâm the ox 53, 243
Balardeu 246
balaur 53
balbal 21, 53
balena 53
balete trees 182, 215
Bali 325
Balios 53, 151, 158, 338
Balius 53
ball tailed cat 53, 124
Ballachulish, Scotland 102
Balongahoy 290
Balthasar 24
the Baltic 186
Baltic Sea 61
balubaale 53, 189
balubaale of death 53
balubaale of war 53, 189
Balzola (Dima) 120
Bamboo Books 188
Bamburg Castle 209
bangma 53
bangmi 53
bangungot 56
Bannocks 243
banshee 54, 216
banshee-like 143, 206
Bantu mythology 173
Banw 53–4, 324
bapet 54
bar juchne 54
bar yachre 54
barbary lamb 55, 202
barbioletes 54
barchad 55
bardha 54
bargeist 54, 154
bargest 54, 154
bargheist 54, 154
barghest 62, 154
bargtjest 54, 154
barguest 54, 62, 63, 132, 154, 228, 249, 266, 291, 295
bariaua 54
Barkley, Sir Moris 61
barmotez 202
barn ghaist 54
barnacha 55
barnacle goose 55
barometz 55, 202
Barraiya 116
Barren Grounds 298
Bartel 195
Bartelor the Wild Bear 195

Barushka Matushka 55
barychnas 170
Bash 50
bashe 50
Basil 313
basil cock 55, 89
basilcoc 55
basili-coc 55
basilicok 55, 56, 89
basilisci serpentis 55
basilisco 90
basilishrkoi 55
Basilisk 55–6, 78, 81, 89, 160, 171, 295
basilisk-like 171
basilisk serpent 55
Basis 50
Basket Monster 173
Basmu 56, 137, 199, 200, 232
Basoga people 180
Basque folklore 20, 171, 336
Basque mythology 21, 34, 28, 120, 140, 141, 171, 216
bat 22, 24, 51, 73, 87, 88, 162, 175, 208, 222, 241, 256, 259, 279, 285, 292, 301, 318, 338, 341
bat-like 17, 45, 106, 107, 109
La Bataille Loquifer 76
Batak folklore 293
Batak mythology 66
Bath-Slough 132
bathtub licker 20
batibat 56
battle magic 329
Battle of Actium 115
Battle of Arcadia 214
Battle of Mag Tuired 63
Battle of Mu 83
Battle on the Lake of Ice 300, 329
battlefield 37, 64, 68, 69, 191, 329
bauba ("bugbear") 56
baubas 56
Baugi 177
Bavaria 38, 195, 309, 337
Bavarian folklore 337
bawa 56
Bay of Cadiz 127
Bay Valley 51
Bayard 56–7, 158, 262
Bayardo 57, 68
Baykok 57
bazalicek 55
beaklike 194
Bean Goose 132
beannach-nimhe 57
bear 16, 34, 37, 38, 41, 52, 58, 63, 75, 81, 82, 111, 133, 146, 152, 17, 187, 195, 219, 236, 250, 252, 253, 259, 268, 274, 285, 288, 308, 322, 335, 339
Bearing Sea, Alaska 193
bearlike 52, 220, 274, 322

beast glatisant 268
Beast Jasconius 57
Beast of Gevaudin 57
beast of Odail Pass 58
Beast of the Apocalypse 106
beast of the Lowering Horn 58
Beathach mbr Loch Odha 57
beaver 12, 26, 60, 130, 225, 266, 281, 337
beaver-like 225, 266
Bebi 49
bed cat 57, 124
Behaiah 40
Behemah 206
Behemoth 206, 346
bei zi 51
Beigad 57–8
Beigadarhill 58
Beigorri 58
Beinvidr 177
yn beisht kione 58, 282
Beithir 58
Beitr 177
Bela Bela Indians 268
Belgian folklore 249
Beli 177
belili 302
Bellerophon 85, 254
Bellzebub 195
Belorussia 334
beloved hare 229
belt, magical 71
Beltaine 63
Belzeniggl 195
Belznickel 195
Ben Bulbain Mountain, Sligo 64
Ben MacDhui 124
ben-varrey 223
Beowulf 127, 138, 143, 240, 280
Beowulf 127, 143, 280
berg-mänlein 113
berg people 321
Bergrisar 177
bergstutzen 301, 309
Bering Sea 20
Berlingr 177
bernaca 55
bernekke 55
bernicle goose 55
bernicle 55
berserkers 335
Beside the Fire 25
Bestia 57, 260
La Bèstia de Gavaudan 57
bestiary, medieval 61, 73, 88, 276
La Bête du Gévaudan 57
Bethlehem 93, 212, 222
betizu 171
Bêvar-Asp 345
Bevis of Southampton 41
Bhainsasura 58
bhakti 83
Bhardra 58, 216, 280, 331
Bhima 52, 192
bi-blouk 58, 149

bialozar 58
biaolozar 196
Biarkarimur 58
Biarki 58
biasd bheulach 58
biasd na srogaig 58
Biast 260
Bibi 49
bicha 59
bicorne 59
bicouaine 59
Bida 59
El Bien Peinado 94
Bifrost 149
big beast of Lochawe 57
Big Dipper 105
Big Ears 59, 73
Big Fish 59
Big Fish of Iliamna 59
big head 59
Big Owl 60
Bilbao 127
billdad 60, 124
biloko 60
Bilvapatha 234
Bilvapatra 234
bimbam 60, 124
binangunan 317
binaye ahani 29, 60, 314, 321
binaye albani 60
Binbinga people 64
la bincouaine 59
bingbuffer 60
bird 13, 15, 20, 21, 22, 27, 31, 33, 43, 44, 45, 46, 51, 52, 54, 55, 56, 60, 64, 67, 68, 72, 73, 75, 77, 79, 83, 85, 87, 88, 89, 93, 100, 107, 111, 112, 119, 120, 123, 124, 125, 127, 129, 130, 132, 134, 135, 141, 148, 149, 150, 153, 155, 156, 158, 160, 163, 164, 165, 169, 175, 176, 178, 182, 183, 184, 187, 192, 196, 198, 200, 202, 204, 212, 213, 217, 220, 225, 226, 234, 236, 239, 240, 242, 243, 245, 247, 249, 250, 254, 255, 256, 257, 258, 259, 264, 265, 267, 269, 270, 273, 274, 276, 277, 279, 283, 284, 285, 287, 289, 290, 293, 295, 297, 301, 304, 312, 314, 317, 319, 320, 324, 325, 326, 327, 330, 331, 332, 333, 336, 337, 341, 342, 343, 344, 345, 346
The Bird Girp 137
bird griffin 60, 297
bird-like 23, 51, 64, 75, 85, 134, 149, 225, 240, 255, 256, 285, 301
bird man 60
Bird of Dawn 153
bird of immortality 273
bird of the dawn 79
birds, king of the 184, 292

birds, magical 14
birds of Mount Gurayu 61
birds of Rhiannon 61
Birth of the Buddha 117
bisan 61
Biscay 253
bisclaveret 335
bishop fish 61, 282
Bishop Harsnet 128
bishop of Castre 219
Bishop of Skalholt 113
Bison Bull 61, 296
Bistern Dragon 61
Bitje 61
bitoso 61–2
bivar-asp 49
biwa-bokuboku 62
biwa monk 62
bixie 62
Bizhan 287
Bjarr 186
Bjorgolfr 177
Bjorn 63
black angus 62, 184
black bog of Hergest 147
black cat 19, 73, 256
black dog 62–3, 73, 76, 129, 139, 143, 147, 154, 186, 228, 249, 250, 256, 264, 295
black dog of Hergest 154
black hodag 159
Black Peterm 195
Black Pit 195
Black Sea 40, 276
Black Shanglan 62
Black Shuck 62–3, 132, 154, 291
black shug 62, 154
black sow 63
black waters of the Underworld, personification of 305
black worm 63
blackbird 164
bladmall 63
Blakk 63
Blakkr 63
Blappvari 177
bledlochtana 63
bledmail 63, 282
bledmall 63, 282
Bleeding Lance 144
bleiz-garo 211
bleiz-garou 211
bleiz-garv 334
Blind King of Kauravyas 101
Blodinghofi 63
Blodug-hofi 63
Bloðughofi 63
Blóðughófi 63
blood dogs 63
Bloody Bones 64, 271
bloody man 143
blue men 224
bmola 64
bo-guest 54, 154
boa constrictor 17, 28, 168
Boanthropy 334, 335

boar 5, 16, 17, 21, 30, 47, 53, 57, 63, 64, 69, 72, 73, 74, 92, 97, 111, 114, 120, 141, 144, 145, 147, 166, 205, 209, 232, 238, 260, 271, 273, 277, 282, 296, 298, 324, 327, 334, 335, 337, 340, 344
boar-like 21, 141, 205
boar of Ben Bulbain 64
boas 30, 64
Bobbi Bobbi 64
bobcat 90
Bobi-Bobi 270
bocanach 65
bockman 65
bockshexe 23
bocksmarte 23
bodhisattva 29, 117
Boeotia 109
bogart 295
bogatyr 55, 187, 194
Bogazkoy 107
bogeyman 50, 65, 71, 72, 93, 94, 194, 281, 291
boggelman 65
bogieman 65
Bohol 226
Boisterer 90
Bokuba 62
Bokwus 65
Bolivia 35, 207, 276
Bolivian folklore 12, 276
Bolla 65, 197
Bolman 65
Bologna, Italy 170
Bolton ass 65
Bolung 270
Bonacho 246
bonachus 66
bonacon 66
bonaconn 66
bonasus 66
Bonhomme Sept-Heures 65
Bonito maidens 65–6
bonnacon 66
Bonnie Prince Charlie 64
boobrie 5, 66, 122
boogerman 65
boogermonster 65
boogeyman 65
boogie man 65
boogyman 65
Book of Creation 140
Book of Deuteronomy 247
Book of Han 261
Book of Heroes 114
Book of Hours 144
Book of Jasher 303
Book of Job 327
Book of Physiognomy 188
Book of Psalms 346
Book of Revelations 31, 96
Book of the Overthrowing of Apophis 36, 235, 283
Book of Tobit 36, 235, 285
bookhas 259
boomerang 64, 236

boon 37, 134, 179, 180, 181, 291, 304
boon of immortality 134, 179
Booyan (Buyan) Island 132, 133
Bor 47
Al Borak 15, 66
borametz 55
Boraq 66
boraro 66
Boraspati Ni Tano 66
Boreas 66, 158, 262
boreyne 67
boroboro-ton 67
boroka 67
borometz 55
Bors 268
Borushka Matushka 55
Bosnia 265, 334
Bouders 67
Boudons 67
Boundary Pound, Maine 60
bovine-like 85
Brahma 179, 180, 191, 197, 236, 270
brahmaparus 67
brahmaparush 67
brahmaparusha 67
brahmeparush 67
brain sucker 217
bramaparush 67
Bran 15, 67, 95, 212, 280, 283
Bran the Blessed 95
Brash 148
Brazil 35, 153, 174, 210, 334, 344
Brazilian folklore 47, 78, 153, 226, 292
bread fruit tree 176
breath, fire 14, 91, 107, 109, 153, 168, 197, 252, 260, 266, 274
breath, poisonous 107, 110, 208
Brenton 113
Breton folklore 33, 341
Brian Boru 259
bride-price 262
Brigadore 67
Brigliadore 67
Brigliadoro 68
Brinsop, England 68
Brinsop Dragon 68
Brisingamen Dwarfs 113
British Columbia, Canada 30, 120, 156, 182, 206, 297, 322, 333
British Columbia folklore 333
British folklore 41, 59, 61, 65, 68, 78, 85, 98, 108, 117, 132, 155, 186, 209, 243, 280, 337, 339
British Guyana (Guiana) 101
Brittany 33, 334, 335
Brize 68

broc sidh 68
Bronie 68
Bronte 16, 44, 68, 119, 158, 204, 256, 257, 267, 300
Brontes 95
bronze bulls 309
Bronzomarte 68
brownies 117
broxa 68
Brucha 68, 210
bruckee 68
Brunei, Borneo 190
Brunhilde 141, 142, 330
buata 69, 73
buba 69
bubak 69
bubák 69
Bucco 105
bucentaur 69
Bucephala 69
Bucephalas 69, 219
Bucephalus (Bucephalas) 219
Bucephalus 69, 219
buckland shag 69
budas 69
Buddhist folklore 36, 193
Buddhist mythology 86, 108, 231
Budli 138
Buecubu 73
Buenos Aries, Argentina 101
buffalo-like 293
Bugal the snake 132
buhlgeist 170, 302
Buhumulaka 234
bujanga 69–70
Bukavac 70
Bukephalos 69
bulaing 70
Bulanj 270
Bulat 184
bulbul hezar 53
bulchin 59
Bulgarian folklore 69, 149, 320
bull 37, 39, 41, 49, 50, 51, 58, 59, 61, 66, 70, 74, 77, 80, 86, 87, 91, 92, 93, 104, 119, 122, 125, 126, 130, 134, 136, 145, 178, 185, 196, 197, 199, 203, 212, 226, 227, 232, 235, 236, 237, 266, 268, 279, 288, 296, 306, 308, 309, 315, 325, 326, 328, 341
bull-men 315
Bull of Heaven 70, 119, 145
Bull of Inde 70
Bull of the Gods 237
bullar 65, 197
bullock 67, 132, 267
bumann 65
bumble tree 199
bumole 64
buneep 70
bunyip 70

Bunyon, John 143
buo 263
bura-bura 70
burach bhadi 70–71
Burak the horse of Abraham 66
Burak 66
Buraq 66
Buri (Bure) 47, 113
Burko 71
Burma 68, 253, 267, 313
Burmese folklore 174, 181, 221, 231, 290, 293, 319, 328, 334
Burmese mythology 47, 157
Burton, Richard 273
buru 71
buruburu 71
Burushko 71
bushtra 71
Busiltjörn River 143
busse 71
bussemand 71
bussemend 71
butatsch-ah-ilgs 71
buxenwolf 71
buzawosj 72
Buzebergt 195
bwcas 259
Bwlch 324
Byakko, Japan 320
Byakko 72, 135, 304, 320
Byelorus 335

Cabal 72, 209, 324, 344
Caballucos del Diablo 72
cablyy-ushtey 308
Cabracan 332
cabyll-ushtey 72, 291
cactus cat 72, 124
Cadair Idris 94
Cadeia 109
cadejo 72–3
Cadissen 203
cadmean Vixen 313
Cadmus (Kadmos) 109
Caeneus 39, 42, 204, 226, 256, 328
Caeneus, Prince 39, 42, 256, 328
Caesar Augustus 75
Cafal 72
Cafall 72
cafre 73, 265
Cagrino 73
Cai (Kay) 76, 144
Cain 143, 335
Caincinde 19
Cairngorm Mountains 124
cait sith 59, 73
Calabria 33
calaca 93
caladre 73
caladrius 73
calag 73–4
la calchona 74
caleps 74
calf 36, 62, 66, 73, 76, 91,

108, 163, 218, 228, 235, 236, 250, 274, 304
Calf of Kamadhenu 304
California, USA 81, 148, 321
Caligula 272
callitrice 74
callitrix 74
calopus 22, 74
Calydonian boar 74, 92
calygreyhound 74
camahueto 74
cambions 74–5, 170
Cambodia 46
Cambrensis, Giraldus 55
camel 15, 23, 43, 75, 86, 99, 108, 185, 247, 257, 268, 343
camel-leopard 75
cameleopardel 75
cameleopardel 75
camelo-pard 75
camelo-pardalis 75
Cameria 331
camp chipmunk 75, 124
Campacti 75
Campe 75, 110
camphor-bearing trees 61
camphor language 61
camphor tree 195, 256
camphurcii 75
campions 74
camros 75
camrus 75
Camulatz 76, 91, 311, 338
Canace 76
Canache 76, 104
Canada 26, 32, 65, 150, 156, 160, 168, 182, 185, 190, 199, 227, 230, 236, 242, 263, 268, 322, 324
cancer 20, 77
canchu 76
Candle Dragon 346
canine-like 145, 282
Canis 201
canis lucernarius 226
Canis Minor 215
cannibal 12, 43, 58, 60, 67, 149, 192, 244
cannibalistic monster 46, 150, 185, 242
Cantabria, Spain 72
Cantabrian region 94
Canterbury Tales 56, 89
cap, magical 104
cap of divinity 328
Capacti 76
Le Capalu 76, 78
Capalus 76, 78
Cape Cod 265
capelthwaite 62, 76, 154
Capitol Hill 77
Capiz province, Philippines 45
Capreus of Haliartus, King 40
Capricorn 18, 76, 77, 281
Capricornus 18, 25, 76, 77
caprine (goatlike) 162, 137, 175, 194

The Capture of Sampo 168
Caraibes folklore 336
Carbuncle Snake 77
Carbunkel 77
carcazonon 183, 229
Carcinus 77, 165
caretyne 77
Carib folklore 269
Caribbean island folklore 28, 178, 211
Caribbean island mythology 46
caristae 77
carnivorous ao ao 35
Carrabuncle 77
Carrier people 120
carrog 77
cartazonon 77, 326, 327
cartazoon 183
Carthage 77
Carthaginian serpent 77
Cas Corach 19
Casar, Francisco de la Vega 127
Caspar 24
Caspar Plautius 281
Cassiopeia 82
Castalian spring 78
castalides 78
Castor 79, 84, 95, 96, 151, 258
cat 19, 28, 32, 38, 52, 53, 57, 59, 72, 73, 74, 76, 78, 79, 81, 88, 93, 98, 124, 125, 126, 138, 145, 146, 167, 180, 191, 205, 216, 233, 238, 240, 243, 253, 256, 266, 269, 278, 295, 269, 299, 301, 309, 311, 326, 333, 334, 335, 341
cat fish 78
cat-fish 78
cat-headed snake 98
cat sídhe 73
cat sith 73
catablepon 78
Catalonian folklore 231, 330
Catalonian mythology 102, 156
caterpillar 39, 273, 287
catfish 176, 181, 235
Cath Balug 78
Cath Balwg 78
Cath Paluc 78
Cath Palug 76, 78
Cathy 203
catlike 59, 98, 114, 177, 239, 316, 322, 342
catoblepas 78
cattle 24, 47, 48, 54, 63, 64, 66, 68, 72, 92, 98, 107, 113, 114, 122, 126, 131, 136, 147, 148, 153, 155, 169, 172, 173, 180, 181, 203, 205, 209, 210, 218, 231, 252, 293, 308, 335, 341
cattywampus 78, 124
catwolfe 74

Caucasus eagle 78, 115
Caucasus Mountains 78
Caucavielha 171
cauchmar 170
Caumas 78
cauquemare 23
Cavall 72
cave 17, 18, 19, 21, 22, 34, 56, 65, 94, 99, 106, 107, 115, 116, 117, 125, 127, 134, 142, 143, 153, 164, 170, 172, 185, 199, 201, 209, 211, 218, 226, 236, 246, 298, 322, 330, 343
Cave Cruachan 19
cave of the sky 56
Caw, King 344
Caw of Scotland 209
Cawthorne dragon 78
Cawthorne wyrm 78
Cawthorner Park, England 78
caypor 78
ccoa 78–9
ce sith 93
ceasg 79
Cecrops 47, 79
Ceffyl-Dwr 79
ceffyl dŵr 79
Cei (Kay) 78
Celadon the Lapith 28
Celaeno 152
Celeris 79
celestial archer 125
celestial being 108
celestial cock 79, 153
celestial creature 37, 127, 327
celestial dog 316
celestial horse 79–80, 316
Celestial Mountains 80
celestial nature spirits 133
Celestial Stag 80
Celestial Water Dragon 315
celphie 80
Celtic folklore 63, 64, 68, 115, 131, 209, 220, 240, 309, 324
centaur 8, 12, 16, 17, 22, 27, 28, 36, 39, 40, 41, 42, 44, 76, 78, 80, 83, 84, 87, 89, 90, 91, 92, 95, 96, 98, 99, 100, 101, 104, 105, 111, 112, 116, 121, 144, 151, 152, 154, 157, 158, 165, 166, 167, 169, 172, 173, 191, 196, 201, 202, 204, 205, 206, 214, 221, 222, 223, 224, 225, 228, 229, 236, 238, 239, 245, 248, 250, 252, 256, 257, 258, 259, 260, 262, 265, 272, 273, 274, 276, 292, 300, 301, 313, 314, 316, 328
centauren 80
centaurides 81, 166
centauro tritons 167
Centauromachy 12, 28, 36,

39, 41, 42, 80, 83, 87, 89, 90, 92, 96, 99, 101, 105, 111, 121, 144, 154, 157, 166, 169, 202, 204, 214, 221, 223, 2224, 229, 245, 248, 256, 272, 273, 328
Centauros 80
centichora 81, 114
centicore 81, 114
centipede 81, 86, 281
centipede of Biwa 81
Central American folklore 72
Central American whintosser 81, 124
centycore 81
Cephalus 201, 313
cepus 82
cerastes 82
Cerberus 82, 85, 115, 165, 238, 304
cercopes 82
Ceres 39, 40
Cerneian Hind 38
Cernel 63
Cerus 82
Cerynean Hind 38
Ceryneia Hind 38
Cerynitian Hind 38
Ceshamain 63
Ceto 99, 115, 121, 141, 201, 221, 300
Cetus 82–3, 254, 275
cetus dentatus 275
Ceylon 140
Chagrin 73
chai tung 188
chain of Cilydd Hundred Holds 111
chakora 83
chaladrius 73
Chaldean mythology 288
Chamba pan 169
Champeya 234
chamrosh 83, 285
chamucho 93
Chan 83
chan chu 315
chancha con cadenas 83
chancho de lata 83
Ch'ang Hao 83
Chaos, personification of 208, 315, 331
Chapalu 76, 78
charadrius 73
Charaxus 83, 90
Chariklo 84
chariot 11, 12, 14, 16, 19, 25, 26, 31, 40, 41, 44, 53, 66, 68, 96, 102, 111, 112, 119, 120, 125, 145, 156, 157, 158, 162, 175, 200, 204, 207, 234, 242, 254, 256, 257, 258, 262, 266, 267, 295, 297, 307, 316, 328, 338
Charlemagne 56, 68, 76
Charles IX 219
charm, magical 52, 190
Charybdis 84, 281
chatloup 74

Chaucer, Geoffrey 56, 89
chauche vieille 23
Chauchevieille 171
Cheiron 8, 16, 17, 22, 42, 76, 84, 96, 104, 105, 111, 116, 151, 152, 165, 166, 167, 201, 205, 206, 214, 222, 223, 228, 236, 238, 248, 250, 252, 257, 262, 265, 300, 301, 314, 316
Chel the python 132
Cherokee folklore 245, 333
Cherruve 84
Cherufe 84
Le Chevalier du Papegau 127
Chhandas 260
chi 206
Ch'I Lin 327
ch'i-lin lin 188
Ch'i-Lung 84
Chi Lung Wang 84
chi mu 342
Chi Po 125
Chi Song-Zi 125
chiai tung 84–5, 179, 212, 327, 339
chiang-liang 85
chiao 85, 108, 189, 344
chiao-lung 85
chichevache 59, 85
chichiface 85
chick charnie 85
Chickasaw folklore 293
chickcharnee 85
chickcharney 85
chickcharnie 85
chicken 89, 159, 200, 207, 217, 262, 295, 301
Chidna 115
Chief of All the Animals 179
Chief of the Fishes 227
chief of the fulmars 32
chiehe'uaehe 85
Chien Ping 72
Chi'en Tang 85
chi'ih-muh 252
Chikura 85
child-like 26
Child of the Waters 29
child-snatcher 265
children 5, 11, 13, 18, 26, 30, 31, 32, 36, 38, 70, 43, 45, 46, 47, 50, 52, 54, 56, 64, 65, 67, 69, 72, 78, 87, 92, 96, 94, 95, 103, 114, 116, 117, 118, 126, 128, 130, 137, 140, 148, 149, 160, 168, 169, 170, 171, 175, 177, 178, 180, 182, 183, 190, 191, 194, 195, 204, 217, 220, 225, 226, 229, 230, 232, 235, 236, 238, 241, 244, 246, 251, 252, 253, 254, 255, 259, 263, 265, 271, 272, 276, 279, 281, 290, 292, 296, 297, 300, 301, 320, 324, 325, 327, 335, 336

Chile 74, 84, 86, 87, 90, 118, 128, 145, 163, 168, 171
Chilean folklore 179, 203, 260, 302
Chilean mythology 22
Chiloc 86
Chilote and Mapuche mythology 256
chiludo 74
Chimaera 82, 85
Chimalmat 332
chimchimen 168
Chimera 62, 85, 115, 165, 238, 242, 254
chimerical animal 124
chimerical creature 2, 20, 32, 51, 67, 71, 80, 83, 85, 87, 108, 122, 134, 137, 143, 145, 151, 157, 159, 162, 175, 178, 202, 220, 225, 227, 229, 232, 233, 242, 252, 267, 274, 277, 285, 299, 301, 306, 324, 337, 339, 340, 343
chimerical hybrid 27, 159
Chin Ming 135
China 29, 35, 42, 54, 86, 96, 109, 112, 125, 141, 162, 163, 176, 190, 212, 216, 236, 257, 275, 283, 314, 326, 327, 334, 335, 344
China Sea 42, 112
Chinese dragon 86, 108, 274, 309, 342
Chinese folklore 72, 83, 84, 85, 109, 123, 124, 129, 135, 159, 161, 162, 163, 164, 165, 175, 176, 188, 191, 198, 204, 212, 214, 222, 239, 256, 259, 260, 261, 262, 267, 268, 269, 284, 289, 290, 304, 315, 316, 319, 320, 334, 338, 339, 342, 343, 344, 345
Chinese fox 86
Chinese lion 183, 194
Chinese mythology 35, 42, 49, 51, 79, 80, 85, 87, 102, 104, 106, 109, 125, 129, 140, 148, 150, 153, 162, 163, 175, 176, 189, 196, 205, 206, 211, 213, 250, 261, 262, 264, 345
319, 342, 344, 346
Chinook Klickitat 337
chinthe 86
chio-tuan 86
chipekwe 117
Chippewa 155
Chirada 134
Chiricahua 60
Chiron 84
chitauli 218
Chitor, India 170
Chitra 234
chivato 86, 118
Chiyou 196

chōchinobake 86–7
chochinobake 86
Choctaw people 184
choin dubh 62, 154
Choko 87, 190
cholera 313
chollima 87
chonchon 87
chonma 87
ch'ou-t'i 87
Chou Wang 83
Chrétien de Troyes 54, 144
Christ, symbol of 143, 327
Christian demonology 123, 307
Christian devil 195
Christian folklore 89, 91, 150, 166, 246, 286, 308
Christian iconography 313
Christian tradition 107, 327
Le christianisme et l'Ex-treme-Orient 86
Christianity 14, 18, 19, 21, 31, 33, 107, 143, 312, 338
Christmas 95, 139, 193, 195
Christmas Eve 138, 139, 178
Christmas nisse 178
The Chronicles of Japan 115
Chronos, the dragon 87
Chrysaor 222, 254
Chthonius 87
Chu-Ya 153
ch'uan-t'ou 87
Chuang Tzu 255
Chudo-Yudo 87
Chukwa 44, 88, 215
chumcho 93
chupacabra 32, 88, 256
church grim 143
Church of Saint Mary Magdalene 193
churchyard dog 132
churning and frothing water, personification of 80
Churning of the Ocean 18, 21, 37, 284, 304, 325, 330
Chyavana 215
cicadas 61
cigouave 88
Cillaros 95
cinnabar 125, 251, 316
Cinnabar Caves 125
cinnamologus 88
cinnamon 54
cinnamon bird 88
cinnamon quills 88
cinnamulgus 88
Cipactil-Caiman 76
Cipactli 88
Cipatli 75
Circe 144, 281
Circhos 89
Cirein Cròin 89
Cirein Croin 89, 282
cirenus bird 88
Cithaeronian Lion 89

Cithaeronian 89, 238
Citraka 234
civet cat 341
clam 39, 83, 128, 273, 312
Clanis 89, 172
Clarion 144
classical Greek and Roman mythology 16, 26, 27, 68, 172, 204, 256, 266, 300
Claudian 95
Claudius Aelian 237
Claudius Aelianus 27, 110
claw-like 43, 61
Claw People 189
Clayoqut 149
Cleopatra 167
Clodion the Long 268
cloud-like 21
cloud of smoke 118
cluricaunes 295
Clytus 89
Cnossus 44
coat-of-arms 143
Coatlicue 339
cobra 20, 171, 234, 276, 330
coca 89, 93, 94
cock-fish 89
cock horse 157
cock of dawn 79
cock of Heaven 79, 89
cockatrice 28, 55, 56, 89, 200, 286
cockatrix 89
cockerel 56, 89, 90
coco 93
coco man 93
coconut tree 310, 333
Codex Borgia 76
Codex Yoalli Ehēcatl 76
Coeur d'Alene 156
cohuleen druith 224
coic biasta mora grannai 90
Colchis dragon 187
Colchis 40
Coll ap Collfrewy 154
collar of Canhastry Hun-dred Hands 111
collie 185
colo-colo 90
colocolo 90
Cologne, Germany 24
Colombian folklore 160, 262, 282, 324
Colorado, USA 296
Columbia River sand squink 90, 124
Columbus, Christopher 282
comb 60, 190, 252, 318, 324
Comb-Rice Field, Princess 116
come-at-a-body 90, 124
Cometes 83, 90
Comography 23
Compendium Maleficarum 37

Compendium of Witches 37
Comrade 90
Comtesse d' Aulnoy 246
con-ma-dau 90
Con Tram Nu' O' C 91
Conabos 19, 91, 158, 258
Confucius 188
Congo, Africa 11, 26, 60, 117, 225, 270, 326
Congo-Gabon boarder 221
Connacht 18, 104, 126
Connecticut, USA 138
conopenii 91
Conrad Lycosthenes 36
constellation 25, 40, 70, 77, 84, 99, 105, 119, 215, 289, 294, 313, 330
constrictor-like 248
contraries 315
Conway Valley 77
Coosa 336
copard phalmant 257
copper cat 326
copper mine 326
corc-chluasask 91
Cordillera 276
Cordoba 83
Cornu 91
cornucopia 25
Cornwall, England 154, 243
corocotta 92
corpan side 6, 91
corpse bird 15
corpse candle 113, 178, 298, 303
Corpus Christi 98
Corynthus 91
cosmic cow 135
cosmic dragon 22, 141, 275
cosmic eagle 188
cosmic elk 187
cosmic golden egg 33, 101, 198, 266, 302, 329
cosmic fish 101
cosmic goose 135
cosmic rainbow serpent 96
cosmic scarab beetle 187
cosmic serpent 315
cosmic turtle 21, 101
cosmic water 199, 249, 319
cosmic whale 268
Costa Rican demonology 249
Cotzbalam 91
cougar 265
cougar fish 91, 124, 231
council of Nicea 31
count p'eng 256
courage, freedom, and love, symbolic of 279
Coventry 16
Cow of Plenty 304
coxcomb 337
Coyolxauhqui 339
Coyote 337
coyote 90
crab-spider 28
crane 52, 225, 249, 302
Crantor 99
Cree 46, 155, 225

Cree folklore 315, 336
Creek folklore 336
Cretan bull 91
Crete 25, 29, 77, 198, 227, 294
crimsonowl 345
crio-sphinx 92
criosphinx 32, 92, 156, 299
Croagh Patrick 232
crocodile 11, 12, 26, 88, 107, 132, 166, 171, 199, 207, 216, 274, 283, 297, 333
crocodile-like 76, 106, 117, 240, 248, 251, 319, 333, 337
crocotta 96, 206, 218
crocotte 92
crocuta 92
crodh mara 92, 122, 147
crodh sidhe 92
Cromis 92, 214
cromlechs 216
Crommyonian Sow 92, 115
cron annwn 131
Cronus (Uranus) 75
crop failure 29
Croque-mitaine (Croquemitaine) 93, 246
le croque-mitaine 93, 246
crossroads 47, 62, 168, 210, 249, 299
crow 79, 83, 126, 146, 154, 183, 191, 262, 270, 277, 292, 298, 311, 341, 344
Cruachan 18, 19, 117
cruelty and evil, personification of 323
crustacean 55, 77
cryptid 2, 7, 260
Ctesias 247
cu bird 93
cu sith 62, 67, 93, 122, 154
cu sìth 93
Cuailnge 126
cuba 93, 124
Cubilon 93, 222
cuca 93
Cúchulainn 47, 112, 207
cuco 93
cucui 93
cucuy 93, 94
el cucuy 94
Cuélebre 94
Cuero 94
Cuero Unudo 94
cughtagh 94
Culebre 94
Culhwch 111, 324, 344
cultural hero 1, 14, 15, 19, 27, 28, 38, 39, 40, 41, 42, 44, 47, 55, 60, 64, 67, 78, 81, 83, 85, 89, 91, 92, 96, 97, 98, 99, 112, 136, 137, 158, 173, 192, 212, 222, 224, 240, 248, 257, 258, 259, 272, 280, 283, 301, 302, 311, 314, 321, 322, 323, 338, 342

curcrocute 92
Curtag Mhor a' Chuain 89
Cusith 93
cute-cuss 264
cutter-cuss 264
cwn annw 33, 62, 94, 95, 131, 147, 154
cŵn annwfn 147, 154
cwn annwfn 94, 95, 131, 147, 154
cwn annwn 33, 94, 131
cŵn annwn 33, 94, 131
cŵn bendith y manau 147, 154
cwn cyrff 94, 157
cwn mamau 94
cŵn toili 147, 154
cwn wyber 94
cŵn wybr 147, 154
Cybele 16, 17
cyclone or whirlwind, personification of 97
Cyclops 21, 34, 74, 75, 95, 346
Cyclops, Elder 95
Cyclops, Younger 95
Cyfwlch 324
Cylhwch 16, 30, 111
Cylla 95
Cyll'aros 95
Cyllaros 95, 151, 158
Cyllarus 95–6, 166
Cyllarus, horse 96
Cymelus 96
Cymry Fu 15
cynamolgus 88
Cynedyr the Wild 16, 30
Cynedyr 324
cynogriffin 83, 285
cynolycus 92
cynoprosopi 96
Cyon Chryseus 198
Cyprian 95
Cyprius 96, 104, 214
Cyrenaica 55

Da 96
da chor 170
Daain 97
dab 170
Dabbatu 'L-Arz 96
Dadhikra 96–7
Dadhikravan 96
Dadhimukha 234
Daedalus 44
daemon 121, 323, 343
Dagr 111, 162, 295
dagwanoёñ'iёn 97
dagwanoenyent 97
Dahag 49, 345
Dahak 49, 345
dahdahwat 97
Dahdk 97
Dahhak 49, 97
Dahomey, West Africa 13, 96, 144, 270
Dahomey mythology 13
dahu 97
dai-dai 101
dai tengu 97, 298

Dai Tengu Sojobo 298
Daidalos 227
Daidarabochi 311
Dain 97, 112, 113
Dainn 97
Dáinn 97
Daire 104, 126
daitengu 97, 298
daitja 302
daitya 293
Daityasena 186
daivres 102
Daksha 196, 233
Daldah 97, 122
Dallwyr, Cornwall 154
Dallwyr Dallben 154
dama dagenda 98
Damavikas 19
Damvaykas 19
danavas 180
Danish folklore 153, 329
Danish mythology 43
Daphnis 27, 39, 98, 112, 158, 173, 222, 248, 259, 314
dard 98
Dardanus 67
Dark Lake 143
Dark Mountain 316
darkness, personification of 22, 222, 318
David, King 40, 271
Day of Judgment 89, 186
dazzelwurm 301, 309
De rerum natura 153
dea 98, 277
Death 33, 87, 240, 371
death omen 15, 33, 54, 62, 63, 73, 94, 112, 132, 148, 171, 197, 216, 250, 254, 268, 272, 295, 311, 334
death worm 23, 98
de Berkeley, Sir Maurice 61
de Berneville, Marie-Catherine Jumelle 246
Decius, Emperor 185
deer 28, 34, 67, 75, 86, 90, 147, 155, 157, 159, 174, 183, 184, 186, 188, 191, 192, 204, 229, 243, 252, 256, 259, 268, 275, 276, 291, 297, 315, 320, 326, 327, 337
Deer Island 181
deer-like 327, 332
Deerhurst, England 98
Deerhurst dragon 98
Degei 270
Deianeira (Mnesimache) 100, 121
Deianira 239
Deimos 98
Deinos 102
Deion 142
de Labarthe, Angela 75
delgeth 99
Dellingr 111, 162, 295
Delphi, Greece 69, 99, 109, 110, 121, 247, 267

Delphin 99
Delphinos 99
Delphinus 99, 119
Delphyne 99, 110, 267
Delphyyna 99
de Mandeville, Sir John 172, 202, 203
Demeter (Ceres) 39, 40
demi-god 6, 27, 38, 39, 40, 69, 78, 83, 87, 91, 92, 96, 98, 102, 105, 110, 112, 115, 116, 120, 133, 137, 158, 165, 173, 191, 198, 204, 214, 219, 222, 238, 239, 248, 249, 257, 258, 259, 301, 314
Democratic Republic of the Congo 60
Demoleon 99
demon 1, 6, 12, 14, 17, 19, 21, 24, 25, 26, 30, 37, 42, 43, 44, 46, 52, 56, 70, 72, 78, 86, 91, 97, 99, 102, 118, 120, 123, 128, 131, 136, 143, 150, 151, 152, 153, 161, 175, 183, 186, 187, 189, 190, 192, 193, 194, 197, 202, 206, 216, 217, 221, 230, 236, 240, 246, 250, 261, 263, 269, 269, 270, 271, 274, 283, 288, 289, 292, 300, 301, 303, 311, 315, 317, 318, 326, 328, 332, 336, 341, 343, 344, 346
démon du midi 118
demon-like 78
demon of disease and sickness 42
demon of drought 197
demon of envy and faith 206
demon of illness 190
demon of lightning 269
demon of the semen, wisdom, and the Watery Abyss 214
demonic creature 12, 14, 16, 19, 21, 26, 51, 56, 58, 62, 70, 84, 131, 141, 145, 148, 150, 153, 154, 170, 174, 176, 180, 183, 190, 192, 193, 194, 218, 235, 265, 269, 272, 274, 280, 285, 286, 289, 292, 300, 301, 307, 317, 318, 332, 334, 336, 341
demonology, medieval 206, 301
demonology of ancient Persia 102
demons of vengeance 120
den-bleiz 334
Den of Nargun 236
den-vleiz 211
dendan 99
dendenbome 311
Dents Rouge 246
de Plancy, Colin 205
Dercetis 99

Derceto 99
Derketo 99, 223
Dermot 64
Derwyn Corph 15
Despoina 40
Despot Vuk, Lord 347
destroying and life-giving elements, personification of 271
destructive forces and evil, personification of 156
de Troyes, Chrétien 144
Deukalion 226
dev 42, 99, 320
devalpa 100
Devas 37, 102, 134, 181
devi 99
devil-bird 100
devil dog 62, 154
devil whale 44, 100, 124
Devil's dandy dog 154
Devil's Hole, Arkansas 142
Devon County, England 69, 231
Devourer 26, 134
Devourer of Amenti 26
dew mink 100, 124
Dexamenos 100
Dexamenus, King 100, 121
dgèrnésiais 259
dhakhan 100, 270
Dhakhan of the Kabi 270
Dhananjaya 100, 234
Dharana 234
Dharanendra 250
dhembesuta 100
Dhinnabarrada 100–101
Dhrana 101, 180
Dhritarashtra 101, 234
Dhuldul 101
Dhumarna 101
dhuraghoo 103
di-di 101
Dia 80
Diana 38, 74, 84, 104, 146, 201, 267, 308, 320
Diarmaid 64
Diarmait 64
diba 50
Dictionaire Infernale 205
Dictys 101, 154
didi-aguiri 101
el dientudo 101
dig-gajas 32, 43, 44, 101, 198, 266, 279, 280, 302, 329, 331
diggajas 18, 101, 216
dik-gajas 101
Dike 120
Dilipa 102, 234
dilong 102, 129
Dimme-Kur 202
Dimmea 202
ding ball 102, 124
Dinga, King 59
dinny-mara 224
Dino 142
Dinos 102, 203, 219, 258, 338

Diomedes of Aetolia, King 102, 203, 219, 258, 338
Dioskouroi 151, 258
Dip 102
dipsa 102
dirae 120, 130
direach 102
direach ghlinn eitidh 102
Dirt Spider 322
disease 13, 18, 29, 32, 42, 52, 90, 139, 156, 169, 262, 310, 332, 339, 341, 345
dismal sauger 102, 124
Dissul 16, 30
Ditaolane 181
dithreach 102
div 99, 102, 136
divine 6, 11, 19, 20, 25, 30, 31, 34, 41, 43, 51, 53, 86, 89, 108, 120, 127, 143, 150, 152, 160, 179, 183, 185, 194, 196, 200, 208, 213, 226, 245, 252, 254, 299, 324, 328, 338, 346
divine creature 41, 213
Divine Laws 31
divine messenger 6, 324
divine protection, symbolic of 183
Divisions of Seasons 189
divs 99, 102–03
diwe 103
djendoes 139
Djieien 103
djinn 18, 67, 99, 143, 150, 152, 221, 236, 269, 271, 282, 292, 346
djude 139
do patkar 112
dobarcu 103
dobhar-chu 103
Dobrynya Nikitich 71
dochje 23
dockele 23
dockeli 23
dog 15, 16, 17, 22, 28, 32, 40, 42, 45, 47, 48, 50, 54, 62, 63, 67, 71, 72, 73, 74, 76, 80, 82, 83, 86, 89, 92, 93, 96, 103, 104, 105, 111, 115, 122, 123, 129, 132, 133, 138, 139, 140, 143, 145, 146, 147, 151, 152, 154, 160, 164, 165, 166, 167, 173, 183, 185, 186, 191, 194, 198, 200, 201, 202, 203, 204, 205, 206, 209, 212, 214, 215, 222, 223, 226, 228, 234, 236, 238, 242, 248, 249, 250, 251, 252, 256, 261, 262, 264, 268, 269, 278, 281, 282, 285, 290, 292, 294, 295, 300, 301, 307, 311, 313, 314, 316, 324, 328, 334, 335, 336, 344
dog foo 183, 194
Dog Husband 103
dog of the Seven Sleepers 15, 103

dog of Tobit 15, 103
Dog Star 89, 215
dogai 103
doggi 23
doglike 102, 120, 259, 292, 322
dogs of Actæon 8, 16, 17, 22, 42, 76, 96, 104, 105, 111, 151, 152, 166, 167, 200, 201, 205, 206, 214, 222, 223, 228, 236, 238, 248, 250, 252, 262, 265, 300, 301, 314, 316
dogs of Buddha 104
dogs of Fo 104, 261
dogs of Hell 131
dokkaebi 104
dokuro-no-kai 134
dolmens 216
dolphin 18, 82, 99, 157, 167, 282
domovoi djedoe 139
domovoi 139
Don Cooley 104
Donegal County 303
Dongo 104
dongus 70
donkey 23, 29, 66, 164, 185, 206, 249, 250, 288
Donn Cuailnge 104, 126
Donn Cúailnge 104, 126
Donn Tarb 104
dooinney marrey 224
doom dog 62, 154
Doorga 104, 105
Dorcaeus 105
Dorceus 104, 105
dorch 113
dorotabo 105
dorotabō 105
dorraghow 103
dorraghowor 103
Dorylas 105
Dossenus 105
doyarchu 103
dracaenae 105, 110, 203, 276
Dracaena Scythia 115
dracaenae-like 276
draccena 110
Draco 105, 110
draconcopedes 106
dracones aethiopicum 110
draconia 106
Draft of Immortality 148
drage 208
dragon, Occidental 5, 106, 108
Dragon, Oriental 106, 108, 344
dragon-carp 108, 188, 344
dragon goddess 21, 148, 190, 202, 220, 221, 228
dragon horse 79–80, 108, 211
Dragon Kings 35, 108–109, 179, 211, 213, 235, 250, 273, 275
dragon lanterns 5, 108
dragon-like 110, 142, 161,

175, 227, 238, 251, 295, 307, 326, 340, 344
dragon of Death 240, 271
dragon of Deerhurst 98
dragon of Delphi 267
dragon of the Abyss 42
dragon of the Apocalypse 260
Dragon of the Lake 109
dragon Son of Ares 109
dragon turtle 109
dragon tygre 109
dragon wolf 109, 347
dragonet 109–10, 337
dragonj 110
Dragon's Gate 102
draguas 110
drak 106
Drakaina Skythia 115
drakaina 75, 92, 99, 110, 115, 216
drake 127, 208
drakon 79, 105, 106, 109, 110, 111, 115, 119, 187, 201, 238
Drakon Chronos 87
drakone 110
drakones aithiopes 110
drakones Indikoi 110–11
drakones Troiades 111
drakones Trôiades 111
drakonet 105
Drapp 195
Drasill 111
drauga 99
drauge 143
draugr 138, 143
draygan 325
Drayton, Michael 247
Dreamtime mythology 136, 199, 270, 334
drek 111
drekalo 111
drekavac 111
dreki 106, 248
drerge 113
Dromas 104, 111
dromedary 343
Drona 175, 279
drop bear 111
dropbear 111
Drosull 111
Drösull 111
drought 17, 36, 42, 87, 107, 120, 162, 163, 173, 197, 213, 270, 309, 325, 332, 339, 343
drought-dragon 17
drought (extreme), personification of 339
dru-didi 101
druckerl 23
drude 23
Drudwas ap Tryffin 14
Drudwyn 16, 30, 72, 111, 324
druid stone 170
druk 107
drut 23
Dryalos 111

Dryalus 111
Dryas 42, 111, 112, 169, 256, 261
dtacontias 120
dû paikar 112
Dub Sainglend 112, 207
Dubb Sainglenn 112
Dubh Saingleann 112
ducci 170
Duck's Pool Meadow, Brinsop, England 68
dudje 139
duende 139, 170, 204
dukun tangka palasik 251
Dulcefal 112
Duldul 122
Dumbshfr 294
dun cow 138
dun cow of Kirkham 138
dun cow of Mac Brandy's thicket 138
dund 112
Duneyr 97, 112, 113
Duneyrr 112
dung beetle 187
dungaven hooter 112
dungavenhooter 112
Dunlyrr 112
dunya mara 224
Dupo 27, 39, 98, 112, 158, 173, 222, 248, 259, 314
Durabror 112
Durathor 112
Durathror 97, 112–13
Duraþrór 112
Durga 58
Durham, England 131, 203
Durínn's Kin 113
Durrinn's folk 113
durugh 99
Dutch folklore 71, 291
Dutch myth 195
Duzyairya 251
Dvalar 113
Dvalin 97, 112, 113, 228
Dvalinn 113
dvergur 139
dwaallicht 113
dware 113
dwarf 6, 12, 113–14, 117, 122, 123, 139, 171, 204, 228, 277, 262
dweeorg 113
dwerger 113
dwergugh 113
dworh 113
Dwyfach 13
Dwyfan 13
Dyffryn Amanw 53, 54, 144, 147, 209
Dyinyinga 318
Dyved 154

Ea (Marduk) 281
eač uisge 114
each uisce 47, 72, 92, 114, 138, 186
each uisge 114, 186, 242, 308

eagle 16, 18, 22, 25, 34, 38, 54, 58, 64, 67, 78, 86, 96, 107, 108, 115, 116, 118, 132, 134, 146, 155, 164, 175, 177, 180, 188, 196, 198, 202, 203, 218, 196, 198, 202, 203, 218, 232, 240, 243, 247, 249, 252, 259, 271, 273, 284, 258, 312, 215, 320, 322, 325, 330, 337, 338
eagle-like 54, 108, 322
eale 81, 114
Earl of Ormande 22
Earth (element), symbol of 247
earth spider 114–15, 322
earthquake 76, 81, 84, 102, 176, 181, 207, 230, 235, 238, 251, 253, 283, 284, 331
earthquake beetle 176
earthworm 47, 225, 226
easg saint 115
East Anglia, England 63
East Indian folklore 276
Easter Morning 57
Eastern Sea of China 35
eater of people 243
Eater of the Dead 26, 49
Eblis 136
The Ecclesiastical History of Iceland 113
ech tened 115
echeneis 115
Echidna 78, 82, 85, 92, 105, 110, 115, 165, 201, 238
eclipse 50, 107, 149, 226, 257, 315, 346
Ecuador 26, 174
Ecuadoran Amazon river basin 174
Edgar, King 41, 116
eel 11, 57, 70, 86, 176, 203, 298, 310
eel-like 11, 242, 298
eenhoorn 326
eer-moonan 115
Eerion 254
Efrasiyab 16
Egder 116
Egdir 116
Egmont 308
Egoir 116, 271
Egypt 43, 61, 76, 152, 154, 166, 187, 203, 222, 258, 286, 299, 303, 314
Egyptian Book of the Dead 20, 36, 49, 272
Egyptian creation mythology 143
Egyptian mythology 11, 12, 20, 26, 30, 33, 34, 48, 50, 92, 108, 135, 143, 152, 153, 154, 155, 156, 170, 171, 187, 215, 216, 222, 223, 235, 237, 238, 247, 248, 272, 276, 277, 283, 284, 285, 286, 289,

299, 300, 310, 311, 312, 314, 325
Egyptian Underworld 49, 299
Eight-Forked Serpent of Koshi 116
eighth section 187, 286
Eikin 116
Eikjjyrnir 116
Eikthyrner 116
Eikthyrni 116
Eikthyrnir 116
Eimgeitr 177
Eimnir 177
Eingana 116
einherjar 146, 276
einhorn 326
eisges 186
ejderha 116
Ekachakrapura 52
Ekhepolos 19
Ekhidna 115
Ekhion 47
Elapatra 234
elastic-like 136
Elatus 116
elb 117
elbe 23
die elben 116
eldjotnar 177
Eldr 177
Electra 151
elemental 110, 115, 116, 139, 277, 305, 340
elementary spirits 116
elephant 11, 18, 19, 28, 31, 32, 43, 47, 49, 51, 58, 74, 81, 88, 99, 101, 106, 107, 110, 111, 114, 120, 132, 165, 144, 163, 172, 199, 215, 216, 229, 234, 243, 245, 250, 252, 253, 260, 266, 267, 273, 278, 279, 280, 283, 292, 302, 305, 319, 327, 329, 331, 334, 340
elephant-like 114
Elephant That Foretold the Birth of the Buddha 117
elephant-tiger 117
eleventh hour 115, 155
elf 117, 141, 174, 177, 208, 210
Elfame 117
elfin 73, 117, 209, 225
elfin cats 73
elfin cow 209, 225
elflike 341
Eli 111
Elias 24
Elis 165
Elixir of Immortality 29, 41, 270, 271, 330
Elixir of Jade 229, 315
elk 21, 103, 187, 251, 259
elk-like 14
ellén trechend 117
ellyll 117
ellyllon 117
elwedritsche 337

Emain Macha 18
Embarr 118
emela-ntouka 117
Emesse 324
emeula natuka 117
emia-ntouka 117
Emianga folklore 38
emperors and kings, symbol of 132
empousai 118
empouse 118, 230
empusa 118
empusae 118
empusas 118
empuse 118
empusen 118
Enabarr 35, 118
Enbarr 118
Enbarr of the Flowing Mane 118
encantada 118
encanto 118
encerrados 86, 118
endrop 118, 186
enen-ra 118
enfield 118
England 1, 14, 54, 61, 62, 63, 64, 68, 69, 76, 78, 97, 98, 113, 117, 129, 132, 143, 147, 148, 203, 243, 246, 250, 271, 288
Engulfer 156
Engur 14
enhjoning 326
Enide 54, 119, 144
Enide's dappled palfrey 119
Enide's sorrel palfrey 119
Enik 119, 223, 285
Enil 107, 200
enkanto 118
Enkidu 70, 119, 145
enko-kappa 289
Enlil 34
Enoch 24, 30
enra-enra 118
Entilaka 234
Enuma Elish 14, 107
Enyo 142
Eoghainn 126
Eoos 119
Eoös 119
Eos 242, 257
Eoten 177
Eous 14, 16, 19, 44, 68, 119, 158, 204, 256, 257, 267
ephélés 170, 302
The Epic of Gilgamesh 119
Epic of the Dausi 59
Epidaurian dragon 119
Epidaurian drakon 119
Epidsurus 119
epimachus 247
epimacus 143, 247
Epistil Isu 68, 90, 115, 210, 237
equine 7, 79, 138, 158, 183, 194, 217, 240, 242, 327
Equuleus 119
Erbus 120

erd-mänlein 113, 19
erdmanlein 139
erdmanleins 139
Erebus (the Underworld) 87
Erec 119, 144
Erec and Enide 119, 144
erefil u 168
Erekhtheus 57, 262
Erensuge 120
Ereshkigal 199
Erigone 215
erinnyes 120
Erinyes 120, 130
erl 117
erotic dreams 24
Errinys 130
Erymanthian boar 120
Erynnes 40, 130
Erythreos 119, 120, 158
Eselarmonde 144
Essay on the Natural History of Chile 128
Essex, England 63, 155
Essex serpent 155
estas 120
Estonia 18, 194
Etasa 120
eternity, symbol of 249
Ethiopia 74, 75, 80, 110, 120, 165, 252, 254, 286, 309
Ethiopian dragon 120
Ethnarchs 145
Ethon 121, 132, 261
Etin 177
Etruscan mythology, ancient 323
Etruscans, ancient 18, 205, 253, 309
Etymologiae 301
Euippe 84
Euippus 89
Eumenides 120, 130
Euos 119, 158
Euphorion of Chalcis 237
Eurei 16, 30
Euripides 106
Europa 92, 102
European folklore 71, 74, 77, 98, 106, 157, 224, 338
European heraldry 27, 28
Euruale 121
Euryale 121, 141, 221, 222, 300
Eurybatus 82
Eurybios 80
Eurynomos 121
Eurynomus, centaur 121
Eurystheus, King 38, 82, 92, 120, 219, 238
Eurytion 100, 121, 133, 249
Eurytus 12, 28, 36, 39, 41, 42, 83, 87, 89, 90, 92, 99, 101, 105, 111, 121, 144, 154, 157, 166, 169, 172, 202, 204, 214, 221, 223, 224, 226, 229, 238, 348, 256, 257, 260, 272, 273, 313, 328

Eve 106, 166, 225
evil, personification of 244, 330, 345
evil eye 30, 183
evran 116
evren 116
Ewa Lagoon 182
Exadius 39, 42, 226, 256, 328
exedra 156
exorcism 68, 170, 271, 300
Explaining and Analyzing Characters 108
extraterrestrial creature 88
Eyfura 122
Eyrgjafa 177
Ezekiel 312

fachan 102
fad felen 121, 339
fad felen 339
Fadda 97, 122
Faerie Queen 67
Fafnir 122
Fáfnir 122
fainthearted, personification of 157
fairies 8, 70, 113, 117, 209, 289, 305, 321, 347
fairy animal 15, 25, 33, 36, 41, 46, 47, 50, 54, 56, 58, 62, 66, 68, 70, 72, 73, 76, 79, 91, 92, 93, 94, 102, 118, 119, 122, 123, 124, 130, 132, 137, 138, 139, 147, 148, 154, 159, 186, 203, 209, 212, 225, 228, 240, 241, 242, 243, 244, 250, 252, 253, 259, 280, 283, 287, 288, 291, 295, 307, 308, 313, 324, 331, 336, 341
fairy-cattle 92
fairy chalice 123
fairy cow 92, 130, 138
fairy creature 122
fairy dog 62, 123, 147, 154
fairy horse 47, 50, 114
fairy hound 67, 148
Fairy Pig of Man 41
fairy swine 154
Fairyland 117, 123, 279
Fakr 122
Fákr 122
Falak 51, 122
falcon-fish 122
Falhofner 122
Falhofnir 122–23
Falhófnir 122
fallen angels 31, 114, 145, 206, 258
falm 123
familiar 7, 19, 52, 123, 161, 169, 193, 207, 217, 218, 247, 262, 266, 317, 332
familiar spirit 123, 247
Family Discourse 188
famine 108, 245
Famine (the entity) 29
faming 123, 175, 304, 343

fananim-pitoloha 123
fanany 123
fandrefiala 123
Fane 247
Fangbodi 177
Fanplant Lake 316
farasi bahari 123
Farbanti 177
Farmanvawa 283
Faroe Islands 159, 321
Farvann 123, 124
fary 117
fastitocalon 44, 124
fat old woman of the post 56
fatal sisters 120
Fate 93, 207, 331
Father Christmas 195
Father of all Turtles 195
Father Time 33
Fatouma, Princess 109
faun 124, 153, 252
Fauna 124, 252
Fauni 252
Fauns 124, 252
Faunus 15, 77, 124, 252, 280, 292
fawn 224
fay 67, 93, 117, 122, 126, 207, 252, 328, 331, 334
Fe-Lian 124, 289
fear liath mór 124
fear liath more 124
fear of using an unlit bathroom late at night, personification of 20
fearsome creature 124
fearsome critter 21, 39, 48, 53, 57, 60, 72, 75, 78, 81, 90, 91, 93, 100, 102, 124, 128, 129, 132, 135, 136, 137, 138, 140, 141, 146, 147, 151, 156, 159, 161, 163, 164, 175, 182, 189, 210, 212, 225, 230, 257, 260, 265, 269, 275, 278, 288, 296, 297, 298, 299, 305, 311, 320, 321, 328, 333, 335, 336, 337
feather-covered snake 125
feathered serpent 125, 247
The Feats and Exploits of Ninurta 42
fée 117
Fei Lian 125
Fei-Lain 125
Feke 128
Feki 128
felicitous yen 213
feline 29, 76, 78, 93, 102, 227, 326, 336
feng 135
feng-bird 125
Feng Bo 125
feng huang 125
feng-huang 125
fêng-huang 125
feng hwang 125
fenghuang 125, 159, 330, 343

fenis 258
fenix 258
Fenja 177
Fenrer 125
Fenrir 125–26, 152, 214
Fenris 125
Fenrisulfr 125
Fenrisúlfr 125
Fenriswolf 125
Fenriswulf 125
fer-las mhór 124
Fergus 253
Fergus mac Leti 231
Feridun 345
ferla mohr 124
ferla mór 124
ferlie more 124
Ferrier's guild 231
La Ferte-Bernard 255
Fertility Diables 195
fertility, symbol of 307
Festival of the Three Kings 24
fey-like creature 73
Fiala 126
Fialar 126, 146
fideal 126
fidealadh 126
Fiery Ones 30
fiery snake 19
fifth section 33, 311, 312
Fijian mythology 239, 264
Filipino folklore 21, 50, 67, 69, 73, 168, 179, 204, 215, 217, 221, 243, 265, 278, 279, 294, 307
Filipino mythology 118, 226, 306
fillyfoo 142
Fimbulthul 116
Final Judgment 33
Findbennach 126
Fine-Ear 90
Fine Oreille 246
Finland 113, 321
Finn Mac Cumhaill 15, 67, 212, 280, 283
Finnbennach 104, 126
Finnbhennach 126
Finnish folklore 18, 168, 250, 332
Finnish mythology 304, 305
Finnish Russian folklore 250
Fionn 64, 67
Fionn Bheannach 126
Fionn MacCumhail 303
Fiorgwyn 177
fire-bird 345
fire-breathing creatures 19, 65, 85, 87, 89, 91, 98, 107, 127, 153, 187, 193, 255, 258, 323, 340, 347
fire drake 127
fire drake of Beowulf 127
fire jotnar 177
firebird 127, 265
firedrake 127
firefly 302

First Branch of the Mabinogi 33
fish 2, 11, 12, 14, 17, 18, 21, 23, 26, 30, 35, 38, 40, 42, 44, 46, 51, 53, 55, 56, 57, 59, 60, 61, 63, 66, 71, 75, 76, 78, 87, 89, 91, 99, 100, 103, 108, 115, 122, 124, 125, 126, 127, 128, 136, 137, 139, 140, 146, 148, 153, 157, 158, 159, 163, 164, 166, 167, 168, 171, 172, 175, 179, 182, 189, 191, 193, 197, 198, 199, 205, 207, 210, 211, 214, 216, 217, 218, 219, 223, 224, 227, 229, 230, 231, 232, 240, 243, 253, 255, 259, 260, 261, 263, 268, 272, 276, 278, 279, 280, 281, 282, 283, 286, 294, 298, 305, 309, 315, 318, 321, 322, 328, 334, 336, 337, 344
fish-knight 127
fish-lion 216
fish man 127
fish-man 127
fish-men 315
fish with one hundred heads 164
fishing tales 14, 173
Fjalar 126
Fjalarr 113, 126
Fjolvarr 177
Fjolverkr 177
Fjorm 116
Fjosvartnir 25
Fleeing Serpent 208
Fleeting Serpent 211
flibbertigibbet 124, 128
flipper-like 196
flittericks 128
floater on ocean streams 44
flock of golden sheep 201
flood 13, 36, 42, 76, 77, 80, 91, 99, 105, 107, 116, 134, 140, 164, 175, 179, 199, 252, 255, 263, 270, 281, 311, 316, 327, 332, 336, 338, 342, 344, 346
Florida, Unites States of America 64, 165, 297
flutelike 276
flying fish 14, 286, 328
flying fox 14, 64
flying heads 97, 128
flying humanoids 87
flying serpent of Isa 186
flying squirrel 128
Fo dogs 104
foamy steed 299
foddenskkmaend 139, 321
Foljambe family 74
Folkvir 7, 128
follet 139
fomor 134
Fon people 96
Foo dogs 104
Fool Dancer 242

Forbidden Fruit 225
force of lightning, personification of 19
forest 5, 15, 18, 21, 32, 37, 43, 47, 48, 54, 60, 69, 71, 82, 85, 101, 102, 111, 126, 134, 135, 139, 141, 145, 149, 151, 155, 169, 174, 175, 179, 180, 181, 182, 183, 184, 191, 192, 204, 205, 206, 207, 210, 214, 215, 218, 221, 231, 236, 239, 245, 250, 253, 254, 269, 274, 281, 283, 290, 291, 293, 299, 304, 308, 309, 311, 316, 318, 321, 323, 324, 328, 329, 331, 332, 344
forest rhinoceros 117
forgotten knowledge 97
Forked Mountain 27
formicaleon 34
formicaleun 34
formula, magical 20, 154, 285, 286, 310, 214, 325, 334
Fornjotr 177
Fortunio 90
Four God principle 74, 135, 284, 304
fourth section 155, 223, 310
fox 86, 87, 88, 108, 118, 128, 135, 145, 146, 162, 168, 190, 192, 200, 201, 204, 239, 241, 252, 291, 312, 313, 320, 334, 343
fox-fairy 162
fox-like 88, 168, 200
fox-maiden 128
fox serpent 128, 168, 239
fox-snake 145
fox spirit 108, 135, 190, 194, 195, 196, 197, 198, 233, 241, 272, 288, 291, 320, 340, 343
Frænir 122
France 1, 57, 75, 89, 134, 194, 211, 301, 313, 330, 334, 335
Francis II 219
Frasier, Duncan 209
Frau Holle 332
Fraueli 23
Freke 128–9, 135
Freki 128
Frekr 177
French Alps folklore 38
French Arthurian folklore 76, 127
French folklore 27, 97, 145, 211, 246, 255, 268, 308, 313, 331
Frenzy of Orlando 268
freshwater, personification of 315
Freybug 129
Freyia 113
Freyr 63, 145, 146, 177, 296

Friesland 114
Frigga 133, 150
frigid cold of winter, personification of 42
frightening figures 244
Frisian folklore 266
Friuch 104, 126
frog 105, 109, 113, 159, 183, 188, 200, 244, 261, 284, 303, 332, 342, 343
frost jotnar 177
Frosti 177
Fu dogs 104
Fu His, Emperor 188
fu-t'sang lung 129
fuath 12, 69, 126, 129, 186, 216, 289, 328, 331
fuath-arrached 129
fuathan 129
Fucanglong 129
fuchi-zaru 182
fuku-riu 129
full moon 26, 45, 50, 210, 217
Fulong 129
fum hwang 125
Funeral Mountain terrashot 124, 129
funeral pyres 142, 196, 239, 266
Fung 130, 165, 213, 319, 342, 344
Fung Hwang 125, 129–30
Fung Po 124
fur-bearing trout 130, 167
fur-seals 70
furi 164
Furiae 120, 130
Furies 22, 120, 130, 222, 318
Fusberta 57
futa-guichi onna 130
Futa Jallon, Africa 173
futakuchi-onna 130
Fuwch Gyfeiliorn 130–31, 147
fylgukona 150
Fyrnir 177

ga-git 131
ga-gorib 131
Gaasyendietha 131
gabble retchets 131
gaborchend 131
gaborchind 131
Gabriel 66, 132, 149
Gabriel hound 94, 131, 132, 154
Gabriel ratchets 131
Gabriel ratchet's hounds 131
gadfly 68
gadungan 214, 215, 334
Gaea 39, 76, 84, 95, 99, 115, 133, 137, 201, 249, 292
Gagalvid 126
gagana 132
Gaganeshvara 134
gainjin 132

Gairloch, Scotland 126
Gaius Julius Solinus 66, 167
Gaius Valerius Flaccus 151
gaja-virala 279
gajasimha 132
Galaffre 246
Galahad 268
Galathe 121, 132, 261
Galati, Asia 246, 308
Galatia 246
Galeru 270
Galician folklore 94
galley-trot 132, 291
galleytrot 62, 132, 154
galliwampus 124, 132
Gallu 202, 328
gally-trot 132
gamayun 132
Gamr 152
gandaberunda 132
Gandan mythology 53, 189
Gandarəβa 132
Gandareva 133
Gandarewa 133
Gandarva 133
gandharva 37, 133, 134
Ganges River 245
Ganglati 177
Ganglot 177
Gangr 177
Ganiagwaihegowa 133
ganj 133
Ganyadjigowa 97
Gao-kerena 75
gara 47
garaboncias 107
Garafena 133
Garafina 133
Garden of Eden 106, 225
Gardrofa 133
Garðrofa 133, 159
Gargittios 133, 249
La Gargouille 133–34
Gargoyle 133
Garguiem 133
garkain 134
garlic 32, 45, 46, 73, 170, 207, 242, 301, 345
garlic oil 12
Garm 134, 152
Garm, the Watchdog of the Dead 152
Garme 152
Garmr 134
Garselid 324
Garsrofa 133
gartenzwerg 139
Garuda 41, 85, 108, 134, 146, 175, 181, 184, 188, 234, 277, 315, 327, 330
Garuda Bird 134
Garula 134
Garutman 134
gashadokuro 134
Gates of Decay 304
Gaungu-Hrolfs 112
Gausinelis 19
Gavaevodata 134
Gawain 144, 268

gazerium 124, 135, 298
Gazu Hyakki Yakō 35
geese 24, 55, 132
Gefjun 159, 167, 271, 272
Geirdnir 135
Geirvimul 116
geis 64, 231
Geitir 177
Gelonus 115
Gem of Life 312
gemlike 86
Genbu 72, 135, 284, 304
General History of Connecti- cut 93, 100, 164
General Seto 287
genetic hybrid 88
Gengen Wer 135
Genghis Khan 86
Genius 145
Genjo 62
genko 135
geraher 135
Gerd 177
Gere 135
gerfalc 22
gergasi 135
Geri 129, 135
Gering 135
gerjis 135
German folklore 37, 47, 52, 62, 65, 71, 116, 139, 228, 229, 272, 281, 294, 295
German mythology 142
Germany 23, 24, 61, 113, 114, 155, 194, 208, 321, 335
Gerr 135
Geryon 133, 165, 249
Gessner, Conrad 100
Gestur 177
Getulia 226
getulian dogge 226
Geush Urvan 135
ghost 37, 52, 58, 65, 71, 74, 170, 181, 183, 190, 241, 272, 274, 288, 295
ghost of fear 71
ghul 136
ghul-like 21, 53
Gian Ben Gian 136
giant 16, 29, 30, 46, 60, 72, 111, 136, 137, 143, 168, 179, 246, 283, 295, 311, 313, 320, 324, 342, 344
Giant Dingo 136
gichi-anami'e-bizhiw 326
giddy fish 124, 136–37, 336
gidyer tree 101
Gifr 128
Gigant Scuttle 213
gigante 38, 76, 102, 133, 137, 219, 249, 265
Gigantomachy 137, 273
gigelorum 137
gigi-hebi 322
Gilgamesh 70, 119, 145
gilikango 317
gilitrutt 132

gillygaloo 124, 137
Ginnungagap 47, 177
Ginnungagap ice 47
giol-daoram 137
Gipul 116
giraffe 159
Girika 234
Girp 137
girtabilli 137
girtablilu 37, 137
girtablullu 137, 199
Gisl 137
Gjere 135
Gjolp 177
Glad 137
Gladr 111, 137
Glaer 137
Glær 137
glaistyn 138
Glamr 137–38
glas gaivlen 138
Glas Ghailbhleann 138, 147
glasgavlen 138
glashan 138
glashtinhe 72
glashtyn 138, 259
Glasir Grove 123, 135, 137, 138, 147, 148, 159, 176, 206, 213, 292, 294, 298, 318, 330
glass snake 176
Glastonbury 138
glastyn 138
glatisaunt 268
Glaukos 226
Glaumr 138
Glaumvor 177
glawackus 124, 138
Gleipnir 126
Glen 137
Glen Aven 123
Glen of Eiti, Scotland 102
Glener 137
Gleneus 80
Glenr 137
Gler 138
Gloso 139
Gluskab 64
gluttony, symbol of 146, 308
glyryvilu 128
Gna (Gnaa) 133, 150
Gnaa 133, 150, 159
Gnan 136
Gnipahellir (Gnypa) 134
gnom 139
gnome 139, 243
gnomiko 139
gnomo 139
gnyan 139
goanna lizard 336
goat 18, 19, 20, 25, 28, 65, 74, 76, 77, 97, 122, 124, 139, 158, 195, 198, 204, 205, 207, 216, 233, 252, 259, 268, 276, 279, 280, 281, 284, 292, 320, 326, 328, 344
goat fish 281
goat stag 158

goayr heddagh 139
gobble-ratches 131
Gobi Desert 23, 98
goblin 93, 104, 139, 193, 181, 207, 246
goblin-like 104
goblin of Adachigahara 246
goblin scarecrow 139
goborchend 131
goborchinu 139, 186
god of asceticism and flesh eaters 192
god of commercial success 190, 320
god of darkness and evil 36
god of fire 134, 140, 339
god of Lake Tritonis 321
god of light, nature, and warriors 331
god of lightning 269
god of prosperity 315
god of rain and sun 63
god of rain 63, 75, 125, 344
god of sea and storms 340
god of storms 209, 325, 341
god of the air 217
god of the forests 149
god of the mountain 79
god of the north wind 66
god of the sea 39, 40, 82, 95, 99, 141, 151, 157, 217, 221, 223, 226, 254, 281, 300, 321
god of the sky 28, 119
god of the sun 14, 80, 83, 137
god of the underworld 8, 12, 16, 82, 242, 248
god of the wind 53, 76, 91, 192, 311, 338
god of thunder 205, 269, 306, 321
god of war 17, 19, 91, 98, 109, 258
god of wealth 8, 191
god of wisdom, education, and calligraphy 290
goddess-like 37
goddess of death 56
goddess of justice 120
goddess of primordial clay, mud, or ocean slit 202
goddess of rice 241
goddess of the sun 341
goddess of the three paths and witchcraft 301
goddess of vegetation and moisture 99
goddess of weaving 38
gods of the Ugaritic pan- theon 341
gogo-me 289
gogome 289
Goidelic Celts 19
Góin 139
Goin 139, 142, 228, 245, 305
Goinn 139

Góinn 139
Göktürks 43
Gokula 17
Gol 346
Gol the Naked 346
Gol the Needy 346
Gol Voyansky 346
gold 21, 22, 38, 59, 63, 72, 86, 94, 113, 122, 127, 133, 140, 146, 191, 208, 229, 253, 261, 306, 313, 321, 344, 345
gold-digging ant 140
Golden Apples of Hesperos 115, 201
Golden Fleece 187, 201
Golden Hound 198
Goldenhorn 346
Goldfax 140
Goldhorn 346
golem 140
golligog 142
Gollinkambi 146
Golltoppr 146
gollygog 142
Gomel 116
gommes 139
Gong-Gong 140, 338
gonibilla 140
Good Buso 306
Good Friday 45, 95
good omen 104, 307
goofang 124, 140
goofus bird 124, 141
goose 23, 55, 71, 132, 135, 143, 295
goose tree 55
gopher 311
Gopul 116
Gor 177
Gorgo the Medusa 141
gorgo 141
gorgone 223
gorgoniy 141
Gorgons 115, 121, 130, 141, 142, 221, 222, 300
Gormand 90
gorri txiki 141
Gorska Makna 241
Goruinich 133
Gorynytch 141
Gosh 135
Gosh Goshuurun 135
Goshuuruan 135
Goshuurvan 135
Gosiute 243
goteface 320
gotho 113
Goti 141
Gou Mang 141, 275
gowrow 142
Graabak 142
Grabak 142
Grábakr 139, 142, 228, 245, 305
Grabakr 142
Grabofc 142
Grabovac 142
Graeae 142
Graes 142

Graftner 142
Grafvitner 142
Grafvitnir 142
Grafvitnit 142
Grafvollud 142
Grafvölludr 139, 142, 228, 245, 305
Grafvolludr 142
Grafvollund 142
graha 47
Graiai 142
Grail Castle 144
Gran Chaco, Bolivia 207, 276
El Gran Moxo 313
granby panther 138
Grand Colin 246
Grane 142
Grani 142
Granni 142
Granny Squanit 265
grasshopper 32, 148, 292
Great Abyss 269
Great Basin, USA 54
great black stag of the Hercynian Forest 155
Great Cackler 143
Great Chi'en Tang 85
great horned snake 161
Great Lakes, USA 57, 227, 298, 299, 326
Great One 171
Great Plains, USA 170, 174
Great Records Made in the Period of Peace and Prosperity 87, 260
great sea serpent 282
Great Spirit 133
great underwater wildcat 326
great unknown of the seas 282
Great Wind Bird 337
Great Woman of the Wood 30
Greatheart 143
Greece 71, 74, 82, 162, 224, 230, 258, 272, 302, 303, 313, 334, 335
greed, personification of 217
Greek folklore 21, 102, 224, 253, 256, 293, 305, 332
Greek mythology 12, 14, 16, 17, 19, 22, 25, 27, 28, 36, 37, 38, 39, 40, 41, 42, 43, 44, 47, 53, 55, 57, 60, 66, 69, 75, 76, 77, 78, 79, 81, 82, 83, 84, 87, 89, 90, 91, 92, 95, 96, 98, 99, 100, 101, 102, 104, 105, 107, 109, 110, 111, 112, 115, 116, 118, 119, 120, 121, 123, 130, 132, 133, 137, 141, 142, 144, 151, 152, 154, 157, 158, 165, 166, 167, 169, 172, 173, 180, 181, 187, 196, 198,

200, 201, 201, 202, 203, 204, 205, 206, 210, 214, 215, 216, 217, 219, 220, 221, 222, 223, 224, 225, 226, 227, 228, 229, 236, 238, 239, 242, 245, 247, 248, 249, 250, 252, 254, 256, 257, 258, 259, 260, 261, 262, 265, 267, 269, 272, 273, 274, 280, 281, 284, 292, 294, 296, 300, 301, 302, 304, 313, 314, 316, 318, 321, 328, 329, 331, 338, 346
green dragon 49, 231, 284
Greenland 169, 190
Gregory of Nazianzus 313
Gregory the Great 313
grek-vleiz 211
Grenada 93, 212, 222
Grendel 143, 280
Grettir 138
Grettis Saga 137
Greyfell 142
greyhound 58, 118
griffin 14, 20, 22, 25, 54, 60, 143, 154, 157, 160, 183, 192, 200, 218, 247, 285, 292, 297, 325
griffin-like 20, 192, 200
griffon 143
griffon 143
grillus 144
grim 143, 186
Grim Reaper 33
Grimlingr 177
Grimliongr 177
Grimnir 177
Grímnismál 123, 137, 148
Grinbulsti 145
grine 143, 144
Gringalet 144
Gringolet with the Red Ears 144
Gringolet 144
Gringuljete 144
Grisons, Switzerland 71
groot slang 144, 172
ground manikins 139
Ground Spider 322
gruagach 259
grubs 101, 315
Grugyn Gwrych Ereint 54, 144, 209, 324
grylio 144
gryllus 144
Gryneus 144
gryp 143
grype 143
gryph 143
gryphon 143, 281, 282
gryphus 143
gryps 143
guanapipi 198
Guaraní Indians 179
Guaraní mythology 263
Guaraníian mythology 313
guardian 11, 56, 58, 60, 62, 82, 87, 94, 99, 101, 107, 110, 123, 129, 143, 144, 145, 152, 160, 167, 172,

183, 186, 194, 198, 201, 207, 208, 216, 217, 227, 232, 261, 276, 279, 280, 283, 286, 290, 292, 299, 301, 304, 307, 312, 318, 328, 331, 340, 346
guardian angel 144–45, 150
guardian of Caliludan 56
guardian of Israel 145
guardian of the sturgeon 227
guarifil u 168
Guazzo, Francesco Maria 37
Gudanna 145
Gudea 61, 147, 197, 211, 251, 287, 294, 296, 301
Guecubu 73
Gugalana 145
guhin 145
gui xian 145
guiaskuitas 264
guild-folk 321
guild neighbors 231
guirivilo 239
guirivilu 128
guirivulu 145
guita 231
guivre 27, 133, 145
Gukumatz 125
Gulben 64
Gulgun 145, 287
Gullfaxi 140
Gullin-Bursti 145
Gullin-kambi 146
Gullinborst 145
Gullinborste 145
Gullinborsti 63, 145, 146, 296
Gullinburste 145
Gullinbursti 145
Gullinbusti 145
Gullinkambe 146
Gullinkambi 146
Gullinkam'bi 146
gullipen 163
Gulltop 146
Gulltopp 146
Gulltoppr 146
gulo 146
gulon 146
Gultopr 146
gumberoo 124, 146
gumiho 146, 198
Gumphinkel 195
Gunakesi 41
Gunnar 160
Gunnarr 141
Gunnthra 116
Gurangatch 164
gurt dog 62, 154
Gurula 164
guruvilu 239
Gusir 177
guyanousa 264, 265
guyascuttus 264
guyascutus 124, 146–47
guyastacuttus 264
Guyon 67

Gwalchmei 144
gwartheg y llyn 92, 147, 209
Gwent 154
Gwiber 147, 399
Gwilenhin 324
Gwragedd Annwn 147, 209
Gwrfoddw 209
Gwydir 147
gwyllgi 62, 147, 154
Gwyllgi the dog of darkness 147, 154
Gwyn Ap Nudd 95
Gwynedd, Maelgwn 121
Gwynn 324
Gwys 147, 324
Gyan 136
Gyan-ben-Gian 136
gyascutus 146, 265
Gylfaginning 123, 137
Gylfi 177
Gyllenbuste 145
Gyllenkambe 146
Gyller 147
Gyllinborste 145
Gyllinger 147
Gyllingr 177
Gyllir 147, 177
gyoryu 188
Gypsum 147, 296
Gypsy 73, 184, 264
Gypsy demonology 73
Gytrash 62, 131, 148, 154

Ha-puu 148, 228
haakapainizi 148
habergeiss 148
Habrok 148
Habrok 148
Hábrók 148
Haddingr 294
Hadentheni 133
Hades (Dis) 121, 222, 300
Hadhayaosh 148
Hadhayosh 148
Hae-Wang 343
haegte 170
haehtisse 170
haetae 162
haf-skrimsl 295
haf-strambr 295
hafaza 145
Hafeti 148
Háfeti 148
haffrii 223
hafgufe 195
hag 22, 23, 71, 170, 204, 207, 222, 230, 241, 246, 289, 305, 318, 339
hag-like 305
hagge 170
Haggis 97
Hāhau-Whenua 148
hai chai 84, 327
hai chiai 84, 188
hai ho shang 148
hai riyo 149
hai-ryu 319
hai-uri 88, 320
hai-uru 149

Haida 131, 315
Haida Indians 131
haietlik 149
Haiti 88, 270, 320, 334
Haizum 149
Haki 122, 177
hakulaq 149
hakutaku 51
hākuturi 149
hala 149
Halesus 204
halfway people 223
Halimaka 234
Hall of Judgment 286
Halls of Valhalla 142
halulu 149
hameh 149–50
hamingja 150
Hammadi 109
Hamme, Belgium 249
hammerlinge 139
Hamou Ukaiou 18, 150
Hampshire, England 61
hamsa 150
Hamshamtsus 150
Hamskerper 150, 159
Hamskerpir 150
Han Dynasty 80, 125, 316
han-riu 84, 150
han-ryu 150
hanadaka tengu 150
Haneo'o fishpond 190
hangdown 124, 151
Hanigongendatha 133
hannya 151
hannya-shin-kyo 151
Hans Muff 195
Hanstrapp 165
Hantharwaddy 157
Hanuman 293, 329
Hanxue Ma 80
Hao Yixing 190
happy auger 102, 124, 151
Haraldr 128
Haranyabahu 234
Hardgreipr 177
härdmandle 113
Hardverkr 177
hare 86, 224, 229, 274
Harginn 73
Haridraka 234
harimau jadi-jadian 273
Harpagium, Phrygia 95
Harpagos 95, 151, 258
Harpalus 104, 151
harpy 39, 53, 60, 67, 151, 152, 265, 338
harpy-like 67
Harpyes 104, 152
harpyia 151, 152
harpyiai 151
harts 97, 112, 113, 116
Harun 152
Haruna 152
hashi hime 152
Hasidic folklore 68
Hastibhadra 234
Hastinapura 306
Hastingue, France 211

hatdedases 97
Hati 152, 162
Hati Hrodvitnirsson 152
hatif 152
Hatuibwari 152
Hau 152, 191
Haustigi 177
havhest 153
havmand 224
havsfru 294
Hawaii, USA 228, 310
Hawaiian mythology 21, 148, 149, 182, 190, 198, 221, 228, 243, 274
hawk 22, 48, 60, 116, 124, 148, 156, 175, 277, 284, 299, 312, 330, 337
Haya-Siras 50
He Who Is Coming Into Being 187
Hea-bani 153
Heabani 153
Headingley Hill, England 54
headless horseman 112
headless mule 153
Heardred 127
heart 30, 33, 45, 46, 49, 70, 96, 103, 110, 123, 130, 163, 166, 169, 173, 184, 187, 193, 231, 245, 276, 279, 284, 290, 301, 311, 326, 329, 336, 337
heath hounds 131
heaven 1, 14, 19, 64, 77, 86, 88, 89, 95, 96, 99, 105, 109, 117, 119, 120, 125, 126, 130, 131, 133, 137, 140, 150, 153, 159, 175, 188, 206, 207, 215, 222, 244, 258, 276, 278, 285, 293, 299, 215, 216, 219, 320, 324, 331, 346
Heaven 15, 31, 66, 70, 106, 132, 144, 170, 182, 184, 185, 208, 274
Heaven Bellower 156
Heaven Breaker 156
Heavenly Cock 153, 314
Hebrew mythology, legend and folklore 55, 206, 288, 306, 333, 346
Hecate 118, 301
Hecatoncheires 95
Hector 19, 121, 132, 261, 268
Hedammu 153
hedgehog 73, 188, 226
heg 178, 298
hegge 170
Heidrun 153
Heidrún 153
heifer 67, 68, 123
Heimdal 146
heinzemannchens 139
heitlik 149
Heitsi-eibib 131
Hek 153
Hekau 153
Hekret 153

Hel 126, 152, 153, 177
hel-kaplein 113
Helblindi 177
The Heldenbuch 114
Helen of Troy 79, 261
Helheim 126
Helheimr 296
helhest 153
Helimus 154
heliodromos 154
Heliopolis, Egypt 158
Helios (Sol) 16, 26, 266, 267
hell 33, 51, 75, 102, 166, 196, 275
Hell 32, 51, 62, 71, 72, 73, 90, 117, 122, 131, 143, 154, 175, 274, 278, 309
hell beast 132
Helle 40
hellhound 62, 63, 102, 154, 304
Helops 154
Helreginn 177
Hemetch 154
Hemth 154
Hen Wen 78, 154
Hen-Wen 154
Hengjankjoptr 177
Henham dragon 155
Henhams 155
Henry II 219
Henry III 219
Henwen 154
Hephaistos (Vulcan) 14, 25, 95, 198, 201
Hera (Juno) 68, 96, 110, 165, 267, 313
herald for the coming of spring 141
heraldic symbology 22, 23, 25, 27, 51, 67, 74, 77, 89, 109, 118, 122, 160, 204, 214, 220, 233, 238, 247, 280, 281, 282, 324, 338, 343
heraldry 27, 28, 44, 51, 78, 109, 114, 145, 160, 204, 214, 233, 247
hercinia 155
Hercules (Heracles) 27, 38, 39, 40, 41, 44, 69, 77, 78, 82, 83, 84, 89, 91, 92, 96, 98, 100, 102, 105, 112, 115, 116, 120, 121, 133, 137, 158, 165, 173, 201, 204, 214, 219, 222, 238, 239, 248, 249, 257, 258, 259, 301, 302, 314, 321, 338
Hercynian Forest, Germany 155
Hercynian stag 155
Hereford map 220
Herkir 177
Herla's Hounds 33
Hermes (Mercury) 40, 68, 77, 79, 99, 258
hermetic 116, 139, 277, 305

hero 5, 14, 15, 16, 19, 20, 27, 28, 34, 35, 38, 39, 40, 41, 42, 44, 47, 48, 49, 50, 51, 55, 56, 57, 58, 60, 64, 67, 68, 70, 71, 74, 77, 78, 81, 82, 83, 85, 89, 91, 92, 95, 96, 97, 98, 99, 100, 103, 105, 107, 109, 111, 112, 114, 115, 116, 117, 119, 120, 121, 122, 127, 131, 132, 133, 136, 137, 138, 141, 142, 143, 145, 148, 154, 157, 158, 162, 163, 165, 169, 172, 173, 176, 181, 184, 185, 187, 188, 192, 193, 194, 199, 200, 201, 207, 208, 212, 214, 219, 222, 224, 226, 238, 239, 240, 248, 249, 251, 252, 253, 254, 255, 257, 258, 259, 264, 270, 272, 273, 276, 277, 279, 280, 281, 282, 283, 287, 294, 297, 300, 301, 302, 303, 310, 311, 313, 314, 320, 321, 322, 324, 329, 335, 338, 345, 346, 347
Herodotus 140, 247
heroes 1, 6, 21, 29, 53, 74, 84, 97, 99, 110, 133, 146, 204, 254, 282, 290, 328, 342
heroism and righteousness, symbol of 205
herok'a 155
hero's accomplishments, symbol of the 254
Hert-Nemmat-Set 155
Hert-Sefu-S 155
Herzegovina 261
Hesiod 39, 42, 82, 85, 141, 151, 201, 238, 256, 258, 280, 328
Hesperian fruit 105
Hesperidean dragon 201
Hesperidean snake Ladôn 201
Hetch-Nau 155, 203, 238
hexendrücken 170
hiai chai 155
hickle snifter 189
hicklesnifer 124, 155
Hidden Land of Kane 228
hide 94, 156
hidebehind 124, 156
Hidesato 81
Hidhaegg 240
hieraco-sphnix 156
hieracosphnix 30, 92, 156, 209
hierocosphinxex 156
High King of Ireland 259
Hilde-svine 145
Hildisvini 145
Hildr 330
hili 156, 317
hill manikins 139
hill men 321
hill-people 321

hill trolls 113, 321
Hilmgareariki 112
Him of the Hairy Hands 213
Himalayan folklore 71
Himalayas 21, 191
Himapandara 279
Himefaxi 156
Himinbrioter 156
Himinbrjoter 156
Himinhriot 156
Himinhrjodr 156
Himinhrjot 156
Hina 274, 310
Hina-arau-riki 274
Hind of Ceryneia 38
Hindu folklore 17, 18, 278, 279, 287, 304
Hindu mythology 15, 17, 18, 19, 21, 28, 32, 41, 43, 44, 50, 53, 58, 83, 85, 88, 96, 100, 101, 102, 112, 120, 132, 133, 134, 146, 150, 174, 175, 186, 188, 191, 192, 196, 197, 198, 199, 210, 215, 216, 233, 234, 235, 236, 250, 252, 253, 260, 264, 266, 267, 269, 270, 275, 277, 278, 280, 284, 293, 302, 304, 306, 318, 325, 327, 328, 329, 330, 331, 340
Hinqumemen 156
Hinthar 157, 167
Hiphinous 157
hippalectryon 157
hippalektryon 157, 158
Hipparchus of Nicaea 119
Hippason 157
hippocambus 157
hippocamp 157, 165
hippocampe 157
hippocampi 157
hippocamps 157
hippocampus 157
hippocentaur 80
hippocerf 157
hippoceros 326
hippocervus 157
Hippocrene 254
Hippodame 12, 28, 36, 39, 41, 42, 83, 87, 89, 90, 92, 96, 99, 101, 105, 111, 121, 144, 154, 157, 166, 169, 172, 202, 204, 214, 221, 223, 224, 226, 229, 238, 248, 256, 257, 260, 272, 273, 313, 328
hippogriff 157
hippogtyph 157
hippoi athanatoi 14, 16, 19, 26, 39, 53, 57, 66, 68, 91, 95, 119, 120, 151, 157, 158, 204, 242, 254, 256, 257, 258, 261, 266, 267, 300, 338
hippoi monokerata 158
hippoi troiades 158
hippokampoi 157
Hippolytos 84

Hipponoe 221
hippopotamus 26, 51
hippotaynes 172
Hippotion 27, 39, 98, 112, 158, 173, 222, 248, 259, 314
hiranyagarbha 172
hircocervus 158
hisa-me 289
hisame 289
Hispanic folklore 319
Histoire Naturelle 225
Histoires ou Contes du temps Passé 246
Historia Animalium 61
The History of Foure-Footed Beasts 226
History of the Northern People 146
Hitachi 235
hitotsume-kozō 35, 158
Hittite mythology 169
Hiyakudori 158
Hizen 233
hizri 158
Hjalmther, horse 159
Hjalmther, person 148
Hkringwan 231
Hlebardr 177
Hlid 159
Hloi 177
hmong 170
hnikur 159, 86
hō-ō 159
ho-oo 159
hobgoblin 220, 295
Hochigan 159
hodag 124, 159
Hoefir 159, 167, 271, 272
hoengaek 160
Hofvarpner 159
Hófvarpnir 133, 150, 159
Hofvarpnir 159
Hofvarpur 159
hog fish 26
hog-nose snake 339
hoga 30
Hoga tree 30
Hogni (Högni) 160
Hokhokw 160
Hokkaido, Japan 21
hōkō 256
Hokuriku, Japan 26
hol 225
holder-folk 321
holedwelling 309
Holkvir 160
hollow-men 321
Holvir 160
Holy of Holies 228
Holy Ones 30
Holy Saturday 57
holy water 221, 308
homa 160
homa bird 160
hombre caiman 160
el hombre caiman 160
el hombre del saco 160
el hombre pex 127
Homer 19, 40, 53, 95, 141,

151, 204, 254, 261, 294, 338
Homeric Hymn to Apollo 110
L'Homme Rouge 246
homocane 160
homunculus 30, 160
homunculus-like 30
honey-dew 97, 112, 113
Honey Island Swamp, Louisiana 211
hongaek 160
Honorius Philoponus 282
Honoyeta 161
Honshu, Japan 48
hoop snake 124, 161
Hopi mythology 251, 290
Hopleus 39, 42, 226, 256, 328
Horae 14
horned alligator 161
horned dragon 85, 145, 161, 175, 189, 191
horned serpent 32, 56, 161, 261, 293, 325, 341
horned snake 32, 161, 227, 247, 310, 331
hornworm 82
horny bunny 174
Horo-Matangi 161
Horomatangi 161
horse 15, 16, 19, 23, 24, 25, 28, 37, 39, 40, 41, 42, 47, 50, 51, 52, 53, 54, 55, 56, 57, 63, 65, 66, 67, 68, 69, 71, 72, 73, 77, 79, 80, 81, 82, 83, 84, 85, 87, 90, 91, 95, 96, 98, 101, 103, 106, 111, 112, 113, 114, 115, 118, 119, 122, 123, 128, 137, 138, 139, 140, 141, 142, 143, 144, 145, 146, 148, 149, 153, 157, 158, 159, 160, 162, 165, 167, 172, 174, 175, 176, 178, 179, 182, 186, 188, 191, 192, 194, 204, 208, 219, 222, 223, 228, 229, 230, 233, 236, 237, 241, 242, 244, 245, 249, 252, 253, 254, 259, 260, 261, 262, 263, 267, 268, 272, 275, 276, 277, 281, 284, 285, 287, 288, 292, 293, 294, 296, 298, 299, 300, 302, 304, 305, 306, 307, 316, 317, 318, 319, 323, 324, 326, 327, 329, 330, 336, 338
horse-like 66, 70, 98, 245
horse stag 158
Horse-Success Mountains 316
horse-whale 275
Horton, England 148
Horus 143, 187
Hothbrodd 223, 229
Hoto-Puku 161–62, 254
hou-ou 159
hound-like head 82

Hounds of Annwn 33, 41, 62, 93, 94, 122, 154
Hounds of the Hills 33
hounds of Zeus 151
household spirit 117, 171, 186
How Culhwch Won Olwen 72, 209, 344
Hoxhogwaxtewae 160
Hoxhok-of-the-Sky 160
Hraudnir 177
Hraudungr 177
Hreggwidur 112
Hreidmar the magician 122
Hrid 162
Hríð 162
Hrim Faxi 11
Hrimefath 156
Hrimfax 162
Hrimfaxe 11, 156, 162
Hrímfaxe 162
Hrímfaxi 162
Hrimfaxi 25, 47, 156, 162, 295
Hrimgrimnir 177
hrimpursar 177
Hrimr 177
Hrimthursars 304
Hringvolnir 177
Hripstodi 177
Hritvitnir 162
Hroarr 177
Hrodr 177
Hrodvitner 152, 162
Hrodvitnir 125
Hrokkvir 177
Hrolf, King 58
Hrosspjoft 177
Hrot, King 143
Hrothvitnir 162
Hrungnir 140, 177
Hrym 177
Hrymfaxe 156, 162
Hrymr 177
hrymthursars 213
hsiao 162
hsieh-chai 162
hsigo 162
hsing-t'ien 162
Hu Gadarn 13
hu hsien 86, 162
hua-fish 163
Hua-Hu-Tiao 163
Hua Yang 128, 163
huallepen 163
Huang Di 125, 196, 342
Huang Long 163
Huanglong 163
huayu 163
Hubei, China 176
huckleberry bush 43
Hudson Bay, Canada 168, 185, 227, 268, 298, 324
Huecu 94
Huecuvu 73
hugao 124, 163
Hugh MacLeod 123
Hugin 163
Huginn 163, 232

hui 163, 164
Huisne River 255
Huitzilopochtli 339
huldrafolk 117
huli jing 86, 87, 108, 135, 192
Huli people 98
huma 164
human-like 15, 341
human pride which destroys the soul, symbolic of 232
human sacrifice 130, 307, 342
human-scorpion hybrids 37
human snakes 164
human speech 14, 39, 40, 53, 63, 90, 92, 106, 185, 232, 306, 338
humanoid 26, 28, 36, 41, 47, 52, 59, 60, 62, 66, 86, 89, 93, 101, 102, 117, 127, 131, 140, 144, 150, 160, 162, 164, 168, 171, 172, 173, 180, 183, 184, 185, 188, 192, 195, 210, 211, 220, 230, 233, 240, 242, 245, 246, 247, 259, 260, 265, 267, 291, 293, 297, 305, 324, 334
humanoid monster 41, 89, 184
humility 124, 164
humility bird 164
Hunahpu 332
Hundolfr 177
hundred-heads 164
Hungarian folklore 107, 207, 242, 279
Hungary 194, 301, 324
Hunin 163
Huorco 246
Hupasiya 169
Hurakan 76, 91, 311, 338
huri 164
Hurricane Township, Maine 60
hurricanes 269
Huru Kareao 164
Huru-Kareao 164
Hurukareao 164
hus Erymanthios 120
Hus Kalydonios 74
Hus Klazomenaios 92
huspalim 165
hustomte 139
huxian 86
Huxwhukw 160
Hvalr 177
hvcko capko 165
Hvergelmir Well 139, 142, 228, 245, 305
hwa yih 165, 213, 319, 342, 344
Hwai nan Tsze 107, 188, 189, 200, 208, 218, 291, 342, 344
Hwanf Ti 188
Hwang 125, 129–30

hybrid 23, 25, 27, 34, 37, 42, 44, 50, 66, 72, 73, 74, 75, 78, 88, 89, 91, 92, 105, 132, 135, 144, 146, 147, 153, 154, 155, 157, 158, 159, 160, 163, 164, 165, 171, 172, 178, 183, 184, 190, 191, 194, 200, 202, 204, 205, 211, 213, 215, 216, 222, 223, 226, 227, 236, 238, 240, 241, 244, 247, 248, 250, 252, 253, 254, 256, 259, 260, 263, 268, 270, 276, 277, 284, 285, 286, 290, 291, 292, 303, 304, 309, 312, 313, 314, 316, 320, 328, 329, 333, 334, 335, 338, 339
hybrid creature 89, 91, 132, 144, 154, 157, 160, 165, 215, 223, 236, 238, 241, 244, 256, 260, 276, 286, 313, 320
hybrid race 37
hybrid women 50
Hyde, Douglas 25
hydra 77, 82, 85, 87, 101, 110, 115, 116, 123, 165, 180, 207, 238, 239, 249, 340
hydra Lernaia 165
hydra-like 87, 116, 249, 340
hydra of Lerna 165
hydra of Lernaea 165
hydrippus 165–66
hydromel 153
hydros 166
hydrus 166
hyena 57, 69, 92, 192, 334, 335
Hyginus 102, 201, 203, 219, 258, 267, 338
Hyk 153
Hylactor 104, 166
Hylaeus 166
Hylaios 166, 274
Hyle 156, 257
Hyles 156, 257
Hyleus 104, 166
Hyllus 239
Hylonome 95, 96, 166
hyman topodes 167
hymche 168
Hymir 156, 248
Hymn to Aphrodite (Venus) 284
hyosube 167
hyosubo 167
hyosue 167
hyosunbe 167
hyphialtes 302
hypnalis 167
hypocrisy, personification of 247
Hyrr 159, 167, 271, 272
Hýrr 167

iaculi 27, 167
iak im 339

Ibanag folklore 279
Iberian folklore 153
ibex 252, 346
Icarius 215
ice giants 192
ice worm 167
Iceland 57, 113, 159, 186, 220
Icelandic folklore 58, 244, 295
ichchadhari nag 167
ichneumon 166
Ichnobates 104, 167, 222
ichthyocentaur 167
Ida 77
Idmon of Colophone 38
idrus 166
iele 167–68
iemisch 168
Ihu-Maataotao 161
Ihuaivulu 168
Ika 168
Ika-O-Te-Rangi 168
Ika-Roa 168
ikalu nappa 168
Ikaroa 168
ikhthyokentauroi 167
Iki-Tursas 168
Iko-Turso 168
Iku-Tursas 168
ikugan 168
Ikuutayuuq 168–69
Ilerion 22
ill fortune 29, 325
ill omen 76, 86, 176, 242
Iliad 19, 39, 53, 204, 261, 338
Illini tribe 259
Illinois, USA 205, 217, 259
Illujanka 169
Illuyanka 107, 169
Ilocano demonology 56
ilomba 169
Ilulange 173
Il'ya Muromets 55
Imap Umassoursa 169
Imbreus 111, 169
Imbrius 39, 111, 121, 169, 214
Imbros 169
Imdugud 34
Imgig Bird 34
immortal 14, 19, 21, 24, 39, 53, 54, 77, 84, 95, 97, 116, 121, 141, 151, 158, 162, 165, 183, 184, 242, 262, 292, 300, 337, 338
immortality 37, 38, 41, 84, 134, 141, 179, 184, 225, 240, 244, 341
Imndugud 34
imoogi 170
Imperfect Mountain 140
impundulu 169–70
Imr 177
imugo 170
Imy-Hemef 170
In Bao A Qou 170
Inari 190, 241, 320

Inari fox 241
Inchiquin, Ireland 68
incubi 170, 303
Incubus 5, 74, 75, 170, 178, 207, 221, 280, 303, 345
incunche 171
indacinga 170–71
India 16, 28, 37, 47, 52, 67, 73, 77, 86, 109, 111, 114, 132, 158, 163, 170, 183, 196, 203, 229, 233, 249, 252, 266, 270, 274, 313, 326, 327, 329, 333
Indian folklore 53, 70, 167, 234, 276, 322, 341
Indian Ocean 123, 227, 320
Indo-China 216
Indonesia 11, 46, 216, 263
Indonesia and Malaya folklore 263
Indonesian folklore 33, 75, 178
Indra 17, 18, 19, 41, 100, 101, 133, 179, 184, 215, 277, 278, 306, 325, 331
Indradyumna, King 21
Indraprastha 100
Indrik 171
Indrik the Beast 171
Indus Valley 326
inet 12, 171
ingkanto 118
inguma 171
Iniguez 253
Inis Cathaig 277
injun devil 138
Inkanyamba 171
Inkarri 79
inkhomi 171
inntxixu 171
Innu people 46
Ino 40
insect 24, 66, 148, 267, 280
insect-like 267
insomnia 21
intigre 69
inttxixu 171
Intulo 171
intxix 171
intxixa 171
intxixu 171
intxixua 171
intxixue 171
intxixui 171
intxixuo 171
intxoxu 171
intxxiu 171
Inuit 6, 17, 20, 26, 32, 41, 46, 48, 168, 169, 171, 172, 173, 180, 185, 186, 189, 190, 193, 243, 251, 262, 267, 268, 318, 324, 325, 336
Inuit folklore 6, 41, 169, 171, 172, 180, 185, 186, 243, 267, 268, 318, 324, 325

Inuit mythology 17, 46, 48, 173, 189, 190, 251, 262
inuragullit 171
Inuus 23
Inventorum Natura 267
invunche 86, 171–72, 321
inxtixu 171
inyoni yezulu 169
Io 68, 219, 335
Iolaols 165
Iole 239
Iorek 172
Iormungandr 176
Iörmungandr 176
Iormungandur 176
Iormuni 172
Iotunn 177
iöunn 136
Iphinous 89, 172
Ipopodes 172
ipotane 172
iqalu-nappa 172
Iranian folklore 103, 182, 283
Iranian mythology 52, 330
Iravat 18
Iravata 101
Irish Christian folklore 91
Irish folklore 18, 25, 47, 62, 63, 91, 103, 114, 118, 126, 131, 138, 139, 231, 232, 246, 251, 254, 259, 260, 277, 303
Irish highlands 46
Irish mythology 15, 35, 104, 117, 212, 283
iriz ima 172
Iromunrek 172
iron 21, 68, 69, 72, 86, 108, 127, 132, 141, 152, 165, 170, 184, 196, 210, 218, 265, 277, 287, 309, 312, 317, 330, 346
Iron Pillar of Delhi 330
Iroquois 59, 97, 128
Iroquois tribes 97
Iroquois mythology 59
irresponsibility and reck-lessness, personification of 231
Isa (Jesus) 51
Isa Bere 173
Isaiah 106
Ishkur 325
Ishmael 66
ishologu 167
ishologu 170
Ishtar 70, 99, 119, 145, 197
Isikqukqumadevu 173
Isiququmadevu 173
Isitoq 173
Isitwalangcengce 173
Islamic folklore 122, 183, 227, 232
Islamic mythology 51, 66, 122, 197, 227, 236, 344
Islamic Turkish literature 116
Island of Birds 157
Island of Molucca 75

island of Samos 237
Island of Sumatra 251
island of the Blessed 14
Island of the Devils 20
Isle of Anglesey 78
Isle of Britain 154
Isle of Man, Great Britain 41, 58, 94, 138, 228, 308, 309
Isle of Skye, Scotland 58, 92, 159, 212
Isle of Thylen 219
isonade 179
Isoples 27, 39, 98, 112, 158, 173, 222, 248, 259, 314
ispolini 136
Istar 153
Isungr 177
Italian folklore 114, 213, 327
Italo-Albanian demonology 300
Italy 64, 84, 120, 170, 216, 252, 281, 323, 330, 335
itcuintlipotzotli 173
itnxixu 171
Ito Soda 233
ittan-momen 173–74
itzcuintlipotzotli 173
Ivan the Fool 71, 294
iwakoshinpuk 174
Iwanci 174
Iwanei 174
Ixion 80, 245
iya 174
iza 106
Izanami 289
izulu 169
Izumo 249

Jacarillo Apache 60
jacinth 66
jack-a-lope 174
jack-o-lantern 70
jack-pine jackelope 174
jackalope 174, 337
jaculus 27, 167
Jade Emperor 108
Jade Moon Rabbit 229
Jade Rabbit 229
jaguar- like 66
jaguar-man 174, 334
jaguareté avá 174
jaguarete ova 174
jala-turga 174
jall 114
Jamaican folklore 274
James, King 40
Jamie 220
jan 172, 231, 246
jan the sun 174
Janamejaya 234, 306
Jancsi 279
János Vitéz 279
Japan 21, 26, 29, 81, 128, 176, 179, 182, 183, 192, 233, 256, 304, 309, 314, 320, 327, 334, 335
Japanese Buddhist folklore 193

Japanese chimera 142
Japanese demonology 192, 242, 246, 269, 274
Japanese fairy tale 20
Japanese fishing folklore 173
Japanese folklore 20, 26, 27, 35, 43, 52, 60, 62, 71, 81, 105, 115, 116, 118, 134, 152, 158, 159, 167, 173, 176, 179, 180, 181, 190, 192, 194, 195, 196, 198, 229, 231, 233, 235, 238, 240, 241, 242, 243, 244, 245, 272, 277, 280, 287, 288, 289, 290, 291, 299, 304, 306, 307, 311, 312, 319, 320, 322, 323, 329, 333, 340, 341, 343, 345, 347
Japanese mythology 48, 49, 52, 60, 67, 87, 97, 129, 130, 135, 145, 149, 150, 151, 155, 178, 179, 181, 183, 184, 190, 192, 194, 197, 227, 230, 235, 241, 246, 249, 269, 273, 275, 288, 303, 310, 314, 315, 325, 340, 342
Japanese Shinto mythology 249
jaracaca 174
jaracas 174
Jaralez 38
Jarapiri 270
Jari 113, 175, 177, 279
Jarita 175, 279
Jaritari 175, 279
Jarnvidr Forest 214
jasconius 57, 100
Jason 84, 187, 201, 262
Jason and the Argonauts 151
Jason the Argonaut 262
Jatayu 175, 277
jättar 136
jättiläiset 136
Java 17, 304, 334
Javanese folklore 69, 214
javelin snake 27, 167
jay hawk 124, 175
jay-hawk 175
Jaya 234
jednorozec 326
jeduah 55, 202
jellyfish 275
jemechim 168
jemisch 168
Jen Fang 188, 189, 213, 342
jenny haniver 282
jerff 146
Jerome 313
Jersey devil 175
Jerusalem 15
Jetunn 177
jeweled eggs 196
Jewish demonology 288
Jewish folklore 31
Jezîrat al–Tennyn 227
jhumbies 178

jiaolong 175
jiaoming 123, 175, 304, 343
Jim Puttock of Wick 193
Jinde 165
Jingwei 175
jinmenju 176
jinshin-mushi 176
jinshin namazu 176
jinshin uwo 176
jinwei hu 162
Jitta-Jitta 136
jiu tou niao 176
jiufeng 176
Jnana 136
Johana 161
Johannaeus, Finnus 113
John Chrysoston 313
John the Valiant 279
joint snake 276
Jokull 177
Joly, Leon 86
Jor 176
Jór 176
Jormindgand 176
Jörmungand 176
Jormungander 176
Jormungandr 126, 156, 176, 177, 249
Jörmungandr 177
Jormungandur 176
Jormungard 176
Jormungrund 162
Jotnar 113, 126, 136, 177
Jöttin 177
Jotun 47, 113, 122, 126, 136, 140, 153, 156, 159, 167, 177, 271, 272
Jotunheimr 126, 177
Jötunn 177
Ju Lai 214
Juan-ch'eng 211
Judgment Day 117, 145, 251, 260
Judgment of the Dead ceremony 26
Judeo-Christian folklore 166, 326, 327
jujak 178
Julemand (Santa Claus) 178
julenisse 178
Julunggul 270
juma 178
jumar 178
jumbee 178
jumbi 178
jumbies 178
jumby 178
Juno 68, 77, 80, 96, 105, 110, 145, 165, 219, 267, 313
Juravale's Marsh 113
Jurik 178
Juruna people 293
justice, purity and righteousness, symbol of 236
Jute 177
jutul 321

Jyotiratha 234
Jyotishka 234

ka-riu 178–79, 273
ka ryu 179
ka-ryu 179
ka wi nulita 170
kaaguy pori 179
Kaahumanu 228
Kabandha 179
kabauter 139
Kabbalistic folklore 140
Kabi people 100
kabouter 139
Kadimakara 179
Kadimurka 179
Kadru 18, 233, 252
kafar 73, 265
kafre 73
Kahashima River 228
Kai Kai 179
kai-tsi 155, 179–80
kai tsu 84, 179
kaibyou 180
Kailasaka 234
kajanprati 70
Kajjutajuk 180
Kakamora 180
kakli besar 180
kakua kambuzi 180
Kala 234
Kalakanjas 180
Kalakeyas 180
Kalapuya Indians 26, 34
Kalasha 234
Kaldgrani 177
Kaleru 270
Kalfsvisa 300, 329
Kali 184
Kalika 234
kalinago 46
Kalindi river 180
Kaliya 101, 180, 234
Kaliyanaga 180
kalku 87
Kallukanxhe 184
Kalmasha 234
kaluk 181
kalumpang trees 317
Kalydonian boar 74
Kamadhenu 181, 304
kamaitachi 181
Kamayusha 134
Kambala 234
Kami 145, 176, 181, 190, 237, 320
kami-kiri 181
kamikiri 181
Kamilaroi peoples 100
kammapa 181
Kammu people 334
Kampe 75
kampos 282
Kamyaka forest 192
kanae 181–82
kaname ishi 176
kaname-ishi 235
kanashibara 170
Kanchil 135
Kane 149

Kane-Kua-Ana 182
kaneakeluh 182
kangaroo 1, 2, 60, 111, 151, 232, 292, 323
kangaroo-like 60, 151
kankagee 124, 182
kanko 196
Kansu provenance, China 80
Kao Yao 162
Kapila 43, 101, 164, 234, 266
kappa 167, 182, 289
kapre 182
Kaptan 217
kar-fish 182
kara fish 182
kara kasa 183
kara-kasa 183
Kara-omo, China 80
kara-shishi 183, 194
kara-shiski 104
Karadjeri mythology 70, 216
karakadan 271
Karakasa 183
karakasa kozo 183
karakasa obake 183
Karapiti blowhole 161
karasu tengu 150, 183
Karavira 234
karawatoniga 183
Kardama 234
karg 183
kargas 183
Karia 270
Karihi 263
karina 183
karkadan 183–84, 229, 326
karkadann 183, 229, 326
karkadanno 183
Karkanxhol 184
Karkara 234
karkedden 183
karkend 183
Karkinos 77
Karkotaka 184, 234
Karl the Yoeman 63
karma 164, 274
karmadan 183
karnmapa 181
Karotaka 234
karrigell an Ankou 33
Karshipta 184
Karsiptar 184
kartajan 183
Karura 184
karv 160
kasa-bake 183
kasa-obake 183
Kashchei 87, 184
Kashchei the Deathless 87, 184
Kashchey 184
kashehotapolo 184–85
Kashima, Japan 176, 235
Kashmire 216
Kashub people 230
Kashyapa 234

Kashyapi 134
Kasna 17
Al Kaswa 185
Kasyapa 18, 180, 196, 233
Katakhanoso 51
Kataore 185
Kathasaritsagara 330
Katmir 103, 185
katoblepon 185
Katonda 53, 189
katraresh 185
Katreus 226
Katsura-otoko 185
katytayuuq 185, 324
Kau You 179
kaukas 19, 78, 186
kaukis 139
Kauravya 101, 186, 234
kawa-zaru 182
Kawaiisu mythology 148
Kawaissu Tubatulabal 240
kawako 182
Kawhia 309
kayman 144
ke-ippai 249
keelut 186
ke'lets 186
Kellas Cats 73
Kelmendi tribe 194
kelpie 47, 50, 79, 114, 118, 129, 186, 225, 243, 285, 308, 331
Kenken-Ur 143
Kennebec River, Maine 135, 298
kentaure 80
kentaurides 81
kentauroi 80
kentauros 80
Kentucky, USA 333
Kenya 218, 231
kepec 139
Kerberos 82
Keresapa 133
Kərəsāspa 132
Keresaspa 251, 297
kergrim 186
kerkes 13, 186
kerkopes 82
Kernites River 38
Kertr 186
Kerynitian Hind 38
Keshi 186–87
Keshimanthana 187
Keshin 186
kesprap kamui 187
Keteus 80
Ketmir 185
Ketos 82, 282
kezkezan 183
Khaga 234
Khageshvara 134
Khalkotauroi 187
Khandava forest 175
Khangay 323
Khara 187
Kharybdis 84
Kheglen 187
Kheiron 84
Khem 30, 299

Kheper 187
Khepere 187
Khepra 187
Khepri 187
Kheti 187
Khimaira 85
Khnathaiti 251
khodumodumo 181
Khoikhoi mythology 131
Khoikhoi people 58, 149
Khoisan 144
Kholkian drakon 187
kholomodumo 181
Khosrau Parvez (Parwiz) 145, 287
khrafstra 21, 22, 41, 42, 49, 52, 102, 103, 112, 132, 133, 183, 187, 188, 218, 273, 283, 293, 315, 326, 345
Khrysomallos 40
Khyung 188
Khyungpo 188
Ki 42
ki-lin 86, 188, 268, 327
k'i-lin 108, 188, 189
ki-man 144
ki-rin 191
ki-tsune 192
Kia-Yu 188
kiai-lin 108, 188–89
kiai-t'an 108, 188–89
kiao 85, 86, 188, 189, 191, 213, 288, 342, 344
kiao-lung 84, 86, 108, 179, 188, 196, 200, 252
kiau 189
Kibi Province 228
Kibuka 53, 189
Kibuuka 189
kickle snifter 124, 189
kicklesnifter 189
kiel-gelal 303
kien-ma 108, 188, 189, 342
kien-sie 108, 189
Kiev, Ukraine 141, 323
Kigatilik 189
Kihawahine 190, 228
Kii-no-kuni-zaka 231
Kijilamuh Ka'ong 270
kikimora 170, 230
kikituk 190
kiko 190
Kiko Myojin 87, 190
Kikuyu people 231
kilbit 206
Kilili 197
kilin 188, 268
Kilyakai 190
Kimanaueze 192
kimono 62, 194, 246, 319
kimpurushas 191
Kin King 130
Kin Ryu 190
Kinabalu 190
Kincaled 144
kindly ones 130
The Kindly Ones 120, 130
Kinepeikwa 224
King Island, Alaska 251

King Lear 128
king of all foxes 87, 190
King of All the Lakes 103
king of Egypt, symbol of the 299
king of Hilmgareariki 112
king of the birds 184, 292
king of the Scythians 115
king of the sea serpents 101
King of the Serpents 101, 180, 270
king of the snakes 83
king of the Underworld 33, 59
King, symbol of 109
Kingdom of Belgium 250
kingmingoarkulluk 190
Kingu 191
Kingugu 191
Kinie Ger 191
kinnaras 134, 191, 236
Kio-Touan 327
kioh-lung 86, 189, 191, 213, 217, 342
kioh twan 191, 327
Kiowa mythology 161
Kirata 191
kirien 191
kirin 188, 191, 192, 327
kirk grim 143
kirkegrim 143
kirkigrim 143
Kirmira 192
kirni 192
Kirtimukha 192
Kishar 202
kishi 192
kissugu 202
kitiaquantj 64
kitsune 108, 190, 192, 194, 195, 196, 197, 198, 233, 241, 272, 288, 291, 307, 320, 340, 343
Kitsune-okuri 192
kitsune-tsuki 86
kitten-like 90
kiwahkw 192–93
Kiyo 193
Kiyohime 193
klabauter 139
Klamath folklore 139
kleine volk 113
kleinmanneken 139
Knecht Ruprecht 195
Knickerbocker Magazine 265
knight 28, 41, 57, 61, 66, 68, 76, 107, 127, 193, 219, 276, 329, 346
knight fish 193
The Knight of the Parrot 127
knowledge and wisdom, symbol of 132
Knucker 193
Knucker Hole 193
koala-like 111
kogukhpuk 193
kohen gadol 288
Kohu 168
Koklikas 19

kokma 170
Kokoua 239
kolivilor 193
Köll 177
Kolonos 296
Kolowisi 193
koma-inu 104, 183, 194
Kompira 193
Konabos 91, 158
konaki-jijii 194, 245
kongamato 279
Konjaku Hyakki Shui 105
Konoha-Tengu 194
el kookooee 194
Korca, Albania 110
kore 194
Korean folklore 11, 104, 106, 146, 160, 170, 178, 200, 217, 229, 236, 277, 258, 342, 343
koresck 194
koresk 326, 327
kornbockes 259
kornwolf 194
koro 322
koro-hebi 322
Koryak 199
koryo 194
Kosala, India 101
Koschei 184
Kościej 184
Koshchei 184
Koshchey 184
Koshchiy 184
Koshi dragon 340
Koshi Road 340
Kosmatushka 55
Kosmatushko 194
kosode-no-te 194
Kostěj 184
kotai 195
Kotanaka 234
kotengu 183
Kothar-wa-Hassis 341
koto (floor harp) 195
koto-furunushi 195
Kottr 177
Kouravya 234
koyemshi 195
kozo 183
krabben 195
krabbern 195
kraken 195
Kramer, Heinrich 203
Krampus 195
Krampuss 195
Krampusz 195
krasnoludek 139
Kratim 185
kravyad 17, 43, 196, 210, 270, 278, 279
kravyada 196, 275
kraxen 195
Krenaios 196
Kreon 313
kreutzer 58, 196
Krios Khrysomallos 40
Krisaka 234
Krishna 17, 53, 180, 187, 199, 234, 304

Krisky 241
Krodha 196
Krodha-Vasa 196
Krodhaa 196
Krodhavasa 196
Krodhavasha 196
kuanthrops 335
Kuanthropy 334, 335
Kubba 16
Kubera 101
Kubile 16
Kublai Khan 274
kucedre 197
kuchisake onna 196
kuda-gitsune 196, 200
kudan 196, 306
Kuen Lun 257
k'uh-lung 196
Kui 197, 197
Kui Yi Zu 196
Kujata 51, 197
kuko 197
kukui 194
Kukulkan 125
Kukuna 234
Kukura 234
Kuli-Ana 197, 196
Kulika 197, 234
kulili 197
Kulilu 197
Kulkulcan 28
kulshedra 65, 110, 197
kulullu 97
kumakatok 197
Kumara 234
Kumarbi 153
Kumarbi Cycle 153
Kumbhakarna 197, 198
kumbur 244
kumiho 198
kumo 198
Kumuda 43, 101, 198, 234
Kumudvati 198
K'un 255
Kun 198, 344
kunapipi 198
Kundrav 133
Kung Kung 140
Kuniya 198, 208
Kunjara 234
Kunmanngur 270
Kunmanngurr 270
Kunti 52
kuntiak 183
kuntilanak 263
Kuon Khryseos 198
Kupe 310
kupua 198, 199
Kur 199
Kurits 199
Kurnugi 37
Kurozuka 246
Kurrea 199
Kurria 199
Kurukadi 334
kusarikku 137, 199
Kushaka 234
Kushiinada-Hime 249
Kushmanda 234
kutabe 51

Kutkinnaku 199
Kuvalayapida 199
Kuvera 19
Kwakiutl folklore 197, 339, 340
Kwakiutla people 150, 160, 199, 236, 242
Kwakwakalanooksiwae 199–200
Kwakwaka'wakw folklore 266
Kwalulu Nata, Africa 171
kwanko 196, 200
kwei 109
Kweku Ananse 28
Kw'en 198
Kwoh P'oh 130
kwun-keng 189, 200
ky-lin 188
Kybele 16
Kyclops 95
kye-ryong 200
kyeryong 200
Kyklopes 95
kylin 268
Kymelos 96
kynolykos 92
kyo 108, 200
Kyoto, Japan 76, 245, 290
Kyr 200
Kyrmir 177
kyubi no kitsune 200

Labashu 202
Labbu 56, 107, 200, 233
Labrador 298
Labros 205
Labu 200
Labuna 51
labyrinth 44, 227
lacertilian 60, 97, 106, 108, 164, 203, 229, 254, 309
Lachne 104, 200, 201
Lacon 104, 201
Ladom 201
Ladon 105, 115, 201
Ladon, dog 104, 201
Ladon river 38
Ladwn 201
Lady Godiva (Godgifu) 16
Lady Kayo 163
Lady of Largo 201
Lady of the Fair Hair 127
Lady of the Land 201
Laelaps 104, 201, 313
Laelaps, dog 201
Lafquen Trilque 94
Lag-na-Paiste 251
Lagafljot 295
lagahoo 211
Lagarre 59
Lagash 61, 147, 197, 211, 257, 287, 294, 296, 301
Lago Lacar, Andes 94
Laguna Bay 217
Lahamu 202, 220
lahmu ippiru 202, 244
Laibolos 202
Laidley Worm of Spindleston Heugh 209

laidly worm 209
laidly worm of Bamborough 209
Lailaps 201, 313
Laird of Lariston 208
Lakalai folklore 331
Lake Bathurst, Australia 70
Lake Biwa, Japan 81
Lake Cuni-Cuni 313
Lake Cwm Ffynnon 13
Lake Darmsee 229
Lake Excess 163
Lake George, Australia 70
Lake Indradyumna 21
Lake Lacar, Argentina 94, 156
Lake Luschersee, Switzerland 71
lake monster 12, 26, 27, 68, 156, 161, 205, 217, 231, 241, 251, 260, 263, 267, 276, 282, 311
Lake of the Beast 268
Lake Pohenegamook 263
Lake Pyramid 29
Lake Rotoaria 164
Lake Stymphalus, Arcadia 302
Lake Superior 227
Lake Tanganyika 251
Lake Tritonis, Liby 321
Lake Ukasima 325
Lake Varukasha 132
Lake Winnapeg 227
Lakhamu 202
Lakota 174, 315, 326, 327
Lakota folklore 174, 327
Lakota Sioux 315
Lalaps 201
lalomena 202
Lama 188, 202, 203
laman lupa 202
Lamassu 202
Lamastu 201
Lamb, Robert 209
lamb tree 202–03
Lambton, John 203
Lambton, Lord of 203
Lambton dragon 203
Lambton worm 203
Lambton wurm 203
Lambton wyrm 203
lamiae 203
lamies 203
lamma 203
Lammassu 202
lammasu 203
lampalugua 203
Lampon 102, 203, 285, 338
lampong 204
Lampos 120, 158, 204, 257, 261, 266
Lamri 209
lamya 204
Lancelot Greaves 68
Land of Magic Water 260
Land of the Dead 23, 319, 332

Landnamabok 57
landslide 207, 296
Langal 270
Lango people 341
langsuir 52
Lanka 278
Laocoon 111
laohu 204
Lapith soldiers 39, 42, 112, 121, 169, 214, 221, 224, 248, 256, 261, 273, 313, 328
Lapland 113
Largo 201
Lariston, Laird of 208
latawiec 204
Latreus 204
Latvia 194
lau-palolo 228
Lauoho Rock 190
laura 204
laure 204
lavellan 205
law of fertility 325
lawn-niao 107
leash of Cors Hundred Claws 195
Lebros 17, 104, 205
lebushter 71
leech 25, 32, 70
Leeds, Daniel, and Jane 175
Leeds, Jenny 175
Leeds, England 250
Leeds Point, New Jersey 175
leeton 23
legarou 334
Lei 205
Lei Chen-Tzu 205
Lei Zhe Zi 205
Leidi 177
Leili 177
Lelaps 104, 201, 205
Lena River 18
Lenape mythology 270
lenapizka 205, 217
Leo 313
leokampoi 205
leokampos 205
leon nemeios 238
leongalli 205
leonine 40, 162, 192, 200, 259, 273, 279, 308, 320, 326, 328
leontophone 205
leopard's bane 205
Lernaean hydra 165
Lernean, Argolis 165
lešak 205
leshak 205
leshii 205
leshiy 205
leshouikha 205
leshy 205
lesiy 205
lesní mužík 205
lesnik 205
lesný mužík 205
lesny mužik/ded 205

Lesotho, South Africa 156, 181, 317
lesovij 205
lesovik 205
lesovy 205
Lesser Dog-Star 215
lesser gods 29
lesun 205
lešy 205
leszi 205
leszy 205
Letfet 206
Letfeti 206
letiche 211
Leto 267
Letteti 206
Lettfeti 206
Léttfeti 206
Leucite 104, 206
Leucon 104, 206
leucrocotta 206
leucrocuta 218
leucrota 92, 206
leukrokotai 206
Leviathan 206, 208, 246, 308, 330, 346
Levitan 206
li 206
li long 206
li-lung 206
liath 124
Liath Macha 207
Libyan folklore 167
Licho 207
licorne 326
lidérc 207
Lierganes, Spain 127
ligaroo 303
Lightfoot 90
lightning 19, 66, 95, 104, 110, 149, 157, 169, 174, 207, 237, 254, 269, 300, 311, 315, 327
lightning monsters 207
lightning serpent 149, 207
lightning snake 207
Liho 207
Liitr 177
lik 207
Likho 207
Likouala 117
lilin 303
lilit 303
Lin 130
lin-che-chi 188
Lincolnshire, England 148, 150, 288
lind-wurm 208
lindorm 208, 261
lindorm snake 208
lindworm 208
lindwurm 208
Ling Guang 330
ling k'uang 330
ling-kwei 108, 208
linguistic pun, personification of 343
Lint-Drache 208
Linton Hill 208
Linton worm 208

Lintrache 208
lintver 106
lintvurm 106
Lintwurm 208
lion 28, 30, 34, 37, 40, 48,
    51, 53, 60, 62, 67, 77, 81,
    82, 85, 86, 87, 88, 89, 92,
    102, 104, 107, 112, 115,
    118, 132, 143, 153, 156,
    165, 167, 179, 183, 192,
    194, 200, 202, 203, 204,
    205, 206, 214, 215, 216,
    218, 219, 223, 232, 238,
    239, 247, 253, 267, 268,
    271, 272, 273, 277, 278,
    279, 283, 284, 285, 290,
    292, 293, 297, 299, 308,
    312, 313, 324, 325, 326,
    328, 333, 334, 335, 339,
    340
lion-dragon 325
lion-like 40, 308
lions of Buddha 104
lios-alfar 208
liosalfar 208
liosálfar 208
Liru 198, 208
Lit 208
Litanu 208–09
Lithuania 19, 334
Lithuanian folklore 186,
    255, 346
Lithuanian mythology 56
Little Dipper 105
little lamb 55
Liu Hai 315
liver 21, 45, 46, 67, 78, 99,
    114, 115, 146, 182, 219,
    246
Livyatan 206
Liwyāṯān 206
lizard 32, 38, 52, 60, 66,
    97, 98, 106, 108, 146,
    159, 161, 164, 171, 203,
    229, 232, 254, 274, 301,
    309, 313, 336
lizard-like 60, 97, 106,
    108, 164, 203, 229, 254,
    309
ljosalfar 208
llama 23
llamhigyn y dwr 209, 334
Llamrei 209
Llgadrudd Emys 209
Llwydawg Govynnyad 54,
    144, 209, 324
Llwydawg the Killer 209
Llyfr Coch Hergest 13
Llyfr Gwyn Rhydderch 13
llyn barfog 12, 130, 209
Llyn Llion 12
Llyn yr Afanc 12
loathly worm 209
loathsome dragon 209
lob ombre 335
lob omem 335
loberia 210
lobis-homem 209–10
lobishomen 209, 210
lobishumen 210

lobisomen 153
lobison 210, 334
lobizon 210
lobombre 335
lobster 27
Loc a' Mhuillidh 58
Loch Ewe 62
Loch Foyle 251
Loch Maree Hotel 126
Loch na Fideil 126
Loch nam Breacan Dubha
    212
Loch Ness Monster 7, 260
Loch Rudrainge 231
Loch Shandangan, Ireland
    68
Lochan an Tarbh-Uisge
    308
locuste 210
Lodinn 177
lof jerskor 210
lofjerskor 210, 269
log gar 124, 210, 231
loha-mukha 210
lohikäärme 106
Lohita 234
lokapala elephants 101
Loki 126, 146, 153, 177,
    296, 304, 305
lone travelers 57, 237, 245,
    266
long ma 211
long-mâ 211
Long Wang 107, 108, 211
longgui 109
Longwang 211
Loo-wit Mountain 283
Lord Despot Vuk 347
Lord Millit Lake 163
Lord of Animals 171
Lord of Lambton 203
Lord of the Abyss 133
Lord of the Rings 247
Lord of the River 259
Lord Samanana 211
Lord's Day 68, 90, 115,
    210, 237
Lorge 248
Lork 23
Lotan 206, 208, 211
lou carcolh 211
Lough Derg, Ireland 91
Lough Swilly 303
Louhi 168
louhikäärme 106
Louisiana, USA 211
loup carou 211
loup garou 211–12, 334
loup-garou 334
loup garpou 335
louweerou 335
Lower Stanks, England 68
LTN 211
Lu 188, 327
lu dja lako 212
lú' dja lâko 212
luan 213
Luath Luchar 15, 67, 212,
    280, 283
lubaale 53

Lubina 93, 212, 222
Lucan 102, 286
lucidius 212
luck 5, 8, 69, 72, 79, 135,
    138, 150, 159, 186, 217,
    235, 240, 246, 259, 275,
    308, 333
luck dragon 129
Lucky Piggies 41
Lucky Piggy 41
lüdérc 207
Ludovico Ariosto 157
luduan 212
luferlang 212
lufferlang 212
Lugal-e u me-lam-bi nir-gal
    42
Lugale 42
lugarhoo 211
Lugbaran mythology 15
luideag 212
luison 210, 212
lumberjack communities
    21, 53, 57, 60, 75, 78, 81,
    90, 93, 100, 102, 124,
    128, 129, 132, 135, 136,
    138, 140, 141, 147, 147,
    151, 155, 156, 159, 161,
    163, 164, 175, 182, 189,
    210, 212, 225, 230, 257,
    260, 264, 264, 269, 275,
    278, 288, 296, 298, 299,
    305, 311, 320, 321, 328,
    333, 335, 336, 337
lumberjack folklore 39, 48,
    137, 146
lumerpa 212–13
lunar eclipse 315
lung 108, 161, 188, 189,
    191, 213
Lung Meng 107
Lung Wang 84, 108, 213,
    250
Lungr 213
lunkus 264
l'uomo nero 327–28
lupo manaro 213, 335
lupo mannaro 213
lupus vesperitinus 92
Lusatia, Germany 114
Lusca 213
Luska 213
Lut 213
Lút 213
lute 62, 330
Luther, Martin 75
Lutr 213
Lútr 213
Luz 343
lwan shui 213
Lybbeals of Prienlascors
    144
Lybia 121, 300
Lycabas 214, 221, 224,
    248, 260, 313
lycanthrope 19, 33, 71, 335
Lycaon 335
Lycetus 214
Lycia 85
Lycidas 214

Lyciday 39, 121, 169, 214
Lycides 214
Lycisca 104, 214
Lycisce 214
lycopodium 55, 202
lycopodium barometz 202
Lycus 92, 154, 214
Lyminister Nucker 193
Lyminster 193
Lyminster Nicor 193
lympago 218
lyon-poisson 214

Ma Yüan-shuai 214
maahinen 139
Maana-Garm 214
Maanegarm 152, 214
Maar 23
mab 170
Mabinogi of Branwen,
    Daughter of Llyr 61
The Mabinogion 72, 155,
    209, 344
Mabon ap Modron 111
macan gadongan 214
macan gadungan 214, 334
mace-like 102
Macedonia 17, 204, 245,
    357
Macedonian folklore 17,
    305
MacEndroe, Ean 62
Macha 18, 207
machi 256, 332
macupo 218
Mad Dog 191
Mada 215
Madagascan folklore 123,
    217, 320
Madagascar 54, 123, 202,
    274, 298, 320
Madai 231
Madambara 18
Maen Du 155
Maera 215
maere 170
maero 215
maeroero 215
mafedet 215
Magauayan 217
Magdalena 260
Magdalena River, Columbia
    160
magic 5, 13, 45, 46, 60, 64,
    104, 136, 143, 156, 172,
    184, 187, 192, 204, 218,
    240, 260, 261, 262, 270,
    273, 290, 301, 315, 317,
    323, 324, 326, 329, 333
Magnus, Olaus 40, 146,
    219, 276
magtitima 215
Magyars of Hungary 324
Maha-Pudma 58, 88, 215,-
    16, 280, 331
Mahabharata 21, 50, 52,
    233, 234, 266, 306, 318,
    325, 329
Mahahanu 234
Mahamucilinda 231

Mahanila 234
Mahapadama 234
Maharaurava 196, 275
Mahasankha 234
Mahavikrama 234
Mahavyutpatti 234
Mahisha 58
Mahmud Khilji of Malwa 170
mahoragas 134, 216
Mahr 23
Mahrt 23
Mahrte 23
Maiangara 216, 270
maide 216
maiden 12, 13, 54, 59, 65, 66, 83, 100, 107, 128, 142, 157, 163, 176, 177, 185, 201, 209, 215, 216, 221, 223, 224, 227, 254, 255, 290, 293, 295, 306
maighdean-mara 223
maighdean mhara 79
maighdean na tuinne 79
maighdean uaine 216
Main Mangi 187
Maine, USA 60
mair 170
mairi 216
mairoero 215
mairu 171
maize 48
Maka 216
makara 216
Makira 180
mako yamo 341
Makua people 237
Malagasy folklore 123, 202, 298, 319
Malagigi 57
Malahas 30
Malak YHWH 30
Malay Peninsula 12, 273
Malay people 61
Malaysia 46, 51, 61, 262
Malaysian folklore 135, 180, 255, 306, 316
maliades 216
maliadus 216
Maliseet-Passamaquoddy folklore 337
Maliseet-Passamaquoddy people 36
Malleus Maleficarum 203
Malyapindaka 234
Mama Dglo 216
Mama D'leau 216
Mama Dlo 216–17
Mama Glow 216
Mamadi Sefe Dekote 59
Maman de l' eau 216
mameleu 217
mamlambo 7, 217
Mammoth 159
man chw'en 188
Man of the Sea 266
Man Scorpion 191
man-tiger 218
man-tigeris 218
Mana-garm 152, 214

Mána-Garm 152, 214
Mána-Garmr 214
Manabozho 224
Mánagarm 214
Managarma 214
Managarmr 214
Mánagarmr 214
mananambal 45
Manananggal 21
mananggal 21
Manannán mac Lir 118
Manas 20
Manasvin 234
Manaul 217
Manchester, England 54
mancomorion 218
Manda-Pala 175, 279
mandarin duck 163
Mandriguiri Mountain 15
Manducus 105
Manetuwi-Rusi-Pissi 217
mang 217
Mangalya 217
mangarisaoka 217
mangarsahoc 217
Mangi 140
mangmangkit 214
Mangōroa 168
Mangōroa I Ata 168
mánguang anak 265
Mani (Maane) 25
Mani-Bhitti 284
Manicuda 234
Manigarm 152, 214
Manikantha 234
manikin 139
Manimat 234
Maninaga 234
Manipur 186, 235
Manito 207
Mannann mac Lir 35
mano 139
manó 139
man's duality of nature, symbol of 69
man's struggle over the elemental forces of nature, symbol of 340
Manta 94
manta ray 156
mantahungal 218
mantegre 218
mantichora 218
manticora 218
manticoras 218
manticore 88, 218
manticory 218
mantikhoras 218
mantindane 218
mantiserra 218
mantygre 218
Manuel I Conmenus 22
Manx folklore 72, 139
mao-tuh 218, 342
Maori folklore 161, 181, 215, 239, 243, 263, 264, 308, 309, 318
Maori mythology 149, 168, 254, 307
Maori people 164

Mapuche mythology 84, 256
Mar 23, 170
mara 23, 170
Mara-garme 152
marakihan 218
Marathonian bull 91
Marco Polo 91, 208, 273, 327
marcupo 217, 218, 219
Marcus Annaeus Lucanus 286
mard-khor 218
Marduk 107, 191, 197, 200, 232, 281, 316, 328
mare 19, 23, 24, 40, 41, 50, 80, 81, 100, 119, 133, 140, 149, 159, 170, 209, 262, 270, 278, 296, 305, 316
mare-hag 170
mareikura 36, 319, 335
Mares of Diomedes 102, 203, 219, 258, 338
Mares of Thrace 219
Margaret 209
Mari 20, 58
maricomorion 218
Marinduque 202
marine boar 282
marine lion 219
marine sow 219, 282
Mark Antony 115
Mark of Cain 335
market hog 209
Marksman 90
marmot 165
Maron 292
marool 219
Marquina 21, 34
Marrakech 18, 271
Marrock 219, 220
Marrock the Good Knight 219
Marrocke 219
marsok 220
Marsyas 220
Marsyas of Phrygia 220
Marsyas River 220
Märt 23
martikhorai 218
martiora 218
martlet 220
Mary Morgan 223
Maryland, USA 161
Massaru Tami 220
mast of the water 207
Master of Darkness 49
master of the fishes 227, 276
Master Stoorworm 220, 282
mastiff dog 54
Mata 104, 126, 220, 238
Matachi 341
Matali 41
matchi-manitou 225
Mathura 186
mati-anak 263
Matlose 220

matruculan 221
Mau-Ola 221, 228
Mau-ola 221, 228
mauari 221
Maugis Renadu 56
Maui 148, 310
Māui 148, 310
Maushop 265
mauthe dhoog 62, 154
Mauthe Dog 228
Mauthe Doog 228
Mawu 96
Maya, Queen 117
Mayan mythology 332, 338
Mayor of Arundel 193
mbōn 221
Mbumba 221
Mbumba Luangu 221
mebeddel 221
Meca 15
Mecca 11, 185
Medb 104, 126
Medea 187, 201
medieval folklore 155, 157, 165, 208, 248, 252, 260, 263, 303
Mediterranean folklore 25, 96
Mediterranean Sea 206
Medon 221, 260
Medusa 83, 121, 141, 142, 221, 222, 254, 300
Megaera 22, 120, 130, 222
Megaira 222
Megareus, King 89
Mehen 222
mei 222
Meinthjofr 230
Melampo 93, 212, 222
Melampus 104, 167, 222
Melanchaetes 222
Melanchaites 225
Melanchetes 27, 39, 98, 112, 158, 173, 222, 248, 259, 314
Melanchetus 104, 222
Melanesia 46, 54, 69, 270, 331
Melanesian folklore 12, 50, 183
Melanesian mythology 11, 152
Melanesian people 65
Melaneus 104, 223
Melaneus, dog 223
Melanion 166
Melanippe 84
Melchior 24
Meleager 74, 84, 92
meliades 216
Melissae 25
Melnir 223, 233
memecoleous 218
Menai Strait 78
Mende tribe 318
Menelaus of Mycenae, King 261
Meneleus 223
Meng Chang 304
mengshou 261

Menik 119, 223, 285
Menmenu 223
menninkäinen 139
Menominee mythology 227
menong 42
mercula 220
Merdas 345
Meritursas 168
merle 220, 336
merlette 220
Merlin 75, 268
merlion 223
mermaid 79, 168, 197, 223, 224, 240, 269, 285, 294, 318
merman 148, 172, 224, 232, 267, 282, 321
Mermeros 214, 224, 248, 313
mermicoleon 34
Merovee, King 268
Merovingian bloodline 268
Merrak 219
merrow 285
mescal 72
Mescalero Apache 60
Meshekenabec 224
Meshkenabec 224
Mesoamerican divinatory and ritual manuscript 76
Mesoamerican mythology 28, 125
Mesopotamia 14, 83, 99, 119, 202, 258, 326
Mesopotamian demonology 21, 202
Mesopotamian mythology 76, 83, 137, 199, 203, 215, 232
Messenger of Indra 278
Mester Stoorworm 220, 282
Metamorphoses 12, 16, 28, 36, 44, 68, 83, 87, 89, 90, 92, 95, 99, 101, 105, 111, 119, 121, 154, 166, 172, 204, 214, 229, 238, 256, 257, 260, 272, 335
meteor 131
Meteor Dragon 131
meteorite 19
metewelen 193
Metis 75
Mewreke 219
Mexican Aztec mythology 319
Mexican folklore 17, 30, 93, 94, 173
Mexico 30, 32, 88
Mi-Ni-Wa-Tu 224
Mial Mhor a' Chuain 89
Michael 7 30, 95, 145, 247, 262
michi-pichi 225
michi-pichoux 225, 326
michipichi 225
Middle Ages 50, 54, 55, 107, 119, 123, 139, 165, 229, 231, 258, 301

Midgard (earth) 116, 156
Midgard Serpent 126, 156, 177
Midgardrsormr 177
Miðgarðrsormr 177
Miðgarðsorm 177
Midgardsormr 177
Miðgarðsormr 177
Midi 118, 177
midnight 62, 69, 212, 244, 287, 307, 315, 337
migas 225
Mikonawa 225
milamo bird 124, 225
milcham 225
milk 15, 19, 24, 47, 52, 54, 66, 68, 77, 82, 96, 97, 98, 110, 123, 130, 138, 147, 174, 181, 218, 221, 225, 228, 234, 242, 304, 317, 320
Milk-White Milch Cow 225
Milton, John 247
Mimas 39, 42, 225, 256, 328
Mimi 226
mimick dog 226
mimike dog 226
Min-Magayi 181
Minamoto no Yoshitsune 298
Minangkabau people 251
Mindanao, Philippines 168
Mindi 270
Mindoro 202
Minghi Ghiamtso 286
minhocão 226
Mini 226
Minnesota, USA 48, 189, 260
minocane 160
Minokawa 226
minor gods 36, 150
minor tengu 183
Minos, King 44, 92, 226
Minotaur 44, 92, 159, 226, 227
Minotaur-like 159
miqqiayuuq 227
mirag 227
Miraj 66, 227
miraj 66, 227
mir'aj 227
al mi'raj 227
mirmicioleon 34
misfortune 29, 30, 43, 160, 207, 240, 262, 281, 304, 307, 317, 326, 332, 339
mishibizhiw 326
mishipeshu 227, 326
mishipissy 227
mishipizhiw 227
miskena 227
Miskena 227
miskitto 230
missipissy 227
Missouri River 224, 327, 332

mitchipichi 225
mite 137
Mithgarth-Worm 177
Mithgarthsorm 177
Mithra 103, 136
mittagsfrau 262
Mizuchi 227, 228
mlokowy smij 228
Mmabon 324
mmoatia 228
mo-ki 281
Mo-Li Ch'ing 163
Mo-O-Inanea 21, 148, 190, 221, 228
Moab 40
Moddey Dhoo 62, 154, 228
Moddey Dhoo of Norfolk 62, 154
Moddey Dohe 228
Mode, Heinz Adolf 60, 297
Modnir 113, 228
Módnir 113, 228
Modred 220
Modsoghir 113
Mohammed 11, 101, 185
Mohawk 332
Mohiriikkwchep 230
mohoao 215
mohowao 215
Moimotaro 20
Moinn 139, 142, 228, 245, 305
Móinn 139, 142, 228, 245, 305
moksin tongbop 236
Molina, Juan-Ignacio 128
molinillo 324
mollusk 211
molong 170
Molossus 104, 228
momiji 319
momonjaa 229
momonjii 229
Momotaro, the Little Peachling 20
monachi marini 61
monachus marinus 282
Mongolia 32, 98, 327
Mongolian Death Worm 23, 98
Mongolian folklore 205, 323
mongoose 56
Monju-bosatsu 290
monk fish 229
monkey 28, 162, 179, 182, 205, 210, 218, 242, 269, 289, 291, 329
monkey-like 17, 82, 101, 171, 226, 240, 263, 317, 329
monkfish 282
mono-no-ke 229
monocentaur 247
monocentaurus 247
monoceros 229, 247, 326
monoceros marinus 229
monocerotem 229

monocerus 229
monokerata 158, 229
monster 7, 12, 17, 18, 19, 20, 26, 27, 30, 35, 41, 42, 46, 47, 49, 52, 56, 57, 60, 63, 67, 68, 71, 73, 76, 77, 81, 84, 85, 86, 87, 88, 89, 91, 94, 96, 98, 104, 105, 110, 114, 115, 116, 118, 123, 127, 128, 131, 132, 133, 135, 137, 138, 141, 143, 145, 149, 150, 151, 153, 156, 157, 161, 165, 171, 173, 174, 176, 180, 181, 184, 185, 192, 193, 197, 199, 203, 205, 207, 211, 214, 215, 216, 217, 219, 220, 224, 225, 227, 229, 230, 231, 232, 239, 240, 241, 242, 243, 245, 251, 254, 260, 263, 264, 267, 270, 275, 276, 277, 281, 282, 290, 291, 294, 301, 303, 307, 310, 311, 316, 319, 322, 324, 325, 326, 329, 332, 333, 336, 338, 340, 341
Monsters of the North Sea 40
Monstrum in Oceano Germanica 40
Montecristo (Mondragon) 120
montegre 218
Montenegro 265
Monychus 204, 229
moogie 142, 229
moolgewanke 70
Moon 22, 25, 26, 39, 50, 76, 91, 107, 140, 152, 162, 171, 185, 192, 197, 210, 214, 217, 223, 225, 226, 229, 245, 259, 273, 274, 276, 282, 289, 290, 292, 311, 315, 316, 328, 331, 332, 333, 338
Moon Rabbit 229, 315
moonbeams 83
Moongarm 152, 214
Moor 23
moose 58, 163, 187, 288
Mopsus 226, 245
Mor 124, 229
Mór 124, 229
Mora 23, 90, 115, 230
Morgan la Fay 252
morgens 223
Morlaix, France 313
mormo 52, 118, 230
mormolikeion 230
mormoliki 230
mormolix 230
mormolykeia 230
Morn (Morginn) 329
Mornir 177
Moro tradition 61, 199
Moroccan folklore 18, 143, 150, 221, 271
Moroccan mythology 18, 143, 150, 221, 271

moromolukiai 230
moromolykiai 118
Morous 23
morphing shuck 62, 154
morrough 223
moruach 223
moruadh 223
morúsi 170
móry 170
Moselantja 230
Moses 21, 96, 106, 166, 288, 303
Moshiriikkwechep 230
moskitto 124, 230, 231
Moslem folklore 185
mosquito-like 338
mosquitoes 23, 332
moss people 113
Mot 211
mother of all monsters 115
Mount Aetna 76, 95
Mount Albur 83, 283
Mount Anie 343
Mount Artemisius 38
Mount Atlas 142
Mount Bell 346
Mount Bita, Philippines 250
Mount Cithaeron 104
Mount Damávand 345
Mount Demavend 49
Mount Erymanthus 120
Mount Helicon 254
Mount Hengshan 51
Mount Inari, Japan 233
Mount Kaf 103
Mount Kalaban 199
Mount Katahdin 64
Mount Katsuragi 114
Mount Kernites 38
Mount Kinabalu, Borneo 190
Mount Kiubo 195
Mount Kurama 97, 298
Mount Lampe 120
Mount Mandara 37, 330
Mount Mazovan 248
Mount Oeta 239
Mount Olympus 40, 254, 273
Mount Parnassus 78, 267
Mount Pelion 84
Mount Pilate, Switzerland 110, 337
Mount Saini 288
Mount Saint Helens 283
Mount Sipylos 198
Mount Triglav 346
Mount Zhangwei 346
mountain lion 53, 326, 333, 334, 335
Mountain of Mashu 137
mountain sheep 243
mouse 148, 200, 316, 325, 334, 336
mouse-like 336
mousedeer 135
mu 83, 202, 231, 342
Mu-Iam 231
Mucalinda 231

Mucilinda 231, 234
Muddy Bath River 316
Muddy Ones 220
Mudgaraparnaka 234
mudheads 195
muera 170
Muidris 231
muir-gheilt 223
Muirdris 231
muiriasc 232
mujina 231, 242, 307
Mukhara 234
Mukil-res-lemutti 328
Mukunga M'bura 231
Mula 153, 202, 231
mula fera 231
mulassa 231
muldarpe 232
Muldjewangk 232
mule 23, 42, 66, 97, 118, 122, 148, 153, 178, 231, 234, 247, 267, 292
mule-like 118, 231, 247
Mulla 202
Mumba 334
Munin 163, 232
Muninn 232
Mura 23
Murawa 23
murdhuch'a 223
murghi-i-adami 232
Murray River, Australia 70, 232, 326
murrisk 232
Mus 251
muscaliet 232
Muses 78, 130, 220, 254
Musheng 231
Mushikada 234
Mushussu 56, 200, 215, 232
Mušhuššu 56, 200, 215, 232
Mušḫuššu 56, 200, 215, 232
musical instrument 62, 195, 288
musilindi 233
musimon 233
musimu 233
Muslim folklore 89, 37, 101, 136, 145, 149
Muslim mythology 13, 44, 66, 103, 185
Musmahhu 287
Muspelheimr 177
Muspellsheim 11, 25
Musrussu dragon 232
Muti 270
Myanmar 253, 267
Mycenae 38, 120, 238, 261
Mylnir 223, 233
Mynydd Amanw 147
myobu 233
Myōbu 233
Myrkwood 223, 233
myrmecoleon 34
myrmecoles 34
myrmekes indikoi 140
myrrh 247

Na-Achia 107
Nabeshima, Cat of 233
Nachtmaennli 23
Nachtmahr 23
Nachtmanndli 23
Nachtmännlein 23
Nachtmerrie 23
Nachtschwalbe 23
Nachttoter 23
Nafnaþulur 112
naga 36, 41, 47, 70, 85, 101, 107, 108, 134, 180, 184, 186, 197, 198, 231, 233, 234, 250, 252, 260, 264, 269, 270, 284, 315, 328, 330
nāga 233
Naga Anantaboga 28
Naga-like 276
Naga-malla 18
naga raja 306
Nagantaka 134
nagaraja 325, 330, 333
Nagenatzani 99
nāgī 234
nagin 167
nagini 233, 234, 235
nāginī 234
nagis 233
Nahemah 303
nahualli 339
Nahusha 234
Nai 234
nains 139
Nak 36, 235, 238, 283
Nakhon Pathom City 117
Nala 184
naluganan 56
nama 144
namahage 26, 235
Namazu 176, 181, 235
namazu 176, 181, 235
namorodo 235
Nan-t'o 235
Nanda 234, 235
Nanda 234, 235
Nandakam 234
Nandi 235
Nandini 181
Nandopananda 234
Nanes Bakbakwalanooksiwae 236
nanggu moksin 236
nanu 139
Nape 70, 104, 236
Nara Prefecture, Japan 304
Narada 184
Naraen-ten 184
naras 236
Nargun 236
Nascopie 155
Nash Harbor Village 103
nashas 236
nasnas 236
Nastrond 240
nathraig luamning 237
Nati 177
National Legends of Roumania 53
Native American mythol-

ogy 48, 103, 142, 251, 315
Natt 162, 295
Natural History 14, 64, 92, 115, 128, 195, 206, 253, 258, 301
Natural Magick 178
natural phenomena, personification of 53, 343
Naturalis Historia 55
nature deities 237
nature spirit 11, 14, 15, 17, 18, 19, 21, 29, 34, 65, 66, 78, 85, 98, 104, 124, 129, 139, 152, 155, 173, 180, 181, 199, 205, 210, 215, 228, 236, 237, 243, 250, 252, 253, 260, 262, 263, 265, 266, 269, 280, 289, 290, 291, 293, 294, 295, 308, 331, 332, 333, 339, 343, 344
Nau 155, 223, 237, 238
Nau-Shesma 237
Nauruan mythology 39, 273
Naut 237
Navajo folklore 29, 99, 311, 316
Navajo people 60, 311, 313, 321, 322, 342
Nayanezgani 29, 322, 342
nayar 319
Nayenezgani 311
Nazha 35
ndogbojusui 237
ndzoodzoo 237, 326
nead 237
Neanderthals 190
Nebraska 174
Nebrophonos 104, 238
Nebrophonus 238
Nedymnus 238
Negative Confession 26, 286
Negeg 135
Negros 226
neguruvilu 128, 239
Neha-Hra 238
Neheb Ka 238
Nehebkau 155, 238
Nehebu-Kau 238
nekke 186
neko-mata 238
nekomata 238
Nemean Lion 85, 89, 115, 165, 238
Nemeian lion 238
Nen 237
Nenechen 332
nennir 244
neo–Platonic doctrine 116, 139, 277, 305
Nepal 216
nependis 238
Neph 92, 299
Nephele 40, 80, 245, 258
Neptune's horse 157
nereis 223
Nereus 99

Nergal 56
nerrefil u 168
nervelu 168
nesnas 236, 289
Nessos 239
Nessus 239
Nestor 84
Netherlands 65, 113, 114
Netherlands folklore 65
neugle 242
Nevada, USA 29, 334
New Britain, Melanesia 69, 73, 331
New England, USA 93
New Galicia 88
New Guinea folklore 339
New South Wales 70, 146
New South Wales, Australia 70, 146
New Year 26, 95, 197
New Zealand 148, 185, 215, 218, 253, 310, 318, 324
newt 25
Nez Perce folklore 337
Nezha 35
Nga Whetu 168
ngakoula-ngou 50
Ngalbjod 270
Ngalyod 270
ngamba-namae 117
ngani-vatu 239, 273
ngarat 239, 273
ngelmu gadungan 215
Ngorieru 15, 239
ngoulou 117
ngurüvil u 168
nguruvilu 239
ngutu-lei 239
niam-niam 244
Nian, the Beast 239
Nibelungenlied 208
Nicander of Colophon 82
Nicholas, Father Louis 225
nick 186
nicker 186
nickur 159, 186
nicor 193, 239, 244
Nidfollr 240
Nidhhogg 240
Nidhhoggr 240
Nidhøg 240
Nidhögg 240
Nídhögg 240
Níðhögg 240
Nidhogg 240, 248, 271
Nidhoggr 240
Nidhöggr 240
Niðhöggr 240
Nídhöggr 240
Níðhöggr 240
Nidhoggur 240
Niðhöggur 240
Nidhug 240
Nielop 23
Nien 239
Niffelheim 126
Niflheim 47, 153
Niflheim ice 47

Niflheimr 139, 142, 228, 245, 305
Niger River 173
Nigeria 13
Night Born Sisters 130
Night Chamber 312
Night Hag 241
night hound 154
Night Terror 23
nightmare 23, 52, 56, 142, 170, 171, 230
nihniknoovi 240
Nihon Shoki 115
nikar 159
nikyr 186
Nila 234
Nile River, Egypt 76, 166
Nindanao 61
nine-headed bird 176
Ningiri 240
ningyo 240
Nini-Ganne 240
Ninki Nanka 240
ninner 159, 186
ninth section 11, 61, 289, 312
Ninurta (Ningirsu) 34, 42, 61, 147, 197, 199, 211, 251, 287, 294, 296, 301, 326
nirgalli 240
niribil u 168
ñirivilo o nirivilo 239
ñirivilu 239
nirribil u 168
Nishakara 277
Nishthurika 234
Nisqually tribe 322
nisse 139, 178
nissen 139
Nisthurika 234
Nithhogg 240
Nithhoggr 240
Nithhöggr 240
ñivivilu 239
nix 186
nixie 244
Njordr 329
Njugals Water 242
Noah's ark 255
nobiagari 241
nobility, power, and strength, symbolic of 324
nobusuma 241
Nocnitsa 241
nocny forman 241
Nocny Hanik 241
Nocny Murava 241
nocturnal creatures 21, 35, 48, 56, 58, 70, 74, 131, 134, 150, 168, 171, 186, 215, 216, 217, 224, 228, 231, 240, 241, 242, 245, 260, 263, 292, 297, 298, 301, 308, 317, 319, 323326, 331, 334, 335
nocturnal emissions 21
nocturnal predator 35, 48, 134, 186, 319, 326, 331
noggle 242, 243

nogitsune 241
nogle 242
nok 159
nokken 241
Nomeion 80
Nomos 12, 16, 121, 242
Nonios 242
Nonius 242
Noolmahl 242
noppera-bo 242
noppera-bō 242
nopperabō 242
nopperabo 242, 246
Nor 177
nora 242
Nordic folklore 137
nore 242
Norfolk, England 62, 63, 154
Norge 248
Norglein 248
Norkele 248
Normandy, France 134
norrgens 246
Norse folklore 117, 134
Norse mythology 6, 25, 47, 63, 97, 111, 112, 113, 114, 116, 122, 126, 128, 133, 134, 135, 136, 137, 138, 140, 141, 142, 145, 146, 147, 148, 150, 153, 156, 159, 162, 163, 176, 177, 178, 186, 206, 208, 213, 214, 223, 228, 229, 232, 233, 240, 245, 248, 249, 296, 298, 299, 300, 302, 304, 305, 307, 318, 329, 330
North Carolina, USA 161, 278, 325
North Devon, England 132
North Gloom 225
North Sea 14, 40, 130, 276, 291
Northern Sea of China 35, 133
Norway 138, 294
Norwegian nisse 178
Nothung 122
Notos 242
Nott (Night) 156
nozuchi 322
La N'Roi Madai 231
nsanga 117
Nu Wa 175
nue 242
nuggie 242, 243
nuggle 243
nuhehho 244
nukekubi 243
nuku-mai-tore 243
Nuli'rahak 243
Number-nip 139
numputol 265
Nun 53, 243
nunda 243
nuno 243
nuno sa punso 243
Nunyenunc 243
Nuozha 35

nuppebbo 244
nuppefuhō 244
nuppeppo 244
nupperabo 244
nure onna 244
nure-onna 244
nurikabe 244
nursery bogie 244
nürüfil u 168
ñuruvilu 239
nutum 244
Nuu-chah-nulth people 220
nyam nyam 244
nyama 117
Nyame 28
nyan 47
nygel 242, 243
nykr 244
nykur 50
nymphs of time 14
nyuggle 243

o-bake 52
o-bakemono 52
o-dokuro 134
o-goa-cho 325
O-gon-cho 245
O Goncho 245
o-mamori 246
O-Tengu 150
O-Toyo 233
Oannes 223
obake 52, 183, 245
obariyon 245
Obere 12
Ocasta 245
ocean men 223, 224
Oceanus 82, 151
octopus 21, 94, 168, 195, 213, 310, 321, 324
Ocypete 131
Ödag 345
Odail Pass 58
Odgar 344
Odin 47, 63, 126, 129, 135, 142, 143, 163, 232, 246, 296, 304, 329, 330
Odites 245
Oditus 245
odontotyrannos 245
odoro-odoro 249
odoroshi 249
Odysseus 40, 84, 95, 144, 281
Oeclus 245
Oeneus 74
oennerbanske 113
Oennereeske 113, 114
Oenoe 38
Offspring of Leviathan 308
Oflugbardi 177
Ofner 245
Ofnir 245
Ogbanje 13
Ogier 76, 252
Ogier le Danois 76
Ogier the Dane 252
Ogkios 39
Ogladnir 177

ogre 246
ogro 246
Ogygian 201
ohaguro-bettari 246
ointment 46, 172, 187
Ojibwa folklore 32
Okiva 239
Oklahoma, USA 164, 300, 301
okubyohgami 71
ol' higue 298
Olaus Magnus 40, 146, 19, 276
Old Bloody Bones 64
Old Hag 23
Old Norse traditions 295
Old Shock 62, 154
Old Shuck 62, 154
Old Sumerian 34
Olenos 121
Olenus 100
olgoj chorchoj 98
Ollipeist 246
ollphiest 254
Olus 82
Olympus 25, 40, 95, 219, 254, 273
Omaha folklore 332
omen 15, 22, 30, 33, 54, 62, 63, 73, 79, 86, 94, 104, 112, 125, 132, 135, 148, 163, 164, 170, 171, 176, 196, 197, 216, 242, 250, 254, 268, 272, 288, 295, 307, 311, 320, 334, 344, 345
omen of death 33
On Monsters and Marvels 30, 219, 248, 267, 275, 313
Onacho 246
Onachus 246, 308
onbu-obake 245
Ondudr 177
One-Eyed Likho 207
One-Thousand and One Arabian Nights 51, 239, 264, 273
Onibaba 246
onocentaur 247
onoi monokerata 229
onokentauroi 247
onoscèles 247
onoscentaurus 247
Ontario, Canada 230
Onuphis 50
onyx monoceros 247
ooer 247
oozlum bird 247
Oph 247
ophies amphipterotoi 247
ophies pteretos 247
Ophion 28
opinicus 247
oracle 53, 82, 109, 267
oracles at Delphi 69
Oraetaona 345
Oraibi 290
orc 22, 80, 247
Orc Treith 324

orca 20, 268, 333
Orch 246, 247
Orchomen Road 302
Il Orco 248
orculli 246
Order of Seraphim 206
Oregon, USA 26, 34
Oreios 248
Oreithyia 262
Oresitrophus 248
Oreus 248, 259
Orge 248
Oribasus 248
Orio 141
Orion 38, 166, 265, 274, 294, 313
Ork 247, 248
orke 247
Orkney 186, 220, 247, 285, 307, 325
Orkney Islands 247, 307
Orlando Furioso 57, 157, 268
Orlo 246
orm 106, 247
Ormar 139, 142, 228, 245, 248, 305
ormr 248
Orneus 248
Ornir 177
ornithomancy 42
Orobios 248
orobon 248
oroboros 249
oroborus 248
Orochi 249
orphan bird 249
Orthaon 80
Orthos 249
Orthus 249
Orusula 249
Osa-gitsune 87
osaki gitsune 200
Oschaert 249
Osgriii 177
Osiris 11, 26, 30, 49, 152, 155, 187, 216, 233, 238, 284
Osiris the Seeker 26, 155, 223, 238
Oskrudr 177
osoroshii 249
ossifrage 164
ostrich 22, 235
Othegwenhda 103
Otherworld 19
otherworld being 13
otoroshi 249, 250
otter 34, 66, 103, 311, 341
Otter, King 103
otter-like 34
Ouatoga 259
ouph 117
oureboros 248
Oureios 248
ouroboros 248
ouzelum 247
ovda 250
Ovid 256, 257, 335
owb 123
Oweynagat 18

owl 45, 60, 93, 183, 198, 269, 300, 301, 315, 317, 322, 341, 345
owl-like 162, 301
ox 13, 26, 36, 39, 53, 66, 69, 70, 74, 75, 128, 133, 148, 153, 156, 159, 162, 167, 172, 173, 179, 188, 192, 200, 202, 208, 225, 249, 252, 268, 271, 272, 298, 306, 308, 312, 313, 320, 344
ox-like 185, 197, 202, 308
oysters 182
Ozark folklore 297
Ozark Mountains, USA 60
Ozark Native American mythology 142

Pa gur yu y Poraru 78
pa snake 250
Pachytos 250
Pacis 50
Pacolet 246
Padfooit 250
Padfoot 250
Padma 234
Padmas 234
Padmavati 250
paean (a song of praise) 197
Pah 250
Pai Lung 108, 250
pairika 250, 251
Paiste 251
Paititi 313
Paiutes 243
paiyuk 251
Pakistan 36
Pakshiraj 134
Pakshiraj 134
Pala 234, 279
Palamedes 84, 268
palasik 251
palfrey 119, 329
palimbing 306
Pallas 99
Palm-Tree-King 251
palraiyuk 251
Palug 76, 78
Palug's Cat 78
palulukon 251
Palulukong 193
pamba 251
Pamir Mountains 316
Pamphagus 252
Pan 252, 280, 292
Pan (Faunus) 77, 252, 292
pan long 252
p'an-lung 252
panacea 252
pananggaln 255
pananggalan 255
Pandara 234
Pandareos 198
Panes 15, 252
Paniski 15
Paniskoi 252
Pannagas 252, 328
Panthalops 22

pantheon 6, 321, 341
panther 85, 88, 102, 106, 163, 326
Pao Shis 163
Papago folklore 316
papal corruption, symbol of 252
Papillon 252
Pappus 105
papstesel 252
Papua New Guinea 190
Papua New Guinean mythology 161
Papuans mythology 132
Paracelsus 139
Paradise 15, 33, 37, 44, 53, 66, 103, 132, 141, 154, 185, 243, 252, 258
Paradise Lost 247
Paraguay 35, 179, 261, 334
Paraguayan folklore 174, 212
Paralda 305
parander 252
parandrus 252
parandus 252
parasol tree 178
parata 253
Paravataksha 253
Pard 75, 253
pardal 253
Pardalo 253
pardalocampoi 253
pardalokampoi 253
pardus 253
Pare, Ambroise 165, 219, 267, 275
Parikshit, King 306
parrot-like 195
Parshvantha 250
Parsva 101
partridge 83, 234
pashu gaung phyat 253
Pasiphae, Queen 44, 92, 226
Passalus 82
Passamaquoddy folklore 337
Passe Brewell 253
Passé Brewell 253
Passetroill 253
pastinaca 253
Patagonian folklore 168, 302
Patala 234, 284
patasola 253, 254
patuljak 139
Pau-Su 163
Paul Bunyan 75, 136, 137
Paul Bunyan tales 75
Paulownia tree 159
Pawnee 207
Peach River 163
peacocks 232
Peallaidh, Pehuda 255
pearl 86, 106, 108, 190
Pearl Harbor 182
Pedair Cainc y Mabinogi 33
Pedasos 254
Peel Castle 228

pegasies 254
Pegasis 254
pegasoi aithiopes 254
Pegasos 254
Pégasos 254
Pegasus 254
Pegasus-like 285
Peissawg the Tall 209
peist 254
Peke-Haua 254
Pelates of Pella 28
Peleus 84, 89, 105, 166, 172, 257
Pellinore 268
Pelops 89
Peluda 255
Pelzeboc 195
Pelzebock 195
Pelznickel 195
Pemphredo 142
pênangal 255
penanggalan 255
penangglan 255
penezny smij 255
peng 255
p'eng 255
p'eng-hou 256
p'eng-niao 255
penghou 256
pénghoú 255
pennanggalan 255
Pennsylvania, USA 139, 299
Penobscot folklore 333
Pentheus 47
Peoria people 205, 217
Perceval 268
Père Fouettard 195, 246
Père Lustucru 246
Peredur 13
Perilous Gorge 144
Perimedes 256
Permet 331
perockius oregoniensis 264
Perrault, Charles 246
perris 102
Perseus 27, 83, 121, 142, 222, 254, 300
Persian and Zoroastrian folklore 187
Persian folklore 21, 22, 41, 42, 44, 49, 91, 164, 184, 194, 272, 273, 276, 283, 285, 287, 293, 315, 326, 330, 345
Persian mythology 75, 83, 99, 112, 136, 160, 187, 285
Peru 78
peryton 256
pesanta 256
Peters, Reverend Samuel 93, 164
Petraeus 256
Petraios 80, 256, 296
Petreus 256
petroglyph 259
peuchen 256
Peukeus 111, 256
Phaea 92

Phaethon 256
Phaeton 256
Phaia 92
Phaithon 256
Phalerus 39, 42, 226, 256, 328
phalmant 257
Phan, King 117
Phanes 80
phantoms 104
Pharaoh 286, 299, 303
Phareus 257
Phaunos 80, 124
pheasant 83, 165, 174, 213, 319, 342, 344
Pheng 257
phénix 258
phenomena 20, 53, 107, 136, 229
Pheocomes 257
Pherecydes of Syros 121
phi kau 170
phi krasue 127
phi um 170
phii krasue 257
philamaloo bird 257
Philip, King 69
Philippine mythology 45, 56
phillyloo bird 257
Philosophers' Stone 229
Philostratus the Elder 81
Philyra 84, 257
Philyrides 84, 257
Phineus 27
Phlegon 257
Phlegraeos 257
Phlogios 258
Phobos 258
Phoenician mythology 157, 248
phoenix 258
phoenix-like 72, 123, 135, 175, 284, 304, 343
Pholgios 258
Pholos 258
Pholus 258
phooka 259
Phorcydes 141
Phorcys 115, 121, 141, 201, 221, 300
Phoroneus 280
phouka 259
Phrixus 40, 259
Phrygia and Sumeria (ancient), mythology of 17
physeter 282
Physiologus 34, 53, 73, 81, 167, 260
pi-his 259
pi xiu 261
P'i-Ya 188
pi yao 259
piasa 259
Piast 254, 260
Picktree Brag 288
Pictish beast 260
Pictish dragon 260
Pier Jan Claes 246

Pig-Dragon 346
piguchen 256
piguechen 87
pihuchen 256
Pihuechenyi 260
pihuichen 256
pihuychen 256
Pilgrim's Progress 143
Pill of Immortality 229, 315
pinari 260
Pindara 234
Pindaraka 234
pine tree 99, 215, 269, 342
ping feng 260
Pingala 43, 101, 234, 260, 329
Pinjaraka 234
pinnacle grouse 260
pipi 182
piranu 260
Pirithous 12, 28, 36, 39, 41, 42, 83, 87, 89, 90, 92, 96, 99, 101, 105, 121, 144, 154, 157, 166, 169, 172, 202, 204, 214, 221, 223, 224, 226, 229, 238, 245, 248, 256, 257, 260, 272, 273, 313, 328
Pirithous, King of 39, 42, 256, 328
Pirithous, Prince of 39, 42, 256
pirobolus 260
Piscean 75, 85, 188, 191, 211, 224, 229, 240, 260, 266, 272, 281
Pisenor 260
pishauchees 303
Pistris 261
Pistris vel Pistrix 261
Pistrix 261
Pisuhand 19
pita-skog 261
Pitaka 162, 185, 254
Pitharaka 234
piuchen 256
Piute mythology 29
piwuchen 256
pixiu 261
plague 20, 29, 98, 122, 139, 201, 323, 332, 340
Plague of sulanuth 303
plakavac 261
Plaksy 241
plant annwn 209
plant of immortality 341
plastic-like 90
plata yryguy 261
Plato 75, 160
Pliny the Elder 14, 55, 64, 66, 78, 92, 115, 155, 205, 206, 229, 247, 253, 267, 272, 309, 320
plon 261
Plutarch 93, 144
pnigalion 170
po-ni-ke 258

po-shan 252
Podarce 261
Podarces 261
Podarge 261
Podargos 258, 261
Podargus 261
Podarkês 261
Podarkes 261, 262
Poemenis 262   *
Pograde, Albania 110
poh 262
poh shan 86
Pohenegamook 263
Poison 15, 20, 23, 49, 56, 57, 67, 75, 81, 102, 122, 127, 144, 180, 184, 193, 198, 205, 209, 215, 218, 219, 222, 228, 234, 238, 239, 267, 281, 291, 315, 316
poisonous 23, 32, 49, 54, 55, 56, 64, 78, 81, 94, 99, 106, 107, 109, 110, 145, 152, 165, 171, 193, 198, 205, 208, 222, 232, 234, 239, 242, 254, 266, 286, 287, 293, 297, 305, 306, 309, 330, 336, 337
poisson chevalier 127
Poland 61, 194, 204
polar worms 262
polednice 262
polevik 262
polevoi 262
Polish and Russian folklore 58
Polish folklore 50, 295
polkonj 80
polkonji 80
pollo malign 262
Pollux 79, 95, 96, 151, 258
polong 262, 263
poludnica 262
poludnitsa 262
polutan 139
Polydeuces 84, 258
Polynesian folklore 310
Polynesian mythology 36, 219, 239, 335
polyp 195
Polyphemus 95
pombero 263
pomegranate tree 17
pomol 64
ponaturi 263
Ponca people 170
pongo 263
Ponik 263
pontarf 263
pontianak 263, 264
pontipinnak 263
pooka 62, 154, 259
Pookonghoy 290
Popol Vuh 48, 76, 91, 311, 332, 338
porcine (piglike) 35, 219, 224
Pordage 151
porpoise-like 298
Porta, John Baptist 178

Portugal 68, 153, 209, 210, 335
Portuguese folklore 94
Poseidon (Neptune) 39, 40, 82, 92, 121, 141, 157, 226, 227, 254, 281, 295, 296
post-medieval European demonology 74
post–Vedic legend 101, 266
Potaka 234
Potentate with Seven Heads 211
potercuk 204
poua-kai 264
pouakai 264
pouka 259
poukai 264
pouke 259
pouki 264
pouque 259
power, symbol of 161, 193, 217, 277, 314
pozoj 106
praatzelwurm 301, 309
pre–Christian folklore 246
pre–Columbian Peruvian mythology 76
prehistoric creatures 179
premog 106
Prester John 22
presteros 264
preyts 170
přezpołdnica 262
Priam 204
priccolitsch 164
pricolic 264
priculics 264
prikolotsch 264
Primal waters 42
primordial bull-cow 134
primordial chaos 269
primordial cow 47
primordial dragon goddess 21, 148, 190, 221
primordial egg 143
primordial god 202
primordial ocean 148
primordial ox 148
primordial Piscean dragon 75
primordial spider 39, 273
primordial void 47
Prinz, H. 60, 297
připołdnica 262
Pristis 261
Pristrix 261
Prithusravas 234, 264
prock gwinter 265
Procris 201
Prodigorum ac ostentorum chronicon 37
progenitor 131, 134, 152, 180, 181, 188, 189, 8, 218, 268, 281, 291, 293, 295, 344
Prolochusc 39, 42, 256, 328
Prolochusm 226
Prometheus 78

proper conduct dragon 342
prophetic bird 132
Prose Edda 36, 39, 63, 97, 111, 112, 113, 116, 122, 123, 128, 129, 133, 134, 135, 137, 138, 139, 141, 142, 143, 148, 150, 152, 153, 156, 159, 160, 162, 167, 172, 186, 200, 206, 208, 228, 230, 232, 240, 245, 248, 271, 272, 276, 292, 294, 296, 300, 302, 305, 307, 329, 330
protector of birds 83
proto-dragon 170
Prthivi 101
pschesponiza 262
pscipolnitsa 262
psoglav 265
psychopomp 35, 54, 62, 63, 73, 94, 112, 132, 148, 171, 197, 216, 250, 254, 268, 272, 295, 334
ptak ohnivak 345
Pterelas 265
Pthah 30, 299
ptitsa sirin 293
ptitsy-siriny 265
Ptolemy 201, 226, 271
Ptolemy Philadelphus 271
Ptoophagos 265
Ptoophagus 265
Pu Songling 339
púca 259
puck 266
Puckwudgie 265
Pugot 265, 266
Pugwis 266
puk 266
púka 259
Pukis 19
pukje 266
pukys 266
Pulang 270
Pulk, Jim 193
Pullangi 270
Pullanj 270
Puloma 180
puma 145, 168
pumapmicuc 67
pumpot 266
Pundarika 234, 266
punyaiama 266
Purlanj 270
Purling 270
Purocis 266
Puroeis 266
Pusat Tasik 270
Pushpa 234
Pushpa-Danta 266
Puspadanta 266
Puuk 19, 266
pwca 259
pyinsa rupa 267
pyong 267
pyralli 267
Pyrallis 267
Pyramid Forty 137
pyrassoupi 267, 326
pyrausta 267

Pyrenees folklore 343
Pyroeis 267
Pyrois 267
pyrotocone 267
pyrotokon 267
Pythia 267
Pythios 267
Pytho 267
python 99, 121, 124, 141, 200, 201, 230, 267, 289, 293, 316
python-like 49, 170, 270

Qatmir 185
qaxdascidi 267
qianli ma 267
qianlima 267
qilaluga-nappa 267
qilalugak-nappa 172
qilin 268
qiqion 268
qiqirn 268
qivittoq 190
qoqnos 258
qoqnus 258
Quadriga 14, 16, 26, 44, 68, 119, 204, 256, 257, 266, 267
Quanekelak 268
Quauquemaire 23
Quebec, Canada 65, 263
Quechua people 75
Queen Charlotte Islands 131
Queensland, Australia 100
questing beast 268
quetzal bird 125
Quetzalcoatl 251
Quicha people 26
Quiche people 76, 91, 311, 338
Quikirnaqu 199
Quinault people 103
quinotaur 268

Ra 11, 12, 36, 216, 222, 238, 258, 269, 272, 283, 286, 289, 310, 311
Rabbi Loew of Prague 140
Rabbi Zera 140
Rabbinical folklore 54, 225
rabbit 32, 109, 147, 200, 229, 232, 249, 292, 337, 342, 343
rabbit-like 147
Rabi Benjamin of Tudela 54
Rabican 268
Rabicano 268
raccoon-dog 242
Rach'aders 269
Rachaders 269
rachet owl 269
Racking One 23
racumon 269
radande 269
Rager 269
Raghava 234, 269
Ragnarock 134

Ragnarok 116, 126, 146, 177, 214, 240
Rahab 31, 269
Rahshi 292
Rahu 192, 293
Rai 23
Raicho 269
Raiden 269
Raigo 312
Raijin 269
raiju 269
Raiko 322
rain bird 269
Rain King 303
rainbird 269
rainbow 96, 100, 107, 132, 216, 221, 231, 252, 270
Rainbow Crow 270
Rainbow Monster 270
Rainbow Serpent 70, 199, 216, 270
Rainbow Snake 96, 221, 270
rainfall 6, 75, 251
Rainseou 240
rainstorms 36
Raja Naga 270
Raja Sulayman 250
Rajah Vikram 51
Rakhsh 270
rakshasas 270, 271
ram 40, 74, 92, 233, 251, 260, 277, 299, 306, 320, 326
Rama, Prince 175
Ramanaka Island 180
Ramayana 58, 175, 191, 216, 252, 270, 280, 328, 331
Raminagrobis 246
Ran Tsu, King 163
Rana Kumbha 170
Rangbein 177
Range of Ares (Mars) 187
Raphael 30
al Raqim 185
Rasatala 181
rasselbock 337
rat 163, 205, 251, 312
rat-like 312, 341
Rata 263
Rataosk 271
Ratatosk 251, 271
Rath Blathmaic, Ireland 68
rattlesnake 125, 275
Rätzel 23
Raudr 271
raukshehs 170
Ravana 175, 197, 278
raven 91, 199, 314, 329, 330
Raven-Big-Quikil 199
ravens 104, 126, 163, 232, 329
Rawhead 271
Re 156, 299
red beans 49
red bird 125
Red Book of Hergest 13
Red Deer 97, 112, 113

Red Dragon of Wales 339
red eyes 46, 52, 63, 64, 66,
85, 94, 116, 128, 217,
224, 228, 239, 298, 299,
344
red fox 312
Red Horn 155
Red Sea 248
redjal el marja 271
re'em 271
reem 271
Regenmöhme 272
Regin 122
Regulus 55, 77
reiko 272
Rekinn 272
Rekinni 272
Reksh 272
reksoso 270
remora 272
Renoart 78
reptile 55, 81, 89, 96, 151,
189, 280
reptilian creature 98, 244
Republic of the Congo 60,
117
Republic of Trinidad and
Tobago 216
Rerek 272
Reretoi 185
revenant 272
revenge 58, 86, 94, 137,
152, 193, 204, 215, 243,
278, 310, 333
Reynard the Fox 252
Rh Ya 129
Rhea 110, 198
Rhiphonos 80
Rhiwgyverthwch 155
Rhode Island, USA 77
Rhoecus 272, 274
Rhoetus 83, 90, 111
Rhoetus, Centaur 272
Rhoetus, Giante 273
Rhoikos 274
Rhone River 308
Rhos church 121
Rhymes 36, 39, 58, 97, 112,
113, 116, 122, 129, 134,
135, 139, 142, 148, 152,
153, 159, 162, 167, 172,
200, 208, 228, 232, 240,
245, 253, 271, 272, 276,
296, 305, 307
ri riu 273
ri-ryu 273
rickaboo racker 264
Righteous Ass 273
Rigi 273
rimau jadi-jadian 273
Rimefax 156, 162
Rimfakse 156, 162
Rimfaxi 156, 162
Rinaldo 57
Rinjin 275
Riphens 273
River, Lord of the 259
River Meuse 56
river-serpent 38
River Thames 186

River Tweed 208
rizos 62
roane 285
roc 215
roc-like 243, 267
rock demons 42
Rocky Mountains 174,
299
Roe Valley 251
roggenmuhme 262
Rogo-Tumu-Here 274
Roikos 274
rok 183, 273
rokuro-kubi 274
rokurokubi 274
Roland 68
rolling calf 274
Roman Catholic folklore
31
Roman Catholic prayers
263
Roman folklore 62, 301,
308
Roman mythology 16, 26,
27, 68, 77, 105, 120, 124,
152, 172, 204, 256, 266,
300, 301
Romania 167, 168, 264,
280
Romanian folklore 54, 118,
280, 331, 345
Romans 19, 75, 98, 157,
258
rompo 274
Romulus and Remus 75
Rondelet, Guillaume 229
rông 274
rongeur d'os 62
Roostem (Rustam) 41, 283
rooster 19, 61, 125, 126,
146, 157, 202, 262, 288,
308, 314
rooster egg 19
roperite 275
roshwalr 275
rosomacha 92
rossamaka 146
rosualt 232
Rotorua 161, 185
rou garou 211
Rou Shou 275
Rouen 134
rougarou 211
Roxburghshire, Scotland
208
Ru Shou 275
Rua 324
Ruapehu 308
rubberado 275
Rübezahl 139
ruby 51, 77, 197, 224, 277,
331
ruc 273
Rucht 104, 126
rucke 273
rugaru 211
rukh 273
rukhkh 273
Ruler of Haddings 294
Rumpelklas 195

rumptifusel 275
Rungnir 275
runt beaver trout 130
Ruprecht 195
rurū 275
Russia 7, 22, 23, 50, 55, 58,
71, 87, 107, 118, 132, 133,
141, 171, 184, 194, 230,
250, 265, 290, 291, 293,
323, 326, 327, 345, 346,
347
Russian and Slavic folklore
22
Russian folklore 50, 55, 58,
71, 87, 107, 118, 132, 133,
141, 171, 184, 194, 250,
265, 290, 293, 294, 345,
347
ruszor 275
ryo 109
Ryo-Wo 275
ryong 274
ryu 108, 179
Ryujin 81, 275
Ryujin, the Dragon God
275

sa-yin 276
Saa-Set 276
saait redjal el marja 271
Saalah 246, 282
saaláh 282
saapin 276
Sabala 234
Sabarifya 123
Sabbath 237, 288
Sacrament of Baptism 263
sacred bull 50
Sacred Bull of Hermonthis
50
sacred goose 143
sacred grove 40, 187
Sada-Dana 18
sadhuzag 276
Saehrimner 276
Saehrimnir 276
Saehrímnir 276
Saekarlsmuli 177
saena 276, 285
safat 276
Sagara 234, 252
Sagittarius 84
sagittary 80
sahab 276
Saharan desert 96
Saikoku, Japan 48
Saingliu 112, 207
Saint Agnes' Day 95
Saint Albertus 28
Saint Attracta's monster
277
Saint Brendan 57, 100, 124
Saint Colum Cille 303
Saint David's Day 95
Saint Eleuthere 263
Saint Elmo's fire 278
Saint Estcourt 263
Saint George 65, 68, 89,
197, 263, 330
Saint George's Day 65, 197

Saint Gudmund 295
Saint Isidore of Seville 27,
155, 301
Saint John's Day 95
Saint John's Eve 72
Saint Lawrence River 225
Saint Martha 308
Saint Martin's Day 95
Saint Michael the
Archangel's Day 95
Saint Mountain 171
Saint Murrough 251
Saint Nicholas 195
Saint Paul 31
Saint Romain (Romanus)
134
Saint Sebastian's Day 160
sak 277
Salamander 98, 115, 116,
139, 144, 277, 278, 305
Salamandra 277
Salfang 177
Salgofni 146
Salgofnir 146
salmon 65, 79, 181, 260,
297, 315, 322
salt 25, 39, 45, 46, 47, 66,
75, 119, 129, 157, 178,
202, 206, 273, 299, 303
Samana, Lord 211
Samba 173
Samebito 277
Samendill 177
samhghubh'a 223
samjogo 277, 314
Sampaati 277, 278
Sampati 277, 329
Sampo 168
samru 273
Samudra Manthana 284,
304
samudraru 318
samurai 233, 287, 290
Samvarta 278
Samvritta 234
San Christobal, Galapagos
239
San thsai thou hoei 257
sandhill perch 125, 278
Sankhacuda 234
Sankhapala 234
Sanku 234
Sanskrit epic 52, 196, 233
Santa Claus 178, 195
santelmo 278
santer 125, 278
Santo Elmo 278
sarabha 239, 278
Saracen Mountain 71
Sarama 278
Sarameya 278
Sarameyas 278
Sarana 234
Sarava 278
Saravha 279
sarce 286
Sardula 279
sargon 279
sarimanok 279

Sarisrikta 175, 279
Sárkánykígyó 106, 279
Sarngika 175, 279
Sarpa-sattra 306
Sarparati 134
Sarpedon 254
sarre 286
Sarsaok 148
Sarva-Bhauma 101, 279
Sarvabhavma 279
sasabonsam 279
Satan 31, 301
satry 279
satyr 80, 82, 124, 220, 252, 279, 280, 284, 292
satyr-like 65, 74, 153, 205
satyral 218
satyre-fish 280
satyrisci 280
Saul 123
Saumanasa 58, 216, 280, 331
Sausga 153
sawfish 14, 88, 286
Saxon folklore 295
Sazae-Oni 280
sburator 280
Scandinavian and Teutonic mythology 208
Scandinavian folklore 50, 89, 114, 153, 246, 332
Scandinavian mythology 12, 195, 239, 321
scarecrow 139, 320
Scattery Island 277
sceadugenga 280
Sceolan 15, 67, 212, 280, 283
Sceolang 280
schachi hoko 149
Schechirion 280
Schmutzli 195
schnellgeiste 151
Schrätlein 23
Schrättel 23
Schrättele 23
Schrätteli 23
schrattl 23, 24, 148
Schrettele 23
Schrötle 23
Schrötlein 23
Schrsttel 23
der schwarze 280, 281
der schwarze mann 280
scie 286
Scipio Africanus 75
scissors 21, 170, 324
scitalis 281
sciu-crak 195
scoffin 295
scolopendra 281
Scorpio 313
scorpion men 37, 137, 153
scorpions 37, 49, 98, 137, 191, 218, 238, 294, 303, 345
scots hounds 63
Scottish folklore 50, 57, 58, 69, 73, 89, 91, 94, 114, 118, 123, 126, 129,

137, 186, 216, 224, 289, 307, 315, 328, 331, 338
Scottish Highlands 47, 57, 58, 59, 66, 73, 92, 147, 205, 260
scrat 295
scrato 295
Scully, Quebec 263
sculpin-like 296
Scylla 84, 110, 115, 281
Scyphius 281
Scythe 33, 43
Scythes 115
Scythia 71, 172
Scythian Dracaena 115
scythian lamb 55
Scythian Monster 115
Scythians, king of the 115
sea-bird 135
sea bishop 61, 282
sea-cow 30
sea creature 11, 23, 74, 75, 100, 169, 172, 206, 213, 239, 243, 253, 268, 273, 276, 282
sea-dog 281, 282
sea goat 281
sea-gryphon 281, 282
sea hog 282
sea horse 153, 157
sea knight 193
sea lion 179
sea monk 61, 282
sea monster 247, 282
Sea of Milk 15
sea satyr 280, 282
sea serpent 11, 12, 14, 21, 23, 26, 27, 29, 40, 46, 48, 53, 63, 71, 75, 82, 88, 89, 100, 101, 111, 115, 124, 132, 153, 161, 168, 169, 177, 195, 211, 213, 217, 218, 219, 220, 224, 225, 227, 228, 229, 230, 231, 239, 240, 247, 255, 260, 261, 263, 267, 268, 269, 274, 276, 277, 286, 282, 286, 295, 307, 308, 318, 319, 320, 322, 325, 333, 337, 339, 340, 342
sea serpents, king of the 101
sea-stag 282
sea-turtle 124, 220
sea wind, personification of 306
sea wolf 281, 282, 333
sea-worm 206
sea-wyvern 282
seabird 32, 179
seabishop 61
seal fairy 285
Seal of Solomon 96
seal people 285
sealáh 282
sealah 282, 283
seals 247, 285
sear dugh 15, 67, 212, 280, 283
Seatco 283

Sebau 36, 155, 235, 238, 283
Sebi 283
Sebu River 18
Sebuit-Nebt-Uaa-Khesfet-Sebau-Em-Pert-F 155
second-generation Titans 14, 16, 26, 44, 68, 119, 226, 256, 257, 266, 267
secret knowledge 71, 128, 234
Sedna 32
Šêdu 202
Seemurg 33, 157, 160, 276, 283, 285
Seemurgh 283
Seesha 284
Sefer 284
Sefer Yetzirah 140
segben 284
seilenoi 284
Seilenos 284
Seine River 134
Seiryu 72, 135, 284, 304
Seker 33, 284, 312
Sekien, Toriyama 35
selchies 285
selkie folk 285
selkies 285
semargl 285
semargl-pereplut 285
Semi 285
semi-divine 20, 53, 254, 338
Seminole people 164, 165, 300
Semitic Ugaritic folklore 208
Sena 42
sena meregha 276
senad 285
senamurv 276
Seneca people 97, 103, 131, 133
Senenahemthet 285
Senik 119, 223, 285
senmurv 83, 157, 283, 285
Senmurw 283, 285
senrima 285
Seps 286
Septuagint 271
Serbia 18, 148, 334
Serbian folklore 111
serou 286, 327
serpent 11, 12, 14, 15, 17, 18, 20, 21, 23, 26, 27, 28, 29, 32, 33, 34, 36, 38, 40, 43, 44, 48, 50, 51, 53, 55, 56, 58, 61, 63, 64, 67, 70, 71, 75, 77, 82, 88, 89, 94, 96, 99, 100, 111, 115, 116, 121, 122, 124, 125, 126, 127, 128, 132, 134, 137, 139, 142, 144, 145, 149, 152, 153, 154, 155, 161, 168, 169, 170, 172, 177, 180, 187, 188, 195, 197, 202, 203, 206, 207, 208, 211, 213, 216, 217, 218, 219, 220, 222, 224,

225, 227, 228, 229, 230, 231, 232, 235, 237, 238, 239, 240, 245, 247, 248, 249, 251, 253, 260, 261, 263, 267, 268, 269, 270, 272, 274, 275, 276, 277, 281, 282, 283, 286, 288, 289, 293, 298, 300, 303, 306, 308, 310, 311, 312, 314, 315, 318, 320, 322, 325, 329, 330, 333, 337, 338, 339, 340, 341, 342, 347
serpent king 28
serpent-like 128, 154, 285, 286, 310
serpent, musical 232
serpent of Isa 286
serpentine creature 27, 47, 69, 107, 111, 123, 166, 171, 262, 322
serpentine dragon 38, 63, 77, 116, 144, 161, 179, 184, 189, 193, 217, 249, 250, 251, 279, 302, 319, 327, 331
serpentine-like 27, 110, 152, 153, 200, 289
Serpents, King of the 101, 180, 270
Serpopard 286
serra 286
serre 286
Seryu 284
Sesha 28, 53, 284
Sesha-Naga 284
Set 20, 56, 107, 155, 216, 272, 276, 286
Set-Hra 286
Set-Qesu 286
Setcheh 287
Sethu 286
Seto Taisho 287
Setotaishō 287
seven-colored horse 287
Seven-Headed Snake 287
Seven Macaw 331
seven sleepers 15
Seven Youths 185
seventh section 11, 20
seventh son 210, 212
sevienda 287
Sgeolaind 280
Shabdiz 287
Shabrang 287
shachi 287
shachihoko 287
shadavar 287
shaddim 288
shadhahvar 287
shadow 29, 46, 69, 85, 132, 170, 210, 212, 241, 269, 284, 292, 317
shag-foal 287, 288
shagamaw 125, 288
Shagfoal 148, 287
Shaggy Beast of La Ferte-Bernard 255
Shah-I Mur Ghan 283
shakko 288

shakujos 183
shaman 29, 32, 98, 189, 190, 251, 332, 334, 335
Shamash 70, 137
Shamash (Utu) 137
shamir 288
Shamiram 38
shamisen-choro 62, 288
Shan Hai King 188, 262
shan kiao 288
shang yang 269
shang yung 269
Shankha 234
Shankhashirsa 234
Shannon river 277
Shannon Valley 246
shanxiao 339
shape-shifting 12, 17, 19, 20, 24, 27, 37, 40, 45, 46, 47, 54, 66, 69, 71, 72, 79, 86, 87, 88, 102, 103, 104, 107, 108, 110, 114, 115, 118, 122, 123, 125, 128, 136, 145, 146, 148, 149, 161, 163, 167, 169, 174, 175, 180, 182, 183, 186, 189, 192, 194, 198, 204, 207, 210, 220, 228, 230, 231, 232, 233, 237, 238, 241, 242, 243, 244, 247, 250, 256, 259, 264, 265, 266, 271, 273, 275, 280, 284, 285, 287, 288, 292, 295, 299, 300, 301, 303, 305, 307, 317, 318, 321, 324, 329, 332, 334, 335, 339, 341, 343
shar khorkhoi 98
Sharama 278
Sharameyas 278
shark 14, 88, 168, 213, 263, 277, 339
shark-like 173, 281
Sharur 42, 199
Shawnee folklore 217
Shawnee myth 224
she-ass of Balaam 44
sheahah 322
shed 34, 40, 224, 281, 288, 298, 299, 300
shedim 288, 289
Sheen-Mane 256
sheep 19, 35, 55, 66, 74, 76, 88, 114, 136, 139, 147, 155, 163, 168, 179, 194, 201, 209, 216, 243, 250, 273, 334, 335
sheep-like 74
sheerree 301
shellicoat 289
shelly coat 289
shellycoat 289
Shemti 289
Shen-Yi 124, 289
Shenendre 184
Shesha 28, 284
Shesha the Endless 28
Shethu 289
Shetland Islands 47, 114, 220, 243, 285, 325

Shetland pony 243
Shetu 289
shibaten 289
shield-maiden 142
Shield of Heracles 39, 42, 256, 328
Shikhi 234
shikk 289
shikkara 340
shiko-me 289
Shikoku, Jaapan 289
shikome 289
Shining-Mane 256, 294
shinseen 289
Shinto charms 134
Shinto mythology 195, 200, 249
shiq 289
shiqq 236, 289
shiri-me 290
shirime 290
Shirin 287
Shirishaka 234
shiro-uneri 290
shirouneri 290
shisa 290
shishi 183, 290
shishi dog 183, 194
shishiga 290
shíta 290
shitta 290
Shiva 67, 236, 269
Shiya 329
Shodieonskon 97
shojo 291
shōjō 291
shokera 291
shoney 186
shoopiltee 47, 114, 186, 291
shoopiltie 291
shooting star 235, 345
Shoshone 243
Shoulderless 331
shre 301
Shriker 148
shrimp 135
Shu Wen 108
shuck 62, 63, 132, 154, 291
shucky dog 62, 154
shudala madan 291
Shug Monkey 291
Shui Ying bird 129
Shukir 62, 63
shurale 291
shuryo 291, 340, 343
Shus I ki 188, 189, 213, 342
Shyeni 175, 277
Si-Kalac 217
Si-Kavay 217
Si Wakandage 332
Si Yang Y Shu 85
Sia Jatta Bari 59
sianach 291
Siang Shu 188
Siberia 32, 321
Siberian mythology 22, 34, 187
Sicilian legends, medieval 263

Sicily 33, 84, 281
Sid 116
side hill dodger 264
sidehill badger 264
sidehill dodger 264
sidehill gouger 264
sidehill sauger 264
sidewinder 264
Siegfried (Sigurd) 122
sien-lung 108, 188, 291, 344
Sierra Leone 318
Sierra Madre Mountain 278
sigbin 284, 292
sign of the Cross 61, 170, 263
Sigurd 122, 142, 160
Sigurd Fafnisbane 142
Sigurdr 142
sijjil stones 11
si'la 292
si'lat 292
Sileni 292
sileni 280
Silenoi 292
Silenus 292
Silfrintop 292
Silfrintopp 292
Silfrintoppr 292
Silfrtoppr 292
silkie 285
Sillus 82
silver 22, 41, 50, 65, 74, 86, 125, 133, 144, 151, 197, 217, 292, 295, 296, 307, 321, 324, 345
silver bullet 103
Simarghu 292
Simargl 283, 285
simian 18, 82, 165, 226, 240, 243, 317, 329
simian-like 17, 101, 168, 171, 226, 329
simmurgh 292
simoorgh 157
Simorgh 292
Simorq 283
Simple Jack 136
Simug 292
Simurgh 33, 157, 160, 276, 283, 292
Simyr 283
Sin 84, 179, 200
sin u 84
sin you 84, 179
Sina Mru 292
Sinaa 292
Sinach Sinach 231
Sinam 283
Sindbad the Sailor 273
Sindri 146
Siner 293
singa 223, 293
Singa Pura 223
Singapore 223
Sinhalese folklore 140
Sinhalese mythology 132
Sinhika 293
Sinir 293

Sinlap 231, 293
sinlap 231, 293
sint holo 293
sinurgh 273
siod brad 91
siodbrad 91
Sion, Llywelyn 121
Siorgh 292
Sioux 224, 315
Sir Bevis of Southampton 41
Sir Bors 268
Sir Cai (Kay) 76, 144
Sir Fergus 253
Sir Galahad 268
Sir Gawain 144, 268
Sir Guyon 67
Sir Hector 268
Sir Lancelot Greaves 68
Sir Palamedes 268
Sir Pellinore 268
Sir Perceval 268
Sir Tristram 253
Sir Yvain the Bastard 268
siren serpent 293
sirena 223, 294, 306
sirin 22, 132, 293
Sirishaka 234
Sirius 293, 294
Sirrush 232
Sirrušu 232
sisiutl 149
Sison, King 318
Sita 175, 179, 198, 278
Sitanana 134
situla 102
Siuko Burko 294
Sivushko 55
Six-Headed Wild Ram 294, 296
siyokoy 294
sjo-orm 282
sjofn 186
sjörå 294
Skaevadr 294
Skævadr 294
Skalli 177
Skanda 58
Skeidbrimir 294
Skeironiles 295
Skeironites 296
skeletal creatures 33, 57, 65, 114, 134, 235
skeletal horses 33
skeleton 33, 93, 134
Skelkingr 294
Skerkir 177
Skinfax 294
Skinfaxi 25, 47, 162, 294
skirimsl 295
Skoedbrimir 295
skoffin 55, 295
skolopendra 281
Skotos 22, 222, 318
skraethins 295
Skramr 178
skrat 295
skrati 178, 295
skratt 295
skratte 295

skratten 295
skriatok 139
Skriker 62, 148, 154, 295
Skrimnir 178
skrimsl 295
skřítek 139
Skroggr 178
skrzat 139
Skserir 178
skunk 32, 93
skvader 337
sky maidens 295
sky women 295
sky yelpers 131
skykraken 195
Skylla 281
Skyphios 295
Slain Heroes 34, 42, 61, 147, 197, 211, 251, 287, 294, 296, 302
Slavic folklore 22, 127, 207, 230, 241, 261, 265, 266, 285
Slavic mythology 70
Slayer's Stone 193
Sleipne 296
Sleipnir 68, 140, 142, 143, 159, 296, 304, 305
slide rock bolter 125, 296
Slidrugtanni 145, 296
Sliorugtanni 145, 296
Slipener 296
sliver cat 296
Slongvir 296
Slöngvir 296
Slovakia 335
Slovenian folklore 80, 346
Slungnir 296
Small Man 194, 296
smallpox 90, 313
småtomte 139
smerkava 297
Smirdris 231
Smith, John 98
Snaer 178
snail 28, 39, 211, 280
snail-like 323
snake creatures 15, 164
snake demon 19
snake griffin 60, 297
snake-people 198, 208
snakes, king of the 83
snallygaster 151
snanaik 322
Snavidhka 297
Snavidka 297
snawfus 297
Snee-Nee-Iq 297
snipe 97, 297
snipe-hunt 97
Snoer 63
snoligoster 125, 297
snollygoster 151
snow snake 125, 297, 298
Snow Spirit 270
snow wasset 125, 298
snydae 125, 135, 298
Sojobo 97, 298
Sokin 116
Sol 11, 14, 16, 25, 26, 44,

68, 119, 120, 195, 204, 226, 256, 257, 266, 267
sol draulen 195
solaris 298
solemn ones 120
Solomon, King 288
Solomon Islands 65, 180, 260, 333
Soma Offering 215
song bird 325
Song of Ilion 6
Song of the Sea 153
Songhay folklore 104
Songhay people 346
songo 50
songomby 298
Sons of God 30
Sophocles 22, 222, 318
sorcerers 26, 45, 46, 47, 51, 75, 87, 169, 190, 271
Sotho people 181
Soti 298
Sóti 298
soucayant 178, 298, 299
soucouyant 298
soucouyen 298
soukoyan 298
soul 11, 13, 15, 19, 26, 32, 33, 37, 46, 48, 49, 65, 73, 79, 86, 96, 110, 117, 134, 145, 150, 154, 166, 184, 187, 214, 222, 230, 232, 237, 304, 309, 322, 324, 343
South America 74, 77, 101, 145, 168, 207, 253, 332, 334, 335, 338
South American folklore 74, 207, 253, 338
South Dakota 174
South Gloom 255
South Tyrolean folklore 248
Southern Sea of China 35
sow 28, 57, 63, 78, 83, 92, 109, 139, 187, 219, 282
sow of Crommyon 92, 115
sow of Dallweir Dallpenn 154
sow of Krommyon 92
Spain 72, 94, 127, 153, 171, 330, 335
spaniel dog 160
Spanish folklore 29, 30, 32, 59, 89, 94, 253, 287
Spargeus 80
Sparinsheith 299
sparrow 68, 86, 125, 249
sparrow hawk 22
Spay-ius 19
spear-like 99, 123
spectral hounds 64, 131, 132
spell, magical 11, 20, 26, 33, 34, 39, 43, 61, 131, 152, 153, 154, 187, 235, 237, 263, 276, 283, 286, 289, 310, 311, 312, 314, 325
Spenta Mainyu 49
sperm whale 324

sphinx, Egyptian 299
spider 28, 38, 39, 49, 103, 113, 114, 115, 198, 273, 299, 322
spider hengeyokai 299
Spider-Woman 322
Spindleston Heugh 209
Spindleston Hills 209
spiny anteaters 115
spirit 5, 11, 13, 14, 15, 16, 17, 18, 19, 20, 21, 24, 29, 30, 34, 36, 37, 43, 48, 51, 53, 55, 57, 58, 61, 62, 65, 66, 70, 77, 78, 85, 94, 95, 97, 98, 103, 104, 107, 108, 116, 117, 123, 124, 129, 130, 133, 135, 139, 141, 143, 145, 146, 149, 150, 151, 152, 155, 160, 167, 170, 171, 173, 174, 175, 179, 180, 181, 186, 187, 188, 189, 190, 193, 194, 195, 196, 197, 198, 199, 200, 202, 205, 210, 214, 215, 216, 217, 226, 228, 230, 231, 233, 236, 237, 238, 241, 242, 243, 245, 247, 248, 250, 252, 253, 255, 256, 259, 260, 262, 263, 265, 266, 269, 270, 272, 280, 283, 284, 288, 289, 290, 291, 293, 294, 295, 297, 303, 304, 308, 318, 320, 321, 322, 324, 326, 328, 329, 331, 332, 333, 334, 339, 340, 341, 343, 344, 346, 347
spirits of the water 221
Spirukas 19
splinter cat 125, 299
splintercat 299
Spornvitnir 299
Sporvitnir 299
Sprenger, Jacob 203
Sprettingr 178
spring worm 309
springwurm 301, 309
sprite 295, 315
Spumador 299
squatina angelus 61
squid 21
squid-like 195
squirrel-like 336
squonk 5, 125, 299, 300
sri 300
Sri-Lanka 100
Sriand 179
srin 300
Srit 251
Srvara 297
Ssu-ma Ch'ien 83
staff of Moses 96
Staffordshire, England 132
stag bunny 174
stags 71, 80, 97, 104, 112, 113, 116, 125, 126, 155, 157, 158, 253, 268, 276, 282, 289
stallion 40, 41, 53, 79, 110,

133, 145, 159, 242, 254, 267, 287, 296, 304, 338
Stamba-mitra 175, 279
Stampare 23
Stampen 23
Stampfen 23
steed of Neptune 157
Stefiu 300
steh-tathl 322
steinbock 346
stele volk 113
stellio 98, 277
Stellio 98, 277
stellione 98
Stempe 23
Stephen the First, King 301
Sterope 158, 300
Steropes 95
Sthenius 300
Sthenno 300
Stheno 121, 141, 221, 222, 300
Sthenusa 300
Sticte 104, 300
Stigandi 178
stihi 300
Stiifr 300
stikini 300, 301
stillborn child 24, 52
Stiphilus 301
stirk 67
stollenwurm 301, 309
Stomach Faces 144
stone-eater 264
Stone of Benn 220
Stoorworm 220, 282
Stoppklos 195
storax 247
storm bird 124, 200
storm-demons 288
storm spirits 95
storm winds and whirl-winds, personifications of 151
storms 16, 23, 25, 32, 37, 64, 79, 94, 95, 107, 110, 116, 124, 125, 127, 149, 151, 162, 169, 197, 200, 207, 209, 219, 223, 231, 287, 237, 239, 240, 269, 270, 283, 285, 288, 289, 294, 315, 316, 320, 325, 326, 330, 338, 340, 341, 342, 345
storms at sea 37
Storverkr 178
Story of the Slaying of Labbu 56, 200, 232
Straits of Messina 84, 281
Stray Cow 130
Stricto 104, 301
strigae 301
striglais 301
strix 301
Strong-Back 90
Strong Copper 296, 301
Strong Ones 130
strong toad 302
Strymon 302
Strymon (river), Trace 302

Stuart, Charles Edward 64
Stufr 300, 302
Stúfr 302
Stumi 178
sturgeon 227
Sturlson, Snorri 111, 122, 128, 138, 141, 142, 148, 186, 228, 229, 294, 296, 302, 329
stvkwvnaya 302
Stymphalian birds 302
su 302
Su-Pratika 43, 101, 302
su shuang 304
Su-Zaku 304
Subahu 234
Subha-Danti 266
Subhadanti 101
Subhradanti 43
succarath 302
succubi 118, 170, 207, 233, 302, 303, 313, 574
succumbus 303
sucoyan 303
Sudhahara 134
Sufah 96
Suffolk, England 63
sughmaire 303
suhur-mas 281
sui riu 179, 273, 303
Sui-Ryu 303
suicide 71, 120, 145, 167, 239, 304
suicide shuck 62, 152
Suiko, Empress 240
suileach 303
suire 223
Sukkubus 23
sukuyan 303, 334
sulanuth 303
Sultan Majnun 243
suman 228
Sumana 234
Sumanomukha 234
Sumargh 292
Sumarr 178
Sumatran folklore 124
Sumer 145
Sumeria 34, 106, 108, 133, 147, 197, 202, 223, 281
Sumerian creation myth 197
Sumerian mythology 34, 37, 42, 61, 133, 147, 197, 199, 200, 211, 251, 281, 287, 294, 296, 301
Summeria 303
Summers, Montague 230
Sumukha 41, 85, 304
sun 5, 11, 12, 14, 16, 18, 19, 22, 24, 25, 26, 29, 33, 36, 39, 41, 44, 45, 47, 50, 60, 68, 69, 72, 83, 96, 101, 119, 120, 123, 133, 137, 140, 149, 151, 152, 153, 154, 159, 161, 162, 171, 174, 179, 180, 187, 198, 199, 204, 208, 213, 216, 222, 223, 226, 238, 239, 250, 256, 257, 258, 259,

266, 267, 272, 273, 277, 282, 283, 285, 286, 289, 294, 299, 300, 302, 310, 311, 314, 316, 329, 332, 331, 345, 346, 349
Sun Bearer 29
Sun Dog 17
sun fish 140
sun god 11, 12, 14, 16, 36, 41, 44, 68, 119, 171, 199, 204, 216, 222, 223, 226, 238, 256, 257, 258, 272, 283, 286, 289, 310, 311
suna-kake-baba 304
sunakake-baba 304
sundal bolong 304
Sunday Express 233
Sunday Letters 68, 90, 115, 210, 237
sundel bolong 304
sundelbolong 304
Sunna, King 12
Suparna 134
supernatural creature 7, 52
Supratika 302
Supreme Commander of War 191
Surabhi 181, 304
Surasa 234, 252
Suraya 41
Surgiva 179
Surinam 334
Suriname folklore 48
Surma 304
Surt 47
Surya 101
Susa-No-O 116
Susawona 340
Susena 234
Susenda 234
sushuang 123, 175, 304, 343
Sussex, king of 193
Sussex folklore 193
Suzaku 72, 135, 284, 304, 330
Svaðifoeri 304
Svadilfare 296, 304
Svaðilfari 304
Svadilfari 304, 305
Svadilföri 304
Svafner 305
Svalin 11, 25
Svanau 278
Svarangr 178
Svarnir 305
Svartr 178
Svasana 234
Svasudr 178
Svathrlfari 304
Sveta 234
Svol 116
svuvara 205
swallowing monster 243
swamfisk 305
swamp auger 125, 305
swamp-gahoon 125, 305
swamp-swiver 305
swan 130, 150, 224, 249, 305

Swan of Tuonela 205
Swat River 36
Sweden 146
Swedish fairies 137
Swedish folklore 178, 210, 269
swiftness, symbol of 74
swimming elephant 260
swine-like 30
Swiss Alps 38, 309
Swiss Christmas folklore 139
Swiss Christmas traditions 195
Swiss folklore 71, 301, 337
Switzerland 110, 114, 337
swooning shadow 132
sword fish 14
sword-like 308
sword ox 306
swordfish 202
Śyena 134
Syfwlch 324
Sylph 305
sylphids 305
sylvan 237
syqenez 305, 306
syren 306
Syrians, ancient 340
sz 306, 327

Tabele 59
Tabernacle 306
Tablets of Destiny 34, 191
tabong 52
taboo 173, 228, 334
tachash 306
Tagalog 45, 182, 202
Tagalog folklore 182
Tagalog people 202
Tagamaling 306
Tagbanua, Philippines 53
Tagbanua people 218
Taghairm 59
Tahmurath 292
T'ai P'ing Kuang Chi 87, 260
tailless black sow 63
tain gou 316
Taipan 270
tairbh uisge 308
tairbh-uisge 91, 308
Takemikazuchi-no-miko 235
Takitimu 324
Takshaka 234, 306
Takshasila 306
takujui 306
Talas 306
talasam 307
Talbot 281
Tale of the Heike 242
Tales of Monsters Then and Now 105
Taliesin 121
talisman 32, 316, 317
Tamrakarna 101, 279
Tamrakarni 43
Tanaina, Alaska 59

Tanaina folklore 267
Tāne 149
Tangaroa 274
Tangaroa-mihi 185
Tanggal 45, 46
tangie 307
tangka palasik 251
Tanihwa 307
Taninim 206
taniwha 161, 162, 164, 185, 253, 254, 307, 309, 324
Tanngiost 307
Tanngniostr 307
Tanngnistr 307
Tanngnjost 307
Tanngnjostr 307
Tanngnost 307
Tanngrisne 307
Tanngrisner 307
Tanngrisni 307
Tanngrisnir 307
Tanngrisnr 307
tanooki 307
Tantalos 198
tanti-gaha 47
tanuki 47, 269, 307
Tanzanian folklore 251
tao tie 307
t'ao t'ieh 308
Taoist Chinese mythology 211
Taoists hermits 205
Taotie 307
Tapopus 22
Tarafe 173
Taranaki 308
tarandrus 308
Taras 308
Tarascon, France 308
Tarasconus 246, 308
Tarasque 89, 308
tarbh uisge 308
Taredd 324
Tarhunna (Tarhunta) 169
Tarkshya 134
Tarmachans Mountains, Scotland 308
tarnkapppe 113
taroo ushtey 308
Tarquinia, Italy 323
tarroo-ushtey 308, 309
tartar 55, 135
Tartaro 246
Tartaros 318
tartaruchi 309
tartaruchus 309
Tartarus (Hell) 75, 95, 99, 115, 120, 309
tartary lamb 55, 209
Tatar mythology 11
Tataswin 134
tatsu 149, 309
tatter foal 287
tatter-foal 287
tatterfoal 287
tatzelwurm 205, 301, 309
Taupo 161
tauri aethiopicum sylvestres 309
tauri silvestres 309

Tauriskos 308
tauroi aithiopes 309
tauroi aithiopikoi 309
taurokampoi 309
taurokampos 309
tauros aithiopikos 309
Taurus 70, 313
Tawake-tara 169, 302
Tawhaki 181, 263
taxim 309
Tcheser-Tep 310
Tchet 310
Tchetbi 310
tchian du bouolay 62, 154
tcinto-saktco 310
te-aitanga-a-hine-mate-roe 215
Te Ikaroa 168
te-no-me 242, 310
te parata 253
Te Tuna 310
Te Waro-uri 254
Te Wheke-a-Muturangi 310
teakettle 125, 311
teapot Samurai 287
tearai oni 311
tebbib 69
Tecumbalam 76, 311, 338
Teehooltsoodi 311
Teelget 311
tehuel che chon 168
T'ein Kou 293
Teka-Hra 311
tele volk 113
Tell Halaf palace 37
Temasek 223
Temeluchus 309
Ten Commandments 288
ten-gu 311
Tenantomwan 199
tengu 97, 145, 150
tenjō-name 312
tenjōname 312
tenko 312
Tennessee, USA 325, 333
tennin 282
tenth section 285, 286, 300, 314
Tepan 33, 312
Tepi 312
Ter 312
Terit 324
terrashot 124, 129
terrestrial devil 205
terrestrial water, personification of 235
Tessub 153
Teton Sioux mythology 224
tetramorph 312, 313
teufelwal 100
teui dog 17
Teumessian fox 201, 313
teurst 313
Teutonic folklore 127
Teutonic mythology 63
Tewkesbury, England 98
Text of Unas 11, 20, 26, 33, 34, 43, 61, 152, 153, 154,

187, 235, 237, 276, 283, 286, 289, 310, 311, 312, 314, 325
Teyu Yagua 313
Tezcatlipoca 319
thabet tase 313
Thai folklore 318
Thailand 117, 257
thanacth 257
thao-thieh 307
Thaumas 214, 221, 224, 248, 313
Thaumus 151
thaye tase 313
Theban 201
Thebes 109, 254, 313
Theia 82
thekwane 169
thelgeth 29, 60, 313, 321
Themistitan, Mexico 30
Therbeeo 14, 158
Thereus 27, 39, 98, 112, 158, 173, 222, 248, 259, 314
therianthropy 20, 23, 27, 40, 47, 52, 58, 66, 69, 71, 102, 128, 145, 148, 169, 174, 175, 180, 182, 210, 216, 230, 232, 233, 335, 347
Theridamas 314
Theron 104, 314
theroo usha 308
Thes-Hrau 314
Theseus 28, 92, 99, 121, 226, 227, 238, 273
Thessalia 121
Thessalian legends 295
Thessaly 281
Thethu 314
Thetis 84
thing-wraiths 322
Thir 213
Thistilbardi 178
Thoas 262
Thobadzistshini 29, 342
thokolosi 317
Thonius 314
Thor 63, 97, 112, 113, 140, 156, 177, 307, 321
Thorgrimr 36, 39, 58, 97, 112, 113, 116, 122, 129, 134, 135, 139, 142, 148, 152, 153, 159, 162, 167, 172, 200, 208, 228, 232, 240, 245, 271, 272, 276, 296, 305, 307
Thorri 178
Thorska-fjord 295
Thous 104, 313
thousand-headed serpent 15
Thrael 213
Thraetaona 49, 345
Thraetona 97
three-headed monster 18, 87
Three-Legged Ass 187
three-legged bird 79, 148, 153, 277, 314

three-legged toad 153, 277, 314
three weasels 181
Thrgan 63
Thrigeitir 178
thrower down 131
Thrudgelmir 177
thrumpin 315
Thu'ban 315
Thuban 315
thunderbird 7, 58, 149, 269, 315, 318, 332
thunderbolts 17, 38, 95, 215, 316, 331
thunderstorm 323, 343
Thurse 177
thyrsus 280
ti-en lung 141, 275, 315
ti-lung 315
Tiamat 14, 56, 107, 137, 191, 197, 198, 199, 202, 220, 232, 315, 326, 328
tian long 316
tian ma 316
tiangou 316
tianlong 129, 316
tianma 79, 316
Tiansi 316
Tiber River, Italy 252
Tibet 188, 216, 286, 300, 327
The Tibetan Book of the Dead 51
Tibetan folklore 139, 188
Tibetian-Mongolian dictionary 286
ticholtsodi 316
Tidal Jewels 275
Tieholtsali 311
Tieholysodi 311
tien-kou 311
t'ien kuo 316
tien-long 315
ti'en-lung 315
tien-schu 316
T'ien-shih 316
tigbalan 317
tigbanua 316
tiger 16, 25, 28, 72, 85, 86, 109, 117, 135, 168, 195, 205, 214, 217, 218, 225, 242, 262, 263, 270, 273, 279, 284, 287, 304, 313, 324, 341
tiger-like 135, 225
tigre capiango 334
tigre de agua 168
Tigris 104, 199, 316
Tigris River 199
Tik-Tik 45, 46, 316, 317
Tikaloshe 317
tikbalan 317
tikbalang 317
tikdoshe 149
tikoloshe 156, 218, 317, 318
timber giants 322
timi-timin-gila 318
timin 318
timin-gila 318
timin-gila-gila 318

timingila 318
tingoi 318
tinmiukpuk 315, 318
tinnin 315, 318
Tipaka 318
tipatshimuns 47
Tippler 90
Tipua 318
Tirana, Albania 69, 204
tire snake 302
tirichik 282
Tirisuk 318
Tishpak 56, 200, 232
Tishtar 75
Tisiphone 22, 120, 130, 222, 318
Titanomachy 198
Tittiri 234
Titus Lucretius Carus 153
tityron 233
tityrus 233
tizheruk, yuk 251
Tjaldari 318
Tjhobadesstchin 99
Tlaltecuhtli 88
Tlatecuhtli 319
To Fu 165, 213, 319, 342, 344
to fu 165, 213, 319, 342, 344
to kas 319
toad 28, 209, 262, 302, 315, 319
toad-like 334
Toad Woman 319
tobi tatsu 149, 319
tobi-tatsu 319
toenayar 267
tofu-kozo 319
tōfu-kozō 319
Toggeli 23
Togrul 324
tohunga 185
tokan-dia 319
tokan-tongotra 319
tokandia 319
tokantongotra 319
tokkuri 287
toko 320
tokolosh 317
tokoloshe 156, 317
tokoloshi 317
Toledo 253
Tolkien, J. R. R. 247
tolosum 307
Tomb of Orcus II 323
tome 261, 320
Tommy Rawhead 271
tompondrano 320
tomte 139
tomte gubbe 139
tomtenisse 139
Tonacatepetl 48
To'nenile 316
Tongariro 308
Tonton Macoute 320
tontti 139
too jon sheu 320
too jor shen 320
too jun 320

too jun shen 320
Toolalla 199
toom ahr 323
Topsell, Edward 66, 226
torbalan 320
Torch Darkness 346
Torch Dragon 346
Toriyama Sekien 35
Tork 320
Tork Angegh 320
Tornadoes 171, 295
torpek 113
Torres Strait Islands 103
tortoise 44, 88, 108, 182,
    188, 208, 215, 259, 289,
    302, 344
tortoise-like 289
Totaro 277
tote road shagamaw 288
Totomi province, Japan
    192
Tou-Kio-Cheou 327
Toulouse, France 75
Tounela 305
Tower of Babel 220
Tower of Victory 170
trace horses 16, 119
Trachmyr 111
tragelaph 158
tragelaphus 320
tragopan 320
Trampling 23, 170, 245,
    299
trash 62, 148, 154
trashalka 69
traveler 44, 53, 73, 75, 165,
    177, 219, 259, 262, 273,
    301, 323, 327
traveler folklore, medieval
    44
The Travels of Sir John
    Mandeville 201, 203
treasure 6, 35, 41, 49, 60,
    63, 94, 107, 109, 122, 127,
    129, 133, 137, 143, 152,
    160, 162, 186, 207, 208,
    211, 234, 261, 278, 300,
    307, 313, 331, 346
Treasure of Truth 49
tree goose 55
Tree of All Healing 75
Tree of All Seeds 182,
    273, 276, 285
Tree of Knowledge 106,
    292
Tree of Life 75, 324
tree squeak 125, 320
treesqueak 320
trelquehuecuve 86, 94,
    172, 321
Trempe 23
trequehuecuve 321
Trevisa, John 106
Triballus 82
trickster 28, 48, 86, 198,
    231, 249, 259, 262, 296,
    307, 310, 337
Triglav Lakes Valley 346
tripoderoo 125, 321
Tristram 253

Trita 17
Triton 321
Tritons 157, 167, 224, 321
Troas 95
Trobriand Islands 46
Troit 324
Trojan War 53, 223, 338
Trojan warrior 19, 39, 204
trold 113, 114
troll 113, 114, 143, 178,
    246, 295, 321
trooping fairies 117
trows 321
Troynt 324
Trud 23, 24
Trude 23
A True Relation of a Mon-
    strous Serpent Seen at
    Henham on the Mount in
    Saffron Walden 155
trulli 321
the Truncated 112
Trutte 23
Tryd 23
tsanahale 29, 60, 314, 321
tsemaus 322
tsenahale 322
tsiatko 322
Tsimshian 30, 149
Tsin-Ssi 153
tsog 170
tsog tsuam 170
Tsohanoai 342
tso'po 188
tsopo 286
Tsuchi Gumo 115, 321
Tsuchi-Gumo 322
tsuchi'gumo 114
tsuchigumo 322
Tsuchigumo 322
tsuchikorobi 322
tsuchinoko 322
Tsukino Usagi 229
tsukomogami 52, 62, 70,
    87, 95, 173, 183, 288,
    322, 343, 347
tsukumo-gami 322
tsukumogami 322
tsukumogamo 229, 322
ts'um'a'ks 322
Tsuna 322
tsunami 176
tsurube-otoshi 323
Tuat 11, 20, 33, 36, 43, 61,
    152, 155, 197, 223, 237,
    276, 283, 285, 286, 289,
    299, 310, 311, 312, 314
tuba 323
tubae 323
tuberculosis 169, 250
Tubetube and Wagawaga
    folklore 54
Tuchulcha 323
Tucky Piggy 41
Tudd 23
Tugarin Zmey 323, 346
Tuhikarapapa 185
Tukano mythology 66
Tulihand 19
tulpar 19, 323

Tulsa 336
tulung 317
Tumu-Ra'i-Fuena 324
la tunda 324
tunerak 336
tunnituaqruk 185, 324
Tuonela 304, 305
Tuonetar 304
Tuoni 304
Tupari people 47
Tupiian people 344
tupilak 190
tupilaq 190
tupilat 190
Turen 67
Turgul 324
Turi-a-faumea 274
Turisas 168
Turkey 71, 331, 335
Turkish folklore 33, 186
Turkish mythology 42,
    183, 323
turquoise 339
Tursas 168
turtle-like 124, 255
Turul 324
tusse 321
Tutara-Kauika 324
tuwung 317
Twelfth Night 184
Twelve Nights of Christ-
    mas 139, 193
twins 60, 74, 99, 151, 258,
    267, 271, 334
Twisting Serpent 208
Twisty Serpent 211
Twrch Trwyth 5, 16, 30,
    53, 72, 144, 147, 209,
    324
tyger 25, 324
tyn-schu 316
Typhoeus 76, 82, 85, 92,
    99, 110, 115, 151, 165,
    201, 238
typhoon 164, 206
Tyr 134
Tyrrhenian Sea 219

U-wa, China 80
Ubangi folklore 50
Ubangi Shari 50
Uchaishravas 324, 325
Uchchaih-Srauas 324
Uchchaihsravas 324
Udayana 234, 325, 330
Ufa 325
Ugallu 328
Uganda, Africa 15, 180, 341
Ugjuknarpak 325
Ugraka 234
Uile Bheisd a' Chuain 89
uilebheist 325
Uirne 280
uisges 280
Uji River 152
Ukasima 325
ukena 326
Ukisima, Kyoto 245
ukomiarik 170
Ukraine 141, 204, 323

uktena 325
ulama 117
Úlfr Fenris 125
Ulmka 234
Uloopi 325
Ulster, Ireland 18, 104, 126
Ulupi 186, 325
Uluru 198, 208
uma na-iru 325
umbilical cord 21, 55, 116
Umm Naush 326
Umu Dabrutu 326
Unaging Chronos 87
Unas, King 11, 20, 26, 33,
    34, 43, 61, 152, 153, 154,
    187, 235, 237, 276, 283,
    285, 286, 289, 310, 311,
    312, 314, 325
unbaptized baby 132
unborn children 45, 246,
    324
unborn fetus 221
Uncle Gunnysack 320
undead 32, 35, 57
underground-people 321
underwater cat 326
underwater panther 326
Underworld 8, 11, 12, 16,
    20, 30, 32, 33, 36, 37, 42,
    43, 49, 54, 59, 61, 82, 87,
    94, 120, 129, 130, 133,
    141, 147, 152, 153, 154,
    155, 165, 187, 199, 222,
    223, 235, 237, 242, 248,
    276, 283, 285, 286, 289,
    299, 300, 304, 305, 310,
    311, 312, 314, 319, 323,
    331, 339
Underworld, King of the
    33, 59
Ungur 270
Unhcegila 326
unicorn 2, 8, 11, 12, 44, 75,
    77, 84, 86, 155, 158, 171,
    183, 187, 188, 191, 192,
    194, 212, 227, 229, 237,
    247, 262, 267, 268, 271,
    286, 287, 302, 306, 319,
    320, 326, 327
Unicorn, Occidental 326
Unicorn, Oriental 158,
    188, 191, 192, 212, 262,
    268
unicorn stag 155
unicornio 326
unicornus 326
unicünio 326
United States of America
    21, 26, 29, 32, 34, 39, 53,
    54, 57, 59, 60, 65, 72, 75,
    77, 78, 81, 90, 91, 93, 97,
    100, 102, 103, 124, 128,
    129, 133, 135, 136, 137,
    138, 139, 140, 141, 146,
    147, 148, 149, 151, 155,
    156, 159, 161, 163, 164,
    174, 175, 182, 184, 186,
    189, 210, 211, 212, 225,
    227, 230, 245, 251, 257,
    259, 260, 265, 269, 275,

278, 283, 288, 296, 297, 298, 299, 300, 305, 311, 313, 320, 321, 322, 325, 328, 333, 334, 335, 336, 337, 342
University of Halle 60, 297
Unktehi 327
Unktehila 327
Unktexi 327
Unnati 327
unnerorske 113
Unseelie Court 113, 117
unterliegerinnen 303
unukornulo 326
Upaka 328
Upananda 234
Upanandaka 234
upir 334
Upland 125, 328, 329
upland trout 125, 328
Upphiminn 329
uraeu 20
uraeus 285
Uragas 252, 328
Uranian Cyclopes 95
Uranus 75, 95, 120, 130, 137
urban legend 280
Ureus 39, 42, 256, 328
Uridimmu 328
urisk 328
Urius 328
Urmahlullu 328
uroboros 248
uroborus 248
Uroo 328
Ursa Major 105
ursidae (bearlike) 52, 220, 267, 274, 322
ùruisg 220, 267, 274, 322
Uruk 70, 119
urum 170
urus 271, 309
Usas 97
ustukhwan kh'ur 164
Ute folklore 54, 251
Utpala 234
Utpalaka 234
Uwabami 329
Uwibami 329

vahan 18, 235
vahana 150
Vainateya 134
Vajrppani 325
Vakr 329
Valaskialf 116, 153
Vale of Towy 225
Valhalla (Valaskialf) 116, 142, 153, 163, 276, 296
Valisikha 234
Valkyrie 142, 330
Valley of the Mata, Ireland 220
Valr 329
Valravn 329
Vamana 43, 101, 234, 266, 304, 329
vampire 1, 8, 17, 24, 25,

45-46, 48, 51, 67, 87, 118, 178, 182, 204, 210, 218, 230, 233, 241, 257, 262, 263, 263¬264, 266, 272, 292, 298-299, 300¬301, 303, 317, 331, 332, 341
vampire bat 341
Vampire: His Kith and Kin 230
vampire-like 45
vampiric animal 32
vampiric celestial creature 37
vampiric creature 8, 12, 13, 23, 25, 32, 45, 59, 60, 82, 88, 90, 128, 143, 169, 178, 182, 204, 207, 210, 211, 218, 222, 230, 241, 242, 244, 247, 251, 255, 256, 261, 264, 266, 271, 279, 280, 284, 298, 300-301, 303, 317, 341, 345
vampiric demonic-creature 51
vampiric dog 47
vampiric Were-Creature 264
vampiric witch 45¬46, 68, 303
Vampyr 23
vanadevatas 329
Vanagandr 125
Vanaheimr 329
vanara 278, 329
Vanargand 125
Vanargandr 125
Vanarganndr 125
Vancouver Island 340
Vaner 329
Vanir 329
Vanr Van 329
varcolaci 264
varengan 330
Vars (Varns) 152
Varuna 101, 216, 234
Vasara 234
vasi pancasadvara 330
vassorm 208
Vasuki 234, 284, 330
Vasunemi 330
vatna-hestur 244
Vatnsdæla 57
Vayu 52, 101
Ve 47
Vedic mythology 102, 133, 180, 216, 264, 269, 329
védomec 170
Vedrfolnir 116, 330
vegetable lamb of tartary 55, 202
vehicle of the Asvins 150
La Velue 255
Venezuelan folklore 221
venom 23, 29, 32, 49, 55, 56, 67, 89, 98, 102, 106, 110, 127, 144, 161, 167, 177, 184, 221, 234, 251, 286, 345
verm 106, 248

vermilion bird 304, 330
Vermont 130
versipellis 335
Vespasian, Emperor 226
Vesteinn 329
Vetal 51
Vetala 51, 266
Vetr 178
la víbria 330
Vid 116
Vidar 126
Vidblindi 178
Viddi 178
Vidgymnir 178
Vidhya mountains 277
Vidofner 146
Víðófnir 146
Vidolfr 178
Víðópnir 146
Vidyujjvala 234
vielfras 146
vienaragis 326
Vietnam 90
Vietnamese dragons 109, 274
Vietnamese folklore 274
Vietnamese mythology 109, 211
Vifill 300, 302
Vigg 330
Viggr 330
vigspa 329
Vijay Stambh 170
Vikram and the Vampire 51
Vikunda 234
Vili 47
vilkatas 334
vilkolakis 334
Vilmeidr 178
Vilvaka 234
Vinata (Diti) 85, 134
Vinayaka 327
Vindhya forest 253
Vindr 178
vine-like 55
Vingrip 178
Vingskornir 330
Vipar 178
viper 82, 98, 115, 168, 222, 330, 338
Viraja 234
Viranaka 234
Virasa 234
vircolac 331
vircolak 335
Virgil 16, 95, 152
virgin 38, 84, 104, 109, 170, 180, 221, 249, 250, 258, 263, 327
Virgin Mary 249
Virginia, USA 333
Virohama 234
Virtra 180
Virupaksha 58, 216, 280, 331
vis 331
Visayan creation legend 217
Visayan folklore 292
Vishapa 49

Vishnu 15, 18, 37, 41, 134, 146, 175, 269, 284
Vishnuratha 134
Visvamitra 181
Visvavasu 179
Vithafnir 146
Vitore 331
Vitra 17, 331
viza 106
Vladimir, Prince 141
vlkodlaks 335
Vodou 88
Voivre 331
volcano 84, 129, 168, 308
Volga Tartars 291
von Gesner, Konrad 61
vookodlaks 335
Vornir 178
vough 331
Vouivre 331
Vourukasa 42, 330
Vourukasa sea 182, 276
Vourukasha 148, 187, 273
vrikshakas 331
Vritra 17, 331
Vritta 234
Vrtra 17, 331
vseslav 334
Vucub Caquix 331¬332
Vuire 331
Vulkodlak 335
Vulpangue 128, 168
vulture 13, 28, 34, 117, 121, 152, 154, 175, 273, 277, 323
Vuokho 332

Wadag 345
Wagadoo, Africa 59
Waheela 26
Wahiero 263
wahwee 332
waillepen 332
Wainamoinen 168
Wak Wak 21
wak waks 118
Wakandagi 332
wakinyan 315
Wakinyan tanka 315
Wakndagi Pezi 332
waldgeist 332
waldgeister 332
Wales, symbol of 339
walichu 332¬333
wallaby 332
Wallach 53
Wallachia 264
Walrider 23
Walriderske 23
walrus dog 48
walrus-like 70, 82
Walton Hill, England 98
Walutahanga 333
Wampanoag people 265
wampus cat 125, 333
wana-games-ak 333
wanagemeswak 333
Wanambi 270
Wanganui River 308
wani 333

wappentier 333
war between Britain and
    Wales 147
War of Heaven 31
Warger the crocodile 132
warhorse 12, 16, 56, 62,
    69, 294, 323
warou 211
wasco 333
wasgo 149, 333
Washington, USA 337
Washo folklore 334
water babies 334
water-boa 26
water buffalo 58, 91, 117,
    306, 327
water devil 50
water dragon 58
water-elephant 334
water fairy 50
water-fowl 44
water-horse 47, 79, 114, 174
water horse 69, 72, 79,
    118, 138, 241, 243, 291
water kelpie 285
water leaper 209, 334
water lynx 227
water monster 17, 114, 161,
    165, 193, 327, 332
water possum 17
water snake 15, 70, 165,
    174, 188, 189, 191, 207,
    213, 216, 328, 342
water-snake 239
water-spirit 186
water, symbol of 179
water worms 126
waterfall 17, 61, 94, 199,
    328, 337
waterhole 100, 146, 240,
    334
Waters of Life and Death
    87
waterspout 106, 108, 171,
    206
Watery Abyss 14
wati-kutjara 334
waukheon 315
wawkalak 335
wayang mythology 29
Wear River 203
weasel 52, 56, 89, 98, 181,
    232, 269, 303, 335
weasel-like 253, 337
weather (bad), personifica-
    tion of 149
wedding of Pirithous 12,
    28, 36, 39, 41, 83, 87, 89,
    90, 92, 96, 99, 101, 105,
    111, 121, 144, 154, 157,
    166, 169, 172, 202, 204,
    214, 221, 223, 224, 226,
    229, 238, 245, 248, 257,
    260, 272, 273, 313
Wee Ping 190
Wee San 190
weewilmekq 337
Wei-te-lun-kai 235, 334
Welsh black cattle 131,
    209

Welsh fairy mythology 94
Welsh folklore 12, 14, 15,
    77, 79, 130, 138, 147,
    154, 209, 225
Welsh mythology 33, 41
Wen Wang 205
Wend folklore 261
Wend mythology 69, 72,
    297
wer-wold 335
were-bear 334, 335
were-being 334
were-boar 334, 335
were-cats 29, 334, 335
were-cow 334
were-creatures 17, 174,
    264, 334–35
were-crocodile 335
were-dog 334, 335
were-fox 334, 335
were-hyena 69, 334, 335
were-jackal 334, 335
were-jaguar 334
were-leopard 334, 335
were-mountain lion 334,
    335
were-tiger 214, 273
werewolf-like 111, 184, 212
werewolves 19, 24, 33, 48,
    52, 57, 69, 71, 119, 153,
    184, 193, 194, 209, 210,
    211, 212, 213, 219, 334,
    335, 347
West Africa 13, 28, 104,
    144, 172, 270
West African coast 26
West African folklore 28,
    237, 240, 346
West African mythology
    59
West African Review 279
West Arnhem Land, Aus-
    tralia 235
West Dorset District
    Council 282
West Indies 299, 303
West Virginia 159
Western Sea of China 35
Westmanland 269
Westmorland, England 76
whale 28, 32, 44, 89, 99,
    100, 124, 177, 179, 206,
    247, 261, 267, 268, 275,
    277, 281, 283, 295, 315,
    318, 324, 333, 346
whappernocker 125, 335
whatukura 36, 219,
    335¬336
whirligig fish 125, 336
whirlpool 29, 84, 89, 164,
    195, 275, 337
whirlwind 15, 16, 20, 36,
    97, 151, 201, 217, 219,
    250, 255, 295, 309, 336
white bear 58
white beard 210, 298
white bird 73, 100, 337
white boar 64
White Book of Rhydderch
    13

white bull 104, 126
white butterfly 24
white charger 56
white chickens 215
white deer 297
white dog 103, 132, 250,
    316
white dog wolf 206
white dragon 42, 106, 108,
    147, 213, 217, 250, 339
white elephant 18, 117,
    163
white fairy-hound 148
white fairy horse 50
white hair 33, 72, 340
white hat 23, 341
white horse 79, 229, 262,
    302, 330
white iguana 334
White Ladies 347
white-like 309
white maidens 54
white mare 305
white marsh 51
white merle 336
White Mountain Apache
    60
white mule 42, 97, 122
white ones 54, 66
white ox-head 69
white pig 41
white rat 163
white rooster 61
white-scaled dragon 325
white scaled serpents 298
white spider 322
white stallion 151, 254
white tiger 72, 135, 284,
    304
white tusk 344
white whale 267
white winder 290
Whore of Babylon 106
whowie 336
wi katca 326
wi katcha 336
wi-lu-gho-yuk 336
Wichtel 23, 139
wichtelweib 113
wichtlein 113
wight 113, 117
Wiglaf 127
wihwin 336
wikatcha 336
Wild Beast of Gevaudin
    57
wild boar of Ben Bulben
    64
Wild Hunt 95, 132, 337
wildcat 73, 74, 326
wildcat-like 316
will am alone 125, 336
will-o'-the-wisp 108
William the Conqueror 75
willopus-wallopus 125,
    337
Willow Mountain 345
Wilser dragon 337
Wilser 110, 337
Winckelriedt 337

wind bird 64, 337
wind eagle 64
Windsingers 305
wine 12, 17, 27, 28, 36, 37,
    39, 41, 80, 83, 87, 89, 90,
    92, 98, 99, 100, 101, 105,
    111, 112, 121, 130, 144,
    154, 157, 158, 166, 169,
    172, 173, 192, 202, 204,
    214, 215, 219, 222, 223,
    226, 228, 229, 238, 248,
    257, 258, 259, 260, 272,
    273, 280, 284, 314
winged horse 14, 16, 19,
    26, 47, 68, 83, 85, 87, 96,
    119, 120, 133, 158, 162,
    204, 222, 223, 254, 266,
    285, 294, 300, 323
winged lion 48, 62, 86,
    240
winged serpent 27, 28, 94,
    107, 166, 249, 306, 329
Wingeecaribee 146
Winnipeg, Canada 227
Winwalite 144
Wirwir 337
Wisconsin, USA 48, 57,
    91, 159, 189, 260, 296
wish hound 131, 154, 337
wishpooshi 337
wisk 131
wisked hound 337
witch doctor 13, 218
witch hunter 75
witch-like 103
Witch of Endor 123
witchcraft 26, 46, 67, 143,
    210, 217, 301, 329
witches 7, 15, 20, 24, 30,
    37, 45, 46, 51, 52, 56, 59,
    67, 68, 73, 86, 87, 97,
    118, 123, 138, 143, 169,
    170, 171, 172, 175, 193,
    203, 217, 218, 245, 262,
    263, 281, 292, 301, 303,
    317, 321
Witiko people 46
wives-tales 176
Wivre 331
Wiwilemekq 337
Wiwilemekw 337
wizard 15, 57, 74, 75, 157,
    185, 241, 295
wizard's shackle 70–71
Wochowsen 337
Woinunggur 270
wolf 20, 26, 33, 42, 67, 71,
    72, 74, 75, 92, 107, 109,
    112, 118, 125, 126, 134,
    135, 142, 155, 162, 177,
    178, 206, 210, 211, 213,
    214, 220, 222, 236, 245,
    248, 250, 264, 269, 281,
    282, 283, 299, 308, 314,
    316, 324, 325, 329, 333,
    335, 338, 347
wolf coat 264
wolf hound 134, 177
wolf hybrid 222, 236, 248,
    250, 335, 338

wolf-like 43, 165, 173, 331, 333, 338
wolf-man 213
wolf-skin 105
wolf-trampler 299
Wollondilly 146
Wollunquain 270
wolperdinger 337
wolpertinger 337
wolverine 298
wombat 232, 332
wonderful pig of the ocean 282
Wonders of the Worlds 167
Wondzad 270
Woodbridge 132
woodchuck 93
woodchuck-like 90
World Serpent 44, 53
World Tree 18, 97, 112, 113
World War II 32
worm 23, 62, 63, 98, 104, 106, 126, 130, 164, 167, 177, 187, 191, 203, 206, 208, 209, 225, 248, 254, 258, 262, 273, 282, 287, 288, 301, 306, 309, 320, 335
wormlike 98, 208, 295
Worms, Germany 208
Wormwood 31
Worombi 270
Wouivre 331
Wreghorn, England 54
Wu Ge Shan Li 261
Wu-ti, Emperor 80
Wuchowsen 337¬338
Wulungen 270
Wulungu 270
wulver 338
Wyandot (Huron) people 32
Wynken de Worde 172
wyrm 78, 106, 203, 248
wyvern 282, 331, 338
Wyvre 331

xan 338
Xanthos 53, 102, 151, 158, 203, 219, 258, 261, 262, 338
Xanthus 79, 261, 338
Xbalanque 332
Xecotcovach 76, 91, 311, 338
Xerxes 302
xexeu 338
Xhosa people 7, 156, 317
Xiang Yao 140, 338
xiao 339
xie chai 339
xie zhi 339
xiezhi 339
Xingu River 293
xiubhcocab 339
Xiuhcoatl 339
Xiuhtecuhtli 339
Xolotl 339
Xuan Wu 135

Xuanwu 145
xueˇ-rén 182

Y Ddraig Goch 147, 339
y fad felen 121
Y Fuwch Frech 130
Y Fuwch Gyfeiliorn 130
y fuwh laethwen lefrith 225
Y Wrach 339
yach 341
yagarua 339
yagim 339, 340
yagis 340
yahmur 34
yakan 340
Yakima 337
yakkha 341
yako 291, 340, 343
yaksa 341
Yakuts people 18
yala 340
yalaka 340
yale 114
yali 114, 340
Yam 211
Yama 101, 278
yama-uba 340
yama-waro 340
yamabito 340
Yamabushi 190
Yamabushi 196, 200
yamabushi tengu 183
yamamba 343
yamanba 343
Yamapura 43
Yamasee Cherokee folklore 245
Yamata 249, 340
Yamata-no-Orochi 249
yamauba 340, 343
Yamm 107, 340–341
Yamo 341
yampee 212
Yan Di, Emperor 175
Yang Chien 83
Yang Ching 163
Yangon, Burma 267
yannig 341
yannig an od 341
yaquaru 341
yaquaruigh 341
yasha 341
yashi 341
Yata Garasu 341
Yatagarasu 314, 341
yato no kami 341
yato-no-kami 341
yatso no kami 341
Yatsukahagi 322
yatu-dhana 271
Ychen Bannog 225
yech 341–342
yedinorog 326¬327
Yegara-no-Heida 329
Ye'iitsho La'I Naaghaii 342
Yeitso 29, 342
Yelafaz 39
Yelapahi 342

yell hound 131
yell-hound 337
Yellow Emperor 51, 108, 344
Yellow River 342
yem'chen 168
Yemen 11, 236
yemische 168
Yeo 140
yeouija 170
Yero 270
yesk 131
yeth hounds 131, 154, 337
Ygdrasil 97, 112, 113, 123, 137, 146, 153, 162, 240, 271, 330
Yi 125
Yi Zu 196
yin chu 165, 319, 342, 344
ying-long 96, 342
ying lung 86, 108, 191, 319, 342
ying-lung 86, 108, 342
ying-ying 188, 189, 213, 342
Yingarna 270
yksisarvinen 326
Ymir 47, 177
Ymsi 178
yn-schu 316
yo 108, 342
yo-naoshi 235
Yofune-nushi 342–343
yoh shoh 343
yohshoh 343
yojanas 17
Yōkai 20, 35, 43, 49, 52, 62, 67, 70, 87, 105, 118, 130, 134, 152, 158, 167, 173, 176, 181, 183, 194, 195, 196, 235, 238, 241, 242, 244, 245, 246, 274, 287, 288, 290, 291, 304, 307, 310, 311, 312, 319, 322, 323, 340, 343, 345, 347
Yōkai creature 130
yokaigaku 343
Yomi 289
yomo-tsu-shiko-me 289
yomotsu-shiko-me 289
yomotsu-shikome 289
yona gorri 343
yonagorri 343
yong 108, 343
Yong-Wang 343
yonglong 342
Yorikata 291, 340, 343
Yorimitsu 115
Yorkshire, England 54, 76, 78, 132, 143, 148, 246, 295
Yorkshire folklore 54, 295
Yosa Buson of Kyoto 290
Youchang 123, 175, 304, 343
Ypocras 201
ypotryll 343, 344
Yr hen Wrach 339

Ysbaddaden 16, 30, 72, 111, 324, 344
Ysgithyrwyn 209, 344
Yspaddaden Pencawr castle 147
Ystral 209
Yu 344
Yu, Emperor 163
Yu Chu 213
yu-kai 107
yu-kia 344
yu-lung 344
Yu Siang 213, 344
Yueh kingdom 125
Yueh-kiu 188, 189
Yuen Kien Lei Han 155
Yuen Kien Lei Hau 191
yuen-yuen 108, 344
Yukon 315, 318
Yulunggu 270
Yup'ik people 20
yurupari 344
Yvain the Bastard 268

Zabava 141
Zagh 344
Zahhāk 345
Zahhak 49, 345
Zahhāk-e Tāzi 345
Zahn, Joannes 202
Zal 276, 283
Zambia, Africa 207
zaratan 44, 100
Zarevna Militrissa 347
zashiki-warashi 345
zburător 280
zburator 280, 345
zebra 178
Zephyros 53, 158, 338
Zephyrus 39, 151
Zeus (Jupiter) 25, 38, 40, 66, 68, 75, 76, 77, 78, 80, 84, 95, 99, 110, 151, 158, 198, 201, 219, 242, 254, 267, 299, 313
zhar-ptitsa 127, 345
Zhejiand 125
zhu 345–346
zhu bird 345
Zhu Long 346
zhū Què 330
Zhu Rong 140
Zhulong 346
ziegenmelker 148
Zig 346
Zilant 346
Zin 346
Zipacna 332
Ziraafa 75
zitny snij 346
ziz 258, 333, 346
Zlatorog 346¬347
Zmag Ognjeni Vuk 334, 347
zmaj 106, 107
Zmei Gorynytch 141
Zmej Goronech 347
Zmey Gorenetch 347
zmij 106
zmin 106

zmora 170, 230
Zodiac 107, 313
Zohak 49, 345
Zohhāk 345
zokuzokugami 71
Zomok 106–107, 279

zoophyle (animal-plant hybrid) 55, 202
zorigami 347
Zoroastrian folklore 187, 250
Zoroastrian mythology 41,

42, 43, 44, 49, 97, 102, 132, 134, 135, 148, 273, 297, 305, 345
zorro-vibora 168
Zu 34
Zulu folklore 173

Zulu people 171
Zululand 173
zunbera-bō 242
Zuni mythology 193, 195
zwerge 113
zzwerg 113

www.ingramcontent.com/pod-product-compliance
Lightning Source LLC
Chambersburg PA
CBHW080547270326
41929CB00019B/3223